1 MONTH OF
FREE
READING

at

www.ForgottenBooks.com

By purchasing this book you are eligible for one month membership to ForgottenBooks.com, giving you unlimited access to our entire collection of over 1,000,000 titles via our web site and mobile apps.

To claim your free month visit:
www.forgottenbooks.com/free786526

ISBN 978-0-483-52492-7
PIBN 10786526

Fabian Tract No. 153.

THE TWENTIETH CENTURY REFORM BILL.

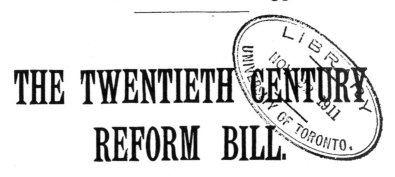

BY

HENRY H. SCHLOESSER.

PUBLISHED AND SOLD BY

THE FABIAN SOCIETY.

PRICE ONE PENNY.

LONDON:

THE FABIAN SOCIETY, 3 CLEMENT'S INN, STRAND, W.C.

JANUARY, 1911.

THE TWENTIETH CENTURY
REFORM BILL.

PREPARED BY HENRY H. SCHLOESSER WITH THE ASSISTANCE OF A.
COMMITTEE APPOINTED FOR THE PURPOSE BY THE EXECUTIVE
COMMITTEE OF THE FABIAN SOCIETY.

INTRODUCTION.

THE first draft of this measure was issued by the Fabian Society as Tract No. 14, "The New Reform Bill," exactly twenty years ago. No single one of the reforms then advocated has since become law ; but at the present moment (January, 1911) the prospects of Electoral Reform are brighter than for many years past, and some of the proposals of our Bill are definitely promised by the first Cabinet within living memory which can reckon on fulfilling its promises without the concurrence of the Upper House.

The present Bill, redrafted throughout and altered in many details (especially by the substitution of the Alternative Vote for the Second Ballot), is intended as a complete scheme of Electoral Reform, with the exceptions noted below. It therefore includes Adult Suffrage and completely removes all existing sex disqualifications in connection with parliamentary elections. It permits women, married or single, to vote for and to be members of parliament as well as all minor governing bodies.

But it should be pointed out that the advocacy of Adult Suffrage in this Tract is not intended to prejudice the highly controversial question whether at the present time the enfranchisement of women should be sought by such partial measures as conferring the parliamentary vote on some or all of the women at present qualified to vote for local governing bodies, or whether nothing less than Adult Suffrage should be accepted. This is a question of immediate parliamentary tactics which is outside the scope of the scheme here outlined.

Since the time of the Chartist agitation, no attempt has been made to formulate a thorough scheme for the reform of the laws regulating our electoral system, if the confused, inconsistent, and often unintelligible mass of Acts of Parliament on the statute book can be dignified by such a name. From the Statute of Edward I., establishing freedom of election, down to the Registration Act, 1908, there have been over one hundred and sixty Acts to regulate the franchise, registration of electors, and procedure at elections, etc. ; of which more than one hundred and twenty have been enacted since the passing of the Reform Act of 1832—a measure intended by Lord John Russell to settle finally the question of reform.

With the single exception of the Corrupt and Illegal Practices Act (1883), no attempt has been made to codify any section of electoral law. One Act of Parliament contradicts another, and a reverence for antiquated modes of draughtsmanship has only made confusion worse confounded. A vote is given to every male householder, only to be taken away from him by a cumbrous and iniquitous system of registration, with a long term of qualification, and an intentionally complex arrangement of claim, objection, and revision.

It is often said that the points of the People's Charter have been embodied in English law; but, as a matter of fact, the ballot alone has been adopted in its entirety. The suffrage has been considerably lowered, and some approach was made, twenty-five years ago, to the establishment of equal electoral districts, but the payment of members and a reduction in the duration of parliament are still promises for the future, though now more likely to be realized than ever before. The abolition of a property qualification for members has been largely a nominal reform, and can only be rendered effective by the payment of election expenses.

In the following draft bill, an attempt has been made to put into practicable legal shape the aspirations of advanced political reformers. Its provisions include the following points:—

ADULT SUFFRAGE.
MINIMUM RESIDENTIAL QUALIFICATION.
EFFICIENT QUARTERLY REGISTRATION BY PAID OFFICERS.
ALTERNATIVE VOTE.
SIMULTANEOUS ELECTIONS.
ABOLITION OF PLURAL VOTING.
EXTENSION OF THE HOURS OF POLLING.

RESTRICTION ON USE OF CONVEYANCES.
PAYMENT OF ALL ELECTION EXPENSES, AND OF NEARLY ALL THE NECESSARY COST OF CANDIDATURE.
PAYMENT OF MEMBERS, AND OF THEIR TRAVELLING EXPENSES.
QUINQUENNIAL PARLIAMENTS.

To make a complete Reform Bill, provision should also be made for the establishment of equal electoral districts, automatically re-adjusted according to population after every census; for the consolidation of the eighty-five statutes dealing with the disqualification of candidates, and of the thirty-one dealing with the procedure at an election; for the further simplification and strengthening of the law relating to corrupt and illegal practices; and for dealing with the whole question of the House of Lords.

Until the electorate consists of the whole adult population, and perfect freedom of choice of members, combined with the fullest control over their legislative action, has been secured through payment of members and their election expenses, and the alternative vote, the people will be seriously handicapped in the promotion and enactment of those measures of social reform which will ultimately result in the establishment of a properly organized community based on the socialization of industry.

THE BILL.

BE it enacted by the King's Most Excellent Majesty, by and with the advice and consent of the Lords Spiritual and Temporal and Commons in this present Parliament assembled and by the authority of the same as follows:

1. This Act may be cited as the Representation of the People Act, 1911.

2. This Act shall come into operation at the end of the present parliament.

Part I.—Adult Suffrage.

3. 1. A uniform franchise shall be established throughout the United Kingdom and every person (including women, whether under coverture or not), save as hereinafter expressly provided, who has during four weeks preceding any registration day, namely the fifteenth day of December, March, June or September, resided within the same constituency shall be entitled on that registration day to be registered as a voter, and when registered to vote at any parliamentary, municipal, county, or other public election held under the provisions of any statute within the area in which he is resident.

2. No person shall be entitled to be registered as a voter or to vote if he
  (1) is an infant or an alien ; or
  (2) is a lunatic within the meaning of the Lunacy Act, 1890 ; or
  (3) has been convicted of a corrupt or illegal practice and has been declared incapacitated for voting during the period of such incapacity.

4. No person shall be entitled to be registered as a voter, or when registered to vote, other than a person duly qualified under section three of this Act, and, save as herein provided, all the Acts conferring franchises and disqualifying persons as electors are hereby repealed.

Registration.

5. For the purposes of this Act the following persons shall be the local registration officers and deputy registration officers.

	Registration Officer	Deputy Registration Officer
a. In every administrative county	The Clerk of the County Council	One person for each county parliamentary constituency to be appointed by the County Council
b. In every county borough returning not more than one member to Parliament, and in every non-county borough returning one member to parliament	The Town Clerk	None
c. In every county and non-county borough returning two or more members to Parliament	The Town Clerk	One person for each parliamentary division to be appointed by the Borough Council
d. In every group of boroughs returning a member to parliament	The Town Clerk of a borough selected by the Local Gov'ment Board	The Town Clerk of every other borough in the group for his county

6. 1. On or before the last day of December, March, June, and September in each year every local registration officer shall either himself or by his deputy prepare and publish lists supplementary to the previous final list (1) of all persons not included in the previous final list who shall have resided for a period of four weeks next preceding the fifteenth day of December, March, June, and September respectively within the constituency and are not disqualified as aforesaid, (2) of all persons included in the previous final list who have not resided in the constituency during the said four weeks.

2. Such lists shall be classified according to locality and shall be prepared in such form and published in such manner as the Local Government Board shall prescribe.

3. It shall be the duty of every person who is rated for the relief of the poor or for any other purpose in respect of the ownership or occupation of any dwelling house or tenement to supply the local registration officer or his deputy at his request with every information within his power respecting the names and addresses of all such persons of twenty-one years of age or over as may have resided in his dwelling house or tenement for the period of four weeks next preceding the fifteenth day of December, March, June, and September respectively.

4. Any person who shall refuse or negligently omit to supply such information when so requested, or who shall wilfully or negligently give false or inaccurate information, shall, upon summary conviction, be liable to a fine not exceeding fifty pounds or to imprisonment, with or without hard labor, for a term not exceeding one month.

7. Any person may, on or before the tenth day of January, April, July, or October, as the case may be, by notice in writing to the local registration officer, object to the name of any person being upon the register on the ground that he is not entitled under this Act to be registered as a voter.

8. Any person entitled under this Act to be registered as a voter and whose name is not in the previous final list or on the first supplementary list may, on or before the tenth day of January, April, July, or October, as the case may be, by notice in writing to the local registration officer, claim to be registered as a voter.

9. 1. On receipt of an objection the local registration officer shall forthwith give notice thereof by post to the person objected to, stating the ground of the objection and the name and address of the person making the objection.

2. A list of names and addresses of the persons objected to and the ground of the objection and a list of the persons claiming to be registered shall be published on or before the fifteenth day of January, April, July, or October respectively by the local registration officer in such manner as the Local Government Board shall prescribe.

10. The office of revising barrister is hereby abolished.

11. The registrar of the county court exercising jurisdiction within the constituency or, if there be more than one county court, of such county court as the Home Office may appoint, or the deputy of such registrar, shall sit and shall determine all objections and claims as soon as may be and within one month after the twentieth day of January, April, July, or October respectively. Any person aggrieved by the decisions of the registrar may appeal to the judge of the county court, whose decision shall be final, save by leave of the judge or of the High Court. A person objected to or claiming to be registered may appeal by any other person appointed in writing on that behalf before the registrar and the judge. No fees shall be charged in such proceedings, and no costs shall be awarded to either party unless it shall appear to the judge that a claim or an objection is not bona fide made.

12. The decision of a registrar shall, pending appeal under section eleven of this Act, be regarded as a final decision.

13. On the twenty-second day of February, May, August, and November in each year every local registration office shall print and publish, in such manner as the Local Government Board may prescribe, lists of electors, classified according to locality, and prepared in such form as the Local Government Board shall prescribe. Such lists shall contain the names of all persons on the previous final list or on the first supplementary list, except those on the second supplementary list or successfully objected to before the registrar or judge, and the names of all persons who have successfully established claims before the registrar or judge, and such lists shall be deemed to be final lists and to be conclusive evidence, until the due publication of the next quarterly final list, of the right of any person whose name appears on such final lists to vote at any election within the constituency for which he is declared in any such list to be entitled to vote.

Expenses.

14. Save as herein expressly provided, one half of the expenses involved in carrying out the provisions of this Act shall be defrayed out of moneys provided by parliament in the form of a grant to the councils of counties and boroughs exercising powers under this Act, and such expenses as are not defrayed out of such grant shall be paid, in the case of a county, out of the county fund, and in the case of a borough out of the borough fund or rate, and the apportioning of all such expenses, whether for parliamentary or municipal purposes, shall be decided by the Local Government Board, whose decision on such questions shall be final.

15. No grant shall be payable under section fourteen of this Act to the council of any county or borough which has not, in the opinion of the Local Government Board efficiently exercised its powers under this Act.

Plural Voting.

16. Any person who shall vote more than once in the United Kingdom at one general parliamentary election or at any two or more bye-elections holden on the same day, or who shall vote more than once in the same constituency for any county, municipal, or other public election held under the provisions of any statute shall be guilty of a misdemeanor, and, **on** being convicted thereof, shall be liable to imprisonment for any term not exceeding one year, with or without hard labor.

The present arrangements for registering the crowded dwellers in populous cities are virtually those which sufficed when the Statute of Henry VI. for the first time restricted the county franchise to forty shilling freeholders. The electoral registration of London's five million inhabitants is left to no better organization than that of a rural hamlet of the last century.

At present only one in seven and a half of London's population is on the register, as compared with one in six of the United Kingdom outside London, and one in five in many provincial boroughs. The term of occupation is absurdly long, and so arbitrarily dated, that a large number of removals in London practically involve from eighteen months to two years disfranchisement.

This part supersedes the cumbrous mass of legal technicalities contained in thirteen Acts of Parliament, and makes the work of registration as simple, economical, and nearly automatic as possible. The present interval of more than four months between the date of claim and the date on which the register comes into force is reduced to rather over two months. The disabilities of women and peers of parliament are removed. Adult suffrage is enacted, with the minimum term of residence necessary for the purposes of registration. Under the existing Registration Acts the work of registration, which is only done *once* a year, commences in April or May, and is not concluded till October 12th, which is the last day for the holding of the Revision Court. Under such a scheme as that proposed, the register would be made up *four* times a year, and the four registrations would cost little more to prepare than the one list under existing regulations. The individual voter is relieved of trouble and expense in claiming and supporting his claim, and provision is made for the punishment of misconduct or wilful neglect on the part of the registration officers. The existing system of revision of the voters' lists is abolished, and a saving effected in the item of revising barristers' salaries in England of £25,000 a year. The work of preparing the register is transferred to the county and borough councils. There will be only one register for all elections, local as well as parliamentary.

Part II.—Elections.

Candidates.

17. Save as in this Act expressly provided, all elections shall take place at the time and in the manner now provided by parliament.

18. 1. Save as hereinafter provided, any person not disqualified under section three, sub-section two, of this Act, for being an elector may be a candidate at any election.

2. Provided that no person who has, within two years of any registration day, been convicted, either on indictment or summarily, of any crime and sentenced to imprisonment with hard labor without the option of a fine, or to any greater punishment, and has not received a free pardon, or has, within or during the time aforesaid been adjudged bankrupt, or made a composition or arrangement with his creditors, and not received his discharge, shall be qualified to be a candidate at any election.

19. No peer of parliament shall, so long as he is a duly elected member of the House of Commons, be entitled to sit or vote in the House of Lords.

Returning Officers.

20. For the purposes of this Act the local registration officer shall be the returning officer for all elections held within his constituency, and the salary of every local registration officer shall be deemed to include his expenses as returning officer, and all fees and charges of returning officers shall be abolished.

Official Poll Card.

21. The returning officer in every constituency shall, three days before the day of any election, forward by post to every elector an official poll card, showing the names of the candidates, the number of the elector on the register, and the place at which he is entitled to poll. Such poll cards shall be transmitted through the Post Office and delivered free of charge.

22. The returning officer in every constituency shall, within three days of the date of nomination, cause to be printed and posted in convenient places throughout the constituency an official placard showing the names of all the candidates, the date of the poll, and the polling places assigned to each district.

Free Election Addresses.

23. Every candidate may at his nomination deliver to the returning officer a copy of his election address, which shall not exceed five thousand words in length. The returning officer shall have all such election addresses printed, and shall deliver to the Post Office a packet directed to each registered elector in the constituency containing copies of all such addresses. The Post Office shall transmit and deliver such packets free of charge.

Free Postage of Election Literature.

24. Every candidate may once between his nomination and the day of election deliver to the returning officer a packet of literature for each elector, folded and addressed in accordance with the regulations of the Post Office relating to inland letters and not exceeding four ounces in weight. The returning officer shall deliver such packets to the Post Office and the Post Office shall deliver them to the addressees free of charge.

In the States of Oregon and Montana, where the Initiative and Referendum are used for State legislation, the voters are "instructed by means of literature furnished by those initiating or opposing a measure and distributed by the Secretary of State" (*Political Science Quarterly*, December, 1908).

Free Use of Schoolroom.

25. 1. A candidate at any election may use, free of charge, for the purpose of public meetings during the period of an election, any suitable room in any school receiving a grant out of moneys provided by parliament, and any suitable room in any building, the expense of maintaining which is wholly or partially payable out of any local rate ; provided that three days' notice of the proposed public meeting be given to the authority responsible for such school or building.

2. The use of the school or building shall be granted in the order of the receipt of the application by or on behalf of the candidates, provided that no candidate shall have the use of the same hall or room on a second occasion should any other candidate desire the use of it for the first time.

Hours of Polling.

26. At every election the poll (if any) shall commence at eight o'clock in the forenoon and be kept open till ten o'clock in the afternoon of the same day.

27. The Local Government Board shall provide an adequate number of ballot boxes for each constituency, materials for voters to mark the ballot papers, and all forms, other than ballot papers, required for use at an election, and shall supply them, free of charge, within ten days of the receipt of the requisition of the returning officer for the constituency in which they are to be used.

28. The returning officer shall furnish all ballot papers and all forms of nomination of candidates at a parliamentary election, and shall provide each polling station with copies of the register of voters, or such parts thereof as contain the names of the voters allotted to vote at such station, for use by the presiding officer and the personation agents of each candidate.

Maximum Expenses.

29. One half of the maximum expenses mentioned in Parts I., II., and III. of the First Schedule of the Corrupt and Illegal Practices Prevention Act, 1883, shall be substituted for the maximum amounts contained in Part IV. of the First Schedule of that Act.

Simultaneous Elections.

30. All writs issued by the Clerk to the Crown to the returning officers of constituencies at a general election of members to parliament shall bear the same date and shall on that date be issued.

The returning officer of every parliamentary constituency shall appoint the day for the nomination of candidates to be not later than the fourth day after the day on which he receives the writ, and the day for taking the poll to be the third Saturday after the date on which the writ is issued.

The cost of a general election, even under the restricted scale of the Corrupt and Illegal Practices Prevention Act (1883), is still such a tax on the candidates as to re-establish for some purposes the property qualification supposed to have been abolished in 1858.

In boroughs the maximum expenditure allowed for one candidate is £350, where the number of electors does not exceed two thousand, and rises by £30 for every succeeding thousand or part of a thousand electors. In counties the maximum is £650, for two thousand electors, and £60 for each thousand or part of a thousand electors above that number. This scale does not include the returning officer's expenses, which, though limited by the Parliamentary Elections (Returning Officers) Act (1875), amounted to £25,000 in January, 1910. The total expenditure, according to the candidates' returns at the general election of 1906 was £1,166,858, and in that of January, 1910, £1,296,382, including returning officer's expenses. The returning officer's expenses would be largely reduced by this part of the Act so far as his old duties are concerned, and the extra expense involved by his new duties would be minimized by having the printing, etc., done on a large scale. By clause 29 these maximum expenses are halved. The schedule of charges at present allowed would be considerably modified, and the amount of personal expenditure by the candidate reduced.

By these provisions everything practicable has been done to place the poorest candidate on an equality with the richest.

In no European country but the United Kingdom is the expense of printing ballot papers, provision of ballot boxes, voting compartments, forms of nomination and return, travelling of presiding officers, and conveyance of boxes, etc., to the place of counting votes and declaration of the poll, placed upon the candidates. In this country the above expenses, known as "the returning officer's expenses," are at present (1911) divided equally between the various candidates.

In France, Austria, Hungary, and Italy the payment is made entirely out of the State Exchequer. In the Netherlands, Portugal, Spain, Sweden, and Japan the burden is thrown on the local rates. In Belgium and Greece the expense is divided, the ballot boxes, desks, and permanent fixtures being provided by the State in the first instance, and stored, renewed, and repaired by the localities to which they are allotted for use. All other election expenses are paid out of the local funds. In Germany the polling expenses are defrayed locally.

In Norway election to the Storthing is absolutely free of expense.

Under the Act Regulating the Procedure at Parliamentary and Municipal Elections (35 & 36 Vict. c. 33), the returning officer may use, free of charge, for the purpose of taking the poll at a parliamentary election, any room in a school receiving a grant out of moneys provided by parliament, and any room the expense of maintaining which is payable out of any local rate. Any such room in a rural district can be used for parish meetings, public enquiries, meetings relating to allotments under the Small Holdings and Allotments Act, 1908, and for meetings "for the purpose of the candidature of any person for the (rural) district council or the parish council." Local Government Act, 1894, section 4.

Alternative Parliamentary Vote.

31. Whenever more than two candidates are nominated for one parliamentary constituency, the following provisions shall take effect.

1. Every elector shall have an ordinary vote (herein called a first vote) and an alternative vote (herein called a second vote).

2. The ballot papers shall be printed in such a way as to allow two defined spaces for voting opposite the name of each candidate.

3. Every voter shall exercise his first vote by marking his ballot paper in the usual manner in the space marked first vote, and shall exercise his second vote by marking the same ballot paper in the usual manner in the space marked second vote.

32. 1. Every vote given as a first or second vote shall be allowed or disallowed and counted in the like manner as if such a vote were a vote given at an election when not more than two candidates have been nominated.

2. The first votes shall be counted first, and if any candidate receive more than one half of the first votes recorded he shall be declared to be duly elected.

3. If no candidate receive more than one half of the total number of first votes recorded, the second votes recorded on those ballot papers on which the first vote has not been cast for the two candidates receiving the greatest number of first votes shall be counted, and such second votes as are thereon recorded for the two candidates receiving the greatest number of votes shall be added to the first votes recorded for such candidates, and the candidate who receives the greatest number of votes when such second votes are so added to the first votes recorded for such candidates shall be and be declared to be duly elected.

4. If no candidate receive more than one half of the total number of first votes recorded, and one, two, or more candidates who receive the highest number of first votes after the candidate who receives the highest number of votes receive an equal number of first votes, the second votes recorded on those ballot papers in which one first vote has been recorded for any candidate receiving less votes than the candidates so receiving an equal number of votes shall be counted, and such second votes shall be added to the votes of the candidates so receiving an equal number of votes, and the candidate who receives the greatest number of votes shall be deemed to be one of the two candidates receiving the greatest number of votes under sub-section three of this section, and thereupon the counting of votes shall proceed and the result of the election be ascertained as in that sub-section provided.

5. If no candidate receive more than one half of the total number of first votes recorded, and the two or more candidates who receive the highest number of first votes after the candidate who receives the highest number of votes receive an equal number of votes, and there are no candidates receiving less votes than such candidates receiving equal votes, the second votes recorded on those ballot papers on which the first vote has been recorded for the candidates receiving equal votes shall be counted and such second votes shall be added to the votes of the candidates so receiving an equal number of votes, and the candidate who receives the greatest number of votes shall be deemed to be one of the candidates receiving the greatest number of votes under sub-section three of this section, and thereupon the counting of votes shall proceed and the result of the election be ascertained as in that sub-section provided.

Our Antiquated System.—" The ' relative majority ' single-member method is in force, besides the United Kingdom, in the United States, Denmark (for the Lower House), Bulgaria and Greece.

" *The Second Ballot.*—The Second Ballot exists in Austria-Hungary, France, Germany (both for the Reichstag and in most of the States), Italy, the Netherlands, Norway, Roumania, Russia, Servia (for single-member districts), and Switzerland (for the Federal Council).

" In France, Norway, Roumania, Russia, and Switzerland all the candidates at a first ballot may stand again at the second, where a relatively small majority suffices ;

in the other countries all candidates are eliminated from the second ballot except the two who received the largest number of votes at the first.

"In some countries a provision is added that a candidate must receive at the first ballot not only an absolute majority of the votes cast, but also a number of votes equal to a definite proportion (one quarter in France, one-sixth in Italy) of the registered electors.

"The intervals between the two elections are frequently fixed by law. Thus, in France the second ballot takes place on the second Sunday after the first—i.e., a fortnight, as elections are always held on Sundays; in Italy, after an interval of not less than four or more than eight days." (Royal Commission, *infra*, 1910, p. 50.)

THE ALTERNATIVE VOTE.

Second ballot is the usual method for determining an election when three or more candidates stand for one seat, and its advantages are obvious, because it prevents the election of a candidate who is voted for by a minority of the actual voters.

Our present system—also the rule in the United States and in nearly all the British Dominions—which only allows one ballot, forces compromise before the election, or splits between the various groups or parties which support the ministry or the opposition, with the result that the seat may go to the most solid and not to the most numerous section.

The presence of an active and important third party in English politics, the Labor Party, makes some form of second ballot imperative.*

The alternative vote here proposed is strongly advocated by the Royal Commission appointed to enquire into Electoral Systems in their Report of 1910, signed by Lord Richard Cavendish, the Hon. W. Pember Reeves, Sir Courtenay Ilbert, and others.

It has precisely the same result as second ballot where there are two or three candidates for one seat, and will have nearly the same result in other cases. It has the great advantage of not involving the delay, expense, and trouble of a second ballot after an interval of a fortnight; it does not give opportunity for bargaining in the interval between the two ballots, a practice likely to lead to objectionable compromises; and it practically prevents small third or fourth parties deciding a contest on illegitimate grounds.

Under second ballot, if the votes were A 1,400. B 800, C 700, D 200, and assuming that B and C were closely allied parties, their joint vote should carry the seat. But D could give the victory to either side, and might easily do so for reasons which may be vaguely termed illegitimate.

The alternative vote practically prevents this, because no one could foresee the result of a complicated election with sufficient certainty to justify bargaining.

The alternative vote has been in operation in Queensland since the Electoral Act of 1892 and in Western Australia since the Electoral Act of 1907.

PROPORTIONAL REPRESENTATION.

We do not propose this widely advertised scheme of reform of our electoral system for reasons admirably set forth in the report of the commission already referred to.

If parliament had merely to discuss and consult, a method of election which gave every section representation in proportion to its numbers would have much to recommend it. But, in fact, parliament has to legislate, and through its executive, the cabinet, to administer our home affairs and to conduct foreign and colonial policy. For these purposes a method of elecion which accentuates the majority at any given time is actually preferable to a method which accurately represents it. Weak governments are the worst governments, because they do least work and do it badly. When the electorate is divided, as it often is, in the proportion (say) of nineteen votes on one side to twenty on the other, it is for the advantage of the nation that the parliament returned by those votes should be in the proportion of fourteen to twenty-five.

---

* The case against it, even under the present system, is stated by Mr. J. Ramsay MacDonald in his "Socialism and Government," though, on the whole, he decides that a change is necessary.

The arguments against proportional representation are, that it would involve large constituencies, not less than ten times the size of our present ones. The cost of elections would be enormously increased, and the difficulty of candidates making themselves and their opinions known to their constituents would be aggravated. In the old London School Board elections the parties had to meet this by dividing the large constituencies then in use into districts and allotting the parts to the several candidates, who devoted themselves to these districts only, and invited the electors thereof to give them all their votes.

The very heavy cost of these elections would increase the advantage which wealthy candidates and parties already have over those with less money at their disposal.

Other objections are the impossibility of devising any satisfactory method of conducting bye elections under a system of proportional representation, and the fact that the expected result, the election of two or more large parties very nearly balanced and a few nondescripts representing special sections or, through their outstanding personalities, representing, in fact, themselves, would give the balance of power, the decision as to the policy of the nation, into the hands of a group of these small, incompatible minorities, such as, at the present moment, Free-Trade Unionists, the Anti-Socialist Radicals, the Anti-Romanists, the Liberal Unionists, the Anti-Labor-Party Socialists, the Women Suffragists, the Independent Nationalists, and the other often estimable, but peculiar, politicians who usually represent worn out creeds or else political parties not yet in being.

Lastly, the difficulties of the imperfectly educated voter would be enormously increased. Instead of having to vote for one of two or, at most (except in rare cases), three candidates, he would be required to select ten names out of a list of twenty, at least, and twenty-five, thirty, forty, or even more in other cases. Chance, notoriety for quite irrelevant reasons, and numerous other factors would come into play. Numbers of persons would be returned to parliament not to represent a definite political policy or a particular view held by a small section, but because they bore a well known name, or owned a Derby winner, or had a son who played in the county cricket eleven or the borough football club.

For these and other reasons set out in the Report of the Royal Commission above referred to, and also cogently stated by Mr. J. Ramsay MacDonald in his "Socialism and Government," we think that no system of proportional representation yet invented could be adopted without gravely impairing effective democratic control.

Proportional representation is in operation in Belgium, Denmark, Finland, Servia, Sweden, Switzerland (in eight cantons), Tasmania, and Wurtemberg.

33. 1. No conveyance or horse or other animal shall be let, lent, or employed by any person for the purpose of conveying any other person, except a bona fide member of his own household, to or from the poll, except as provided in section 14 (3) of the Corrupt and Illegal Practices Prevention Act, 1883.

2. Any person who shall so let, lend, or employ a conveyance or horse or other animal contrary to the provisions of this section shall, on summary conviction, be liable to a fine not exceding £100.

The section above named permits an elector or several electors at their joint cost to hire a public stage or hackney carriage for the purpose of being conveyed to or from the poll.

Part III.—Parliament.

34. 1. Each of the parliamentary boroughs returning two members to parliament shall for the purpose of returning members to serve for such borough in parliament be divided into divisions.

2. The number, names, contents, and boundaries of such divisions respectively shall be those specified by the Local Government Board.

35. No university or group of universities shall return a member or members to serve for such university or group of universities in parliament.

36. 1. Every member duly elected to parliament, who has duly taken the oath required to be taken by members of parliament, or who has duly made affirmation in lieu thereof in the manner required by law, shall from the time of taking such oath or making such affirmation, so long as he remains a member of any parliament, be entitled to a salary of three hundred pounds per annum, which salary shall be paid out of moneys provided by parliament.

2. Every such member shall likewise be entitled to an allowance, to be paid out of moneys provided by parliament, for travelling expenses at the following rate, namely, when in the opinion of the Speaker :

> *a.* The furthest boundary of the constituency is over 500 miles from the Palace of Westminster : £100 per annum.
>
> *b.* The furthest boundary of the constituency is over 250 miles, but not over 500 miles, from the Palace of Westminster : £75 per annum.
>
> *c.* The furthest boundary of the constituency is 250 miles or under from the Palace of Westminster : £50 per annum.

37. Five years shall be substituted for seven years as the time fixed for the maximum duration of parliament under the Septennial Act, 1715.

Prior to the Revolution of 1688, with the exception of a few years during the Commonwealth, the duration of parliaments was entirely within the control of the Sovereign. One of the parliaments of Charles II. sat eighteen years. The Triennial Act was passed in 1694. Its preamble declares "that frequent and new parliaments tend very much to the happy union and good agreement of King and people." The Septennial Act, one of the earliest measures of the first parliament of George I., was nominally based on a desire to relieve the country of the "grievous and burdensome" expense of elections, and also from "the violent and lasting heats and animosities among the subjects of the realm," but was really aimed at the "restless and Popish faction," which was "designing and endeavoring to renew the Rebellion within this Kingdom and an invasion from abroad." The dangers of 1714 have passed away, and the Septennial Act should therefore have been repealed more than a century and a half ago, but all attempts at repeal have been unsuccessful. Parliaments rarely last longer than five years, and the average length is considerably less. A legislative assembly of the Union of South Africa may sit for five years ; the House of Representatives of the Australian Commonwealth for three years, and these are among the newest parliaments created. The German Reichstag is elected for five years.

The proposal to pay members of parliament is not an untried and new-fangled innovation, but a reversion to old constitutional custom, both in England and Scotland. "The custom began," says Dr. Henry, in his work "Greater Britain," "with the commencement of representation from a principle of common equity." In Scotland the payment was made in accordance with the terms of a statute dated 1427, which has been preserved, and is supposed to have been copied from an English statute that has been lost. Professor Thorold Rogers says that in the reign of Edward I. "the member of parliament had daily wages; the knights or county members receiving more—the amount is not invariable—than the burgesses. When the parliament was prorogued or dismissed, the writs for payment were made out, and the time during which the house sat exactly calculated." A judgment of Lord Chancellor Nottingham after the dissolution of parliament in 1681 proves that the payment was not merely a voluntary contribution by the constituencies. Thomas King, M.P. for Harwich, presented a petition stating "that he had served as burgesse in parliament for the said borrough severall yeares, and did give his constant attendance therein; but that the said borrough had not paid him his wages, though often requested so to do." Notice being given to the Corporation of Harwich and the facts being verified, a writ was ordered to be issued, de expensis burgensium levandis. This was probably the last order so made. "I know no reason," said Lord Campbell, commenting on this judgment, "in point of law why any member may not insist on payment of his wages. For this point in the People's Charter—payment of wages—no new law is required." An Act of 1541 made the payment of wages depend upon attendance in the house throughout the whole session. Payment of members is required to enable constituencies to choose freely their representatives, to give the public complete control over them, and to compel them to perform their duties with diligence and efficiency. The poor candidate would thus be put upon an equality with the richest. An equitable and convenient adjustment of burdens is made by the payment of members out of the state, and the election expenses out of the local, exchequers. Payment of members is the law in almost every country where representative government prevails. A table of existing laws on the subject will be found opposite.

The declaration of Mr. Asquith, in November, 1910, as Prime Minister and Leader of the Liberal Party, to the effect that payment of members and payment of election expenses would be established in 1911, if he was again returned to power, makes clause 36 the first likely to be adopted at Westminster.

Clause 37 is the last clause of the Parliament Bill, 1910.

LIST OF BOOKS.

KING, J.—Electoral Reform: an Enquiry into our System of Parliamentary Representation. 1908. Unwin. 2s. 6d. net.

MacDONALD, J. R.—Socialism and Government. 1909. I.L.P., 23 Bride Lane, E.C. 2s. and 3s. net.

Report of Royal Commission on Electoral Systems. Cd. 5163, 1910. 6½d.

Reports from His Majesty's Representatives in Foreign Countries and in British Colonies respecting the Application of the Principle of Proportional Representation to Public Elections. Cd. 3501. 1907. 1s. 3d.

Table of Existing Laws as to Payment of Members of Legislatures.

COUNTRY.	PAYMENT TO MEMBERS OF LEGISLATURE.	OTHER ALLOWANCES.
AUSTRIA	16s. 8d. per day while the House is in session.	Travelling expenses paid
BELGIUM	Deputies receive 4,000 francs (£160) per year.	Free travelling on State railways. Free travelling on private railways between residence aud capital.
BAVARIA	Members of Upper House are unpaid. Deputies receive 10s. per day during session.	Free railway travelling during session and eight days before and after.
BULGARIA ...	Members of National Assembly living in capital receive 12s. per day during session ; members resident out of capital receive 16s. per day, which includes travelling expenses.	
DENMARK ...	Members receive 11s. 1d. per day during the first six months of the session and 6s. 8d. per day for every additional day.	Free railway travelling (second class).
FRANCE	Senators and deputies receive £600 per year.	An annual payment of £2 entitles members of both Chambers to travel free on all railways.
GERMANY ...	Members of the Reichstag receive £150 per year. A sum of £1 is deducted for each day's absence.	Free railway travelling during session.
GREECE	Deputies are paid £72 for each ordinary session. For an extraordinary session only travelling expenses are allowed, but reimbursements for extra expenses, varying from £60 to £80, are generally voted.	Free railway and steamship travelling during session.
HUNGARY ...	Members of the Lower House receive £200 per year, with £66 13s. for house rent.	
ITALY	Members are not paid.	Free railway travelling and postage.
NETHERLANDS	Members of the First Chamber not residing at the Hague are paid 16s. 8d. per day while in session. Members of the Second Chamber receive £166 per year.	Free railway travelling.

Country.	Payment to Members of Legislature.	Other Allowances.
Norway	All members of the Storthing receive 13s. 4d. per day during session.	Travelling expenses as follows : 2½d. per kilometre for pony or cariole. 5d. per kilometre for rowboats. 1¾d. per kilometre for train. 5d. per sea mile for steamers. Free medical attendance during session. Funeral expenses paid if member dies during session.
Portugal	Colonial deputies receive £20 per month while the Cortes is sitting and £10 per month at other times. Ordinary deputies have been unpaid since 1892.	
Prussia	Members receive 15s. per day during session.	
Roumania	Deputies receive 16s. 8d. per day of actual attendance during session.	Free railway travelling.
Russia	Elective members of the Council of the Empire receive during the session £2 13s. per day. Members of the Duma receive £1 13s. per day during the session.	Free railway travelling to and from St. Petersburg.
Saxony	Members of both Houses resident in capital receive 6s. per day during the session. Other members receive 12s. per day and travelling allowance.	
Servia	Deputies receive 12s. per day during session.	Travelling allowance.
Spain	Neither senators nor deputies are paid.	
Sweden	Members of both Chambers receive £66 for each session of four months and 11s. per day for an extra session.	Travelling expenses paid
Switzerland	Members of the National Council and Council of States receive 16s. 8d. per day during session.	Travelling expenses paid at rate of 20 centimes per kilometre (2½d. per mile).
United States	All members of Congress receive $7,500 (£1,500) per year.	Travelling allowance of 20 cents (10d.) per mile.

COUNTRY.	PAYMENT TO MEMBERS OF LEGISLATURE.		OTHER ALLOWANCES.
UNITED STATES (*continued*)			Senators allowed $2,000 (£400) per year for clerical assistance ; congressmen allowed $1,500 (£300) per year. All members allowed $125 (£25) per year for stationery. Free postage. Private room (furnished, lighted, and heated free) provided in Congressional official building for each member. Free seed samples from Agricultural Department for farmer constituents, etc.
WURTEMBERG	Members of both Chambers receive 15s. per day.		Free railway travelling.
CANADA	Members of Senate and House of Commons receive £500 each session of more than 30 days. If session lasts less than thirty days, £4 per day is paid. The leader of the opposition receives £1,400 per year extra.		Travelling expenses paid
AUSTRALIAN COMMONWLTH	Members receive £600 per year.		Free travelling on Government railways.
VICTORIA	Members of Legislative Council (Upper House) are unpaid. Members of Legislative Assembly (Lower House) receive £300 per year.		Ditto Ditto
QUEENSLAND ...	Ditto	Ditto	Ditto Ditto
NEW SOUTH WALES	Ditto	Ditto	Ditto Ditto
SOUTH AUSTRALIA	Members of each House receive £200 per year.		Ditto Ditto
WESTERN AUSTRALIA	Ditto	Ditto	Ditto Ditto
TASMANIA ...	Members of each House receive £100 per year.		Ditto Ditto
NEW ZEALAND	Members of Legislative Council (Upper House) receive £200 per year. Members of House of Representatives (Lower House) receive £300 per year.		Ditto Ditto

FABIAN SOCIETY.—The Fabian Society consists of Socialists. A statement of its Rules and the following publications can be obtained from the Secretary, at the Fabian Office, 3 Clement's Inn, London, W.C.

FABIAN ESSAYS IN SOCIALISM. New Preface by BERNARD SHAW. Paper 6d. net; cloth 1/6; postage 2½d. and 4d.

WHAT TO READ on Social and Economic Subjects. Fifth edition, revised to October, 1910, and enlarged. Interleaved, paper, 1s. n. cloth 2s. n., post. 2d.

THIS MISERY OF BOOTS. By H. G. WELLS. 3d., post free 4d.

TRACT INDEX AND CATALOGUE RAISONNÉ. 3d.

FABIAN TRACTS and LEAFLETS.

Tracts, each 16 to 52 pp., price 1d., or 9d. per dos., unless otherwise stated.
Leaflets, 4 pp. each, price 1d. for six copies, 1s. per 100, or 8/6 per 1000.

The Set of 78, 3s.; post free 3/5. Bound in Buckram, 4/6 n.; post free 5s.

I.—General Socialism in its various aspects.

TRACTS.—151. The Point of Honour: a Correspondence on Aristocracy and Socialism. By RUTH CAVENDISH BENTINCK. 147. Capital and Compensation. By EDW. R. PEASE. 146. Socialism and Superior Brains. A reply to Mr. Mallock. By BERNARD SHAW. 142. Rent and Value. 138. Municipal Trading. 121. Public Service versus Private Expenditure. By Sir OLIVER LODGE. 113. Communism. By WM. MORRIS. 107. Socialism for Millionaires. By BERNARD SHAW. 139. Socialism and the Churches. By Rev. JOHN CLIFFORD, D.D. 133. Socialism and Christianity. By Rev. PERCY DEARMER (in cover with portrait of the author). 78. Socialism and the Teaching of Christ. By Dr. J. CLIFFORD. 42. Christian Socialism. By Rev. S. D. HEADLAM. 79. A Word of Remembrance and Caution to the Rich. By JOHN WOOLMAN. 75. Labor in the Longest Reign. By S. WEBB. 72. The Moral Aspects of Socialism. By SIDNEY BALL. 69. Difficulties of Individualism. By SIDNEY WEBB. 51. Socialism: True and False. By S. WEBB. 45. The Impossibilities of Anarchism. By BERNARD SHAW (price 2d.). 7. Capital and Land (7th edn. revised 1908). 5. Facts for Socialists (11th ed., revised 1908). 132. A Guide to Books for Socialists. LEAFLETS—13. What Socialism Is. 1. Why are the Many Poor? WELSH TRACTS—143. Sosialaeth yng Ngoleuni'r Beibl. Gan J. R. JONES (Caernarfon). 141. Translation of 139. 87. Translation of 78. 38. Translation of 1.

II.—Applications of Socialism to Particular Problems.

TRACTS.—152. Our Taxes as they are and as they ought to be. By ROBT. JONES, B.Sc. In cover, 2d. 150. State Purchase of Railways. By EMIL DAVIES. In cover, 2d. 149. The Endowment of Motherhood. By H. D. HARBEN. In cover, 2d. 145. The Case for School Nurseries. By Mrs. TOWNSHEND. 144. Machinery: its Masters and its Servants. By H. H. SCHLOESSER and C. GAME. 140. Child Labor under Capitalism. By Mrs. HYLTON DALE. 136. The Village and the Landlord. By EDW. CARPENTER. 131. The Decline in the Birth-Rate. By S. WEBB. 130. Home Work and Sweating. By Miss B.L. HUTCHINS. 128. The Case for a Legal Minimum Wage. 122. Municipal Milk and Public Health. By Dr. F. LAWSON DODD. 125. Municipalization by Provinces. 119. Public Control of Electrical Power and Transit. 123. The Revival of Agriculture. 118. The Secret of Rural Depopulation. 115. State Aid to Agriculture: an Example. 112. Life in the Laundry. 98. State Railways for Ireland. 124. State Control of Trusts. 86. Municipal Drink Traffic. 84. Economics of Direct Employment. 83. State Arbitration and the Living Wage. LEAFLET.—104. How Trade Unions benefit Workmen.

III.—Local Government Powers : How to use them.

TRACTS.—137. Parish Councils and Village Life. 109. Cottage Plans and Common Sense. By RAYMOND UNWIN. 76. Houses for the People. 99. Local Government in Ireland. 82. Workmen's Compensation Act. New edition for the Act of 1906. 62. Parish and District Councils. 54. The Humanizing of the Poor Law. By J. F. OAKESHOTT. LEAFLETS.—134. Small Holdings, Allotments and Common Pastures: and how to get them. 20. Questions for Poor Law Guardians. 68. The Tenant's Sanitary Catechism. 71. Ditto for London. FABIAN MUNICIPAL LEAFLETS (Nos. 32, 37 and 90 to 93). Municipalization of the Gas Supply. A Labor Policy for Public Authorities. Municipalization of Milk Supply. Municipal Pawnshops. Municipal Slaughterhouses. Women as Councillors. 1/- per 100.

IV. –General Politics and Fabian Policy.

127. Socialism and Labor Policy. 116. Fabianism and the Fiscal Question: an alternative policy. 108. Twentieth Century Politics. By

Fabian Tract No. 154.

THE
CASE FOR SCHOOL CLINICS.

BY

L. HADEN GUEST, M.R.C.S. (Eng.)
L.R.C.P. (Lond.)

PUBLISHED AND SOLD BY

THE FABIAN SOCIETY.

PRICE ONE PENNY.

LONDON:
THE FABIAN SOCIETY, 3 CLEMENT'S INN, STRAND, W.C.
MARCH 1911.

THE CASE FOR SCHOOL CLINICS.

*Reprinted with additions and corrections by the courtesy of the
"Daily News."*

IF we were really a practical nation instead of an obscurantist nation, we should do some very simple things for school children. We should, to begin with, treat them as individual boys and girls and not as administrative units, with the possibility of a decimal point thrown in. The things that children need are known to very many thousands of English men and women ; they comprise good food, good clothing, good housing, and loving care. In educational matters educationists are so far agreed that in a genuinely representative congress, expressing unfettered opinions, there would be no serious differences of opinion on essentials. But we are not a practical nation, and I do not propose to discuss the detail of these practical things. There is a huge gap between what we know how to do and what we immediately proceed to do on any extensive scale. The why and wherefore of this is another matter ; at present my concern is with the things that we can immediately proceed to do for the school child.

On the roundabout route by which we approach common sense, the medical inspection of school children is a long step. By this inspection the problem is displayed and made graphic before our eyes. Before medical inspection theorists could argue ad infinitum, after medical inspection the argument must at least centre round the facts discovered.

What Inspection Shows.

The main subdivisions and groupings of children which medical inspection enables us to make, are, broadly speaking, the same for all schools. In every school the bulk of the children show an average health which is comparatively satisfactory. And among the children presenting defects of mind and physique there are two main groups. In both of these medical defects are present, but in the one the family circumstances are average or above the average, in the other group the circumstances are below the average. The first may be said to present simply medical defects, the second medical defects plus poverty.

The children who are average must not be thought by any means to be satisfactory. The average of one school is of necessity made for that school, and applies to the particular children drawn from the homes round about it. The average of a school in a slum neighborhood would be below the average for a school in a district of well-paid artizans. In London, for instance, parts of Lambeth may be well below parts of Battersea.

The average is in no case very high, in the London County Council schools three decayed teeth are charted as normal, many slight eye defects, many slight degrees of feeble nutrition, and many slight deformities are "normal." None the less these things are handicaps in schoolwork, and in after life. Such average children are very "average" in general capacity, in character, and in grasp of the duties of citizenship and of their part in life.

To raise the average of child life in all schools to the level of the school with the highest average among children drawn from the same social stratum, to raise the average of all slum schools to the average of the best slum school, is a non-utopian ideal with a very concrete measure of its success, which we might well adopt into our municipal politics.

The problem of the average child is largely a problem for the statesman and social reformer ; medical knowledge has made the problem concrete and definite, and can suggest some needed reforms. But the problem of the child with defects, whether purely medical or medical plus poverty, is predominantly a doctor's question.

The Medical Group and the Poverty Group.

The division into two groups is important from the standpoint of treatment. The purely medical cases can get cured comparatively easily, the poverty cases only with difficulty. To treat a child with obstructed breathing and adenoids who is otherwise fairly sound and who comes from a decent home, is simple, and cure is probable. The parents of such a child will take trouble to see that the defect is remedied when it is pointed out to them. The decent home and the child's fairly sound condition are an indication that the parents have the desire and probably the time to see that proper treatment is applied. In every large town and accessible for most small towns and villages there are hospitals and dispensaries supplying facilities for treatment which can be taken advantage of by those having the desire and the time to do so. On the whole the great bulk of children presenting medical defects pure and simple will have those defects attended to by existing institutions when the parents become aware of what is needed. In this respect medical inspection puts the child of the poor man on a level with the child of the rich man, by giving him an expert opinion on what should be done to put the child in the fittest possible condition. Medical inspection does a great work if it makes medical knowledge available to the parents of all children.

Difficulty of the Poverty Group.

In the case of children presenting medical defects plus poverty, the case is far different. To begin with, such children often present not one or two but a group of defects, and complicated and continuous treatment may be required. The general condition of such children is not good, and the children do not give good results from treatment. Discharging ears in a badly nourished poor child for instance, take longer to get well than in a decently nourished average child. But, worst of all, the parents of such poor children do not take them for medical treatment. Sometimes the parents will not take them—these, I think, are the rarer cases—sometimes the parents do not think medical treatment necessary, these are commoner cases. Sometimes the parents cannot spare time to get the children treated. This last class is as large as either of the two others, and may in certain localities be larger. In the first group come the children from drunken and vicious homes, in the second from feckless homes, in the third from overworked and underworked homes. We might call them the vicious, the feckless, and the poor homes.

The remedy for these conditions lies outside the scope of school organization, but the recognition of the existence of these conditions is very much a matter for school authorities. For the plain A B C of the facts is this, that it is no use treating defects of nose and throat, eye and ear, unless you treat the underlying debility of constitution produced by the home conditions. That means remedial school feeding firstly and open-air schools, school baths and gymnasia among other things as secondary methods. This state of things means also a new organization for getting the children treated.

It may, in theory, be highly desirable to " insist " on the parents getting remedied the defects pointed out to them by medical inspection. In practice the parents will either not do so, or only pretend to do so, for in the matter of getting treatment it is fatally easy to pretend. If the poverty group children are to have their illnesses and ailments remedied, they will have to be (a) fed on a diet designed to improve their physique, and (b) sent to hospital or school clinic in charge of someone from the school by the authority of the school.

The home conditions of such children also need tackling ; the necessity of open windows and soap and water need pointing out, and all kinds of complicated little details need discussing with the parents. These are the duties of the care committee, but if they are to be effectively carried out, if remedial feeding is to become a reality instead of a pretence, and if medical defects are to be cured, there is only one effective way of doing these things—all of these activities must centre round a school clinic. And the school clinic, the school doctors, and the school nurses must be as much a part of the school organization as the school teachers.

The average children in council schools (who are nevertheless below the standard of their own possibilities), and the children with medical defects only, may be put aside for the moment ; the children with defects plus poverty are an urgent problem demanding instant attention.

The Morass of Destitution.

Children belonging to the poverty group, as already defined, are the children sprung from the morass of destitution which quakes and shivers around the foundations of our civilization. These children come from definitely localized neighborhoods, from particular streets, and from special blocks of "model" dwellings. The poverty of destitution and demoralization is spotted over the surface of our towns as concretely as smallpox is spotted over the face of a man sick from this disease. The poverty spots are, however, mouths of the abyss into which human life and our civilization sink away out of sight of man. And to children coming from the poverty spots, it is no use giving a box of ointment or a bottle of lotion to cure their diseases ; these things make no impression thrown into the abyss.

A mother equipped with patience, the desire of cleanliness, and the wish for health, may get some good out of a hospital out patient department, even if the interview accorded by the doctor after hours of waiting be very brief. The mother from the demoralized poverty spot, even if she does arrive at the hospital, will get usually no help of which she can avail herself.

The doctor's point of view needs to be considered. A busy man, seeing very many similar cases, giving very frequently the same instructions, and meeting constantly with the same failure to get those instructions adequately carried out, may sometimes get a little hopeless as to the value of his out patient work.

A Typical Slum Mother.

The advent of a typical slum (poverty spot) mother increases the doctor's feeling of hopelessness ten or twentyfold. Take a concrete case, that of a child with discharge from the ears. The mother of the case I have in mind is a person with tattered, frowsy, and safety-pinned raiment, conforming generally to the blouse and skirt type ; the sleeves are torn to a conveniently free length, the waist is commodiously ample. Neither face nor hands are especially clean, the face is coarse in feature and grinningly amiable. Conversation reveals much surface plausibility, with much genuine and deep laid sloth and inertia. The home is in two or three dark, semi-basement rooms, low, hung with lines on which hang flapping clothes, cumbered with backless chairs, decayed tables, peeling veneer chests of drawers, and iron bedsteads heaped with brownish coverings.

Is it wonderful that, faced by the problem of treating the child of such a mother, living in such a home, the doctor may get a little despairing? Treatment which consists partly of syringing out the ears must inevitably fail of being carried out under cleanly conditions (aseptic is pure utopianism). Regularity is not understood ; any directions given, except with the most labored simplicity, are not understood. For unexplained reasons such a patient will frequently not attend to see the doctor and report progress. For other unexplained reasons the patient will try "a bottle of medicine" from some private dispensary or from some other public institution. On other occasions the patient will attend in charge of an incompetent person to whom it is useless to give instructions and from whom it is impossible to expect reasonable information. In the particular instance the person in charge was sometimes a drunken grandmother, and once or twice a sister only a year or two older than the patient.

In such cases it may be possible to get parental consent to an operation for removal of tonsils or adenoids. That involves very little trouble to the parents, and is besides by way of being fashionable, and has proved of benefit to neighboring children. But an operation is the first part of the treatment and not the end. A child operated upon needs medical supervision and careful training before it may be pronounced cured. And this supervision and training it does not get.

Deeper Deeps.

The case cited above is by no means an especially bad one; it may even be thought to belong to the aristocracy of the poverty group. It is still possible to treat a child of this kind by the united effort of school nurse, school teachers, school doctor, dispensary doctor, with the casual intervention of the clergyman, the district visitor, and a member of the care committee. But there are many children beyond these agencies. There is (I take examples at random as they occur to me from my own experience) the case of the blind woman, a widow, with verminous and ringworm smitten children. Medical treatment comes and goes, according to the aberrations of the patient's mother, but the conditions persist. To expostulate with such a woman for sewing her child's clothing tightly upon its back is to get a glib explanation (glaringly denied by the conditions) that this is done regularly every night after the equally regular bath. Nevertheless, however glaringly obvious the condition, the cure is not obvious under existing circumstances. To give a complete outfit of clean clothes is no remedy; it has been tried more than once and failed.

Another case is that of a child attending a school for mental defectives. The school nurse noticed the discharging ears, and managed, after considerable trouble with minor arrangements, to get the child specially medically examined. At the examination the mother stated that the child was "under treatment." This, it appeared, meant one attendance in six weeks at a hospital out patient department, where she was given some lotion and some rapid and half-comprehended instructions. The mother then consented for a special arrangement to be made whereby the child was to be sent from school to a public dispensary every day, in order that the ears might be properly syringed out and attended to by a nurse. The school doctor gave the mother a letter for the school teacher to the effect that the mother agreed to this, to be given to the school teacher by the child. Three days afterwards a teacher called on the dispensary doctor to enquire when treatment might begin, as she had heard about it from the nurse. It then appeared that the letter had not been delivered. Another teacher then visited the child's home and secured the school doctor's letter. "It had been forgotten." After this the child attended at the dispensary most days, but never on Saturdays, when it "minded the baby." As soon as the summer vacation began, the child also ceased attending. After the summer holiday the ears, which were in a most serious and foul condition, were found just as bad as they ever had been. The same thing occurred at the Christmas vacation. And these measures taken to get treatment were quite independent of numerous official letters and enquiries about the child, involving the labor of clerks and other officials on a fruitless task.

Even when with great and, compared with the results, disproportionate exertion, such a child has been cured of one definite ailment, it very often presents another. Frequently a poverty group child shows more than one defect, often several defects, and the cure of one may leave the others unaffected. While the cure of all definite ailments may still leave the groundwork of anæmia and a debilitated constitution unaffected. To get a poverty group child into a good state of health often involves prolonged and expensive treatment, one or more operations on ear, glands in the neck, tonsils or adenoids, a stay in hospital and at a convalescent home, and perhaps a prolonged three to six months holiday in some country cottage, all of which means much money and very much expenditure of time and energy.

The Necessity of the School Clinic.

To continue the present methods of dealing with the poverty group children is to perpetuate the diseases and defects from which they suffer. Nothing but a special organization to meet the special case will be of any great service. What is done at present is of immense help in ameliorating disease, in easing pain, in keeping the worse worst conditions from spreading too widely ; but what is done at present is costly, cumbrous, involves great labor, and effects little permanent result, in the poverty group often none.

When medical treatment is as much a part of the school work as manual training or housewifery, then it will have a chance to be effective. The educated observation of the teacher will be at hand and at the doctor's disposal to supplement the haphazard observation of the parent, the report of the school medical inspector and the observation of the school nurse will be available, and the machinery of the school organization, with school nurse, attendance officer, and children's care committee, will be able to be used for the purpose of carrying out necessary instructions in the home and out of school hours. In a word, instead of endeavoring to treat an ailing child by the agency of half a dozen badly co-ordinated or entirely separate institutions, with no effective grip anywhere, we shall be treating the same ailment as a part of the school life, with the necessary means entirely at our disposal, and with all the other agencies adequately co-ordinated and properly effective.

All the activities controlled and directed by the care committee should be worked in the closest co-operation with the school clinic. This is especially true of the provision of meals for necessitous children, but it is also true of the provision of boots and of clothing and of the arrangement of country holidays.

In describing the suggested organization of the school clinic I am relying on my experience at the St. George's Dispensary in Blackfriars, where for some time past the medical staff have been experimenting in the direction of the school clinic. The patients at this dispensary are women, school children, and infants; the dispensary is free to those too poor to pay for medical advice, and some 6,000 patients, a large number of whom are school children, are seen every year. This figure probably represents the full number of patients who can be seen in the space available and during the time the doctors are in attendance.

Judging from this experience and that of others who have been pioneering on school clinic lines, one gets a very actual view of the conditions to be met.

The Clinic Required.

In every thickly populated locality schools are built fairly close to each other, and fall into groups. To supply the need of such a group only one clinic is required, and may well serve for sixteen or twenty schools, with a school population of something under a thousand each.

To start a clinic the first necessity is to find a convenient building situated in the centre of the group, or as near this as may be. It is desirable, especially for small children, to have the clinic not more than twenty minutes' walk from any school. Greater distances are inconvenient, and much smaller distances highly desirable. The St. George's Dispensary is established in an old public house less than ten minutes' walk from nearly a dozen schools.

A clinic must have a large waiting-room, one or two rooms for consultation with the doctor, and a room for treatments and dressing by the nurse.

A doctor should be in attendance at the clinic during school hours, and the head teachers of the schools belonging to the group should send there, in charge of the school nurse or other responsible person, all the children who are to have treatment. These children will be roughly those of the poverty group, but they will also include cases of discharging ears and other chronic ailments which need daily care, and cannot be attended to at a hospital. The children sent to the clinic would be normally those examined by the school doctor, whose parents were recommended to get them treatment, but who failed to obtain it on their own initiative, after a reasonable period, say a month. In some acute and urgent cases the clinic should render first aid, as it were, and the teachers should be encouraged to send children for examination whenever there was uncertainty as to its condition.

A Sorting Out Centre.

When a medical inspection of a school is made the defects discovered fall into very definite classes. Among them some children, for instance, will have defects of vision, some obstruction at the back of the nose caused by adenoids, some have discharging ears, and others threatening or incipient phthisis. Which of these ailments can the school clinic properly treat? Partly this must depend upon the situation of the clinic. If it is near to a good special hospital for eye diseases or for those of nose, throat, or any other special ailments, and if satisfactory arrangements can be made for treatment at that hospital, then it is a waste of energy to multiply treatment centres. But the clinic should always reserve to itself the power to treat any kind of case in the event of a child for any reason failing to go to the special hospital. This does not mean that a recalcitrant eye case should be treated at the clinic, but that the child not getting treatment should be sent to the clinic and arrangements made, through the clinic organization, for the special treatment needed. All that is often wanted, when parents refuse or fail to get the suggested treatment, is a medical talk, giving them information or reassuring them about some not understood medical mystery.

This hypothetical instance gives the key to the line of treatment which must be adopted. The clinic will be the organization which sees that the child gets treatment. A large number of cases, those of diseases of ear, nose, and throat, many skin diseases, chest troubles, digestive troubles, and others, would be actually treated at the clinic. But the very severe ear trouble would be sent to hospital, the serious phthisis to the sanatorium, and the serious bone tuberculosis to the special hospital. The clinic, in fact, while acting as a treatment centre for those defects and diseases which can be con-veniently and economically treated in an institution fitted up in a simple and inexpensive way, would also act as a sorting centre, and draft off serious and special cases to the institution where their appropriate treatment could be obtained.

Co-operation with Hospitals.

The school clinic should work in the closest co-operation with the hospitals and dispensaries, and have standing arrangements whereby certain classes of cases could be sent direct to them as soon as discovered. Some of the arrangements made at present with hospitals for treatment would fit in well. This means in practice that the clinics would only need the simplest apparatus, and that for the complex cases the costly and elaborate hospital organization would be made use of.

Existing Clinics.

In Germany, of course, school clinics for the treatment of all varieties of school diseases have been in existence for some years, with the greatest possible benefit to the health of the children con-cerned. But it is not necessary to go to Germany for examples. These institutions are in existence already in various towns in England, the Board of Education having power to sanction their establishment under section 13 of the Education (Administrative Provisions) Act, 1907, under which medical inspection is carried on. In London voluntary agencies have established clinics at Bow, Deptford, and Blackfriars. In Cambridge a dental clinic established on a voluntary basis has now been taken over by the municipality and is run as a publicly supported institution. In London a dental clinic is working at Deptford on two afternoons a week, and one is being established, as the result of a private experiment, to work on five afternoons a week at the St. George's Dispensary, Blackfriars. Bradford, Brighton, Sheffield, Southampton and York are among other towns where school clinic treatment is provided. The clinic at Bradford is open six days a week and treats children requiring spectacles, skin diseases, including X-ray treatment for ringworm, children referred from medical inspection, and for admission to special schools, including open-air schools, cases of discharging ears (syringed daily by the nurses), and children who have been in contact with, or are recovering from, infectious disease. At Bradford the clinic is found not to interfere with ordinary medical practice, and it is significant in this respect that a clinic has been established at Wandsworth, under the auspices of the local branch of the British Medical Association, and a treatment centre opened in Hampstead under the control of local medical practitioners. Probably the London County Council will be forced by pressure of circumstances to establish clinics in lieu of their present hospital system, a sub-committee of the Education Committee having reported strongly in favor of the system in 1908.

Part of the reason for the establishment of school clinics lies in the fact that without them the large poverty group of ailing children cannot be adequately treated because their parents have not time to, cannot, or will not, take their children to private doctors or hospitals. Nevertheless a clinic may look forward to frequent visits from the parents and every possible endeavor should be made to get the parents to attend. There are very few of even the most demoralized slum dwellers who do not wish to do what they can for the good of their children. But when not only means, but all knowledge is lacking, it is idle to expect the observance of hygienic common sense. Many parents who cannot afford to wait for a whole morning or afternoon, or even the larger part of a day at a hospital, could manage to get to the clinic if a definite hour was fixed.

The Clinic and Common Sense Hygiene.

The clinic should, in fact, become the instruction centre for parents in the art of hygiene, the concrete examples being provided by their own children's ailments. Such concrete hygiene teaching, supplemented, perhaps, by special demonstrations and talks for parents—on the care of the teeth, on breathing and on feeding, for instance—would do more for slum districts and poverty spots than years of abstract lectures in evening schools, admirable as these are.

Above all the clinic must be simple, straightforward, and human. A laughing and a smiling child should be the rule, a solemn or a weeping child the exception. The doctors' and nurses' rooms should be places of happiness and kindliness. In this way the confidence of child and parent will be gained easily, treatment will be facilitated and the parents will try to obey and understand rules of treat-

,ment and hygiene. In my own experience I have met very few people incapable of following simple hygienic and medical instructions.

The Clinic and Poverty.

In the preceding paragraphs I sketched the organization of the school clinic on its medical side, and indicated how it would deal with medically and surgically remediable ailments and defects. But among the poverty group children the worst disease, upon which the others do indeed largely depend, is poverty itself. Lack of boots, lack of clothing, and lack of food are not matters which the doctor can professionally remedy. But the school clinic should work in the closest touch with the care committee, and when the doctor has done all that is possible to put the ailing child straight from his point of view, the care committee agency must be called in to remedy poverty defects which otherwise would render (and do now render under present circumstances) all the medical labor in vain. The underfed child must be fed, the underclothed child clothed. The doctor will certify what social factors are likely to cause or allow a relapse of the illness or defect, and it must be the business of the care committee to take precautions accordingly.

Remedial Feeding.

This will mean in practice that the care committee must have a fund for supplying the needs of school clinic cases. The committee must go even further. The chief need of poverty group children often is carefully adjusted feeding, adjusted, that is, to their damaged and deteriorated digestive systems. This remedial feeding will inevitably be an important part of the school clinic's prescriptions, and will have to be something very different from the present haphazard meals, frequently all that is now provided under the Provision of Meals Act. These meals will be framed on the lines of a medical prescription, and might well (in some cases, at least) be distributed on the plan used by the excellent invalid kitchen in Southwark, which provides meals of different kinds to suit invalid digestions.

Used in this way it will be essential to see that the meal serves its purpose of feeding the child adequately and not of merely staving off starvation. If the school meal was improved so as to become a really physiologically good meal, it would be unnecessary to have invalid cookery for special cases. If the meals are not so improved, it is difficult to see how otherwise the proper feeding of ailing and debilitated poor children is to be obtained.

When one turns from feeding to consider the question of boots and clothes, it is clear that very much requires to be done. A school clinic will have only one answer to the conundrum as to whether it is better to treat recurrent attacks of bronchitis and throat trouble or provide a stout pair of boots and warm clothing. The drug bill and the bill of salaries and general expenses will be balanced against a bill for clothes and boots, and found to be much heavier. The bill is heavier now, but different pockets pay the different bills ; and the hospitals that appeal for subscriptions do not consider it part of their duty to prevent the need for some of their work by subsidizing boot and clothing clubs for schools ; nor would they, as long as they are separated institutions, do much good by their subsidies, if given.

Country Holidays.

It is the same with another important aspect of care committee work, that of providing for country holidays. The knowledge gained at the school clinic will be of immense help in determining what children need this kind of holiday and what that. At the present time the question of country holidays and of convalescence after illness or sanatorium treatment are in a rather unorganized condition. Multitudes of children who would benefit by country holidays do not get them, many children who need seaside convalescence or sanatorium treatment do not get it, while, at the same time, financially unsuitable children are allowed to take advantage of charities which are needed by others less well able to pay. The conditions at present are unavoidable, but a school clinic would make it easier to apply the charities to the best result. Given, then, that the care committee is working in close touch with the doctors, it should be possible to arrange for the optimum use of the agencies at the committee's disposal and probably for the holidaying of all those children whose condition urgently required it, and especially those threatened with tuberculosis.

Very much valuable work is done by voluntary and paid health visitors, who endeavor by home visits and by plain talks to impress on the homes of poor people the common sense lessons of modern hygiene. The school clinic will do much to fortify and reinforce this health missionary work. For the clinic will not only act as a centre, a rallying point, and a reference on all questions connected with the health of the school child, but it will train the children and the parents themselves as health missionaries on their own account. As I have before mentioned, the discussion of a practical point of hygiene, say, that of open windows or of personal cleanliness, becomes not only concrete, but vital, when it is discussed with the parents with the ailment or delicacy of a beloved child as its object lesson. The lesson (it is a way with lessons) may have to be repeated, but ultimately it will be effective. A school clinic properly conducted should spread principles of hygiene very rapidly throughout its district.

The Main Points.

I have above pointed out how the school clinic will enable all cases of ailment or defect in school children to be adequately treated, how it will link the school organization with the present school doctors and school nurses and with the special and general hospitals.

How, again, all the activities which have to do with feeding, clothing, holidaying, and convalescence may be naturally grouped and co-ordinated with the clinic's medical work. And how, further, the activity of the clinic and its co-ordinated helpers will stretch outside the clinic, outside the school, and penetrate by means of its missionaries into the home itself, bringing the sweetness and light of health to the parents of school children (particularly of the poverty group), clothed in the garb of their own thoughts and ideas, and exemplified by the occurrences of their daily lives.

Nothing here suggested is utopian, nothing advocated is more than the grouping together of isolated and unco-ordinated practical activities already existing in one form or another. The school clinic, by medically studying the child, provides the natural centre and rallying point for all these activities. The agencies which are now working in a scattered and unco-ordinated way for the helping of school children will be centralized by the clinic, organized, and made a hundred per cent. more effective than they can now be. And we may hope for great and almost unrealizable changes when the school clinic pours out health and help and kindliness in every congested and poor district, for then the growth of child life, which now sinks down into the abyss, will spring up and grow healthily into the light and air of good human existence.

Pure Utopianism.

What I have spoken of above is practical to-day; that which follows will not be "practical" until to-morrow, when some of the preliminary work of clearing out the awful morass of slum child life shall have been performed. To-day it is only a dream, a dream of the time when the child at school shall grow as sweetly and as happily as a flower in a garden, when it shall stretch up its mind for knowledge as a flower for sunlight, and when all the strange and impish deformities and etiolations medical inspectors have to catalogue are relegated to infrequent hospitals and sanatoria with but very few beds in their wards.

The school clinic will aim to get the level of all children up to the low "average" or "normal" of the relatively healthy in present council schools, and when that is accomplished we can begin our real work of devising means whereby that low, that all too low, average may be transcended; the lethargic body grow supple, nimble, and good to look upon; the dulled senses quick, true, and responsive; and the narrow mind actively growing and expanding. All these things are within the sphere of the school doctor, all these things are within the scope of present day medical knowledge. The knowledge is here in reality; it is only the accomplishment in fact that is in Utopia—to-morrow.

In the good time when the poverty group child has grown into a sound average and the present average become robust, I look forward to a new kind of standard being introduced in schools—standards of imagination. In the present day children are only sent to the doctor when they are obviously deaf, or blind, or halt, or maimed. In the future the tests will be more subtle, and I confidently anticipate the time when "Peter Pan" or "The Blue Bird," or some such fairy tale, will be a compulsory subject of the ordinary council school curriculum. At that day any child failing to reach, at any rate, the "Peter Pan" standard of imagination will promptly be sent to the school clinic. It is, after all, a rather serious reflection that there are many thousand "average" children to-day who do not reach this level.

The first step towards the raising of the standard must be taken by raising the lowest, and by pouring so much health, help, and kindliness into the poverty group children that their all too low grade finally disappears.

BIBLIOGRAPHY.

Report M.O. (Education), L.C.C., p. 52, 1907 ; p. 21, 1908 ; p. 41, 1909.

Report M.O., Dunfermline, 1909.

Medical Inspection of Schools. DR. HOGARTH. Henry Frowde. 1909. 6s.

Medical Supervision in Schools. E. M. STEVENS. Ballière, Tindal & Cox. 1910.

Medical Inspection of Schools and Scholars. Edited by T. N. KELYNACH, M.D.
    P. S. King. 1910. 10s.

Treatment of School Children. R. H. CROWLEY, M.D. Methuen. 1910. 3s. 6d.

Public Health, 1909, p. 462, "A School Clinic for Contagious Skin Diseases."

    „   „   1910, p. 120, "Treatment of Teeth in Public Elementary Schools in
        relation to Public Health."

    „   „   1910, p. 295, "The Need for School Clinics for Defective Eyesight."

    „   „   1910, p. 370, "Report on School Clinics."

    „   „   1911, p. 226, "Administrative Control of Ringworm."

"A Plea for School Clinics." MARGARET MCMILLAN. *Progress*, October, 1909,
    p. 243.

FABIAN SOCIETY.—The Fabian Society consists of Socialists. A statement of its Rules and the following publications can be obtained from the Secretary, at the Fabian Office, 3 Clement's Inn, London, W.C.

FABIAN ESSAYS IN SOCIALISM. New Preface by BERNARD SHAW. Paper 6d. net; cloth 1/6; postage 2½d. and 4d.

WHAT TO READ on Social and Economic Subjects. Fifth edition, revised to October, 1910, and enlarged. Interleaved, paper, 1s. n. cloth 2s. n., post. 2d.

THIS MISERY OF BOOTS. By H. G. WELLS. 3d., post free 4d.

FABIAN TRACTS and LEAFLETS.

Tracts, each 16 to 52 pp., price 1d., or 9d. per doz., unless otherwise stated.

Leaflets, 4 pp. each, price 1d. for six copies, 1s. per 100, or 8/6 per 1000.

The Set of 78, 3s.; post free 3/5. Bound in Buckram, 4/6 n.; post free 5s.

I.—General Socialism in its various aspects.

TRACTS.—151. The Point of Honour: a Correspondence on Aristocracy and Socialism. By RUTH CAVENDISH BENTINCK. 147. Capital and Compensation. By EDW. R. PEASE. 146. Socialism and Superior Brains. A reply to Mr. Mallock. By BERNARD SHAW. 142. Rent and Value. 138. Municipal Trading. 121. Public Service versus Private Expenditure. By Sir OLIVER LODGE. 113. Communism. By WM. MORRIS. 107. Socialism for Millionaires. By BERNARD SHAW. 139. Socialism and the Churches. By Rev. JOHN CLIFFORD, D.D 133. Socialism and Christianity. By Rev. PERCY DEARMER (in cover with portrait of the author). 78. Socialism and the Teaching of Christ. By Dr. J. CLIFFORD. 42. Christian Socialism. By Rev. S. D. HEADLAM. 79. A Word of Remembrance and Caution to the Rich. By JOHN WOOLMAN. 75. Labor in the Longest Reign. By S. WEBB. 72. The Moral Aspects of Socialism. By SIDNEY BALL. 69. Difficulties of Individualism. By SIDNEY WEBB. 51. Socialism: True and False. By S. WEBB. 45. The Impossibilities of Anarchism. By BERNARD SHAW (price 2d.). 7. Capital and Land (7th edn. revised 1908). 5. Facts for Socialists (11th ed., revised 1908). 132. A Guide to Books for Socialists. LEAFLETS—13. What Socialism Is. 1. Why are the Many Poor? WELSH TRACTS—143. Sosialaeth yng Ngoleuni'r Beibl. Gan J. R. JONES (Caernarfon). 141. Translation of 139. 87. Translation of 78. 38. Translation of 1.

II.—Applications of Socialism to Particular Problems.

TRACTS.—154. The Case for School Clinics. By L. HADEN GUEST. 153 The Twentieth Century Reform Bill. By H. H. SCHLOESSER. 152. Our Taxes as they are and as they ought to be. By ROBT. JONES, B.Sc. In cover, 2d. 150. State Purchase of Railways. By EMIL DAVIES. In cover, 2d. 149. The Endowment of Motherhood. By H. D. HARBEN. In cover, 2d. 145. The Case for School Nurseries. By Mrs. TOWNSHEND. 144. Machinery: its Masters and its Servants. By H. H. SCHLOESSER and O. GAME. 140. Child Labor under Capitalism. By Mrs. HYLTON DALE. 136. The Village and the Landlord. By EDW. CARPENTER. 131. The Decline in the Birth-Rate. By S. WEBB. 130. Home Work and Sweating. By Miss B. L. HUTCHINS. 128. The Case for a Legal Minimum Wage. 122. Municipal Milk and Public Health. By Dr. F. LAWSON DODD. 125. Municipalization by Provinces. 119. Public Control of Electrical Power and Transit. 123. The Revival of Agriculture. 118. The Secret of Rural Depopulation. 115. State Aid to Agriculture: an Example. 112. Life in the Laundry. 98. State Railways for Ireland. 124. State Control of Trusts. 86. Municipal Drink Traffic. 84. Economics of Direct Employment. 83. State Arbitration and the Living Wage. LEAFLET.—104. How Trade Unions benefit Workmen.

III.—Local Government Powers: How to use them.

TRACTS.—137. Parish Councils and Village Life. 109. Cottage Plans and Common Sense. By RAYMOND UNWIN. 76. Houses for the People. 99. Local Government in Ireland. 82. Workmen's Compensation Act. New edition for the Act of 1906. 62. Parish and District Councils. 54. The Humanizing of the Poor Law. By J. F. OAKESHOTT. LEAFLETS.— 134. Small Holdings, Allotments and Common Pastures: and how to get them. 20. Questions for Poor Law Guardians. 68. The Tenant's Sanitary Catechism. 71. Ditto for London. FABIAN MUNICIPAL LEAFLETS (Nos. 32, 37 and 90 to 93). Municipalization of the Gas Supply. A Labor Policy for Public Authorities. Municipalization of Milk Supply. Municipal Pawnshops. Municipal Slaughterhouses. Women as Councillors. 1/- per 100.

IV. - General Politics and Fabian Policy.

127. Socialism and Labor Policy. 116. Fabianism and the Fiscal

Fabian Tract No. 155.

THE CASE AGAINST THE REFERENDUM.

BY

CLIFFORD D. SHARP.

PUBLISHED AND SOLD BY

THE FABIAN SOCIETY.

PRICE ONE PENNY.

LONDON:
THE FABIAN SOCIETY, 3 CLEMENT'S INN, STRAND, W.C.
APRIL, 1911.

THE CASE AGAINST THE REFERENDUM.

THE proposal to establish the Referendum in this country seems to have entered, temporarily at least, the sphere of practical politics. How long it will remain within that holy of holies probably depends upon how long its official sponsors continue to cherish the illusion that, once established, it can be so restricted as to make it a reliable instrument for the defence of hereditary privilege. It is never wise, however, to count upon the early dissipation of a political illusion, no matter how fragile, and for the present we must assume that the Conservative leaders seriously intend to incorporate the Referendum in our political system at the earliest opportunity.

The proposition has been so little discussed that it is not easy to estimate the forces which will be ranged on either side. So far the Liberals have found no difficulty in making up their minds, since it is fairly obvious that at the moment they have all to lose by the Referendum and nothing to gain. But whether their minds will remain made up in the same sense under all political circumstances may be doubted. The experience of other countries seems to have been that whilst the party in opposition generally favours any proposal to introduce or extend the use of the Referendum, the party in power is always hostile to it—which, indeed, is precisely what one would expect. At all events, there is no reason why Liberals as Liberals should be permanently opposed to the Referendum. Sooner or later the proposal is likely to find friends and enemies in every political camp ; and if we are to form any sort of stable judgment upon the worth of the Referendum as an instrument of democratic government we must ignore as far as possible its bearings upon current politics, and examine its intrinsic worth, not as a bar to Home Rule or Tariff Reform, but as a part of some definite and intelligible theory of government. That, at all events, is what is attempted here.

Definition of Terms.

The subject is not sufficiently familiar in England for definitions to be unnecessary.

The REFERENDUM is a popular vote for or against a law or an alteration of the constitution which has already been passed by the legislature. It may be " compulsory " or " optional," according as to whether it has to be applied as a matter of course or only on the demand of a certain proportion of the electorate.

The POPULAR INITIATIVE is a device by which a certain number of electors can demand the adoption of a law or constitutional amendment. The demand may (1) be in general terms, or (2) take the

.form of a Bill already drafted. In the first case, if the legislature approves it proceeds to draw up a Bill embodying the proposal, which is then submitted to the popular vote; if it disapproves, it may call for the decision of the electorate before it drafts the Bill. In the second case (which is distinguished as the " formulated initiative "), the law which is demanded must be submitted at once to the popular .vote in the exact form and phraseology in which it has been drafted by its promoters. Not so much as a comma must be altered by the legislature, which, however, generally has the right, if it wishes, of submitting at the same time an alternative Bill of its own.

DIRECT GOVERNMENT (as opposed to Representative Government) may be said to exist where the Referendum and the Initiative are both freely used by the electors without restriction as to time or subject. By its chief advocates in the United States it is accurately described as " majority rule," pure and simple.

History of the Referendum.

Historically the Referendum is the offspring by unbroken descent of the primitive mass meeting of self-governing citizens. Both in Switzerland and in the United States, the only countries where it flourishes to-day, the whole body of citizens were from the earliest times (in the Swiss cantons from the thirteenth century, and in the American colonies from their foundation) accustomed to exercise all the functions of government for themselves in open assembly. This direct control over the affairs of State was never entirely surrendered, and when the assemblies of all the citizens became impracticable and more and more powers had to be delegated to representative councils, the Referendum came into being gradually and naturally, not as an accession of popular power, but as a mere retention by the sovereign people of certain important powers in their own hands. In its. earliest form, in both countries, the Referendum consisted simply in the reference of a law from the Legislative Council to the communes or townships, the citizens of which thereupon met together and decided what answer they should send to the Council. It is thus not easy to say precisely when the Referendum as we know it came into existence.

The United States.—It is clear, however, although it was advocated by Victor Considérant and many of the " men of 1848," that it cannot be described as an invention of modern democracy. It was included in the programme of constitutional reform (the " Agreement of the People ") which the Levellers tried to force upon Cromwell in 1647 ; and it was certainly in use in the Puritan colonies of America in something very like its present form during the earlier half of the seventeenth century.* Throughout the eighteenth century it continued to

* One of the first recorded instances of its use took place in Massachusetts on May 29th, 1644, when the legislative body of this Puritan colony conveyed an earnest request to the elders and freemen to " take into serious consideration whether God do not expect that all the inhabitants of the plantation allow to magistrates and all that are called to country service a proportionate allowance. . . ." This seems to have been an early demand for " payment of members."

Subsequently the Declaration of Independence was agreed to in this and other colonies by Referendum, and the number of votes given for and against the new constitution of 1780 after the war, is definitely on record.

be employed occasionally, and when, after the War of Independence, the young States set about the business of drafting constitutions for themselves they nearly all included as a matter of course a provision whereby the first draft itself, and all future amendments which might be proposed, should be confirmed by a direct vote of all the citizens. One State at least (Georgia) included also a provision for the employment of the popular Initiative for constitutional amendments.

From that time onwards the Referendum has been in regular use for constitutional purposes in all the States of the Union except Delaware. But it was not until almost the end of the nineteenth century that it began to be applied to ordinary legislation. This development was partly due to propaganda, partly to the fact that ordinary laws were so often held to amount to alterations of the constitution that the distinction between the two became uncertain and unimportant.*

In 1898 South Dakota led the way to a still more important development by formally adopting not only the Referendum, but the Popular Initiative as well, for all legislative purposes. Its example has since been followed by ten or twelve other States, and there is no reason to suppose that it will end with these. It appears, indeed, that we are about to witness throughout the United States an experiment in Direct Government on an immense scale, a scale restricted only by the not very important limitations of State, as compared with Federal, legislative activity. Already in a single decade a mass of material has been accumulated which, as soon as it is made available for the political student, will cause him to forsake for ever the little Swiss Republic which has hitherto so monopolized his attention.

Switzerland.—At present, however, Switzerland cannot be ignored. The history of the development of the Referendum and Initiative in Switzerland is remarkably similar to their history in America, and need not be detailed. The Initiative has been in use rather longer in the Cantons than in the States, but otherwise the differences are merely those due to the different character of the populations. At the present time the position in Switzerland is briefly as follows. In the Federal Government the Referendum is compulsory for constitutional amendments, and is applied to ordinary laws upon the demand of thirty thousand electors. The Popular Initiative (for which fifty thousand signatures are necessary) is applicable in either the "formulated" or general form to constitutional amendments, but not to ordinary laws. The distinction, however, here, as in America, is of little consequence, since practically any law can be drafted as an amendment of the constitution. In all the Cantonal Governments the Referendum is compulsory for constitutional amendments, and in some places for all ordinary legislation that is not expressly excepted. The Initiative is also freely used, though its form differs from canton to canton.

* This distinction, which was formerly the basis of the whole political system of the United States, was founded on the consideration that the constitution alone possessed the high sanction of a direct vote of the people. The extended use of the Referendum, by giving all sorts of laws the highest possible sanction, has now practically obliterated the distinction in most of the States. In Federal affairs, however, where there is no Referendum for any purpose, it is still of the utmost importance.

Australia.—The only country outside Switzerland and the United States in which the Referendum is in use is Australia. It appears to have been tentatively introduced in an advisory form in South Australia in 1896, when the Government called for a popular vote on the question of religious teaching in the State schools. The purpose of this vote was not to confirm any law, but merely to elicit the opinion of the electors, and the experiment has not been repeated. When Federation took place, however, the Referendum was definitely adopted in the Constitution of the Commonwealth, which provided that any future amendment must be confirmed both by a majority of all those voting in the Commonwealth and by a majority of those voting in a majority of States. The new Constitution was itself submitted to a popular vote in 1898 and rejected. It was then modified and accepted by another vote in 1900. The first amendment was submitted and passed in 1906, and two further amendments were submitted in April, 1910, one of which was accepted and the other rejected.*

It will be noticed that the three countries in which the Referendum has established itself—if, indeed, it can be said to be yet established in Australia—are all of them federations of States with a very large measure of local autonomy. This is a very important fact, the significance of which will be apparent when we come to consider the practical merits and defects of Direct Legislation as applied to a large and centralized sovereign State.

English Local Government.—All that need be added here to complete the brief descriptive summary which has been given is a reference to the fact that a form of Referendum has long been in use in this country—and possibly elsewhere—in local and municipal affairs. Certain adoptive Acts, such as the Public Libraries Act, have required a poll of the ratepayers to be taken before they could be put into force in any district ; and upon various other questions of local government, like the purchase or lease of tramways, the electors have the right of demanding a poll after a Town or Parish meeting has been held.† The public interest, however, attached to the Referendum as a municipal institution has never been very great, and with the growth of large and fully responsible local authorities it seems likely to fall more and more into disuse.

The Inevitable Corollary of the Referendum.

We now come to the real subject of this paper : the pros and cons of the proposal to introduce the machinery of the Referendum

* The amendment which was rejected concerned certain complicated adjustments between the Federal and State finances which had been agreed to at a special conference of the Premiers of the different States. It is improbable that more than a very few of the electors understood the proposal which they voted against—which may have been the reason why they voted against it.

† It is interesting to notice that as with Referendum in America and Switzerland, so with this English practice of taking a " poll of the parish " : at no time did it appear as a democratic innovation, it arose as a perfectly natural development when parish meetings and " open vestries " of the ratepayers grew to an unwieldy and impossible size. It was, indeed, in law, merely an adjournment of the vestry meeting in order to take a vote of those whose presence was presumed. See " The Parish and the County," by Sidney and Beatrice Webb.

for use in this country in national and Imperial affairs. The first important point to be considered is whether it would be possible, having once introduced the Referendum, to restrict its application or to prevent the development of a system of Direct Legislation as complete as that which exists in Switzerland and America.

The experience of America goes to show that as long as the use of the Referendum is confined to questions which can properly be described as constitutional there is no marked tendency on the part of the electors to demand its extension to other purposes ; but as soon as for one reason or another it begins to be applied to matters of ordinary legislation the momentum of its development becomes irresistible, and cannot be checked until its scope has been widened to include all possible subjects of legislation, and its inherent limitations corrected by the addition of the Popular Initiative.

Now the actual proposal which has been put forward in this country is clearly to apply the Referendum to ordinary legislation, to anything which the House of Lords or some other undefined authority chooses to regard as " revolutionary " ; it may be a Budget, a Church Disestablishment Bill, or even a mere Licensing or Education Bill. There is, therefore, good reason to suppose that if this proposal is carried out by any future Government it will either prove abortive, because incompatible with the spirit of our political institutions, and shortly be repealed ; or else within a comparatively few years the rest of the machinery of Direct Legislation will be added unto it and it will become possible to submit "Right to Work" Bills, and "Conciliation" Bills and the like, to a vote of all the people by means of the formulated Initiative. Moreover, quite apart from the experience of other countries, there are strong reasons why this should happen. It is scarcely likely at the present juncture, when new legislation is being demanded on all hands and the chief complaint that is heard is of the slowness and the comparative barrenness of the Parliamentary machine, that the mass of the electors will remain content with the mere power of checking their representatives. The chief Conservative advocate of the Referendum, Professor Dicey, habitually refers to it as the "National Veto," apparently regarding the description as a tacit recommendation. But it may be safely asserted that the majority of electors at the present time are far more interested in the abolition than in the creation of vetoes upon the action of Parliament. Moreover, it would need but a short experience of the Referendum to teach the electors that the power of framing the question is scarcely less important than the power of voting upon it.

For all these reasons it is impossible to consider the establishment of the Referendum in this country except as a first instalment of a more or less complete system of Direct Legislation which, although it would not of course displace, would modify fundamentally the whole of our representative system. We are therefore justified in treating the issue as one not merely between the adoption or non-adoption of a restricted and rarely used Referendum, but between the essential principles of Direct and Representative Government.

The Case for Direct Government.

Let us consider first the chief arguments in favor of Direct Legislation. The general contention of its advocates is, of course, that by no other means is it possible to ensure that "the will of the people" shall prevail. Thus Mr. J. A. Hobson urges that "there is no certain way of determining this fact (i.e., whether a law is 'acceptable to the body of the people') unless an opportunity is afforded to ask the people." This assertion plainly begs the whole question at issue, namely, whether the people should be asked to give their judgment upon a Bill, a mere legal document, or upon an Act, the practical merits or defects of which they have experienced. The same may be said of all arguments which refer to "the will of the people" as a definite and easily ascertainable fact. They all beg the question of how the real "will of the people" may be discovered, which is, of course, the crux of the whole matter. Instances might be adduced from the experience of the American States of laws having been enthusiastically adopted by large majorities which turned out to represent in practice anything but "the will of the people."

Another argument for Direct Legislation, an argument which in the United States carries decisive weight with the mass of the people, is that it destroys the power of vested interests by making corruption practically impossible. This no doubt is true. Where the representatives of the people not only have their price, but can find some one eager to give it to them, there you have, not democracy at all, but plutocracy in its worst form, and every democrat in such circumstances becomes of necessity a staunch advocate of the Referendum. But it must be remembered that it is only certain flagrant forms of corruption obvious to the elector that can be effectively checkmated by the Referendum, and that the argument has therefore little application in this country. Moreover, it is worth noting that if the possibility of securing honest representatives be granted, the point of the argument is immediately reversed. For it is clear that wealthy vested interests which can control the Press must always be able to influence the electors far more easily than they can influence any reasonably honest and public-spirited representative assembly.*

---

* In 1890 an amendment of the Swiss Constitution providing for the subsequent establishment by law of universal accident and invalidity insurance was enthusiastically adopted by an enormous majority (283,328 ayes, and 92,200 noes). But before the law itself could be drafted and passed through the legislature a campaign was organized by the insurance companies and wealthy employers regardless of expense. A special paper was started to oppose the law, and posters were showered all over the country. As a result when the voting day came the law was rejected. (*The Swiss Democracy*, H. D. Lloyd and J. A. Hobson.)

This incident is interesting, because it is always contended by advocates of the Referendum that in so far as the electors may require education on any subject which they have to vote upon, it will be effectively provided by the various propagandist societies and leagues and by Members of Parliament anxious to get their measure through. A Referendum is referred to as if it would be like a General Election in miniature, except that, as Lord Courtney puts it, "there would in fact be no candidates, and their hopes and fears and personal interest would not arise." Lord Courtney apparently regards this absence of the hopes and fears of personal interests of candidates as a great advantage. In fact it would be likely to prove the reverse, since there would be no one to spend money on "educating" the electors, except persons who were financially interested in the passage or rejection of the submitted measure.

An argument of far greater force in Great Britain is the contention that the Referendum acts as an immense stimulus to the political education of the people by forcing them to think about their laws and to realize their privileges and responsibilities as citizens of a self-governing State. Only so, it is urged, can they become the "free and enlightened" persons they are expected to be. This argument ignores, of course, the corruptibility of what must always be the chief instrument of such education, namely, the Press; but after making full allowance for that unfortunate circumstance, it remains undeniable that a series of popular votings on important questions would be calculated to have some extremely valuable educational results—results which might startle many of the present advocates of the "National Veto." All that can be said on the other side is that even education may be bought too dearly.

But perhaps the most appealing of all the arguments for the system of Direct Legislation is the sobering and altogether healthy effect which the mere existence of the Referendum and Popular Initiative inevitably has upon revolutionary movements of all kinds. The fact that any reasonably substantial section of the electors can at any moment demand an effective popular verdict upon any legislative project which they like to bring forward, deprives the disappointed propagandist of all those excuses for failure with which he sometimes strives to conceal even from himself the real cause. Socialists need scarcely to be reminded of the forms these excuses take; they are only too familiar. Sometimes it is "the party system" that gets the blame, sometimes the consoling bogey is "a conspiracy of the governing classes," and occasionally we hear significant whispers about some powerful ring of Jewish financiers or, it may be, in Lancashire, of Roman Catholic prelates. Anything is apt to be good enough to explain away the unpleasant fact that the right sort of legislation is not forthcoming.

The moment the Popular Initiative becomes an established fact all these comfortable theories have to be abandoned, and the breath that is wasted in propounding them diverted into more fruitful channels. Far too many Socialists to-day are plainly obsessed with the idea that Parliament itself is the great obstacle to Socialism, and that if only the people could make their will directly effective all would be well—the Utopia would be at our doors. Twenty or thirty years ago when Socialism was young such errors were perhaps permissible, almost necessary; to-day they are deadly. Nothing is more vital at the present moment to the continued advance of Socialism than a clear realization of the facts, that the working classes of England are not yet Socialists; that, until they are, Socialist legislation is impossible and undesirable; and that in the meantime no energy can be spared from the work of education for mere abuse of political machinery. That it automatically keeps all revolutionary propagandists in clear and continuous touch with the hard facts of the situation is one of the most attractive features of Direct Legislation.

The Case Against Direct Government.

The system of Direct Legislation is always identified by its advocates with " majority rule." The issue which they raise is therefore a perfectly clear and straightforward one, namely, whether " majority rule " is superior or inferior to " government by consent." The difference between these two forms of government is, of course, essentially a question of how minorities are to be treated. Under a system of majority rule the only right possessed by a minority is that of complete submission. A system of government by consent, on the other hand, recognizes the claim of any minority to be granted all such rights as do not seriously conflict with rights *of an equally important nature* of the majority.

An imaginary example will illustrate the point. Suppose that a small group of persons dwelling in a certain street enjoy a sincere conviction that it is necessary to their eternal salvation that they should sing hymns at the top of their voices between nine and ten o'clock every Sunday morning, and at no other time. And suppose that that is exactly the time which the other inhabitants of the street, who form a considerable majority, have selected for a pleasant extra hour of sleep. How is the issue between the two parties to be settled? If it is settled on the principles of government by consent the noisy minority will be allowed to continue their matins, with a strong suggestion that they should moderate their tones as much as ever their consciences will allow. The majority will no doubt grumble until they get hardened to the disturbance, but comparative peace will reign. If, however, the dispute is settled by a majority vote, the singers will be suppressed, and from thenceforward will constitute an outraged, and therefore dangerous, minority, whose respect for the justice of the law is gone for ever. Both solutions may be called " democratic " ; but one is a good solution, and the other a very bad one.

This is an illustration of the first great argument against any system which approximates to pure majority rule : that it takes no account, and can take no account, of the quality or intensity of the feeling behind any individual vote. For it is just that intensity which matters, and which must constantly be considered and allowed for if any form of government is to be satisfactory. The primary, indeed the only, object of having any government at all is that it may reconcile conflicting interests and conflicting desires and arrange a general *modus vivendi*. And the only test of whether a Government is good or bad is whether or not the *modus vivendi* which it has arranged secures the voluntary respect and adhesion of the great mass of the community. No law can fully satisfy everybody. The most—and the least—we must ask is that the inevitable dissatisfaction should be reduced to a minimum, and especially that no section of the people should be given cause to regard themselves as unjustly treated. The greatest crime which any Government can commit is to deal with any section of the citizens in such a way as to alienate their loyalty towards the common institutions of the nation and make them feel that resistance to the law is a moral duty. For such action must endanger the very foundations of civilized human society.

The ideal of those who uphold majority rule is apparently that upon every separate subject of legislation the will of the majority should be made to prevail. So simple a definition of the problem of democracy begs every question and shirks every real difficulty. Ultimately any form of democratic government must stand or fall not so much by its perfect subservience to majorities as by its just treatment of minorities—a far more difficult condition to fulfil. That minorities must not rule is only the first canon of good government ; the second is that they must not be ignored. Yet how, under a system of Direct Legislation, can they be other than ignored ? It must handicap them in two ways. In the first place, it is obviously far easier for a minority to submit their claims to a representative assembly than to the whole body of electors ; and in the second place, representatives are far more likely than are the electors to give such claims adequate consideration. An individual elector in casting his vote for or against any proposal has naturally and properly no other object than to give expression to his own individual opinion upon the matter as it affects himself. But the same individual voting on the same proposal in the capacity of a representative would approach the question in quite a different way, and would feel it his duty, on account of the trust reposed in him, to take into account claims which as a mere elector he would ignore.*

Apart, however, from this sense of duty towards the community as a whole, there are factors which tend to make representatives duly sensitive to the claims of minorities. The average Member of Parliament holds his seat by a fairly steady party vote. Once he has got it, he can generally count upon keeping it, provided he does not arouse violent and active resentment amongst any section of his constituents. Consequently, where the feelings of the majority about any issue are lukewarm, whilst those of the minority are deep and strong, he will probably be guided rather by the latter than by the former. In other words, he will attempt to go behind mere numerical votes and take into account the *relative intensities* of conflicting desires. He will thus tend to support such solutions of the various problems which arise as satisfy the fundamental requirement of good government, that popular dissatisfaction should be reduced to a minimum with a view to the maintenance of universal respect for the law.

---

* The difference of attitude here referred to is the essential factor in the distinction, often misunderstood, between a delegate and a representative. The former has nothing to do but to carry out the instructions actually given to him by the majority of his constituents, and is responsible to that majority alone. The latter is responsible to *all* his constituents, and has the semi-judicial function to perform of deciding how far it may be right that the wishes of this or that minority should receive consideration. In other words, whilst the representative is a device for securing the presence, as it were, of all the people at the making of their laws, the delegate is a mere telephone to which the majority in any given constituency alone has access.

Territorial Minorities.

In considering the application of majority rule to this country a question of immense practical importance arises. Any given law is to be decided by a majority ; that is clear. But by a majority of whom ? Of the persons who are directly affected by the law, or of all the adult inhabitants of the United Kingdom ? This difficulty is fundamental with a system of government so centralized as ours. Take, for example, the question of Welsh Disestablishment. What is the value upon this issue of the vote of, say, a Kentish farm labourer or a Yorkshire manufacturer ? What does either of them know or care about the subject ? They will be no more affected by the disestablishment of the Anglican Church in Wales than they are now by the establishment of the Presbyterian Church in Scotland—a fact of which, by the way, they are both of them most probably unaware. By what conceivable theory of government could a Referendum of the United Kingdom on such an issue be justified ? The result of the vote outside Wales would be merely irrelevant, that is to say, would afford no guide whatever to the statesman as to the decision which he ought to take in the interests of *good democratic government.*

The same reasoning applies to Irish Home Rule. The fact that the mass of the Irish people have been in rebellion for a century against the government under which they live may be deplorable, but it is the only fact in the whole situation which can carry any weight with the democrat. Home Rule may have bad results for Great Britain, and even for Ireland herself. Union may have been worth trying, but it has failed because it has not secured the assent of the Irish people. They do not respect the law because they do not feel it is their own law. Home Rule, in short, appears to be the only plan by which this unconquerably romantic race can realize the blessings and responsibilities of self-government ; and that, as far as the democrat is concerned, is the last word on the rights and wrongs of the problem. A knowledge of the views of the electors of Great Britain would not contribute to its right solution in the least degree.

These two cases are of course rather exceptional. They belong to the category of questions, mainly or exclusively affecting a single locality, to which the Referendum has never been applied in any part of the world, and has never been regarded as applicable by any of its advocates outside the English Conservative party. The very significant fact has already been noted that the Referendum has only been adopted where a very complete system of local autonomy already exists. Consequently one of the most obvious dangers of Direct Legislation, the oppression of territorial minorities, has in practice been largely avoided.

Racial, Religious, and other Minorities.

But the danger to other minorities, more or less permanent, which are *not* concentrated in one locality, and which, therefore, can enjoy no autonomy, remains, and has proved to be very real. Two instances may be cited.

First, there is the well-known case in Switzerland where the Popular Initiative was employed by an anti-Semitic faction to introduce a Bill imposing pains and penalties on all persons slaughtering animals in a certain manner, namely, the manner prescribed by the Jewish law. Under cover of a humanitarian agitation, and in the face of the opposition of both Houses of the Legislature, the Bill was carried into law. Fortunately its drafting was imperfect, so that the Executive authorities in the Cantons have been able largely to ignore its tyrannous provisions. It should be added that this is the only case up to the present where the Federal Initiative in Switzerland has been successfully employed.

The second instance refers to America and is much more serious. It is that in State after State at the present time the Referendum is being used to disfranchise the negroes ; not, of course, by actually laying down a colour line—that is prohibited by the Federal Constitution—but by imposing qualifications which are quite as effective a bar to the black man, and the purpose of which is understood by every one.*

Now is there any democratic advocate of "majority rule" who would defend this application of its principles? *And if not, why not?* There is no question but that in these States there are large majorities in favour of the disfranchisement of the negroes. Why should not the will of the majority prevail? The answer to that question strikes at the very root of the principles of Direct Legislation, because it must involve an admission that laws are of different sorts, some properly requiring much more than a bare majority of votes, and some much less. Mr. J. A. Hobson, arguing in favour of the Referendum, urges that "experienced statesmen . . . know that many laws . . . fail to work chiefly because of their unpopularity among the people." Surely what experienced statesmen know is that when laws fail to work it is generally due, not to a majority, but to an active minority, of malcontents. The Referendum only intensifies the danger. Witness the history of Prohibition in the United States. Laws actually passed by a majority vote forbidding the use of alcohol have notoriously failed to work, simply for the reason that such an interference with individual liberty requires something approaching unanimity amongst the electors before it ought to be enacted. There are lots of similar questions upon which from time to time legislation is proposed, and which ought not to be dealt with by anything less than, say, a 75 per cent. majority.

On the other hand, there are propositions for which a majority ought not to be required at all. Laws of a type already referred to affecting mainly or solely the inhabitants of a single locality come

* It may be urged that in some States the feeling against the negroes being allowed to exercise the rights of citizenship is so strong that the Representative Assemblies would have been, and in fact have been, obliged to adopt these measures on their own initiative. This may be true, but on the other hand it is unlikely that a representative body would consent to such an abuse of power without a really overwhelming mandate. The danger, therefore, is much less under a representative than under a direct legislative system.

under this heading together with others affecting minorities of different sorts. Broadly, it may be said that if a substantial minority want something very badly indeed, whilst the majority are mildly opposed, then the minority ought to have their way. This proposition is but the corollary of the proposition laid down earlier in this paper, that legislation must not so outrage the feelings of any section of the electors as to make them rebels against the law. Faults of omission may have as serious results in this respect as faults of commission. The Trades Disputes Bill of 1906 is a case in point. Whether the majority of voters were behind that Bill may be doubted, but about the intensity of feeling and the moral force behind it there can be no doubt at all ; and it is to be noted as a signal instance of the success of our representative system that the Bill did actually become law. That is the answer to those people who complain that the present machinery of legislation enables the will of the people to be ignored. The truth is that where any substantial section of the electors know clearly and definitely what they want, they get it. The real difficulty is that generally they do not know what they want.

What is " The Will of the People " ?

This brings us back to the question already asked : what is "the will of the people"? It is not a question which can be answered offhand, but this much is certain, that you cannot discover the will of the people by any system of counting heads that was ever invented. The ideal elector who always knows exactly what laws he wants and always deliberately uses his vote to obtain them, is unknown to the practical politician. He is, indeed, every whit as much a figment of the academic imagination as was the "economic man" with whom the *laisser-faire* economists used to juggle. The votes of most electors, whether they be educated or uneducated, wise or foolish, are influenced by a hundred and one considerations entirely foreign to the merits of the matter in hand.

Thus the experience of both Switzerland and America is conclusive on this point, that proposals submitted to a popular vote at the same time tend to stand or fall together. "An unpopular proposal will frequently carry down to defeat proposals which if submitted alone might easily have been adopted; and a popular proposal will aid others submitted at the same time." * On one occasion in Switzerland an entirely harmless Bill for amending the law as to patents happened to be submitted at the same time as a law to establish compulsory vaccination. The latter was extremely unpopular, and both proposals were decisively rejected. Subsequently the law about patents was put forward in better company and accepted by an enormous majority. Astute politicians will no doubt soon learn how to turn this tendency to account for their own ends, but the existence of such a tendency shows how uncertain is the relation between the vote and the real will behind it. And this is

* *Revision and Amendment of State Constitutions.* By W. F. Dodd. U.S.A. 1910.

but one instance out of a hundred that might be adduced of that uncertainty.*

The Necessity of Compromise.

But even if it were always possible to discover the will behind the individual vote, the problem of discovering "the will of the people" would not be solved. For clearly where there is a definite and serious cleavage of opinion on any subject the will of a bare majority must be a very different thing from "the will of the people," if any intelligible meaning is to be attached to that phrase. "The will of the people" would be best interpreted in such a case by some sort of compromise representing, not merely the resultant of so many conflicting wills, but their greatest common measure, their substantial agreement.

The writer happens to have the honour to serve upon the Executive Committee of the Fabian Society, a body whose methods of transacting business may or may not be unique, but are certainly instructive. There is an unwritten rule or custom, almost invariably observed, that divisions should never be taken upon really important questions, except in the very last resort. The use of divisions is to clear away unimportant matters so that time may not be wasted in discussing them at length. In matters of real consequence when there are two diverse opinions it is clearly absurd to divide and adopt the one which happens to have the odd vote behind it. The reasonable course is to go on discussing the question until a solution is discovered which everybody is ready to accept as a compromise. That compromise represents the substantial agreement of the Committee, and by the time it is reached the chances are that most of the members will regard it not in the light of a compromise at all, but as the best possible solution, and will be ready to give it active support without feeling that they have sacrificed to it any part of their better judgment.†

No one surely will deny that the character of all legislation ought to be determined by some such process as this. At all events a system under which nothing of the kind is possible must stand condemned.

The subject of compromise, however, vital as it is to the success of any kind of government, is too wide to be pursued here. It must suffice to suggest that, after all, the device of counting heads is at best a very crude and unsatisfactory method of deciding important or complicated issues in accordance with "the will of the people." We may be obliged to resort to it from time to time, but we need not glorify it as if it were in itself the pure quintessence of democracy. For in reality it is its *reductio ad absurdum*.

* An interesting sidelight is thrown on the practical working of Direct Legislation by the Constitution of North Dakota, U.S.A., which contains a provision to the effect that if two conflicting measures dealing with the same subject should be submitted at the same time and both should be passed (!) the one with the greatest number of affirmative Votes behind it is to be taken as accepted, and the other as rejected.

† This, in point of fact, is the usual custom of a body much older than the Fabian Society, the Society of Friends ; and is also the way in which the Mir manages the affairs of every Russian village.

Public Opinion v. Popular Opinion.

There is another point connected with the determination of the real will of the people which demands brief reference. Every one who has paid any attention to political history knows that from time to time laws have been passed which would have been emphatically rejected by the people at the time of their enactment, but which would have been equally emphatically accepted if submitted after being in operation for a year or two. Obvious instances are Catholic Emancipation and compulsory Education. It would seem that certain propositions can never hope to be "popular" until *after* they have become accomplished facts. At the present moment there are at least two issues before the country which are probably of this character: Women's Suffrage and the raising of the school age. Public opinion—which is not necessarily the same at any given moment as the opinion of the majority—supports both these proposals. Both will certainly be adopted within a few years, and a little later will be fully, if tacitly, endorsed by the people. Yet if they were submitted to a popular vote before enactment they would just as certainly both be rejected, even if in the case of Women's Suffrage women were allowed to vote.

These statements in regard to the particular questions selected may be doubted, but it cannot be denied that there are questions about which they would be true. We have here a definite political phenomenon which theoretical advocates of Direct Legislation must find some means of dealing with. There appears to be only one way of meeting the difficulty, and that is to legislate through representatives, and throw upon them the responsibility of deciding—on penalty of losing their seats in case of error—not what Bills but what Acts will secure the approval of the people. To discover the real will of the people, writes Mr. Ramsay MacDonald, "is the task of the statesman who knows how far expressed desire is not real desire, who understands how he is to speak for what is in the heart but not on the lips of the people, and who, without mandates, and even against mandates, does what the people really want." *

The Responsibility of the Representative.

Most, if not all, of the simple issues of modern politics belong to one of the categories described above. Either because they deal solely with small minorities, or for some other reason, they are obviously unsuitable for the application of the Referendum. But what of those more complicated issues and projects which form the bulk of our legislative output at the present time?

The average elector may be able to judge principles, but he has neither the time nor the knowledge nor the will to consider details. It is common knowledge amongst State politicians in America that a Bill which exceeds certain very narrow limits of length and complexity is almost certain to be rejected by the electors. Advocates of

* *Socialism and Government*, Vol. I., p. 9. No student of Socialism, or, indeed, of any aspect of modern politics, can afford to miss this original and really masterly study of political theory.

Direct Legislation, indeed, constantly cite this as one of the great advantages of the system, that it leads to a simplification of the laws. But whatever may be the advantages of simple drafting, they are surely insignificant compared with its drawbacks. For not only must it largely exclude concessions to minorities, but it carries with it as a necessary corollary that the executive officials should be given a free hand to deal with points of administration which in England, for example, would be dealt with in the Act itself and settled by Parliament. Both in Switzerland and in America the officials do, in fact, exercise unheard of powers which, if administration were anything like as centralized as it is in this country, would be intolerable.

This difficulty becomes overwhelming in regard to that large class of modern legislation in which details are everything and principles comparatively nothing. The creation or alteration of duties on imported articles is an example. It is impossible to conceive a more insane or a more dangerous proposal than that Tariff Reform should be decided by popular vote. Apart from objections to indirect taxation *per se*, not one elector in a thousand, be he wage-earner or University don, is in a position to form an opinion of any intrinsic value upon the question of whether Tariff Reform is likely to do the nation more harm than good. If the object be to reach a right decision you might almost as well save the cost and trouble of a Referendum by tossing a halfpenny instead.

Suppose that, dismissing all preconceived theories of government, the reader were called upon to devise a satisfactory method of settling such a question. What would he propose? Would he not say something like this? "Let us select a number of men, as intelligent as possible, representing all classes in the community; let us insist that they shall have access to every possible source of information and opportunity of weighing expert opinion on all sides; and then let us leave the decision to them, *holding them responsible for the consequences.*" If he were wise, he would add that the representatives should not be allowed, upon any pretence whatever, to shift the responsibility for the decision on to the electors by referring the matter to a popular vote at the last moment. That is to say, he would choose the representative method and the representative method alone.

It may be argued that Tariff Reform is a very exceptional case. But it is the case chosen for the first application of the Referendum. Besides, an ever-increasing proportion of our most important legislation is of a similar character, that is to say, its merits and defects are so much a matter of details that they can only be appreciated with the assistance of experts, and pronounced upon by persons who have devoted much attention to the art of legislation. If Great Britain were governed by counties it might be otherwise, but it is governed as a single community, and the consequences of that fact must be accepted. It is often asserted that all opposition to the Referendum is inspired by the belief that representatives are wiser than the people, and know better what is good for them. In other words, that the arguments against the Referendum might equally be employed to justify a system of oligarchy. Such assertions, ignorantly or intentionally, are altogether wide of the mark. No doubt it is true, though one can call to mind many exceptions, that a representative is usually superior in general intelligence and ability to the average of the persons who have chosen him to represent them ; and this is an important fact. But the case against the Referendum requires no such assumption. The point is that the representative has opportunities which in the nature of things are denied to the individual elector of hearing not some, but all, of the evidence for or against any proposal ; and it would be just as valid if representatives were chosen by lot instead of by election. A representative body is " superior " to the electors for the purpose of legislation in precisely the same sense as a jury is superior to the general newspaper-reading public for the purpose of giving a just verdict. Inherently there is no more " oligarchy " about one than about the other.

There is, however, one essential condition which is by no means always fulfilled at present but must be fulfilled if representatives are really to represent ; and that condition is that they should be held strictly responsible for the consequences of their action or inaction on any subject. The right of the elector must be recognized even to give his representative a mandate for a certain policy and then to blame him if it turns out badly. Otherwise there can be no security for the proper exercise of those powers which under any system of democracy must be entrusted to the representative assembly. The experience of Switzerland proves, if proof be necessary, that the habitual use of the Referendum does, in fact, destroy this safeguard. Elections are rarely contested except for some personal reason, and the representative becomes in effect an irresponsible official, acting as he pleases in regard to all those matters which are not submitted to a popular vote. In Switzerland the volume and importance of the legislation not so submitted are small, and the danger of excessive bureaucracy is so far mitigated. But in England the bulk of the legislation must under any circumstances be left to the discretion of Parliament, and the evils that would surely flow from any diminution of its responsibility to the electorate are hard to exaggerate.

The Practical Working of Direct Legislation.

There is no space here for any sort of detailed analysis of the actual results of the Referendum and Initiative where they have been adopted. Nor is it likely that such an analysis would afford a basis for judging the effect of the same machinery in this country. The total population of Switzerland is less than half that of Greater London, and is divided amongst twenty-five cantons, each of which is autonomous for almost all the ordinary purposes of government. For Great Britain to adopt the Referendum on the strength of Swiss experience alone would be about as reasonable as for the House of Commons to adopt the principle of co-option on the strength of the experience of a Board of Guardians. In America the unit of government is larger ; but there Direct Legislation is still in the early experimental stage, and neither the triumphs which it has achieved nor the absurdities which it has been responsible for afford. a fair basis for generalization at present.*

It should be said, however, that the widely prevalent notion that the Referendum has a conservative effect upon legislation appears to be based on very insufficient evidence. It is true that in Switzerland a disproportionate number of measures submitted by the Federal Government are rejected, but this may be explained by the deep-rooted preference of the Swiss elector to be governed by his Canton rather than by the Federation. The proposals of the Federal authorities are thus always more or less suspect, and opposition to them is no proof of conservatism In America, on the other hand, the weight has been deliberately thrown into the other scale in some of the States, by allowing new measures to be placed on the ballot-paper as affirmative propositions, which must be crossed out by those who object to them ; that is to say, the non-voter is counted on the affirmative side. Elsewhere a definite anti-conservative bias has appeared without any such artificial aid, owing to the increasing number of proposals submitted at one time. In Oregon in 1906 the ballot-paper contained the names of thirty-seven candidates and the titles of thirty-two measures. Very few electors take the trouble to go more than halfway down the paper. Consequently proposals put forward by a small active minority tend to get passed, because the affirmative is organized and the negative is not. The only people who understand or are interested in the proposition sufficiently to vote upon it at all are mostly its supporters.†

To sum up, there seems no particular reason to suppose that the adoption of the Referendum in this country would result in special advantage to any party. A certain conservatism would no doubt become apparent amongst the electors in regard to large constructive schemes of social reorganization. But to balance this there would be the unquestionable popularity of land taxes, supertaxes, heavy death duties, and the like.‡ The case for and against the introduction of the beginnings of Direct Government rests, therefore, solely upon the merits of that system compared with the Representative System as a

* The experience of the English Trade Unions has provided data as valuable perhaps as any for a study of the working of Direct Legislation. In this connection the reader is directed to *Industrial Democracy*, by Sidney and Beatrice Webb, where he will find an analytical account of how the Referendum and Initiative were adopted and enthusiastically employed by some of the largest Trade Unions during the nineteenth century, and how they fell steadily into disuse and discredit, until finally it was seen that the practice of taking a general poll was practically useful only for some such purpose as that of discovering whether the members might be relied upon to support individually a proposal requiring concerted voluntary action, e.g., a strike.

† It might be suggested that this tendency meets the objection urged above, that the Referendum tends to the oppression or neglect of minorities. But it is to be observed (1) that it is only a safeguard upon issues of little public interest, and (2) that to give minorities an improper influence in certain matters is no remedy for allowing them none in others.

‡ A vote taken in the Canton Grisons on Sunday, March 6th, 1911, suggests the possibility of other sorts of anti-capitalistic legislation. By a majority of more than three to one the electors decided to prohibit absolutely the use of motor cars upon any public road within the area of this Canton.

satisfactory instrument of democracy. It must be admitted that when the unit of government is small and the population homogeneous in character, the advantages of the Referendum (as also, when practicable, of the mass meeting of citizens) are very considerable. But when the unit of government is large and the population heterogeneous, the inherent defects of "majority rule" assume overwhelming importance.

The choice which must be made is a momentous one, fraught, perhaps, with the most profound consequences in relation to the future prospects of democracy. For democracy is still upon its trial. Nowhere in the world as yet can it be said to have worked to the complete satisfaction of everyone. Everywhere still there are doubters, even in the foremost ranks of the democratic movement itself; people who despair of their faith and are turning to alternative theories, to Plato, to government by the best, government by a semi-ascetic voluntary order or government by a specially trained, or even specially bred, class. No great attention need be paid to the views of such pessimists, but they suffice to illustrate a fact which does deserve consideration, that the permanent success and stability of democracy have not yet been conclusively demonstrated. Developments are perfectly conceivable which would lead to such widespread disgust with popular government as to cause a revolt in favour of some other alternative, possibly a personal dictatorship.

How can these dangers best be avoided? By following the ideal of "majority rule" or the ideal of "government by consent"? In other words, is legislation to be determined by a mere counting of heads or by methods which allow of a more or less accurate estimation, both quantitative and qualitative, of all the forces and currents of opinion in the community? It may be that upon the answer to that question hangs the fate of democracy itself.

SELECT BIBLIOGRAPHY.

STODDART, JANE T. Against the Referendum. 1910. Hodder. 1s.
DEPLOIGE, S. The Referendum in Switzerland. 1898. King. 7s. 6d. n.
BRYCE, JAS. The American Commonwealth. New Edition. 1910.
OBERHOLTZER, E. P. The Referendum in America. 1893. New York. 2 dols.
DODD, W. F. Revision and Amendment of State Constitutions. 1910. Johns Hopkins Press, U.S.A.
LLOYD, H. D , and J. A. HOBSON. The Swiss Democracy. 1908. Unwin. 6s. n.
Reports from His Majesty's Representatives Abroad respecting the Institution known as the Referendum. 1911. Cd. 5522.
United States Senate. Papers communicated by Jennings and Pomeroy. 1898.
   Note.—The literature of the Referendum in the United States may be divided into two classes : (1) Propagandist literature, which is very extensive but of little value to the student. The United States Senate paper referred to above is of great length, and may be regarded as exhaustive in this class ; (2) analytical literature, which mostly consists of articles in the numerous political and sociological reviews, for example :
The Political Science Quarterly. (U.S.A.)
The Arena. (U.S.A.)
The American Journal of Sociology.
The American Political Science Review.

FABIAN SOCIETY.—The Fabian Society consists of Socialists. A statement of its Rules and the following publications can be obtained from the Secretary, at the Fabian Office, 3 Clement's Inn, London, W.C.

FABIAN ESSAYS IN SOCIALISM. New Preface by BERNARD SHAW. Paper 6d. net; cloth 1/6; postage 2½d. and 4d.

WHAT TO READ on Social and Economic Subjects. Fifth edition, revised to October, 1910, and enlarged. Interleaved, paper, 1s. n. cloth 2s. n., post. 2d.

THIS MISERY OF BOOTS. By H. G. WELLS. 3d., post free 4d.

FABIAN TRACTS and LEAFLETS.

Tracts, each 16 to 52 pp., price 1d., or 9d. per doz., unless otherwise stated.
Leaflets, 4 pp. each, price 1d. for six copies, 1s. per 100, or 8/6 per 1000.

The Set of 78, 3s.; post free 3/5. Bound in Buckram, 4/6 n.; post free 5s.

I.—General Socialism in its various aspects.

TRACTS.—151. The Point of Honour: a Correspondence on Aristocracy and Socialism. By RUTH CAVENDISH BENTINCK. 147. Capital and Compensation. By EDW. R. PEASE. 146. Socialism and Superior Brains. A reply to Mr. Mallock. By BERNARD SHAW. 142. Rent and Value. 138. Municipal Trading. 121. Public Service versus Private Expenditure. By Sir OLIVER LODGE. 113. Communism. By WM. MORRIS. 107. Socialism for Millionaires. By BERNARD SHAW. 139. Socialism and the Churches. By Rev. JOHN CLIFFORD, D.D. 133. Socialism and Christianity. By Rev. PERCY DEARMER (in cover with portrait of the author). 78. Socialism and the Teaching of Christ. By Dr. J. CLIFFORD. 42. Christian Socialism. By Rev. S. D. HEADLAM. 79. A Word of Remembrance and Caution to the Rich. By JOHN WOOLMAN. 75. Labor in the Longest Reign. By S. WEBB. 72. The Moral Aspects of Socialism. By SIDNEY BALL. 69. Difficulties of Individualism. By SIDNEY WEBB. 51. Socialism: True and False. By S. WEBB. 45. The Impossibilities of Anarchism. By BERNARD SHAW (price 2d.). 7. Capital and Land (7th edn. revised 1908). 5. Facts for Socialists (11th ed., revised 1908). 132. A Guide to Books for Socialists. LEAFLETS—13. What Socialism Is. 1. Why are the Many Poor? WELSH TRACTS—143. Sosialaeth yng Ngoleuni'r Beibl. Gan J. R. JONES (Caernarfon). 141. Translation of 139. 87. Translation of 78. 38. Translation of 1.

II.—Applications of Socialism to Particular Problems.

TRACTS.—154. The Case for School Clinics. By L. HADEN GUEST. 153. The Twentieth Century Reform Bill. By H. H. SCHLOESSER. 152. Our Taxes as they are and as they ought to be. By ROBT. JONES, B.Sc. In cover, 2d. 150. State Purchase of Railways. By EMIL DAVIES. In cover, 2d. 149. The Endowment of Motherhood. By H. D. HARBEN. In cover, 2d. 145. The Case for School Nurseries. By Mrs. TOWNSHEND. 144. Machinery: its Masters and its Servants. By H. H. SCHLOESSER and C. GAME. 140. Child Labor under Capitalism. By Mrs. HYLTON DALE. 136. The Village and the Landlord. By EDW. CARPENTER. 131. The Decline in the Birth-Rate. By S. WEBB. 130. Home Work and Sweating. By Miss B. L. HUTCHINS. 128. The Case for a Legal Minimum Wage. 122. Municipal Milk and Public Health. By Dr. F. LAWSON DODD. 125. Municipalization by Provinces. 119. Public Control of Electrical Power and Transit. 123. The Revival of Agriculture. 118. The Secret of Rural Depopulation. 115. State Aid to Agriculture: an Example. 112. Life in the Laundry. 98. State Railways for Ireland. 124. State Control of Trusts. 86. Municipal Drink Traffic. 84. Economics of Direct Employment. 83. State Arbitration and the Living Wage. LEAFLET.—104. How Trade Unions benefit Workmen.

III.—Local Government Powers: How to use them.

TRACTS.—137. Parish Councils and Village Life. 109. Cottage Plans and Common Sense. By RAYMOND UNWIN. 76. Houses for the People. 99. Local Government in Ireland. 82. Workmen's Compensation Act. New edition for the Act of 1906. 62. Parish and District Councils. 54. The Humanizing of the Poor Law. By J. F. OAKESHOTT. LEAFLETS.— 134. Small Holdings, Allotments and Common Pastures: and how to get them. 20. Questions for Poor Law Guardians. 68. The Tenant's Sanitary Catechism. 71. Ditto for London. FABIAN MUNICIPAL LEAFLETS (Nos. 32, 37 and 90 to 93). Municipalization of the Gas Supply. A Labor Policy for Public Authorities. Municipalization of Milk Supply. Municipal Pawnshops. Municipal Slaughterhouses. Women as Councillors. 1/- per 100.

IV.—General Politics and Fabian Policy.

127. Socialism and Labor Policy. 116. Fabianism and the Fiscal

WHAT AN EDUCATION COMMITTEE CAN DO. (ELEMENTARY SCHOOLS.)

WE are spending, in the United Kingdom, something like forty millions sterling out of the rates and taxes and public endowments on our educational system, and nobody is yet satisfied with the result. On all sides critics and educational reformers are asking for this or that alteration in what we teach our children and how we teach them. The ideal system will be reached only in the ideal State. In the meantime, whilst the educationalists are discussing what sort of education we should have, the practical administrator has to carry on such schools as exist. The present pamphlet represents an attempt to supply the men and women who find themselves on local education authorities, bodies of school managers, or children's care committees, with some useful information as to how to make the schools committed to their charge more efficient. At present, it is not too much to say, nearly all the twenty thousand schools in Great Britain are quite unnecessarily imperfect. The bulk of them fall as far below the best specimens as these best specimens themselves fall short of our ideal. To bring your own particular school—taking all local circumstances into account—up to something like the standard of the best contemporary school is as useful an achievement in our own day and generation as raising the standard of the ideal.

The following pages are therefore devoted to such humdrum matters as accommodation and staffing, equipment and curriculum, pictures and scholarships. The enormously important subject of medical inspection and treatment, and the physical condition of the child, must be dealt with separately.

Accommodation.

It is incumbent upon an education authority to provide sufficient school accommodation for every child of school age within its area, but a rising standard of efficiency, together with occasional fluctuations in population, prevents this from becoming a matter of undue simplicity. During the past forty years nearly every detail of school planning has changed. A modern well equipped school has a central hall for general assembly ; class rooms not less than four hundred square feet in area, to seat forty children, well lighted from the left of the pupils, well ventilated, and warmed ; wide corridors ; safe and efficient staircases and exits ; adequate cloak rooms, where wet clothes can be dried ; well provided lavatories for necessary washing ; a good supply of drinking water ; sanitary offices ; and sufficient playground accommodation, with a portion covered for shelter in wet weather.*

* Redman's Road L.C.C. Elementary School, Stepney, London, has class rooms to hold forty pupils ; ample halls, staircases, and exits ; is lit by electric light ; heated by low pressure hot water apparatus ; and its playgrounds provide thirty square feet to each pupil.

Such a school finds no counterpart among those erected before 1870, and is far in advance of many erected before 1900. At the time when some of the older voluntary schools were built, the Education Department of the day did not insist upon receiving complete and detailed plans before sanctioning the building ; and these often did not provide the eight square feet per child, including corridor and cloak room space, in the estimate which was first exacted. This provision has increased, and for some time past ten square feet in senior schools, and nine square feet in infant schools, counting only class rooms, have been enforced in all new buildings ; and the demand is now made that all old buildings shall be also raised to this standard.

Hence it is not surprising to find that in its last Report (1908-9) the Board points out that in England and Wales two thousand school premises, nearly one tenth of the whole, are still unsatisfactory. Of these, six hundred and sixty have been condemned, a time limit having been given for their recognition. It is to be noted that the standard adopted by the Board in thus condemning schools is by no means a high one compared with modern ideas on school planning ; and, further, that when a time limit is given, often of two or three years, during which condemned premises are allowed to continue in use, at the end of that time frequently no new building is available, and the time is extended until five or six years may elapse before satisfactory accommodation is provided, the health and efficiency of pupils and teachers alike suffering in the meantime. And such inadequate school buildings appear to be most common in the North of England.*

Some local authorities have arranged to rebuild or remodel systematically a certain number of schools each year. Thus in London a list of schools, arranged in order of urgency, has been prepared, with which it is proposed to deal at the rate of nine each year. One hundred and eighteen of the one hundred and ninety-seven council schools built 1870-80, and thirty-four of the one hundred and fifty-one built 1881-90, have so far been dealt with, leaving yet many defective buildings, some of which have been condemned in reports year after year for defects in lighting, warming, ventilation, cloak rooms, staircases, and playground accommodation, in strange contrast to the excellent provision made in new school premises.†

Of old, class rooms were built to seat from sixty to ninety pupils, often with one large room in which four or more classes could be taught together. Many such still remain, particularly in rural districts. The large room is still favored because of its convenience for purposes of Sunday school and evening meetings. One of the greatest commercial cities of the North has a non-provided school with a room eighty feet by twenty-five feet, in which one hundred and ninety children are taught in four classes. But in most districts

---

* Report, Board of Education, 1909.

† As the result of a careful survey by the London County Council in 1905 of the four hundred and thirty-three non-provided schools, closure was required in twenty-three cases and improvements in three hundred and forty-nine cases.

these are being gradually partitioned off, two large class rooms for sixty or seventy pupils being sometimes divided into three smaller rooms. Thus in London during 1907-8 five hundred and forty-three class rooms, with an average accommodation for sixty-seven pupils, were changed into five hundred and ninety rooms, with an average of fifty-two ; but in January, 1909, there still remained one thousand two hundred rooms accommodating more than sixty pupils.

Many schools, in some districts the majority, are still unprovided with halls in which no classes are taught, now recognized as essential for efficient work under modern methods. Thus there are fourteen schools in Colchester, seventeen in York, seventeen in Burnley, fifteen in Reading, without halls. In Darwen only two schools out of twenty are so provided, and West Bromwich has none, its schools resembling in this respect the majority in rural districts.

The question of safe exits in case of fire and provision of fire alarms has come to the fore of late. Some schools would prove veritable death traps in the event of a panic. Some authorities, as London, have recently been reconstructing and providing new exits, rehanging doors so that all shall open outwards, and providing fire alarms to ensure safety. In many districts, particularly in congested town areas, playgrounds are inadequate, giving insufficient room for adequate exercise—in one such the infants play in a continual gloom with no open air, whilst the boys play in instalments, in what is little better than an enlargement of the sanitary offices—deficiency here also adding to the difficulty of remodelling the premises where this is necessary.*

There is a general consensus of opinion that three hundred pupils is the number that can be most adequately provided for in one department, this number being large enough to admit of due classification and small enough for adequate supervision by the head teacher.

In many cases, for purposes of economy, much larger schools are administered. Some London council schools provide for five hundred and sixty pupils, and some districts in the North of England, as Burnley, have schools with more than eight hundred children under one head teacher. But higher elementary schools are restricted to three hundred and fifty pupils, and this number is the proposed limit for the new central elementary schools in London. If such a number is large enough in schools where classes are small and the premises exceedingly well equipped, there appears no reason why it should be exceeded in the ordinary schools, which are in other respects less well off.

Fluctuations in school population often cause considerable difficulty in providing sufficient school accommodation. Rapidly growing residential districts, sometimes already heavily rated, often fail to keep pace with the demand, with disastrous results. Thus, in a letter to the Tottenham Education Committee, sent in February,

---

* In Manchester it has recently been decided to build a new school in a corner of one of the public parks. The Edinburgh School Board has bought a large playing field for the common use of the schools with insufficient playgrounds.

1910, the Board of Education pointed out that nearly every school had too many children, that some class rooms were overcrowded to the extent of forty or fifty children, that passages and exit corridors were used for teaching purposes, and that the resulting overcrowding was bad for health and education. Such a case is fortunately extreme, though the conditions are not unknown elsewhere. On the other hand, some districts have an accommodation considerably in excess of present needs ; whilst again in some large areas, with a total excess of accommodation, there may be deficiency in certain parts of the area. Thus, for example, the London Authority, with a total accommodation greater than its needs, has recently given notice of its intention to build or enlarge schools for nearly ten thousand children in East and North London, where for some time past there have been insufficient school places.*

Staffing.

In considering the question of the relative values and sufficiency of staffs the different grades of teachers now employed must be remembered.

Over one hundred and fifty-nine thousand teachers were engaged in the elementary schools of England during the year 1908-9, of whom only eighty-nine thousand were certificated, and of these only forty-seven thousand had spent two or three years in a training college and were technically known as "trained" ; whilst forty-two thousand had received the certificate without having been through a training college. Of the remaining seventy thousand, nearly forty thousand have had some experience as pupil teachers, but having failed to pass the necessary examinations are known as uncertificated ; whilst the remaining thirty thousand are composed of pupil teachers, student teachers, and the anomalous, unqualified class known as supplementary teachers.†

In no satisfactory scheme of education would an unqualified teacher be allowed to be responsible for the education of children, any more than an unqualified medical student is allowed to be responsible for their physical well being. In the following statistics, therefore, only certificated teachers are considered, and the average number of children in average attendance for which such certificated teacher is responsible has been taken as the best basis of comparison. In this connection, however, two points have to be borne in mind : first, that amongst these certificated teachers are included the head

* In connection with this question the Board of Education has recently published the report of a committee on the provision of school buildings which, whilst efficient, shall be less costly and permanent in structure. Report of Departmental Committee on the Cost of School Buildings (Cd. 5534), 1911.

† It is noteworthy that, excluding pupil teachers, ninety-one per cent. of the non-certificated teachers are women, often very badly paid ; also that whilst so many unqualified teachers are allowed to be responsible for a class, a very large number of fully qualified young people, again mostly women, who have been trained at considerable expense to the State, have either been unable to obtain employment, or have had to accept employment as uncertificated teachers. It is said that in Lancashire alone there were recently (1910) two hundred and ninety-six certificated teachers employed as, and at the wages of, uncertificated teachers.

teachers, who are always for a part or the whole of their time engaged in administrative or executive duties, and who thus can never give their undivided attention to a class, and are often not expected to, therefore the number of pupils per certificated *class* teacher is always greater than that given ; whilst, in the second place, this number is still further increased by the fact that the teacher is actually responsible for the number of children *on the register*, for the irregular, who are often the greater burden, as well as for the regular. Thus in a school of three hundred pupils in average attendance, staffed by six certificated teachers, the number of children on the registers would be about three hundred and thirty, and in a school of this size the head teacher should be entirely freed from responsibility for a class ; hence the remaining five certificated teachers would be responsible for. sixty-five pupils each, instead of fifty, as would appear at first glance. This needs to be borne in mind when considering the following figures.

If school provision varies at all, it might be expected to vary in proportion to the wealth of a district. The best basis of wealth comparison for school purposes is that taken by the Government, the amount yielded by dividing the total product of a penny rate for the district by the number of children in average attendance. But it should be noted that by the Special Aid Grant, which is distributed in inverse proportion to this product of a penny rate, some approach to equality of burden is attempted.

The following table gives for the years 1907-8 and 1908-9 respectively the number of adult teachers per thousand pupils in average attendance in county boroughs, boroughs and urban districts, and in rural areas under county councils, in England and Wales.*

No. of Teachers per 1,000 Children in Average Attendance

ENGLAND

	Certificated		Uncertificated		Others		Totals	
	1907-8	1908-9	1907-8	1908-9	1907-8	1908-9	1907-8	1908-9
London...	23·6	24·2	1·57	1·2	0·78	0·39	25·95	25·79
County Boroughs	18·65	19·28	7·66	7·19	1·28	0·99	27·59	27·46
Bor. & Urb. Dist.	16·63	17·2	9·18	8·76	2·09	1·74	27·9	27·7
County Areas ...	14·69	15·08	10·17	10·59	7·24	6·59	32·1	32·2

WALES.

	Certificated		Uncertificated		Others		Totals	
County Boroughs	16·95	17·52	10·19	9·91	2·86	2·06	30·0	29·49
Bor. & Urb. Dist.	15·46	16·34	12·08	12·39	4·23	3·67	31·77	32·4
County Areas ...	13·34	13·89	12·65	13·17	8·65	8·51	34·54	35·57

* It may be noted that the more progressive areas maintain a certain number of higher grade or higher elementary schools, more liberally staffed than the ordinary schools. In such a district, though the average be below fifty, the size of classes may vary from twenty-five in a higher elementary school to seventy in an ordinary school at the beginning of the school year. On the other hand, nearly all authorities have a number of "supply ' teachers available in case of the absence of permanent teachers, and have also some teachers of special subjects who are not technically "certificated," and do not count for staffing purposes. Thus London in 1910 had one hundred and twenty-six visiting teachers, mainly for French ; three hundred and thirty-four teachers of domestic economy ; and two hundred and ninety-seven teachers of handicraft under this last head.

In order that there should be one certificated teacher for every forty pupils, with a head teacher freed from responsibility for a class for every three hundred pupils, 28·3 certificated teachers for every thousand pupils would be necessary. From this table it will be seen how far we are from that quite modern ideal. But there has been steady improvement in the number of certificated teachers employed, approximating generally to ·6, being lowest in the English rural areas, whilst the number of uncertificated and others tends to get less. Further, it may be noted that the quality of the teaching provision decreases as we go from county boroughs to rural districts; that Wales makes distinctly worse provision than England; and that the number of "teachers of a sort" provided is not an indication of the quality of the teaching staff, unless taken inversely.

The second table gives for certain education areas the product of a penny rate (ppr.) and the education rate for 1907-8, together with A, the number of children in average attendance to each certificated teacher, including the head teacher, and B, the percentage of certificated teachers in the total number of adult teachers employed, for 1907-8 and 1908-9 respectively. The instances given are typical of many that might be cited, and are arranged in order of column A for 1908-9.

Area	Ppr.	Rate	A 1907-8	A 1908-9	B 1907-8	B 1908-9
COUNTY AREAS.						
Middlesex	4/4	10·7	49·7	50·5	66·0	71·0
Surrey	5/6	10·1	55·4	56·0	49·9	56·5
Kent	3/4	10·9	64·7	63·3	44·7	50·8
Lancashire... ...	3/0	9·8	67·0	65·0	40·8	47·5
West Riding ...	2/8	10·4	69·0	65·1	40·4	48·5
Norfolk	2/4	9·0	71·1	70·2	33·8	40·0
Essex	2/8	11·3	75·0	73·3	39·5	44·2
Holland (Lincs.) ...	3/8	5·6	75·8	76·5	36·6	36·7
SOME WELSH TOWNS.						
Barry	3/4	20·8	30·8	29·	84·2	84·4
Cardiff	3/2	13·9	55·7	51·	62·4	69·3
Newport	2/6	17·2	58·4	58·	60·9	62·6
Swansea	2/2	19·7	64·4	6 5·3	53·2	53·0
ENGLISH TOWN AREAS.						
Hornsey	6/8	15·2	33·2	33.0	95·0	95·0
Tottenham ...	2/2	24·2	41·0	40·8	82·4	94·0
London	5/4	17·0	43·2	41·6	81·5	92·8
Birkenhead ...	2/10	15·5	49·3	45·9	70·4	74·6
Leyton	2/2	24·9	47·0	48·7	67·2	83·5
Manchester ...	3/6	14·9	51·5	49·1	56·7	61·2
Oldham	2/2	20·1	52·6	50·1	66·7	68·0
Stockport	2/4	11·2	66·0	63·2	57·6	60·5
Preston	1/10	7·6	68·0	66·6	50·6	54·9
Eastbourne ...	6/4	5·6	72·0	69·6	47·0	55·4
Worcester	2/4	10·4	71·4	70·5	38·2	46·1
St. Helens	1/8	10·0	76·5	71·4	42·0	46·6

Together with general improvement very considerable variation will be noticed. The counties ranged from 50·5 to 76·5 pupils per certificated teacher. There seems no reason why the Holland Division of Lincolnshire should be so poorly equipped and spend so little. In the towns, too, the teaching provision of heavily rated Tottenham and Leyton will bear comparison with that made in London and Birmingham. Nor are these two exceptional among the poorer residential districts around London. In Ilford, Leyton, East Ham, West Ham, Walthamstow, and Edmonton, the rate varied from 19·8 to 24·9 pence, and the provision of certificated teachers varied from one to forty-seven to one to fifty pupils. Wealthier Manchester is at last coming into line with them. Oldham and Preston, two towns very similar in character, afford an interesting contrast, Oldham raising an education rate nearly three times as great as Preston and providing thirteen per cent. more certificated teachers. Birkenhead and Stockport form another interesting pair, and the comparison is somewhat odious for Stockport. But if Preston and Stockport were not well equipped, wealthy Eastbourne and the dignified cathedral city of Worcester could at least cast no stones at them, whilst the poverty of St. Helens cannot justify its lack of qualified teachers. If, indeed, the head teachers of schools large enough for them to be relieved from responsibility for a class had been excluded from the computation, some of these authorities would, as already explained, make a much worse appearance. Thus in Eastbourne, excluding the head teachers of each of its twenty-five departments, there was in 1908-9 only one certificated class teacher for every one hundred and three pupils in average attendance. But Eastbourne had its reward in having one of the lowest education rates in the kingdom.*

The issue of Circular 709, which, whilst reducing the numbers of pupils for which non-certificated teachers will in future be allowed to be responsible, insists that the number of scholars on the register of a class under the instruction of one teacher shall not exceed sixty, is justified by such instances as have been, and others that could be, quoted ; as is also the wish of the Board of Education that "the arrangements of certain authorities should be levelled upwards to the standard already attained, or in process of attaining, in other parts of the country, and that a more uniform observance of the fundamental conditions of educational efficiency should be secured."† But, in order to attain that, there needs to be also some readjustment of the financial burden to relieve the discrepancy between such rates as that of 24·9 pence in the pound in Leyton and that of 5·6 pence in Eastbourne.‡

* The proportions of non-provided schools in these districts is suggestive. Oldham had sixteen non-provided out of thirty-eight schools ; Preston, thirty-six out of thirty-eight ; Worcester, sixteen out of eighteen ; Eastbourne, ten out of thirteen ; and St. Helens, thirty-three out of thirty-nine. Eastbourne is also the favored abode of a large number of proprietary schools.

† Prefatory Memorandum, Code of Regulations, 1909.

‡ Ilford in 1891, had a population of ten thousand nine hundred and eleven and an education rate of twopence ; in June, 1909, its population was seventy-nine thousand four hundred and thirty-six and its education rate for 1909-10 is one shilling and ten-pence in the pound. Since 1894 it has built thirteen schools, and two more are planned.

Desks.

Let us now turn to the subject of equipment of school premises. For children under six it seems to be agreed that low tables and small chairs are better than any form of desk. The children sit in small groups, six or eight at a table, and the mistress moves easily among them. These little chairs and tables can be procured from any good makers of school furniture at the following prices : chairs, two shillings and threepence to three shillings and fourpence each ; tables, ten shillings to sixteen shillings, according to size.

For older children also separate seats should be used. Doctors and teachers alike agree on this point. For reasons of hygiene and of order there should be a clear space between children engaged in school work. The long benches once in use, and still used in many country schools, are therefore to be condemned. The single seat is best provided by single desks. Chairs are sometimes used with these for reasons of economy. The desk without seat costs about eighteen shillings, and the chair may be had for two shillings ; while a desk with attached seat costs from twenty-two shillings and six-pence to twenty-five shillings, according to varieties of pattern. The small saving, however, effected by the use of chairs is reported to be inadvisable, since the chairs are noisy in use ; and with them it is not so easy to secure that the child sits in a good position for reading, writing, or drawing. And if the growing child sits in a dis-torted position for four or five hours of five days in the week, the effect on his immature body is disastrous.

The cost of providing single desks for many hundreds or thousands of children is evidently a matter for serious consideration to many educational authorities. New schools can be fitted out with tables and separate chairs for baby classes, and with single desks for the standards, at no very great addition to the cost of the old fashioned and unhygienic double desks. But to "scrap" an existing supply is the difficulty of many administrators. A com-promise between the worst system and the best can be found and cost lessened by desks such as the " Sheffield," in which a long slope for books is backed by separate seats at satisfactory distances from each other. These have also the merit, shared by the single desk, of preventing overcrowding. A dual desk can easily be made to seat three and a form a very indefinite number, but only one child can sit on a separate seat.

Flat desks are objectionable, because the child must bend over them to write in a position which cramps the body. This objection does not apply to the tables for babies, who do not write.

It may be well to suggest here that all desks should be cleansed once a week with a disinfectant solution.

We have made enquiries of makers of school furniture and of workmen whether it is advisable to convert dual desks already existing in a school into single ones. So far as our enquiries have gone, all authorities agree that this is not worth while. The cost, they say, of providing the necessary iron supports would amount to almost that of new single desks. The desk so made would be inferior to the new desk made to a better pattern, and therefore it does not appear that the adaptation can generally be recommended. Local conditions, however, might make such a plan possible in some places, where the necessary labor is easily obtainable and where cost must be very rigidly calculated.

Pictures.

Every room in the school should have some pictures. Some of these are for decoration purely, since we want to give our children in the schools something of beauty and color, which unluckily many of them cannot find in their own poverty stricken homes. Others are for use in teaching, and are a most valuable aid to the teacher.

Of the first class are landscapes, reproductions of famous pictures, and photographs of statuary. A fine set of landscapes in color lithography, produced in Germany, can be had at six shillings (unframed) each. Frames with movable backs can be had, thirty-three by twenty-six inches, for three shillings and sixpence each.* Reproductions of the pictures of great artists will not only decorate the class room, but give the children the beginning of an acquaintance with the masterpieces of human achievement in beauty. One can get, for example, admirable color prints of Turner's pictures of Venice or his Fighting Téméraire, in frames, at prices varying from five shillings and sixpence to eight shillings and ninepence. Seemann's Masterpieces, published by Asher, include photographs of friezes from the Parthenon, the Venus of Milo, reliefs from the famous Baptistry Door at Florence, thirty-one by twenty-five inches, at ninepence unframed and three shillings and sevenpence framed.

The school should contain also pictures of such places and scenery as do not come within the child's own experience. Some of the lithographed color landscapes are useful in this connection, such as those of Autumn Leaves (Otto), A Daisy Field, Windermere (Luther Hooper), to be had framed at about nine shillings each. Pictures of the unfamiliar animals must be added to these. The Woodbury phototypes, seventeen by nineteen inches, three shillings and sixpence in frames, are good examples.

Little children should have the simplest pictures in their rooms, in flat color, with simple outlines, and little detail. Cecil Aldin's Friezes, Caldecott's Nursery Rhymes, are good examples of what they need. They love pictures of the domestic animals.

In every case pictures should be hung low, so that they can be easily seen by the children in the room. The more easily they can be handled and their places changed by the teacher the better. They may with advantage be moved from room to room at intervals of a few months, so that the interest of the children may be roused by new pictures in their rooms. The frames with movable backs are also very useful for the purpose of changing pictures, either as they are wanted to illustrate lessons or because the pupils are no longer interested in a picture which they know by heart.

* From Asher & Co , 13 Bedford Street, Covent Garden, W.C.

Buckinghamshire has a voluntary organization, recognized by the County Education Committee, which, on receipt of subscriptions from school managers (allowed in the yearly estimates), lends pictures to a school and changes them yearly. The number of pictures sent is proportionate to the subscription. By this excellent plan a constant variety is secured, and the interest of the children roused in the new picture on the wall. Where this plan is adopted, frames of standard sizes might be used, so that the pictures might be forwarded unframed and cost of carriage lessened. Frames should be simple ; broad dark ones are generally best. White might be used for children's pictures. The frame should fit the edge of the picture itself, leaving none of the white margin visible.

Closely connected with the supply of pictures is the use of a good school lantern. Many authorities provide these, whilst some have organized loan collections of slides for use with them, of which the largest is to be found in London. Here during the past few years the lantern has become increasingly popular as an aid to teaching, while the list of slides on loan has increased from a few hundred to several thousand.

Series Recommended.

Teubner Series (Asher & Co.), four shillings to six shillings, unframed.

Voigtländer Series (Asher & Co.), two shillings and sixpence to six shillings, unframed.

Caspari Friezes, for small children (Asher & Co.), three shillings and sixpence to four shillings and sixpence, unframed.

Scholars' Cartoons (Haufstängl), seven shillings and sixpence, unframed.

Britannia Historical Pictures (Arnold), two shillings and sixpence, unframed.

Fitzroy Pictures (G. Bell, Covent Garden), two shillings and sixpence to five shillings and sixpence.

Historical Portraits (Art for Schools Association, Queen Street, Bloomsbury, W.C.), one shilling and sixpence to ten shillings and sixpence.

These prices are generally subject to discount.

School Libraries.

A good library is an indispensable adjunct to a school. Beyond the interest and intellectual stimulus it provides, it offers also a training for the right use of leisure, not less important than training for work.

Hence it is disappointing to find how very few schools, except in the more advanced districts, are well equipped in this respect. In many no library exists. One advanced city has libraries only in eighty-eight out of one hundred and forty-four senior departments. In others there is one for the older scholars only. In some schools a library is provided, but is never used, or its use is restricted to the top class or to the most regular scholars. Even in London these varieties may be found. That there should be books on loan accessible to every child in the school who is able to read, not merely as a reward, but as an essential part of his education, is for many a distant ideal. What, too, is often overlooked is that the books should be such as to arouse a spontaneous interest, graduated to the ages of those who shall read them, not the cast off works of the last generation, more strongly and less invitingly bound.

In London provision is made for library books for the children in Standard Three and upwards, but facilities may be extended to children below the Third Standard. For the annual replenishing of the library, expenditure is allowed at the rate of one halfpenny per head per child in average attendance up to a general limit of twelve shillings for each senior department.

But however good the school library may be, there should be co-operation with the public library. In Sheffield, in seventy-four senior departments, four thousand three hundred and seven pupils have borrowed, on an average, two thousand four hundred and eighty-five books from the public library per week. In many London boroughs also such co-operation exists. In Stepney and Poplar, for example, the teachers recommend pupils as borrowers on forms provided for the purpose, advise as to the selection of books from the special catalogue, and co-operate with the librarian in ensuring their due return and proper use.

It is evident, too, that very few authorities make any grant towards the provision of a teachers' reference library in each school ; and this is, perhaps, the more necessary just where they are least often found—in the rural districts. The London authority not only does this, but is forming its own educational circulating library for the use of teachers and officers ; and is, moreover, inviting the local libraries to place similar pedagogical works upon their shelves. The Surrey County Council has also a central reference library for teachers, from which books are lent to schools at the rate of one per month for each department having less than one hundred and fifty pupils, and two where there are more.

Some of the best schools, too, have formed a small reference library for the use of the older pupils, to train them in the habit of consulting larger books of reference. In some cases this can be amalgamated with the teachers' reference library.

Curriculum.

The broad outlines of the elementary school curriculum are laid out in the annual Code of Regulations,* but these permit of considerable variety of interpretation, depending mainly upon the quality of the teaching staff and the nature of the equipment provided. The latter is often the determining factor ; the complaints that certain work, which would be desirable, cannot be carried out from lack of suitable rooms and appliances are very general.

* See Code of Regulations for Public Elementary Schools; also Suggestions for the Consideration of Teachers.

Of late years considerable improvements in the methods of teaching the long recognized school subjects—writing, arithmetic, English, history, and geography—have been introduced ; whilst other subjects have been added to the curriculum, with the object, on the one hand, of making school life more interesting and healthful ; on the other, of bringing the knowledge and skill acquired more directly into touch with life activities. Thus the teaching of freehand drawing has in the best school systems developed into brush drawing, clay modelling, and design. Nature study is becoming more general. An improved system of physical exercises has been introduced, with which often goes some instruction in personal hygiene, in swimming, and in organized games. These changes have raised another difficulty, that of the overcrowded curriculum. The solution of this problem must be found both by lessening the time given to the older subjects and by introducing a closer co-operation between subjects such as history, English, and geography, nature study and drawing, arithmetic and domestic science or handicraft, in such a way that the teaching of one may help in the comprehension of the other.

In order to provide some preparation for the more specifically after-school activities, through subjects and by methods in themselves educationally valuable to children, grants are paid by the Board of Education for satisfactory courses of instruction in cookery, laundry work, combined domestic subjects, handicraft, and, in rural districts, gardening and dairy work. But the grants paid do not cover the whole cost of such instruction even when provided with the minimum of equipment, hence the frequent lack of provision. Such subjects are usually taught at centres which children from neighboring schools attend one half day in each week, and they all involve some amount of manual as well as mental training. But they have in the past been taught without any connection with the other subjects in the curriculum, a defect which some attempts are being made to remedy. In London some centres are being allocated to the exclusive use of the pupils of one school and placed under the control of the head teacher, as in the central elementary schools ; in others conferences are arranged between the heads of the contributory schools and the teachers of these special subject centres. The fact that in England, unlike America, handwork, except in the form of drawing, is usually non-existent during the four or five years between the infant school and the upper classes of the elementary school has also attracted attention of late. In many advanced schools some form of educational handwork has been introduced in those years ; and, partly to encourage this, the Board of Education has recently arranged that a grant should be paid in a limited number of cases for a lighter and less expensive form of woodwork than is ordinarily practised.

HANDICRAFT.

This subject is confined to boys, and usually consists of some form of woodwork, though in some of the larger industrial areas metalwork is included. In 1908-9 it was taught to over two hundred thousand pupils in nearly three thousand seven hundred schools in England and Wales; yet out of sixty-two autonomous counties, no satisfactory provision for its teaching had been made in eighteen, including Cornwall, Dorset, Lincoln, Northumberland, Nottinghamshire, and the East Riding. Even though the distances to be traversed present difficulties in rural districts, the table appended shows that this difficulty is not insuperable.

DOMESTIC SCIENCE.

This, for girls, more than supplies the place which handicraft fills for boys. It includes cookery, taught in 1908-9 to nearly three hundred thousand girls; laundrywork, taught to ninety-three thousand; and combined domestic subjects, comprising cookery, laundry, and housewifery, taught to sixteen thousand girls in England alone. For this last there is usually provided a cottage or flat fitted as a workman's home. Some interesting developments are taking place in these subjects. The Hull Education Committee has recently decided to provide for girls about to leave school a half time course of three and a half months, to include four weeks cookery, two weeks laundrywork, and eight weeks in an artizan's house; whilst London has established twelve domestic economy day schools, where a year's full time training is to be given to selected girls between the ages of thirteen and sixteen years. But there are still many districts where no facilities are provided for practical training in domestic subjects during school years, and few where the accommodation is sufficient to provide for all the girls old enough to profit by such training.

An essential part of domestic science is the instruction in needlework, which for many years has formed an important, and often very irksome, subject in the ordinary school course. The barbarous practice, so long continued, of forcing infants to engage in needlework drill long before the fine muscles used would have been normally developed, is fast dying out; but in many girls' schools slow and obsolete methods and unnecessarily fine stitching are still exacted. The Board of Education has recently permitted the use of the sewing machine to be taught in girls' schools, and some authorities are already providing machines for this purpose.

GARDENING.

This is almost entirely confined to rural districts. In 1908-9 twenty-eight thousand pupils were receiving instruction in England alone in twelve hundred schools, of which one hundred were in urban areas. The number of pupils had nearly doubled during the previous three years. The Board of Education, writing to the Lancashire Education Committee, recently suggested that "the work of a rural school should centre round such practical subjects as are suited to the occupations of the locality, namely, gardening, handicraft, and domestic economy; and associated with these should be subjects teaching the principles underlying the practical instruction, such as arithmetic, drawing, and rural science." Yet there has been great diversity in the provision made for the teaching of so eminently rural a subject as gardening ; for whilst Staffordshire and Surrey headed the list in 1908-9 with one hundred and thirty-eight and one hundred and eight schools respectively receiving grants for it, Rutland had none.*

The following table gives the number of pupils who qualified for Board of Education grants in these subjects, in the various areas noted, during the year 1908-9. The ppr. (see page 6), the rate in pence, and the average attendance of pupils of *five years and over* are given for purposes of comparison. The columns refer respectively to cookery, laundry, combined domestic subjects, handicraft, and gardening, and the figure in the last column shows what percentage the sum of these forms of the average attendance. It is suggested that even though instruction in these subjects is confined to pupils over eleven years of age, this figure gives a good basis of comparison as to the extent of provision made under these heads.

As in the preceding table, considerable variations will be found, and there appears no reason why among the counties Berkshire, Northumberland, and the East Riding should be so seriously in default. Nor are these the worst. Rutland, comparatively wealthy, with ppr. 3s. 10d. and nearly three thousand pupils, earned such grants on *ten*, and rejoiced in an education rate of 3·8d., whilst the Holland division of Lincolnshire, ppr. 3s. 8d. and rate 5·6d., earned these grants on fourteen of its more than nine thousand pupils. In the town areas there are also some notable differences. Why should Manchester and Liverpool make worse provision than Reading, and West Ham eclipse the wealthier districts below it? And there are too many urban areas where no better provision is made than in Peterborough, Bury, and Dover, and some quite prepared to dispute with Dover for the privilege of being the worst. Yet improvement in the past year has been general. Surrey, London, and Manchester have increased the percentage in the last column by four, Essex by six, and Middlesex by 10·5. Some towns, however, have made little progress, and the East Riding has done worse, from ·9 to ·6. Fortunately it cannot do much worse.

---

* Among recent developments it may be noted that in 1908 9 one hundred and nine boys qualified for grants in cookery in Essex, East Suffolk, and the North Riding, and fifty-four girls in dairy work, of whom fifty were in Cornwall.

Area.	Ppr.	Rate.	Average Attendance Five Years.	No. of Pupils Receiving Grants (1908-9) in:					
				Cookery.	Laundry.	Domestic Subjects.	Handicraft.	Gardening.	Per cent.
COUNTY AREAS.									
Surrey	5/6	10·1	53,525	3,443	933	—	2,191	1,824	15·6
Gloucestershire	2/6	11·3	41,696	2,015	1,042	141	1,002	892	12·2
Essex	2/8	11·3	59,375	4,630	260	—	680	1,042	11·1
Kent	3/4	10·9	71,979	2,406	241	—	548	664	5·3
Lancashire	3/0	9·8	127,960	2,992	345	11	507	629	3·6
West Riding	2/8	10·4	165,267	3,981	537	—	707	360	3·4
Berkshire	3/4	11·5	22,664	141	—	—	90	164	1·3
Northumberland	3/2	10·5	42,933	117	—	—	—	260	·9
East Riding	3/8	7·5	17,768	—	—	—	—	100	·6
TOWN AREAS (ENGLAND).									
Hornsey	7/2	15·2	6,833	776	196	54	758	—	26·1
Reading	2/10	18·7	10,632	960	626	64	951	—	24·4
London	5/4	17·0	604,842	49,650	33,425	7,861	57,812	20	23·1
Birkenhead	2/10	15·5	17,876	2,122	358	—	1,368	—	21·5
Manchester	3/6	14·9	91,100	6,368	1,209	169	7,613	14	16·8
West Ham	1/10	22·7	50,517	3,377	2,123	—	2,710	—	16·2
Liverpool	3/0	16·0	112,293	7,936	1,870	—	5,730	—	13·9
Stockport	2/4	11·2	14,763	1,061	—	—	339	54	9·8
Northampton	2/2	19·9	12,566	1,023	56	—	—	—	8·6
Peterborough	2/2	8·8	5,292	360	—	—	—	26	7·3
Bury	2/10	9·4	6,430	234	—	—	176	—	5·9
Dover	2/10	11·6	5,527	180	—	—	—	—	3·3

So far as the elementary school is concerned, the vocational value of such subjects should be subsidiary to their educational value, as giving more play to the muscular activities of childhood and, through their direct dealings with concrete matter, providing a good basis for intellectual activities. Somewhat similar in nature is the increased attention now given to the teaching of elementary science in schools—another subject often starved for lack of the necessary equipment—together with the rapid growth of late years of the nature study movement. I he same spirit has entered into the teaching of other school subjects. London puts aside about five hundred pounds per annum to help in paying the expenses of pupils visiting, during school hours, places of educational interest having some bearing on the class lessons, and is prepared to expend another one hundred pounds per year towards the expenses inci- dental to school journeys on which, during a week or more, pupils from certain schools study the topography, geology, history, climatic conditions, etc., of some country district. All such work has its effect upon the teaching of other parts of the curriculum, the his- tory, geography, English, mathematics. No part of the school system has felt the effects of this wider view of educational respon- sibility more than the infant school, within the walls of which a revolution, still uncompleted, has been silently proceeding these ten years past. But all these new developments make heavy calls upon the skill and intelligence of the teachers, and need a more generous equipment than was formerly found necessary. Hence those dis- tricts where necessary equipment is refused, or where unskilled teachers are engaged, are refusing their children a fair chance as compared with those of more favored districts, where the essentials of satisfactory preparation for modern conditions are more justly provided.

Scholarships.

No public authority had power to incur expenditure on scholar- ships prior to the Technical Instruction Act of 1891 ; the Acts of 1902-3, placing elementary and secondary education in the hands of the county and borough councils first explicitly permitted general schemes to be made. Many varieties of such are now in process of evolution. Here we shall deal in the main with scholarships open to pupils in the elementary schools, and not, as in the case of the " probationer " scholarships, earmarked for those' intending to be- come teachers.

London (average attendance 650,554) now offers about 1,800 junior county scholarships to pupils between eleven and twelve years of age, tenable for three years, but renewable for a further two years in the case of those pupils who show ability to profit by the extension. It has been decided that, in view of the generally rising standard of attainments of the pupils in London elementary schools, no definite limit shall be placed upon the number to be awarded in future. Nor is any distinction of sex to be made ; formerly girls had the preference, in 1907 by seventeen to ten, in 1908 by thirteen to ten ; but it is proposed that in future the numbers shall be approximately equal, and this year, 1910, there have been awarded 865 to boys and 846 to girls. It is to be noted that in addition to those granted by the Council there are about 325 trust fund scholarships open to competition by children in London elementary schools.

Manchester (average attendance 97,068) offers twenty junior scholarships, tenable for five years, with a varying number of bursaries of £10 per annum for two years, limited to boys of fourteen to fifteen years already in the higher elementary schools, and ten bursaries of £10 for three years awarded to pupils who have obtained foundation scholarships at secondary schools. Differentiation here is in favor of the boys, who receive twelve of the twenty scholarships, eight of the ten bursaries, in addition to all the higher elementary bursaries. Liverpool (average attendance 117,255) offers fifty junior scholarships for two years, renewable for a third or fourth year, and equally divided between boys and girls. Ilford (average attendance 9,824) gave sixty-one scholarships in 1909. Coventry (average attendance 14,444) gives forty-five ; whilst Burnley (average attendance 15,151) provides only twenty.

As examples of what is being done in the rural areas under the county councils, we may note that Lancashire (average attendance 137,791) offers 350 junior exhibitions restricted to children in the elementary schools, and 100 open junior scholarships, all tenable for four years ; candidates must be between eleven and thirteen years of age. Kent (average attendance 76,840) gives 200 to boys and girls of eleven years of age. Warwickshire (average attendance 37,309) offers twenty-four, whilst Hertfordshire (average attendance 42,754) provides twenty.

Though there is some variation in methods of award the written competitive examination seems to hold general sway as yet, as for example in Lancashire. In some districts, as in Liverpool and Warwickshire and Wiltshire, this is followed by an oral examination of selected candidates, a method which is said to have given general satisfaction ; but here, even more than in the written test, much depends upon the conditions under which this is carried out. In other places the head teachers of the elementary school have some power of recommendation, and it is possible that this is more often influential than printed schemes would testify. But in London the head teachers are specially instructed to send in for the written examination all boys and girls between eleven and twelve years who are working in the fifth or higher standard ; the examiners, however, in conjunction with the results of this examination, consider the position of the pupil at the previous school term examination.

The amount of the grants made towards maintenance shows considerable variation, and this is a matter of vital importance, for where these are insufficient one of two things happens : either the children of poor parents fail to compete, or, should they obtain a scholarship, relinquish it long before its term has expired. The income of the parent also needs consideration, otherwise grants may go where they are not needed, or an undue proportion may go to those who can afford to pay for extra tuition for their children preparatory to the examination. In London junior scholarships may be held by children of parents having incomes up to £300 per annum, but two-thirds of the total must go to those having less than £160 per annum. Only the latter obtain grants during the first three years of £6 per annum; for the fourth and fifth years, whilst these receive £15 per annum, those whose parents' income falls between £160 and £300 get only £10 per annum. In each case free education and books are provided.

In Manchester grants for the five years range from £10 to £20, with £2 10s. increases; but from these the ordinary fees of the secondary schools have to be paid. In Liverpool the grants made are £6, £9, £12 and £15 per annum, with free education and half the cost of books. The county (Lancashire) is, however, less generous. It gives free education up to £6 per annum, travelling expenses in excess of £1 per annum, an allowance for books not exceeding £1 per annum, and a maintenance grant only during the third and fourth years, and then strictly where circumstances render this necessary. Hence it is not surprising to hear that the scholarships are frequently relinquished. This appears also to be the case in Wiltshire, where, in addition to free tuition, £5 only is granted towards maintenance, whilst Warwickshire gives £10 in addition to travelling expenses. This last item is important in rural districts, where some pupils travel upwards of ten miles to school, whilst others are deterred by distance or difficult access from competing. In Devonshire the heads of the secondary schools have suggested the provision of conveyances to gather the pupils from outlying districts, and the authority has promised to consider any scheme to that end that may be submitted. In other places it has been suggested that lodging-houses might be registered near the schools, where pupils coming from a distance could reside during the school days of the week; but for these maintenance grants would need to be adequate if this suggestion were adopted.

The evils of inadequate grants to which reference has been made have of late become acute in relation to other classes of pupils. By Section 20 of the Regulations for Secondary Schools, 25 per cent. of free places have to be provided in all secondary schools receiving grants from the Board of Education. With these, however, there goes no financial help for the poorer pupils, for whom they were doubtless intended, towards maintenance, books, or travelling. Similarly, many of the endowed charity, or trust fund, scholarships provide only free education, or with this a quite inadequate money grant. Beyond these two classes lies another, the existence of which has called for comment in many parts of the country, made up of pupils who, on account of late development or temporary illness, or some other reason, miss the junior scholarships at the early age at which they are awarded, but whose general abilities are such as to justify the belief that they should have received one. For all these classes the London County Council propose this year to provide 300 supplementary county scholarships, graduated in value in accordance with the income of the parent and the age of the pupil, and tenable from thirteen to sixteen years of age.*

But there has been of late a growing feeling that the education provided at the secondary schools through the scholarships above described does not meet all the requirements of the case, and some authorities have begun to provide trade scholarships for elementary school pupils.† Of such London has now 158 available for boys and 168 for girls, and it is hoped that within the next few years, after further experience has helped to solve some of the difficult problems connected with this question, some 600 will be available. These are tenable for two or three years, and carry maintenance grants varying from £6 to £15, with free education in such trades as building, engineering, book production, silversmithing, etc., for boys, and dress-making, tailoring, upholstery, millinery, etc., for girls. In addition there are 300 domestic economy scholarships granted to girls of fourteen years of age for one year—to be increased in some cases to two—with a maintenance grant of £4.‡

Medical Inspection.

The Education (Administrative Provisions) Act, 1907, has made it compulsory on all local education authorities to provide for the medical inspection of school children. The Board of Education at present requires that the examination shall include all children admitted to the school and all expected to leave during the year.§ As a rule also special cases selected by the teachers are seen by the school doctors.

Who should be appointed School Medical Officer?

The Board of Education has strongly recommended that in counties, county boroughs, and where practicable in non-county boroughs, the medical officer of health should be appointed school medical officer. The former has various responsibilities with regard to infectious diseases, school closure, and sanitary condition of schools ; he is responsible, too, for the hygiene and sanitary conditions of the homes, which are of primary importance to the health of the child, but over which the school medical officer, as such, has at present no control. It is most desirable, therefore, that the two services should be closely co-ordinated, and that the chief responsibility for both should, where practicable, rest on one and the same

* The new scheme for Durham provides for scholarships in proportion of one to 3,000 of the population for pupils under thirteen years (approximately 250), and one to 20,000 of population for pupils between thirteen and fifteen (approximately thirty-five to forty), and this same number will be offered to pupils in secondary schools between thirteen and fifteen years of age.

† It is worthy of note that grants may now be made to parents of children in ordinary elementary schools to enable them to keep their children at school beyond the age of exemption from school attendance.

‡ The Gloucestershire Education Committee has since 1907 been interested in such problems and has established a craft school at Brimscombe, whilst several counties, as Dorset and Hertfordshire, offer agricultural scholarships.

§ Minute of Board of Education, June 25th, 1910 (Cd. 5231).

person. When the medical officer of health is appointed school medical officer, medical inspection is usually carried out by assistants, as at Colchester, where an assistant woman medical officer of health and school medical officer devotes her whole time to medical inspection and work in the schools.

In Hertfordshire and Derbyshire the county medical officer of health was appointed school medical officer, and the medical officer of health of each local sanitary authority assistant school medical officer, thus still further co-ordinating the work of the doctor in the school and in the home. Though the scheme is said to work well in Hertfordshire it has the drawback that medical inspection and supervision of hygiene in the schools are specialized work which the local officer may not be particularly well qualified to undertake. It is noteworthy that the tendency generally among education authorities is to abandon the system of part time in favor of that of whole time school medical officers,* and where school clinics are established at which treatment is carried out by school medical officers, the plea of monotony of work sometimes urged against whole time appointments ceases to have any force.†

It is well to appoint a duly qualified medical woman for the inspection of the girls and infants. Up the end of 1908 sixty-eight women had been appointed as school medical officers, or assistants, by local education authorities.

The Routine of Medical Inspection.

The Board of Education has issued a schedule of medical inspection, which specifies the information that should be obtained by the inspector and his assistants. This schedule is being generally followed by local education authorities with little alteration.‡

The amount of time given by the medical officer to the examination of each child varies enormously under different local authorities. At a council school in Coventry the doctor gave an average of twenty minutes per child, while in a village of Kent an average of 2·4 minutes only was allowed for the doctor's examination. It would seem, from a comparison of instances and reports, that seven to ten minutes is the time considered necessary in an ordinary way for the examination of normal cases, while longer is allowed for special cases. A shorter time than this is clearly insufficient for the prescribed stock-taking of the special conditions of teeth, nose, throat, and eyes, hearing, speech and mental condition, plus examination for any abnormal condition of heart, lungs or nervous system, even if the formal preliminaries and the weighing, measuring, eye-testing and examination as to general cleanliness are performed by school nurses or teachers.

---

* Annual Report for 1908 of Chief Medical Officer of the Board of Education, p. 19.

† See Report of School Medical Officer, Bradford, 1908, p. 42.

‡ Annual Report for 1908 of the Chief Medical Officer of the Board of Education, p. 30.

The head teachers of each department are usually present at the medical examination in addition to undertaking, in many districts, part of the preliminary work. This co-operation of the teachers though in many ways very desirable is open to grave objections in localities where the schools are not fully staffed ; as, for example, in Kent, where the staffing is low and where it also appears that the briefest period is given to examination by the medical officer.

Co-operation of Parents.

There is much to be gained by having parents present at the medical examination of their children. It should be recognized that in case of a defect being discovered it is the doctor's duty to place his knowledge at the disposal of the child's parents and convey to them a realization of the conditions present. The doctor may then point out that treatment is required, but detailed consideration (e.g., the recommendation of operation for adenoids) should be left to the doctor who will undertake the case. Furthermore, though this is not part of his duties, he is sometimes able to point out simple remedies for any small ailments discovered, give hints as to the clothing, which is apt in the case of girls to be excessive in quantity and at the same time unhygienic, and give general advice as to hygiene and cleanliness. He does this whilst conducting the examination, without much loss of time, and were school clinics established where the examining doctor also administered treatment, this could be made part of his recognized duty, thereby vastly increasing the value of the inspection.

In any case, if the parent is present there is greater probability that he or she will go to the trouble and expense of carrying out treatment which the doctor's examination has shown to be required.

The majority of education authorities invite parents to attend ; some further encourage them by providing a comfortable waiting place, by having children accompanied by a parent examined first, and by generally endeavoring to put them to as little inconvenience and loss of time, and to make things as agreeable to them as possible.

The percentage of parents' attendance varies very much from place to place. At a school in Lancashire none were present at the examination of their children, though all were invited. At a village in Warwickshire nearly every child was attended by a parent. In a Coventry school parents attended with their girls but not with their boys. In the county of Worcester 61 per cent. of the children examined were attended by a parent, and judging by other examples this is probably not far above the average.

Value of Medical Examination.

There can be no question as to the value of medical examination. Prevention is better than cure, and routine inspection brings to light many incipient maladies which teachers and parents had not suspected. For example, in Worcestershire cases were discovered of incipient spinal curvature,* to correct which it is necessary the desks should be high enough and suitably placed. Cases were found of "dilated heart" due to cycling up steep hills, which became normal when on the doctor's advice this practice was given up.† Various school medical officers have found it necessary to warn parents and teachers in cases where a child was being punished for apparent stupidity or naughtiness which was really the result of disease or defective eyesight or hearing,‡ also where the condition of the heart rendered the child unfit to take part in the ordinary physical exercises,§ or to walk or run long distances, carrying a father's dinner.‖

The discovery of cases of incipient phthisis in time to check the development of the disease must also be of great value.

But apart from these less common and less obvious diseases there is a vast amount of preventible ill health among school children for which, as the medical inspection has shown, nothing is as a general rule done. Adenoids, enlarged tonsils, discharging ears, deafness, sore eyes, sore heads, and defective teeth are among the ailments commonly left untreated, although they are a serious menace to the health and efficiency of the children.

When children thus suffering are medically examined, it is at least pointed out to the parents that treatment should be sought.

Medical Treatment.

The percentage of school children found in need of medical treatment who actually obtain it varies very much from district to district, according to the facilities which exist for it and the amount of trouble taken in the matter by the education authority or some voluntary society.

It is reported that in Surrey satisfactory treatment was obtained for the children by their parents in 28·3 per cent. of the cases where treatment was recommended.

In Derbyshire 63·6 sought medical advice, and of the eye cases 33 per cent. provided themselves with spectacles.

In the Lindsay division of Lincolnshire 24·8 per cent. of the children were taken to a doctor.

In several towns and counties there is evidence that the medical charities and hospitals have been largely drawn upon for treatment by school children as a result of school medical inspection, and in some districts it is said the work of the private practitioner has increased.¶

Sir George Newman states that in many districts 20 to 60 per cent. of the children requiring treatment have been treated; but satisfactory

---

* Annual Report of School Medical Officer for 1908, p. 64.

† Ibid, p. 37.

‡ Herts Annual Report of School Medical Officer, 1908, pp. 26-7, and Bristol Report of Education Committee, 1909, p. 63.

§ Ibid, also Manchester Report of Education Committee, 1908-9, p. 185.

‖ Worcester Report of School Medical Officer, 1908, p. 37.

¶ Annual Report for 1908 of Chief Medical Officer of the Board of Education, p. 34.

as it is that medical inspection should already have produced such practical results, it cannot be a matter of complacency that there are still in our schools in these districts from 40 to 80 per cent. of children known to be in need of ameliorative treatment for whom nothing is being done.

The Act of Parliament not only makes medical inspection compulsory, but also permits education authorities to make arrangements for attending to the health and physical condition of the children, subject to sanction by the Board of Education.

Examples of such arrangements already sanctioned by the Board of Education are the appointment of school nurses, the free provision of spectacles, arrangements with hospitals, dispensaries, or private practitioners, and the establishment of school clinics.

School Nurses.

It is hardly possible to over estimate the value of the school nurse, and for assistance in medical inspection local education authorities have power to appoint nurses without asking permission of the Board of Education. Many local authorities employ them specially for the examination as regards general cleanliness and condition of heads.

But as an arrangement for attending to the health of the children, the Board of Education cordially encourages the appointment of school nurses to carry out treatment " on the understanding that the nurse will act under the supervision and authority of the school medical officer." *

Sir George Newman, in his report, says: "Such matters as the antiseptic treatment of discharging ears, the maintenance of cleanliness, the treatment of sores and minor skin diseases or minor diseases of the eye, such as blepharitis and conjunctivitis, and the treatment of slight injuries, seem to fall within the scope of the school nurse."† The school nurse can furthermore do much to promote the health of the children by visiting the homes, encouraging the parents to obtain medical treatment recommended by the school doctor, and instructing the mother where home care is needed.

In certain localities, notably Worcestershire and Bradford, children absent from school are reported by the attendance officers and brought up for examination by the school medical officer; in the latter case at the school clinic. Dr. Mary Williams, in her report to the Worcestershire County Council, says: "There is considerable loss of grant from children absent from school on account of ill health, and much of this might be prevented if (a) children were not allowed to be absent unless really ill, and (b) if the parents were compelled to begin to treat the ailment causing absence so soon as the children were at home."‡ Such prompt examination is

* Annual Report for 1908 of Chief Medical Officer of Board of Education, pp. 26 et seq., 92.

† Ibid. p. 26.

‡ First Annual Report of the School Medical Officer, Worcestershire, 1908, p. 53.

further a step towards securing that in cases of serious disease the child is not being neglected, as too often happens.

Nurses as Attendance Officers.

If, as this report suggests, nurses were appointed as attendance officers, such officers would be prompt to detect cases of shamming, would see that treatment prescribed by the doctor was carried out without loss of time, and in cases of neglect could give valuable evidence in court. There seems to be no reason why such a scheme, combining the office of school nurse and attendance officer, might not be universally adopted, in rural districts as well as in the towns, with very great benefit to the children and a financial gain to the ratepayer by the increase of grant, which greater regularity of school attendance, due to prevention of both illness and shamming, would secure.

Cleansing Schemes.

At present the school nurse is employed by many education authorities to examine children's heads for pediculosis under cleansing schemes, and great reforms have thereby been achieved. In Gloucestershire, Worcestershire, and other districts, parents are warned and instructions for cleansing sent when their children's heads are found "dirty." After a certain interval each child's head is re-examined, if necessary a second and a third time, and if still dirty the child is excluded from school. If after a further period the child does not return cured, the parents are prosecuted for not sending the child to school in a proper condition. In some districts the nurses visit the homes and assist the mother to effect the cleansing.

The standard of cleanliness has by such means been greatly raised * and the much more extensive operation of cleansing schemes is called for. Rural schools often suffer from "dirty heads" as well as urban schools.† For example, in a certain rural Kentish school complaint is made that a large proportion of the children are thus infected.

In London an elaborate cleansing scheme is in operation, and up to December, 1909, had been applied to 288 schools, whereby the standard of what constitutes cleanliness was raised ; and even with this more stringent standard, the percentage of children with verminous heads was reduced to 20·9. ‡

An interesting experiment was tried in the autumn of 1909 at three schools in which there were hot water baths.§

While the children were cleansed at school, the sanitary authority undertook the cleansing of home and bedding. The experiment was eminently successful, meeting with the approval of children and

* London County Council, Report of Medical Officer (Education) for 1909, p. 32.

† Annual Report for 1909 of the Chief Medical Officer of the Board of Education, p. 29.

‡ London County Council, Report of Medical Officer (Education) for 1909, p. 32.

§ "Chaucer," Bermondsey; "Pulteney," Soho; Finch Street, Whitechapel. Ibid. p. 32.

parents, and in a large proportion of cases effecting what might be hoped would prove a permanent cure.

Where satisfactory cleansing stations for children are not already established, that is, stations where there is no risk of their being associated in any way with the ordinary verminous person, nor with infectious disease contacts, and where their efficient supervision is provided for, it is most convenient, effective, and economical to establish the cleansing station at the school. A hot water bath and vermin destroyer for clothing comprise the necessary apparatus.*

School Baths.

In the interests of health and cleanliness alike it is to be hoped that the example of those authorities who have installed school baths will be widely followed.

Dr. Crowley, in his report to the Bradford Education Committee, 1908, says :

"Good use is made of the six excellent school baths under the authority, and the children attend also the public baths. It is difficult to speak too highly of the value of the school swimming bath, the place and function of which is far from being sufficiently appreciated. . . . Swimming baths should be available for all school children and reserved exclusively for them. One has only to watch the children in the baths to appreciate what an excellent physical effect this form of bathing has, and swimming is one of the finest forms of physical exercise. No part of the school curriculum is more educational. . . . How valuable this may be, even for quite small children, and how educational to the mothers, may be seen in one of the school baths in the city, where the water is let down at the end of each week and the little ones splash about to their hearts' content.

"Failing the swimming bath, the shower bath, at any rate, should be available in all schools. A system of showers is inexpensive to instal, economical to work [provided there is an abundant water supply], and a large number of children can be bathed in a comparatively short time. . . .

"It is important that the part of the building devoted to the shower bath should be airy and well lighted, and the dressing room should be separated from the bath proper. Such baths must on no account be looked upon as installed for dirty children only. . . . Their effect is educational, is a mental and moral one as well as a physical; and the school bathing should be looked upon by the children as part of the ordinary school curriculum." †

At Sheffield special arrangements have been made by the Education Committee for the school children to attend public swimming baths both in and out of school hours. At Sunderland also public swimming baths are used by the boys. At Bristol nearly 4,000 boys were taught swimming during the summer of 1908. At Glasgow

* Ibid. pp. 33-36.

† Report of the School Medical Officer, 1908, to the City of Bradford Education Committee, pp. 45-6.

spray baths have been fitted in two of the schools, and in Liverpool the school children during the summer months use two free open air baths. In London children attend the public swimming baths, and a few schools have private baths of their own.

Spectacles.

Sanction for the free provision of spectacles to school children, out of the rates, was obtained in 1908-9 by twenty-one local authorities.* A large number of other local authorities are endeavoring to secure that all children in need of spectacles shall obtain them, whatever the position of the family, by means of charitable funds to supplement parents' payments. Such funds, however, as in the case of London, are apt to fall short in meeting the growing demand.

Arrangements with Hospitals.

The sanction by the Board of Education of arrangements under which local education authorities pay hospitals or other voluntary institutions for the treatment of some of the miscellaneous assortment of diseases and ailments that inspection reveals among school children, can only be regarded as a temporary expedient. There are a number of reasons why such arrangements are unjust, costly and inefficient. It is customary at hospitals to grant treatment free or at a nominal charge to the poor. But the Local Education Authorities (Medical Treatment) Act, 1909, has made it obligatory for local education authorities to make a charge for the treatment given to school children, though they need not enforce payment if the parent is unable "by reason of circumstances other than his own default," or, in other words, poverty, to pay. Under such arrangements, therefore, it comes about that instead of facilitating the medical treatment of children of school age the intervention of the Education Authority debars the parents from the benefit of the free use of the hospitals for children of school age. This hardship is now widely felt in London in consequence of the arrangements made between the London County Council and certain hospitals.

But apart from the perversion of voluntary institutions from the uses intended by their benefactors, the treatment at a large institution with its necessarily expensive upkeep is absurdly extravagant in the case of many of the minor ailments. Hospital treatment is suitable for certain diseases and operations, and for these possibly their use should be continued in the case of school children. But not only is hospital treatment expensive, but what is more important, it is usually ill adapted and inefficient for such conditions as sore eyes, discharging ears, ringworm, and skin diseases, which require not one visit, nor even a weekly visit, but treatment daily, and sometimes twice or thrice daily to effect a cure. Moreover, it is hardly possible so to organize visits to hospitals that all the cases receive immediate attention, and the danger to the health of the child, and inconvenience, loss of time, and loss of work to the parent entailed by the

---

* Annual Report for 1908 of Chief Medical Officer of Board of Education, p. 93.

long hours of waiting, are hardly realized by those sections of the community who in illness are attended at their homes by a private practitioner. The journeying to and fro moreover is often an expense to be considered.

School Clinics.

The best method of dealing with the minor ailments, and indeed of sorting out all cases for reference to the appropriate agency or institution, whether it be hospital, open air school, baths, free dinners, playground classes, or whatever health promoting means may be available, is the establishment at or near a school or group of schools of a health centre or clinic. Here a nurse is in constant attendance to treat sore eyes, discharging ears, skin diseases, and such ailments generally as require attention daily. A doctor is also in attendance (at regularly certain times), and all cases are kept under supervision until they are cured.

A large and expensive establishment is unnecessary and out of place for the school clinic. At the privately established clinic at Deptford, in one room dentist, doctor, and nurse all do their work, each in their own corner of the room, without in any way hindering one another. Another room serves as waiting room for a large number of parents and children, since this clinic is not on school premises, and the work cannot be carried on here during school hours. Where the clinic is on school premises and open during school hours even less accommodation is necessary.

The Board of Education has already sanctioned the establishment of clinics by various education authorities ; for example, a fully equipped one at Bradford, and arrangements on a smaller scale at Brighton, Reading, Abertillery, Southampton and York (for ringworm only).* A dental clinic was established by private generosity at Cambridge, and the education authority has since taken it over.†

School dentists have also been engaged by the London County Council at Deptford, and by the education authorities at Bradford and Norwich.

At Bradford during the last six months of 1908, 841 children were treated at the clinic, 546 being cured and 295 retained for treatment.‡ The diseases at that time treated were defective vision and diseases of the eye, ringworm, pediculosis, skin diseases, and discharging ears.

The success of school clinics, where established by education authorities or by private benefaction has been most marked, and they are undoubtedly the most efficient as well as the most economical method of treatment for a large class of ailments. Their establishment should be very general.

---

* Annual Report for 1908 of Chief Medical Officer of the Board of Education, p. 97.

† Ibid, pp. 100-1.

‡ Report of School Medical Officer for 1908, pp. 98, 99.

Ringworm.

Clinics for the X-ray treatment of ringworm should also be every-where available in order that this disease may be dealt with in the speediest and therefore the most economical manner. The loss of grant for children absent with ringworm and their loss of education is at present considerable.

Teeth.

It is practically certain that unless special measures are taken by education authorities little will be done by parents to get treatment other than extraction for their children's defective teeth, and inspec tion has shown that from 20 to 40 per cent. of the children examined, except the babies' classes, have four or more decayed teeth.*

Perhaps this is the most serious of all the conditions medical inspection has brought to light, since debility, indigestion, anæmia and even phthisis are all traced to decayed teeth.

Toothbrush clubs have been established in Worcestershire† and London,‡ but we must look in the main to the establishment of dental clinics for the remedy of this state of things. At the Deptford clinic, a voluntary institution, the L.C.C. dentist already alluded to has his equipment, and is at work on certain days and hours, stopping and otherwise attending to the teeth of the children from the ele-mentary schools of the neighborhood. A dental clinic is also to be established at the St. George's Dispensary, Surrey Row, Blackfriars, for children from the neighboring schools.

Breathing and Physical Exercises.

In the treatment of adenoids, so common in our schools, operation alone is not sufficient, but proper breathing must also be taught.§ At the school clinic established by private benefaction at Deptford a teacher is frequently in attendance to train such children, and her work has met with great success. Such teaching may also be given by an instructor who goes round to the schools and shows the teachers how to give breathing and physical exercises. Special exercises may also benefit children with a tendency to spinal curva-ture. But physical training should not be restricted to the ailing. Breathing and physical exercises and the cultivation of hygienic habits generally, as in handkerchief drill, are of the greatest value in promoting the health and vigor of children from the infant classes upwards, and the extension of their judicious use both as preventive and curative means is much to be advocated.

Home Conditions.

But for large numbers of ailing children no treatment by doctor, nurse or teacher will alone suffice. It is their home conditions which are at fault. Lessons to parents, and children too, as to right

* Annual Report for 1908 of Chief Medical Officer of the Board of Education, p. 53.
† Worcestershire Aftercare Committee Report. p. 6.
‡ Report of Medical Officer (Education) for 1909, p. 16.
§ Report of Chief Medical Officer of Board of Education, pp. 58-9.

feeding, the value of open windows, cleanliness and such matters may do much. But there are still many to whom a different mode of living, or more nourishment than the parents can afford to give them, are essential for improvement in health.

The Open Air School.

One of the most promising of all forms of treatment for ailments and diseases such as anæmia, incipient phthisis, nervousness, malnutrition and general debility with its numerous manifestations, which doctoring alone cannot cure, is the open air school.

The idea was introduced from Germany, and the first English open air school was established in 1907 by the London County Council, who kept three such schools open in the summers of 1908 and 1909.

In 1908 open air schools were set up also at Bradford, Halifax and Norwich.

These schools were recognized under the Elementary Education (Defective and Epileptic Children) Act, 1899, thereby securing that admission shall be by the selection of the medical officer of the local education authority, that the children are taught in small classes, that hours of instruction shall be short, that the curriculum includes manual training, and that the schools can be kept open during ordinary school holidays. There might, however, be difficulties in establishing such schools permanently in number sufficient to the need under this Act.

Except in London it is not usually hard to obtain a suitable site within the area of the local education authority.

In choosing a site the main points to bear in mind are the desirability of plenty of fresh air and as much sunshine as possible, healthy soil, plentiful water supply, and pleasant surroundings ; a small wood is an attractive feature in connection with some of the outdoor classes.

The buildings should be slight and airy, since the classes are held in the open air, but verandahs, sheds, or even class rooms are needed for protection in rain or strong sunshine. It is necessary to have kitchens, bathrooms, offices, and rooms for the teachers, school doctor and nurse attached to the open air school.

Desks and seats are not used so much as in ordinary schools. It is best to have single desks, and they should be easily portable. The seats or chairs must have proper backs, since most of the children are delicate.

Every child should be given some form of hammock chair for the afternoon rest which forms so important a part of the curriculum. The ordinary deck chairs sometimes used are not suitable, as they do not allow a sufficiently recumbent position.*

As regards the size of the school it seems to be generally agreed that a school for about one hundred and twenty is more economical and more generally satisfactory than several smaller ones. It is said to be a great advantage to have children of all sizes at the same

* Annual Report of Chief Medical Officer of Board of Education, 1908, p. 123.

school, provided they are sufficiently numerous for suitable classification, and with the larger school it is worth while to provide for the daily attendance of a nurse, which is nearly always required for some of the cases.

Though certificate from the school medical officer is essential for admission to open air schools under the 1899 Act, the London County Council in 1909 further limited admission by strictly requiring certain payments (from 1s. to 3s. per week) from the parents, with the result that a large number of the children selected were afterwards rejected * and their places filled by children less in need of such treatment, but for whom their parents were able to contribute.

At Bradford it was advocated that no such condition should be made, suitability for admission to be the ground of selection irrespective of the social position or ability of parents to contribute.†

At both the Bradford and London schools the children attend daily, in time for breakfast, and leave again after tea ; they therefore receive three good meals. One to two hours sleep or rest in the afternoon is always insisted on. Strict cleanliness is required, and baths are usually given. It should, especially in summer, be possible to give every child a daily bath as part of the treatment. Shower baths are advocated for this purpose. It is strongly urged‡ that the children should take part in the domestic work of the school, even at the expense of some inconvenience to the adult helpers, for this and the gardening work do much to enhance the family feeling which is so desirable in a school of this kind. §

All classes are small and of short duration to avoid mental fatigue. They are usually given in the open air, and practical demonstration is much used. For example, in the geography lesson miniature rivers, lakes, and mountains may be constructed, and arithmetic is taught by the taking of actual measurements. A large part of the class time is occupied with such subjects‖ as nature study, local history, geography, practical arithmetic, school journeys, physical exercises, organized games, and visits to museums, with lessons upon them. Time is also allowed for ordinary play.

All reports show the immense benefit derived by the children from sojourn in open air schools,¶ both in mental and moral tone, and in physical effect, measured by general bearing, the cure of ailments, increase in weight, and increased proportion of hæmoglobin in the blood. It was found at Charlottenburg, the pioneer of open air schools, during the first three years, that delicate children after a spell there, notwithstanding the small amount of time given to lessons, were able not only to take their proper place, but often to pass

* London County Council Report of Medical Officer (Education) for 1909, p. 87.
† Report of School Medical Officer to Bradford Education Committee, December, 1908, p. 79, etc.
‡ Annual Report for 1908 of the Chief Medical Officer of Board of Education, p. 126.
§ Ibid, p. 127.   ‖ Ibid, p. 124.
¶ For example, Annual Report of Chief Medical Officer of Board of Education for 1908 ; Report of School Medical Officer for 1908, Bradford ; London County Council, Report of School Medical Officer for 1909.

their school mates on their return to the ordinary schools ; and in England the teachers testify that the results on the work are excellent.*

It appears from reports that the period for which children are kept at the open air school is not always long enough. The London County Council School Medical Officer, in his report, urges that the London schools should be kept open all the year round, as at Bradford ; and this would be an economy, as providing a number of permanent school places instead of merely temporary ones.

There are children who are unfit to attend any but open air schools and a large number whom a temporary sojourn in such schools would enormously benefit ; it is therefore to be hoped that the extension of this form of school will be rapid.

The establishment of residential open air schools in addition to the day school is also greatly needed.

Both Dr. Kerr and Dr. Crowley urge the provision also of special "tuberculosis" schools or sanatoria, which should be permanently open and carried out on open air school lines.

Another experiment is being tried by the London County Council, who have decided to maintain for three years a special tuberculosis school in connection with the Paddington Dispensary for the Prevention of Consumption, where children suffering from or predisposed to tuberculosis, or in an infective environment, or discharged from sanatoria or convalescent homes can be educated. The majority of these children are not fit to attend the ordinary schools, and all will benefit by the open windows, hygienic measures, and special adaptation of the work to their physical condition.†

Playground Classes.

So great has been the success of the open air school that experiment has been made in utilizing school playgrounds for open air classes. In the autumn of 1909 this was tried in six London County Council schools, in some cases specially delicate children being selected, in others whole standards, or all standards in rotation being taken irrespective of health conditions.

The results in both types of open air class appear to have been good.

In the case of the delicate children, the classes were arranged on lines similar to those of the open air schools, and were held continuously out of doors. Such classes are not, however, an adequate substitute for the open air school, with its organized feeding, rest, and longer hours out of doors, though considerable benefit was derived by the children.

Where ordinary classes, not selected for health reasons, as at Stockwell Road School, occupied the playground in succession, excellent results were also attained. In addition to ordinary class

* Annual Report of Chief Medical Officer to Board of Education for 1908, p. 128.
† See London County Council Minutes, March 1st, 1910, p. 465, and London County Council, Report of School Medical Officer for 1909, p. 94.

work, physical exercise and breathing exercises were arranged for. Dr. Kerr says : " The alertness and bracing effect of the day in the open was quite noticeable on the following days, and an important negative result was that the discipline of the school did not suffer in any way." * With reference to this type of playground class the report continues later : " Its special function is to act as a kind of tonic to the ordinary drawbacks of classroom work, such as the fatigue and inattentiveness resulting from a vitiated atmosphere and want of sufficient movement. The direct curative effect on delicate children is likely to be disappointing. Type D [rotation of classes] seems more suited for the boy of average or fair physical condition than for the sickly or debilitated ; but one day in ten in the open air, although better than none at all, is insufficient to meet his needs. It seems preferable that each standard should have one whole day in ten rather than one session every fifth day, but it would be better still if one whole day in each week could be spent in the open air." †

Holiday Colonies.

Little has yet been done in England in the way of organizing holiday colonies which are a feature in some Continental countries, notably Sweden, where whole classes of town children, together with their teachers, migrate for part of the summer to the country. Manchester has made an experiment in this direction by establishing a country school,‡ which was opened in June, 1904, as a voluntary institution, and later taken over by the education authority. Classes of forty children are transferred to this school for a fortnight each during the summer months.

Vacation Schools.

During the summer of 1910 the London County Council have opened two vacation schools in poor districts during the holidays.

Such a school was first started nine years ago at the Passmore Edwards Settlement.

" The aim," says Miss D. M. Ward,§ " of the vacation school is twofold : (1) to draw the children out of the loafing, demoralizing life of the streets, and give them wholesome and happy occupation under an ordered, but sympathetic, control ; and (2) to give them different occupations from their ordinary school work of the rest of the year. Hence our insistence on all forms of manual work, on physical exercises, dancing, and games."

The teachers at the Passmore Edwards vacation school are mainly students who have finished their course at the training college and some secondary school and kindergarten teachers and drill instructors. The classes include carpentering, cobbling, wood-wook, cookery, basket making, drill, and games.

* London County Council, Report of Medical Officer (Education) for 1909, p. 92.
† Ibid. p. 93.
‡ Annual Report of Education Committee, 1908-9, pp. 74-82.
§ *The School Child*, October, 1910, p. 12.

There is great competition among the children of the neighborhood for admission to the school, which is by ticket, the head teachers of the elementary schools assisting in the selection of children specially in need of the vacation school. Some of the children have been to the school three or four years running.[*]

The Bristol Education Committee made a grant to a voluntary vacation school in the summer of 1908. [†]

Though most needed in congested centres of population, the vacation school may be a source of great pleasure and benefit to the children in rural districts also as was shown by the vacation school at Newport, Essex.[‡]

School Feeding.

Among the various forms of remedial treatment school feeding takes an important place.

It has long been known that in the poor districts of our cities many children came to school in such a condition from want of food that they were quite unfit to do any lessons.

School teachers and other kindly people therefore began organizing breakfasts and dinners for the starving children. The Education (Provision of Meals) Act, 1906, enabled such local authorities as adopted the Act to provide meals for school children out of the rates so long as their expenditure did not exceed a halfpenny rate. Up to 1909 10 over one hundred local education authorities appear to have adopted the Act and drawn on the rates for school feeding,[§] and many other local authorities are either expending voluntary funds on this work or having their scholars fed by voluntary agencies. During 1908-9 116,840 children were reported to the Board of Education as receiving meals through the education authorities in England and Wales.[||]

London, having fed a large number of children by means of voluntary funds, adopted the Act early in 1909, and during 1908-9 an average of 39,632 children were fed weekly.

Though malnutrition is frequently reported by the school doctors, this condition is difficult of diagnosis and may be due to improper feeding and other causes, as well as insufficient feeding; but it is no longer necessary to point out that there are large numbers of families where the wage earner is unemployed, or receives such low wages that it is impossible, with the most careful management, for him to feed all his children adequately. Rowntree's standard,[¶] allowing an average of three shillings for an adult and two shillings and threepence for a child for food materials, in addition to all other necessary expenses, such as rent, fuel, and

---

[*] *The School Child*, October, 1910, p. 12.

[†] Report, Bristol Education Committee, March, 1909, p. 21.

[‡] See "Our Village Vacation School," by Mrs Carl Meyer, in the *British Health Review*, May, 1910.

[§] Report on Working of Education (Provision of Meals) Act, 1909, pp. 26-9.

[||] Ibid. p. 21.

[¶] B. Seebohm Rowntree. "Poverty : a Study of Town Life," p. 105

clothing, is a low one, as is also the standard taken by the London County Council organizers in their report on twelve necessitous schools,* allowing fifteen shillings per week for a standard family of two adults and four children, after deducting all outgoings on rent and thrift ; and it may be assumed that families whose true incomes from all sources fall below this standard are unable to obtain sufficient food. There will be few education authorities—in fact it may be asserted that there will be none—who have not children in need of school feeding by reason of poverty alone ; and there are other causes which often make school meals requisite, such as distance of children's homes from the school, especially in the rural districts, absence of parents, as when the mother, whether or no widowed, goes out to work, or when the mother is dead, inability of the parents, through illness or any other cause, to prepare suitable home meals, or special delicacy of children making it advisable to allow milk or cod liver oil as an extra.

Among the local authorities who are feeding school children there is great variety in the kind of meal given and in the manner of giving it. Under the purely voluntary system it was often considered that a basin of soup on certain days in the week met all requirements.

The larger local education authorities have now for the most part drawn up menus, usually with the assistance of school medical officer or domestic economy superintendent, allowing for the best value in proteids, fats and other needful constituents, and arranging for a different meal at least on each day of the week, and usually limiting soup meals to twice weekly.

Education authorities have adopted various plans for providing their school dinners, such as arranging with a large contractor or with local caterers, or having the meals cooked on the premises where they are served. All these methods are being tried for different London schools.

But the plan which appears to be both most satisfactory and most economical, is the establishment of large central kitchens under the direct control of the education authority. Bradford, Manchester, Bristol, Middlesborough, and Bury are among the towns which have adopted this plan.

At Bristol a large kitchen and store room was adapted and equipment installed at a cost of some £344 at the end of 1908, and over two thousand dinners daily can be supplied at a total cost of three farthings each, another three farthings being expended for administration. The menus cover a wide range of variety, and are nourishing and appetizing, though it must not be supposed that a really sufficient meal can be provided without greater expenditure on food materials.

The food is distributed, usually in cans which keep it quite hot, to the different feeding centres. At Manchester and Bristol tradesmen's carts are utilized for the purpose, at Bury the corporation trams distribute the food.

* London County Council Report on " Home Circumstances of the Children in Twelve Necessitous Schools."

The children are served either in the schools, in halls or other premises hired for the purpose, or at restaurants.

The latter plan must almost invariably be condemned, as satisfactory arrangements can very rarely be made to keep the children entirely apart from miscellaneous customers, or to ensure adequate supervision both of the children and of the food supplied to them.

Feeding in mission halls, chapels, and other hired premises may be satisfactory if the hall or room is really suitable, well lighted, warmed and aired, clean and cheerful, but there are many attendant drawbacks, children often having to cross crowded thoroughfares to get to their dinners and wait about in all weathers, and moreover the halls actually used, and the attendance necessarily engaged with the halls, are too often by no means satisfactory or suitable.

Feeding on school premises does away with the drawbacks of promiscuous company, dangerous crossing of streets, and waiting about, but in many of the schools there is at present no suitable accommodation for school dinners. It may be hoped that in future dining rooms may become an essential part of the school premises and "table manners, materials provided" part of the curriculum; and in the meantime many of our schools have spacious halls where meals can with proper organization be served without interference with ordinary school work.

In addition to helpers who serve food, lay the tables, wash up, etc., supervisors should always be appointed, as the school dinner may become highly educational or thoroughly demoralizing according to the manner in which it is conducted. Wherever they are willing to assist, teachers are the best supervisors, and some education authorities, for example Bristol, have secured their co-operation, without making such service compulsory, extra payment being made for supervision of the dinners. Monitors and monitresses from among the children can hand round the food and help generally at the dinners.

To make the meal as educational and civilizing as possible clean white table cloths should be supplied. Education authorities can hardly be expected to provide flowers unless they can be grown in the school gardens, but they may encourage friends to adorn the tables with them.

Payment for school dinners can be recovered under the Act from the parents where they are able to pay, but this provision has not been largely enforced. Were arrangements made, and the dinners conducted in such a fashion that no parent could object to his child being so fed, there would probably be many well-to-do parents who would be glad to pay and so avail themselves of school dinners for their children. This is especially the case in rural districts where children come one, two or even four miles to school, and thus on five days of the week dine off the bread with jam, dripping or butter which they bring with them, and eat wandering about the playground or lanes. At Easebourne, near Midhurst, Lord Egmont provides a hot dinner at school during the winter months for children residing more than one mile from the school, and such a system needs to be extensively adopted by rural education authorities if the full advantages of country rearing are to be enjoyed by the children of agricultural workers and rural artizans.

The Place of the Voluntary Worker.

The work of volunteers has been enlisted by many local education authorities to " arrange for the individual treatment of poor children by voluntary agencies or otherwise."* The London County Council have made it part of the duty of the children's care committees established by them " to endeavor to induce parents to obtain the advice and treatment recommended in the medical register of the school." † The Somerset County Council have utilized the district education committees for a similar purpose.‡ It is inadvisable and in the end costly to employ volunteers for work which the nurse or health visitor is alone fitted to undertake, unless the authority is able to ensure that its voluntary helpers are duly qualified by the necessary training. If trained and organized, volunteers might find a permanent place in the scheme of public assistance, and render most valuable service by giving expert advice on feeding and hygiene generally in the homes. Meantime the co-operation of the intelligent though untrained worker can be turned to account in following medical inspection, by interviewing, visiting, and re-visiting the parents, and endeavoring to overcome any prejudice, indolence or ignorance on their part which stands in the way of the doctor's recommendations being carried out. In initiating a new scheme, such as the present one to care extensively for the health of our future citizens, a large amount of patient attention to each individual case is necessary, which may well be undertaken by anyone possessed of tact and sufficient intelligence to carry out instructions. Time is thus gained for plans to mature and to receive full consideration before the official organism which may eventually be necessary for their permanent and harmonious working is completely developed.

---

* Annual Report for 1908 of Chief Medical Officer of Board of Education, p. 94.

† London County Council Handbook for Care Committees, p. 19, No. 1,332. P. S. King & Son.

‡ Annual Report for 1908 of Chief Medical Officer of Board of Education, p. 94.

THE W

Fabian Tract No. 157.

THE WORKING LIFE OF WOMEN.

BY MISS B. L. HUTCHINS.

PUBLISHED AND SOLD BY

THE FABIAN SOCIETY.

Fabian Women's Group Series, No. 1.

PRICE ONE PENNY.

LONDON:

THE FABIAN SOCIETY, 3 CLEMENT'S INN, STRAND, W.C.

JUNE 1911.

THE WORKING LIFE OF WOMEN.

IT is still the custom in some quarters to assert that "the proper sphere for women is the home," and to assume that a decree of Providence or a natural law has marked off and separated the duties of men and women. Man, it is said, is the economic support and protector of the family, woman is its watchful guardian and nurse; whence it follows that the wife must be maintained by her husband in order to give her whole time to home and children. The present paper does not attempt to discuss what is in theory the highest life for women; whether the majority of women can ever realize their fullest life outside the family, or whether an intelligent wife and mother has not on the whole, other things equal, more scope for the development of her personality than any single woman can possibly have. The question I am here concerned with relates to the actual position of the women themselves. Is it the lot of all women, or even of a large majority of women, to have their material needs provided for them so that they can reserve themselves for the duties that tend to conserve the home and family?

Let us see what the Census has to tell us on the subject. We find that in 1901 there were in round numbers 15,729,000 men and boys, and 16,799,000 women and girls, in England and Wales. This means that there are 1,070,000 more women than men, and if we omit all children under fifteen there are about 110 women to every 100 men. This surplus of women has increased slowly but steadily in every Census since 1841; that is to say, in 1841 there were in every 1,000 persons 489 males, and 511 females; but in 1901 there were in every 1,000, 484 males, and 516 females.

The disproportionate numbers of women are no doubt partly due to the Imperial needs which compel a large number of men to emigrate to our actual or potential colonies and dependencies. It is impossible to say how many are thus to be accounted for, probably not a very large proportion, save in the upper classes. The Census shows figures for the army, navy, and merchant seamen serving abroad, but if these are added to the population of the United Kingdom the excess of women is still considerable. There seems to be no means of estimating the numbers of men who are absent on private business.

The main cause of the surplus of women seems to be their lower death-rate, and this is popularly accounted for as the advantage resulting to women from their comparatively sheltered life and less exposure to accident and occupational disease. This assumption no doubt accounts for some part of the difference; women do not work on railways or as general laborers, or usually in the most unhealthy processes of trades scheduled as " Dangerous " under the Factory Act. There can be no doubt either that the death-rate of women has been lowered by the operation of the Factory Act in improving conditions of employment. The death-rate of men has also been lowered, but in a less degree, because although men benefit by improved conditions in the factory just as women do, the proportion of men employed in factories and workshops is small comparatively with women, so many men being employed in transport, building, laboring, docks, etc. These latter occupations so far have obtained very little legal protection from the risks and dangers run by the workers, although many of these dangers are notoriously preventible.

Still it is doubtful whether the lower death-rate of women can be entirely accounted for by the greater degree of protection enjoyed. Women often work longer hours even under the Factory Act than most men do under their trade union ; much of the work done by women in laundries, jam factories, sack factories, and others, is extremely laborious. Again, the enormous amount of domestic work accomplished by women in their homes, without outside help, in addition to the bearing and caring for infants and young children, must be equal in output of energy to much more than all the industrial work of women, especially when the rough, inconvenient, and inadequate nature of the appliances common in working-class homes is considered, and the still more painful fact is remembered that the very person responsible for all this work is often the one of the family who in case of need is the first to go short of food.

It is true that more men than women die of accidents. But let us add to the accidental deaths the deaths of women from childbirth and other causes peculiar to women. We find that in 1907 10,895 males died from accidents ; 4,890 females died from accidents ; 4,670 from causes peculiar to women, 9,560 altogether, about 1,300 less than men. But the total deaths of men in 1907 exceeded the deaths of women by 14,297, an excess more than ten times as great.

There is also the question of age, which is important in connection with the death-rate. The number of boys born is larger than the number of girls, about 104 to 100. The death-rate of boy babies is almost always higher than that of girls, and in 1907 the death-rate of boys under four was higher than that of girls, but the death-rate of boys from four to fifteen was lower than that of girls at the same age ; then at fifteen the male death-rate again rises above the female and remains higher at all later ages.

DEATH-RATES, 1907, PER 1,000 LIVING.

	Under 1 Year per 1,000 births	aged 1	2	3	4	under 5	5	10
Males ...	130	38·4	15·5	10·1	6·9	44·8	3·3	1.9
Females...	104	36·2	14·8	9·7	7·6	37·0	3·4	2·0

	15	20	25	35	45	55	65	all ages
Males ...	2·9	3·8	5·6	9·5	16·9	33·7	94·1	16·0
Females. ...	2·7	3·2	4·6	7·8	13·1	26·0	85·9	14·1

Now if the lower death-rate of girls and women is due to their being taken more care of, how inexplicable are these figures. There is little enough difference in the care and shelter given to boys and girls under four, yet the boys die much faster; between four and fifteen, on the other hand, girls usually are a good deal more sheltered and protected than boys, and less likely to run into dangerous places and positions, yet from four to fifteen the male death-rate is slightly lower than the female. At fifteen when, as we shall see, a very large proportion of girls begin industrial work, the death-rates are again reversed, the male death-rate being thenceforward the higher. Nor does it appear that the death-rate of young women is much influenced by the fact of industrial employment. It is true that in Lancashire, where many women and girls work, the death-rate of women is higher than in England and Wales; but in Durham, where comparatively very few women and girls are employed, the death-rate is higher still.

PERCENTAGE OF FEMALES OCCUPIED.

	LANCASHIRE.			DURHAM		
	Ages 15	20	25-34	15	20	25-34
Single	78	80	76	40	49	49
Married or widowed	24	25	19	1	2	3
Death-rates, 1907—						
Male...	3·3	4·2	6·1	3·8	4·7	5·6
Female	3·0	3·5	5·4	3·7	4·4	6·3

The contrast seems to indicate that it is not the fact of employment, but the conditions, both of life and employment, that are prejudicial to women in these industrial centres, for although death-rates have generally fallen, they are still higher in most of the mining and manufacturing districts, notably in Lancashire and Durham, than the average of England and Wales.

It will be agreed that the greater average duration of life among women is sufficient to account for a large excess number of women over men, over and above the emigration of many young men, which contributes to the same result. The surplus of women is distributed very differently in different districts: it is greater in London and the Home Counties, and also in Lancashire; less in the mining districts and the rural districts; and generally much greater in town than country. In the urban districts women over fifteen number 112, in the rural districts only 102, to every 100 males. This is perhaps partly due to the girls going to towns as domestic servants; for although the percentage of domestic servants is rather higher in the country than in town, the actual numbers are much less, and particular towns and residential urban districts—Bournemouth, Hampstead, and the like—show a very high percentage of servants. But the higher proportion of males in the country must in part be due to the fact that babies born in the country have a better chance of life. Although the number of boys born is greater than the number of girls (it was about 1,037 to 1,000 in 1891-1900, and slightly higher since 1901), the boy babies are on the average more difficult to bring into the world and more delicate for the first few years of life, as is shown by the male infant death-rate being higher than the female. It follows that though boy babies are more numerous at the outset, the girls steadily gain upon them, and at some point in early life the numbers are equal. If infant mortality is high, the surplus boy babies are very soon swept out of existence, and there may be " superfluous women " even under five years old! But in healthy districts, especially in the country, where infant mortality is low, the boys survive in greater numbers, and exceed the girls in numbers up to the age of twenty; thus in later life the disproportion of women is not so great in the country as it is in towns. This fact constitutes one important reason (among others that are better known) for improving the sanitary conditions in towns. A diminution in infant mortality will tend to keep a larger proportion of boys alive, and thus by so much redress the balance of the sexes. To give an instance : in rural districts of Lancashire the boys under five were 1,018 to every 1,000 girls ; in the urban districts, which include many towns with a high infant mortality, the boys under five were only 989 to every 1,000 girls. It is impossible here to give many details on this point, but fuller statistics are given in the *Statistical Journal*, June, 1909, pp. 211-212.

Marriage and Widowhood.

But it is evident that one way or another we must face the fact of a large excess number of women, even though we may hope that improvement in the people's life and health may prevent some of the waste of men and boys' life that occurs at present. How are women provided for ? Marriage is still the most important and extensively followed occupation for women. Over 5,700,000 women in England and Wales are married, or 49·6 per cent. ; nearly one-half of the female population over fifteen.

In every 100 women aged 15-20 ...... 2 are married.
      ,,   ,,   ,, 20-25 ...... 27 ,,
                     ,, 25-35 ...... 64 ,,
                     ,, 35-45 ...... 75 ,,
                     ,, 45-55 ...... 71 ,,
                     ,, 55-65 ...... 57 ,,
      ,,   ,,   ,, 65-75 ...... 37 ,,
      ,,   ,,   ,, 75 ...... 16 ,,

In middle life—from thirty-five to fifty-five—three-fourths of the women are married. In early life a large proportion are single ; in later life a large proportion are widowed. Put it in another way. From twenty to thirty-five, only two out of every four women are married, most of the others being still single ; from thirty-five to fifty-five, three in every four women are married ; over fifty-five, less than two in every four are married, most of the others being already widowed. It is only for twenty years (between thirty-five and fifty-five) that as many as three-fourths of women can be said to be provided for by marriage, even on the assumption that all wives are provided for by their husbands.

As we have seen, women exceed men in numbers, and not only that, but the age of marriage is usually for economic reasons later for men than women, and some men do not marry at all, consequently it is utterly vain to assume that women *generally* can look to marriage for support, and to talk of the home as "women's true sphere." Mrs. Butler wrote, now many years ago, that, like Pharaoh who commanded the Israelites to make bricks without straw, "these moralisers command this multitue of enquiring women back to homes which are not, and which they have not the material to create." Although about three-fourths of the women in the country do get married some time or other, at any given time fully half the women over fifteen are either single or widowed. Women marry younger and live longer than men, consequently the proportion of widows is considerable, something like one woman in every eight over twenty years old. The largest proportion occurs, as might be expected, at advanced years.

In every 100 women aged 35-45 ...... 6 are widows.
,, ,, ,, 45-55 ...... 16 ,,
,, 55-65 ...... 31 ,,
,, 65-75 ...... 52 ,,
,, 75 ...... 73 ,,

Occupation.

The number of women and girls over fifteen returned in 1901 as occupied was 3,970,000, or 34·5. This figure can only be regarded as an approximate one, as there is little information to show how many of the numerous women who work occasionally, but not regularly, do or do not return themselves as occupied, and even if this information were forthcoming, it is difficult to see how any precise line of demarcation could be devised to distinguish the degree of regularity that should constitute an "occupied" woman. The figure is again obviously inadequate in regard to women's *work* (as distinguished from occupation), as no account is taken of the enormous amount of work done at home—cooking, washing, cleaning, mending and making of clothes, tendance of children, and nursing the sick done by women, especially in the working class, who are not returned as belonging to any specific occupation.

It is misleading, however, to take the percentage 34·5 as if it meant that about one-third of all women enter upon a trade or occupation.

In every 100 women aged 15 ...... 66 are occupied.
,, ,, ,, 20 ...... 56 ,,
,, 25 ...... 31 ,,
,, 35 ...... 23 ,,
,, 45 ...... 22 ,,
,, 55 ...... 21 ,,
,, ,, ,, 65 ...... 16 ,,
,, ,, ,, 75 ...... 7 ,,

These figures show what is a very important point to remember, viz., that the majority of women workers are quite young, and this is one great difference in the work of men and women. The Census shows that over 90 per cent. of the men are occupied till fifty-five, and 89 per cent. even from fifty-five to sixty-five. But for women, especially in the industrial classes, the case is different. Their employment is largely an episode of early life. The majority of young working women work for a few years and leave work at marriage, as is shown by the rapid fall in the percentage occupied from the age of twenty-five. It is often stated by social investigators that the prospect·of marriage makes working girls slack about trade unions, and indifferent about training. Many girls seem for this reason to fail in some degree to realize their full possibilities or to achieve their full industrial efficiency. In the case of those who do marry, and whose best years will be given to work socially far more important than the episodic employment carried on by them in mill, factory or workroom, this alleged lack of industrial efficiency is not perhaps of much consequence. But although a large proportion of women are married before thirty-five, and as we know, the proportion married is greater in the working classes than among the middle and upper classes, yet it is a mistake to suppose that the mature single woman in industry is so rare as to be a negligible quantity. There are, for instance, nearly a quarter of a million single occupied women between thirty-five and forty-four. They include 88,000 domestic servants, 32,500 professional women (teachers, doctors, etc.), 30,000 textile workers, and 40,000 workers in making clothes and dress. These figures show that self dependence is a necessity for many even at the age when, and in the class where marriage is most frequent. The importance to the single self-supporting woman of a skilled occupation which she can pursue with self-respect and for which she can be decently remunerated, need hardly be emphasized here.

Married and Widowed Women Occupied.

The proportion of married or widowed women who are occupied is about 13 per cent., but, unlike the single women, whose percentage of occupation steadily falls as age increases, the percentage of married or widowed occupied is low at first, highest between thirty-five and fifty-five, and then falls to old age.

In every hundred married or widowed women occupied, six are under twenty-five; forty-four are between twenty-five and forty-five; forty are between forty-five and sixty-five; ten are over sixty-five.

The figures in our Census unfortunately do not separate the married or widowed occupied, so it is difficult to estimate from the above figures what proportion falls in to either class, but there can be little doubt that the high percentage of middle-aged women is due to widowhood. Frau Elizabeth Gnauck-Kühne, who has made a very able study of the life and work of German women,* tells us that in Germany, of married women only 12 per cent. are occupied, of widowed women as many as 44 per cent. The proportion of occupied widows is probably lower with us, as we have much less small farming, which in Germany is often carried on by women after the

* " Die Deutsche Frau."

husbands' death ; but there can be little doubt that the proportion of widows working is higher than the proportion married. In a very interesting passage Madame Gnauck points out the peculiar handicap suffered by a woman who is thus forced to renew industrial activity in middle life. The industrial life of women, she writes, is not continuous, but is split in two. Woman is normally provided for by marriage, let us say, for twenty or thirty years. But marriage is not a life-long provision for the average woman, it is only a provision for the best years of life, those years, in fact, in which a woman is ordinarily most capable of taking care of herself. The husband is, in many cases, swept off in middle life, and in the industrial classes he has usually not had very much chance of saving a competence for his widow. A certain proportion of women, therefore, we cannot say exactly how many, are forced to re-enter the labor market by widowhood, or by other economic causes—illness of the husband, desertion, and so on. Once more the woman appears in the industrial arena, with all the disadvantage of a long period of intermitted employment and loss of industrial experience. Having lost the habit of industrial work, having very usually children to look after and a home to find, she has to compete with girls and young women for wages based on the standard of life of a single unencumbered woman. It may be that the inferior technical skill often attributed to women as compared with men is largely due to this fact, that while a man gives his best years to his work, a woman gives precisely those years to other work, and therefore returns to industry under a considerable handicap. We can hardly doubt that this is a chief cause of pauperism.

The late Mr. Kirkman Gray, in his interesting unfinished work, "Philanthropy and the State," wrote :—" The theory is that the male can earn enough for a family and the female enough for herself. But this theory, even if we accept it as correct, makes no allowance for the fact that every eighth woman is a widow. Here then is the bitter anomaly of the widow's position in the economic sphere. As head of a family, she ought to be able to earn a family wage ; as woman she can only gain the customary price of individual subsistence." The Minority Report of the Poor Law Commission recognizes the same anomaly. " It is to the man that is paid the income necessary for the support of the family, on the assumption that the work of the woman is to care for the home and the children. The result is that mothers of young children, if they seek industrial employment, do so under the double disadvantage that the woman's wage is fixed to maintain herself alone, and that even this can be earned only by giving up to work the time that is needed by the care of the children."

Even the Charity Organization Society, which usually inclines to ignore the social aspect of economic hardship and treat every case as merely individual, is forced to recognize the anomaly of the widow's position. "We must look the poor woman's troubles in the face. . . . She has to do the work of two people ; she has to be the breadwinner and go out to work, and she must also be the housekeeper. She has to wash, clean, and cook, make and mend clothes, care for and train her children. Can one pair of hands manage all this? And, secondly, when she goes out to work our poor widow will probably only earn low wages . . . about 10s. a week, and she will certainly not be able to support herself and her family on that." *

The reflection here occurs that the life of women is inseparably connected with the life of men, and we may well pause to ask whether it is necessary so large a proportion of women should be widows at all. There is an excellent saying, that "we can have as many paupers as we like to pay for." It has an intimate bearing on the toleration of preventible disease and accidents as well as on administrative laxity in the Poor Law. The comparative mortality figure for the general laborer is more than double that of occupied males generally, and it is true the Registrar-General ascribes some of this mortality to confused returns, but even if some allowance, say 25 per cent., be made on this ground, the excess is still great. A pamphlet by Mr. Brockelbank † shows that in 1907 one shunter in thirteen was killed or injured at his work on the railway. The same writer gives reasons for supposing that the published returns of fatal accidents to railway servants fall far short of the truth, only those accidents which cause death within twenty-four hours being reported as fatal.

Many other occupations have a deplorably high death-rate, and it would seem that there is still a good deal to be done in improving the conditions of those workers who are not under the Factory Acts or protected by any effective organization. The protection of women by factory regulation has gone on the lines of protecting the individual woman worker at her work. Surely protection is also needed for the woman at home who sees her husband go off daily to some dangerous trade, where, for want of the necessary technical means for the prevention of disease or accident, he may be killed, maimed, or incur disease, and she and her children be left desolate.

It is notorious that a great deal of industrial disease and many accidents are due to causes largely preventible and within control. A very interesting report was issued last year in regard to dangers in building operations, which affect a large number of men—over a million. The report states that laborers are the principal sufferers from accidents, and have the most dangerous part of the work to do. One trade union secretary stated that 9 per cent. of his members had accidents in 1905. On this scale in eleven years each member would have an accident. Another union official said that a large number of accidents were preventible, and asked for more Government inspection. An employer stated that accidents were, in his belief, largely due to the lack of competent foremen and skilled supervision ; he had only had three accidents in thirty years' experience, and attributed this immunity to his engagement of a really competent man. He thought the building trade got into bad odor with the public owing to the tendency to save in wages and put

* "How to Help Widows," by A. M. Humphrey, p. 1. (Published by the Charity Organization Society.)

† "A Question of National Importance." (Hapworth and Co., 1909.)

incompetent men to work that needs really expert supervision. Another witness complained that accidents were caused by putting unskilled men to skilled work for the sake of cheapness.

Dr. Young stated before the Physical Deterioration Committee in 1903 that factories contributed to the spread of phthisis, and that he considered that while a great deal had been done to combat the special dangers and diseases incidental to special trades in general industrial conditions, a great deal remained to be done, and legislative interference had by no means reached its limit. From the Registrar-General's report we find that very high rates of phthisis occur among men in early manhood and middle life. In 1891-1900 of the total deaths among men twenty-five to thirty-five, nearly one-half were due to phthisis and respiratory diseases. The comparative mortality figure for certain occupations in 1900-02 was as follows :—

	Phthisis.	Other Respiratory Diseases.
All occupied males	175	78
All occupied males in agricultural districts	125	38
Tin miners	838	653
General laborers	567	268
General laborers (industrial districts)	450	171
File makers...	375	173
Lead miners	317	187
Dock laborers	291	161

It is in the light of such figures as these, it seems to me, that we have to study the problem of married or widowed women's work and the pauperism of able-bodied widows and their children. As women become better instructed, better organized, able to take more interest in politics, and especially when they obtain the Parliamentary franchise, it is to be hoped that they will agitate for drastic legislation and stringent inspection in the industries carried on by men and unregulated by Factory Law.

In the mining and industrial counties the death-rate is markedly above that of England and Wales as a whole, and it is somewhat curious that while a great deal of attention has been given to the infant mortality of Lancashire, which is usually explained as being due to married women's employment, much less notice has been taken of the fact that the *corrected* death-rate of Lancashire is even more above the average than is the mortality of infants.* In 1907, which was an exceptionally healthy year, the death-rates of Lancashire, though diminished, showed themselves still conspicuously above the average ; which can be most simply shown by taking the death-rate for the whole country as 100.

* See Corrected Death-Rates in Counties, Registrar-General's Report for 1907, pp. 12-20, cf. p. 14.

COMPARATIVE DEATH-RATE, 1907.

	Infants.	General Death-Rate, corrected for age-constitution.	
		Male.	Female.
England and Wales ...	100	100	100
Lancashire	117	124	126

A large part of this excess mortality, which is not by any means peculiar to Lancashire but can be paralleled in some mining districts and exceeded in the Potteries, is made up of deaths from phthisis and respiratory diseases, which are now considered to be largely traceable to unhealthy conditions of houses and work places, and in very great measure preventible. It is impossible in the limits of this paper to give full statistics, but those who desire further information are referred to the Reports of the Registrar-General, especially the two parts of the Decennial Supplement, published in 1907 and 1908 respectively, which are an invaluable mine of facts and figures, and also to the *Statistical Journal* (*loc. cit.*)

The Woman's Handicap.

It is not very easy to summarize briefly the facts of woman's life and employment, which demand a treatment much fuller than is possible within our limits. But there are several points which seem to be of special importance. First, there is the curious fact that women, though physically weaker than men, seem to have a greater stability of nerves, a greater power of resistance to disease, and a stronger hold of life altogether. It is notorious that there are more male lunatics, and very many more male criminals than female, and much fewer women die from alcoholism, nervous diseases, suicide, and various complaints that indicate mental and physical instability, while more women than men die of old age. On the other hand, there are more female paupers and more female old-age pensioners than male, and these facts seem to indicate that women on the whole are handicapped rather by their economic position than by physical disability. We have seen that in this country women are more numerous than men, and that for various reasons they cannot all be maintained by men, even if it were theoretically desirable that they should be so maintained, a point which I am not here discussing. It follows that (quite apart from the question of economic independence as an ideal) economic self dependence is in a vast number of cases a necessity. It is impossible to estimate in how many cases this occurs, but it is safe to say that many women do in fact support themselves and others, and that many more would do so if they could.

Normally working women seem to pass from one plane of social development to another, not once only but in many cases twice or thrice in their lives. We might distinguish these planes as status and contract, or value-in-use or value-in-exchange. All children, it is evident, are born into a world of value-in-use ; they are not, for some years at all events, valued at what their services will fetch in the market. At an age varying somewhere between eight and eighteen or twenty the working girl, like the boy, starts on an excursion into the world of competition and exchange ; she sells her work for what it will fetch. This stage, the stage of the cash nexus, lasts for the majority of girls a few years only. If she marries and leaves work, she returns at once into the world of value-in-use : the work she does for husband, home, and children is not paid at so much per unit, but is done for its own sake. This accounts on an average for say twenty-five years ; then she, in numbers at present unknown, is forced again to enter competitive industry on widowhood. This is what Madame Gnauck has called the "cleft" (*Spalte*) in the woman's industrial career. The lower death-rate of women is actually a source of weakness to them, in so far as it leaves a disproportionate number of women without partners at the very time when owing to the care of young children they are least capable of self-support, and it increases the competition of women for employment. Their use-value in the home, however great, will not fetch bread and shelter for their children. Professor Thomas Jones, in his deeply interesting report to the Poor Law Commission (Appendix XVII., Out-Relief and Wages) has been impressed by the pitiful fact that outside work should be forced on women whose whole desire is usually to be at home. He writes in reference to the well-intentioned efforts made by the Charity Organization Society to train widows for self support, efforts which, unfortunately, have not met with much success : "The widow whom it is sought to train is no longer young. It is rather late to begin. . . . Further, many women are domestic by instinct, and dislike factory life. More important still in explaining failure . . . . is the conflict between the bread-winner and the house-mother. Many a mother is distracted during the training time with anxiety for the children at home who may or may not be properly cared for."*

Many serious discourses and amiable sermons are delivered in public and in private on the supreme beauty and importance of woman's influence, the necessity of maintaining a high standard of home life, and the integrity of the family. All this may be true, but for many women it is singularly irrelevant. *Il faut vivre.*

A woman may possess all the domestic virtues in the highest possible degree, but she cannot live by them. Value-in-use is subordinated to value-in-exchange. Mrs. Brown may be much more useful, from the point of view of her family and the community, when she is engaged in keeping her little home clean and tidy and caring more or less efficiently for the fatherless little Browns' bodily and spiritual needs, than she is when fruit-picking, sack-making, or washing for an employer's profit. But the point is that these kinds of work do at worst bring her in a few shillings a week, and the former—nothing at all. In the face of such facts it is absurd to tell women that their work as mothers is of the highest importance to the State. We may hope, however, that public opinion will ere long be convinced that the present system of dealing with indigent widows, as described in Professor Jones's Report, is wasteful of child life, destructive of the home, and cruelly

* Poor Law Commission, Appendix, Vol. XVII.

burdensome to the most conscientious and tender-hearted mothers. The truly statesmanlike course will be to grant widows with young children a pension sufficient for family maintenance, on the condition that the home should be under some form of efficient inspection or control to ensure the money being properly laid out and the children cared for.* In the case of those women who are not naturally adapted to an entirely domestic life and prefer to work for themselves, it might be arranged that some portion of the pension should be diverted to pay a substitute. These cases would probably not be numerous, but it is as well to recognize that some such do exist.†

Socialists will not fail to realize that the case of the mother of small children forced under a competitive system to do unskilful and ill-remunerated work and neglect the work that is all-important for the State, viz., the care and nurture of its future citizens, is only an extreme instance of the anomaly of the whole position of woman in an individualist industrial community. This is not a place to enter on a discussion of the lines on which the economic position of women may be expected to develop under Socialism. I desire here merely to emphasize the importance of the distinction between value-in-use and value-in exchange which seems to me to lie at the root of the whole social question ; but most especially so as regards women. Our present industrial system, and therewith largely our social system also, is continually balanced perilously on the possibility of profit. Production is directed, not towards satisfying the needs and building up of the character of the nation's citizens, but merely towards what will yield most profit to the individuals who control the process. Except to the extent of the regulations of the Factory, Public Health, and Adulteration Acts (often inadequate and imperfectly enforced), it makes no difference at all whether the objects produced are useful or poisonous, beautiful or hideous, whether the conditions are healthy or dangerous, ennobling or degrading ; profit is the only test. The special anomaly of the woman's position is that while the pressure of social tradition is continually used to induce her to cultivate qualities that, so far from helping, are a positive hindrance to success in competitive industry, yet when circumstances throw her out into the struggle there is little or no social attempt made to compensate her for her deficiencies. Her very virtues are often her weakness.

No sane person can argue that adaptability to the conditions of profit-making industry can afford any test of a woman's merit *quâ* woman, yet it is all that many women have to depend on for their own and their children's living. The position ought at once to be frankly faced that women's work at home is service to the State, and it may be hoped that ere long some practical step may be taken to put in force the Minority Report suggestions regarding allowances to widows with young children.

* See Minority Report Poor Law Commission, Part I., p. 184 (Longmans' edition).

† I am not here alluding to cruel, depraved, or drunken mothers. In those cases children should obviously be entirely removed from the mother, and she herself dealt with penally or curatively, as may be deemed advisable.

Votes for Women and the Public Health.

BY

Dr. L. HADEN GUEST, L.R.C.P., M.R.C.S.

(of the Fabian Society).

EVERY FABIAN WOMAN SHOULD READ IT.

To be obtained from

THE LITERATURE DEPARTMENT,

WOMEN'S FREEDOM LEAGUE,

1 ROBERT ST., ADELPHI, W.C.

THE FABIAN SOCIALIST SERIES.

In attractive wrappers at **6**d. each net, and in quarter cloth boards, gilt top, at **1**s. each, net. Postage: 1d. and 2d. each.

VOLUMES NOW READY:

IX. **THE THEORY AND PRACTICE OF TRADE UNIONISM.**
By J. H. Greenwood. Preface by Sidney Webb.

VIII. **SOCIALISM AND SUPERIOR BRAINS.**
By Bernard Shaw. With new portrait of the author.

VII. **WASTAGE OF CHILD LIFE.**
By J. Johnston, M.D. A study of Lancashire towns.

VI. **SOCIALISM AND NATIONAL MINIMUM.**
By Mrs. Sidney Webb, Miss B. L. Hutchins, and others.

V. **THE COMMONSENSE OF MUNICIPAL TRADING.**
By Bernard Shaw. With new Preface.

IV. **THE BASIS AND POLICY OF SOCIALISM.**
By Sidney Webb and the Fabian Society.

III. **SOCIALISM AND INDIVIDUALISM.**
Contents: By Sidney Webb, Sidney Ball, G. Bernard Shaw, and Sir Oliver Lodge.

II. **SOCIALISM AND AGRICULTURE.**
Contents: By Edward Carpenter, T. S. Dymond, Lieut.-Col. D. C. Pedder, and the Fabian Society.

I. **SOCIALISM AND RELIGION.**
Contents: By the Rev. Stewart D. Headlam, the Rev. Percy Dearmer, the Rev. John Clifford, and John Woolman.

London: THE FABIAN SOCIETY, 3 Clement's Inn, Strand, W.C.

Tracts, each 16 to 52 pp., price 1d., or 9d. per doz., unless otherwise stated.
Leaflets, 4 pp. each, price 1d. for six copies, 1s. per 100, or 8/6 per 1000.
The Set of 78, 3s.; post free 3/5. Bound in Buckram, 4/6 n.; post free 5s.

I.—General Socialism in its various aspects.

TRACTS.—151. The Point of Honour: a Correspondence on Aristocracy and Socialism By RUTH CAVENDISH BENTINCK. 147. Capital and Compensation. By EDW. R. PEASE. 146. Socialism and Superior Brains. A reply to Mr. Mallock. By BERNARD SHAW. 142. Rent and Value. 138. Municipal Trading. 121. Public Service versus Private Expenditure. By Sir OLIVER LODGE. 113. Communism. By WM. MORRIS. 107. Socialism for Millionaires. By BERNARD SHAW. 139. Socialism and the Churches. By Rev JOHN CLIFFORD, D.D 133. Socialism and Christianity. By Rev. PERCY DEARMER (in cover with portrait of the author). 78. Socialism and the Teaching of Christ. By Dr. J. CLIFFORD. 42. Christian Socialism. By Rev. S. D. HEADLAM. 79. A Word of Remembrance and Caution to the Rich. By JOHN WOOLMAN. 75. Labor in the Longest Reign. By S. WEBB. 72. The Moral Aspects of Socialism. By SIDNEY BALL 69. Difficulties of Individualism. By SIDNEY WEBB. 51. Socialism: True and False. By S. WEBB. 45. The Impossibilities of Anarchism. By BERNARD SHAW (price 2d.). 7. Capital and Land (7th edn. revised 1908). 5. Facts for Socialists (11th ed., revised 1908). 132. A Guide to Books for Socialists. LEAFLETS—13. What Socialism Is 1. Why are the Many Poor? WELSH TRACTS—143. Sosialaeth yng Ngoleuni'r Beibl. Gan J. R. JONES (Caernarfon). 141. Translation of 139. 87. Translation of 78. 38. Translation of 1.

II.—Applications of Socialism to Particular Problems.

TRACTS.—155. The Case against the Referendum. By CLIFFORD D. SHARP. 154. The Case for School Clinics. By L. HADEN GUEST. 153. The Twentieth Century Reform Bill. By H. H. SCHLOESSER. 152. Our Taxes as they are and as they ought to be. By ROBT. JONES, B.Sc. In cover, 2d. 150. State Purchase of Railways. By EMIL DAVIES. In cover, 2d. 149. The Endowment of Motherhood. By H. D. HARBEN. In cover, 2d. 145. The Case for School Nurseries. By Mrs. TOWNSHEND. 144. Machinery: its Masters and its Servants. By H. H. SCHLOESSER and C. GAME. 140. Child Labor under Capitalism. By Mrs. HYLTON DALE. 136. The Village and the Landlord. By EDW. CARPENTER. 131. The Decline in the Birth-Rate. By S. WEBB. 130. Home Work and Sweating. By Miss B. L. HUTCHINS. 128. The Case for a Legal Minimum Wage. 122. Municipal Milk and Public Health. By Dr. F. LAWSON DODD. 125. Municipalization by Provinces. 119. Public Control of Electrical Power and Transit. 123. The Revival of Agriculture. 118. The Secret of Rural Depopulation. 115. State Aid to Agriculture: an Example. 112. Life in the Laundry. 98. State Railways for Ireland. 124. State Control of Trusts. 86. Municipal Drink Traffic. 84. Economics of Direct Employment. 83. State Arbitration and the Living Wage. LEAFLET.—104. How Trade Unions benefit Workmen.

III.—Local Government Powers: How to use them.

TRACTS.— 156. What an Education Committee can do (Elementary Schools). 137. Parish Councils and Village Life. 109. Cottage Plans and Common Sense. 76. Houses for the People. 99. Local Government in Ireland. 82. Workmen's Compensation Act. New edition for the Act of 1906. 62. Parish and District Councils. 54. The Humanizing of the Poor Law. LEAFLETS.— 134. Small Holdings: and how to get them. 68. The Tenant's Sanitary Catechism. 71. Ditto for London. FABIAN MUNICIPAL LEAFLETS (Nos. 32, 37 and 90 to 93). Municipalization of the Gas Supply. A Labor Policy for Public Authorities. Municipalization of Milk Supply. Municipal Pawnshops. Municipal Slaughterhouses. Women as Councillors.

IV.—General Politics and Fabian Policy.

127. Socialism and Labor Policy. 116. Fabianism and the Fiscal Question: an alternative policy. 108. Twentieth Century Politics. By SIDNEY WEBB. 70. Report on Fabian Policy. 41. The Fabian Society its Early History. By BERNARD SHAW.

Printed by G. Standring, 7 Finsbury St., London, E.C., and published by the Fabian Society, 3 Clement's Inn, Strand, London, W.C.

Fabian Tract No. 158.

The Case Against the Charity Organization Society.

BY MRS. TOWNSHEND.

PUBLISHED AND SOLD BY

THE FABIAN SOCIETY..

PRICE ONE PENNY.

LONDON:
THE FABIAN SOCIETY, 3 CLEMENT'S INN, STRAND, W.C.
JULY 1911.

The Case against the Charity Organization Society.

The Charity Organization Society Blocks the Way.

It is surprising to find that the most strenuous opposition to almost every scheme for social betterment comes from a body of people who are devoting their lives to that very purpose. Why have charity organizers resisted and denounced the proposals of General Booth's "Darkest England" scheme; of Mr. Charles Booth's Old Age Pensions scheme; of all the various schemes for providing meals for hungry school children; of the Old Age Pensions Act of 1908; of every scheme for "school clinics"; of every scheme for providing for the unemployed? Why did they object to the proposals of the Minority Report of the Poor Law Commission, the most masterly scheme ever brought forward for co-ordinating the forces against destitution, the very object they have themselves in view?*

Those of us who are keen that the public sense of responsibility should be awakened with regard to destitution must feel that this opposition on the part of "charity experts" is of the utmost importance, and I want if possible to trace it to its source and to see what it has to do with the organization of charity.

"The Greatest of These is Charity."

And first of all, what do we mean by charity? It is hard to say how much the Christian laudation of the virtue has to answer for. The current misinterpretation of the thirteenth chapter of the First Epistle to the Corinthians has set a seal of merit and respectability on free gifts that becomes very mischievous if it serves to accentuate the human weakness of preferring impulse to science and generosity to justice.

When the question arises as to whether it is better to fight destitution out of the rates by means of a series of preventive measures aimed not at results but at causes, or on the other hand, to leave it to be dealt with, so far as possible, by free will offerings administered by volunteers, those beautiful familiar words form a very real handicap in favor of the obsolete and more slipshod alternative. But how much of the virtue that "vaunteth not itself" is really to be found in the modern subscription list?

* For their own answer to these queries, see "The Social Criterion," Dr. B. Bosanquet. Blackwood.

Charity and Commercialism.

As long as the ties between men were largely personal, as long as production took place in the workshop of the craftsman and the household of the lord of the manor, almsgiving was a natural healthy expression of human love and sympathy. As such it is still to be found among the poor. One sees sometimes in the slums a certain generous happy go-lucky community of interests which comes far nearer to the charity that "suffereth long and is kind" than any that can be organized. The virtue still inheres in such rash and ill-considered acts as the hasty adoption of motherless children or the sharing a scanty meal with a starving neighbor, but it tends to be squeezed out by the machinery of investigation that becomes necessary, if almsgiving is to be placed on a scientific basis.

The beneficence of to-day is not to be blamed because the element of love has evaporated from it. The loss is inevitable. It is due to the complexity of modern life, to those dissociating forces that have reduced all mutual service to a basis of cash payment. The swiftly rising tide of industrial change, sweeping away all the old landmarks of service and responsibility, has left a chasm between rich and poor. A capitalist class with a civilization of its own cannot enter into the everyday life of the wageworker, who lives from hand to mouth, with habits, necessities, and pleasures entirely different.

It is this separation that cuts at the root of charity, severing the outward act from the inward grace. Robbed of close personal contact, the relationship of giver and receiver is bound to lose its beauty.* I can without loss of dignity accept help from a friend who loves me, but not from a stranger. Among the rich the warm impulse to help a friend in distress is replaced by a sentimental pity for seething humanity, and the act of devotion or loving service by a donation to a charitable institution ; while among the poor, glad acceptance of friendly aid in time of need is apt to degenerate into cringing dependence, for gratitude is not a wholesome emotion unless it be vitalized by love. All the specific defects with which we are familiar—misdirection, waste, overlapping, professional parasitism—arise out of this separation.

Origin of the C.O.S.

It was to fight these evils that the C.O.S. was founded. By the middle of the nineteenth century England, having outstripped her neighbors in industrial change, had become enormously rich. The contrast of the wealth of the capitalist class and the poverty and insecurity of the worker had become pronounced, and the blood money of charity flowed freely in an ever increasing stream.

---

* It may be mentioned here that the C.O.S. does all it can to prevent almsgiving from becoming purely impersonal by sending to each donor a report on the cases helped by his subscription and enabling him to take some interest in their individual circumstances. But this artificial contrivance for generating sympathy at a distance, away from the sights and sounds and smells of destitution, is far from restoring the ancient community of feeling.

But thoughtful people were becoming dissatisfied with charitable methods and results. In the later months of 1860, a time of much poverty and distress, sundry letters to the *Times* gave expression to this feeling and led to the formation of the "Society for the Relief of Distress," which aimed at establishing a more personal relation between giver and receiver and a more careful administration of charity. In March, 1868, Mr. Hicks, a member of this society, brought forward a proposal for establishing a central board of charities, to classify them, analyze and compare their accounts, and present an annual report. In June of the same year the "Association for the Prevention of Pauperism and Crime" was founded, with the Rev. Henry Solly as Hon. Secretary, Lord Shaftesbury, Lord Lichfield, and many other well known people as members. This society, though it began by aiming at big constructive schemes, such as that of employing "waste labor on waste land," gradually decided to limit its work to organization and propaganda. A paper read by Dr. Hawksley on December 17th, 1868, seems to have brought about this decision. It was issued as a pamphlet, entitled "The Charities of London and Some Errors of their Administration, with Suggestions of an lmproved System of Private and Official Charitable Relief." Dr. Hawksley estimates the total annual expenditure in London on the repression of crime, relief of distress, education, and social and moral improvement, at over seven millions, but points out that little good was being done by the expenditure of this great sum, because neither poor law nor charity aimed at *preventing* destitution. His recommendations are practical and far reaching. They include a central office for the control and audit of charities and for the inspection of annual reports, and a large staff of voluntary district visitors to carry out the necessary investigation of cases and applications. These suggestions formed the starting point of the C.O.S. "The movement began," writes Dr. Hawksley, in a letter dated October 22nd, 1892, and quoted in an editorial article on the origin of the society in the *C.O.S. Review,* "with Mr. Solly and the Association for the Prevention of Pauperism and Crime, and after a laborious existence of some months ended in accepting Lord Lichfield's suggestion to concentrate all our forces on charity organization, etc., as proposed in my pamphlet." *

The Object and Methods of the C.O.S.

are thus stated in its "Manual":—

"The main object of the society is the improvement of the condition of the poor. This it endeavors to attain (1) by bringing about co-operation between charity and the poor law, and between charitable persons and agencies of all religious denominations amongst themselves; (2) by spreading sound views on charitable work and creating a class of almoners to carry them out ; (3) by securing due investigation and fitting action in all cases ; (4) by repressing mendicity." †

* "Origin of the London C.O.S.," *C O.S. Review*, No. 94, October, 1892. See also "Philanthropy and the State," B. Kirkman Gray, Appendix to Chapter VIII.

† "Relief and Charity Organization," Occasional Paper No. 8, Third Series C.O.S. Papers.

With regard to No. (1), it must be admitted that the society has met with no marked success. London charities are still unorganized and new bodies, called "Guilds of Help" and "Councils of Social Welfare," are springing up to attempt once more what it has failed to accomplish.

Valuable Work of the C.O.S.

With regard to (2), (3), and (4), it has been more successful. There is no doubt that its influence on public opinion has been very important and, to a large extent, excellent. "The repression of mendicity" appealed forcibly to the well-to-do classes. The hideous inconvenience to the public at large of street begging and of the begging letter ensured a welcome for any proposal for putting a stop to such nuisances, especially one which issued from high benevolence and claimed to further the well being of the destitute. The views and methods of the society, though they never became really popular, were listened to with respect ; and it has certainly done a great work in training public opinion concerning the duties and responsibilities connected with almsgiving and in initiating orderly and efficient methods of social work. It has checked well meaning muddlers, has taught how to sift for helpable cases, and how to choose the right modes of help. It may lay claim to initiating in England the reign of the enquiry form and the "dossier." Even the country parson and the district visitor are falling into line, while many of the paid investigators for Royal Commissions and the London County Council have owed their efficiency to its training.

The society's want of success as an organizer of charity may perhaps be accounted for by the fact that it soon found itself largely occupied in the actual bestowal of relief, thus entering the lists with the various benevolent societies which it had set itself to investigate and to organize, and offering a concrete example of the actual working of those rules and principles on which the verdicts of the society were based. These soon became a strict and clearly formulated creed.

Principles of the C.O.S.[*]

1. Full investigation into the circumstances of the applicant to be undertaken in every case.

2. No relief to be given that is not adequate, that cannot hope to render the person or family relieved self-supporting.

3. No relief to be given to cases that are either so "bad" in point of character or so chronic in their need as to be incapable of permanent restoration.

4. All "hopeless" cases, however deserving, to be handed over to the poor law.

This creed, which, like all sets of working rules, arose out of temporary conditions, many of them badly needing alteration, has gradually acquired a kind of sacred character, and a strange structure of social theory has been built on it that is almost grotesque when compared with everyday experience.

* Cf. "Principles of Decision," C.O.S. Paper No. 5.

The very excellence of the society's work has served to make this theory more mischievous, for it comes before the public backed by the honored names of devoted workers.

Fundamental Errors of the C.O.S.

I.—Limitation of State Action with Reference to Destitution.

The first step towards organization seemed to be to draw a clear line between the province of the State in dealing with destitution and that of private charity. Unfortunately the early leaders of the society stumbled in taking this first step, and their initial blunder, never having been corrected by their followers, has tainted all the valuable work which they proceeded to set on foot.

They misread the facts that lay before them. They stoned the prophets of their own day and built the sepulchres of those who had preached to their fathers. In other words, they neglected the signs of the times (easy for us to read in the light of the years that have elapsed since 1869), such signs as the agitation for public education, for the decent housing of the poor, and for factory legislation, and they harked back to the decisions of the wise men of 1834. They failed to see that laissez faire was giving way all along the line before the phenomena of modern capitalism. They stuck to the theory of individual independence and of the danger of State interference in a world where man-made laws were enabling the rich to grind the faces of the poor. So long as the relative amounts of rent, interest, and wages were believed to be beyond human control, generosity in the rich, fortitude in the poor, seemed indeed the virtues called for ; but those very investigations incidental to the careful bestowal of charity must have brought to light a gross disparity of distribution, a hideous waste of national resources that no charity could stem or cure. If only the leaders of the society had recognized this, had seen that the efficacy of charity for the redress of social grievances was at an end, and that the time had come when the community as a whole must shoulder its responsibilities, the C.O.S. might have begun work of great national importance in preparing the way for modern social legislation. But they did not see this. Habitually oblivious of any department of State action except the Poor Law, they saw merely that the more humane and the more lax of poor law administrators were overstepping the limits which had been legally assigned to them, and they traced the increase not only of pauperism, but also of destitution, to this relaxation of the principles of 1834. These principles—that the poor law should be a stern measure, seeking not the prevention, but merely the relief, of dire necessity, and that the condition of the pauper should never be "more eligible" than that of the lowest grade of self-supporting laborers, however insufficient for decent life that might be—they were prepared to adopt without modification, in the belief that the diminution of poverty which followed the reforms of 1834 is to be traced exclusively to those reforms, and that similar results might be

confidently expected from a return to them. The exclusive importance attached to this one period of history and to this one among
many possible causes for the improvement which took place at that
time is very characteristic of C.O.S. thought as we know it. It is
interesting, therefore, to discover from the writings of Dr. Hawksley,
to whom rather than to any other single person the origin of the
society is due, and from those of Dr. Devine, the Secretary of the
New York C.O.S., that these particular views have no necessary connection with the organization of charity. Dr. Devine, in the " Principles of Relief," points out that there were many changes going on
in the thirties to which the improvement of the people may have
owed quite as much as to that stricter administration of the poor law
on which so much stress has been laid.*

Dr. Hawksley goes still further, expressing the warmest disappro-
bation of the reformed poor law, " which in spirit sought to deal
with destitution only in its completed state—it did not attempt the
prevention of pauperism by seeing that the children of the
dependent, or the idle, or the vicious, were trained for industry and
virtue—it did not entertain the question of individual merit or
demerit, but it adopted a uniform system of relief which was to be
so ingeniously balanced that, on the one hand, its recipients might
be prevented dying of starvation or want of shelter, but, on the
other hand, that the kind and mode of the relief should be so hard,
painful, and humiliating, that none but the very helpless and hard
pressed should seek for it. The system was to be a test, and the
idea was that if you drive away poverty out of your sight, you would
cure it, as if the charnel house could be changed by screening it
with a whited sepulchre. The system did not contemplate visiting
' the fatherless and widow in their affliction,' but it set itself up in
the broad way of misery and destitution, and to every applicant, as a
rule, it refused the recognition of any domesticities. It treated with
contempt the humanizing influences of hearth and home, and with
stern voice, pointing the way to the dreary portal of ' the House,' it
said : ' Enter or depart without aid.' The result has been the
creation of an abject, miserable race." †

The society that Dr. Hawksley was to some extent instrumental
in founding has departed widely from these views. Its members
have fully agreed with him that paupers are " an abject and miserable race," but instead of attributing this, as he did, to " maladmin-
istration," to the fact that grudging relief was given instead of treatment and that it was given too late, only after destitution had set in,
they attributed the evil results of poor relief entirely to the fact that
it was given by the State, ignoring altogether the very different
results of other forms of State action.

Instead of recognizing that the poor law was already obsolete and
was bound to become more anomalous with every succeeding

<hr />

* See " Principles of Relief," Professor Devine, pp. 276-7. The Macmillan Co.

† " The Charities of London," etc., T. Hawksley, M.D. Published by the Association for Preventing Pauperism and Crime, London, 1868.

measure of social legislation, they accepted it as immutable and made it the corner stone of their system. Their line of argument was very singular. They admitted that the poor law was demoralizing; that its action was merely palliative, not restorative; that at best it could only prevent the worst horrors of destitution, but could not prevent its occurrence and its recurrence; and yet they never proposed any change in the application of public funds! They insisted that private funds should always be expended with a view to prevention and cure, but that public funds should be strictly reserved for those who were already in the last stage of destitution, and therefore already beyond curative measures.

Taking for granted that State action must demoralize, they assigned to private charity the task of preserving from pauperism all those persons or families whose need was only temporary or accidental, or easily remediable, especially where such need was accompanied by good character and record.

It is interesting to find this limitation of State action in a book published in 1868 by Mr. Charles Bosanquet. He was not one of the group who started the society, but he was an early member of it and became secretary in 1870.

" It would not be difficult," he says, " to classify cases between the poor law and voluntary charity. The former would take the ordinary chronic cases, the latter, perhaps, some of the more deserving chronic cases, but especially those temporary cases which, it might be hoped, judicious help would save from sinking into pauperism." *

Whether Mr. Charles Bosanquet was or was not the first to introduce this system of classification into the C.O S. creed, there is no doubt that he continued to preach it after he became secretary and that it has taken a permanent place. " It is an essential difference between charity and the poor law," he writes, " that the former can direct its energies to preventive and remedial action. As the poor law is bound to give necessary existence to all destitute persons, charity is only doing the work of the law if it take up such cases without special reason." †

An authoritative statement of the same view is to be found in the introduction to a recent number of the very valuable Charities Register and Digest which is published annually by the society.

" The claim for poor law relief rests, it may be broadly stated, upon the destitution of the claimant. . . . On the threshold of the question then we see the boundary lines of charity and the poor law. To charity it is not a question of primary importance whether a person is destitute or not. For it destitution is no test. It has more chance of helping effectually if a person is not destitute. It has to prevent destitution and indigence. It may have to supply actual necessaries, but to place the poor beyond the reach of need or to

---

* " London : Some Account of its Growth, Charitable Agencies, and Wants," by C. B. P. Bosanquet, M.A., Barrister-at-Law, pp. 199-202. Hatchard, 1868.

† " History and Mode of Operation of the C.O.S.," C. B. P. Bosanquet.

prevent the recurrence of need is its true vocation. It is unlimited in its scope and gives as a free gift. From the point of view of the poor law the question of destitution is all important. It is the passport to relief. Its administration is tied and bound with restrictions. Its supplies are drawn from a ratepayers' trust fund. Its main purpose is not to prevent or remove distress, but to alleviate it. It is a stern alleviative measure. It helps only when it must ; charity always when it wills."*

It is singular that in these utterances, and hundreds of similar ones that could be adduced, the charity organizers give no reason (other than the present condition of the law) for this hard and fast distinction between the principles which should guide public and private administrators in dealing with destitution. Presumably they think the reasons *sautent aux yeux*, but surely much might be said for entirely reversing their decision. The prevention of destitution implies that we should search out those who are on the downward road and arrest their progress before they become "destitute." Such action demands a many-sided and far-sighted policy, for the roads that lead to destitution are many and gradual. It demands a considerable outlay, producing distant and not always obvious results. Above all, it demands disciplinary powers.† Where are we to look for the statesman who will co-ordinate and maintain such a policy, for the Exchequer to supply capital for such a purpose, for the authority to wield such powers, if not the Government of the country ? And yet, according to Dr. Loch and Dr. Bosanquet, this is precisely where we are not to look.

If they wished to lay down a hard and fast rule, one might have expected that it would be that great remedial and preventive measures should be left to the national and local executive, the collective wisdom of the nation, while private charity should concern itself with the pitiable, but apparently hopeless cases, should indeed humbly take up the work of palliation with instruments of love and religion and personal self-sacrifice that the State can with difficulty command, as, in fact, the Salvation Army and the Church Army profess to do. On the contrary, their decision is, as has been shown, exactly the reverse ; charity is to be remedial, the State is to confine its action to palliation.

This decision accords perfectly, no doubt, with facts as they are. It is a statement of the theory behind the existing poor law, but in the writings of the charity organizers there is acceptance and approval as well as statement. Dr. Bosanquet emphasizes and explains that approval in his essay on "Socialism and Natural Selection " " We should never forget," he says, " that the system," i.e., State "interference," "is a necessary evil, nor ever handle our

---

* Introduction to Annual Charities Register and Digest, 1909, "On the Functions of the Poor Law and Charity." Cf. "Charity and Social Life," C. S. Loch, p. 349. Macmillan, 1910.

† The experiments already tried in the operations of the Local Health Authority, the Local Education Authority, and the Local Lunacy Authority have been—in marked contrast with the Poor Law—highly promising in their success.

national initiative, whether through the poor law or through more general legislation, so as to relieve the father of the support of the wife and children or the grown up child of the support of his parents. We should raise no expectation of help or of employment invented ad hoc which may derange the man's organization of life in view of the whole moral responsibilities which as a father he has accepted." *

A good example of the actual mischief wrought by this pernicious doctrine that public action weakens private resource is to be found in the C.O.S. attitude towards the agitation for school clinics. The absolute futility of school inspection unless followed by treatment is obvious. At least fifty per cent. of the children in our schools are suffering from defects which, if not dealt with, will seriously handicap them in after life. These defects require treatment from a nurse under medical supervision. It is simply ridiculous to suppose that the mother of a family living on a pound a week in two rooms can find leisure to take her child suffering from adenoids to a distant hospital, can wait for it to recover consciousness, and then bring it back, still bleeding, in a public omnibus ; that she can afterwards superintend the breathing exercises that are as important as the operation, or if the child's ears are affected, can spend half an hour daily in syringing them. The position becomes still more impossible if a second child requires spectacles and a third has decayed teeth to be stopped or extracted ; yet such a case is not impossible or even unusual. It is perfectly clear that if the men and women of the next generation are to start life with a fairly sound physique, the preventive measures which are taken for the rich man's child in the nursery must be taken for the poor man's child in the school.

Advice, nurses, nursing appliances must be provided collectively, since it is a sheer impossibility that they can be provided in the

bers of care committees, and even county councils outside of London, are beginning to see that the difficulty can be met only by means of medical centres in connection with the schools. One might expect that a society whose aim is " the improvement of the condition of the poor " would guide public opinion towards such a conclusion. We find instead that the C.O.S. has been acting, as usual, not as a pioneer, but as a powerful, though fortunately insufficient, brake.

At this last stage of the controversy (March 21st, 1911) nothing authoritative has been issued by the society. In default of it we may quote from the Occasional Paper on " The Relief of School Children " (No. 8, Fourth Series). Such measures "teach him" (the child) "to look to outside help for the things he has a right to expect from his parents, a lesson he will not be slow to remember when he himself is a parent. The child needs before all things in the present day to learn the lessons of self-reliance and self-respect." †

* " Aspects of the Social Problem ": XVI. " Socialism and Natural Selection," Dr. B Bosanquet, p. 304.

† Occasional Paper C.O.S. No 8, Fourth Series.

And from an essay of Dr. Bosanquet's entitled " The Social Criterion " : " Granting a complete system of inspection at schools and of sanitary supervision through the health authorities and advice from health visitors, the normal mode of medical attendance should be for the wage earner as for ourselves, attendance by his family doctor, whom the head of the family chooses, trusts, and pays. On a provident system this is in many places successfully arranged, to the complete satisfaction of the doctor and of the patient. When, however, we should go to the specialist or to expensive nursing homes, the wage earner will be referred by his family doctor to the appropriate hospital or infirmary. . . . Thus the division of labor is properly maintained, the all important relation of trust and confidence between the family and the family doctor is not interfered with, the general practitioner's position is secured, and the hospital also is secured in the acquisition of interesting cases and in the fullest exercise of its powers of helpfulness." *

With regard to proposals for free medical treatment, Dr. Bosanquet says : " Such a policy is calculated to ruin the medical clubs and provident dispensaries, and to substitute visits of an official who, however good, is not the people's choice for the family doctor whom they like and trust and pay." †

This question of school medical treatment is for the moment, perhaps, more under discussion than any other question of social reform, and for that reason affords the most striking example of the C.O.S. policy of obstruction ; but that policy is perfectly consistent and perfectly general in character. It erects a barrier in the face of every attempt to lighten that pressure on the wage-earner which results from existing industrial conditions.

II.—THAT UNEARNED INCOME INJURES THE POOR BUT NOT THE RICH.

Another arbitrary assumption of the charity organizers is that for any man to enjoy any benefits which he has not definitely worked for and earned is injurious to his character. The naïveté with which they take this for granted is really preposterous when one remembers that nearly all the more respectable and refined members of the community are themselves living chiefly on wealth which they have not earned. One begins to wonder how those of us whose income is derived from dividends have any independence of character left. Dr. Bosanquet points out that the recipient of charitable help is injured because it comes miraculously and not as the natural result of personal effort ; ‡ but what effort do I make in connection with my dividends from the North Eastern Railway, and

---

* "The Social Criterion," a Paper read by B. Bosanquet, M.A., LL.D, November 15th, 1907, before the Edinburgh C.O.S., p. 23.

† Ibid. p. 24.

‡ "The point of private property is that things should not come miraculously and be unaffected by your dealings with them, but that you should be in contact with something which in the external world is the definite material representation of yourself." "Aspects of the Social Problem," p. 313.

what can be more miraculous than my waking up one morning to find that certain shares that were worth £100 yesterday are now worth £105?

Dr. Bosanquet must really find some other reasons for objecting to doles, unless he is prepared to return to the ancient canon law with reference to usury.

III.—"Character is the Condition of Conditions."*

The third grave error in C.O.S. theory is like the first, in that it arises out of the acceptance of human arrangements as if they were heaven-sent and unchangeable.

Accepting the individual ownership of land and capital and a competitive wage system—all with exactly the same limitations and mitigations that are to-day in force, and no more—as the inevitable basis of society, the charity organizers are driven to an easy optimism that sees a satisfactory opportunity open to every virtuous worker, and looks forward with composure to a future when the working class, having been taught thrift, industry, and self-control, will do its duty in that state of life to which modern industrial processes shall call it.

Poverty, even extreme poverty, seems to them unavoidable. "Destitution," says Dr. Loch in his last book, "cannot disappear. Every group of competing men is continually producing it." † Not to abolish destitution, but to improve "social habit," should be, he thinks, the aim of the philanthropist. It is for this reason that he looks coldly at all recent schemes for social betterment.

"The remarkable and well known investigations of Mr. Charles Booth and Mr. Seebohm Rowntree, which have stirred public thought in many circles, were, in our judgment," he says, "faulty from this point of view. They were not analytical of social habit, but of relative poverty and riches. They graded the population according as they were 'poor,' or 'very poor,' or above a poverty line. Their authors aimed at marking out such a line of poverty, forgetful, as it seems to us, of the fact that poverty is so entirely relative to use and habit and potential ability of all kinds, that it can never serve as a satisfactory basis of social investigation or social reconstruction. It is not the greater or lesser command of means that makes the material difference in the contentment and efficiency of social life, but the use of means relative to station in life and its possibilities. Nevertheless, in these investigations it was on the possession of means that stress was laid. Hence the suggestion that the issue to be settled by the country—the line of social reform—was the endowment of the class or classes whose resources were considered relatively insufficient.

"But to transfer the wealth of one class to another, by taxation or otherwise, is no solution of social difficulty." ‡

---

* "Aspects of the Social Problem," Dr. Bosanquet, Preface, p. vii.
† "Charity and Social Life," C. S. Loch, p. 393. Macmillan, 1910.
‡ Ibid. pp. 386-7.

For a clear statement of the opposite view we cannot do better than turn to the writings of Dr. Devine, General Secretary of the New York C.O.S., and thus discover that the views of Dr. Loch are not inseparable from the aims of the society. "I hold," says Dr. Devine, "that personal depravity is as foreign to any sound theory of the hardships of our modern poor as witchcraft or demoniacal possession ; that these hardships are economic, social, transitional, measurable, manageable. Misery, as we say of tuberculosis, is communicable, curable, and preventable. It lies not in the unalterable nature of things, but in our particular human institutions, our social arrangements, our tenements and streets and subways, our laws and courts and gaols, our religion, our education, our philanthropy, our politics, our industry and our business." *

Even more definitely Dr. Devine, towards the end of the same book, expresses the view "that distress and crime are more largely the results of social environment than of defective character, and that our efforts should therefore be directed toward the changing of adverse social conditions, some of which can be accomplished only by the resources of legislation, of taxation, of large expenditure, or by changes in our educational system, or in our penal system, or in our taxing system, or even in our industrial system." †

If we turn to the writings of Mrs. Bosanquet, perhaps the most popular exponent of what we are accustomed to look on as the C.O.S. view, we find that though she is more willing than Dr. Loch to admit the drawbacks of extreme poverty, yet she is equally certain that the aim of the philanthropist should be to stimulate the energy and improve the character of the sufferers, rather than to make any change in "adverse social conditions."

"How can we bring it about," she asks, "that they (i.e., 'those whom we may call the very poor') shall have a permanently greater command over the necessaries and luxuries of life ? The superficial remedy is that of gifts. . . . But this is a policy which has no tendency to remove the evil. . . . The less obvious, but more effective, remedy is to approach the problem by striking at its roots in the minds of the people themselves ; to stimulate their energies ; to insist upon their responsibilities ; to train their faculties. In short, to make them efficient." ‡

"Wherever there are people in want," she continues, "there lies the possibility of a new market and an increased demand for workers. The key necessary to open it is the efficiency which will enable them to buy by their services, what before they only needed." §

This theory—that the root of the problem must be sought in the minds of the people themselves ; that the key to the industrial impasse of unemployment is the efficiency of the worker ; that, in short, the poor need not be poor if they choose to exert themselves ;

* "Misery and its Causes," E. T. Devine. Macmillan & Co., 1909.
† Ibid. p. 267.
‡ "The Strength of the People," Helen Bosanquet, p. 114. Macmillan, 1902.
§ Ibid. p. 115.

and that the only way effectually to help them is to drive home their personal responsibility—is indeed the keynote of the C.O.S. philosophy ; and yet, we may remark in passing, that, as in the case of the first " error," it is markedly absent from the utterances of the actual founders of the society.

The Rev. Henry Solly, in his address on " How to Deal with the Unemployed Poor of London," * alluding to recent riots in Wigan, quotes from the *Spectator* for May 2nd, 1868 : " Five hundred lives ought to have been taken in that town rather than five hundred laborers should have been robbed by violence and with impunity of their labor, rather than the law should have been made ridiculous and authority contemptible," and adds : " True, most sorrowfully and unanswerably true ; but what about the responsibility resting on owners of property in the neighborhood for allowing twenty thousand colliers to live in a state of semi-barbarism ? What about the responsibility of persons of property and education in this metropolis, if the question of preserving the reign of law and order were to be decided some day by slaughtering five hundred miserable semi-savage fellow citizens in the streets because we would not adopt remedial and preventive measures in time ? "

We find the same frank acknowledgment of collective responsibility in Dr. Hawksley's address already quoted from : " When we think," he says, " of the suspended murderer, let us ask ourselves whether we took pains to educate and train him for virtue and usefulness ; and if we have not, let us bow our heads and be silent in the overwhelming sense of our responsibility. Or when we view the sad state of the poor—their overcrowded and filthy dwellings, the foul air, the bad and adulterated food, the disproportion between the present expenses of living and the wages that such darkened minds and feeble bodies can earn—let us again be mute and grateful that our own state is better, let us remove these stumbling blocks in the way of health and virtuous industry. Before we venture to judge these people, let us rather ask ourselves how much more are we to blame than they." †

Nothing could be further removed from the tone of virtuous superiority which characterizes the writings of later exponents of C.O.S. views, and yet these two men may be said to have first formulated the aims of the society.

It may perhaps be claimed that the new theory is due to experience, that it is founded on poor law statistics and on the observation of C.O.S. investigators, who find that there is nearly always some moral defect associated with cases of dire poverty.

The argument from poor law statistics may be ruled out at once. It is simply misleading to speak as if pauperism and poverty were interchangeable terms. Pauperism can be diminished, or even

---

* " How to Deal with the Unemployed Poor of London, etc." Paper read by the Rev. H. Solly at the Society of Arts, June 22nd, 1868, which brought about the formation of the " Association for the Prevention of Pauperism and Crime."

† " The Charities of London, etc.," T. Hawksley. M.D. Read at a meeting of the Association for Preventing Pauperism and Crime, December 17th, 1868.

quenched altogether, by a change in the poor law which would leave poverty just where it was.

The fallacies that underlie the other argument are a little more subtle. First, the ancient fallacy of "any and all." One may say with truth to the last dozen people who compose the queue outside the pit door of a crowded theatre, "if you had been here half an hour earlier you would have got good seats," but if one says it to the whole crowd it is obviously untrue, for the amount of accommodation remaining the same, the number of disappointed people would also remain the same. In Mr. Hobson's words, "the individualist argument by which our charity organization thinkers seek to show that because A, B, or C in a degraded class is able, by means of superior character or capacity, to rise out of that class, no one need remain there, contains the same fallacy. It assumes what it is required to prove, viz., that there are no economic or other social forces which limit the number of successful rises. It assumes that every workman can secure regularity of employment and good wages · · · and that all can equally secure for themselves a comfortable and solid economic position by the wise exertion of their individual powers. Now if there exist any economic forces, in their operation independent of individual control, which at any given time limit the demand for labor in the industrial field . . . these forces, by exercising a selective influence, preclude the possibility of universal success. All economists agree in asserting the existence of these forces, though they differ widely in assigning causes for them. All economists affirm the operation of great tidal movements in trade which for long periods limit the demand for labor, and thus oblige a certain large quantity of unemployment. The C.O.S. investigator naturally finds that the individuals thrown out of work in these periods of depression are mostly below the level of their fellows in industrial or in moral character, and attributes to this 'individual' fact the explanation of the unemployment. He wrongly concludes that if these unemployed were upon the same industrial and moral level as their comrades who are at work, there would be work for all. He does not reason to this judgment, but, with infantile simplicity, assumes it." *

We find a similar assumption underlying the argument with regard to underpayment in "The Strength of the People." Mrs. Bosanquet takes for granted that payment is determined by quality of work, and concludes, quite logically, that the cure for a man's poverty is to make him do good work. To a casual observer the argument receives some support from appearances, as in the case of unemployment, for just as the unemployed are usually less steady and skilful than the employed, so is the sweated worker less efficient than the well paid worker.

To conclude that efficiency would secure good wages is, however, quite unwarrantable, for wages are determined in a state of free competition not by the intrinsic value of the work, but by the relative needs of the worker to sell and the employer to buy. Unfortu-

* "The Crisis of Liberalism," J. A. Hobson, p. 205.

nately, however, though good work does not always secure good wages, bad wages will usually produce bad work. " The father of a family who receives eighteen shil.ings a week and pays seven shillings for lodging cannot, if he also feeds his wife and children, either remain or become a very good workman. Before he can do better work he must be better paid. Mrs. Bosanquet thinks otherwise. Efficiency and, consequently, prosperity might, she appears to believe, be enforced upon the poor by the withdrawal of such help as is now accorded them. . . . The hunger and hardship of their daily lives do not furnish an adequate spur, but perhaps despair might do so. We seem to hear Mrs. Chick exhorting the dying Mrs. Dombey ' to make an effort.' " *

This attempt to abolish sweating by improving the sweated worker is on a par with that perennial crusade against prostitution, which consists in " rescue work " and the inculcation of personal chastity, leaving entirely out of consideration the economic conditions which give rise to prostitution. Both are attempts to eradicate social evils by improving the moral character of their victims, *without arresting the causes*, and therefore both are as useless as Mrs. Partington's mop.

But even if we grant that efficiency is the true cure for sweating or, to put it more broadly, that a man's social position depends on his character, we have still to consider what his character depends on. Does it not depend largely on his physique, his upbringing, and his general surroundings? Even if we admit that all energetic individuals may make satisfactory lives for themselves, how can we expect that the requisite moral energy shall be generated in the environment of poverty? It may be true, as Dr. Bosanquet says, that material conditions are largely independent of " the energy of the mind which they surround," but it is at least equally true that the energy becomes impossible under certain material conditions. The driving force of individual effort is a realization of higher wants. How are these wants to grow in such an atmosphere?

It is indeed hard to understand how this theory that the moral elevation of the masses must precede in point of time all successful reforms of environment can have survived the impact with fact which C.O.S. methods imply. With the slum child before their eyes, born with low vitality, reared by ignorant and poor parents, breathing bad air, wearing foul clothes, tormented with vermin, how can they assert that the problem is a moral one, that " in social reform character is the condition of conditions " ? † " Only give scope of character, it will unfailingly pull us through." Of course material improvements will be of no use unless they react on character, but have we any reason to suppose that they will fail to do so? Is it not likely that the child bred in cleanly habits will wish to be clean, and, in general, is not the way to raise the standard of living to accustom the young to higher ways of life? Even if it is true that character is the most important element in social reform, it

* " Sweated Industry," Clementina Black, p. 155.
† " Aspects of the Social Problem," B. Bosanquet, Preface, p. vii.

is equally true that habit is the most important element in the formation of character, and habits of life are conditioned by environment.

But in all this talk about character it is well to consider whether the characteristics on which Dr. Loch and his followers lay so much stress are the most important for the future of our country.

It has been said that the C.O.S. holds a brief for the independence of the workers. Certainly this is the virtue on which these writers chiefly insist. The constantly recurring argument against old age pensions, against school feeding or school clinics, is that such State aid will tend to relax the effort to be entirely self-supporting. The C.O.S. ideal is that every head of a family should provide for his children, and even for his collateral relatives if they happen to be incapable of providing for themselves. "That terrible pressure of the poorer upon the poor, which Mr. Booth regards as so serious an evil, appears to Mrs. Bosanquet * an element of hope and strength. Morally the charity of the poor to one another is undoubtedly a beautiful thing ; economically it is assuredly one of the causes that increase and aggravate poverty, and such diminution of pauperism as is produced by the maintenance out of the workhouse of an aged or sick relative may, in the long run, lead to the destitution of a whole family The last result of such maintenance may, if widespread, be far more nationally expensive than if all the sick and aged were supported out of the public purse." †

But apart from the question whether it is cheaper for us to support the sick and the aged or to bind that burden exclusively on the wage earner, it remains for us to enquire whether a thrifty, calculating habit of mind, a tendency to count the cost to the uttermost farthing before giving way to a generous or æsthetic impulse, to prefer always the solid necessaries of life before its joys and delights, to limit one's outlook to the material wellbeing of oneself and one's blood relations, whether such a disposition is the one and only basis of national prosperity. What becomes of the graces of life under such a régime, what becomes of the search after beauty and knowledge, what becomes of that training in corporate action on which all successful administration depends and of the sense of human solidarity which lies at the root of citizenship ?

But now, apart from theory, let us test this statement as to the all-importance of character by what we see around us. Is it true or is it not true that a man's personal character determines the comfort and wellbeing of himself, his wife, and family ? If so, the agricultural laborer at twelve shillings a week, whose family cannot have clean skins, clean clothes, and enough to eat, must be a worse man morally than the fox hunting squire who is his landlord, and the house mother, toiling early and late to keep her children decent, a worse woman than the squire's wife waited on by five servants.

Is it true or is it not true? If not, then not character, but the accident of birth is the condition of conditions, together with the laws and customs of the time and country into which a man is born.

* See "The Strength of the People."
† "Sweated Industry," Clementina Black, p. 155.

Now these laws and customs are after all of human origin. We, the governing classes, are responsible for them. The C.O.S. philosopher appears to think that they are God ordained and came down from heaven ready made, but does not attempt to reconcile such a view with his studies of history and of the varying laws and customs of different countries at the present time.

Social conditions are amenable to human action. In a democratic country laws and customs are modified by public opinion acting on and through the Government. What becomes then of this terror of State interference, with its debilitating effect on individual character? It stands revealed as a satisfaction with social conditions as they exist at the present time in England and a dislike to any proposed modification of them. "We like things very well as they are. We have much and you have little; but you must cut your coat according to your cloth, as we do. If you are very thrifty, very sober, very industrious, if you put off marrying till you have insured your life and built yourself a really nice cottage with a bath room, and put by a nice little annuity for your old age, there will still be time for you to produce two or three strong healthy sons to work for our children. We may go to our clubs, our dinner parties, and our theatres, but you must not frequent the village alehouse. We may send up our sons for scholarships at Oxford, but you must pay out of your hard earned wages for any higher education that your children may desire. You must pay your rates and taxes as we do. There is no reason why we should bear a disproportionate amount of the burden; for though our wealth is greater, more is expected of us and our needs are greater. Any attempt, however, on your part to secure for yourselves any special return for your expenditure is most mistaken. It is true that the vast sums spent on the army and navy provide convenient and respectable careers for the less brilliant of our sons; while the more brilliant can obtain official posts at home or in India, well paid out of public money. It is true that it is the streets where we live that are well lighted and paved out of the rates, but this is all as it should be, and any attempt on your part to have your children fed when you are out of work or medically treated at the public cost is most ill judged. School meals and nursery schools would relieve your wife of part of her unceasing toil and might enable her to keep your home and your children cleaner, while school clinics might make a vast change in the health and wellbeing of the coming generation and in the future of our country; but what are these advantages compared with the sacredness of individual responsibility and of family life? It is the duty and privilege of every man to organize his life in view of the whole normal responsibilities which as a father he has accepted, and any State assistance which interferes with that duty and privilege is a cruel kindness. So important is your individual independence that it must not be jeopardized even to improve the health and save the lives of your children. It is better for England that her citizens should grow up crooked, diseased, and undersized than that they should believe in mutual aid and learn to look upon State funds as common funds, to be wisely administered for the common good."

Such, in plain words, is the C.O.S. attitude towards poverty. So stated the theory sounds offensive and absurd ; but when we meet with it interwoven with high sounding philosophical phrases and also with the record of many years of unselfish and benevolent effort, we are apt to be hoodwinked as to its real character. There is, moreover, insidious attraction for the well-to-do in this notion that destitution is but the natural working out of human character. If the present condition of affairs suits us, much satisfaction is to be derived from the assurance that any alteration of outward conditions, any change in human laws or institutions, would be worse than useless. The theory thrives and spreads among our upper and middle classes because it strikes root into the indolence and self-satisfaction of an, easy and sheltered life.

BIBLIOGRAPHY.

How to Deal with the Unemployed Poor of London, etc. A paper read by the Rev. H. Solly at the Society of Arts, June 22nd, 1868.

The Charities of London. T. Hawksley, M.D. 1868.

London : Some Account of its Growth, Charitable Agencies, and Wants. C. B. P. Bosanquet. 1861.

The Origin of the London C.O.S. *The C.O.S. Review*, Vol. 8, No. 94, October and November, 1892.

Aspects of the Social Problem. By various Writers. Edited by Bernard Bosanquet, M.A., L.L.D. Macmillan. 1895.

Democracy and Social Ethics. Jane Addams. The Macmillan Company. 1902.

The Strength of the People. Mrs. B. Bosanquet (Helen Dendy). Macmillan. 1902.

History of Philanthropy in England. B. Kirkman Gray. P. S. King and Son. 1905.

Newer Ideals of Peace. Jane Addams. The Macmillan Company. 1907.

The Social Criterion ; or, How to Judge of Proposed Social Reforms. B. Bosanquet, M.A., LL.D. Blackwood. 1907.

The History and Mode of Operation of the C.O.S. By the Secretary of the Council, C. B. P. Bosanquet.

Sweated Industry and the Minimum Wage. Clementina Black. Duckworth. 1907.

Philanthropy and the State. B Kirkman Gray. Edited by E. Kirkman Gray and B. L. Hutchins. King. 1908.

The Principles of Relief. E. T. Devine, Ph.D., LL.D. (New York) The Macmillan Company. 1909.

Misery and its Causes. E. T. Devine, Ph.D., LL.D. (New York) The Macmillan Company. 1909.

Tha Majority Report [of the Poor Law Commission]. By Prof. B. Bosanquet, M.A., LL.D., in *Sociological Review*, April, 1909.

The Silver Box. Plays by John Galsworthy. Duckworth and Co. 1909.

The Break-Up of the Poor Law and the Remedy for Unemployment. Sidney and Beatrice Webb. National Committee for Prevention of Destitution, 37 Norfolk Street, Strand, W.C.

The Crisis of Liberalism. J. A. Hobson. P. S. King and Son. 1909.

The Minority Report for Scotland. Scottish National Committee for the Prevention of Destitution, 180 Hope Street, Glasgow.

Charity and Social Life. C. S. Loch, LL.D. Macmillan. 1910.

The Prevention of Destitution. Sidney and Beatrice Webb. Longmans. 1911.

The C.O.S. Review. Published monthly. Longmans and Offices of the C.O.S., Denison House, Vauxhall Bridge Road, London, S.W.

Fabian Tract No. 159.

THE NECESSARY BASIS OF SOCIETY.

By SIDNEY WEBB.

PUBLISHED AND SOLD BY

THE FABIAN SOCIETY.

PRICE ONE PENNY.

LONDON:
THE FABIAN SOCIETY, 3 CLEMENT'S INN, STRAND, W.C.
JULY, 1911.

THE NECESSARY BASIS OF SOCIETY.[1]

IN choosing for my subject "The Necessary Basis of Society," I shall not deal with any plank of the platform of the Liberal, the Conservative, or the Labor Party. Nor is it my intention to argue the more fashionable thesis of to-day, that either Socialism or Individualism, according to taste, is the more desirable principle on which to organize society. My aim is the more limited and, I venture to hope, the more practically useful one of bringing to your notice certain considerations on which all political parties can agree ; considerations without attention to which, I believe, it is impossible to expect to have, on any principles whatsoever, even a decently successful social order. However much the rival partisans may quarrel among themselves as to what sort of social order they wish to have —however much in this respect the Liberal may differ from the Conservative, the Republican from the Royalist, the Democrat from the Aristocrat, the Trade Unionist from the Capitalist, the Socialist from the Individualist—there are, as I venture to believe, certain fundamental matters of social organization which they can (and, if they are well-informed, reasonable beings, must) accept as indispensable to any successful carrying out of their own projects and ideas.

I invite you, in the first place, to consider for a moment some of the characteristics of popular government. It has been, in a sense, the special task of the nineteenth century, in our conceptions of social organization, to bring into prominence the claims, and needs, and rights of the average man, the typical citizen, the normal human being. I do not need to expatiate on the triumphant progress round the world of what we may call the ideas of 1789 ; on the rout and extermination of the notion that society ought or can even properly be governed for the advantage of a privileged class ; or on the universal acceptance of the Democratic assumption that it is by its results upon the life of the whole body of citizens that every government must stand or fall. One effect of this triumph of Democracy has been to influence us all in favor of large and sweeping applications of governmental administration. That which is used or enjoyed or participated in by every citizen alike has necessarily come to seem much more "Democratic" than that which can only be used or enjoyed or participated in by a few people. Seeing that all have to pay for governmental action, we get into the habit of thinking it exceptionally appropriate—even, we may say, specially fair—to employ the forces of government in such ways only, and for

---

[1] These pages contain the substance of an Address given to the Social and Political Education League in London, May 14th, 1908, and of an article in the *Contemporary Review* for June, 1908.

such ends only, as concern us all. So much is this the case that there are actually people to-day, thinking themselves educated, who make this a test of legislation. If a measure does not extend to the whole population they denounce it as "class legislation," the implication being that "class legislation" is bad, or wicked, or, at any rate, undemocratic. It is characteristic of the infantile condition of American political thought that in some of the United States "class legislation" is actually forbidden by the State Constitution. The result of this conception has been that the work of government, so far as it has been based on Democratic ideas, has so far reminded us rather of the crude and clumsy proceedings of an army of occupation than of any fine adjustment of services to needs. It has, even in the most advanced countries, progressed little further—to use a pregnant phrase of Mr. H. G. Wells—than dealing with things in a wholesale sort of way. But the wholesale method of supplying human needs is very far from ensuring accurate adjustment. We are apt 'to forget that the average citizen or the normal human being is a mere abstraction, who does not exist. You and I have never seen him in the flesh. So varied is our individuality that whatever is handed out to all alike must necessarily fail to meet our requirements with any exactness. This is not a valid objection to nineteenth century achievements. A regiment of naked men needs clothing too urgently to allow us to grumble that the standard sizes of the regimental contractor make all the uniforms, if closely scrutinized, nothing better than misfits. The Early Victorian community, bare of schools, or drains, or Factory Acts, had to get itself supplied with the common article of standard pattern, so to speak, by wholesale, in order to be able to survive at all. But this necessity ought not to blind us to the fact that, when we come to scrutinize them closely, all these governmental products, supplied on the conception of Democracy as necessarily a wholesale provider, are, one and all, like the army contractors' uniforms, nothing better than misfits.

My first proposition is, therefore, the paradoxical one that, whilst it may have been the most pressing business of nineteenth century governments to deal with the whole people, or, at any rate, with majorities, by far the most important business of twentieth century governments must be to provide not only for minorities, but even for quite small minorities, and actually for individuals. We are no longer content with the army contractors' standard sizes. The regimental boots and uniforms must be made to fit each individual soldier. This, when you come to think of it, is just as "Democratic" in any sense whatsoever, as the merely wholesale method. "Class legislation," in short, is not only not bad, or wicked, or undemocratic, but actually the only good, the only useful, and the only really effective legislation. Of course, it is not necessary to confine legislative advantages to one minority any more than to one individual. Every minority—every citizen, in fact—has to be supplied, under the one system as under the other, just as every soldier in the regiment has to have his suit of clothing and his pair of marching boots. Only, on the one method, the fit is so bad that the soldier is galled, and his marching and fighting capacity falls far short of what can be attained. On the other method, an improved fit so much increases freedom of action that both comfort and efficiency are greatly increased.

An actual example of progressive government action may serve to make my meaning clearer. A century ago the provision of schools formed in England no part of governmental activity. The first need was to get supplied in sufficient quantity the most universal and least specialized type of school. The Democratic program was simply "schools for all." The ideal of advanced reformers was the universal provision of the "common school," the school common to all, in which, in every group of a few hundred families, all the boys or girls—some said all the boys *and* girls— should sit side by side, receiving whatever their intellects, whatever their idiosyncracies, whatever their opportunities, the same kind and degree of education. We may agree that these enthusiastic Democrats were right in desiring to get rid of purely artificial class distinctions in education. Moreover, a lonely village, like the cluster of homesteads in the early American backwoods, has necessarily got to put up with a single undifferentiated school. But we do not to-day, in any highly organized community, provide or expect to have provided, any monotonous array of such "common schools." We recognize now that children have infinitely varied needs and capacities in education. Where many thousands of children are together in the same locality, we have learnt how to avoid the more atrocious of the misfits that were involved in the "common school." And thus an Education Authority such as that of London already provides not one kind of school, but several dozen different kinds—not merely the ordinary boys' school and girls' schools and infants' schools, but also special schools for the quick and precocious, and special schools for the backward and feeble-minded ; blind schools and deaf schools and cripple schools ; day schools and boarding schools ; truant schools and industrial schools ; domestic economy schools and three or four kinds of trade schools ; and half-a-dozen different types of secondary schools. The "schools for all," for which Bentham and James Mill and Francis Place strove a century ago, have become differentiated into these dozens of different kinds of school for differently situated groups of children. What was originally a common universal provision has become a highly specialized meeting of the needs of a series of minorities—many of them quite small minorities. And the end is not yet. We don't yet know how to provide each individual child with exactly the kind and grade and amount of education that its individuality requires. This, however, and not "common schools," has already become, in education, the Democratic ideal.

Or consider, in another sphere of government, how far we have already travelled in a quite analogous differentiation and specialization of Poor Relief. Originally the dominant conception of the Poor Law was the relief of destitution, visualized as the handing out of bread or other necessaries of life, just to keep people from dying of starvation. Nowadays we ought not to think of dealing with our million of paupers in any such simple and uniform way. When you come to think of it, there is no average pauper any more than there is an average man. Hence the very notion of the simple undifferentiated "relief" of the destitute—the very conception of herding them all together in one common institution—is to-day quite comically obsolete, though we still find dear, good people, who really date back to before 1834, unable to imagine anything else, and still discussing little details about the horribly demoralizing mixed general workhouse poorhouse, as if it were not a scandal and a disgrace to us that this dreadful building, unknown in any other country, has not long ago been razed to the ground. What the modern enlightened administrator has learnt, though the average Poor Law Guardian cannot understand what it means, is that there is no category of the destitute ; that the people with whom he has to deal do not, in fact, form a single class at all, but a whole series of distinct classes, differing widely in their requirements. Thus, what we have to aim at providing to-day is not relief at all, but appropriate treatment for each class—foster parents or nurseries for such of the destitute persons as are infants, schools for such of them as are children, specialized infirmaries for such of them as are sick, highly equipped asylums for such of them as are of unsound mind, pensions or suitable homes for such of them as are permanently invalided or merely aged, farm colonies or training homes for the able-bodied for whom work cannot be found, and of dozens of more minutely specialized forms of treatment appropriate to such sub-classes as the blind, the deaf, the crippled, the candidates for migration or emigration, the feeble-minded, the sane epileptics, the chronic inebriates, and so on, most of which are actually now being undertaken, in rivalry with the Poor Law Authority, by the specialized Local Authorities established in connection with the Town or County Council. It is really ludicrous to think that, in this twentieth century, there are still people who think that all these different services, each requiring it own specialized technique, can be administered in each locality by a single body, the Board of Guardians in England and Ireland, and the Parish Council in Scotland, which can thus never possess either the knowledge or the competent staff to deal properly with any one of them. The survival down to the present day of such an anomaly as a special Poor Law Authority, with such an entirely obsolete institution as the mixed general workhouse, established to deal in an undifferentiated way with such an unreal abstraction as the "destitute," is a striking example of how imperfectly we have yet realized that government action of this "universal" character is entirely out of date.

From my fundamental paradox that governmental action, to be successful, must henceforth necessarily take the form, more and more, of provision for minorities, various inferences follow. We see at once how needful becomes, in every branch of administration and legislation, a high degree of specialized knowledge and expertness.

The provision for the average man, whether in the way of pro-
hibitions or in matters of supply, is a comparatively simple matter.
The draughtsmen of the American Declaration of Independence and
the author of the "Rights of Man," writing as they did for the
Political Man—quite as unreal a being as the Economic Man—
found no difficulty in deducing from first principles all the government that they contemplated. I sometimes think that those who
object to any other kind of legislation are often unconsciously
biassed by a haunting suspicion that they, at any rate, are un-
equipped for it. In our own time it does not require much knowledge to draw up, let us say, a Factory Law on the lines of universal
application still customary in the legislation of France. "Clause 1 :
The hours of labor shall not exceed eight per day. Clause 2 : The
Minister of the Interior is charged with the execution of this law."
This is scarcely an exaggeration of the type of legislation to which
the conception of governmental action as concerned with the whole
people inevitably leads. What we in England have learnt is that
not until factory legislation has been broken up and sub-divided into
highly specialized regulations, each affecting a particular trade or
a group of trades—in short, not until government becomes a matter
of dealing with minorities—becomes, in fact, nothing but "class
legislation "—does it become either effective in itself or other than a
clanking fetter and incumbrance upon our personal freedom. But
well-fitting clothes involve skilled tailoring. Accordingly legislation
and governmental administration necessarily become, in all highly
organized communities—however Democratic they may be—more
and more the business of persons elaborately trained and set apart
for the task, and less and less the immediate outcome of popular
feeling. Nothing was more inexact than the forecast that so
alarmed our fathers, that Democracy meant government by the
mob. The more strong and effective becomes the Democratic feeling, the more will legislatures and governments be driven to grapple
seriously with the real grievances and needs, not of the people in
the abstract, but of the people as they really are ; the more will it
become clear that the only way to do this is to provide what is
actually required by the series of small minorities of which the
people as a whole is composed ; and the more this continuous series
of class legislation, dealing successively with every class in the community, will necessarily involve, not the sweeping generalities and
political abstractions which mark to-day the political thinking both
of mobs and college common-rooms, nor even the comparatively
simple, broad general issues that can be submitted to direct popular
vote, or formulated by the merely amateur member of Parliament,
but the highly elaborated technicalities by which the really experienced departmental administrator seeks to carry out the orders of
the legislature. Already we come to recognize that it is neither the
street-corner orator nor the Fellow of All Souls who makes the
most successful member of a twentieth century Cabinet.

But this inference is not the one on which I want here to lay
most stress. Nor do I wish to do more than glance in passing at

another consequence of government more and more concerning itself with minorities. It is almost impossible to get out of the heads of fastidious people of the last generation a shrinking terror of Democracy as involving the sacrifice of all that is delicate, all that is refined, all that is distinguished, to the needs and passions of the "vulgar herd." But the "vulgar herd" is, as we have now seen, no indissoluble whole, necessarily swamping any small minority. It is, in itself, nothing but a congeries of small minorities—each of them by itself quite as weak and powerless politically as the "remnant" of refined and distinguished folk, which may therefore quite comfortably reassure its timid soul. The most Democratic government of the ensuing century—based, as it must necessarily be, on the very idea of providing for each of the series of minorities of which the world is made up—is as capable of providing for one minority as for another, for its poets as for its apprentices, for its scientists as for its soldiers, for its artists as for its artificers, and with the advance of actual knowledge in the administration is even more likely to know how they can be fostered and really well provided for than the irresponsible plutocratic patron ever did.

And here I come at last to the proposition which I am more particularly concerned to press upon you to-night. As it is coming more and more to be the business of government to deal with minorities, to provide what is required for minorities, to legislate for minorities, because minorities are what the people as a whole is composed of, so we are discovering in one department of life after another, that it is upon the specialized scientific treatment of minorities—often of quite small minorities—that social well-being depends. It is curious to remember that practically all past Utopias seem to contemplate a world made up entirely of healthy adults! But it is not enough to provide the government that we might imagine would be required for a community of average, normal healthy citizens—that way, in the actual world in which we live, made up as it is entirely of citizens who are not average or normal at all, lie degeneration, disease and death. Consider first the case of physical health. If the community provides no exceptional provision for the sick—no special care of the tuberculous, no isolation hospitals for zymotic diseases, none of the social elaborations of modern preventive medicine—we know that disease will arise, and will spread, not to the weakly alone but also to the strong; that not only will the yearly toll of death be heavier than it need be, but that sickness will drag down and incapacitate also the average man, and abstract unnecessary days from social service; and, worse than all, even if it do not affect adversely that mysterious germ plasm on which the race depends, that it will, at any rate, generation after generation, impair the vitality and lower the efficiency of the community as a whole. Hence, every civilized government finds it imperative to provide elaborately for the quite small minority of the sick—to deal with them, in fact, individually, one by one—to insist on extensive precautions against disease; to press, indeed, upon everyone, so far as we yet know how, the obligation to be well—

that is to say, to promulgate and enforce what may be called a National Minimum of Health, below which, in the interest of the community as a whole. no one is permitted to fall.

Carry the conception a stage further. The past century has seen a gradual and empirical adoption of the principle of the segregation of persons of unsound mind—of special provision by appropriate institutions for even harmless lunatics and idiots, for epileptics and chronic inebriates, now about to be extended to the merely feeble-minded—partly, no doubt, out of humanity to the unfortunate individuals themselves, but more and more because of a recognition of the fact that their indiscriminate presence in the competitive world has a tendency to deteriorate the sane, to drag down the standard of intelligence and self control, to lower the level of order as well as of intellect in the community as a whole. We now, in short, enforce a National Minimum of Sanity, below which no denizen of the world of free citizenship is allowed to fall.

And we have already gone much further. With the support—now unanimous, if somewhat belated—of the economists, we have recognized that the conditions of the wage contract can no more safely be left uncontrolled by law than any other department of civilized life, and we have the constantly growing series of Factory Acts, Mines Regulation Acts, Merchant Shipping Acts, Shop Hours Acts, Railways Regulation Acts, and now even a Trade Boards Act —all proceeding on the principle that it is absolutely necessary for social well-being that there should be an inflexible inferior limit below which the conditions of employment must not be permitted to fall.

And now at last the meaning of my title will, I hope, be clear. My thesis is that the Necessary Basis of Society, in the complications of modern industrial civilization, is the formulation and rigid enforcement in all spheres of social activity, of a National Minimum below which the individual, whether he likes it or not, cannot, in the interests of the well-being of the whole, ever be allowed to fall. It is this policy of a National Minimum which, in my judgment, is going to inspire and guide and explain the statesmanship and the politics of the twentieth century.

I have already described some of the ways in which this policy of a National Minimum has, usually without much comprehension of its bearing, influenced our social and industrial legislation. But it is clear that various other applications of the policy lie near at hand, to some of which we may, in conclusion, give our attention. In the Democratic politics of to-morrow we may expect to see the policy of the National Minimum translating itself into four main branches of legislative and executive activity. There will clearly have to be a legal minimum of wages, as there is already in Australasia, and as we have now, in the Trade Boards Act, already adopted in principle for the United Kingdom, with the general agreement of all parties. The employers will be under no legal obligation to employ any person whatsoever; but if they do employ him or her it will be a condition of every contract, not to be waived or ignored, that its terms shall not be such as will impair the efficiency of the citizen or diminish the vitality of the race. To engage labor at wages insufficient to repair the waste of tissue caused by the employment is demonstrably to injure the community as a whole, and will be prosecuted as such in the criminal courts. Those whose labor, in the judgment of the employers, is not worth the National Minimum —the aged, the permanently invalided, the crippled and the blind, the mentally or morally deficient, the epileptic and the chronically feckless and feeble-minded—will be maintained by the community, as, indeed, they are now. But as every economist knows, of all the ways of maintaining those unable to earn a full livelihood, by far the most costly and injurious is to allow them to compete in the labor market, and thus to drag down by their very infirmity those who are whole. There are still people, of course, who simply cannot imagine how a legal minimum wage could possibly be enforced, just as there were, sixty years ago, economists who demonstrated the impossibility of factory laws. I don't think we need waste time tonight over their ignorance—for it is simply ignorance.

There will be a National Minimum of Leisure and recreation time secured by law to every wage earner. It will certainly be an implied condition of every contract of employment, rigidly enforced by law, that it shall leave untouched fourteen or sixteen hours out of each twenty-four, for needful sleep, recreation, exercise of mind or body, and the duties of citizenship and family life. Any attempt by man or woman to sell for wages any part of the fourteen or sixteen sacred hours will be blamed as virtual embezzlement, since this part of the twenty-four hours' day must be regarded as necessarily reserved for the purpose of maintaining unimpaired the efficiency of the race. Any employer purchasing them, or allowing them to be spent in his mill or mine, will be prosecuted and punished, just as if he had incited to embezzlement or had received stolen goods. This, indeed, is already law in principle, again with the general assent of all parties, though very imperfectly applied and enforced, in our Mines Regulation Acts, our Railway Regulation Acts, our Shop Hours Acts, and our Factory Acts. And with this will go the campaign for the actual prevention of Unemployment, and for securing to everyone full provision, along with training, whenever we have failed to prevent involuntary idleness.

There will be a National Minimum of Sanitation, enforced not merely on land or house owners or occupiers, but also on local governing authorities. The nation will find it preposterous that any parish or city, merely out of stupidity, or incapacity, or parsimony, should foster disease, or bring up its quota of citizens in a condition of impaired vitality. The power of the community as a whole will, somehow or other, be brought to bear upon every backward district, compelling it to bear its part in the constant campaign for the actual prevention of disease, to lay on pure water, to improve its drainage, and to take such action, even by municipal building, if need be, that no family in the land shall have less than "three rooms and a scullery" as the minimum required for health and decency. Along with this must come the adequate provision of medical attendance, skilled nursing, and hospital accommodation for all the sick. White infants, in particular, are getting too scarce to be allowed to die at their present quite unnecessary rate. Within a generation of the adoption of such a policy the death-rate and sickness experience would show a reduction of one-third of what is at present endured as if it were the decree of Providence.

There will obviously be a National Minimum of Child Nurture —not merely of education in the sense of schooling, not merely in the provision of teaching, but in everything required for the healthy, happy rearing of the citizen that is to be. Besides schools and colleges of every grade, effectively open to all who can profit by them, there will have to be an adequate "scholarship ladder," securing maintenance as well as free tuition, right up to the post-graduate course, for every scholar proving himself or herself fitted for anything beyond ordinary schooling. And this provision will be enforced by the national power upon local school authorities, as well as upon parents and employers. What right has any part of the community to allow any part of its quota of citizens to be lost to the community by carelessness or neglect, or to be reared in ignorance, or to suffer even one potential genius to be snuffed out by hardship or privation? The next few years will see not only a great improvement in ordinary schooling, but also the doubling or trebling of our collective provision for child nurture from infancy to adolescence.

The lesson of economic and political science to the twentieth century is that only by such highly differentiated governmental action for all the several minorities that make up the community— only by the enforcement of some such policy of a National Minimum in Subsistence, Leisure, Sanitation, and Child Nurture—will modern industrial communities escape degeneration and decay. Where life is abandoned to unfettered competition, what is known to the economists as "Gresham's Law" of currency applies—the bad drives out the good : evolution means degeneration. To prevent this evil result is, as both Europe and America are discovering in the twentieth century, the main function of government.

Now, I dare say that some of you, knowing that I am a Socialist, will imagine that they see in this proposition nothing but a cunningly devized form of Socialism, put skilfully in a way not to shock the timid. On my honor I have no such guile. In my view, this policy of the National Minimum is a necessary condition of a healthy social order, whether you adopt the Individualist or the Collectivist principle in the organization of your State. You cannot have a successful and healthy Individualist State—whether of millionaires and wage slaves, or of peasant proprietors and small masters—without it. In fact, it is the necessary *basis* of Society, whether you intend the *superstructure* to remain Individualist or whether you wish it to become Collectivist. You will notice that to enforce the National Minimum will not interfere either with the pecuniary profits or with the power or the personal development of the exceptional man. The illimitable realm of the upward remains, without restriction, open to him. The policy of the National Minimum does not involve any attack upon, or any diminution of, either rent or interest—the whole differential advantage of superior sites, and soils, and machines, and opportunities remains absolutely unaffected. That, by the way, is why I, as a Socialist, describe it only as the basis of social organization ; it does not, like the " nationalization of the means of production, distribution, and exchange," deal with the superstructure.

Nor does this Policy of the National Minimum abolish competition, which, as we may confidently reassure timid Individualists, can no more be abolished than gravitation. But in the wild anarchy of unregulated modern industry, competition is apt to be as indiscriminately destructive as was the fall of the Tower of Siloam. It is, I need hardly remind you, quite a mistake to suppose that the bracing and invigorating action of competition, or any other social force, is proportionate to its intensity. We do not nowadays plunge our babies into cold water in order to harden them, or deliberately bring up our sons—whatever we may do with those of the poor— between a gin-shop and a brothel, in order to strengthen their characters. In the domain of human experience and social organization generally, as I have read of biology, " Weak stimuli kindle life activity, medium stimuli promote it ; but strong stimuli impede it, and the strongest bring it altogether to an end." [1] What the enforcement of a policy of the National Minimum does to competition, as we see by a whole century of experience of factory legislation, is to change its form and shift its incidence. By fencing off the downward way, we divert the forces of competition along the upward way. We transfer the competitive pressure away from a degradation of the means of subsistence of the mass of the people (where it does little but harm), to the intellect of everyone who has any, in the degree that he has it (where it quite usefully sharpens the wits). Only by constructing this Necessary Basis can the twentieth century community go forward—only in this way, in fact, can it, whether Individualist or Collectivist in its leanings, avert social degradation and decay. [2]

[1] Rudolf Arndt.

[2] For further explanation of the Policy of the National Minimum and answers to economic and other objections, see "Industrial Democracy," by S. and B. Webb (Longmans, 12s. 6d.), or "Socialism and National Minimum" (Fabian Socialist Series : Fifield, 6d. and 1s.).

FABIAN SOCIETY.—The Fabian Society consists of Socialists. A statement of its Rules and the following publications can be obtained from the Secretary, at the Fabian Office, 3 Clement's Inn, London, W.O.

FABIAN ESSAYS IN SOCIALISM. Paper 6d.; cloth 1'6; post. 2½d. and 4d.

WHAT TO READ on Social and Economic Subjects. Fifth edition, revised to October, 1910, and enlarged. Interleaved, paper, 1s. n. cloth 2s. n., post. 2d.

THIS MISERY OF BOOTS. By H. G. WELLS. 3d., post free 4d.

FABIAN TRACTS and LEAFLETS.

Tracts, each 16 to 52 pp., price 1d., or 9d. per doz., unless otherwise stated.
Leaflets, 4 pp. each, price 1d. for six copies, 1s. per 100, or 8 6 per 1000.

The Set of 78, 3s.; post free 3 5. Bound in Buckram, 4,6 n.; post free 5s

I.—General Socialism in its various aspects.

TRACTS. –159. The Necessary Basis of Society. By SIDNEY WEBB. 151. The Point of Honour: a Correspondence on Aristocracy and Socialism By RUTH CAVENDISH BENTINCK. 147. Capital and Compensation. By EDW. R. PEASE. 146. Socialism and Superior Brains. By BERNARD SHAW. 142. Rent and Value. 138. Municipal Trading. 121. Public Service versus Private Expenditure. By Sir OLIVER LODGE. 113. Communism. By · WM. MORRIS. 107. Socialism for Millionaires. By BERNARD SHAW. 139. Socialism and the Churches. By Rev JOHN CLIFFORD, D.D 133. Socialism and Christianity. By Rev. PERCY DEARMER. 78. Socialism and the Teaching of Christ. By Dr. J. CLIFFORD. 4 . Christian Socialism. By Rev. S. D. HEADLAM. 79. A Word of Remembrance and Caution to the Rich. By JOHN WOOLMAN. 75. Labor in the Longest Reign By S. WEBB 72. The Moral Aspects of Socialism. By SIDNEY BALL 69. Difficulties of Individualism. By SIDNEY WEBB. 51. Socialism: True and False. By S. WEBB. 45. The Impossibilities of Anarchism. By BERNARD SHAW (price 2d.). 7. Capital and Land (7th edn revised 1908). 5. Facts for Socialists (11th ed., revised 1908). 132. A Guide to Books for Socialists. LEAFLETS—13. What Socialism Is :. Why are the Many Poor? WELSH TRACTS—143. Sosialaeth yng Ngoleuni'r Beibl. Gan J. R JONES (Caernarfon). 141. Translation of 139. 87. Translation of 78. 38. Translation of 1.

II.—Applications of Socialism to Particular Problems.

TRACTS. – 157. The Working Life of Women. By Miss B. L. HUTCHINS. 155. The Case against the Referendum. By CLIFFORD D. SHARP. 154. The Case for School Clinics. By L. HADEN GUEST. 153. The Twentieth Century Reform Bill. By H. H. SCHLOESSER. 152. Our Taxes as they are and as they ought to be. By ROBT JONES, B.Sc. In cover, 2d. 150. State Purchase of Railways. By EMIL DAVIES. In cover, 2d. 149. The Endowment of Motherhood. By H. D. HARBEN. In cover, 2d. 145. The Case for School Nurseries. By Mrs. TOWNSHEND. 144. Machinery: its Masters and its Servants. By H. H. SCHLOESSER and C. GAME. 140. Child Labor under Capitalism. By Mrs. HYLTON DALE. 136. The Village and the Landlord. By EDW. CARPENTER. 131. The Decline in the Birth-Rate. By S. WEBB. 130. Home Work and Sweating. By Miss B. L. HUTCHINS. 128. The Case for a Legal Minimum Wage. 122. Municipal Milk and Public Health. . By Dr. F. LAWSON DODD. 125. Municipalization by Provinces. 119. Public Control of Electrical Power and Transit. 123. The Revival of Agriculture. 118. The Secret of Rural Depopulation. 115. State Aid to Agriculture: an Example. 112. Life in the Laundry. 98 State Railways for Ireland. 124. State Control of Trusts. 86. Municipal Drink Traffic. 84. Economics of Direct Employment. 83. State Arbitration and the Living Wage. LEAFLET.—104. How Trade Unions benefit Workmen.

III.—Local Government Powers: How to use them.

TRACTS.— 156. What an Education Committee can do (Elementary Schools', 3d. 137. Parish Councils and Village Life. 109. Cottage Plans and Common Sense. 76. Houses for the People. 99. Local Government in Ireland. 82 Workmen's Compensation Act New edition for the Act of 1906. 62. Parish and District Councils. 54 The Humanizing of the Poor Law. LEAFLETS.— 134. Small Holdings: and how to get them. 68. The Tenant's Sanitary Catechism. 71. Ditto for London.

IV. General Politics and Fabian Policy.

TRACTS.—158. The Case against the C.O.S. By Mrs. TOWNSHEND. 127. Socialism and Labor Policy. 116. Fabianism and the Fiscal Question: an alternative policy. 108. Twentieth Century Politics. By

Fabian Tract No. 160.

A NATIONAL MEDICAL SERVICE.

BY

F. LAWSON DODD,

M.R.C.S., L.R.C.P. (Lond.), L.D.S., D.P.H. (Eng.)

PUBLISHED AND SOLD BY

THE FABIAN SOCIETY.

PRICE TWOPENCE.

LONDON:

THE FABIAN SOCIETY, 3 CLEMENT'S INN, STRAND, W.C.

NOVEMBER 1911.

A NATIONAL MEDICAL SERVICE.

THE final aim of Socialism includes the socialization of the national wealth. But before coming to close quarters with this great problem we have to recognize that a large amount of spade work, of a nature less dazzling, perhaps, than direct Socialist propaganda, but not less necessary, must take the shape of organizing for social purposes those services called the professions, which contain a large proportion of the intellectual and trained members of the community, by whose efforts, even though hitherto only to a small degree secured for public ends, the cause of social reform has been so consistently helped forward. It is certain that long before the democracy is ready to undertake its widest responsibilities the educational profession will have to be organized in its service, and the nationalization of the medical service should be considered a prior step to that of the great routine industries. Working for Socialism along these lines we have the advantage of securing the sympathy and active help of a larger section of the population than any mere industrial propaganda would bring to our aid. The provision of good secondary schools by the County Council, for instance, has begun already to bring home to the poorer middle classes the economy and efficiency of State action. The application of the principles of Socialism to the profession of medicine would be another powerful demonstration of the sanity of our ideals to working and middle classes alike, and would put into the hands of the Socialists the most powerful weapon they could possess. There exists in relation to this branch of Socialist effort an abundance of those forces which make for a radical transformation of structure and function. There is widespread discontent with the present system, both inside and outside the profession ; there is a crying need for economic co-ordination, for collective and individual efficiency ; and reforming zeal is likely to be none the less active, because no one will seriously lose by the change, while both the profession and the public welfare will stand to gain.

It may be necessary at the outset to remind the layman that the present system—or want of system—in the medical service is but a temporary phase in its history. There have been three stages in medical progress. First, the *mysterious*, when the practitioner was found in the garb of the medicine man, the druid, and the witch, leading up to the ecclesiastical, which led to a medico-theological sway in Europe throughout the Middle Ages, when the recognized medical work was performed by the monks. The second stage may be described as the *commercial* or *guild* system, which developed

with the downfall of the monasteries, when the function of the healing art was assumed by the smiths and barbers, as servants of the
monks ; and later the establishment of apothecaries, surgeons, and
physicians, who were organized into guilds, and who sold their services to those who could pay for them. The growth of science,
combined with the natural repugnance towards selling professional
service to the person in need, and the beginnings of a State medical
service, have ushered in the third stage, which may be called the
professional. At all times there has been a mingling of these main
features, but the growing feeling that medical service cannot be
appraised in terms of cash : the disability on suing for fees voluntarily accepted by Fellows of the Royal College of Physicians : the
suppression of ordinary advertisement : the tacit recognition of only
one medical status in the eyes of the law : the gradual rise of a
medical civil service : the professional ban placed on the patenting
of remedies discovered by the individual : are all signs that the
third stage is well upon us. In fact, one of the most distinguished
physicians of to-day * recently declared : "The healing of the sick
was never a business. It was in early times attached to religious
rites, and more or less sanctified as a divine calling. Hippocrates,
St. Luke, Christ himself were examples. The monasteries in the
Middle Ages were the great centres of medical treatment : to each,
or to most of them, were attached infirmaries. The great hospitals
—St. Bartholomew's, St. Thomas's, Bethlehem—were priories in the
twelfth and thirteenth centuries, and were only secularized at the
time of the Reformation. The practical result was that any money
equivalent for medical services had from all time been more or less
of the nature of an offering, an offering to the gods at one time, an
offering to the servants of the gods at another, and still offerings,
honoraria, voluntary offerings rather than exacted payments."

The best description of the blending of the commercial with the
professional man is given us by Thackeray : "Early in the Regency
of George the Magnificent there lived in a small town in the heart
of England, called Clavering, a gentleman whose name was Pendennis. There were those alive who remembered having seen his
name upon a board, which was surmounted by a gilt pestle and
mortar, over the door of a very humble little shop in the city of
Bath, whence Mr. Pendennis exercised the profession of apothecary
and surgeon, and where he not only attended sick gentlemen in
their sick rooms and ladies at the most interesting periods of their
lives, but would condescend to sell a brown paper plaster to a
farmer's wife across the counter or to vend tooth brushes, hair
powder, and ladies' perfumery."

At the time here described, and for many years after, there was
connected with medicine competition enough to please the most
enthusiastic member of the Manchester School. Many corporate
bodies had been granted special rights with regard to the conferring
of licences to practise medicine—societies of apothecaries, colleges of

* Sir R. Douglas Powell, at Meeting of Marylebone Division B.M.A., November
30th, 1906. Vide *British Medical Journal*, December 15th, 1906, p. 337.

surgeons and physicians, and several universities in different parts óf
the kingdom possessed these powers, and the competition for the
licentiates' fees resulted in an alarming reduction of the standard of
qualification. There was no reciprocity between the licensing authorities, and at the same time no effective authority to put down illegality.
Hence there were many spurious diplomas and licences, and numerous
quacks both inside and outside the profession, while, at the same
time, an ignorant public possessed no means of distinguishing the
good from the bad ; qualified men were frequently only persons who
had " walked the hospitals " for a few months, and had finally
bought a diploma from a body that knew well that if not granted it
would be easily purchased elsewhere. But competition reigned also
among the qualified, and the effect of this on not very scientific
doctors is described by George Eliot in the persons of the practitioners of Milby : " Mr. Pilgrim looked with great tolerance on all
shades of religious opinion that did not include a belief in cures by
miracle." " Pratt elegantly referred all diseases to *debility*, and, with
a proper contempt for symptomatic treatment, went to the root of
the matter with port wine and bark. Pilgrim was persuaded that the
evil principle in the human system was *plethora*, and he made war
against it with cupping, blistering and cathartics."

This state of chaos continued well into the middle of the nine-
teenth century, but was being undermined mainly by two influences :
First, the immense advance of science in relation to medical practice,
and second, the movement, led on the one hand by Wakley of the
Lancet, and on the other by Sir J. Simon, Medical Officer to the
Privy Council, which aimed at the establishment of medicine on a
State basis. The two forces making for reform may be described as
(1) State interference or control, and (2) State organization.

State Interference.

The first great step towards the co-ordination of the medical
profession and its control by the State was taken in 1858 by the
passing of the Medical Act of that year, followed in 1876 by the Act
admitting women to qualification for the register. This measure of
1858 was carried primarily in the interests of the public, although
the profession has reaped its reward also. Its main purpose was to
enable persons to distinguish between qualified and unqualified
practitioners. Mr. S. H. Walpole, the Home Secretary of the time,
and the chief supporter of the Bill, stated expressly that it was not
intended to prevent the public from consulting whomsoever it wished
—whether qualified or unqualified—and that any advantage that
might accrue to the profession was quite secondary to the main
object of the Bill, viz., the protection of the public from fraud.
Under its provisions was created, as an offshoot of the Privy Council,
that body which is becoming daily of greater importance in all
matters affecting the relations between the medical profession and
the public—the *General Medical Council*. This is a statutory body
including representatives of the profession, but principally charged
with its regulation and control for purposes of public protection.

At the present time it is composed of thirty-four members, five representing the Privy Council, five the profession, and twenty-four the educational bodies. It is not even incumbent upon (although generally the practice of) the educational bodies and the Privy Council to select medical men as representatives. The functions of the General Medical Council are as follows : (1) The keeping of a register to enable qualified men to be distinguished from unqualified ; (2) the controlling of medical education and the raising of its standard by preventing down-grade competition between the educational bodies (with this end in view it carries out a systematic and careful inspection of all medical examinations) ; (3) to act as a professional court of justice and remove from the register the names of those convicted of crime or of "infamous conduct in a professional respect," such as "covering," "canvassing," the employment of unqualified assistants, etc. ; and (4) the drawing up of a pharmacopœia.

The General Medical Council is the authority which brings the community into touch with the profession, and gives it an enlightened means of control. Its creation is an admission of professional rights, it is true ; but much more does it lay down the principle that the medical service exists for the public interest, and should be administered, controlled, and governed with that idea. It is a recognition of medicine as a trade union, and also of the need for adequate control by the community of such a powerful organization. By the creation of the General Medical Council we have laid the foundation for that State organization of the medical service which it will be the work of the future to carry out.

Great as was the advance made by the Act of 1858, strengthened later by the Dentists' Act of 1878, and the Amending Act of 1886, yet all authorities are agreed that the work of co-ordination and organization has only just commenced. There are too many varying examinations which alike qualify for the register, though their value differs widely. There is great overlapping of educational institutions in single areas such as London. There is scandalous underpayment of professional teachers in connection with medical education. Finally, the relation between the charity-supported hospitals and the medical schools is not clearly defined, and is far from satisfactory. It is not surprising, then, that amendments of the Acts of 1858 to 1886 are contemplated by Bills now before Parliament, promoted by the British Medical and British Dental Associations, the former of which aims at (1) the reduction of the personnel of the General Medical Council and an addition to its representative character ; (2) the institution of one State examination for entrance to the profession, and (3) the legal prohibition of practice by any but qualified men ; while the Dentists' Bill aims at prohibition of unqualified practice. It will thus be seen that from the profession itself there is a widely voiced demand for further State interference, and for a more uniform system ; and it is for the public to see that the general interests of society are at the same time carefully safeguarded. In view of the measures relating to medical matters that are likely to come up for solution during the next few years, it is well to realize that the probity and efficiency of the medical service is of the utmost importance to all classes. Socialism has had most effective support from scientific members of a profession whose whole tendency is towards reform, whose daily study makes for an equalized conception of human nature, and who are taking an increasing interest in Socialist propaganda. The influence of quackery, with its secret remedies, its advertisement, its ignorant audacity, and its intense commercialism, is essentially anti-social; and the widespread use of patent medicines must be regarded as a form of exploitation of the ignorant and weak, as hateful and injurious as that represented by the individual appropriation of rent and interest. The denunciation of the qualified man is no part of Socialist propaganda. He does not necessarily represent the reforming element in society, nor does he enter his profession for propagandist reasons, but, as a rule, he compares very favorably with his fellow citizens in the matter of humanity, enlightenment and sympathy.

State Organization.

We have glanced at the chief step which the community has taken towards controlling the profession from without; it remains for us to consider to what degree its organization directly as a State service has already been carried out. In order to make this clearer, let us review the present constitution of the whole profession. There are at present (1911) 40,642 registered practitioners, who may be classified as follows:

London	6,415
Provincial England	17,721
Wales	1,336
Scotland	3,958
Ireland	2,724
Resident Abroad	5,188
The Services	3,300

Few people realize to what a large extent the medical service is already socialized. The Army and Navy and Indian Services account for 3,300 practitioners, excluding a numerous and ever growing Colonial Service. In addition there are the full time public health officers, to the number of about 400 in England and Scotland; the medical staff of the Local Government Board and the Board of Education; the prison surgeons; medical inspectors under the Factory Acts; medical visitors in lunacy; poor law medical officers; the medical staff of the Metropolitan Asylums Board; medical officers of lunatic asylums; and school doctors.

These services represent the growing needs of an organized community; most of them are of recent origin, and all are increasing in numbers from year to year. But they do not represent the whole scope of publicly controlled medical work. A large amount of official duty is also done by practitioners who, to the number of 1,423 in Great Britain, add to their own practice the duties of medical officer of health, the 4,000 poor law doctors, the Post Office medical officers, certifying factory surgeons, medical advisers under the Workmen's Compensation Act. It will not be denied that the combination of public functions with private practice is viewed with a growing distrust, which will end in forcing more and more of the official work into the hands of the whole time man, a change that would be easily accomplished by means of co-operation between different local government areas, and one which would greatly improve the administration, as it should raise the standard of the officials affected. In any case, a large and growing proportion of medical practitioners is already removed from the sphere of competitive practice. This proportion is working as a civil service under such conditions as any Socialist would approve of, nor can it be doubted that the public services compare favorably with any branch of the profession. Their popularity is proved by the great competition there is for such posts as happen to become vacant or are created for fresh necessities. Removed from the petty worries of fee collecting (a kind of tax gathering which is in no way connected with medicine, and which to the average medical man is wholly distasteful), there is ample opportunity for scientific work over and above the routine duties; and that such opportunity is taken advantage of, the records of the Local Government Board and the annual reports of the medical officers of health will clearly prove.

State Insurance.

There is taking place at the present moment a movement for the partial nationalization of the medical profession which, according to many, is likely to surpass all the steps that have hitherto been taken in that direction, viz., the Scheme of Compulsory National Insurance against Sickness and Invalidity. If this bill become law, nearly half the medical work of the nation will henceforth be paid for in part out of public funds administered for that purpose through the agency of the trade unions, the friendly societies, and the Post Office. This will, no doubt, commence in the form of a vast system of well paid club medical work, but as its scope extends to a wider circle of persons and the State continues to buy control through its increasing contributions, it is likely that an ever increasing number of private practitioners, becoming freed from competitive practice, will find the advantages of regular salaries with emancipation from the many calls to gratuitous work, amply compensate them for the gamble for success which medical practice has too often been in the past. The organization of a majority of medical men in the different localities again, will bring the possibility of arranging for hours of duty, will obviate the scandal of the twenty-four day for the doctor and make for complete organization, with ultimate nationalization.

The Private Practitioner.

The bulk of medical men, however, are still private practitioners, either consultants or in general practice, and it remains to analyze the conditions under which their work is carried on, so that we may find out to what degree Socialist opinions and social development will modify them. The medical student spends his five or six years at the hospital or medical school, passes his final examination, registers his name, and, if he chooses to be a consultant—for which money as well as brains will be necessary—he gets a series of hospital appointments and bides his time. If he select general practice he buys or starts such a practice in a chosen locality and waits for work. He has been for years devoting himself to scientific study, too much influenced by the approaching examination, it is true, yet largely disinterested. He now finds himself in a new world : he has to compete for patients with others in the same calling. His work and ways are now appraised by persons who are in no way qualified to discern the *best* man. The public judge of the qualities *they* can appreciate, and, needless to say, the prize of practice too often goes to the man whose manner, establishment, social intercourse, religion, amusements, motor-car, etc., most favorably impress his would-be patients. Up to the time of starting, all his work was subject to professional valuation. Now he is thrown on the mercy of public opinion—often the opinion of the very persons whose diseases he is called upon to treat, and from whom he may, or may not, get that mysterious reputation implied in the epithet " clever."

Whatever competition may do for trade, it has nothing but a thoroughly bad influence on professional work. It often brings rewards to the least worthy ; it tends to drive down fees below a level compatible with efficiency, as is shown by the sixpenny and shilling dispensary practices. It tends to crush out that fraternal feeling that should always exist in such a service as medicine ; it undermines that co-operation which is of great importance in practice, both to patient and doctor ; and it places an educated man at the mercy of each individual member of an unenlightened public, on whose ailments he is made dependent for his living. There is a further blot on the present chaotic condition of the medical profession, namely, the fact that when the student starts in practice—unless he is one of the favored minority who happens to get a hospital appointment—he surely, if slowly, loses touch with the more methodical and scientific side of his profession, and stands in danger of drifting into a routine manner of looking at things, from which even the occasional opportunity of post-graduate lectures and the excellent medical periodicals cannot save him, if his practice is a small one ; while if his clientèle grows to fairly large proportions, sheer fatigue, emphasized by the continuous nature of his work and the pressure on his time, acts equally effectively.

In the matter of over-work, all branches of the medical and allied professions are worse off than any other calling, and the results are shown in the high mortality among doctors, ranging above all others, except the three somewhat closely related occupations of wine merchants, innkeepers, and cabdrivers.* There is no more useless waste of valuable human life and energy than that which

* Mulhall's "Dictionary of Statistics," 4th edition, p. 181, and "Vital Statistics," by Wm. Farr, 1885 edition, p. 401.

competitive commercialism has attached in the form of day and night work to the practice of medicine, and there is just as good a case for legal interference in this matter as in any of those instances in which Acts of Parliament have regulated the hours of labour. The medical men do not like the arrangement ; it is injurious to the public interest in that it may lead to individual disaster just as surely as the over-employment of a signalman or engine-driver may lead to a collision, and yet nothing is done because we regard commercialism as inevitable.

Other Hardships of the Competitive System.

Slowly the evils of competition are revealing themselves to the profession, but there are certain other hardships which are more obvious. The first of these to be noted is the constant tendency on the part of the public to impose on the physician or surgeon in the matter of gratuitous work. A well-known surgeon* has said : " The well-to-do philanthropist is so moved by the sight of suffering that he is impelled to ask the doctor to cure it gratis." Practically all hospital appointments (except those under the control of the State) are unpaid, and although the *éclat* of a position on the staff of a large city hospital is in some ways its own reward, yet there are endless posts held in connection with small provincial hospitals, orphanages, epileptic colonies, etc., etc., which bring to the holder of them neither the reward of education nor any professional distinction, and which are filled without fee by the long-suffering profession. Then, again, there are countless reports and certificates (some of which, such as the death certificates, are matters of compulsion), which the doctor is asked to sign, and for which he is unpaid ; and there are those who, regarding his calling as a noble one, consider that it would be demeaned by the settlement of their quarterly or half-yearly accounts, which for social reasons it is almost impossible for the creditor to recover in the legal manner. No body of men is more imposed upon in these ways, and if ever a doctor asks for his fee in advance, or refuses to get up at night to attend a case without the assurance that it will be forthcoming, he is regarded by the public almost in the light of a criminal.

Hospital Competition (" Abuse.")

There is another factor that tells heavily against the average medical man, especially in the poor and populous localities, that is hospital competition—or "abuse," as it is called. The immense increase in free hospital, or assisted dispensary treatment is making this more and more serious. Although some hospitals—notably the London—are trying to carry out a selective process with regard to their patients, the temptation for statistical and educational reasons is all in the direction of encouraging them to come. It is hard for a democratically minded doctor to refuse hospital treatment to an interesting case whose income is £5 a week, and take under his care

* J. F. Fuller, M.A., M.B , F.R.C.S.   Paper read at Southampton, 1893.

an alcoholic dyspeptic whose average wage is £1. The impossibility of any effective selection of patients according to appearance and wages, is apparent to anyone who thinks. If you put up a barrier of appearance, you exclude the tidy and penurious clerk, and include the skilled artizan, whose comfortable circumstances make him careless as to his appearance. If, on the other hand, you erect a maximum wage barrier, then you admit a bachelor with twenty-five shillings a week, and exclude a married man with a family of five who earns thirty shillings. The most superficial observer knows, in fact, that there are thousands of the small shopkeeper or poor professional class who need free hospital treatment just as much as those imaginary persons for whom hospitals are intended, and yet who would be excluded as unfit. That this competition is really serious is shown by the growth in the number of patients annually treated in the London hospitals. These were, according to Sir H. Burdett :

1895	...	...	...	...	1,753,611	patients.
1902	...	...	...	...	2,098,905	,,

The same authority concludes that, in spite of the fact that each visit to the hospital, with the journey and the waiting, took five to six hours, counting the whole population of London, one out of every two persons gets free medical advice, while thirty years ago the figure was one in every four. The same condition, only less acute, holds good in the provinces, as the following table shows.*

In Portsmouth	1 out of	14·0	people received free medical relief.†	
Cardiff	1	7·1	..	..
Glasgow	1	5·3		
Manchester	1	3·5		
Liverpool	1	3·4		
Birmingham	1	3·2		
Brighton	1	3·1		
Bristol		2·9		
Edinburgh	1	2·8	,,	
London	1	2·2		
Newcastle	1	1·9	,	,,
Dublin	1	1·3	,,	,,

This question is being further complicated by the fact that working men are becoming collective subscribers to hospitals in urban areas, and it is not unreasonable to suppose that they will fall into the same error as members of the middle class in considering that a donation entitles them to free treatment. Whatever may be said with regard to out-patients, there is no doubt whatever that the in-patients belong to a large extent to a class above the necessitous

* Speech of Sir H. Burdett, *British Medical Journal Supplement*, December 15th, 1906.

† This means that the proportion of cases to the population is as stated ; but one person may be counted as several cases or may attend several hospitals in the course of a year.

poor ; and one is not surprised that sick members of the middle and lower middle classes should use all their ingenuity to get admitted to a hospital when they cannot afford the best treatment at home. Nor is this surprising when it is remembered that modern medical treatment implies the use of expensive apparatus, such as those used for the X Rays, for bacteriological diagnosis, etc., as well as all the necessities of modern aseptic surgery. With the growth of hospitals there is an increasing opportunity of education for those on the staff, making them a more dangerous competitive class in the eyes of the majority of their colleagues, while at the same time that efficiency is gained in the treatment of patients who would normally fall to the share of the poorer practitioners.

Hospital competition as a source of discontent is supplemented by that of the optician, who poaches in the preserves of the ophthalmic surgeon ; the chemist, who prescribes as well as dispenses remedies, and even does minor surgery ; the herbalist and all kinds of quack healers as well as patent medicine vendors, who make the lives of the less fortunate members of the profession a story of respectable penury. Circulated a few weeks ago among the members of the Marylebone Branch of the British Medical Association was a pamphlet written by one of the victims of this competition. He says, addressing his more fortunate West End brethren : " We do not 'hunger and thirst' after your righteousness ; our needs are food, clothing, house rent, and wherewithal to pay our taxes, or for our house, or carriage, or motor, or even a new bicycle. This is our 'economic' question, to be worked out on the basis of 'advice and medicine for sixpence,' 'a visit for one shilling,' 'a labour for ten shillings.' We cannot afford Westminster or Charterhouse for our sons, but even we struggling doctors must educate our daughters. In short, it is the old schoolboy heading : 'Edendum est vivere.' This is our economic need. Change places with us for one week. Come away from your carriages and motor cars, your butlers and retinues of servants, your houses furnished like palaces. Forget your shooting lodges and fishing lettings and come to 'poverty, hunger, and dirt,' where 'women's lives are wearing out' and the men are weaving their shrouds. Come to the factories and the coal mines. Live sandwiched in between a butcher and a pawnbroker, and feel that they both are more independent than you are."

The only inaccuracy of this picture is the exaggerated idea of financial success which, according to the writer, Marylebone offers to its professional population. If we are to believe writers such as the late Sir James Paget and others, we are forced to the conclusion, in the words of a well known surgeon,* that " in London the position of the young consultant is tragic in the extreme."

" The Battle of the Clubs."

There is one other evil resulting from the present circumstances of the medical man that must be noted, because it has caused a very great outcry in the profession,—namely, the sweating of doctors by

* Dr. J. F. Fuller.

the working classes organized as friendly societies and burial clubs. Such organizations represent the attempts of the people to obtain collective medical service at a small weekly rate per member. This has represented a new form of collective bargaining. On the one hand a single medical man, and on the other an organized, ready-made clientèle. Under these circumstances, the individual professional man has been powerless to escape overwork and gross underpayment. Tempted by a fixed nucleus of salary, or the threat of seeing a stranger called in to do his work, the unfortunate individual has been driven to accept the most unfavorable terms, and has been at the same time subject to that kind of treatment which the aggrieved always receive at the hands of the aggressor.

Two shillings to five shillings per member per annum is a common sum for the doctor to receive, the average fee for each attendance working out at 10·6od.* ; in the case of one club a fee of 1od. per member per year was received by the club doctor. Attempts have been made by the doctors to combine against this kind of thing, but, for obvious reasons, with only partial success. When local men *have* combined successfully a man from a neighboring town has been imported, and in some instances, where this has failed, a substitute has been tempted away from the remoter parts of Ireland. This sweating of medical men and the way they are treated by clubs (trade union and otherwise) is similar, except that it is worse, to blacklegging in industrial trades, and shows that the working classes have still a good deal to learn in the matter of meting out fair conditions to their employees.

False Remedies.

Of course, remedies for the above-mentioned grievances are being constantly suggested by those who see the evil, or feel the pinch, but most of them are based upon the idea that the present order is from everlasting to everlasting, and often the treatment suggested is of the most futile and symptomatic kind. The suggestion, for instance, of cutting down hospital attendance, as well as those other remedies mentioned already in connection with "hospital abuse," display a great ignorance of human nature, as well as a total incapacity to realize the grievances bound up with the general problem in the matter of medical attendance. It need only be said that for thirty years the cry of "hospital abuse" has been heard, and has been accompanied by a steady rise in the number seeking relief from hospitals. Co-operation between the general practitioner and the hospital has been suggested, with equal lack of insight into the problem. Combination among the profession is, from its very economic conditions, only partially possible, and, indeed, under present circumstances, anything like a thorough combination would be a public danger. Other palliatives might be named, but it is well before looking for a remedy, to bear in mind that any solution

* "An Investigation into Economic Conditions of Medical Practice in the United Kingdom," Brit. Med. Assoc., 1905.

of the problem, to be satisfactory, must take into consideration the case of the public as well as the profession, and briefly to consider the hardships which result to the lay community from the present individualism in medicine.

Public Grievances.

It will be seen at once that the most serious hardships resulting from the present system of medical service fall upon the middle classes. The small tradesman, for instance, when he happens to visit the local hospital, sees a finely equipped machinery for the cure of disease, staffed by the most able and scientific members of the profession, offered freely for the treatment of the poor, to which category he knows secretly that he belongs, but dares not acknowledge it for prudential reasons. He sees hospitals endowed and adapted for every purpose of treatment, with polished teak floors, glazed tile walls, ample cubic space and ventilation, perfect operating theatres, well kept instruments, with a highly skilled and specialized staff of physicians, surgeons, ophthalmic surgeons, gynæcologists, dental surgeons, nurses, dispensers, and attendants, all ready and willing to receive the first member of the submerged fifth who happens to contract disease or meet with accident. He knows, too, that paupers in the large cities, and—to a greater degree than was the case formerly—throughout the provinces, are getting a care which is almost as good. While *he* has to call in his medical man, and to be treated (if seriously ill) in a room above his shop, which is in no way suitable for prolonged treatment, and where wall-paper, carpet, curtains, want of proper ventilation, all make for a prolongation of his misery. If an operation be required he must have the man on the spot to perform it, or pay a large fee to get a specialist from a neighboring city who knows that everything is against the patient whose only operating theatre is his own bedroom, or whose operating table is the one on which dinner is usually served! If the patient happens to be the bread-winner, he finds the procuring of efficient medical treatment, which implies each year, in place of physic, a growing need for skilled nursing and costly therapeutic appliances, a very costly affair, and that, too, at a time when he can least afford the money. If his illness becomes more serious, even though he cannot afford it, his family spend their last twenty pounds to call in one of the consultants who attended his general servant when she was in the hospital of the neighboring town. He knows, too, that in the matter of the best medical treatment the very rich, who can afford the expensive nursing home and the many appliances necessary for restoring health to the diseased, share these advantages with the poor, and he is apt to ask himself why he should not have his share of the good things. But with all the disadvantages mentioned above, there is another from which the poor patient is often delivered—he alone does not *employ* his medical man, and hence his treatment is likely to be unbiassed by those little concessions to a client which this relationship of employer and employed so often calls forth. If the poor man is alcoholic, is suffering from the need for occupation, is inclined to excesses of any kind, he is told so more plainly by his hospital doctor than is the average patient in private practice. A further advantage of the hospital patient, whether "out" or "in," consists in the fact that he is treated at a sort of medical exchange, where there is co-operation between a staff numbering among them specialists of all kinds. I have seen two leading London surgeons consulting with two physicians of equal eminence over a poor old woman in a hospital ward. This kind of professional co-operation contrasts singularly with private practice on a competitive basis, which always tends to shut the profession into water-tight compartments, and puts beyond the reach of all but the hospital patient that free, unbiassed and many-sided consultation which in serious illness is of so much importance. Only a complete re-organization of the profession will put proper specialist treatment within the reach of the middle-class man, and make his chance of recovery as good as that of the pauper in the State-managed hospital.

There is one further disadvantage from the present system of practice which accrues to the middle-class public : namely, the fact that the power of life and death, the decision as to serious operation, or critical treatment, is too much confined to the judgment of the one—or at most two—medical men which the members of that class can afford to call in. It is high time that the public should appoint in its own interest Inspectors of Surgery, whose duty it would be to give an independent opinion, whenever possible, in cases of serious operations, both as to their advisability for the patient, and as to the competence of the surgeons to carry them out.

Transition.

It is clear that a co-ordinated State service of medicine, in its widest aspect, is the only solution that offers itself to the student of sociology as in any way satisfactory, whether from the standpoint of the doctor or the patient. The sociologist has come to realize that that ideal will not be attained by any short cut ; much public education will be required, both of Socialists and non-Socialists ; certain departments of professional work will have to grow and others atrophy before the change will be complete. The important thing is to realize the phenomena of transition so that we may effect the change along the line of least resistance.

In this connection it should be our aim to increase the efficiency of the public departments of medicine. We know that the 1,800 local sanitary authorities of England and Wales, together with the county councils, have among them about 1,500 medical officers of health, and that out of these only 350 (including those of London, the county councils, and county boroughs) are salaried "full-timers," whilst about 400 are private practitioners to whom the health authority pays a stipend of from £3 to £30 per annum. Further, in Scotland the 313 local authorities have among them about 120 medical officers of health, of whom 40 devote all their time to their duties, whilst about 80 are engaged in private practice and receive salaries varying from £2 2s. to £200. All reformers should work for the appointment of one whole-time medical officer of health at least for each county council. The larger cities and towns have appointed medical officers, and it is a public duty to see that their tenure of office is secure, and that they have ample qualified assistance. Large numbers of small boroughs and urban districts have at present only part-time officers, and these are paid salaries ridiculously inadequate. The policy here should be the appointment as opportunity offers of whole-time men, and the pooling of small urban and rural districts so as to make the work important enough and the salaries sufficient for a whole-time public health officer. Preventive medicine is bound to take a more important place in the future, as faith in cures is dwindling, and even the costly sanatoria for consumption are now regarded as doubtful palliatives which restore the consumptive to apparent health, only that he may die more quickly when he returns to his unhealthy occupation or ill-ventilated cottage. The individual demand for curative advice and medicine is likely to be largely replaced by a collective demand for information as to how to suppress or improve the callings and home conditions that kill and maim. Thus the centre of gravity of medicine will leave the curative and tend more towards the side of preventive medicine. It is around the public health service that all the other branches of medicine will tend to group themselves, and this department has been steadily undergoing a change of function since its establishment by the Act of 1875. For twenty-five years it mainly dealt with the environment of the individual—refuse disposal, drainage, disinfection of houses, ventilation, air space, food adulteration, and kindred matters; recently the change has been in the direction of personal hygiene. The idea that accumulations of refuse can be injurious is supplemented by the conviction that verminous persons may similarly be destructive of social welfare. The public health officer now enters a realm which may be called that of preventive treatment. He draws up placards on the dangers of alcohol, the social risks of the spitting habit; he issues cards of advice for poor mothers as well as pamphlets to consumptives; he is entrusted with the supervision of midwives, whose disinfection may be enforced by him under certain circumstances; he administers the "Cleansing of Persons Act," and may prescribe a bath for a verminous person; he is commencing the inspection of school children, and has to arrange not only for advice to teachers and parents, but prescribes ointment and other media of treatment; he organizes a staff of health visitors to superintend the newly born, and is not infrequently head of an infants' milk depôt. It will thus be seen that the medical officer of health is beginning to widen his boundaries, that prevention, in short, needs to be supplemented by a personal attention that is curative as well; in other words, the line of distinction between prevention and cure is tending to disappear.

The strengthening of the departments will be supplemented in another direction by the co-ordination of those State medical services which at present overlap and frequently are in conflict with one another. Take, for instance, the poor law medical service, which costs £5,000,000 a year and has a staff of 4,000 medical officers. With its restriction to persons proved to be destitute, its tardy application of treatment, with consequent waste of life and health to the nation, its failure to reach a large amount of illness even amongst the destitute themselves, its unconditioned grants of so-called medical relief, which inculcate no healthy habit in the recipients, it is clear that this service must be co-ordinated with public health administration. For it is the business of the latter service to seek out illness, to treat at the earliest possible moment, to remove injurious conditions; to apply specialized treatment, and, above all, to educate the public, with the end of preventing disease at its source. The mere "relief" of the individual must give way to a method of dealing with disease based upon wider social aims. The recommendations in favor of a unified medical service so ably put forward by the Minority of the Poor Law Commissioners, and supported by the responsible medical heads of the great departments concerned, viz., the Local Government Boards of England and Wales, Scotland, and Ireland, and the Board of Education, mark one great step forward in the direction of a State medical service based on public health principles. In such a unified medical service, organized in suitable districts, the existing medical officers of health, hospital superintendents, school doctors, district medical officers, workhouse and dispensary doctors, medical superintendents of poor law infirmaries, would find their appropriate places under the administrative control of a county medical officer chosen for his experience and knowledge in this direction.

There are many public appointments which, to the advantage of the community, might be filled by medical men. As governors of prisons, for instance, they would generally be more suitable than military men, and their training adapts them for such posts as inspectors of factories. When it is said that the profession is overcrowded—a statement which is only true of urban areas—it is forgotten that there is abundant medical work waiting to be done before the community has utilized the energy that is at present being wasted.

The Ultimate Solution.

However perfect may be the system of preventive medicine, it will always seem unfair to the average man that the only persons to get the very best treatment of a curative kind should be the pauper, the lunatic, the criminal, and the millionaire. A growing sense of social justice will demand that the best medical service be placed within the reach of all; and that implies a very high degree of excellence on the part of the qualified medical man, with an equal facility on the part of the patient for obtaining the most scientific appliances. Now the only way to put them within the reach of the many is to organize the medical service from the ambulance bearer to the consulting surgeon; and to keep that organization vital it must, in the case of the curative arts at least, be built around a public hospital. Every medical man must be connected with his hospital to the end of his career, i.e., his opportunities for scientific study must be constant. The Army and Navy are recognizing this need in the facilities offered to their officers for intermittent hospital study ; and it is one of the fundamental reasons for nationalizing medicine. The maintenance of all hospitals out of Imperial and Local funds,* and their management by the community, will be the first step towards educational efficiency in the profession. Under the provisions of the Public Health Act of 1875 ratepayers may provide themselves with hospitals of any kind. They are already supporting fever hospitals, asylums, sanatoria for tuberculous patients, and inebriates' homes. With these institutions in their hands there are no arguments left to oppose the abolition of all so-called charity in connection with the treatment of disease. Socialist finance will certainly reduce the number of millionaire donors, but it will regard the charge for hospital accommodation as a most necessary form of national insurance against sickness to impose on the people. If the cost of treatment is heavy at the outset this will only demonstrate more clearly the relative economy of prevention. The change from charitable to publicly controlled hospitals will at once place medicine on a collectivist basis. The staffs will have to be paid just as the Metropolitan Asylums Board now pays its officers, and the right of free treatment will determine the ultimate connection of all doctors with the hospitals of their respective districts. The extravagant charges of cruelty and wanton experimentation brought against hospital treatment and so often shown to be groundless on investigation, are, where true, due to the lack of public control and the social status of the patient. Both of these wrongs are characteristic of all present social institutions, and it is our duty to remedy them. By this, or some similar method of organization, we should not only remedy those evils of private practice which have already been referred to, but also obviate the hopeless waste of time involved in the waiting for a practice. The working hours of the profession could be regulated, and all its members kept in touch with scientific progress. Skill and capacity could then be made the criteria of success and promotion, while a certain freedom of choice with regard to their medical attendants would at the same time be left to the members of the public.

In a community where the health of the citizens was regarded as of equal importance with its trade statistics, the creation of a Ministry of Health would not long be delayed. This department of the Central Government would be assisted and advised by the General Medical Council, just as the Secretary for War is advised by the Army Council. The Minister of Health† would be responsible to Parliament for the following departments : registration of births, diseases, and deaths ; meteorology ; coroners' returns ; central and local sanitary and other medical work ; adulteration reports ; factory supervision and reports ; veterinary supervision ; prison and police inspection ; the oversight of all public sanitary works. In short, what is needed is a co-ordination of the health functions of the

* *Vide* Fabian Tract No. 95, " Municipal Hospitals."
† "A Ministry of Health," Sir B. W. Richardson. Chatto and Windus, 1879.

Local Government Board and a separation of those of its present activities which are alien to these. With regard to local administration, each county borough or other large and populous district would have its health office, with a principal medical officer of health, having under him the various branches of preventive medicine, such as sanitray inspectors, health visitors, and school inspectors, and the organized hospitals and departments for medicine, surgery, midwifery, ophthalmology, dermatology, dentistry, etc. Each department would have its senior medical officer, with a staff under him. There would be a visiting staff to see patients at their homes, an out-patient department connected with the public hospital for the treatment of minor ailments and accidents, a hospital with wards for the treatment of serious illness, divided according to the class of disease to be treated. Under the same administration should be placed the special hospitals for the insane, the inebriate, the persons suffering from infectious disease, epileptics, etc. These hospitals would continue their work as at present, but with a further degree of co-operation. The social and scientific value of co-ordination between all departments of medicine cannot be overstated, but the prevailing idea underlying all should be prevention. Every opportunity would be given for consultation between the members of the staffs throughout the whole service. At · the large central hospitals students would be taught their profession and, when qualified to treat disease, would be drafted to those places in need of help.

In each locality the district health office would keep records of disease and of the means employed for its prevention or cure. Such a register of sickness would enable the student for the first time to find out the extent of the incidence of disease, both qualitatively and quantitatively, and the effect of the methods of treatment employed over the largest possible area.

The cost of the State medical service should fall in part on the national Exchequer, and partly on local taxation, in order to encourage efficiency in prevention. The economy of organization, the greatly lessened cost of illness due to the increase in sanitary control, the immense amount saved in the reduced number of working days lost through illness—computed at the present time at £7,500,000 per annum—would make the health tax seem light, and it would be regarded as a profitable form of insurance. The doctor's bill comes now at the worst time, especially when the head of the family has been ill ; then the small tax in time of health would save many an illness from its most painful side. It is true that the efficient treatment of disease would cost more than the present inefficient methods—in the case of the lower middle class, for instance, the provision of skilled nursing assistance, drugs, dressings, and suitable food would be a fresh charge on the community—but it should not be any part of Socialist policy to lessen the expenditure on preventing disease. If all the broken-down members of society, all its mentally defective persons, all those suffering from debility, incipient phthisis, alcoholism, or heart disease were to be properly taken in hand by the comparatively small residue of moderately healthy persons, it would begin to dawn upon us that these evils are largely due to the waste and folly of present-day commercialism. It is voluntary neglect and blindness that makes things as they are tolerable, and compulsory charges for treatment levied socially would effectively counteract neglect, and would open the eyes of the most blind. From the point of view of the public, it has been argued that the ample and free provision of medical assistance would mean an unnecessary demand for drugs and treatment on the part of an increasing number of people. "The poor," wrote Sir William Gull, "have an idea that disease comes from Providence, and that it must be cured by drugs. Now, if there is any idea that ought to be rooted out it is this"; and the practice of modern medicine is becoming more and more a matter of advice as to methods of living and general regimen. In a word, it is becoming educational, and fulfilling the words of Sir John Simon : * "In proportion as medicine has become a science, it has ceased to be the mystery of a caste." The enormous consumption of drugged sweets and patent medicines of all kinds is but a reflection of the impotence of the genuine practitioner to cure disease, whose cause is of daily recurrence, and which a change of environment or habit can alone effectually remedy. The patient seeks advice which the doctor dare not give—it is too Utopian—he receives a drug which fails, and in despair turns to those patent remedies which are advertised to cure all ailments, until finally he falls a victim to some parasitic industry or insanitary home condition.

A New Army Organization.

The work of co-ordinating and organizing the medical service is perhaps the most important piece of Army reorganization which awaits the statesman of the twentieth century; for disease is an enemy with which we are daily at war, whose victims number annually five hundred thousand in dead alone, while the wounded are ten times as numerous. Something has been done by organization ; yet while the nation seems so indifferent to the story told by the death-rates of adults and infants, and only deigns to register a few of the ailments that affect its members, but little can be expected. It is the duty of the Socialist to teach people to think, not only imperially, but in communities, and also, perhaps, to feel in communities as well. Our forty thousand doctors need the guiding hand of a statesman who will do for the health of the people what War Ministers desire to do for its external security.

The falseness of the conception of Socialism as a disintegrating force, and as a dividing up of wealth or material advantages, will be again demonstrated by its application of the problems of public health and medicine. From the provision of surgery to that of sewers its tendency is towards a unification and an amalgamation of interests, and wherever this has taken place it has brought immense social benefit in its train. The water supply, when co-ordinated and municipalized, was no longer the source of disease and death that it

* English Sanitary Institution. Cassell and Co., 1890.

was in the days of individual enterprise, and the provision of an organized body of medical officers of health has already accomplished a steady reduction in the death-rates, as well as in the incidence of disease,—to mention only two instances.

Medicine and Statecraft.

The individual practitioners of the country, acting against that class interest which a commercial age has bound up with the misfortune of their fellows, have done much to improve the lot of the people ; but when the medical man has been at the same time something of a statesman, the results of his work have been enormous. The work of Sir G. Baker and many others in the eighteenth century was followed by that of Chadwick, Southwood Smith, and Sir J. Simon in the nineteenth. The secret of their success was the fact that they realized that sickness was a burden on the rates which had to be prevented, and they diagnosed a diseased condition of society which lay beneath the individual suffering they saw around them. They realized that there was a social pathology very analogous to that of the individual organism, that health was a *national* asset, and that the poverty of masses of the population was but a symptom of a disease—a circulatory disease—that might end in social destruction. While the marriage between medicine and statecraft opens up immense possibilities for the development of the race both physically and morally, it is none the less important, now that the work of the statesman is becoming more and more that of the organizer of economic social conditions, that he too, should be imbued with the same spirit that characterizes the physician or surgeon. He will have to apply or administer remedies distasteful to the sufferer ; to perform operations upon a living society, such as the removal of vested interests and social abuses, which have become closely bound to the life of the people ; and in doing this it will be well for him to avoid unnecessary pain, using to this end such anæsthetics as compensation and the time limit in his operations for nationalizing health. But the statesman as physician will also realize where and in what degree society is undeveloped, and he will constantly aim at the building up of industries and professions into orderly and organized service. The complete socialization of medical practice will at once raise it from the commercial level to which the modern world has brought it to the height of a profession whose powers for usefulness will be fuller and wider than ever before, so making it one of the greatest forces in the emancipation of humanity from the horrors of modern competitive industrialism.

For List of Books see Cover.

Fabian Tract No. 161.

AFFORESTATION AND UNEMPLOYMENT.

BY ARTHUR P. GRENFELL

(LATE INDIAN FOREST SERVICE).

PUBLISHED AND SOLD BY

THE FABIAN SOCIETY.

PRICE ONE PENNY.

LONDON:

THE FABIAN SOCIETY, 3 CLEMENT'S INN, STRAND, W.C.

JANUARY, 1912.

THE SOCIALIST YEAR BOOK

AND

LABOUR ANNUAL for 1912.

BY

J. BRUCE GLASIER.

Every student of Socialism, every Socialist speaker, and every intelligent Socialist, *should* have a copy. In a word, there should be a copy in every home.

IT IS THE SOCIALIST BOOK OF THE SEASON,
and will be in season during the whole year.

IT READS LIKE A ROMANCE.

PRICE SIXPENCE.

Post free **9d.** Bound in Cloth, **1s.** Post free **1s. 3d.**

ORDER DIRECT FROM

THE NATIONAL LABOUR PRESS, LIMITED,
30 BLACKFRIARS STREET, MANCHESTER.

I.L.P. HEAD OFFICE, ST. BRIDE'S HOUSE, SALISBURY SQUARE, FLEET STREET, LONDON, E.C. ; 100 JOHN BRIGHT STREET, BIRMINGHAM ; AND 5 WORMALD ROW, ALBION STREET, LEEDS.

AFFORESTATION AND UNEMPLOY-
MENT.

THE United Kingdom is remarkable amongst civilized nations in two respects: it has a smaller area of forest than any other in similar latitudes; and though it has a Government Department called "Woods and Forests," that Department is not much more than an office for the State gardeners and gamekeepers. The science and the art of forestry, studied and practised by every other important nation and by ourselves in our Indian Empire and in our colonies, is so utterly neglected at home that people of ordinary intelligence rarely know that the science and art exist.

No doubt statistics afford us some excuse. By forests we do not mean the deer forests of Scotland and the heath-clad.hills and moorlands which in England are known as Ashdown Forest and Dartmoor Forest and so on. We mean land covered with trees, and the percentage of forest in this sense is in Ireland 1·5 of the area, Wales 3·9, Scotland 4·6, and England 5·3, compared with 17 per cent. in France, 17·3 per cent. in Belgium, the most thickly populated of countries, 25·9 in Germany, 32·6 in Austria, 35 in Sweden and in Hungary, 42 in Russia, and 48 in Servia.

Our national want of attention to forestry is therefore accounted for by the scarcity of our forests. But, for reasons about to be explained, the time has come to establish in our country both forests and the science and art of forestry.

Report of the Royal Commission.

Such, at any rate, is the opinion expressed in the Report on Afforestation (Cd. 4460) of the Royal Commission on Coast Erosion, etc., issued in 1909.

The nineteen Commissioners comprised six professional men (two of whom were experts in forestry) and four officials (two State and two municipal); while of the nine politicians five were Liberals, including a Trade Unionist, two Conservatives, and one each from the Nationalist and Labor Parties. The Report was unanimous, with some reservations from one Commissioner, and proposed that the State should purchase suitable land in order to plant 150,000 acres yearly, at an average annual cost of £2,000,000, until a national forest estate of 9,000,000 acres had been created. In times of trade depression some of the labor required would be drawn from the ranks of the unemployed, a fair number of whom are fit to carry out the work with but little preliminary training.

As a piece of Collectivism the scheme is a striking one. No body of men as representative as were the Commissioners would have produced it unless a very strong case had been made out.

With but few exceptions, the Report was received with a chorus of approval by the press. The organ of the country gentlemen, the *Field*, in its issue of January 23rd, 1909, wrote :

The opinion of the Commission upon Afforestation is emphatic. In effect they say : " Yes, afforestation is both practicable and desirable." It would be passing strange if the decision had been otherwise. For many years the authorities best able to form an opinion have been urging not only the wisdom, but the national necessity, of safeguarding our timber resources.

We may reasonably hope that the work of this Commission will be positive, and not in the direction of that shunting which is so frequently the conclusion of costly official enquiries. To be effective, however, there should be no delay in the beginning. Nor is there any reason for hesitation. Upon the facts as to the necessity of systematic afforestation there is universal agreement, and the portions of the Report containing it may at once be taken as read. The existence of unemployed men is also too obvious for dispute. The real points of debate are : (1) Are the men fit for work ? (2) Will the work be profitable ? The assurances of the Commission upon these questions we cannot but regard as wholly satisfactory.

With this declaration on the part of progressive landlords little fault need be found, but the difficulty in practice will be to hold them and their agents to it.

Proposed National Forests.

The Commission report that 6,000,000 acres in Scotland, 2,500,000 in England and Wales, and 500,000 acres in Ireland, 9,000,000 acres in all, are fit for afforestation and should be afforested. They point out that the world supply of timber is being steadily depleted, that the price is constantly rising, and that (in 1907) we imported 8,315,937 loads of timber, valued at £20,127,943, from countries of similar climate and character to our own. This quantity of timber could be grown on 9,000,000 acres, planted to cut on a regular rotation, and the Commission report that exactly this area of suitable land is available for the purpose. This, of course, is a mere coincidence, and there is no reason to suppose that our imports will be constant at the figure of 1907.

There is, therefore, a clear primâ facie case for the promotion of afforestation ; but this is one of those services which private enterprise has not yet undertaken, and, indeed, is unfitted to undertake. The initial outlay is substantial. The Commission estimate of cost of land and planting is £13 6s. 8d. per acre. Interest and management expenses have to be added annually. For twenty years there is no direct return whatever, and for another twenty years the thinnings yield but a small income. When forty years have elapsed the crop can be sold at £60 per acre, and if left for eighty years it will realize £175 per acre. But the investment of a substantial capital which will cost money to protect for twenty years, will yield very little for forty years, and between that and eighty years will give in lump sums, according to the acreage cut, a return of £3 16s. 6d. per cent. on the whole outlay is not a business proposition for an individual, however young and however wealthy. The State, which can borrow cheaply, which lives for ever, and can therefore afford to take long views, is the only body which could undertake afforestation on a large scale.

Germany has had State forest departments for a century. Saxony. has 429,300 acres of State forests and obtains a net return of 22s. an acre. In Prussia, Bavaria, and four other States, the net revenue of the State forests is between 10s. and 15s. an acre, whilst in Wurtemburg the return is as high as 25s. 3d.*

Nearly every important nation not only owns and works State forests, but undertakes the systematic teaching of forestry, the science and art of the profitable growing of timber for sale.

In Switzerland 71 per cent., in Hungary 68 per cent., in Russia 60 per cent. of the forests, 25 per cent. of the whole area, belongs to the State, and in Germany 52 per cent. of the forest area is State or municipal. In other countries the proportion is considerable, though smaller, save in British India, where it is nearly 100 per cent., and in the United Kingdom where it is 2 per cent.

Climate and Soil.

Yet our climate and soil are suitable for the growing of timber; and English wood is as good as or better than that of other countries, if it is properly grown. In practice our home grown timber is usually inferior, because our woods are used primarily for ornament and sport. We grow fine trees with spreading branches and abundant space for underwood ; the timber merchant wants tall trees with no big branches, and for this purpose they must be grown close together, as in natural forests.

Why Afforest at all?

The Commission demonstrate that 9,000,000 acres of land, now used to little purpose, employing scarcely any labor, and producing nothing but game and a little mutton, could be purchased and planted by the State, would yield in a generation or so a very large amount of wealth, larger, indeed, than the estimate if the price of timber continues to rise in the future as it has in the past, and would in the end return what is for the State a fair profit on the whole enterprise.

But there are the special reasons for undertaking it. Commercially the proposition is sound but it is not exactly attractive. It is the expected social results which determined the Commission to recommend afforestation to the nation.

Forestry and Unemployment.

Afforestation has an important bearing on the problem of unemployment in two main ways.

1. It can be advantageously used as a direct palliative, or, to put it more correctly, a preventive of unemployment both during trade depressions caused by cyclical fluctuations and in the slack periods of seasonal trades.

* These figures are, presumably, the net annual income, that is the difference between receipts and working expenses per acre averaged over the whole area. The forests are mostly natural, and no doubt State property from time immemorial. These figures therefore have little relation to the finances of the scheme proposed for the United Kingdom.

2. Its permanent effect will be to help in, what is an essential part of the organization of the labor market, the better distribution of labor.

Everyone knows what the "casual labor system" means. Round the dock gates in London and Liverpool and Hull, and all our other great ports, to take only one example, there is constantly hanging an army of "under employed" men fighting for a bare existence, and that army is partly recruited by country-born men who have drifted away from the rural villages and farms. Now, if unemployment is to be satisfactorily dealt with, it is necessary, as the Minority Report of the Poor Law Commission has shown, that the casual labor system should be abolished, the recruiting of the "casual" army stopped, and the present congested masses of the "under employed" dispersed. The men who are squeezed out in the process of decasualization will have to be absorbed eventually into regular and self-supporting employment, and one of the forms of that employment will be the work of afforestation. Thus afforestation will play an important part both as a preventive of the "drift to the towns" and as an absorbent of much labor which is at present unemployed or "under employed."* Incidentally, of course, the creation of forests would develop other industries beyond the mere growing and felling of timber, e.g., its conversion and manipulation, and the wood-working trades generally. It has been estimated by a high authority that the afforestation of a million acres would afford regular work on the land for 100,000† men, which means, to put it another way, life in the country for half a million persons, counting five to the family.

The peculiar value of afforestation as a preventive of unemployment is, however, its applicability to times of great industrial depression and to seasonal slackness. It is hardly necessary to say that it must not be used for relief works, which are thoroughly unsound, and can have no place in a well organized system. But the peculiarity of afforestation is that it lends itself admirably to temporary work. Planting can, to a great extent, be put in hand at intervals according to the state of the labor market, without detriment either to the work itself or to the interests of the community.‡ In giving evidence before the Royal Commission, Professor Schlich was asked, "If you had to regard periods of depression in the labor market,

---

* This does not mean that every under employed dock porter or builder's laborer could go straight to tree planting. Training will be a necessary part of such reorganization of industry. It is worth remembering, however, in this connection, that the Report on Afforestation found that "there are sufficient unemployed persons willing to submit to and able to satisfy ordinary labor tests, who could advantageously be employed without a period of special training." This is a conclusion based on the experience of a number of practical foresters and others who have actually used the "unemployed" in their work. (See the Report, 1909, Cd. 4460, pp. 15 foll.).

† The discrepancy between these figures and those at the end of the section is due to the deduction of labor displaced allowed for in the latter estimate.

‡ Provided that, as in India with famine relief works, schemes are carefully elaborated to this end beforehand.

would it very seriously interfere with systematic operations if you had to do little planting for two or three years, and had a correspondingly increased quantity once in three or four years, we will say?" His reply was: "I think it would make very little, if any, difference, provided you did a certain amount within a certain number of years, say within every ten years approximately the same amount. . . . Generally speaking, I can say it does not matter whether you do a double amount in one year and nothing in the next year in the shape of planting—really it makes no difference in the long run so long as you do every five years, or every ten years at the outside, approximately the same amount."

It is clear, then, that a large part of the work in the national forests could be (and ought to be as the Minority Report of the Poor Law Commission suggests) "executed out of loans on a ten years' program, and within the decade, made to vary in volume in such a way as to ebb and flow in a manner complementary to the flow and ebb of private industry."

It is clear, also, that another part of the national (or municipal) forests can be used to prevent seasonal unemployment. The actual planting of trees is confined to the winter months (roughly from October to April), whilst preliminary work, such as fencing, clearing the ground of brushwood, draining, etc., may be done either in winter or summer. Obviously, therefore, sylvicultural operations will fit in with agriculture. Thousands of men who will be busy during the summer at haymaking, harvesting and the hoeing of roots, can find employment in the woods when ordinary farm work is slack during the winter. Moreover, with a proper organization of the labor market, that is to say, with national labor exchanges and training establishments in full working order, there is no reason why forest work—the rougher and less specialized departments of it at any rate —should not be the alternate trade of many urban laborers, men in the building trade for instance. There is afforestable land in the neighborhood of many great cities (such as London, Portsmouth, or the towns of the West Riding), while several of the great municipalities (e.g., Birmingham, Leeds, Liverpool), have water catchment areas, which really need afforesting.

Two and a half million acres is England's share of the area proposed to be planted. It is here that forestry has its principal bearing on the unemployed question. In Surrey, Kent, and Sussex, not to speak of Essex, there are 36,000 acres of afforestable land, about 90,000 acres in Hampshire, nearly 300,000 * in the South-West of England. Here are demonstration areas and training grounds close at hand, where men can be tested and, if necessary, trained until they are fit to be drafted to the Yorkshire moors or the highlands of Scotland. In Scotland there would not be enough men unemployed in times of depression to do the work on the large areas proposed to be acquired unless men previously trained in England could be drawn upon.

* Moreover, out of 28,000 acres of hill and heath land in Suffolk about three quarters, or 20,000 acres, could be successfully planted.

Enough has been said to show the special value of afforestation in dealing with the unemployed problem. Important questions then arise as to the number of men employable on any given area of woodland and the amount of supervision and training necessary.

This is what the Commissioners arrive at in the way of employment :

(a) *Temporary.*—Temporary employment is afforded annually to 18,000 men during the winter months. Subsidiary occupations would employ as many more. This is equivalent to the labor of 12,000 men for one year and increases gradually as the scheme matures.

(b) *Permanent.*—Permanent employment is afforded to one man per 100 acres afforested, rising to 90,000 men when the whole area has been dealt with. The scheme is a "snowball." At first the labor of 12,500 men will be required ; ultimately it will rise to 90,000. The subsidiary industries will absorb a much larger number, so that finally this new industry will support an additional population of about two to two and a half millions.

Forestry and Small Holdings.

A large forest scheme started at several centres in England will greatly assist the development of many land reforms. For, to quote from the Report, "the conversion of comparatively unprofitable lands into forests enhances the productiveness of adjacent areas and should promote the development of the small holdings movement." This is fairly well understood in Scotland, and it should be the business of all south of the Tweed to see that it is equally well understood in England.*

The English Small Holdings Act on its introduction aroused great expectations among the rural population, which have since in many counties been disappointed. With the help of well considered afforestation schemes, the hopes of those fortunate enough to live in their neighborhood stand more chance of being realized. As an instance of the way in which a system of small holdings can be set upon a sound financial basis the evidence of Mr. Rawlence is much to the point. He stated that in Dorset, Wilts, Hants, and Kent (to which may be added Devon, Somerset, Yorkshire, Wales, and many other areas), there "must be hundreds of thousands of acres, taking that land the normal [annual] value of which would be less than five shillings per acre." He also gave instances of estates sold or for sale at £10 or less per acre, and added: "If you want to buy land of that sort, the better plan will be to buy an estate of 700 acres, taking my illustration ; and you would probably let several small holdings for almost as much as the whole farm is let, and you would have the residue left [for forestry purposes] practically for nothing."

---

* The Commission report that only half a million acres need be acquired for forest purposes in Ireland. This is a timid recommendation ; but to analyze the situation there, which is complicated by all kinds of political issues, would require too much space.

The advantage to the small holder of being able to earn good wages during the winter in the adjoining State forests is too obvious to need enlarging on. It will serve to tide him over the period it takes for his farm to become economically self-supporting, and afford him ready money for rent and the interest on the capital required for stock. If the county councils do not fall in with this idea, there is no reason, save the defects of the present Board of Agriculture, why the State itself should not establish the subsidiary small holdings, under section 20 of the Small Holdings and Allotments Act, 1908. There will be a further advantage in that co-operation, which is so essential to the success of the small holder, ought to be initiated and fostered by central State action, and these "national" small holdings will provide an invaluable opportunity for this purpose.

Opposition to be Overcome.

In England: for Hunting and Sheep Farming.

In England, apart from the grouse shooting on the Yorkshire moors, the hunting rather than the shooting interest is to be feared. For example, there are, according to the Commissioners, many suitable areas in the West of England; for instance, in Somerset alone the Mendips, the Quantocks, and Exmoor. Now the prosperity of the present rather scanty population of Exmoor is based on two things—sheep grazing and the existence of the Devon and Somerset stag-hounds. It is true, as the Report points out, that much land could be devoted to forestry that is now being used as pasture for sheep, and that the system of farming could, without difficulty, be adapted thereto. If the poor upland pasture were improved by suitable cultivation and the use of artificial manures, as is being done with great success in Belgium and Denmark, and to a lesser extent in England itself, the diminished area of grazing could easily carry the same number of sheep as before. If additional land were required to be given up to the forester, great stock would be substituted for small, and cattle breeding and dairy farming would replace the production of mutton.

But the opposition of the stag hunters is more serious. In England the ownership of land in many cases, if not most, does not imply the management of a business, but rather the enjoyment of a luxury. Consequently, even though it could be proved as a matter of estate management that a landlord who lent himself to a large scheme of afforestation on Exmoor would benefit himself materially, it does not follow that this would move him to support locally unpopular improvements. Still less would he or his agent be influenced by the fact that such a scheme could indirectly benefit the unemployed of Bristol, Bridgwater, and Taunton during times of trade depression. For if new work were started on a large scale in his neighborhood, there would be a demand not only for comparatively unskilled labor from the towns, but also for skilled woodmen, planters, and men brought up on the land from the neighborhood. This would inevitably send up the wages of the rural proletariat; and however much some of us may wish to see that (as it is the necessary antecedent from a financial point of view of most land reforms), it would for that very reason be opposed by the existing territorial interests. Increased wages, though they would ultimately pay for themselves in the better quality of the work done, might at first lead to reductions in rent ; and whereas rents are now rising, the rise might be stopped. Changes in husbandry—even changes which would ultimately increase rents—are not often welcomed by the landowner. His immediate interest "is in getting the utmost possible rent, which may (and often does) come from such a use of the land as involves its producing a smaller quantity of foodstuffs than some other use"; just as "the farmer's pecuniary interest lies in getting the highest possible percentage on the capital he employs, which may (and often does) lead him positively to restrict the intensity of his labor and the product of the farm."*

In Scotland : Grouse and Deer.

Scotland, where the Commission recommends that 6,000,000 acres be acquired for plantations, is where afforestation is likely to be carried out on a large scale. In that country, outside the fertile lowlands, all classes of the country population are well aware that the rural economy is based almost entirely on the use of the land for sport. And this is a very unsafe position. Fashions in shooting change. Just as pheasant shooting is losing the esteem of sportsmen because over preservation has made it too artificial (and as a table bird the tame hand-reared pheasant is little, if at all, superior to a barndoor fowl), so in deer forests, where the ground is often overstocked and the beasts' range limited, the stalker will seldom get such fine trophies as he can in Germany and Eastern Europe, where the deer live under more natural conditions. But the conversion of bare mountain land and heath into forest will not destroy the shooting. Except for rabbits (which are incompatible with afforestation, but which in any case are of no account in the Highlands), game will still flourish, though its character may be changed. As a well informed article in the *Academy* puts it : "People can make shooting for black game, capercailzie, and pheasants instead of grouse at no pecuniary loss. They can keep deer from destroying the young trees by giving them fodder, as they do in the German deer forests." Pheasants reared in large areas of dense forest would be wild and gamey enough to satisfy the most critical shot or maître d'hotel, and this kind of shooting would soon recover its value. The able writer of the *Times* articles on British forestry, published between February and May, 1908, observes upon game preservation that "Any misgivings as to the effect of forestry upon pheasant shooting may be allayed by recollecting that the battue system is a fashion imported from Germany, where scientific forestry has been longer established than in any other country."

* Sidney Webb : preface to the English translation of Hasbach's "History of the English Agricultural Laborer."

It may seem strange to devote so much consideration to un-economic sports hitherto enjoyed only by the leisured rich. But, according to the Royal Commission, the sporting rights would serve to cover the expense of local taxation and part of the upkeep of the woods until they began to pay expenses. In fact they are an economic asset of immediate value ; and their exercise need not interfere with the proper tending and profitable exploitation of the forests, although perhaps their enjoyment in a more democratic fashion than at present will have to be deferred until the national income is more equably distributed. In the near future the State might let shootings to co-operative societies of sportsmen, upon trustworthy guarantees of fair usage.

The Scots will, therefore, be well advised to accept the Commissioners' scheme ; for they will be in the pleasant position of eating their cake and having it too, at least a part of it. And on points like these those who wish to see the scheme carried through in its entirety do well to be posted. There are differences of opinion as to the best scale for a start. Mr. R. C. Munro Ferguson, M.P., who has been a conspicuous advocate of forestry in Scotland, said, in July, 1910: "The agricultural interest is exceeding sensitive as regards the afforestation policy of the Commission on the ground that it may absorb some undue proportion of the available resources." This would be perfectly true if he had stopped there, but he con-tinued : " That, however, is a groundless fear, because it must be a matter of some years before any large scheme of afforestation can be undertaken, and an expenditure averaging £50,000 for the first six or eight years is probably as much as could be well laid out on the requisite preliminary machinery." Here his view entirely conflicts with the view of most experienced men. They are of opinion that too much time is being spent in talk, and that there are plenty of men and sufficient experience accumulated in the United Kingdom to allow the work to be begun on a far larger scale with every promise of success.

THE OPPOSITION OF LAND AGENTS.

Even if landowners were less unprogressive than is often alleged, and many were prepared to support a large development of State forests in their neighborhood and run the risk of the increased value of the adjoining estates being largely absorbed by taxation, there would remain another very formidable class to be reckoned with.

Compare the amount received by the landlord and his agent. The landlord does 5 per cent. of the work and receives 95 per cent. of the rent ; that is to say, the work of the landlord is rewarded 361 times as highly as that of the agent. Here is a disproportion that exists in no other business. If we turn to the provisions of the Commissioners' larger scheme, we find that the administration charges required to produce a net revenue of £17,500,000 amount to no less than £1,800,000, or nine and a half per cent. on the total of the two sums. The inference is obvious : either the agent is very much underpaid, or the work is often badly done. Both conditions are true at once in varying degree. The result is that the land agent, as compared with other professional men, can only make a living by managing a very large tract of land in a routine fashion. He has not the time, even if he had the knowledge to do his part in adapting the husbandry of the estate to changing conditions. Were he to do so he would lose in two ways. Firstly, he would manage less land and get a correspondingly smaller income ; secondly, until the improvement on the land he still managed became productive he would lose a part of his percentage on that. This is particularly true of forestry, because farm land given up to plantations would hardly become productive during the agent's lifetime. The consequence is that English land agents as a class (since they are but human) are quite ignorant of scientific forestry. Hence if their business were curtailed in one direction by the creation of large State forests, they could hardly hope, under any proper system of administration that is likely to be set up, to expand it in another by assuming the direction of these forest estates. Nor do they show any serious signs of improving. Only a few years ago the lecturer in estate agency and forestry at a well known college, which has been compared in efficiency with the Agricultural University at Copenhagen, qualified for his duties in teaching forestry by a short visit to Germany. And a few months ago a very capable land agent in charge of some large woods in the south of England told the writer that he was ignorant of the art, and more than hinted that it did not matter in the least.

Artists and Scenery.

There remains a final objection which, as it is often raised by those who profess to love "natural" scenery, must be met and answered. It is said that afforestation will destroy the "natural" beauty of the moors and mountains, and that economic forests must necessarily be ugly. This is not so, for 2,500,000 acres devoted to forests in England will leave plenty of open space, while the additional charm of real forest scenery will be added. The author of the very able series of articles on "British Forestry" in the *Times* (February to May, 1908), completely disposes of the objection :

> If woods are to be preserved they must be managed on an economic basis. We hope to convince readers that this can be done without sacrifice to sylvan beauty— that the best æsthetic results indeed can only be obtained as the outcome of sound forest treatment. The most delectable and special characteristic of English scenery consists in richly timbered parks, the finest of which owe their origin to ancient forests. Take as an example in the South the park at Ashridge. Nowhere else shall you see such statues of beeches in dense masses, in detached groups, and standing singly—the very perfection of tree growth. But do not imagine that such a result can be attained by dotting beeches about on open ground. The Queen beech at Ashridge had never attained her height of 135 feet with 90 feet of clean bole unless she had shared with ten thousand sisters the discipline of high forest.

Similarly Maeterlinck has waxed eloquent on the beauties of serried ranks of forest trees. Dealing with arboriculture in a park he says :

Plant it with beautiful trees, not parsimoniously placed as though each of them were an object of art displayed on a grassy tray, but close together like the ranks of a kindly army in order of battle. . . . Trees never feel themselves really trees nor perform their duties unless they are in numbers. Then at once everything is transformed—sky and light recover their first deep meaning, dew and shade return, silence and peace once more find a refuge.

Of the common Scots pine he adds :

You can picture nothing to compare with the architectural and religious alignment of the innumerable shafts shooting towards the sky, smooth, inflexible, pure. . . .

It is to be hoped that the town councils of England will lay the words of the practical man and the poet to heart, so that we, too, may have nobly timbered woods close to our big towns such as give a distinctive charm to many Danish, Belgian and German cities.

A New Department Wanted.

The Commissioners appear to have recognized this, for they advise that their scheme be administered by Commissioners specially appointed for the purpose. This is an admission that the Departments of Woods and Forests and of Agriculture, as at present organized, are unfit for it. With one or two exceptions, the officials capable of executive work have only the ordinary land agent's training. Mr. Munro Ferguson, in a letter to the *Times* in 1910, pleaded that we are not in a position to find offhand skilled subordinate officials and working foresters for executive duties. But this plea must not be exaggerated. "Offhand" does not mean five to eight years. The first essential step is a properly constituted Forestry Department. It would be idle to try developing this out of the Office of Woods and Forests, if "development" implied retaining anything more than the name of the department. Its first duties will be to secure demonstration forests, provide the necessary sylvicultural training for the executive staff, make a survey of lands suitable for forests, and prepare schemes for planting them. So soon as this new department is ready to act, the Commissioners' scheme should be entrusted to it for execution. It may well have recourse to the large water "catchment" areas which several municipalities possess in the Midlands and the North of England, and which are being planted in a tentative fashion. These will be very useful as demonstration areas and training grounds. Moreover, since the representatives of these towns have already asked for expert advice and financial aid, the new Forest Department should be able to secure efficient management. We must not forget the recommendation of the Royal Commission that "this form of State work can best be performed by a central authority," a recommendation which all Progressives, with the object lesson of the administration of the Small Holdings Act before them, will cordially endorse.

Conclusion.

In conclusion, what is now needed in this matter is not enquiry, but agitation and definite State action. The experts have done their part. The case is made out. The only danger is lest a scheme which has few, if any, open enemies should, through public apathy and official incompetence, be allowed to lapse. Reformers should press for proper .publicity on matters of afforestation and especially for :

1. A well equipped executive Forest Department under the reformed Board of Agriculture, with an expert body to make a proper return of the land suitable for afforestation, to give advice, and to prepare schemes.

2. A settled policy of steady acquisition of land by the State and local authorities to be used for afforestation ; the local authorities to be advised by and, if necessary, subsidized and controlled by the Forest Department.

3. Proper technical instruction in forestry, both in rural schools and colleges and in the universities.

It is only by these means that this important measure of national reconstruction can be brought into being.

BOOKS FOR REFERENCE.

On Afforestation. Second Report of the Royal Commission on Coast Erosion, Reclamation of Tidal Lands, and Afforestation in the United Kingdom. Cd. 4460. Wyman. 1909. 6d. Minutes of Evidence and Appendices ; being Vol. II., Part II. Cd. 4461. Wyman. 1909. 5s. 3d.

FORBES, A. C.—Development of British Forestry. Arnold. 1910. 10s. 6d. n.

FORBES, A. C., and Prof. W. R. FISHER.—Two Prize Essays on the Adaptation of Land for Afforestation. Loughton and Co., 1 Essex Street. 1904.

MUNRO-FERGUSON, R. C.—Afforestation. An Address. London : National Liberal Club.

NISBET, JOHN.—Our Forests and Woodlands. Dent (Haddon Hall Library). 1900. 7s. 6d. n.

————— The Forester. Practical Treatise on British Forestry and Arboriculture for Londoners, Land Agents, and Foresters. Two vols. Blackwood. 1905. 42s. n.

SCHLICH, Sir W.—Forestry in the United Kingdom. Bradbury. 1904. 2s. n.

————— Manual of Forestry. Vol. I. Forest Policy in the British Empire. Bradbury. 1906. 6s. n.

SCHWAPPACH, ADAM.—Forestry. Dent. 1904. 1s. n.

SUMMERBELL, T.—Afforestation. I.L.P. Pamphlet. 1908. 1d.

THE FABIAN SOCIALIST SERIES. 15

VOLUMES NOW READY.

I. SOCIALISM AND RELIGION.
CONTENTS: (1) Christian Socialism, by the Rev. Stewart D. Headlam. (2) Socialism and Christianity, by the Rev. Percy Dearmer. (3) Socialism and the Teaching of Christ, by the Rev. John Clifford. (4) A Word of Remembrance and Caution to the Rich, by John Woolman.

II. SOCIALISM AND AGRICULTURE.
CONTENTS: (1) The Village and the Landlord, by Edward Carpenter. (2) State Aid to Agriculture, by T. S. Dymond. (3) The Secret of Rural Depopulation, by Lieut.-Col. D. C. Pedder. (4) The Revival of Agriculture, by the Fabian Society.

III. SOCIALISM AND INDIVIDUALISM.
CONTENTS: (1) The Difficulties of Individualism, by Sidney Webb. (2) The Moral Aspects of Socialism, by Sidney Ball. (3) The Impossibilities of Anarchism, by G. Bernard Shaw. (4) Public Service v. Private Expenditure, by Sir Oliver Lodge.

IV. THE BASIS AND POLICY OF SOCIALISM.
CONTENTS: (1) Facts for Socialists, by the Fabian Society. (2) Capital and Land by the Fabian Society. (3) Socialism: True and False, by Sidney Webb. (4) Twentieth Century Politics, by Sidney Webb.

V. THE COMMONSENSE OF MUNICIPAL TRADING.
By Bernard Shaw. With new Preface. "Whether you agree with it entirely or not, you are bound to admit its intellectual power and persuasive eloquence."

VI. SOCIALISM AND NATIONAL MINIMUM.
By Mrs. Sidney Webb, Miss B. L. Hutchins, and others.

VII. WASTAGE OF CHILD LIFE.
By J. Johnston, M.D. "Passing from one count to another, he puts together his huge indictment of national extravagance; showing also how the practice of thrift might ensure to the nation the possession of healthy and efficient citizens."—*Daily News.*

VIII. SOCIALISM AND SUPERIOR BRAINS: A Reply to Mr. Mallock.
By Bernard Shaw.

IX. THE THEORY AND PRACTICE OF TRADE UNIONISM.
By J. H. Greenwood. Preface by Sidney Webb.

The first four volumes consist of a revised, collected, and classified edition of some of the most valuable of the famous "Fabian Tracts" in a style more suitable for the general reading public. Each booklet is printed on good paper with good type, and is supplied in two forms, viz., in attractive wrappers at 6d. each, net, and in quarter cloth boards, gilt top, at 1/- each, net. Postage: 1d. and 2d. each, except for No. 5, 1½d. and 2d.

THE FABIAN SOCIETY, 3, CLEMENT'S INN, STRAND.

FIFTH EDITION. REVISED.

WHAT TO READ

ON SOCIAL AND ECONOMIC SUBJECTS.

AN UP-TO-DATE, SELECT BIBLIOGRAPHY, DEALING WITH SOCIALISM, SOCIAL AND INDUSTRIAL PROBLEMS, ECONOMICS AND ECONOMIC HISTORY, POLITICAL SCIENCE, GOVERNMENT AND ENGLISH HISTORY.

Compiled by the Fabian Society for Students of University Extension Lectures and Classes, for persons investigating Social Problems, and for the general reader.

**Interleaved, in Paper Cover, 1s. net; postage 2d.
Bound in buckram, 2s. net; postage 3d.**

THE FABIAN SOCIETY, 3 CLEMENT'S INN, STRAND, LONDON; or of P. S. KING & SON.

FABIAN SOCIETY.—The Fabian Society consists of Socialists. A statement of its Rules and the following publications can be obtained from the Secretary, at the Fabian Office, 3 Clement's Inn, London, W.C.

FABIAN ESSAYS IN SOCIALISM. Paper 6d.; cloth 1/6; post. 2½d. and 4d.

WHAT TO READ on Social and Economic Subjects. Fifth edition, revised to October, 1910, and enlarged. Interleaved, paper, 1s. n. cloth 2s. n., post. 2d.

THIS MISERY OF BOOTS. By H. G. WELLS. 3d., post free 4d.

FABIAN TRACTS and LEAFLETS.

Tracts, each 16 to 52 pp., price 1d., or 9d. per doz., unless otherwise stated. Leaflets, 4 pp. each, price 1d. for six copies, 1s. per 100, or 8/6 per 1000.

The Set of 78, 3s.; post free 3/5. Bound in Buckram, 4/6 n.; post free 5s.

I.—General Socialism in its various aspects.

TRACTS.—159. The Necessary Basis of Society. By SIDNEY WEBB. 151. The Point of Honour: a Correspondence on Aristocracy and Socialism. By RUTH CAVENDISH BENTINCK. 147. Capital and Compensation. By EDW. R. PEASE. 146. Socialism and Superior Brains. By BERNARD SHAW. 142. Rent and Value. 138. Municipal Trading. 121. Public Service versus Private Expenditure. By Sir OLIVER LODGE. 113. Communism. By WM. MORRIS. 107. Socialism for Millionaires. By BERNARD SHAW. 139. Socialism and the Churches. By Rev. JOHN CLIFFORD, D.D. 133. Socialism and Christianity. By Rev. PERCY DEARMER. 78. Socialism and the Teaching of Christ. By Dr. J. CLIFFORD. 42. Christian Socialism. By Rev. S. D. HEADLAM. 79. A Word of Remembrance and Caution to the Rich. By JOHN WOOLMAN. 75. Labor in the Longest Reign. By S. WEBB. 72. The Moral Aspects of Socialism. By SIDNEY BALL. 69. Difficulties of Individualism. By SIDNEY WEBB. 51. Socialism: True and False. By S. WEBB. 45. The Impossibilities of Anarchism. By BERNARD SHAW (price 2d.). 7. Capital and Land (7th edn. revised 1908). 5. Facts for Socialists (11th ed., revised 1908). 132. A Guide to Books for Socialists. LEAFLETS—13. What Socialism Is. 1. Why are the Many Poor? WELSH TRACTS—143. Sosialaeth yng Ngoleuni'r Beibl. Gan J. R. JONES (Caernarfon). 141. Translation of 139. 87. Translation of 78. 38. Translation of 1.

II.—Applications of Socialism to Particular Problems.

TRACTS.—160. A National Medical Service. By F. LAWSON DODD. 2d. 157. The Working Life of Women. By Miss B. L. HUTCHINS. 155. The Case against the Referendum. By CLIFFORD D. SHARP. 154. The Case for School Clinics. By L. HADEN GUEST. 153. The Twentieth Century Reform Bill. By H. H. SCHLOESSER. 152. Our Taxes as they are and as they ought to be. By ROBT. JONES, B.Sc. In cover, 2d. 150. State Purchase of Railways. By EMIL DAVIES. In cover, 2d. 149. The Endowment of Motherhood. By H. D. HARBEN. In cover, 2d. 145. The Case for School Nurseries. By Mrs. TOWNSHEND. 144. Machinery: its Masters and its Servants. By H. H. SCHLOESSER and C. GAME. 140. Child Labor under Capitalism. By Mrs. HYLTON DALE. 136. The Village and the Landlord. By EDW. CARPENTER. 131. The Decline in the Birth-Rate. By S. WEBB. 130. Home Work and Sweating. By Miss B. L. HUTCHINS. 128. The Case for a Legal Minimum Wage. 122. Municipal Milk and Public Health. By Dr. F. LAWSON DODD. 125. Municipalization by Provinces. 119. Public Control of Electrical Power and Transit. 123. The Revival of Agriculture. 118. The Secret of Rural Depopulation. 115. State Aid to Agriculture: an Example. 112. Life in the Laundry. 98 State Railways for Ireland. 124. State Control of Trusts. 86. Municipal Drink Traffic. 84. Economics of Direct Employment. 83. State Arbitration and the Living Wage. LEAFLET.—104. How Trade Unions benefit Workmen.

III.—Local Government Powers: How to use them.

TRACTS.—156. What an Education Committee can do (Elementary Schools), 3d. 137. Parish Councils and Village Life. 109. Cottage Plans and Common Sense. 76. Houses for the People. 99. Local Government in Ireland. 82. Workmen's Compensation Act. New edition for the Act of 1906. 62. Parish and District Councils. 54. The Humanizing of the Poor Law. LEAFLETS.—134. Small Holdings: and how to get them. 68. The Tenant's Sanitary Catechism. 71. Ditto for London.

IV.—General Politics and Fabian Policy.

TRACTS.—158. The Case against the C.O.S. By Mrs. TOWNSHEND.

Fabian Tract No. 162.

FAMILY LIFE ON A POUND A WEEK.

BY

MRS. PEMBER REEVES.

PUBLISHED AND SOLD BY

THE FABIAN SOCIETY.

Fabian Women's Group Series, No. 2.

PRICE TWOPENCE.

LONDON:

THE FABIAN SOCIETY, 3 CLEMENT'S INN, STRAND, W.C.
PUBLISHED FEBRUARY 1912. SECOND REPRINT APRIL 1914.

Family Life on a Pound a Week.

WHO are the poor? Are only those people counted poor who are driven to sleep on the Embankment or to throng the casual wards? Or does the term cover all cheap labor? If so, at what wage does poverty begin? Attention is often diverted from the condition of an individual or of a class by the perfectly accurate announcement that there are "plenty of people worse off than that," to which statement would probably be added the generally accepted formula that the poor should be divided into the "undeserving" and "deserving." Deserving of what? Nobody likes to say "of sufficient pay for the work they do." And yet if they do not deserve that, what do they deserve?

It is the purpose of this tract to describe the resources of London working men and their families when the wages range between 18s. and 24s. a week. These men are often somebody's laborers, or they may be carters, horse-keepers, porters, railway carriage washers, fish-fryers, and perhaps one may be a borough council street sweeper on half time. They are in regular work and receiving a regular wage, which means that they are not in any sense casuals, though they suffer at times from unemployment and live in the dread of it. Whole streets are inhabited by this class of family. They "keep themselves to themselves" with as much anxiety and respectability as the dwellers in a West End square. They generally live in the upper or lower half of a small house, for the whole rent of which either they or the other family are responsible to the landlord. A kind of sordid decency is the chief characteristic of their horribly monotonous streets. Mile after mile of them, every house alike except for the baker's or greengrocer's shop at the corner, they cross and recross, broken occasionally by big thoroughfares where trams, omnibuses, and public houses are. A church, a chapel, or more often a school, makes a welcome oasis in the architectural desert. The ordinary visitor seldom finds access to these houses, where the people are jealously respectable and make no claim on any charity or institution other than the hospital.

The Cost of Houseroom.

How does a Lambeth working man's wife with four children manage on a pound a week? If ordinary middle class persons were to attempt the calculation, they would stop with a sense of shock and come to the conclusion that everything, from rent to food, must be very cheap in Lambeth. Now is this so? The chief divisions in a twenty shilling budget are rent, insurance, light and heat, food. To begin with rent, a good unfurnished room in Lambeth, measuring twelve feet by fifteen feet, costs 4s. a week. A house of eighteen rooms, with storage for coal, with hot and cold water system, and sinks and waste pipes throughout, can be obtained in Kensington, rent, rates, and taxes included, for £250 a year. If the tenant of this house paid 4s. a week for every twenty square yards of his floor space, he would, roughly speaking, pay £385 a year. But if he paid 4s. a week for the same amount of cubic space that the Lambeth man gets for his 4s., the West End householder would pay about £500 a year instead of £250. These figures are approximate, but they are calculated from real instances. Add to this that the large house has better air, greater quiet, and healthier surroundings. The man who pays a rent of 7s. or 8s. in South London may be paying over one third of his income, for which he may get three tiny rooms in a four roomed dwelling, with a mother or other relative occupying and paying for the fourth room. The living room may be ten feet by eight feet, and three of its walls may be pierced by doors, the room itself being the passage way to the back yard. Two slightly larger rooms are bedrooms. A family of eight persons divides into two parties, four elder children sleep in one bed in one room, while the parents and two younger children sleep in the other. The four elder children go, perhaps, to three different schools. When one of them brings home measles from its school measles go round the bed ; when another brings home whooping cough from its school the same course is pursued by whooping cough. The afflicted children are kept away from school, but the baby and the two year old, who are both teething, have no chance of escape. The distracted mothers do what they can, but in many cases the rooms are terribly damp, and in many the chimneys smoke continually. The convalescence of the children—if they do convalesce—is difficult and prolonged. For one third of his income then the man with £1 or 22s. a week cannot afford space enough for health. His wife may have to carry all her water upstairs and, when it is used, carry it down again. There is no storage for coal ; perhaps no room for the humblest mailcart for the baby. Add to this that as likely as not the walls are old and infested with bugs, which defy the cleanest woman, and can only be kept under by constant fumigation and repapering. It is obvious that the well-to-do man for less than a third of his income can afford a better bargain than this for the housing of his family.

Coal is another necessary which the poor cannot afford to buy economically. The woman with 20s. a week must buy by the hundredweight. She pays from 1s. 4d. in the summer to 1s. 7d. or 1s. 8d. in the winter. The same quality of coal can be bought by the ton in Kensington for less than 1s. per cwt: in the summer and for 1s. 1d. in the winter. Gas also is dearer by the pennyworth than by the 1,000 cubic feet.

Certain kinds of food can be bought cheaply in Lambeth Walk of a Sunday morning—meat which would not be saleable on Monday—vegetables in the same plight. But sugar has risen as ruthlessly for the poor as for the rich, milk has done the same, and even the tinned milk which is separated before being tinned, and which is the only milk a woman with 20s. a week can afford, is now a halfpenny more a tin. Bread is no cheaper in Lambeth than in Kensington, but the Lambeth woman buys hers at the shop because she is then entitled to the legal weight, whereas the " delivered."

bread of the West End is known as "fancy" bread by the trade and is generally under weight.

Insurance for Funerals.

Insurance in Lambeth (up to the time of writing) means burial insurance. The middle class man does not need to pay out something like a twentieth part of his income in order to provide for the possible burials in his family. The poorly paid working man is driven to this great expense for two reasons. First, he is likely to lose one or more of his children, and the poorer he is the more likely he is to lose them ; second, the cost of a funeral, including cemetery fees, is out of all proportion to his means. It is generally supposed that poor people, rather than miss the delight of a gorgeous funeral, will dissipate money which ought to be spent on rent or food or thrift. As a matter of fact undertakers in Lambeth or Kennington will bury an infant for the sum of 28s. or 30s. This includes the cemetery fee of 10s. An older child will cost according to size, a child of three perhaps £2 5s., until the length of the body is too great to go under the box seat of the funeral vehicle, when a hearse becomes necessary and the price leaps to something like £4 4s. At a later stage the cemetery fee goes up. Under these circumstances the poor man has as alternatives burial by the parish and insurance. It is the insurance which is the extravagance—not the way he manages his funerals. But his fear of being made a pauper or of being driven to borrow the price of a child's funeral keeps his wife paying a weekly sum, varying with the number of children, of from 6d. to a 1s. or even over. One penny a week from birth barely covers the funeral expenses at any age in childhood. Adults commonly pay 2d. a week. A peculiar hardship which often befalls the poor man is that, owing to periods of unemployment, his payments are interrupted and his policies may therefore lapse. His children are at those times less well fed and more likely to die, and he may quite well be driven to the disgrace of a pauper burial after having paid insurance for many years. Burial by the parish is taboo among the poor. It is no use arguing the case with them. The parents fiercely resent being made paupers because of their bereavement. Moreover they consider the pauper burial unnecessarily wanting in dignity and respect. They say that as soon as have the parish they would have the dustman call for their dead. The three years' old daughter of a carter out of work died of tuberculosis. The father, whose policies had lapsed, borrowed the sum of £2 5s. necessary to bury the child. The mother was four months paying the debt off by reducing the food of herself and of the five other children. To reduce the food of the breadwinner is an impossibility. The funeral cortège consisted of one vehicle in which the little coffin went under the driver's seat. The parents and a neighbour sat in the back part of the vehicle. They saw the child buried in a common grave with twelve other coffins of all sizes. "We 'ad to keep a sharp eye out for Edie," they said ; "she were so little she were almost 'id."

The following is an account kept of the funeral of a child of six months who died of infantile cholera in the deadly month of August, 1911.

The parents had insured her for 2d. a week, being unusually careful people. The sum received was £2.

Funeral	...	...	...	...	£1	12	0
Death certificate	...	...	...	...	0	1	3
Gravediggers	...	...	...	...	0	2	0
Hearse attendants ...	...	...	...	0	2	0
Woman to lay her out	...	...	...	0	2	0
Insurance agent	...	...	...	...	0	1	0
Flowers	...	...	...	...	...	0	0	6
Black tie for father ...	...	...	...	0	1	0

£2 1 9

This child was buried in a common grave with three others. There is no display and no extravagance in this list. The tips to the gravediggers, hearse attendants and insurance agent were all urgently applied for, though not in every case by the person who received the money. The cost of the child's illness had amounted to 10s.—chiefly spent on special food. The survivors lived on reduced rations for two weeks in order to get square again. The fathers's wage was 24s., every penny of which he always handed over to his wife. Until burial can be made an honorable public service there seems to be no hope of relief in this direction for the family living on any sum round about £1 a week.

How the Budgets were obtained.

In order to explain how the family budgets given further on were obtained, it is necessary to state that an investigation has been carried on for three years by a small committee formed of members of the Fabian Women's Group. The investigation has for its object observation of the effect on mother and child of proper nourishment before and after birth.

To further this enquiry it was found necessary to take down each week in writing the whole family expenditure for that week. The budgets thus collected began before the birth of the child and continued until the child was a year old. The names of expectant mothers were taken at random from the out-patient department of a well known lying-in hospital. Only legally married people were dealt with because the hospital confined itself to such persons. The committee decided to refuse cases where virulent disease in the parents might outweigh the benefits of proper nourishment, but it was considered that moderate drinking on the part of the parents would probably be a normal condition and must therefore be accepted. As a matter of fact, tuberculosis in some form or other was found to be so common that to rule it out would be to refuse almost half the cases. Respiratory and tuberculous disease was therefore accepted. With regard to drink, on the contrary, only one instance did we find of a woman who drank. A few men were supposed to take a glass, but in every case but one they faithfully rendered over to their wives the agreed upon weekly allowance. Out of fifty cases taken at haphazard this is a good record.

As may well be imagined, the visitors did not find accounts in being. The women "knew it in their heads," they said, but to write it down was absurdly impossible. Gradually, however, the interest grew, and with patience a few weeks generally saw some kind of record of the family expenditure. The first attempts taught the investigator far more than they taught the mother. A book was supplied to each woman, and week after week she entered in it every penny she received and spent. Wednesday was the great day when, with her floor scrubbed and her hair as tidy as she could manage, she disentangled these accounts with the aid of the visitor. Her spelling was curious, but her arithmetic was generally correct. "Sewuitt . . . 1¾" was as serious an error as the figures often knew. "Coul . . thruppons" is Lambeth for "cow-heel . . 3d." Seeing the visitor hesitate over the item "yearn . . . 1d," the offended mother wrote next week, "yearn is for mending sokes." Eight women were found who could neither read nor write. Sometimes they had only forgotten, and were capable of being coaxed back into literary endeavour, but in a few stubborn cases the husband came to the rescue, and in three, eldest sons or daughters, aged ten or twelve, were the scribes. One wrote in large copper-plate, "peper . . . apeny," which threatened to remain ambiguous till his return from school. Fortunately the mother had a burst of memory. Another entry, "earrins , . too d" gave a lot of trouble, but turned out to mean "herrings . . . 2d." A literary genius of thirteen kept her accounts as a kind of diary, part of which ran as follows.

"Mr. D, ad too diners for thruppence, wich is not mutch e bein such a arty man."

Pages of this serial had to be reduced, though with regret, to the limits of ordinary accounts. Many of the women enjoyed their task, and proudly produced correct budgets week after week.

A typical budget is that of Mrs. X. Her husband is a railway carriage washer, who earns 18s. for a six days week and 21s. every other week when he works seven days. He pays his wife all that he earns. There are three children. The two budgets were taken on March 22nd and March 29th, 1911.

A 21S. WEEK.

				s.	d.	
Rent	...	...	...	7	0	
Clothing club	...	...	...	1	2	for two weeks.
Insurance ...	...	...	...	1	6	for two weeks.
Coal and wood	...	...	...	1	7	
Coke	...	...	...	0	3	
Gas ...	...	...	...	0	10	
Soap, soda ...	...	...	...	0	5	
Matches	...	...	...	0	1	
Blacklead, blacking		...	...	0	1	

12 11

Left for food 8s. 1d.

				s.	d.
11 loaves ...	...	...	. .	2	7
1 quartern flour ...	...	...		0	5½
Meat ...	...	...		1	10
Potatoes and greens	...	...		0	9½
½ lb. butter...	...	...	...	0	6
1 lb. jam ...	...	...	...	0	3
6 oz. tea ...	...	...	...	0	6
2 lb. sugar ...	...	...	...	0	4
1 tin milk ...	...	...	...	0	4
Cocoa ...	...	...	...	0	4
Suet ...	...	...	...	0	2
				8	1

Average per head for food 1s. 7½d. a week, or less than 3d. a day all round the family. But a working man cannot do on less than 6d. a day, which means 3s. 6d. a week. This reduces the average of the mother and children to 1s. 1¾d. or less than 2d. a day.

An 18s. week.

						s.	d.
Rent ...	...	...	...	...	...	7	0
Coal and wood	...	...	...	...	...	1	7
Gas ...	...	...	...	...	...	0	10
Soap, soda ...	...	...	...	...	...	0	5
Matches ...	...	...	...	...	...	0	1
						9	11

Left for food 8s. 1d.

						s.	d.
11 loaves ...	...	...	...	...	...	2	7
1 quartern flour	...	...	...	...	...	0	5½
Meat ...	...	...	...	...	...	1	9½
Potatoes and greens	...	...	...	...	0	9
½ lb. butter ...	...	...	...	...	...	0	6
1 lb. jam ...	...	...	...	...	...	0	3
6 oz. tea ...	...	...	...	...	...	0	6
2 lb. sugar ...	...	...	...	...	...	0	4
1 tin milk ...	...	...	...	...	...	0	4
Cocoa ...	...	...	...	...	...	0	4
Suet ...	...	...	...	...	...	0	3
						8	1

Average per head for food 1s. 7½d. a week, or less than 3d. a day.

In the same street lives Mrs. Y, whose husband is a laborer who works at Hackney Marshes, a long way off. He earns 24s. and gives his wife 19s. 6d. His fares cost 3s. 6d. a week. There are three children. Date of visit October 25th, 1911.

						s.	d.
Rent ...	...	...	...	...	...	7	0
Insurance	...	...	...	...	...	0	7
Calico club ...	...	...	...	...	...	0	6
Coal club ...	...	...	...	...	...	1	0
Soap, soda ...	...	...	...	...	...	0	4½
Gas ...	...	...	...	...	...	0	8
Blacklead and blacking	...	...	...	...	0	1
Mangling	...	...	...	...	...	0	2
Wood	...	...	...	...	...	0	1
1 yard flannelette	...	...	...	...	0	2¾
Hearthstone...	...	...	...	...	...	0	½
						10	8¾

Left for food 8s. 9¼d.

						s.	d.
7 loaves and 7 loaf bottoms	...	...	...	2	7½
¼ quartern flour	...	...	...	...	0	2¾
Meat ...	...	...	...	...	...	2	9½
Potatoes and greens	...	...	...	...	0	10
1 lb. butter ...	...	...	...	...	0	10
¼ lb. tea	...	...	...	...	...	0	7
3 lb. sugar ...	...	...	...	...	0	7½
Fish ...	...	...	...	...	...	0	3
						8	9¼

Average for food per head 1s. 9d. a week, or 3d. a day.

Mr. Y. is rather a bigger man than most Lambeth workers, and requires at least 4s. a week spent on his food. Hardly too large an allowance for a working man. But that reduces the average spent on the rest of the family to 1s. 2¼d. a week per head or 2d. a day.

The housekeeping allowance is often all that the man earns. The wife either allows him a few coppers for fares, or not, as she can afford. Where the wage is regular, but below £1 a week, this is usually the case. A man with 24s. will keep 2s. or 2s. 6d., and will dress, drink, smoke, and pay fares out of it. A very usual amount for a man to pay his wife is 20s. a week. It almost looks as though there were an understanding that, where possible, that is the correct sum. The workman earning 20s. a week often pays it all over to his wife. If his wages rise to 22s. he goes on paying the 20s. and keeps the extra money. Given, then, the 20s. a week it entirely depends on how many children there are, whether the family lives on insufficient food or on miserably insufficient food—whether the family is merely badly housed or is frightfully crowded as well as badly housed.

To illustrate this, here are the budgets of three women with varying numbers of children, each of whom is allowed 23s. a week— an amount which generally means that the husband is earning about 25s. In one of these cases this is so, but in the other two it will be noticed that the 23s. is the whole family income. In spite of this, and in spite of the fact that it is above the average allowance, the amount spent a week per head on food falls to 1s. 1¼d. all round when there are six children. If 3s. 6d. be spent on the man, the average for the woman and children is 9¼d. per week.

Mr. A, horsekeeper, wages 25s., gives wife 23s., three children born, three alive, five persons to feed. March 24th, 1909.

	s.	d.
Rent	6	6
Insurance	0	10
1 cwt. coal	1	6
Lamp oil	0	5
Boots...	1	6½
Soap and soda	0	4
Wood	0	2
	11	3½

Left for food 11s. 8½d.

	s.	d.
11 loaves	2	6¼
Meat	3	11
Potatoes	0	10
Greens	0	2½
1 lb. margarine, 1 lb. jam	0	9
8 oz. tea	0	8
2 tins milk	0	6
2 lbs. sugar	0	4½
½ quartern flour	0	3
Bacon and fish	0	11
Rice	0	3
Suet	0	2¼
Pot herbs	0	4
	11	8½

Average for food per head a week 2s. 4d. or 4d. a day.

Mr. B sells on commission, earns about 15s., boy earns 2s., girl 6s., wife gets in all 23s., five children born, five alive, seven persons to feed. July 6th, 1910.

	s.	d.
Rent	7	6
Insurance	0	7
½ cwt. coal	0	7½
Gas	1	0
Boots...	2	6
Soap and soda	0	4¼
Hat	1	0¾
Saved	0	2¼
	13	9¾

Left for food 9s. 2¼d.

	s.	d.
9½ loaves	2	3
Meat	2	6
Potatoes	0	7
Greens	0	2½
1 lb. butter	1	0
7 oz. tea	0	7
1 tin milk	0	3½
3 lbs. sugar	0	6¾
½ quartern flour	0	2½
Bacon	0	4½
Cornflour	0	2½
Currants	0	1½
½ lb. cheese	0	3½
	9	2¼

Average for food per head a week 1s. 3¾d. or 2¼d. a day.

Mr. C, carter, wages 23s., gives wife 23s., seven children born, six alive, eight persons to feed. April 21st, 1910.

	s.	d.
Rent	8	6
Insurance	1	0
1 cwt. coal	1	6
Gas	0	11
Boots mended	1	8¼
Clothing club	0	6
	14	1¼

Left for food 8s. 10¾d.

	s.	d.
14 loaves	3	2½
Meat	2	0¼
Potatoes	0	9
Greens	0	3
2 lb. margarine	1	0
4 oz. tea	0	4
No milk.		
4½ lb. sugar	0	9
½ quartern flour	0	3
No bacon.		
Dripping	0	4
	8	10¾

Average for food per head a week 1s. 1¼d. or almost 2d. a day

In these three budgets the women housed their families as well as they could and economized in food when the family increased. The rooms were as large and light as they could get—inadequate and bad, of course, but not specially dark or damp. Mrs. B needed les coal in July, so she laid out extra money on clothes. She always saved, if it were only a farthing. It is curious to note how with the larger family the first set of expenses goes up and the amount left over for food goes down. On the whole these families were about equally housed. The first two women have so far reared all their children. Mrs. C has lost one. Compare this result with the second and third of the following budgets, where the women economized in rent in order to spend more on food.

Mr. D, emergency 'bus conductor, wages 4s. a day, four or five days a week, five children born, five alive. August 25th, 1910.

							s.	d.
Rent ...	...	...	...	...	...	...	9	0*
Insurance	...	...	...	...	...	...	0	7
$\frac{1}{2}$ cwt. coal	...	...	...	...	...	...	0	8
Gas ...	...	...	...	...	...	...	0	4
Soap, soda	...	...	...	...	...	...	0	2
Matches	...	...	...	...	...	...	0	1
							10	10

* Three light, dry, airy rooms at top of model dwelling. ...

Left for food 6s. 6½d.

							s.	d.
10 loaves	...	...	...	...	...	...	2	$3\frac{1}{2}$
Meat ...	...	...	...	...	...	...	1	8
Potatoes	...	...	...	...	...	...	0	6
Vegetables ...	...	...	...	...	...	...	0	2
1 lb. margarine	...	...	...	...	...	...	0	$7\frac{1}{2}$
6 oz. tea	...	...	...	...	...	...	0	6
2 tins milk...	...	...	...	...	...	...	0	6
1½ lb. sugar ...	...	...	...	...	...	...	0	$3\frac{1}{2}$
							6	$6\frac{1}{2}$

Week's average per head for food 11¼d. or 1¾d. a day.

Mr. E, fishmonger's assistant, wages 24s.; seven children born, four alive. March 24th, 1910.

							s.	d.
Rent ...	...	...	...	...	...	...	5	6*
Insurance	...	...	...	...	...	...	0	7
1¾ cwt. coal ...	...	...	...	...	...	...	2	3
Gas ...	...	...	...	...	...	...	1	0
Starch, soap, soda ...	...	...	...	...	...	...	0	5
Wood	...	...	...	...	...	...	0	1
Newspaper ...	...	...	...	...	...	...	0	1
							9	11

* Two fair sized, but very dark, damp rooms in deep basement.

Left for food 12s. 7½d.

						s.	d.
10 loaves ...	...	...	...	...	...	2	3½
Meat ...	...	...	...	...	...	5	2
Potatoes ...	...	...	...	...	...	0	6
Greens ...	...	...	...	...	...	0	4
1 lb. butter, 1 lb. jam	...	...	...	...	...	1	3½
8 oz. tea ...	...	...	...	...	...	0	8
6½ pints fresh milk ...	...	...	...	...	...	1	1
2½ lb. sugar ...	...	...	...	...	...	0	5¼
½ qrtn. flour ...	...	...	...	...	...	0	2¾
Bacon ...	...	...	...	...	...	0	6
Currants ...	...	...	...	...	...	0	1½
						12	7½

Week's average per head for food 2s. 1¼d. or 3¾d. a day.

Mr. F, carter, wages 22s., nine children born, four alive. July 14th, 1910.

						s.	d.
Rent ...	...	...	...	...	...	4	6*
Insurance ...	...	...	...	...	...	0	8½
1 cwt. coal ...	...	...	...	...	...	1	6
Lamp oil ...	...	...	...	...	...	0	8
Starch, soap, soda ...	...	...	...	...	...	0	5
Boot club ...	...	...	...	...	...	1	0
Clothing club ...	...	...	...	...	...	0	6
						9	3½

* Two tiny rooms in very old one storey cottage below level of alley way.

Left for food 10s. 8½.

						s.	d.
11 loaves ...	...	...	...	...	...	2	6
Meat and fish ...	...	...	...	...	...	3	0
Potatoes ...	...	...	...	...	...	0	8
Vegetables ...	...	...	...	...	...	0	5
1 lb. margarine, 1 lb. jam ...	...	...	...	...	...	0	10½
8 oz. tea ...	...	...	...	...	...	0	8
1 tin milk ...	...	...	...	...	...	0	3½
4 lb. sugar ...	...	...	...	...	...	0	10
1 qrtn. flour ...	...	...	...	...	...	0	6
Bovril ...	...	...	...	...	...	0	6½
2 lb. rice ...	...	...	...	...	...	0	4
Salt, pepper ...	...	...	...	...	...	0	1
						10	8½

Week's average per head for food 1s. 9½d. or 3d. a day.

All the children in these three families are delicate. Perhaps there is a worse heredity in the case of Mrs. D's children than in the other two. Mrs. D, who had only 17s. 4½d. to spend and a child more to spend it on, paid 3s. 6d. more in rent than Mrs. E, and 4s. 6d. more than Mrs. F. She spent less on coal and gas than either of the others—even taking into account that July is a warm, light month. She spent less on cleaning and nothing on clothes. She fed her family—her husband, herself and five children—on 11¼d. a head a week. All her children were living.

Mrs. E, who lives in very damp, dark rooms, has to spend heavily on coal and gas to keep them warm and lighted Even for the time of year she takes an unusual amount of coal. She spends more on cleaning, and takes in a Sunday paper. She had 22s. 6½d. to spend, and was able to allow 2s. 1½d. a week a head for food. She has lost three children.

Mrs. F economizes in food as well as rent, and spends 1s. 6d. a week on clothing. She has lost five children.

Each of these families had lived a very long time in the rooms described. The three women were clean, hardworking, and tidy to a fault. The men decent, kindly, sober and industrious. The comparison of the two tables seems to show that air, light and freedom from damp are as necessary to the health of young children as even sufficient and proper food. In fact, the mother who provided good housing conditions and fed the family on 11¼d. a head per week, did better for her children than the mother who lived in the underground rooms—spent plenty of money on coal, and fed her family on 2s. 1½d. a head per week. The poor mother who economized on both food and rent in order to clothe decently did worst of all.

Another budget which compares interestingly on this point with Mrs. F's is that of Mrs. G. She has slightly over 20s. a week, sometimes a few pence over, sometimes more than a shilling over. She houses her children better than Mrs. F does, and spends much less a week on food. She has reared all her six children.

Mr. G, printer's laborer, wages 24s., six children born, six living. He goes a long distance to his work and is obliged to spend on fares. Date of budget, September 20th, 1911.

Mrs. G.	s.	d.
Rent	8	0
Insurance	1	8
¾ cwt. coal	1	0
Gas	0	11
Starch, soap, soda	0	5
Boot club	1	0
Clothing club	0	6
Boot laces	0	1½
Matches	0	1
Blacking	0	0½

Left for food 7s. 11d.

						s.	d.
14 loaves	...	...	...	...	...	2	11
Meat ...	...	...	...	...	...	2	0
Potatoes	...	...	...	...	...	0	6
Vegetables ...	...	...	...	...	...	0	4
1 lb. margarine	...	...	...	...	...	0	6
No tea							
2 tins milk ...	...	...	...	...	...	0	7
2 lb. sugar ...	...	...	...	...	...	0	5
1 qrtn. flour ...	...	...	...	...	...	0	5
Salt ...	...	...	...	...	...	0	1
Pot herbs ...	...	...	...	...	...	0	2
						7	11

Week's average per head for food 1s.

Mrs. F.

						s.	d.
Rent ...	...	...	...	...	...	4	6
Insurance ...	...	...	...	...	...	0	8½
1 cwt. coal ...	...	...	...	...	...	1	6
Lamp oil ...	...	...	...	...	...	0	8
Starch, soap, soda ...	...	...	...	...	...	0	5
Boot club ...	...	...	...	...	...	1	0
Clothing club	...	...	...	...	...	0	6
						9	3½

Left for food 10s. 8½d.

						s.	d.
11 loaves ...	...	...	...	...	...	2	6
Meat and fish	...	...	...	...	...	3	0
Potatoes ...	...	...	...	...	...	0	8
Vegetables ...	...	...	...	...	...	0	5
Margarine and am ...	...	...	...	...	...	0	10½
8 oz. tea ...	...	...	...	...	...	0	8
1 tin milk ...	...	...	...	...	...	0	3½
4 lb. sugar ...	...	...	...	...	...	0	10
1 qrtn. flour ...	...	...	...	...	...	0	6
Salt, pepper ...	...	...	...	...	...	0	1
Bovril ...	...	...	...	...	...	0	6½
2 lb. rice ...	...	...	...	...	...	0	4
						10	8½

Week's average per head for food 1s. 9½d.

It will be seen that Mrs. G spends a regular 1s. 6d. a week on
clothes, the same amount that Mrs F does. She has 21s. 8d. to
spend, where Mrs. F has 20s., but she has six children, whereas Mrs.
F has four. She spends 3s. 6d. a week more on rent, and certainly
houses her family better, having three small, inconvenient, crowded,

but fairly light, dry rooms, in place of Mrs. F's terrible little abode. She buys cheaper bread and flour, and spends but 1s. a week a head on food. She has lost no children, whereas Mrs. F has lost five. It is not to be supposed that the surviving children of Mrs. F, or the children of Mrs. G are robust and strong. Poverty has killed Mrs. F's five weakest children and drained the vitality of her four stronger ones. Poverty has prevented any of Mrs. G's children from being strong. The malnutrition of school children, which was so conspicuously mentioned in the published report of Sir George Newman, Chief Medical Officer of the Board of Education, seems to be explained by these budgets. The idea that mothers who have to feed man, woman and children on 1s. a head a week can do anything else than underfeed them must be abandoned. But it is also evident that the mothers who in desperation try economizing in rent in order to feed better are doing unwisely.

The question of food values is much discussed in connection with ignorance and extravagance on the part of the poor. It is possible, of course, that a shilling, or elevenpence farthing might be laid out to better advantage on a week's food than is done in the foregoing budgets. But superior food value generally means longer cooking—more utensils—more wholesome air and storage conveniences than can be commanded by these women. To take porridge as an instance. When well cooked for an hour and eaten with milk and sugar, most children would find it delicious and wholesome. But when the remainder of last night's pennyworth of gas is all that can be allowed for its cooking, when the pot is the same as that in which fish or potatoes or meat are cooked, when it has to be eaten half raw without milk and with but a hint of sugar, the children loathe it. They eat bread and dripping with relish. No cooking is required there, for which the weary, harassed mother is only too thankful—so they almost live on bread and dripping. A normal menu for a family of seven persons living on £1 a week is as follows :—

Breakfast for seven persons.

1 loaf ; 1 oz. dripping or margarine ; ¼ oz. tea ; ½ oz. sugar ; ¼d. worth tinned milk.

Dinners.

Sunday, 3 lb. meat ; 3 lb. potatoes ; 1 cabbage.
Monday, any meat left from Sunday, with suet pudding. The father on weekdays taking a chop or other food with him to work.
Tuesday, Thursday, Friday, Saturday, suet pudding, with treacle or sugar, or gravy and potatoes.
Wednesday, 1 lb. meat and potatoes stewed with onions.

Tea for seven persons.

1 loaf ; 1 oz. dripping or margarine ; ¼ oz. tea ; ½ oz. sugar; ¼d. worth of tinned milk ; Saturday evening may see a rasher or a bloater for the man's tea.

It will be noticed both from the budgets and from this menu that tinned milk is the only milk which the mother can afford. Each of these threepenny tins bears round it in red letters the words "This milk is not recommended as food for infants." Nevertheless it is the only milk the infants get unless their mother can nurse them. If the mothers are able to nurse they always do for two very convincing reasons—it is cheaper—it is less trouble. But the milk of a mother fed on such diet is not the elixir of life which it could be, and which, under different conditions, it should be. Very often it fails her altogether. Then the child is fed on tinned milk. When it is fractious, because it is miserably unsatisfied, it is given a dummy teat to suck or a raisin wrapped in a bit of rag. This is not because the mother is ignorant of the fact that she could nurse much better if she took plenty of milk, or that if her child must be brought up by hand it were better to feed it from the M.B.C. milk depôt. It is because milk usually costs 4d. a quart, and just now costs 5d., and either price is prohibitive. The milk depôt feeds a new baby for 9d. a week till it is three months old, when 1s. 6d. is charged. The price rises regularly till it reaches something like 3s. at the age of a year. In a family where the weekly average is 1s., or even 1s. 3d., 1s. 6d. cannot be devoted to the new baby without cutting down the average for everybody else. So baby often has "jest wot we 'ave ourselves." It is all there is for him to have.

Meals and Manners.

The diet for the other children is chiefly bread, with suet pudding for a change. Often they do not sit down for a meal ; it is not worth while. A table is covered with newspaper and as many plates as there are children are put round with a portion on each. The eating of this meal may take ten minutes or perhaps less. The children stand round, eat, snatch up caps and hats, and are off to school again. Breakfast and tea are, as often as not, eaten while the child plays in the yard or walks to school. A slice of bread, spread with something, is handed to each, and they eat it how and where they will. In some cases the father comes home for a meal at some inconvenient hour in the afternoon, such as half past three or four or five. This may mean that the children's chief meal takes place then in order to economize coal or gas and make one cooking do. This is not because the mother is lazy and indifferent to her children's well being. It is because she has but one pair of hands and but one overburdened brain. She can just get through her day if she does everything she has to do inefficiently. Give her six children, and between the bearing of them and the rearing of them she has little extra vitality left for scientific cooking, even if she could afford the necessary time and appliances. In fact one woman is not equal to the bearing and efficient, proper care of six children. She can make one bed for four of them, but if she had to make four beds, if she had to separate the boys from the girls and keep two rooms clean instead of one, if she had to make proper clothing and keep those clothes properly washed and ironed and mended, if she had to give each child a daily bath, if she had to attend thoroughly to teeth, noses, ears, and eyes, if she had to cook really nourishing food, with adequate utensils and dishes, and if she had to wash up these utensils and dishes after every meal, she would need not only far more money, but far more help. The children of the poor suffer from want of light, want of air, want of warmth, want of sufficient and proper food, and want of clothes, because the wage of their fathers is not enough to pay for these necessaries. They also suffer from want of cleanliness, want of attention to health, want of peace and quiet, because the strength of their mothers is not enough to provide these necessary conditions.

Clothing.

It is easy to say that the mothers manage badly. If they economize in rent the children die. If they economize in food the children may live, but in a weakened state. There is nothing else that they can economize in. Fuel and light are used sparingly ; there is no room for reduction there. Clothes hardly appear in the poorer budgets at all. In the course of fifteen months visiting, one family on 23s. a week spent £3 5s. 5½d. on clothes for the mother and six children. Half of the sum was spent on boots, so that the clothes, other than boots, of seven people cost 32s. 9d. in fifteen months, an average of 4s. 8d. a head. Another family spent 9d. a week on boots and 9d. a week on clothes in general. There were four children. Other families again only buy clothes when summer comes and less is needed for fuel. Boots are the chief expense under this heading, and few fathers in Lambeth are not able to sole a little boot with some sort of skill. Most of the body clothing is bought third and fourth hand. How it is that the women's garments do not drop off them is a mystery. They never seem to buy new ones, and yet the hard wear to which the clothes are subjected ought to finish them in a month. It is obvious that clothing can hardly be further reduced. Remains insurance. It has been shown that steady, hardworking people refuse to have their dead buried by the parish. If they should change their attitude to this question and decide to ' economize here, it is difficult to imagine the state of mind of the "parish" when confronted by the problem.

How then is the man on a pound a week to house his children decently and feed them sufficiently? How is his wife to care for them properly? The answer is that, in London at least, be they never so hardworking and sober and thrifty, the task is impossible.

But there is a large class who get less than a pound a week. There is also a large class who get work irregularly. How do such people manage ?

A small proportion of the cases undertaken in the investigation, from ill health and other causes, fell out of work. Their subsequent struggles afford material with which to answer this question.

Mr. H, carter, out of work through illness, gets an odd job once or twice in the week. Wages 24s. when in work. Six children born. five alive.

July 7th, 1910, had earned 5s. 5d.

							s.	d.
Rent ...	...	...	...	...	...	goes	unpaid	
Insurance	...	...	...	...	...	...	lapsed	
Coal ...	...	...	...	...	...	...	0	2
Soap, soda	...	...	...	...	...	...	0	4
Gas ...	...	...	...	...	...	...	0	6
Matches	...	...	...	...	...	...	0	1
Blacklead	...	...	...	...	...	...	0	$0\frac{1}{2}$
							1	$1\frac{1}{2}$

Leaving for food 4s. 3½d.

							s.	d.
9 loaves	...	...	...	...	...	...	2	$0\frac{3}{4}$
Meat ...	...	...	...	...	...	...	0	9
Potatoes	...	...	...	...	...	...	0	3
Vegetables	...	...	...	...	...	...	0	1
Margarine	...	...	...	...	...	...	0	$1\frac{3}{4}$
3 oz. tea	...	...	...	...	...	...	0	3
Tinned milk...	...	...	...	...	...	none	
1¼ lb. sugar ...	...	...	...	...	...	0	3
Dripping	...	...	...	...	...	...	0	6
							4	$3\frac{1}{2}$

Or an average per head for food of 7¼d. a week, or 1d. a day.

July 14th had earned 15s. 10d.

						s.	d.
Rent (two weeks) ...	...	...	...	...	11	0	
Insurance ...	...	...	...	...	...	lapsed	
Coal ...	...	...	...	...	...	0	2
Gas ...	...	...	...	...	...	0	5
Soap, soda, blue	...	...	...	...	0	$4\frac{1}{2}$
Wood	...	...	...	...	...	0	$0\frac{1}{2}$
						12	0

Leaving for food 3s. 10d.

						s.	d.
7 loaves	...	...	...	...	...	1	$7\frac{1}{4}$
Meat ...	...	...	...	...	...	0	6
Potatoes	...	...	...	...	...	0	$3\frac{1}{2}$
Vegetables	...	...	...	...	...	0	1
Margarine	...	...	...	...	...	—	
4 oz. tea	...	...	...	...	...	0	4
Tinned milk...	...	...	...	...	...	—	
1½ lb. sugar ...	...	...	...	...	0	3
Dripping	...	...	...	...	...	0	6
1 lb. jam	...	...	...	...	...	0	$3\frac{1}{4}$
						3	10

Or an average per head for food of 6¼d. a week, or less than
1d. a day.

Mr. I, bottle washer, out of work through illness, wife earned what she could. Wages 18s. when in work. One child born, one alive.

August 10th, 1910. Mrs. I had earned 2s. 6d.

		s.	d.
Rent	went unpaid		
Insurance	... lapsed		
Coal	—		
Lamp oil	—		
Soap, soda	—		
		nothing	

Mrs. I was told by **infirmary** doctor to feed her husband up.

	s.	d.
3 loaves	0	8¼
Meat	1	1
Potatoes	0	3
Vegetables	0	0¾
3 oz. tea	0	3
1 lb. sugar	0	2
	2	6

Average per head for food 10d. or 1⅓d. a day.

August 17th. **Mrs. I** had earned 3s. 6d.

		s.	d.
Rent	went unpaid		
Insurance	—		
Coal	0	4	
Lamp oil	0	2	
Soap	0	2	
Firewood	0	1	
		0	9

Mrs. I still feeding her husband up.

	s.	d.
4 loaves	0	11
Meat	1	0
Potatoes	0	2
Vegetables	0	1
1 oz. tea	0	1
1½ lb. sugar	0	3
Margarine	0	3
	2	9

Average per head for food 11d. or 1⅘d. per day.

When Mr. I could earn again, his back rent amounted to 15s. He found work at Finsbury Park, he living south of Kennington Park. He walked to and from his work every day, refusing to move because he and his wife were known in Kennington, and rather than see them go into the "house" their friends would help them through a bad spell. People in that class never write, and to move away from friends and relations is to quit the last hope of assistance should misfortune come. Mr. Y, who works on Hackney Marshes while living at Kennington, is another instance of this. A fish fryer who had to take work at Finsbury Park declared that he walked eighteen miles a day to and from his work.

Mr. J, carter out of work through illness, took out an organ when well enough to push it. Wages 18s. when in work. Six children born, six alive.

Jan. 26th, 1910, Mr. and Mrs. J had earned between them 9s.

Feb. 2nd,	„	..	..	..	7s.
Feb. 9th,	„	„		..	8s. 10d.
Feb. 16th,	„				9s.
Feb. 23rd,	„	„	„	„	7s. 6d.

	Jan. 26th		Feb. 2nd		Feb. 9th		Feb. 16th		Feb. 23rd	
	s.	d.	s.	d.	s.	d.	s.	d.	s.	d.
Rent ...	5	6	3	0	5	6	5	6	3	6
Coal ...	0	6	0	6	0	4	0	6	0	6
Wood ...	0	1	0	1	0	1	0	1	0	1½
Lamp oil...	0	1	0	1	0	1	0	1	0	1½
Soap, soda..	0	2	0	2	0	2	0	2	0	4
	6	4	3	10	6	2	6	4	4	7
Leaving for food ...	2	8	3	2	2	8	2	8	2	11
Average for food per head a week in holidays	0	4	almost 5		0	4	0	4	0	4½

Those children who were of school age in these three families were fed once a day for five days a week during term time. None of the children were earning. The three women were extremely clean and, as far as their wretched means would allow, were good managers. It is impossible to lay out to advantage money which comes in spasmodically and belated, so that some urgent need must be attended to with each penny as it is earned. After a certain point of starvation food must come first, though before that point is reached it is extraordinary how often rent seems to be made a first charge on wages.

It is an undoubted fact that the great majority of babies born to this class of parent come into the world normal as regards weight ; osy fat little creatures who should flourish and thrive in decent conditions. At the end of a year they show many signs of delicacy most of which have been created by lack of warmth, lack of air, lack of light, lack of medical care, lack of food. It seems certain that could these children have what is necessary to a healthy child they are capable of growing up into healthy men and women. Baby clinics, school clinics, free public baths, free public wash-houses would seem to be but the beginning of a scheme of national care for the nation's children. The argument that the conditions described in this tract are useful in that they kill off the sickly children and allow the stronger to survive is an argument which is not followed by its supporters to a logical conclusion. The conditions which kill a weak child drain and devitalize strong children. For every one who dies three or four others live to be in need later on of sanatorium or hospital, or even asylum. It would surely pay the nation to turn its attention to the rearing of its children. It is no use urging that parents are drunken, and lazy and vicious ; where that is true all the more do their children need protection and care; in fact, they only have to be drunken and lazy and vicious enough, for their children to be boarded out by the local authority, and four shillings paid weekly for their food alone, a sum undreamed of by the ordinary decent mother on a pound a week. If the parents, with all the strength, with all the industry, with all the thrift, with all the anxious care shown by these budgets, can only lodge their children as they do, and feed them as they do, what is the use of appealing to the parents for what only money can procure, money being the one thing they have not got? If this rich and powerful nation desires to have strong, healthy children, who are worthy of it, what is to prevent it? There is no reason why the school children should suffer from malnutrition, or why an unusually beautiful summer should kill off the babies like flies.

What Can be Done?

The remedy for this state of things is not easy to devise. Advance is likely to be made along two lines where it has already begun—the growing demand for a national minimum wage and the responsibility for the nation's children which is being increasingly assumed by the State. Trade boards are a beginning, piecemeal and tentative, which should make a starting point for a strong effort to attain a national minimum wage throughout the kingdom. It would be comparatively simple to define a fair wage for the individual worker. In Fabian Tract No. 128, "The Case for a Legal Minimum Wage," the difficulties and limitations, as well as the advantages, of that bed of Procrustes, a family minimum wage, are very fully dealt with. But, after all, the whole question raised by these budgets is one of children. A wage which was a tight fit for three children would be miserably inadequate for six or seven. Add to this that there is no certainty that the wage earner, man or woman, would always spend the whole wage upon actual necessaries. If amusements, however innocent, were brought into the budget, something already in it would have to go. Very moderate drinking would upset the balance altogether. It is not reasonable to expect

working class men and women never to spend on other things than
rent, insurance, clothing, firing, and food. Middle class people do
not expect from themselves such iron self-control. Children, once
an economic asset, are now a cause of expense, continually increased
by legislation, which tends more and more to take children and
young persons out of the labor market. The State, which has
wisely decreed that children shall not be self-supporting, has no
more valuable asset than these children were they reared under conditions favorable to child life instead of in the darkness and dampness and semi-starvation which is all that the decent, hardworking
poor can now afford. Any minimum wage which is likely to be
wrung from the pockets of the employing class during the next few
years would not affect the question raised by the earlier budgets in
this tract where the wage is already over £1 a week. Therefore,
along with a strenuous demand for a national minimum wage,
advance must be made on the line already laid down by the State in
its provision of free and compulsory education for its children and in
its statutory endorsement of the principle of school feeding. The
establishment of school clinics, which is a step likely soon to become
general, ought to be followed by a national system of compulsorily
attended baby clinics. It is obvious from official reports already laid
before the public that by the time they can be received into a
national school many children have already suffered for want of
medical attention. The doctors in charge of baby clinics, knowing
that what a hungry, healthy infant wants is milk, and being confronted week after week with the same hungry infants gradually
growing less and less healthy as their need was not satisfied, would
collect and tabulate in their reports an amount of evidence on the
subject which would revolutionize public opinion on the question of
the nation's children and their needs.

If men, already in steady receipt of wages as high as any minimum wage likely to be attained for years to come, can only feed and
house their families after the strictest personal self-denial, as these
budgets show, the State, if it is to concern itself with its most vital
affairs, should recognize its ultimate responsibility for the proper
maintenance of its children. That this responsibility might eventually take the shape suggested in "The Case for a Legal Minimum
Wage," for the children of widows or unmarried women, is quite
possible. Some form of child maintenance grant might be placed in
the hands of parents who, as joint administrators, would be answerable for the well-being of their children. It would be easy to discover through the clinics whether this duty was in each case being
efficiently performed. A child, presented happy and well cared for,
would be a sufficient guarantee, and a child whose condition appeared
to be unsatisfactory would be noted and all necessary steps would be
taken to secure its welfare. The country has faced the dead weight
of Old Age Pensions ; it is not impossible that the creative and repaying task of building up the nation's youth should be collectively
undertaken.

WAGE EARNERS' BUDGETS. BOOKS RECOMMENDED.

BELL, LADY.—At the Works. A Study of a Manufacturing Town. Arnold. 1907. 6s.

CHAPIN, ROBERT COIT, Ph.D.—The Standard of Living among Working Men's Families in New York City. New York, Charities Publication Committee. 1909. Contains a useful bibliography of methods of budget keeping and tabulation, and of printed collections of budgets.

DAVIES, M. F.—Life in an English Village. 1909. Unwin. 10s. 6d. net.

LE PLAY, FRÉDÉRIC.—Les Ouvriers européens. Paris. 1855-1879. Contains a large number of elaborate monographs on working class families, including several in England.

Liverpool Joint Research Committee.—How the Casual Laborer Lives. 1909. Liverpool, Northern Publishing Company. 1s.

MANN, H. H.—Life in an Agricultural Village in England. Sociological Papers, Vol. I., p. 163. 1905.

MORE, LOUISE BOLARD.—Wage Earners' Budgets. A Study of Standards and Cost of Living in New York City. New York, Henry Holt & Co. 1907. A detailed study of two hundred budgets.

PATON, DUNLOP and INGLIS.—Study of the Dietary of the Working Classes in Edinburgh. o.p. Contains probably the most thorough and scientific examination of food yet available.

ROWNTREE, B. S.—Poverty: a Study of Town Life. 1901. Macmillan. 1s. net.

The Life of the Railway Clerk. Some Interesting Facts and Figures. Prepared by Three Experienced Railwaymen. 1911. Railway Clerks Association. 3d. Gives budgets of thirty-three railway clerks.

United States Bureau of Labor. Sixth Annual Report, 1890. Cost of Production: Iron, Steel, Coal. Gives returns from 3,260 families in these industries, including 770 families in Europe.

WILLIAMS, ETHEL, M.D.—Report on Children on Poor Relief. Poor Law Commission. Vol. XVIII. 1910; Cd. 5037. P. S. King & Son. 2s. 4d.

WILSON, FOX.—Wages and Earnings of Agricultural Laborers. 1900; Cd. 346. 1905; Cd. 2376.

Accounts of Expenditure of Wage Earning Women and Girls. Board of Trade (Labor Department). 1911; Cd. 5963. 5d.

Report on Cost of Living of the Working Classes in Large Towns. Report of an Enquiry by the Board of Trade. United Kingdom: 1908; Cd. 3864. 6s. Germany: 1908; Cd. 4032. 4s. 11d. France: 1909; Cd. 4512. 4s. 1d. Belgium: 1910; Cd. 5065. 2s. 2d. All can be procured from P. S. King & Son.

FABIAN SOCIETY.—The Fabian Society consists of Socialists. A statement of its Rules and a complete list of publications can be obtained from the Secretary, at the Fabian Office, 3 Clement's Inn, London, W.O.

FABIAN ESSAYS IN SOCIALISM. Paper 6d.; cloth 1/6; post. 2½d. and 4d.

WHAT TO READ on Social and Economic Subjects. 1s. n. and 2s. n.

THE RURAL PROBLEM. By H. D. HARBEN. 2s. 6d. n.

THIS MISERY OF BOOTS. By H. G. WELLS. 3d., post free 4d.

FABIAN TRACTS and LEAFLETS.

Tracts, each 16 to 52 pp., price 1d., or 9d. per doz., unless otherwise stated.
Leaflets, 4 pp. each, price 1d. for six copies, 1s. per 100, or 8/6 per 1000.

The Set of 77, 3/6; post free 3/11. Bound in buckram, 5/-n.; post free 5/6.

I.—General Socialism in its various aspects.

TRACTS.—169. The Socialist Movement in Germany. By W. S. SANDERS. In cover, with portrait of Bebel, 2d. 159. The Necessary Basis of Society. By SIDNEY WEBB. 151. The Point of Honour. By RUTH C. BENTINCK. 147. Capital and Compensation. By E. R. PEASE. 146. Socialism and Superior Brains. By BERNARD SHAW. 142. Rent and Value. 138. Municipal Trading. 121. Public Service versus Private Expenditure. By Sir OLIVER LODGE. 107. Socialism for Millionaires. By BERNARD SHAW. 139. Socialism and the Churches. By Rev. JOHN CLIFFORD, D.D. 133. Socialism and Christianity. By Rev. PERCY DEARMER. 78. Socialism and the Teaching of Christ. By Dr. J. CLIFFORD. 42. Christian Socialism. By Rev. S. D. HEADLAM. 79. A Word of Remembrance and Caution to the Rich. By JOHN WOOLMAN. 72. The Moral Aspects of Socialism. By SIDNEY BALL. 69. Difficulties of Individualism. By S. WEBB. 51. Socialism: True and False. By S. WEBB. 45. The Impossibilities of Anarchism. By BERNARD SHAW (price 2d.). 7. Capital and Land (revised 1908). 5. Facts for Socialists (revised 1908). 132. A Guide to Books for Socialists. LEAFLETS—13. What Socialism Is. 1. Why are the Many Poor? WELSH TRACTS—143. Sosialaeth yng Ngoleuni'r Beibl. 141. Translation of 139. 87. Translation of 78. 38. Translation of 1.

II.—Applications of Socialism to Particular Problems.

TRACTS.—173. Public versus Private Electricity Supply. By C. A. BAKER. 171. The Nationalization of Mines and Minerals Bill. By H. H. SCHLOESSER. 170. Profit-Sharing & Co-Partnership: a Fraud and Failure? By E. R. PEASE. In cover. 164. Gold and State Banking. By E. R. PEASE. 163. Women and Prisons. By HELEN BLAGG and CHARLOTTE WILSON. 2d. 162. Family Life on a Pound a Week. By Mrs. REEVES. In cover, 2d. 161. Afforestation and Unemployment. By A. P. GRENFELL. 160. A National Medical Service. By F. LAWSON DODD. 2d. 157. The Working Life of Women. By Miss B. L. HUTCHINS. 155. The Case against the Referendum. By CLIFFORD SHARP. 154. The Case for School Clinics. By L. HADEN GUEST. 153. The Twentieth Century Reform Bill. By H. H. SCHLOESSER. 152. Our Taxes as they are and as they ought to be. By R. JONES, B.Sc. In cover, 2d. 150. State Purchase of Railways. By EMIL DAVIES. In cover, 2d. 149. The Endowment of Motherhood. By H. D. HARBEN. In cover, 2d. 131. The Decline of the Birth-Rate. By SIDNEY WEBB. 145. The Case for School Nurseries. By Mrs. TOWNSHEND. 140. Child Labor under Capitalism. By Mrs. HYLTON DALE. 136. The Village and the Landlord. By EDW. CARPENTER. 128. The Case for a Legal Minimum Wage. 122. Municipal Milk and Public Health. By Dr. F. LAWSON DODD. 125. Municipalization by Provinces. 124. State Control of Trusts. 83. State Arbitration and the Living Wage. LEAFLET.—104. How Trade Unions benefit Workmen.

III.—Local Government Powers : How to use them.

TRACTS.—172. What about the Rates? or, Municpal Finance and Municipal Autonomy. By SIDNEY WEBB. 156. What an Education Committee can do (Elementary Schools), 3d. 62. Parish and District Councils. (Revised 1913). 137. Parish Councils and Village Life. 109. Cottage Plans and Common Sense. 76. Houses for the People. 82. Workmen's Compensation Act. LEAFLETS.—134. Small Holdings: and how to get them. 68. The Tenant's Sanitary Catechism. 71. Ditto for London.

IV.—General Politics and Fabian Policy.

TRACTS.—158. The Case against the C.O.S. By Mrs. TOWNSHEND. 108. Twentieth Century Politics. By S. WEBB. 70. Report on Fabian Policy. 41. The Fabian Society: its Early History. By BERNARD SHAW.

V.—Biographical Series. In portrait covers, 2d. each.

Fabian Tract No. 163.

WOMEN AND PRISONS.

BY

HELEN BLAGG & CHARLOTTE WILSON.

PUBLISHED AND SOLD BY

THE FABIAN SOCIETY.

Fabian Women's Group Series, No. 3.

PRICE TWOPENCE.

LONDON:
THE FABIAN SOCIETY, 3 CLEMENT'S INN, STRAND, W.C.
MARCH, 1912.

WOMEN AND PRISONS.

DRAFTED BY MISS HELEN BLAGG AND MRS. CHARLOTTE WILSON FROM
MATERIAL COLLECTED DURING 1910-11 BY A COMMITTEE OF
THE FABIAN WOMEN'S GROUP, WHICH ALSO INCLUDED MISS
ATKINSON, MRS. BOYD DAWSON, MRS. MAPPLEBECK, MRS.
RUTH RIDSDALE, MISS ELLEN SMITH.

PART I.—DEVELOPMENT OF THE ENGLISH PENAL SYSTEM.

Introduction.

WOMEN suffer under the criminal law and its administration as men
do and in other ways besides. In order to understand what specially
relates to women it is necessary to consider our penal system as a
whole. The penalty of imprisonment is now its central feature ; but
the predominance of the prison is a comparatively new thing, co-
incident with the growth of our present economic conditions, and as
they change it seems likely to cease. The instinct of self-preservation in a community is the source of all penal systems ; but that instinct has intermingled with a variety of passions, and striven to
explain and express itself by very dissimilar ideas and methods at
different periods in our history. Fragments of all of these compose
the underlying strata of our penal system to-day.

Revenge and Restitution.

The original form of punishment was retribution—an eye for an
eye and a tooth for a tooth—really the fundamental childish instinct
of hitting back when struck. Later, as an alternative to retribution,
came the idea of restitution, that is of payment in money or kind
for personal damage done or for goods appropriated. In Anglo-
Saxon customary law each man and each part of a man had a price,
which was paid as compensation direct to the injured person and his
kin. Later his lord and his king demanded compensation as well.
Ultimately the State annexed the whole in criminal cases on the
plea that the wrongdoer had broken the king's peace. An attenu-
ated remnant of the ancient custom of restitution has come down to
us in the form of fines, and of the damages and costs awarded in
civil cases. But it is believed by some criminologists that a return
to the old idea, recast to suit modern conditions, might be a
valuable agency in the reform of the criminal.

Revenge and Expiation.

Ideas of revenge and restitution have been allied from time immemorial with that of expiation. The wrongdoer must be made to atone for his crime by undergoing some form of personal suffering. Under the influence of mediæval theology revenge and restitution merged in the expanding force of this ancient doctrine till it became the dominating factor in criminal procedure. Hanging, burning, beheading, dismemberment, crushing, branding, ducking, whipping, mutilation, the stocks, and the pillory were favorite modes of punishment in England almost down to modern times. Banishment from city, village, guild, or hundred, which often meant in the Middle Ages outlawry * and starvation, was succeeded early in the seventeenth century by transportation to our plantations across the Atlantic, the transported being sold as servants to free settlers.† After the revolt of the American Colonies Australia was substituted for America as a dumping ground for our convicts, male and female ; and the plight of most of them there in "hulks" or "factories," in chain gangs, or as "assigned servants," was little better than that of servitude in the plantations.‡ Transportation finally came to an end in 1867 with the refusal of West Australia to receive convicts.

Up to the beginning of the last century death or transportation were the usual forms of punishment even for trivial offences. A child might be hanged for stealing a pocket handkerchief. But since 1838 the death penalty has rarely been exacted for any offence save murder.§ Since 1868 executions have taken place in private. In earlier times they were public, and people used to make up parties to see criminals hanged.

Little mercy was shown to women in the matter of punishment ; indeed burning, one of the most cruel of deaths, was a frequent penalty for their offences. A woman was burnt for coining in 1789. The penalty was abolished the following year. A woman was flogged through the streets of London for the last time in 1764. Whipping for female offenders was finally abolished only in 1820.

Whilst the idea of expiation dominated society mere imprisonment was too mild a final penalty for anything but debt or lesser political offences. Gaols were fever haunted, pestiferous dens, sometimes underground, where men, women, and children awaiting trial or execution of sentence were fettered and huddled promiscuously together. They got food and drink by bargaining with their gaoler, who received no wages, but made his living out of the prisoners and could retain them in bondage until they paid him. There were also Houses of Correction for rogues and disorderly persons and

* Outlawry, i.e., being out of the king's protection, is still a possible penalty for crime ; abolished for civil cases 1879. Pollock and Maitland, "History of English Law," Vol. I., p. 49, note. For imprisonment in the Middle Ages and penalties incident to exile, Ibid., Vol. II., pp. 516-8. Banishment from the village was practised in Scotland in the nineteenth century. Andrews, "Old Time Punishments," p. 114.

† "White Servitude in Virginia" (Ballagh); "Slavery and Servitude in North Carolina" (Bassett). Johns Hopkins University Studies, xiii. and xiv.

‡ See Report of Select Committee on Transportation, 1838.

§ 1,601 persons were condemned to death in 1831 ; in 1910-11 only 25.

the Bethlehem Hospital (Bedlam) for obstreperous lunatics, where the public paid to go on Sundays to see the insane, like animals in the Zoo, behind the iron bars of their cages.

Deterrence and the Reform of the Criminal.

A note of coming change was struck during the eighteenth century. The Society of Friends in America and in England were pleading against the death penalty, and urging that room for repentance be given to the criminal ; while Howard* and Bentham were formulating schemes of punishment which might deter from crime, whilst reforming instead of merely torturing the evil doer. The agency they proposed was imprisonment in isolation, and the cellular penitentiary at Millbank was built in 1816 to try an experiment for which, however, public opinion was not yet ready. For more than thirty years Millbank was the white elephant of prison reform.

The movement initiated by Romilly and Mackintosh for the substitution of the penalty of imprisonment for those of death or barbarous misusage, progressed side by side with the efforts to improve the state of local prisons initiated by Howard, and carried on by Elizabeth Fry, Nield and Buxton and their Society for the Reform of Prison Discipline. The reforms it strove to effect were the classification and separation of prisoners, at all events of the sexes ; a bed for each person, if not a separate cell ; some attempt to preserve health ; the appointment of prison chaplains and the moral instruction of prisoners ; continual and arduous employment ; the use of fetters only as an " urgent necessity " ; and female officers for female offenders. For many years the reformers were ridiculed as " ultra-humanitarians " endeavoring to " pamper the criminal classes," but they succeeded in provoking a series of Parliamentary enquiries and some enactments, which, like the efforts of the eighteenth century, remained a dead letter until public opinion overtook legislation.

General progress, including the establishment of a regular police force in 1829, and the more efficient lighting of towns, combined with the abandonment of the worst barbarities of our criminal law, resulted in a gradual diminution of crime. This reassured the public, and when the Australian Colonies made their first resolute stand against transportation in 1840, England was ripe for a new development of the penal system.

The building of the model prison at Pentonville, with 520 separate cells, was followed by the promulgation by Sir George Grey, Home Secretary 1846-52, of a new scheme, in which the prison was the main agency for dealing with all classes of criminals—except those condemned to capital punishment or let off with a fine. (1) A limited period of separate confinement in a penitentiary or local prison, accompanied by industrial employment and moral training. (2) For long sentence prisoners hard associated labor at a public works prison. (3) A ticket-of-leave, curtailing the sentence of well-behaved

---

* Howard first called attention to the subject in his "State of Prisons in England and Wales," 1777. Mrs. Fry started the "Association for the Improvement of Female Prisoners in Newgate" in 1817. Like Howard she afterwards carried on a widespread agitation for prison reform at home and abroad.

industrious convicts, but leaving them under police supervision. National uniformity in the discipline and diet of local prisons was finally secured by the Prisons Act of 1877, which placed gaols throughout the country under the jurisdiction of the Home Secretary with Prison Commissioners (Prison Board) under him, and Prison Inspectors. Thus the ideal of a method of punishment which should deter by its severity, while reclaiming the criminal by its moral suasion, has been reduced to practice and subjected to the test of experience for nearly three-quarters of a century. Those most convinced of its necessity will hardly contend that it has justified the high hopes and noble enthusiasm in which it originated.

The Modern Point of View.

The scientific study of criminal psychology and pathology and of social conditions in relation to crime, combined with an enlarging sense of collective responsibility, has made the twentieth century thoroughly impatient of the results produced by the penal reforms of the nineteenth. The statistics of recidivism (i.e., the recurrence of convictions of the same person) demonstrate failure to reclaim the individual, whilst the inadequacy of deterrence is suggested by high premiums against burglary and larceny, by country roads infested with rogues and vagabonds, streets with prostitutes, drunkards and pickpockets, hotels and clubs with cardsharpers and "kleptomaniacs," and commercial centres with swindlers and embezzlers, most of whom never come within the reach of the law. It is scarcely needful to add that women suffer even more than men from this continuance of social insecurity.

Modern criminologists regard the attempt to combine aims so incompatible as deterrent punishment and a serious attempt to reform the criminal as the makeshift of a period of transition. The path of penal reform is seen to lie towards the prevention of crime by removal of causes, the classification of criminals for the purpose of dealing with them in the manner most for their own interest, as well as for the public good, the protection of society by the segregation, under beneficent conditions, of the insane, the deficient and the hopelessly anti-social, and the systematic effort to restore the erring to mental health by humane curative and educational treatment.

These proposals of reform are based on an alteration in our view of the incidence of personal responsibility, and the part played by the individual will in conduct. The old idea of penal as of educational discipline was to crush and break , the modern idea is to fortify and build up force of character. Kropotkin, writing twenty-two years ago of his own experience gained "In Russian and French Prisons,"* drew attention to weakness of will and a natural but misdirected desire for approbation, as common characteristics of criminals, whose show of dangerous anti-social energy is often a result of sheer desperation; and his opinion has been confirmed by our best English observers. The remedy indicated by modern thought lies in a development of the personal sense of responsibility for self-direction, which can only exist where scope is afforded for some freedom of action and oppor-

* Page 354.

tunity given for the exercise of bodily and mental powers. The old idea was that the collective force of society should be used to suppress the will and stultify the faculties of every person of whose activities custom or authority disapproved. The modern idea is that the collective force of society should be used to stimulate and support the exercise of individual will power under a sense of personal and social responsibility, and to make every effort to strengthen and restore it where it is enfeebled or lost, combined of course with opportunity for the free exercise in a useful and healthy direction of such powers as the individual may possess. In a word our present inclination towards a positive rather than a negative method for the solution of such social problems as destitution, ignorance or sickness is extending likewise to the treatment of crime.

Such changes would involve nothing less than the abolition of our present prison system, and the movement towards them is as yet but partial and tentative. Our judicial and administrative authorities are aware that the present state of things is by no means satisfactory, but they are still befogged by the idea of safeguarding us by means of punishment as a deterrent, if not as an expiation. They are still trying to reconcile this attitude with the partial adoption of methods likely to be effectual in forestalling crime by preventing its causes and in humanely reclaiming the criminal or gently rendering him innocuous. The two radically incompatible points of view clash at every step, and consequently our latest reforms tend to be halting, inadequate and self-contradictory. Nevertheless they are paths leading up to the coming change.

PART II.—PRISONS.

The prison being the main penal agency of recent times most men and women who come under our criminal law are to be found within its walls. Though the death penalty still stands on the statute book for offences other than murder, it is many years since it has been so applied. The present method of inflicting it is less cruel,* and even for murder there is a growing tendency to extend the limits of the mental irresponsibility or extenuating circumstances which permit incarceration to be substituted for hanging, e.g., in cases of maternal infanticide.†

The Prison System.

Solitary confinement as a part of imprisonment was first introduced by Sir James Graham as Home Secretary in 1842, with the intention that it should be accompanied by definite training. Till 1898 each long-sentence prisoner underwent this confinement, at first for eighteen and afterwards for nine months; it was then reduced to six months, and now to only one for those condemned to hard labor or penal servitude. In the case of women it is only

* A jerk causing instant death by breaking the neck is said to have been first tried as a substitute for slow suffocation by hanging in 1760.

† Three females were condemned to death during 1910-11, but in each case the sentence was commuted.—Report of the Commissioners of Prisons, Part I, p. 103.

undergone by convicts (New Rules, July, 1910). Silence is however insisted upon during associated labor and exercise. A prisoner is supposed to speak and to be spoken to only by officials, and then as little as possible.

Penal servitude was devised in 1853 as a substitute for transportation. It has been applied since 1891 to all prisoners (convicts) with sentences of three years and over. These convicts are employed in associated labor, the men in public works, in building, quarrying, farm work or trades ; the women in baking, bookbinding, sewing, knitting, tailoring, mattress making, twine making, gardening, cooking, washing, and general service for the prison. There is but one convict prison for women, that at Aylesbury. Only forty-two women convicts were admitted during 1910-11, of whom thirty-two are classified as " recidivists " and ten as " star " prisoners.* Solitary confinement takes place first in the local prison, in which those with shorter sentences spend their whole time.

Local prisons, in which far the larger number of women are confined, usually accommodate both men and women prisoners in different wards ; and, generally speaking, there is one prison to each county. A number of unsuitable local prisons were closed by the Prisons Acts of 1877 and 1898, but in many places there is still room for much improvement in sanitary and other arrangements.

The court, on passing a sentence of imprisonment without hard labor, may direct the prisoner to be treated as an offender of either the first or second division. In the absence of direction he or she is treated as a prisoner of the third or ordinary division, with or without " hard labor." The first division implies detention merely, the second penal discipline much mitigated. Besides short sentence prisoners in these three divisions, local prisons contain those sentenced to death, those awaiting trial, and those imprisoned for debt, all kept separately and under special rules. There is also a star class for first offenders of good previous character who are willing to give their respectable relations as references, which many refuse to do.

In local prisons a matron, and at Aylesbury a lady superintendent, has charge of the women's side. Since the revelations of the suffrage prisoners in 1908-9, a medical woman Inspector of Prisons has been appointed.

Hard labor for a man means labor in solitary confinement, but for a woman associated labor for the same length of time daily (six to ten hours excluding meals), unless the doctor objects, " regard being had to any advice or suggestions from the Visiting Committee or Discharged Prisoners Aid Society."

In both local and convict prisons there is a system of marks for industry and good conduct, whereby prisoners may earn remission of sentence and also various privileges attained by stated grades and a gratuity before discharge.

Convicts are classed in three categories :—

> A. Ordinary, including (1) star class, as in local prisons ; (2) intermediates i.e., other first offenders ; (3) recidivists.

* Report of the Commissioners of Prisons and Directors of Convict Prisons, 1910-11, p. 78.

B. Habitual offenders sentenced to preventive detention, who can earn privileges and also gratuities to spend in prison, but not remission of sentence.

C. Long sentence prisoners, who after serving ten years and earning all privileges ordinarily possible, may earn special privileges and gratuities, together with remission of sentence.

The prison staff consists of a governor, doctor, chaplain, and their assistants, and of warders. There are also nurses in the prison hospital, ministers and priests who visit Nonconformist and Roman Catholic prisoners, and skilled instructors. There is a visiting committee of local magistrates for local prisons, and a board of visitors appointed by the Home Secretary for convict prisons, also unofficial ladies' visiting committees and societies which aid discharged prisoners.

Prison regulations * are alike for men and women, with the exceptions here noted. Women prisoners are dealt with by female officers and a female officer accompanies any male official, even the governor, when he visits the women's quarters.

"The labor of all prisoners shall, if possible, be productive, and the trades and industries taught and carried on shall, if practicable, be such as shall fit the prisoner to earn his livelihood on release"; but "a prisoner may be employed in the service of the prison," and short sentence women are so employed, as technical instruction cannot usefully be given to them.

A man over 16 and under 60 condemned to hard labor sleeps on a plank bed without a mattress for the first fortnight, but a woman is allowed a mattress.

All non-technical instruction is under the control of the chaplain, and must include reading, writing and arithmetic, and religious exhortation, for which purpose the chaplain often visits the cells. The prison library consists of books sanctioned by the commissioners (in convict prisons by the directors). During the first month prisoners may only read books of instruction—religious and secular.

"Prisoners who do not do their best to profit by the instruction afforded them may be deprived of any privileges in the same way as if they had been idle or negligent at labor," or be punished according to the general rules. (Regulations in Cells, 1911.)

The main difference between men and women is in diet. All females are allowanced with juveniles. Males over 16 have larger rations.

Analysis of Dietary in Local Prisons.

Diet A. For all prisoners sentenced to less than four months, during the first seven days of imprisonment. Bread (men 8 oz., women 6 oz.) and gruel (1 pt.) daily for breakfast and supper. Dinner: Bread (men 8 oz., women 6 oz.) and porridge (1 pt.), or potatoes (8 oz.) or suet pudding (men 8 oz., women 6 oz.).

Diet B. After first seven days for whole term if not exceeding four months. Bread and gruel (same amounts as A) daily for breakfast and supper for women, porridge substituted for gruel for men's supper. Dinner: Bread (6 oz.) and potatoes (8 oz.) daily, together with soup (1 pt.), or cooked meat (men 4 oz., women 3 oz.), or suet pudding (men 10 oz., women 8 oz.) on two days a week each. Beans (men 10 oz., women 8 oz.) and fat bacon (men 2 oz., women 1 oz.) on the remaining day.

Diet C. After first four months for rest of term. Breakfast: Bread (8 oz.) and porridge (1 pt.) for men, bread (6 oz.) and tea (1 pt.) for women. Supper: Bread and cocoa in the same relative amounts. Dinner: As in Diet B, slightly larger quantities of potatoes, suet pudding, meat or beans being given.

Juvenile prisoners may, in addition to the above diet, be allowed milk, not exceeding one pint per diem, at the discretion of the medical officer, and one pint of porridge in lieu of tea for breakfast.

* The following particulars are taken from the "Prisons Rules for Local and Convict Prisons in England, issued 1898, and revised to December, 1903," compared with later administrative orders and the experiences of prisoners down to 1912.

The dietary for convicts is like C, but somewhat more varied, and sweet things are not excluded.

" The diet for special classes of prisoners, viz. :—(a) Prisoners on remand or awaiting trial who do not maintain themselves, (b) Offenders of the First Division who do not maintain themselves, (c) Offenders of the Second Division, (d) Debtors, shall be Diet B ; provided that they shall receive for breakfast one pint of tea in lieu of gruel, and for supper one pint of cocoa in lieu of porridge or gruel ; and that when detained in prison more than four months they shall receive C Diet at the expiration of the fourth month."*

Women, like men, are punished for offences against prison discipline by close confinement, by three days on bread and water, or a longer period on low diet in special cells on a plank bed. They may be put in irons but not flogged. Punishments are awarded by the governor or the visiting committee under strict regulations. Prisoners may make complaints to either of these authorities. If a prisoner takes advantage of the privilege, such boldness is said often to result in loss of marks or privileges.

A mother may keep with her an infant at the breast until it is nine to twelve months old.

Such in rough outline is the existing prison system as applied to both sexes.

The Prison System as it Appears to Those Immediately Concerned.

The Prison Commissioners every year issue a report which shows how seriously they take their responsibilities and how anxiously they endeavor to make the best of a system which they still look upon as inevitable. Prison officials whilst holding office are debarred from publishing their views, but on retirement inspectors, governors, doctors, matrons, and chaplains have done so. Their testimony is, intentionally or unintentionally, amongst the most damning evidence against things as they have been and still are.

" The working of prison systems, whether at home or abroad," says Dr. Morrison, late Chaplain at Wandsworth Prison, " teaches us that any person, be he child or man, who has once been in prison is much more likely to come back again than a person who, for a similar offence, has received punishment in a different form."— " Crime and its Cause."

The experience of prisoners themselves is necessarily rare and difficult to obtain. Very occasionally an unfortunate more able to express himself than most publishes such a book as " Five Years. Penal Servitude, by One who has Experienced It." Amongst these the splendid and terrible " De Profundis " and " Ballad of Reading Gaol " of Oscar Wilde stand alone. Occasionally a political prisoner like Michael Davitt publishes a thoughtful appreciation of what he has observed. When anyone who has experienced imprisonment does speak it is to condemn the system.

" Penal servitude," said Michael Davitt in 1885 (" Leaves from a Prison Diary ") " has become so elaborate that it is now a huge punishing machine destitute, through centralized control and responsibility, of discrimination, feeling, and sensitiveness ; and its non-success as a deterrent from crime and complete failure in reformative effect upon criminal character are owing to its obvious essential tendency to deal with erring human beings, who are still men despite their crimes, in a manner which mechanically reduces them to a uniform level of disciplined brutes."

* Ibid.

Women in Holloway.

Since Elizabeth Fry described the "hell above ground" at Newgate few women have written of prison from close personal observation. No female prisoner recorded her experiences until suffragists in large numbers were sent to Holloway (1907-11). Their criticisms are therefore worthy of careful consideration even on that ground alone. The letters or statements of twelve women are here quoted. All are first hand and carefully verified.

First Experiences Summarized.

Received into prison from the van the prisoners are stripped, deprived of all personal possessions, even a name—henceforth they are known by number only—bathed, and dressed in prison clothes, each one wearing clothes exactly similar to those of every other female prisoner of the same division. The three classes wear clothing of different color and texture. The dress has been very much improved during the last two years by the woman Inspector of Prisons. Until 1910 the outfit was that in use by the working classes of 1860, but it is now chosen with a view to hygiene and to the individual needs of the prisoners. A cloak is provided, which may be kept in the cell as an additional wrap. One handkerchief (a duster) is allowed each week, and only one towel is provided.

Daily Routine.

Called at 5.30-6 a.m. Breakfast, about 7 (one rarely knows the exact time). Chapel, 8.30. Associated labor (under skilled instructors for long sentence prisoners). Exercise (about one hour). Dinner, about 12 o'clock. Associated labor. Supper, 5 p.m.

The cell door is then closed for the night and, except in the case of serious illness, is not allowed to be opened again until the next morning. The prisoner may read until the light is turned out (about 8.30), or may go to bed directly she has eaten her supper. All prison work has been taken from her and she is allowed to do no work for herself, nor are mothers with infants allowed to make the baby's clothes.

Between rising and chapel the bed has to be made, the cell scrubbed, and all tin utensils polished. Associated labor under instruction includes needlework, dressmaking, laundry work, or gardening. The rule of absolute silence is in force the whole day. When out at exercise the prisoner must walk all the time, to stand still or to sit down is not allowed. On Sunday the prisoner attends chapel twice and, unless she is allowed out for exercise, is confined to her cell the rest of the day, no work being done.

Food and Hygiene.

"The food may be sufficient to ward off the actual pangs of hunger, but the monotony of the diet amounts, after a time, to positive torture."

"The food is scanty, the ventilation totally inadequate; the result is to make prisoners dull and stupid, unfit to earn their living when they come out, yet the reason that many are there at all is chiefly from their inability to earn an honest living."

"The food of third division prisoners consists of gruel of no flavor whatever, and of the consistency of paste, and coarse brown bread. This is served at 7 a.m. and 5 p.m. At mid-day meat and potatoes are served. I believe the food allowances are worked out so that if they are all consumed a sufficient quantity of the various necessary foodstuffs is taken. But it is now generally admitted that food consumed with a sense of distaste cannot be assimilated, and the bad air and lack of exercise, and the fact that the meals are taken alone, naturally reduce the prisoners' appetites so that they cannot eat the uninviting food, or if they do so, it is of little use to them. Moreover the bread is so hard and dry and is so irritating to the stomach as frequently to set up gastric disorders, so that few of the women can eat half the amount supplied. Therefore it will be readily seen that the women are habitually underfed, their vitality is low, and they are an easy prey to all diseases."

Many other prisoners speak of the prevalence of diarrhœa, which is very weakening, and, with prison conditions, is most inconvenient and distressing in every way. The "convenience" supplied in the cell is totally inadequate, and even if it be of a proper size and does not leak, the fact that it remains unemptied from evening till morning is, in case of illness especially, very insanitary and dangerous to health. "Lavatory time" is permitted only at a fixed hour twice a day, only one water-closet being provided for twenty-three cells.

"I slept in one of the ordinary cells, which have sliding panes, leaving at the best two openings about six inches square. The windows are set in the wall high up, and are 3 by 1½ or 2 feet area. Added to this they are very dirty, so that the light in the cell is always dim. After the prisoner has been locked in the cell all night the air is unbearable, and its unhealthiness is increased by damp. The cells are washed at six in the morning, and the corridors are washed at the same time. In spite of the fact that any adequate through ventilation is impossible, owing to the height of the windows and the small area that opens, the prisoners are locked into the cells again at seven for breakfast, so that they sit in a wet cell and are forced to breathe the evaporating moisture which cannot escape. A great number of the prisoners suffer from chronic catarrh, and anyone with a tendency to consumption could hardly fail to contract the disease." *

In this connection it must be borne in mind that when mental and physical vitality are at a low ebb and impressions from without few and monotonous, the physical facts of existence loom gigantic in the mind and physical discomfort may cause mental agony, especially if the suffering is inflicted by others against whose will the victim has no appeal. Enforced privations produce exactly the opposite of the spiritual uplifting, sometimes a result of voluntary asceticism.

DISCIPLINE AND ITS EFFECTS.

A matter on which the suffrage prisoners lay much stress is the inhuman way in which the wardresses address the prisoners, and the lack of all human intercourse between them. This was explained by an official in the prison service as being necessary in order to avoid any possibility of favoritism, and to avoid jealousy among the prisoners. To maintain order among such a heterogeneous collection of rebels as a crowd of prisoners, it is found necessary to accustom them to obey a sharp word of command.

"The prison system is not calculated to reform criminals. It induces deceit above all things—the rule of silence being one that everybody breaks whenever possible. It reduces people to mere numbered machines, thus doing away with any sense of personal responsibility. It suppresses all initiative and undermines all self-reliance, whereas I take it that the desirable thing is to build up a sense of self-reliance

* Next to heart disease the most frequent causes of deaths in prison are pneumonia and phthisis.—Medical Report of Commissioners, 1910-11, Part I., p. 40.

and respect, and to encourage people to have a stronger sense of individual responsibility towards the rest of mankind."

" The whole system is one to destroy anyone's self-respect and moral control."

" I observed the gradual hardening of certain of the prisoners who were quite obviously full of grief and shame on arrival. . . . . The principal effect of the prison system as it now exists seems to me to be the destruction of self-respect and initiative. I believe many of the wardresses who come into closer contact with the prisoners than any of the other officials, take what opportunity they find of urging the women to a better way of life, but since the system works in the other direction, their influence cannot be very great. The wardresses are as much prisoners as we are."

" To be continually in disgrace ; to never hear a kindly tone or a word of encouragement, is sufficient to crush those who are already weak, and who have fallen in the battle of life. . . . . There is an atmosphere of fear and suspicion throughout a prison that weakens the character and engenders deceit."

" Every endeavor is made to render the life dull, monotonous and dreary ; all the surroundings are as hideous as human ingenuity can make them, the food unappetizing, and the whole tone brutalizing and hardening."

PUNISHMENTS.

" When you are put into the punishment cell you feel as if you were absolutely cut off from the rest of the world, the echoes of footsteps along the stone corridors, the banging and locking of doors become so magnified as to have a gruesome and horrible effect on your nerves."

" Hour after hour, day after day (seven days) I spent sitting on the wooden bed, doing nothing, hardly thinking, staring into vacancy. I could well imagine the loneliness, silence (for two doors close this cell), darkness and cold, sending women mad. The horror of it is still with me, and night after night, unable to sleep, I go through it all again. . . . . I tried walking about to obtain exercise, but the cell echoed so weirdly and horribly I was obliged to desist."

This prisoner was in " close confinement," i.e., no exercise, chapel, or anything that takes a prisoner out of her cell is permitted.

" The punishment cell is longer and higher, though not so wide as the ordinary cell. . . . . The furniture consisted of two shelves in one corner, a wooden bed three inches high with wooden pillow, also fixed into the ground, with the top and one side against the wall, and a tree trunk clamped into the wall was the only seat. A few tin utensils, every one of which leaked. . . . . The cell was damp, and any water spilt took days to dry up."

Most prisoners complain of want of ventilation, especially in punishment cells, but one says :—

" The punishment cell is bitterly cold and very draughty. And all punishment cells are very dark, light only shining in on bright days, and in the middle of the day."

Handcuffs, another form of punishment, are described as

" A brutal torture, especially when placed behind, as the arms have to be forced back and twisted before they can be fastened, and they are fastened in such a manner as to give cramp ; after a time your arms are dead and numb."

As to the infliction of punishments the same prisoner says :—

" The way the punishments are dealt out by the visiting magistrates is really too callous. The sentences, you know, are already arranged before they have heard your side of the question "

Punishments may be given for not completing the task set. In undetected cases of incipient insanity or imbecility, the effect of such punishment is too hideous to contemplate.

What wonder then that the women who go to prison become hardened criminals, and that the problem of the female recidivist haunts the brains of the conscientious commissioner ?

The root of the matter seems to be that there is no attempt at individual treatment, and no effort to draw out the best that is in each prisoner. Goodness, kindness, humanity are crushed out by the deadening life. The high grim walls, the iron bars, the hard bed, and all the bare surroundings are but outward signs of the essential fact of the absence of love and beauty. In the piteous words of the " Ballad of Reading Gaol " :—

> " For neither milk-white rose nor red
> May bloom in prison air ;
> The shard, the pebble and the flint,
> Are what they give us there :
> For flowers have been known to heal
> A common man's despair."

PART III.—CRIMINALS AND CRIME.

I.—Relative Statistics for Men and Women.*

According to the last Annual Report of the Prison Commissioners the number of prisoners received under sentence in His Majesty's Prisons amounted to 186,395 during the year, a decrease of 13,870 from the year before (p. 4). Some of these moreover were committed several times during the year, so that this total is in excess of the actual number of fresh offenders received. The total numbers in custody during the year were 194,037 males and 42,581 females in local prisons, and 4,559 males and 164 females in convict prisons (p. 29).

AVERAGE DAILY POPULATION OF PRISONS, 1910-11 (p. 5).

	Males.	Females.	Total.
Local	14,596	2,386	16,982
Convict	3,195	114	3,309
Borstal	508	27	535
State Inebriate Reformatories ...	24	54	78

Note that the number of women prisoners is very much smaller than that of the men. Nevertheless records of recidivism show that of the males a percentage of 58·8 only had been previously convicted and as many as 77·2 of the females (p. 17).

These figures seem to lead to the following conclusions :—Either (a) Crime among women, while confined to a much smaller class than among men, proceeds from an ineradicably unmoral nature ; in other words, those women who commit crimes are much worse morally and therefore less reclaimable than men criminals ; or (b) Prison treatment is better suited to men than to women, reforming a percentage of 41·2 of them, while only 22·8 of the women are deterred from committing further breaches of the law ; or (c) Owing to the state of public opinion imprisonment affects the future social and economic life of women more adversely than that of men, and further crime results from bad company, poverty and despair.

* Reference, unless otherwise stated, is to " The Report of the Commissioners of Prisons and the Directors of Convict Prisons for the year ended March, 1911," Part I.

The period of detention and the method of treatment naturally affect the whole question.

PERIODS OF DETENTION IN LOCAL PRISONS.*

The total number of prisoners committed to local prisons from ordinary courts during 1910-11 was 166,230. (Males 130,350, females 35,880.) The length of sentences was as follows :—

	Males.	Females.
Over 2 years	3	0
Over 18 months and under 2 years (inclusive) ...	235	11
Over 12 months and under 18 months ,, ...	1,044	33
Over 3 months and under 12 months ,, ...	7,967	1,143
Over 1 week and under 3 months ,, ...	74,896	21,606
1 week and under	46,205	13,087

Thus it will be seen that while the majority of prisoners of both sexes are convicted for three months or less, the average length of sentence is even shorter for women than for men, and only 44 women out of 35,880 were convicted for twelve months during the year.

The Prison Commissioners† give a "typical case" of a girl of 20 committed for a month or less thirteen times in two years for prostitution, vagrancy or indecency. The Lady Inspector says of such cases "a stream of bright, childish girls passes in and out of the prisons many of whom are in the power of older and worse people than themselves. . . . In spite of their dreadful experiences they do not differ greatly in (natural) mental and physical development from the better class girls who are growing happily at school and hockey-field while they are qualifying as prison habituals." Their stunted minds, she continues, are gradually perverted, enfeebled or unhinged unless they can be removed from the influences that are destroying them, but short sentences for purposes of educational treatment are well-nigh useless.

AGES OF CONVICTED CRIMINAL PRISONERS COMMITTED TO LOCAL PRISONS ON CONVICTION DURING THE YEAR ENDED MARCH, 1911.

	Male.	Per centage of total.	Female.	Per centage of total.
Under 12	—	—	—	—
12 to 16	32	—	2	—
16 to 21	10,380	7·0	1,163	3·2
21 to 30	36,555	27.7	7,831	21·8
30 to 40	36,626	27·8	12,569	35·0
All ages	131,746	—	35,949	—

The question of the age incidence of crime is important. It appears from these statistics and others that the age incidence is higher in women than in men. The proportion of youths to girls under 20 is about nine to one, the number of men between the ages of 20 and 40 are much the same, but far the largest proportion of women criminals are aged from 30 to 40. (Appendix V, p. 67).

* Ibid, p. 64.
† Ibid, pp. 11 and 34-6.

DIFFERENCES IN THE NATURE OF CRIME.[*]

		Convictions on Indictment.	Summary Convictions and in default of Sureties.	Total.
(a) Offences against the person (murder, wounding, cruelty, including cruelty to and neglect of children, assault and immoral offences)	Males 939	9,067	10,003
	Females 84	1,877	1,961
(b) Offences against property with violence (burglary, robbery, etc.)	Males 2,475	—	2,475
	Females 36	—	36
(c) Offences against property without violence (chiefly larceny, stealing and fraud, including forgery)	Males 4,626	16,234	20,858
	Females 412	2,575	2,987

The above table gives the figures for the three main divisions of serious crime. The most noticeable fact in it is the comparative rarity of crimes of violence among women; except for cruelty to children, including neglect,[†] the proportion is markedly less than amongst men. It may also be taken as a certainty that there is a much smaller skilled professional criminal class among women than among men. There are few professional criminals in class (a); probably the largest number, chiefly men, belong to class (b).

A barrister tells us that in his many years' experience at the criminal bar, practically all women convicted of indictable offences are (1) prostitutes or (2) married women convicted of neglecting their children through drink, or (3) domestic servants who have succumbed to their peculiar facilities for stealing clothing or jewellery; usually girls in poor households and themselves physically and mentally below par. Of these three categories prostitutes are immensely the largest, from 85 to 90 per cent. of the whole. "It would be almost true to say that indictable crime among women is confined to women who are prostitutes. This is, I fancy, the main explanation of the greater irreclaimability of women criminals."

It is interesting to compare these facts with those of the older system before penal servitude took the place of transportation for long sentence prisoners. From 1787 to 1837, 43,506 men and 6,791 women were transported to New South Wales, and 24,785 men and 2,974 women to Van Dieman's Land from 1817 to 1837. The largest consignment in any one year occurred in 1833, when 2,310 men and 420 women were sent to New South Wales, and 1,576 men and 245 women to Van Dieman's Land. The evidence before the Select Committee[‡] stigmatized the conduct of the women convicts as being "as bad as anything could well be." They were "ferocious," "drunken and abandoned prostitutes," "more irreformable than male convicts." When assigned as servants "from negligence they turn to pilfering, from pilfering generally follows drunkenness, and from drunkenness generally debauchery, and it is very rare indeed,

---

[*] Statistics brought together from same Report, Tables pp. 104-7.

[†] During 1910-11, males convicted summarily and otherwise for cruelty to children 870, females 675. Compare proportion with that for common assault, males 4,416, females 821. Ibid.

[‡] From "Report from the Select Committee on Transportation communicated by the Commons to the Lords, 1838."

that a woman remains a few months in service before she goes to the factory for punishment." " The proportion of women reformed is much smaller than amongst men," but " those who have good mistresses turn out well." In some places convict women servants could only obtain some sort of protection from brutal ill-usage by prostituting themselves. (Evidence of Rev. Dr. Ullathorne, Vicar-General of New Holland). Women convicts "contaminated all around them, and it was impossible to reform them," " they are so bad that settlers have no heart to treat them well," nevertheless, marriage sometimes reformed them. (Evidence of P. Murdock, Superintendent of Emu. Plains).

The comparison of these observations upon the results of a bygone method with observations upon the methods of to-day seems to indicate that whilst women are less likely to become criminals, they react still more disastrously than men under penal severity ; also that there is an intimate connection between prostitution and crime amongst women.

II.—Causes of Crime.

It must be borne in mind that "crime" is an arbitrary legal term. "There is an enormous mass of so called crime in England which is not crime at all. . . . Eighty-three per cent. of the annual convictions, summarily and on indictment, followed by committal to gaol, are for misconduct that is distinctly non-criminal, such as breaches of municipal byelaws and police regulations, drunkenness, gaming, and offences under Vagrancy Acts ";* also the peculiarly feminine offence of prostitution.†

The large proportion of brief sentences (p. 14 infra) are in themselves enough to indicate the triviality of the offences, and, as Major Griffiths says, " the question will arise some day whether it is really necessary to maintain fifty-six local prisons, with all their elaborate paraphernalia, their imposing buildings, and expensive staff to maintain discipline in daily life and insist upon the proper observation of customs and usages, many of them of purely modern invention." He might have added "or of dubious social value." We have nearly always some men and women in our prisons who are there for zeal in social reform or individual experiment distasteful to custom or to the powers that be, though the future may regard it as harmless or even acclaim it as beneficial.

* Major A. G. F. Griffiths, H.M. Inspector of Prisons 1878-96, article "Prisons," Encyclopædia Britannica. For Major Griffiths's larger works see Bibliography. Compare Kirkman Gray, " Philanthropy and the State," pp. 161-4.

† 8,642 women were sent to local prisons for this offence during the year March 1910-11 ; 6,013 of them in default of fine. During the same year out of the 123,172 males and 35,378 females received into local prisons, 3,614 males and 149 females were sentenced as disorderly paupers, 2,115 males and 134 females for neglect to maintain a family, and 926 males and 44 females for stealing or destroying workhouse clothes and other offences against the Poor Law. Under the Vagrancy Acts 20,988 males and 1,061 females were sentenced for begging, and 5,087 males and 381 females for sleeping out of doors. During this year altogether 60,386 males and 24,499 females were imprisoned simply in default of payment of fine, and 17,437 as debtors or under civil process. 910 males and one female were committed under the Game Laws. Report of Commissioners of Prisons, Part I., pp. 28, 109-10.

Turning to crimes of more serious character, one of the most important determining causes appears to be mental disease or deficiency. Besides the considerable number of criminals certified insane before conviction there is an even larger proportion found to be insane on reception in prison or at some period during imprisonment.

The Report of the Medical Inspector for 1910-11[*] gives the number of prisoners certified insane in local prisons during the year as 136, of whom 121 were males and 15 females.

We select the following as typical cases :—[†]

Age.	Degree of Education, Standard.	Occupation and Offence.	Sentence.	Supposed Cause.
27	I	Servant, neglecting children.	3 months hard labor.	Recurrent melancholia (puerperal) due to trouble.
35	Nil	Rag Sorter. Drunk and Disorderly.	1 month hard labor.	Melancholia, due to intemperance.
28	IV	Dressmaker. Prostitution.	1 month imprisonment.	Insane on admission. Melancholia, due to stress.
29	Imperfect	Laundress. Burglary	3 years penal servitude.	Recurrent mania, probably congenital.

Congenital mental deficiency appears in the statistical table as the main cause of insanity leading to crime. Other causes appearing with regularity are alcoholism, epilepsy and syphilis. Among criminologists hereditary predisposition is also generally accepted as an operative cause.

The congenitally feeble-minded form a much larger proportion of the prison population than actual lunatics. During 1910-11 "the number of prisoners formally recognized as being so feeble-minded as to be unfit for the ordinary penal discipline was 359 in local prisons and in convict prisons 120."[‡]

In this class must also be included the moral imbeciles, chiefly congenital. Here is a typical instance :—[§]

No. 1191, aged 27, education imperfect, a hawker, who committed an indecent assault, sentenced to three months hard labor, was found on reception to be of "unsound mind" in the form of "congenital mental deficiency, moral," from "congenital syphilis."

Again, there are a certain number of mentally unusual persons, possibly of exceptionally brilliant gifts, who need special conditions to develop healthily, and not obtaining them may become criminals. Add to these, and to the mentally unsound and deficient, all those normal persons who are goaded or led into crime as a result of preventible social causes, such as extreme poverty, or negligence and misusage in youth, and a very small proportion of our criminal population remains to be accounted for as individuals by nature so anti-social as to be a perennial danger to their fellow men. ‖

[*] Ibid, pp. 28, 42.
[†] Ibid, Appendix 18, Table D. pp. 130-143.
[‡] Ibid, p. 28.
[§] Ibid, pp. 132-3.
‖ As an example of such take the poisoner Palmer, as described by Sir James Fitzjames Stephen in "A General View of the Criminal Law of England," p. 272.

PART IV.—PATHS OF CHANGE.

It is abundantly evident that the causes of crime above indicated have their root deep in our existing social organization. Any adequate preventive measures must be inextricably bound up with such wide issues as security of employment, a living wage, housing and sanitation, and national responsibility for the nurture and training of youth, for the care of the feeble and sick in body and mind, and for the prevention of destitution.

Furthermore, the difficulties created by existing law are, as the Prison Commissioners observe, "well-nigh insuperable." Our Common Law is an obscure tangle of custom and precedent ; our confused mass of Statutes, Bye-laws and Regulations, sometimes actually provocative in character, is bewildering to the most astute of lawyers, and incomprehensible to the plain citizen.

These large issues can be but alluded to here, gravely as they affect the causes of crime. We pass to the attempts now being made to transform the penal system itself from a mechanism aiding and abetting the manufacture of criminals, into an agency for the prevention of crime and the reclamation of the erring.

A burning question of the moment is the length of sentences. If crime is to be prevented by effectively segregating or reforming criminals they must be put, and kept for some considerable time, under skilled care and supervision, directly they first begin to go wrong ; but to inflict long sentences of punitive imprisonment for trivial offences is sheer cruelty. Here lies the crux, and the nation for the nonce is Mr. Facing-both-ways. Nevertheless many changes now in progress are heading straight for the transformation of definite terms of rigorous imprisonment apportioned to the heinousness of the offence into indeterminate terms of humane institutional or external treatment apportioned to the needs of the offender. Such changes fall mainly into two divisions. (I) Further classification and correlative specialized treatment, accompanied by mitigation of the hardships of imprisonment in general. (II) Improvements in official administration.

I.—Classification and Special Treatment.

THE PROBATION SYSTEM.

The probation system, "a system of liberty under supervision," originated in Massachusetts, U.S.A., about 1880, for children, and has now been adopted in at least nineteen of the States. It was recommended strongly at the Prison Congress at Buda Pest, September, 1905, and by the Probation of Offenders Act (1907) came into force in England, January, 1908. By this Act an offender may be discharged, and enter into recognizances to be of good behavior, being liable to be called upon for conviction and sentence at any time during the next three years.

The system properly worked is primarily educational rather than punitive. It is an elastic combination of officialism and philanthropy, and therefore depends for its success mainly on efficient administration. The offender is usually placed by the magistrates under the control of a specified probation officer, who has to be obeyed, who may make compulsory regulations, and who reports monthly to the magistrate. In America, in places where it is worked to great perfection, 70 to 90 per cent. of successes are claimed for the system.

It appears from the criminal statistics for the year 1909 that 8,962 persons in England and Wales were put on probation under the Act, of whom only 624 had subsequently to appear for sentence. Of these 133 were discharged, and only 184 were ultimately sentenced to imprisonment, the others (307) being variously dealt with—in many cases sent to homes or reformatories. Of the total number placed on probation 6,862 were males and 2,100 females. Amongst the females 394 were less than 16 years old, 665 between 16 and 21, and 1,041 above that age.*

In its main idea the probation system is almost a return to the law of Anglo-Saxon England, in many ways superior to our own, where the community, i.e., the hundred or the kindred was held responsible for the good behavior of the individual. Modern society is too complicated for an exact return to this idea, but under the Probation Act the community deputes its duties to its representative, i.e., to the probation officer, because that is the best way in which, as a society, it can fulfil its duty to the unfit. And the probation officer who understands the duties of the office will see that the family, i.e. the parents or guardians are made to fulfil their duties. In the case of young offenders the parents quite as much as the children are "put on probation." Working through the family and the home this system gives the unfortunate a strong friend from outside who can often provide education and training and employment. It is better than prison from the economic as well as from the humane point of view, for the offender is not removed from work in the outside world, so need not be maintained by the State, nor is the wage earner's family thrown upon the Poor Law. There is no criminal taint, no loss of status, no association with other offenders ; on the contrary in the most successful cases the whole tone of the home is raised. The system aims at making both the unit and the family more useful to society.

To do all this successfully the probation officers must be experienced men and women with insight and tact. They must combine force of character and firmness with gentleness and sympathy. In London existing agencies, such as Mr. Wheatley's St. Giles's Christian Mission, the Police Court Mission of the Church of England Temperance Society, and the Church and Salvation Armies, undertake the greater part of the probation work, in which, on the whole, they seem to have great success. There is, however, room for development and improvement in the system, especially in two directions :—

    (a) Pressure brought to bear on magistrates, especially in country districts, to make use of the Act and, except for the very gravest offences, to refrain entirely from sending to prison any person under twenty-one, or any first offender.

* Criminal Statistics for 1909, pp. 166, 167, Table 4, III.

(b) Improvement in the training, salary, and status generally of the probation officer, and the appointment of a larger proportion of women.

It seems possible in the future that an increasing number of men and women with a wide outlook and greater culture may find in this work their true vocation. In the United States of America it is often taken up by settlement workers.

REFORMATORY AND INDUSTRIAL SCHOOLS.

When all possible use has been made of the probation system, there will still remain a certain number of boys and girls who are homeless or "incorrigibles." Such children are now sent to industrial schools and reformatories. By the Children Act of 1908 reformatory is to be preferred to prison for all young persons (fourteen to sixteen years), no child under fourteen is to be sent to penal servitude, and sentence of death may not be pronounced on anyone under sixteen. Practically, therefore, imprisonment is abolished for all girls under sixteen, and for juvenile adults (sixteen to twenty-one) the Borstal system is now in force.

BORSTAL SYSTEM.

Amongst the 10,380 male and 1,163 female juvenile adults convicted during the year 1910-11, 489 males and 35 females were selected for treatment in Borstal institutions.[*]

The system is so called from the village of Borstal, near Rochester, where the primary institution stands. The ruling principle is training—physical, mental, and manual. Much use is made of physical drill, of work in the open air, of lectures, of music, instruction in skilled trades, and education generally, and of progress from grade to grade. The upper grade, "Blues," dine in a large hall, sleep on spring mattresses in dormitories, and play cricket or football on Saturday afternoon. The food, though plain, is plentiful, and apparently appetizing. There is nothing degrading in the routine ; on the contrary, everything is uplifting. The inmates do not show the same recidivist tendency as ordinary prisoners because they have been taught to desire "something better." The Governor of Borstal reports 82 per cent. of his boys as satisfactory, and of the 303 youths discharged last year only 13 have been reconvicted. Since July, 1909, this institution has ceased to rank as a prison, and four similar institutions for youths have been opened, as well as one at Aylesbury for girls. They are not meant for first offenders, but to reclaim young people of really bad character. Those in Borstal last year averaged about three previous convictions apiece.[†]

OFFENCES OF BORSTAL INMATES, 1910-11.

	Males.	Females.
Against persons	11	1
Against property with violence	219	—
Against property without violence	214	—
Malicious injury to property	6	1
Other offences	9	33

[*] Report of Prison Commissioners, Part I., 1910-11, p. 24.
[†] Ibid., Part II., p. 192.

Sentences of twelve months are insufficient to reclaim young hooligans who on arrival are practically below the normal, physically and mentally. Sometimes it takes eighteen months to make any impression. "There are many boys here whose wits are dulled by neglect and bad treatment, and this is the first time they have experienced a combination of kindness and discipline." * Two years is the minimum useful sentence, and three is far better ; but last year 150 of the Borstal boys were sent for less than two years. The Medical Officer is more and more struck by "the importance of physical unfitness as a determining factor" in the downfall of these youths.† The feeble minded or incorrigibly vicious are not retained in Borstal institutions.

AYLESBURY BORSTAL FOR GIRLS, 1910-11. (STARTED IN AUGUST, 1909).

In custody at the beginning of the year	...	...	...	...	23
Received during the year	...	...	...	...	35
Recommitted (forfeiture of licence) ...	...	...	...	•••	2
			Total	...	60
Released during the year ...	...	...	...	...	34

Average age 18 years and 7 months. Education—12 had reached Standard IV, and two Standard VII at school. None were wholly illiterate. (The majority of Borstal youths had been in Standards II. and III).

Employment : 11 needlework, 8 cleaners and jobbers in and about the prison, 7 gardeners. It is hoped to add training in laundry work and cooking. The Borstal girls like hard manual labor better than sewing, and "it is surprising to see the vigor they put into rough work. They are full of energy and apparently tireless." They enjoy drill and gardening, and the medical officer notes the marked effect of physical exercise in improving not only the physique and carriage, but "mentally their power of attention and concentration." The chaplain has been teaching history, geography and other general subjects, and finds the girls "quicker and more elastic mentally," "with much improved powers of observation and thought."

"A minimum of three years is needed to eradicate bad habits of want of self-control and inconsequence caused by years of bad environment," but only five of the girls were committed for this period, and 12 of them for less than one year."‡

MODIFIED BORSTAL RULES IN LOCAL PRISONS.

This experiment began in 1900, and by the Prevention of Crimes Act (1908) all juvenile adults (16-25 years in this case), except those sentenced to less than one month or more than three years, are dealt with, as far as possible, on Borstal lines under the superintendence of a Special Borstal Committee. Those sentenced to more than four months are sent to special collecting centres. During 1910-11 there were 1,810 juvenile adults treated under modified Borstal rules in local prisons, and of the 651 discharged from special centres, 56 per

* Ibid., Part II., p. 200, from Report of Governor of Feltham Borstal Institution.
† Ibid., Part II.
‡ Ibid, Part II, pp. 188-90, Report of Officers of Aylesbury Borstal.

cent. are known to be doing well, and only 8 per cent. are known to have been re-convicted.*

PRISONERS AID AND AFTER-CARE ASSOCIATIONS.

Under the Borstal system every case is carefully followed up after leaving the institution by the Borstal Association. There are also voluntary committees, certified by the Home Office, for prisoners' aid at most local and convict prisons. A sum of £7,500 was recently assigned by the Chancellor of the Exchequer for the development of this work in relation to convicts, and since April, 1911, after care for them has been undertaken by one central agency called the " Central Association for the Aid of Discharged Convicts," which repres the Government and various Prisoners' Aid Societies, including the Church and Salvation Armies, and the Borstal Association.† It will henceforth exercise supervision over the discharged convict. The hated ticket-of-leave system is abolished. A prisoner who has earned a licence which entitles him or her to remission of sentence, is removed from all connection with the police, as long as he or she behaves properly. The Central Association has been at work too short a time for any result to be chronicled, but it should be remembered that the work of obtaining employment, lodging, etc., for discharged prisoners, and giving them encouragement to make a new start is quite as important as that of the probation officer. In this work women are taking a large share.

PREVENTIVE DETENTION.

The habitual criminals who, under the Prevention of Crime Act, 1908, constitute the special convict class (B) should rather be termed " professionals." The special treatment was intended for those " competent, often highly skilled persons who deliberately, with their eyes open, preferred a life of crime and knew all the tricks and turns and manœuvres necessary for that life." By the new rules (February, 1911) the criminal presented by the police to the Director of Public Prosecutions for preventive detention, must be over thirty years of age, have already undergone a term of penal servitude and be charged anew with a substantial and serious offence. Convicts under preventive detention cannot earn a licence for any remission of sentence, but must serve their whole time. Instead they earn special privileges in prison, where they are kept under separate rules. Since the Act came into operation 250 males and 3 females have been received in this class.‡

The experiment is of great interest to criminologists and penal reformers. It is a test of the curative effect upon healthy but anti-social persons of prolonged segregation, and also of segregation under conditions deliberately intended not to produce suffering, but to reform.

The Home Office has also recently been endeavoring to mitigate the suffering of imprisonment for convicts in general. The monotony

* Ibid, Part I, p. 25.
† Ibid, Part I, pp. 100-1.
‡ Ibid, pp. 113-6.

for long sentence prisoners is relieved by periodical lectures and concerts. The Commissioners in their latest report mention with gratification the pleasure (Oh, shades of our grandparents !) which the convicts take in these entertainments. Aged convicts have been placed in a special class and allowed some comforts.

INEBRIATES.

" Over one-half of the women and nearly one-third of the men sentenced to imprisonment in this country are committed for drunkenness, and repeated convictions in both cases, and especially in the case of women, constitute one of the saddest and most unprofitable features of prison administration."* The Inebriates Act of 1908 was an attempt to separate habitual drunkards from other offenders for curative treatment. It provided for the establishment of two classes of institutions, certified reformatories and state reformatories. Any person convicted of drunkenness four times in one year may be detained in one of these institutions for a period not exceeding three years. Those with a three years sentence are usually liberated at the expiration of two years and two months, and if they break out again are sent back to finish the remaining ten months.

The scheme as hitherto administered has turned out a costly failure. The cures are few, the drawbacks many. A woman, for instance, may be liberated to find her home broken up and herself alone and adrift. Two cases were reported recently of women who within three months of their discharge from an inebriate reformatory were re-committed in a state of pregnancy and remained comfortably housed until after confinement, when they were once more allowed to depart, their fatherless babies being sent to a children's home. Such a system is obviously faulty both from the moral and economic point of view, and many magistrates are refusing to make further use of inebriate reformatories. The state reformatories at Warwick (men) and Aylesbury (women) were intended for drunkards convicted of other crimes but have become scrap-heaps for the "weak-minded, degraded, and more or less irresponsible" persons found unmanageable in certified reformatories. The Medical Inspector of Prisons has some grave words to say of the danger to society of losing all hold over these unfortunates "simply because a sentence happens to have expired."† The period of detention in such cases should be indeterminate, and the inebriate on release should be placed in the charge of a probation officer. Mental deficients should not be classified or treated with inebriates, but permanently segregated with those afflicted in like manner.

Alcoholism is pre-eminently a "crime" that can only be effectually checked amongst the poor, as it has been amongst the rich, by a change both in conditions and in opinion. Imprisonment is worse than useless as deterrent or cure. So are fines as at present levied upon family necessities rather than upon the offender's drink money.

* Report of Prison Commissioners, 1908-9, Part I.
† Report of Prison Commissioners, 1910-11, Part I., p. 57.

Possibly home treatment under the care of a probation officer, combined in some cases with compulsory work or physical drill, might give the best chance of reformation to many delinquents in their noviciate.

THE MENTALLY UNSOUND.

About 400 feeble-minded prisoners are received by local prisons each year. " For the last four or five years a record has been kept of their convictions, etc., and there are now nearly a thousand individuals on this register," writes the Medical Inspector of Prisons, in his report for 1909-10. In 1910-11 he says " the distressing feature of conviction and re-conviction of weak-minded prisoners shows no abatement "; and the Commissioners again urge their removal from prison to special institutions under medical care.

An attempt is being made to segregate males of unsound mind (not certified lunatics), sentenced to penal servitude, at Parkhurst Convict Prison, and to study them carefully. The medical officer reports 120 convicts classified as weak-minded, and 27 others under observation. The following extracts from his report need no comment.

Classification of 120 weak-minded convicts : — Congenital deficiency with epilepsy 10, without epilepsy 36, imperfectly developed stage of insanity 26, mental debility after attack of insanity 13, senility 3, alcoholic 9, undefined 23.

List of crimes for which they have been sentenced to penal servitude :—False pretences 1, receiving stolen property 2, larceny 24, burglary 13, housebreaking 19, blackmailing 1, manslaughter 5, doing grievous bodily harm 2, wounding 7, shooting 3, wilful murder 10, rape 2, carnal knowledge of little children 8, arson 17, horse stealing 3, killing sheep 1, obstruction on railways 1, unnatural offence 1.

Of these 62 committed their first crime before the age of 20, and the total number of convictions against the whole 120 feeble-minded convicts amounts to 91 penal and 1,306 other.*

At Aylesbury the feeble-minded convict women are also segregated in a special ward (daily average 12 during 1910-11).

There is, however, as yet no legal enquiry before conviction as to the pathological cause of crime, and these hapless creatures are still subject to penal discipline in convict prisons, and are discharged when their sentence is served ; whilst in local prisons they still drift ceaselessly in and out. It is a crying social need to retain under permanent humane supervision beings whom it is as cruel to punish as it is dangerous to society to leave to their own devices.

IMPRISONMENT IN DEFAULT OF FINE.

In cases where a fine is imposed time should always be given for its payment.† In 1910-11, of the total number received on conviction 84,885 (or 50 per cent.), 60,386 males and 24,499 females, were committed in default of fine. Obviously there is every reason to avoid sending persons to prison who fail to pay fines through poverty, and who might do so if given a reasonable period in which to earn or borrow money. To refuse them time is economically unsound, and increases the disparity of treatment of rich and poor. It should

* Ibid., Part II, p. 219.

† This is one of the reforms which the Home Secretary promised in 1910 to inaugurate at once.

be noticed that there is not the same law for rich and poor in this matter, for the fine is imposed in proportion to the offence committed, and not to the income of the offender. A fine of 10s. to a work girl travelling without a ticket would equal £10 or even £1,000 to the careless rich committing the same offence, though the penalty imposed would be nominally the same ; and, as a matter of fact, in many cases, the girl would go to prison, which entails her moral and economic ruin, while the rich man would not even be caused a momentary inconvenience by the payment of his fine.

Awaiting Trial.

It is obviously advisable to avoid any association of the potential criminal with criminal surroundings. Children's Courts are a move in the right direction. It is a regulation of the Children Act, 1908, that the trials of boys and girls under fourteen must be held in a court separated by place or day from that used for adult offenders. Children must also now be kept apart from adult offenders during detention ; but it is very undesirable that young girls and boys should be kept in gaol on remand for long periods, " awaiting trial," as is now the case, even though ultimately they may not be committed to prison. There can be very little distinction in the mind of a girl as to whether she is technically undergoing a sentence of imprisonment, or only awaiting a trial at which she may be acquitted, especially as her treatment in gaol differs comparatively little from that of a convicted prisoner. She obtains that familiarity with the inside of a prison which above all things ought to be avoided.

The whole system of rigorously confining accused persons in such a manner as to cripple their mental activity will presently be recognized as an arrant injustice.

The classification of offenders and the break up of the prison into a series of specialized institutions and services to deal with various classes has begun, but the movement has still far to go.

II.—Improvements in Administration.

The Need for Special Training.

Changes of method such as those above indicated carry with them a need for the special training of officers of all grades connected with the penal service. There are now two grades for wardresses as for warders, and a training school for female officers has been formed at Holloway, where probationers are to be taught hygiene and Swedish drill, and some of them educated as technical teachers. There is no reason why the profession of prison wardress should not rank as high as that of trained hospital or asylum nurse. What is needed is that a woman, with a vocation like that of Florence Nightingale, shall come forward and show by her example that work in prisons is of equal importance with the tending of the sick, or the care of the mentally afflicted.

The post of prison doctor cannot satisfactorily be held by one who practises outside, as it requires very special study and training in pathology and mental science, and should give scope and work enough for a full-time post. In America criminal laboratories are

being established for research into the pathology of crime. There
are in this country men well equipped to undertake such work, and
if, at the same time, statistics could be collected on scientific lines,
much might be done towards elucidating the problem of recidivism.
These laboratories could be utilized as lecture centres for the training
of prison officials. At present only the medical officers are required
to have any scientific training at all, and it is quite possible that even
they have never studied criminal pathology or psychology. Public
opinion should be educated to require at least as much scientific
knowledge and special experience from prison officials as from the
head and staff of a lunatic asylum.

The absence of specialized preparation for dealing with the delicate and difficult problems of criminal psychology is even more
painfully apparent on the bench than amongst prison officials.
Admirably efficient as the English judge usually is in eliciting
evidence and procuring a just verdict, when he comes to consider
the sentence, he is nearly always as complete an amateur as the
average magistrate, who knows nothing of criminology or of prison
life. Moreover, the whole bias of the English law of criminal
evidence (which at every point insists on accentuating the facts of
the particular crime and not drawing inferences from the antecedents
of the criminal) handicaps the judge. He is led thereby "to make
the punishment fit the crime," whereas the whole work of reform is
to make it fit the criminal. Most of our judges are either "merci-
ful," which means they revel in short sentences, or "stern," which
means they give flogging when they can. The judge's work might
well stop when the verdict is found, and sentence be passed, after
careful, unhurried consideration of the record both of the case and
of the criminal, by officials whose experience and expert training is
of another sort.

THE NEED FOR WOMEN OFFICIALS.

It is exceedingly desirable that women should be on the medical
staff of prisons where women are confined. The medical woman
Inspector has already done much to improve the conditions of
women prisoners, and it is greatly to be hoped that this appointment will be followed by those of other women as medical officers
as well as inspectors. The office of spiritual or moral adviser also
is one which some women are particularly well-qualified to fill in a
prison. Again, in a woman's prison it seems desirable that the
governor should be a woman. In the small local prison at Aigle, in
the Rhone Valley, a woman is governor in charge of both men and
women prisoners ; why not at Holloway or Aylesbury, where all
prisoners are women? And why is not one at least of the Prison
Commissioners a woman?

Women are already employed in this country in the detective
service. When the whole police force is employed more extensively
in the prevention than the detection of crime, as it surely will presently be, women's help will be increasingly needful. A women's
auxiliary to the police force, as already in operation in Germany,
would be invaluable.

Undoubtedly where girls or women are concerned in cases connected with indecency or immorality the courts might well be cleared of all men, except those officially concerned, as is done in children's courts ; but if any of the public are allowed to remain, the court should not be cleared, as is now the case, of all women. It is obviously unfair in such cases that a woman should be obliged to give evidence or to be tried alone before a general audience of men. It would be an advantage if it were made compulsory for a police court matron or woman probation officer to be in charge of young women offenders .to prevent their contamination by hardened criminals, and to be present when their cases are tried. It has been suggested that there should be special courts for women as for children, but these will hardly serve any useful purpose unless there are women magistrates and the women's auxiliary to the police force to deal with women and children, innovations which would do more than anything perhaps for the reform of police court procedure, especially as it concerns women and young persons. It seems probable that women would be more likely than men to understand and to enter into cases concerning their own sex. The same qualities which have made women invaluable in poor law, educational, and municipal administration, and in the large and increasing amount of voluntary work which they are doing in connection with prisons, are likely to make them invaluable on the magistrates' bench.

It is probable that in the future women will be appointed as judges and magistrates, as well as summoned to serve on juries ; and this is, in our opinion, a consummation most devoutly to be wished in the interests of society.* There is no path of change along which women are more particularly concerned to press forward than that which leads them to an official share in judicial procedure and in the administration of the penal system.

* A measure qualifying women to exercise judicial functions is now before the Norwegian Parliament. In Mrs. Wolstenholme Elmy's pamphlet, "The Criminal Code in Relation to Women," 1880, the cause of the disuse of the ancient "jury of matrons" is described.

BIBLIOGRAPHY.

I.—History.

ANDREWS, WILLIAM, F.R.H.S. Old Time Punishments. 1890. Simpkin, Marshall.
BALLAGH, DR. J. C. White Servitude in the Colony of Virginia : a Study of the System of Indentured Labor in the American Colonies. Johns Hopkins University Studies, Series XIII. 1895. Baltimore.
BASSETT, DR. Y. S. Slavery and Servitude in the Colony of North Carolina. Johns Hopkins University Studies, Series XIV. 1896. Baltimore.
BENTHAM, JEREMY. Panopticon ; or, the Inspection House, 1791. Works. (Ed. Bowring.) Vol. IV. 1843. Tait.
BONNER, HYPATIA BRADLAUGH. Gallows and Lash. (Cruelties of Civilization Series. Vol. III.) 1897. Reeves.
FRY, MRS. ELIZABETH. Journals and Letters. Edited by her Daughters. 1847. Gilpin.
——— Reports (a) on Prisons of Northern England and of Scotland; (b) on Prisons of Ireland (with F. J. Gurney), 1827. 1847. Fletcher, Norwich.
HOWARD, JOHN. State of Prisons in England aud Wales. 1777.

HOWARD, JOHN. Works. 5 vols. 1792.
———— Letters, etc. Edited by W. Tallack. 1905. Methuen.
POLLOCK AND MAITLAND. History of English Law before the Time of Edward I.
Second edition. 1898. Cambridge University Press. 40s.
PIKE, L. O. History of Crime in England: Illustrating Changes in the Law with
the Progress of Civilization. 2 vols. London, 1873-76. Smith and Elder.
STEPHEN, SIR JAMES FITZJAMES. A General View of the Criminal Law of England.
1863 and 1890. Macmillan.

II.—Criminology and Penal Theory.

ANDERSON, SIR ROBERT. Criminals and Crime. 1907. Nesbit.
CARLYLE, THOMAS. Model Prisons. (Latter Day Pamphlets.)
CARPENTER, EDWARD. Prisons, Police and Punishment. 1905. Fifield.
CARPENTER, MARY. Reformatory Prison Discipline as Developed by Sir W. Crofton
in Irish Convict Prisons. 1872. Longmans.
DEVON, JAMES (Medical Officer at H.M. Prison, Glasgow). The Criminal and the
Community. 1911. Lane. 6s. net.
DU CANE, SIR ED. F. Punishment and Prevention. 1895.
GRAY, B. KIRKMAN. Philanthropy and the State. Edited by E. K. Gray and B. L.
Hutchins. 1908. P. S. King & Sons. 7s. 6d.
LOMBROSO, C., and FERRERO, G. The Female Offender. (Criminology Series.)
1895.
LOMBROSO, C. Crime: Its Causes and Remedies. Translated by Maurice Par-
melee, Ph.D. 1911. Heinemann. 16s. net.
MAUDSLEY, DR. H. Responsibility in Mental Disease. (International Science
Series.) 1874.
MORRISON, W. D. Crime and its Causes. 1891. Sonnenschein. 2s. 6d.
———— Juvenile Offenders. 1896.
RUSSELL, C. E. B., and RIGBY, L. M. The Making of the Criminal. 1906. Mac-
millan.
RUSSELL, C. E. B. Young Gaol Birds. 1910. Macmillan.
TALLACK, WILLIAM, Secretary of the Howard Association. Penological and Pre-
ventive Principles. 1889. Wertheimer. 8s.

III.—Prison Life and Experience.

BALFOUR, J. S. My Prison Life. 1907.
DAVITT, MICHAEL. Leaves from a Prison Diary. 2 vols. New York, 1885.
Five Years Penal Servitude. By One Who Has Endured It. 1882. Routledge.
GRIFFITHS, MAJOR ARTHUR (Inspector of Prisons). Memorials of Millbank.
2 vols. London, 1875.
———— Chronicles of Newgate. 1884. Chapman & Hall.
———— Secrets of the Prison House. 2 vols.
KROPOTKIN, P. Russian and French Prisons. 1887. Ward & Downey.
"W. B. N." (LORD WILLIAM BEAUCHAMP NEVILL). Penal Servitude. 1903.
QUINTON, R. F., M.D. (late Governor and Medical Officer of H.M. Prison, Holloway).
Crime and the Criminal, 1876-1910. 1910. Longmans.
ROBINSON, L. W. Female Life in Prison. By a Prison Matron. 1862. Hurst &
Blackett.
WILDE, OSCAR. De Profundis, 1905, and The Ballad of Reading Gaol, 1898. (As
published in Works of Oscar Wilde.) 1908. Methuen.

IV.—Official Reports and Statistics.

Report from the Select Committee on Transportation, communicated by the Commons
to the Lords, 1838.
Report of the Departmental Committee on Prisons, 1895.
Report of the Commissioners of Prisons and the Directors of Convict Prisons for
1910-11. Part I. Cd. 5891. Price 7½d. Part II. Cd. 5892. Price 11½d.
Criminal Statistics for 1909. Judicial. Part I. Cd. 5473. Price 1s. 10d.

Fabian Tract No. 164.

GOLD AND STATE BANKING

A Study in the Economics of Monopoly.

BY

EDWARD R. PEASE.

PUBLISHED AND SOLD BY

THE FABIAN SOCIETY.

PRICE ONE PENNY.

LONDON:
THE FABIAN SOCIETY, 3 CLEMENT'S INN, STRAND, W.C.
JUNE, 1912.

GOLD AND STATE BANKING.

A STUDY IN THE ECONOMICS OF MONOPOLY.

PREFATORY NOTE ON CURRENCY CRANKS.

Currency cranks are the most foolish of theorists, and their schemes the most futile of Utopias.

The following pages, read as a lecture to the Fabian Society in April, 1911, contain some speculations about the place of gold in the machinery of commerce which the writer puts forward with diffidence, precisely because of his distrust of the company he is keeping.

His speculations lead up to a remarkable conclusion, which, however, is not necessarily dependent on them. And the reader is particularly requested to note that what is here outlined is not a scheme, but a forecast. Neither the Government nor any individual is asked to adopt any proposals or to follow any advice. The writer invites them only to accept Mr. Asquith's well-known policy—" Wait and see." In his view, the almost inevitable effect of economic causes will be that our banks will continue to amalgamate : when there is only one bank, or virtually one, its power will be too enormous for private persons to wield ; hence it must be controlled by the State.

The remarkable consequences of this monopoly are briefly indicated in the following pages, which to some extent are based on ideas set forth in Fabian Tract No. 147, " Capital and Compensation."

The connection between Socialism and currency is ancient and respectable.

Labor Notes.

Robert Owen, the father of Socialism, devised the simple expedient of labor notes, which, like a will-o'-the-wisp, if such a thing exist, has ever since lured Socialist theorists to destruction.

He established a series of stores, one, the most famous, in Gray's Inn Road, at which commodities, chiefly boots and clothes, were received and were paid for in hour notes on a valuation in money, an hour being reckoned at sixpence. The introduction of time was therefore purely nominal and for purposes of edification. The time value of an article had no necessary relation to the time spent in its production, except in so far as it has at present, that is, in so far as it regulates the cost of production.

Nothing which Owen devised in Utopian reconstruction seems to have lasted longer than a few months, or at most a year or two, and his labor exchanges all promptly failed, though exactly why does not appear. All one can learn from Frank Podmore's exhaustive biography is that they began with apparent success and sprang up in crowds, but in a year or two had all faded away.

In his labor notes, as in his co-operative communities, Owen got hold of a right idea, but he tried to do by private enterprise what can only be properly and completely accomplished by the State, and therefore he failed.

The idea of labor notes is simple enough. It is that labor, added to raw materials, creates wealth. Trade is simply barter. All that is wanted is some authorized indication that the laborer by his labor has created wealth. Constitute an authority with power to apprise the value embodied in the article and to grant certificates therefor, and you have at once a currency which is based on actual wealth and which cannot exceed it in amount.

Where the Theory Fails.

But there is one big flaw in this theory. The mere addition of labor to raw material does not necessarily create wealth. The product must be such as to satisfy some human desire. Moreover, the amount of the labor is no measure of the amount of wealth. And the human desire must be a desire for the product *here and now*, in exactly the right form and quantity. Without this correspondence no amount of labor produces wealth. Finally, not only does desire fluctuate and change, but also it has the very awkward feature that it automatically and inevitably diminishes in intensity as the quantity of the product increases. Thus it is impossible to measure wealth in terms of labor.

Moreover, where do services come in? The work of tramwaymen and busmen and cabmen is moving about people. It may be argued that I am of more value to the community when by the labor of numerous railway servants I am removed each day from the Surrey village in which I live to my office in London, but their labor embodied in me has no exchange value, and it may be said to be cancelled by more labor on the part of the railway servants in conveying me home again at night.

A moment's reflection will show that only some labor is so embodied in commodities as to have a more or less permanent exchange value. Therefore the theory breaks down. The Marxian law stipulates that the labor which creates value shall be socially valuable, but the difficulty is that this can only be ascertained long after the labor has been expended. The labor embodied in commodities cannot be valued with any certainty because the value of the commodity fluctuates, whilst the value of the labor note, if it is to be useful as currency, must be rigidly fixed. The labor note, in fact, comes to be merely an attractive name for a paper currency; the idea that its amount will be automatically regulated by the available wealth of the community vanishes. The notion that it has some special security in the object created by the labor it pays for is unsound because the object created has itself no certain value.

It may be thought that the labor note project is as dead as the wages fund theorem, and it is waste of time to demonstrate its fallacies. This is not so. A recent book, entitled "Twentieth Century Socialism,"* by the late Edmond Kelly, an American lawyer, and a most capable and intelligent man, describes a mixed system of currency, according to which gold will be used for export purposes and labor notes for internal trade, and this project is set out in all seriousness as the most up to date device for settling currency problems.

But any ardent advocate of labor notes who reads this is no doubt already burning to point out that the advantage of labor notes would be that, unlike gold, they cost virtually nothing to produce, and unlike some other forms of currency, they earn no interest, whilst bills and mortgage bonds and overdrafts all carry interest, a charge on industry for the benefit of the capitalists.

The Guernsey Market Notes.

Socialists who take up finance have at intervals since Socialism began, discovered the Guernsey Market House, and they tell us with glee how the States of Guernsey, being short of the needful, resolved to build a market and to pay the workpeople, not in gold but in labor notes, which were to be legally current till the profits of the market enabled them to be redeemed. Why should not our municipalities build their markets, lay their tramlines, construct their waterworks by the same method, and thus escape the necessity of paying ransom to the monopolists of gold or, in simpler words, interest on the capital borrowed.

Mr. Theodore Harris, a member of our Society, not exactly orthodox in his opinions or, indeed, practice, in the matter of currency, has rendered a great service by investigating this famous transaction in the archives of the island ; † and alas, the bright illusion vanishes ! The labor notes were not, so far as evidence goes, given in exchange for labor, but were put out as currency, just as Argentina or Honduras, or Venezuela does to-day. They were not secured on a market in building, but on an excise of spirits, just as any borrowing State with bad credit hypothecates its customs or its railway receipts as special security for its loan. In fact, the notes have not been repaid yet, and these same notes, though the Market House was built in 1820, still circulate in the island.

What the States of Guernsey actually did was to issue paper money, in small amounts, intended to be redeemed after short periods ; and the scheme came to an end apparently, precisely as the economists predict. Guernsey found the facile descent into paper currency as attractive as all States find it. It set its printing

* Longmans; 1910. 7s. 6d. net.

† "An Example of Communal Currency : the Facts About the Guernsey Market House." Compiled . . . by J. Theodore Harris. P. S. King & Son. 1911.

press humming till its paper notes amounted to £55,000. Then the bankers kicked. The account of their difficulties is obscurely worded, and the editor makes no attempt to elucidate it. But it seems clear that foreign commerce and finance could not go on with a currency incapable of export. The market notes were driving out the gold, because gold alone was valuable for sending abroad. So the bankers persuaded the States to retrace their steps. The £55,000 was reduced to £41,000, and at this figure it has remained ever since.

It is obvious that any Government by the issue of paper money, can make once for all, a profit to the amount of the gold replaced by the paper which has no appreciable cost. To that extent it is always possible for a Government to obtain a supply of capital free of cost. It can only do it once. In the United Kingdom the value of our gold coins in circulation is £113,000,000.* Theoretically we could let the foreigner take these, and replace them by inconvertible paper. Practically every nation which can afford it uses gold in preference to inconvertible paper, because experience shows that a currency of, or based on, gold is worth as an instrument of exchange far more than its cost. Inconvertible paper is only used by nations who have blundered financially and have failed hitherto to recover their losses.

The Stability of Gold.

Gold, then, is universally regarded as the best basis for currency, because it is the most stable. But it is said by some that the alleged stability of gold as a measure of value is not a fact. Other things, it is said, exchange with gold in proportion to its quantity. An increase in the supply of gold means a rise in prices, because there is more gold available to exchange against products in general. It is pointed out that the gold production of the world has increased enormously, from £22,000,000 in 1885 to £95,000,000 in 1911, and in fact the rise in commodity prices in most countries of the world, and recently England, is a marked feature of present day politics.

Let us consider what actually happens. Every month the Transvaal mines produce some 800,000 ozs. of gold, worth roughly £3,400,000. The greater part of that gold is shipped to London. When £1,000,000 of gold is landed from South Africa, let us suppose that it is taken, as much or most of it is, by the Bank of England. When in the Bank it is actual or potential money, and is available as currency or floating capital. Its immediate effect is to increase the supply of loanable capital, to decrease the rate of interest on such capital by increasing the supply, and also by increasing the gold reserve. (It must be remembered that the Bank rate is largely determined by the amount of gold reserve ; the rate is put up when gold is scarce, in order to attract floating capital to England, and therefore to check the outflow of gold and sometimes to bring gold.)

---

* Report of the Deputy Master of the Mint, 1911. Of this sum £44,214,173 was held by bankers, including the Bank of England, on June 30th, 1910. Gold bullion to the value of £20,000,000 also in the Bank is not included in the above.

But low rates of interest mean cheap trading and low prices. So the first effect of more gold is not to raise but to lower, even if only a little, the range of prices.*

Now has it any other effect? Does anybody who has a bank account, in the savings bank or any other bank, ever fail to get gold when he asks for it? Obviously not. Whether the Bank of England has much gold or little, it always pays in gold any person who has a claim upon it. Even if ten or twenty millions in gold were brought into the Bank, no person would use another sovereign than he uses now.†

It therefore seems to be clear that for currency purposes we have in England, and have had for fifty years past, every ounce of gold we want to use. Whether the Transvaal or Mysore or Westralia or the Jungle produce from their mines ounces of gold by the million or no ounces at all, we in England do not use one half sovereign more or less of currency. If I owned a private mine, and took its proceeds, 100,000 ounces, to the Mint, and got it coined into sovereigns, I could only pay these into a bank; in a few hours they would be in the coffers of the Bank of England, and the currency would be at exactly the same level as before.‡

The inference is that the quantity of gold in use in England as currency is not determined by the quantity of gold produced in the mines, because currency in England is the first claim on the world supply of gold, and is relatively a small claim. A mere fraction of the ninety-five millions in value produced annually (the figure is for 1911) is all that is required to supply the wear and tear, and to meet the demands (if there are any) of our growing population, and increasing commerce and industry. If half a million or one million is all we need annually for our currency, it is immaterial whether the total production is fifty or seventy-five or one hundred millions.

What becomes of the rest? Large amounts are used in the arts, for jewelry and watches and gold leaf. For the rest, it seems probable that other countries are not, as we are, full up with gold. Twenty years ago, when I was in the United States, I saw a gold coin in the Eastern and Middle States in the course of three months only once or twice. There was no gold in circulation, and I believe there is very little even now.§ Only a few years ago, in 1907, America

---

* Some economists argue that a low rate of discount encourages loans for the purchase of commodities and so raises prices. But the new loans may also be applied to the production of more commodities and so lower prices. In fact during the present century, with its unparalleled gold production, the Bank rate has on the average been markedly higher than it was at the end of the last century. From 1892-7 it varied between 2 per cent. and 3 per cent. (average 2·46); from 1898-1911 it varied between 3 per cent. and almost 5 per cent. (average 3·61). The recent effect of the great output of gold on prices through its tendency to lower the Bank rate has therefore been at the utmost only negative.

† For confirmation of this view see de Launay, "The World's Gold," quoted by W. W. Carlile, "Monetary Economics" (Arnold, 1912), p. 6.

‡ Gold in circulation is currency; gold in the Bank is floating capital.

§ The United States Currency Department has taken a great deal of gold in recent years and held early in 1912 £247,000,000.

ran out of currency and had to borrow gold and anything else as quickly as possible from all the world over. India, again, is on a gold basis, but has no gold currency. It is said that the gold coinage melts away into hoards. Here too it is probable you could not get gold anywhere and everywhere, if you want it and have negotiable currency to give for it.

I am not prepared to say whether the rise of prices* in India, which is enormous, or in the United States, which is notorious, or in Germany, where it is affecting the fortunes of political parties, is or is not due to the increased supplies of gold or to what extent it is due to this cause among others in each case, because I am not familiar with the banking and currency system of those countries. They may in the past have had available less gold than they could use, and the increase of the world supply may be having some effect on their prices.

In England the only possible effect † of increased output of gold seems to me to be to lower prices, and that perhaps is why England has largely escaped that great rise in the cost of living of which so many other nations are complaining.

In foreign countries, it may be that the gold reservoir, so to speak, is not yet full, and its gradual filling from the produce of the mines may be affecting the level of prices. In England our reservoir has been full for the past half century at least, the level varies slightly from month to month or from year to year, but that is a matter of internal and external trade, and bears no sort of relation to the gold supply of the world.

The Local Value of Gold.

What, then, determines the value of gold? Why does half an ounce of gold (say £2) exchange, roughly, for a ton of iron, or a quarter of wheat? Why is it reckoned a bare living wage for a fortnight in London? Why in all these cases is the weight of gold half an ounce, and not a quarter of an ounce or two ounces?

* The increase of prices abroad must affect the prices of imported goods and raw materials in England.

† One accepted explanation of the effect of increased gold production on prices attributes the rise to the increased demand for commodities caused by the wealth of the mineowners. But in this connection gold is in no way different from any other commodity, except in so far as a bountiful harvest or a big cotton crop tend to depress the prices of wheat and cotton; and the increase of wealth in terms of gold is not necessarily proportionate to the increase of commodities. According to this theory, the settlement of new countries (as in Canada or South America) should affect prices quite as much as the discovery of new gold fields. Stanley Jevons made an investigation of prices in the years 1845-62 and calculated, by taking "unweighted" prices (i.e., considering a rise of 10 per cent. in the price of corn as practically equivalent to a fall of 10 per cent. in the price of black pepper), that prices on the average had risen 9½ per cent. coincidently with an increase in the production of gold. All his forecasts based on this induction have proved wrong, and he made no attempt to check his conclusion by ascertaining that no such alteration of prices had occurred in previous decades when there had been no change in gold production. Moreover he did not attempt to show *how* the increased output of gold had affected prices. ("A Serious Fall in the Value of Gold," by W. Stanley Jevons; Stanford, 1863. This is said to be still the classical authority for the generally accepted doctrine.)

Well, the first thing to notice is that the value of gold not only varies from century to century—that is well known, and economists write books about it—but from place to place.

By one of those odd blindnesses common amongst economists, the fact that the exchange value of gold varies from place to place is commonly disregarded : the professors are aware of the phenomenon but it does not fit into their theories, and so they only speak of it as a variation in real wages, or the cost of living. But if the value of commodities varies in terms of gold, it is necessarily and equally true that the value of gold varies in terms of commodities.

I read recently that in the remote interior of China a European missionary can live in comfort on 12s. 6d. a month. That is an extreme case. Wages in Belgium are, according to Seebohm Rowntree,* about half those in England. In America, according to a recent Board of Trade Report,† wages are more than twice our rate, and it is commonly said that a dollar is the equivalent of a shilling. Now I do not see that it can be disputed that this means that the value of gold in terms of commodities and services varies. Impossible, it is sometimes said : merchants would buy where commodities are cheap, people with fixed incomes would rush to live where their gold purchases much. Well, they would and they do. The coast towns of France swarm with our half-pay officers, who live there precisely because their gold has a higher value in France than in England. And as for the merchants, their business in the main does consist in buying where many commodities are given for little gold, and selling where more gold is given for the same commodities. Would eggs be brought from Denmark and Siberia and Ireland to sell, not in London only, but throughout England, in towns and villages and farms, if eggs and gold interchanged on equal terms in Siberia and in Surrey ?

Now the prices of certain articles, of corn and cotton, of iron and copper and tin, are more or less international. Apart from tariffs, corn and iron must fetch practically the same prices in London and Hamburg, in Marseilles and in Constantinople, because cargoes can be sent to one or the other at practically the same cost ; they are one market for international produce, and goods in one market can have but one price.

But for land and houses and labor, and innumerable other things, the effective market is measured by half-miles, and for the great bulk of things it is bounded by a frontier. Our home trade, as all the world knows, is enormously greater than our foreign trade and enormously more valuable. Only a mere fraction of the people can select their places of residence in accordance with the purchasing power of their incomes, because most incomes are earned. Only a tiny fraction will exercise this choice, because most people are bound

---

* In some trades ; in others the difference is less. "Land and Labor : Lessons from Belgium" (Macmillan, 1910), p. 561, etc.

† The precise ratio is as 100 to 232. "The Cost of Living in American Towns." Cd. 5609, 1911.

by stronger attractions than a high purchasing power of gold. Finally, only a few of the things which are bought and sold can be transferred from one country to another.

Since, then, gold has different values according to locality, it is clear in the first place that its value is not determined by any cause connected with gold itself. For gold is indisputably international and flows with hardly a trace of resistance from one country to another, across oceans and mountains from Arctic beaches and Australian deserts, to the strong rooms in London and Paris and Berlin.

Hence we are forced to the apparently absurd conclusion that the value of gold in any given locality is not determined by any general cause at all, but depends on local custom. In other words, agricultural labor is paid 10s. a week in Dorset and 20s. a week in Northumberland largely because it was paid, let us say, 9s. a week in Dorset and 18s. a week in Northumberland ten years ago, and the laborers have managed to get a rise of 1s. and 2s. respectively in the interval. If you ask why wages are not 18s. a week in Dorset also, there is no reason in the nature of things. It is custom.* Northumbrians have been able to raise their wages because of the neighboring coal mines. Dorset men have not. But it is misleading to use special illustrations. A dozen explanations can be given why wages vary in different countries. But it is not so easy by any means to explain why the general level of prices varies so enormously from Belgium or Russia to New York or Pittsburg.

Take Belgium again. According to Mr. Rowntree wages are low because house rents are low.† Rents are low because building is cheap. Building is cheap because wages are low. A complete circle! In other words wages are low in Belgium because wages are low. That in my opinion is the correct explanation. In terms of gold it is equivalent to saying that the value of gold in relation to commodities is high in Belgium. In fact, labor is not, as used to be said, the source of all wealth, but a factor in all wealth of overwhelming importance. The cost of labor largely determines the range of prices. Wherever labor is or has been scarce and that scarcity has forced wages up and prices with them : or wherever labor is organized and intelligent, and demands high wages, prices also are high, and gold is relatively cheap. On the other hand where labor is ignorant or degraded, or remote from the world market, wages are low, prices are low, and gold is dear.

* By custom I mean that which exists owing to the habits of thought of the people of a district. The value of gold in terms of labor, for example, is fixed locally because people have been and are in the habit of offering and accepting certain rates of wages, certain rents for cottages and, to some extent, for farms, and even prices for commodities. Within the limits of these customs, rates are kept relatively stable by competition. No man can obtain much more than the customary rate because of the competition of his neighbors.

† This is not intended as a criticism of Mr. Rowntree, and in fact he does *not* explicitly include low rents amongst the causes of low wages in Belgium, though it is implied on pp. 72 and 529. See also pp. 445, 527 and 528 of " Land and Labor."

But remember, labor benefits by high wages even if accompanied by high prices, because the world market controls the prices of world commodities, such as corn and meat, and therefore, notwithstanding high prices, the American and Australian and English workmen are better off than the Belgian and Italian, the Hindu and the Chinee.

Is Gold a Monopoly?

Socialists sometimes object to gold as a basis of currency, because they say that the bankers and financiers have a monopoly of gold, and by that monopoly make great wealth for themselves.

Now the idea that in England bankers and financiers have a monopoly of gold, or desire a monopoly of it, is singularly perverse. In fact, it is the one commodity of which by law there is, and can be, no monopoly. Our whole monetary system is based on free gold, and it is this free gold which makes London the financial clearing-house of the world. By law, every bank or other debtor must make payment in Bank of England notes or in gold, and every holder of Bank of England notes can by law get gold for his notes at the Bank. A monopoly of gold, if it means anything, means a monopoly, not against the poor, but against the rich. De Beers have a virtual monopoly of diamonds because they control the sales to the rich, who are able and willing to buy. There is no monopoly in motor cars, though comparatively few are wealthy enough to be buyers.

There is, by law, no monopoly of gold, because any man who can command three pounds' worth of saleable property, or can do three pounds' worth of saleable services, and therefore has a claim on the world, can demand payment in gold, and, in fact as well as law, can get it in gold.

But there is another consideration. The odd thing is that gold, supposed to be desired by all men, is in fact the one thing bankers dislike and detest.

A banker keeps a large part of his assets in investments of various sorts, stocks, bills and loans, and a small part in gold. The stocks and bills and loans all yield interest, and it is from them that he pays the interest on his deposits, and makes his working expenses, and his dividends. His gold yields no return whatever, and requires safe custody, for which he has to pay. Every additional £1,000 in gold is so much interest lost, and so much extra coin to be cared for. Every thousand sovereigns he pays away reduces his dead capital. That is why there is a constant rumble of complaint going on that the bankers do not keep a sufficient reserve of coin, and trust too much to the Bank of England. The financial critics, always half a century out of date, as I shall subsequently show, are full of the terrible risks the banks run in keeping their stocks of gold so low. Why this perversity if their "monopoly" of gold is so precious? On the contrary, what is precious to them is to get rid of every sovereign they can possibly spare, and to foist on to the Bank of England, a semi-public body, the duty of keeping for the country the enormous stock of idle and useless gold, which from generation to generation reposes in its vaults, as a fetish for the City to worship, a sort of golden ark of the covenant, kept in the holy of holies of Thread-needle Street, never to be seen or touched by the ordinary mortal, but in some mysterious way essential to the stability and endurance of the mighty fabric of our commerce and industry.

During the past twenty years there has never been less than 20 millions sterling of gold in the Bank, rusting, so to speak, idly in its strong rooms. During the last forty years there has never been less than $17\frac{3}{4}$ millions. Even in 1866, the year of the great panic, when half the banks were toppling and credit was shaken to its core, the Bank never had less than $11\frac{3}{4}$ millions, and this was only about a million under the average of several previous years.

Our Banks too Big to Fail.

The fact, which surely everybody knows and hardly anybody ventures to state, is that the stability of our great banks—and all our banking system which now matters a tittle consists of great banks—is based not on the supply of gold in their vaults, nor on the reserve in the Bank of England, but on the fact that they are too big to fail, too big commercially and far too big politically. If Lloyds, or the London County, or the National Provincial stopped payment, the consequences would far exceed a San Francisco earthquake, a Chicago fire, or any other catastrophe within the memory of man. The Chancellor of the Exchequer with a word could avert the catastrophe as Richard Seddon did in New Zealand,* and so saved his country from the panic which desolated Australia ; or as an alternative, a dozen bank managers in conclave could save the situation, as they saved it when reckless speculation in Argentine loans wrecked the fortunes of the house of Barings.

Is it credible that both the Ministry and the banking community would stand aside in face of an impending calamity certain to bring them irretrievable misfortunes ?

Even in America at the financial crisis of a few years ago the banks, when they had time to think about it, refused to resign when defeated by the scarcity of currency, considering it wiser simply to decline to honor cheques till the clouds rolled by, rather than follow the traditionally correct course of closing their doors and winding up in bankruptcy because they happened to have run short of gold or paper currency.

The ultimate security of our banks is, then, dependent not on a stock of gold, but on the political and commercial common sense of our country. The economists still talk about commercial crises because they read Mill and Ricardo—who wrote about what they saw around them—instead of observing what happens now. All the first class finance of the empire is and has for years been centred in London, and there has been no bank failure in London of the traditional sort since the failure of Overend, Gurney & Co. in 1866,

* By an Act passed in one day, June 30th, 1894, the Government lent the Bank of New Zealand £2,000,000 in return for a share of control. A further loan was made in 1895.—"Newest England," by H. D. Lloyd. (New York), Doubleday. 1900. Page 276.

an event which but few bankers nowadays will be old enough to recollect. *Industrial* crises—periods of declining trade—we still have, and shall have no doubt for years to come. *Financial* crises are matters of ancient history, which are described in the classical economists, who, I understand, are chiefly studied by the occupants of bank parlors.

Bankers, old fashioned people who follow tradition with great reverence, still believe that their five per cent. or ten per cent. of gold is their sole salvation. They compare their banks to a mighty pyramid of credit standing upside down, poised on its tiny apex of gold ; they flatter themselves that it is their extraordinary caution, their admirable system, their almost superhuman dexterity, which alone accomplish this perennial miracle.

The Basis of Currency.

In fact it is all a delusion, because the security of the credit system does not depend on gold, but on public good sense ; and gold is to the system merely the small change, as silver and copper are to the individual. The only proper explanation of our system of currency with which I am acquainted is to be found in John A. Hobson's important book, "The Industrial System," although it is in my opinion marred by a curious error of some £15,000,000,000 sterling! The great bulk of our currency consists of bankers' credit, but it does not seem to be commonly recognized that the potential substance of bank credit is the total tangible wealth of the country, which is estimated at something between fifteen and twenty thousand millions sterling.*

The realized property of the nation consists of all sorts of things —land, houses, machinery, products, raw or manufactured, all the miscellaneous property summed up in the case of individuals only at their death for the beneficent operation of the death duties.

Our banking system is an enormous federated pawnshop. Those who have things—traders with goods bought on credit, or in warehouses, or on the high seas, or in process of manufacture, landowners requiring money to build or improve, householders desiring to buy a house and pay by instalments, all who want to use and control property which they cannot at the moment fully pay for, deposit the documents representing that property, deeds, bills, bonds, etc., at a bank as security for loans. On the other side is the class who keep their spare money at the bank, current accounts or deposit accounts. What the banker borrows he lends. What the depositors possess is really and ultimately the goods which the borrowers have pledged.

Our currency consists in the main of crossed cheques, that is, orders on the bankers to transfer claims on the goods in pawn from

---

* He considers the effect on prices of a given increase of the output of gold in relation to the national income (£2,000,000,000). My view is that gold, except for use in the arts, is of the character of capital and not income, since it is necessarily saved, and cannot be spent. Hence the increased output has relation to the national capital, which is fifteen to twenty thousand millions. See Chapter xvi,

one account in a bank to another account in the same or another bank. As I have said before, the whole of the realized and saleable wealth of the country or, to speak more accurately, the whole less the margin of safety which the prudent banker would deduct, is potentially available to be thus turned into currency ; and under a perfect system, a monopoly, it would actually be available.

One State Bank.

Our banking system can, however, never be perfect till it is not merely a series of trusts, but an actual monopoly, which of course must be under the State.

If all banking were done at one bank, the problem would be infinitely simplified, and people would realize that our paper currency, bank notes, cheques and bills are not, in truth, based on gold alone, but on all other forms of realized wealth. Moreover, they would further perceive that the real limitation of a banker's operations is not the amount of his deposits, but the amount of his loans.

The assets of the bank are the goods pawned with it. Whilst we have a number of independent banks, each one can only lend in proportion to its deposits, because one bank might hold the property, and another bank might hold the credits or currency secured on it. If we had but one bank, and all cheques were drawn on it, and had to be paid back again into it, banking, so far as internal commerce was concerned, would be reduced to book-keeping. A supply of gold would have to be kept for small change, but beyond that, for the purposes of internal transactions, no gold basis would be dreamt of ; no banking panic could be feared, because what was withdrawn with one hand would have to be paid back with the other.

The Uselessness of Deposits.

A universal State bank could convert into currency any property lodged with it, and would not have to consider its deposits of currency, that is, its deposits in the ordinary sense. What good, then, would the deposits be ? Why should the bank accept and pay interest on deposits ? The only possible answer is in the negative. Under a régime of competition, bankers must pay interest on deposits because their loans are limited by their borrowings. Under a monopoly conditions are wholly altered. The "laws" of political economy and the rules of commerce, elaborately worked out in theory as well as in practice on the assumption of competition vanish into nothing as soon as a monopoly supervenes.

The economics of monopoly have not yet been even sketched, but at first glance one can see surprising results.

With a strict banking monopoly all crossed cheques would be drawn on and paid into the same bank. Therefore, all cheque transactions would be book transfers from one customer to another.

Under the competitive banking system, if I have £1,000 at my credit in Parr's Bank, the bank will pay me £20 or £30 a year to leave that deposit there, because if I spent it, I should pay it away to persons who had accounts in other banks. But if there was only one bank, I could only pay it away to other customers of that bank ; the £1,000 could only be transferred from one customer to another. That, obviously, would make no sort of difference to the bank. Therefore, the bank would not pay me £30 a year for refraining from transferring my £1,000 to other accounts in the bank's ledgers.

It is easy to explain why, under competitive banking, a banker's loans are limited by his deposits, and under a unified banking system there would be no such limit. When a bank accepts, say, warrants for goods in dock warehouses as security for a loan, it in effect promises to pay gold, if demanded, to the agreed amount. For most purposes this promise does not take effect, because transactions are in cheques balanced against one another.

But at the end of the day each banker squares up through the Clearing House, and if in any case the amount due *to* other banks exceeds the amount due *from* other banks, the bank which owes actually does pay in gold or in notes or drafts on the Bank of England, which are equivalent to gold.

Deposits in a bank are made in gold or cheques on other banks. The bank which receives £1,000 in deposits, can lend that sum, because its payments out will equal its payments in. But it cannot lend in excess of its deposits to any large extent, because it would have to pay away the difference in gold or its equivalent, at the end of the day.

But if there were only one bank there would be no settling up in the evening ; no other bank would exist to demand a balance in gold. All the elaborate Clearing House business, which is in effect, a balancing up in order to arrange that each particular bank shall have at the end of the day the proper amount of assets to balance its liabilities would cease, because the claims on the goods would always be in the possession of clients of the bank which held the goods. The bank, it is true, would undertake to pay gold against goods as before, but gold for internal circulation—and for the moment I exclude foreign trade—varies in amount slowly and between well-ascertained limits ; and on the average, if one borrower took his loan in gold, other depositors would bring in gold to the equivalent amount.

Remarkable Consequences Thereof.

I confess this proposition is simply staggering. There are our enormous bank deposits, the pride of the City, fifteen hundred millions in all. Banks are amalgamating every day. There are only some sixty or seventy left which do home business in the United Kingdom. If those amalgamate, the need for these enormous deposits suddenly, so to speak, vanishes. The universal banker drops a note to each depositor : " Dear Sir or Madam, The National London Midland County Capital Joint Stock Bank of England has resolved to amalgamate with Messrs. Lloyds, Parr, Barclay, British Linen Co., its remaining competitor, as from the 25th inst., and I beg to inform you that we shall no longer be able to pay interest on your deposit. You may take it somewhere else *if you can.* Your obedient servant, General Manager."

But this suggests a misconception. The interest-bearing value of deposits ceases, not by the fiat of a monopolist, but in actual fact. Bank deposits are only a shadow, so to speak, of wealth. Take a case. If I possess £1,000 of Great Western Railway five per cent. debentures (that is a part of the land, stations, engines, etc., of a railway company) any bank will lend me, say, £1,000 on them at, say, four per cent. If I choose to be so foolish, I can deposit that £1,000 in the same bank and the bank will pay me, say, two and a half per cent. on it.

We have then

(a) Certain tangible things, railway lines, and buildings and engines,
(b) Debenture stock representing them at five per cent.,
(c) A loan from the bank on them at four per cent.,
(d) A deposit at the bank of the loan at two and a half per cent.,

all three latter based on the railway, and consisting of nothing else than the railway. The action of the bank in lending £1,000 on the debentures is to make the railway, to the extent of £1,000, available for currency. For the time it is as much currency as gold or notes.

Now the point I want to make clear—and it is not very simple—is that deposits in banks are based on things like railways or bales of cotton, have no value apart from those things, have no power apart from those things of earning interest, and are not in themselves of any value, but merely represent claims of one set of people on wealth apparently held by another set.

It is all a system of double entry. Every item appears at least twice. So long as we have competing banks this system must be kept up, and a bank must make its claims on the general stock of wealth, that is, its deposits, balance its loans, that is the claims it gives to others, on the particular wealth pawned with itself.

But as soon as it becomes the universal pawnshop, the sole creator of bankers' currency, it cannot be called upon (as any one bank can at present) to pay against property lodged in another bank. Therefore the value of deposits ceases.

Effect on the Rate of Interest.

Another consideration arises. If the unified bank has not to pay interest on deposits,* what rate of interest would it charge on loans? On the whole I do not see why it should charge more than enough to earn the necessary working expenses and interest on its working capital, say one and a half per cent. It will really in practice be much less. But let us say one and a half per cent. for the present. Take a simple case. I buy ten acres of land for £5,000 in order to build houses for sale. I deposit that land—in the form of deeds—with the universal bank, which advances me £4,000. That £4,000

---

* Banks hold large deposits on current account for which they pay no interest. But this is really a concealed "cross entry." The customer pays the bank for keeping his account by letting it have a loan without interest.

is paid away in cheques to timber merchants and brick merchants, and artizans of all sorts, and all the cheques obviously are paid in again to the bank, so that the £4,000 stands in other names than mine. Presently I sell the houses for £10,000 which comes into my account out of some other account all in the one bank. Then I pay off the loan: get my land transferred to the purchasers, and the transaction is closed. I started with £5,000 and end up with £6,000. The bank is out of pocket by the cost of the clerical labor, the valuation of the land and other working expenses, and that is all. These I must pay. Beyond these working expenses, there is no necessary reason why anything should be charged at all.

Further, the effect of this on the rate of interest on borrowed money would be remarkable. If the State bank lent on good security at one and a half per cent. fixed, it would obviously pay me to buy £1,000,000 Consols returning about three per cent., and get the money from the bank at one and a half per cent. The security would be perfect, and the profit £15,000 a year. Everybody would do this. And at once the price of all gilt-edged securities would rise till they returned to an investor only a shade over one and a half per cent. Our two and a half per cent. Consols could be reduced at once to one and a half per cent. Our town and county councils could borrow in future at one and a half per cent. The toll taken by the idle possessors of capital would in future borrowings be only half what it has hitherto been, though existing obligations would continue for a time.

A Bank Monopoly in Sight.

We are already within an easily measurable distance of a banking monopoly. In the Stock Exchange Year Book for 1898 the number of banks recorded which did a home trade, in the United Kingdom and the Isle of Man, is one hundred and twenty. In the volume for 1908 the number is seventy-nine. In ten years forty-one banks have disappeared.

The latest list of joint stock banks,* omitting one or two quite insignificant in size, is sixty-eight, some of them quite small ones. At the present rate of decrease there will be only sixteen in 1924, and only one in 1929! It is not the small banks only which disappear. Only recently the London and County and the London and Westminster, both first rank concerns, joined their forces. It is, moreover, inevitable because large banks almost invariably pay a higher rate of interest on their capital than small ones.† It is an advantage to big banks to buy small ones, and to small ones to sell to big. In another ten years everybody will be discussing what the

---

* "Stock Exchange Year Book," 1912. I have not included the very large number of foreign and colonial banks, which no doubt conduct a little home trade, or the discount houses. The Co-operative Wholesale Bank is not in the list, but I doubt if there are any other omissions.

† The Bank of England is an exception; it has a relatively low rate of dividend because it keeps so large a part of its capital in gold.

effects of a banking monopoly will be. This, then, is no speculation, such as the familiar puzzle, How will newspapers run under Socialism? This banking monopoly is coming so near that it is actually in sight, and its arrival can be calculated almost as accurately as the next total eclipse of the sun.

Moreover, this monopoly cannot be left in private hands. Finance is the life blood of commerce, of industry, and of politics. Any board of directors which possessed exclusive power to grant or withhold credit would be the virtual dictators of the Government and of the lives of the people. No community could endure such a monopoly for an hour in any other hands than its own representatives. And the control over industry which such a monopoly would give to the State must have far reaching consequences.*

International Banking.

But unfortunately this attractive forecast can scarcely be realized in one country alone. If the United Kingdom no longer gave interest on deposits and America maintained her antiquated system of tiny banks, currency would tend to float over where it would earn interest, and this would mean in the long run a demand by America for our gold. In fact competition between countries is on the same lines as competition between banks in one country.

But there is already in existence a piece of machinery expressly designed to maintain our stock of gold. The Bank rate is put up when there is too big a demand for our gold because a relatively high rate of interest attracts floating capital from other financial centres, Paris, or Berlin, or New York, and the influx of capital means either the influx of gold or the cessation of its efflux.

Under the unified banking system this machinery would necessarily be retained, in order to preserve the balance of gold actually required for our international and internal trade.

But this retention of the Bank rate means that interest would continue to be paid on floating capital, that is, amongst other things, bank deposits ; and so it may be said the whole idea of cheap loans vanishes. I think this is not necessarily the case.

Bankers' deposits vary in their depth, so to speak, from day to day money, lent for twenty-four hours only, to loans, mostly taken by bankers trading abroad, for periods up to a year. Now day to day money cannot move far. A lender who may require repayment in a day or even a week will not send his money even as far as Paris. Probably by far the greater part of bankers' deposits is money

---

* The State already participates in the business of banking through the Post Office Savings Banks and the Postal Order and Money Order business. In Austria, Switzerland (1906), Japan (1906), and Germany (1909) Postal Cheque systems have been in operation for some years which in effect convert every post office into a branch bank for the purpose of the transfer of money. (Report by the Postal Clerks Association, 39 Gainsborough Street, Higher Broughton, Manchester. "The Post Office : the Case for Improvement, Development, and Extension," ? 1911. ? free.) Progress in England on these lines may be anticipated, and ultimately the State will doubtless work the Post Office Banking business and the Unified Bank in co-operation. But it is not possible here to deal with the problem of their amalgamation.

required at very short notice, which would in no case be sent abroad. It is true that the rate of interest paid on deposits varies with the Bank rate, but it always lags one and a half per cent. behind that rate, and that rate itself is quite often below the market rate. It is therefore clear that floating capital is attracted from abroad by the rate of discount on bills, and not by the rate of interest on deposits. When the Bank rate is four per cent. in London and three per cent. in Paris, the London holder of a bill who wishes cash for it discounts it in Paris at three per cent. rather than in London at four per cent. In other words he sells the bill in Paris and gets the money (floating capital) sent over to London for him. But the merchant with more money than he wants for the moment does not as a rule deposit elsewhere than with his own bank, and he takes the two per cent. or three per cent., whatever it is, according as fate determines.

It is difficult to foresee exactly what would happen under a unified banking system, that is, under conditions very different from our own. But so far as I can judge the continuance of the protection of our gold reserve by means of a varying Bank rate does not involve the maintenance of our present payment for money placed on deposit. It must be remembered that already the bankers hold enormous sums on current account on which they pay no interest at all. Further, at present Colonial and other banks accept deposits for terms of months at substantially higher rates than the London banks pay, and therefore deposits fixed for long periods tend to go abroad. This tendency of deposits would be promoted if our unified bank paid no interest at all, and perhaps payment of interest on deposits for substantial terms might be necessary, at any rate at first, in order to help to keep our gold at home and prevent our Bank rate from maintaining too high a level.

All this is only a special example of the general rule that industrially the world is rapidly becoming a unit. It is practically impossible for one country greatly to outstrip the others in even such rudimentary instalments of Socialism as factory legislation or such elementary approximations to common sense as reduction of armaments.

As I have said before, it is difficult to see precisely how near we can approach to an ideal banking system in England so long as other countries remain as they are. But of one thing we may be sure. Other countries will advance, as we are advancing ; and if the international difficulty is the only one this forecast has to face, it may be regarded with confident equanimity.

Socialist Theorists Justified.

One point in conclusion. The old Utopian Socialists invented labor notes because they dimly saw that currency should be founded on wealth and not alone on gold. Commerce and finance have spontaneously carried out their idea in a practical form and created the cheque system, which is, in fact, an almost perfect currency, based on wealth, the product of labor.

So, too, these forerunners dimly dreamed that interest was an unnecessary charge on labor and was somehow created by our system of finance. That dream, too, will come true, in so far as the interest is now unnecessarily charged on the simple transaction of making the-realized wealth of the country available for our currency.

·NOTE:

It may be worth while to answer in anticipation two criticisms of a general character on the argument advanced in the foregoing paper.

If the quantity of gold produced bears practically no relation to its present value as currency, how, it may be said, can the enormous prices (i.e., the low value of gold) on goldfields be accounted for, and what is the explanation of the changes in the levels of prices in Tudor and other periods?

The answer is that my paper deals with currency in England, now, under a system of universal banking. In Tudor times and indeed at any time up to about half a century ago, there was no such banking system, and prices, in Tudor times at any rate, *were* determined by the quantity of gold or silver available for currency. The currency system I analyze is very modern and very local, and of other times and places I say nothing.

Again, it may be asked why we should not use silver or copper for our currency if the quantity of gold produced bears no relation to its value in currency. Would the discovery of a method of transmuting lead into gold have no effect on the exchange value of the sovereign?

The answer is this. If any one person possessed the secret of turning lead into gold and used it only to supply gold for his own needs as currency, his great wealth, increasing *pro tanto* the demand for commodities, would infinitesimally raise the general level of prices. Gold, for him, would be more easily obtained than commodities, and he would spend it freely. If many or most people obtained gold with relative ease (as was recently the case at Klondyke, or at any other placer goldfield), the general level of prices *is* raised because gold dust is relatively easier to obtain than bottles of whisky: and gold is in fact used rather for primitive barter than as an adjunct to a modern banking system.

If (as might conceivably happen) a cheap method of extracting gold from sea-water were discovered, the company exploiting the secret would for a while earn enormous profits, and those profits would, by increasing the demand for products, raise, perhaps sensibly, the level of prices. But apart from this the currency value of gold in England would not be directly affected *so long as the whole output was freely absorbed*. (Elsewhere, in the absence of a complete banking system, prices might be greatly raised, and this would *indirectly* affect prices here.) But the time would ultimately come when nobody would want gold at the Mint price : the Bank of England would have enough, and all nations would have what they required for currency and for the arts at the fixed price. Then something would begin to happen. The sea-gold company of the hypothesis would get its gold turned into sovereigns at the Mint in accordance with the law, and these, put into circulation by the company, would be paid into banks and ultimately into the Bank of England. The Bank could not get rid of them because other countries, by hypothesis, already had all the gold they wanted. Our financial system would therefore be clogged with surplus gold which locked up the bank capital in a form yielding no interest. · At this point, if not before, our system of free coinage of gold would no longer work, and the whole problem of currency would have to be reconsidered.

·, · In other words, our present currency system (and incidentally the reasoning of the foregoing paper) is dependent on the fact that the demand for gold exceeds the supply. The output, however great, is absorbed somehow, and there is always room for more. The moment the demand is satisfied, a new factor, so it seems to me, will appear on the scene, the effects of which are not easily calculable.

Finally, I desire to emphasize that the distinction between capital (actual things which earn interest) and currency created out of this capital by banks (which can be used as capital for some purposes) is vital to my argument, and has been as yet insufficiently recognized by economists. It is the interest now charged on this form of currency which under an altered system could be largely and permanently reduced.

Fabian Tract No. 165.

FRANCIS PLACE

THE TAILOR OF CHARING CROSS

BY

ST. JOHN G. ERVINE

PUBLISHED AND SOLD BY

THE FABIAN SOCIETY

Biographical Series No. 1

PRICE TWOPENCE

LONDON
THE FABIAN SOCIETY, 3 CLEMENT'S INN, STRAND, W.C.
OCTOBER 1912

FRANCIS PLACE,

THE TAILOR OF CHARING CROSS.

FRANCIS PLACE was born on November 3rd, 1771, in a "sponging-house," or private debtors' prison, in Vinegar Yard, near Drury Lane, kept by his father, Simon Place, who was at that time a bailiff to the Marshalsea Court. He died on January 1st, 1854, at a house in Foxley Terrace, Earl's Court, at the age of eighty-two. His death attracted almost as little attention as his birth. He might have passed out of the memory of men had not Mr. Graham Wallas dug out the facts of his career from a mass of unattractive manuscripts, and printed them in his admirable " Life of Francis Place." Yet no man of his century was more necessary to the establishment of democracy in England than he. He was essentially the practical man in politics. Other men saw visions and dreamed dreams, but he, when they related their visions and retold their dreams, turned the visions into acts and the dreams into laws. He was an agitator of a totally different type from the agitator of common imagination. He had not the gift of oratory, and was a little distrustful of those who had; he could not stir an audience by emotional appeals, nor did he aspire to do so; he could not force men to deeds by finely written statements, though he tried to do so: he was too prolix, too eager to state all that there was to state, whereas the art of writing consists in knowing what to omit; but he could prepare plans for using to the best advantage the emotion which orators evoked. He made ways for the safe passage of democracy, and devised schemes for its protection while it was still weak. When the visionaries came to him and said, " The people must be free," he replied: " Yes, but how shall we make them free ? " And then, so practical was he, instantly set about discovering a means to this end. The idealist and the practical man too frequently work in opposition to each other. It was fortunate for the cause of democracy that Francis Place, entirely practical, should always have desired to work with the idealists who were setting up the structure of a commonwealth in England in the early nineteenth century.

Boyhood and Education.

His father was a rough, careless, and sometimes brutal man, whose habitual method of communicating with his children was to assault them. " If he were coming along a passage or any narrow place such as a doorway, and was met by either me or my brother, he always made a blow at us with his fist for coming in his way. If we attempted to retreat he would make us come forward, and as certainly as we came forward he would knock us down." Mr. Place, after a number of years' service as a keeper of a sponging-house, took a tavern, but he spent so much of his money in the State lotteries that he frequently had to resort to his old trade as a journeyman baker in order to retrieve his losses, his wife in the meantime maintaining their family by needlework. From the age of four until he was nearly fourteen Francis was sent to one of the private adventure schools which abounded in the neighborhood of Drury Lane and Fleet Street in the eighteenth century. The instruction given to him was of poor quality, but he was quick-witted and eager to know, and he easily became head boy in his school. His thirst for learning, however, did not prevent him from taking part in the street life of his day. He was, writes Mr. Graham Wallas, skilled in street games, a hunter of bullock in the Strand, an obstinate faction fighter, and a daily witness of every form of open crime and debauchery.

When the time came for him to leave school, he being then about fourteen years old, his father decided to apprentice him to a conveyancer, but he refused to become a lawyer; and his father, thus flouted, strode into the bar-parlor and offered him as an apprentice to anyone who would have him. A drunken breeches maker, named France, accepted the offer, and to him the boy was formally bound. During this time he became associated with a "cutter club"—an eight-oared boat's crew—who used to drink and sing together in the evening. The coxswain of this crew was subsequently transported for robbery, and the stroke oar was hanged for murder. A certain quality of pride saved Francis Place from dissoluteness, and in 1790, when he was eighteen, and had given up his indentures, he met his future wife, Elizabeth Chadd.

Marriage.

The effect of this meeting was to check any tendency to viciousness he ever had. He then began the career of extraordinary endeavor, which lasted for the remainder of his life. His fortunes at this time were not happy. His trade was a declining industry, and, although he was a highly skilled workman, he could not earn more than fourteen shillings a week. His family was impoverished; his father, in ill-health, had sold his tavern and had lost the proceeds in a lottery, and his mother was obliged to work as a washerwoman. The time did not seem propitious for marriage; but Place, always indomitable and always hopeful, was prepared to take risks which Elizabeth Chadd, unhappy at home, was willing to share, and in March, 1791, when he was nineteen and a-half, and she was not quite seventeen, they married and went to live in one room in a court off the Strand. Their joint earnings were under seventeen shillings a week. "From this we had to pay for lodgings three shillings and sixpence a week, and on an average one shilling and sixpence a week for coals and candles. Thus we had only twelve shillings a week for food and clothes and other necessaries."

When he was twenty-one, and the father of a child, a strike took place in the leather breeches trade. At this time the Combination Laws were still in force. There were, however, a number of societies of a purely benevolent character in existence, and to one of these, the Breeches Makers' Benefit Society, Francis Place belonged. He has left an interesting account of this society and the strike which it caused : " The club, though actually a benefit club, was intended for the purpose of supporting the members in a strike for wages. It had now, in the spring of 1793, about £250 in its chest, which was deemed sufficient. A strike was agreed upon, and the men left their work."

The conditions of labor in this trade were exceedingly bad. A skilled workman, regularly employed, could earn a guinea a week ; but regular employment was seldom to be had, and, generally speaking, wages for good workmen, often employed, were never more than eighteen shillings a week, and frequently a good deal less. Unfortunately for the leather breeches makers, the employers made a counter move, which eventually destroyed the strike. They urged their customers to buy stuff breeches instead of those made of leather, and at the same time organized a boycott of all leather breeches makers, whether they were concerned in the strike or not. The Combination Laws theoretically applied to all members of the community, to employers as well as to workmen, but although they were rigorously enforced against workmen, Place, in after life, was unable to discover a single instance of their having been enforced against employers.

First Efforts at Organization.

Although Place was a member and a regular subscriber to the funds of his society, he seldom attended any of its meetings, and he was unaware of the fact that a strike had been decided upon, or that it had actually taken place, until he received his dismissal from one of his employers. The moment he heard of the strike he went to the club house, where he was informed that every man out of work would receive seven shillings a week from the funds. He made enquiries, and learned that there were as many members of the society as there were pounds in the chest, and saw that the funds would be exhausted in three weeks. His genius for organizing began to stir. The stewards of the club had no plans laid. It seemed to them that all that was necessary was to declare a strike and pay out seven shillings a week to the members until the funds were depleted. They hoped that by that time the employers would also be exhausted. Place changed all that. He suggested that those members who were prepared to leave London, undertaking not to return for one month, should receive a week's payment in advance. These men would not receive any further sum. A number of the members accepted the offer because of the custom of the trade that a tramping journeyman should receive a day's keep, a night's lodging, and a shilling the next morning, and in some of the larger towns a breakfast and half-a-crown from country leather breeches makers' shops to help him along until he had obtained work.

When this matter was settled, and the fund was thereby relieved, Place proposed another scheme of an ingenious character, whereby each man remaining in London, instead of receiving seven shillings per week, should make up two pairs of breeches of a particular quality, for which he should be allowed four shillings each pair. These breeches were sold in a shop taken for the purpose, Place being employed as manager for twelve shillings a week. The effect of these proposals was that the fund, instead of being exhausted at the end of three weeks, lasted for three months. The strike, however, was unsuccessful. When the money was expended the men had to return to work on the employers' terms, and those of them, like Place, who had been conspicuous in the strike, were refused employment of any sort by any leather breeches maker. The failure of the strike was due to the facts that the industry was a declining one and that the masters, being few in number, were able to combine with little trouble against their workers.

A Time of Acute Poverty.

To this time of strike organization there succeeded, for Place, a time of acute poverty. For eight months he could not obtain work of any kind. He had expended his small savings during the period of the strike and so was without resources. His only child had sickened of smallpox and died. He and his wife suffered every privation that comes from lack of food and adequate shelter. They had pawned all that they had to pawn, obtaining for this purpose the services of an old woman who lived in the same house; for, though they were actually enduring hunger, neither he nor she would go to the pawnbroker in person. When they could no longer find pledgable goods, the old woman, guessing their state, informed the landlord of the house, and he offered them credit for everything he sold, whilst his wife almost forced them to accept bread, coals, soap and candles. "And at the end of our privation, notwithstanding we were only half fed on bread and water, with an occasional red herring, we were six pounds in debt to our landlord."

When it seemed that the boycott upon him would not be removed, Place decided to leave his trade, and sought employment as overseer of parish scavengers at eighteen shillings a week. He obtained the post, but a few days before he was expected to begin his duties, one of his former employers sent for him. He declined to go, suspecting that this was a trap, such as had already been laid for him, to obtain an admission from him of the existence of a trade club, in order to secure his prosecution under the Combination Laws. Mrs. Place, however, went in his stead, "and in a short time she returned and let fall from her apron as much work for me as she could bring away. She was unable to speak until she was relieved by a flood of tears." He and she set to work, laboring sixteen and sometimes eighteen hours a day. "We turned out of bed to work, and turned from our work to bed again." In a short time they were able to redeem their furniture and to purchase necessaries. They moved to a more convenient home, and so prosperous did they become that Place was able to assist his mother to some extent.

Self-Education.

During this terrible period of his life Place read a great many hard books, "many volumes in history, voyages and travels, politics, law and philosophy, Adam Smith and Locke, and especially Hume's Essays and Treatises. . . . . I taught myself decimals, equations, the square, cube and biquadrate roots. I got some knowledge of logarithms and some of algebra. I readily got through a small school book of geometry, and having an odd volume, the first of Williamson's Euclid, I attacked it vigorously and perseveringly." Prior to this time he had read "the histories of Greece and Rome, and some translated works of Greek and Roman writers ; Hume, Smollett, Fielding's novels and Robertson's works, some of Hume's Essays, some translations from French writers and much on geography, some books on anatomy and surgery, some relating to science and the arts, and many magazines. I had worked all the problems in the introduction to Guthrie's Geography, and had made some small progress in geometry." In addition he had read "Blackstone, Hale's 'Common Law,' several other law books, and much biography." He obtained these books partly through the good offices of an old woman who acted as caretaker of chambers in the Temple—she borrowed the books from the rooms she cleaned—and partly through hiring them from a book shop in Maiden Lane, Charing Cross, "leaving a small sum as deposit and paying a trifle for reading them."

After a few months of prosperity his work slackened, and again he found himself unemployed. He immediately set about reorganizing the Breeches Makers' Benefit Society, set it up in 1794 as a Tontine Sick Club, himself the secretary at a salary of £10 per annum, and was able to obtain in the spring of 1795, without a strike, the increase of wage which had unsuccessfully been demanded in 1793. This success, apparently, was too much for the members of the society. They seemed to imagine that their labor troubles were for ever at an end, and they dissolved the society, sharing the funds among the members. Place lost his post. For a time he was employed by other trade clubs to draft rules and articles, and was appointed secretary and organizer of the carpenters, plumbers, and other trade clubs. He was now twenty-three years of age.

The State of Europe.

The history of the world at that time was one of change and revolution. Ancient institutions were toppling, and great traditions were dissolving. In America and in France, republics had been established. In England, the old order was speedily giving place to the new : the aristocrat and landed proprietor was collapsing before the plutocrat and factory owner. In Ireland, discontent was about to swell into rebellion. The naturalistic philosophers had dealt stout blows to religion and the divine right of kings—the whole social theory was being revised and restated. The spirit of Voltaire and Rousseau was abroad in England, preparing the way which later on was to be trodden by Byron and Shelley. Thomas Paine had lately published "The Rights of Man," the most famous of all the replies to Burke's " Reflections upon the French Revolution," and a million and a half copies had been sold in England alone. Later came the " Age of Reason," which, shattered Place's Christianity.

It was natural, therefore, that in the great recasting of the world's beliefs which then took place, Francis Place should turn his mind towards those who were identified with the building of a democracy in England. In 1794 he became a member of the London Corresponding Society—"the mother," as Burke called it, "of all the mischief.'' It was characteristic of Place that he joined the society at a time when many of its members had been frightened into resignation through the persecution of some of its officers. " Many persons, of whom I was one, considered it meritorious and the performance of a duty to become members now that it [the society] was threatened with violence." It seems incredible that this society, with mild intentions, should have so terrified the oligarchy as it apparently did. Its political program consisted of universal suffrage, annual parliaments, payment of members, and its object was to " correspond with other societies that might be formed having the same object in view, as well as with public-spirited individuals." The title of the society led many persons to believe that its function was to correspond with the Government of France : the state of the public mind at that time was so panicky that such correspondence was instinctively assumed to be of a treasonable character. The society, however, had no relationship with the French Government. Its constitution was framed for the purpose of enabling working class organizations throughout the country to communicate with each other by letter without violating the law against the federation of political bodies.

The London Corresponding Society.

In May, 1794, Thomas Hardy, the secretary and founder of the society, together with ten other persons, was arrested for high treason. Place became a member of one of the committees which were formed to arrange for the defence of the accused men. The result of the trial was that the prisoners were acquitted, and instantly there came a great accession to the membership of the society. Place became a person of consequence, generally taking the chair at committee meetings. He began to urge that method of political agitation which remained his method for the rest of his life, and which he practised with singular success. He opposed himself to those who were continually urging that public demonstrations should be held chiefly to scare the oligarchs into granting reforms. Place did not believe in the excessive susceptibility of the governing classes to terror. " I believed that ministers would go on until they brought the Government to a standstill—that was until they could carry it on no longer. It appeared to me that the only chance the people either had or could have for cheap and good government was in their being taught the advantages of representation, so as to lead them to desire a wholly representative government ; so that whenever the conduct of ministers should produce a crisis, they should be qualified to support those who were the most likely to establish a cheap and simple sort of government. I therefore advised that the society should proceed as quietly and privately as possible." His advice at this date was disregarded, and the scarifying demonstrations were held; but the oligarchy, instead of frantically passing ameliorative Acts, promptly passed Treason and Sedition Bills, suspended Habeas Corpus, and clapped the agitators into gaol without trial. The effect of this was almost to destroy the society, the more timid members scurrying out of it in that panic which they had hoped would fall upon the governing classes. It lived on in a state of depressed vitality, but Place, finding his advice several times foolishly disregarded, resigned from it, and in 1798, the year of the Irish rebellion, it died.

Attempts to Establish a Business.

While Place was engaged in these political adventures, he was also endeavoring to raise his status from that of a journeyman to that of an employer. He thought of a method of doing this which he calculated would take six years to execute, although, as the event showed, he was able to do it in four years. The success of the scheme depended upon patience, much knowledge of human nature, very hard work and an indomitable will. Place possessed all these qualities. He began to build up a connection by getting a few private customers, and then he set about obtaining credit from drapers and clothiers. " I knew that by purchasing materials at two or three shops, however small the quantities, and letting each of them know that I made purchases of others, each would sell to me at as low a price as he could, and each would after a time give me credit." He did this, and soon found, as he had anticipated, that offers of credit were made to him. " From this time I always bought on short credit ; instead of paying for the goods, I put by the money, taking care always to pay for what I had before the term of credit expired. I thus established a character for punctuality and integrity . . . . and, as I foresaw, I should, if I could once take a shop, have credit for any amount whatever."

Misfortune in Business.

Unfortunately, his fortune did not flourish as well at first as he had hoped. His charges were low and his customers were few, and some of them neglected to pay for the goods with which he supplied them. His family, which now consisted of himself, his wife, and two children, began to suffer hardship again, and his wife, whose nerve had been shattered in the bad time that succeeded the strike of the leather breeches makers, urged him to give up his hope of becoming a master and resume his occupation as a journeyman. He steadfastly refused to do this, insisting that he would work himself into a condition to become a master tradesman. During this period, one of " great privation," he displayed that immense strength of purpose which distinguished him always, and which, a little later than this, was to endure a greater trial still. Only a man of unbounded self-confidence would have faced the chilly, grey view which lay before

Francis Place at that time. Only a man of unquenchable spirit would have thought, when he was half-starved, of learning French so that he might give his children "the best possible education which my circumstances could afford." He propped his French grammar before him while he worked, and learnt it by rote. He spent his evenings in reading Helvetius, Rousseau and Voltaire, and despite his acute poverty, men of advanced views began to seek him out in order that they might talk to him on the topics of the time.

. His fortune improved a little, and in 1799 he and a fellow-workman entered into partnership and opened a tailor's shop at 29 Charing Cross. The stock was obtained on credit, and the joint cash funds of the partners on the opening day were one shilling and tenpence ! In two years they were employing thirty-six men ! It was now, when prosperity seemed to be leaping upon him, that Place suffered his greatest trial. His partner married a woman who could not agree with Place, and, apparently at her suggestion, and on the strength of the promise of a large loan, he forced the business into liquidation and bought the goodwill for himself. Poor Mrs. Place lost her spirit altogether. "She saw nothing before her but destruction. . . . Industry was no use to us, integrity would not serve us, honesty would be of no avail. We had worked harder and done more than anybody else, and now we were to suffer more than anybody else." For the rest of her life she was haunted by the fear of poverty. But this sudden disaster did not destroy Francis Place. He convinced his creditors that he had been vilely served by his partner, and they offered him so much assistance that, in 1801, three months after he had first learnt of his partner's perfidy, he opened a finer and bigger shop on his own account at No. 16 Charing Cross. From this time onwards his affairs prospered, and in 1816 the net profits for the year from his business were more than three thousand pounds. He retired from trade in 1817, his age being forty-six years, and devoted himself to politics.

Place had one very notable quality—the power to concentrate on a particular piece of work—and during the first five years that he was tenant of the shop in Charing Cross, he devoted himself entirely to the task of building up his business. The time, as has been said, was troublous, and the borough in which he lived, that of the City and Liberty of Westminster, was the vent of discontent. By arrangement, the two seats for the borough were shared by the Whigs and the Tories. Radical candidates sought election without success. At the end of five years' tenancy of his shop, Place began to relax his attention from business considerations and revived his interest in politics. At first he found his friends among the well-to-do Whig tradesmen, most of whom were electors of the borough and great admirers of Charles James Fox, Sheridan and Erskine. Place, who "never had any respect for Fox or Sheridan, and not much for Erskine," bantered his friends on their regard for the Whigs, " who cared little for the people further than they could be made to promote their own interests, whether those interests were popular or pecuniary." Indeed, his hatred of the Whigs was almost excessive.

Always they were " the dirty Whigs," the sole difference between them and the Tories being that " the Tories would exalt the kingly power that it might trample upon the aristocracy and the people, while the Whigs would establish an aristocratical oligarchy to trample on the king and the people." About this time Cobbett, for whom Place had very little respect, was endeavoring, in his *Political Register*, to revive the democratic movement, and seeing in the borough of Westminster a likely seat for a democratic representative, he wrote four " Letters to the Electors of Westminster," which were printed in his journal. The last of these letters was published just after Lord Percy, eldest son of the Duke of Northumberland, and " a very young man, without pretensions to talents of any kind," had, through a ministerial trick, been returned unopposed for the borough. The letter bitterly reproached the electors for allowing themselves to be hoodwinked as they had been, and it had considerable effect upon those who read it.

Westminster Politics.

But the reproaches of Cobbett were not the only force which set going a movement among the electors to secure independent representation for Westminster. The conduct of the Duke of Northumberland during the sham election was one factor, Sir Francis Burdett was another. The duke ordered his servants, clad in showy livery, to distribute bread and beer and cheese among a number of ruffians who congregated about his house. The servants tossed chunks of bread among these men and women, who were, of course, alleged to be the free and independent voters of Westminster. The spectacle of these people clawing at the bread and lapping up the beer, which had been upset from the barrels and was running through the gutters, filled the electors themselves with disgust. In 1807 Sir Francis Burdett, a very wealthy man, sick of the intrigues of parties, was nominated, almost against his desire, as a candidate for the borough, together with one James Paull, who had polled a respectable number of votes at a previous election. Place, who had begun to extend his circle of acquaintance in the district, took charge of the electoral arrangements, and, despite the fact that the two candidates quarrelled four days before the date of the poll and fought a duel in which they were both seriously wounded, managed to get Burdett elected. Paull's candidature had been dropped. For three weeks Place worked at the committee rooms from seven o'clock in the morning until twelve o'clock at night. The difficulties seemed almost insuperable, and the discouragements offered to the Radicals were enormous. They had decided not to have any " paid counsellors, attorneys, inspectors or canvassers, no bribing, no paying of rates, no treating, no cockades, no paid constables, excepting two to keep the committee-room doors." They simply informed the magistrates of what they were doing, and left the responsibility of keeping the peace to them.

Place had organized this election so remarkably that he was resorted to by all sorts of persons for advice in connection with demonstrations, and the Westminster Committee became the recognized political authority in the borough. Sir Francis Burdett, sincerely democratic, was not a very able man, and a few years later he allowed himself to be convinced that Place was a Government spy. The grounds for this charge were too flimsy to bear examination, but for nine years Place and Burdett did not speak; and, owing to the aspersions made upon him, Place withdrew from active association with his former friends, although he always gave his advice to them when they asked for it, which was frequently. What follows explains why.

Imprisonment of Sir Francis Burdett.

It happened in the course of time that Burdett came into collision with the Government in defence of free speech. He had made a speech in the House of Commons protesting against the imprisonment of one John Gale Jones, who had been committed to Newgate for organizing a discussion at a debating society on the action of the Government in prohibiting strangers from the House during the debate on the Walcheren expedition. Burdett printed his speech in Cobbett's *Register*, and this act was held to be a breach of privilege. A motion to commit Burdett to the Tower was carried by a majority of 38, but Burdett, barricading himself in his house at Piccadilly, announced that he considered the Speaker's warrant to be illegal, and that he would resist its execution by force. The soldiers were called out, the mob became agitated, and the City authorities, who were antagonistic to the Government, tried, without success, to convince the Government that their conduct was illegal. A council of war, to which Place was invited, was held in Burdett's house. A number of half-crazy people were present, one of whom had devised a plan for defending the house from the attack of the soldiery. Gunpowder mines were to be laid in front of the house, so that the attacking soldiers might easily be blown to a place where there is neither war nor rumors of war. The common sense of Place was obviously necessary to restrain these wild conspirators. "It will be easy enough," he said, "to clear the hall of constables and soldiers, to drive them into the street or to destroy them, but are you prepared to take the next step and go on?"

They were not prepared to take the next step; they knew that it was impossible for them to do so; and so the crazy scheme crumpled up. Place did not object to the proposal to resist the soldiers by force because it was a proposal to declare civil war, but because it was impossible for the rebellious Radicals to make any sort of a fight. "There was no organization and no arms, and to have resisted under such circumstances would have been madness." All they could do, he urged, with any hope of success was to use the police forces of the City against the Government. For various reasons, the City forces were unavailing, and Burdett was arrested and conveyed to the Tower. Whilst he was in prison, Place was called upon to serve on the jury which inquired into the circumstances in which Joseph Sellis, valet to the Duke of Cumberland, died.

Charged with Treachery.

The duke was very unpopular with the populace, and most people desired that the jury should return a verdict to the effect that the valet had been murdered by his master. Place, having carefully investigated the evidence, came to the conclusion that Sellis died by his own hand, and succeeded in bringing the other jurymen to the same conclusion, although they were all prejudiced against the duke. It was because of his conduct on this occasion that Place was accused of being a Government spy, and through it, with the help of the malicious, he lost the friendship of Burdett. For ten years the word " spy " was the favorite taunt thrown at him by those whom he displeased.

The effect of this on his career was partly good and partly bad: bad, because it led to his abstention from movements in which he would have been of the greatest service; good, because the leisure he now had enabled him to get into contact with men who had other points of view than mere Radicalism. He became acquainted with Thomas Spence, the land nationalizer, and with Robert Owen. Spence was a very honest, very poor, and very single-minded man, who loved mankind in the abstract so passionately that when he contemplated mankind in the concrete he lost his temper. He had fixed his mind so completely on land nationalization that he could not see or think of anything else. He suffered very great privations in propagating his views, getting his living by trundling a barrow about London, from which he sold saloup and pamphlets denouncing landlords and their villainies. He was John the Baptist to Henry George. The nationalization of land meant to him the establishment of the kingdom of heaven on earth and the birth of a new race of men. The man who is optimistic about the future is invariably pessimistic about the present, and it was so with this poor Spence. No man loved humanity so purely as he, and no man lashed his fellows with his tongue so bitterly. He reviled the men about him because they were not the men of his dream . . . . Contact with this one-idea'd man sharpened Place's belief that the men of the vision can only be brought to reality out of the flesh and blood of the men of fact.

Robert Owen.

Robert Owen, that curious compound of a man of vision and a man of affairs, came to Place in 1813 with his " New View of Society." He was " a man of kind manners and good intentions, of an imperturbable temper, and an enthusiastic desire to promote the happiness of mankind." Like all men who have discovered the secret of human ills, Owen was convinced that his project, so " simple, easy of adoption, and so plainly efficacious . . . . must be embraced by every thinking man the moment he was made to understand it." It is, perhaps, the fundamental defect of the idealist mind that it forgets that human nature is not a rigid, measurable thing, and that the charm of human beings is not in their resemblances, but in their differences. Owen looked upon the world and saw it peopled by millions of Robert Owens ; and, since he knew what Robert Owen desired, he imagined that he also knew what all men needed and desired. Once, after he had seen Owen, Place wrote in his diary : "Mr. Owen this day has assured me, in the presence of more than thirty other persons, that within six months the whole state and condition of society in Great Britain will be changed, and all his views will be carried into effect."

Place also became acquainted with many of the Utilitarian philosophers. James Mill, the father of John Stuart, and Jeremy Bentham became his close friends, and from them he derived an amount of knowledge which he could not otherwise have obtained. James Mill was a man of notable austerity of manner, as those who have read John Stuart Mill's Autobiography will know. He must have been an uncomfortable sort of man to live with, for he could not, as Place could, comprehend the value of idleness. He saw the world as an enormous schoolroom, and all the men and women merely scholars, but he did not appear to see any place in which the knowledge when obtained would be used. Like St. Francis of Assisi, he despised every worldly thing ; but, unlike St. Francis, he had no hope of a better place. He simply acquired knowledge for knowledge's sake. Whenever Place visited the Mills, he, like all who stayed with them, was put through his lessons as relentlessly as John Stuart and Willie and Clara Mill. For four hours every day he was compelled to grind at Latin, repeating the declensions afterwards to the inexorable Mill. Out of this tremendous industry, this search for knowledge, there came that spirit which tests and is not afraid to reject. The Utilitarians had for their watchword "the greatest happiness of the greatest number." James Mill did not believe in happiness at all, but he was prepared to make the best of a hopeless case, and so he and his friends set themselves to the task of delivering England from the mess in which they found her.

Malthusianism.

Place saturated his mind with the writings of the political economists, and about this time he got the one bee which he ever had in his bonnet. He read Malthus's "Principle of Population," and became a Neo-Malthusian in theory, for in practice he had fifteen children. Until he died he believed that the redemption of the people from poverty could only be brought about by the limitation of families. Laws wisely administered might do much, but they would only be so much trifling with a great problem. It is astonishing, when one reflects upon the fact that he possessed rather more common sense than is generally given to men, that he should so easily have believed this economic fairy tale. But although he held this belief very firmly, he did not, as the one-idea'd do, preach it exclusively. He saw that Neo-Malthusian doctrines were not likely to impress ignorant and impoverished men, and he set about the work of creating an instructed and prosperous race. There was an enormous amount to be done. The Combination Laws were still in force, and these alone made it impossible for the working class to improve their status. The theory of individualism at that date had completely gone out of its mind. There were no trade unions, no Factory Acts, no Public Health Acts, no Education Acts, no Workmen's Compensation Acts ; the Corn Laws were still unrepealed ; the franchise was a limited one; the Poor Law was that of Elizabeth. The agricultural laborer was in a state of frightful demoralization, and the town laborer was little better. There was such a state of affairs in England as should have inspired any self-respecting deity to fury, and have reduced the most optimistic of men to a state of chronic depression. The odd thing about human nature is that it never despairs, and although that terrible time in England seems to us, who stand at this distance from it, to have been one in which obstacles were piled so high in the way of the reformer that progress was almost impossible, the reformers of the day regarded them with as good heart as we regard the comparatively trifling obstacles that lie strewn about the field of endeavor to-day. If Carlyle, who came later, saw men as "mostly fools," Place saw them as "mostly ignorant," and so that this description might no longer be applicable to his countrymen he devoted himself to the business of education.

Elementary Education.

It is commonly alleged by the Church educationists that the system of elementary education in England was started by members of the Established Church. "There is a sense," the *Church Times* says, "in which every Christian is a member of the Church of England . . . but a Quaker is an unbaptized person, and therefore not a Christian at all." In 1798, a young Quaker, named Joseph Lancaster, began to teach poor boys in a shed adjoining his father's house in the Borough Road. Lancaster was one of those men with whom Place frequently came in contact, a mixture of pure genius and pure folly. He could conceive big ideas, but he could not rear them after delivery. Place was the divinely-inspired foster-parent to the ideas of such men. He could not himself conceive large schemes, but he had the rare faculty of knowing a good idea when he saw it, and the still rarer faculty of being able to develop the idea and bring it to adult life. Lancaster was a wild creature, extraordinarily extravagant, somehow convinced that he had only to spend enough money for his difficulties to disappear. He was continually in danger of being committed to the debtors' prison. His proposal was to establish schools in which the pupils should be taught by older pupils—monitors. The whole education theory at that time, so far as working class children were concerned, was very hazy. The idea that the task might be undertaken by the State does not appear to have penetrated even Place's mind : he and his colleagues saw the Lancastrian schools resting for ever on a voluntary basis. In these circumstances, economy was essential. Subscriptions were not likely to be large or many, for a large number of influential persons were opposed to education for the working class. Lord Grosvenor, whom Place approached, "said he had a strong desire to assist the institution, but he had also some apprehension that the education the people were getting would make them discontented with the Government . . . . *we* must take care of ourselves." He did not subscribe. It must not be thought, however, that the necessity for economy was the cause of the monitorial system being employed. Place himself was of opinion that the teaching of children by children was a better way of educating them than having them taught by trained men and women. On this basis the schools were started after a great deal of wrangling between Lancaster and the trustees whom he had persuaded to provide the funds needed. In 1811 the "National Society for the Education of Poor Children in the Principles of the Established Church" was formed, and elementary education, so to speak, found its legs.

The Lancastrian Schools.

The history of the Lancastrian schools is a saddening one. Lancaster quarrelled interminably, aud finally he had to be pensioned off. The society was dissolved and a fresh one was formed, Place being a member of the committee. In drawing up the bye-laws of the new society he displayed his intense dislike of patronage of poor people. He deleted the words "poor" and "laboring poor" and any expression which "could give offence or hurt the feelings of anyone." He never at any time forgot that he, too, had suffered poverty ; and even in connection with his fad, Neo-Malthusianism, he retained undiminished his loyalty to his class. "Mr. Malthus," he writes, concerning "Principle of Population," "denies to the unemployed workman the right to eat, but he allows the right to the unemployed rich man. He says, 'Every man may do as he will with his own,' and he expects to be able to satisfy the starving man with bare assertions of abstract rights. Mr. Malthus is not speaking of *legal right*, for, he says, the poor have a *legal right*, which is the very thing he proposes to destroy. It is an abstract right, which is denied to the poor man, but allowed to the rich ; and this abstract, which has no meaning, although dignified with the title of the 'law of nature, which is the law of God,' is to be explained and taught to the poor, who are to be fully convinced."

Place worked with great assiduity for the success of the Lancastrian schools, and endeavored to start a series of higher schools on a similar basis, for which Jeremy Bentham devised a scheme of education. He mapped the whole of London into districts, in each of which there was to be a school to which poor parents could send their children on payment of a penny a week. This payment was to save the pupils from the stigma of charity. But all his educational plans failed. The monitorial system was a bad one ; Lancaster was plotting against Place ; and, worst of all, the committee began to quarrel among themselves. Place was an atheist, and he made no secret of his disbelief in God. Lancaster wrote to members of the committee, alleging that Place secretly designed to remove the Bible from the schools, and succeeded in creating so much ferment that, although he personally was discredited, Place found it no longer possible to work with his colleagues, and so he resigned his position.

Joseph Hume.

By this time he was well acquainted with Joseph Hume, whom he supplied with facts and material for argument in favor of reforms in the House of Commons. The combination of talents that here took place was a remarkable one. Hume, a very sincere Radical, had enormous vitality and was absolutely impervious to discouragement. He could not be put out of countenance by anyone. Place was industrious and certain. He could draw up rules and schemes easily. When he presented a document to a member of Parliament, the member could be assured that it contained facts and not fancies. These two men in conjunction, the one in the House, the other outside, both of them the butts of the wealthy and the powerful, between them compelled the oligarchy to do their will. But Place was the greater man of the two. Hume had the sense to do what Place told him, though now and then, as in the case of the Combination Laws, he had to be urged somewhat strenuously to action. When Hume had to speak in the House, he went as a matter of course to Place for instructions, and Place primed him so well that he always made a mark in the debates.

Reference has several times been made in this short sketch to the Combination Laws. During the eighteenth century there had been passed a series of statutes directed against combinations of journeymen in particular trades. The first of the series was an Act of 1721 "for regulating the journeymen tailors within the bills of mortality," and the last the General Act of 1799 "to prevent unlawful combinations of workmen." A unanimous refusal to work at reduced prices was regarded as sufficient evidence of unlawful combination, and the non-acceptance by an unemployed journeyman of work offered to him by an employer in his trade meant liability to undergo a long period of imprisonment or to be impressed into His Majesty's sea or land forces. These laws were the most serious obstacle that lay in the way of labor. So long as they were on the statute book the condition of the working class nearly approached that of slavery. It was to remove them from the statute books that Francis Place worked, and in 1824-5, working almost single handed, he managed to do it. "The Labor Question," wrote Mr. Gladstone in 1892, " may be said to have come into public view simultaneously with the repeal, between sixty and seventy years ago, of the Combination Laws, which had made it an offence for laboring men to unite for the purpose of procuring by joint action, through peaceful means, an augmentation of their wages. From this point progress began."

The Combination Laws.

In 1810, the *Times* prosecuted its journeymen compositors for belonging to a combination and taking part in a strike. This is the text of the sentence inflicted upon them by Sir John Sylvester (Bloody Black Jack), the Common Serjeant of London :

" Prisoners, you have been convicted of a most wicked conspiracy to injure the most vital interests of those very employers who gave you bread, with intent to impede and injure them in their business ; and, indeed, as far as in you lay, to effect their ruin. The frequency of such crimes among men of your class of life, and their mischievous and dangerous tendency to ruin the fortunes of those employers which a principle of gratitude and self-interest should induce you to support, demand of the law that a severe example should be made of those persons who shall be convicted of such daring and flagitious combinations in defiance of public justice and in violation of public order. No symptom of contrition on your part has appeared, no abatement of the combination in which you are accomplices has yet resulted from the example of your convictions."

Bloody Black Jack thereupon sentenced the prisoners, who had asked for higher wages, to terms of imprisonment varying from nine months to two years.

In the same year that this happened the master tailors tried to obtain an Act of Parliament to put down a combination of their workmen, and Place, who was a master tailor, was invited to join the committee. He refused to join the committee, but they elected him a member of it against his will. He attended one meeting and told the masters as plainly as possible why he would not join them, and why they ought to abandon their project. They declined to do this, and a committee was appointed by the House of Commons to take evidence. Place went before the committee and offered to give evidence, which was accepted, and succeeded in bringing to the ground the proposal to quash the union. He now began seriously to get the laws repealed. He could not hope for assistance from the workmen themselves, who had made up their minds that the laws were irrevocable. Whenever a dispute took place between employers and workmen, he interfered, "sometimes with the masters, sometimes with the men, very generally, as far as I could, by means of one or more of the newspapers, and sometimes by acting as a pacificator, always pushing for the one purpose, the repeal of the laws." He wrote letters to trade societies, sent articles to newspapers, interviewed employers and workmen, and collected as much evidence as possible to assist him in his purpose. He lent money to the proprietor of a small newspaper in order that he might propagate his views in it, and he had copies of the paper distributed among people who were likely to be affected by it. He induced Hume to take interest in the proposal, and in five years had worked up so much feeling on the subject that he began to think the repeal of the laws was now certain. He was too optimistic, however, and it was not until 1822 that Hume gave notice of his intention to bring in a Bill for that purpose. This Bill was mainly intended to be a demonstration. "I was therefore in no hurry to urge Mr. Hume to proceed beyond indicating his purpose. I supplied him with a considerable quantity of papers, printed and manuscript, relating to the subject, advised him to examine them carefully, and promised my assistance to the greatest possible extent for the next session. These papers were afterwards sent to Mr. McCulloch, at Edinburgh, who was at this time editor of the *Scotsman* newspaper, and he made admirable use of them in that paper. This gave a decided tone to several other country papers, and caused the whole subject to be discussed in a way, and to an extent, which it had never been before."

The Repeal of the Combination Laws.

Unfortunately, a Mr. Peter Moore, member for Coventry, in 1823 produced a rival Bill, which so scared the House of Commons that when Hume introduced Place's measure in 1824 it met with considerable opposition. In view of the temper of the House, Place advised Hume to abandon the Bill and move for a Select Committee to enquire into the working of the laws. The timidity of the general body of the House spread to some of Hume's supporters, who induced him to whittle the motion to nothing. Place began to stir. He lectured Hume at great length, wrote a letter to him to be shown to his wavering friends, and drew up memoranda for Hume's own benefit. The upshot of the affair was that Hume was bullied by Place into moving for the committee, which was appointed. A great deal of publicity was given to the fact that the committee was sitting, and delegates from workmen's societies began to arrive in London from all parts of the country. Place interviewed them all. "I heard the story which everyone of these men had to tell. I examined and cross-examined them, took down the leading particulars of each case, and then arranged the matter as briefs for Mr. Hume, and, as a rule, for the guidance of the witnesses, a copy was given to each." Place had to encounter great difficulties in preparing matter for this committee. The members of the committee would not allow him to assist Hume officially, and they professed great indignation at finding Hume's briefs made out in Place's handwriting. They talked of calling him before them for tampering with the witnesses, a course of action which would have pleased him immensely, but, preserving their sanity, they did not do so. The witnesses, too, were difficult. Many of them had pet theories of their own to expound, and Place was hard put to it to induce them to keep their theories to themselves. All of them expected that wages would instantly rise when the Combination Laws were repealed. "Not one of them," says Place, "had any idea of the connection between wages and population." Presumably Place, who spent three months in arranging the affairs of this committee, did a little unobtrusive propaganda on Neo-Malthusianism on discovering this.

His tactics in connection with the Select Committee seem to have been extremely able. The mere secretarial work which he performed was enough to try the strength of several men ; but, in addition to this, he found time to think out the best way of circumventing the upholders of the laws. He had to make it clear to his friends that speechmaking would be a mistake, and that instead of the committee presenting a report in the customary manner, it would be better to submit their recommendations at first in the shape of resolutions, and then, when argument had been expended and members of the House were tired of the subject, present the report.

This was done, and all went well until the Attorney-General persuaded Hume to allow a barrister, named Hamond, to draft the Bills. Hamond made a sad mess of the business, and the reformers were now in a difficulty. The Bills were not what they wanted, but if they were not careful they might lose even those. The difficulty was surmounted by Place, who simply redrafted the Bills as he desired them to be and said no more about it. Hamond, having received his fee, did not bother further, and in due course the Bills were passed through the Commons without anyone quite understanding what had happened, and, after a period of peril in the Lords, they became statutes. The Combination Laws were repealed and working men were free to combine for their own protection.

After the Combination Laws.

Place, having soaked his mind in the economics of the time (he had too much respect for economists) naturally enough failed to appreciate the necessity for Trade Unions. He imagined that the repeal of the Combination Laws would make them unnecessary. "The combinations of workmen are but defensive measures resorted to for the purpose of counteracting the offensive ones of their masters. . . . Combinations will soon cease to exist. Men have been kept together for long periods only by the oppression of the laws. These being repealed, combinations will lose the matter which cements them into masses, and they will fall to pieces." He had not at that date discovered that the securing of victory is not nearly so important as the maintenance of victory. When the Combination Laws were repealed the country was enjoying great prosperity, and the freed workmen speedily set about demanding a more adequate share in it. Strikes broke out everywhere. A section of the employing class began to agitate for the re-enactment of the laws, and Place, fearful lest this should happen, urged the workmen to desist from striking. But the workmen were not going to be persuaded even by good friends like Place to desist from enforcing their demands. They were profoundly convinced that the law had been used for the purpose of keeping down wages, and they were determined to get them raised, particularly as the cost of living was rapidly increasing. In the cotton trade a great lock-out by the masters took place. The shipbuilders refused to confer with their workmen on the question of grievances, and issued a note to the effect that members of the Shipwrights' Union would not be employed by them. "The conduct of both the sailors and shipwrights was exemplary, no disorderly acts could be alleged against them. But as the shipping interest . . . had the ready ear of ministers, they most shamefully misrepresented the conduct of the men, and represented the consequences as likely to lead to the destruction of the commerce and shipping of the empire. Ministers were so ignorant as to be misled by these misrepresentations, and were mean and despicable enough to plot with these people against their workmen. The interest of the unprincipled proprietors of the *Times* newspaper was intimately connected with the 'shipping interest,' and it lent its services to their cause. It stuck at nothing in the way of false assertion and invective; it represented the conduct of Mr. Hume as mischievous in the extreme, and that of the working people all over the country as perfectly nefarious; and it urged ministers to re-enact the old laws, or to enact new ones, to bring the people into a state of miserable subjection." It will have been observed by those who read the press carefully during the Railway Strike in 1911 and the Coal Strike of 1912 that capitalist journalism has not changed its character.

Attempt to Re-enact the Combination Laws.

To this agitation there followed something which is one of the most discreditable of the many discreditable things that politicians have done. The shipbuilders, lying hard, induced Mr. Huskisson and Mr. (afterwards Sir Robert) Peel to give notice of their intention to re-enact the Combination Laws. Huskisson had already solemnly assured Hume that he had no intention whatever of doing this, and Hume, believing Huskisson to be a man of honor, had accepted his word, and so was unprepared to counter his motion for a committee. Fortunately, Huskisson had drafted his motion clumsily. He asked for a committee "to enquire *respecting the conduct of workmen*" Hume and Place were quick to see that such an enquiry could only be adequately conducted if the persons into whose conduct enquiry was to be made were given an opportunity of rebutting the charges made against them, and, to the astonishment and disgust of Huskisson, they demanded that the workmen should be brought before the committee and examined. Another factor in favor of Hume and Place was that the Easter holidays were approaching and the committee could not meet for at least a fortnight. Place used the time to great advantage. He wrote to the trade societies, urging them to send delegates and to collect money for the payment of parliamentary agents and expenses; he collected money himself; he wrote a pamphlet exposing Huskisson's speech, and had it carefully distributed. He and Hume "nobbled" the Attorney-General and succeeded in persuading him to refuse to draft Huskisson's Bill. They filled the passage leading to the committee room with workmen demanding to be examined. Place wrote letters here and letters there, put witnesses through their paces, interviewed members, induced witnesses to demand payment for their services, which had been refused, although it was made to employers without cavil, and annoyed the committee so intensely that they talked of having him brought to the bar of the Commons. He and Hume could not prevent a new measure from being passed, but they were able to mould it to so great an extent that it differed very slightly from the previous measure moved by Hume. In the Commons,

during the committee stage, the ministers attacked them grossly.
"Wallace gave loose to invective and was disgracefully abusive.
Huskisson became enraged and most grossly insulted Sir Francis
Burdett and Mr. Hobhouse. Mr. Peel stuck at nothing. He lied
so openly, so grossly, so repeatedly, and so shamelessly, as even to
astonish me, who always thought, and still do think, him a pitiful,
shuffling fellow. He was repeatedly detected by Mr. Hume and as
frequently exposed. Still he lied again without the least embarrassment and was never in the smallest degree abashed."

Agitation for Reform.

The repeal of the Combination Laws was not the only service
which Place rendered to the cause of democracy, but it was the
greatest. He might then reasonably have desisted from his labors,
for he was growing old, and had suffered a great loss in the death of
his wife, but he was of that order of men for whom there is no rest
in life. There was work still to he done which he, better than other
men, could do. The entire system of parliamentary representation
needed reforming, and Place threw himself into this work with as
much vigor as he had displayed over the Combination Laws.

George IV, a man of ungovernable temper, who was likely, said
one of his tutors, to be "either the most polished gentleman or the
most accomplished blackguard in Europe, possibly an admixture of
both," died on January 26th, 1830. He was a god with clay feet,
from the point of view of Whigs and Radicals ; for his sympathy
with Whiggery during the time that he was Prince of Wales was an
affectation chiefly for the purpose of annoying his father. The
movement for reform, begun in the reign of George III, was
opposed, with the King's concurrence, by the ministers of George
IV. A few months before he ascended the throne, the massacre of
Peterloo took place. He opposed, on religious grounds, the passing
of the Catholic Emancipation Bill until the Duke of Wellington
informed him that either he would have to compromise with his
religious conscience or make ready for civil war in Ireland. The
King compromised. All compromise denotes friction and ill temper,
and the circumstances of the time made it inevitable that the conduct of the State should be difficult. The Duke of Wellington, who
as a politician lost the reputation he had gained as a soldier, was of
the damn-your-eyes type of statesman, a type which, while picturesque, is unpleasant to live under. He rigidly opposed himself to
any reform of the parliamentary system, and soon after the accession
of William IV he was forced to resign the premiership. The state
of Europe was again disturbed. The Three Days Revolution had
taken place in Paris, and Louis Phillippe, a constitutional monarch,
had supplanted Charles X, a despot. This change heartened the
reformers in England. A little later came another revolution ;
Belgium broke away from Holland, but here there was less hearten-
ing for the reformers, who feared that the King's ministers, in con-
sort with the governments of Prussia and Holland, might make war
on France. Had such an alliance been formed for such a purpose,

there might have been in England a revolution approaching in fearfulness that which took place in France in 1793. Place, indeed, was prepared for this to happen. In the towns the housekeepers were banding themselves together and threatening to refuse to pay taxes should war be declared. In the country the laborers were burning hayricks in thirteen counties. In London, workmen, stirred by Robert Owen and Thomas Hodgskin, the forerunner and inspirer of Karl Marx, were in that mood of sullenness which is the prelude to revolt. Reform had to be, and so the Duke went out of power and the Whigs, under Earl Grey, came in.

The Reform Bill.

The Whigs, always valiant and progressive when the prospect of office was remote, were strangely reticent about their principles when the prospect of office was near. Place conceived it to be his duty to make them voluble again, and so he began once more his old task of organizing agitation. Letters were written here, there, and everywhere; deputations were arranged; public opinion was moulded through the press and from the platform; and at length backbone was put into ministers, who would much rather have been spineless. The Reform Bill was introduced into the House of Commons on March 1st, 1831. It was a better Bill than Place had expected. Its sponsors thought it was worse than he expected, and they were prepared for his rage; but while he proceeded to agitate for more, he was fairly content with what he had received. The Bill received a second reading on March 21st, by a majority of one, which meant that defeat in committee was certain. On April 19th and 21st the Government were defeated, and on April 22nd the King prorogued Parliament, which immediately dissolved. The new Parliament met on June 14th, having a majority of over a hundred in favor of the Bill, which was at once reintroduced. The Tories so successfully obstructed its passage through the Commons that it did not reach the Lords until September 21st. On October 8th the motion for the second reading in the Upper Chamber was rejected by a majority of forty-one. It was now that Place's fighting instinct was thoroughly aroused. On the day following the rejection of the Bill he organized a demonstration in its favor, which was held on October 13th, and was a great success. On Monday he attended four public meetings, and on Tuesday, hearing that the Whigs were likely to compromise over the Bill, he wrote a letter, which he hoped would be shown to the ministers, in which he hinted that a riot would probably take place. He addressed meetings, drew up a memorial to the ministers declaring that if the Bill were not passed in its original form "this country will inevitably be plunged into all the horrors of a violent revolution," and immediately took a deputation to see Lord Grey. The deputation was received by that lord at a quarter to eleven at night in a very holty-toity manner. "Any disturbances would be put down by military force." Dissensions began to separate the reformers themselves. The middle class reformers were prepared to compromise on the

Bill, they to be included in it, the working classes to be excluded from it. The fury of Place on this occasion was remarkable. He wrote to Grote, the historian, "they [the working-class] proved that they were ready, at any risk, and at any sacrifice, to stand by us. And then what did we do? We abandoned them, deserted, betrayed them, and shall have betrayed them again before three days have passed over our heads. . . . We, the dastardly, talking, swaggering dogs, will sneak away with our tails between our legs."

The amount of work he did was almost as great as he did when he organized the campaign for the repeal of the Combination Laws ; and it was as effective, for the Government introduced a new Reform Bill which was as good as, if not better than, the old one. The troubles of the reformers were not yet over, for the Bill had to be forced through the Lords. Before the Bill reached that House there was an outbreak of cholera in England, which made political agitation almost impossible. "The King, under the influence of his wife, his sisters, and his illegitimate children," writes Mr. Graham Wallas, "was now nervous about the Bill, and disinclined to secure ministers a majority by creating peers." The Whigs were ignorant of this, although the Tories were aware of it. On March 26th, 1832, the second Reform Bill was introduced into the House of Lords. Place had drawn up a petition to the peers in favor of the Bill, and this petition, "quietly offensive," was printed in many newspapers. Contrary to expectation, the Lords seemed willing to read the Bill a second time, and this fact caused suspicion to grow in the minds of the reformers that an intrigue to spoil the Bill was being carried on. Place discovered that the intrigue was to substitute a twenty pound franchise for the ten pound franchise in London. On April 17th the Bill was read a second time by a majority of nine, but was wrecked in committee, by a majority of thirty-five, on May 7th. The King declined to create the peers demanded by Lord Grey, who resigned, and the Duke of Wellington was called again to power. This in itself was sufficient to inflame the people. A bishop was mobbed in church and the King was hooted on Constitution Hill. Queen Adelaide was publicly execrated. People made preparations for the revolution which they felt to be at hand, and military men set about drilling the reformers for the fight.

"Go for Gold."

A far simpler means of breaking the opposition than that of bloodshed was found by Place. He caused a number of bills to be posted about the country which bore this legend : To stop the Duke go for gold. The people were advised to draw their balances from the Bank of England and to demand payment in gold. The depletion of the reserve was not a thing to be contemplated by the directors of the bank with equanimity. The King, a poor creature, gave way, Lord Grey obtained his guarantees, and the Bill was safe.

Its passage, however, made small difference to the working class, in whose minds the doctrines of Robert Owen and Thomas Hodgskin began to develop. A new word was added to the language—

Socialism—and in 1833 Owen, with others, endeavored to form a national federation of trade unions. The originators of the movement, which quickly attracted half a million members, proposed to begin their work by declaring a general strike for an eight hours day on March 1st, 1834. This strike, however, did not take place, the funds of the federation having been wasted on a number of sectional strikes, and the movement almost died. On March 17th, 1834, six agricultural laborers were sentenced to seven years transportation for "administering illegal oaths" while forming a branch of the Grand National Trades Union. The declining movement was restored to strength, and strong efforts were made to secure the remission of this brutal sentence, but without success. There followed to this a period of industrial unrest, and then gradually the Grand National Trades Union drooped and died. But if the thing itself was dead, the discontent which caused it to be was still potent.

The Passing of the Reform Bill.

The enactment of the Reform Bill, after a discussion spread over a period of nearly a century, only added half a million persons to the list of electors. Almost the whole of the laboring class was still unenfranchised. On August 14th, 1834, destitution legally became a crime. The new Poor Law, with its principle of deterrence, was the instrument to this end. The Poor Law Commissioners asserted that, in the interests of the independent poor (a phrase without meaning), the condition of the pauper should be less eligible than that of the worst situated independent laborers, on the ground that if this were not so, there would probably cease to be any independent laborers. Two things were then operating on the working class mind : one was the treachery of the middle class, which, with the aid of the working class, obtained enfranchisement for itself, and then refused to assist the working class to similar political freedom ; the other was the poverty brought about by the failure of the harvests and the depression of trade in 1837. Dear food, low wages, and scarcity of work made the difficulty of devising a condition of life for paupers which would be less eligible than that of the worst situated free laborer one which the administrators of the Poor Law could not surmount. They did their best, however, and the result was an agitation against the Poor Law, a demand for factory legislation and for political reform. Out of this discontent came Chartism.

Chartism.

In 1838 Francis Place drew up the "People's Charter," in which were set forth the famous six points : Manhood Suffrage, Equal Electoral Districts, Vote by Ballot, Annual Parliaments, Abolition of Property Qualification for Members of the House of Commons, and Payment of Members of Parliament for their services. The Chartist movement in England resembled the Fenian movement in Ireland, in that a great deal of fuss was made about nothing. The proposals contained in the "People's Charter," seem to us to be mild enough, but to the oligarchy of that time they seemed to denote the end of all things ; and men went into the streets and fought with the soldiers for the sake of the Charter. In 1839 ten men were killed and many were wounded in Newport, Monmouthshire. Three of the leaders were sentenced to death, their punishment being afterwards commuted to transportation. In 1842 there were riots in the northern and midland parts of England, and in 1848 the Chartists scared the wits out of England with a proposal to hold a demonstration at Kennington Common, which demonstration turned out to be as futile as the Fenian invasion of Canada.

Francis Place had little to do with the Chartists. His habit of mind was different from that of Lovett, Vincent, Cleave, and the other leaders of the movement. He was a Malthusian economist, they were Socialists and angry class warriors ; and so, although he respected them and maintained friendly relations with them, particularly with Lovett, his association with them was of small account. His chief work was to draft the Charter and to secure the commutation of the death sentences into sentences of transportation. They belonged to the order of pioneers ; he belonged to the order of men who come after pioneers. But though he could not work easily with pioneers, he was fully conscious of their utility. "Such men," he wrote, "are always, and necessarily, ignorant of the best means of progressing towards the accomplishment of their purpose at a distant time, and can seldom be persuaded that the time for their accomplishment is distant. Few, indeed, such men would interfere at all unless they imagined that the change they desired was at hand. They may be considered as pioneers who, by their labors and their sacrifices, smooth the way for those who are to follow them. Never without such persons to move forward, and never but through their errors and misfortunes, would mankind have emerged from barbarism and gone on as they have done, slow and painful as their progress has been."

Old Age and Death.

Place was now an old man. Misfortune closed in on him towards the end of his life. He had married a second time and the marriage was unhappy. He separated from his wife. He lost some of his money ; and then, last scene of all, paralysis fell upon him and his brain became affected. Death came to him quietly in the night, when no one was by. He passed out, almost forgotten. "Can death," wrote Marcus Aurelius, "be terrible to him to whom that only seems good which in the ordinary course of nature is seasonable ; to him to whom, whether his actions be many or few, so they be all good, is all one ; and who, whether he beholds the things of the world, being always the same, either for many years or for few years only, is altogether indifferent ?"

Francis Place was not of that order of democrats who believe that the common man knows more than the rare man. He had not the Chestertonian trust in instinct ; he was an early Victorian Fabian. "We want in public men," he wrote, "dogged thinking, clear ideas, comprehensive views, and pertinacity, i.e., a good share of obstinacy or hardheadedness." Kind hearts might be more than coronets, but good brains were better than either. On the other hand, he knew enough of rare men to know that they were fallible. Politicians with careers to fashion and reformers who have gone mad on their theories, these were creatures against whom the common man must always be on his guard. He could not suffer fools gladly, but he was not that worst of fools, the fool who will not learn from fools. Spence and Owen were fools in his eyes because they allowed themselves to become obsessed with one idea, but he was not oblivious of the fact that that idea was of value. It was his fortune not to possess a sense of humor ; he could not joke. No man who can see the ridiculous can possibly be a leader ; no man with a sense of humor can ever head a revolution, for the absurdities of enthusiasm will stand up before him so prominently that he will not be able to see the goal towards which the enthusiasts are marching. Keir Hardie leads men ; Bernard Shaw laughs at them. Although Place had spent so many years of his life in pulling strings and had frequently seen men's motives laid bare before him, he did not become cynical. "I take the past," he wrote to Lovett, "and comparing it with the present, see an immense change for the better." In the same letter he wrote : "I saw that to better the condition of others to any considerable extent was a long uphill piece of work ; that my best efforts would produce very little effect. But I saw very distinctly that I could do nothing better, nothing indeed half so good." He was full of rare courage and rare faith. I have called him a Neo-Malthusian, although that term did not come into use until the time of Bradlaugh and Mrs. Besant, because his views were identical with those who were so named. He propagated his Neo-Malthusianism to his own detriment and loss. It was sufficient for him to believe in a thing to nerve himself to bring it to be ; but he had to be convinced that the thing was worth while. He saw men as brains wasted. Great masses of people were born, passed through the world, and died without conferring any advantage on their fellows ; not because they were indolent or indifferent, but solely because use was not made of them. It was his desire so to order the world that every man and woman in it could move easily to his or her place. That man is a democrat who believes in a world where the wise man may be wise and the fool may be foolish, and no one will call him out of his name or demand more from him than he can give ; who believes in diversity rather than uniformity, knowing that it is the variations from type which make type tolerable. Fools and wise men have their place in the world ; the one may be the inspiration of the other. Plato and Aristotle were the fulfilment of each other. Owen and Place made it possible for democracy to be in England.

> Bring me my bow of burning gold !
> Bring me my arrows of desire !
> Bring me my spear : O clouds unfold !
> Bring me my chariot of fire !

I will not cease from mental fight,
Nor shall my sword sleep in my hand,
Till we have built Jerusalem
In England's green and pleasant land.

So wrote William Blake. If Owen wielded the sword and stretched the bow of burning gold, Place forged the one and made the other. It was that men might know that Place worked without ceasing; he made mistakes, but he had the right vision, and in good time men came to know more than possibly he had expected. It is our vision that matters, not the mistakes we make. We may go forth like Columbus, to discover a new way to the Indies, and fail in our endeavor. But what matter? We may discover the Americas.

The only book on the subject is : " The Life of Francis Place, 1771-1854," by GRAHAM WALLAS, M.A. Longmans, Green & Co.; 1898. Published at 12s. and subsequently reprinted at 2s. 6d. Both editions are out of print, and another cheap reprint is under consideration.

FABIAN SOCIETY.—The Fabian Society consists of Socialists. A statement of its Rules and the following publications can be obtained from the Secretary, at the Fabian Office, 3 Clement's Inn, London, W.C.

FABIAN ESSAYS IN SOCIALISM. Paper 6d.; cloth 1/6; post. 2½d. and 4d.

WHAT TO READ on Social and Economic Subjects. Fifth edition, revised to October, 1910, and enlarged. Interleaved, paper, 1s. n. cloth 2s. n., post. 2d.

THIS MISERY OF BOOTS. By H. G. WELLS. 3d., post free 4d.

FABIAN TRACTS and LEAFLETS.

Tracts, each 16 to 52 pp., price 1d., or 9d. per doz., unless otherwise stated.
Leaflets, 4 pp. each, price 1d. for six copies, 1s. per 100, or 8/6 per 1000.

The Set of 81, 3s.; post free 3/5. Bound in Buckram, 4/6 n.; post free 5s.

I.—General Socialism in its various aspects.

TRACTS.—159. The Necessary Basis of Society. By SIDNEY WEBB. 151. The Point of Honour: a Correspondence on Aristocracy and Socialism. By RUTH CAVENDISH BENTINCK. 147. Capital and Compensation. By EDW. R. PEASE. 146. Socialism and Superior Brains. By BERNARD SHAW. 142. Rent and Value. 138. Municipal Trading. 121. Public Service versus Private Expenditure. By Sir OLIVER LODGE. 113. Communism. By WM. MORRIS. 107. Socialism for Millionaires. By BERNARD SHAW. 139. Socialism and the Churches. By Rev. JOHN CLIFFORD, D.D. 133. Socialism and Christianity. By Rev. PERCY DEARMER. 78. Socialism and the Teaching of Christ. By Dr. J. CLIFFORD. 42. Christian Socialism. By Rev. S. D. HEADLAM. 79. A Word of Remembrance and Caution to the Rich. By JOHN WOOLMAN. 75. Labor in the Longest Reign. By S. WEBB. 72. The Moral Aspects of Socialism. By SIDNEY BALL. 69. Difficulties of Individualism. By SIDNEY WEBB. 51. Socialism: True and False. By S. WEBB. 45. The Impossibilities of Anarchism. By BERNARD SHAW (price 2d.). 7. Capital and Land (7th edn. revised 1908). 5. Facts for Socialists (11th ed., revised 1908). 132. A Guide to Books for Socialists. LEAFLETS—13. What Socialism Is. 1. Why are the Many Poor? WELSH TRACTS—143. Sosialaeth yng Ngoleuni'r Beibl. Gan J. R. JONES (Caernarfon). 141. Translation of 139. 87. Translation of 78. 38. Translation of 1.

II.—Applications of Socialism to Particular Problems.

TRACTS.—164. Gold and State Banking. By E. R. PEASE. 163. Women and Prisons. By HELEN BLAGG and CHARLOTTE M. WILSON. 2d. 162. Family Life on a Pound a Week. By Mrs. PEMBER REEVES. In cover, 2d. 161. Afforestation and Unemployment. By ARTHUR P. GRENFELL. 160. A National Medical Service. By F. LAWSON DODD. 2d. 157. The Working Life of Women. By Miss B. L. HUTCHINS. 155. The Case against the Referendum. By CLIFFORD D. SHARP. 154. The Case for School Clinics. By L. HADEN GUEST. 153. The Twentieth Century Reform Bill. By H. H. SCHLOESSER. 152. Our Taxes as they are and as they ought to be. By ROBT. JONES, B.Sc. In cover, 2d. 150. State Purchase of Railways. By EMIL DAVIES. In cover, 2d. 149. The Endowment of Motherhood. By H. D. HARBEN. In cover, 2d. 145. The Case for School Nurseries. By Mrs. TOWNSHEND. 144. Machinery: its Masters and its Servants. By H. H. SCHLOESSER and C. GAME. 140. Child Labor under Capitalism. By Mrs. HYLTON DALE. 136. The Village and the Landlord. By EDW. CARPENTER. 131. The Decline in the Birth-Rate. By S. WEBB. 130. Home Work and Sweating. By Miss B. L. HUTCHINS. 128. The Case for a Legal Minimum Wage. 122. Municipal Milk and Public Health. By Dr. F. LAWSON DODD. 125. Municipalization by Provinces. 123. The Revival of Agriculture. 118. The Secret of Rural Depopulation. 115. State Aid to Agriculture: an Example. 112. Life in the Laundry. 98. State Railways for Ireland. 124. State Control of Trusts. 86. Municipal Drink Traffic. 83. State Arbitration and the Living Wage. LEAFLET.—104. How Trade Unions benefit Workmen.

III.—Local Government Powers: How to use them.

TRACTS.—156. What an Education Committee can do (Elementary Schools), 3d. 137. Parish Councils and Village Life. 109. Cottage Plans and Common Sense. 76. Houses for the People. 82. Workmen's Compensation Act. 54. The Humanizing of the Poor Law. LEAFLETS.—134. Small Holdings: and how to get them. 68. The Tenant's Sanitary Catechism. 71. Ditto for London.

IV. -General Politics and Fabian Policy.

Fabian Tract No. 166.

ROBERT OWEN

SOCIAL REFORMER

BY

B. L. HUTCHINS

PUBLISHED AND SOLD BY

THE FABIAN SOCIETY

Biographical Series No. 2

PRICE TWOPENCE

LONDON:
THE FABIAN SOCIETY, 3 CLEMENT'S INN, STRAND, W.C.
NOVEMBER 1912

Robert Owen, Social Reformer.

I have never advocated the possibility of creating a physical and mental equality among the human race, knowing well that it is from our physical and mental varieties that the very essence of knowledge, wisdom, and happiness, or rational enjoyment is to arise. The equality which belongs to the new, true, and rational system of human existence is an equality of conditions or of surroundings which shall give to each, according to natural organization, an equal physical, intellectual, moral, spiritual, and practical treatment, training, education, position, employment according to age, and share in local and general government, when governing rationally shall be understood and applied to practice.—" Life of Robert Owen," by Himself, p. iii.

ROBERT OWEN is a figure of great significance in the social history of the nineteenth century. It is easy to show the limitations of his educational theories ; it is child's play to explode his particular form of Socialism ; and it is not difficult to demonstrate that his style was ponderous and he himself something of a bore. Yet, when all these admissions have been made, " whatever his mistakes, Owen was a pathfinder." *

He was born into a time of crisis and convulsion,

> " Wandering between two worlds, one dead,
> The other powerless to be born."

The Industrial Revolution was ignored by some contemporary thinkers, and was a hopeless puzzle, a dark enigma, to others. It is Owen's glory that while still young, with little education, and all the cares of business and commercial responsibility on his shoulders, he saw his way to the solution of some of the most pressing social difficulties and anomalies, and put his ideas in practice in his own factory and schools with astonishing success. There are personalities, such as William Morris, or even Lord Shaftesbury, who in their different ways are more attractive, more affecting, more sympathetic, but the remarkable fact about Owen is that his ideas on social legislation were at once original and practical. Our factory legislation is still based upon his suggestions more than upon those of any other man ; and if the unspeakable horrors of child labor under the early factory system have been mitigated, and the disgrace of England in this matter to a large extent removed, it should not be forgotten that Robert Owen showed the way.

Early Life.

Robert Owen was born in Newtown, Montgomeryshire, North Wales, on May 14th, 1771, and was baptized on June 12th following. His father, also a Robert Owen, was brought up to be a saddler,

* Helene Simon.

and probably an ironmonger also, the two trades being, in small towns, then often combined. The mother's name was Williams, and she belonged to a respectable family of farmers living near Newtown, where the couple settled on marriage. The elder Owen, in addition to his two trades, filled the office of postmaster, and had much of the management of parish affairs in his hands. There were seven children, of whom the subject of this memoir was the sixth. Two died young. The most characteristic of Owen's reminiscences of childhood is the incident, as related by him, of accidentally swallowing some scalding "flummery" or porridge when quite a little boy, which so damaged his stomach that he was always incapable of digesting any but the simplest food, and that in very small quantities. "This," he remarks, with an optimism all his own, "made me attend to the effects of different qualities of food on my changed constitution, and gave me the habit of close observation and of continual reflection ; and I have always thought that this accident had a great influence in forming my character."

The boy attended the school of a Mr. Thicknesse, who appears to have had no very remarkable qualification for his office, but to have been on friendly terms with his pupil, whom (at the age of seven !) he associated with himself as assistant "usher." Owen was a voracious reader, and devoured all the books his father's friends in the town could lend him. Among these were "Robinson Crusoe," "Philip Quarle," "The Pilgrim's Progress," "Paradise Lost," Richardson's and other standard novels. He also read, he says, "religious works of all parties," being a religiously inclined child ; but this multifarious reading gave him cause for surprise in the immense hatred and opposition he found between members of different faiths, and also between the different sects of the Christian faith. These studies were diversified by games and dancing lessons, in all which amusements he records complacently that he excelled his companions, adding, rather comically, that "the contest for partners among the girls was often amusing, but sometimes really distressing." He also remarks in this connection that "the minds and feelings of young children·are seldom duly considered, and that if adults would patiently encourage them to express candidly what they thought and felt, much suffering would be saved to the children and much useful knowledge in human nature would be gained by the adults." There is, perhaps, here a touch of over sentimentality ; but, considering how brutal the treatment of children at this period frequently was, it is interesting to find a man who was himself so signally successful in the discipline and management of children, urging thoughtfulness and consideration upon the adult mind of his time.

Apprenticeship.

The experiences of this baby usher lasted about two years. At ten years old, at his own earnest wish, he was sent to London, to be under the care of his elder brother, who, having worked with a saddler, had settled himself comfortably by marrying his master's widow and taking over the business. A situation was found for little Robert with a Mr. McGuffog, who had begun life with half a crown, which he laid out in the purchase of "some things for sale," for hawking in a basket. The basket had been exchanged for a pedlar's pack, and subsequently the pack for an establishment at Stamford, "for the sale of the best and finest articles of female wear." Robert was domesticated with the McGuffog family for some years, treated like their own child, "carefully initiated into the routine of the business, and instructed in its detail." "Many of the customers . . . were amongst the highest nobility in the kingdom, and often six or seven carriages belonging to them were at the same time in attendance at the premises." He recalls of his master and mistress that the husband belonged to the Church of Scotland, the wife to that of England ; but so placable and tolerant were the two, that they went every Sunday first to the one church, afterwards to the other, and he "never knew a religious difference between them." This observation early inclined him to view dogmatic differences as unimportant.

After a few years he left these good friends, and took a place as assistant in an old-established house on Old London Bridge, Borough side. Being now arrived at the mature age of fifteen, he says, " My previous habits prepared me to take an efficient part in the retail division of the business of serving. I was lodged and boarded in the house and had a salary of twenty-five pounds a year, and I thought myself rich and independent. . . . . To the assistants in this busy establishment the duties were very onerous. They were up and had breakfasted and were dressed to receive customers in the shop at eight o'clock—and dressing then was no light matter. Boy as I was then, I had to wait my turn for the hairdresser to powder and pomatum and curl my hair, for I had two large curls on each side, and a stiff pigtail, and until all this was very nicely and systematically done, no one could think of appearing before a customer. Between eight and nine the shop began to fill with purchasers, and their number increased until it was crowded to excess, although a large apartment, and this continued until late in the evening, usually until ten or half past ten, during all the spring months. Dinner and tea were hastily taken—two or three, sometimes only one, escaping at a time to take what he or she could the most easily swallow, and returning to take the places of others who were serving. The only regular meals at this season were our breakfasts, except on Sundays, on which day a good dinner was always provided and was much enjoyed. But when the purchasers left at ten or half past ten . . . . a new part of the business began. The articles dealt in as haberdashery were innumerable, and these when exposed to the customers were tossed and tumbled and unfolded in the utmost confusion and disorder, and there was no time or space to put anything right and in order during the day. . . . . It was often two o'clock in the morning before the goods . . . . had been put in order. . . . . Frequently at two in the morning, after being actively engaged on foot all day from eight on the previous morning, I have scarcely been able with the aid of the bannisters to go upstairs to bed. And then I had but five hours for sleep." This strain and overwork seemed to Owen more than his constitution could bear, and he obtained another situation, in Manchester. Here he found good living, kind treatment, and reasonable hours of work. He received £40 a year, with board and lodging, and considered himself to be "overflowing with wealth."

In Business at Eighteen.

When he was eighteen years old, he heard from a mechanic who supplied the firm with wire bonnet frames that some extraordinary inventions were "beginning to be introduced in Manchester for spinning cotton by new and curious machinery." The maker of bonnet frames after a time succeeded in getting a sight of these machines at work, and told Owen "he was sure he could make and work them," if only he had capital. He thought that with a hundred pounds he could make a beginning, and offered Owen half profits and partnership if he would lend him that sum. Robert immediately wrote to his brother William in London to ask if he could make the advance required, which request was granted. Robert gave notice to his employer and told him he was going into business for himself. So far as we can learn from his autobiography, no one seems to have been particularly astonished at this lad of eighteen starting on his own account. Meantime a large workshop had been obtained, and about forty men set to work making machines, the necessary materials, wood, iron, and brass, being obtained on credit. Of this light-hearted pair of partners, one, Owen, "had not the slightest knowledge of this new machinery—had never seen it at work." The other, Jones, the mechanic partner, knew little about "book-keeping, finance matters, or the superintendence of men," and was without any idea how to conduct business on the scale now projected. Owen's experience in drapery establishments had given him some idea of business management. As he sagely remarks, he knew wages must be paid, and that if the men were not well looked after, the business must soon come to an end. He kept the accounts, made all payments and received monies, and closely observed the work of the different departments, though at this time he did not really understand it. He managed to maintain order and regularity, and the concern did far better than he had expected. The firm made and sold mules for spinning cotton, and did a fair amount of trade, though as Robert confesses, the want of business capacity in his partner caused him some fear and trembling.* After some months of this, a man possessed of a moderate capital offered to join Jones and put some money into the business. They offered to buy out Robert Owen, and he separated very willingly from his partner. By agreement with them he was to receive six mule machines for himself, three of which only were actually handed over, with a reel and a making-up machine.

At this time Arkwright was starting his great cotton-spinning mill, but the manufacture of British muslins was still in its infancy.

Autobiography, p. 23.

Owen says that before 1780 or thereabouts no muslins were for sale but those made in the East Indies, but while he was apprenticed to McGuffog a man called Oldknow, of Stockport, in Cheshire, began to manufacture what he described as "British mull muslin." It was less than a yard wide, and was supplied to Mr. McGuffog for 9s. or 9s. 6d., and retailed by the latter to his customers at 10s. 6d. the yard. It was eagerly bought up by McGuffog's aristocratic customers at that price, and Oldknow could not make it rapidly enough. This incident no doubt helped Owen to realize that there were considerable possibilities in the new machines. Although employing only three hands he was able to make about £6 a week profit. A rich Manchester manufacturer called Drinkwater had also built a mill for finer spinning, and was filling it with machinery, but being entirely ignorant of cotton spinning, although a first-rate merchant, was somewhat at a loss to find an expert manager.

Manager of a Large Mill.

Owen, hearing of Drinkwater's dilemma, went to his counting house, and, inexperienced as he was, asked for the vacant situation. The great capitalist asked what salary the youth required, and was amazed at the cool reply, "Three hundred a year." His protest, however, being met by a demonstration that this surprising young man was already making that sum by his own business, Drinkwater agreed to take up Owen's references, and told him to call again. On the day appointed he agreed to the three hundred a year, and took over Owen's machinery at cost price.

Robert Owen was now installed as manager in authority over five hundred men, women, and children, and his predecessor having already left, and his employer understanding nothing of the work, he entered upon his new duties and responsibilities without any instruction or explanation about anything. Much of the machinery was entirely new to him. He determined, however, to do the best he could, inspected everything very minutely, examined the drawings and calculations of the machinery left by Lee, was first in the mill in the morning, and locked up the premises at night. For six weeks he abstained from giving a single direct order, "saying merely yes or no to the questions of what was to be done or otherwise." At the end of that time he felt himself master of his position, was able to perceive the defects in the various processes, and the incorrectness of certain parts of the machinery, all then in a rude state, compared with later developments. Owen was able to greatly improve the quality of the manufacture, and appears to have been very successful in the management of the workpeople. Drinkwater, who cared nothing for personal supervision of his mill, was much pleased to find his responsibilities taken off his shoulders. He raised Owen's salary, and promised to take him into partnership in three years time.

Life at Manchester.

The next three or four years were a time of mental growth and stimulus for this strange lad. He made friends among the staff at

Manchester College, and joined in evening meetings for the discussion of "religion, morals, and other similar subjects." He met Coleridge, who had wished to discuss with him, and became a member of the celebrated "Lit. and Phil.," or the Literary and Philosophical Society of Manchester, which gave him an introduction to the leading professional men of the town, especially those of the medical profession. He was shortly afterwards invited to become a member of what he describes as a "club or committee" of this society, which included the celebrated Dr. Thomas Percival as its president, Dr. Ferriar, and others. Dr. Percival invited Owen to speak at a meeting, a suggestion which embarrassed and confused the young man, who succeeded only in stammering a few incoherent sentences. On a later occasion, however, Owen read a paper on the subject of fine cotton spinning, which was well received by the society ; and his name appears in 1796 as a member of the Manchester Board of Health, a body formed by Dr. Percival to devise remedies for the evil and unhealthy conditions incidental to factory employment.

His connection with Mr. Drinkwater came to a sudden end. Oldknow proposed to marry Drinkwater's daughter, and wished to be taken into partnership. As he had the reputation of being a wealthy, rising man, Drinkwater was eager to accept him both as a son-in-law and a partner, and asked Owen to abandon the agreement for partnership and remain on as manager at an increased salary. Owen's pride was aroused by this rather shabby attempt to break the previous contract, and he at once resigned, not only the prospect of partnership, but also his existing situation. He received more than one offer of partnership from capitalists who doubtless knew of his technical knowledge and business capacity, and after declining one rather haughtily because its conditions seemed to him not sufficiently favorable, he accepted another, which was, in fact, less advantageous. He became managing director of the Chorlton Twist Company, and had to superintend the building of its new factory and the installation of the machinery.

Marriage.

In the course of a business visit to Glasgow, where his firm had many customers, Owen made the acquaintance of Miss Dale, destined later on to become his wife. Her father was David Dale, owner of the New Lanark Mills, a man of great wealth, and at that time probably the leading merchant in Glasgow. Not only was his worldly position greatly superior to Owen's, but there was a further obstacle to be overcome in his religious opinions. Dale was an extremely pious and narrow-minded Nonconformist ; Owen was already a Freethinker, taught by determinism that a man's religious beliefs were irrevocably fixed by his antecedents and circumstances, and therefore could be the subject neither of blame nor praise. Having discovered that the young lady was not unresponsive to his affection, but that her father was unlikely to receive him favorably, Owen determined nevertheless to obtain an introduction to Dale, and, with his usual curious mixture of simplicity and audacity, conceived the idea of calling on him with a proposal to purchase the mills. Dale was somewhat astonished by such a proposal from so young a man, but advised him to journey to New Lanark and inspect them. The previous negotiations that had been going on between the young people subsequently came to Dale's ears, and at first displeased him. Owen was a stranger, an Englishman, and unknown to him. Owen, however, was backed up by his partners, John Barton and John Atkinson, who arrived at Glasgow to go into the matter in person. The upshot of the matter was that their offer was accepted by Dale, who eventually consented also to the marriage of Owen and his daughter. In 1798 or '99 (the dates are somewhat confused in the Autobiography) Owen found himself at twenty-eight manager and part proprietor of the New Lanark Mills and a married man.

At New Lanark.

This event forms the turning point in Owen's career. His extraordinarily rapid success in winning an assured position at an early age was no doubt due in part only to his own ability, since some part of it can be accounted for by the peculiar circumstances of the time, the introduction and development of steam power and machinery having made it possible to obtain profits on a startling scale. But Owen was a junior partner, and his own capital was but small. His first concern was to secure an ample dividend for the firm, this being the necessary condition of liberty to carry out the measures of reform in the works that he was already considering in his own mind. An isolated remark in the Autobiography (which is written in a rambling and unsystematic manner) gives the clue to his cogitations. Early in the time of his association with Drinkwater he " noticed the great attention given to the dead machinery, and the neglect and disregard of the living machinery," or, in plainer language, of the workers employed. Owen's peculiar power of detachment from the merely personal aspect of his affairs preserved him from the egotistic optimism characteristic of many manufacturers of that date, who, having greatly increased their own wealth through the Industrial Revolution, could not see its attendant evils. He had associated with Dr. Percival in Manchester, and had heard of the diseases and other terrible evils that were caused by the herding of pauper apprentices in insanitary dens in the neighborhood of the mills. In some of the mills, especially those in secluded valleys removed from any check of public opinion, little children were made to work night and day, in heated rooms, uncleansed and unventilated, with little or no provision for teaching, care, or education. In the worst cases there were cruel beatings and other brutal punishments, and in most, probably, little thought for means of safeguard against and prevention of terrible accidents from machinery. Owen's intention was "not to be a mere manager of cotton mills, as such mills were at this time generally managed, but to . . . change the conditions of the people, who were surrounded by circumstances having an injurious influence upon the character of the entire population of New Lanark."

The Mills.

A considerable amount of information as to the state of these mills before Owen took them in hand is accessible, but it is not all unanimous. Owen, in his Autobiography, paints a gloomy picture ; while visitors, who made excursions to New Lanark, professed themselves impressed by Mr. Dale's liberality to the factory children and his zeal for their morals and education. The discrepancy of evidence is, however, more apparent than real. According to the standard of those days the New Lanark Mills were models. They were kept much cleaner and were far better ventilated than the ordinary cotton mill, and the pauper children, whom Mr. Dale was obliged to obtain from a distance, were, as Owen himself told Sir Robert Peel's Committee in 1816, well fed and cared for. But, in spite of these advantages, Owen, who made himself intimately acquainted with the condition of the operatives, found much that was objectionable. Five hundred children were employed, who had been taken from poorhouses, chiefly from Edinburgh, and these children were mostly between the ages of five and eight years old. The reason such young children were taken was that Mr. Dale could not get them older. If he did not take them at this early age, they were not to be had at all. The hours of work were thirteen a day (sometimes more), including meal times, for which intervals, amounting to an hour and a half in all, were allowed. Owen found that, in spite of the good food and relatively good care enjoyed by the children when out of the mills, the long hours of work had stunted their growth and, in some cases, deformed their limbs. Although a good teacher, according to the ideas of the time, had been engaged, the children made very slow progress, even in learning the alphabet. These facts convinced Owen that the children were injured by being taken into the mills at so early an age and by being made to work for so many hours, and as soon as he could make other arrangements, he put an end to the system, discontinued the employment of pauper children, refused to engage any child under ten years old, and reduced the hours of work to twelve daily, of which one and a quarter were given to rest and meals. He would have preferred to raise the age of full time employment to twelve years and to reduce the hours of work still further, but, being more or less in his partners' hands, he was compelled to initiate these reforms gradually. He soon, however, arrived at a conviction, based on the experience gained by watching his own factory at work, that no loss need be incurred, either in home or foreign trade, by reducing work to about ten hours employment daily. The improvement in health and energy resulting from increased leisure was so remarkable as to convince him that more consideration for the operatives, more attention given to their conditions of work generally, especially shorter hours, so far from increasing expenses, would tend to promote efficiency, and as he also pointed out, would effect a great improvement in the health of operatives, both young and old, and also improve their education, and tend to diminish the poor rates of the country.*

* See Parliamentary Papers, 1816, Vol. III, Peel's Committee, Evidence of Robert Owen.

It is, indeed, hardly credible that the schooling which was supposed to be given to the children after their seven o'clock supper till nine, could have been of much use after so many hours at work in the mill. Owen's view was that " this kind of instruction, when the strength of the children was exhausted, only tormented them, without doing any real good ; for I found that none of them understood anything they attempted to read, and many of them fell asleep during the school hours."

The Village.

Owen also did a great deal to improve the village houses and streets, and build new houses to receive new families to supply the place of the paupers, and to re-arrange the interior of the mills, and replace the old machinery by new.

"The houses contained at that time no more than one apartment, few exceeded a single storey in height, and a dunghill in front of each seems to have been considered by the then inmates as a necessary appendage to their humble dwelling." Owen rebuilt or improved the houses, and had the streets daily swept and cleansed and refuse removed by men employed for the purpose. The next difficulty was to induce habits of domestic cleanliness, which at first Owen tried to achieve by means of lectures and persuasive talks. Finding more urgent measures were necessary, he called a public meeting and advised the people to appoint a committee from amongst themselves to inspect the houses in the village and report as to cleanliness in a book kept for the purpose. This suggestion at first nearly produced a revolution among the women, but it is stated nevertheless that the measure was put in operation, by Owen's orders, in so conciliatory a manner that hostility soon subsided.* Stores were opened to supply the people with food, clothing, milk, fuel, etc., at cost price. Previously the credit system prevailed, and all the retail shops could sell spirits. The quality of the goods was most inferior, and the charges high to cover risk. The result of this change saved the people twenty-five per cent. in their expenses, besides giving them the best, instead of very inferior, articles.†

It is, however, in his plans for mental and moral improvement that Owen is seen at his most characteristic and singular aspect. The factory population of that date, it must be remembered, was usually imported away from its own place of abode. Prejudice against cotton mills was very strong among the laboring classes of Scotland, who disliked the close confinement and long hours of

* "Owen at New Lanark." By One formerly a Teacher at New Lanark. Manchester. 1839. Pp. 4, 5.

† There are risks in connection with shops run by employers for profit which are now well known, and have been the occasion of many Truck Acts; but in this case the profits of the stores were not taken by Owen, but were used for the benefit of the workpeople themselves and for the upkeep of the schools, the scheme resembling a consumers' co-operative store rather than a shop for private profit. Compare Report of Peel's Committee, Robert Owen's evidence, p. 22.

labor incidental to factory life. The people working at New Lanark had "been collected from anywhere and anyhow, for it was then most difficult to induce any sober welldoing family to leave their home to go into cotton mills as then conducted."

It is evident that the factory population thus recruited might not be altogether easy people to deal with. Owen says that he had at first "every bad habit and practice of the people to overcome." Drinking, immorality, and theft were general; and Dale, who had given but little time to personal supervision of the mills, had been freely plundered. But Owen was not disheartened. In a curious passage he shows his views on the subject of human nature and his characteristic confidence that with his methods all would be well. "There were two ways before me by which to govern the population. First, by contending against the people, who had to contend against the evil conditions by which, through ignorance, they were surrounded; and in this case I should have had continually to find fault with all, and to keep them in a state of constant ill will and irritation, to have many of them tried for theft, to have some imprisoned and transported, and at that period to have others condemned to death; for in some cases I detected thefts to a large amount, there being no check upon any of their proceedings. This was the course which had ever been the practice of society. Or, secondly, I had to consider these unfortunately placed people as they really were, the creatures of ignorance and vicious circumstances, who were made to be what they were by the evil conditions which had been made to surround them, and for which alone society, if any party, should be made responsible. And instead of tormenting the individuals, imprisoning and transporting some, hanging others, and keeping the population in a state of constant irrational excitement, I had to change these evil conditions for good ones, and thus, in the due order of nature, according to its unchanging laws, to supersede the inferior and bad characters, created by inferior and bad conditions, by superior and good characters, to be created by superior and good conditions." Success in this great undertaking could only be obtained by the knowledge "that the character of each of our race is formed by God or nature and by society, and that it is impossible that any human being could or can form his own qualities or character."

Owen drew up a set of rules to be observed by the inhabitants of New Lanark for the maintenance of cleanliness, order and good behavior. Every house was to be cleaned at least once a week and whitewashed at least once a year by the tenant; the tenants were further required, in rotation, to provide for cleaning the public stairs, and sweeping the roadway in front of their dwellings, and were forbidden to throw ashes and dirty water into the streets, or to keep cattle, swine, poultry or dogs in the houses. There were provisions for the prevention of trespass and damage to the company's fences and other property. A rather extreme view of authority inspired a rule requiring all doors to be closed at 10.30, and no one to be abroad after that hour without permission. Temperance in the use of liquors was enjoined. Toleration was urged upon the members of different religious sects and the whole village was advised "to the utmost of their power as far as is consistent with their duty to God and society, to endeavor both by word and deed to make everyone happy with whom they have any intercourse."

The "Silent Monitor."

A singular device was adopted by Owen as an aid to enforcing good behavior in the mills, punishment of any kind being contrary to his principles. A four-sided piece of wood, the sides colored black, blue, yellow, and white, was suspended near to each of the factory workers. The side turned to the front told the conduct of that person during the previous day, the four colours being taken as by degrees of comparison, black representing of course bad, blue indifferent, yellow good, and white excellent. There was also a system of registering marks for conduct. The superintendent of each department had to place these "silent monitors" every day, and the master placed those for the superintendent. Anyone who thought himself treated unjustly by the superintendent had the right of complaining to Owen, but such complaints very rarely occurred. With his usual simplicity, Owen attributes much of his success to this quaint little device, which probably, apart from his own character and influence, and the beneficial measures introduced, would have had but little effect. His humanity to the people is illustrated by the fact that at one time, when owing to trade conditions the mills were at a standstill for several months, he expended £7,000 in wages rather than turn the people adrift.

Financial Success.

As a matter of business, the mills were highly successful. From 1799 to 1809, over and above interest on capital at five per cent., a a dividend of £60,000 was cleared, which, however, includes the £7,000 spent on payment of wages as just indicated. Owen's partners, however, in spite of this financial success, took alarm at his schemes for social betterment. They came down from London and Manchester to inspect what had been done, expressed themselves highly pleased, listened to his plans, but eventually presented him with a silver salver bearing a laudatory inscription, and decided they could go no further with him. Owen offered to buy the mills of them for £84,000, and they gladly consented. A second partnership, formed to purchase the mills, resulted again in strain and tension. Owen then drew up a pamphlet describing his work at New Lanark, and the efforts he had made and hoped still to make for furthering the cause of education and improving the position of the people concerned, and making an appeal to benevolent and wealthy men to join him in partnership and purchase the business, not only for the sake of the immediate good of the employees, but in order to set up a model of what a manufacturing community might be. Among those who responded to the invitation were Jeremy Bentham, the philosopher, and William Allen, the Quaker and philanthropist. When Owen had completed his arrangements for taking over the business, and returned to New Lanark, the work-people were so overjoyed to see him that they took the horses out of the carriage and drew him in it home, in spite of his expostulations.

On balancing the accounts of the four years partnership now dissolved, it was found that after allowing five per cent. for the capital employed, the concern showed a net profit of £160,000.

A New View of Society.

Owen came before the world as an educational reformer in 1813, when he published his " New View of Society : or, Essays on the Principle of the Formation of the Human Character." Education in England, as most people know, was grossly neglected at this time, especially in regard to the children of the working class. The grammar schools endowed by mediæval piety were appropriated to the instruction of middle-class children, and the charity schools founded in the eighteenth century were, though numerous, utterly inadequate for the needs of a growing industrial society, nor was the education offered in those schools planned on lines that could by any stretch of imagination be called liberal. William Allen, Owen's partner, estimated the number of children in London who were wholly without education at over 100,000. From the very begin-ning of the nineteenth century education was already a battlefield. The Liberal Nonconformists, led by Lancaster, and the Church party, inspired by Dr. Bell, were each responsible for plans for cheap popular education. Owen gave generous assistance to both, but in the schools he established at New Lanark he went beyond either. The schemes of Bell and Lancaster were little but plans for economising the teacher, that is to say, by setting the older children to teach the younger. Owen distrusted the system of teaching by rote, and laid great stress on the personality of the teacher and the individual attention given to children.

A building was erected at New Lanark, to be used exclusively for school classes, lectures, music and recreation. There were two schoolrooms, one hung round with pictures of animals, shells, minerals, etc., and with large maps. Dancing and singing lessons were given, and the younger classes were taught reading, natural history, and geography. Both boys and girls were drilled, formed in divisions led by young drummers and fifers, and became very expert and perfect in their exercises. The children all wore white garments, given them by Owen, tunics for the boys, frocks for the girls, which were changed three times a week.

Before the shortening of the hours of work, the average attend-ance at the evening schools was less than 100 a night ; but after the reduction on January 1, 1816, the attendance rose rapidly, and was 380 in January, 386 in February, and 396 in March.

The basic principle of Owen's educational system was that man is before all things a social or gregarious being, from which it follows that the happiness of the individual is most intimately bound up with that of the community of which he is a member. The practical corollary of this principle was the exclusion of all artificial rewards or punishments. No child got a prize for industry and good conduct, none was punished for idleness and disobedience, Owen holding the belief that such incentives are bad for the character, introduce false ideals and erroneous notions, and generally leave the will weak and unfortified against temptation when the artificial stimulus is removed. The scholars were taught to feel that the best incentive to industry is the pleasure of learning, and the best reward for kindliness and good behavior the friendly feeling of companionship set up. Instead of being scolded or punished for being untruthful or disobliging, the children at New Lanark were taught that sincerity and good fellowship are the means to a happy life.* A child who did wrong was considered to deserve pity rather than blame. Owen's son, Dale, who was a convinced believer in his father's system, points out that though children educated on the old-fashioned method, "over-awed by the fear of punishment and stimulated by the hope of reward," might appear very diligent and submissive while the teacher's eye is on them, habits formed by mere mechanical inducements would not be rooted in the character, not to mention that obstinacy and wilfulness may even be fostered by feeling that there is something courageous and independent in thus rejecting baits offered to their lower nature and daring to choose the more perilous path. However that may be, there is a general testimony of those who visited the schools that the children were singularly gentle, happy looking, and well behaved ; which, indeed, is markedly the case in a school of the present day, run on similar principles, and known to the writer.

Methods of Education.

As regards the teaching itself, every effort was made to make every subject attractive and interesting ; to teach as much as possible by conversation and by maps, pictures, and natural objects ; and not to weary the children's' attention. A special feature of the system was the lecture on natural science, geography, or history, which would be illustrated, as the subject might permit, by maps, pictures, diagrams, etc., and, as occasion might serve, made to convey a moral lesson. Thus a geography lesson would be combined with descriptive detail and made to illustrate Robert Owen's favorite thesis that character is the product of circumstances. These lessons, the value of which obviously would depend mainly on the teacher's personality, seem to have given immense pleasure to the children, and to have greatly interested strangers, who were now visiting New Lanark in increasing numbers.

Instead of reading in a mechanical fashion or learning mere words by rote, the children were questioned on what they read, and encouraged to discuss, ask questions, or find illustrations of what they read. Thus the habit was formed of endeavoring to understand what is read or heard, instead of conning a mere jingle and patter of unmeaning words, which, it is to be feared, make up the

* R. Dale Owen, " System of Education at New Lanark," 1824, p. 13.

idea of "lessons" to many hapless little scholars even up till now. On this point Dale Owen asks pertinently whether a chemist, being anxious that a child should be able to trace and understand some valuable and important deductions, which with great study and investigation he had derived from certain chemical facts, would act wisely in insisting that the child should at once commit to memory and implicitly believe these deductions? The answer is obvious; that any wise man would first store a child's mind with facts and elementary knowledge, and only gradually, as judgment and intelligence became matured, make him acquainted with theory and principle.*

In the training both of the character and of the intelligence, the aim of the school was to awaken the will and observation in the child to act and reflect for himself, rather than drive him by mere mechanical compulsion.

Many were the distinguished strangers who at this time made a pilgrimage to New Lanark. Griscom, an American Professor of Chemistry and Natural Philosophy, visited Owen in the course of a tour, and was most favorably impressed with the school. He records that the children appeared perfectly happy and fearless, and would take Owen by the hand or the coat to attract his attention. The Duke of Kent (father of Queen Victoria) was deeply interested in Owen's experiments, and sent his physician to visit and report upon New Lanark. Many others—statesmen, philanthropists, reformers, and humanitarians, enthusiasts of all kinds—also found their way to the factory and school.

Condition of the People.

About 1815 Owen began to turn his attention to measures of a public character which should improve the condition of the operatives employed in the now rapidly increasing textile industry. He visited many mills in various parts of the country, and was much struck by the wonderful machines employed in these factories and the improvements that were constantly being made in them. But he was also painfully impressed, as he had been years before, by the deteriorating effects on young people of the conditions of employment. He saw that the workers were almost literally the slaves of the new mechanical powers, and later on he asserted that the white slavery of English manufactories under unrestricted competition was worse than the black slavery he had seen in the West Indies and the United States, where the slaves were better cared for in regard to food, clothing, and conditions as to health than were the oppressed and degraded children and workpeople in the factories of Great Britain. It is true that some of the worst evils were tending to disappear, e.g., with the introduction of steam power night work was considerably discontinued; and as employers were no longer obliged to place their factories in out of the way spots for water power, the need for employing parish apprentices had therefore largely ceased. The factories were placed in populous centres

* "System of Education at New Lanark," p. 55.

and to some extent at least under the check of public opinion ; whilst the children were living at home with their parents, under more human and natural conditions than the unhappy apprentices who had been lodged at the mills. It also appears that the factories of the new type were larger and better kept than the old, and the operatives of a higher social grade. But, in spite of these influences, which made for good, the evidence before Peel's Committee shows that conditions were still very bad. Children were employed at a very early age, and for terribly long hours. Even the better class manufacturers usually kept the mill open for thirteen hours a day, and allowed an hour off for dinner, breakfast and tea being brought to the children in the mill and snatched at intervals, the machinery going all the time. Sometimes even a dinner interval was not given, and some mills were kept going for fifteen or even sixteen hours a day. Many of the children had to attend for several hours on Sunday to clean the machinery. It was asserted by the manufacturers that these long hours did not really mean the same duration of actual work ; that the children were merely in attendance to watch the machines and piece the broken threads, no physical exertion being required. This description conveniently ignored the fact that the children had practically to stand the whole time, and the bad effects of such long standing and confinement were heightened by the close and heated atmosphere. The finer qualities of yarn, at all events, needed a warm atmosphere, and in many factories the temperature, summer and winter, was kept up to about eighty degrees. Sir Robert Peel told the House of Commons that he employed nearly a thousand children in his cotton mill, and was seldom able to visit it, owing to press of engagements ; but whenever he could go and see the works, he was struck with " the uniform appearance of bad health and, in many cases, stunted growth of the children. The hours of labor were regulated by the interest of the overseer, whose remuneration depending on the quantity of work done, he was often induced to make the poor children work excessive hours and to stop their complaints by trifling bribes."

Factory Children.

In 1815 Owen called a meeting of Scottish manufacturers, to be held in the Tontine, Glasgow, to consider, first, the necessity and policy of asking the Government, then under Lord Liverpool's administration, to remit the heavy duty then paid on the importation of cotton ; and, secondly, to consider measures to improve the condition of children and others employed in textile mills. The first proposal, to remit the import duty on raw material, was carried unanimously. He then proposed a string of resolutions for improving the condition of the workers. In the course of his remarks he 'pointed out that the cotton manufacture, vast as were its profits, was not an unmixed benefit to the nation, but, under existing conditions, was destructive of the " health, morals, and social comforts" of the mass of the people engaged in it. He urged those present not to forget the interests of those by whom their profits were made, and suggested a Factory Act. Not one person in the meeting would second the motion. Subsequently Owen published a pamphlet,* dedicated significantly "to the British Legislature," in which he described the position of children under the manufacturing system, and suggested a remedy. "The children now find they must labor incessantly for their bare subsistence. They have not been used to innocent, healthy, and rational amusements. They are not permitted the requisite time, if they had been previously accustomed to enjoy them. . . . Such a system of training cannot be expected to produce any other than a population weak in bodily and mental faculties, and with habits generally destructive of their own comfort, of the wellbeing of those around them, and strongly calculated to subdue all the social affections. Man so circumstanced sees all around him hurrying forward, at a mail coach speed, to acquire individual wealth, regardless of him, his comforts, his wants, or even his sufferings, except by way of degrading parish charity, fitted only to steel the heart of man against his fellows or to form the tyrant and the slave. . . . The employer regards the employed as mere instruments of gain."

The legislative measure he suggested was to limit the hours of labor in factories to twelve per day, including one and a half for meals; to prohibit employment of children under ten in factories; to require that employment of children from ten to twelve should be for half time only; and that no children should be admitted to work in factories at all until they could read and write, understand elementary arithmetic, and, in the case of girls, sew and make their clothes. The arguments used by Owen in support of this suggested measure are such as have been amply confirmed by the experience of those in touch with industry; but they were then new and startling, and, it is to be feared, even at the present day are unfamiliar to many of the dwellers in Suburbia. In regard to the objection then commonly raised that the quantity produced would be decreased by shorter hours, he explained that by making the proposed Factory Act uniform over the United Kingdom, any increase of cost, supposing such to ensue, would be borne by the consumers, not by the manufacturers; but he doubted much whether any manufactory, arranged so as to occupy the hands twelve hours a day, would not produce its fabric nearly, if not altogether, as cheap as those in which work was prolonged to fourteen or fifteen hours a day. Even should this view not prove to be entirely justified, the improved health and comfort of the operative population and the diminution of poor rates would amply compensate the country for a fractional addition to the prime cost of any commodity. "In a national view, the labor which is exerted twelve hours a day will be obtained more economically than if stretched to a longer period. . . . Since the general introduction of expensive machinery human nature has been forced far beyond its average strength, and much, very much, private misery and public injury are the consequence."

* "Observations on the Effect of the Manufacturing System." London. 1815.

The Human Machinery.

In an address to the superintendents of manufactories, written about the end of 1813, Owen thus voices his appeal for the operatives :—

"Experience has shown you the difference of the results between mechanism which is neat, clean, well arranged, and always in a high state of repair; and that which is allowed to be dirty, in disorder, without the means of preventing unnecessary friction, and which therefore becomes and works much out of repair. In the first case the whole economy and management are good; every operation proceeds with ease, order, and success. In the last the reverse must follow, and a scene be presented of counteraction, confusion, and dissatisfaction among all the agents and instruments interested or occupied in the general process, which cannot fail to create great loss.

"If, then, the care as to the state of your inanimate machines can produce such beneficial results, what may not be expected if you devote equal attention to your vital machines, which are far more wonderfully constructed? When you shall acquire a right knowledge of these, of their curious mechanism, of their self-adjusting powers; when the proper mainspring shall be applied to their varied movements—you will become conscious of their real value, and you will readily be induced to turn your thoughts more frequently from your inanimate to your living machines; you will discover that the latter may be easily trained and directed to procure a large increase of pecuniary gain, while you may also derive from them high and substantial gratification.

"Will you then continue to expend large sums of money to procure the best devised mechanism of wood, brass, or iron; to retain it in perfect repair; to provide the best substance for the prevention of unnecessary friction, and to save it from falling into premature decay? Will you also devote years of intense application to understand the connection of the various parts of these lifeless machines, to improve their effective powers, and to calculate with mathematical precision all their minute and combined movements? . . . . Will you not afford some of your attention to consider whether a portion of your time and capital would not be more advantageously applied to improve your living machines? . . . Far more attention has been given to perfect the raw materials of wood and metals than those of body and mind. . . . . Man, even as an instrument for the creation of wealth, may be greatly improved. . . . . You may not only partially improve these living instruments, but learn how to impart to them such excellence as shall make them infinitely surpass those of the present and all former times."*

In the course of this campaign for the remission of the cotton duties and for the regulation of child labor, Owen sent copies of his proposals to the members of both Houses of Parliament, and went up to interview members of the Government. In regard to the first

* Appendix B, Autobiography, p. 259.

proposal he met with a favorable reception from Vansittart, the Chancellor of the Exchequer, but his efforts on behalf of the children were not so immediately fruitful, although they excited considerable interest and sympathy in the minds of some. Sir Robert Peel was asked to take charge of Owen's draft Bill. The choice was an appropriate one, the Act of 1802, for regulating the conditions of pauper apprentices in cotton and woollen mills, having been due to the same statesman's initiative. This Act, the only Factory Act then on the statute book, had become out of date owing to technical and economic changes which had caused the employment of pauper apprentices to be largely discontinued. The new Bill was more, comprehensive, and applied to all children in mills and factories. Its main provisions were that no child should be employed in a mill or factory below the age of ten; that no person under eighteen should be employed for more than twelve and a half hours per day, of which only ten were to be given to work, half an hour to instruction, leaving two hours for rest and meal times. The justices were empowered to appoint duly qualified inspectors and to pay them for their services. It was explicitly provided that these inspectors were not to be interested or in any way connected with the mills and manufactories they were to inspect, and they were given full powers to enter the mills for purposes of inspection at any time of day they chose.

It is interesting in considering this Bill to recall that the institution of factory inspectors was not effected till 1833, the ten hours day did not become law till 1847, and the prohibition of work under ten years old did not come into force until the year 1874.

Peel's Committee.

Nothing more was done in 1815, the Bill having been introduced and published as a tentative measure to evoke discussion and criticism. In 1816, however, Sir Robert Peel returned to the subject, and moved for the appointment of a committee to take evidence and report upon the state of children employed in manufactories. Some of the evidence given before this committee by Owen has already been quoted above. Perhaps the most remarkable point is the hostility shown by some members of the committee to Owen's ideas and proposals, which, so far as the Factory Bill went, would nowadays be considered very mild. When he said he thought it unnecessary for children under ten to be employed in any regular work, and considered instruction and education at that age were enough exertion, he was asked by some moralist, whose name is unfortunately not handed down to fame, "Would there not be a danger of their acquiring by that time (*ten years old*) vicious habits for want of regular occupation?" and replied that his own experience led him, on the contrary, to find that habits were good in proportion to instruction. When he was pressed to explain his contention that a reduction of hours had resulted in a greater proportional output, he showed that a larger quantity might be produced by greater attention or by preventing breakage, and by not losing any time in beginning or leaving work. This evidently surprised some of the committee, who appeared incredulous that he, "as an experienced cotton spinner, or a spinner of any kind," could think that machines could produce a greater quantity save by the quickening of their movement. Owen again repeated that greater attention by the workpeople in avoiding breakage or waste of time might increase output, and that in his experience the shorter hours work did result in closer attention.*

The Factory Act, 1819.

The Factory Bill was delayed for some reason till 1818, when Sir Robert Peel introduced it again. The second reading was carried in the Commons by ninety-one to twenty-six, but the Bill was again delayed by the action of the House of Lords, who professed themselves not satisfied that the need for any such legislation had been demonstrated. They appointed a committee of their own, which took evidence during 1818 and 1819. A great deal of evidence was produced, which was intended to show that factories were ideally healthy and the death-rate much below that in ordinary places; that England's place in the markets of the world would be endangered; that wages must be reduced in a proportion equal to or greater than the proposed reduction of hours; that the morals of the "lower orders" must be deteriorated by so much free time. Doctors were found to testify, e.g., that it need not hurt a child to work at night, or to stand twelve hours a day at work, or to eat their meals while so standing! The evidence of 1816, however, had not been forgotten, and other evidence was produced before the Lords' Committee which amply proved the conditions to be highly injurious to the children's health. The Bill became law in the summer of 1819, but, in order to conciliate the millowners and the House of Lords, the original provisions were deprived of much that was valuable. Woollen, flax, and other mills were omitted, the Act applying to cotton only; the age limit for child labor was fixed at nine years instead of ten; the hours of labor were to be twelve instead of ten or ten and a half hours. Worst of all, the provision for inspection in Owen's draft was deleted and nothing was put in its place, the supervision of factories being left, as before, in the hands of the justices, although it was perfectly well known that they had not enforced the Act of 1802.

Owen's direct influence on the development of English factory legislation thus suffered a check. The fact nevertheless remains that the Act of 1819, mutilated and imperfect as it was, was the first real recognition of responsibility by the State for industrial conditions. The Act of 1802 had been merely an extension of the State's care for Poor Law children; the Act of 1819 recognized the

* The present writer has been told the same by several manufacturers. One of these remarked that " in nine hours the girls had done all the work it was in them to. do," and that the attention could not be satisfactorily maintained longer. Another remarked that overtime in the evening generally meant bad work next morning. See also instances described in "History of Factory Legislation," Hutchins and Harrison, Chapter VII.

employed child as such. It was not until 1833 that an effective measure was placed upon the statute book, and the guidance of this movement had long before this passed out of Owen's hands. But he it was who first compelled the State to recognize the changes made by the growth and concentration of capital ; he it was who tried practical experiments in the way of shorter hours and improved conditions ; and, much as he had done himself as a model employer, it was he who recognized the fact that, under the conditions of modern industry, State intervention was necessary, because the forces of competition are too much for the manufacturer, single and unaided, to resist, save in especially favorable circumstances.

International Agitation.

Owen was also fully conscious that in years to come the problem of social reform would have to be faced internationally. In 1818 he addressed a memorial, on behalf of the working classes, "to the Allied Powers assembled in Congress at Aix-la-Chapelle." This document is characterized by extraordinary optimism and a pathetic conviction that society was, in actual fact, moving rapidly to a state of harmony and co-operation. It also shows a curious ignorance of recent history in assuming that child labor was but a recent introduction, whereas we know now from other sources that child labor had been general, and in some cases excessive, in textile industry carried on under the domestic system. In spite of these misconceptions, the document makes some valuable and important points. It shows that by the introduction of machinery and the factory s stem an enormous increase in productive power had been achievedy By the aid of science Great Britain could now produce many times as much wealth in a given time as she could previously. This surplus of wealth might be either wasted in war, dissipated in competition with the nations, or applied directly to improve her own population. Moreover, the existing productive power was but trifling compared with that which might be obtained in the future. Capital and industry were unemployed or misapplied which might be used to create more wealth. "Already," said Owen, " with a population under twenty millions, and a manual power not exceeding six millions,* with the aid of new power, undirected, except by a blind private interest, she supplied her own demand, and overstocks with, her manufactures all the markets in the world to which her commerce is admitted. She is now using every exertion to open new markets, even in the most distant regions ; and she could soon, by the help of science, supply the wants of another world equally populous with the earth. . . . The grand question now to be solved is, not how a sufficiency of wealth may be produced, but how the excess of riches which may be most easily created may be generally distributed throughout society advantageously for all, and without prematurely disturbing the existing institutions or arrangements in any country." Owen's estimates were based on manufacturing

* This figure is arrived at by comparison with the era before machinery. The exact figure is unimportant. The increase of productive power is an undoubted fact.

industry, and he did not give sufficient weight to the consideration that mechanical science was not likely (so far as we can see) to effect so rapid and startling an increase in the production of food or other necessaries obtained from the soil itself.* The really important point made by Owen here and elsewhere is his insistence on the problem of distribution. It is still the case that much wealth which might be used to enrich life is squandered in the war of armaments and the war of competition. There is no way of avoiding that destructive waste save by co-operation and mutual control.

Owen died in 1858. It might seem that his life was a failure, his immediate efforts having been sorely disappointed over the Factory Act of 1819, and his wonderful forecasts of universal peace and prosperity having been sadly falsified by events. But the real results of Owen's work are to be seen in the long series of factory legislation, which, slowly and imperfectly, it is true, has yet built up a system of protection for the worker, and in the efforts which, in the twentieth century, have at last achieved some beginnings of success for international regulation of labor. In 1900 the "Union Internationale pour la Protection légale des Travailleurs" was formed. Through its initiative, influence, and suggestion, conventions have already been accepted by a large number of the leading Powers, under which the night work of women is forbidden and the use of white phosphorus, a deadly poison, formerly employed in matchmaking with great dangers to the workers, is prohibited. Other measures with regard to the night work of boys and the control of other industrial poisons are being considered. This is a work which is as yet in its infancy, but is likely to be fraught with great results in the future.

Conclusion.

It is difficult in a few words to sum up the singular career and personality of Robert Owen. The so-called "usher" of seven, the boy who, with powdered hair, waited on his master's customers in the old warehouse on London Bridge, has a curious old world air, which clings to him even when a dozen years later finds him face to face with the intricate problems of the modern industrial world. It will not have escaped readers of the extracts given above from Robert Owen's works that he wrote a painfully long winded style, and that his thought is often uncritical and obscure. In a candid passage his son, R. Dale Owen, reminds us that Owen was without any real educational or scientific training. As a child he managed to read a good many books, but had neither time nor opportunity to be a student. "In this way he worked out his problems for human improvement to great disadvantage, missing a thousand things that great minds had thought and said before his time, and often mistaking ideas that were truly his own for novelties that no human being had heretofore given to the world." †

* Podmore, I, p. 261.
† "Threading My Way," p. 66 *et seq.*

Owen's personal temper and character appear to have been of unusual sweetness. His "ruling passion," his son records, "was the love of his kind, individually and collectively." An old friend said of Owen, jokingly, that "if he had seven thousand children instead of seven, he would love them all devotedly." He was, in fact, to his own children a most affectionate and careful parent, but had none of the selfish narrowness that sometimes goes with strong domestic instincts. The whole human race was to him the subject of warm, even indulgent, affection. He simply brushed aside the impression then general that the best way to manage children was to bully them, and the best way to get work out of factory operatives was to keep them incessantly at it. He did not believe in sin and wicked-ness, and saw in the sinner only the victim of untoward circum-stances. He was sometimes misled by the illusion, characteristic of many eighteenth century thinkers, that the human race, if surrounded by a healthy and comfortable environment, and properly instructed in the advantages of social, as opposed to anti-social, conduct, must inevitably go right of itself, and he left out of account the whole array of inherited weaknesses of character and constitution, the strength of passions (which probably his own temperament left him almost unaware of), and the temptation to greed and tyranny offered by almost any known form of organized social life. It is easy to indicate the limitations of his thought. The fact remains that within those limits there is an immensely fruitful field for the application of his ideas, as he proved by the almost startling results of his training and influence on a set of operatives and their children who were by no means picked members of society to start with.

The importance of Owen's life and teaching does not lie in his social philosophy, which was crude and already somewhat out of date, but in the practical success of his experiments as a model employer, and in his flashes of social intuition, which made him see, as by inspiration, the needs of his time. Leslie Stephen said of him that he was "one of those intolerable bores who are of the salt of the earth," but it is evident that he must have possessed a large measure of the undefinable attribute known as "personal magnetism." Thus we find him achieving an entrance into good posts early in life with little aid from capital or influence, able to control and manage workpeople in the factory, to banish drunkenness and disorder, to win the affection of the children in the schools, to persuade the teachers to adopt his new and unfamiliar methods, and to excite the active sympathy and interest of men, like the Duke of Kent, greatly above him in social station. Owen could see and act far better than he could think, and his views have been justified by events. His Life, by Frank Podmore, is a great book, one of the most fascinating of English biographies, but perhaps even Mr. Podmore hardly does justice to the clearness of Owen's vision in the human side of economics. Owen found the politicians and economists obsessed by a mechanical conception of industry. An hour's work was an hour's work, and in the debates and pamphlets of the time there is an almost entire omission of any reference to the personality of the worker, or to the possible effect of his health, strength, and efficiency on the output. Manual labor was then taken as a constant quantity, the only means of augmenting the output being by increasing the hours or by improving the machinery. Later economists have given more attention to the personality of the operative, and modern scientific investigation has shewn that Owen's conception of industry is a true one, solidly based on the facts of life. There is much evidence now accessible to show how eminently susceptible to influences the human worker is, and how shortsighted it is to regard him or her as a mere pair of hands. Better food, better air, more rest, teaching, and recreation, improve the human machine, even regarding him merely as a machine. From the point of view of the State or the community it is hardly necessary to say the case is tenfold stronger. The State can by no means afford to have its citizens, actual or potential, endangered by unhealhy, dangerous, or demoralizing conditions of work. This statement is becoming almost a truism now, though its full implications have not yet been adopted as part of practical politics. But the measure of recognition it has obtained, both at home and abroad, is a measure of the greatness of Robert Owen, the pathfinder of social legislation, who had a vision for the realities of modern industrial life when they were as yet dim, strange, and unknown to his contemporaries. No one has yet done so much as he did to show that man must be the master of the machine if he is not to be its slave.

NOTE.—Robert Owen, disappointed in his scheme for social reform through the State, turned his attention to the formation of communities in which, as he hoped, his theories might be carried out. This part of his life, which is very distinct from his services to social reform, will be treated in a separate paper.

BIBLIOGRAPHY.

Report of Committee on the State of Children in Manufactories. Parliamentary Papers. 1816. Vol. III. Evidence by ROBERT OWEN.

Statement Regarding the New Lanark Establishment. By ROBERT OWEN. Published Anonymously. Edinburgh. 1812.

Observations on the Effect of the Manufacturing System. Dedicated to the British Legislature. By ROBERT OWEN. Third Edition. London. 1818. (Also included with his Autobiography, see below.)   [1824.

Outline of the System of Education at New Lanark. By R. DALE OWEN. Glasgow.

Life of Robert Owen. By HIMSELF. Including Essays on the Formation of Character and many other papers and documents. London. 1857.

Threading My Way. By R. DALE OWEN. London. 1874.

Robert Owen. By LESLIE STEPHEN. Dictionary of National Biography.

Robert Owen : Sein Leben und seine Bedeutung fur die Gegenwart. Von HELENE SIMON. Fischer, Jena. 1905.

Robert Owen : a Biography. By FRANK PODMORE. Two vols. Hutchinson. 1906. (By far the most important work on the subject.)

Fabian Tract No. 167.

ı

WILLIAM MORRIS & THE COMMUNIST IDEAL

By MRS. TOWNSHEND

Published and sold by the Fabian Society.
Biographical Series No. 3.　　　Price 2d.

LONDON:
THE FABIAN SOCIETY, 3 CLEMENT'S INN, STRAND, W.C.
DECEMBER 1912

WILLIAM MORRIS
AND THE COMMUNIST IDEAL.

Boyhood.

WILLIAM MORRIS was born in 1834 and died in 1896. His working life therefore fell in the latter half of the nineteenth century, exactly the period when Commercialism was most rampant. It was a time of peace and prosperity. Manufacturers were raking in profits from the great discoveries of the beginning of the century, railways and steamships had given fresh impetus to trade. The long reign of a virtuous and narrow-minded sovereign favored the growth of vulgar self-complacency. It was a smug age, an age of rapidly increasing wealth ill-distributed and ill-spent.

Morris was a member of a well-to-do middle class family. His childhood was spent in a large house on the edge of Epping Forest, looking over a great stretch of the pasture land of Essex, with the Thames winding through the marshes. He passed a happy boyhood in a peaceful, old-fashioned, essentially English home. At fourteen he was sent to Marlborough. He entered but little, however, into the life of the school, took no part in school games, and is remembered by his school-fellows as a strange boy fond of mooning about by himself and of telling long stories "full of knights and fairies." He was "thickset and strong-looking, with a high color and black curly hair, good-natured and kind, but with a fearful temper." He was fond of taking long walks and collecting birds' eggs, and he was always doing something with his hands, netting if nothing else.

Like man like boy! The strangely diverse characteristics of this remarkable man were already noticeable, a poet without a poetic temperament, patient and industrious, kindly and gentle yet hasty and choleric, a lover of solitude for all his abounding sympathy with mankind. It was not at school but at home that he found congenial surroundings. "I am sure you must think me a great fool," he writes to his sister, "to be always thinking about home, but I really can't help it, I don't think it is my fault for there are such a lot of things I want to do and say."

Oxford Life and Friendships. Cult of the Middle Ages.

But though it is easy in his later life to trace the influence of his peaceful home between the forest and the plain, it was at Oxford that his genius found or formed the channels it was to flow through. At his own college (Exeter) and among the undergraduates of his own year he was fortunate enough to find a man with whom he was able to share his inmost thoughts. The tie between Morris and Burne-Jones was no ordinary college friendship. It lasted till death and affected the lives of both, but though (or perhaps because)

Morris was the greater of the two men the intercourse between them had more important results on his career than on that of his friend.

At twenty Morris, full of vitality and with many markedly diverse characteristics, would have been singled out as a man certain to make his mark in the world, but the kind of work that lay before him would have been hard to foretell. Like his friend, he was destined for the Church. Both alike had felt the influence of that wave of mystical theology which had swept over the dry bones of Anglican Christianity, and both alike suffered a severe disillusionment during their first year at Oxford. Their readings in theology served to extinguish gradually in both the fire of religious enthusiasm, and to kindle in its stead a devotion to ideal beauty, curiously remote and exotic. It was associated with a passion for the Middle Ages and for the particular types and forms of Art that flourished in them, and of course with a contempt and loathing for contemporary life with all its seething confusion of industrial progress. In these quiet Oxford days, spent in poring over ecclesiastical poetry, mediæval chronicles and church history, it was no wonder that these youths should look at the world through a narrow peep-hole: the wonder is that in the case of one of them the peep-hole was never widened throughout a long industrious life of artistic production. Morris was too big a man to have his outlook on the world permanently circumscribed in this way, but in the output of his early years, and indeed in the artistic work—whether literary or plastic—of his whole life, we find the narrowing influence of his first introduction to the world of thouhgt and emotion, and of his lifelong intercourse with Burne-Jones and the school to which he belonged.

Morris was by nature an artist. He was full of enthusiasm and vital energy, quick to see and to feel, eager to create. The pre-Raphaelite movement, with its worship of beauty and its atmosphere of rarity and remoteness, influenced him, not by making him an artist, but by cutting him off from the life of his day and generation, the true source of inspiration for living art. His life is the story of a pilgrimage out of a world peopled by shadows into the daylight world of his fellow-men. Unfortunately, his dearest friends continued to live in the world of shadows, and from time to time they ·drew him back into it.

Poetry.

The impulse towards self-expression found vent first in poetry, and, to the end, painter and craftsman though he was, his chief gift was literary. The gift seems to have been a sudden discovery during college days. Canon Dixon gives an amusing account of how he and Price went to Exeter one night to see the two friends. "As soon as we entered the room, Burne-Jones exclaimed wildly: 'He's a big poet!' 'Who is?' asked we. 'Why, Topsy'—the name which he had given him. We sat down and heard Morris read his first poem, the first that he had ever written in his life. It was called 'The Willow and the Red Cliff.' As he read it, I felt that it was something the like of which had never been heard before. . . . . I expressed my admiration in some way, as we all did, and I remember his remark : 'Well, if this is poetry, it is very easy to write.' From that time onward he came to my rooms almost every day with a new poem."*

He was rapid and prolific, and his poems filled many books. The best known is, perhaps, the long series of stories in verse called "The Earthly Paradise." " In all the noble roll of our poets," says Swinburne, " there has been since Chaucer no second teller of tales comparable to the first till the advent of this one." The stories, told sometimes in verse, sometimes, and even better, in prose, continued to pour forth from his fertile brain right on to the end of his life, with the exception, as we shall see, of seven years that were devoted to sterner work.

Choice of a Vocation.

But though his strongest and most enduring impulse was towards imaginative writing, it is not as a writer that his light shines before men. If he had poured the full stream of his creative vitality into this one channel, England might have added a new name to the list of her great poets, but there are things that the English of to-day need more than poetry. They need to learn that sordid labor degrades not merely those who perform it, but those who reap the fruits of it ; that to enjoy cheap machine-made luxury is as degrading as to produce it ; that a brutalized laboring class is sure to have for its master an unrefined, uncivilized plutocracy. These are the things Morris made clear to those who would look and listen. He could not have learned and taught them if he had sat in studious leisure producing poetry. His activity was many-sided, and he put heart and brain into it all. The real significance of his life story is that he created a fine career, a splendid personality out of the every-day experiences that come to all of us. He saw the outside world, the works of men and God, not with half-shut eyes and sleepy indifference as we most of us see them, but with vivid curiosity and wonder. Friendship and love, the home-building impulse and the sense of universal brotherhood visited him in turn as they visit every decent human being, but he received them not sluggishly, still less with stubborn resistance, but with alert and whole-hearted enthusiasm. Each new stage of experience was marked by a new departure in activity ; but, and this was the most remarkable characteristic of all, the new enterprise did not supersede the old. In a prose romance, written while he was at Oxford, he has given us some suggestive touches of autobiography. " I could soon find out," says the hero, " whether a thing were possible or not to me ; then, if it were not, I threw it away for ever, never thought of it again, no regret, no longing for that, it was past and over to me ; but if it were possible and I made up my mind to do it, then and there I began it, and in due time finished it, turning neither to the right hand nor the left till it was done. So I did with all things that I set my hand to."†

* " Life of William Morris," by J. W. Mackail, Vol. l., pp. 51, 52.
† " Frank's Sealed Letter." " Oxford and Cambridge Magazine," I.

Architecture.

This was Morris's ideal, and this, too, was his practice. It describes the tenor of his whole life, as well as the bent of his character, although the bare recital of these early years might convey a very different notion. We have seen that his intention of taking orders did not long survive his first term of study and discussion at Oxford, and that Art in various forms, and especially the Art of the Middle Ages, began to fill the horizon of his mind. In the glow of enthusiasm roused by the cathedrals of northern France, where he spent two delightful holidays, it was natural enough that he should choose architecture to replace the Church as his future profession, the work by which he should earn his living. Though his apprenticeship to Street was of short duration, and though he never became an architect, yet the purpose that underlay this change of profession never altered. His business through life—a business pursued with unflagging industry which reaped a substantial worldly success—was to make modern houses worth living in. All the crafts that he turned his hand to—painting, furniture-making, dyeing, weaving— all were subservient, and consciously subservient, to this end: all with the one exception of the printing of books, the beloved Benjamin of his industries, which grew, not so much out of his life-long love of the house beautiful as out of a passion equally enduring for literature —the thoughts and words of men.

Painting.

It was under the influence of Rossetti, whose strange power of fascination altered many lives, that Morris took to painting, first as a pastime, then, dropping architecture, as his regular profession. " Rossetti says I ought to paint," he writes soon after his move from Oxford to London, in his twenty-fourth year ; " he says I shall be able. Now, as he is a very great man, and speaks with authority and not as the scribes, I *must* try. I don't hope much, I must say, yet will try my best . . . . not giving up the architecture, but trying if it is possible to get six hours a day for drawing besides office work. One won't get much enjoyment out of life at this rate, I know well ; but that don't matter : I have no right to ask for it, at all events— love and work, these two things only. . . . . I can't enter into politics, social subjects, with any interest ; for, on the whole, I see that things are in a muddle, and I have no power or vocation to set them right in ever so little a degree. My work is the embodiment of dreams in one form or another."* In this land of dreams Morris lived for a year or two, in daily intercourse with those inveterate dreamers who were his friends ; but it was not to such a world that he really belonged, and he was restless and unsatisfied. " He has lately taken a strong fancy for the human," says one of his companions at this time ; and not long after, in his twenty-sixth year, marriage and the need of making a home brought him back into touch with the life of the world.

* Mackail, vol. I., p. 107.

House Decoration.

The act of becoming a householder was for him a new departure, and the building and garnishing of his home a kind of sacrament. He could not endure base surroundings. A fair orderly garden, a house wisely planned and solidly built, and within it chairs, tables and utensils that were a pleasure to make and to use—these were to him the necessary background of a decent life. His friend Philip Webb could build the house for him, and there were others among the younger architects who were of the true faith, but where was he to turn for his furniture and his wall-hangings? The domestic arts were extinct—killed by the factory system, by machinery, by steam and by industrial enterprise. Clothes, jewellery and all kinds of household gear were made, not for use, but for profit. They gave pleasure no longer either to those who fashioned them or to those who used them, but only to the hucksterer who made money out of transferring them from the one to the other, and whose interests it was that they should be cheap and showy and flimsy. All this was borne in on Morris just as he was beginning to feel sure that he was not meant for a painter any more than for an architect, and it helped him to find work that he *was* suited for, work that he could earn his bread by, and that needed doing.

How Morris became Tradesman and Manufacturer.

"The first thing that a man has to do," Ruskin had written ten years earlier, "is to find out what he is fit for. In which enquiry he may be very safely guided by his likings, if he be not also guided by his pride. People usually reason in some such fashion as this : 'I don't seem quite fit for a head manager in the firm of — & Co., therefore, in all probability, 1 am fit to be Chancellor of the Exchequer'; whereas they ought, rather, to reason thus : 'I don't seem to be quite fit to be head manager in the firm of — & Co., but, I daresay, I might do something in a small greengrocery business : I used to be a good judge of pease'; that is to say, always trying lower instead of trying higher until they find bottom. . . . . I do not believe that any greater good could be achieved for the country than the change in public feeling on this head which might be brought about by a few benevolent men, undeniably in the class of gentlemen, who would, on principle, enter into some of our commonest trades and make them honorable." When Morris and his friends started a firm of decorators as Morris, Marshall, Faulkner and Co., it was not with any such benevolent motive. The undertaking was nevertheless destined to become even more important to the cause of social progress than to that of Art. It began quite humbly, with a ridiculously small capital, but Morris threw himself wholeheartedly into the work, for which he was extraordinarily well fitted. "From the first the firm turned out whatever anyone wanted in the way of decorative material—architectural adjuncts, furniture, tapestries, embroideries, stained glass, wall-papers and what not. The goods were first-rate, the art and the workmanship excellent, the prices high. . . . You could have the things such as the firm chose

that they should be, or you could do without them. . . . There
was no compromise. Morris, as senior partner, laid down the law,
and all his clients had to bend or break."* We cannot here pursue
the fascinating story of the firm through its early struggles to the
financial success that crowned them, and of the long list of industries
undertaken, first at Queen Square and then at Merton, in which
Morris was not merely manager but working foreman, giving to each
in turn the insight of the artist, the skill of the craftsman, and the
patience and industry which were so peculiarly his own, and which
combined so strangely with his boyish vehemence. The mere
amount of work he got through is amazing. We read of days spent
in designing wall-papers and chintzes, and contriving how they
ought to be printed, in watching over dyeing vats, and working at
looms, and reinventing the lost art of tapestry weaving, while all the
time, in moments of leisure, the stream of poetry flowed on, and yet
his friends agree that he always had time for talk and laughter and
for little feasts and holidays. Many new and delightful glimpses into
his home life are to be found in Miss Morris's introduction and notes
to the fine edition of his works now in course of publication. Of
any little family festival he was the centre and mainspring, and to
any public cause that seemed to him important he was always ready
to give time and energy. His love of fun was as strong as his love
of work, and his knowledge of common things and interest in them
was unfailing. He was a clever cook, and enjoyed an opportunity of
proving his skill. " I always bless God," he once said, " for making
anything so strong as an onion."

" A Master Artizan."

If one wants to understand Morris, and especially the path that
led him to Socialism, one must realize how much he identified himself with his shop, and especially with his factory. This was the
work that he faced the world with—his " bread-and-cheese work," as
he called it. In an intimate letter he speaks of himself as " a master
artizan, if I may claim that dignity." That it was no empty claim
one may gather from such passages as this from his letters : " I am
trying to learn all I can about dyeing, even the handiwork of it,
which is simple enough ; but, like many other simple things, contains
matters in it that one would not think of unless one were told.
Besides my business of seeing to the cotton printing, I am working in
Mr. Wardle's dye-house in sabots and blouse pretty much all day long."
And again : " This morning I assisted at the dyeing of 20 lbs. of silk
for our damask in the blue vat. It was very exciting, as the thing
is quite unused now, and we ran a good chance of spoiling the silk.
There were four dyers and Mr. Wardle at work, and myself as dyers'
mate. The men were encouraged with beer, and to it they went,
and pretty it was to see the silk coming green out of the vat and
gradually turning blue. We succeeded very well as far as we can
tell at present. The oldest of the workmen, an old fellow of
seventy, remembers silk being dyed so long ago. The vat, you

* "D. G. Rossetti: His Family-Letters." With a Memoir by W. M. Rossetti.
Vol. I., p. 219.

must know, is a formidable-looking thing, 9 feet deep and about 6 feet square, and is sunk into the earth right up to the top. To-morrow I am going to Nottingham to see wool dyed blue in the woad vat, as it is called." His toil at the dye vat was not in vain. There is plenty of testimony that he became an expert dyer. "When he ceased to dye with his own hands, I soon felt the difference," writes a lady who embroidered very skilfully for the firm. "The colors themselves became perfectly level and had a monotonous prosy look; the very lustre of the silk was less beautiful. When I complained, he said: ' Yes, they have grown too clever at it. Of course, it means they don't love color, or they would do it."

The Germ of Morris's Socialism.

That a man should put his heart into his work, and that the work should be of a kind that he can care about : this was a fixed belief with Morris, and it lay at the root of his Socialism. Of himself it was true right through every detail of his many crafts. "Lord bless us," he breaks out, when he had been worried by having to write tiresome letters, "how nice it will be when I can get back to my little patterns and dyeing and the dear warp and weft at Hammersmith." His work was done for the love of it, but there was nothing amateurish or unpractical about it. "I should very much like," he writes, "to make the business quite a success, and it can't be unless I work at it myself. I must say, though I don't call myself money-greedy, a smash on that side would be a terrible nuisance. I have so many serious troubles, pleasures, hopes and fears that I have not time on my hands to be ruined and get really poor: above all things, it would destroy my freedom of work, which is a dear delight to me." It is noticeable that the work he is thinking of here is not the " bread-and-cheese work," but that "pleasure work of books " that never ceased, for he goes on to lament that for the moment he was doing nothing original, and to express the hope that he was not going " to fall off in imagination and enthusiasm "* as he grew older. He need not have feared, for it was only in later life that he entered fully upon the inheritance of northern story and legend that inspired his best work. It was a curious case of discovered kinship. His hatred of modern civilization was part cause and part result of his passion for the early sagas. He saw in them a picture—far enough, no doubt, from the actual facts at any period, near or remote—of the brotherhood of man that he longed for. He was strangely out of place in artificial modern society, and the comradeship, the adventure, the freedom of these tales were like the breath of life to him, and one cannot doubt that they served to fan the smouldering sense of revolt that flamed out later into open rebellion against the sordid slavery of the workers as he knew them.

"I had been reading the Njala in the original before I came here," he writes from Leek, where he was busy among his dye vats. "It is better even than I remembered ; the style most solemn : all men's children in it, as always in the best of the northern stories, so

* Mackail, vol. I., p. 291. Letter, dated Feb. 11th, 1873.

venerable to each other and so venerated : and the exceeding good temper of Gunnar amidst his heroism, and the calm of Njal : and I don't know anything more consoling or grander in all literature (to use a beastly French word) than Gunnar's singing in his house under the moon and the drifting clouds. What a glorious outcome of the worship of courage these stories are."*

Already in the "Earthly Paradise" we can perceive the hold they had on his mind. There is a zest and glow in "The Lovers of Gudrun" that are not to be found in the other tales. But it is in "Sigurd the Volsung," his most important literary achievement, that the influence of the north finds full expression. It was in the year 1876, when he was forty-two, that this great epic was written. One realizes the extraordinary vigor and many sidedness of the man at this middle period of his life when one remembers that it was the very time when, as we have seen, his craft work seemed to occupy every scrap of leisure. But this was not all. Great as he had proved himself as poet and craftsman, he was greater yet as man, too great to be shut in by study or workshop. Courage, energy, and patience personified, he was certain to come out into the open when the time was ripe and take his share in shaping events. It was not until middle life that the moment came. Two causes called him. In the one case the response came from his profound and growing sense of human solidarity, in the other from his reverence for the past and the work of the great men who were dead and whose art had died with them.

The "Anti-Scrape."

Indignation against the ruthless tide of restoration which was fast submerging the last traces of noble mediæval architecture finds expression again and again in the private letters transcribed by Mr. Mackail. At last, when one of the ancient parish churches that he loved so well close to his own country home was threatened, and just afterwards the beautiful Minster of Tewkesbury, indignation found vent in action. He wrote a letter to the *Athenæum*, explaining the urgency of the need, and begged all thoughtful people to join him in trying to meet it. "What I wish for is that an association should be set on foot to keep a watch on old monuments, to protest against all 'restoration' that means more than keeping out wind and weather, and by all means, literary and other, to awaken a feeling that our ancient buildings are not mere ecclesiastical toys, but sacred monuments of the nation's growth and hope." The appeal was not in vain. Within a month the Society for the Protection of Ancient Buildings (the Anti-Scrape as he nicknamed it) was founded, with Morris for its secretary. Until his death his zeal for the cause never waned. He wrote for it a prospectus, a model of terse and simple English, which was translated into French, German, Italian, and Dutch ; he poured out freely both time and money ; and he gave in its interests the first of those public lectures which, fine as they were, never became a really congenial task.

* Mackail, vol. I., p. 335 ; 1877.

"Bulgarian Atrocities."

This was in the spring of 1877, a few months before Morris had been roused to his first political utterance by the terrible accounts of cruelty in Bulgaria and the dread lest England might take up arms against Russia in support of Turkey. "I who am writing this," he wrote in a letter to the *Daily News*, "am one of a large class of men —quiet men—who usually go about their own business, heeding public matters less than they ought, and afraid to speak in such a huge concourse as the English nation, however much they may feel, but who are now stung into bitterness by thinking how helpless they are in a public matter that touches them so closely. . . . I appeal to the working men and pray them to look to it that if this shame falls on them they will certainly remember it, and be burdened by it when their day clears for them and they attain all and more than all they are now striving for." *

I have quoted from this letter because it represents, together with the Manifesto to the Working Men of England issued a few months later, when war seemed imminent, Morris's first public utterance of Socialism. It is interesting to see that it was already tinged with distrust of a central representative government. The movement into which he threw himself with so much vigor was, however, Liberal, not Socialist, in its origin. Some leading Socialists, Hyndman for one, were indeed in the opposite camp. Long afterwards he described his surprise on meeting Morris in 1879 for the first time. "It was many years after I had enjoyed his poetry and mocked a little, as ignorant young men will, at his asthetic armchairs and wallpapers that I met the man himself. . . . I imagined him as a refined and delicate gentleman, easily overwrought by his sentiments. That was not his appearance in the flesh, as we all know. Refinement undoubtedly there was in the delicate lines of the nose and the beautiful moulding of the forehead. But his hearty voice, his jolly, vigorous frame, his easy, sailorlike dress, the whole figure, gave me a better opinion of the ' atrocity mongers,' as I considered them, than anything I have seen before or since." †

But though the Eastern question led him to act for a time with the Liberal Party, it served also to show him that it was not an organization to which the welfare of the workers could be trusted. "Working men of England," he writes in the Manifesto already mentioned, "one word of warning yet. I doubt if you know the bitterness of hatred against freedom and progress that lies at the hearts of a certain part of the richer classes in this country. . . . These men cannot speak of your order, of its aims, of its leaders, without a sneer or an insult. These men, if they had the power (may England perish rather !) would thwart your just aspirations, would silence you, would deliver you, bound hand and foot, for ever to irresponsible capital."

* Letter to the *Daily News*, October 26th, 1876, signed William Morris, Author of " The Earthly Paradise."

† *Justice* for October 6th, 1896.

Every word of the Manifesto proves that he had become a Socialist by conviction, as he had always been one by temperament, and we shall do well to pause a moment in this brief narrative of his life in order to reckon up the debt we owe to the greatest Englishman who has passed away out of our ranks.

What Socialism Owes to William Morris.

When our children's children recall the great names of the Victorian Age, there is not one will kindle a warmer interest than that of William Morris. They will remember him for his stories and poems and for his pioneer work in the revival of handicraft, but above all for the vigor and charm of his personality. He was the sort of man who impressed his friends so strongly that the impression survives, a man who excelled the ordinary man in almost every direction of human activity and was typical nevertheless of his race and his country. He was a man of genius, but his genius irradiated not merely his craftsmanship and his poetry, but everything he turned his hand to. He was an expert not merely in literature and manufacture, but in life. A robust power of enjoyment was his most marked characteristic. He insisted on enjoying things. The very utensils in his house must give joy in the using or he would not use them. Work that brought no joy was fit only for slaves. It is this abundant vitality, this love of life and the world; it is the fact that he had eyes to see and ears to hear and a heart to perceive; it is, in short, because he was an artist and a genius, that his contribution to Socialism is of outstanding value, although he proved himself but a shortsighted leader and never grappled closely with the problems we have to face. Economic reasoning was not in his line, nor details of administration, but he knew a great deal about the world we live in and how to use it to the utmost advantage. The sense of brotherhood was strong in him, and it was illuminated by insight and sympathy. We can learn, therefore, far more from the story of his approach to Socialism, of the way in which he was driven to adopt it as the only hope, than from any formal statement that he ever made of its doctrines.

The Path to Socialism.

That approach can best be traced in his popular lectures on Art, which began in the year 1877. In these lectures his sympathies are with the craftsman. He recognizes no essential difference between the artist and the workman. As a contrast to the modest ideal of a 20s., or even a 30s. minimum wage, there is something delightfully inspiriting in his claim that the hire of the workman should include " Money enough to keep him from fear of want or degradation for him and his ; leisure enough from bread-earning work (even though it be pleasant to him) to give him time to read and think, and connect his own life with the life of the great world; work enough of the kind aforesaid, and praise of it, and encouragement enough to make him feel good friends with his fellows ; and, lastly, not least (for 'tis verily part of the bargain), his own due share of Art, the chief part of which will be a dwelling that does not lack the beauty which Nature would freely allow it if our own perversity did not turn Nature out of doors." "I specially wished," he writes, in answer to a complaint that he had strayed beyond the question of "mere Art," "to point out that the question of popular Art was a social question, involving the happiness or misery of the greater part of the community. The absence of popular Art from modern times is more disquieting and grievous to bear for this reason than for any other, that it betokens that fatal division of men into the cultivated and the degraded classes which competitive commerce has bred and fosters; popular Art has no chance of a healthy life, or indeed, of a life at all, till we are on the way to fill up this terrible gulf between riches and poverty. . . . It may well be a burden to the conscience of an honest man who lives a more manlike life to think of the innumerable lives which are spent in toil unrelieved by hope and uncheered by praise ; men who might as well, for all the good they are doing their neighbors by their work, be turning a crank with nothing at the end of it. . . . Over and over again have I asked myself, why should not my lot be the common lot ? My work is simple work enough ; much of it, nor that the least pleasant, any man of decent intelligence could do if he could but get to care about the work and its results. Indeed, I have been ashamed when I have thought of the contrast between my happy working hours and the unpraised, unrewarded, monotonous drudgery which most men are condemned to. Nothing shall convince me that such labor as this is good or necessary to civilization." * It was this " burden on his conscience," growing heavier as experience and character ripened, that drove Morris to Socialism. That very insight into the happenings of human life, into joy and grief and desire which inspired his stories, enabled him to see society as in truth it was.

To him the vulgar luxury of the rich was even more hateful than the squalor of the poor. "Apart from the desire to produce beautiful things," he says, " the leading passion of my life has been and is hatred of modern civilization. . . . . What shall I say concerning its mastery of and its waste of mechanical power, its Commonwealth so poor, its enemies of the Commonwealth so rich, its stupendous organization—for the misery of life ; its contempt of simple pleasure, which everyone could enjoy but for its folly ; its eyeless vulgarity, which has destroyed Art, the one certain solace of labor ? " " The hope of the past times was gone," he goes on, telling the story of his conversion ; " the struggle of mankind for many ages had produced nothing but this sordid, aimless, ugly confusion ; the immediate future seemed to me likely to intensify all the present evils by sweeping away the last survivals of the days before the dull squalor of civilization had settled down on the world. This was a bad lookout, indeed, and, if I may mention myself as a personality and not as a mere type, especially so to a man of my disposition, careless of metaphysics and religion, as well as of scientific analysis,

* Letter to the *Manchester Examiner*, March, 1883.

but with a deep love of the earth and the life on it, and a passion for the history of the past of mankind. Think of it ! Was it all to end in a counting-house on the top of a cinder-heap, with Podsnap's drawing-room in the offing, and a Whig Committee dealing out champagne to the rich and margarine to the poor in such convenient proportions as would make all men contented together, though the pleasure of the eyes was gone from the world and the place of Homer was to be taken by Huxley ! Yet, believe me, in my heart, when I really forced myself to look towards the future, that is what I saw in it ; and, as far as I could tell, scarce anyone seemed to think it worth while to struggle against such a consummation of civilization. So, then, I was in for a fine pessimistic end of life, if it had not somehow dawned on me that, amid all the filth of civilization, the seeds of a great change, what we others call Social Revolution, were beginning to germinate. The whole face of things was changed to me by that discovery, and all I had to do then in order to become a Socialist was to hook myself on to the practical movement."*

Avowal of Socialism. The S.D.F.

This "hooking on" took place in the autumn of 1882, when Morris, at the age of forty-eight, joined the Democratic Federation (which became subsequently the Social Democratic Federation, and eventually took the title of the British Socialist Party). "For my part, I used to think," he writes to a friend who remonstrated with him at this time, "that one might further real Socialistic progress by doing what one could on the lines of ordinary middle-class Radicalism. I have been driven of late into the conclusion that I was mistaken ; that Radicalism is on the wrong line, so to say, and will never develop into anything more than Radicalism—in fact, that it is made for and by the middle classes, and will always be under the control of rich capitalists : they will have no objection to its *political* development, if they think they can stop it there; but, as to real social changes, they will not allow them if they can help it." †

"The contrasts of rich and poor," he writes, again to the same friend, a few days later, "are unendurable and ought not to be endured by either rich or poor. Now it seems to me that, feeling this, I am bound to act for the destruction of the system which seems to me mere oppression and obstruction. Such a system can only be destroyed by the united discontent of numbers : isolated acts of a few persons of the middle and upper-classes seeming to me (as I have said before) quite powerless against it : in other words, the antagonism of classes, which the system has bred, is the natural and necessary instrument for its destruction." ‡

There was nothing half-hearted in Morris's acceptance of Socialism. He threw all his vigor, all his enthusiasm into propaganda, though it was not a kind of work that gave scope for the rarest

* "How I Became a Socialist." W. M. Reprinted from *Justice.*

† Letter to Mr. C. E. Maurice, June 22nd, 1883. See "Life of William Morris," vol. II., p. 103.

‡ Ibid.

powers of his mind and heart. It is pathetic to hear how he schooled himself to study Marx and tried to grasp economic problems, for it is only now and then, when he uses his gift as seer, that his Socialist writings spring into life and are of lasting value. His friends were grieved, naturally enough, that the poet should be lost in the lecturer, especially as he had no gift for oratory, but he made light very characteristically of any possible loss to the world. "Poetry goes with the hand-arts, I think," he says to an intimate friend, " and, like them, has now become unreal. The arts have got to die, what is left of them, before they can be born again. You know my views on the matter—I apply them to myself as well as to others. This would not, I admit, prevent my writing poetry, any more than it prevents my doing my pattern work, because the mere personal pleasure of it urges one to the work ; but it prevents my looking at it as a sacred duty. . . . . Meantime the propaganda gives me work to do which, unimportant as it seems, is part of a great whole which cannot be lost, and that ought to be enough for me." *

The Socialist League.

But it was not only the toughness of economic theory that made his new duties distasteful. From the first there were dissensions in the camp. " I find myself drifting," he says, " into the disgraceful position of a moderator and patcher up, which is much against my inclination." Worse still was to follow. The patching up was unsuccessful, and Morris found himself, in the beginning of 1885, the leader of a small body of seceders who took the name of the Socialist League.

For six years he gave much time and money to the internal management of the League, as well as to the revolutionary propaganda, which was its avowed object, and which was carried on chiefly by means of the *Commonweal*, first a monthly and afterwards a weekly paper, edited † and to a large extent written by Morris. Surely no Socialist paper can show a record so brilliant. " The Dream of John Ball" and " News from Nowhere" appeared in it as serials, and a long poem, " The Pilgrims of Hope," of which some portions stand high among his finest work—" Mother and Son," for instance, and " The Half of Life Gone."

In addition to these weightier contributions, few numbers are without some paragraph from his pen, all the more arresting from its simple familiar wording, that brings us directly into touch with his views on life and events.

Take this explanation, for instance, of the revolutionary attitude of the League from the first weekly issue, May 1st, 1886 :—

" We believe that the advanced part of the capitalist class, especially in this country, is drifting, not without a feeling of fear and discomfort, towards State Socialism of the crudest kind ; and a certain school of Socialists are fond of pointing out this tendency

---

* Letter to Mr. C. E. Maurice. See "Life of William Morris," vol. II., pp. 106, 107.
 † E. Belfort Bax was joint-editor with William Morris.

with exultation. . . . . But there is another thing besides bourgeois stumbling into State Socialism which shows which way the tide is setting, and that is the instinctive revolutionary attempts which drive them into these courses. What is to be said about these? They are leaderless often and half blind. But are they fruitful of nothing but suffering to the workers? We think not; for besides the immediate gain which they force from the dominant class as above said, they are a stern education for the workers themselves. . . . . The worst thing that we have to dread is that the oppressed people will learn a dull contentment with their lot. . . . . The rudest and most unsuccessful attempts at revolution are better, than that." "The real business of Socialists," writes Morris in another number, " is to impress on the workers the fact that they are a class, whereas they ought to be society. If we mix ourselves up with Parliament, we shall confuse and dull this fact in people's minds, instead of making it clear and intensifying it." * And again, under the heading "Unattractive Labour": " It is no real paradox to say that the unattractiveness of labor, which is now the curse of the world, will become the hope of the world. As long as the workman could sit at home working easily and quietly, his long hours of labor mattered little to him, and other evils could be borne. . . . . But now that labor has become a mere burden, the disease of a class, that class will, by all means, try to throw it off, to lessen its weight, and in their efforts to do so they must of necessity destroy society, which is founded on the patient bearing of that burden. . . . . True, their masters, taught prudence by fear, will try, are trying, various means to make the workers bear their burden ; but one after the other they will be found out and discredited. Philanthropy has had its day and is gone, thrift and self-help are going; participation in profits, parliamentarianism and universal suffrage, State Socialism will have to go the same road, and the workers will be face to face at last with the fact that modern civilization, with its elaborate hierarchy and iron drill, is founded on their intolerable burden, and then no shortening of the day's work which would leave profit to the employer will make their labor hours short enough. They will see that modern society can only exist as long as they bear *their* burden with some degree of patience; their patience will be worn out, and to pieces will modern society go."

After a visit to Leeds and Bradford he writes : "The constant weight of drill in these highly organized industries has necessarily limited the intelligence of the men and deadened their individuality, while the system is so powerful and searching that they find it difficult to conceive of any system under which they could be other than human machines." † Elsewhere we find the same idea condensed into an epigram : " Individual profit makers are not a necessity for labor, but an obstruction to it." ‡

* "Socialism and Politics." Supplement to *Commonweal*, July, 1885.
† *Commonweal*, May 8th, 1886.
‡ Ibid, July 2nd, 1887.

Speaking of "Education under Capitalism" he says : "My heart sank under Mr. McChoakumchild and his method, and I thought how much luckier I was to have been born well enough off to be sent to a school where I was taught—nothing, but learned archæology and romance on the Wiltshire Downs." *

Under the heading "How We Live and How We Might Live" he writes : "Often when I have been sickened by the stupidity of the mean, idiotic rabbit warrens that rich men build for themselves in Bayswater and elsewhere, I console myself with visions of the noble Communal Hall of the future, unsparing of materials, generous in worthy ornament, alive with the noblest thoughts of our time, and the past embodied in the best art which free and manly people could produce ; such an abode of man as no private enterprise could come near for beauty and fitness, because only collective thought and collective life could cherish the aspirations which would give birth to its beauty or have the skill and leisure that could carry them out." †

Popular Control of Administration.

These cuttings from the *Commonweal* show that the views of the League were definitely revolutionary, and this is clearly stated in its Manifesto. There was to be no tinkering, no half measures ; the basis of society was to be changed. "No number of merely administrative changes, until the workers are in possession of all political power, would make any real approach to Socialism." "By political power," Morris goes on to explain, "we do not mean the exercise of the franchise or even the fullest development of the representative system, but the direct control by the people of the whole administration of the community whatever the ultimate destiny of that administration is to be." ‡

Communism.

One seeks in vain in the Manifesto for any definite suggestions as to the method in which this "direct control" was to be exercised, but Morris's lectures throw some light on the ideal of social organization that he had formed. "Those who see this view of the new society," he says, "believe that decentralization in it would be complete. The political unit with them would be not a nation, but a commune. The whole of reasonable society would be a great federation of such communes. . . . A nation is a body of people kept together for purposes of rivalry and war with other similar bodies, and when competition shall have given place to combination the function of the nation will be gone." "I will recapitulate," he continues, "the two views taken by Socialists as to the future of society. According to the first, the State—that is, the nation organized for unwasteful production and exchange of wealth—will be the sole possessor of the national plant and stock, the sole

---

* *Commonweal*, June 30th, 1888.　　　† Ibid, July 2nd, 1887.

‡ Manifesto of the Socialist League. A new edition, annotated by W. Morris and Belfort Bax. 1885.

employer of labor, which she will so regulate in the general interest that no man will ever need to fear lack of employment and due earnings therefrom. . . . According to the other view, the centralized nation would give place to a federation of communities, who would hold all wealth in common, and would use that wealth for satisfying the needs of each member, only exacting from each that he should do his best according to his capacity towards the production of the common wealth. . . .

"These two views of the future of society are sometimes opposed to each other as Socialism and Communism ; but to my mind the latter is simply the necessary development of the former, which implies a transition period during which people would be getting rid of the habits of mind bred by the long ages of tyranny and commercial competition, and be learning that it is to the interest of each that all should thrive. When men had lost the fear of each other engendered by our system of artificial famine, they would feel that the best way of avoiding the waste of labor would be to allow every man to take what he needed from the common store, since he would have no temptation or opportunity of doing anything with a greater portion than he really needed for his personal use. Thus would be minimized the danger of the community falling into bureaucracy, the multiplication of boards and offices, and all the paraphernalia of official authority, which is after all a burden, even when it is exercised by the delegation of the whole people and in accordance with their wishes." *

Any detailed scheme of State Socialism roused ire and repugnance in Morris, though one does not deny that towards the end of his life he was brought in a chastened spirit to bow his neck to the Fabian yoke. Still, his submission had the unreality of a death bed repentance. The creed was, in truth, alien to his nature. His hopes and wishes for the future were dominated by the glorious visions of free human activity, of pride and joy in the work of one's hands and brain, which he associated, rightly or wrongly, with the past. It was not only capitalism which he hated. The tameness and elaboration of modern mechanical production would be just as odious to him if the plant were in State ownership and the management in the hands of Government officials. His delightful rural idyll, "News from Nowhere," was written, Mr. Mackail tells us, as a protest against the apotheosis of centralization and of urban life held up as the social ideal by Mr. Bellamy in his "Looking Backward." Characteristically enough the land of Morris's prevision was a Utopia for the worker rather than for the consumer. The production of wealth interested him more than its enjoyment, the joy of making more than the joy of spending.

"Mr. Bellamy worries himself unnecessarily," he wrote in the *Commonweal* for June, 1889, "in seeking, with obvious failure, some incentive to labor to replace the fear of starvation, which is at

* "The Labor Question from the Socialist Standpoint." W. Morris. (One of a Course of Lectures on " The Claims of Labor.") Edinburgh Co-operative Printing Company, Limited. 1886.

present our only one ; whereas it cannot be too often repeated that the true incentive to useful and happy labor is, and must be, pleasure in the work itself." How to preserve, or rather how to recover, that incentive is for Morris the problem of problems ; but it is one that the orthodox Socialist is apt to overlook, although the man in the street, that much underrated critic, is always ready to remind him of it. It is the old story once more of being led astray by that mythological person, the economic man. The social reformer constructs, or rather designs, an organization of industry which threatens to totter as soon as it is built for want of just this foundation stone, the significance of which was instantly apparent to the eye of the poet, though to the economist it seemed a negligable detail. And here we come upon the real mission of William Morris to his generation, his special function in the Socialist movement. A craftsman himself, he thought of the worker not as an abstraction, but as a comrade, with motives more or less like his own. This vital sympathetic outlook led him, no doubt, into blunders from time to time, especially in his dealings with individuals, but it preserved him from some serious and common errors. His view of the future, of the new social structure for which we are all working, may have been one sided, but the side he saw was the side unseen by men immersed in questions of administrative reform or in organizing the class war. Fabians and Social Democrats were alike in this. They were apt to leave out of their calculations the humanization of the worker in and through his work, of bringing home to him the realization of his own place in the social economy. A decent life for the workman, the recognition on his own part of the dignity of his work, seemed to Morris not merely the end for which we were striving, but the only means of attaining it. "It is necessary to point out," he writes, "that there are some Socialists who do not think that the problem of the organization of life and necessary labor can be dealt with by a huge national centralization, working by a kind of magic for which no one feels himself responsible ; that, on the contrary, it will be necessary for the unit of administration to be small enough for every citizen to feel himself responsible for its details and be interested in them ; that individual men cannot shuffle off the business of life on to the shoulders of an abstraction called the State, but must deal with each other ; that variety of life is as much an aim of true Communism as equality of condition, and that nothing but an union of these two will bring about real freedom ; that modern nationalities are mere artificial devices for the commercial war that we seek to put an end to, and will disappear with it ; and, finally, that art, using the word in its widest and due signification, is not a mere adjunct of life which free and happy men can do without, but the necessary expression and indispensable instrument of human happiness." *

Distrust of Political Action.

In his own day Morris stood almost alone among Socialists in his distrust of political action, of a "huge national centralization working

* Review of "Looking Backward" in the *Commonweal* for June, 1889, by W. M.

by a kind of magic." It is true that there were in England two antagonistic types of Socialism, but their opposition was one of method rather than of aim. Both intended to capture the Government of the country, in the one case by revolutionary, in the other by more insidious methods. Morris, on the other hand, was inclined to throw the government of the country to the winds and to scorn the notion of a democratic control of industry exercised by means of a parliamentary vote. He never committed himself, so far as I know, as to the actual means by which any other kind of control by the " useful classes" was to be brought into being, but there seems little doubt that, if he were alive now, we should find him in the Syndicalist camp. A deep distrust of salvation by means of the vote would lead him there, and a profound belief that revolutionary activity in the working class can be more effectively evoked and fostered by bringing home to them the sense of their social responsibility as workers than as parliamentary constituents. In the one case interest is focussed on party politics, usually in their crudest form, and the lesson learned by the worker is a lesson in docility: he is taught to function smoothly as a wheel in the party machine. In the other case he is brought face to face with the actual problems of industrial production and organization; he learns to be resourceful and self-reliant and to take his place consciously and intelligently in the great enterprise of providing for the needs of mankind. I have said that Morris never committed himself as to the method in which this direct connection between the worker and the organization of industry was to be effected, but a private letter of his, written in 1888, gives a naif and vivid picture of industrial society as he visualized it in the future and the supercession of government: "Our present representative system," he writes, "is the reflection of our class society. The fact of the antagonism of classes underlies all our government, and causes political parties. . . . . The business of a statesman is to balance the greed and fears of the proprietary class against the necessities and demands of the working class. This is a sorry business, and leads to all kinds of trickery and evasion, so that it is more than doubtful whether a statesman can be a moderately honest man. Now, the control of classes being abolished, all this would fall to the ground. The relations of men to each other would become personal; wealth would be looked upon as an instrument of life and not as a reason for living, and therefore dominant over men's lives. Whatever laws existed would be much fewer, very simple, and easily understood by all; they would mostly concern the protection of the person. In dealing with property, its fetish quality having disappeared, its use only would have to be considered, e.g., shall we (the public) work this coal mine or shut it up? Is it necessary for us to lay down this park in wheat, or can we afford to keep it as a place of recreation? Will it be desirable to improve this shoemaking machine, or can we go on with it as it is? Will it be necessary to call for special volunteers to cultivate yonder fen, or will the action of the law of compensation be inducement enough for its cultivation? And so forth. . . .

"To return to our government of the future, which would be rather an administration of things than a government of persons. Nations, as political entities, would cease to exist. Civilization would mean the federalization of a variety of communities, great and small, at one end of which would be the township and the local guild, and at the other some central body whose function would be almost entirely the guardianship of the *principles* of society. . . . Between these two poles there would be various federations, which would grow together or dissolve as convenience of place, climate, language, etc., dictated, and would dissolve peaceably when occasion prompted. Of course public intercourse between the members of the federation would have to be carried on by means of delegation, but the delegates would not pretend to represent anyone or anything but the business with which they are delegated, e.g., 'We are a shoemaking community chiefly, you cotton spinners. Are we making too many shoes? Shall we turn, some of us, to gardening for a month or two, or shall we go on?' And so forth. . . . To my mind the essential thing to this view . . . is the township, or parish, or ward, or local guild, small enough to manage its own affairs directly. And I don't doubt that gradually all public business would be so much simplified that it would come to little more than a correspondence. 'Such are the facts with us ; compare them with the facts with you. You know how to act.' So that we should tend to the abolition of all government, and even of all regulations that were not really habitual ; and voluntary association would become a necessary habit and the only bond of society." *

It will be noticed that Morris differs both from Kropotkin with his " groups" and from most of the modern Syndicalists with their industrial guilds in localizing the communities that are to constitute his social framework. Notwithstanding his conviction that men must be organized as producers, his home loving nature refused to conceive a society which made light of the ties of neighborhood, of growth in a common soil. England was very dear to him as a land, though not as a nation ; and still dearer was the corner of England where he was born and bred. If we understand Morris and his attitude towards the future, we shall see that his Socialism was revolutionary and uncompromising just because he was conservative at heart. The transition period, as he called it, of State Socialism was distasteful to him because it seemed to substitute a dull uniformity for the detail and variety of the past. He admitted eventually that it was bound to come, he saw that it was coming by means of humdrum agitation followed by humdrum legislation, but he could never feel any enthusiasm about it.

Education towards Revolution.

We have seen that the split with the Social Democratic Federation, in so far as it was not due merely to personal misunderstandings, was a protest against circuitous and indirect methods of

* Letters on Socialism by W. Morris to Rev. G. Bainton. London. Privately printed. 1894. (Only thirty-four copies.)

advance. His desire was to found a Socialist Party which should begin to act at once not by permeating cultivated people, nor by gaining representation in Parliament, but by raising a standard of revolt to which the oppressed could rally. His one encouragement in making a new attempt had been the signs of discontent among the masses. To focus this discontent and render it articulate was his purpose in forming the Socialist League. A passionate hatred had grown up in him of a society which seemed to him " mere cannibalism," " so corrupt, so steeped in hypocrisy, that one turns from one stratum of it to another with hopeless loathing." In one direction only did he see hope, the road to revolution ; but that road, as he saw it, was gradual and arduous. To educate a strong party of workers in the aims of Socialism, so that when the seething forces of popular discontent could no longer be restrained, leaders should be forthcoming among the people to tell them what to aim at and what to ask for. An aimless revolt, leading to counter revolution, seemed to him a threatening calamity. Looking back to that period, a quarter of a century ago, we see that Morris over estimated the danger of a premature upheaval. Society was not ripe for it. Education was needed not merely to guide, but to produce that impatience of injustice and oppression which must be the motive power in such an upheaval. He believed that the new birth of society was at hand, and that the work for Socialists was to strive to help it forward, so that it might come with as little confusion and suffering as might be. "Education towards revolution seems to me," he said, " to express in three words what our policy should be." It was a policy which separated him on the one hand from Parliamentarians and Opportunists, and on the other from Anarchists ready for all risks of immediate revolution ; and so it came about that the League grew but slowly, and steered with difficulty between Scylla and Charybdis. Morris held the helm as long as he could, but from the first the road to revolution that he saw had little attraction for most of his comrades. After a few years a policy of high handed robbery, of bombs and barricades, came to be openly advocated by many voluble members of the League, and in 1889 these views were so much in the ascendant that Morris was actually deposed from the control of the *Commonweal*, dependent as it still was on him both for matter and money. He continued to write for it until November, 1890, when he published in it a final statement of his views under the title "Where Are We Now ?" After reviewing the seven years that had elapsed since Socialism had "come to life again," he goes on to describe the two lines on which the " methods of impatience " profess to work, the line of " palliation " and the line of " partial inconsequent revolt," and then explains his own policy, which differed as much from one as from the other. " Our business," he concludes, " is the making of Socialists, i.e., convincing people that Socialism is good for them and is possible. When we have enough people of that way of thinking, they will find out what action is necessary for putting their principles in practice."

This dignified protest was ill received by the majority of the members of the League, and Morris had no choice but to sever his connection with a body whose policy he disapproved.

Hammersmith Socialist Society.

After his withdrawal it struggled on for eighteen months, and then ended dramatically with the arrest of the printer and publisher of the *Commonweal.* Meanwhile Morris and the little group who shared his views organized themselves as the Hammersmith Socialist Society, and issued a circular drafted by Morris to the provincial branches of the League explaining their action.

The membership was very small at first, and never became large. Mr. Emery Walker was secretary and Morris treasurer, and the meetings took place in Kelmscott House.

Until the end of his life Morris relaxed no whit in enthusiasm for the cause, and his opposition towards Anarchism grew stronger rather than weaker. " It is not the dissolution of society for which we strive," he writes in December, 1890, " but its reintegration. The idea put forward by some who attack present society of the complete independence of every individual, that is, of freedom without society, is not merely impossible of realization, but, when looked into, turns out to be inconceivable." *

Seven Years of Peaceful Work.

But though his belief in Socialism was as strong as ever, he became convinced, as time went on, that the active work immediately called for was work unsuited to his taste and to his powers.

" In all the wearisome shilly shally of parliamentary politics I should be absolutely useless, and the immediate end to be gained, the pushing things just a trifle nearer to State Socialism, which, when realized, seems to me but a dull goal, all this quite sickens me. Also I know that there are a good many other idealists (if I may use that word of myself) who are in the same position, and I don't see why they should not hold together and keep out of the vestry business, necessary as that may be. Preaching the ideal is surely always necessary. Yet, on the other hand, I sometimes vex myself by thinking that perhaps I am not doing the most I can merely for the sake of a piece of ' preciousness.' " †

To make use of Morris for organizing meetings and speaking at street corners was to dig with a damascened sword blade. He was here to show how life, even in the nineteenth century, could be full of variety and delight. The revival of the lost art of printing, the engrossing occupation of his latest years, was a return to the true work of his life. We are glad to remember that the seven years of stress and turmoil, when he fought so nobly for the ideal that lay always before him, were succeeded by seven years of serene and happy work, which has left the world richer in all the crafts that subserve the making of books.

* Manifesto of the Hammersmith Socialist Society.
† Letter to Mrs. Burne-Jones, dated July 29th, 1888, quoted in Mackail's " Life of William Morris," vol. ii, p. 206.

To the last, however, he went on lecturing from time to time on Socialism. On October 30th, 1895, just a year before his death, he gave an address to inaugurate the Oxford Socialist Union. A few months later he was present at the New Year's Meeting of the Social Democratic Federation, and made there a short but noble and touching speech on behalf of unity. Two days afterwards he gave his last Sunday evening lecture at Kelmscott House, again on the same subject, the title being "One Socialist Party."

One more year marked by failing strength but unfailing industry was spent in seeing through the press the greatest of his printing achievements, the Kelmscott Chaucer, and in composing the last of his long series of stories, " The Sundering Flood."

He died on October 3rd, 1896, aged 62, and was buried in the little churchyard at Kelmscott. The body was borne to the grave in an open haycart, festooned with vines, alders, and bulrushes, and driven by a countryman.

WORKS OF WILLIAM MORRIS ON SOCIALISM.

Architecture, Industry and Wealth. Collected papers by William Morris. 1902. Longmans. 6s. net.
Hopes and Fears for Art. 1882. Longmans. 4s. 6d.
Signs of Change. 1888. Longmans. 4s. 6d.
Architecture and History and Westminster Abbey. 1900. Longmans. 2s 6d. net.
Art and its Producers. 1901. Longmans. 2s. 6d. net.
Poems by the Way. Sq cr. 1891. Longmans. 6s.
A Dream of John Ball and a King's Lesson. 1888. Longmans. 1s. 6d.
News from Nowhere. 1890. Longmans. 1s. 6d.
How I Became a Socialist. Reprinted from *Justice*. 1896. 1d.
The Claims of Labor. A Course of Lectures, one only by W. M. 1886. Co-operative Printing Company, Edinburgh. 1d.

BIOGRAPHICAL AND CRITICAL BOOKS.

Life of William Morris. By J. W. MACKAIL. 2 vols. 2nd edition. 1901. Longmans. 4s.
Socialism: Its Growth and Outcome. W. MORRIS and BELFORT BAX. 1908. Swan Sonnenschein. 3s. 6d.
William Morris, Socialist-Craftsman. By HOLBROOK JACKSON. 1908. Fifield. 6d. and 1s.
William Morris: His Art, his Writing, and his Public Life. A record, by AYMER VALLANCE. 1897. George Bell and Sons. . 25s. net.
The Books of William Morris described, with some account of his doings in Literature and the Allied Arts. By H. BUXTON FORMAN. 1897. Frank Hollings. 10s. 6d. net.
William Morris: Poet, Craftsman, Socialist. By E. L. CARY. Illustrated. 1902. G. P. Putnam and Sons. $3.50.
A Bibliography of the Works of William Morris. By TEMPLE SCOTT. 1897. George Bell and Sons. 5s. net.
Morris as Workmaster. W. R. LETHABY. 1901. John Hogg, 13 Paternoster Row, E.C. 6d. net. ———

The Collected Works, edited by Miss MAY MORRIS, are in course of publication by Longmans and Co., in 24 volumes, at £12 12s. the set. The volumes are not sold separately. ———

Extracts from the works of William Morris have been made by the kind permission of his literary executors; the right to reprint extracts from J. W. Mackail's "Life" has been purchased from Messrs. Longmans, Green & Co.

FABIAN SOCIETY.—The Fabian Society consists of Socialists. A statement of its Rules and a complete list of publications can be obtained from the Secretary, at the Fabian Office, 3 Clement's Inn, London, W.C.

FABIAN ESSAYS IN SOCIALISM. Paper 6d.; cloth 1/6; post. 2½d. and 4d

WHAT TO READ on Social and Economic Subjects. 1s. n. and 2s. n.

THIS MISERY OF BOOTS. By H. G. WELLS. 3d., post free 4d.

FABIAN TRACTS and LEAFLETS.

Tracts, each 16 to 52 pp., price 1d., or 9d. per dos., unless otherwise stated.
Leaflets, 4 pp. each, price 1d. for six copies, 1s. per 100, or 8/6 per 1000.

The Set of 81, 3s.; post free 3/5. Bound in Buckram, 4/6 n.; post free 5s.

I.—General Socialism in its various aspects.

TRACTS.—159. The Necessary Basis of Society. By SIDNEY WEBB. 151. The Point of Honour. By RUTH C. BENTINCK. 147. Capital and Compensation. By E. R. PEASE. 146. Socialism and Superior Brains. By BERNARD SHAW. 142. Rent and Value. 138. Municipal Trading. 121. Public Service versus Private Expenditure. By Sir OLIVER LODGE. 107. Socialism for Millionaires. By BERNARD SHAW. 139. Socialism and the Churches. By Rev JOHN CLIFFORD, D.D. 133. Socialism and Christianity. By Rev. PERCY DEARMER. 78. Socialism and the Teaching of Christ. By Dr. J. CLIFFORD. 42. Christian Socialism. By Rev. S. D. HEADLAM. 79. A Word of Remembrance and Caution to the Rich. By JOHN WOOLMAN. 72. The Moral Aspects of Socialism. By SIDNEY BALL. 69. Difficulties of Individualism. By S. WEBB. 51. Socialism: True and False. By S. WEBB. 45. The Impossibilities of Anarchism. By BERNARD SHAW (price 2d.). 7. Capital and Land (revised 1908) 5. Facts for Socialists (revised 1908). 132. A Guide to Books for Socialists. LEAFLETS—13. What Socialism Is 1. Why are the Many Poor? WELSH TRACTS—143. Sosialaeth yng Ngoleuni'r Beibl. 141. Translation of 139. 87. Translation of 78. 38. Translation of 1.

II.—Applications of Socialism to Particular Problems.

TRACTS.—164. Gold and State Banking. By E. R. PEASE. 163. Women and Prisons. By HELEN BLAGG and CHARLOTTE M. WILSON. 2d. 162. Family Life on a Pound a Week. By Mrs. REEVES. In cover, 2d. 161. Afforestation and Unemployment. By A. P. GRENFELL. 160. A National Medical Service. By F. LAWSON DODD. 2d. 157. The Working Life of Women. By Miss B. L. HUTCHINS. 155. The Case against the Referendum. By CLIFFORD SHARP. 154. The Case for School Clinics. By L. HADEN GUEST. 153. The Twentieth Century Reform Bill. By H. H. SCHLOESSER. 152. Our Taxes as they are and as they ought to be. By R. JONES, B.Sc. In cover, 2d. 150. State Purchase of Railways. By EMIL DAVIES. In cover, 2d. 149. The Endowment of Motherhood. By H. D. HARBEN. In cover, 2d. 145. The Case for School Nurseries. By Mrs. TOWNSHEND. 140. Child Labor under Capitalism. By Mrs. HYLTON DALE. 136. The Village and the Landlord. By EDW. CARPENTER. 130. Home Work and Sweating. By Miss B. L. HUTCHINS. 128. The Case for a Legal Minimum Wage. 122. Municipal Milk and Public Health. By Dr. F. LAWSON DODD. 125. Municipalization by Provinces. 123. The Revival of Agriculture. 115. State Aid to Agriculture: an Example. 124. State Control of Trusts. 86. Municipal Drink Traffic. 83. State Arbitration and the Living Wage. LEAFLET.—104. How Trade Unions benefit Workmen.

III.—Local Government Powers : How to use them.

TRACTS.—156. What an Education Committee can do (Elementary Schools), 3d. 137. Parish Councils and Village Life. 109. Cottage Plans and Common Sense. 76. Houses for the People. 82. Workmen's Compensation Act. 54. The Humanizing of the Poor Law. LEAFLETS.—134. Small Holdings: and how to get them. 68. The Tenant's Sanitary Catechism. 71. Ditto for London.

IV.—General Politics and Fabian Policy.

TRACTS.—158. The Case against the C.O.S. By Mrs. TOWNSHEND. 108. Twentieth Century Politics. By S. WEBB. 70. Report on Fabian Policy. 41. The Fabian Society: its Early History. By BERNARD SHAW.

V.—Biographical Series. In cover, 2d. each.

165. Francis Place. By ST. JOHN G. ERVINE. 166. Robert Owen, Social Reformer. By Miss B. L. HUTCHINS.

Printed by G. Standring, 7 Finsbury St., London, E.C, and published by the Fabian Society, 3 Clement's Inn, Strand, London, W.C.

Fabian Tract No. 168.

JOHN STUART MILL

By JULIUS WEST

Biographical Series No. 4.   Price 2d.
Published and sold by the Fabian Society,
3 Clement's Inn, Strand, London, W.C.
January 1913.

JOHN STUART MILL.

BIOGRAPHICAL.

ACROSS the bleak desert of intellect which coincides with the first fifty years of the reign of Queen Victoria there run numerous uncertain pathways, all starting from the Temple of Mammon. These pathways meet and mingle in all sorts of unexpected, complicated fashions, and the majority of them lead nowhere. One, known as Carlyle, for example, appears ever to be getting more distant from the Temple, but in the end goes no farther than Chelsea. Another, called Ruskin, leaves the Temple of Mammon with a grand blazing of trumpets, but, going a little way, stops before a Gothic Temple, and the call of the trumpet is converted to the dronings of an organ. Of all the pathways, Mill is perhaps the clearest. It sets out from the front parlour of a man, Bentham, of whom more will be said ; it leads down a steep precipice called the Wages Fund Theory (where danger notices have been but lately erected) ; it traverses a bit of boggy ground which is marked on the maps as the Law of Population ; it turns a few curious corners, when, lo, the Promised Land is in sight.

Now, as to this man Bentham. About 1800 there was in existence a body of philosophers who believed that the purpose of all human effort should be the increase of the sum total of human happiness ; with real, perfervid energy and emotion they sought, in their own words, "the greatest good of the greatest number." Of these Bentham was the founder, and when he died, in 1832, he left a particularly unpleasant prison at Westminster (the Millbank Penitentiary) as a monument to his endeavours to increase human happiness. In 1808, when Bentham was sixty years of age, he made the acquaintance of a rigid and logical Scotsman named James Mill. Mill sat at Bentham's feet, assimilated his doctrines, made them a shade more rigid, and finally became Bentham's lieutenant. And Mill dedicated his (at that time) only son, John Stuart, that the youngster, who was only born in 1806, should be a worthy successor to the two friends, and should continue to proclaim the truths of Utilitarianism to all the world. The history of the intellectual life of J. S. Mill is contained in his efforts to escape from the narrow individualistic creed of his progenitors, real and spiritual, and his gradual approach towards Socialism.

We need not close our eyes to the fact that Bentham was a power, that he profoundly influenced the evolution of the law and of public administration, to be nevertheless extremely critical of his influence upon J. S. Mill. At this distance from the Benthamites it is difficult to realize how starkly intense was their individualism. "Laissez faire" with them was more than a theory ; it was a faith. Bentham, who wrote on almost everything, produced a small

"Manual of Political Economy," from whose dark, unfathomed depths the following gem has been extracted: "With the view of causing an increase to take place in the mass of national wealth, or with a view to increase of the means either of subsistence or enjoyment, without some special reason, the general rule is that nothing ought to be done or attempted by government. The motto or watchword of government on these occasions ought to be—*Be quiet.*" * He died in 1832, at the age of eighty-four, leaving behind him one hundred and forty boxes of manuscript. For many years his life had been that of a tabulating machine with a mania for neologizing. He invented, for example, seven classes of "Offences against the positive increase of the National Felicity." † These include the heinous crimes of offending against epistemo-threptic, antembletic and hedomonarchic trusts. He is at present probably tabulating and renaming the numerous varieties of asbestos.

The Misfortunes of Mill: His Father.

But long before his death James Mill, observing that the mantle of Bentham was in danger of being soiled by continual dragging through the muddy waters of the elder's verbiage, took it from his shoulders and placed it upon his own. (This is no mere figure of speech; for the unpruned language of Bentham's later days was incomprehensible to the public, and so his notes had to be edited and his books written by his disciples.) With James Mill there is little need for us to tarry. He is best remembered by his character and his eldest son.

James Mill came to London from Scotland, and having for some years earned a precarious living by journalism, proceeded to write a History of India. It appeared in 1817, the result of nine years hard work. That he had no first hand knowledge of his subject was, he considered, all to the good. It permitted full play to the objective attitude. But the three substantial resultant volumes of conscientious drought brought him a reward. Established as an authority on the country he had never seen, he succeeded in obtaining a post in the office of the East India Company. In 1836, the year of his death, he was drawing a salary of £2,000.

The Misfortunes of Mill: His Upbringing.

In the intervals of his journalistic work, and, later, in the leisure accorded by his official duties, James Mill educated his son. The course of instruction prescribed and administered by this, the most ruthless of all parents, was encyclopædic in its scope and devastating in its character. John Stuart Mill, while yet infant and amorphous, was destined by his father for leadership and educated accordingly. In his "Autobiography" (p. 3) he says, "I have no recollection of the time when I began to learn Greek; I have been told it was when I was three years old." At the age of seven he had read the first six dialogues of Plato, and subsequently acted as teacher to his younger brothers and sisters. Such inexorability as his

* Works, Ed. Bowring, 1843.
† "Principles of Morals and Legislation," Chap. XVI.

father's in teaching young minds to shoot would lead many to suicide. There is little need to detail. The practice of long walks with his father, in which instruction was combined with exercise, was perhaps the principal reason for J. S. Mill's physical survival. Intellectually, his persistence to years of discretion must be credited to his heredity. Of boyhood he had none. Says Mill: "He was earnestly bent upon my escaping not only the corrupting influence which boys exercise over boys, but the contagion of vulgar modes of thought and feeling; and for this he was willing that I should pay the price of inferiority in the accomplishments which school-boys in all countries chiefly cultivate."* It is astonishing that this system did not convert his brain into a sort of *pâté de foie gras*. But he survived. The worst efforts of his father failed to affect the stability of his marvellous brain. Having left his child-hood with his cradle, he proceeded to absorb all that there was to be absorbed of Greek and Latin, mathematics, history, both ancient and modern, and the remaining subjects prescribed by convention and his father's views. At the age when, nowadays, he might be qualifying for a Boy Scout, Mill took to philosophy, psychology and logic. In 1823 (age 17) his father obtained him a clerkship in the India House, where he remained until 1858. About this time he began to write for the *Edinburgh* and *Westminster Reviews*. In 1825 he " edited," in manner aforesaid, Bentham's " Rationale of Judicial Evidence," much to his own edification.

The Strenuous Life.

Of this period of his life, when the rigidity of parental control had been somewhat relaxed, it would have been not unreasonable to expect that Mill, like Richard Feverel, might have rebelled against the "system." Far from it; the process had been too thorough. Mill never sowed any wild oats of any species whatsoever; he did not even cut down the familial apple-tree. At the age of twenty he virtually founded the " London Debating Society," which seems to have been something like the Fabian Society would have been if it had no Basis and no external objects. To this belonged, amongst others, Macaulay, Edward Bulwer Lytton, a large number of incipient reputations, and the *élite* of the Oxford and Cambridge Unions. Concurrently with the existence of this society, Mill and Grote, the future historian, formed a study circle which met twice a week at the latter's house for the discussion of Economics. When this subject contained no more unexplored regions, the circle took up Logic and Analytical Psychology. In all the meetings extended over five years, giving Mill an additional stratum upon which to base his subsequent work. As one result of these meetings, we should note the " Essays on Unsettled Questions in Political Economy," which was written about 1830-31, but not published until 1844.

Throughout this whole period Mill was a frequent contributor to the Reviews. His literary output previous to 1843 was voluminous, but consisted almost entirely of criticism. In that year he published his first classic, "A System of Logic, Ratiocinative and Inductive; being

"Autobiography," p. 20.

a connected view of the principles of evidence and the methods of scientific investigation." To this portentous work belonged all the characteristics enumerated above of his father's "India"; it was perhaps the most important book of its time, and its merits were such that eight editions were exhausted in the author's lifetime. Having completed this, Mill shortly turned his attention to his next classic work, which appeared in 1848. Of this, the "Principles of Political Economy," more will be said later, when some of its points will be examined. These two books are Mill's most substantial contributions to human thought. Of those of his smaller works with which we shall be concerned the most important are the "Representative Government" and the "Subjection of Women." These each contain, roughly, the full development of a single idea, and, although by no means trivial, are scarcely entitled to rank with his "classic" works. Before allowing his books to speak for themselves, the outstanding features of the remainder of his life must be stated.

His Marriage.

In the first place, as to Mill's marriage. At the age of twenty-three Mill became acquainted with a Mrs. Taylor, wife of a City drysalter. He sat at her feet some sixteen years, when she became a widow, and two years afterwards Mill and she were married. He continued to sit at her feet for seven more years, until 1858, when she died. Of her he writes throughout in terms of extreme admiration, which, coming from a man of Mill's dispassionate temperament, approach rhapsody. For example, in dedicating his "Liberty" to her, the year following her death, he concludes with these words: "Were I but capable of interpreting to the world one half the great thoughts and noble feelings which are buried in her grave I should be the medium of a greater benefit to it than is ever likely to arise from anything that I can write, unprompted and unassisted by her all but unrivalled wisdom." Mill's biographers, Leslie Stephen and Bain, are somewhat sceptical. Bain writes, "Grote used to say 'only John Mill's reputation could survive such displays.'"[*] There is no point in endeavouring to estimate the accuracy of such declarations; we must take Mill's word and leave it at that, perhaps with the added comment that a woman capable of inspiring such depths of feeling would also be capable of affecting the quality of Mill's work; of improving it without necessarily herself touching it.

In the year of her death the East India Company ceased to exist. The Indian Mutiny had convinced the Government that it was, on the whole, inadvisable to run an empire by private enterprise, and the business of administering India was nationalized. The Company, of course, was unwilling, and resisted the divestment of its interests. It fell to Mill, by this time virtually in command at India House, to draft the Company's petition for reprieve, in a document which was pronounced by Earl Grey "the ablest State paper he had ever read."[†] But all in vain; the India Office superseded the India House. and Mill was retired on a pension of £1,500.

* Bain, "J. S. Mill: a Criticism," p. 167.
† Bain, p. 96.

M.P. for Westminster.

Then Mill went into Parliament. The story of his election, which took place in 1865, is strikingly characteristic of Mill's tenacity of opinion and undeviating pursuit of whatever path of conduct he held to be right. In these days the term "principle" is in danger of obliteration, save only in so far as it enters into the adjective "unprincipled," and Mill's own account of the election has a distinctly humorous touch. Westminster was the favoured constituency. He writes, for example, "I was convinced that no numerous or influential portion of any electoral body really wished to be represented by a person of my opinions. . . . It was, and is, my fixed conviction that a candidate ought not to incur one farthing of expense for undertaking a public duty. . . . I felt, therefore, that I ought not to seek election to Parliament, much less to expend any money in procuring it."* Authors are not generally gifted with such a degree of self-effacement, not to mention politicians. However, a body of electors came and asked Mill to stand, and he, having "put their disposition to the proof by one of the frankest explanations ever tendered, I should think, to an electoral body by a candidate,"† consented. A well known "literary man was heard to say that the Almighty himself would have no chance of being elected on such a programme."‡ The result of this amazing election was that Mill secured a majority of 700 over W. H. Smith, his Conservative competitor. He attached himself to Gladstone, but in fact retained his independence, and not infrequently opposed his own party. He remained in Parliament for three years, during which he took a prominent part in the troublous passage of the Reform Bill of '67, and otherwise. It was on an occasion connected with this Reform agitation that the Hyde Park railings were pushed down. Mill appears to have mediated between the demonstrators and the Government with the result that serious collisions were prevented. It was not to be expected that the miracle would happen twice; Mill was not re-elected. He himself does not seem to have greatly regretted losing his seat.

The Last Years.

So he went back to his books and to Avignon, to pass the remaining years of his life near his wife's grave. He there wrote the "Subjection of Women," and planned a book on Socialism, which was left unfinished. These and voluminous replies to correspondents appear to have been the principal occupations of the years 1868-73. In the latter year he died, at Avignon, as the result of a local epidemic disease.

This is but the briefest sketch of Mill's life. The four aspects of his work most likely to interest Socialists will be studied separately. Until his work has been discussed it is useless to attempt framing an estimate of his influence. Moreover, we shall not be dealing at all with some of perhaps his most important aspects. As a Rationalist and as a Philosopher he takes a high place amongst the world's thinkers, but we need only study him in his relation to society.

* "Autobiography," p. 160.   † Ibid, p. 161.   ‡ Ibid, p. 162.

In 1865, the year Mill went into Parliament, he published his substantial " Examination of Sir William Hamilton's Philosophy," a work from which most Englishmen drew their philosophy for the subsequent decade. He had already (1863) published "Utilitarianism," wherein the opinions of Bentham and his father were rendered with more qualification than sympathy. "On Liberty" (1859), in which he and his wife collaborated, is a fine piece of writing, but curiously inconsequent, and does not advocate anything more exciting than non-interference, and not always that.

Mill was an honourable, upright man, capable of commanding firm friendships and the greatest respect. "Saint of Rationalism" was the title bestowed on him by Gladstone. Herbert Spencer gives many instances of Mill's generosity, and wrote an almost emotional obituary notice.* His was a noble, unselfish life, and with it passed perhaps the greatest purifying force of the last century.

ECONOMIST.

Economics in 1836.

Roughly speaking, Mill's work as an economist may be summed up by saying that he found economics a body of doctrines and left it a body of doctrine. For the first time the mass of theories evolved by and since Adam Smith were integrated into a coherent and, on the whole, a moderately consistent statement. Adam Smith popularized economics; that is to say, for all practical purposes he founded it. A little later Malthus added the theory of population with considerations arising therefrom. Sir Edward West introduced the notion of the margin of cultivation. Ricardo stated the idea of economic rent. Nassau Senior evolved the quaint " abstinence " theory—abstinence being " a term by which we express the conduct of a person who either abstains from the unproductive use of what he can command, or designedly prefers the production of remote to that of immediate results."† They took this sort of thing very seriously in 1836. It will be readily understood therefore that the seventy years following the publication of the " Wealth of Nations " (1776) had literally made a hash of economics. It had appeared with certain pretensions to be a science; it had degenerated into a gallimaufry. Hence the importance of Mill's work.

The Perils of Population.

Yet the result was not altogether satisfactory. Mill's unfortunate education was to blame. He had started life upon a Ricardian diet, and absorbed Malthus with depressing avidity. Hence he was incapable of seeing facts for himself: he could squeeze out the full content of other writers' syllogisms, but himself refrained from stating new premises. To the end of his days he was haunted by the bogey of population; he despaired of ever achieving a state where the distribution of wealth should be equitable; multiplication

* See Appendix G. Spencer, "Autobiography," Vol. II.
† Senior, " Political Economy," p. 58.

would hinder division. It is seldom that philoprogenitiveness was dealt with as severely as by this son of a philoprogenitive father. Sinking for a moment his accustomed humanitarianism, he descends to the level of a hardened official of the Charity Organization Society. "Poverty," he declares, "like most social evils, exists because men follow their brute instincts without due consideration." In a footnote he adds: "Little improvement can be expected in morality until the producing of large families is regarded with the same feelings as drunkenness or any other physical excess."* His whole attitude towards social reforms is tempered by the fear that, perhaps, they would only increase man's unfortunate liability to be born; that generosity would merely induce generation.

Hence Mill's condemnation of a minimum wage, legal or moral. "If nothing more were necessary than a compulsory accumulation (*i.e.*, of money to be available for wages), sufficient to provide employment at ample wages for the existing numbers of the people, such a proposition would have no more strenuous supporter than myself. Society mainly consists of those who live by bodily labour; and if society, that is, if the labourers lend their physical force to protect individuals in the enjoyment of superfluities, they are entitled to do so, and have always done so, with the reservation of a power to tax those superfluities for purposes of public utility, amongst which purposes the subsistence of the people is the foremost. Since no one is responsible for having been born, no pecuniary sacrifice is too great to be made by those who have more than enough for the purpose of securing enough to all persons already in existence." † All of which shows how Mill's progress towards Socialism was turned aside by an optical illusion. He could not realize, as Sadler had already realized, that comfort was a very potent preventive check, and that Malthus, whose anxieties were justifiable at the time he wrote, would be disproved by the lapse of time.

Wages and Welfare.

Of Trade Unions and their future development Mill does not seem to have had much idea. On the first occasion when he refers in his published works to unions, in a pleasantly amusing letter to Carlyle, written from Paris, he slightly jests at their expense. On the authority of an "impartial" person, he states of French Unions, that "their object is not so much more money as to elevate their rank in society, since at present the gentlemen will not keep company with them, and they will not keep company with the common labourers." ‡ That was in 1833. In later years his views were softened. He could never recognize that trade unions were of much positive utility, even though he would not admit they were actually harmful. But Mill's keen sense of justice made him actually befriend the unions, without admitting their efficiency. Wages, he believed, were settled for the individual by competition between masters and workers. So long as the masters could do as they pleased in order

* " Principles," Book II., Chap. XIII.
† "Principles," Book II., Chap. XII.
‡ " Letters," p. 74.

to lower wages, so long was it unjust to forbid workers to combine in order to raise wages. He inveighs against combination laws, "laws enacted and maintained for the declared purpose of keeping wages low," because "such laws exhibit the infernal spirit of the slave master, who, to retain the working classes in avowed slavery, has ceased to be practicable."[*] He goes even further: "The best interests of the human race imperatively require that all economical experiments, voluntarily undertaken, should have the fullest licence, and that force and fraud should be the only means of attempting to benefit themselves which are interdicted to the less fortunate classes of the community." This last passage was added in the third edition of the "Principles" four years after the original appearance of the book, and illustrates Mill's advancing views.

Holding, as he did, the Malthusian theory of population, it would have been illogical on Mill's part to have definitely gone over to the support of trade unionism. For this theory held a corollary, the wages fund theory, and the two were inseparable: vicious doctrines have extraordinary powers of cohesion. We need not excite ourselves over the esoteric aspects of this particular dogma. Briefly and exoterically they are as follows. Malthus and his followers believed that overpopulation was the cause of most misery, as a quotation made above has illustrated. From this it was permissible to deduce, subalternately, that overpopulation was the cause of low wages. Hence there was supposed to be a connection between population and wages, and the more there was of one, the less there would be of the other. A step further, and we have the idea stated, to quote Senior, "that wages depend" on "the extent of the fund for the maintenance of labourers, compared with the number of labourers to be maintained." This is the celebrated Wages Fund theory, to which Mill was a subscriber. In these enlightened days, when everybody disbelieves in Malthus's theory, but is hyper-Malthusian in his practice, the sister doctrine of the Wages Fund is no longer with us. Moreover, it has been pointed out that wages are not paid out of a fund earmarked, as it were, for that purpose. Wages are paid out of the produce of labour, which can be increased indefinitely until the point is reached when all human wants are satiated and machinery can do no more to stimulate desires, either by producing things cheaper or by producing anything at all that man has not got, but would like to have if he saw it.

Holding this theory, Mill could not but believe (1) that if anybody of workers succeeded, by means of a trade union or otherwise, in raising their wages, it could only be at the expense of other workers; (2) that any permanent improvement in the wage position of all the workers must await the time when their rate of multiplication would be considerably decreased.[†]

[*] "Principles," Book V., Chap. X., § 5.

[†] For full discussion of the Wages Fund Theory see Cannan, "A History of the Theories of Production and Distribution in English Political Economy from 1776 to 1848," *passim*; Marshall, "Principles of Economics," Appendix J; Taussig, "Wages and Capital, an Examination of the Wages Fund Doctrine"; and Webb, "Industrial Democracy," Part III., Chapter I.

It was a distinctly uncomfortable theory and so plausible that it was universally believed. Lassalle's "Iron Law of Wages," emanating from a fervent Socialist, is a restatement of the theory, before which Socialists, as well as the orthodox, were forced, in default of an alternative theory, to prostrate themselves. Mill's is the glory of upsetting the car of Juggernaut, although Frederic Harrison had already noted the fallacy. In a review of a work of Thornton, a fellow economist, in the *Fortnightly Review* in May, 1869, the theory was solemnly stated, examined, and disproved. Economics was never the same after this inroad into its hitherto unquestioned sanctities. Mill himself died shortly afterwards, and it was left to others, notably to Jevons, to collect the tattered fragments of political economy; and by the publication of the "Theory of Political Economy" in 1871, with an exposition of his theory of marginal utility, once more to give the science an appearance of respectability, not to say probability.†

The Future of Labour.

There are discrepancies between the first and second halves of the "Principles." Mill began as an individualist advocate of peasant proprietorship, converted himself as he went on, and ended almost as a Socialist. But, as nobody held out to the end of the book, and very few got beyond the first half, its influence was in favour of peasant proprietorship.

No essay upon the economic principles of Mill is exempted from referring to Book IV, Chapter VII, of his "Principles." For that bears the title "On the Probable Futurity of the Labouring Classes." In 1817 the House of Commons appointed a "Select Committee on the Education of the Lower Orders." In 1848, in his chapter on the "labouring classes" (the term itself shows an advance), Mill says he uses the term in the conventional sense, as "I do not regard as either just or salutary a state of society in which there is any class which is not labouring, any human beings exempt from bearing their share of the necessary labours of human life, except those unable to labour, or who have fairly earned rest by previous toil" (§ 1). The interest of this passage lies in the change of attitude indicated, not the change which had taken place between 1817 and 1848, but the expressed possibility of social transformation. And this possibility is presented in a description which, if it suffers somewhat from Malthusian squint, yet also contains something of a prophet's vision. The relation between rich and poor is to vanish. Just as feudalism is now dead, so must the poor of to-day emerge from their tutelage. Independence is the key to the future of the workers. "Whatever advice, exhortation, or guidance is held out to the labouring classes must henceforth be tendered to them as equals, and accepted by them with their eyes open." Then he proceeds briefly to survey profit sharing. The results have sometimes been favourable, but the capitalist is not eliminated ; in fact his hold is strengthened over his

† See Mill's "Principles of Political Economy," edition Ashley, Appendix O. Longmans, 1910.

employees. "The form of association, however, which, if mankind, continue to improve, must be expected in the end to predominate, is not that which can exist between a capitalist as chief, but in . . ." (§ 6), and Mill proceeds to narrate the history and the results of co-operative production. Here the prophet's voice was speaking. The future of co-operation is hidden from us, but who knows how far it will evolve? Once the great mass of the people begin to produce the necessaries of life for themselves without the needlessly insinuated mediation of predatory capital, the future state will evolve with a swiftness and a certainty unprecedented in the annals of civilization. With the displacement of the capitalist will come, not the millenium, but at the least a society whose basis is not that of our own, capital needlessly deviated from production to advertisement, advertisement, and ever more advertisement. Mill's great position as an economist does not rest, as he considered it to rest, upon a discovery of his concerning distribution, nor, as other persons have considered, upon his treatment of value. It rests upon his humanity and the introduction of the element of humanity into economics. He attempted to apply to what others had regarded as an art, to be treated entirely for art's sake, the saving grace of human fellowship.

FEMINIST.

The abuse of power and the detrimental effects of involuntary subordination are themes which recur more frequently in Mill's work than any other. It is because he objects to the dominance of capital that he becomes so nearly a Socialist. It is because government by the few is a system too apt to ally itself with tyranny that he is so strong a democrat. It is because he realizes the peculiar evils which arise from the subjection of women that he is a feminist.

There are two species of prophets. One is the man who utilizes the historical method, the inductive method, or what not, and foretells a fragment of the events of the coming year, or perhaps of the next few years—he sees, but has no vision. The other species has no use for the inductive method, and regards a telescope as an anachronism. He sees far ahead and is emphatic. Isaiah belonged to this class, Marx to the former. Mill we may class with Marx in this respect, save only in a single direction. Where the future of women is concerned he ceases to rely on the creaking machinery of the syllogism, and with no thought of inconsistency, speaks the truth that is in him. Although "The Subjection of Women," his most extended statement on the subject, was the last work to be published in his lifetime, yet in every one of his earlier works he had dwelt on the subject, wherever opportunity arose, with insistence, with indomitable iteration. He wished to see the status, legal, political and social, of women raised to that of men, but concentrated on endeavouring to obtain for women the vote on the same terms as men had it, claiming throughout that as men had no abstract right to decide for women, women should be put into a position to decide for themselves. In a letter to Florence Nightingale, written in 1867, he says: "I will confess to you that I have often stood amazed at what has seemed to me the presumption with which persons who think themselves humble set bounds to the capacities of improvement of their fellow creatures, think themselves qualified to define how much or how little of the divine light of truth can be borne by the world in general, assume that none but the very élite can see what is perfectly clear to themselves, and think themselves permitted to dole out in infinitesimal doses that daily bread of truth upon which they themselves live, and without which the world must come to an end."*

The Truth about Women.

His "Liberty" bears as its text a quotation from Humboldt's "Sphere and Duties of Government," concluding with "the absolute and essential importance of human development in its richest diversity." The whole case against the present position of women was just that this diversity of development was prohibited, and that even undiversified development was stunted. In a diary he kept for a few months in 1854, wherein Mill inscribed a curious mixture of platitude and epigram, he states his "deliberate opinion that any great improvement in human life is not to be looked for so long as the animal instinct of sex occupies the absurdly disproportionate place it does therein," and that firstly, in order to attain any improvement, "that women should cease to be set aside for this function, and should be admitted to all other duties and occupations on a par with men." † He develops in this place, in fact, an epigram he had put to paper three weeks before, that "What is called morality in these times is a regulated sensuality."‡ Sex is an accident, and should not be a determinant. In the drama of life it is illogical that women should never enact more than a secondary rôle—especially to Mill, who believed that they are usually "of far greater versatility than men."§ Sex is considered "as entirely irrelevant to political rights as difference in height or in the colour of the hair."‖ Again, "The ideas and institutions by which the accident of sex is made the groundwork of an inequality of legal rights, and a forced dissimilarity of social functions, must ere long be recognized as the greatest hindrance to moral, social, and even intellectual development."¶ To the objection (how tenacious are these barnacles!) that women are as a matter of fact unequal to men in the character of their achievements, that history, novels, art, etc., proceed from men alone, for all practical purposes, Mill had the reply that women are going along the same paths as men; they have not yet left their leading strings. They have always had men's works set before them; when they cease to copy them, your objections will fall to the ground and you will see that, after all, sex *is* an accident. Besides, "how many of the most original thoughts of male writers came to them from the suggestion and prompting of some woman."** The same case is stated in great

* "Letters," Vol. II., p. 104.
† Ibid, Vol. II., p. 382.   ‡ Ibid, Vol. II., p. 376.
§ "Principles," Book I., Chapter VIII., § 5.
‖ "Representative Government," Chapter VIII.
¶ "Principles," Book IV., Chapter VII., § 4.
** "Letters," Vol. II., p. 381.

detail in " The Subjection of Women." In brief, it may be sum marized : " Women's work is not, at present, equal to men's work. But women have never been allowed to be original. Release them from their subjection, and the consequences will prove .whether or not women are essentially inferior. But don't punish them for their inferiority before they have had a chance to demonstrate their relative worth. And, my dear sir, if I may be permitted to express a personal opinion, I should not be at all surprised if your own morals did not benefit somewhat by such a demonstration."

So much for Mill's attitude. Now as to his acts.

The Invasion of Westminster.

In 1866 Gladstone introduced a Reform Bill, was defeated on it, and resigned. Lord Derby formed a Conservative Government, and Disraeli became the Leader of the House of Commons. In due course he, too, introduced a Reform Bill to enfranchise the small town householder and the lodger. Long and tiresome were the debates, and countless amendments marked the tortuous, serpentine progress of the Bill to the Statute Book. Here Mill had his opportunity. Woman Suffrage was no longer to be a thing unuttered in Parliament. On May 20th, 1867, he moved an amendment to omit " man " and insert " person " in place thereof, and so to make the Bill apply to both sexes. Mill made a long and eloquent speech, which, perhaps, suffered from lack of precedent. He was not to be contented with the mere verbal substitution, but proceeded to dilate on the position of women, economic and legal, to describe the educational disadvantages under which they lived, in short, to give a lecture on the Woman Question. The following is an example ; it illustrates his somewhat ponderous style no less than his matter : " The notion of a hard and fast line of separation between women's occupations and men's—of forbidding women to take interest in the things which interest men—belongs to a bygone state of society which is receding further and further into the past. We talk of political revolutions, but we do not sufficiently attend to the fact that there has taken place amongst us a silent domestic revolution—women and men are, for the first time in history, really each other's companions." * The result was the usual one. There were the immemorial asseverations adduced in opposition, that the amendment, if carried into law, would set a premium upon spinsterhood, that the law was not really unjust to women on the whole [" If an hon. gentleman married a widow with ten children, he had to support every one of them," said one of the hon. gentlemen], that God never intended women to vote, and so on. A " great man who flourished about 500 years before Christ " and the court of Dahomey were brought up and used in evidence against Mill. Gladstone was asked to express an opinion. He said nothing, but voted against the amendment. Seventy-three voted in favour and 196 against. True to posterity, a Lord something Hamilton voted against the proposal. But, including pairs and tellers, at least eighty Members of Parliament forty-five years

* " Hansard," 30 Vict., 1867, Vol. III., p. 821,

ago found themselves in favour of Woman Suffrage. It was not a triumph, but a highly successful initiation. The London Woman's Suffrage Society was started, and Mill's motion developed into a movement.

A Summary.

It is no easy task to collect and integrate all Mill's scattered dicta on women. Nor indeed would much interest be attached to the performance, for many of the evils, against which he stormed with his greatest energy, have been lessened, if not eradicated. Property rights have been granted, and the law has generally receded from its former implicit tenet that women form a criminal class. Custom (call it convention, if you will) no longer holds women in thraldom to the extent of forbidding any voluntarily undertaken remedy for economic dependence. It is permitted to women to become educated. Previously, curious as it may appear, women had only been permitted to educate. The self-supporting woman of the middle class is no longer the mid-Victorian governess, anæmic and, perhaps excusably, ready to descend upon the marriageable younger sons of her employers, pictured in many novels of the period. To what extent these changes may be attributed to Mill is only conjecturable. What-ever may be said to minimise his work, it cannot be disputed that he has been the inspirer of progressive women in every country where there are such women to a degree untouched by any predecessor.*

Generally speaking, Mill's attitude was a very simple one. The well-worn metaphor of the ivy twined lovingly about the sturdy oak was no doubt picturesque and the rights of publication were enjoyed by a thousand minor poets. But the ivy is a parasite, and nobody but a decadent sentimentalist can extract much pleasure from the contemplation of parasitism practised upon a national scale. Let the law treat men and women as equals, and all the rest will follow. Writing on divorce, for example, he says, "I do not think that the conditions of the dissolubility of marriage can be properly determined until women have an equal voice in determining them, nor until there has been experience of the marriage relation as it would exist between equals. Until then I should not like to commit myself to more than the general principle of relief from the contract in extreme cases."† Let women be admitted to qualifying examinations for occupations on the same basis as men, then it will be seen whether women are capable of practising as doctors, lawyers, and the like. If they are found incapable, not much harm has been done; presumably there would be few women anxious to enter a profession, knowing that their predecessors in that profession had been unsuccessful by reason of their inherent and ineradicable sexual qualities. But, on the other hand, if they are successful, then the sources are doubled of the supply of skill, of knowledge, of energy to produce necessary services, to alleviate sufferings, and to add to the positive

---

* See Dr. Stanton Coit's introduction to the 1909 edition of the " Subjection of Women,"

†" Letters," Vol. II., p. 212,

goods of life. They are more than doubled, for the introduction of fresh skill will be accompanied with a new and keener competition waged between equals and beneficial in its outcome. With the improvement in the position of women, men too would gain. Then and then only will it be possible to imagine an ideal liberty, a state where the vague aspirations of to-day would be translated into achievements and facts enduring and powerful.

DEMOCRAT.

There are persons to whose mental eyes democracy best presents itself as a great quasi-religious service. Such are Whitman, Carpenter and their followers. The conception lends itself to criticism because to attain good government it is highly undesirable that all the governed should worship at the same shrine; dissent is the very life-blood of harmony in things political. There are other persons, such as Mr. Asquith, for whom democracy is a limited liability affair, with an undistinguished coat of arms, bearing for its device a registration official, couchant, except in the first fortnight of July. Both these conceptions are sincerely held by a large number of excellent people, who firmly believe that the sovereign power resides in the people, and that it is desirable that it should continue to reside there.

It is, however, possible for a man to be a staunch democrat and yet to have the greatest possible detestation for the numerical majority—the "compact majority" at which Ibsen jibes so vigorously. England is, from a numerical point of view, governed to-day by the working classes. The working classes allow government to be conducted along lines which, frequently enough, are detrimental to their own interests, and, as we all believe at times, to the country's interests.

The distinction between the general idea of democracy and Mill's lies in this: by democracy is generally meant one active and combined majority, while Mill preferred to regard it as an agglomeration of minorities.* The problem of democracy was to him, how to provide for the adequate expression of the different minorities. The greatest minority of all was, and still is, the women. The next greatest minorities were, then more than now, the several sections of the manual workers; and, after that, there were the numerous political minorities for whom the exigencies of parliamentary government prohibited representation in Westminister. For, to Mill, the free and unrestricted discussion of ideas was all-important. A person might hold any opinions under the sun—he might conceivably be a mad eugenist favouring unnatural selection in the form of mating by *ad hoc* state officials—but it was not for any man or any institution to forbid the discussion of such ideas.

Labour Representation.

It has just been mentioned that Mill held views on Labour Representation. Indeed, they circumstanced the genesis of the Labour Party. Mill had always maintained the friendliest relations with the

* See Chapter VII., " Representative Government."

trade union leaders of his time, especially with George Odger. In 1857 we find that he was encouraging and aiding Holyoake to put up one of the first parliamentary candidatures of a working man.* John Bright was of opinion that Parliament was above classes and represented all; that the introduction of a labour element would add a class spirit of an unfortunate description. It was all very well to have extreme Radicals, who preached revolution, republicanism, etc., and were at times even punished for treasonable behaviour. But Bright knew very well that Horne Tooke, John Wilkes, and the rest were middle-class men (and Charles James Fox was an aristocrat!), whose sentiments, even in their most vehement moments, were not those of the multitude, and at times shared equally with Burke a certain academicism. Holyoake stood for the Tower Hamlets, but withdrew before the polling took place.

Mill realized, too, that government would not remain as it then was, a hobby of the wealthier class. "We are now, I think, standing on the very boundary line between this new statesmanship and the old, and the next generation will be accustomed to a very different set of political arguments and topics from those of the present and past."† The representation of the unrepresented was all-important. The presence of working men in the House of Commons seemed to him "indispensable to a sufficient discussion of public interests from the particular point of view of the working classes."‡ The policy he favoured was one of "keeping the Liberal out." In a letter written to Odger in 1871, when the latter was standing for Southwark, Mill says: "The working men are quite right in allowing Tories to get into the House to defeat this exclusive feeling of the Whigs (then in office), and may do it without sacrificing any principle. The working men's policy is to insist upon their own representation, and, in default of success, to permit Tories to be sent into the House until the Whig majority is seriously threatened, when, of course, the Whigs will be happy to compromise and allow a few working men representatives in the House."§ Well has experience justified this advice.

The Heritage of Hare.

As to smaller minorities, for them he strongly supported a plan of proportional representation invented by Thomas Hare, in which Mill found the salvation of "independent opinion." "I saw in this great practical and philosophical idea the greatest improvement of which the system of representative government is susceptible, an improvement which, in the most felicitous manner, exactly meets and cures the grand, and what before seemed the inherent, defect of the representative system. . . . This great discovery, for it is no less, in the political art, inspired me, as I believe it has inspired all thoughtful persons who have adopted it, with new and more sanguine hopes respecting the prospects of human society; by freeing

* See A. W. Humphrey, "A History of Labour Representation," and Holyoake's Biography (McCabe) and Autobiography.
† "Letters," Vol II., p. 56.
‡ Ibid, p. 268.
§ Webb's "History of Trade Unionism," p. 272.

the form of political institutions towards which the whole civilized world is manifestly and irresistibly tending, from the chief part of what seemed to qualify or render doubtful its ultimate benefits. Minorities, so long as they remain minorities, are, and ought to be, outvoted ; but under arrangements which enable any assemblage of voters, amounting to a certain number, to place in the legislature a representative of its own choice, minorities cannot be suppressed. . . . The legislature, instead of being weeded of individual peculiarities and entirely made up of men who simply represent the creed of great political or religious parties, will comprise a large proportion of the most eminent individual minds in the country, placed there, without reference to party, by voters who appreciate their individual eminence." * This much-belauded plan was a simple variant of the proportional representation idea : to secure election only a quota of votes are necessary, the remainder polled by a successful candidate are transferable to another candidate whose name the voter might himself put on the ballot-paper. Any elector is at liberty to vote for any candidate in any part of the country. These are the main provisions of the scheme. Mill's conversions to new ideas were always of the thoroughgoing nature. He appears to have preached the new invention in season and out of season, and, no doubt, made himself unpopular thereby.

Proposed Improvements.

Mill subjected the entire Parliamentary system to a fairly searching analysis, both in his " Representative Government " and in a pamphlet " Thoughts on Parliamentary Reform." It must be confessed that he placed rather too high an estimate on the values of various points in the electoral machine. He believes that voting should be public and opposes the ballot. "The *spirit* of an institution," he comments, "the impression it makes on the mind of the citizen, is one of the most important parts of its operation." †
Money payments of any sort should not be required of the candidate ; they should be borne by his constituents. Members of Parliament should not be paid If a Member is poor and requires pecuniary aid, his constituents should subscribe for the purpose. Perhaps the most curious of his efforts to tinker with the legislative machine is his recommendation that plurality of votes should be given, "not to property, but to proved superiority of education." This recommendation, however, he pathetically admits, did not meet with widespread approval. "As far as I have been able to observe, it has found favour with nobody." ‡ Possibly even Mill had his doubts about it, for he says it was a suggestion "which I had never discussed with my almost infallible counsellor, and I have no evidence that she would have concurred in it." Another suggestion was that Parliament should not be burdened with the details of law making. "Any government fit for a high state of civilization would have as one of its fundamental elements a small body, not exceeding

* "Autobiography." p. 148.
† "Representative Government," Chapter X.
‡ "Autobiography," p. 148.

in number the members of a Cabinet, who should act as a Commission of legislation, having for its appointed office to make the laws. . . . The Commission would only embody the element of intelligence in their construction; Parliament would represent that of will." * Parliament was to issue instructions (presumably in the form of general resolutions), the Commission was to draft a Bill accordingly, which Parliament could either accept, reject, or refer back for amendment. Similarly Mill wished to separate the executive and administrative functions. "Instead of the function of governing, for which it is radically unfit, the proper office of a representative assembly is to watch and control the government." †

These suggestions—or, at any rate, some of them—may be considered as of nugatory importance and hardly worth discussing. But although their intrinsic worth may be nominal, they afford an excellent insight into the spirit inherent in all Mill's theories. The mental attitude of the bulk of mankind, so far as it has any, on the subject of democracy is, granted amiability and the absence of political discord, "There are wonderful things latent in democracy. May they remain so." Experimentation in democracy is now inextricably connected with the name Pankhurst. Pressed on the subject, the Bulk of Mankind develops distrust and party views. Mill is different. Believing, too, that there are wonderful things latent in democracy, he wishes them to be made patent. To secure this object no possible method is too minute, too circuitous. To develop every personality to its utmost was his ideal, and democracy was the most obvious of the many means by which that ideal was to be attained. The rights of the individual soul arose with Bentham; Mill adapted the patriarch's ideas to the requirements of his age.

SOCIALIST.

In the course of its century-old career, the word Socialism has continually been changing its connotation. But, whatever might be its precise meaning about the time when Mill wrote his "Principles of Political Economy," there can be no possible doubt that the revolutions of 1848 gave the word a popular meaning synonymous with the terms applied to political behaviour of the most abominable character. And the sister-term Communism shared the opprobrium. Yet Mill, who always sought the truth, gave the schemes of Fourier, Saint-Simon and Louis Blanc careful attention in his "Principles of Political Economy"; and when the 1852 edition appeared the following extraordinary expression of opinion was included in his study of Communism: "If, therefore, the choice were to be made between Communism with all its chances, and the present state of society with all its sufferings and injustices; if the institution of private property necessarily carried with it as a consequence that the produce of labour should be apportioned as we now see it, almost in an inverse ratio to the labour—the largest portions to those who have never worked at all, the next largest to those whose work is almost

* "Representative Government," Chapter V.
† Ibid, loc. cit.

nominal, and so in a descending scale, the remuneration dwindling as the work grows harder and more disagreeable, until the most fatiguing and exhausting bodily labour cannot count with certainty on being able to earn even the necessaries of life; if this or Communism were the alternative, all the difficulties, great or small, of Communism would be but as dust in the balance."* It is almost necessary to remind oneself that the writer was the son of James Mill, and the spiritual heir of the individualists.

On the subject of State enterprise he maintains silence, although, generally speaking, he is opposed to any extension of government interference, on the grounds that a multiplicity of functions must lead to inefficiency. Yet he is always anxious to learn by experiment; on no account will he have an experiment hindered because it does not fit in with his views. Writing to Edwin Chadwick in 1867 he says: "I think there is a chance that Ireland may be tried as a *corpus vile* for experimentation on Government management of railways."† In 1898 the Fabian Society published Tract No. 98, "State Railways for Ireland." In 1910 the Vice-Regal Commission on Irish Railways declared by a bare majority in favour of nationalization. The mills of God grind slowly.

The Individual and the State.

Mill was for ever insisting upon the necessity for a moral as well as an economic improvement. Writing to Auberon Herbert the year before his death, Mill said: "My idea is (but I am open to correction) that, for some time to come, politics and social and economic questions will be the absorbing subjects to most of those working men who have the aspirations and the mental activity to which the appeal would have to be made. . . . . You wish to make them feel the importance of the higher virtues. I think this can be most effectually done by pointing out to them how much those virtues are needed to enable a democracy, and above all any approach to Socialism, to work in any satisfactory manner."‡

It is not unfair to suggest that, before the last few years of his life, when Mill made a special study of Socialism, he was by no means clear as to what Socialists wanted, and whether or not he was one of them. The following passage, for example, while it teems with the utmost philanthropy, at the same time reveals a curious indecision. It refers to Mrs. Mill and himself: "While we repudiated with the greatest energy that tyranny of society over the individual which most Socialistic systems are supposed to involve, we yet looked forward to a time when society will no longer be divided into the idle and the industrious; when the rule that they who do not work shall not eat will be applied not to paupers only, but impartially to all; when the division of the produce of labour, instead of depending, as in so great a degree it now does, on the accident of birth, will be made by concert on an acknowledged principle of justice; and when it will no longer either be, or be thought to be, impossible for human

---

* "Principles," Book II., Chapter I., § 3.
† "Letters," Vol. II., p. 194.
‡ "Letters," Vol. II., p. 328.

beings to exert themselves strenuously in procuring benefits which are not to be exclusively their own, but to be shared with the society they belong to. The social problem of the future we considered to be how to unite the greatest individual liberty of action with a common ownership in the raw material of the globe, and an equal participation of all in the benefits of combined labour."* He consistently affirmed what he denied, and it is difficult to place him with absolute accuracy.

Reference has already been made to a work on Socialism planned by Mill in his last years. Of this only four chapters came to be actually written, and were first published in 1879 in the pages of the *Fortnightly Review*. Mill begins by showing that the gradual arrival of manhood suffrage in all countries would lead sooner or later to the thorough discussion of the subject of property. In fact, the Labour Congresses and the " International Society " (probably the International Working Men's Association) were already discussing the subject, and so formulating the future courses of action of the working classes of the different countries of Europe. He then proceeds to study the Socialist indictment. It is curious that he makes neither here nor elsewhere any mention of Marx or the Communist Manifesto.

The Socialist Indictment.

The Socialist indictment constitutes, he admits, "a frightful case, either against the existing order of society or against the position of man himself in this world." He believes that Socialists generally placed too much emphasis on the evils of competition, without noticing its beneficial consequences. Nevertheless, on this subject " Socialists have really made out the existence not only of a great evil, but of one which grows and tends to grow with the growth of population and wealth." He then himself gives at some length some of the less obvious evils of fraud, bankruptcy, etc., but thinks that in production fraud could be largely " overcome by the institution of co-operative stores." Yet, having examined the expressions of Socialists, and convicted them of exaggeration, he admits that that by no means settles the whole matter, and concludes a chapter with the words, " . . . . the intellectual and moral grounds of Socialism deserve the most attentive study, as affording in many cases the guiding principles of the improvements necessary to give the present economic system of society its best chance." It is instructive to make an analysis, paragraph by paragraph, of his final summing-up. It is then seen that the favourable and unfavourable dicta alternate in an uninterrupted sequence throughout. The conclusion is as follows: " The result of our review of the various difficulties of Socialism has led us to the conclusion that the various schemes for managing the productive resources of the country by public instead of private agency have a case for a trial, and some of them may eventually establish their claims to preference over the existing order of things, but that they are at present workable only by the *élite* of mankind, and have yet to prove their power of training

* " Autobiography," p. 133.

mankind at large to the state of improvement which they pre-suppose." As to taking over the whole land and capital of the country and centralizing its administration, that is "obviously chimerical." The revolutionary plan of taking over everything by one blow meets with no grace whatever.

But this does not conclude Mill's survey. He realizes that the root of the matter is the conception of property. He agrees that the right of holding property, and to a still larger extent of trans-mitting it, is conferred and maintained by the State. Hence this conclusion: "A proposed reform in laws or customs is not necessarily objectionable because its adoption would imply, not the adaptation of all human affairs to the existing idea of property, but the adapta-tion of existing ideas of property to the growth and improvement of human affairs. . . . . Society is fully entitled to abrogate or alter any particular right of property which, on sufficient consideration, it judges to stand in the way of the public good. And assuredly the terrible case which, as we saw in a former chapter, Socialists are able to make out against the present economic order of society, demands a full consideration of all means by which the institution may have a chance of being made to work in a manner more beneficial to that large portion of society which at present enjoys the least share of its direct benefits."

What does all this come to? It may at first sight appear feeble, tentative, undirected. But before pronouncing a final judgment, a glance at Mill's material will be instructive. This consists mainly—almost exclusively—of the visions of Owen, the far-fetched schemes of Fourier, and the aspirations of Louis Blanc.

Yet, in all this amorphous and inchoate matter, Mill was able to discern many of the stable elements. He exclaims against cen-tralization just as he had doubted the possibility of any great growth of joint stock enterprise merely because he could not foresee the extent of its future development. But he sees behind all the cloudi-nesses of the Socialists of 1848 something substantial, something real. He is able to sketch something very near the actual line of the future evolution of Socialist thought. Had he lived another ten years he would almost certainly have been amongst the founders of the Fabian Society.

Back to Mill.

The Socialist movement to-day, or rather, the evolutionary sec-tion, stands far from the field of combat selected by its progenitors. To-day many ideas are regarded as of secondary importance, or nugatory or actually wrong, which a generation ago were held as dogma, beyond criticism or attack. And the evolutionary Socialist of to-day may find himself opposed to land nationalization, or even to any accepted *ad hoc* nationalization. He may be opposed to the multiplication of State officials ; he may support or he may, on the whole, oppose the Labour Party, preferring to throw in his lot for the attainment of his ideals with a party until recently unanimously denounced as bourgeois capitalist. And even then he will, and does, sincerely believe himself to be a Socialist. The idea of what constitutes Socialism and a Socialist is changing. What is the direction of the change? It appears well within the bounds of probability that the attitude of the evolutionary Socialist upon matters connected with society (granted some few exceptions) is approximating to that of Mill. To the present writer it seems probable that the history of the next few years of the Socialist movement will accentuate the changing attitude. It is almost safe to predict the development of the movement. The next few years of its history will be marked by the augmented value attached to the "moral factor," which will be used by Socialists as a touchstone in matters of legislation. The co-operative movement will meet with support from Socialists, and will probably extend its scope. The Socialist programme will shrink to the dimensions of a single session's possibilities, and will refuse to discuss the nationalization of any services not already, as it were, upon the list. A larger share of attention will be given to problems specially affecting women. These are but a few of the salient probabilities : their derivation is obvious. And long before they emerge as things accomplished Mill will have received his rightful share of recognition as one of the moulders of modern Socialism and the future State.

Conclusion.

Perhaps the most important point about Mill is his attitude. He was the son of his father in more senses than one. There is an extraordinary parallelism between their works. The father wrote an "Elements of Political Economy," the son wrote the "Principles of Political Economy, with Some of their Applications to Social Philosophy." The father wrote an essay on "Government," the son an "Essay on Representative Government." The father wrote "An Analysis of the Problems of the Human Mind," the son wrote his "Logic" as a sort of introduction and the "Examination of Hamilton" as a sort of supplement. As we have seen, both hereditary and environmental influences were applied in the most thorough manner possible. The mental attitude of J. S. Mill therefore is individual only so far as it differs from his father's. Very largely the broadness of his views, even when they appear opposed to his father's, is simply to be ascribed to the gradual exploitation of the elder's theories. But to whatever degree his work is put down to paternal influence, there can be no doubt that J. S. Mill exerted a wonderfully broadening effect over English political thought. Mill translated the notion of police, as held by Bentham, into the notion of a polity. The study of the affairs of the State was held to be the study of the means of attaining the greatest cheapness. Mill changed the idea of economy into the idea of economics. In Mill's childhood the greatest importance was attached to the study of the humanities ; he made the greatest importance attach to the study of humanity. It is as a broadening influence that he is most important, infusing the doctrines of Liberalism with something more approaching liberality, and directing, for the first time, to the claims of labour a substantial portion of public attention.

Another point is worth briefly discussing. There are two lines along which changes in the body politic may arrive : by gradual evolution and by cataclysmic revolution. The method of evolution is slow, sure, and unattractive. The other method is attractive because of its pyrotechnic qualities, and windy philosophies will ever sway the imagination of the politically uninstructed. Mill is noteworthy principally as an excellent doubter. He had no originality ; he hesitates always. But out of his hesitations come great things. If his direction be zigzag, nevertheless he marks a path ; and in his case, at any rate, his end was worth more than his conclusions.

BIBLIOGRAPHY.

ABOUT MILL.

BAIN, PROFESSOR. John Stuart Mill : a Criticism. 1882.

COURTNEY, W. L. Life of J. S. Mill. (Great Writers Series.) 1889.

STEPHEN. LESLIE. The Utilitarians. Three Vols. Vol. I. Bentham ; Vol. II. James Mill; Vol. III. J. S. Mill. And Article in the Dictionary of National Biography.

GRAHAM, WILLIAM. English Political Philosophy. 1907.

BY MILL.

All the following are published by Longmans, unless the contrary is stated.

A System of Logic, etc. 1843.

Essays on Some Unsettled Questions in Political Economy. 1844.

Principles of Political Economy. 1848.

On Liberty. 1859.

Dissertations and Discussions. Four Vols. 1859-1876.

Considerations on Representative Government. 1861.

Utilitarianism. 1863.

  (The last two, with On Liberty, can be had in one volume in Dent's Everyman Series.)

Examination of Sir William Hamilton's Philosophy. 1865.

Auguste Comte and Positivism. 1865.

Inaugural Address at the University of St. Andrews. 1867.

England and Ireland. 1868.

The Subjection of Women. 1869.

Autobiography. 1873.

Three Essays on Religion. 1874.

Letters. Edited by HUGH S. R. ELLIOTT. Two Vols. 1910.

F ABIAN SOCIETY.—The Fabian Society consists of Socialists. A statement of its Rules and a complete list of publications can be obtained from the Secretary, at the Fabian Office, 3 Clement's Inn, London, W.C.

FABIAN ESSAYS IN SOCIALISM. Paper 6d.; cloth 1/6; post. 2½d. and 4d

WHAT TO READ on Social and Economic Subjects. 1s. n. and 2s. n.

THIS MISERY OF BOOTS. By H. G. WELLS. 3d., post free 4d.

FABIAN TRACTS and LEAFLETS.

Tracts, each 16 to 52 pp., price 1d., or 9d. per doz., unless otherwise stated.
Leaflets, 4 pp. each, price 1d. for six copies, 1s. per 100, or 8/6 per 1000.

The Set of 81, 3s.; post free 3/5. Bound in Buckram, 4/6 n.; post free 5s.

I.—General Socialism in its various aspects.

TRACTS.—159. The Necessary Basis of Society. By SIDNEY WEBB. 151. The Point of Honour. By RUTH C. BENTINCK. 147. Capital and Compensation. By E. R. PEASE. 146. Socialism and Superior Brains. By BERNARD SHAW. 142. Rent and Value. 138. Municipal Trading. 121. Public Service versus Private Expenditure. By Sir OLIVER LODGE. 107. Socialism for Millionaires. By BERNARD SHAW. 139. Socialism and the Churches. By Rev JOHN CLIFFORD, D.D 133. Socialism and Christianity. By Rev. PERCY DEARMER. 78. Socialism and the Teaching of Christ. By Dr. J. CLIFFORD. 42. Christian Socialism By Rev. S. D. HEADLAM. 79. A Word of Remembrance and Caution to the Rich. By JOHN WOOLMAN. 72. The Moral Aspects of Socialism. By SIDNEY BALL. 69. Difficulties of Individualism. By S. WEBB. 51. Socialism: True and False. By S. WEBB. 45. The Impossibilities of Anarchism. By BERNARD SHAW (price 2d.). 7. Capital and Land (revised 1908) 5. Facts for Socialists (revised 1908). 132. A Guide to Books for Socialists. LEAFLETS—13. What Socialism Is. 1. Why are the Many Poor? WELSH TRACTS—143. Sosialaeth yng Ngoleuni'r Beibl. 141. Translation of 139. 87. Translation of 78. 38. Translation of 1.

II.—Applications of Socialism to Particular Problems.

TRACTS.—164. Gold and State Banking. By E. R. PEASE. 163. Women and Prisons. By HELEN BLAGG and CHARLOTTE M. WILSON. 2d. 162. Family Life on a Pound a Week. By Mrs. REEVES. In cover, 2d. 161. Afforestation and Unemployment. By A. P. GRENFELL. 160. A National Medical Service. By F. LAWSON DODD. 2d. 157. The Working Life of Women. By Miss B. L. HUTCHINS. 155. The Case against the Referendum. By CLIFFORD SHARP. 154. The Case for School Clinics. By L. HADEN GUEST. 153. The Twentieth Century Reform Bill. By H. H. SCHLOESSER. 152. Our Taxes as they are and as they ought to be. By R. JONES, B.Sc. In cover, 2d. 150. State Purchase of Railways. By EMIL DAVIES. In cover, 2d. 149. The Endowment of Motherhood. By H. D. HARBEN. In cover, 2d. 145. The Case for School Nurseries. By Mrs. TOWNSHEND. 140. Child Labor under Capitalism. By Mrs. HYLTON DALE. 136. The Village and the Landlord. By EDW. CARPENTER. 130. Home Work and Sweating. By Miss B. L. HUTCHINS. 128. The Case for a Legal Minimum Wage. 122. Municipal Milk and Public Health. By Dr. F. LAWSON DODD. 125. Municipalization by Provinces. 123. The Revival of Agriculture. 115. State Aid to Agriculture: an Example. 124. State Control of Trusts. 86. Municipal Drink Traffic. 83. State Arbitration and the Living Wage. LEAFLET.—104. How Trade Unions benefit Workmen.

III.—Local Government Powers : How to use them.

TRACTS.— 156. What an Education Committee can do (Elementary Schools), 3d. 137. Parish Councils and Village Life. 109. Cottage Plans and Common Sense. 76. Houses for the People. 82. Workmen's Compensation Act. 54. The Humanizing of the Poor Law. LEAFLETS.—134. Small Holdings: and how to get them. 68. The Tenant's Sanitary Catechism. 71. Ditto for London.

IV.—General Politics and Fabian Policy.

TRACTS.—158. The Case against the C.O.S. By Mrs. TOWNSHEND. 108. Twentieth Century Politics. By S. WEBB. 70. Report on Fabian Policy. 41. The Fabian Society: its Early History. By BERNARD SHAW.

V.—Biographical Series. In cover, 2d. each.

165. Francis Place. By ST. JOHN G. ERVINE. 166. Robert Owen, Social Reformer. By Miss B. L. HUTCHINS. 167. William Morris and the Communist Ideal. By Mrs. TOWNSHEND. 168. John Stuart Mill. By JULIUS WEST.

Fabian Tract No. 169.

\

THE SOCIALIST MOVE-MENT IN GERMANY . .

By W. STEPHEN SANDERS.

Published and sold by the Fabian Society,
3 Clement's Inn, Strand, London, W.C.
February 1913.   Price 2d.

THE SOCIALIST MOVEMENT IN GERMANY.

"THE workers of Germany have always looked to the English working class for example and inspiration, and we hope that our teachers are now satisfied with their pupils." In these words Herr Hermann Molkenbuhr, secretary of the German Socialist Democratic Party and one of the 110 Socialist members of the Reichstag, responded to a vote of congratulation passed at the British Labor Party Conference at Birmingham, in January, 1912, on the occasion of the striking victories of his party at the general election for the Reichstag then just completed. This flattering tribute to the influence on the masses in Germany of English ideas and methods in political and industrial organization should afford lively gratification to the workers of this country; for it was tendered by one of the leaders of the most efficiently organized political party in the whole world. In both the spheres of politics and industry the German workman has adopted the principle of combination evolved in England, adapting it with the patience and persistence characteristic of his race to the peculiar conditions of his own land, and by its means he has attained results which are astounding when the enormous difficulties to be contended with are taken into account.

These results cannot be fully and accurately estimated by simply studying the statistics of the growth of the twin movements of Social Democracy and Trade Unionism, striking and eloquent though these statistics are. Behind the giant numbers there is a powerful feeling of solidarity among the working classes, coupled with a strong sense of responsibility for the moulding of their own future, both created by the unceasing agitation and education of the two movements. The disciplined faith and self-confidence, together with the multifarious opportunities for practical activities, given by the Socialist and Trade Union organizations have prevented their members from becoming mere vague and dreamy idealists or purely destructive critics. Although apparently still believing in the coming of the great day prophesied with magnificent fervor in the Communist Manifesto of 1848 when capitalism will be overthrown at one blow, in reality the German Social Democrat relies on no economic or political miracle for the attainment of his ultimate aim, but steadily, day by day, toils at the task of underpinning the foundations of the present individualistic social order, and replacing them bit by bit with Socialist material preparatory to the gradual rebuilding of the whole superstructure.

The Founders.

The German Socialist movement possesses the great advantage of having for its founders the two great personalities, Ferdinand Lassalle and Karl Marx. The names of these two men have become the banners and battle cries of the organized masses, giving to their movements the glamor and appeal that comes from historic associations. Lassalle, in the words of one of their songs, forged the sword of the German workers ; Marx taught them the purpose for which the weapon should be used.

Ferdinand Lassalle was born in 1825 at Breslau. His father was a prosperous Jewish merchant, who desired that his son should also be a man of commerce. Lassalle, however, declined to follow in his father's footsteps, and decided to enter upon a career of academic training. He studied at the university of his native city and Berlin, passing his examinations with distinction. At the early age of twenty he impressed his friends and acquaintances, including Alexander von Humboldt and Heinrich Heine, with his brilliant intellectual powers and dominating will. During the revolutionary year of 1848 he became acquainted with Marx, and contributed to a newspaper edited by him. In 1849 he was arrested and tried for urging the people to offer armed resistance to the autocratic Prussian Government, and was sentenced to six months' imprisonment. The speech he had prepared for his defence, which was not delivered in court owing to the action of the judges in excluding the public from the trial, but published afterwards, earned for him considerable reputation owing to its logical force and telling rhetoric.

During the fifties he dropped out of public life, but kept up a correspondence with Marx, now exiled for ever from his native country. He resumed his philosophical and literary studies, the outcome of which included the completion of a learned book on Heraclitus begun in his student days ; a big book entitled " System of Acquired Rights "; and a historical drama of indifferent merit. In these and other writings he showed himself to be a thorough disciple of Hegel, especially in his attitude towards the State, expressing the great philosopher's view " that the State is the march of God through society " in equally strong but less theological language. In this close adherence to Hegelianism he differed strongly from Marx, who, though heavily indebted to Hegel for the dialectic of which he was both master and servant, was dogmatically materialist in his philosophy.

Lassalle's Agitation.

In 1862 Lassalle left his study for the platform in response to an invitation to lecture to a Berlin Liberal Club. He was now completely out of sympathy with the Liberals, or Progressists, as they were then called, owing to their want of courage and enterprise. He chose for his theme the timely subject of " The Nature of Constitutions." The King of Prussia was at that moment endeavoring to rule without a Parliament, because that body had proved itself, for a German legislative assembly, remarkably intractable and insubordinate to the royal authority. This lecture, given in two parts, was repeated three times. It annoyed the Progressists exceedingly, mainly because it laid down the doctrine that questions of constitutional right are questions of power, and that if the Progressists wished to defeat the King and his Government it was no use merely arguing about the justice of their position and the illegality and injustice of that of the monarch and his ministers. Action was necessary. The Parliament, he contended, ought to refuse to meet until the King consented to behave constitutionally. This would compel him either to surrender or to rule as a despot ; the latter course the sovereign would not dare to adopt. The conservative and reactionary elements were delighted with the disappointment and disgust of the Progressists at Lassalle's derision of their futility ; but the Government, displeased with the bold advice given in the second part of the lecture, confiscated it at Königsberg when it appeared in pamphlet form. No proceedings, however, were taken against the author.

Brought into public notice again, Lassalle received a request to lecture to another Berlin audience of a different type—the members of an artizans' club. He complied, and described the subject of his address in a ponderous title containing twelve words, which was afterwards shortened to "The Workers' Program." This lecture, although almost unnoticed at the moment, had great propagandist influence later, when published as a pamphlet, and was, moreover, the direct cause of Lassalle undertaking his famous agitation among the working classes.

"The Workers' Program."

"The Workers' Program" sets forth in a manner suited to the time most of the ideas of the Communist Manifesto. Its economic doctrines, its view of history, its presentation of the fourth estate—the proletariat—as the revolutionary factor in society, as the class whose interests would dominate the future, are almost pure Marxism. But Lassalle does not keep consistently to the materialist conception of history ; and in his insistence that the true function of the State is "to help the development of the human race towards freedom," he breaks entirely with Marxian political philosophy. He attacked the *laissez faire* Liberal view, the " night watchman " idea of the State, that it should be nothing more than a protector of property from robbery and housebreaking. But the true function of the State could only be fulfilled by a State which adequately represents the interests of all ; in a word, by a State based on the will of the majority operating through equal and universal suffrage.* Economic change, the invention of machinery, and the growth of the factory system had made the wage earners potentially the most powerful class in the modern State : the next necessary step was to make them legally the most powerful by instituting complete democracy. By achieving this the legal recognition of the revolution which had already taken place would be secured. The French Revolution of

* Manhood suffrage was called universal suffrage at this period.

1789 was the revolution of the middle class against the feudal aristocracy, of trade and industry against landed property. The revolution which began in 1848 is the revolution of the proletariat against the rule of the capitalist. The victory of the proletariat, unlike previous class victories, will be the victory of all mankind ; the freedom obtained will be the freedom for everyone. Lassalle closed his address with the impressive exhortation : " The great world-historical importance of this mission must absorb all your thoughts. The vices of the oppressed, the idle dissipation of the thoughtless, even the harmless frivolities of the unimportant must find no place in your lives. You, the proletariat, are the rock on which the Church of the present must be built."

It is easy to find errors in Lassalle's presentation of the economic situation in Germany in the early sixties and to point out that the development of capitalist industry had not reached the stage when it could be said that capitalism on a grand scale was dominating politically a vast, potentially powerful proletariat. It is true that in Prussia half the population were then engaged in agriculture ; the town workers were largely employed in handicrafts, and only ten per cent. of the whole people were dependent on wages earned in factories. Lassalle made the assumption that the capitalistic indus-trial, and social conditions then rapidly ripening in England were at the same advanced stage in his own country, and the assumption was of course wrong ; hence the small immediate results of his cam-paign among the workers. But taken as prophecy, the substance of his lecture was remarkably correct ; for the astonishing industrial and commercial growth of modern Germany, the beginnings of which were then causing politicians and social students to take thought, has indeed largely created, with the aid of the teachings of Lassalle and Marx, a great and ever increasing army of the prole-tariat in disciplined revolt against organized capitalism.

Lassalle and Schultze-Delitzsch.

On the publication of "The Workers' Program" the Berlin police suppressed it and instituted criminal proceedings against Lassalle for "exciting the non-possessing classes to hatred and con-tempt of the possessing classes." He was sentenced to four months imprisonment in spite of his trenchant and able defence, in which severe castigation was meted out to the court and the prosecuting counsel. On appeal the punishment was reduced to a fine, but the confiscation of the pamphlet was upheld. Nevertheless a new edition was printed in Switzerland and circulated among the work-ing classes.

It was issued at an opportune moment. The growth of indus-trialism, relatively small though it was, had produced the crop of social problems common on capitalist soil, together with the usual well meant philanthropic proposals for their solution. Among the methods popular with Liberals and Progressists of the period for the improvement of the material conditions of the wage earner was that of voluntary self-help associations for production and distribution, coupled with free competition, advocated by Herr Schultze-Delitzsch. Although he had a considerable following, especially among small masters whose existence was threatened by the factory system, numbers of thoughtful workmen were not enamored of this rather dull and chilly gospel. Moreover, they were desirous of having a direct share in political activity, and were urging the middle class Progressists to admit the workers to full membership of the Progressist Union. The response to their request was that " all workers might consider honorary membership of the Union as their birthright," that is to say, "they might have the honor to remain outside it." * The chief centre of this movement was Leipzig. In that city a local Workmen's Association had appointed a committee to undertake the task of establishing an association on national lines and to summon a conference at Leipzig for that purpose. This committee, struck with the ideas formulated in " The Workers' Program," invited Lassalle to express in any form he might think fit his views of the movement and the policy it should pursue, and of the value of the Schultze-Delitzsch proposals. They had no doubt that " other ways and means than those put forward by Schultze-Delitzsch might be suggested for attaining the ends of the working class movement, namely, the political, material, and intellectual improvement in the condition of the workers"; and as Lassalle's pamphlet had met with great approval in their ranks, they would be thoroughly able to appreciate further communications from him on these points.

The Universal Workmen's Association.

With Lassalle's reply, on March 1st, 1863, to this invitation begins the actual Socialist agitation which led ultimately to the formation of the present German Social Democratic Party. In his letter known as the " Public Reply" he laid down definitely and concisely the policy a working class movement should adopt. The question had been discussed whether the supporters of the Workmen's Association should abstain from politics altogether or join the Progressists. Lassalle advocated a third course : they must concern themselves with politics, but as a separate, independent Labor Party. Voluntary co-operation, thrift, and self-help on the Schultze-Delitzsch plan would inevitably fail because of the iron law which keeps the worker down to the bare minimum of existence. The only way of overcoming this law was to get rid of the capitalist by establishing a system of co-operative production, and thus secure to the actual worker the gains of the entrepreneur. But no industrial undertaking in modern days could succeed without large capital, and it was hopeless for the worker to expect to secure this absolute necessity by adopting the principles of Schultze-Delitzsch. Where could the capital be obtained ? Lassalle's answer was, from the State. The State could lend the required funds at the normal rate of interest, and the workers could then compete with private

* "Ferdinand Lassalle," E. Bernstein, p. 14.

capitalists on equal terms. How was this State credit to be ensured ? By the workers becoming the dominating factor in the State through the conquest of political power. Let them form an association throughout Germany on the analogy of the English Anti-Corn-Law League, with the sole object of achieving universal suffrage. With every workman in possession of a vote it would be easy to acquire State aid for the establishment of productive co-operative societies and thus abolish the iron law.

The publication of Lassalle's letter of counsel roused a veritable storm of indignation and resentment in Progressist circles. The struggle of the Prussian Diet with the Government seemed to be reaching a revolutionary stage, and Lassalle's advice "to split the progressive forces" appeared to the Liberals to be that of a traitor. They denied the validity of the iron law ; but Lassalle, with a tremendous display of economic learning, defended it brilliantly in spite of its fallaciousness. Defeated in argument, they turned round and maintained that the iron law was a natural law which nothing could alter. Again Lassalle scored an easy victory in debate. In May, 1863, he delivered two great speeches in support of his policy to a conference of Workmen's Associations held at Frankfort-on-the-Main and attended by thirteen hundred delegates. He carried his audience with him in face of strong opposition from the followers of Schultze-Delitzsch, and a resolution was passed in favor of forming a new organization with the Lassallean program. On May 23rd, 1863, at Leipzig the Universal Working Men's Association was formed. Lassalle was elected President, with dictatorial powers. He was now launched on his career as working class leader and agitator.

An Unpromising Beginning.

The new association grew but slowly. Lassalle had expected that the issue of his "Public Reply" would have an effect similar to that produced by the nailing of Luther's theses to the door of the Church at Wittenberg ; but, to his keen disappointment, the working classes remained indifferent. Three months after its foundation there were scarcely nine hundred members of the Association, and Berlin, of which Lassalle had had great hopes, refused to be stirred. His energy, although tremendous, was spasmodic. After six weeks of intense activity he left Germany for three months, continuing his work for the Association, however, by means of correspondence. On his return he undertook a campaign on the Rhine, addressing great meetings at Barmen, Düsseldorf, and other towns. He was now at the height of his power as an orator ; his speeches, full of fiery, passionate rhetoric, added to his fame as the evangelist of democracy. He then concentrated on Berlin, but the antagonism of the Progressists, at that time all powerful in the Prussian capital, and the action of the police in rendering it impossible for him to obtain halls for meetings and in confiscating his pamphlets, made the situation overwhelmingly difficult. Twice he was prosecuted ; on one occasion the charge was high treason. But although these actions were the cause of much worry and waste of time, they nevertheless assisted Lassalle considerably in his agitation. The law court was his element. His carefully prepared speeches in defence, or rather defiance, were splendid propaganda ; and his knowledge of the law, learned in long legal battles, enabled him to triumph over prosecuting counsel, judges, and juries. The charge of high treason resulted in an acquittal ; the other process ended in a sentence of imprisonment which Lassalle did not live to serve.

The Progressist hatred of Lassalle was heartily reciprocated by him. He attacked them mercilessly, contrasting their feeble flabbiness with the stern resolution of their adversary Bismarck. At this period he began negotiations with the Iron Chancellor, which gave grounds for further suspicion that he was playing the game of the reactionaries. Lassalle no doubt hoped to win Bismarck's support for his scheme of universal suffrage and State credit for productive co-operation. The Progressists were then securing good majorities in the Prussian Diet in spite of the undemocratic, indirect, three class electoral system (which obtains to this day), and had therefore no strong desire for a reform of the franchise. What actually took place at the interviews between Lassalle and Bismarck remains a matter of conjecture. Years afterwards the Chancellor, challenged to explain the remarkable acquaintanceship, declared that there were no political negotiations because Lassalle had nothing to offer. He, Bismarck, was glad to have met such a man of genius, who was highly gifted and exceedingly ambitious, "a great man, with whom one might be delighted to converse." But whether there were negotiations or not, Lassalle in his speeches declared more and more positively that the Prussian Government would grant universal suffrage, and wrote of Bismarck as being "my plenipotentiary," whom he thought to use only so long as he should be useful. Three years later, in 1867, when the Reichstag of the North German Confederation was established, Bismarck insisted, in opposition not only to Conservative but also to Liberal politicians, that manhood suffrage should be its basis.*

Lassalle's Romantic End.

In May, 1864, Lassalle went on his last tour of agitation. He chose again the Rhine district, which had proved highly favorable soil for the seed of his propaganda. His progress was a continuous triumphal procession. Workmen greeted him with such enthusiastic jubilation that he wrote, "The impression made upon me was that such scenes must have attended the founding of new religions." But his speeches during this final campaign were not on the same high level of quality and power as those of the previous year. They are marked by a tendency to demagogy, hitherto held under control, and a strain of egoistic self-praise. On May 22nd, at Ronsdorf, he gave his last address, the most sanguine and extravagant of all. He concluded with a dramatic appeal to his hearers not to let the great movement fall with him. Three months later, on August 31st, he died from the effects of a shot received in a duel.

*"Cambridge Modern History," Vol. XI, p. 459.

The strength and glamor of Lassalle's magnetic personality keep for him the first place in the gallery of German Socialist leaders. The intellectual contribution of Marx to the movement is un--doubtedly greater than his. Indeed, Lassalle himself owed no small part of his economic theories and his insight into modern social and industrial conditions to the man who shares with him the veneration of millions of German workmen. But it was through Lassalle's overpowering will, titanic energy, and inspiring influence as a man of action that the thoughts of Marx became embodied in the aims of a great party. The profound intellectual and personal devotion of Marx to the cause of the masses has earned for him the deep reverence of the German Socialists. His writings are still conned by many of them as the Covenanters conned the Scriptures. He remains the philosophic father of German Socialism, although his authority weakens as the movement broadens. But while Marx is honored as a great thinker, Lassalle is adored as a great leader. His striking figure and meteoric career have made a deep impression upon the hearts and minds of the organized masses; his romantic, though foolish, end, his human failings, even his egoism, endear him to them. They have enshrined his memory in poetry and song, while it appears to be as impossible for them to be lyrical over Marx as it is to set "*Das Kapital*" to music.

Marx and the International.

At Lassalle's death the Universal Workmen's Association had a membership of between four and five thousand. The leadership of this small body passed into the hands of Bernhard Becker, who had been nominated by Lassalle as his successor. He was an incompetent and ineffectual person. Through his mismanagement the Association lost ground until, in 1867, he was replaced by Jean Baptista von Schweitzer, who had been largely responsible for the issue, in 1865, of the *Sozial Demokrat*, the first journal of the organization, the forerunner of the present multitude of German Socialist organs. The paper began with an able staff of contributors, including Marx, Frederick Engels, Wilhelm Liebknecht, and Georg Herwegh, but most of these severed their connection with it on the publication in its columns of a series of articles glorifying Prussia and Bismarck. Von Schweitzer, who had been intimately acquainted with Lassalle, was a man of considerable ability. He revived the Association, and remained at its head until 1871, when he retired. He was expelled the following year on a charge of treachery. By this time a rival body, the Social Democratic Workmen's Party, founded on Marxian principles, had arisen, which, after many storms and quarrels with the Association, amalgamated with it in 1875, and formed the existing German Social Democratic Party.

The Social Democratic Workmen's Party was the outcome of the International Working Men's Association, known as the "International," inaugurated in 1864 at St. Martin's Hall, Long Acre, London. Karl Marx, an exile from Germany since 1849, when he was thirty-one years old, had taken a prominent part in the formation of the International and soon became the most powerful influence in its counsels. At the first conference of the organization, held at Geneva in 1866, the statutes and program drawn up by Marx were adopted. The program, like that of Lassalle, was an adaptation of the Communist Manifesto of 1848. It called to the workers to unite internationally in order to become masters of their economic destiny through the conquest of political power. But Marx, unlike Lassalle, appeared to have had faith in the possibility of raising the condition of the workers even under a capitalist *régime*. This is expressed in his inaugural address to the International, where he speaks of the Ten Hours Act as being, " not merely a great practical result, but the victory of a principle. For the first time the political economy of the *bourgeoisie* has been in clear broad day put in subjection to the political economy of the working class." He further declared that the success of co-operation had spread the hope that wage labor was a transitory form, destined to be replaced by the associated labor of free men, and it was the aim of the International to promote this hope.

The Social Democratic Workmen's Party.

In Germany the ground had been prepared for the Marxist gospel. In 1863, very soon after the foundation of Lassalle's Universal Association, a number of workers' educational societies— in reality political bodies — combined into a league to support Schultze-Delitzsch and oppose Lassalle. The headquarters of the league were at Leipzig, and one of the most important members was August Bebel, then working in that city. Wilhelm Liebknecht, an exile of 1848, who had lived in London for thirteen years, and become an ardent disciple of Marx, learned to know Bebel and helped to win him over to Socialism. In 1868 they succeeded in persuading the annual congress of the league to accept the main items of the program of the International. They received an accession of strength from a number of dissentients from the Universal Association who were dissatisfied with von Schweitzer's policy and rule. In 1869, at Eisenach, the league dissolved, and, after a vain attempt at union with the Universal Association, formed the Social Democratic Workmen's Party, which became known as the Eisenach, or " honorable," Party, and which declared itself, as far as the law allowed, affiliated to the International. Meanwhile both sections scored their first electoral victories by returning, in 1867, seven members to the North German Reichstag, of whom Bebel and Liebknecht and two others represented the Marxian section.

The Union of the Eisenachers and the Lassalleans.

Bitterness between the two groups increased owing to difference of attitude in the Reichstag towards the Franco-Prussian War. The Eisenachers, true to their international principles, voted against supplies for the German army ; the representatives of the Universal Association, or Lassalleans as they were now called, more nationalist in spirit, took the opposite line. When France was defeated, Bebel and Liebknecht urged that peace should be made on generous terms, and without annexation of Alsace-Lorraine. For this they were denounced as traitors, tried, and sent to prison for two years and nine months and two years respectively. The Lassalleans violently attacked the Eisenachers in the streets of Leipzig, thereby reflecting the general sense of outraged patriotism aroused by the conduct of Bebel and Liebknecht.

The tremendous wave of self-conscious national sentiment which followed the German triumph over France naturally swept back both currents of the Socialist movement. To the first Reichstag of the newly created German Empire only two Socialists were elected, of whom one was Bebel. But in a few years the patriotic tide had ebbed, and the working classes were suffering through the economic crisis that arose after the war. The discontent of the masses renewed the strength of the Socialists, who secured ten seats at the Reichstag elections of 1874, of which seven were held by Eisenachers. These successes roused the Government to repressive action, and it declared the organizations of both sections illegal. Attacked in this fashion, the Lassalleans and the Eisenachers drew together, and, as already related, they combined in 1875. The fusion took place at a Congress held at Gotha in May. The official figures of the membership of the two sections at the time of the unification, eleven years after Lassalle's death, appear tiny compared with the mighty host enrolled to-day under the banner he was the first to unfurl. The Lassalleans numbered 15,322, and the Eisenachers 9,121.*

Unity, as usual, was only obtained by compromise. Included in the program of the new combination was Lassalle's proposal for State-aided productive associations, but under democratic guarantees. This and other "unscientific" and crude demands and principles called forth strong opposition from Marx, who considered the program "utterly condemnable and demoralizing." He contended characteristically that common action was of far greater importance than a common creed or program; but if one were adopted, it should not be theoretically unsound and otherwise unsatisfactory. In other words, it should be Marxian or nothing. But the Eisenach leaders were wise enough and strong enough to disregard the advice of their imperious mentor. They replied that it was impossible for him to judge the situation aright from London, and that, although they had great respect for his opinion, they were unable to follow it in this instance. Further, in order to prevent Marx's communication from being used by either section as a means for preventing unity, they decided to treat it as confidential, and it was not laid before the Congress. Marx's inflexible temper was roused to fury at the rejection of his counsel, and he was exceedingly bitter towards Liebknecht, his special pupil. Later, however, he acknowledged he had been mistaken, and that Liebknecht, Bebel and the other Eisenachers had acted rightly in sacrificing orthodoxy to united action.

* The name taken by the unified party was Die Sozialistische Arbeiterpartei (The Socialist Workmen's Party). The title Social Democratic Party was adopted in 1890.

Although Marx objected so strongly to the compromise program, the spirit of his doctrine prevailed therein. On the other hand, Lassalle's organizing genius embodied in the Universal Association brought to the combined party the stern discipline and the knowledge of the importance of incessant agitation, well ordered finances and constant attention to detail which are to-day the outstanding features of the German Social Democratic Party.

The Period of Persecution.

The effect of the union of the two sections was soon apparent. In the Reichstag elections of 1877 the Socialist vote reached nearly half a million, an increase of 40 per cent. on that of 1874. This rapid growth naturally stimulated the reactionary forces to further repressive efforts. The civil law was stretched to the utmost in the attacks made by the Government upon the Socialist movement. The support given to the Government in its anti-Socialist campaign was not confined to the Conservative politicians. The Progressists, weak and pusillanimous as ever, were terrified at the spread of Socialist views, and fled in masses to the camp of reaction. The conduct of German Liberalism completely justified the Marxian principle of *Klassenkampf* (class struggle), and explains the weak position the Liberal parties have since occupied in the politics of the Empire. Among the measures used by the Government to dam back the "red flood" was the issuing of a letter to employers of labor advising them, for their own good, to employ no persons who were suspected of being Social Democrats. In 1876 the party was solemnly declared to be dissolved for offences against the Coalition Laws; but, as individual members could not be suppressed under the existing legal code, exceptional legislation was decided upon. The Government was assisted in its designs by two foolish attempts, made early in 1878, on the life of the Emperor. The perpetrators were obviously lunatics, but the opportunity was too good to be missed. Although there was not the slightest evidence that Socialists were concerned in these feeble outrages, the Government spread the report that the madmen were Social Democrats. Between the dates of the two attempts repressive proposals were laid before the Reichstag, but they were thrown out. A few days after the second attempt the Reichstag was dissolved, and the ensuing election resulted in a majority in favor of the Government's desires. The Social Democratic vote fell for the first time in the history of the party.

The Exceptional Law.

The Exceptional Law against Social Democracy passed in October, 1878, was of the most drastic character. It rendered illegal any association having Socialist aims. Any meeting which displayed Socialist tendencies was to be summarily disbanded, and those which indicated by their purpose that they were likely to promote such tendencies were forbidden. Collection of funds for Socialist purposes was prohibited. No meetings of any kind were allowed without the previous permission of the police, excepting election meetings for the

Reichstag and for the Diets of the various German States. Socialists could be forbidden residence in places where the police considered their influence to be dangerous. All literature or printed matter with Socialist tendencies was interdicted, and persons discovered circulating newspapers or documents of this nature could be deprived of the right to distribute any literature whatever, either by way of business or otherwise. Punishments for breaking the law ranged from fines of £25 or three months' imprisonment for minor offenders to long terms of imprisonment for leaders. The law was to run for three years but successive Parliaments prolonged it, with slight alterations, until October, 1890.

Owing to the enormous powers possessed by the German police, the Exceptional Law was in reality far more harsh than even its draconian provisions indicate. An executive, subject to hardly any checks, could and actually did use these powers to their fullest extent and with very little regard to precise details of legality. Knowing that the authorities were hoping that the Socialists would be driven to desperation, the Social Democratic leaders warned their followers against committing acts of violent resistance and to avoid unnecessary infringements of the law. The Socialist journals dropped their propagandist note, and became mere recorders of news and facts. But the police were not to be foiled. They judged the newspapers by their past, and suppressed all except two of the fifty which were then published. The minor state of siege was declared in Berlin, and sixty-seven prominent Socialists were banished from the city one month after the law had been promulgated. Similar steps were taken in other large towns, including Leipzig, Frankfort and Hamburg. All open agitation and organization was, of course, entirely suppressed, and the movement was driven underground, where, in spite of the keen watchfulness of the all-powerful police, propaganda was carried on quite effectually, chiefly by the means of cleverly arranged secret distribution of newspapers and other literature printed abroad and smuggled over the borders of the Empire. Persecution and imprisonment failed to intimidate the growing multitude of grimly earnest disciples of Lassalle and Marx ; instead of daunting them, it spurred them on to greater activity and higher ingenuity in spreading their views.

Futile Sops to Cerberus.

Bismarck's openly confessed attempt to reconcile the working classes to the loss of the small amount of political freedom they had possessed by granting doles of social reform in the shape of measures of State Insurance was equally unsuccessful. It is true the Socialist vote in 1881 fell again, and more heavily than in 1878; but in 1884 and 1887 it grew with extraordinary rapidity, rising in the latter year to over three-quarters of a million. In 1890 it jumped up to nearly a million and a half. It was now evident that the law had been not only an iniquitous crime but a colossal blunder. Instead of destroying the Social Democrats, its blows had hammered and welded the political and industrial discontent of the masses into a solid and tenacious Socialist movement. The party had been tried as by fire, and had stood the test magnificently. During the twelve years of brutal coercion its members, including the chief leaders, had suffered in the aggregate 831 years imprisonment, not to mention fines, banishments and other forms of persecution. Yet the Socialist vote had more than trebled itself and the representation in the Reichstag had grown from nine to thirty-five. Still more important, there had been created in every industrial centre a nucleus of determined men who had proved by suffering their devotion to the Socialist cause and who were prepared to give the best of their tried capacities to its service. The experiment in Russianizing Germany had brought about the very conditions its authors had sought to prevent. When Bismarck was dismissed in 1890 by the present Kaiser the Exceptional Law went with him. An attempt was made in 1895 to revive it in a new form, but it was defeated in the Reichstag. Since that date no distinctively anti-Socialist legislation has been put forward by the Government, although Conservative politicians still clamor for strong measures against the "Red Peril."

Although the Socialist movement flourished in defiance of the Exceptional Law, it went through many internecine conflicts and encountered many internal difficulties which could not be fought out or overcome until the law had lapsed. The extreme elements demanded militant action, and when their agitation met with no response, the leaders, as is usual under such circumstances, were charged with cowardice and with being corrupted by futile and enervating parliamentarianism. But after 1890, when annual congresses could again be held on German soil without police interference, frank discussion of the situation ended in a complete vindication of the old leaders Bebel, Liebknecht and Singer, and the final overthrow of their critics. In 1890 the organization of the party was reconstructed as far as the Coalition Laws would permit, that is to say, in a very restricted fashion. Then, in 1891, at Erfurt, the present program of the party, in which Marxian principles have swept the remnants of the Lassallean proposals for State-aided cooperation off the field, was drawn up and agreed upon.

The Erfurt Program.

But although the Erfurt Program is binding upon the party as a whole, and influences very largely its political policy, there is a wide divergence in the ranks with regard to the significance to be attached to its various parts. The orthodox section, who cling with passionate intensity to the Marxian prelude as though it were an inspired document which should determine the actions of the party for ever, have constantly to meet the criticisms of another section, heterodox and opportunist, who, while recognizing to the full the greatness of Marx, are not prepared to allow the dead hand of a fallible philosopher to guide them in new and unforeseen circumstances. This section is known as the Revisionists, while the strict Marxists are called Radicals. The two groups have always existed in the party, and they are the products of differing social, industrial, and political conditions. In Prussia, the home of unbending, autocratic, and able bureaucracy, the Radical section naturally flourishes, for there the *Klassenkampf* theory appears to be absolutely in accord with facts. Contempt for democracy is the prevailing element in the stifling, police ridden atmosphere. The masses are shown on every possible occasion how little the governing class cares for their opinions or respects their wishes. Reforms, social or otherwise, when granted are given in the shape which pleases the authorities and are administered in a manner which arouses keen resentment among thoughtful, self-respecting people. Hence any suggestion of enlarging the power of the present bureaucratic State, even for useful purposes, is looked upon with distrust and suspicion by the Socialists of Prussia as likely to lead to further unwarrantable limitations of personal liberty. The lamentable history of North German Liberalism has also helped to strengthen the hard, uncompromising spirit of the Radical section, and has prevented any successful working agreement between Socialists and Liberals for securing popular control of the Government.

The Revisionists and the Radicals.

Revisionism has its home in South Germany, where industry is less developed and political and social life is far more free and democratic. Georg von Vollmar, the leader of the Bavarian Social Democrats, has always declined to accept the dogma of the inevitable concentration of the ownership of capital and land in fewer and fewer hands, especially with regard to the latter. Furthermore, he has maintained that the party should drop its irreconcilable attitude and endeavor to win immediate reforms, contending that by doing so it would win support from the agricultural population of small proprietors, who naturally find nothing attractive in the Marxian view that they must first be ruined before they can be helped.

The Revisionist School received a great impetus when, in 1899, Eduard Bernstein published "*Die Voraussetzungen des Sozialismus und die Aufgaben der Sozialdemokratie*," * in which he criticized Marxian economics and philosophy, and denied that Socialism was dependent upon economic necessity, or that it was necessary to found it solely on materialism. He pointed out that the German Social Democratic Party had grown great through acting in opposition to the theoretical basis of its program, and urged that it should openly declare itself to be what it really is, a democratic socialistic reform party. It is interesting to note in passing that just as "*Das Kapital*" was the result of Marx's studies in England, so the intellectual basis of Revisionism was formulated by Bernstein during his stay in this country when banished from Germany on account of his Socialist activities.

Although the struggle between the Revisionist and Radical wings of the party is still undecided, there can be no doubt that the influence of the former has gained ground in recent years. This is

* Translated and published by the Independent Labor Party under the title of "Evolutionary Socialism."

shewn in the greater emphasis now laid upon the practical side of the Erfurt Program and the tacit abandonment of the idea that nothing short of the Social Revolution can prevent "the increase of the insecurity of the existence of the proletariat, small masters and peasants, and the intensification of misery, oppression, slavery, humiliation, and exploitation" under capitalism. The contradiction between the theoretical argument of the program, which propounds the fatalistic view that the present social order offers no hope of improvement for the masses, and the demands which follow for immediate political and social betterment provides ample justification for the position of the Revisionists. The logic of circumstances and the illogicalness of the strict Marxists are factors on their side. Trade Unionism, formerly held to be useless in face of the iron law of wages, has refused to accept the validity of the law, and has grown so tremendously that the party has been compelled to admit the need for and efficacy of industrial combination, and gradually to concede it equal importance with political organization. Fortunately this attitude was adopted in time; otherwise antagonism would most probably have arisen between the two movements. With a wise indifference to consistency, the party has encouraged the formation of fighting Trade Unions, the *Freie Gewerkschaften*. Most of the leaders of these bodies are well known Social Democrats, chiefly of the Revisionist school. There is a close connection between these so-called Social Democratic Unions, which now have a membership of close upon two and a half millions, and the party itself; and frequent consultations take place between the heads of the two organizations, although the unions are not allowed by law to take part in politics. Further, the growth of co-operation has been aided by the party, and the great bulk of the members of distributive societies are now Social Democratic in opinion.

Compromise and Compacts.

In the political sphere the Social Democrats began to practise very early in their history the art of compromise, which is decidedly out of keeping with their revolutionary phraseology. It had been decided at the Congress held in 1887 at St. Gall, during the period of the Exceptional Law, that Social Democrats should vote for no Reichstag candidates except those run by the party. But in 1890 the party leaders issued instructions in connection with the elections of that year, that, in the absence of Social Democrats, candidates of parties pledged to oppose the renewal of the Exceptional Law were to be supported. This advice was bitterly attacked by the ultra-revolutionary elements, the "*Jungen*," who soon after 1890 split off, developed Anarchistic tendencies, and died of them. Since then the party has voted in second ballots for various other parties. For instance, in 1907 it supported its most able and bitter opponent, the Centre (or Catholic) Party, because for the moment, and for the moment only, the Centre had gone into opposition. In the election of 1912 it threw its weight on the side of Liberalism, and the Executive Committee even went so far as to instruct its members in sixteen constituencies, where there were second ballots between Social Democrats and *Freisinnige* (Liberals), not to be too enthusiastic in support of their own candidates, and to let the *Freisinnige* win, thereby securing Liberal aid in thirty-one other constituencies for Social Democrats who were fighting Conservatives or Catholics. Naturally this daring order, although successful, in that it probably gained seats for the party, caused considerable resentment among the Radical section, but it was endorsed afterwards at the party congress.

In Bavaria have occurred still greater departures from rigid adherence to the principle that all "bourgeois" parties being capitalist in origin must be equally opposed. There being no second ballots for the State Parliament, the Bavarian Social Democrats, in 1912, made a compact with the Liberals for a division of the constituencies, and agreed that there were to be no opposing candidatures, but mutual support. This glaringly opportunist alliance excited only a few murmurs of reproach from the stern cohorts of North Germany. On the other hand, the recent action of the Social Democrats in the Parliaments of South Germany in voting for the State budgets has been condemned by the party congress; but, nevertheless, the offenders have openly stated that in this question they intend to be guided by their own State organizations rather than by the congress.

Other Aspects of Revisionism.

Another change has taken place in the party which may be considered to be of a Revisionist character, namely, in its attitude towards nationalism. It is no longer the general opinion that under the present capitalist system it is a matter of indifference to the workers whether their capitalist masters and rulers are German, Russian, or English. Even Bebel has declared that he is prepared to fight for his Fatherland in a defensive war, and the party congress of 1907 refused to censure another Socialist member of the Reichstag for an even more militant patriotic declaration. Here the spirit of Lassalle has conquered Marx. While still distinguished for its efforts to maintain peace and goodwill among the nations and its opposition to militarism and the demand for a larger German navy, the party has become, if not less international, less cosmopolitan in its outlook, especially during the last decade.

The stress now laid by the party on immediate reforms is nowhere so pronounced as in the domain of local government. There are over 10,000 Socialist members of town and village councils acting, not merely as propagandists, but as administrators with a practical program of municipal Socialism. To their efforts are due, as their opponents sometimes admit, much of the rapid extension of municipal activity and the remarkable improvements which have taken place in the big cities of the empire. Here the Social Democrats have found a valuable and almost inexhaustible field for their energies, and one which is increasingly engaging their attention. A special organ, *Kommunale Praxis*, is published by the party to educate and inform its members on subjects appertaining to municipal and other forms of local government.

The Strength of the Party.

The conflicts of various currents and differing opinions as to policy and tactics within the party, leading often to fierce literary and vocal battles, have not prevented the rapid continuous increase either of the Social Democratic vote or of the Socialist organization. Industrialism, in its swift advance during the last fifteen years, has drawn huge numbers of workers from the rural regions to urban areas, converting small quiet centres into large and important manufacturing cities. ' Free from the tyranny of the Prussian Junker, the despot of the countryside in North Germany, the mass of this new population quickly comes under the influence of the ceaseless agitation of the Socialists, who claim support for the party as the only one that demands for the people those political rights which in England are either the achievements or the program of ordinary Liberalism. No other party can be relied upon to defend the workers' industrial organizations from attack or to advocate further extensions of the right of combination. Moreover, all other political groups stand more or less for a continuance of the present policy of Protection, which has brought about a big increase in the cost of living. The disunited remnant of German Liberalism, which at one time aspired to be the voice of democracy, suffers from a chronic inclination to bolt to the enemy at the slightest encouragement or patronizing attention from the Kaiser's ministers. Hence the workmen and even middle-class democrats have come to look upon the Social Democratic Party as the only faithful champion of their interests and aspirations.

Since the expiration of the Exceptional Law in 1890 the party has gained nearly three million votes, securing four and a quarter millions in January, 1912, over one-third of the total number cast. The Social Democratic Party in the Reichstag has grown in the same period from 35 to 110, and is now the largest group in that chamber, which has a membership of 397. The organization has developed even more remarkably. In 1875, when the party was formed by the fusion of the Lassalleans and the Eisenachers, it had, as we have seen, barely 25,000 members ; in 1912 it could boast of a membership roll of 970,112, of which 130,371 were women, though they were only in 1906 permitted by law to belong to it. In 1890 the income of the Executive Committee was about £5,000 ; in 1912 it had risen to close upon £100,000. These figures do not, of course, include the incomes of the local organizations existing in nearly every constituency, which together make up a far larger sum. These local organizations are of tremendous strength in the large cities and other thickly populated areas. In six mammoth constituencies there are organizations each with over 20,000 paying members : namely, Hamburg III., 42,532 ; Teltow (near Berlin), 32,885 ; Leipzig-Land, 32,219 ; Berlin VI., 31,408 ; Berlin IV., 25,267 ;

Nuremberg, 20,118.* The yearly incomes of these several bodies, made up chiefly of monthly subscriptions of about fourpence per member, each attain the respectable sums of five to seven thousand pounds. These financial statistics are all the more noteworthy when it is remembered that the money is given entirely for political purposes and, in most cases, in addition to contributions paid to trade unions.

The Social Democratic Press.

The party possesses 91 newspapers and journals, of which 86 appear daily. All but eight are printed in establishments owned by the party. The total circulation of the Social Democratic press in 1912 was about one and a half million. The income derived from sales and advertisements amounted in the same year to nearly £800,000. The central organ, *Vorwärts*, published in Berlin, has a daily circulation of 170,000, costs about £98,000 per annum to produce, and yielded a net profit to the party of £15,000 in 1912. The humorous, illustrated party journal, *Der Wahre Jacob*, has a circulation of close upon 400,000, costs about £14,000 per annum to produce, and earned a profit of £2,500 in 1912. *Die Gleichheit*, the women's journal, has a sale of 107,000, costs £3,500 to print and publish, and made a profit of £500 in 1912. The more or less academic weekly review, *Die Neue Zeit*, circulates to the extent of 10,000, costs £3,000 per annum, and, unlike most party reviews has a balance to the good amounting in 1912 to £160.

In addition to the party newspapers and journals, of which one appears daily in every large German town, the numerous local party presses issue countless books, pamphlets and leaflets, especially during election times. For the electoral agitation of 1912 it is estimated that eighty million copies of Socialist leaflets were printed and distributed. In the same year the central press at Berlin alone issued seventy different publications, ranging from complete editions of Schiller and Heine and other books to tracts and leaflets of a few pages, amounting in all to 2¾ million copies.† The turnover of this department reached £40,000 in 1912, with a profit of £2,500.

Organization and its Results.

Since 1905, when the Coalition Laws were amended to allow greater freedom of political combination, the organization of the party has been placed upon a firm foundation. The basis is the local organizations in the Reichstag constituencies. These are linked up into twenty-nine district federations, and the district federations into

---

* The Reichstag constituencies are all single member divisions, and they vary tremendously in size, from Teltow, with 338,798 electors, to Bückeburg, with 10,709. The Government refuses to redistribute the seats because it fears this would lead to a large increase in the Social Democratic representation.

† As an instance of Social Democratic publishing enterprise it may be mentioned that the *Partei Vorstand* commissioned Herr M. Beer, until recently London correspondent of the *Vorwärts*, to write an exhaustive history of British Socialism, which was issued in one large volume in January, 1913, under the title of " *Geschichte des Sozialismus in England.*"

State organizations in the various States of the Empire. The chief authority is the annual Congress, which consists of delegates from the local organizations, the number from each depending upon the size of membership, together with the Social Democratic members of the Reichstag and the members of the Executive Committee. The Congress elects annually the Executive Committee, which consists of the *Partei Vorstand* (comprising a chairman, vice-chairman, a treasurer, six secretaries, one of whom must be a woman, and two assistants) and the *Kontroll Commission*, or Committee of Control, consisting of nine members. The *Vorstand* are mainly paid officials; nearly all of them devote their whole time to party business. They are responsible for the heavy detail work of the party, and have a large clerical staff at their disposal. In order to assist the Executive in arriving at decisions on political policy and other important matters a Council, consisting of representatives from the executive committees of the various district federations, was instituted in 1912. This was done, it was said, "to check the growing bureaucratic tendencies" of the *Partei Vorstand*. There are now forty-nine paid secretaries of district and state federations and eighty-four paid secretaries of local organizations.

There is no doubt as to the efficiency of this ably officialled organization. The rank and file members are not allowed to remain mere passive payers of subscriptions. They are expected to be active in the distribution of literature, in making converts by constant argument and discussion among their workmates, and in sharing the heavy toil of electioneering and the organizing of meetings and demonstrations. In the big industrial regions at election times the Social Democratic battalions work like a machine. Hence in Berlin and Greater Berlin, with its eight Reichstag divisions, there is now only one which has not gone "red," and that, the West End division, in which are situated the Kaiser's palace and the houses of the wealthy, was only saved to the Liberals in 1912 by nine votes on a poll of over 11,000. In the seven other constituencies at the same election the Social Democratic vote was 559,678 out of a total of 805,730, or nearly 70 per cent. In the purely working class divisions of these seven the proportion reached 80 per cent. Results almost equally startling were obtained in other big centres of population, including Munich, Hamburg, Leipzig, Dresden, Nuremberg, Stuttgart, Cologne, Hanover, Frankfort, Königsberg, Strassburg, Breslau, and the like. With few exceptions every large German city throughout the empire has now a Social Democrat representing it in the Imperial Parliament.

Socialism and Philosophy, Science and Art.

The political sphere, however, is not the only one to which the party devotes time, energy, and money. " We German Socialists," says Engels, " are proud of our descent not only from Saint Simon, Fourier, and Owen, but also from Kant, Fichte, and Hegel. The German Labor movement is the heir of German classical philosophy." Lassalle claimed that he wrote every line armed with the entire culture of his century. These proud boasts have doubt-less helped to inspire the Social Democrats to become the bearers of art, philosophy, and science to the masses. One of the most active branches of the organization are the education committees, which have been established in 317 localities. Of these the greater num-ber are formed in conjunction with the trade unions. There is also a central education committee, whose duty is to promote and assist the local committees. The expenditure of these bodies amounted to more than £32,000 in 1912. They arranged about 2,000 lectures on economics, history, literature, art, socialism, philosophy, co-operation, trade unionism, political science, and technical subjects; and innumerable concerts, entertainments, and dramatic and operatic performances. These are, of course, in addition to the ordinary propaganda and election meetings, of which about 30,000 were held. The musical and dramatic performances are carried out on a large scale. Theatres, with complete companies of actors, actresses and orchestras, are engaged to perform plays of Shakespeare, Goethe, and Schiller, as well as modern dramas of a propagandist type. The Education Com-mittee of Hamburg reports successful renderings of Beethoven's symphonies to large audiences of working men, and the Cologne Education Committee found that Bach can secure good attendances from working class members of the party. The cinematograph has also been brought into the service of Socialist instruction.

One of the most interesting institutions connected with the edu-cational work of the party is the Socialist School or College at Berlin. Here every year 31 selected men and women of various ages are given instruction in general, social, and constitutional his-tory; political economy; history and theory of Socialism; social and industrial law; the art of speaking and writing; journalism; and other subjects. Each scholar is allowed a full maintenance grant during the school period. By this means a steady supply of trained agitators and officials is provided for the party. The cost of the School is £2,000 per annum, of which £1,000 is spent in main-tenance grants.

Socialist Women and Young People.

A special department, the Women's Bureau, deals with the work of the 130,000 women of the party. One day a year, May 12th, the Social Democratic Women's Day, is specially devoted to demonstra-tions and meetings to demand the extension of the suffrage to women. Special pamphlets, leaflets, and other publications are pre-pared for the agitation among women, and a special women's confer-ence is held just before the annual congress of the party. A valuable social service is carried on largely by the women of the movement through the medium of Committees for the Protection of Children. These purely voluntary bodies are established in 125 localities. They seek to prevent breaches of the various laws to protect children, especially those connected with child wage earners; and they are said to be more effective than the State factory inspectors.

Although young persons are forbidden by law to belong to the Social Democratic organization, steps are taken by the party to provide means for keeping them in touch with Socialist ideas. Committees for this purpose exist in 574 localities, through which a special journal, *Arbeiter Jugend*, is sold to the number of over 80,000 copies. Libraries for young persons are also provided in 138 districts. The committees, in 1912, held 3,500 lectures and 1,623 concerts and entertainments, and organized 384 visits to museums and picture galleries and the like, and 4,682 walking and other excursions. In these various functions many tens of thousands of young people took part. The Central Bureau, which directs these activities, issues special literature for the young. In 1912 about 650,000 copies of various books, pamphlets and leaflets of this nature were published. The local committees have powerful enemies in the various organizations established by religious and other societies to protect youths and girls between fourteen and eighteen years of age from Socialist infection ; but, in spite of all opposition, the recruiting to the army of the " Reds " grows at a pace that strikes terror to the hearts of the anti-Socialists, who, in their panic-stricken attacks upon the Social Democrats, descend to the lowest depths of misrepresentation and vituperation.

The Party and the Trade Unions.

It will be readily understood that the manifold operations of the Social Democratic organization require in every city quarters of no inconsiderable magnitude. In most large German towns, and in some of the smaller ones, the Socialists and trade unionists have joined hands and built splendidly equipped offices and meeting-places for the two movements. These *Gewerkschaftshäuser* or *Volkshäuser*, as they are called, are notable features of Berlin, Hamburg, Leipzig, Chemnitz and other big centres. In their erection many thousands of pounds, subscribed by the organized workers, have been invested. The *Volkshaus* usually contains the offices of most of the trade unions and other labor organizations of the city, halls for large meetings, a restaurant, recreation and reading rooms, and sometimes lodging rooms and baths for trade unionists travelling in search of work. In Berlin the Social Democratic activities are so numerous and extensive that a separate establishment has always been required for them. In 1911 the *Partei Vorstand* acquired, at a cost of £225,000, four large blocks of buildings in Lindenstrasse, one of the main thoroughfares of the capital. Here in due course will be housed all the central agencies of the party : the executive committee, the central committees of the education, women's and young persons' departments, the party school, the archives, the *Vorwärt's* printing and publishing works, and the book store. These new headquarters will be worthy of the mighty and marvellously organized movement to which they belong. It is interesting to note that, by a curious stroke of irony, among the present tenants of the buildings now paying rent to the hated Social Democrats are two strongly Conservative newspapers.

Equipment for Conquest.

The secret of the extraordinary achievements of the German Socialists lies in their remarkable combination of idealism and practicality. Though their heads are sometimes among the stars, their feet are always on the solid earth; though many of them still believe in the early Marxian myth of a final collapse of capitalism from which Socialism will rise in full splendor, they never use the plea " that nothing but Socialism is of any use " in order to shirk the task of grappling with immediate problems. So multifarious are the ways in which they are equipping themselves for the conquest of political power, and so intent are they on the making of their organization equal to the great mission which Lassalle declared destiny had laid upon the working classes, that to many thousands, as to Eduard Bernstein, " the movement is everything, the ultimate aim is nothing." The movement is a constant, many-sided struggle for political, economic and social emancipation in which, more and more, experience is replacing abstract theory as a guide. And the training and discipline induced by the ceaseless battling of the movement with opponents and obstacles of all kinds is producing a self-respecting, self-confident and purposeful democracy which, when it does attain political power, will have learned to use it soberly and with judgment in the tremendous task of changing the German Empire into the German Co-operative Commonwealth.

PROGRAM OF THE SOCIAL DEMOCRATIC PARTY OF GERMANY.

(ADOPTED AT THE ERFURT CONGRESS, 1891.)

From "German Social Democracy," by Bertrand Russell, and "Modern Socialism,"
by R. C. K. Ensor.

The economic development of bourgeois society leads necessarily to the disappearance of production on a small scale (*Kleinbetrieb*), the principle of which consists in the workers owning the means of production. This economic development separates the worker from his means of production, and transforms him into an unpropertied proletarian, while the means of production become the property of a comparatively small number of capitalists and great landlords.

Hand in hand with the monopolizing of the means of production goes the supplanting of scattered small businesses by colossal businesses, the development of the tool into the machine, and a gigantic growth of the productivity of human labor. But all the advantages of this change are monopolized by the capitalists and great landlords. For the proletariat and the declining intermediate classes—small masters, peasants—it betokens growing increase of the insecurity of their existence, of misery, oppression, slavery, humiliation, and exploitation.

Ever greater grows the number of the proletariat, ever more extensive the army of surplus workers, ever sharper the contrast between exploiters and exploited, and ever bitterer the class warfare between bourgeoisie and proletariat, which divides modern society into two hostile camps, and is the common characteristic of all industrial countries.

The gulf between propertied and unpropertied is further widened through the crises, rooted in the essence of the capitalistic method of production, which constantly become more far-reaching and more devastating, which make general insecurity into the normal condition of society, and furnish the proof that the productive powers of modern society have outgrown its control, that private property in the means of production is irreconcilable with the due application and full development of those powers.

Private property in the means of production, which was formerly the means of securing to the producer the possession of his own product, has to-day become the means of expropriating peasants, handicraftsmen, and small producers, and of putting the non-workers, capitalists, and great landlords in possession of the product of the workers. Only the conversion of capitalistic private property in the means of production—land, quarries, and mines, raw material, tools, machines, means of communication—into common property, and the change of the production of goods into a Socialistic production, worked for and through society, can bring it about that production on a large scale, and the ever growing productiveness of human labor, shall develop, for the hitherto exploited classes, from a source of misery and oppression, into a source of the highest well being and perfect universal harmony.

This social change betokens the emancipation, not only of the proletariat, but of the whole human race, which is suffering under the present conditions. But it can only be the work of the working classes, because all other classes, in spite of conflicts of interests among themselves, take their stand on the ground of private property in the means of production, and have, for their common aim, the maintenance of the foundations of existing society.

The struggle of the working class against capitalistic exploitation is of necessity a political struggle. The working class cannot carry on its economic contests, and cannot develop its economic organization, without political rights. It cannot bring about the transference of the means of production into the possession of the community without acquiring political power.

To give to this fight of the working class a conscious and unified form, and to show it its necessary goal—that is the task of the Social Democratic Party.

The interests of the working classes are the same in all countries with a capitalistic mode of production. With the extension of the world's commerce, and of production for the world market, the position of the worker in every country grows ever more dependent on the position of the worker in other countries. The liberation of the working class, accordingly, is a work in which the workmen of all civilized countries are equally involved. In recognition of this, the Social Democratic Party of Germany feels and declares itself to be *one* with the class conscious workmen of all other countries.

The Social Democratic Party of Germany does not fight, accordingly, for new class privileges and class rights, but for the abolition of class rule and of classes themselves, for equal rights and equal duties of all, without distinction of sex or descent. Starting from these views, it combats, within existing society, not only the exploitation and oppression of wage earners, but every kind of exploitation and oppression, whether directed against a class, a party, a sex, or a race.

Proceeding from these principles, the Social Democratic Party of Germany demands, to begin with:

1. Universal, equal, and direct suffrage, with secret ballot, for all elections, of all citizens of the Empire over twenty years of age, without distinction of sex. Proportional representation and, until this is introduced, legal redistribution of electoral districts after every census. Biennial legislative periods. Holding of the elections on a legal holiday. Compensation for the elected representatives. Abolition of every limitation of political rights, except in the case of legal incapacity.

2. Direct legislation through the people, by means of the rights of proposal and rejection. Self-determination and self-government of the people in realm, state, province, and parish. Election of magistrates by the people, with responsibility to the people. Annual voting of taxes.

3. Education of all to bear arms. Militia in the place of the standing army. Decision by the popular representatives on questions of war and peace. Settlement of all international disputes by arbitration.

4. Abolition of all laws which limit or suppress the right of meeting and association.

5. Abolition of all laws which place women, whether in a public or a private capacity, at a disadvantage as compared with men.

6. Declaration that religion is a private matter. Abolition of all expenditure of public funds upon ecclesiastical and religious objects. Ecclesiastical and religious bodies are to be regarded as private associations, which regulate their affairs entirely independently.

7. Secularization of schools. Compulsory attendance at the public national schools. Free education, free supply of educational materials, and free maintenance in the public schools, as well as in the higher educational institutions, for those boys and girls who, on account of their capacities, are considered fit for further education.

8. Free administration of justice and free legal assistance. Administration of the law through judges elected by the people. Appeal in criminal cases. Compensation of persons unjustly accused, imprisoned, or condemned. Abolition of capital punishment.

9. Free medical attendance, including midwifery, and free supply of medicines. Free burial.

10. Graduated income and property tax for defraying all public expenses, so far as these are to be covered by taxation. Obligatory self-assessment. Succession duties, graduated according to the amount of the inheritance and the degree of relationship. Abolition of all indirect taxes, customs, and other economic measures, which sacrifice the interests of the community to those of a privileged minority.

For the protection of the working classes, the Social Democratic Party of Germany demands immediately:

1. An effective national and international legislation for the protection of labor on the following principles:—

   (a) Fixing of a normal working day, which shall not exceed eight hours.
   (b) Prohibition of the employment of children under fourteen.
   (c) Prohibition of night work, except in those industries which, by their nature, require night work, from technical reasons or for the public welfare.
   (d) An unbroken rest of at least thirty-six hours in every week for every worker.
   (e) Prohibition of the truck system.

2. Inspection of all industrial establishments, investigation and regulation of conditions of labor in town and country by a central labor department, district labor bureaus, and chambers of labor.

3. Legal equality of agricultural laborers and domestic servants with industrial workers. Abolition of the special regulations concerning servants.

4. Assurance of the right of combination.

5. Taking over by the Imperial Government of the whole system of working people's insurance, though giving the working people a controlling share in the administration.

6. Separation of the Churches and the State.

(a) Suppression of the grant for public worship.

(b) Philosophic or religious associations to be civil persons at law.

7. Revision of selections in the Civil Code concerning marriage and the paternal authority.

(a) Civil equality of the sexes, and of children, whether natural or legitimate.

(b) Revision of the divorce laws, maintaining the husband's liability to support the wife or the children.

(c) Inquiry into paternity to be legalized.

(d) Protective measures in favor of children materially or morally abandoned.

GROWTH OF THE SOCIAL DEMOCRATIC VOTE IN GERMANY.

Year.	Social Democratic vote (First Ballot).	Percentage of total vote.	Social Democrats Returned.
1871	124,655	3	2
1874	351,952	6·8	10
1877	493,288	9·1	13
1878	437,158	7·6	9
1881	311,961	6·1	13
1884	549,990	9·7	24
1887	763,128	10·1	11
1890	1,427,298	19·7	35
1893	1,786,738	23·2	44
1898	2,107,076	27·2	56
1903	3,010,771	31·7	81
1907	3,259,020	28·9	43
1912	4,250,329	34·8	110

The Reichstag is composed of 397 members. If the Social Democrats were represented in proportion to their vote of 1912 they would have 138 members.

BIBLIOGRAPHY.

ENGLISH.

Ferdinand Lassalle as Social Reformer. E. BERNSTEIN. 1893. Sonnenschein. 2s. 6d.

Ferdinand Lassalle. G. BRANDES. 1911. Heinemann. 6s. net.

Karl Marx : his Life and Work. JOHN SPARGO. 1910. National Labor Press. 8s. 6d.

The Evolution of Modern Germany. W. H. DAWSON. 1908. Unwin. 21s. net.

Evolutionary Socialism. E. BERNSTEIN. 1909. I.L.P. 1s. 6d. and 1s. net.

Modern Socialism as Set Forth by Socialists in their Speeches, Writings, and Programs. R. C. K. ENSOR. 1907. Harper. 5s., 2s., and 1s. net.

German Social Democracy. BERTRAND RUSSELL. 1896. King. 3s. 6d.

History of Socialism. THOMAS KIRKUP. 4th ed. 1909. Black.
7s. 6d.
Socialists at Work. R. HUNTER. 1908. Macmillan. 6s. 6d. net.
German Socialism and Ferdinand Lassalle. W. H. DAWSON. 1891.
Sonnenschein. O.P.
Bismarck and State Socialism. W. H. DAWSON. 1890. Sonnen-
schein. 2s. 6d.
Socialism and the Social Movement. W. SOMBART. 1909. Dent.
3s. 6d.
Manifesto of the Communist Party. K. MARX and F. ENGELS.
1888. W. Reeves. 2d.
The Working Man's Program. FERDINAND LASSALLE. 1884.
Modern Press. 6d.
The Social Revolution and On the Morrow of the Revolution.
K. KAUTSKY. 1903. Twentieth Century Press. 6d.
Socialism : a Critical Analysis. O. D. SKELTON. 1911. Constable.
6s. net.
My Life. AUGUST BEBEL. 1912. Unwin. 7s. 6d. net.

GERMAN.

Unsere Ziele. AUGUST BEBEL. Mk. 0.75.
Der Revisionismus in der Sozialdemokratie. E. BERNSTEIN. Mk.
0.75.
Geschichte der Berliner Arbeiter Bewegung. E. BERNSTEIN. 3
Bände. Mk. 19.50.
Das Erfurter Programm in seinem grundsätzlichen Teil. K.
KAUTSKY. Mk. 2.
Grundsätze und Forderungen der Sozialdemokratie. K. KAUTSKY
und B. SCHÖNLAUK. Mk. 0.50.
Protokolle der Parteitage (Reports of Annual Party Conferences).
From Mk. 0.25 to Mk. 2.50. [*Invaluable to students of the
movement.*]
Ferdinand Lassalle. Reden und Schriften, herausgegeben von E.
BERNSTEIN. 3 Bände. Mk. 14.50.
Aus meinem Leben. AUGUST BEBEL. Mk. 5.
Wilhelm Liebknecht, sein Leben und Wirken. Mk. 1.50.
Geschichte der deutschen Sozialdemokratie. F. MEHRING. 4
Bände. Mk. 20.
Das Kommunal Programm der Sozialdemokratie Preussens. PAUL
HIRSCH. Mk. 3.
Die bürgerlichen Parteien des deutschen Reichstags. L. FRANK.
Mk. 1.

(*The above can be had from the Vorwärts Buchhandlung, Berlin.*)

Die politischen Parteien. F. NAUMANN. Buchverlag der Hilfe,
Berlin. Mk. 2.
Die Heutige Sozialdemokratie. R. BRUNHUBER. 1906. Fischer,.
Jena. Mk. 2.

Fabian Tract No. 170. |

PROFIT-SHARING AND CO-PARTNERSHIP: A FRAUD & A FAILURE?

By EDWARD R. PEASE.

Published and sold by the Fabian Society,
3 Clement's Inn, Strand, London, W.C.
April 1913.   Price 1d.

Profit-Sharing and Co-Partnership :

A fraud and a failure?

THE capitalist employer as a factor in the machinery of production is a comparatively modern phenomenon. The English landlord is as old as England : the princely merchant venturer appeared in the sixteenth and seventeenth centuries, but he was a buyer and seller of goods and not in the main an employer of labor. It was only about a century ago that the capitalist manufacturer, the wealthy owner of huge works employing thousands of "hands," began to emerge, with the steam engine which was the author of his being.

And the curious thing is that no sooner had he made his appearance than the best of our social thinkers set themselves to discover how he could be eliminated. Nobody really welcomed him : nobody wholly admired him : whilst the thinkers and dreamers began to devise schemes for getting rid of him altogether.

Robert Owen, himself one of the foremost of the cotton-capitalists, spent his later years in planning, crudely and vaguely, his ideal communities at New Harmony, Queenwood, and elsewhere, whose basic principle was the production of wealth without the intervention of the employer—organized communities which should own their capital in common, and where the profit on the capital employed would go to those who did the work.

Co-operative Associations of Producers.

After him, in England, came the Christian Socialists, Maurice, Kingsley and Ludlow, whose ideal was a sort of peaceful Syndicalism, a society composed of co-operative producers, groups of men living the individual life of citizens but all possessing shares in the machines they worked, whereby the interests of capital and labor would be completely harmonized, because the laborer would always be a capitalist and the capitalist a laborer. All these projects were plans for eliminating the capitalist and distributing his profits, obviously vastly in excess of the value of his services to society, amongst the workers, who again were as obviously underpaid for their all-important share in the process of production. Owen and the Christian Socialists were at any rate whole-hearted in their plans for the reform of the system of distribution ; their intentions were excellent ; they failed because they did not recognize that the capitalist director of industry performs a necessary function : labor by itself is in practice insufficiently supplied with capital and is inexpert in the art of management. Co-operative productive societies had the advantage of magnificent advertisement, but this did not compensate for inadequate capital and a form of organization extremely difficult to manage. The employer, driven by the competition of his rivals, must make profits his first concern. He can dismiss inefficient workmen ; put his men on short time or order wholesale discharges when business is slack, and, subject to the risks of a strike, reduce wages when profits decline. For the manager of a co-operative production concern (and *à fortiori*, of any Communistic community), who is the servant of the men he superintends, such drastic measures, at times vital for commercial salvation, are well-nigh impossible.

Hence co-operative production, organized on the basis of an association of producers, is a feeble plant, and half a century of active propaganda leaves it as incapable as ever to cope with the other forms of industrial enterprise.

The Advent of Profit-Sharing.

Realizing this difficulty, a new idea presented itself to certain well-meaning capitalists, who recognized the social defencelessness of their position and sought some way of salvation which should not lead to commercial destruction.

Let the capitalist keep his control and provide the capital as of old ; but let him share out a part of his surplus profits, voluntarily, as an act of grace, amongst the workpeople who create his wealth. Here surely is a solution to the age-long antagonism of labor and capital. Let one side contribute capital and organizing ability and in return receive interest at a reasonable rate, and an agreed sum as wages of management ; let the other get their weekly wage for their work as of old ; when times are reasonably prosperous there will still be a balance left, which can be divided, on terms to be arranged, between owners and workers. All will then be partakers in the profits of industry ; industrial warfare will be replaced by industrial peace ; and the paternal employer surrounded by his contented and loyal workpeople will reproduce in the industrial world the happy picture of the kindly landlord and devoted tenantry which existed or was supposed to exist throughout Merrie England in the good days of old.

Profit-Sharing Good for Employers.

But the introduction of this millennium had to be set about in a different manner from that appropriate to co-operative undertakings. Owen and Maurice had to convert the working classes ; the re-organisation of society was to grow up from below. Well-intentioned friends might help, but the workers themselves were to act. In profit-sharing, on the other hand, the employer takes the lead ; it rests with him to formulate the scheme ; the profits are his, and he alone can consent to share them. Therefore the appeal must be attuned to his ears, and the trap baited with lures which will attract his appetite. Hence we find that the promoters of profit-sharing make haste to explain that the capitalist employer has everything to gain and nothing whatever to lose by the new panacea. He is to share out his profits amongst his men, no doubt, but all the bread he casts upon the waters of labor will come back to him forthwith bearing abundant increase.

"It is related that when John Marshall of Leeds was showing Robert Owen over his mills he remarked, 'If my people were to be careful and avoid waste they might save me £4,000 a year.' Owen replied, 'Well, why don't you give them £2,000 to do it? and then you would be richer by £2,000 a year.'"[*] That is the key-note. Share the profits with the men, but see that they themselves produce extra profits which will more than cover their "shares."

The picture drawn in all innocence by the advocates of profit-sharing is in truth most alluring to the intelligent capitalist. By a neat re-arrangement he is to get :—

1. Additional profits on his capital, since only a *part* of the savings of extra zeal and care is to be returned as dividend on wages to the workpeople.

2. His hands are to be loyal, contented, diligent, trustworthy and better paid, and this last, according to modern economics, is in itself a source of profit. Good pay means good work.

3. The trade union agitator is to be kept outside the door : no strikes, no organized demands for shorter hours, better wages, improved working rules. All chance that his men will go out on a sympathetic strike, a catastrophe the good employer justly fears and excusably resents, is averted. No labor unrest will disturb his oasis of industrial peace.

4. A saving of supervision, and reduction of all those worries incidental to bad work, waste of material, and industrial in-efficiency. The employer is often an artist in production : quite apart from mere profits, he prefers to see his work done properly ; waste annoys him for its own sake ; com-plaints from customers of bad work touch his sense of honor as well as his pocket. All these will be averted when every workman is a foreman to his fellows, each interested in saving material, in devising little plans for doing things better and cheaper, and each on the look out that no one of the scores or hundreds of co-partners wastes the time for which he is paid and so diminishes the margin of profit in which all alike are to share.

All these advantages will yield the profit-sharing enterprise profits substantially in excess of what otherwise would have been earned. Part only need be ceded to the workers ; the other part falls to the employer as the reward of his enlightened self-interest.

Surely here is a project for making the best of both worlds ! Let us now consider its history.

Statistics.

"Co-partnership in Industry," by Charles Carpenter, Chairman of the South Metropolitan Gas Company,[†] gives a chronological list of "over two hundred notices of attempts in the direction of improved relations between capitalist and laborer. . . . . Most of the schemes

---

[*] D. F. Schloss, " Methods of Industrial Remuneration," 3rd edn., 1898, p. 255 n.

[†] Co-partnership Publishers, 79 Southampton Row, London. 1912. 6d. net.

have come to an end. In some cases the business has ceased to exist or has [changed hands]. Sometimes the scheme has failed because the workmen failed to see its possibilities . . . the great majority of failures are in connection with cash bonus schemes. . . ." The prefatory note adds more about the failures and their causes which we have not space to quote, but adds not a word about the successes !

The first recorded scheme dates from 1829. Three were started in 1831-2, two in the fifties, one in 1864, sixteen in 1865-7, and then any number up to half a dozen yearly till 1889, when the active propaganda of Professor Sedley Taylor and the industrial unrest of the dock strike period brought the yearly total to twenty or more. By 1893 the boom was exhausted, and only three cases are recorded, and the good trade years 1905 and 1906 yield not a single case. Since then the movement has been looking up, though the crop of 1911 is no more than five.* If we take the Board of Trade 1912 List for the period 1865-1896, that is from the beginning (omitting an Irish scheme started in 1829) up to 15 years ago, 177 schemes have been started, of which 134 have come to an end, whilst 43 remain in operation, and the fate of 2 is unknown. In the four years 1889-1892, when profit-sharing had a boom, 87 schemes were started, of which 66 have stopped, 2 cannot be traced, and only 19 are known to exist still. The average duration of the 76 schemes formed between 1867 and 1890 inclusive which have ceased and of which precise particulars are known was about 9 years and 9 months.

What is the explanation of this slow progress constantly dogged by failure? Why does this attractive scheme, apparently beneficial to all concerned, end so constantly in disappointment? Where is the flaw in the reasoning? How is it that ardent advocacy of benevolent enthusiasts such as Sedley Taylor, the blessings of the economists—the professorial exponents of the science seem nearly all to regard profit sharing with approval†—and the active propaganda of the Labor Co-partnership Association, whose annual meeting of 1908 for example was addressed by the Right Hon. A. J. Balfour, Mr. Christopher (later Lord) Furness, and Professor A. C. Pigou, all come to so little ?

What is Profit ?

In order to answer this riddle we must more closely examine exactly what is meant by profit-sharing. In the first place, what is profit? The answer to this is, in effect, under the modern industrial system, whatever you please. The return on capital embarked in industry is quite properly divided into two parts, the first called interest, say three to four per cent., the rate which the investor can obtain from safe securities, and which is therefore the minimum he

* Since this was printed the Board of Trade Report on Profit-sharing and Labor Co-partnership (Cd. 6496, 1912) has been published, which gives a list of 133 schemes in operation, 164 abandoned schemes, and 3 doubtfuls. The list includes nearly 100 cases omitted by Mr. Carpenter, and should be consulted if more complete figures are desired.

† An exception is Professor J. W. Ashley of Birmingham : see his Preface to Edward Cadbury's "Experiments in Industrial Organization." Longmans. 1912.

expects from any enterprise; and next, the amount, whatever it may be, in excess of this sum, which capital embarked in risky enterprises—and all business is risky—obtains. The latter is profit in the narrower sense. But there are two sorts of capital commonly dealt with in business. The one is the actual things, whether money or machinery or goods, which are used in any enterprise. These are the tangible assets of a company and this is the capital which earns the profit. The other is the nominal capital, usually, but not always, considerably in excess of this amount, either because the company has purchased the tangible assets as a going concern, along with the goodwill, and often has paid a price, in shares, far in excess of its actual cost, or because there are promotion expenses, legal expenses, commissions, discounts, and services of all kinds, which may be greatly in excess of the genuine minimum. In one sense this does not greatly matter to anybody. The capital of a company is, in many cases, no more than a method of determining at what rate the profits shall be divided. After the company is started it makes little difference whether a profit of £1,000 is paid away to the owners of 10,000 £1 shares, earning ten per cent., or 10,000 £2 shares, earning five per cent. But since the shareable profit is calculated according to the rate and not according to the amount, it makes all the difference in the world in the case of a company which shares with its workpeople everything over four per cent. If the company is capitalized at £10,000, the profit over four per cent. in which the workers share is £600: if it is capitalized at £20,000, the shareable profit is only £200. Now it may be positively stated that there is no definite basis whatever on which a going concern turned into a company should be capitalized. Occasionally the owners of a business have sold it to the public at much below its true value, so that the shares (as those of Bryant & May, Limited, for example) have stood at a very large premium ever since the day of issue. More often company promoters sell at too high a price, so that the shares quickly drop to a discount and remain there ever after. But if the workers are to share in the profits after a minimum rate of dividend is paid, they will want to be satisfied in every case that the nominal capital of the company is not in excess of its real value; and, on the other hand, should profit-sharing become, as its promoters hope, a widespread custom, a real factor in the industrial system, any business man who desired to conform to the letter of the principle whilst escaping its consequences, has only to capitalize his company on such a generous scale as to avoid making profits above the minimum rate, and so to escape the obligation of sharing anything with his employees.

What is "Sharing"?

If profits are difficult to determine, "sharing" is equally vague and shifting. The varieties in the method of sharing might be described as infinite, if the total number of cases were sufficient to justify the appellation.

The essence of the whole thing is that it is a gift from the employer to the employed ; and obviously the gift may take any form that commends itself to the employer, may be in cash or in shares, or in a provident fund, or an old age pension, payable at once or on departure, to all employees or only those who have served a minimuu period ; may be dependent on non-membership of a trade union or on contracting for a term of service ; may be forfeited by a strike, and so on.

Then as to the amount payable, we find there is no fixed plan. There is usually a minimum rate of interest on capital before the shareable profit is reached ; depreciation is usually provided for, and sometimes reserves to whatever amount the employer thinks fit ! *

The minimum interest may be cumulative (i.e., payable out of good years if passed in bad ones) or it may not. Finally, there is no fixed proportion in which the surplus, whatever it be, is divided between the workers. Profit-sharing is, in fact, the antithesis of collective bargaining. The profit shared out is a gift horse, and the workmen have no right to look it in the mouth. Clearly, then, with so diverse and elusive an arrangement, the causes of failure may be innumerable ; and the thing itself may vary from a genuine and generous scheme by which an employer hands over to his workpeople everything above a legitimate salary to himself as manager —there have been such cases—to the dishonest dodge of a clever hypocrite for getting bigger profit from his hands in exchange for promises that never materialise.

Co-partnership.

The early profit-sharers adopted the crude und unsuccessful method of cash bonus, that is a percentage of profits payable in cash. But it seemed a pity to let good money go out of the concern. Why not keep the money, encourage thrift, turn the workpeople into small, very small, shareholders, and, in addition, drop the old name, with its melancholy associations, and call the new variety Co-partnership ?

This novel plan involves, it is true, some concession to the workpeople. They are to be placed, after a fashion, on a level with the proprietors ; they are to have a voice, if only a small one, in the management ; they may even be allowed a director or two on the board. On the other hand, their alliance with the company is cemented more firmly than ever. The cash bonus is soon paid and soon spent. The slowly acquired share is a stake in the concern which cannot be pulled up without effort. With every workman tied up to such a stake, industrial rebellion is improbable, and even labor unrest will fail to disturb.

---

* A famous scheme, Henry Briggs, Son & Co.'s Collieries, which divided £40,151 amongst its employees in nine years to 1874, was terminated partly because the men struck against a reduction of wages and partly because in 1873 £30,000 was taken from profits for the purchase of a new mine, and large sums were placed to reserve, in all of which the workers considered themselves entitled to share. (Report, etc., Cd: 6496, pp. 43-6.)

It must here be remarked that the term co-partnership is nowadays applied to two other forms of industrial enterprise with which this paper is not concerned. The housebuilding companies of co-partnership tenants are schemes whereby persons combine as tenants to erect and then purchase collectively out of their savings the houses they occupy. This industrial device is, in fact, a species by itself, altogether distinct from the profit-sharing co-partnery dealt with in this paper, and equally distinct from the "self-governing workshop," which used to be called a co-operative productive company, and is now frequently classed as co-partnership. When the capital of a company is owned, in whole or to a substantial extent, by the workers in the establishment, and the control of the concern is vested in them and their elected delegates, the profits belong to them to share amongst themselves in such a manner as by their rules they determine.

The self-governing workshop has its merits and demerits, which are not considered in this paper. But although it is often classed as co-partnership, it is, in fact, a very different sort of industrial enterprise, and to describe by one term the South Metropolitan Gas Company and some little group of struggling operatives formed into a co-operative society to make boots or bind books simply leads to confusion of thought.

The pioneer of co-partnership profit-sharing was

The South Metropolitan Gas Company.

The strange history of this company's relations with its men sums up the pros and cons of profit-sharing. The matter was one of acute controversy at the time and is so, in a sense, still. We cannot therefore be accused of unfairness if we quote at length the account of it given by Mr. Aneurin Williams, Hon. Treasurer of the Labor Co-partnership Association, in his pamphlet "A Better Way." *

Speaking of cases in which the workman becomes a shareholder, he says :

"Certainly the most striking example of this kind of partnership is to be found in the South Metropolitan Gas Company in London, a business with a capital of £8,325,340, and employing some 5,459 workmen ; and there can hardly be a better introduction to the subject than the history of what that company has done.† It will be remembered how, in the winter of 1889-90, it was engaged in a life and death struggle with the National Union of Gasworkers and General Laborers. It was just at that time that the organizations of unskilled labor in this country were beginning to feel their strength and to try, no doubt in a somewhat blind and desperate way, to gain for their members some of those advantages which had been so successfully won during the preceding generation by the great unions of skilled workers. The

* Labor Co-partnership Association, 6 Bloomsbury Square, London, n. d., ? 1911, price 2d.

† See also Sir George Livesey's "Paper on the Profit-Sharing Scheme of the South Metropolitan Gas Company." (London: Labor Co-partnership Association.)

late Sir George Livesey, for so long chairman of the South Metropolitan Gas Company, has given more than one graphic account of the danger the company found itself in, of losing altogether control over the management of its own business. The company, upon the initiative of Sir George (then Mr.) Livesey and of his father before him, had over a considerable period of years adopted various schemes for the special benefit of its employees, and had also considered some scheme of profit-sharing. In 1889, therefore, the directors decided to carry out this idea, with a view to more closely identifying the workers' interests with those of the company, and of avoiding the friction and great losses to which they found themselves more and more subject. They therefore offered the workers a profit-sharing scheme under certain conditions. By law, the amount of profit which this company may distribute to its shareholders rises as the price at which it sells gas to the public falls. When gas is 3s. 1d. per 1,000 cubic feet, the company may pay, if it earns it, a dividend equal to ten per cent. per annum upon its old unconverted stock, or four per cent. on its present converted stock. For every penny per 1,000 cubic feet which the price of gas is reduced below 3s. 1d. the rate of dividend which may be paid rises 2s. 8d. per cent on its converted stock. Thus, at 3s. per 1,000, £4 2s. 8d. per cent. may be paid: at 2s. 6d. per 1,000 £4 18s. 8d. per cent., and so on. Thus the interests of the public and the shareholders both lie in cheapening the selling price of gas. The company now offered to its employees of every class a similar arrangement, which, as since modified, is that for every 1d. the price of gas falls below 3s. 1d. per 1,000 cubic feet a bonus of 1½s. per cent. is paid on their wages or salaries. This, however, was subject to the condition, among others, that each person accepting the profit-sharing scheme should sign an agreement to serve the company for one year. These agreements were to be dated on different days, so that a strike would become practically impossible, inasmuch as the workers could only strike all together by an illegal conspiracy to violate their agreements. To these agreements the trade union took violent objection, saying at the same time, however, that they did not object to a scheme of profit-sharing under fair conditions. The result, as is well known, was a great strike, its end being a complete victory for the company. The places of the strikers were supplied by new men, and the best terms they could get in the end were that they would be taken back if and as vacancies arose. I may mention, incidentally, that the Labor Co-partnership Association, for which I am now writing, offered its friendly services during this lamentable conflict, and I am told all terms might have been, if indeed they were not, satisfactorily arranged, except the question of re-instating the strikers and dismissing the newcomers. This was a point of honor on one side and the other, and an absolute split took place.

"When, however, the strike was all over, it might have been hoped that things would settle down into harmony. Unfortunately, the most prominent labor leader concerned made a speech in which he threatened that the next time the men would not give notice, but would lay down their tools on the minute. The company retaliated by posting a notice that no member of the trade union concerned would be employed, though Sir George Livesey told the Labor Commission this notice had not been strictly adhered to. However, every workman accepting the profit-sharing scheme was, until 1902, required to declare himself not a member of that trade union. Thus, and from other causes, the feud between the company and the trade union was continued. In 1902, however, the company at the suggestion of the Labor Co-partnership Association withdrew this restriction. It is no part of my duty here to try to apportion the blame for this lamentable state of affairs continuing over so many years. The company, no doubt, felt it absolutely necessary to keep control of its business, and to provide against the public calamity of South London being some night reduced to darkness, and thereby delivered over a prey to the worst elements of its population. On the other hand, in the absence of any other form of efficient protection (whether by the action of the State or otherwise), the trade union no doubt felt that to prevent the workers striking if necessary, and to prevent them joining the union of the trade, was to deliver them over helpless into the hands of their employers.

" It will be seen, therefore, that the South Metropolitan Gas Company is not in every respect a good instance of those better relations between capital and organized labor which we desire. It must, however, be carefully noted that, as between the company and those employed since the strike, the relations have left nothing to desire in the matter of good feeling. The ill feeling has been solely between the company and the trade union and its sympathisers. It should be pointed out also that though two unions were concerned in this quarrel, the company never denied the principle of trade unionism.

" For several years simple profit-sharing on the basis I have described went on. The workers were encouraged to leave their bonus on deposit with the company at four per cent. About one half of the money was so left, but by less than one half of the men. In 1894 the company was so satisfied with the results that it made a move forward, and offered to increase the rate of bonus by one half (i.e., from one per cent. to one and a half per cent. per penny on the price of gas) to those workmen who would agree to leave half their profit as shares in the company. For carrying out this plan trustees were appointed to purchase shares represented by the total of the small sums belonging to the employees. Each man became an independent shareholder when his stake in the company reached a nominal value of £5 stock,* costing at that time about £13, and yielding at that price about five per cent. to the investor. This development

---

* That is, old unconverted stock, equivalent to £12 10s. nominal of the present stock.

also was a great success, and in the years 1896-1897 the company took a further step and sought and obtained power from Parliament to add to its board of directors representatives of its employees. This power was somewhat later carried out : the manual workers who are shareholders now elect two directors, and the salaried staff who are shareholders one, while the ordinary shareholders elect six. Of course this gives the employees (who now hold shares and deposits to the value of about £401,038), an amount of representation on the directorate very largely in excess of the proportion of their shares. It was, however, felt that while shareholding must be a condition precedent to a voice in the affairs of the company, it was not the only interest of the employees which ought to be represented on the directorate. In addition to the partnership arrangements, and partly growing out of them, there are other arrangements, for a conciliation board, for social purposes, for enquiries into such accidents as occur, for provident purposes, and so forth, in which the representatives of the company and of the employees act together for their mutual advantage. Sir George Livesey declared again and again that the large sum of money (£427,000) which had been paid over the period of eighteen years in the form of profit to the employees has not meant a penny reduction of profit to the shareholders, inasmuch as the workers have more than earned it by their better and more economical working. It should be clearly understood that the worker shareholder remains just as liable to dismissal and in every way just as subject to the officials of the company as ever he was under the wage system pure and simple.

"This is by far the biggest experiment in partnership between capital and labor which has been carried out in this country, and it is certainly a highly successful one, in spite of the deplorable conflict between the company and the trade union."

Co-partnership in Gasworks.

The example of the South Metropolitan Gas Company has been followed, slowly at first, and rapidly in recent years, so that in 1912 there were 33 companies working on this system. But there is a strange and very obvious reason why co-partnership succeeds in gas concerns and in gas alone. All gas companies are established by Act of Parliament, and all are regulated by the peculiar sliding scale system already mentioned. The Act fixes a basic price, in the case of the Gas Light and Coke Company of London of 3s. 2d. per 1,000 feet in 1910. The company is forbidden by law to increase its dividend above the minimum unless it reduces the price to the customers. For every penny reduction in the price of gas the shareholders may receive an extra quarter per cent. dividend.

The effects of this are complicated. The company is always apt to be loaded up with profits which it cannot make use of. Money is sometimes no object to it. When profits grow large enough, roughly speaking four fifths of them have to be conceded to the consumer in reductions of price and only one fifth can be paid to the shareholders. What above all things the company desires is reductions in the cost of production, which will allow the price to be reduced and the dividend to be increased. Moreover, in view of this arrangement, the law takes very good care that there is no hocus pocus about the capital account. There is no chance for the shareholders to get allotments of valuable stock for less than the market price, and anything like "watering" the capital is out of the question.* If a gas company wants more capital, it must notify the local authority, advertise in the local press, and sell the new stock at public auction. The whole business must be carried out under the public eye, and full returns rendered to the Government of every pound of capital received and every penny of dividend paid.

The Gas Light and Coke Company of London, probably the largest gas company in the world, pays a bonus to its men on the price of gas, which corresponds to the dividend payable, thus :

Price of Gas.	Bonus.	Dividend.
3s. 2d.	nil	£4 0 0 per cent. per annum.
3s. 1d.	½ per cent.	£4 2 8† „ „
3s.	1 per cent.	£4 5 4† „ „

And so on, the bonus increasing at a higher rate till it reaches :

2s. 6d.	5 per cent.	£4 17 4 per cent. per annum.

which is the figure at present.

Lastly, in the gas industry, the operatives are by law virtually compelled to give long notice of any proposed strike. For reasons of public safety Parliament enacted, at a time when gas was the sole illuminant, that for gasworkers to leave work in breach of their contract of employment and without due notice should be a criminal offence punishable by as much as three months hard labor.

Gas companies and their employees are therefore in a very peculiar legal position, and it is probably owing to this, together with the legal monopoly which frees them from the risks of competition and makes regular profits virtually a certainty, and also to their necessary geographical isolation, that profit-sharing has, for the moment at any rate, succeeded in this industry and in this alone.

"The Treaty of Hartlepools." ‡

The most famous of recent co-partnership schemes was started in the autumn of 1908 by the late Lord (then Sir Christopher) Furness in his Hartlepools Shipyards.

Annoyed by what he regarded as needless friction with trade unions, he made a public offer either to sell his works to the unions

* "Watering" by Act of Parliament does not matter. The Gas Light and Coke Company has £14,451,145 of "water" in its £28,632,925 capital, but the amount is recorded in every balance sheet for the information of all concerned.

† These figures are temporarily modified by a special provision for redemption of stock.

‡ See *The Magazine of Commerce* (Souvenir Co-partnery Edition), December, 1908, 155 Cheapside, E.C.

or to establish the following scheme in the Middleton and Harbour Dockyards of Irvine's Shipbuilding and Dry Docks Company, Limited.

He proposed to create 50,000 four per cent. preference shares, with a first charge on the profits of the company, to be called Employees' Shares, and to be held by persons employed in the yards. These were to be allotted to employees, and paid for by a five per cent. deduction from wages and by capitalizing the dividend. Profits, after providing for this preference interest, were to be allocated to pay a five per cent. cumulative dividend on ordinary capital, and the directors were to have a free hand to put away reserves, depreciation and development funds. Anything left was to be divided pro rata on the ordinary and the employees' capital.

Anybody leaving the service of the company " would be able to sell his shares " at an assessed price, or at the market value, to other employees only.

The wages and conditions of labor were to remain matters of negotiation between trade unions and the directors, and the holders of employees' shares were to have no voice at all in the management of the company and no right to attend the shareholders' meetings.

But a Works Council was established, consisting of delegates of the employers and employed, with power to advise on anything in dispute ; and a proposal was even made, not very definitely, that trade union officials from outside might be co-opted to this council as aldermen.

The whole scheme involved a complete recognition of trade unions. The treaty was referred to the unions concerned, discussed by them, and finally accepted by a vote, in the aggregate, of ten to one.

It was tried for a year and then it failed. The men resolved, by a decisive vote, to abandon it. What precisely weighed with them in coming to this decision must necessarily be a matter of conjecture, but the chief complaint appears to have arisen from the fact that although shipbuilding is a very irregular trade, and men constantly change from one firm to another, by this scheme each move from the Furness yards involved the sale of Furness stock.

Moreover, apart from the Works Council, which had no essential connection with the co-partnership scheme, it is difficult to see what there was particularly attractive in the proposal. The men were kindly permitted to purchase out of their wages a four per cent. preference stock at par, with the chance of a further dividend, if earned, but with no voice in the management of the business. It is, to say the least, doubtful if the company could have raised capital so cheaply in the market or, in other words, if the market value of the stock offered would be as high as the price asked for it.*

* The Irvine Shipbuilding Company is a subsidiary company in the Furness, Withy, & Company combine. The latter paid ten per cent. in 1905, fifteen per cent. in 1906, ten per cent. in 1907, five per cent. in 1908, 1909 and 1910 (during which the scheme was in operation), and seven and a half per cent. in 1911.

We do not suggest that the scheme was, in fact, a dodge for getting cheap capital, but undoubtedly it was not anything in the nature of a gift to the workmen. They were asked to pay full value for what they got. The only concession was in the form of a method of purchase by small instalments, which was no doubt troublesome and expensive to the company.

Anyway, the scheme, in spite of the glamor of its inception and the ability and good faith of its founder, was quickly added to the long roll of co-partnership failures.

A Limited Sphere.

Destitution cannot be remedied by doles, and almsgiving is no cure for poverty. But it does not follow from this that no one should help a neighbor in distress or that the squire should be blamed if he gives Christmas gifts to the laborers on his estate.

Profit-sharing is no remedy for the poverty of the workers, and offers no solution of the problems of modern industry, no sleeping-draught for industrial unrest. None the less, it cannot be said that all profit-sharing is bad, far less that all employers who adopt it are pious frauds. It is essentially a gift, and when an employer resolves to give his workpeople a supplement to their regular wages calculated on a fixed basis, no one can complain, provided that it is a genuine gift taken from his legitimate profits and not earned by their own excess of labor and, above all, that it does not destroy their class solidarity. This last condition bars out all staple and all organized trades. Few trade unionists do, and none should, countenance any such proposal. Cotton and coal and iron workers should have nothing to do with such schemes. But the case is otherwise with unskilled employees in some isolated works, say a jam factory in a remote village, or the laborers on a farm, where trade unionism is, apparently, impracticable.

The desire of the idealist, that the worker should take an interest in his work, and feel himself to be not a mere hand employed by a master but a co-partner, a part owner of the concern, is well founded, and indeed is largely the root of all industrial co-operation. To this extent the idea of profit-sharing is sound, and appeals to every intelligent student of social conditions. Provided, then, that the share of profit given by the employer is a genuine gift for which no return is asked either in extra exertion or in "loyalty," and that the solidarity of labor is not broken, the benevolent employer may properly adopt this method of benefitting his workpeople, just as the landlord may properly distribute blankets and beef to the cottagers on his estate. But neither of them must pretend that his beneficence is a solution of any social problem.*

* The statistics of profit-sharing in all the concerns in which it has been tried are significant. The "profit" shared (after the deduction of rent, interest on capital, wages of management, depreciation and reserves) has averaged about 10 per cent of the amount given in wages; and the worker's share has been, on an average, just about 5 per cent. addition to his wages, or about a farthing an hour! Out of a total national income in 1912 of about 2,100 millions, the total of wages was under 800 millions. Universal profit-sharing might have made it 840 millions out of 2,100.

The Causes of Failure.

Probably if the truth be known profit-sharing schemes have failed because the workmen have studied too carefully the publications of the advocates of the system. The fraud on the workers is too palpable. The men have found out that they are like the dog fed off his own tail. They earn the bonus (if there is any), and their employer returns them a fraction of what they have produced. Moreover they may easily earn it and yet receive none of it. Profits depend on the trading skill of the employer and the chances of the market, even more than on the special diligence of the men. The return they receive for their extra exertions is determined by factors over which they have no control. One or two miscalculated contracts may deprive them of all the profits for which they have labored. They properly object to let their remuneration depend on the skill or luck of the heads of the business.

Working Class Solidarity.

But the final and conclusive objection to profit-sharing is that it necessarily tends to working-class disintegration. Wherever the capitalist system continues, dividing society into private employers on one side and private employees on the other, the employer and workman must be armed for a fight, even if, like the Great Powers of Europe, they maintain cordial relations for generations. Organization alone places the worker on the same plane as his employer. All intelligent workmen recognize that industrial solidarity is the basis of all working class progress ; and profit-sharing is, intentionally or incidentally, destructive of this solidarity. The workers must be free to combine in trade unions and in federations of unions in whatever manner they think fit, and must be able to strike as a trade, as an industry, or indeed as a class, as often as is necessary for the protection and advancement of their interests. Profit-sharing splits up trades and industries into coteries of privileged workers, each group with interests different from, and perhaps antagonistic to, the others. In some cases, as has been already indicated, profit-sharing and co-partnership schemes have been adopted deliberately with the object of smashing up trade unionism ; in other cases it has been recommended to employers because of its value for this purpose; in all cases it has this effect, unless there is no solidarity to disintegrate, no unionism to destroy.

The employees of a profit-sharing firm are bound to their employer more closely than to their fellows. It is their interest to stand aloof from the industrial combat, because they have privileges to lose or a tiny share of capital to consider.

Collective bargaining, the common rule, trade union wages and conditions, are the protection of the workers against sweating and oppression in all their forms ; and in these safeguards lie their hope for material advances in wages, and ultimately an increase in their share in the product of industry and their control over its management.

Profit-sharing and co-partnership may be properly called a "piffling palliative," which assumes the permanent continuance of the antithesis between employer and employed. This relation is out of date and no longer in accord with our sense of the fitness of things. There can be no true fellowship between the employer and his hands, the master and his men. We have come to see the truth in the old command, "Call no man master." In the industrial organization of the future there will be no master, but all will be servants one of another, and yet all owners of the wealth which together they create.

That is the fellowship of the future, which, as Morris said, is life.

LIST OF BOOKS.

Incomparably the best collection of British data is :

Report on Profit-sharing and Labor Co-partnership in the United Kingdom. Board of Trade (Labor Department), Cd. 6496. 1912. 8½d. (Chiefly compiled by the late DAVID F. SCHLOSS.) It contains an elaborate bibliography.

A particularly valuable analysis is to be found in :

D. F. SCHLOSS. Methods of Industrial Remuneration. 3rd Edn. Williams & Norgate. 1907. 3s. 6d.

Publications of the Labor Co-partnership Association, 6 Bloomsbury Square, London, W.C., e.g., A Better Way : some facts and suggestions as to introducing the partnership of labor with capital into established businesses, by ANEURIN WILLIAMS, M.A. (? 1911), 2d., and Annual Reports, Leaflets, etc.

Co-partnership in Industry. By CHARLES CARPENTER, M.Inst. C.E., Chairman of the South Metropolitan Gas Company. Co-partnership Publishers, Limited, 73 Southampton Row, London, W.C. 1912. 6d. net.

EARLIER BOOKS.

BUSHILL, T. W. Profit-sharing and the Labor Question. Methuen. 1893. *O.p.*

GILMAN, N. P. Profit-sharing. Macmillan. 1892. 7s. 6d.

LLOYD, H. D. Labor Co-partnership in Great Britain and Ireland. Harper. 1898. 5s.

TAYLOR, SEDLEY. Profit-sharing. Paul. 1884. *O.p.*

Fabian Tract No. 171.

The Nationalization of Mines and Minerals Bill.

BY

HENRY H. SCHLOESSER.

PUBLISHED AND SOLD BY

THE FABIAN SOCIETY.

PRICE ONE PENNY.

LONDON

THE FABIAN SOCIETY, 3 CLEMENT'S INN, STRAND, W.C.

JULY 1913.

THE FABIAN SOCIETY supplies to Trade Union Branches, Socialist Societies, Co-operative Societies, Labor Representation Committees, Trade Councils, Labor and Liberal Clubs, C. O. S. and C. S. U. Branches, Reading Societies, and Study Classes,

BOXES OF BOOKS

on Political, Historical, Economic and Social subjects: both up-to-date new books, and well-established classical works. Each box contains from twenty to twenty-five volumes, selected from a library of 5,000 books, in accordance with the desires of the subscribers. For ten shillings a year, any subscribing society is kept supplied with a box for a year, and four changes of box are allowed. The Society has had eighteen years' experience in arranging these libraries, and has now over two hundred boxes in use.

For prospectus and application form write to
THE FABIAN SOCIETY, 3 CLEMENT'S INN, STRAND, LONDON, W.C.

THE FABIAN SOCIALIST SERIES.
VOLUMES NOW READY.

I. SOCIALISM AND RELIGION.
CONTENTS: (1) Christian Socialism, by the Rev. Stewart D. Headlam. (2) Socialism and Christianity, by the Rev. Percy Dearmer. (3) Socialism and the Teaching of Christ, by the Rev. John Clifford. (4) A Word of Remembrance and Caution to the Rich, by John Woolman.

II. SOCIALISM AND AGRICULTURE.
CONTENTS: (1) The Village and the Landlord, by Edward Carpenter. (2) State Aid to Agriculture, by T. S. Dymond. (3) The Secret of Rural Depopulation, by Lieut.-Col. D. C. Pedder. (4) The Revival of Agriculture, by the Fabian Society.

III. SOCIALISM AND INDIVIDUALISM.
CONTENTS: (1) The Difficulties of Individualism, by Sidney Webb. (2) The Moral Aspects of Socialism, by Sidney Ball. (3) The Impossibilities of Anarchism, by G. Bernard Shaw. (4) Public Service v. Private Expenditure, by Sir Oliver Lodge.

IV. THE BASIS AND POLICY OF SOCIALISM.
CONTENTS: (1) Facts for Socialists, by the Fabian Society. (2) Capital and Land by the Fabian Society. (3) Socialism: True and False, by Sidney Webb. (4) Twentieth Century Politics, by Sidney Webb.

V. THE COMMONSENSE OF MUNICIPAL TRADING.
By Bernard Shaw. With new Preface. "Whether you agree with it entirely or not, you are bound to admit its intellectual power and persuasive eloquence.

VI. SOCIALISM AND NATIONAL MINIMUM.
By Mrs. Sidney Webb, Miss B. L. Hutchins, and others.

VII. WASTAGE OF CHILD LIFE.
By J. Johnston, M.D. "Passing from one count to another, he puts together his huge indictment of national extravagance; showing also how the practice of thrift might ensure to the nation the possession of healthy and efficient citizens."—*Daily News.*

VIII. SOCIALISM AND SUPERIOR BRAINS: A Reply to Mr. Mallock.
By Bernard Shaw.

IX. THE THEORY AND PRACTICE OF TRADE UNIONISM.
By J. H. Greenwood. Preface by Sidney Webb.

The first four volumes consist of a revised, collected, and classified edition of some of the most valuable of the famous "Fabian Tracts" in a style more suitable for the general reading public. Each booklet is printed on good paper with good type, and is supplied in two forms, viz., in attractive wrappers at 6d. each, net, and in quarter cloth boards, gilt top, at 1/- each, net. Postage: 1d. and 2d. each, except for No. 5, 1½d. and 2d.

THE FABIAN SOCIETY, 3, CLEMENT'S INN, STRAND.

THE NATIONALIZATION OF MINES AND MINERALS BILL.

THE following draft Bill for the Nationalization of Mines and Minerals, prepared by the writer of this Tract on the instructions of the Executive Committee of the Miners' Federation of Great Britain, was adopted by the Annual Conference of that body at its meeting at Swansea in October 1912, and subsequently introduced by the Labor Party in the House of Commons.

As the first Bill prepared by a Trade Union for the " Nationalization " of its industry, the measure is one of no small interest. The Fabian Society accordingly publishes it in a convenient form, with the consent of the Executive Committee of the Miners' Federation, for public information.

The Bill is the Bill of the Labor Party and the Miners' Federation; the Fabian Society is responsible only for the notes which have been added for convenience of reference.

A Bill to Nationalize the Coal Mines and Minerals of the United Kingdom and to provide for the National Distribution and Sale of Coal.

WHEREAS it is expedient that the coal mines and coal of the United Kingdom should be taken into the possession of the State.

Be it enacted by the King's Most Excellent Majesty, by and with the advice and consent of the Lords Spiritual and Temporal and Commons in this present Parliament assembled, and by the authority of the same, as follows:

1.—MINISTER FOR MINES.

(1) There shall be a Minister for Mines to be appointed by His Majesty and to hold office during the pleasure of His Majesty.

(2) The Minister for Mines shall at the same time be capable of being elected to and of sitting in the Commons House of Parliament, and his office shall be deemed to be an office included in

Schedule H of the Representation of the People Act, 1867 ; Schedule H of the Representation of the People (Scotland) Act, 1868 ; and Schedule E of the Representation of the People (Ireland) Act, 1868.

(3) The Minister for Mines shall take the oath of allegiance and official oath, and shall be deemed to be included in the First Part of the Schedule to the Promissory Oaths Act, 1868.

(4) The Minister for Mines shall appoint one secretary, such assistant secretaries, and such other officers and servants as the Minister for Mines may with the sanction of the Treasury determine.

(5) There shall be paid to the Minister for Mines, out of money provided by Parliament, a salary at the rate of two thousand pounds a year, and to the secretary, assistant secretaries, officers, and servants such salaries or remuneration as the Treasury shall from time to time determine.

(6) All expenses incurred by the Minister for Mines under this Act, to such amount as may be sanctioned by the Treasury, shall be paid out of money provided by Parliament.

(7) The Minister for Mines shall have an official seal, which shall be officially and publicly noticed, and such seal shall be authenticated by the Minister or the secretary or one of the assistant secretaries, or some person authorized by the Minister for Mines to act on his behalf.

(8) Every document purporting to be an order, licence, or other instrument issued by the Minister for Mines, and to be sealed with his seal, authenticated in manner provided by this Act, or to be signed by the secretary or by one of the assistant secretaries, or any person authorized by the Minister for Mines to act on his behalf, shall be received in evidence and be deemed to be such order, licence, or other instrument without further proof, unless the contrary be shown.

(9) A certificate signed by the Minister for Mines that any order, licence, or other instrument purporting to be made or issued by him is so made or issued shall be conclusive evidence of the fact so certified.

(10) There shall be transferred and attached to the Minister for Mines such of the persons employed under any Government department in or about the execution of the powers and duties transferred by or in pursuance of this Act to the Minister for Mines as the Government department may with the sanction of the Treasury determine.

These are the usual formal clauses required for the establishment of a new Ministerial office. The salary (£2,000) proposed to be assigned to the Minister for Mines is the same as that now paid to the President of the Board of Education, the Chancellor of the Duchy of Lancaster, and the First Commissioner of Works and Buildings. It is less than that paid to the Postmaster-General (£2,500), and much less than that (£5,000) paid to the various Secretaries of State, the President of the Board of Trade, and the President of the Local Government Board.

2.—Transference of Coal Mines and Minerals to Minister for Mines.

On and after the appointed day :

(a) Every colliery and coal mine, whether in actual work or discontinued, or exhausted, or abandoned, and every shaft, pit, level, or inclined plane in course of being made or driven for commencing or opening any such colliery or coal mine, including every patent fuel plant, coke oven, coal washery, railway rolling stock, and all other works belonging to or connected with such colliery or coal mine, and every house belonging to the owners of any such colliery or coal mine which is occupied by workmen employed at such coal mine (all of which are herein included in the expression "coal mine") and ;

(b) All coal, anthracite, lignite, or other mineral used for fuel, whether at present being worked or not worked, or connected or not connected with any coal mine, beneath the surface of the ground (all of which are herein included in the expression "minerals")

shall be vested in and held by the Minister for Mines in his corporate capacity and his successors.

This "vesting" clause enables the Minister for Mines to enter into possession on the appointed day (see clause 18), without waiting to obtain separate conveyances from all the owners of all the various interests. For the compensation to owners, see clauses 4 to 7 ; and for its distribution among them, see clauses 7 and 11.

3.—Purchase of Coal Mines.

The Minister for Mines shall purchase the coal mines of the United Kingdom (other than those which are the property of the Crown at the time of the passing of this Act) at the price and in the manner provided by this Act. Provided always that the value of any minerals or right to work minerals or mineral way leave shall not be taken into account in computing such price, for all of which no compensation shall be paid.

According to the recent Commission on the subject, the coal supplies thus acquired are estimated to last 100 years in the North of England, and in the rest of the United Kingdom 250 years.

The owner of minerals, mineral rights, or mineral way leaves, would be compensated only in so far as he was also the owner or part owner of a colliery, which was either working, or had ceased working, or was in course of preparation for working (see clause 2 a); but it is probable that practically all persons owning minerals, mineral rights, or mineral way leaves, other than surface way leaves, are also interested in collieries, past, present or future.

The annual income from mining royalties (i.e., "rights to work and way leaves"), which is, however, not all from coal, was, in 1911-12, £8,763,916, on which sum the Mineral Rights Duty (an additional income tax of one shilling in the pound) was paid (House of Commons Returns, Nos. 190 and 317 of 1912). Of this total, perhaps four-fifths is in respect of coal. This estimate agrees with that of Mr. T. Mardy Jones in the *Economic Review*, 1908.

On the Continent, royalty rents are practically non-existent. In France the surface owner of the land does not own the minerals beneath his property. French law does not recognize any private ownership of minerals which are not the subject of a lease or concession.

The State may grant a concession to a person for a nominal royalty to work minerals, and in this case the concessionaire may have to pay a small royalty to the surface owner, but the amount of the royalty is fixed by the State and is fixed permanently in the first instance, the amount, which is small, being determined by custom and local usage. Similar systems obtain in Belgium, Germany, and Spain.

In early years in England it was doubtful whether coal belonged to the Crown or private individuals. It was held, however, in 1568 that gold and silver mines belonged to the Crown, but "base" metals to the landowner.—Bainbridge, " Law of Mines and Minerals."

The growth of the value of royalty rents may be illustrated by the following case. In 1748 the Marquis of Bute leased to Anthony Bacon eight miles of mineral property at Merthyr for 97 years at an annual royalty of £100. In 1848 the same property was re-leased at £20,000 a year.

4.—MINES COMMISSIONERS.

(1) For the purposes of assessing the purchase price of coal mines it shall be lawful for His Majesty, by warrants under the sign manual, to appoint ten commissioners, to be styled the Mines Commissioners (herein called the Commissioners) of whom one, appointed by His Majesty, shall be Chairman.

(2) Three of the said Commissioners shall be nominated by the Mining Association of Great Britain, three of them shall be nominated by the Miners' Federation of Great Britain, and two of them shall be nominated by the British Trade Union Congress.

(3) At the expiration of twelve months from the passing of this Act, in the event of a majority of the Commissioners failing to agree as to the purchase price of a particular coal mine, it shall be lawful for the Chairman himself to fix the purchase price of such coal mine, but, save as herein expressly provided, the finding of the Commissioners as to the purchase price of coal mines shall be final and conclusive and binding on all parties.

(4) It shall be lawful for the Minister for Mines to remove any Commissioner for inability or misbehavior. Every order of removal shall state the reasons for which it is made, and no such order shall come into operation until it has lain before the Houses of Parliament for not less than thirty days while Parliament is sitting.

(5) The Commissioners may appoint and employ such assessors, surveyors, valuers, clerks, messengers, and other persons required for the due performance of their duties as the Treasury on the recommendation of the Minister for Mines may sanction.

(6) There shall be paid to the Commissioners and to each of the persons appointed or employed under this section such salary or remuneration as the Treasury may sanction ; and all such salaries and remuneration and the expenses of the Commission incurred in the execution of their duties, to such amount as may be sanctioned by the Treasury, shall be paid out of moneys provided by Parliament.

5.—VALUATION OF COAL MINES.

(1) The Commissioners shall, as soon as may be after the passing of this Act, cause a valuation to be made of all coal mines in the United Kingdom, showing respectively the total ascertained value of the coal mine and its profitable rights, and the total ascertained

value of the coal mine exclusive of such rights ; and the owner of every coal mine and any person receiving any rents, interest, or profit from any coal mine, on being required by notice by the Commissioners, shall furnish to the Commissioners a return containing such particulars as the Commissioners may require as to his property, rent, interest, or profits in such coal mine.

(2) The Commissioners may likewise cause any coal mine to be inspected, require the production of documents, or do any other thing which may in their opinion be necessary to fix the purchase price of the coal mine.

The powers given to the Commissioners under this clause resemble those which are now possessed by the Land Valuers under the Finance Acts.

6.—ASCERTAINMENT OF PURCHASE PRICE.

(1) The purchase price of the coal mine shall be computed by ascertaining, and on the basis of the average annual number of tons of minerals actually raised during the five preceding years, provided that in no case shall the maximum purchase price be taken to be more than the following :

	s.	d.
When 100,000 tons or less have been raised per annum on the average during the five preceding years, a capital sum equal to one such year's output at	12	0 per ton
When more than 100,000 tons have been raised per annum on the average during the five preceding years, a capital sum equal to one such year's output at	10	0 per ton

(2) Subject to the provisions of sub-section (1) of this section, the Commissioners in arriving at such computation shall also have regard to the actual gross and net profits which have been made in the coal mine during such years and to the amounts which may have been set aside from time to time for depreciation, renewals, or development, and to the probable duration of the life of the mine, and to the nature and condition of such coal mine, and to the state of repairs thereof, and to the coke ovens, washeries, and other works and houses which may for the purposes of this Act be deemed to be a part of the coal mine, and to the liabilities of any coal mine undertaking existing at the time of purchase which are transferable to the Minister for Mines under section 11 of this Act.

(3) Provided further that where a coal mine, in the opinion of the Commissioners, has not been fully developed, the amount which would be raised under full development shall be taken as the average annual number of tons raised, and the maximum purchase price in such case shall be taken to be a capital sum equal to the product of such number of tons and 12s. or 10s. per ton respectively, for the purpose of ascertaining the maximum value per ton under sub-section (1) of this section.

The purchase price is to be based, in the main, on the annual output of each colliery ; and ten or twelve shillings per ton of such output is named as the maximum price. This is a common method of valuing colliery property. Thus, when the late

Sir George Elliott proposed that all colliery owners should unite in one great National Coal Trust, the basis at which they were to come in was fifteen shillings per ton of annual output. He considered in 1893 that all the collieries in the country could be converted into one concern at a capital cost of £120,000,000. For present assessment purposes, the rateable value is based upon the gross vend and selling price of the usually preceding year.

The average annual output for the years 1906-10 was 261,726,945 tons, so that the maximum purchase price would be (at ten shillings per ton) about £130,863,475, say £140,000,000, that is £20,000,000 more than Sir G. Elliot's estimate of twenty years ago, a difference which would include the cost of colliers' houses, etc., taken over by the Bill.

7.—Issue of Coal Mine Stock.

(1) The purchase price of coal mines, as ascertained under the provisions of this Act, shall be paid by the Minister for Mines in Coal Mines Purchase Stock to the persons who in the opinion of the Commissioners have established their title to such stock. Provided that an appeal shall lie to the High Court from the decision of the Commissioners as to the title of any such persons, but for no other purpose.

(2) For the purpose of paying such purchase price the Treasury shall, on the request of the Minister for Mines, by warrant addressed to the Bank of England, direct the creation of a new capital stock (to be called "Guaranteed Three Per Cent. Coal Mine Stock") and in this Act referred to as "the stock," consisting of perpetual annuities, yielding dividends at the rate of three per cent. per annum on the nominal amount of capital.

(3) The annuities shall be payable by equal half yearly or quarterly dividends at such times in each year as may be fixed by the warrant first creating the stock.

(4) The stock shall be redeemed at the rate of one hundred pounds sterling for every one hundred pounds of stock at such times and in such amounts and manner as may be fixed by the Treasury.

(5) The stock may be issued at such times and in such amounts and subject to such conditions as the Treasury may direct.

(6) The dividends on the stock shall be paid out of the income of the Coal Mines Fund, and if that is insufficient shall be charged on and paid out of the Consolidated Fund of the United Kingdom and the growing produce thereof.

(7) The stock shall be transferable in the books of the Bank of England in like manner as other stock is transferable under the National Debt Act, 1870.

Payment is to be made in Three per Cent. Government Stock at par. The exact terms would doubtless be settled according to the state of the market at the date of passing the Bill. At the present price of Consols, it may be doubtful whether £100 of such stock would sell for more than 85.

The annual profits of all sorts of mines averaged during the five years ending March, 1910, £11,697,120; and of this it is estimated that eleven twelfths, or £10,500,000, is from coal mines (Sir A. Markham). The interest on £140,000,000 at three per cent. under the Bill would amount annually to about £4,200,000. A sinking fund which would redeem the capital debt in twenty years would amount to £5,000,000 annually.

There would be a surplus of £7,300,000 in the hands of the Minister for Mines if the £6,000,000 a year now paid to the royalty owners, which the Bill proposes to terminate, be added to the £1,300,000 saved in interest after £5,000,000 for redemption has been paid.

The difficulty of distributing the compensation by the Commissioners is greatly lessened by the fact that the great bulk of the capital held in mines is held in companies, where the respective rights of shareholders are easily ascertainable. The following calculations show that, in fact, only one-fifteenth of the total capital held in mines is held by private individuals. The capital value (of all the individual, non-company property interests in all sorts of mines) passing by death in 1909-10 (there being 128 such estates) was £560,424 net, the value being taken at thirteen and two-fifths years' purchase. (Fifty-fourth Report of Commissioners of Inland Revenue, Cd. 5833 of 1911.)

Assuming that one-twentieth of the total property passes each year by death, the aggregate capital value of all kinds of property in all sorts of mines in the United Kingdom not owned by joint stock companies is, on this Government valuation, which is accepted by the owners for taxation purposes, about £11,200,000. That of coal mines alone must, of course, be less, perhaps, four-fifths of these totals—*i.e.*, about £10,000,000, or only one-fourteenth of the total capital held in mines.

Evidence of the extent of company ownership is also shown by the fact that the total number of separate coal mines at work in the United Kingdom is about 3,500. The number of separate firms or companies is, of course, much smaller : it has been estimated at 1,500.

8.—WORKING OF COAL MINES AND SALE OF COAL BY MINISTER FOR MINES.

(1) Subject to the provisions of this Act, it shall be lawful for the Minister for Mines on behalf of His Majesty, to open and work coal mines and generally to carry on the business of coal mining and vending in all its branches, together with all other industries usually carried on in connection therewith. Provided that it shall not be lawful for the Minister for Mines to lease any mine or mines to any person.

(2) The Minister for Mines may compulsorily purchase land or acquire such rights over land as he may require for the purpose of this Act, and shall have, with regard to the compulsory purchase of land, all the powers of purchasers acting under the Land Clauses Acts.

(3) For the purposes of this section the Minister for Mines may from time to time, in such manner and on such terms as he thinks fit :—

(a) Appoint managers, engineers, agents, workmen, and servants ; and

(b) Construct, erect, or purchase, lease, or otherwise acquire, buildings, plant, machinery, railways, tramways, hulks, ships, and other fixed or movable appliances or works of any description, and sell or otherwise dispose of the same when no longer required ; and

(c) Sell, supply, and deliver coal and other products the result of coal-mining operations ; and

(d) Enter into and enforce contracts and engagements ; and

(e) Generally do anything that the owner of a coal mine might lawfully do in the working of the mine, or that is authorized by regulations under this Act.

(4) In addition to the powers conferred on the Minister for Mines by the last preceding sub-section he may, in such manner as he thinks fit, work any railway, tramway, hulk, ship, or other movable appliance acquired by him for the purpose of supplying and delivering coa .

The Minister for Mines is to work the mines by his own staff. Coal mines are worked by the State in Germany, Austria, Sweden, Russia, and several other countries in connection with their military and ordnance departments.

The German Government owns eleven coal mines in Westphalia, employing about 5,000 men. The coal is used for the State railways and navy.

New Zealand and Australia provide the only instances where coal mines have been nationalized, and are worked by the State for the supply of community needs. In New Zealand, in 1912, of 271,629 tons of State coal, 60,847 were sold for State purposes and 184,412 tons to the public.

The Victoria State Railway Department owns the Plowett coal mine and sells coal to the Melbourne Metropolitan Board, and whatever can be spared to the public.

In this country a number of municipalities own coal mines, as also do the Ecclesiastical Commissioners, but in every instance the mines are leased out to private companies.

The power to purchase land is necessary in order to enable the Minister for Mines to open new coalfields. As mineral rights, under the Bill, are to lose their value, the compensation awarded under the Lands Clauses Acts would of course not take account of this particular right. The recent Royal Commission on Coal Supplies estimated the available supplies of British coal at a depth of 4,000 feet in unproved coalfields at about 40,000,000,000 tons, compared with about 100,000,000,000 tons in proved coalfields.

9.—ACCOUNTS.

(1) The Minister for Mines shall cause full and faithful accounts to be kept of all moneys received and expended under this Act, and of all assets and liabilities and of all profits and losses, and shall annually lay such accounts before Parliament.

(2) The Minister for Mines shall annually cause a balance sheet of accounts to be made, including a capital account and a profit and loss account for each mine worked under this Act.

(3) Such balance sheet and statement shall be so prepared as to show fully and faithfully the financial position of each such mine, and the financial result of its operations for the year.

10.—COAL MINES ACCOUNT.

(1) All moneys raised under the authority of this Act shall, as and when raised, and all other moneys received hereunder shall, as and when received, be paid into a separate account called "The National Coal Mines Account."

(2) All moneys withdrawn from the National Coal Mines Account constituted under this Act shall be withdrawn only by the order of the Minister for Mines or such other person as the Minister may from time to time appoint, countersigned by the Treasury.

(3) All moneys in the National Coal Mines Account, or payable into that account by any person whomsoever, and also all moneys owing by any person under this Act, are hereby declared to be the property of the Crown, and recoverable accordingly as from debtors to the Crown.

11.—TRANSFERENCE OF EXISTING ASSETS AND LIABILITIES.

(1) There shall be transferred to the Minister for Mines all the existing assets and liabilities of coal mine undertakings, other than liabilities for royalty rents, wayleave rents or any other underground rents or charges, payable or due at the time of the passing of this Act to any person.

(2) On the passing of this Act, there shall be ascertained by the Commissioners the amount of all moneys due to or from all coal mine undertakings, and the finding of the Commissioners as to the amount of such moneys shall be binding and conclusive on all parties.

(3) The net amount of all moneys due to any coal mine undertaking, after all debts due from any such undertaking have been deducted, as ascertained under sub-section (2) of this section, shall be paid by the Minister for Mines to the persons to whom in the opinion of the Commissioners such debts are due and shall be deemed to be expenses incurred under this Act. Provided that an appeal shall lie to the High Court from the decision of the Commissioners as to the title of any such person but for no other purpose.

The sums now payable as royalty rents, way leave rents, and other underground rents or charges will cease to be payable as from the appointed day.

12.—PAYMENTS OUT OF MONEYS PROVIDED BY PARLIAMENT.

(1) All sums expended or payable under this Act in the construction, erection or acquisition of buildings, plant, machinery, railways, tramways, hulks, ships or other appliances or works, or for other expenses required for the working of any mine, shall be payable out of moneys provided by Parliament.

(2) Provided that moneys received under this Act in respect of the sale or supply of coal (including the moneys received from the Government Departments) may be directly expended in or towards carrying out the purposes of this Act.

The effect of paying out of "moneys provided by Parliament" is to make parliamentary criticism more effective than if such expenses are paid out of the Consolidated Fund.

13.—PAYMENT OUT OF CONSOLIDATED FUND.

(1) After full provision has been made for all outgoings, losses, and liabilities for the year (including interest on securities created and issued in respect of moneys raised as aforesaid, and on moneys paid out of the Consolidated Fund), the net surplus profits then remaining shall be applied in establishing a sinking fund and, subject thereto, in establishing a depreciation fund in respect of capital expended.

At present, taking the average of twenty prosperous companies, ten per cent. of the net profit is set aside annually for depreciation and development.

Assuming the profits, after interest and redemption have been met, to amount to about £9,500,000, about £1,000,000 should be allocated annually to the depreciation and development fund.

14.—MANAGEMENT.

Every coal mine worked under this Act shall be managed and worked subject to the provisions of the Coal Mines Regulation Act, 1908, the Coal Mines Act, 1911, and any other Act regulating the hours, wages, or conditions of labor in coal mines.

The "Eight Hours Act," the various Acts regulating labor in mines consolidated in the Coal Mines Act, 1911, and the "Minimum Wage Act," 1912, are formally unaffected by this measure. It may be assumed that the responsibility of the Minister for Mines for casualties, etc., in mines will be made far more direct and effective than is that of the Home Secretary at the present time. Thus in 1909 over 150,000 men and boys were seriously injured in mines ; in 1910 nearly 160,000. In 1910, 1,769 persons were killed in mines. Under this Bill, for all these deplorable accidents the Minister for Mines would be answerable to Parliament. In New Zealand in 1911 only four fatal accidents occurred in State coal mines, having an output of 281,525 tons.

15.—TRADE UNIONS. PARTICIPATION IN POLITICS.

Notwithstanding anything in any Act or Order any society of workers employed in a National coal mine may be registered or constitute themselves as a Trade Union, and do anything individually or in combination which the members of a Trade Union or a Trade Union may lawfully do. Provided further that notwithstanding any regulation to the contrary, it shall be lawful for any person employed under this Act to participate in any civil or political action in like manner as if such person were not employed by His Majesty.

The persons employed under this Act are to be free to join trade unions—a right not expressly, though often in fact, denied to other Government employees—and they are expressly not to be subject to the political disabilities to which, for instance, the employees in the Customs, Inland Revenue and Post Office Departments are, whether by custom or departmental regulation, now subjected. The freedom from political disability does not extend to *legal* as distinguished from *customary* disability. Thus, notwithstanding this clause, it would be as illegal for an employee of the Minister for Mines as for any other civil servant to sit in the House of Commons.

16.—REGULATIONS.

(1) The Minister for Mines may, from time to time, make such regulations as he thinks necessary for any of the following purposes :—

    (*a*) The management of coal mines under this Act ;

    (*b*) The functions, duties, and powers of all persons acting in the management and working of coal mines under this Act ;

    (*c*) The form of the accounts to be kept and the balance sheets to be prepared in respect of coal mines under this Act ;

    (*d*) The mode in which the sinking funds and other funds connected with coal mines under this Act shall be held and administered ;

    (*e*) Generally any other purpose for which, in the opinion of the Minister for Mines, regulations are contemplated or required.

(2) The Minister for Mines, before making or altering any of such regulations or conditions of employment, including wages, as

affect workmen engaged in the mining industry, shall consult with the duly accredited representatives of the workmen, and, in the event of such representatives and the Minister for Mines failing to agree, the matter in dispute may be referred to arbitration on such terms as may be mutually agreed.

17.—Duty of Minister for Mines to Supply Coal.

It shall be the duty of the Minister for Mines to ensure that there is a sufficient supply of coal at reasonable prices throughout the United Kingdom, and for this purpose it shall be the duty of the Minister for Mines to establish stores and depôts and to employ vehicles and to use all other necessary means for the selling of coal within the area of every local authority, and further for this purpose it shall be the duty of the railway companies of the United Kingdom to provide such facilities for the conveyance of coal as the Minister for Mines may deem necessary to enable him to carry out the duties imposed upon him by this section at rates not greater than such railway companies are now entitled to charge for the conveyance of coal.

Clause 17 "nationalizes" the wholesale, retail, and export trade in coal, besides giving the Minister for Mines a monopoly in the getting of coal. This is a novel provision of far-reaching scope. Provision is made in Clause 8 for the Minister for Mines to take over the premises, stocks of coal, and business arrangements of existing coal merchants, exporters, dealers, retailers and hawkers.

In the reign of George II. the price of coal in Manchester and its environs was fixed for forty years at 4d. per cwt. Under this clause the State would once again fix the price of coal.

Under the existing system the very poor pay for their coal anything from 7s. to 10s. above the current rate for larger quantities ; that is, in the aggregate, nearly half as much again as the wealthier classes. There is also much overlapping in distribution. In London alone there are 420 coal merchants ; their average profit is considerable.

In the country the profits and prices are both greater. In Dearham, a mining village, the miners now pay 1s. 2d. per cwt. ; 35 years ago, in the same place, the price was 5d. per cwt. According to Councillor Phillips, of Manchester, the working class families of this city are paying 10½d. per cwt., or 17s. 6d. per ton. In the same town the Corporation buys superior coal for 12s. per ton.

The present average selling price of coal at the pit-head may be taken at 3s. to 5s. per ton for small and dust, 10s. for best steam, and 11s. for best household. The Government Coal Tables give an all-round average for 1910 of 8s. 2¼d. per ton.

According to Sir Hugh Bell, the price realized for one ton of coal being 100d. (8s. 4d.), the cost would be distributed as follows :—Royalty, 4½d. (according to other authorities, 6d.) ; wages, 56d. ; administrative expenses, 2d. ; railway dues, taxes, cottage rents, 27½d. If £2,300,000, approaching one third of the sum of royalty rents, were placed to the reduction of the price of coal, the pit-head price would be reduced to about 8s. per ton average. Working on this pit-head minimum, the economies of distribution, and saving of overlapping and middlemen's profits might further reduce the average price to the consumer.

Five shillings out of the present price of 25s. coal in London is to be ascribed to middlemen's expenses, apart from wagon hire and railway rates According to Mr. Hylton Dale, the wastage due to retransferring coal and reweighing is about 20 cwt. to the truck of ten tons. "After the coal arrives in London," he says, "it is necessary to add an average of 5s. a ton to its price for general expenses before any profit is seen by the merchants."

In New Zealand, before the State acquisition of mines, the average price of coal was 35s. per ton ; it is now as low as 25s. In Germany the Westphalian Syndicate, which is partially under Government control, has abolished the dealer and vends to the public direct at a low price.

18.—Transference to Minister for Mines of Powers and Duties of Home Secretary.

There shall be transferred to and be vested in the Minister for Mines all the powers and duties of the Secretary of State imposed upon him by the Coal Mines Regulation Act, 1908, the Coal Mines Act, 1911, or any other Act regulating or affecting coal mines or the hours or conditions of labor therein.

The Nationalization of Mines may be expected to entail a revision of minimum wages under the 1912 Act.

Trustworthy estimates put the average earnings of all the workers in the coal mines at 28s. per week per adult man, making a total wage-bill for the 1,067,213 persons employed (both above and below ground, and including boys and women) of about £60,000,000. In New Zealand in 1911 the average wage per person employed in a State coal mine was £140 per annum, or 17s. per day shift.

To ensure a minimum wage to every adult male worker in or about coal mines of 30s. per week would involve an increase on the present wage bill of about £4,000,000, or more than half the sum now paid in royalties. This £4,000,000, together with £2,300,000 spent in reducing the price of coal (clause 17), and £1,000,000 in depreciation (clause 13), and £5,000,000 in redemption (clause 7), could all be paid out of the annual profits, which amount to £16,500,000 (£9,500,000 existing profits and £7,000,000 saved in royalty).

19.—Title and Commencement.

This Act may be cited as the Nationalization of Coal Mines and Minerals Act, 1912, and this Act and the Coal Mines Regulation Acts, 1887 and 1908, and the Coal Mines Act, 1911, may be cited together as the Coal Mines Acts, 1887-1912, and shall come into operation on the first day of the sixth month after the passing of this Act, and all valuations, purchase, and transference of coal mines and minerals to the Minister for Mines and all other arrangements for the carrying out of this Act shall be concluded on or before the first day of the fifth year after the coming into operation of this Act.

BIBLIOGRAPHY.

Apart from the mass of literature on Coal and Coal Mining all over the world, it is not easy to find works dealing expressly with "nationalization." The following list of works bearing on Coal Monopolies, Mining Royalties and the Nationalization of the Coal Supply is the best that it has been found possible to compile. There is mentioned in the American *Readers' Guide* a Bibliography, by P. M. Pearson, on the Government Ownership of Coal Mines (Intercollegiate Debates, 435-57; Hinds; 1909; U.S.A.), a copy of which is in the British Library of Political Science (London School of Economics), Clare Market, W.C.

Annales de la Régie Directe (Geneva, Switzerland). Articles on the Nationalization of Coal in :
   Note on La Nationalisation des Mines de Houille en Hongroie. (No. 3, 1909.)
   Recommendations of the Commission des Mines de la Chambre des Députés (France). In favor of nationalizing all mines. (No. 10, 1910.)
   Government Ownership of Coal Mines in Servia. (See *Yovanovitch*, No. 15, 1910.)
BOSENICK, A.—Der Steinkohlenbergbau in Preussen. 114 pp. Zeitschrift für die gesammte Staatswissenschaft. Ergänzungsheft 19.

Commission des Mines ·de la Chambre des Députés (France). Report· of Recommendations of. In faVor of Nationalization of French Coal Mines. 1910.

DALE, HYLTON B.—Coal and the London Coal Trade. 1912.

DEFUISSEAUX, ALFRED.—Mr. Emile Lewy's Scheme for the International Regulation of the Output·of Coal. 1896.

ELLIOT, SIR GEORGE.—Letter . . . in *Times* of September 20th, 1893.

Fabian News. Municipalization of Coal Supply   October, 1910.

JAMES, C. A.—Mining Royalties. 277 pp. 1893.

JEANS, J. S.—Trusts, Pools, and Corners. Methuen. 1894.

JEVONS, W. S.—The Coal Question. 467 pp. 1906.

JONES, T. I. MARDY.—Mining Royalties and all about them. I.L.P. 1908.

LARGE, F. D.—The Coal Strike. *Economic Journal*, March, 1894, p. 27 ; Remedies.

LAUR, F.—La Mine aux Mineurs. 142 pp. 1887.

LEVY, HERMANN.—Monopoly and Competition. Macmillan. 1911. Much about the "Limitation of the Vend" and other monopolies in coal.

LEWY, E.—A Scheme for the Regulation of the Output of Coal by International Agreement. 115 pp. 1896.

LEWY, E.—International Regulation of the Output of Coal in Western Europe. 16 pp. Giard et Brière (Paris). 1912-3.

MACROSTY, H. W.—The Trust Movement in British Industry. Longmans. 1907.

MYERS, TOM.—The State and the Coal Mines. I.L.P. Pamphlet. 1911.

"MYNER COLLIER."—Miners and Poverty. Pamphlet. Forward Publishing Company (Glasgow). 1911.

NIEDER, L.—Die Arbeitsleistung der Saar-Bergleute in den k. preussischen Steinkohlgruben bei Saarbrücken zeit dem jahre 1888. 97 pp. 1909. *Munchener volkswirtschaftliche Studien ;* Bd. 90.

OLIVIER, SIR SYDNEY.—The Miners' Battle—and after. *Contemporary Review*, Nov., 1893.

RICHARDSON, THOMAS, M.P., and WALBANK, JOHN A.—Profits and Wages in the British Coal Trade (1898 to 1910). 96 pp. Newcastle, 1911.

Royal Commission on Mining Royalties : Report and Evidence of.

SABINI, C.—Economic Enquiry into the Coal Industry (Report presented to the Italian Minister of Public Works on the Coal Industry in Germany). Newcastle, 1901.

Socialists and State Ownership in "New Belgian Coalfields." *Economic Journal*, 1903, p. 641.

SNOWDEN, PHILIP.—How to Nationalize the Coal Mines. I.L.P. Pamphlet. 1909.

Socialist Year Book, 1913. I.L.P.

SORLEY, W. R.—Mining Royalties and the Iron and Coal Trades. 39 pp. 1889.

THOMAS, D. A.—Some Notes on the present state of the Coal Trade. 85 pp. Cardiff, 1896.

WALKER, F. A.—Monopolistic Combinations in the German Coal Industry. 334 pp. (American Economic Association, 1904.)

See also—

Annual Report on State Mines of Victoria.

The New Zealand Year Book, for Government Mines in that country.

Annual Report on Government Coal Mines in Prussia.

Various pamphlets published by the Colliery Guardian Company, 30 and 31 Furnival Street, E C.

———————

. The statistics as to coal mines in the United Kingdom are published in the "Coal Tables," those from 1886 to 1910 being given in the House of Commons Return, No. 284 of 1911 (6d.). Fuller particulars are given in the Home Office Report on Mines and Quarries, published annually. Particulars of income from (all sorts of) mines, of the capital value passing at death each year of (all) interests in (all sorts of) mines, and of the annual income from rights to work (royalties) and way leaves will be found in House of Commons·Returns on Inland Revenue, Nos. 190 and 317 of 1912, and the Fifty-Fourth Annual Report of the Commissioners of Inland Revenue (Cd. 5833 of 1911).

FABIAN SOCIETY.—The Fabian Society consists of Socialists. A statement of its Rules and a complete list of publications can be obtained from the Secretary, at the Fabian Office, 3 Clement's Inn, London, W.C.
FABIAN ESSAYS IN SOCIALISM. Paper 6d.; cloth 1/6; post. 2½d. and 4d.
WHAT TO READ on Social and Economic Subjects. 1s. n. and 2s. n.
THIS MISERY OF BOOTS. By H. G. WELLS. 3d., post free 4d.
FABIAN TRACTS and LEAFLETS.
Tracts, each 16 to 52 pp., price 1d., or 9d. per doz., unless otherwise stated.
Leaflets, 4 pp. each, price 1d. for six copies, 1s. per 100, or 8/6 per 1000.
The Set of 77, 3s.; post free 3/5. Bound in Buckram, 4/6 n.; post free 5s.

I.—General Socialism in its various aspects.

TRACTS.—169. The Socialist Movement in Germany. By W. S. SANDERS. In cover, with portrait of Bebel, 2d. 159. The Necessary Basis of Society. By SIDNEY WEBB. 151. The Point of Honour. By RUTH C. BENTINCK. 147. Capital and Compensation. By E. R. PEASE. 146. Socialism and Superior Brains. By BERNARD SHAW. 142. Rent and Value. 138. Municipal Trading. 121. Public Service versus Private Expenditure. By Sir OLIVER LODGE. 107. Socialism for Millionaires. By BERNARD SHAW. 139. Socialism and the Churches. By Rev. JOHN CLIFFORD, D.D. 133. Socialism and Christianity. By Rev. PERCY DEARMER. 78. Socialism and the Teaching of Christ. By Dr. J. CLIFFORD. 42. Christian Socialism. By Rev. S. D. HEADLAM. 79. A Word of Remembrance and Caution to the Rich. By JOHN WOOLMAN. 72. The Moral Aspects of Socialism. By SIDNEY BALL. 69. Difficulties of Individualism. By S. WEBB. 51. Socialism: True and False. By S. WEBB. 45. The Impossibilities of Anarchism. By BERNARD SHAW (price 2d.). 7. Capital and Land (revised 1908). 5. Facts for Socialists (revised 1908). 132. A Guide to Books for Socialists. LEAFLETS—13. What Socialism Is. 1. Why are the Many Poor? WELSH TRACTS—143. Sosialaeth yng Ngoleuni'r Beibl. 141. Translation of 139. 87. Translation of 78. 38. Translation of 1.

II.—Applications of Socialism to Particular Problems.

TRACTS.—171. The Nationalization of Mines and Minerals Bill. By H. H. SCHLOESSER. 170. Profit-Sharing & Co-Partnership: a Fraud and Failure? By E. R. PEASE. In cover. 164. Gold and State Banking. By E. R. PEASE. 163. Women and Prisons. By HELEN BLAGG and CHARLOTTE WILSON. 2d. 162. Family Life on a Pound a Week. By Mrs. REEVES. In cover, 2d. 161. Afforestation and Unemployment. By A. P. GRENFELL. 160. A National Medical Service. By F. LAWSON DODD. 2d. 157. The Working Life of Women. By Miss B. L. HUTCHINS. 155. The Case against the Referendum. By CLIFFORD SHARP. 154. The Case for School Clinics. By L. HADEN GUEST. 153. The Twentieth Century Reform Bill. By H. H. SCHLOESSER. 152. Our Taxes as they are and as they ought to be. By R. JONES, B.Sc. In cover, 2d. 150. State Purchase of Railways. By EMIL DAVIES. In cover, 2d. 149. The Endowment of Motherhood. By H. D. HARBEN. In cover, 2d. 145. The Case for School Nurseries. By Mrs. TOWNSHEND. 140. Child Labor under Capitalism. By Mrs. HYLTON DALE. 136. The Village and the Landlord. By EDW. CARPENTER. 130. Home Work and Sweating By Miss B. L. HUTCHINS. 128. The Case for a Legal Minimum Wage. 122. Municipal Milk and Public Health. By Dr. F. LAWSON DODD. 125. Municipalization by Provinces. 123. The Revival of Agriculture. 115. State Aid to Agriculture: an Example. 124. State Control of Trusts. 86. Municipal Drink Traffic. 83. State Arbitration and the Living Wage. LEAFLET.—104. How Trade Unions benefit Workmen.

III.—Local Government Powers: How to use them.

TRACTS.—172. What about the Rates? or, Municpal Finance and Municipal Autonomy. By SIDNEY WEBB. 156. What an Education Committee can do (Elementary Schools), 3d. 137. Parish Councils and Village Life. 109. Cottage Plans and Common Sense. 76. Houses for the People. 82. Workmen's Compensation Act. LEAFLETS.—134. Small Holdings: and how to get them. 68. The Tenant's Sanitary Catechism. 71. Ditto for London.

IV.—General Politics and Fabian Policy.

TRACTS.—158. The Case against the C.O.S. By Mrs. TOWNSHEND. 108. Twentieth Century Politics. By S. WEBB. 70. Report on Fabian Policy. 41. The Fabian Society: its Early History. By BERNARD SHAW.

V.—Biographical Series. In portrait covers, 2d. each.

What about the Rates?

Or,

Municipal Finance and Municipal Autonomy ..

By SIDNEY WEBB.

Published and sold by the Fabian Society,
3 Clement's Inn, Strand, London, W.C.
July 1913.   Price 1d.

WHAT ABOUT THE RATES?

Municipal Finance and Municipal Autonomy.*

WHAT is it that to-day most hinders municipal progress? I am afraid that most elected persons would say that it is the ratepayers' fear of any increase in the burden of rates. It is this fear that damps the ardor and hinders the work of the enthusiastic reformer who has been elected to a town or district council. What is even more important, it is this very real feeling that strengthens the hands of those members of every council who are anyhow not enthusiastic for social change.

The Rising Rates.

It seems to us always as if the rates were perpetually " going up" and never coming down ! And in the large and growing cities and urban districts this is, in the main, true. We expect a great deal more from our local government in the way of the amenity of life than ever before. The sanitation and the paving and lighting, the provision for the sick and the care of the children, all cost more. But it is a mistake to suppose that rates were never so high at any previous time. In many a country district in the South of England the rates are to-day actually lower than they were a hundred years ago, when the average rate of all the Sussex parishes was 8s. 7½d. in the pound, and that of all the Monmouthshire parishes was 7s. 11¾d. in the pound. I wonder what the Manchester citizen would say to-day if he were asked for two successive rates of five shillings in the pound within not many weeks of each other, as happened in the Manchester of 1796.† Even to-day there are towns in which the rates in 1912-13 were over

Ten Shillings in the Pound

for the year. We are few of us quite so hard hit as the ratepayers of Ilkeston and East Ham, who had to pay 10s.; those of Lowestoft, 10s. 1d.; Merthyr Tydvil, 10s. 2½d.; Stoke, an average of 10s 6d.; West Ham, 10s. 6d.; and Norwich no less than 10s. 7d. in the pound.‡ In a few of the London districts, such as Poplar and Ber-

---

* Enlarged from a paper read at the Conference of Socialist and Labor Elected Persons, held at Manchester on Good Friday, 1913, under the auspices of the Joint Committee of the Fabian Society and Independent Labor Party.

† See "The Parish and the County," by S. and B. Webb, p. 73; "Grants in Aid," by S. Webb, pp. 12, 13.

‡ Table by Mr. James Carter, Borough Treasurer of Preston, in *Municipal Year Book* for 1913, p. 1044.

mondsey, the total rates often exceed 12s. in the pound, in spite of large subventions from the wealthier parts of London under the Equalization of Rates Act.

Nevertheless, as we are only too painfully aware, the rates have risen, and progress is hampered thereby. The fact that any new service, even any improvement in an existing service, would raise the rates still more, stands in the way of our getting more done for the public good.

The Electors Must Pay.

Now, let me say at once, we must not delude ourselves with the hope that we can ever get rid of this obstacle to reform. It seems to me inevitable that the electors should have to feel that, whenever any new or increased expenditure is to be incurred, it is they themselves who will have to pay. This is the price that we pay for local self-government. It would be very nice if we could have, without check or limitation, the pleasure of spending public money on all sorts of desirable improvements : wide streets, lighting, cleansing, and paving up to the very pitch of perfection ; the best schools and school clinics, meals for all the hungry children, and a broad highway to the highest education for all who were capable for it ; complete provision for the sick, the orphans, the widows, and the aged ; and the wisest possible treatment of the unemployed. But if we are going to have all these things in our own city, and to manage them ourselves as we think fit, the citizens of our own locality must be made to feel their responsibility for the expenditure. **We cannot have local autonomy without local finance.**

We Cannot Stop the Grumbling!

Nor can we prevent the ratepayers from grumbling, even if we reduce their present burden. There was just as much grumbling when the education rate was only twopence or threepence as there is now when it is anything between ninepence and two and ninepence. There is just as much complaint of the "extravagance" of the education committee in towns where the amount spent on education is only fifteen or eighteen pence in the pound as there is at Hull, where it is 2s. 2d.; at Crewe and Norwich, where it is 2s. 2¼d.; at Rotherham, Swansea, and Merthyr Tydvil, where it is 2s. 3d.; at East Ham, where it is 2s. 4½d.; or at West Ham, where it is 2s. 8¾d.* Even if it were possible, by finding some new sources of revenue or otherwise, to arrange matters so that the ratepayer only paid half what he now pays, he would, the very next time that there was any increase of his lower rate, grumble just as much as he does now at any increase on the present high rate. The only way to satisfy the ratepayer and prevent him from grumbling would be to arrange that there should never be any increase in his rates. This would mean that the local council would never be able to advance beyond the present position. My first proposition, accordingly, is that it is impossible, consistently with a continuance of local self-government,

* Ibid.

ever to get rid of the ratepayers grumbling at every increase of the rates.

But, even if we cannot hope to get rid of the ratepayers grumbling at every new development of local services, may we not expect to get some immediate relief from the present burden? There is, first of all, as some will say, the profit to be derived from municipal enterprises.

Municipal Trading.

Some municipalities make a large profit on their gasworks, or on their tramway service, or on their electric lighting concerns; and they devote this profit to keeping down the rates. For instance, in 1912-13 Manchester made £50,000 profit out of gas; Leicester, £32,000; Nottingham, £31,183; Leeds, £25,000; whilst even smaller places like Chorley made £2,469; Colne, £2,500; Nelson, £3,532; and Stafford, £3,500. Out of tramways Manchester made £100,000; Leeds, £60,000; Liverpool, £38,244; Salford, £20,000; and Sheffield, £19,238. From electricity Liverpool drew £25,000; Manchester, £24,500; Leeds, £15,000; Nottingham, £14,850; and even such a smaller town as Chesterfield, £1,000; and Luton, £800.

Profits in Relief of Rates.

Altogether, in relief of the rates, from these and similar sources, Manchester drew no less than £188,500; Liverpool, £167,399: Leeds, £115,235; Nottingham, £85,713; and Leicester, £62,807. The greatest reduction in the rate made by these means was at Dewsbury and Wallasey, where the ratepayer benefited to the extent of no less than 1s. 8½d. in the pound; Nottingham, where it was 1s. 6½d.; Macclesfield and Darlington, where it was 1s. 6d.; Halifax, 1s. 5¼d.; Stockport, 1s. 5d.; Stafford, 1s. 4½d.; Yarmouth, Warrington, and Burnley, 1s. 4d.; Leicester, 1s. 3¾d.; Bolton, 1s. 2¾d.; Lancaster, 1s. 2½d.; and Carlisle, 1s. 2d. The Manchester Corporation, for all its large profits, lowered the burden to the ratepayers by only 10¾d. in the pound.

A Doubtful Boon.

What are we to think of municipal profit making to this extent? There may be something to be said for the policy up to a certain point. The municipality may fairly take for the common good such part of its trading profits as arise from the fact that they are derived from monopoly. But this is usually a very small part, often indeed no more than a necessary margin between receipts and expenditure. Where the Town Council (as in the towns mentioned) makes a large profit out of its gasworks, or out of its tramway service, or out of its electrical installation, it is almost always getting that profit unfairly at the expense either of its employees or else of its customers. It is unfair to pay bare subsistence wages to the corporation employees, and work them long hours, and subject them to degrading conditions of labor, merely with the object of earning a profit for the relief of the ratepayer.

Sweating the Worker.

I was shocked to find some years ago, when I visited one of the great gasworks of the Manchester Corporation, that nothing whatever seemed to have been done, after a whole century of municipal ownership, with the object of making the Manchester gasworker into a Manchester citizen. It was not merely that he seemed to be paid no better and to be worked no shorter hours than if he were serving a joint stock company. What was even more startling was that he seemed to be treated by the foreman or manager with no more consideration, to be thrown every summer out of work as callously, to be granted no more holidays on full pay, to be accorded no greater sick leave or superannuation, to be given no more opportunity for changing his clothes and taking a bath, to be allowed no more comfort and amenity in the places where he had to work and wait and eat his food—in a word, provided with no more of the conditions of civilized life than the gasworker under the ordinary capitalist company. And what seemed to me even more grievous was that nobody on the gas committee, nobody on the corporation, nobody in Manchester even, thought that there was anything wrong in this.* It does not seem to occur to a municipal gas committee that they are open to criticism for treating their employees, as regards the amenity of their lives, and especially as regards the regularity of their employment, no better and no worse than private employers. I assert that it is the duty of every public authority to take care that all the conditions of employment of all its wage earners are such as, not only to permit of, but also actively to promote, a decently civilized life, before it takes a penny of the so-called profits of its enterprises in relief of the ratepayer.

Taxing the Gas Consumer.

Moreover, there is no sense in charging an unduly high price for any public service in order merely to benefit the ratepayer. For instance, when the Manchester or Leicester Town Council makes, year after year, a large profit out of its gasworks, it is really taxing the consumers of gas, in proportion to their consumption of gas, for the benefit of the owners and occupiers of house property roughly in proportion to their wealth. For we must remember that whenever

* A brief newspaper report of this statement seems to have made the chairman of the gas committee very indignant, so that we have, by 1913, perhaps made a little progress! In an interview (*Manchester Courier*, March 26th, 1913) he declared that the criticism was "rubbish"; that the Manchester laborers were paid [26s. a week] as well as any others; that there was "no earthly reason why the 1,100 or 1,200 men working for the department should receive treatment better than that received by their fellow citizens or ratepayers."

But apparently social compunction is at work even here, because the Manchester Gas Committee, we are told, has just completed (*at one only of its works*) "one of the finest suites of dining rooms, lavatories, etc., for the use of the men"; far superior to the accommodation afforded to many of their fellow citizens or ratepayers in private employment. Without questioning the chairman's consistency, I am contented to hope that, before the next critic visits Manchester, equally satisfactory accommodation will have been afforded to *all* the men in the employment of the gas department of the corporation, irrespective of the fact that many capitalist employers do not afford such civilizing amenities!

we give any relief to the rates we necessarily give most relief to those who inhabit the largest houses, or who own the greatest amount of house property, and who therefore need it least. Moreover, a very large part of the benefit goes to the railway companies, who now have to contribute to the rates on assessments based mainly on their local traffic, and whom we should thus be subsidizing at the expense of the gas consumers. The consumers of gas in any large city are now, for the most part, either the industrial users of power gas (which is usually supplied at a specially low price very little above cost), or else the tens of thousands of small homes unable to afford the electric light, or using gas for cooking, often by the " penny in the slot " machine. Why tax these in order to make the rates lower for the more opulent ratepayer and for the shareholders of the railway companies? It is even a short-sighted policy to charge an unnecessarily high price for gas when a great many of the smaller homes are not yet up to the gas level, and—to the profit of the private capitalist—still use coal and petroleum. It does not seem sensible for one department of the Manchester Corporation to be trying to diminish the smoke nuisance, whilst another department of that same corporation is, by charging unnecessarily high prices for gas, actively promoting the use of coal fires. And it is a short-sighted policy, as well as a narrow-minded one, to penalize the use of gas in a great city. The opportunities for municipal expansion in the popular use of gas—notwithstanding all the encroachments of the electric light—are still great. The gas committee ought to be playing for the enlargement of its business, until not a single family is left unsupplied. We ought therefore everywhere to urge a reduction in the price of gas—better still the free grant of greater facilities for its use by small consumers—rather than any reduction of rates out of gas profits.

A Tax on Tramway Rides.

And it is much the same with tramway profits. Any large profit derived from a tramway service for the relief of the rates means usually that the tired girls and women, boys and men, who throng the cars night and morning are being charged threehalfpence or twopence for a journey that they might have been allowed to take for a penny. We might even have, as in London and Glasgow, halfpenny fares. We must here remember that the fact that the tram fares are thus unnecessarily kept up means that the railway and omnibus companies are able also to keep their own fares up on all the competing routes. We thus put money into the shareholders' pockets at our own expense!

Sweating the Tramwaymen.

On the other side of the question we find the humbler workers in the municipal tramway service, such as the washers or cleaners—together with the women employed at the manager's office, and even some of the younger clerks—are still far below a thirty shilling wage. The "spare hands" or relief men, whose occasional services are of the greatest use to the management, are paid only for the trips they take without any consideration of how they and their families are to live on the days when there is no job for them; and even the motormen and conductors, who are in most towns taken on at the rate of sixpence an hour only (rising gradually to sevenpence-halfpenny) find their hours so cut up by separate turns as to make it difficult for them to have any home life. The Liverpool Town Council, which makes the third largest profit out of tramways in relief of the rates, still works its tramwaymen as much as 60 hours per week, and allows no extra pay for Sundays or holidays; whereas the Glasgow tramwaymen work only 51 hours a week; and those of Manchester, Leeds, Birmingham, and many other towns work only 54 hours a week. Manchester, which makes actually more profit out of its tramways than any provincial city, gives its tramwaymen various privileges, but it takes the motormen on at no more than sixpence an hour (27s. for a full week), and advances them to no higher maximum than seven and a third pence per hour, with no extra rates for Sunday or holiday work. The Manchester Tramways Committee, instead of putting so much money into the pockets of the Manchester property owners, might well copy Cardiff, Dover, Leith, and Swindon, which give "time and a half" for Sunday work, or the many towns which give "time and a quarter"; whilst it would be a graceful concession to imitate Chester, Doncaster, Lincoln, Leeds, Huddersfield, and other towns, which give "double time" on Christmas Day and Good Friday. Above all, it is not very generous in a corporation making £100,000 a year net profit, that it should be taking on motormen at lower rates than Leeds (7d.); Sheffield, Leicester, and Huddersfield (6¾d.); Stockport, Sunderland (6½d.); Birmingham (6·44d.); or Burnley. Rotherham, Birkenhead, and Liverpool (6¼d.); or that its maximum for such men (7·33d.) should be below those of Liverpool and Birmingham (7·55d.), and Huddersfield, Leeds, Sheffield, and Darwen (7½d.). Similar invidious comparisons might be made as regards conductors and inspectors. Are the Manchester ratepayers morally justified in reducing their own rates in this way?

What Ought to be Done with the Profits.

My conclusion therefore is, that whilst it is usually advantageous for a local authority to own and work as many public services as it can efficiently manage, and whilst it is practically necessary to have the balance on the right side in each case and thus make even a pecuniary profit of this municipal trading, we ought not to look to this source for any substantial relief of the rates. Such municipal profits ought to be devoted first to the really just and generous treatment of all the corporation employees, not only in respect of wages—not even principally in respect of wages, except as regards the lowest grades—but mainly in respect of proper consideration of their circumstances and needs as human beings, and of the security, comfort, and amenity of their lives. These matters are of even more importance than the rate of wages. Secondly, there should come the improvement of the service itself, for the maximizing of the public convenience, especially as regards the mass of the people.

Thirdly comes the reduction of the prices charged for the service, especially all the irritating extra charges, such as gas meter rents, stove rents, payments for connections or installations, and so on ; and especially also those which (like the charge for " penny in the slot " gas and tramway fares) amount, in the main, to taxation of the incomes of the families existing below a decent standard of civilized life. There is accordingly no substantial relief of the rates to be looked for out of the profits of municipal trading. The object of " municipal trading " is not profit, but the service of the public, on the one hand ; and, on the other, such a collective control of the means of production as to prevent them being used either to oppress the workers or tax the consumers.

The Transfer of National Taxes.

It is a vain dream to expect that the Chancellor of the Exchequer will impoverish himself by handing over any national taxes —the Inhabited House Duty or what not—merely in order to benefit the local authorities. Why should he? We, at any rate, have no grounds on which we can ask for this most unsatisfactory and most undesirable step. So long as any tax remains on sugar and tea and coffee and cocoa and currants, at any rate, any proposal for a transfer of national taxes for the relief of the local ratepayers means continuing to tax the children's food, in proportion to consumption, for the benefit of the occupiers of the largest houses, the railway companies, and the property owners, roughly in proportion to their wealth.

New Local Taxes.

If we look for any relief of the rates by new local taxes, I am afraid that we shall be equally disappointed. All the fancy taxes that imagination can suggest—taxes on advertisements, taxes on cats, licences for this or that trade, percentages on the takings of picture palaces and music halls, and all the rest of them—are, in my judgment, illusory. If we could examine each of them in detail, we should find that their actual yield in cash would be so small, so unevenly distributed between town and town, so uncertain, and so inconvenient and costly to collect, that it would not be worth undertaking. There is, of course, the possibility of a local Income Tax or local Death Duties, but here again we find ourselves up against a dead wall.

Why a Local Income Tax is Impossible.

The Chancellor of the Exchequer—even a Socialist Chancellor of the Exchequer—is not likely to allow any town council to be a competitor with him in this rich field. Moreover, a local Income Tax, locally assessed and locally levied, presents difficulties in our own complicated country which seem to me insuperable. Our present Income Tax is successful because no less than four-fifths of it is not assessed directly on the payers, and not collected from them where they happen to live, but is *assessed and collected at the source*, and is thus stopped by deduction from the income before this is paid over.

With a local Income Tax this would be impossible, and the Finance Committee of the Manchester Town Council would have to do what the Chancellor of the Exchequer cannot do, namely, get separately and directly at each Manchester citizen, and ask him to make a correct return of all his income. But who, for this purpose, would be a Manchester citizen? Where is the local Income Tax, where are the local Death Duties, to be paid of all the crowd of rich men who throng the Manchester Exchange or the Liverpool Flags? They have tiny offices at high rents near their daily haunts, but ninety per cent. of them sleep outside the cities in which they make their money. Moreover, *where* do they make their money, at the factory or at the office in the city? Is the Income Tax on the Liverpool millionaire or the Manchester magnate to be enjoyed by the picturesque village in Cheshire or Derbyshire in which he has the mansion in which he sleeps? If so, what does Manchester or Liverpool get out of it? Is it suggested that he can be made to pay on all his income at each of all his many houses? Moreover, what Income Tax would be collected from each of the "multiple shops," in which gigantic companies are now carrying on the sale of meat, groceries, clothing, boots, and what not, in many hundreds of towns and villages? How could it possibly be estimated how much of the profit of the company—profit which comes mainly from its capacity to manufacture and distribute on a large scale—was made at each of its retail shops? Is it suggested that the whole of the company's profits could be taxed by every local authority in whose district it had a shop? The same sort of difficulty arises with the railway and canal companies, who are "occupiers" in practically every parish and borough of their own parts of the kingdom; with the great banks and their tens of thousands of branches; and indeed with all businesses carried on in more than one place. Are all these to be let off, or are they to be charged everywhere on the total income of the concern as a whole, or how can their profits be allocated among the districts of the different taxing authorities? It is of no use saying that *something called a Local Income Tax* exists in other countries, unless we are prepared to answer these questions. In my own judgment, the only way in which we can, in this complicated country, get relief for local taxation out of Income Tax or Death Duties is to assess and collect them nationally—perhaps as an addition or surtax on the imposts already levied by the Chancellor of the Exchequer—and then to distribute the aggregate proceeds among the local authorities according to some deliberately settled scale. To this proposal I shall return later.

We Must Not Sell Our Local Liberties.

I pass over the despairing suggestion that local authorities should be "relieved" of some of their duties by the National Government; that they should give up their schools or their high roads, their police or their hospitals, or their asylums, to a centralized Government department. Let us leave such proposals to the enemy. It is curious that it is always the Socialists who have to stand up for liberty against central government. We, as Socialists, must cherish local government, and aim always at its expansion, not at its contraction.

Tax the Rent.

Let us now consider the subject from the standpoint of economic theory. The view of the best economists is that the source from which the greater part of the cost of public services should be drawn is the annual rent or, as the German Social Democrat would call it, "surplus value" of the community. This does not mean merely the rent of land, but all that part of the product of industry which would otherwise be taken by the owners of the factors of production superior to the worst in use. For instance, the mills in which Horrocks's longcloth is made are more profitable than the ordinary mills; the owners of that flourishing business get what is really economic rent. The factories at Lancaster in which Lord Ashton makes the floorcloth for the world are more profitable than the ordinary factory. Lord Ashton draws a huge sum in economic rent. Now the economist, as I have said, points out that this differential advantage in production, whether due to superior land, superior plant, or to any kind of monopoly, cannot be got in higher wages by the operatives concerned however strong may be their trade union, or however effective may be a minimum wage law. It necessarily goes as tribute to the person who owns these differentially advantageous factors of production. This tribute of economic rent to private owners, as the economists point out, is not necessary to the continuance of industry. It arises only after full remuneration at the market price has been paid for every man's labor by hand or brain. Theoretically, the whole of it could be skimmed off without interfering with the normal return to every person who co-operates in production, whether as manager or inventor or operative. These swollen profits, which make up, the statistician tells us, something like one third of the total national income, ought to be specially drawn upon for the expense of managing the country in the way which alone makes them possible. This is the view of the orthodox economic professor, though he usually shrinks from putting it so plainly. It is also the Socialist view, because here, as elsewhere, the Socialist is only telling the world what the economist preaches in more involved language.

Taxation of Rent must be National.

Now the only equitable and practicable way that can be recommended for getting at economic rent, whether it be rent of specially advantageous pieces of land, or the rent of other specially advantageous factors of production, is by national ownership or national taxation. You cannot have Manchester levying its own tax on its own site values without throwing back all the districts less favorably situated upon their own inferior resources. Is even Manchester prepared to forego its equitable share in the still more advantageous factors of production? Is it prepared, for instance, to give to South

Wales all the profits of the anthracite coal mines, and to the inhabitants of London all the monopoly value of that supremely advantageous position for taxing the world? It is plainly inequitable, as
well as politically impracticable, to get at the economic rent except
nationally.

Grants in Aid.

Thus we come back to Grants in Aid as the really practicable
and effective source of relief to the ratepayers' burden. At present
these Grants in Aid amount to only about 30 millions a year
towards a local expenditure which is rapidly approaching 100 millions. They are at present given in the most foolish way, with the
least possible consideration of either economy or efficiency, or even
equality of relief to local burdens. I have described in a little book,
called " Grants in Aid," which any councillor can get for five shillings, and which he can ask his council to buy for public use, both
what the system now is and what, in my opinion, it ought to be. I
will only say that now that Old Age Pensions, like the prisons, have
become a national charge, there ought to be grants for each of the
five great local services : for (1) education and all that is done for
children ; for (2) sanitation, including drainage, and the whole provision for the sick and infirm, including that now under the board of
guardians ; for (3) police and all the expenses of justice ; for (4) all
the cost of lunacy and the provision for the feeble minded ; and for
(5) streets and highways, including paving. These grants should be
payable, not as lump sums, or in proportion to ratable value or to
population, but (like the old Police Grant) *in proportion to the actual
expenditure on the service*. And, in order not to interfere with the
National Budget, the aggregate amount of all the grants might be
fixed, and revised only every seven years, only the fixed sum being
annually apportioned among the local authorities according to their
several expenditures on the different services. I should like to see
the aggregate fixed at one half of the present local expenditure on
the services to be aided.

Taxation of Site Values.

This is where the Taxation of Site Values comes in. As an
economist I do not myself limit the proposal to the special taxation
of exceptional land, and I should wish to see it extended, as far as
practicable, to all those factors of production which, by their superiority over those at the margin of cultivation, yield an " economic
rent " or surplus value. Even simpler would it be for the Chancellor of the Exchequer to put a " surtax," or addition for local purposes, on the Income Tax and Death Duties, which now yield him
eighty millions a year. To make the Grants in Aid one half of the
cost of the services recommended above would involve—with all the
existing exemptions and abatements—a " surtax " of nearly fifty per
cent. On the other hand, with such a surtax, the Chancellor of the
Exchequer, no longer having to find the existing Grants (thirty millions a year) out of his ordinary revenue, might abolish the Tea and

Sugar Duties and greatly reduce the Income Tax rate. But it is not our business here to-day to trouble much about the Chancellor of the Exchequer's Budget, or the source from which he will pay the Grants in Aid. To the local authorities it matters not whence the Grant comes. All we want is the Grants themselves.

Danger of Reducing Rates.

But we must bear in mind that although we want to facilitate additional expenditure, and perhaps—just by way of greasing the wheels—to effect a small reduction in the hardest cases, we ought not to try generally to reduce the local rates to any great extent. Whatever may be the truth as to the real incidence of rates, nothing is more certain than that any great reduction benefits the landlord, and the landlord almost exclusively. Reduce the rates in Ancoats by twenty-five per cent. and the laborer in the Ancoats slum will pay not a farthing less for the weekly rent of his wretched hovel—the slum owner will get the whole benefit of the reduction. Reduce the rates on agricultural land, as the Conservatives and Tariff Reformers are always proposing—does anyone suppose that the agricultural laborer will pay less for his cottage, or get a rise of wages? Reduce the rates in the coal mining districts, so that the colliery companies have to pay less on the miners' cottages—is there any reason to suppose that the miner will be charged a lower rent, or that he will get a higher price per ton for hewing? A reduction of rates may help the peasant proprietor or the man who owns a freehold house. But so long as we are nearly all in the position of having to pay rent to a private landlord or house owner—especially where, as is the case with regard to more than half the population (and the poorest half), the rent is collected weekly—to expect that the wage earner will benefit by reducing the charge made on the owner is like looking to get butter out of a dog's mouth. The wage earners should demand Grants in Aid to facilitate municipal progress, not in order to reduce existing rates.

The Real Profit of Municipal Enterprise.

Thus, my final conclusion is that we must meet the ratepayer face to face and educate him on the question. Courage and clear thinking, and some capacity for popular explanation, must remain a necessary part of the equipment of the elected councillor. The ratepayer, after all, gets far more in return for his rates than he does for any other part of his expenditure. If you won't pay an adequate Education Rate, you will have to pay a higher Poor Rate and Police Rate. If you won't pay a proper Public Health Rate, you will certainly pay tenfold in Sickness Rate and Death Rate. Mr. Chamberlain successfully fought his municipal battles at Birmingham forty years ago on the war cry of " Higher Rates and a Healthy City." Can anyone doubt that this policy has been proved to " pay " at Birmingham ; to pay even the Birmingham ratepayer and the Birmingham property owner? What city is going to own that it is less enlightened than Birmingham?

Fabian Tract No. 173.

Public versus Private Electricity Supply.

By C. Ashmore Baker,
A.M.I.E.E.

A Paper prepared for the Fabian Research Department, and published on its behalf by the Fabian Society.

Price One Penny.

The Fabian Society, 3 Clement's Inn, Strand, London, W.C. September 1913.

THE FABIAN RESEARCH DEPARTMENT

devotes itself to the collection of information and the investigation of economic and social problems. For convenience, it has its own separate offices (37 Norfolk Street, W.C.) and staff, and its expenses are defrayed entirely by the donations made for its special work. Membership is open to all members of the Fabian Society, whilst other persons willing to help in the work may be co-opted for particular researches as Consultative Members.

An example of the work undertaken is the Report on Land and Rural Problems, prepared by a special Committee (H. D. Harben, Chairman). This is published, complete and with appendices, by Constable and Co. (2s. 6d. net).

The Report of the Committee on the Control of Industry (Mrs. Sidney Webb, Chairman) is now in preparation, and will be published in 1914.

It is proposed to form a Committee on Industrial Insurance.

PUBLIC v. PRIVATE ELECTRICITY SUPPLY.

ONE of the most remarkable economic developments of modern times has been the rapid growth of what is called municipal trading, and perhaps few economic questions have been discussed with more rancour and ignorance on both sides; for it is seldom that even the supporters of the movement advance much in the way of argument beyond sentiment, or vague generalities for the faith they profess.

The general ignorance on the subject is the less pardonable in view of the great mass and ready accessibility of the material available by which the success or failure of the movement may be gauged.

Can a public service be provided better by a public body than by a private enterprise? And how are we to define "better"?

Many defenders of municipal trading argue their case on ethical and even on æsthetic grounds, but the man who has to foot the bill requires something more concrete, and asks: Can a municipality supply as good an article at as low a price as can, say, a public company; and if so, how can we be sure of it both in regard to price and quality?

Now in many fields of activity it is difficult to compare the results produced under the two rival systems we are considering. This difficulty arises frequently from the absence of generally accepted criteria of "goodness."

One party insists on cheapness regardless of economy, another on efficiency regardless of cost, and so on; and there is heard

"Great argument
About it and about."

What is required at the moment is a comparison based on the production of some definite commodity whose value and cost can be readily and accurately gauged.

Now a Board of Trade unit of electricity is a pretty definite thing from a commercial point of view. It cannot be adulterated; its quality cannot vary much from definite standards; it can be accurately measured; and whether we buy it from a company or a town council we can be fairly certain of obtaining an identical article.

Here also we have an article the cost of production of which, by the judicious investment of twopence at any railway bookstall, can be ascertained in the case of a large number of separate undertakings, both publicly and privately owned.

The *Electrical Times* publishes in nearly every issue tables showing the analysed yearly returns of some 300 of the statutory undertakings, and as these returns are made out in a form prescribed by Act of Parliament they are readily comparable.

In addition to the above, the publishers produce an annual reprint of these tables, usually containing in addition to the figures relating to the separate undertakings group analyses giving the results produced by the companies as a whole and by the municipalities as a whole. Let us see what these figures have to say to us.

TABLE I.

	Local Authorities.	Companies.
Capital Expenditure per Kilowatt of Maximum Load	£96	£153
Working Expenses per Unit sold ...	0·80d.	1·27d.
Average Price charged per Unit ...	1·70d.	2·52d.
Amount provided for Depreciation and Reserve per £100 of Capital ...	—	£1·32
Amount provided for Sinking Fund per £100 of Capital	£3·15	—
Load Factor*	20·68 %	18·53 %

Table I. gives us the position of affairs as shown in the last (1910-11) issue of these annual tables, and the figures crudely as they stand appear to present an overwhelming case for the municipalities.

Thus, as regards capital expenditure, for each kilowatt of maximum load (that is to say, for a given capacity for meeting the demand for energy at any time) the companies have expended in cash or credit 60 % more than have the municipalities. In working expenses they spent 59 % more per unit sold; their consumers paid them on an average 48 % more per unit.

And here arises one of the loudest and most persistent of the charges levelled against municipal economics. "They are living on their capital," say the objectors; "in a few years their plant will be obsolete or worn out, and notwithstanding this they will still be obliged to go on paying interest on the capital invested, while new loans will have to be raised for the renewal of their machinery."

Now, if this is true, in what a parlous condition must be the electric supply companies in view of the fact that whereas the municipalities are hastening to perdition on sinking funds averaging 3·15 %, not to mention any additional reserves they may be accumulating, the companies are only providing 1·32, or less than half the amount set aside by the municipalities for the protection of their capital, and this notwithstanding the fact that whereas the companies' statutory powers are virtually terminable at the end of forty-two years, those of the local authorities are to all intents and purposes perpetual.

And yet the companies' shares and debentures are readily saleable at quite substantial prices !

Many other voices are raised in refutation of the evidence crudely set forth in Table I. "The municipal undertakings are much larger than those owned by companies, wherefore they work more cheaply."

The municipalities make large paper profits by selling energy to themselves for street lighting, etc., at exorbitant prices. They charge working expenses to capital account. They sweat their workers.

* Ratio of actual to possible output of units by the plant installed.

They pay extravagant wages for the purpose of vote catching. They have invented a whole calendar of new crimes in addition to the old ones doubtless practised by such enterprising local authorities as may have ruled those "Cities of the Plain."

These things obviously want looking into. Let us make an investigation in order to ascertain what of truth may be in them.

The first of these charges has an appearance of reason, inasmuch as the biggest yearly loads of the municipalities' undertakings averaged 2,000 kilowatts, while that of the companies averaged only 1,440 kilowatts during the year we are considering. We must therefore compare our undertakings size for size.

If the list of authorities given in the *Electrical Times* table be taken, and each group (municipal and company) arranged, not in alphabetical order, but in a table commencing with the largest undertaking (as measured by its maximum load) and ending with the smallest, and if we plot on squared paper the figures given, the abscissæ representing the size of the undertaking and the vertical ordinates any other column of figures, such as the total cost of production per unit or the capital expenditure per kilowatt of maximum load, we shall find that we get a series of dots distributed like the tail of a comet about a mean curve.

What we want is to find the mean trend of that curve.

N.B.—The exposition here following of the method of analysis used is not necessary to the main argument; it is given in order that anyone sufficiently interested to do so may verify for himself the results obtained.

A higher degree of regularity may be obtained by further sub-dividing our towns into groups of ten each, and again plotting our co-ordinates; they now fall into a much more orderly arrangement, but it is still not easy to draw a curve which shall represent their mean. (See Fig. 1.)

FIG. 1.

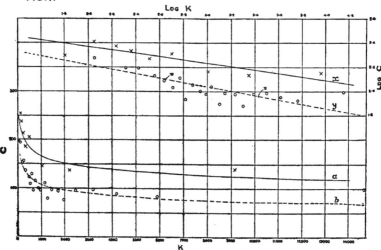

MAXIMUM OUTPUT IN KILOWATTS = K AND CAPITAL COST PER KILOWATT . C

If, however, we take these co-ordinates and instead of plotting them directly we plot their logarithms, we shall find that they lie roughly along a straight line (see *y*, Fig. I), and it is a very easy thing to find the mean of a number of co-ordinates following a straight line law : all we have to do is to separate them into two groups, one containing, say, all the figures of the first half of the table, and the other all the figures of the second half. We then find for each group the average of all the ordinates, and likewise the average of all the abcissæ ; thus we get two separate pairs of co-ordinates, one for the top half of our table and the other for the bottom half. (See *m* and *n*, Fig. I.) Plotting these two points on our squared paper, we draw a line through them which represents the mean of all our separate co-ordinates.

Now what does this straight line mean ?

Having taken as an example the relation between maximum load and capital expenditure for municipal undertakings, if our abcissæ represent logarithms of maximum loads in kilowatts, and our ordinates logarithms of capital cost per kilowatt in £, the line would start from an ordinate measuring 2·58 above the zero point and slope downwards toward the right at the rate of 0·179 inches of vertical height for every inch measured along the horizontal, or in other words :

$$\text{Log C} = 2\text{·}53 - (\text{Log K} \times 0\text{·}179),$$

FIG.2.

CAPITAL COST IN £ PER KILOWATT OF MAXIMUM LOAD

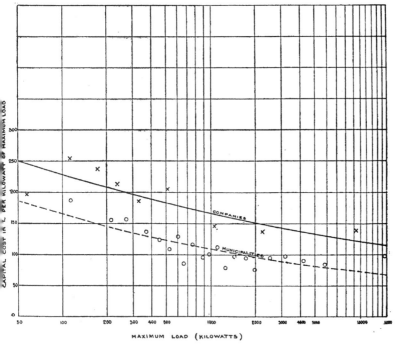

MAXIMUM LOAD (KILOWATTS)

COMPANY OWNED UNDERTAKINGS SHOWN THUS ——————— X
MUNICIPAL   "   "   " ———————— O
EACH X OR O REPRESENTS THE MEAN OF 10 UNDERTAKINGS

or to express our formula numerically: $C = \frac{340}{K^{0 \cdot 179}}$ from which formula we can calculate the mean curve for our co-ordinates already plotted. (Fig. 1, a.) The full line x is the corresponding logarithmic line for companies, and gives us the formula

$$\text{Log } C = 2 \cdot 63 - (\text{Log K} \times 0 \cdot 136), \text{ or } C = \frac{430}{K^{0 \cdot 136}} \text{ as shown in } b, \text{ Fig. 1.}$$

Although these formulæ represent hyperbolas it is not to be argued therefrom that the relation between the size of an undertaking and the cost of its installation or working follows a true hyperbolic law. All that is claimed in the present paper is that for the purposes of comparison, and within the limits of the data available, the mean relation is sufficiently nearly an hyperbola to render any departure from such law negligible.

It will be observed that in curves a and b, Fig. 1, most of the co-ordinate points are grouped at one end of the diagram, that is to say in the region of the most usual size (1,000 to 2,000 kilowatts). In order to make our comparison clearer it will be well to draw our diagrams in such a way that the mean of the ascertained co-ordinates (as represented by circles and crosses respectively) comes nearer the middle of the diagram, while at the same time the extremes are included in the picture. This can be done by graduating our abcissæ in such a way that equal distances represent equal *proportions* instead of equal quantities, that is to say by making our horizontal scale a scale of logarithms as in Fig. 2, which represents the same curves as are shown in Fig. 1. (Compare Figs. 1 and 2.) The abcissæ of this and the succeeding figures, with the exception of Figs. 9 and 12, are graduated in this way, not with any ulterior motives of hanky-panky but for the sake of clearness only.

The method of analyses above described has been followed in all cases in the following curves with the exceptions of that representing "Rent, Rates and Taxes" and of the graph illustrating the relations between "price" and "user," Fig. 12.

Having obtained a means of comparing the results size for size of publicly and privately owned undertakings, let us proceed to make our comparisons and discover what is to be learned therefrom and what justice may be in the accusations brought by its opponents against municipal trading in electricity.

Fig. 2, as already stated, represents capital expenditure per kilowatt of maximum load; the full line being the curve for companies and the dotted line that for municipalities.

It is obvious from these curves that, in the matter of capital expenditure at least, public bodies have proved on the average better buyers than companies, and not merely for large undertakings but better size for size from one end of the scale to the other.

This result was of course to be expected to some extent, inasmuch as the municipal capital contains no water, and moreover a public body can raise money at a cheaper rate than can a limited company who have not the guarantee of public rates behind them. It was hardly to be anticipated, however, that the difference would be so great, averaging as we have already seen 60 %.

Could this result have been obtained if it were to any marked extent customary for those in control of municipal undertakings to burden their capital accounts with items properly chargeable to revenue ? The answer is self-evident.

Now what about those dearly bought units applied to public lighting by means of which the ratepayers' money is filched for the purpose of bolstering up moribund municipal fads ?

Fig. 3 tells us something about this, and what it tells us is that there is " not much in it." The companies' charges are lower by a small percentage for the smaller undertakings and higher for the larger ones, the two curves crossing at a point representing a maxi‑mum load of 2,000 kilowatts.

If therefore the ratepayers are badly off under the municipal régime as regards the cost of electricity for public lighting, they are on the average very seldom better and generally worse off under the companies ; moreover, inasmuch as the municipal undertakings pro‑

FIG. 3

CHARGES FOR ENERGY FOR PUBLIC LIGHTING

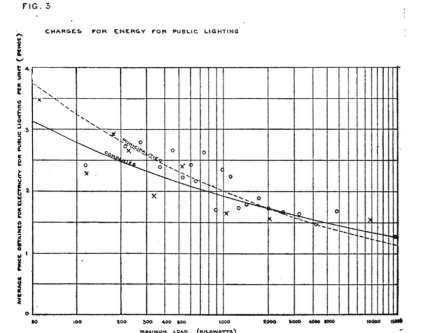

duce at a considerably lower price than do the companies, much of the cost of public lighting must obviously come back to them in the form of profit or in reduced charges for general supply.

Fig. 4 gives us the respective wages curves for the two classes of undertaking, and we must decide from these curves whether "sweat‑ing" or "extravagance" is to be charged against the municipalities.

The municipal curve lies somewhat higher than the company curve up to about 350 kilowatts, and above this limit follows a lower trend, so that of the two counts sweating perhaps more nearly fills the bill. But is it not at least arguable that wise expenditure of capital and able management have resulted in a saving in the

9

IG.4.

COST OF WORKMENS WAGES PER UNIT SOLD

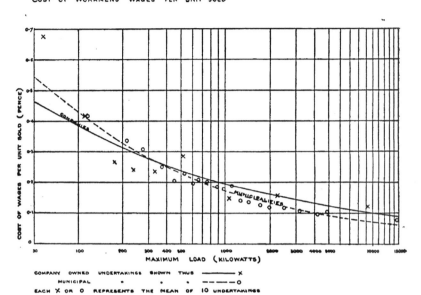

COMPANY OWNED UNDERTAKINGS SHOWN THUS ———— X
MUNICIPAL " " " —————o
EACH X OR O REPRESENTS THE MEAN OF 10 UNDERTAKINGS

amount of labor required? The whole tendency of the evidence supports this view. Indeed, to judge by the comparatively small difference between the respective wages curves and the large differences between those representing other items of expense, it is reasonable to deduce that the municipalities pay on an average a higher rate of wages than the companies but more than make up the difference by judicious management.

Fig. 5 gives us the relative amounts spent per unit sold on " Repairs and Maintenance." Here surely we have the municipalities " on the hip."

To the meanest intelligence it must be obvious at first glance that the plants of the municipalities are rapidly qualifying for the scrap heap, owing to neglect of the elementary duty of preserving the machinery intact.

The difference is remarkable ; the amount per unit spent by the companies being of the order of 50 % higher than that provided by the municipalities.

But it is *only at first glance* that this charge appears justifiable ; for the difference is of much the same order as those between the respective expenditures on management and capital, items of expense which cannot be avoided by the simple method of neglecting to provide them. It is fair to claim therefore that the muncipalities are doing at least as much, if not more, than the companies (in view of their excellent showing on other items) in the way of maintaining their plant in efficient working order.

FIG. 5.

COST OF REPAIRS & MAINTENANCE PER UNIT SOLD

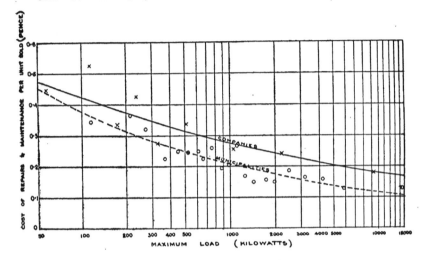

COMPANY OWNED UNDERTAKINGS SHOWN THUS ————————— x

MUNICIPAL   "   "   "   ————————— o

EACH X OR O REPRESENTS THE MEAN OF 10 UNDERTAKINGS

Fig. 6 shows the relative cost of coal per unit sold for the two classes of undertaking. It is only fair to the engineers of the companies to point out that the difference in this case is not in reality as great as would appear from the diagram, and that the apparent difference is largely though not entirely due to the fact that a larger relative percentage of the municipal undertakings is situated in the coal areas.

In Fig. 7 are given the relative amounts spent on management and establishment charges.

What can be the explanation of the extraordinary divergence between these curves? Why should companies have to pay, on an average, anything from 75 % to 300 % more for the management of their undertakings than have the municipalities?

The answer to this question probably lies in the realm of psychology.

The municipalities sweat their officials? Probably they do; certainly the average pay of municipal electrical engineers is extremely low. But it is open to the economist of the cynical "Manchester school" to retort, "If we can get the best men for the rates we pay, why pay more?" and in view of what has gone before, the rejoinder can scarcely be made that the service obtained is of the "nasty" as well as of the "cheap" variety. The general result produced by the municipal engineers is of itself a magnificent testimonial to their efficiency.

The companies have directors' fees to meet? This is, of course, true. You cannot get brains or energy for nothing when your object is private profit. The municipalities, on the other hand, do get the services of their "boards of directors" for nothing; and this brings us to a fundamental proposition of the highest importance in the psychology of public service, namely, *"that men will do better work at a cheaper rate when working for the public good than when working for private gain."* If the figures I am quoting prove anything at all, they prove this.

Figure 8 is rather remarkable for the fact that, as it indicates, the cost of water, oil, and stores like that of coal is, other things being equal, little, if at all, less in the case of the municipalities than in the case of the companies, phenomena so unusual that one feels compelled to look about for an explanation.

FIG. 8.   COST OF COAL AND OTHER FUEL PER UNIT SOLD

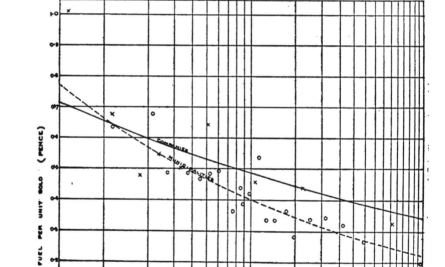

COMPANY OWNED UNDERTAKINGS SHOWN THUS ——————— ×
MUNICIPAL   "   "   ——————— ○
[EACH × OR ○ REPRESENTS THE MEAN OF 10 UNDERTAKINGS

This will probably be found in the fact that where technical as apart from financial matters are concerned there is probably not much to choose between the two classes of undertakings. The companies' engineers would doubtless produce quite as good results as their municipal brethren under equally favorable economic conditions. It is obviously in the board room that the chief differences between public and private trading arise.

Rents, rates, and taxes are presented in Fig. 9, and here will be found some possible explanation of the often heard complaint that the companies are not fairly treated in the matter of rating. The item in question does not appear to follow any law analogous to those governing output and cost under other heads of expenditure (or, indeed, any law at all, except such as under providence may guide the inscrutable workings of the minds of the assessment authorities). They commence equally at or about 0·15d. per unit, and rise and fall respectively to about 0·2d. per unit in the case of the companies and about 0·1d. per unit for the municipal undertakings.

A large proportion of the item in question is due to local rates, which are of the nature of an income tax ; and inasmuch as the companies charge far higher prices for their energy than do the municipalities, it is reasonable to expect their rateable value to be correspondingly higher.

FIG. 7.

MANAGEMENT, SALARIES, OFFICE & LEGAL EXPENSES INSURANCE ETO.

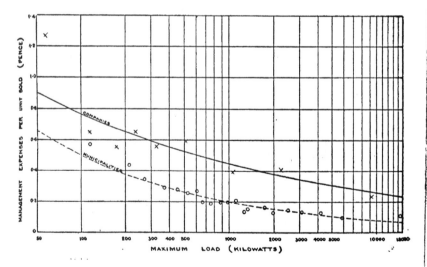

COMPANY OWNED UNDERTAKINGS SHOWN THUS ———— x

MUNICIPAL " " " ——————— o

EACH X OR O REPRESENTS THE MEAN OF 10 UNDERTAKINGS

The remainder of the difference is probably to be accounted for by the obviously superior economic efficiency which the municipalities evince, on the whole, throughout their operations.

In Fig. 10 we have curves representing the grand totals of the preceding curves, and it is an interesting check on the method of

FIG. 8.

COST OF OIL, WASTE, WATER, AND STORES PER UNIT SOLD

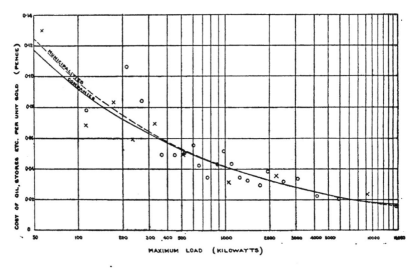

COMPANY OWNED UNDERTAKINGS SHOWN THUS ——————— x
MUNICIPAL " " " — — — — — o
EACH X OR O REPRESENTS THE MEAN OF IO UNDERTAKINGS

analysis employed to find that the respective values of these curves agree to within about 2 % or less with the sums of the preceding curves for items of working cost. Beyond this observation Fig. 10 requires no further comment.

The consumers' point of view is touched upon in Fig. 11, which shows the average price received per unit for publicly and privately owned undertakings respectively of various sizes. It is obvious from these curves on which side the consumers' bread is buttered.

Having, as I submit, effectively shown that the figures given in Table I. present a true comparison between the respective results of public and private ownership, and that they are not to be whittled away by the criticisms with which I have dealt so far, let us return to the consideration of this table. The four essential points in the economics of electricity supply are here presented, and in all of these the municipalities make a far better showing than do the companies. But for the purpose of making a more simple comparison these may be combined into one figure for each class of undertaking.

For this common figure we may take the gross profit per £100 of capital on the assumption that both classes of undertaking charged their consumers the same average price for energy.

In the return we are considering, the number of units of energy sold per kilowatt of maximum load is for municipalities 1,811. The average price charged by the companies, including meter rents, etc., is 2·69 pence.

Had the municipalities charged the same average prices, their gross profit per unit would have been this figure less their cost of production, or 1·89d. per unit, which multiplied by the number of units sold per kilowatt, namely 1,811, gives us a gross profit of 14·9 % on our capital expenditure of £96 per kilowatt.

$$\text{Thus} \quad \frac{1\cdot89 \times 1,811}{240} \times \frac{100}{96} = 14\cdot85$$

Now the difference between the companies' average price and working expenses is only 1·25d., while the number of units sold per kilowatt of maximum load is 1,624, which gives a gross profit of only 5·53 % on a capital of £153 per kilowatt.

$$\text{Thus} \quad \frac{1\cdot42 \times 1,624}{240} \times \frac{100}{153} = 6\cdot28\ \%$$

Thus the municipalities would have earned more than two and a third times the amount of gross profit per £ of capital that the companies have gained.

FIG. 9.

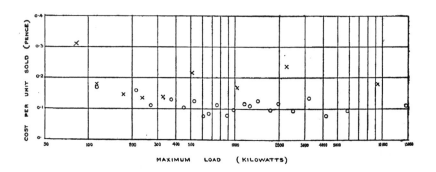

RENTS   RATES   AND   TAXES

COST PER UNIT SOLD (PENCE)

MAXIMUM   LOAD   (KILOWATTS)

COMPANY   OWNED   UNDERTAKINGS   SHOWN   THUS   X
MUNICIPAL   ,,   ,,   ,,   O
EACH   X   OR   O   REPRESENTS   THE   MEAN   OF   10   UNDETAKINGS

If we take nett profit as the basis of comparison, still keeping the two classes of undertaking on an equal commercial footing, the greater success of the municipalities from the purely commercial point of view becomes still more strongly marked.

Thus, accepting the companies' provision for depreciation and reserve as a sufficient allowance in both cases (and there is no commercial reason why if it is sufficient in the case of the companies whose powers are terminable it should not be sufficient in the case of the municipalities who have perpetual powers), we find the nett

FIG.10.

TOTAL WORKING COST PER UNIT SOLD

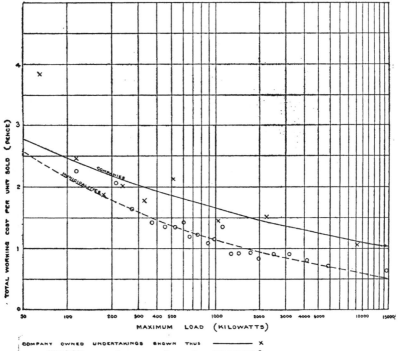

MAXIMUM LOAD (KILOWATTS)

COMPANY OWNED UNDERTAKINGS SHOWN THUS ————— X
MUNICIPAL " " " ————— O
EACH X OR O REPRESENTS THE MEAN OF 10 UNDERTAKINGS

profits are 13·53 % in the case of the municipalities, and 4·95 % in the case of the companies ; the former figure being about two and three fourths times the latter.

If, then, the two systems are compared on the usual basis of profit, it is evident that the municipalities have beaten the companies by the handsome margin of nearly three to one.

So far the municipalities have been on their defence, but we now come to a set of facts justifying a prompt and vigorous attack upon the claim of private enterprise to toleration even, let alone encouragement, in the field of public service.

The "sale" of an article depends largely on its selling price, and this is as true of electrical energy as it is of any other commodity.

The retarding influence of private ownership upon the development of the electrical industry becomes evident from an examination of Fig. 12, in which are depicted the average prices charged and the average sale in units per head of population for provincial undertakings, as derived from the *Electrical Times* annual tables for the years 1903-4 to 1911-12 inclusive; the company returns being given in full and those of the municipalities in dotted lines as before. The inverse relation between the prices charged and the rate of increase is particularly noteworthy.

FIG. 11.

.AVERAGE PRICE OBTAINED (TOTAL SUPPLY)

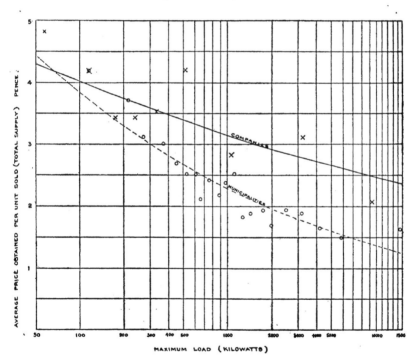

MAXIMUM LOAD (KILOWATTS)

COMPANY OWNED UNDERTAKINGS SHOWN THUS ————— X

MUNICIPAL " , " " – – – – – – O

EACH X OR O REPRESENTS THE MEAN OF 10. UNDERTAKINGS

Compare the development in the one case with that in the other and consider what an intolerable drag on the electrical industry universal company ownership would have been. Thus in the provinces instead of an annual output of some 790 million units for the year 1910-11, we should have been fobbed off with only 460 million.

Instead of a capital of £36,000,000, earning for the public 11·3 %, we should have spent in its place some £28,000,000, plus 60 % or so of water, in order to earn 4·3 % thereon for private investors. Note also the tendency of the companies to maintain their average selling prices at the highest permissible figure and the tendency of the local authorities to reduce theirs to the lowest.

It may be suggested that the supply of electrical energy is an exceptional industry, and that arguments deduced therefrom are not applicable to other industries.

This is not the case, however, as will be seen from an examination of the Parliamentary Returns of gas undertakings.

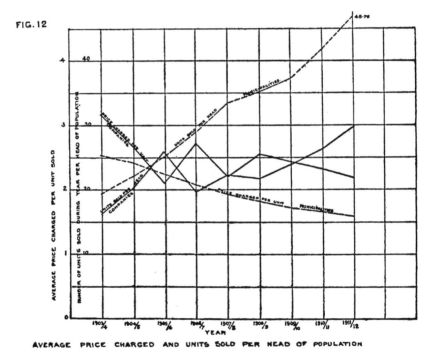

FIG. 12

AVERAGE PRICE CHARGED AND UNITS SOLD PER HEAD OF POPULATION

COMPANY OWNED UNDERTAKINGS SHOWN THUS ————
MUNICIPAL   •   •   • -----------

PROVINCIAL UNDERTAKINGS ONLY.

That for December, 1911, shows the following results :

TABLE II.

	Companies.		Municipalities.
Capital per 1,000 cubic feet of gas sold per annum	16s.	...	12s. 7d.
Working expenses per 1,000 cubic feet sold	31·86d.	...	28·1d.
Revenue per 1,000 cubic feet sold ...	42·56d.	...	38·5d.

Thus, on the basis of equal conditions as before, the gross profits of the municipalities would have been 1s. 2½d. on a capital of 12s. 7d., or 9·58 %, as compared with the gross profit of 5·57 % earned by the companies.

In addition to the above, the municipalities have provided sinking funds, etc., to the amount of nearly a third of their capital. It would be interesting to know what proportion of their capital the companies have written off.

Here also it is interesting to note that whereas the sales in the case of the companies increased to the extent of 2·7 %, in the case of the municipalities they increased by nearly 3·3 %, i.e., the municipalities' business is growing 20 % faster than that of the companies.

In electric traction also the municipalities compare advantageously with the companies. Thus, in the *Electrical Times* annual tables for the year 1910-11 the following figures are given :

TABLE III.

	Companies.		Local Authorities.
Capital cost per mile of track ...	£15,000	...	£16,100
Traffic revenue per car mile ...	9·90d.	...	10·58d.
Operating cost per car mile ...	6·00d.	...	6·52d.
Operating cost per passenger ...	·79d.	...	·64d.
Average fare per passenger ...	1·30d.	...	1·05d.
Depreciation and reserve ...	£1·43	...	£2·70
Nett profit per £100 of capital...	£5·58	...	£6·66

These figures are not strictly comparable, inasmuch as the districts served by the municipalities are usually better suited to tramway traction than those served by the companies.

There can be no doubt, however, that under level conditions, the economic laws which render other categories of municipal enterprise so much more successful commercially than the corresponding private enterprises would in a few years tell as markedly in favor of the municipal traction undertakings as they have already done in the case of municipal electricity and gas supply.

Doubtless the figures I have quoted and the conclusions I have deduced therefrom will be met by the protest (that final refuge of the destitute controversialist), " Statistics can be made to prove anything "; but I have not much fear that statistics (real statistics) can be produced which will suffice to refute my proposition that our municipalities can "beat to a frazzle" the private companies working in the same fields of enterprise.

The question here suggests itself, in what fields of commercial activity is private enterprise likely to succeed better than public enterprise?

It is not the province of the present paper to discuss the relative merits of the two rival systems from the sociological or politico-economic aspects. These have been and will continue to be dealt with by other pens. My object has been to clear the field of some of the more common and immediate misconceptions and super-stitions concerning municipal enterprises which are still widely believed in, and I must now leave it to my readers to judge how far this object has been successfully attained.

F ABIAN SOCIETY.—The Fabian Society consists of Socialists. A state-
ment of its Rules and a complete list of publications can be obtained from
the Secretary, at the Fabian Office, 3 Clement's Inn, London, W.C.
FABIAN ESSAYS IN SOCIALISM. Paper 6d.; cloth 1/6; post. 2½d. and 4d.
WHAT TO READ on Social and Economic Subjects. 1s. n. and 2s. n.
THIS MISERY OF BOOTS. By H. G. WELLS. 3d., post free 4d.
FABIAN TRACTS and LEAFLETS.
Tracts, each 16 to 52 pp., price 1d., or 9d. per doz., unless otherwise stated.
Leaflets, 4 pp. each, price 1d. for six copies, 1s. per 100, or 8/6 per 1000.
The Set of 77, 3s.; post free 3/5. Bound in Buckram, 4/6 n.; post free 5s

I.—General Socialism in its various aspects.

TRACTS.—169. The Socialist Movement in Germany. By W. S. SANDERS.
In cover, with portrait of Bebel, 2d. 159. The Necessary Basis of Society.
By SIDNEY WEBB. 151. The Point of Honour. By RUTH C. BENTINCK.
147. Capital and Compensation. By E. R. PEASE. 146. Socialism and
Superior Brains. By BERNARD SHAW. 142. Rent and Value. 138. Municipal Trading. 121. Public Service versus Private Expenditure. By Sir
OLIVER LODGE. 107. Socialism for Millionaires. By BERNARD SHAW.
139. Socialism and the Churches. By Rev. JOHN CLIFFORD, D.D. 133.
Socialism and Christianity. By Rev. PERCY DEARMER. 78. Socialism
and the Teaching of Christ. By Dr. J. CLIFFORD. 42. Christian Socialism. By Rev. S. D. HEADLAM. 79. A Word of Remembrance and Caution
to the Rich. By JOHN WOOLMAN. 72. The Moral Aspects of Socialism.
By SIDNEY BALL. 69. Difficulties of Individualism. By S. WEBB. 51.
Socialism: True and False. By S. WEBB. 45. The Impossibilities of
Anarchism. By BERNARD SHAW (price 2d.). 7. Capital and Land (revised 1908) 5. Facts for Socialists (revised 1908). 132. A Guide to
Books for Socialists. LEAFLETS—13. What Socialism Is 1. Why are
the Many Poor? WELSH TRACTS—143. Sosialaeth yng Ngoleuni'r Beibl.
141. Translation of 139. 87. Translation of 78. 38. Translation of 1.

II.—Applications of Socialism to Particular Problems.

TRACTS.—171. The Nationalization of Mines and Minerals Bill. By H. H.
SCHLOESSER. 170. Profit-Sharing & Co-Partnership: a Fraud and Failure?
By E. R. PEASE. In cover. 164. Gold and State Banking. By E. R. PEASE.
163. Women and Prisons. By HELEN BLAGG and CHARLOTTE WILSON. 2d.
162. Family Life on a Pound a Week. By Mrs. REEVES. In cover, 2d. 161.
Afforestation and Unemployment. By A. P. GRENFELL. 160. A National
Medical Service. By F. LAWSON DODD. 2d. 157. The Working Life of
Women. By Miss B. L. HUTCHINS. 155. The Case against the Referen-
dum. By CLIFFORD SHARP. 154. The Case for School Clinics. By L. HADEN
GUEST. 153. The Twentieth Century Reform Bill. By H. H. SCHLOESSER.
152. Our Taxes as they are and as they ought to be. By R. JONES, B.Sc.
In cover, 2d. 150. State Purchase of Railways. By EMIL DAVIES. In cover,
2d. 149. The Endowment of Motherhood. By H. D. HARBEN. In cover, 2d.
145. The Case for School Nurseries. By Mrs. TOWNSHEND. 140. Child
Labor under Capitalism. By Mrs. HYLTON DALE. 136. The Village and
the Landlord. By EDW. CARPENTER. 130. Home Work and Sweating
By Miss B. L. HUTCHINS. 128. The Case for a Legal Minimum Wage.
122. Municipal Milk and Public Health. By Dr. F. LAWSON DODD. 125.
Municipalization by Provinces. 123. The Revival of Agriculture. 115.
State Aid to Agriculture: an Example. 124. State Control of Trusts.
86. Municipal Drink Traffic. 83. State Arbitration and the Living
Wage. LEAFLET.—104. How Trade Unions benefit Workmen.

III.—Local Government Powers : How to use them.

TRACTS.—172. What about the Rates? or, Municpal Finance and Municipal Autonomy. By SIDNEY WEBB. 156. What an Education Committee
can do (Elementary Schools), 3d. 137. Parish Councils and Village Life.
109. Cottage Plans and Common Sense. 76. Houses for the People.
82. Workmen's Compensation Act. LEAFLETS.—134. Small Holdings:
and how to get them. 68. The Tenant's Sanitary Catechism. 71. Ditto
for London.

IV.—General Politics and Fabian Policy.

TRACTS.—158. The Case against the C.O.S. By Mrs. TOWNSHEND. 108.
Twentieth Century Politics. By S. WEBB. 70. Report on Fabian Policy.
41. The Fabian Society: its Early History. By BERNARD SHAW.

V.—Biographical Series. In portrait covers, 2d. each.

Fabian Tract No. 174.

CHARLES KINGSLEY & CHRISTIAN SOCIALISM

By COLWYN E. VULLIAMY.

Biographical Series No. 5.   Price 2d.
Published and sold by the Fabian Society,
3 Clement's Inn, Strand, London, W.C.
January 1914.

Charles Kingsley and Christian Socialism.

The Christian Socialists.

"All great poets," says Kingsley's Chartist hero, "are by their office democrats." Perhaps it may be said with equal truth that all real Christians are by their profession Socialists. The vital religions never have fought shy, and never can fight shy, of the social problem. The existence of poverty and evil is contrary to the religious ideal, and is in continual opposition to the religious doctrines. The founders of the Christian Church were very clear on this point. The poor and oppressed were in a special sense God's children, and their presence in society indicated a state of affairs which the Church was foremost in denouncing and in seeking to correct. Maurice, the originator of modern Christian Socialism, never hesitated to affirm the necessity for the co-operation of Church and State in any sound scheme of social reform, and his teaching lays stress on the "radical affinity" between the principles of religion and the practice of Socialism. More, he believed in the direct action of the Church in politics and industrial regulation. That the Christian Socialist Movement has exercised considerable influence in both directions is beyond dispute.

Before considering the position of Charles Kingsley in this movement and his special influence, it will be well to give, first, some idea of the movement itself, and then a short account of the man whose teaching and personality led to its formation—Frederick Denison Maurice.

English Socialism and the Co-operative Idea may be regarded as of twin birth. The work of Robert Owen has been already dealt with in this series; it is not necessary here to describe his theories and reforms in detail. The wonderful, almost quixotic, romance of the New Lanark mills, raised wages, reduced hours, free education and amusements, cheap provisions, and habitable dwellings—all this is well known, and so are Owen's magnificent schemes for the general organization of industries and the free instruction of the whole community. Had the more reasonable of Owen's proposals been peacefully and persistently urged, it is likely that democratic advance during the first half of the last century would have been much more rapid. Unfortunately, the democratic cause fell into the hands of O'Connor and his "physical force" Chartists, and with the fiasco of April 10th, 1848, when the Charter was trundled to its doom in a hackney cab and its heroes dispersed by the householder constables, it seemed as though the rights of the people had suffered a crushing defeat. But this was not so. Stimulated largely by the success of the Rochdale experiment, the co-operative schemes again came to the fore, and plans for industrial and social reform were both voiced by the new movement, which, a year or two later, was known as Christian Socialism. Realizing the finer elements of Chartism, and deeply conscious of the suffering of the people, a group of devoted workers gathered round their leader, Maurice, and by means of an extremely vigorous propaganda, untiring personal labor, and the launching and financing of co-operative concerns, sought to "assert God's order," and to establish a system of brotherhood and mutual help.

The Christian Socialists were by no means revolutionary. They were in some respects conservative—Kingsley always asserted the value of an aristocracy—and believed rather in a restoration than in a reformation of society. They did not seek to reconstruct society, but to avail themselves of the resources of the existing society, which they considered as a divine institution, soiled and corrupted by the evil practices of men, and above all by the spirit of competition. Their strength lay in the noble ideals which they set before the working men. Their weakness lay in the obvious limitations of their dogma, and perhaps also in their conception of the natural goodness of men and in a false theory of society. By 1850 they had already promoted twelve co-operative associations, all of them in trades which were then untransformed by the use of machinery—tailors, shoemakers, builders, piano-makers, printers, smiths, and bakers. It should be pointed out that the Christian Socialist theory of co-operation differed from the Rochdale plan in its fundamental principle. The Rochdale co-operatives adopted the Owenite "elimination of profit" scheme, and formed an association of consumers, with benefits according to the amount purchased ; the Christian Socialists advocated the association of producers, with benefits according to labor. The commercial failure of their enterprises was mainly caused by the fact that in small co-operative concerns run on these lines it was impossible to destroy the competitive element.

The idea of the movement was the application of the religious principle to economic problems, with special emphasis on *the supreme importance of individual character.* The life of the movement was short. After some four years of admirable and heroic effort, and the sacrifice in some cases of health and fortune, they were compelled to abandon their schemes for the regeneration of industry. But although they had failed as a working organization, they had set an example which profoundly influenced the trend of English Socialism and has yielded a richer harvest than any of them could have foreseen. And it may be questioned whether, continuing their individual efforts independently, they did not accomplish more than they could have done had they remained united, and possibly restricted, in close association.

Taken from the religious standpoint, they differed from the great Anglican Revival—the Oxford Movement—in this respect : that instead of bringing the people to the Church, they were concerned rather with bringing the Church to the people.

.. The literature of the Christian Socialists will be dealt with in the course of this essay ; it is time now to give attention to their leader and prophet.

F. D. Maurice.

Frederick Denison Maurice has been described as " certainly the most typical theologian of the nineteenth century." In addition to his great theological and metaphysical learning, he possessed what was then a rather unusual thing in a clergyman—a sturdy democratic spirit. His literary career began early. When a Cambridge undergraduate in 1825 he edited a paper, called the *Metropolitan Quarterly Magazine*, with his friend Whitmore. Most of the contributors were fellow undergraduates, and among them John Stuart Mill, who wrote an attack on *Blackwood's Magazine*, under the title of " The New School for Cockneyism." The *Metropolitan* ceased publication after four issues. After having contributed to the *Athenæum*, he became editor, in 1828 (at the age of twenty-three), but resigned the following year. By 1830 he had completed a novel, " Eustace Conway," which was published about four years later. It was at this period that he removed to Oxford and made the acquaintance of Gladstone, who was then an undergraduate. In 1834 he took orders, and was soon drawn into the pamphleteer controversies which characterized the theological history of that period. " Subscription No Bondage " was written in 1835. From this period he broke away from the Oxford School. Pusey's writings contained " everything he did not think and did not believe," and Pusey, on his part, was " exceedingly angry " with Maurice's tract on Baptism, published in 1837. This year he married Miss Anna Barton, the daughter of General Barton, of the 2nd Life Guards.

In 1838 began a bitter warfare on the part of the religious newspapers, which continued, with little intermission, during his entire lifetime. Carlyle's influence was at this period affecting all ranks of intellectual society. Maurice attended his lectures, but his agreement with Carlyle was only partial, and he sometimes denounced his words and manner as " wild pantheistic rant." The inefficiency of the Church saddened him. " The Church is in a sad state ; we all know that—little light, little life." In 1840 he edited the *Educational Magazine*. He became Professor of Theology at King's College and Chaplain of Lincoln's Inn in 1845. The following year he was visited by Ludlow, who sought his aid in a scheme " to bear the leisure and good feeling of the Inns of Court upon the destitution and vice of the neighborhood," a phrase which leaves one in doubt as to its exact meaning. He was active in the establishment of Queen's College, and was assisted by Kingsley, at a later stage, on the committee.

Politics for the People, the first periodical issued by the new Socialists (the term Christian Socialist was not currently employed until two years later), was first published under Maurice's direction on May 6th, 1848. It ran through three months of publication, and came to an end in July, having reached a weekly circulation of two thousand copies. Maurice now held meetings of his friends once a week at his house in Queen Square; he also organized bible classes and night schools. Ludlow had persuaded the Chartist tailor, Walter Cooper, to hear Maurice preaching at Lincoln's Inn, and this, in April, 1849, led to his first meeting with Chartist working men at the Cranbourne tavern. These meetings were continued and were attended by several clergymen. The period of full activity was about to commence. "The time had come in my father's life," writes his son, "when it was certain that a movement of which he would be the leader must begin."

The little band of workers were formally organized as the Christian Socialists in 1850, and the first number of their organ, the *Christian Socialist*, with Ludlow as editor, was published on November 1st. Maurice's contributions were not numerous.

Both Maurice and his friends were subjected to a wild and bitterly unjust attack from the pen of one Croker in the *Quarterly* for September, 1851. In spite of its manifest exaggeration and open malignity, it did much to inflame public opinion against the Socialists. During the great Iron Trades Strike of 1852 the Christian Socialists were energetic on behalf of the men. The strike was a failure; the men were forced to return to work at the old terms and to abandon their union.

After a prolonged discussion, Maurice was expelled from King's College in 1853 (November), owing to certain opinions expressed in his "Theological Essays"—a publication which could not fail, at such a juncture, to provoke controversy. The whole affair gained a wide publicity. The opinions of the press wavered: Maurice was condemned on the one hand and applauded on the other; to the Broad Churchmen he was a victim, to the High Churchmen a heretic. From conscientious motives he resigned his position at Queen's College the following month—a position to which he returned, in reply to the solicitation of the entire Council, three years later. The survey of his last years must be condensed. He was particularly interested in the instruction of women of the working classes and in the Working Men's College. A series of "Tracts for Priests and People" was written by Maurice and his friends during 1861-2, and published in the latter year. At the same time, after many years of labor, his great work on "Moral and Metaphysical Philosophy" was printed. Towards the close of his life he became more and more absorbed in polemical and theological discussions and in every kind of doctrinal controversy. He died in 1872, at the age of sixty-six.

Maurice possessed a vast personal influence over the men with whom he was brought into contact, and especially over the leaders of the Christian Socialist Movement, who were in turn led by his unanswerable resolution, his loyalty, and his calm endurance. For example, he was able to suppress Lord Ripon's pamphlet on Democracy ("The Duty of the Age") by the mere weight of his objection, even after the pamphlet had been printed and was ready to be distributed. He was the intellect and the scholar of the movement ; his disciple, Kingsley, humanized his ideas and set them in a form " understanded of the people." *

Charles Kingsley—Early Years.

Descended from men who had fought at Naseby and Minden, the son of a country gentleman whose mismanaged fortune was the cause of his entering the Church, Charles Kingsley was born at Holne Vicarage, in Devonshire, on June 12th, 1819. His father was a man of many talents and a keen sportsman, and it was from him, doubtless, that Kingsley inherited that open-air temperament which was always so characteristic. Kingsley's child-play seems to have been divided between the Army and the Church. He was either engaged upon fortification work or he was preaching in his pinafore to an imaginary congregation. His first poem, a very solemn reflection on human mortality, was written at the age of four years and eight months. It is not possible to give his boyhood in detail, but one episode must certainly be dwelt upon.

When a lad of twelve he was sent to school at Clifton, and it was here that, to use his own words, he " received his first lesson in social science." The Bristol riots had begun in the autumn of 1831, and it was in the following year that Kingsley, fascinated, as schoolboys are wont to be, by the horror and excitement of a " row," evaded supervision and went forth to see for himself. It was a nauseating affair. Demos, in true Caliban mood, had broached casks of spirit upon the paving-stones, had defied the soldiers, who sat motionless, orderless on their horses, the blood streaming from their faces ; had plundered, burned and violated in full sight of trembling and hesitating authority. The flames from a burning house ignited the spirit in a gutter ; in one instant a blazing torrent of fire rushed down upon the drunken wretches and left behind it a line of blackened corpses— Demos, to the accompaniment of outrage and suicide, continuing his frenzied debauch. The scene produced the one possible effect on a questioning and intelligent mind : " That sight," he said, " made me a Radical."

College Days and Curacy.

After a two-year's course as a day student at King's College (his father at that time having the living of Chelsea), he gained a scholarship—much to his own surprise—at Magdalene, Cambridge. He was extremely popular with his fellow-undergraduates of every description. Like all imaginative men, he found enjoyment in all kinds of society. His life was one of extraordinary mental and physical activity, though, in the academic sense, he never distinguished himself. In Kingsley, a young man possessed of a vehement and challenging spirit, the restlessness of his age became at times a veritable fever. The Tractarian Movement was in full force. It was a period of fierce and disquieting controversies. His sense of religion

---

* Unlike Kingsley, Maurice was never at his ease when talking to individuals of the manual working class. His manner on such occasions was timid and conventional.

was overclouded. To escape from the strain of his own searching and wearing thoughts he "went in for excitement of every kind "—horses, duck-shooting, fencing, boxing, boating, and so forth. His acquaintance, through his writings, with Carlyle and his philosophy helped to ballast his unsteady and wavering opinions. It is probable, too, that friendship with another undergraduate, Charles Mansfield, proved a good influence.

The story of Mansfield's short life is particularly touching. He possessed an unusual brilliance of conversation, the most intense faith that right was might, and that there was indeed a God in the heavens. He was a student of chemistry, and became so distinguished in this science that men saw in him the successor of Faraday. In due time he became one of the Christian Socialists, and his death, which occurred as the result of an accident in the laboratory, was a grievous loss to the movement, and especially to Kingsley. From Mansfield Kingsley acquired that zeal for sanitary reform and for the institution of a sound national hygiene which became pronounced in his later activities.

Kingsley had at one time considered the law as a profession, but in 1841 he decided upon entering the Church. In striking and very significant words he announces his devotion to "the religion which I have scorned," begins a course of desperately hard reading for his degree, cramming three years' work into six months of unceasing labor, emerges from the trial with a first in classics and senior optime in mathematics, reads for Holy Orders, and is ordained in the July of 1842. During this period of preparation, and, indeed, ever since the summer of 1839, when he first met her, Miss Pascoe Grenfell, the lady who was to be his wife (a *summum bonum* which he then despaired of), was the confidant of his thoughts, hopes and perplexities, and the kind admonitress of his troubled spirit. It was she who introduced him to the writings of Carlyle, Coleridge, and Maurice ; it was she who consoled and strengthened him in the midst of doubt ; and we may be pretty certain that it was for her sake that he worked so hard and so manfully when once the clear road lay before him. During the interval between leaving Cambridge and entering upon his curate life, he began his " Life of St. Elizabeth of Hungary," illustrated with his own drawings. " It was not intended for publication, but as a gift to his wife on his marriage day, if that day should ever come." On July 17th he first ministered in Eversley Church—the church which was destined to be his for more than thirty years.

He seems to have found the parish of Eversley in a lamentable condition. The population were traditional smugglers and poachers. The squire had been a Prince Regent's man—a hard-riding, hard-drinking person, and "a strict game preserver." Of Kingsley's rector I can learn little. Available records are silent. Perhaps we may form a sufficient judgment of his character from the fact that he absconded in 1844. Kingsley's manliness, his plain speaking and preaching, and his skill at fisticuffs rapidly gained him the friendship and respect of the villagers. The poacher and the poet, two

democratic products, have always fraternized in spirit. Here was·
a parson who was some good at last: the empty church began to·
fill.

At the end of 1843 Kingsley took leave of his bachelor quarters
at the corner of Eversley Green, having been offered the curacy of
Pimperne. In January, 1844, he married Miss Grenfell, and, the
living of Eversley becoming unexpectedly vacant, he received the
appointment, and the newly married pair took up their abode in
Eversley Rectory.

The Working Classes in 1844.

. It is by no means unimportant that we should try to form some
idea of the industrial and rural conditions of this period. Chartism
was rampant. The strikes of 1842, when wheat stood at sixty-five
shillings a quarter, and sabotage and violence were general, had
ended, but now (1844) a fierce dispute was in progress between the
masters and men of the northern collieries. The men were beaten,
but their defeat led to the enlistment of 30,000 as physical-force
Chartists. The misery of the industrial workers was almost beyond
belief. The treatment they received from their employers was so·
barbarous and so overbearingly despotic that the facts read like some
black and impossible fantasy of the imagination. A very remarkable
young man of twenty-three was collecting material for his book on
the working classes of England. He was a German, and his name
was Frederick Engels. From his book—the saddest and most terrible
record of that period—I must give one or two typical illustrations.
. Of the London slums he says : " The streets are generally
unpaved, rough, dirty, filled with vegetable and animal refuse, without sewers or gutters, but supplied with foul, stagnant pools instead.
. . . . Scarcely a whole window-pane can be found, the walls are
crumbling, doorposts and window-frames loose and broken, doors of
old boards nailed together. . . . . Heaps of garbage and ashes lie
in all directions, and the foul liquids emptied before the doors gather
in stinking pools. Here live the poorest of the poor ; the worst paid
workers with thieves and the victims of prostitution indiscriminately
huddled together. . . . ." But this is nothing compared with the
state of the factory hands. The facts with regard to the employment
of women are too horrible to be detailed ; vice and disease, the
criminal tyranny of overseers, the violation of every right of womanhood and motherhood—it is as well to pass by these things in silence.
Let me quote from his indictory paragraph : " Women made unfit
for child-bearing, children deformed, men enfeebled, limbs crushed,
whole generations wrecked, afflicted with disease and infirmity . . . .
children seized naked in bed by the overlookers and driven with
kicks and blows to the factory, their clothing over their arms . . . .
their sleepiness is driven off with blows. . . . ." Turn to the country
districts : " The laborer lays snares or shoots here and there a piece
of game. It does not injure the landlord . . . . for he has a vast
superfluity. . . . But if he is caught he goes to jail, and for a
second offence receives *at the least seven years' transportation.* From.

the severity of these laws arise the frequent bloody conflicts with gamekeepers, which lead to *a number of murders every year.*" The general misery was greatly increased by the influx of Irish laborers, especially to the towns, and the consequent lowering of wages. It is not to be wondered at that even the *Times* spoke with a democratic accent!

Pastor in Parochia.

Kingsley was an ideal parish priest. He came to a sorely neglected village, and won first of all the good will, and finally the deep affection, of his parishioners. This was due less to the admirable series of village institutions which he founded than to his real sympathy with the people. He could talk to them, with understanding and interest, on subjects that are seldom within the scope of the ecclesiastical mind—the crops, the weather, the hunting field, pike fishing, the ways of birds and animals, nature lore, and shrewd maxims of sport. His sermons were manly and direct. His care for the suffering was less the performance of a duty than a free act of devotion. There was little incident outside the home circle during the first years of Eversley life. His first child, a daughter, was born in 1846, and his eldest son in 1847. With the crash of 1848 Kingsley began his Socialist work, and the disastrous April 10th found the Rector of Eversley in London.

Chartism.

Kingsley was already known to Maurice. He had attended the meetings of bible scholars at Maurice's house in 1847, and they had corresponded extensively. To Maurice he went therefore to see what could be done to prevent a collision between troops. and Chartists. Maurice was confined to the house with a severe cold, but he sent Kingsley to Ludlow with a letter of introduction. The two men set out for Kennington Common, where the Chartists were to assemble, but at Waterloo Bridge they heard of the ignominious dispersal of the demonstrators and returned to Maurice with the news. From this moment we may trace the inception of the Christian Socialist Movement. The band of men who were to lead the movement had already met—Maurice, Hare, Ludlow, Mansfield, Scott, Parker, Hughes, Kingsley, and, later on, E. Vansittart Neale.

The day following the Chartist fiasco Kingsley wrote to his wife : " All as quiet as a mouse as yet. The storm is blown over till to-morrow, but all are under arms—specials, police, and military. Mr. Maurice is in great excitement, and we are getting out placards for the walls, to speak a word for God with. You must let me stay up to-night, for I am helping in a glorious work. . . ." Kingsley's placard, which may be considered as an attempt to dissuade the workers from direct political action and from the belief that a political remedy would suffice for the evils of the times, was posted all over London on the 11th. "Friends, you want more than Acts of Parliament can give. . . . Workers of England, be wise, and then you must be free, for you will be fit to be free."

However little Maurice and his friends sympathized with physical force Chartism, they recognized that Chartism in general, as an act of insurgency against the fearful social iniquities of that period, did actually represent the claims of an oppressed and degraded people. Kingsley, addressing a meeting of workmen some time later began : "I am a Church of England parson "—a long pause ; then, defiantly—" and a Chartist." Accordingly the pages of their first periodical (or, rather, their first series of tracts) made a special appeal to Chartists, whilst seeking to convince them of the folly and wrong of open violence, and glorying in the success of the house-holder constables. The first number of this publication (consisting of sixteen quarto pages, and issued weekly at one penny) came out on May 6th, and was called *Politics for the People*. The paper was jointly edited by Maurice and Ludlow, and, in addition to their con-tributions, papers were written by Archbishop Whately, Archbishop Trench, Bishop Thirlwall, Dean Stanley, Professor Connington, Dr. Guy, Charles Mansfield, A. J. Scott, Lord Sydney Godolphin Osborne, Sir Edward Strachey, and Charles Kingsley. Maurice's chief contributions were : "Dialogues in the Penny Boats "; "Liberty : a Dialogue between a French Propagandist, an English Laborer, and the Editor "; "Equality," another dialogue ; papers on historical subjects and education ; and a Chartist story. Kingsley, besides "Parson Lot's Letters to Chartists," wrote articles on the National Gallery and the British Museum. All the articles were unsigned or signed by a *nom de plume*. Although short-lived, as we have seen, *Politics for the People* had considerable influence, and did good work in consolidating the new movement, in spreading its ideas, and in gaining enthusiastic recruits.

Socialist Activities.

Their activities were now chiefly directed to the work of educa-tion ; classes were formed, and the friends met each week for study and discussion. Kingsley's first novel, " Yeast," came out during the autumn in *Fraser's Magazine*. This book, which at once established his reputation as a novelist, attracted a great deal of notice, partly hostile and partly appreciative, and was the means of arousing an interest in the sporting parson of Eversley which continued and increased during his whole lifetime. This is not the place for literary comment. The book is still widely read, and, in spite of a rather outworn sentimentalism and the tiresome character of its heroine, remains a very vital piece of work, endeared for ever to sportsmen by its wonderfully observant and broadly painted descriptions. Worn out by the mental and emotional strain of the past months, Kingsley spent the early part of 1849 recovering his health in Devonshire, and did not resume work at Eversley until the summer. Before returning to his parish he visited London, attended several meetings of working men, and joined in the activities of the Christian workers. Maurice was now addressing the Chartist leaders and other working men at the Cranbourne Coffee Tavern. "I was abashed," he wrote, " by the good opinion they had formed of me on no evidence." And later, writing to Kingsley, "They seem to think it a very wonderful thing that a clergyman should be willing to come among them—a sad proof how far we have gone from our proper position." It must be remembered that at this time there was a lamentable want of sympathy between the Church and laboring men, and that the very fact of a man being a "parson" was enough to drive him off the platform at a public meeting. Sometimes there were stirring scenes at the Cranbourne Tavern. On one occasion the National Anthem was hissed. Hughes, like an evangelical Desmoulins, sprang on a chair, vowed that any man who insulted the Queen would have an account to settle with him personally (he was a proficient pugilist), ordered the pianist to play on loudly, and himself led the singing of the Anthem, which was continued so vociferously that interruption was either quelled or was drowned by the mere tumult.

The idea of co-operation, which was oddly associated in the minds of the workmen *with anti-Christian views*, began to make progress, and the Socialists were occupied with schemes for the launching of the small co-operative concerns to which I have referred. Ludlow had visited Paris, and had been greatly interested in the success of the *Associations Ouvrières*. He was convinced that a similar scheme of association would go far towards solving the industrial problem in England, even if it did not offer the complete solution. The workmen were equally anxious for an effective form of co-operation : the Tailors' Association had been launched, and other organizations were speedily planned.

Towards the autumn of 1849 cholera broke out in London and in other parts of the country. What is remarkable is that, with sanitary affairs in such a deplorably neglected condition, the outbreak was not more disastrous than was actually the case. Eversley seems to have escaped, but a formidable low fever to which many of his parishioners fell victims kept Kingsley hard at work during the summer, until, worn out by the anxiety of bed-side vigils—for the rector himself often undertook the duties of a sick nurse—he was obliged to seek health once more on the Devonshire coast. He returned to his parish in September, and set to work with magnificent energy. The cholera was now causing great uneasiness in London. An inquiry into the state of the metropolitan water supply revealed the most scandalous things. In the poorer quarters of London conditions still remained as Engels had described them five years previously. The people had no water fit for drinking. The common sewers were filled with stagnant horrors, in which floated the putrefying bodies of cats and dogs, dead fish, and filth unspeakable. With the cholera at its height the poor wretches dipped cans into the sewer-water—and drank it. In Bermondsey (which Kingsley visited) the distress was terrible. Such a man as Kingsley could not witness these scenes without being stung to the heart, and his efforts for sanitary reform were redoubled. Much of the subsequent improvement in these matters was due to his persistent—one might well say impassioned—labor.

He was at this time writing reviews for *Fraser's Magazine*, and was shaping "Alton Locke"—a book written in a white-heat of excitement and zeal. "Yeast" had made a deep appeal to the younger minds and the universities, and Eversley Rectory was already sought out by scholars and young men with problems.

In the Fulness of Power.

The year 1850 marks the flood-tide of the Christian Socialist Movement. Individualist co-operation was risking its decisive experiment. Mainly under the guidance of E. Vansittart Neale, and the general supervision of the Society for Promoting Working Men's Associations, the twelve co-operative enterprises were organized and financed.* Neale was the hero and the practical director. Until his death, in 1893, he devoted life and fortune to the cause of industrial unity.

The failure, in a few years time, of the Christian Socialist experiment was due to a misconception of the real economic conditions of the time, an exaggerated belief in the spirit of brotherhood, and the absence of a thorough knowledge of the market. It was found impossible to eliminate competition. Each association was perfectly autonomous with regard to its own management. The result was that the men quarrelled with their managers, were slow to admit new members, and, finally, sought to compete with the other groups. I may as well anticipate matters by stating that the Society of Promoters dissolved in 1854, having completely drained their financial resources.

1850 was a hard year for Kingsley and for all classes. Feeling deeply for the local farmers, who found it difficult enough to struggle against high rates and poor prices, Kingsley, by an impulse of generosity which was never forgotten (for he was himself a poor man), gave them back 10 per cent. of the tithe money. At the same time he decided upon that unfailing resource of the country rector—a private pupil. The stress of money matters induced him to proceed apace with "Alton Locke"—whether the last chapters of this book bear evidence of having been written in a hurry I leave for others to decide. He rose at five every morning and slaved at the MS. until breakfast time. The printer's copy was prepared by his wife, and he supervised her work in the evening. The difficulty was to find the printer. Kingsley was attracting too much attention for the more timorous and conservative publishing houses, and the publishers of "Yeast" fought shy of the offer. To his rescue in this predicament came Thomas Carlyle with an introduction to Messrs. Chapman and Hall.

"Alton Locke."

"Alton Locke," the commemorative novel of the Chartist period, and a burning comment on trade conditions, gave rise to so much discussion, and is of such importance to the subjects dealt with in

* The zeal of the Promoters is well illustrated by the fact that they were accustomed to hold their meetings at six o'clock in the morning.

this essay, that we must give it rather more attention than was accorded to "Yeast." In incident and style it conforms to the early Victorian heavy weight model. Few of the standard essentials are lacking. We are even treated to the classic drawing-room-piano scene, and the touches of sentiment are laid on in liberal brushfuls. None the less it is a production of great force and eloquent appeal. Professing to have been written by a working man, the crudeness mentioned by Carlyle is not out of place, and it certainly contains one splendidly drawn character—that of the old Scotch democrat, Mackaye. It was a very clear and disquieting exposure of the "slop trade," and directed the public mind to unsuspected evils. It appealed for greater efficiency in the Church, greater respect for the workman, and a more qualified regard for the "scented Belgravian" and the aristocrat. Above all, it enlisted the sympathies of a sentimental but potent *bourgeoisie*. It was mocked by the elegant reviewers, made light of by the High Churchmen, but was bought and read by thousands. Carlyle has summed up the book admirably when he describes it as ". . . a fervid creation still left half chaotic."

Publication of the "Christian Socialist."

Maurice's workers had now officially announced themselves as the Christian Socialists, and had renewed their literary activities. They were publishing a series of "Tracts on Christian Socialism" as a means of circulating their teaching, and on November 15th they issued the first number of their new periodical, the *Christian Socialist*. Kingsley had written "Cheap Clothes and Nasty" for the tract series under the pseudonym of Parson Lot, and became a contributor to the magazine.

The *Christian Socialist* was edited by Ludlow, and was beset with difficulties from the very start. The newspapers had attacked the movement in the most violent and apparently scandalized manner. It was no easy business to obtain a circulation for the new venture. The booksellers took up a prudish and circumspect attitude, and refused to stock copies. Writing to a friend in December, Kingsley stated that the circulation had risen to 1,500, and was increasing. It is doubtful whether these figures were greatly exceeded. So little interest was at first evinced by the public that the press was almost silent with regard to the magazine, and its influence was imperceptible. Maurice, it would seem, had never looked upon its publication with much favor. He had attempted to dissuade Ludlow from the undertaking—possibly because he feared its political character would become too pronounced—though he realized the importance of possessing some medium through which the whole movement might be linked together and its scattered workers kept in touch with the central idea.

Maurice himself wrote very little for it. Beyond some letters on education, written in the form of a correspondence between himself and an M.P., and the story of "Thomas Bradfoot, Schoolmaster," his contributions were of no great significance. He was anxious that other opinions besides his own should find expression in the paper, although when the difference was too decided, he always interfered, and his objection was sufficient to ensure the withdrawal of the offending article.

There were at this time monthly conferences between the leaders of the movement and the workmen associates for the discussion of all vital points.

The Act of Parliament.

In Parliament, Slaney was using every endeavor to procure an Act legalizing the new co-operative and investment schemes, and securing them the protection, if not the encouragement, of the State. He obtained a Special Committee to enquire into the "investments for the savings of the middle and working classes." It was natural that this Committee should turn to the Christian Socialists for information on a subject to which they were known to have given a very close attention, and on which they had ascertained the exact views of the working men. Ludlow was accordingly the first witness examined. Hughes, Neale, and other members of the Society of Promoters followed, amongst them Walter Cooper, the Chartist. Some of the most weighty and conclusive evidence was given by John Stuart Mill, who spoke in vehement terms in favor of the scheme, i.e., the investment of working men's savings in co-operative concerns. The report of this Committee had been published in July, and, along with its promoters, had drawn upon itself the fire of both great and little guns in the journalistic batteries. The history of this Parliamentary agitation is interesting.

The Home Secretary, Labouchere, requested Ludlow to draft a Bill for legalizing co-operative associations. Nothing could have given him greater pleasure, but the draft demanded such an alarming legal reformation that Labouchere grew timid, expressed his admiration both for Ludlow and the Bill, but did not proceed any further with the matter.

In 1851 Mr. Slaney obtained a new Committee "to consider the Law of Partnership and the expediency of facilitating the limitations of liability, with a view to encourage useful enterprise and the additional employment of labor." All this sonority seems to have had little effect, for it was not until a year afterwards that Slaney finally succeeded in getting the Bill once again to the fore, and it was safely passed by both Houses (under a Conservative Ministry) on June 11th, 1852. Such, in brief, is the story of the first "Industrial and Provident Partnerships Bill," a private measure introduced by Slaney and Tufnell, Liberals, and Sotheron, a Conservative.

Eversley in 1850.

It was in the autumn or early winter of 1850 that the celebrated attack on Eversley Rectory took place. A neighboring clergyman had been murdered by a gang of housebreakers, who were at that time terrorizing the countryside, and the Rectory had scarcely been barricaded and its weapons of defence made ready before it was attacked by the same gang. In the middle of the night the marauders were heard trying to force the back door. Down the stairs rushed the male inmates, with pistols, guns, and a gaping blunderbuss; the "coolest man among them," and the only one unarmed, being F. D. Maurice, who was then paying a visit to Kingsley. Maurice strode out into the darkness in pursuit. He was recalled by Kingsley, and the two men spent the remainder of the night over the study fire, their discourse continuing until the dawn.

Already Kingsley had to deal with a vast correspondence. Young men who could not make up their minds with regard to eternal punishment and other stumbling-blocks of dogma; good fellows in the services who wished for a word of advice or prayers for camp and shipboard; men whose hearts had been stirred by his books. Never, I suppose, was a country rector the recipient of so much appreciation and questioning. No genuine letter was left unanswered. Kingsley had the tenderest sympathy for these corresponding disciples, and his replies show the thoroughness with which he answered their doubts or satisfied their requirements. All the time he was working hard for the welfare of his parish and was much occupied with his pupil, Martineau.

A letter written from Dr. Jelf, the Principal of King's College, to Maurice, in 1851, shows the attitude of the orthodox and outraged mind with regard to Kingsley's books and essays. Archdeacon Hare had accused him of conceit and irreverence a few years before, but Dr. Jelf is even more outspoken. He cannot express too much horror and indignation. Kingsley is a dangerous and reckless writer. He is indescribably irreverent. His arguments are in a high degree inflammatory. "In fact," says Dr. Jelf, rising to the height of his denunciation, "his language is *almost insurrectionary.*" And, moreover, he is associated with "several notorious infidels," and has actually mentioned Tom Paine. It was largely on account of his friendship with Kingsley that Maurice was expelled from the College.

Towards the end of 1850 Kingsley resigned his post as Lecturer at Queen's College, in consequence of an attack in the *Record*.

"Hypatia" was begun as a serial in *Fraser's Magazine* in 1851. He contributed largely to the *Christian Socialist*—fifteen articles—besides a story and some ballads and sonnets. He would have written more for this paper were it not for the fact that he was obliged to earn as much as possible with his pen, and the *Christian Socialist* did not pay its contributors. He reprinted "Yeast," which was published anonymously. The Christian Socialist Movement was hotly attacked by the press, and notably by the *Edinburgh* and *Quarterly Reviews*. Kingsley would not trust himself to read the more personal of these attacks. He was a man whose quick temper and great sensitiveness were sure to lead him into the temptation of violent retort. The *Guardian*, however, had fallen foul of "Yeast" in no measured terms, and had brought such preposterous charges against the author that he wrote a furious denial. In May he delivered a lecture for the Society of Promoters on "The Application of Associative Principles and Methods to Agriculture," and 'in the summer was invited to preach one of the special sermons to working men who had come to London for the Great Exhibition.

"The Message of the Church."

This sermon—"The Message of the Church to Laboring Men"—led to the most extraordinary results. It was preached to a large congregation, mainly of the working classes, and produced a powerful effect. Kingsley had concluded his sermon and was about to give the blessing, when the incumbent of the church, whose name, I believe, was Drew, approached the reading-desk and denounced the preacher before the entire congregation. He agreed with much that had been said, but it was his " painful duty" to characterize portions of the sermon as "dangerous and untrue." This unheard-of scene caused a great sensation. Murmurs were heard ; the workmen pressed forward to the pulpit steps and grasped Kingsley by the hand. As the sermon itself was judged to be the best defence, it was decided in the vestry that it should be printed at once without the alteration of a single word. The affair was taken up by the press ; Kingsley was forbidden by the Bishop of London (Blomfield) to preach in the metropolis ; large numbers of the clergy and of his admirers sent messages of sympathy to Eversley ; and a meeting of workmen, held at Kennington Common, expressed their allegiance to the parson who spoke so manfully on their behalf, and invited him " *to start a free church independent of episcopal rule*, with the promise of a large following." The sermon was now printed, and Blomfield, when he saw the truth of the matter, not only sent for Kingsley (and apologized, we may hope), telling him that he actually approved of the discourse, but immediately withdrew his prohibition.

Trade Unionism.—"Hypatia."

The Christian Socialists were naturally well known to the leaders of Trade Unionism, and it followed that, when the great strike of engineers and iron-workers took place in 1852, impetuous men like Hughes and Ludlow felt their fingers tingling for the conflict. The views of the promoters were varied : some urged one thing and some another. Maurice was fearful lest they should commit themselves to a desperate and ill-judged action. At the beginning of the year the *Christian Socialist* had boldly cast off its disguise and changed its title to the *Journal of Association*, under the editorship of Hughes. The *Journal* lost no time in appealing to the " self-sacrifice, pluck and character " of the men of the amalgamated trades. Ludlow and Hughes sought to agitate public opinion by all possible means : they lectured, wrote to a great number of newspapers, and supported the strike by subscriptions. Although the strike ended in disaster, the hand of friendship had not been extended to the trade unionists in vain, and the sympathy thus established between the more important trade associations and the Christian Socialists led to extremely practical results when, in 1854, the Working Men's College was founded.

Fraser's Magazine for January had contained a criticism of the Socialists, which Kingsley decided to answer. He was, perhaps, somewhat annoyed that his enemies should find a means of expression in the very magazine which was publishing " Hypatia " as a serial— it was a new aspect of journalistic etiquette. After conference with Maurice, who cooled the first transports of his resentment, Kingsley finally evolved "Who are the Friends of Order? A reply to certain observations in a late number of *Fraser's Magazine*." It was printed by E. Lumley and J. J. Bezer, the latter "a man who had been set up as a publisher by the promoters, no living publisher venturing to commit himself to the risk of publishing . . . either the *Christian Socialist* or the Tracts." Bezer was described by Hughes as Μονοψ, or "the one-eyed Chartist costermonger."

The *Journal of Association* came to an end this year, and Kingsley, in a final letter by "Parson Lot," urged his fellow-workers to "say little and work the more." Eversley and its democratic parson were now gaining notoriety. Kingsley seems to have been a popular man with soldiers, and officers from Sandhurst would frequently walk over to see him. His sermons were so vigorous and so powerfully delivered that he always preached to a full church, and, although a man of great rhetorical ability, his discourses were as keenly followed by the farm hand or the stableman as by the scholar. " Hypatia " was published in book form in 1853. As a literary attainment it must rank before any of his other works. To a modern reader, fascinated by the color and graphic detail of the story, it seems remarkable that, when published first, the book caused angry excitement among the High Churchmen, by whom it was regarded as a kind of masked attack, which, indeed, it was. Ten years later, when Kingsley's name had been suggested for the D.C.L. of Oxford, the High Church party raised the voice of protest. Dr. Pusey was scandalized to a degree. Why, good gracious ! This was the fellow who had written " Hypatia," a most vile and profligate book inciting the youth to heterodoxy, and worse, if worse were possible, an *immoral* book. Under threat of a *non-placet* the name was withdrawn. Maurice's "Theological Essays " were published the same year (1853), and outraged the doctrines of the Puseyites even more than Kingsley had outraged their self-respect. His expulsion from King's College followed, and Kingsley was vehement in defending his "dear master " and in scourging his enemies.

Disbanded.

With the collapse of the Society for Promoting Working Men's Associations and the failure of the co-operative businesses, the first Christian Socialist movement came to an end in 1854. The Socialists had failed in their experiment, but they had accomplished a great work. They had given an intellectual expression to the new democratic tendencies. They had striven to popularize and humanize what was then a rather unpopular and inhuman thing—the teaching of the English Church. They had shown (Kingsley in particular had shown it) that a clergyman must think more of the actual needs and nature of the people than of his embroideries and rituals. They had inaugurated a new phase of national thought. Neither were immediate practical results wanting. They had collected a vast amount of evidence on industrial questions; they had exercised an unmistakable influence on political subjects, and had been largely instrumental in gaining sanitary and other improvements. Their writings—more especially Kingsley's novels—had made an appeal to all classes of readers and had stirred the national conscience. And if further proof of their power is wanting, let it be given in the furious attentions paid them by their opponents—never has a popular movement been more violently assailed by a foe made aware of his moral insecurity.

The spirit of the movement was not in reality checked by its disorganization, and, although there was no formal association of Church Socialists until twenty-three years later, the force of the present social movement in the churches is certainly a consequence of the early Christian Socialist labors. The very year which saw the disbanding of the Christian Socialists saw the founding of the Working Men's College, with Maurice as president. It is only necessary to glance at a few names on the teachers' list (taking a period of several years) to see in what direction the finest intellect of that age was tending. Here are some of the names : Ruskin, D. G. Rossetti, Huxley, Tyndall, Madox Brown, Frederick Harrison, Professor Seeley, ·Arthur Hughes, Val Prinsep, the Lushingtons, and C. H. Pearson.

The winter and spring of 1854 was spent by Kingsley and his family at Torquay. The clergy of this place were thrown into panic at his approach, and he was denied the courtesy of the pulpit in all their churches. It is doubtful whether this caused him much disappointment. He spent the greater part of his time on the shore, indulging his naturalist and poetic passions and greatly benefiting in health. Kingsley is so well known as a nature student and as a writer of charming and thoughtful essays in natural research that there is no need to speak in detail of these wanderings on the seashore, when each withdrawing tide left a store of things wonderful, many-coloured and new. It was here that visions of old sea romance gave him the first ideas of " Westward Ho!"

He was busy this year agitating on behalf of sanitary reforms, and was a member of the deputation to Lord Palmerston on this subject. The condition of Eversley as regarded drainage, etc., weighed heavily upon him. He did all that was possible to secure improvements, but the parish was poor and landlords (as landlords are) indifferent. He himself, and all England with him, was at this time profoundly stirred by the Crimean War.

The Midway of Life.

It is not possible for me to give more than a very condensed account of Kingsley's later activities. The ·purpose of this essay is the study of Kingsley as a democratic Christian and a reformer. Those who wish to read of his family life, and to form a closer acquaintance with a most lovable and virile character, must read the standard biography, "Letters and Memories of His Life," edited by his wife, from which I have drawn much of the information set forth in this paper. Some brief survey of character I must necessarily give before the conclusion of the present study, but only a few facts and only those which most nearly concern my subject can be selected from the years of crowded activity following 1854.

We do not find Kingsley writing much on the Crimea. The war was to him "a dreadful nightmare," though it awoke the soldier-spirit in him, and his enthusiasm for the heroes of Sebastopol was intense. In a few hours' time he wrote a tract, "Brave Words to Brave Soldiers and Sailors," many thousands of which were distributed in the Crimea, and must have proved a wholesome alternative to the usual "goody-goody" pamphlets which the soldiers treated as so much waste paper. Cholera was still making an appearance here and there in 1855, and in the winter an outbreak occurred at Bideford, where Kingsley had taken a house. During this visitation he took charge of a district. The outbreak does not appear to have been very serious, and we find him, the same winter, instituting an evening drawing-class for the young men of Bideford, of which he was himself the instructor. The sureness and rapidity with which he drew flowers or symmetrical figures on the blackboard won the admiration of his pupils. The classes became popular, and many a young loafer was enticed from the street corner to become more and more fascinated by the kindly manner and (to him, at any rate) almost unearthly accomplishments of the strange "parson."

As years went by the Rector of Eversley gained a popularity which was at times almost embarrassing. He disliked the parade of carriages and the "talking after church" on Sundays. But for those who came to him privately to discuss his books or confide in him their perplexities and sorrows he had a warm affection. After the founding of the camp at Aldershot, the "dear fellows"—officers of all grades besides rank and file—paid frequent visits to the church and the rectory. One of these became a familiar friend of the Kingsleys. He had been out in the Crimea, and had read "Yeast" when lying grievously stricken in the hospital at Scutari. The hunting scene had made an especial appeal—one can imagine the effect of such a vivid home-picture on a wounded man in Scutari—and he resolved that if ever he got back to England he would go and hear the parson who could write such fine sporting descriptions. He came, still on crutches. Such episodes show very clearly one aspect of Kingsley's appeal to his contemporaries—the appeal of a strong man to strong men. "He loved men and manly pursuits," to quote the words of an officer who used to walk over from Aldershot, and who shall say that he was not himself a tried and battle-worn fighter? Kingsley was a welcome guest at mess ; he entered into the studies and organization of the Staff College with the deepest interest, and his advice to sportsmen—" He told us the best meets of the hounds, the nearest cut to the covers, the best trout streams, and the home of the largest pike "—must have made him extremely popular.

But the real significance of all this soldier intercourse was this : Charles Kingsley was the very man to present religion in a form acceptable to the soldier temperament. To a soldier, manhood is the greatest thing in the world, and the greatest qualities of manhood are courage, physical prowess, endurance, kindness without weakness or wordiness, loyalty, honesty, and a sane patriotism. All these qualities were to be found in Kingsley, with the spirit and mind of a Christian teacher superadded. We can picture such a man casting a net with the first apostles, and proving himself as hard-working a fisherman as any of them, not afraid of soiling his hands with the common labors of common men. Kingsley, in fact, preached the *manliness* of his creed, a sin unpardonable to the High Church exquisites of that time. He spoke, never as a superior person to inferior sinners, but as a man who respected and loved all men. He was thus loved and respected by all who came within the circle of his influence. The soldier loved him for his vigor and sincerity (the soldier cannot analyse, but he can appreciate character, and knows the true from the false) and listened to him because he was no humbug, and always dealt boldly with the truth. His influence among all grades of the service at Aldershot and Sandhurst was therefore strongly marked. He taught the men what is none too much in evidence in the Church of to-day—that manliness and Christianity are not merely reconcilable, but are positively essential to each other.

Soldiers were by no means his only visitors. One is glad to notice that clergymen figure in the visitors' list—of various denominations and opinions. All sorts of men came. Beneath the fir trees on that little sloping lawn they discussed all manner of things. Kingsley was fitted for conversation with every type of man and for sympathy with every kind of nature. He loved and understood them all.

His scientific repute gained him the membership of the Linnæan Society. Literary folk were delighted with the "Prose Idylls" and other essays.

Meanwhile the Christian Socialists, working independently or in other organizations, were assisting in the advance of democracy. Trade depression was severe in 1857, and a committee of enquiry was formed, known as the "Association for the Promotion of Social Science." Maurice, Hughes, and Ludlow all took part in this work. Maurice was a member of the committee, and the report, which was published in 1860, contained contributions from the Christian Socialists. It must be understood that, although I still employ the original term as a matter of convenience, there was not at this time any organized group of Church Socialists, and the public no longer recognized the existence of any special doctrine or activity known as Christian Socialism.

Kingsley became more and more devoted to the cause of sanitary reform. In his opinion, physics and theology should go hand in hand, and he regarded a certain amount of scientific knowledge as a thing indispensable in a clergyman. I am convinced that this opinion foreshadows the future development of the Church, and points the way to a new meaning and efficiency.

In 1860 Kingsley was appointed to the Regius Professorship of Modern History at Cambridge. In the autumn of the same year he and his family entered into residence. It was natural that the same qualities in Kingsley which had appealed to the soldiers should appeal to the undergraduates. He became the hero of the young men. Never has Cambridge known a more popular lecturer or one more sincerely worshipped by his disciples. He began in the smaller rooms of the Schools. They were not big enough. He had to lecture in the biggest room of all, and that was not big enough. Strange scene at professorial lectures, enthusiasm would run high. The lectures were interrupted by irrepressible cheering. Kingsley would stammer, with emotion, "Gentlemen, you must not do it." It was no good, they *would* cheer. The men were not merely interested in the great personality of their lecturer ; they were interested in his subjects. The University Librarian was asked for books which seldom left the shelves. Kingsley made them think, and he made them work, too. There was never yet, I suppose, a really great man who failed to gain the younger sympathies of the age. It is very clear that Kingsley had gained them, for all the groans and sneers of the Puseyites.

The Last Ten Years.

Newman's attack on the English Church could not pass unnoticed by such a loyal Churchman as Kingsley. Newman was, no doubt, his superior in sheer intellect, in theological subtlety, and in the ponderous resources of academic style. In the controversial sense Kingsley was beaten, though we are assured that it was out of a courteous regard for Newman's health, his disinclination for argument, and other personal reasons, that he forbore to attack with vehemence. This may be partly true. It is certain, however, that he had found his match. Probably no living theologian could have gained a victory over one whose craft and scholarship were unequalled, and who was as certain to maintain his defence with vigilance and caution as he was to attack with resistless weight and infallible sagacity. Maurice, who respected the learning and character of Newman, however widely he dissented from his views, " would have given much " to have withheld Kingsley from the dispute.

Hughes, Neale, Ludlow, and others of the Christian Socialist band were active in industrial affairs in 1866. The Cobden Mills were founded by Neale, Greening, Ludlow, Hughes, and Morrison. After some twenty-four years of a rather disastrous existence, the business was disposed of, and thus ended the largest, and in some ways most celebrated, experiment of Christian Socialism. Kingsley does not appear to have taken an active interest in these affairs (his former comrades were zealously fighting on behalf of trade unionism for many years), though he was always in favor of associative principles in trade. It is probable that three causes were responsible for this apparent withdrawal : first, the cooling (though only to a certain extent) of his early democratic ardor ; second, the necessarily changed and enlarged sphere of work, the result of public recognition and celebrity ; and third, a gradual decline in health which marks these last years of his life.

Science absorbed his attention to a greater and greater degree. He was a member both of the Linnæan and Geological Societies, had evolved a theory of raised beaches, and was a keen Darwinian. The Knightsbridge Professorship falling vacant in 1866, he wrote to Maurice, urging him to accept this appointment. It was only with difficulty that Maurice could be persuaded. "At sixty-one," he said, "I am perhaps past such work." The question of election depended on the votes of the seven electors. Four of them voted for Maurice, one for a man of his own college, and the two others abstained, but expressed satisfaction with the result. It must have been with huge personal delight that Kingsley (himself an elector) sent him a telegram announcing his triumph. He wrote later : " Your triumph could not have been more complete. My heart is. as full as a boy's. I thought I should have been ' upset ' when I saw the result." The two friends (or the master and the disciple, as Kingsley would have said) were thus associated in professorial work, both honored by the same university, and both happy in this latter-day closening of their friendship.

Kingsley had won recognition among all classes as a man of honest purpose, gifts approximating to genius, a sound theology, and the talents of a skilled author and graceful poet. He was none the less, perhaps for this very reason, ferociously assailed by the press. In consequence of these attacks he was on the point of resigning the professorship, but he was advised to retain it for at least another year. Accordingly, after nine years' experience as a Cambridge professor—years which had seen his greatest intellectual attainments and the most fruitful expression of his teaching—he resigned the post in 1869. ' His last series of lectures made a great impression.

The close of this year is marked by the fulfilment of one of his great ambitions, a voyage to the West Indies. It was the great holiday of his life. This world could not have supplied such a man as Kingsley—a poet-naturalist—with anything more perfectly enjoyable. He saw " enough to last him his life." He was mad with delight. He was actually moving in the land of romance he had dreamed and written of. He was a boy, full of wonder and surprise. He was an adventurer in tropical forests. He was a sea rover. The Regius Professor was buried !

Parish work, scientific work, three months' residence as Canon of Chester, a discussion with John Stuart Mill on Woman Suffrage, and a huge correspondence with various men on various subjects give a summary of 1870. He was a Teuton in sympathy during the war of 1870-71. He condemned the French policy and the French leadership : it was a righteous and even necessary war for Germany. In 1871 we find him again asserting the need to include physical learning in the general theological course. He realized that the older school of natural theology would be compelled to abandon many of its positions, or, rather, to develop in accordance with the great scientific revolutions of the nineteenth century. He saw that the religion of the future would lay stress on the scientific basis of modern thought, and that the priest of the future would deal less with fable and more with fact. Whether he was right in seeking to unite the functions of preacher and sanitary inspector quite as definitely as he proposed we need not stop to consider. He was certainly right in supposing that religion must pass from a superstitious to a scientific phase. His lectures at this period, particularly those on geological and natural history subjects, were very remarkable. The death of Maurice, in 1872, was a sad loss to Kingsley, and a certain despondency—partly the result of an over-worked and continuously active brain—seems more or less evident in his letters and conversation. But in the autumn of this year he achieved a great practical triumph for the cause which was so dear to him. As President of the Midland Institute he delivered the inaugural address (on the "Science of Health") at Birmingham. One of his listeners immediately placed the sum of two and a half thousand pounds at the disposal of a scheme for classes and lectures on this subject, with a low rate of payment for artizans. The project was successful, and the impetus was thus given to a very noble and necessary work. In 1873 he accepted the Canonry of Westminster, where he preached the well-known series of sermons. 1874 was largely taken up by a tour in America, crammed full of all manner of activities, and ending with a severe illness and a slow recovery in Colorado. He returned to Eversley in August. It was a hot, dry month, there was much sickness in the village, and he was busy attending to the people at all hours, and apparently with all his energy restored. But his health was rapidly failing. After his return to Westminster in the autumn he was again ill; he was now able only to preach once a week, and, although his sermons were still powerful and forcibly delivered, men were shocked to see the change in him, the worn cheeks and the bent figure. His wife's dangerous illness caused him the greatest suffering. On Advent Sunday he preached his last Abbey sermon "with intense fervor." The next day he caught a chill after dining at the Deanery, probably the direct cause of his death. The return journey to Eversley proved too much for his wife, and the happiness of a Christmas home-coming, so dearly longed for, was turned to a sad ministering in what seemed then to be the chamber of death. Kingsley himself grew rapidly worse. Eventually he was unable to bear the terrible strain of carrying on a pencilled intercourse with his wife, who was supposed by all to be dying. His illness (pneumonia) was fast gaining the mastery, yet his fortitude and superb courage remained unshaken. He died on the morning of January 23rd, at the age of fifty-five. His wife recovered.

His Character and Teaching.

In discussing the Socialism of Charles Kingsley, which is identical with that of the Christian Socialist group, we must bear in mind two very important facts: First, that he was remarkably constitutional in principle and method, and by no means revolutionary ; and, second, that his conception of Democracy was one that accepted the existing order of society with all its grades and traditions, and believed that the healthy functioning of that society was all that was needed to ensure the communal welfare. If anything was wrong—and a great deal was wrong—then the fault lay, not with the class, but with the individual. And even if the majority of individuals composing a class were at fault, that was no argument against the class itself, or, rather, against the necessity for the existence of the class. With a majority at fault, the class was *not* performing its true functions ; it was not, therefore, to be abolished, but called back to its duty ; the diseased organ was to be cured, by surgical steel at the worst, but not removed. There was, as I have mentioned, a divine purpose and order in the system of classes. A landed aristocracy was not only a necessary thing, it was "a blessing to the country." The House of Lords represented all that was noble and permanent in the national character (observe, *permanent!*) ; it represented the hereditary instinct, which bound together men of the past, present, and future ages. Royalty was a thing to be revered, because it was royalty. In short, the organization of the unproductive classes was very beautiful, useful, and necessary ; many individuals who belonged to these classes might fail to observe their duties, or, worse still, undertake duties which were not their own, but the class itself was a needful prop of the social fabric ; and, if the tendencies of its components had to be corrected, the thing itself must be preserved at all costs.

The Socialism of Kingsley.

Where then, you may say, is the Socialism in all this? Of modern Socialism there is little trace, and yet it was in this urging of the duty of classes, especially as regarded the treatment of the poor, provision for the health and security of the laboring classes, and the effective ministering of the Church, that Kingsley proved himself a powerful democratic force. His accusation was so vehement that his conservative principles were frequently drowned beneath a full tide of revolt. The organization of trade (which in his mind was a thing apart from the organization of classes) seemed to him to need immediate reform. If, therefore, he was a Conservative as regarded the blessing of an aristocracy, he was an extreme Radical where the working classes were concerned. It is impossible for a man of strong and observant character not to possess democratic tendencies. In Kingsley those tendencies were invigorated by the scenes and events of a revolutionary period, and became the dominant force of his career. He was deeply aware, too, of the fact that the Church was in danger of losing the sympathy of the people ; that she was becoming an exclusive and mystic organization, unduly given to the study of rituals, and not noticing the bad drains and worse morality of the "lower orders" ; for the Christian Socialist ideal for the Church was that it should work *with*, and not apart from, the secular workers. When he signed his Chartist placard as "A Working Parson," he knew that he implied a pretty obvious distinction. Kingsley was a Conservative by birth and tradition, a Chartist through force of circumstances, and a Socialist through sheer manliness and force of character. He belonged to a period when the English gentleman, though growing rare, was not obsolete, and when the middle classes did really advocate what they understood to be progressive measures. He aimed, not at a reform of society in general (which would have struck him as a blasphemous subversion of "God's order"), but at the reform of industrial life and of the Church, the first to be made wholesome and the latter efficient.

The views and methods of Kingsley and his friends have now been sufficiently commented on by the actual passing of time and the development of modern thought. We see the clearer for their mistakes, and are the richer for their noble examples and the fine courage of their teaching. It would be entering upon a fruitless controversy to discuss here the ethics of association, the question of the self-governing workshop, or the future position of the Church. Kingsley's power is to be found, not in the startling or original nature of his views, but in his manly and uncompromising advocacy of those views, and in the example of a most living and vigorous personality.

His Personality.

Like all poets, he was immensely receptive. His emotions were frequently and profoundly stirred by a suggestive fact or a touching scene. He was in love with Nature—every leaf, every cloud, the storm song of winter, rain, sun, the moorland, and the seashore, everything was wonderful and loveable. He possessed the most astounding vitality. It is not recorded of any man that he was more *alive*. His life was one continual excitement. In speech his vehemence was extraordinary. He would begin with a slight stammer and hesitation, but when fairly started, his oratory was fluent and impressive. His sense of the dramatic was unusually keen. He was one of the most influential and celebrated preachers of the time, and as a lecturer his repute was equally great.

He was a man of rare humor, and dearly loved anything that was laughable or even "broad." He could enjoy a page of Rabelais or a sly anecdote of Sterne's as much as anyone. His letters are full of pleasantry, and serve well to illustrate his versatile nature. For instance, he is writing to Tom Hughes, and is giving him some fishing experiences, with all sorts of expert comments on brass minnows, March browns, and so forth, when all at once, and without the least pause for breath, we find him talking of a poor parishioner who is lying on his deathbed. Cant or falseness of any kind were abominable to his sincere nature. A tramp who saw fit to assume the attitude and contortions of a religious zealot was seized by the collar, soundly shaken, and hurried outside Eversley gates with no little wrath.

Two answers of his, written in one of those horrible albums so typical of the Victorian drawing room, are interesting. "The character you most dislike?—Myself. Your ambition?—To die."

He was not a man who cared for distinction or notoriety. He acknowledged a "hankering after" the D.C.L. of Oxford, which was denied him ; but he realized his two "great ambitions," membership of the Linnæan and Geological Societies.

Kingsley did much to popularize the study of physics and natural science, and presented the facts of advanced scientific thought in a way calculated not to hurt religious sensitiveness. I have mentioned that he foresaw the alliance which must some day openly take place between science and religion, and that he was anxious for the education of clergymen in other matters besides those which relate solely to theology. His own religion cannot be said to come under any of the recognized categories. No party of the Church could claim him. He was opposed to the extreme mysticism of the High Church, but had little sympathy with the severe ritual of the Moderates. He was no friend to dogmatism of any sort. He was described by his curate, Harrison, as "a free lance in the ecclesiastical field."

The most immediate and most practical results of his activity are unquestionably to be found in the improvements in sanitary affairs and in the general education of working men. The latter is less directly due to his influence than the former (in which he was said by a great London doctor to have "led the way"), but it was certainly greatly advanced by his teaching and lectures.

The charge of inconsistency has been brought against him with regard to his democratic faith. "In later years," says Martineau, " his convictions became more in accord with *the natural tendency of his mind*" (whatever that means), "and he gradually modified or abandoned his democratic opinions." I can see no trace of all this. The burning enthusiasm of youth may have left him ; his opinions never did. From first to last Charles Kingsley was a democrat—and *that*, I take it, was the "natural tendency of his mind"—and he never proved false to his social creed. The multiplicity of affairs and a life overcrowded with interests and duties prevented him from devoting himself to a special and continuous work on behalf of Socialism. None the less, the author of "Alton Locke" and "The Message of the Church" was no changed man when, in 1866, he welcomed Maurice to Cambridge.

It is not the place here to speak of his home life, of his chivalrous devotion, his intimate sympathies, pictures of the lawn or the fireside, scenes typical of the English rectory. His love for animals, for all living things, with the exception of spiders, is well known. Like Agassiz, he believed in their *post mortem* existence. Those who wish to read a detailed, though necessarily partial, account of his life must turn to the "Letters and Memories."

The Present and the Future.

We cannot doubt that Socialism in the Churches represents a very powerful and very necessary expression of social democracy. Religious Socialism is gaining rapidly in numbers and efficiency, and may quite possibly modify the whole course of religious thought in the future. Whatever significance the movement may have to-day, whatever power it may have in the future, the names of its two great founders, Frederick Denison Maurice and Charles Kingsley, their noble examples of courage, manliness, and faith, will always figure large on the first pages of its history.

For the above summary of Kingsley's life and his relations with the Christian Socialist Movement I am indebted very largely to the standard biography referred to, and also, in addition to his own writings, to the "Life of F. D. Maurice," edited and partly written by his son, Woodworth's "Christian Socialism in England," Stubbs's "Charles Kingsley and the Christian Socialist Movement," Rose's "Rise of Democracy," and Engels' "Condition of the English Working Classes."

THE PRINCIPAL WORKS OF CHARLES KINGSLEY.

Various papers contributed to the *Christian Socialist, Politics for the People*, and the *Journal of Association*. 1848-54.

The Saint's Tragedy. 1848.

Yeast. Published as a serial in *Fraser's Magazine*, 1848. Published in volume form (anonymously), 1851.

Alton Locke 1850.

Cheap Clothes and Nasty. 1850.

Hypatia. Published in *Fraser's Magazine*, 1851. In volume form, 1853.

Westward Ho! 1855.

The Heroes. 1855.

Two Years Ago. 1857.

Poems. 1858.

The Waterbabies. 1862.

Hereward the Wake. 1866.

Collected Essays, Sermons, and Lectures.

Prose Idylls.

Letters; contained in Letters and Memories of his Life. Edited by his Wife. Two Vols. Also abridged form in one vol.

The principal works are all published by Macmillan.

OTHER BOOKS.

KAUFMANN, Rev. M.—Charles Kingsley, Christian Socialist. 1892. Methuen. 5s.

———— Christian Socialism. 1888. Paul. 2s. 6d.

MAURICE, Rev. F. D.—Social Morality. 1869 Macmillan. *O.p.*

NOEL, Rev. CONRAD.—Socialism in Church History. 1910. Palmer. 5s. net.

WESTCOTT, Right Rev. B. F. (Bishop of Durham).—Social Aspects of Christianity. 1887. Macmillan. 6s.

POTTER, BEATRICE (Mrs. Sidney Webb).—Co-operative Movement in Great Britain. 1899. Sonnenschein. 2s. 6d.

McCARTHY, JUSTIN.—Short History of our own Times [1837-1901]. 1904. Chatto. 2s. 6d. and 6d.

ROGERS, J. E. THOROLD.—Industrial and Commercial History of England. 1894. Unwin. 2s. 6d. net.

GAMMAGE, R. G.—Chartist Movement. 1894. Truslove. 15s. net.

CARLYLE, THOMAS.—Chartism. (See complete works.)

FABIAN SOCIETY.—The Fabian Society consists of Socialists. A statement of its Rules and a complete list of **publications can be obtained from**
the Secretary, at the Fabian Office, 3 Clement's Inn, London, W.C.

FABIAN ESSAYS IN SOCIALISM. Paper 6d.; cloth 1/6; post. 2½d. and 4d.
WHAT TO READ on Social and Economic Subjects. 1s. n. and 2s. n.
THE RURAL PROBLEM. By H. D. HARBEN. 2s. 6d. n.
THIS MISERY OF BOOTS. By H. G. WELLS. 3d., post free 4d.

FABIAN TRACTS and LEAFLETS.

Tracts, each 16 to 52 pp., price 1d., or 9d. per doz., unless otherwise stated.
Leaflets, 4 pp. each, price 1d. for six copies, 1s. per 100, or 8/6 per 1000.

The Set of 77, 3s.; post free 3/5. Bound in Buckram, 4/6 n.; post free 5s.

I.—General Socialism in its various aspects.

TRACTS.—169. The Socialist Movement in Germany. By W. S. SANDERS.
In cover, with portrait of Bebel, 2d. 159. The Necessary Basis of Society.
By SIDNEY WEBB. 151. The Point of Honour. By RUTH C. BENTINCK.
147. Capital and Compensation. By E. R. PEASE. 146. Socialism and
Superior Brains. By BERNARD SHAW. 142. Rent and Value. 138. Municipal Trading. 121. Public Service versus Private Expenditure. By Sir
OLIVER LODGE. 107. Socialism for Millionaires. By BERNARD SHAW.
139. Socialism and the Churches. By Rev. JOHN CLIFFORD, D.D. 133.
Socialism and Christianity. By Rev. PERCY DEARMER. 78. Socialism
and the Teaching of Christ. By Dr. J. CLIFFORD. 42. Christian Socialism. By Rev. S. D. HEADLAM. 79. A Word of Remembrance and Caution
to the Rich. By JOHN WOOLMAN. 72. The Moral Aspects of Socialism.
By SIDNEY BALL. 69. Difficulties of Individualism. By S. WEBB. 51.
Socialism: True and False. By S. WEBB. 45. The Impossibilities of
Anarchism. By BERNARD SHAW (price 2d.). 7. Capital and Land (revised 1908). 5. Facts for Socialists (revised 1908). 132. A Guide to
Books for Socialists. LEAFLETS—13. What Socialism Is 1. Why are
the Many Poor? WELSH TRACTS—143. Sosialaeth yng Ngoleuni'r Beibl.
141. Translation of 139. 87. Translation of 78. 38. Translation of 1.

II.—Applications of Socialism to Particular Problems.

TRACTS.—173. Public versus Private Electricity Supply. By C. A.
BAKER. 171. The Nationalization of Mines and Minerals Bill. By H. H.
SCHLOESSER. 170. Profit-Sharing & Co-Partnership: a Fraud and Failure?
By E. R. PEASE. In cover. 164. Gold and State Banking. By E. R. PEASE.
163. Women and Prisons. By HELEN BLAGG and CHARLOTTE WILSON. 2d.
162. Family Life on a Pound a Week. By Mrs. REEVES. In cover, 2d. 161.
Afforestation and Unemployment. By A. P. GRENFELL. 160. A National
Medical Service. By F. LAWSON DODD. 2d. 157. The Working Life of
Women. By Miss B. L. HUTCHINS. 155. The Case against the Referen-
dum. By CLIFFORD SHARP. 154. The Case for School Clinics. By L. HADEN
GUEST. 153. The Twentieth Century Reform Bill. By H. H. SCHLOESSER.
152. Our Taxes as they are and as they ought to be. By R. JONES, B.Sc.
In cover, 2d. 150. State Purchase of Railways. By EMIL DAVIES. In cover,
2d. 149. The Endowment of Motherhood. By H. D. HARBEN. In cover, 2d.
131. The Decline of the Birth-Rate. By SIDNEY WEBB. 145. The Case
for School Nurseries. By Mrs. TOWNSHEND. 140. Child Labor under
Capitalism. By Mrs. HYLTON DALE. 136. The Village and the Landlord.
By EDW. CARPENTER. 130. Home Work and Sweating. By Miss B. L.
HUTCHINS. 128. The Case for a Legal Minimum Wage. 122. Municipal
Milk and Public Health. By Dr. F. LAWSON DODD. 125. Municipaliza-
tion by Provinces. 123. The Revival of Agriculture. 115. State Aid to
Agriculture: an Example. 124. State Control of Trusts. 83. State
Arbitration and the Living Wage. LEAFLET.—104. How Trade Unions
benefit Workmen.

III.—Local Government Powers : How to use them.

TRACTS.—172. What about the Rates? or, Municipal Finance and Municipal Autonomy. By SIDNEY WEBB. 156. What an Education Committee
can do (Elementary Schools), 3d. 62. Parish and District Councils.
(Revised 1913). 137. Parish Councils and Village Life. 109. Cottage
Plans and Common Sense. 76. Houses for the People. 82. Workmen's
Compensation Act. LEAFLETS.—134. Small Holdings: and how to get
them. 68. The Tenant's Sanitary Catechism. 71. Ditto for London.

IV.—General Politics and Fabian Policy.

TRACTS.—158. The Case against the C.O.S. By Mrs. TOWNSHEND. 108.
Twentieth Century Politics. By S. WEBB. 70. Report on Fabian Policy.

Fabian Tract No. 175.

THE ECONOMIC FOUNDA-TIONS OF THE WOMEN'S MOVEMENT . . . By M. A.

Price Twopence.

Fabian Women's Group Series, No. 4.

Published and sold by the Fabian Society, London. June 1914.

The Economic Foundations of the Women's Movement.

The Spiritual Aspect of the Women's Movement.

PURELY economic causes are never sufficient to account entirely for any great revolt of the human spirit. Behind every revolution there lies a spiritual striving, a grasping after an ideal felt rather than seen. Most emphatically is it true that there is a social impulse independent of economic conditions, which has over and over again asserted itself in the demand for the emancipation of women. All the greatest seers and prophets have insisted on the equal value of men and women, and on the right of women to control their own lives. Four centuries before Christ, Plato claimed that in the life of the State women, as well as men, should take their place ; and in all the records of Christ's conversations, which the Gospels have handed down to us, there is not one hint that he advocated that subordination of women on which his disciples later on insisted. In Rome also, at the Renaissance, and at the time of the French Revolution, powerful voices were raised in denunciation of the subjection of women.

These demands were, however, only sporadic. At most they affected a small class. It was not until the nineteenth century that the demand of women for political, economic, and educational freedom was heard among any considerable mass of the people. This extension of the demand for emancipation was due to economic changes, to those alterations in human control over environment which are associated with the substitution of mechanical power for human energy in the making of commodities, and with the development of powerful and smoothly working machines in place of human hands and simple tools.

The Effect of the Industrial Revolution.

Probably when Hargreaves invented his spinning jenny, and when Arkwright established his first cotton mill, in which the power of water took the place of the easily wearied arms of humanity, they had no conception of the fact that they were preparing the way for the greatest revolution in human society which has ever taken place since man learnt the use of fire. Yet nothing less was the truth, for then first men learnt how to utilize for their service the energies of the universe without previously absorbing them into their own bodies or into the bodies of domesticated animals in the form of food. Before the end of the eighteenth century man did indeed use water power on a small scale for grinding corn, and the capricious force of the wind for the same end and for propelling sailing vessels.

But the energies of steam and electricity and petrol were lying dormant or running to waste all around him, while he sweated at the forge or the loom, and was hauled slowly over badly made roads by the straining sinews of horses. Now throughout human society inanimate forces are at work, harnessed at last successfully to the service of man, shaping iron and steel plates, setting to work looms and printing presses, propelling enormous trains of waggons, urging leviathan ships across the ocean.

Before this mighty revolution, whatever alterations man wanted made in his world must be made through his own physical exertions ; now he sets to work the energies of his environment to remould that environment according to his needs. From himself there is demanded merely the brain work of planning nnd directing and the nervous strain of tendence on the marvellous machines. It is true that in our badly arranged social system (all of whose concepts of property, contract, wages, and labor are still adjusted to the pre-machine era) the increased control over nature has brought but little advantage to the mass of the workers. But the full effects of the substitution of inanimate for human energy have not yet been seen, and will ultimately work themselves out into conditions of life vastly different from those which we know at present.

Women Before the Industrial Revolution.

Of all the changes introduced by the industrial revolution there is none greater than the alteration brought about in the position of women. Many people believe that it was only in the nineteenth century that women began, on a large scale, to work for their living. There could be no greater mistake. All the evidence goes to show that before the eighteenth century women, with few exceptions, worked as hard and as long as men did. In the sixteenth century women not only helped their husbands in farm work, but they toiled at spinning and carding of flax and wool as a by-industry of their own. Few nineteenth century women could work harder than the wife of a sixteenth century husbandman, whose duties are thus described by Fitzherbert, writing in 1534 :

"First swepe thy house, dresse up thy dysshe bord, and sette all thynges in good order within thy house. Milk thy kye, suckle thy calves, sye up thy mylke, take uppe thy children and array them, and provide for thy husband's brekefaste, dinner, souper, and thy children and servants, and take thy part with them. And to ordayne corne and malt to the myll, and bake and brue withal whanne nede is. And meet it to the mill and fro the mill, and se that thou have thy measure again beside the toll, or else the miller dealeth not truly with the or els thy corn is not drye as it should be. Thou must make butter and cheese when thou maist, serve thy swyne both morning and evening. and give thy poleyn [i.e., poultry] meat in the morning ; and when tyme of the year cometh thou must take hede how thy hennes, duckes, and geese do ley, and to gather up their eggs, and when they wax broodie to set them there as no beasts, swyne, or other vermin hurt them. . . .

And when they brought forth their birds to see that they be well kept from the gleyd, kites, crowe, polecats, fullymarts, and other vermin. And in the beginning of March or a little before is tyme for a wife to make her garden, and to gette as many good seedes and herbes as she canne, and specially such as be good for the pott and to eat. And also in March is tyme to sowe flax and hemp . . . but how it should be sown, weded, pulled, rippled, watered, washen, dryed, beaten, braked, tawed, heckled, spon, wounded, wrapped, and woven, it needeth not for me to show, for they be wise enough. And thereof may they make shetes, bordclothes, towels, sherts, smocks, and such other necessaries ; and therefore let thy distaff be always ready for a pastime, that thou be not idle. . . . May fortune sometime that thou shalt have so many things to do that thou shalt not well know where is best to begin. . . . It is convenient for a husband to have shepe of his owne for many causes, and then maye his wife have part of the wool to make her husband and herself some clothes. And at the least way she may have the locks of the sheep either to make clothes or blankets and coverlets, or both. And if she have no wool of her own, she may take wool to spyn of clothmakers, and by that means she may have a convenient living and many tymes to do other works. It is a wife's occupation to wynowe all manner of corns, and make malt, to wasshe and wrynge, to make haye, shere corn, and in tyme of nede to helpe her husband fyll the muckwain or dungcart, drive the plough, to load hay, corn, and such other. And to go or ride to the market to sell butter, cheese, milk, eggs, chekyns, capons, henns, pigs, geese, and all manner of corns. And also to bye all manner of necessary things belonging to the household, and to make a trewe reckoning and account to her husband what she hath paid. And if the husband go to the market to bye or sell, as they oft do, he then to show his wife in like manner." *

About two hundred years later a realistic Scotch novelist makes his hero write thus of his second marriage :

" I had placed my affections, with due consideration, on Miss Lizy Kibbock, the well brought up daughter of Mr. Joseph Kibbock, of the Gorbyholm . . . whose cheeses were of such excellent quality that they have, under the name of Delap cheese, spread far and wide over the civilized world. . . . The second Mrs. Balquhidder that was had a genius for management . . . for she was the bee that made my honey. There was such a buying of wool to make blankets, with a booming of the meikle wheel to spin the same, and such birring of the little wheel for sheets and napery, that the manse was for many a day like an organ kist. Then we had milk cows and the calves to bring up and a kirning of butter and a making of cheese. In short, I was almost by myself with the jangle and din . . . and I for a time thought of the peaceful and kindly nature of the first Mrs. Balquhidder with a sigh ; but the outcoming was soon manifest. The second Mrs. Balquhidder sent her butter on the market days to Irville, and her cheese from time to time to

* Fitzherbert's " Book of Husbandry." English Dialect Society. 1882.

Glasgow to Mrs. Firlot, that kept the huxtry in the Salt Market ; and they were both so well made that our dairy was just a coining of money, insomuch that after the first year we had the whole lot of my stipend to put untouched into the bank." *

The Family as the Economic Unit ; Marriage an Industrial Partnership.

These extracts—and many like them could be quoted †—show clearly that before the industrial revolution women took a full share in industrial work. The basis of their work, however, was quite different from what it is to-day. Speaking generally, before the industrial revolution the economic unit was the family, and not the individual. So much was this the case, that in the censuses of 1811, 1821, and 1831 it was assumed that all the members of the family would practise the same occupation. Much of the work done by women in the family was of a domestic nature for the immediate service of their husbands and children, and not for profit. In technical language it was the production of use values, and not of exchange values. This can be illustrated from the inventory of the furniture of a middle class house at Brook, near Wingham, in 1760, which is preserved in an auctioneer's catalogue in the British Museum. The equipment of the establishment included a bolting room, where were kept " one large neading trough, one meal tub and sieve, and one quilting frame"; a bottle house, which contained, among other things, " one brine tub, one syder stock and beater, one pickling trough"; a milk house, where were kept " milk keelers, churns, a butter board, and a butter printer." In the " larder" were " pickling pans and stilling tubs"; in the brew house " a mash tub, five brewing keelers, and one bucking tub" (whatever that may have been).

But it would be a mistake to assume that women never worked for profit. The second Mrs. Balquhidder obviously did. It is common to find a woman carrying on the farm or shop of her husband after his death, and the farmer's wife, who has been already described, was her husband's working partner in his business enterprise as well as his housekeeper and servant. In fact, before the nineteenth century marriage was an industrial partnership as well as a relation of affection. The women worked, and worked hard, contributing much to the wealth of England, which was sold in her

* Galt. "Annals of the Parish," Chapter VI. Pages 38-9 of edition in Routledge's Universal Library.

† " The staff consisted of the general manager, John Dalton ; a collier, who prepared the charcoal from the brushwood of the neighboring forest ; a ' blomesmyth,' or ' smythman,' in charge of the ' blomeharth'; and a ' faber,' working at the stryng hearth. . . . The employment of the wives of the foreman and smith lends an air of domesticity to the little settlement. The wife of John Gyll, the ' blomesmyth,' seems to have been a general factotum, sometimes helping her husband or the laborers, then working at the bellows. At first her employment was intermittent and her payment irregular, but later she seems to have settled down to fixed employment at a regular rate of a halfpenny a blome. i.e., a weight of fifteen stones of thirteen pounds each." "Durham County History," Vol. II, p. 279, quoting Account Roll of John Dalton, first Durham ironmaster (about 1410).

markets. This situation must have served to modify considerably the harshness of the common law, which decreed the husband's entire control of his wife's property. Fitzherbert's husbandman, depending as he did on his wife's energy in poultry yard, garden, and spinning room, would not be likely to insist upon his legal rights to take absolute possession of her earnings. And in one way the law recognized the wife's partnership. A husband could not leave his property entirely away from his wife. The widow's ancient right to one third of her husband's property was only abolished in England by the Reform Parliament,* that Parliament which was called together on the basis of the Franchise Act, which for the first time introduced the word " male " into the qualifications of the parliamentary elector.

The Alteration of the Economic Basis of the Family.

Before the industrial revolution, then, the household was, as a general rule, the unit of industry, and women worked in it as members of the family for the production of exchange as well as of use values. Now what was the effect of the industrial revolution on the position of women in relation to these economic activities of the family? Briefly, the answer is that the introduction of machinery, by taking work out of the home and establishing the factory, the railway, and the mine as the organs of industry, broke up the family as an economic unit and diminished the amount of production for use carried on within the home. Brewing, baking, butter-making, spinning, weaving, even—to a large extent—the making of clothes, have ceased to be activities of the family ; and increasingly house-wives are finding that it is cheaper and more convenient to hand over jam making, laundry work, even window cleaning and floor polishing, to agencies that exist independently of the home. This is an inevitable development. Modern machinery and the use of artificial sources of power immensely cheapen production, but they can only be used by organizations bigger than the family group. So that the economic basis of the family has altered more within the last hundred years than in the whole course of Christian civilization preceding that time.

Inevitably this has reacted on the position of women, whose relation to the family was always closer than that of men ; and the changes in the nature and aspirations of women, which have developed in the nineteenth century, are very largely, though not entirely, due to these altered economic conditions.

The Changed Position of Women.

But different classes of women were affected very differently. Among the wealthier people attempts were made to preserve the subordination of women to the family unit, although the economic justification for that dependence had ceased. Among the poor the necessity for the women's contribution to the family income was so strong that they were drafted into the new forms of industrial life

* Dower Act, 3 & 4 Will. IV., c. 105.

without any consideration of their powers or capacities. To put it shortly, parasitism became the fate of the middle class women, ruthless exploitation that of the working class women. The latter were absorbed in large numbers by the new factories, as were also the children, who equally had worked as parts of the family unit ; and the first stage of machine production saw the women and children workers cruelly and shamelessly sacrificed to the demands of profit.

The Exploitation of the Working Women.

There is no need to repeat this oft told story, but it may be pointed out that the previous close relation of the women and children to the family unit had rendered them incapable of asserting themselves against the powers of capital and competition. And the low wages which they received made them dangerous rivals of the men and no longer co-operators with them. No one during the first agitation for the Factory Acts seems to have realized that the general labor of women and children pulled down the wages of men. The conditions became so bad that dead in the face of a public opinion more strongly individualistic than has ever been the case either before or since, the State was forced to constitute itself the established guardian of the women and children, and to bring into existence all the machinery of the Factory Acts, by which, first in the textile industries and in mining, later on in in all branches of machine production, and still later in practically the whole field of industry, an attempt was made to preserve women and children from the degradation and suffering due to over long hours and work in unsanitary conditions. The problem is, of course, not yet fully solved. In the industrial world the cheap labor of women is continually threatening new industries. Since these women believe themselves inferior to men, and since most of them expect to marry early and regard their occupation only as a makeshift, they are naturally willing to work more cheaply than men, and so constitute a perpetual menace to the masculine standard of life, while they themselves are subjected to conditions unfit for human beings. It cannot be wondered at that under these circumstances many social reformers regard the work of women outside the home as an evil development. For women in the industrial world are frequently forced to be blacklegs. Moreover, the conditions of modern large scale industry are determined not by the needs of the human beings who work in it, but by the demands of the machinery, and are therefore often unsuitable for women (equally so, in all probability, for men). In the early days of the movement for State regulation of industry, that innovation on the doctrine of *laissez faire* which then prevailed was justified on the ground that women were not free agents. Men, it was asserted, could and should stand out for themselves against the power of their employers. The State ought never to interfere in the wages contracts formed by its citizens among themselves, but women and children were not citizens. They were weak, ignorant, easily exploited. Further, they represented in a special way the human capital of the nation. The men might be used from generation to generation and the life of the race would still continue, but a nation which lived upon the labor of its women and children was doomed to degeneration.

The Parasitism of the Middle Class Women.

In this view there is, of course, a truth which must never be forgotten. But it ignores another part of the problem, that which confronted the other class of women. The middle class women had so awful and so bitter an experience that for a time they were quite unable to appreciate the need of State protection for women. The result for them of the introduction of machinery was altogether opposite to the effect produced upon the industrial women. As the economic functions of the family diminished, the daughters of lawyers, doctors, wealthy shopkeepers, and manufacturers did not work out new forms of activity for themselves. It would have been against the dignity of their fathers and brothers to permit them to do so. Moreover, it would have diminished their chances of marriage, and would have involved a breach with the people who were nearest and dearest to them. They remained within the family group, occupied in the insignificant domestic duties that still remained and in the futilities of an extraordinarily conventional social intercourse. Dusting, arranging the flowers, and paying calls were the important duties of their existence. The married middle class woman had indeed, as wife and mother, a definite place and important responsibility, though the decay of household activities and the growing habit of living in suburbs, quite apart from the man's business, lessened at every point her contact with the social world and cut even her off more than had ever been the case previously from intercourse with the spheres of industry and commerce. But the unmarried woman, forbidden during her years of greatest vitality and strongest desire for new scenes and fresh interest to find any channels for her energies, save those of "helping mamma" and "visiting the poor," suffered intensely from the inactive parasitism forced upon her. Exploitation brings great suffering; but suffering as acute, though more obscure, is experienced by those whose growing powers and growing need for human contacts are dammed within them by an incomprehensible social fiat, resting really on conditions that had passed away a generation earlier. The only escape from this enforced inactivity and dependence was through marriage. The middle class woman, in fact, was regarded solely from the standpoint of sex. There was no way by which she might satisfy her natural wish to use the welling energies within her other than by becoming the mistress of a household. Naturally, therefore, she often regarded " to be settled " as an end to be aimed at, quite apart from the personality of the man who offered to make her his wife. And the irony of the situation was that to the finer spirits who refused to acquiesce in this degradation of love to the economic plane, there was no other alternative than an existence which became " that useless, blank, pale, slow-trailing thing " of which one of Charlotte Bronte's heroines so bitterly complains.

The Surplus of Women.

As the nineteenth century wore on other tendencies came into play which further increased the hardships of middle class women. The presence of a surplus of women in the middle classes made itself more and more apparent. Probably the cause of this is the emigration of young men, rendered necessary by our enormous colonial development ; but it may be that some other and more subtle cause is at work. Exact statistics are difficult to give, as our statistics are not based on class distinctions. But certain conclusions can be drawn, as Miss Clara Collet first pointed out, from the distribution of unmarried males and females over certain ages in different boroughs of London, which to some extent are peopled by different classes of the community. The following table shows how striking the difference is, and how the surplus of females tends to accumulate in the better off districts. Some have urged that these surplus females are really domestic servants. But the number of female unmarried domestic servants over thirty-five is comparatively small.

Number of unmarried males and females between the ages of thirty-five and fifty-five in three wealthy and three poor London boroughs, as given in the Census of 1911.

				Males.			Females.
Hampstead	...	...	...	1,559	...	...	4,655
Kensington	...	...	...	2,785	...	...	11,395
Chelsea	...	...	...	1,414	...	...	3,688
Woolwich	...	...	...	1,861	...	...	1,526
Shoreditch	...	...	...	1,689	...	...	1,004
Bethnal Green		...	...	1,635	...	...	1,320

Putting the same facts in another way, for every 100 unmarried men between thirty-five and fifty-five there are in Hampstead 291 unmarried women of the same ages, in Kensington 409, and in Chelsea 260 ; while in Woolwich to every 100 unmarried men of these ages there are 81 unmarried women, in Shoreditch only 59, and in Bethnal Green 81.

We can cite also an article by Miss Hutchins in the *Englishwoman*, June, 1913, in the course of which she says : "Another means of comparing the prospects of marriage in different social strata is by comparing the proportion of single women in the age group 25-45 in rich and poor districts respectively. In making this comparison we must allow for the numbers of domestic servants, who of course very considerably augment the proportion of single women in the wealthy residential districts. The following table shows that, even if we subtract all the domestic indoor servants from the single women in the age group (which is over-generous, as a small but unknown proportion of them are certainly married or widowed), the single women in Hampstead, Kensington and Paddington are a considerably higher proportion than in Stepney, Shoreditch and Poplar. These districts have been 'selected' only in the sense that they were the first that occurred to the writer as affording a marked contrast of wealth and poverty."

Number and proportion of single women and domestic indoor servants in every 100 women aged 25-45 in certain London boroughs.
(Census of 1911.)*

	Number	Per cent. of Women aged 25-45	Difference of percentage
HAMPSTEAD.			
Single Women ...	11,483	57·3	24·7
Domestic Servants	6,534	32·6	
KENSINGTON.			
Single Women ...	21,967	56	21·8
Domestic Servants	13,431	34·2	
PADDINGTON.			
Single Women ...	13,711	46·6	24·5
Domestic Servants	6,473	22·1	
POPLAR.			
Single Women ...	4,406	19·5	17·3
Domestic Servants	506	2·2	
SHOREDITCH.			
Single Women ...	2,923	18·1	15·9
Domestic Servants	340	2·2	
STEPNEY.			
Single Women ...	7,158	18·4	15
Domestic Servants	1,207	3·4	

This table also brings out the extraordinary difference between
the proportions of women of the most marriageable period of life
married in rich and in poor districts. The same fact is illustrated by
the following table, comparing the number of married, single and
widowed women among the population living " on private means "
and among the general population. The comparison is suggested
by Miss Hutchins, but the table used by her in the *Englishwoman*
cannot be reproduced here as the new Census does not give the information in the same way.

Number and percentage of single, married and widowed women over
20 years of age in the population living on private means and in
the general population in England. (Census of 1911.)

	Living on Private Means		General Population	
	Number	Percentage	Number	Percentage
Unmarried .	136,705	46·5	3,448,442	30·2
Married ...	23,724	8·1	6,610,173	57·9
Widowed...	133,698	45·4	1,364,715	11·9
Total ...	294,127	100	11,423,330	100

No doubt the figures in this table are distorted by the number of
widows who owe their private means to their widowhood, but even
allowing for this it is remarkable to discover that the percentage of

* Miss Hutchins's original figures, which were taken from the Census of 1901,
have been brought up to date.

married women in the general population is so much greater than in the population living on private means.

But statistical evidence is really not necessary. All hostesses and organizers of middle class social functions know well that one of the constant difficulties with which they have to contend is the over supply of women.

The Salaried Middle Class.

Another new element in the position of the middle class woman arises from the fact that her men relations tend to become salaried officials in place of independent merchants and employers. This means not only that the women can no longer take part in the economic activities of their men relations, but that, in the event of the death of the latter, their position is far more precarious. A business or a shop goes on even after the death of a husband or father who established or inherited it, but when a salaried official dies his family are altogether deprived of the support which he afforded them.

Can He Afford to Get Married ?

And again, if a wife is no longer of any direct economic value, if, on the contrary, she is an expense, then men, in many cases probably with reluctance, must defer marriage until they can afford that luxury. To a middle class man before the industrial revolution, as indeed to the men of the working class at present, marriage was not a thing "to be afforded." A wife was a partner, bringing to the relation of wedlock economically, as well as in other and more emotional ways, as much value as she received. But the middle class bachelor contemplating marriage to-day realizes that he must be prepared to double, or more than double, his expenditure, while his wife adds nothing to the income. Therefore he defers marriage, finding often an outlet to his emotions in other directions (it would be interesting to endeavor to trace the relation between prostitution and the use of machinery), and the girl who should be his mate withers unwanted in the "upholstered cage" of her parents' home. Therefore in the nineteenth century the middle class woman had fewer chances of marriage, was less needed in the family life if unmarried, and was liable to find herself when that family life came to an end through the death of a father or brother stranded resourceless on the world.

The Tragedy of the Surplus Women.

It is heartrending to think of the hidden tragedies which these sociological changes brought in their train, the mute sufferings of the women, who, unmated and workless, felt themselves of no value or importance to the world around them. What wonder that in the end a revolt came, and women insisted that in the great world of human activities outside the family they, too, must have place and power. Some echo of this unhappiness found its way into the literature of the Victorian era. Charlotte Bronte utters it in the repinings of poor Caroline Helston.

"Caroline," demanded Miss Keeldar, abruptly, "don't you wish you had a profession—a trade?"

"I wish it fifty times a day. As it is, I often wonder what I came into the world for. I long to have something absorbing and compulsory to fill my head and hands, and to occupy my thoughts."

"Can labor alone make a human being happy?"

"No; but it can give varieties of pain, and prevent us from breaking our hearts with a single tyrant master torture. Besides, successful labor has its recompense; a vacant, weary, lonely, hopeless life has none."

"But hard labor and learned professions, they say, make women masculine, coarse, unwomanly."

"And what does it signify whether unmarried and never-to-be-married women are unattractive and inelegant or not? Provided only they are decent, decorous, and neat, it is enough. The utmost which ought to be required of old maids in the way of appearance is that they should not absolutely offend men's eyes as they pass them in the street. For the rest, they should be allowed, without too much scorn, to be as absorbed, grave, plain looking, and plain dressed as they please."

"You might be an old maid yourself, Caroline; you speak so earnestly."

"I shall be one; it is my destiny. I will never marry a Malone or a Sykes, and no one else will ever marry me." *

"Look at the numerous families of girls in this neighborhood: the Armitages, the Birtwhistles, the Sykes. The brothers of these girls are every one in business or in professions. They have something to do. Their sisters have no earthly employment but household work and sewing; no earthly pleasure but an unprofitable visiting; and no hope in all their life to come of anything better. This stagnant state of things makes them decline in health. They are never well, and their minds and views shrink to wondrous narrowness. The great wish, the sole aim, of everyone of them is to be married. But the majority will never marry; they will die as they now live. They scheme, they plot, they dress to ensnare husbands. The gentlemen turn them into ridicule; they don't want them; they hold them very cheap; they say—I have heard them say it with sneering laughs many a time—the matrimonial market is overstocked. Fathers say so likewise, and are angry with their daughters when they observe their manœuvres. They order them to stay at home. What do they expect them to do at home? If you ask, they would answer, sew and cook. They expect them to do this, and this only, contentedly, regularly, uncomplainingly, all their lives long, as if they had no germs of faculties for anything else. A doctrine as reasonable to hold as it would be that the fathers have no faculties but for eating what their daughters cook, or for wearing what they sew." †

The same restlessness, unconscious as it usually was of its cause, was expressed even more fully by George Gissing in that wonderful

* "Shirley," Chapter XII.   † "Shirley," Chapter XXII.

book, " The Odd Women." But to most people the elderly spinster was no more than an occasion for mocking, and yet the same people were most bitter against the women who demanded the right to work, the right to education, and the right to enter politics, those three demands of the disinherited women of middle class Victorian England.

The First Feminist Movement.

The first feminist movement emerged into the open at the time of the Reform Bill of 1867. If its origin is grasped, its peculiar characteristics will be easily understood. It was on the whole a demand of elderly unmarried women for the right to freer activities, as the alternative to an impracticable ideal of marriage and motherhood for every woman.* Therefore it is not astonishing that these early feminists tended on the whole to ignore differences of sex, since those differences had been made the pretext for condemning them to a condition of parasitism, against which a healthy human being was bound to revolt. It was natural enough that these pioneers of the women's movement should insist upon their likeness to men, should demand the right to the same education as men received and the entrance to the same professions as men followed. In their revolt against the degradations which sex parasitism had brought in its train, it was not unnatural that in their dress and bearing they should neglect the grace and charm which a normal man will always desire in women. It was not unnatural either, when they found a section of the public advocating in industry special protection of women by law, that they should regard this as another form of the masculine exclusiveness from which they themselves suffered, so that to them the right of a woman to be a doctor and the right of a woman to work underground in a mine should present themselves as similar demands. Being but middle class women, influenced by the progressive ideals of their class, they were mostly Liberals, and to their special dread of the exclusion of women from human activities, other than those conditioned by sex, was added the strong individualism of the Liberalism of the period. Therefore they naturally set themselves in opposition to the demand for factory legislation, and there arose in consequence misunderstandings between two sections of reformers, the echoes of which have persisted to our own time.

Its Attitude towards Marriage.

The attitude towards marriage of these early feminists has also been much misunderstood. There were, no doubt, a certain number among them who were indifferent or opposed to marriage ; but most of them found themselves driven into hostility to normal family relations, mainly because these were used as an argument to convince them that the alterations in the position of women which they desired were impossible. When a woman, struggling for education and the right to work for herself, was met by the objection : " If you

* Lydia Becker, one of the earliest agitators, is reported to have replied to a married woman, who said that she, too, would like a vote, " My dear, a good husband is much better worth having than a vote,"

learn Greek or if you become a doctor no one will marry you," is it astonishing that she answered, " I don't care if no one does "? Moreover, as has been already said, the pioneers came mostly from the class of "superfluous women." They knew well that marriage was far from being the certainty or the likelihood which their opponents always assumed it to be. The alternative for them was not work *or* marriage, but work and money of their own *or* a spinstered existence in their fathers' houses. Therefore, naturally most of them put out of their minds, with what bitterness few people have realized, the possibility of marriage and motherhood, and turned instead to develop their own intellectual and spiritual forces, devoting themselves to public work and to the struggle for that independent living which is so sweet to the woman who has revolted against parasitism.

Economic Independence.

Few men understand what importance the modern middle class woman attaches to her economic independence. To men the right to earn a livelihood does not present itself as a hardly won and cherished privilege, but as a tiresome necessity. They may have earned an income with difficulty, but, at least, when they earned it it was theirs to spend as they would. But many women, even wealthy women, dressed in gorgeous raiment, with servants and horses and carriages at their command, never know what it is to be able to spend a guinea on the gratification simply of their own tastes. The money that they receive comes from father or husband, and must be spent as father or husband approve. Workers in the feminist movement are perfectly familiar with the well-dressed and prosperous-looking woman who declares, " Yes, I quite agree with you. I have often thought these things myself, and I wish I could help, but my husband does not approve of Women's Suffrage, and I have no money except what I get from him."* The life of the professional woman is often toilsome and often lonely, but the power of self-direction and self-activity which economic independence brings with it counts for much, and few women who have realized what sex-parasitism means, and have succeeded in emerging from it will ever willingly return to it.

The Two Sections of the Women's Movement.

So, at the present time there are two main sections in the modern women's movement—the movement of the middle class women who are revolting against their exclusion from human activity and insisting, firstly, on their right to education, which is now practically

---

* The personal experience of the writer will illustrate this point. She was once staying with the wife of a millionaire, and was going on after her visit for a walking tour with a friend in the Lake district. Mrs. D., when she heard of the plan, said: " Are you two going off by yourselves just where you like ? That must be delightful. All my life I have never been able to do that kind of thing. Before my marriage I had to go where mamma said, and now, of course, Mr. D. always decides about our holiday." Many a wealthy lady is as much subservient to the whims of her husband as though she were one of his upper servants, which, indeed, in many cases, she is, with the difference that they have holidays and she has none.

conceded on all sides ; secondly, on their right to earn a livelihood for themselves, which is rapidly being won ; and, thirdly, on their right to share in the control of Government, the point round which the fight is now most fiercely raging. These women are primarily rebelling against the sex-exclusiveness of men, and regard independence and the right to work as the most valuable privilege to be striven for.

On the other hand, there are the women of the working classes, who have been faced with a totally different problem, and who naturally react in a different way. Parasitism has never been forced on them. Even when the working class woman does not earn her own living in the world of industry—though practically all the unmarried girls of the working classes do so—her activities at home are so unending, and she subconsciously feels so important and so valuable, that she has never conceived of herself as useless and shut out from human interests, as was the parasitic middle class woman. What the woman of the proletariat feels as her grievance is that her work is too long and too monotonous, the burden laid upon her too heavy. Moreover, in her case that burden is due to the power of capitalistic exploitation resulting from the injustice of our social system. It is not due, or not, at least, to any considerable extent, to the fact that the men of her class shut her out from gainful occupations. Therefore, among the working women there is less sex consciousness. Evolving social enthusiasm tends to run rather into the channel of the labor revolt in general than into a specific revolution against the conditions alleged to be due to sex differences. The working woman feels her solidarity with the men of her class rather than their antagonism to her. The reforms that she demands are not independence and the right to work, but rather protection against the unending burden of toil which has been laid upon her. A speaker at a working women's congress said once, " It is not work we want, but more love, more leisure to enjoy life, and more beauty." These facts explain the relative lukewarmness of working class women in the distinctively feminist movement, and one of the possible dangers of the future is that the working class women in their right and natural desire to be protected against that exploitation which the first development of machinery brought with it, should allow themselves to drift without observing it into the parasitism which was the lot of middle class women. If the exclusion of married women from all paid work were carried out ; if the unmarried women were at the same time prevented from following all those occupations which reactionary male hygienists choose, without adequate investigation, to assume to be bad for women ; if at the same time the growth of the public supply of schools and other agencies for the care of children were to go on and the number of children in each family were to continue to diminish ; if the home, by reason of the development of machinery and large scale production, were to lose all those remaining economic activities which are carried on within it, then working women might come to live through the same experience as the middle class women have already known.

Sex-consciousness among Working Women.

But changes are proceeding in this situation. The consciousness of their rights and wrongs as a sex is arising among the working class women. They are beginning to see the possibility that even in the fight against capitalist exploitation, on which the men of their class are now entering, their specific interests may be overlooked. The shocking disregard of the needs of women by the Insurance Act has given them a clear proof of this. The great calamity against which the working class woman needs insurance is the death of her husband and bread winner; yet it is commonly stated that in the bargain with the big insurance societies the Government simply threw overboard the plans for a form of insurance which would make more secure the position of widows and orphans. Again, the home-staying working class woman finds that the Government cares little for her health, and makes practically no provision for her care should she fall ill, save in the one case of maternity benefit, and that, by curious irony, was originally to be paid to the husband and not to herself, save where the woman was herself a wage earner. Moreover, the development of social legislation is throwing heavier burdens on the working woman, and is yet making scant provision for her special needs. There are clubs, lectures, holidays provided for men, for boys, for young girls; but for the married working woman how little is done? A few schools for mothers, still mainly supported by private charity, in the poorest districts is about the sum total; yet all the while it is she who bears the burden of the insurance paid by her husband, for it comes in nine cases out of ten out of her housekeeping money. It is she who has to send the children to school clean and tidy and has to keep the great appetites of growing boys satisfied; it is she who is regarded as responsible for buying inflammable flannelette, for not providing fireguards or separate cradles for the babies, and whatever else a Government of men may choose to impose on her. So that there is appearing also among the working women an understanding of the fact that their interests are not altogether safe in the hands of men, though the working class women will never probably arrive at the intense consciousness of sex antagonism which characterizes some sections of the middle class feminists, and is due to men's callous disregard of their claims as human beings.

Changed Views among the Middle Class Women.

At the same time among the middle class women, too, the situation is altering. Many of them are realizing that to earn their own living is not always the joy it had appeared at first, for the living may be so meagre as to provide, at the cost of perpetual toil, only the merest food and shelter. Although the number of girls among the middle classes who are working for their living is steadily increasing, every now and then one comes across a young woman who finds the rigor of her work and the fierce competition too much for her, and hastens back gladly to the parasitic shelter of her relatives' roof. The lower sections of professional women, in short, are coming to understand the possibilities of exploitation, and are dimly beginning to feel rather than to comprehend the fact that work may be so monotonous and so ill-paid that even their human qualities, and much more their feminine attractiveness, will be beaten out of them in the process of earning their living.

And among the whole community the growth of collectivist feeling is bringing us to realize that State regulation of the conditions of labor is a necessity, and therefore we seldom find now among the feminists that embittered opposition to factory legislation which caused so many difficulties in the seventies and eighties. It is realized on all hands that the position of women in industry is not an exceptional one; that men, too, need protection against over-long hours of work, low wages, and insanitary conditions; and that, therefore, women are not accepting an inferior position in demanding the intervention of the State to secure for them suitable conditions of work.

They Want both Work and Marriage.

An even more momentous change is occurring in the attitude towards marriage. The first generation of feminists did not so much oppose marriagé as ignore it; but there is now coming into existence a second generation of advanced women, few at present, but destined to increase. Most of them know nothing at first hand of the old struggles. They have gone to high schools and colleges, and education has come to them as naturally as to their brothers. Many under the care of feminist relatives have been carefully trained to win the economic independence for which their mothers and aunts agonized in vain. And now these younger women find themselves face to face with a new set of problems. The fierceness and bitterness of the old struggles caused the first set of feminists to put the question of marriage and the supposed special disabilities of their sex altogether on one side. To-day many of these elder women, looking at their young relatives in receipt of independent incomes, doing work that is of real value to the world, and enjoying in such matters as foreign travel, theatre and concert going, and the cultivation of friendships a degree of freedom which they had longed for as unattainable, wonder what difficulties the young women of to-day can possibly have to contend with. But there are fundamental human instincts which can be disregarded only for a time. The problem of the modern professional woman is that she is forced to reconcile two needs of her nature which the present constitution of society make irreconcilable. She wants work, she wants the control of her own financial position, she wants education and the right to take part in the human activities of the State, but at the same time she is no longer willing to be shut out from marriage and motherhood. And the present organization of society means that for most women the two are alternatives. In almost all occupations the public acknowledgement of marriage means for a woman dismissal from her post and diminished economic resources. This is the case in practically all the Government posts: women civil servants, including even factory inspectors and school inspectors, are compelled to resign on marriage. Even the women school medical officers of the L.C.C.

are now forced to sign a contract stating that they will retire on marriage,* and although the same rule is not so strict in private business, there, too, it is rare for married women to be employed. Most women, that is to say, can only continue to preserve that economic independence, so keenly appreciated and won by such fierce struggles, on condition of compulsory celibacy and, what to many women is far worse, compulsory childlessness. Against this state of things a revolt is beginning which so far is barely articulate, but which is bound to make itself heard in public before long. What women who have fully thought out the position want, is not this forced alternative between activity in the human world and control of their own economic position on the one hand and marriage and children on the other, *but both*. The normal woman, like the normal man, desires a mate and a child, but she does not therefore desire nothing else. Least of all does she desire to sink back into a state of economic dependence and sex parasitism. Women do not want either love *or* work, but both ; and the full meaning of the feminist movement will not develop until this demand becomes conscious and articulate among the rank and file of the movement.

Can Child-bearing Women Earn their Living?

Now there can be no denying the fact that this demand will raise many difficulties. Some writers, chief of whom is that extra-ordinarily suggestive and interesting American, Charlotte Perkins Gilman, assume that with improved conditions of household management and the development of large scale housekeeping and publicly managed crèches and nursery schools it will be possible even for childbearing women to continue to earn their own living in such a way that they will be able not only to keep themselves during this period, but to contribute their share towards the bringing up of children, and this without any injury to the children. To the writer this seems a very optimistic attitude. It may, perhaps, be practicable for a few exceptional women, who possess sufficient ability to earn large incomes and have sufficient energy to endure, without breaking down, the twofold strain of working for a living and bringing children into the world. But it is obvious that for the vast majority of women regular work on exactly the same terms as those which men now submit to in office or factory is most undesirable for women during at least six months of the pre-natal and post-natal life of each child. If the child is to be nursed by its mother, as it should be, probably in most cases an even longer period of rest should be taken. The common sense of mankind knows well that just as increasing civilization leads to an increasing protection of children, so, too, it should mean more care for young mothers. During the child-bearing years the welfare of the child should have the precedence over all other considerations. But this does not mean that the woman need be incapacitated for earning her own living during her whole married life. It is not marriage that prevents a

* As these pages pass through the press, the desirability of requiring women doctors to retire on marriage is again being raised on the L.C.C.

woman from working. On the contrary, the married woman who is leading a normal and healthy life is likely to do better work and be a more satisfactory person than the spinster. The real hindrance is not marriage, but motherhood. Most people assume that the two are identical ; but should absorption in maternal duties extend over the whole of married life ? The days have gone past (one hopes never to return) when the married woman had a child every one or two years during the whole of the fertile period of life. The modern family, it seems probable, will not consist in the future of more than three or four children, and even if one made the assumption * that the woman should devote herself entirely to the care of the children until the youngest reached school age, there would still remain many years of her life during which she would be strong and fit for work. Indeed, one of the most pathetic sights of to-day is the middle aged woman whose children have ceased to afford her complete occupation. They are absorbed in school life and in the training for their future occupations. The husband, too, gives up his time to his work and his sport, and the woman of forty or fifty, still at the height of her maturity, stronger perhaps, and certainly wiser, than she was in her youth, is left stranded by the current of life, with no interests outside her family ; whilst by the family the necessary task of being "company to mother" is resented and evaded.† How much happier would such women be if, when their children no longer needed all their time, they could return to activities outside the household ; and how much richer would humanity be if it could avail itself of the services of such women. A type might come into existence, of which only one or two instances have yet appeared, of mature women who, as girls, had worked for themselves and known what human life, as opposed to sex life, meant ; who then had lived through the normal feminine experiences of being sought in marriage, loved, and made mothers of children ; and who, ripened and enriched by these experiences, returned in middle age to the activities of the world, knowing—because they have lived through—both sides of life. How enormously valuable such women would be in education and in the medical profession, where, indeed, even now a few of them may be found.

The Problem of the Future.

So, then, the problem before the future is to secure for women freedom and independence, the right to control their own destinies, and yet to make it possible for the same women to be wives and mothers. The solution of this problem will not be easy. It cannot

* The writer is not prepared to admit that this assumption is true in every case, or indeed in many cases. Many women who can *bear* splendid children are not necessarily fit to care for all the details of their health and rearing, and in many cases it would be well that the mother should return to her normal occupation as soon as ever the child no longer required to be nursed every two or three hours, and should use her earnings to pay for the skilled care given in crèche or nursery, resuming charge of the child in the non-working hours. But that this is possible cannot yet be considered as established beyond a doubt.

† See the serial story "Won Over," which appeared in Mrs. Gilman's magazine *The Forerunner* during 1913.

be attained through the methods advocated by either of the schools of thought that now hold the field ; neither by the feminists of the more old fashioned sort, on the one hand, who simply demand for women the same rights as men possess, ignoring all the inevitable differences of sex ; nor, on the other hand, by those who believe that sex is the only characteristic of women that matters, and disregard in her the human nature that she shares with man. Neither independence alone nor protection alone will meet the case. The whole problem is still so new that it is perhaps best to be cautious in dealing with it, and to avoid committing oneself too soon to any specific solution.

Women in Unpaid Public Work.

It may be that some women after the days of active motherhood are past will find a sufficient sphere in unpaid public work of various kinds, though at present our electoral laws shut out in practice the vast majority of married women from membership of all our public bodies except the less important ones.*

* I am indebted to the Secretary of the Women's Local Government Society for the following note on the electoral laws as they affect the position of married women on public bodies :

For candidature for county and town councils in Great Britain it is necessary to have an electoral qualification, and the candidate's name must appear either on the burgess roll or on the list of county electors. In England and Wales (outside London) married women are in general excluded from standing, as they are not entitled to have their names placed on the register. The Qualification of Women (County and Borough Councils) Act, 1907, removed the disabilities of sex and marriage in regard to candidates, but it did not amend the statute law which demands that candidates for county and town councils shall be electors. Married women can stand in London for the County Council, as the London County Council Electors Act, 1900, gave parochial electors the right to vote for the County Council.

In Scotland and Ireland women owners, women lodgers and women service voters are entitled to be registered, and therefore to stand for county and town councils. In England and Wales these three classes of women cannot have their names placed on the register.

Since 1894 in England and Wales, and since 1898 in Ireland, there has existed a residential qualification alternative with the electoral qualification for the following local government bodies :

ENGLAND AND WALES.	IRELAND.
Metropolitan Borough Councils.	Urban District Councils.
Urban District Councils.	Rural District Councils.
Rural District Councils.	Boards of Guardians.
Parish Councils.	
Boards of Guardians.	

It is in virtue of this residential qualification that at least two-thirds of the women guardians in England and Wales are now serving, and at the triennial elections for Metropolitan borough councils last November three-fourths of the women candidates were qualified by residence only.

In Scotland the school board is the only local authority for which the residential qualification is available. A change in the law is urgently needed in all three countries, so as to permit of an alternative residential qualification for candidates to all local government bodies.

It should be observed that even where there is no legal barrier against the candidature of married women for local bodies, few married women can in practice stand where it is neecssary for candidates to be electors, as married women seldom have qualifications as occupiers or owners, their houses being naturally hired or possessed by their husbands.

The new President of the Local Government Board has undertaken to introduce a Bill abolishing some of these anomalies.

The Legal Claim to Half the Husband's Income.

But it would be unreasonable to insist that the older married women as a whole should be confined to unpaid activities of this specific kind. Moreover, the objection which many of the noblest women feel to an undefined dependence on a husband would not be met at all by this suggestion, and we should find that if marriage means the complete relinquishment of a cherished occupation many of the finest women will refuse to marry. Some thinkers advocate that the difficulty should be met by giving to the married woman a legal claim to half her husband's income, and making her jointly responsible with him for the necessary expenditure on the family. There will be cases where the care of the household and children takes up the whole of a woman's time, in which such an arrangement would be quite legitimate, and it may be that it should be a possible legal settlement for those who care to adopt it. But it certainly should not be compulsory on all married couples. In the first place, it would obviously increase the tendency to evade legal marriage, and so would defeat the very purpose which it has in view. Again, dependence is not any the less dependence if definite legal provision is made for the endowment of it. Moreover, it would endow childless women equally with the child-bearing women, and it would continue the endowment during the years when the woman might reasonably return to ordinary economic activities. Therefore (although there will be cases where women will be supported by husbands who can afford to do so, and so will be set free either for the parasitic activities of fashion, sport and charity, or will use their leisure and freedom to carry on work for which no financial return may be expected, such as scientific research or the agitation for social reforms), yet the whole line of development should be in the direction of decreasing and not increasing the legal right of woman to be kept by the man, save when child-bearing and ·child-nurture are in question.

The Endowment of Motherhood.

Now, these are really specific activities of the greatest possible importance. No act of citizenship is more fundamental than the act of bringing into the world and protecting in his helpless infancy a new citizen, and therefore the most reasonable solution of the problem, though it may not be applicable in every case, is that women during the period when these activities must absorb their whole energies should be supported by a State endowment, but that this State endowment should not continue longer than the time during which they are so absorbed, and that at the end of that time they should be free to return to their former vocations.*

* It is neither possible nor desirable that we should at this stage adopt a dogmatic attitude as to the length of time during which an expectant and nursing mother should be freed from ordinary industry and be supported by a State grant. It will certainly vary from industry to industry. No pregnant woman should follow any occupation where the lifting of heavy weights is necessary or the raising of her arms above her head (obviously ordinary house work should be one of the first industries to be barred).

. Such a system would at one blow solve innumerable difficulties. If childbearing is protected by the State, it would not be unreasonable for the State to impose on the women who are possible mothers certain restrictions with regard to the activities which they may follow. Moreover, if the husband is no longer solely responsible for the support of his wife and her children, marriage will become easier among precisely those classes where we desire to encourage it. At the same time, if the dependence of women on marriage disappeared, and with it the inevitable accompanying subordination of their own wishes to their husbands' marital demands, we should establish the most reasonable check on the increase of the population, namely, the woman's natural dislike to excessive and unwished-for childbearing. That decline of the birth rate among the classes with the highest standard of comfort which exists at present would be checked by the greater facilities for marriage, yet, on the other hand, there would be no danger of the too large families which are due to the dependence of women, and which give rise to over population. At present the distribution of children presents the same inequality as the distribution of wealth ; some people have far too many at the same time that others have too few. Another problem which would in time disappear is the inequality of the wages of men and women. The great argument which now weighs with the popular mind in favor of this inequality is the alleged fact that, most men have dependants, while most women have not. Unfortunately, this is by no means always true ; and, moreover, this theory overlooks the fact that in a certain number of instances, at all events, women compete with men, and therefore if a lower level of payment is established for women, they will drive the men out altogether, as they have done in typewriting, and are in process of doing in elementary school teaching. What we want to work towards is a system whereby all adult human beings not incapacitated by some specific cause shall work for their living and be paid for it, no distinction of sex being made where similar work is done by men and women. Then the young, the aged, and those adults who for some special reason are unable to earn their living, should be supported by the State from the surplus funds available when rent and interest have been absorbed by the community ; a system of which we have already made a beginning in old age pensions on the one hand, and maintenance scholarships on the other. And among the most honored and respected of all those endowed by the State should be the women who are rendering to it the greatest possible service, that, namely, of ushering into the world its future citizens. But their reward for this service should only cover the time when their maternal duties prevent them from taking any part in industry.

On the other hand, most doctors advocate light out-door occupations. Women during these periods need work and interests and activities quite as much as the single or childless women : especially do they need what is now often denied them—some amount of social life. It would be easy under a properly organized state of Socialism to set aside excellently appropriate work for expectant mothers, and the State maintenance might then only need to cover a few weeks.

This is coming to be realized more and more clearly as the ultimate ideal of the feminist movement, and what we have to do at present is, while not straining our adhesion to it unduly in the face of the conflicts of the present situation, to attempt no changes in the law which will make our ultimate attainment of it impossible ; so that we should watch very carefully any development which may result in intensifying the dependence of women outside the childbearing years. It cannot be denied that the demands of some eugenists who are unable to believe that the necessary protection for motherhood can be given save through absolute dependence on a husband may make in this direction, and the increasing tendency of local authorities and government departments and of some philanthropic employers to exclude women from employment simply because they are legally married is equally a danger.

Socialism and Feminism.

It will be seen that these changes in the status of women cannot come about in our present individualistic society. In the first place, under the existing state of competition in business a woman who drops out for the childbearing period can hardly expect to be reinstated, and the world will probably honestly have to face the fact that certain readjustments, not otherwise desirable, must be made in order that the mother may not be penalized in her later economic life by reason of her motherhood. Even among elementary school teachers to-day a married teacher who frequently demands leave of absence because of her approaching confinement finds herself at a serious disadvantage. The absence and subsequent return of the married women to their work will no doubt be inconvenient, but the inconvenience must be faced, and the women as far as possible be placed at no disadvantage, if we are to put a stop to our present practice of the deliberate sterilization of the ablest and most independent women.*

Such a system could be deliberately and consciously introduced into the public services ; it could be imposed on private enterprise by factory legislation, though with much greater difficulty. But it is the development of Socialism, and that alone, which can make it possible throughout the whole fabric of society for the normal woman to attain her twin demands, independent work and motherhood. It is only Socialism which can make the endowment of the women during the maternal years a possibility, that endowment being one of the first charges on the surplus value or economic rent which the State will absorb ; and until the State has made itself master of the land and the capital of this country, it will not have an income big enough to enable it to provide adequate endowments for the childbearing women. Therefore it becomes clear that the only

* Cf. Shaw, "Man and Superman," p. 220. "Mr. Graham Wallas has already ventured to suggest, as Chairman of the School Management Committee of the London School Board, that the accepted policy of the sterilization of the school mistress, however administratively convenient, is open to criticism from the national stockbreeding point of view."

path to the ultimate and most deep lying ends of the feminist movement is through Socialism, and every wise feminist will find herself
more and more compelled to adopt the principles of Socialism. But
the wise Socialists must also be feminists. The public spirit of willing-
ness to serve the community which will be necessary if the Socialist
principles are to work must be inculcated into children from their
earliest days. Can they be so, inculcated by women who know
nothing of the activities of the world beyond the four walls of their
homes? Women, too, must be citizens and fully conscious of the
privileges and duties of their citizenship if Socialism is to. be
attained. Not least among the duties of that citizenship should. be
what Plato long ago demanded of his women guardians :—that they
should bear children for the service of the State.

SHORT BIBLIOGRAPHY.

BEBEL, AUGUST. Woman in the Past, Present, and Future. Reeves. 1893. 1s. net.

BONDFIELD, MARGARET. The National Care of Maternity. Women's Co-operative
Guild. 1d.

BRAUN, LILY. Die Frauenfrage; ihre geschichtliche Entwicklung und wirtschaft-
liche Seite. Leipzig : Hirzel. 1910.

BRONTE, CHARLOTTE. Shirley.

BROWNLOW, J. M. E. Women in Local Government in England and Wales. Nutt.
1911. 2s. 6d. net.

GILMAN, MRS. CHARLOTTE PERKINS. Women and Economics. Cheap edition.
Putnams. 1910. 1s. net.

GALT. Annals of the Parish. Routledge. Universal Library. 1s. net.

GISSING, GEORGE. The Odd Women. Cheap edition. 7d.

HUTCHINS, B. L., and HARRISON, A. History of Factory Legislation. Second
edition. King. 1911. 6s net.

HUTCHINS, B. L. Conflicting Ideals : Two Sides of the Woman's Question. Murby.
1913. 1s. 6d. net.

JAMES, EMILY. The Lady : Studies of Certain Significant Phases of Her History.
Putnams. 1910. 10s. 6d. net.

KEY, ELLEN. The Woman Movement. Putnams. 1913. 6s.

MARTIN, ANNA. The Married Working Woman. N.U.W.S.S. 1911. 2d.

MEISEL-HESS, GRETA Die Sexuelle Krise unserer Zeit : Eine sozial-psychologische
Untersuchung. Jena : Eugen Diederich. 1909.

MILL, JOHN STUART. The Subjection of Women. Popular edition. Longmans.
6d. net.

MORLEY, EDITH J. (Editor). Women in Seven Professions. Issued by the Studies
Committee.of the Fabian Women's Group. Routledge & Sons. 6s.

SCHREINER, OLIVE. Women and Labor. Unwin. 1911. 8s. 6d. net.

VILLIERS, BROUGHAM. The Case for Woman's Suffrage. Unwin. 1907. 2s. 6d.
net.

WOOD, G. H. The Woman Wage Earner. Church League for Woman Suffrage.
1910. 2d.

THE WAR
AND THE WORKERS

Handbook of some Immediate Measures to
Prevent Unemployment and Relieve Distress.

BY

SIDNEY WEBB.

"Obviously, the best way to provide for persons thrown out of their usual employment as a result of the war is to provide them with some other work for wages. . . . . Where the demands of the normal labor market are inadequate the Committee should consult the Local Authorities as to the possibility of expediting schemes of public utility, which might otherwise not be put in hand at the present moment. Whatever work is undertaken by Local Authorities . . . . should be performed in the ordinary way. . . . The men engaged . . . . should, of course, be paid wages in the ordinary way."—*Local Government Board Circular, P.R.D.7, August 20, 1914.*

PRICE ONE PENNY.

THE FABIAN SOCIETY, 3 CLEMENT'S INN, STRAND, LONDON, W.C.
(after Sept. 29th, 1914, 25 Tothill Street, Westminster, London, S.W.)

SEPTEMBER 1, 1914.
(SIXTEENTH THOUSAND, REVISED: SEPTEMBER 21, 1914.)

THE WAR AND THE WORKERS.

HANDBOOK OF SOME IMMEDIATE MEASURES TO PREVENT UNEMPLOYMENT AND RELIEVE DISTRESS.*

WAR finds the nation unprepared for the terrible dislocation of industry, unemployment and distress that is bound to occur. Everybody wants to know what can best be done. The following pages seek to supply authentic information and practical suggestions.

1.—Local Organization.

The Government has directed the formation of a local Citizens' Committee (now styled "Local Representative Committee ") in every Borough and Urban District exceeding 20,000 in population, and in every County for the parts exclusive of these areas. These Committees, which are to be made representative of all sections, and to be presided over by the Mayor or Chairman of Council, are to act in conjunction with the existing Local Authorities. Their duty is to be prevention, even more than relief.

This policy of concentrating the responsibility for emergency measures in a single representative Local Committee is a good one and ought to be loyally supported. But the Committee should be made thoroughly representative of all sections, including especially working men and women. The Government attaches great importance to this latter point. In some places the Committees are too much restricted to "prominent citizens " (always of the male sex), friends of the Mayor or Chairman, and professional philanthropists. Such influential organizations as the local Co-operative Societies, the local Trades Council, the local branches of the leading Friendly Societies and Trade Unions, and the local Socialist Societies have sometimes no members on the Committee. Especially do the local organizations of working women (such as the Women's Trade Unions, the Women's Co-operative Guild, the Women's Labor League, etc.) tend to be ignored. *This is a fatal mistake*, which the Mayor or Chairman or Secretary would do well promptly to correct, if he wishes the Committee's applications for money, or for sanction of schemes to receive official approval. The organization to which you belong should at once apply to the Mayor (or Chairman of County or District Council) for representation. If the Committee is already formed, ask that these representatives may be added. If representation is refused, write or telegraph at once to the President of the Local Government Board, London.

Take care to nominate a representative who can and will attend all the meetings (there will of course be no payment even for travelling expenses), and who will make himself or herself of use.

* This pamphlet embodies and supersedes the "Memorandum" issued August 17, 1914.

Send all your suggestions and offers of help to the Local Committee; and communicate to them at once, without rushing to put them in the newspaper, any complaints, or any information as to things not working properly.

The Committee will at once appoint Sub-Committees—perhaps one to devise schemes for keeping up the volume of employment, and one for each ward or parish to undertake to look out for every case of distress. Remember that the Government lays it down emphatically that no one in distress through the war is to be forced to the Poor Law.

Clerks should be engaged and paid proper wages to carry out the regular office work of the Committee. (The L.G.B. announced, by Circular of August 17th, 1914, that the establishment and incidental expenses of the Committee may be paid out of the local rates.) The Committee must certainly not start on its work of preventing unemployment by actually increasing the very serious unemployment among clerks and typists! Volunteers should be used only for consulting, advising, organising, and supervising the paid staff; for visiting cases; and for the actual dispensing of relief.

2.—Keep Up the Volume of Employment.

The declared policy of the Government—quite rightly—is, *first and foremost*, to use every effort to maintain undiminished the total amount of wage earning employment in the Kingdom as a whole. This is to be the guiding policy of each Local Committee. Therefore don't go to the Committee with the idea that its main business, or the most urgent duty, is to organize measures for the relief of distress. It ought first to set its mind on *preventing the occurrence* of unemployment. It is immensely more valuable to prevent men from being discharged from employment than to relieve them when they are unemployed.

Let your first suggestions to the Committee be to keep up (at standard Trade Union rates of wages) the volume of paid employment carried on in the ordinary way. It is the first time that the Government has adopted so wise a policy. See that your Committee understands it. It has nothing in common with "starting Relief Works" or "employing the unemployed."

3.—How to Keep Up the Volume of Employment.

The first effect of war is to dislocate industry. All sorts of trades carried on by private enterprise will inevitably be diminished, and some even stopped. Many employers will be driven to reduce their staffs of artizans and laborers, clerks and shop assistants, men and women. To fill this void, as the Government rightly declares, it is the duty of every Public Authority to be actually increasing its wages bill. The Government is doing its share by taking some 800,000 men off the Labor Market, and maintaining them and their families; besides giving extraordinarily large orders for army and navy stores, and thus keeping hundreds of firms busy. But every Local Authority ought to be doing its part. The Local

Government Board (Circular of August 20th, 1914) makes it the first duty of the Committee to press this on all the Local Governing Bodies (Borough, Urban, Rural, County, and Parish Councils; Boards of Guardians; Harbor and Port Authorities; School Boards (in Scotland); Education, Asylum, Hospital, or Water Authorities). Therefore, make a point of getting your Committee to write to every such Authority, to enquire what steps it is taking in this matter. Here are some specific suggestions for Local Authorities.

(a) It is not enough to decide to keep places open for Reservists and Territorials called away; to treat them liberally as to pay, etc.; and to make provision for their families. Urge strongly on your Local Authorities that they ought to maintain their staffs at full strength by taking on temporary men; that no public services should be reduced; that no officials should be recalled from leave, or denied their holidays; and that no systematic overtime should be worked. It would be well to get returns for all departments showing the actual numbers on the pay-roll (apart from men called to the front) now, and at the corresponding week last year.

(b) Increased work should be promptly started by all the Local Authorities. The first step should be to put in hand at once all the works of building, repairing, cleaning and improving provided for in the estimates for the current year. Do it all now, in order to absorb the men and women thrown out of work by the war. "Now is the winter of our discontent."

(c) But much more should be done. The Government is prepared to help most liberally with money those Local Authorities that undertake at once new works of public utility, in order to maintain the volume of employment. Urge all the local Councils to draw up at once a list of the buildings that ought to be built, the repairs that ought to be executed, the public improvements that ought to be made in connection with each and all of the departments of their work during the next few years, specifying which of them could be started at once if Government funds were available, so as to involve no rise in the rates. *Every Local Authority should send, at once, such a list to Mr. Herbert Samuel.* Don't think yet of "relief works": think of the following:

    (i) Elementary schools, provided and non-provided, that need to be enlarged, remodelled for smaller classrooms, improved or built (don't forget equipment and school furniture).

    (ii) Additional secondary schools, training colleges, hostels, domestic economy centres, technical institutes, etc., that are required.

(iii) Further buildings and equipment for university colleges, science laboratories, etc. (don't forget to ask the local university what work it could put in hand, or what new buildings it could put up, if money were found; also ask how much is required to do all necessary bookbinding and cataloguing of the Public Libaries).

(iv) Roads, bridges, footpaths, etc., that need bringing up to the standards of the Road Board (the Road Board will be prepared to contribute very largely to the cost of new main roads, as well as for improvements).

(v) Tramways called for to complete the local system ; new car-sheds, waiting-shelters, car-repairing workshops, etc.

(vi) Light railways required in the rural districts, for which the Development Commissioners would gladly find money, if County Councils or other Local Authorities would submit schemes.

(vii) Housing enterprises, including the improvement of slum areas, the erection of additional cottages, etc. Why should not the Pensions Committee seek Government assistance to build cottages, or what used to be called "almshouses," specially for old age pensioners? The Government is prepared to advance up to four millions sterling for housing, charging only such interest as it has itself to pay. Get the Town or District Council to put in a scheme at once. Failing applications from Local Authorities, the Government will fall back on Public Utility Societies, advancing them nine-tenths of the cost.

(viii) Hospitals for all diseases (which every Local Sanitary Authority has already full statutory power to erect and maintain, under the Public Health Act) : these are urgently required in every county of Great Britain, as the voluntary hospitals (where such exist) are nowhere sufficient for the needs revealed by the Insurance Act. Many even of the existing hospital beds are being reserved for the wounded, and civilian patients are already being refused admission in some places. The Government is alive to this need, and will gladly receive suggestions for additional municipal hospitals; especially as every insured person whose admission to hospital is delayed is now costing ten shillings or seven and sixpence a week to the National Insurance Fund, and thereby increasing the deficit on the Approved Societies. Representatives of Approved Societies should therefore move for this, and insist on immediate action.

(ix) Tuberculosis sanatoria, which County and County Borough Councils are called upon, with extensive Government aid, to provide for the tuberculous. In some places plans and schemes for these are being suspended, and it is even alleged that the officers of the L.G.B. and Insurance Commission are delaying sanction for them, in order to save money! This is in direct disobedience of the Cabinet's orders to increase employment and press on all works. See that your own County or County Borough presses forward its own scheme ; and that it appeals to the Prime Minister himself in the event of official obstruction.

(x) Pathological laboratories for the aid of the doctor's diagnosis, especially for tuberculosis. Every County and County Borough Council was called upon by Parliament a year ago to provide these ; and Parliament has voted the money to enable a 50 per cent. grant of the cost to be paid. Now is the time to push forward this work. The L.G.B. is only waiting for proposals to hand out the money in pursuance of the Cabinet policy.

(xi) Street improvements, paving works, main drainage schemes, extensions of the water supply or of the gas and electricity works and plant.

(xii) Afforestation of the municipal water catchment area, or other waste lands—in fact, any planting of trees, for which the Development Commission will find money on liberal terms, for large schemes or small.

(xiii) Additional parks and open spaces—now is the time to move to lay them out.

(xiv) Waste lands (including "drowned" or flooded lands), whether in public or private ownership, for the draining, reclamation or planting of which the Development Commissioners might be asked for grants.

(xv) Harbor improvements, improvement of sea walls and other coast defences, prevention of floods, etc.

The Government has taken statutory power to pay the whole or part of the cost of all the foregoing works ; and any part of the £100,000,000 of money voted by the House of Commons can be made available, if the Government think fit, for any of them. Do not be put off with Departmental refusals to sanction schemes or supply funds on the ground that the money is not provided for in the Department's estimates. Appeal, in need, direct to Mr. Herbert Samuel. It is understood that the Cabinet has decided that no technical difficulties are to be allowed to obstruct the immediate undertaking of desirable works : indeed, the Cabinet realizes keenly that it is a military necessity that the people must be maintained, and if they are not kept employed now in the above legitimate and healthy way, they will have to be presently fed at the public expense! It is better to build schools or hospitals than to pay for either "relief works" or a gigantic system of soup kitchens! Applications with regard to No. iv should be made to the Road Board; with regard to Nos. vi, xii, xiv, and xv to the Development Commission; and with regard to the others to the President of the Local Government Board, who is the Chairman of the Cabinet Emergency Committee. Time presses: get all the Local Authorities to act at once.

There can be no doubt that, with almost all Local Authorities, the wheels would be greased if they could be assured there would be no rise in the rates. The way to do this is for the Government to *suspend all municipal sinking funds* for the period of the war. Press for this to be done. Every Local Authority should at once pass a resolution asking the Government to enact it.

Remember that the Government has laid it down in principle that the "Fair Wages Clauses," insisted on by the House of Commons, are to apply also to contracts for works made by other than Government Departments, provided that they "involve the expenditure of public money or other consideration granted by the Department, or which have to be approved by a Government Department. In all these cases the Government Department is to require the insertion in such contracts of Fair Wages Clauses." (Report of the Official Advisory Committee on Fair Wages Clauses, transmitted by the Lords Commissioners of the Treasury, November, 1912.)

The usual Government "Fair Wages Clause" must therefore be inserted in any contracts entered into for the above works. This is certainly no time for any relaxation in this respect. Let the workmen be taken on through the Labor Exchange on the conditions customary in each trade, without any reference to being in distress.

4.—Remember the Women.

It is inevitable that the works put in hand to increase the volume of employment should operate most directly on men's trades, especially the various branches of the building industry. This is no reason against their being undertaken. Every man kept in receipt of wages helps to keep others in employment in all sorts of occupations.

But something special is needed for the four million wage earning women and girls, many of whom, from "jam hands" to typists, will find themselves discharged. Press the following suggestions on the Local Authorities:

(a) Take care that the staffs of women in public employment (teachers, typists, clerks, charwomen, school cleaners, lavatory attendants, etc.) are kept at full strength.

(b) Do not postpone any orders for uniforms, asylum clothing, or other garments: rather increase stocks.

(c) Increase the elementary school staffs of women teachers, so as to bring the classes down, where accommodation permits, at any rate to the extent of taking on at once the whole year's supply of trained teachers leaving college, or otherwise available.

(d) Now is the time to start, or to increase the staff of, Health Visitors and Women Sanitary Inspectors.

Moreover, don't let the Insurance Committees delay the starting of the scheme for home nursing, for which Parliament has actually voted the money. Every day's delay in providing nursing for insured persons means an unnecessary drain on the funds of the Approved Societies, and a steady increase in the deficits. It will be said that nurses are scarce. But this is mainly because thousands of them, of various degrees of training, have offered their services to tend the wounded—to the extent, it is said, of several nurses to each expected patient! In a few weeks there will be nurses available—partly rejected volunteers, partly trained women who had left the profession, glad now to resume nursing on the suspension of their present occupations or incomes, partly women whose training was interrupted and can now be completed, and partly probationers ending their training. The full staff of probationers must everywhere be maintained. We must remember that the civilian sick have to be nursed equally with the wounded soldiers and sailors. See that the local Insurance Committee takes steps without delay; and that it does not allow the Insurance Commissioners to obstruct the policy of Parliament (which has decided to have the nursing) and of the Cabinet (which has determined to increase employment).

The following ingenious suggestion is commended to all Police Authorities (Watch or Standing Joint Committees) : "Now is the time, when the urban police forces are everywhere working under great pressure, and the Cabinet is anxious to keep up the volume of employment, for the Home Secretary to start the much needed 'police women.' Great Britain has over a hundred thousand policemen and no female constables, though at least one per cent. of the total strength might with advantage be women, if only for use in the protection of women and children. In the United States no fewer than twenty-five cities have now one or more policewomen, Chicago having twenty, whilst Baltimore, Seattle, and Los Angeles have five each, Pittsburgh four, and San Francisco and St. Paul each three." (*The New Statesman*, 15 August, 1914.) Two women have just been appointed unpaid special constables at Sandgate, Kent. Why withhold the paid posts?

More, however, will have to be done. Why should not the Local Education Authority seek authority and funds to enable it to provide maintenance scholarships and appropriate training for all girls under sixteen (or for all such now at school who are willing to stay on), so as to avoid flooding an already overstocked Labor Market? The same might usefully be done for the boys, especially where juvenile unemployment increases. Accommodation could be found temporarily, in London in the Polytechnics, and elsewhere in the technical institutes, which are not fully occupied in the daytime; or in buildings temporarily hired for the purpose. The Board of Education would, it is understood, favorably consider such applications. The Prince of Wales's Fund can find the money. It is a case for local initiative and insistence.

5.—The Three Dont's.

Don't let your Committee be misled by some well meaning, but economically ignorant, person who suggests that the rate of wages should be lowered, "in order to enable more hands to be taken on," etc. Employers will be eager enough to have "cheap labor." This is bad economics. Trade Union wages must be upheld. Wages should be rather raised than lowered, to meet the rising prices.

Don't favor any idea of setting benevolent ladies or school children to make clothes for the poor or necessaries for the troops. This is very apt to increase unemployment. All such work should be done on commercial lines, by properly qualified workers, and paid for by wages. Those who have means should be encourged to pay unemployed women workers to do the work that they wish done. Children are at school to be taught, not to be set to produce. People willing to give gratuitous service should confine themselves to the work that is never paid for.

Don't give food or doles of money until you are face to face with actual want—and even then don't advertise it! Rather hire people to do some work that you want done without any assumption of giving relief. "Invent a service if you have it not."

6.—Temporary Emergencies.

There are a lot of people who will find themselves temporarily "in a hole," where there need be no lasting distress. Intelligent personal assistance is invaluable in such cases. Every Local Committee ought to set apart some man or woman of knowledge and ingenuity from whom such persons can seek advice at stated hours, both morning and evening. Here are some examples :

(a) Wives of Men Called to the Front.

These are now entitled to quite substantial "separation allowances" from the Government, rising up to 25s a week. But it is inevitable that some remittances should be delayed, and some not properly applied for. The help most needed (beyond any necessary emergency relief) is to ensure the future arrival of these remittances.

The wives of Soldiers (including Reservists, Territorials and civilians enlisted for temporary service) should all be drawing, for privates, corporals and sergeants, 16s. od. per week in London postal area, and 12s. 6d. per week elsewhere, together with an additional 2s. 6d. a week for each child (boy under 14 and girl under 16). Motherless children, widowed mothers, and other dependents are now properly provided for in the same way. Payments are now to be made weekly by the Post Office like Old Age Pensions. Wives "not on the strength" are now to get the same ; *but they need to be helped to establish their claims* (marriage certificate and birth certificates of children are required, for which the Local Registrar should be urged to charge only nominal fees).

The wives of Sailors (including Naval Reservists and Marines) are now to get separation allowances on similar lines.

There are also advances on mobilisation, allotments of pay, remittances from the soldiers or sailors themselves, and so on—some of which may not have come to hand. Full particulars can be obtained from the Local Government Board.

The Soldiers' and Sailors' Families Association (23 Queen Anne's Gate, Westminster) will advise as to how the wives can establish their claims and will help any cases of distress. Keep in touch with its branch in your town, and see that any such are promptly dealt with. Do not seek to relieve the Government from its obligations. There ought to be no need for the wife or child or other dependent of anyone called to the front to come on the general relief funds, *which, except in emergency, are not for them.*

(b) FOREIGNERS NOT RECEIVING THEIR REMITTANCES.

Up and down the country there are men and women depending on remittances from abroad, which now fail to arrive. Especially are Germans, Austrians and Hungarians—frequently here as governesses, clerks, teachers, etc.—in this condition. They need to be helped to get to the nearest Consul in temporary charge of their nationality (usually the American Consul); advised how to get their remittances if this is anyway possible; advised as to the societies that can help them; and perhaps assisted by loans.

There are also many foreign waiters and workmen in distress, who need similar personal assistance. They are not at war with us!

(c) INSURED PERSONS.

Remember that all men usually employed in the building, ship-building or engineering trades, in the making of vehicles or sawmilling, and in works of construction are normally " insured " against unemployment, and ought to be in receipt of 7s. a week, irrespective of their means. Ascertain in any case why that sum is not being received; and help the applicant to establish his claim, or to appeal.

Members of Trade Unions and Friendly Societies who have run out of benefit ought to have their arrears paid up for them, or anything else done to enable them to get into benefit again according to the rules.

Every person sick, or incapable of work by physical or mental disablement (including blindness or other affliction; also pregnancy or maternity) ought normally to be entitled to ten shillings (seven and sixpence if a woman) per week from the National Health Insurance Fund; or to five shillings where permanently disabled. Ascertain in any case why that sum is not being received, and help the applicant to establish his claim. Don't easily be put off by a refusal to pay from the Approved Society. It is the experience of those who have pressed such claims that many refusals to pay have been converted into payments by judicious insistence! If necessary, get the co-operation of the claimant's doctor, appeal to the chairman of the society or company, and telegraph or write to the Insurance Commissioners. Claims for actual incapacity to work due merely to pregnancy are often (quite unlawfully) refused.

Arrears of Health Insurance may be paid up voluntarily. But no one ought yet to be out of benefit on account of arrears (except as regards deficiencies in the initial 26 weeks needed for Sickness or Maternity Benefit, and in the initial 104 weeks needed for Disablement Benefit. Every expectant mother ought to see to it that the full number of stamps have been affixed to ensure receipt of Maternity Benefit; if not, it is best to make up the number at once. Wives of men called to the front are entitled to this benefit, whether or not their husbands had joined an Approved Society.

7.—When Distress Comes.

Unfortunately, we cannot hope, whatever we may do, to prevent the occurrence of all distress. When it comes, avoid to the last the mere doling out of relief, whether in money or in bread. What the unemployed man or woman wants is wages, not charity. Do your utmost to get every applicant taken on at regular wages, at some occupation or other, whether or not his accustomed work, or near his present home. Make the fullest possible use of the Labor Exchange, in order that jobs of all sorts, in all parts of the country, may be promptly heard of.* Get railway fares paid where necessary. It is better to get men jobs in other places (helping them to move), or in occupations new to them (treating them temporarily as "improvers"), than to put them on relief.

It is an imperative duty of the community at all hazards to prevent suffering from lack of the necessaries of life. But the worst form that our provision can take is that of the mere charitable dole. The evil effects of this so-called "charity" are not avoided by giving it only after elaborate investigation, or out of public funds, or under the influence of "war fever."

(a) Nobody to be Driven to Poor Relief!

The Government has expressly pledged the honor of the nation that no one brought to destitution as a result of the war shall be driven to the shame and demoralization of the Poor Law. And the Government has lost no time in starting to redeem this pledge. When it was brought to the notice of the Cabinet Committee that the wives of men called to the front had, owing to the non-arrival of the Government allowances due to them, been driven to apply to the Relieving Officer, the Government unhesitatingly decided (*for the first time in Poor Law history*) (i) to repay to the Boards of Guardians their shameful doles; (ii) to erase from the records the names of those thus relieved, and entirely to cancel the transaction; and (iii) to write officially to each woman, informing her of what had been done, and explaining that she had not become a pauper!

This precedent is to be followed in other cases. No distinction was made in the Government's pledge between the dependants of

* In country villages, and other places where is no Labor Exchange (or any effective agency thereof), Local Committees, besides registering all local applicants for relief, may usefully ask all employers to inform them at once of any vacancies or opportunities for employment of local men and women. No one realizes how much employment can be afforded locally, with good will, until the attempt is made.

those called to the front and those serving the community in other ways. *No destitution caused by the war is to be a fit subject for Poor Relief.* Urgent cases must, of course, be attended to as heretofore ; but Boards of Guardians should at once claim repayment from the Local Government Board, and regard themselves only as making temporary advances for the Government. *Local Relief Committees must therefore see to it that no person coming to destitution on account of the war is left without help, or driven to apply to the Relieving Officer.*

(b) FEED THE CHILDREN.

The first thing to be done in distress is to feed the children. The Board of Education is urging every Local Education Authority to undertake to feed, in connection with the elementary schools, every child in need of food, whether actually on the school roll or not, on Saturdays, Sundays, and other holidays, as well as on school days, including children above school age, or under school age—even the infants in connection with Schools for Mothers, etc.)—promising fifty per cent. of the amount spent on those on the school roll. The Prince of Wales's National Relief Fund will make grants towards expenses not authorized from the rates. See that your Local Education Authority, if it has not already done so, *immediately* takes the formal step of passing the resolution necessary " to adopt" the Education (Provision of Meals) Act. Write to your County or Borough Councillor at once, asking whether this has been done. Urge the Local Education Authority to do its full duty in this respect—if not, complain to the Board of Education. If it does, all relief for children had better be concentrated there ; and (except in emergencies and special cases) nothing issued for children by any other agency. Above all, keep the children away from the Board of Guardians : the Poor Law should never have anything to do with children.

(c) PROVIDE FOR MATERNITY AND INFANCY.

The Local Government Board has just pointed out to all County and Borough Councils, and Urban and Rural District Councils, in a Circular of July 30th, 1914, that it now falls within their scope—really in supersession of the Poor Law—to make systematic and gratuitous provision for Maternity and Infancy. Parliament has voted money for a Fifty per Cent. Grant in Aid of their expenditure on this service. The scheme of work suggested includes (i) local supervision of midwives; (ii) an ante-natal clinic for expectant mothers (where provision may be made, out of voluntary funds, or a grant from the Prince of Wales's Fund, for supplying meals); (iii) the home visiting of expectant mothers, to which the Government says it attaches particular importance : this should bring to light any cases needing help ; (iv) a Maternity Hospital, which the Council is authorised to provide ; (v) assistance to the mother to ensure skilled attendance at confinement ; (vi) medical attendance at confinement in all difficult cases ; (vii) hospital treatment after confinement where required ; (viii) treatment of the infant up to school age at a " Baby

Clinic," which the Council is authorised to provide ; (ix) systematic home visiting of infants until they get on the school register.

The very best way to deal with distress among mothers and infants is for the Town or District Council to do its duty in carrying out this scheme. Get your Committee to urge this on the Council. See that the Medical Officer of Health brings up the proposal at once ; and that the Health Committee presses it on the Council. The L.G.B. will, of course, be eager to approve such schemes, in pursuance of the Cabinet's policy. Now is the appropriate time !

This is, in effect, the policy advocated by the Women's Co-operative Guild, which presses strongly for the provision by the Health Committee of (a) medical advice for mothers : this can legally be done under the Public Health Acts at a public dispensary (which is included in the term hospital) ; (b) midwifery at confinement—this may require further authority, but might at once be provided out of voluntary funds ; (c) free dinners for expectant and nursing mothers—this could be organized, out of voluntary funds, in connection with the Maternity Clinic ; (d) free milk for mothers and young children on doctor's recommendation—this can be given out of the rates at the Baby Clinic, as ancillary to medical treatment ; (e) free dinners for children under school age—this can be done, out of voluntary funds, by the Local Education Authority.

If the Local Health Authority and the Local Education Authority both do their duty, as the Government has directed, with the aid of the Government grants promised, and of grants from the Prince of Wales's Fund, the Medical Officer of Health will know of every expectant mother or mother of infants, and there ought to be no cases of distress among them throughout the whole area.

In some places, an energetic Town or District Council actively increasing its public enterprises so as to prevent unemployment, an energetic Education Authority feeding all children in need, and an enlightened Health Committee providing thoroughly for all mothers and infants, might, otherwise than for particular cases of exceptional distress, find no need for any further measures. The emergency would have been met in the best possible way.

(d) EXTENSION OF UNEMPLOYMENT BENEFIT.

(i) *The Trade Union Benefit.*

In a large number of trades, the Trade Union members subscribe liberally whilst in full work in order to provide for themselves "Out of Work Pay" of 8s. to 12s. per week whilst out of employment. The Government now assists this self-help by repaying to any such Trade Union one-sixth of what it has disbursed in this way. About one million Trade Unionists are thus in ordinary times provided for. It would be of the greatest value if similar Unemployment Benefit could be adopted by the other Trade Unions (numbering nearly three million members). The repayment of so small a proportion as one-sixth of the cost—an extremely limited encouragement, far below what is given in other countries—is not sufficient to enable this to be done. Why not offer to increase the proportion to one-half, in order to make it possible for other Trade Unions to institute a system of Out of Work Pay?

But the Government might well go further during the continuance of the war. A Trade Union which can promise that none of its unemployed members shall trouble the Local Committees, or come on public relief, is doing a valuable service to the State. A Trade Union knows its own members, and can judge better than any Distress Committee of their need. The Parliamentary Committee of the Trade Union Congress asks that, in this crisis, every Trade Union giving Out of Work Pay, and thus undertaking the support of its own unemployed members, shall be granted, week by week, in lieu of all other assistance from the State, what it finds necessary to expend in this way according to its rules, subject to a maximum weekly rate to be fixed by the Board of Trade.

(ii) *The Government Unemployment Insurance.*

This (securing 7s. a week for fifteen weeks in each year, with certain limits) extends only to two and a half million men (and 10,000 women), in arbitrarily selected trades, covering only one-sixth of the wage earners. It is suggested (a) that the period of benefit is already proving quite insufficient, and ought to be extended; (b) that the scheme ought at once to be extended to many other trades, employing women as well as men, the workers being, in this emergency, made immediately eligible for benefit. These reforms would, of course, in order to maintain the solvency of the Fund, involve a Parliamentary Grant in lieu of the initial waiting period.

(iii) *Loans to Trades.*

If unemployment becomes widespread, desolating whole industries, something more will have to be done. Yet it is difficult for Parliament actually to give more to one section than to another. It is suggested that, where no Trade Union Out of Work Pay exists, the offer might be made by the Government to the operatives in any trade—preferably through the Trade Union, but enabling non-unionists also to vote, as is the practice among the coal-miners for a checkweighman—to advance to the trade *on loan* the amount necessary to institute and maintain Out of Work Pay weekly throughout the whole war, under the administration of the Trade Union, on the understanding that the loan should be gradually repaid by the proceeds of a deduction to be made under statutory authority from the wages of all the operatives in the trade who might now or hereafter be working full time, with a corresponding payment by the employers (exactly as if made under the Insurance Act, Part II.), these deductions and payments lasting only until the total sum advanced (less the one-sixth or whatever other proportion that the Government might be contributing to other Trade Unions) had been wholly repaid. This plan might suit the circumstances of such industries as the textiles and the miners; and if agreed to at ballots of the whole trade, would involve the Government ultimately in no loss.

(e) Look After the Women.

Think, next, of the case of the unemployed women, because they are generally thought of last. The lot of the women and girls thrown out of employment—jam hands and bottle washers, charwomen and box makers, "hands" from the tea and tobacco factories, and what not—is a particularly hard one. They are excluded from the Government Unemployment Insurance, and their little Trade Unions have no funds. They have a right to honorable maintenance just as much as the men. No one can think of municipal employment for them. The Government agrees that they are not to be driven to Poor Relief. The best thing to do for them is to *take them on as "learners"* or improvers, in some big, empty warehouse, at making and repairing all sorts of garments, hats and boots, not to be put on sale, but for the use of themselves and their children. A certain number every day should be taught to cook the dinner for all, in the very best way. The work will be totally unskilled, even bad; and the result at first will be small. But if competent instructors are provided, the women will, in a few weeks, not only have improved in health, but also have gained a training of the greatest value in their homes. The necessary outlay on premises, equipment, material and instructors (who are themselves thus found paid employment) though, like the women's pay, a dead loss, is more than repaid by the training gained, if not by the utility of the clothes they retain for themselves.

In some cases, large employers of women, whose workshops have to be closed owing to cessation of orders, have offered to place their premises and forewomen gratuitously at the disposal of any Local Committee which would set the girls to work at domestic dressmaking and millinery, interspersed with lessons in cookery, etc. This might be a good way of starting the Training Centres.

The Government has now agreed to let Local Committees start Women's Training Centres on these lines and to find all the necessary funds.

As the object is not to convert these women and girls into professional tailoresses or milliners, but merely to train them to make garments for themselves and their children, it is not desirable that steam power should be used, or factory methods adopted. What should be taught is "domestic" cutting-out, simple dressmaking, the making of undergarments and of children's clothes, and hat trimming, partly by hand and partly with the ordinary domestic sewing machine.*

Failing any such organization, women and girls in distress might, where possible, be required, as a condition of the receipt of pay, to attend regularly for instruction in Domestic Economy and Hygiene

---

* Women's Workrooms have for some years been conducted by the Central (Unemployed) Body for London, under the Unemployed Workmen Act, 1905. These, however, by an unfortunate L.G.B. decision, which is understood to be now officially repented of, have had to be conducted on commercial lines, as if the object were production for profit! The commodities have to be produced for the market and sold—thus actually tending to throw other seamstresses out of work! The women, moreover, are kept to what they can do well, as being most profitable—not put successively to one task after another, so that they may get the utmost possible training. All this is uneconomic and mistaken, and must not be repeated.

—for which unemployed teachers should be engaged and paid, and suitable temporary premises obtained. Remember the successful educational classes for the unemployed during the Lancashire Cotton Famine—undertaken at the suggestion of the operatives themselves.

Consider, in this connection, the special needs of the many thousands of women and girls working only "half-time." To them, often earning 8s. to 12s. per week when in full work, "half time" is starvation. Many casual workers may presently be getting only a few hours' wages in a week. Yet, as they are not wholly "out of work," they may be excluded from all the schemes. They should be eligible to attend the Women's Training Centres on their off days, or Domestic Economy Classes in their free hours; receiving adequate subsistence for these periods.

Consider, too, the widowed home-worker, getting only a few hours work a week; and yet sometimes tied to home by the care of children under school age. The Government insists that, in so far as her distress is caused by the war, the Local Committee must see to it that she is not driven to the Poor Law. She must be given maintenance merely in return for attending to the infants; if possible, in connection with the municipal Baby Clinic or School for Mothers.

Applications for approval of schemes for women, for which grants will be made both from the Queen's and the Prince of Wales's Fund should be made to Miss Macarthur, Hon. Secretary of Central Committee on the Employment of Women, Wimborne House, Arlington Street, London, S.W.

(†) Use the Distress Committee.

Unfortunately, we must contemplate that many Local Authorities will have been slow to understand the important new policy of actually preventing the occurrence of unemployment which the Government has laid down: they will not, in many places, have started enough new enterprises of the kinds already mentioned, nor yet sufficiently enlarged their wages bill, to save their localities from disastrous unemployment. Any such failure of the County, Borough or District Councils to prevent unemployment is not economical, because it compels resort to the worse and more costly alternative of relieving the unemployed who are not in receipt of Unemployment Benefit. The Local Relief Committee must then use the machinery of the Distress Committee, which can everywhere be appointed by the Borough or District Council under the Unemployed Workmen Act, 1905 (in London, such Distress Committees are federated in the "Central (Unemployed) Body," Temple Avenue, Whitefriars, E.C.). The reasons why the actual provision for unemployed workmen should be left to the Distress Committee are (i) because we must not have two overlapping sets of "relief works"; (ii) because there is £100,000 already voted by Parliament for such work, and *only the Distress Committee can draw this grant from the L.G.B.* Hence, see that your Distress Committee is as actively at work as if this were hard winter weather—if it has not yet sprung into activity, complain to the L.G.B. All ablebodied men in distress should be referred to the Distress Committee, and be by that Committee provided for. All needy applicants for whom the Labor Exchange can find no situation anywhere, should be referred to the Distress Committee. (But they should all be registered by the Local Relief Committee, kept in view, and no case lost sight of, to ensure that the Distress Committee neglects none of them.) The Distress Committee will be able to get grants from the L.G.B. towards the cost of all approved schemes. As the Government has made it clear that persons in distress through the war are not to be driven to the Poor Law, it follows that the necessary grants will have to be forthcoming to any extent that the emergency requires.

(g) Find Really Educational Employment for the Men.

It is hopeless to expect the Distress Committee to be able to organize employment at their own trades for this mixed crowd of men—tailors, jewellers, waiters, dockers, carmen, clerks, porters, cabmen. To do this, indeed, would be equivalent to throwing other men out of work. The very best use to which the men can be put, for whom no situation can anywhere be found, and for whom the Distress Committee has to provide, is to put them to work for themselves in some way that promotes their own improvement. The human engine is temporarily out of use—let us utilise the interval to bring it up to the highest possible health and activity. *The Distress Committee can far more profitably pay the unemployed to work at raising their own condition than to work at their old jobs.* The men for whom no situations can be found are, practically always, physically "out of condition" (which of us is not?) ; the occupation to which they have been accustomed is, at least for the present, not required, and hence has no value ; they do not know how to produce food and clothing for themselves, nor yet how to do anything that the nation for the moment wants—let us teach them ! Some can be put to work on the land (that is, can be *taught the processes of agriculture and gardening*) ; others can be put to work at the cooking and cleaning, and other household duties that any set of men require, repairing their own clothes and mending their own boots (that is, *taught how to cook and to sew and to cobble*) ; others can be put to do the necessary alterations and painting and decorating the premises (that is, *taught to use all the ordinary tools*). Every man ought, moreover, to be able to read a plan, and draw to scale, and expert at practical workshop arithmetic. Some few will actually want to learn something by which they think they can earn a living in a new way, or in a different locality—let us meet their laudable desires. What is essential is to realize that the men will, at any rate at first, produce next to nothing, and will need skilled instruction. The result will be, not much value in the way of material product—for "employing the unemployed" is always the costliest of processes—but great advantage to the men themselves in improved health and new training. What is important is that they will have been maintained and improved, instead of being starved and demoralized. This, as the Local Government Board now advises, is the best form of " work for the unemployed," though one difficult to organize for all. The L.G.B. will gladly help with any such scheme of training, which ought to be got ready at once.

(h) Fall Back on Relief Works in the Last Resort.

Some people are impatient of the idea of putting men to work at anything that requires them to be trained : they revolt against the idea of expecting grown men to learn anything new ! Well, if we are so prejudiced that we insist on keeping our unemployed in the same helpless condition as that in which we find them, we shall be driven to the costly futilities known as Relief Works. Pay on Relief Works is better than doles without work ; and if the augmented municipal enterprises already suggested have not kept everybody in regular wage-earning employment, and if we won't train them to better things, we must put them to the only work they can do. The Distress Committee must exhaust its ingenuity to invent Relief Works suitable for " employing the unemployed "—improving parks and open spaces, making roads, digging up waste land to bring it under cultivation, planting waste places and spoil heaps, filling in disused pits or raising the level of low-lying land, strengthening sea walls, raising river banks, preventing floodings, restoring to some sort of beauty the spots which industrialism has made hideous, and so on.

One of the drawbacks to Relief Works is that employment at them never brings a workman again "into benefit" for Government Unemployed Pay. Making a road for the Town Council is working at an insured trade, and counts for Unemployment Benefit. Making a road for the Distress Committee is not working at an insured trade, and does not so count. This is a strong reason for doing works in the ordinary way, and not "to employ the unemployed."

(i) Relief is Not Wages.

But when we have failed to prevent the occurrence of unemployment by the Local Authorities setting on foot enough useful works at standard Trade Union wages—if there are then still unemployed men in distress for whom the Distress Committee has to provide either at educational occupations or on the so-called "Relief Works" —what the Distress Committee pays to the men cannot be deemed wages: it is only an allowance for maintenance, or relief. We cannot pretend to pay, for the common task of practical instruction or digging to which all have to be put, the different Trade Union rates which the several men would have got if they had been working at their respective trades ! We ought to insist, considering present prices, on a minimum rate for the allowance or relief of not less than sixpence an hour for the time the men are in attendance, irrespective of what may be done for the wives and children. No deduction should be made in respect of anything done by the Health or Education Committees. But don't let us pretend that this is wages, or that it has any relation to what the men will "produce" (which in commercial value will be next to nothing).

(j) One Combined Register Only.

One indispensable thing in every locality must be a single register of all kinds of public provision being made for the relief of distress. A dozen different public bodies will be dealing with distress in each locality—to say nothing of all the private charities—and to prevent overlapping (and the chance of some unscrupulous families accepting help simultaneously from half a dozen different sources to the detriment of others more scrupulous) it is of vital importance that each authority or committee affording assistance should have some means of ascertaining, quickly and accurately, what is being done by the others. This register (which had better be kept by a special sub-committee of the Local Committee for the Prevention and Relief of Distress,* and be arranged as a card catalogue of families) ought to include any assistance afforded by (a) the Local Committee itself; (b) the Distress Committee; (c) the Board of Guardians; (d) the Local Education Authority; (e) the Old Age Pensions Committee; (f) the Prince of Wales's Fund, or National War Relief Committee; (g) the Committee for the Relief of Soldiers' and Sailors' Families; (h) the Queen Mary's Needlework Guild; and (i) any philanthropic societies or relief agencies willing to co operate. It would be useful to have the clerk or secretary of each such organization on the sub-committee, together with a representative of the Labor Exchange. Get your Committee to start such a combined register at once. It will, of course, have to be the work of one or more clerks, who ought to be engaged and paid regular wages—no amateur blacklegging! The L.G.B. allows all this expense to be charged to the rates.

(k) Watch Your Local Committee.

Local organizations, such as Fabian Societies; Co-operative Societies; Branches of the I.L.P. and B.S.P.; of Trade Unions and Friendly Societies; of the Women's Co-operative Guild, and of the Women's Labor League; local "Brotherhood" Societies and Adult Schools, etc., might usefully watch the progress of unemployment and distress in their localities, and the proceedings of the several Authorities; and might, from time to time, press on their notice by resolution any points needing attention. It would be a good thing for such organizations to form locally a joint committee for this purpose, with its own secretary, so that it is properly attended to. The War Emergency: Workers' National Committee (28 Victoria Street, Westminster) should be informed of any cases in which the

---

* Not by the Labor Exchange, which ought to keep itself to its own duty of helping men and women, *whether or not in any need*, to find regular wage earning situations, and not be mixed up with the registrati n of applicants for relief *because of their distress*. The Labor Exchange has no more to do with distress than the Post Office has. Its business is only to bring together demand and supply. Of course, such of the applicants for relief as are ablebodied persons ought to be required to keep themselves continuously on the "live" register of the Labor Exchange, which ought to inform the Local Committee of any other distressed persons for whom it cannot find situations.

interests of any section of the wage earners are being neglected, or of any Local Committees that are not working satisfactorily.

8.—How to Help Personally.

Many people in comparatively easy circumstances, or whose salaries are not yet affected, are asking : " What can I do to help ? " To this the first answer is, *go on with your accustomed work, and continue your ordinary life.* Do not, out of panic, or from an egotistical " fussiness," or because of a hypersensitive conscience (which is perhaps not unconnected with personal vanity), aggravate the inevitable dislocation that war causes, by wanton dislocations of your own. Continue at any useful occupation in which you are engaged. Before you change, pause to think what harm you may be doing.

We must all bear our share of the money cost. Economy is a good thing, and thrift a better. But let your economy (which should begin at once) be in your own personal consumption—*not, until your income is actually reduced, in your expenditure.* First, see that you pay all your bills, and henceforth pay cash for everything—it assists trade. You would, of course, not think, without finding something else for them to do, of dismissing any servants, or reducing your domestic establishment at this moment of dreadful danger of unemployment. If you can dispense with their services to yourself, set them to attend to the needs of others. But it is part of the world tragedy of riches, and of the personal luxury to which they lead, that all our daily expenditure maintains, and unwittingly specializes to our service, hosts of unseen workers, who are in effect just as much our body servants as the footman and the lady's maid, and who starve if our expenditure on luxuries is suddenly suspended. Therefore, do not stop orders to dressmakers and tailors, or give up travelling *—merely change the character of your order.* If you can forego the new dress or the new suit of clothes, the holiday excursion or the visit to the theatre, *spend the same amount* on clothes for those who need them badly, or on a holiday for the men or women who would otherwise go without. Don't put down your motor car and dismiss the chauffeur : lend the car for the service of the Local Committee. Exercise thrift by all means ; but thrift means, not stopping expenditure, but its wisest possible allocation among different needs. You will not be wrong if you aim at *restricting your personal use or consumption of other people's labor, or the fruits thereof* (down to what seems to be needed for the maintenance of your utmost efficiency for service) ; *provided that you transfer that use or consumption to others who require it more than you do.*

If you are a person without any useful occupation (which, of course, is not at any time a reputable mode of life)—or if your occupation has been temporarily suspended by the war—you will rightly feel bound at this crisis to give your personal service to the State. Healthy young men of this sort might well enlist or join the Territorials, and thus get trained and mobilized for the military defence of the country. On no account must you do any work gratuitously that would or could otherwise be paid for—leave that to go to the men and women of all grades whose livelihood has been destroyed. But your first duty is to *be helpful to those nearest to you*, especially to all the needy persons with whom you or your family are in any way in contact. What can you do to assist (i) friends or acquaintances whose livelihood has stopped ; (ii) your household establishment and its connections ; (iii) those in your own village, or those with whom you are brought in personal relations? Beyond that, there is an unexciting but useful unpaid service to be rendered in (a) serving on the many committees and sub-committees that are needed ; (b) organising and supervising particular parts of the work ; (c) running about, under instructions, to get information that is needed ; (d) visiting the applicants ; (e) dispensing relief. The organization and provision of useful work and training for the unemployed always hangs fire for lack of competent instructors and directors, and requires all possible help. But don't "fuss" ; send in your name to the Local Committee, to be called on when and for whatever required. "They also serve who only stand and wait."

It is equally evident that we must not, in zeal for "helping the war," sacrifice any of the existing services. What can be more foolish, or more suicidal, than the proposal to close schools and colleges, in order to convert them into hospitals for the wounded? As though there were no building operatives unemployed, no means of very quickly putting up temporary buildings ; no teachers to be cruelly thrown out of work ; and no children to be made to suffer all their lives long, because of panicky haste! What could be more shortsighted—just when shirtmakers and seamstresses are being thrown out of work in all directions—than for unoccupied ladies and their daughters actually to start making shirts and other articles of clothing, with the result of throwing still more women out of work ? (Whoever advised the Queen to call on all the branches of Her Majesty's Needlework Guild to start these amateur sewing centres did a foolish and an utterly mischievous thing. Experience actually shows that the garments made could be bought in the market for less than the cost of cutting out, packing and despatching of materials in small quantities ; so that the result of the good ladies' ineffective labor is literally to waste some of the available money. It has been made abundantly clear that Her Majesty now deeply regrets the precipitate action that she was allowed to take. Do your utmost to stop all such work.)*

* At any rate, make it known that the Queen begs that ladies will on no account make any of the following articles : viz., flannel shirts, socks, and Cardigan jackets ; flannel vests and jerseys, pyjama suits, serge gowns, underclothing, flannel gowns and flannel waistcoats. All these would, in the ordinary course, be bought by the War Office and Admiralty, and every one of them made in the branches of the Queen Mary's Needlework Guild, or by other well-meaning amateurs, is "doing some poor woman out of a job." Even with regard to other garments, the Queen much prefers ladies to purchase them in the shops, or to organize groups of paid women workers to make them. (Her Majesty's official communication to the Press, August 21st.) The War Office actually begs that no one will burden it with such things. "It is unnecessary to send shirts, socks, or underclothing, *as there are ample reserves of these and all other articles of clothing at the base.*" (W.O. official notice, August 28th.)

Unoccupied women and girls should not rush to nurse the wounded soldiers and sailors. Nursing is only for the trained—mere womanly kindness and domestic experience is of no use—and it is said that there are already more volunteers than the War Office and the Red Cross Society know what to do with! There are those at home who, in consequence of the war, equally need volunteer help. The great extension of school feeding and of medical inspection and treatment at school will involve the appointment, throughout the country, by the several Local Education Authorities, of literally tens of thousands of additional members of Children's Care Committees and School Canteen Committees; with endless opportunities for most valuable service to the children. Apply at once to the Clerk of the Education Committee of your County or Town Council. Similarly, the new development of provision for Maternity and Infancy by the Public Health Committees of County and Borough Councils will call for a greatly increased voluntary staff. The Association of Infant Consultations and Schools for Mothers (4 Tavistock Square, London, W.C.), would be glad to hear of voluntary workers for Infant Welfare Centres. The services of the following are required: (a) consultative medical officers; (b) home visitors; (c) helpers with dinners; (d) helpers at sewing, knitting or cooking classes. There are already schools for mothers in over 300 localities throughout the United Kingdom, and these all require additional help now; whilst many new ones will be established.

But it is part of the punishment for a misspent youth that emergency finds you useless! Perhaps the most useful thing that the inexperienced, unoccupied young woman can do is first to put herself through a systematic course of training for social work.*

Conclusion.

The nation has to face a great emergency. At all costs the people must be kept fed. If the war is prolonged, it will tax all the powers of our administrators to avert the most widespread distress. The suggestions contained in this Handbook, if adopted at once and to the full, would, it is believed, prevent such a calamity, without waste of money or demoralization of character. Yet, let us not forget the fact that, in dire necessity, all our economic scruples and philanthropic pedantries will, perforce, have to give way. The people will have to be fed. If we do not find money for wages, and useful provision for those thrown out of work, we shall have eventually to find it, even more of it, for unconditional weekly doles, or the universal soup-kitchen. The money—of which there is really no lack—will have to be found. The question is, how can the emergency most advantageously be met; how can the money be best laid out. Spend it now in prevention: it will actually save you later much more in relief!

* For *suggestions for* such a course of training, see the special prospectus of the London School of Economics (Department of Social Training), Clare Market, Portugal Street, Kingsway, London, W.C.

USEFUL NAMES AND ADDRESSES.

The **Cabinet Emergency Committee** (sometimes called **Central Committee for Prevention and Relief of Distress**) consists of Mr. Herbert Samuel (chairman), Mr. Wedgwood Benn, Mr. Birrell, Mr. John Burns, Mr. J. Herbert Lewis, Mr. Walter Long, Mr. J. Ramsay MacDonald, Mr. Masterman, Sir George Murray, Mr. J. W. Pease, Mrs. H. J. Tennant, Mr. McKinnon Wood.
Address: Local Government Board, Whitehall, London, S.W.

The **Executive Committee of the Prince of Wales's National War Relief Fund** consists of Mr. Wedgwood Benn, M.P. (chairman), Mr. A. J. Balfour, M.P., Mr. A. Birrell, M.P., Duke of Devonshire, Mr. Hayes Fisher, M.P., Mr. A. Henderson, M.P., Lady Kerry, Mr. Walter Long, M.P., Miss Mary Macarthur, Mrs. McKenna, Mr. McKinnon Wood, M.P., Miss Violet Markham, Mr. Masterman, Sir George Murray, Sir George Riddell. (Mr. Warren Fisher, secretary.)
Address for contributions: York House, St. James's Palace, London; for administration: 3 Queen Anne's Gate, London, S.W.

The **Central Committee for Women's Employment** consists of the Marchioness of Crewe (chairman), Mrs. H. J. Tennant (hon. treasurer), Miss Mary Macarthur (hon. secretary), Lady Askwith, Miss Margaret Bondfield, Mrs. Austen Chamberlain, Mrs. Gasson, Miss R. E. Lawrence, Miss Susan Lawrence, L.C.C., Miss Violet Markham, Viscountess Midleton, Hon. Lily Montagu and Dr. Marion Phillips.
Address the Hon. Sec., at Wimborne House, Arlington Street, London, S.W.

The **Committee for London** consists of Mr. John Burns, M.P. (chairman), Miss Adler, Sir John Benn, Sir Vansittart Bowater (Lord Mayor), Lord Devonport, Mr. W. H. Dickinson, M.P., Mr. Gosling, L.C.C., Mr. Brinsley Harper, Mr. Cyril Jackson, L.C.C., Captain Jessel, M.P., Mr. Masterman, Viscount Peel (Chairman L.C.C.), Mrs. Sidney Webb.
Address: Local Government Board, Whitehall, London, S.W.

The **Local Government Board Intelligence Department** has in hand all enquiries as to the prevalence of unemployment and distress. It is assisted by two committees, one for London (chairman, Mr. Cyril Jackson, L.C.C.; hon. sec., Mr. J. St. George Heath), and the other for the rest of England and Wales (chairman, Mr. Seebohm Rowntree).

The Board of Agriculture (Whitehall Place, S.W.) and the Local Government Board are assisted, as regards the £4,000,000 for housing, by two merely consultative committees for agricultural districts and urban areas respectively. With regard to Scotland or Ireland, address the Local Government Board, Edinburgh or Dublin.

The **National Health Insurance Commissioners for England** (Sir R. L. Morant, chairman) are at Wellington House, Buckingham Gate, London, S.W. Those for Scotland and Ireland may be addressed simply at Edinburgh or Dublin respectively.

The **Board of Trade** (**Labour Exchanges and Unemployment Insurance**) is at Queen Anne's Chambers, Broadway, Westminster.

The **Road Board** (Sir George Gibb, chairman; Rees Jeffreys, secretary) is at Queen Anne's Chambers, Broadway, Westminster.

The **Development Commission** (Lord Richard Cavendish, chairman; Mr. Vaughan Nash, C.B., vice-chairman; Mr. H. E. Dale, secretary) is at 6A Dean's Yard, Westminster.

The address of the local "Mayor's Committee," or "Citizens' Committee," or "Local Committtee for the Prevention and Relief of Distress" is, almost certainly, the Town Hall, or Municipal Offices, or Office of County or District Council, of your locality.

The **War Emergency: Workers' National Committee** (Mr. Arthur Henderson, M.P., chairman; Mr. J. S. Middleton, hon. secretary) is at 28 Victoria Street, Westminster.

FABIAN SOCIETY.—The Fabian Society consists of Socialists. A statement of its Rules and a complete list of publications can be obtained from the Secretary, at the Fabian Office. 3 Clement's Inn, London, W.C. after September 1914, 25 Tothill Street, Westminster, S.W.

FABIAN ESSAYS IN SOCIALISM Paper 6d.; cloth 1/6; post. 2½d. and 4d.

WHAT TO READ on Social and Economic Subjects. 1s. n. and 2s. n.

THE RURAL PROBLEM. By H. D. HARBEN. 2s. 6d. n.

THIS MISERY OF BOOTS. By H. G. WELLS. 3d., post free 4d.

FABIAN TRACTS and LEAFLETS.

Tracts, each 16 to 52 pp., price 1d., or 9d. per doz., unless otherwise stated.
Leaflets, 4 pp. each, price 1d. for six copies, 1s. per 100, or 8/6 per 1000.
The Set of 77, 3/6; post free 3/11. Bound in buckram, 5/-n.; post free 5/6.

I.—General Socialism in its various aspects.

TRACTS.—169. The Socialist Movement in Germany. By W. S. SANDERS. In cover, with portrait of Bebel, 2d. 159. The Necessary Basis of Society. By SIDNEY WEBB. 151. The Point of Honour. By RUTH C. BENTINCK. 147. Capital and Compensation. By E. R. PEASE. 146. Socialism and Superior Brains. By BERNARD SHAW. 142. Rent and Value. 138. Municipal Trading. 121. Public Service versus Private Expenditure. By Sir OLIVER LODGE. 107. Socialism for Millionaires. By BERNARD SHAW. 139. Socialism and the Churches. By Rev. JOHN CLIFFORD, D.D. 133. Socialism and Christianity. By Rev. PERCY DEARMER. 78. Socialism and the Teaching of Christ. By Dr. J. CLIFFORD. 42. Christian Socialism By Rev. S. D. HEADLAM. 79. A Word of Remembrance and Caution to the Rich. By JOHN WOOLMAN. 72. The Moral Aspects of Socialism. By SIDNEY BALL. 69. Difficulties of Individualism. By S. WEBB. 51. Socialism: True and False. By S. WEBB. 45. The Impossibilities of Anarchism. By BERNARD SHAW (price 2d.). 7. Capital and Land (revised 1908) 5. Facts for Socialists (revised 1908). 132. A Guide to Books for Socialists. LEAFLETS—13. What Socialism Is 1. Why are the Many Poor? WELSH TRACTS—143. Sosialaeth yng Ngoleuni'r Beibl. 141. Translation of 139. 87. Translation of 78. 38. Translation of 1.

II.—Applications of Socialism to Particular Problems.

TRACTS.—175. Economic Foundations of the Women's Movement. 2d. 173. Public versus Private Electricity Supply. By C. A. BAKER. 171. The Nationalization of Mines and Minerals Bill. By H. H. SCHLOESSER. 170. Profit-Sharing & Co-Partnership: a Fraud and Failure? By E. R PEASE. In cover. 164. Gold and State Banking. By E. R. PEASE. 163 Women and Prisons. By HELEN BLAGG and CHARLOTTE WILSON. 2d. 162. Family Life on a Pound a Week. By Mrs. REEVES. In cover, 2d. 161. Afforestation and Unemployment. By A. P. GRENFELL. 160. A National Medical Service. By F. LAWSON DODD. 2d. 157. The Working Life of Women. By Miss B. L. HUTCHINS. 155. The Case against the Referendum. By CLIFFORD SHARP. 154 The Case for School Clinics. By L. HADEN GUEST. 153. The Twentieth Century Reform Bill. By H. H. SCHLOESSER. 152. Our Taxes as they are and as they ought to be. By R. JONES, B.Sc. In cover, 2d. 150. State Purchase of Railways. By EMIL DAVIES. In cover, 2d. 149. The Endowment of Motherhood. By H. D. HARBEN. In cover, 2d. 131. The Decline of the Birth-Rate. By SIDNEY WEBB. 145. The Case for School Nurseries. By Mrs. TOWNSHEND. 140. Child Labor under Capitalism. By Mrs. HYLTON DALE. 136. The Village and the Landlord. By EDW. CARPENTER. 128. The Case for a Legal Minimum Wage. 122. Municipal Milk and Public Health. By Dr. F. LAWSON DODD. 125. Municipalization by Provinces. 124. State Control of Trusts. 83. State Arbitration and the Living Wage. LEAFLET.—104. How Trade Unions benefit Workmen.

III.—Local Government Powers: How to use them.

TRACTS.—172. What about the Rates? or, Municpal Finance and Municipal Autonomy. By SIDNEY WEBB. 156. What an Education Committee can do (Elementary Schools), 3d. 62. Parish and District Councils. (Revised 1913). 137. Parish Councils and Village Life. 109. Cottage Plans and Common Sense. 76. Houses for the People. 82. Workmen's Compensation Act. LEAFLETS.—134. Small Holdings: and how to get them. 68. The Tenant's Sanitary Catechism. 71. Ditto for London

IV.—General Politics and Fabian Policy.

TRACTS.—158. The Case against the C.O.S. By Mrs. TOWNSHEND. 108. Twentieth Century Politics. By S. WEBB. 70. Report on Fabian Policy.

SOCIALISM AND THE ARTS OF USE.

By A. CLUTTON BROCK.

Price One Penny.

The Fabian Society, 25 Tothill Street, Westminster, London, S.W.   January, 1915.

Socialism and the Arts of Use.

Government and the Arts of Use.

THE question whether Socialism is likely to encourage or to discourage art is of practical importance to Socialists because many people believe that it would make an end of all art, and are therefore opposed to it. Their belief is based upon the fact that our present Government is seldom successful when it tries to encourage art. They point to our Government offices, our memorials to deceased monarchs, and the work of our art schools, as examples of Socialist art, and they ask whether that is better than the art produced in answer to a private demand.

Certainly it is not ; and the Government failure in the matter of architecture has aroused a very strong prejudice against Socialism among architects. They practise the most important of all the arts, and they tell us, from their own experience, that the Government is usually unfortunate in its choice of architects and that it prevents them from doing their best after it has chosen them. This I do not deny—one has only to look at our Government buildings to see that it must be true—but these opponents of Socialism assume that in a Socialist State all art would be at the mercy of the conscious patronage of the Government. They do not ask themselves whether in a Socialist State there might not arise conditions as favorable to the natural growth of architecture and all the arts of use as our present conditions are unfavorable. They assume that those arts, in the modern world, can only be kept alive by the abnormal interest of a few individuals, and they think that Socialism would deprive those few of their power of patronage.

Socialism will not Produce an Immediate Improvement.

This assumption I believe to be wrong. Socialism might destroy the patronage of the abnormal few ; but it might also make an interest in art, and particularly in the arts of use, normal. And my aim now is to explain why I believe it would do this.

But first. I will admit that, if we could suddenly start now with any complete system of Socialism in full working order, I do not for a moment believe we should have an immediate improvement in our pictures or Government offices or public statues or in the memorials to deceased monarchs. There would, no doubt, be more money spent upon public art and less upon private ; but the public art for a time would be just what it is now, and the artists chosen would be those who have an ill-deserved eminence in our present society. It is the general taste that makes art good or bad. It does not produce artists of genius, but it uses them or wastes them.

Whistler said that art happens, by which he meant, I suppose, that people like himself happen : that no society, by taking thought, can cause them to be born. But it is not true that works of art, like Bourges Cathedral, happen, any more than Dreadnoughts happen. They are the results of a long, common, and well directed effort. That kind of effort does not exist now, and in the most favorable circumstances it could only begin slowly, and would continue for some time before it could produce any great results.

Art Manifests Itself First not in Ornament but in Design.

At present the art of building and the art of all objects of use is commonly supposed to be an art of ornament. Architecture means to most of us a kind of ornamented building. Gothic is distinguished from Renaissance by its ornament, by traceried windows and cusps and crockets and so on ; and we are always complaining that we hlave no style of our own in architecture or furniture or anything e se.

But the artistic instinct when it works in the making of objects of use does not first show itself in ornament, but in structure, and it may express itself triumphantly without any ornament.

The artistic instinct, when it first begins to move in the making of an object of use, is not consciously artistic at all. It shows itself mainly in a desire to make that object as well as it can be made, and of the closest possible adaptation to its function. But this desire must be in itself disinterested if it is to produce art. It pays, no doubt, at least in healthy societies, to make things as well as they can be made. But the artistic instinct will not grow out of a mere desire to make them well so that they may sell. For the next stage in the development of that instinct is a recognition of the beauty of a thing that is well adapted to its function ; from which follows an effort to insist upon that beauty for its own sake while at the same time preserving the perfect adaptation to function. It is upon this recognition and this effort that all architectural excellence depends, and indeed all excellence of design. When art is growing and vigorous, it is because men see the natural functional beauty of the things which they make for use and because they try to increase that beauty, perhaps with ornament but certainly with pure design, which does not disguise function but emphasizes it. But the beauty must be seen before it can be heightened with art.

The Recognition of Functional Beauty.

We are amazed at the beauty of the great French Gothic cathedrals, and we think of it as a romantic thing of the past that we can never attain to. But how did the builders of the Middle Ages attain to it ? Not in the least by their facility in designing and carving ornament ; not by their tracery or stained glass or statues. Those things were only the overflow of their energy. A church might have them and yet be bad. It might lack them all, even the stained glass, and yet be noble. What they did was to be aware of the natural functional beauty of a plain building well built, and to see how that beauty might be heightened and emphasized step by step, until they attained to the cathedrals of Bourges and Chartres. All the time their building was engineering, and a great part of its beauty remained engineering or functional beauty, a beauty like that of a fine animal or a great tree. This functional beauty was at last almost perfectly fused with expressive art in the greatest French churches, but both beauties were always present up to the climax of Gothic. And in that great age of art which culminated in the thirteenth century, there is the same artistic impulse applied to most objects of use that have come down to us from that age. It is altogether an architectural age, an age of design, one which recognized the functional beauty of its handiwork and tried to emphasize it. And so it has been in other ages famed for their prevailing artistic excellence. The Chinese pottery of the Sung dynasty, for instance, has often no ornament at all; the beauty consists in the exquisite refinement of form, which is always expressive of function, and in the exquisite quality of glaze, which, like the form, had first a functional purpose. It was merely recognition of the beauties of a well-made pot and a desire to improve upon which produced those miracles of art.

Now the societies which produced this wonderful art were not Socialist according to our ideas; but they had one condition necessary to the vigor of art which our present society almost entirely lacks, and which we can regain, I believe, only by means of Socialism. For it was possible with them for men to build buildings and to make objects of use as well as they could build them or make them, and so it was possible for them to recognize the beauty of such things and to refine upon it generation after generation and man by man. The great churches, whether built for a monastery or for a city, were not built to pay. The Sung pottery was made to sell, but it was made by individual potters for customers who recognized its beauty like the potters themselves, and who therefore encouraged the potters to do their best and to refine and refine until they reached the unequalled height of excellence. I do not suppose that with Socialism our whole system of production would be altered at once, or that we should have pottery like the Sung instead of our present crockery. But let us consider for a moment the manner in which most of our modern buildings are built and most of our more important objects of use are made. I am not now speaking of the objects which we think of as artistic, such as churches or public buildings, but rather of private buildings of all kinds, of lamp posts, pillar boxes, trams, railway bridges and viaducts and stations. Such things are more numerous and important in our lives, they are often larger and more conspicuous, than objects of use have been in any former civilization.

With Us the Art of Design is Checked from the Start.

Yet we never think of all these important objects of use as works of art or as capable of becoming works of art. We never recognize any beauty in them to begin with, and of course we do not attempt to refine upon the beauty which we do not recognize. If any designer of such things saw beauty in them and tried to increase it in a new design, he would be asked at once if the new design were more expensive than the old and if it had any greater practical value. And if it were more expensive and had no more practical value, he would be warned, if he were not dismissed at once as a lunatic, not to waste his time or his employers' money. With us the art of design is checked at its very start by the general attitude towards all objects of use, since for us they are merely objects of use, and so we never think of looking for any beauty in them whatever. According to our present notion, art is art and business is business ; the first is unbusinesslike and the second inartistic, and that is the plain commonsense of the matter.

Machinery is not Necessarily Hostile to Art.

Now that is quite a modern notion and most people believe that it prevails because we live in an age of machinery ; that things made by machinery cannot be beautiful and that therefore it is useless to attempt to heighten their beauty. But on this point there is a great confusion of thought. There was a sudden decay of all the arts of design which began about 1790 and was complete by about 1840. And this happened at the same time as the great increase in the use of machinery. Also in that period there was a production of machine-made ornament of all kinds which did help to destroy the production of hand-made ornament and to corrupt the design of all ornament, whether machine or hand-made. Now I will not lay it down as an absolute dogma that all machine-made ornament must be bad. But it is certainly a fact that most of it is bad and not ornament at all but mere excrescence. Yet to say that is not to say that all machine-made things are necessarily ugly or that they cannot have the same functional beauty as other objects of use. The fact is that the sense of functional beauty was weakening just when machinery began to prevail. It was not that machinery destroyed art or made it impossible, but that we have made a wrong artistic use of machinery and have failed to see its artistic possibilities. Our great mechanical inventions were made just when, for other reasons, art was at its weakest. Therefore, so far as art has been concerned with them at all, they have been used merely to produce imitations of the art of the past. If art had been vigorous it would have mastered machinery instead of being mastered by it. As it is, machinery was used to imitate art, because, since ornament was anyhow ceasing to be expressive, it could be produced just as well by machinery as by hand. With the decay of the sense of design people also lost all sense of the meaning and purpose of ornament. They did not see beauty in what they had made and therefore they tried to add beauty to it instead of drawing beauty out of it. They painted the lily, which is what no one would do who saw that the lily was beautiful to start with.

The significant fact about the decay of the sense of design is that it came with the industrial age, not that it came with machinery.

It came, that is to say, with a new set of ideas, not with a new set of implements. And the idea that was fatal to art was not a refusal to recognize its abstract importance. The dominant capitalists were ready then, as now, to spend money on pictures and other works of art, but they drew a sharp distinction between works of art and objects of use. They might even be ready to add art to objects of use ; but they were not ready to draw art out of them. And the reason was, as Morris pointed out long ago, that they were making objects of use to sell, and merely to sell ; and that they had no disinterested desire to make them as well as they could be made.

The Ideas of the Industrial Age are Hostile to Art.

I spoke a moment ago of a new set of ideas, but the ideas of the industrial age were really only the result of the complete triumph of one instinct. The instinct of gain became all-powerful, and it assumed, contrary to all experience, that it always had been and always must be all-powerful. That in fact it was the only true instinct concerned with the making of things, and that the artistic instinct was merely a bye-play of idleness. That was why all art was conceived to be ornament, since art itself was thought to be purely ornamental. But art, as I have said, is not ornament but design ; and design is the expression of an instinct, the suppression of which destroys all sense of design and with it all the health and vigour of art.

Well, this instinct, to make things as well as they can possibly be made, was suppressed by that other triumphant instinct of gain ; and by the instinct of gain working, not in the actual people who made things, but in those who set them to make things ; not in the designer or the workman, but in the capitalist. He could not exercise the artist's instinct if he would ; it was only possible for him to encourage it in others. And this he did not attempt to do because he conceived of himself merely as a producer of things to sell, competing with other producers. He might honestly try to produce a good article. He might be as moral as you please ; but the artistic instinct is not moral. It aims at excellence for its own satisfaction, not through a sense of duty to the public. The conscientious capitalist might try to give his best, but it is not an artistic best. He was never spurred on to make things more beautiful by a recognition of the beauty of what he had made. So, if in the way of trade he wished to produce a beautiful thing, he did not encourage his designers to refine upon their designs, but he imported an artist to ornament them. And that is why we have schools of ornamental art at South Kensington and elsewhere, and why we talk of applied art as if it were something added to things, like a flounce to a dress. And meanwhile no one ever expects an engineer or any kind of practical designer to have any artistic instinct at all. He is a man of business, and business is inartistic as art is unbusinesslike.

The best example I can give of this view of art is a public not a private enterprise, but for that very reason it will enforce the moral I wish to draw.

The Lesson of the Tower Bridge.

The Tower Bridge is a great work of engineering, and while it remained that and only that, it looked like the gates of the sea. But no one recognized its beauty as a work of engineering, that is to say as a piece of design. On the contrary, since it was a public work, it was thought necessary to cover its indecent nakedness with art. So an architect was imported to do this ; and he made it look like two Gothic towers with a bridge between them. Not only are these towers ugly in themselves, but they make the bridge look ugly, partly because of its incongruity, partly because it seems too heavy for the towers, which, of course, do not really support it at all, and have indeed no function whatever except to be artistic.

Now in this case if the engineer had been conscious of the functional beauty of his design, and if he had tried to heighten that beauty and had made a more costly design in doing so, he would no doubt have been told to mind his own business and leave art to artists. It would never have entered into anyone's head that the art of a bridge is the engineer's business just as much as the art of a statue is the sculptor's business. It would not even enter the engineer's head, for he has been taught by public opinion to suppress his own natural artistic instinct just as the engineers of the great Gothic cathedrals were taught to develop it. By nature very likely he was just such a man as they were ; and we may be sure that they would admire his work as much as they would despise the architectural imitations of their own.

The Tower Bridge was not built to pay, but it was built by a public body still subject to all the capitalist ideas about art and its incompatibility with business. Hence the absurd incompatibility of the art and the business of the bridge. We cannot expect those ideas to disappear all in a moment, or that a capitalist, when he acts as a member of a public body, will escape therefore from their influence. The revival of art, if it does come, will be a long and slow business, and it can only happen when the natural artistic instinct is no longer suppressed by the natural instinct of gain and by all the ideas which that instinct of gain, in its evil supremacy, has imposed upon us.

Art is not Necessarily Doomed in Our Civilization.

Our notion about art now is that it is always and everywhere fighting a losing battle, and that it can only be kept alive by the efforts of the cultured few. And there is truth in that so long as the cultured few impose their own conception of art upon a puzzled and indifferent world. Art will only begin to fight a winning battle when the mass of men rediscover it for themselves without even knowing that what they have discovered is art ; when they find that they can take a pleasure and pride in objects of use as natural and instinctive as the pleasure which they take in flowers or trees now.

It is not, I think, merely visionary to hope for such a change ; for men have taken such a pleasure and pride in objects of use, not once or twice only at favored periods of history, but nearly always until the end of the eighteenth century ; and all our present restlessness and discontent about art proves that we feel the want of this pleasure and would regain it if we could. But how could Socialism help us to regain it ? Certainly not by any conscious State patronage of art such as we have at present, not by giving us more and more sumptuous memorials to deceased monarchs or larger Government offices designed by scholarly architects, but rather, I think, in a manner which I can best illustrate by examples.

The Case of Waterloo Station.

It is natural to men, as I have said, to recognize the functional beauty of things of use ; and our present failure to recognize it is unnatural, and produced not by any decay of the senses, but by a set of ideas and associations which prevent us from using our senses. Let us take, for instance, the case of the new Waterloo Station. That is a piece of engineering which has a very real functional beauty, far more, for instance, than the Hall of the Law Courts. But people see nothing beautiful in it because their eyes are blinded by their ideas about the station ; they think of it as a prosaic work of mere utility, built by a prosaic company for its own profit. And this is the view of it which the company themselves take and are forced to take. They never for one moment suppose that their station could be a work of art or could have any beauty, because it is for them merely a means of earning money. They may, for the sake of advertisement, be ready to spend money upon an architectural façade to it, and they may employ an architect to apply some art to that façade. But art means to them, as to most other people, ornament, pilasters and capitals and cornices and mouldings and such things ; and they regard it as an advertisement, as a means of drawing attention to their station. But art, being by its nature disinterested, will not live on these terms ; and architectural façades of this kind are a mere collection of artistic features that once had life and meaning and now have none whatever. Some are better than others, but there is no growth or development of art in them ; and we can look for none so long as the motive which causes money to be spent on art is merely advertisement or even a vague belief that art ought to be patronized.

To the railway company their station is, inevitably, merely an object of use ; not only have they no motive for making it beautiful, but they do not even see that it has any beauty. If, for some reason, they were in a lavish mood and determined to spend money upon making it beautiful, they would probably give all the columns Corinthian capitals of wrought iron. Indeed there is an absurd hint at capitals on the top of these columns, and that is the only ugliness in the structure of the station.

But if anyone were to suggest to the directors of the company that their station had already a functional beauty and that they ought to have spent money on emphasizing this functional beauty, that they ought to allow their engineer to indulge his natural artistic instinct, they would of course reply that their business was to earn dividends, not to spend money on art which no one would recognize.

Art and the Engineer.

All real art, from the point of view of a profit earning company, is sheer waste ; and that is the point of view which has been forced upon all of us, so that we neither see real art in its shy beginnings and possibilities, nor do we expect any money ever to be spent on it.

Waterloo Station, as I have said, has a beauty of its own already. But that beauty tantalizes one with hints and suggestions of a much greater and more conscious beauty that might have been obtained by emphasis of structural features, and could only have been obtained by the designer of the station with his sense of structure. And the art of station design could only grow and develop if one engineer improved upon the design of another, recognizing its beauty and seeing how that beauty might be further increased ; if, in fact, there was incessant experiment of the same kind as that which culminated in the great French cathedrals of the thirteenth century.

We have already incessant experiment in purely engineering problems, but the further artistic experiment cannot even begin. The engineering beauty is there, the designer's instinct to refine upon it must be there, for man's nature has not been utterly changed in a hundred years ; and so, too, the ordinary man's sense of beauty must be there if he could but be aware of it. It is only a certain set of ideas and associations which prevent both designer and public from asserting their instinct and their sense, and these are the ideas and associations of capitalism.

The Relation of Lender and Borrower.

You cannot have a living and growing art unless you are ready to spend money upon it, not as an advertisement or as a luxury, for money so spent will give you merely ornament, but as something which is worth having for its own sake. And no capitalist enterprise will ever spend money upon art in that spirit, nor will the public ever demand that a capitalist enterprise shall do so.

For the buildings or objects of use provided by a capitalist enterprise belong to the capitalists, and the public have no interest in them except in the use they make of them. To the public at present a railway station is a mere convenience, and they ask nothing of it except that it shall be convenient. They take no pride in it, for they have no part or lot in it. They only use it as we use books from a circulating library, in which we have no pride of possession, and of which therefore we expect no beauty either of binding or of type.

Indeed our relation to all works of capitalist enterprise is exactly the relation of subscribers to the books of a circulating library. We use them, but we have no further interest in them ; and that is the reason why we neither recognize any beauty which they may already possess, nor have any desire that that beauty shall be increased. Under our present system we all, at least those of us who have any money, are subscribers rather than owners ; and the owners themselves are shareholders with no sense of possession, except of dividends. If I own some South Western Railway Stock, I do not feel that Waterloo Station belongs to me, or that I have any interest whatever in making it more beautiful. I enter it not as an owner, but as a subscriber, and I forget my ownership as soon as I begin to travel on the line. So there is no consciousness of ownership anywhere, and ownership itself is a kind of abstraction. No one can say, in any sense or with any meaning, that Waterloo Station is his station. It and a thousand other buildings and objects of use are merely things that people make use of, and we are all living more and more in a world of things with which we have an utterly inhuman and indifferent relation.

Our Artistic Parsimony and How it Might be Removed.

But this relation to things of use, again, is not natural to man. And that other relation, in which men took a pride in them, recognized their beauty, and tried to increase it, was in the past the rule rather than the exception ; and in ages when there was great poverty, when there were plagues, famines, wars, and other disasters, men have not grudged the money necessary to glorify objects of use. That kind of parsimony, which we see everywhere, is peculiar to modern times. And it is the result of our peculiar relation between those who own objects of use and those who use them, a relation always of lender and borrower. If this could come to an end we might confidently expect that our parsimony and indifference would gradually cease. Of course, if our railways were nationalized, we should not all at once begin to feel towards our railway stations as men in the Middle Ages felt towards their cathedrals. Indeed at present we are just as parsimonious and indifferent towards things made by the State as towards those made by private enterprise. No one, for instance, seems to notice the beauty of the trams on the Embankment, or to consider how much more beautiful they might be made ; but that is because public enterprise is still so rare that the ideas associated with private enterprise still cling to it. When the County Council runs trams, we think of it as a private company, and we use the trams without any sense of possession in them, just as we use the 'busses of the London General Omnibus Company. And a public body, too, when it engages in any kind of trade, is still, to itself, a private trader. That is to say, it has the attitude of the private trader towards his own stock in trade, the attitude dictated by competition and by the determination to make as much money as possible. But we may expect, I think, that the more public enterprise prevailed, the more would the influence of private enterprise weaken. The facts would change and the state of mind with them. I do not mean that in this matter of trams, for instance, the County Council would suddenly say, " Our trams must be made more beautiful," and would therefore engage an artist to design them. That is not the way in which art grows. That is the way in which it is patronized and perverted by connoisseurs. What I do mean is that the County Council and the public itself would gradually begin to take a pride in their tramways. They would no longer think of them merely as money making machines and conveniences. Gradually the tram designer would begin to express his own natural artistic instinct in his design, and he would not be instantly checked by the cry of expense. Then the public would notice his new trams and like their design. They would not say that they were more artistic ; they would simply find that they took the pleasure which we all take in a design that expresses function and emphasizes it. Then other designers would notice those improvements and improve upon them, and the public would notice these further improvements and take a pride in them, the people of one town saying to the people of another : "Yes, your Hull trams are well enough, but have you seen our new trams at Halifax ? They beat everything." Then the Hull designer would go and look at the Halifax trams, and would be spurred to improve upon them in his next design. And so a new kind of competition would arise in trams and in a thousand other objects of use, or rather that old kind of competition which helped to produce the cathedrals of the Middle Ages, a competition not of cheapness, but of excellence.

Poetry and Prose in Art.

We think of trams and railway stations as very prosaic things, having nothing in common with those cathedrals ; and I do not suppose that any great general emotion could express itself in a station as the religious emotion was expressed at Chartres or Bourges. But we, with our loss of art in all things of common use, have acquired a vicious notion that all art must be pure expression, and expression of the highest and most passionate emotions. For us there is nothing between the meanness of a workhouse that looks as if it had been designed by Scrooge, and the irrelevant splendor of a new monster hotel. Both of those have the same defect manifested in different ways ; in neither is there any recognition of the beauty of functional design, but one of them tries to make up for it by the use of ornament that is like the flowers of speech of a bad prosaic writer. The good writer of prose knows that it has its beauties too, and that they are spoilt by incongruous poetic ornament. He may not call himself an artist, yet there is art and the beauty of art in his prosaic excellence, in the structure of a sentence which says exactly what it means; and he too recognizing this beauty unconsciously perhaps, is always trying to heighten it. So, whenever art flourishes, there is a recognition of the beauty of all design and an effort to increase it, even though the object designed has no association with the higher emotions. There is in fact a prose of art as well as a poetry, and whenever its poetry is sublime its prose is also beautiful. But we have forgotten that there is a prose of art at all. To us art is all poetry which we plaster irrelevantly on the most prosaic objects as if we were ashamed of them. And indeed we are ashamed of them just because they are prosaic to us, just because we never recognise or try to heighten their natural beauty of design. In an age of healthy art, objects of use may be the prose of art, but they are not prosaic in one sense, for they are made as beautiful as the emphasis of their function can make them. And design can flouish nowhere unless it flourishes in the prose as well as in the poetry of art. It is not a faculty that a few specially trained artists can suddenly apply to a church or a palace or a Victoria memorial. It is a faculty that must be exercised by all designers and the value of which must be recognized by the public, whether it be applied to churches or palaces, or to railway stations, or to trams or pillar boxes.

What we call design now is all remembered from the art of the past ; but art, when it is alive, lives not on the admiration of past art but on discovery. To the artist reality suggests something finer than itself, and yet itself. To the great builders of the Middle Ages a cathedral did not suggest a great avenue of stone, but a finer, more completely organized cathedral—which they proceeded to build. So a railway station should suggest, not some vaguely romantic hall of vapors and hurrying crowds, but a finer, more highly organized railway station, which we too should proceed to build.

There must be a prose of life, but if it becomes merely prosaic to us, merely routine, that is because of our failure to make anything of it. We cannot be always in a high and passionate state of emotion, like the bright seraphim in burning row ; and art for us is not all a touching of celestial harps with golden wires. Rather it is, or might be, in the mass of its achievements, a symptom of our triumph over routine in the prose of life. And the peculiar weakness of our present society is that it fails utterly to triumph over this routine, and betrays that failure in all objects of use. For us nearly every object of use is a platitude, and that means that a great part of life itself is a platitude ; that in all our commercial and industrial relations with each other we are dominated by a belief, at once platitudinous and untrue, that we must take as much and give as little as we can. Where that belief prevails, there can be no art of design ; for the art of design comes into being through the designer's impulse to give more than he need give ; and that impulse is checked at once where he works for employers who tell him to give as little as he can.

Machinery and Functional Beauty.

The fact that we make many things with machinery has nothing to do with our failure to recognize their beauty. If things made by machinery could have no functional beauty, machinery would of course be fatal to art, and we should have to make up our minds whether we would give up art or machinery. But, as I have tried to show, many machine-made things have great beauty, and our failure to recognize it is the result merely of associations which prevent us from taking the pleasure we ought to take in such things. An artistic person will, for instance, admire some fantastic, ancient fowling piece. It is old and highly ornamented, and therefore he thinks of it as a work of art. But he will not admire a modern sporting gun by a good maker because he thinks of it as an article of commerce. And yet the modern gun has a beauty of design, a functional beauty, far beyond that of the old one. It has an almost miraculous elegance, which is heightened, not spoilt, by the precision of the mechanical finish. In this case an extreme beauty has been achieved because the wealthy sportsman does take a pride in his weapon. He does not call it beautiful any more than the people of the Middle Ages called their cathedrals works of art. But without knowing it he recognizes the beauty of fine design and workmanship and is ready to pay for it. So it is also with motor cars, which become more beautiful in design every year. But it is not so with the mass of objects of use which are made for the larger public and it cannot be so as long as the public has no sense of possession of those objects and no control over them, and so long as the designers of them are prevented from expressing their natural sense of design.

We have lost control by an accident, through a conjunction of circumstances that has never happened before in the world's history; and, since Socialism is an effort to regain this control, it is also an effort to produce those conditions which will be favorable to the arts of use. In respect to art it is not a very conscious effort; but the conscious efforts to encourage art have not been very successful. What art wants is not the patronage of superior persons but a fair chance with the ordinary man; and that Socialism would give it, if it gave to the ordinary man a fair chance of enjoying those things which his ancestors enjoyed.

FABIAN SOCIETY.—The Fabian Society consists of Socialists. The Annual Report with the Rules and a list of publications can be obtained at the Office, 25 Tothill Street, Westminster, London, S.W.

FABIAN ESSAYS IN SOCIALISM. Paper 6d.; cloth 1/6; post. 2½d. and 4d.
WHAT TO READ on Social and Economic Subjects. 1s. n. and 2s. n.
  THE RURAL PROBLEM. By H. D. HARBEN. 2s. 6d. n.
THIS MISERY OF BOOTS. By H. G. WELLS. 3d., post free 4d.
  FABIAN TRACTS and LEAFLETS.
  Tracts, each 16 to 52 pp., price 1d., or 9d. per dos., unless otherwise stated.
   Leaflets, 4 pp. each, price 1d. for six copies, 1s. per 100, or 8/6 per 1000.
The Set of 77, 3/6; post free 3/11. Bound in buckram, 5/- n.; post free 5/6.

I.—General Socialism in its various aspects.

TRACTS.—169. The Socialist Movement in Germany. By W.S.SANDERS. 2d. 159. The Necessary Basis of Society. By SIDNEY WEBB. 151. The Point of Honour. By RUTH C. BENTINCK. 147. Capital and Compensation. By E. R. PEASE. 146. Socialism and Superior Brains. By BERNARD SHAW. 142. Rent and Value. 138. Municipal Trading. 121. Public Service v. Private Expenditure. By Sir OLIVER LODGE. 107. Socialism for Millionaires. By BERNARD SHAW. 139. Socialism and the Churches. By Rev. JOHN CLIFFORD, D.D. 133. Socialism and Christianity. By Rev. PERCY DEARMER. 78. Socialism and the Teaching of Christ. By Dr. J. CLIFFORD. 42. Christian Socialism. By Rev. S. D. HEADLAM. 79. A Word of Remembrance and Caution to the Rich. By JOHN WOOLMAN. 72. The Moral Aspects of Socialism. By SIDNEY BALL. 69. Difficulties of Individualism. By S. WEBB. 51. Socialism: True and False. By S. WEBB. 45. The Impossibilities of Anarchism. By BERNARD SHAW (price 2d.). 7. Capital and Land. 5. Facts for Socialists. 132. A Guide to Books for Socialists. LEAFLETS—13. What Socialism Is. 1. Why are the Many Poor? WELSH TRACTS—143. Sosialaeth yng Ngoleuni'r Beibl. 141. Translation of 139. 87. Translation of 78. 38. Translation of 1.

II.—Applications of Socialism to Particular Problems.

TRACTS.—175. Economic Foundations of the Women's Movement. 2d. 173. Public versus Private Electricity Supply. By C. A. BAKER. 171. The Nationalization of Mines and Minerals Bill. By H. H. SLESSER. 170. Profit-Sharing & Co-Partnership: a Fraud and Failure? By E. R. PEASE. In cover. 164. Gold and State Banking. By E. R. PEASE. 163. Women and Prisons. By HELEN BLAGG and CHARLOTTE WILSON. 2d. 162. Family Life on a Pound a Week. By Mrs. REEVES. In cover, 2d. 161. Afforestation and Unemployment. By A. P. GRENFELL. 160. A National Medical Service. By F. LAWSON DODD. 2d. 157. The Working Life of Women. By Miss B. L. HUTCHINS. 155. The Case against the Referendum. By CLIFFORD SHARP. 154. The Case for School Clinics. By L. HADEN GUEST. 153. The Twentieth Century Reform Bill. By H. H. SLESSER. 152. Our Taxes as they are and as they ought to be. By R. JONES. 2d. 150. State Purchase of Railways. By EMIL DAVIES. 2d. 149. The Endowment of Motherhood. By H. D. HARBEN. 2d. 131. The Decline of the Birth-Rate. By SIDNEY WEBB. 145. The Case for School Nurseries. By Mrs. TOWNSHEND. 140. Child Labor under Capitalism. By Mrs. H. DALE. 136. The Village and the Landlord. By EDW. CARPENTER. 144. Machinery: its Masters and Servants. By H. H. SLESSER and C. GAME. 128. The Case for a Legal Minimum Wage. 122. Municipal Milk and Public Health. By Dr. F. LAWSON DODD. 125. Municipalization by Provinces. 124. State Control of Trusts. 83. State Arbitration and the Living Wage. LEAFLET.—104. How Trade Unions benefit Workmen.

III.—Local Government Powers : How to use them.

TRACTS.—176. The War and the Workers: Handbook of Measures to Prevent Unemployment and Relieve Distress. By SIDNEY WEBB. 172. What about the Rates? By S. WEBB. 156. What an Education Committee can do (Elementary Schools), 3d. 62. Parish and District Councils. (Revised 1913). 137. Parish Councils and Village Life. 109. Cottage Plans and Common Sense. 76. Houses for the People. 82. Workmen's Compensation Act. LEAFLETS.—134. Small Holdings. 68. The Tenant's Sanitary Catechism. 71. Ditto for London.

IV.—General Politics and Fabian Policy.

TRACTS.—158. The Case against the C.O.S. By Mrs. TOWNSHEND. 108. Twentieth Century Politics. By S. WEBB. 70. Report on Fabian Policy. 41. The Fabian Society: its Early History. By BERNARD SHAW.

Fabian Tract No. 178.

THE WAR; WOMEN; AND UNEMPLOYMENT

I.—UNEMPLOYMENT.
II.—WOMEN AND INDUSTRY.

By the Women's Group Executive.

Price Twopence.

Fabian Women's Group Series, No. 5.

Published and sold by the Fabian Society,
London.   March 1915.

THE WAR;
WOMEN; AND UNEMPLOYMENT.

MANY social problems have presented themselves to us in a fresh light and in changed relations in consequence of the experience brought by war. One of these problems is that of woman's economic position in this country.

Two aspects of that position are discussed in the two separate parts of this Tract. The first is the immediately practical question of the present wide-spread distress among women workers owing to lack of employment. The second is the helplessness of woman in face of the now pressing economic needs of the nation, owing to her lack of training and want of experience in business and organization.

PART I.—UNEMPLOYMENT AMONG WOMEN WAGE-EARNERS, AND HOW TO DEAL WITH IT.

We are only now slowly coming to realize that "unemployment" in industry affects women as well as men, and often differently from men. How often do we not still find the state of the labor market treated as if it were solely a matter of the relative supply of and demand for *men?* If not many men are out of work, Government officials, Ministers of the Crown, and newspaper writers take it for granted that all is well. The Board of Trade Monthly Index Number (based on the unemployed members of certain trade unions), and the statistical return of unemployed among the trades coming within Part II. of the Insurance Act, are quite commonly accepted as fairly measuring the amount of distress from unemployment. Yet the three million persons covered by these two returns include scarcely any women. There is no Index Number with regard to women's unemployment. Hardly any statistics are published about it, or, when published, they are hardly ever given anything like the same prominence as those relating to men. The result of all this is that the great and terrible distress suffered by women wage-earners thrown out of work, whether owing to ordinary trade depression or to dislocation of war, and the consequent suffering to those whom these women wage-earners are helping to support, are very largely overlooked.

It is, perhaps, partly in consequence of this lack of statistical information about unemployment among women that the measures taken to prevent, or mitigate, or relieve unemployment nearly always result in benefit to men. Thus, when it is thought advisable to prevent unemployment by increasing the amount of work put in hand by town councils and other local authorities, it is always in men's trades that the additional volume of employment is created—the town council expedites some work of building, or drainage, or paving, or painting and decorating in order to take on men at wages. When distress becomes acute, the "relief works" started by the Local Distress Committee, such as road-making, or digging, or tree planting, are nearly always for unemployed men.

What is often forgotten, too, is that statistics with regard to the industries in which men are employed may give quite a wrong impression as to the state of employment in those trades in which women are engaged. Thus, during the months of September and October, 1914, when only a relatively small percentage of men were registered as unemployed, largely owing to the enormous number taken into Government pay or employed on municipal works, the percentage of women thrown out of work and standing idle without wages *was at least three times as great.* Yet the small percentage of men registered as unemployed was constantly being cited during that period as evidence that things were going on quite well, and that no exceptional measures were required. If as large a percentage of men had been registering as unemployed as there were women thrown out of work much more energetic steps would have been taken.

In the following pages we shall seek to prove the need for definite and distinct consideration, both by Government and the local authorities, not forgetting local relief committees of all sorts, of the needs of the women wage-earners who are unemployed, and to explain what ought to be done to help them, together with the part which might and should be taken in this matter by women themselves.

Who are the Women Wage-earners.

Few people realize to what an enormous number the women wage-earners have grown in the United Kingdom. Never before have we had such a host. From the 1911 census we learn that no fewer than 5,8~~39,158~~ females of ten years and upwards were engaged "in gainful occupations" in England and Wales alone. This total of close upon ~~six~~ *five millions of working women and girls* excludes all those wholly engaged in unpaid domestic work at home. About 80,000 out of the total are working employers; about 313,000 more are "individual producers" working on their own account; the remainder, comprising the vast majority, are serving for salaries or wages. It is high time that we realized that industrial wage-earning is not an exceptional thing for women. More than half the entire female population of these islands between the ages of 15 and 25 is thus at work for hire. In fact, the great majority of British women are wage-earners during some part of their lives; at the most employed age 70 per cent. are employed.

Here are the " gainful occupations " at which the bulk of approximately ~~six~~ five millions in England and Wales were working in 1911 :—*

	Domestic service (indoors)	1,260,673
	Cotton manufacture	372,834
	Dressmaking	333,129
	Teaching (all branches)	211,183
	Local Government (including Police and and Poor Law Services	176,450
Net totals in industries or services.	Wool and Worsted manufacture ...	127,637
	Tailoring	127,527
	Drapery	110,955
	Inn or hotel service	110,506
	Agriculture	94,841
	Printing, bookbinding and stationery ...	87,609
	Grocery	58,935
	Boot and shoe making	45,986
	National Government	34,089
Totals in Occupation Tables.	Medical and nursing	87,699
	Art, music, drama...	49,998
	Laundry	167,052
	Metal trades	101,050
	Charwomen	126,061

If the female workers of Scotland (593,210) and of Ireland (430,092) be added to those of England and Wales, the total reaches 6,877,338. By 1915 the number of women and girls working for gain in the United Kingdom must have risen to at least ~~seven~~ over six millions.

It may be worth while to add a statistical estimate—the most accurate that can be framed until the Board of Trade deigns to give as much attention to women as to men—of what such of these women earn as belong to the manual working wage-earning class, omitting the professionals, such as doctors, artists, teachers, journalists, managers, clerks, and municipal or national Government officials, and to compare their earnings with those of men of the manual working wage-earning class. The estimate includes the value of board and lodging, when supplied, and of all extras, but deducts an estimated percentage for unemployment, holidays, and short time.

Table prepared for the Fabian Women's Group by Mr. Sidney Webb showing estimated earnings of Employed Manual Working Wage-Earners in the United Kingdom in the year 1912:

* Valuable summary tables of the occupations of women in England and Wales, prepared by Miss Wyatt Papworth and Miss Dorothy Zimmern, are published by the Women's Industrial Council. Price 6d.

MALES.

Class.	Numbers.	Average earnings in full week, including emoluments.		Average Wages Bill for a full week.	Yearly Wages Bill.*
		s.	d.	Million £.	Million £.
Men in situations :					
Below 15s. ...	320,000 = 4%	13	0	0·21	10
15s. to 20s. ...	640,000 = 8%	18	0	0·58	27
20s. ,, 25s. ...	1,600,000 = 20%	22	6	1·80	85
25s. ,, 30s. ...	1,680,000 = 21%	27	6	2·31	109
30s. ,, 35s. ...	1,680,000 = 21%	32	6	2·73	128
35s. ,, 40s. ...	1,040,000 = 13%	37	6	1·95	92
40s. ,, 45s. ...	560,000 = 7%	42	6	1·20	56·5
Over 45s. ...	480,000 = 6%	50	0	1·20	56·5
Men in situations	8,000,000 = 100%	30	0	12·00	564
Casuals	700,000	12	0	0·42	18·5
Adult males ...	8,700,000	28	4	12·42	582·5
Boys	1,900,000	10	0	0·95	44
All males ...	10,600,000	25	3	13·38	626·5

Average earnings per adult employed manual working man through-

out the year $\frac{582·5}{8·7}$ £66·95, or £1 5s. 9d. per week.

* Allowing five weeks for short time, sickness, involuntary holidays and unemployment.

FEMALES.

Class.	Numbers.	Average earnings in a full week.		Average weekly Wages Bill for a full week	Yearly Wages Bill (net, as above).
		s.	d.	in £100,000.	£.
Women in situations :					
Below 12s. ...	1,000,000	9	0	450	21,150,000
12s. to 15s. ...	1,500,000	13	0	975	45,825,000
Over 15s. ...	500,000	17	0	425	19,975,000
Women in Situations	3,000,000	12	4	1,850	86,950,000
Casuals	100,000	3	6	17½	822,500
Adult women ...	3,100,000	11	7	1,867½	87,772,500
Girls	1,500,000	7	6	565	26,550,000
All females ...	4,600,000	10	7	2,432½	114,322,500
Total Wages Bill ...	...	...	...	...	£740,875,500

Average earnings per adult employed manual working woman

throughout the year $\frac{87·772}{3·1}$ £28·31, or 10s. 10½d. per week.

NOTE.—The difference between 4,600,000 (the estimated number of female manual working wage-earners in 1912) and 6,000,000 (the estimated number of women and girls gainfully occupied in 1915) is to be accounted for partly by the increase in numbers between 1912 and 1915, but mainly by (a) the women employers ; (b) the women working on their own account in industrial occupations ; (c) the women and girls gainfully occupied but non-manual working wage-earners, such as doctors, artists, teachers, journalists, managers, clerks, local and national government employees. Domestic servants are included as manual working wage earners.

The estimate allows for an average of five weeks' wages lost in a year through short time, sickness, involuntary holidays, and unemployment. This "ordinary" amount of unemployment, though it makes a big hole in a woman's scanty wages, is not that about which we are now concerned. What is serious is the continued inability to get another situation, prolonged perhaps for many weeks ; the weary search for a vacancy that takes the very heart out of a woman ; the drain on the scanty savings so difficult to accumulate, which brings her face to face with the worst that fate can have in store for her.

How to Prevent Unemployment.

The first thing to be done, when prolonged and widespread unemployment is imminent or apprehended, is to seek to prevent it. In this case prevention is ever so much better than cure. If private employers are beginning to turn off their "hands," it is the duty of public employers—that is to say, the Government Departments and the various local authorities—to do all that they can to increase their own staffs. When there is a falling off in the amount of employment in the way of trade, whatever work or service useful to the community can be undertaken by the public authorities ought then to be deliberately undertaken. Labor should be engaged at the standard rates of wages in the ordinary way, with the object of maintaining undiminished, as far as possible, the total volume of wage-earning employment. Nor need we be too careful that the augmentation of public employment is exactly in those particular crafts or specialized occupations in which a diminution of private employment is likely to occur. Coincidence in this respect, in so far as it is practicable, greatly facilitates matters, and it is not suggested that discharged clerks or jewellers can become navvies or cooks ; but in the ever-changing tides of the vast labor market, the broadening of any channel has an effect in carrying off some of the flood, and of thereby relieving the pressure elsewhere. Any increase in demand for labor, by lessening the number of possible competitors, helps indirectly every kind of labor that is seeking employment.

This policy of actually preventing unemployment by augmenting public employment, in order to counterbalance the diminution of private employment—a policy quite distinct from that of letting people fall into unemployment and then providing "relief works" on which to set them to work just because they are unemployed and in distress—is now what is advised by the political economists. It has been definitely adopted as the policy of the State. In the Development and Road Board Act, 1909, it was expressly laid down by Parliament that, in creating employment under that Act, the Commissioners were to "have regard to the state of the labor market"; the implication being that they were to do little when trade was good, and as much as possible when trade was bad.

In August, 1914, when so much unemployment was caused by the war, we saw the various Government Departments (such as the

Office of Works in particular) under the direct instructions of the Cabinet, frankly recognizing the public responsibility for preventing as much unemployment as possible, and racking their brains to discover what work they could put in hand. Finally, we had the Local Government Board quite explicitly enjoining this policy on the local authorities as a general principle.

"Obviously the best way to provide for persons thrown out of their usual employment as a result of the war is to provide them with some other work for wages. . . . Where the demands of the normal labor market are inadequate, the committee should consult the local authorities as to the possibility of expediting schemes of public utility, which might otherwise not be put in hand at the present moment. Whatever work is undertaken by local authorities . . . should be performed in the ordinary way. . . . The men engaged . . . should, of course, be paid wages in the ordinary way."—(Circular P.R.D. 7, August 20th, 1914.)

Note the words "the men"! Unemployment among seven millions of gainfully occupied women and girls needs to be prevented just as much as unemployment among the thirteen millions of gainfully occupied men and boys, and no doubt the Local Government Board meant their advice to be taken as regards both sexes equally ; but, unfortunately, those in charge of our Government Departments and those who run our town councils are almost exclusively men. When they put in hand schemes for increasing the volume of public employment, what is thought of is, practically always, employment for men. This, of course, comes easiest to them ; and, moreover, few unemployed women wage-earners have even a municipal vote.

Women should see to it that, when unemployment is threatened, or has actually occurred, this policy of augmenting the volume of public employment is applied in the case of women, as it is in the case of men. The local authorities ought everywhere to be pressed to increase their staffs of women and girls, as some partial set-off to the new employment that they seek to provide for men. As there were no fewer than 176,450 women and girls in the Local Government service in England and Wales alone in 1911, the addition of only five per cent. (or one for every twenty already employed) would mean that nearly 9,000 unemployed women would be taken off the labor market. What town councillors are apt to do, if they are not reminded of women's needs in this respect, is rather to leave accidental vacancies unfilled among their women teachers or clerks, so that the staff falls off by five per cent. or more, and unemployment is actually increased.

We ought to urge on the borough and urban councils—also upon the county councils—that, in times of trade depression, they should take special care that their staffs of women and girls (teachers, typists, clerks, inspectors, health visitors, nurses, asylum attendants, charwomen, school cleaners, lavatory attendants, etc.) are kept at full strength, and, wherever occasion arises, promptly increased. We should press for the fullest possible number of learners or probationers to be taken on in every department, so that an increased number of women might be trained for higher work ; that, for instance, all possible opportunities should be taken to increase the numbers of scholarships for girls, girl student-teachers, and female teachers in training; that additional training colleges and hostels should be established; that the number of probationer-nurses in the public health hospitals and workhouse infirmaries should be augmented; we should insist that the elementary school staffs of women teachers should be increased—at any rate to the extent of all the trained teachers available, even taking on at once the whole year's supply leaving college in July—so as to effect the very desirable reform of reducing the size of the classes, wherever accommodation permits; we should demand that the opportunity be taken to introduce, among the council's staff, women sanitary inspectors and women health visitors; or to increase their number if already instituted, up to the limit of the local requirements.

We might very well press the local police authority (in London, the Home Secretary; in the City of London, the Corporation; in counties, the Standing Joint Committee; in boroughs, the Watch Committee) to appoint the police matrons who are so urgently required at all police stations. Why should they not appoint, too, some women as police constables, in order that they may be employed in various directions where they are more suitable than men? In the United States no fewer than twenty-five cities have now one or more "policewomen," Chicago having twenty, whilst Baltimore, Seattle and Los Angeles have five each, Pittsburgh four, and San Francisco and St. Paul each three. Canada, too, is beginning to utilize its women as police assistants, Vancouver setting the example in this direction. In at least thirty-five towns in Germany women police assistants have been appointed; in Mainz, Munich, Dresden, and ten other towns, they are appointed by the State and municipal authorities. Women police have also been appointed in Austria, Denmark, Holland, Norway, Switzerland and Sweden. Even in England, in order to meet the conditions arising from the war, women are now serving on the patrols organized by the National Society of Women Workers, and as voluntary policewomen organized by the Women's Freedom League, but they are not appointed on oath, and, therefore, have no power of arrest; moreover, the work is of a voluntary character. The police patrol work has already been abundantly justified, and should be extended in many directions. Police and military authorities alike are welcoming, and in some cases asking for, this co-operation on the part of women. If women can do the work, why withhold either the official status or the pay? The latest published report of the Commissioner of Metropolitan Police, for 1913, reveals the fact that London, at all events, employs one paid woman police officer, whose business it is to take the depositions of women and children in certain cases. By this time it may be hoped that there are more than one. In Southampton two women police constables were appointed in January, 1915.

Again, the local education authority might well take this opportunity to keep back from the overstocked labor market as many as possible of the girls about to leave school at thirteen or fourteen, and secure to them a year or two more educational training, wherever possible of a technical character. To enable such girls to abstain from wage-earning, it would be necessary to provide them with maintenance whilst under training. This it is within the legal powers of the local education authority to do by awarding them maintenance scholarships, carrying not only full education but also a payment of the necessary few shillings a week. The number of such scholarships for girls compares very unfavorably with that for boys.

The idea might be carried further. It would be distinctly advantageous if the local education authority would, at times when women are exceptionally unemployed, offer maintenance scholarships pretty freely to selected girls of sixteen or eighteen, who are willing to put themselves under training, either for any skilled craft at which they could eventually get employment, or for sick nursing, for which there is a rapidly growing permanent demand; or, indeed, for any of the higher openings for women. A patriotic education committee might be moved to agree to such a proposal by offering special scholarships to the daughters of "men at the front," or of killed or wounded.

The present provision of technical education for girls by local authorities is extremely inadequate. In London, since 1904, trade schools have been established for limited numbers of girls, including, at present, schools for dressmaking, ladies' tailoring, millinery, upholstery, trade embroidery, corset and lingerie making, waistcoat making, cookery, domestic service, laundry work and photography; but outside London trade schools for girls hardly exist. At Manchester and Plymouth schools for dressmaking have been established, though in the former city there is provision for only twenty-four students; Reading has a school for domestic economy, the Birmingham education authority has lately opened a school for the training of girls as children's nurses, and the Brighton education authority has just decided to start a school for laundry work. This exhausts the list.

Trade schools apart, in the recent general development of technical instruction under the auspices of the Board of Education and local education authorities, whether by means of evening classes or of "vocational training" in secondary schools, there has been a strong tendency to confine the instruction of girls, other than intending teachers, to housecraft and needlework, or else preparation for clerical work, or, in evening classes, dressmaking.

Now is the time to provide more schools and more classes teaching new trades and promoting efficiency in trades already followed, which will make women competent wage-earners in the future. To this end it will be essential to provide a large number of scholarships with maintenance grants for girls, which grants would help to educate parents in the idea that immediate employment of a boy or girl on leaving school is detrimental to his or her future welfare, and that the school age must be raised so as to secure an adequate and thorough training in some trade or profession. Why should there not be opportunities for women to enter certain skilled and lucrative trades in which at present provision is made only for men? Further, it is necessary to convince parents and local authorities that an educational training would be valuable in avocations not heretofore supposed to require it. A shop assistant, for example, would find her work more interesting, be more efficient, and be able to command better pay if she had a sound knowledge of the nature and provenance of the goods she sells.

Again, the local health committees should certainly see to it that the maternity centre and baby clinic, which every town needs, is at once started and developed. In this connection the sanction given by the Local Government Board for the training and employment, at fourpence per hour, either from relief funds or otherwise, of a staff of "mothers' helps" or "sick room helps" to visit the homes of women who are sick or being confined, in order to keep their households going, should certainly be utilized.

Local insurance committees should lose no opportunity to press for a beginning of the scheme for the home nursing of the sick, for which Parliament voted the money in the summer of 1914. The Insurance Commissioners do not want to take action on this decision of Parliament, and they are pleading for delay on grounds of economy and shortage of nurses. But unless a start is made with the training of probationers there will never be enough nurses. The sick need the nursing as much now (and are costing the approved societies as much through lack of nursing) as they did when the House of Commons passed the vote. The Government should be pressed on this matter.

Furthermore, local authorities should find and directly provide work at wages for unemployed women, analogous to the new buildings or the additional furniture by which these authorities can relieve the labour market as regards men. We ought to see to it that local authorities do not postpone any orders for uniforms, asylum clothing, or other garments; they should rather take the opportunity to increase stocks. They can sometimes properly take on a few women in the sewing rooms of the asylums or other institutions. Many women clerks and secretaries who are unemployed might be given work in public libraries. In February, 1913, 59 women were employed in the public libraries of eight metropolitan boroughs, and 314 in those of provincial towns, including 114 in Manchester. The women assistants who are thus employed are of various grades, and the salaries are from £1 a week, rising to 25s., and from £80, rising to £130. The work is particularly suited to women, and if more women were members of public library committees, it is reasonable to believe that the appointment of women librarians would be more frequent. It may not be generally known that women can be co-opted as additional members of such committees.

The local education authority might equip all the children at school with gymnasium and swimming costumes, and see to it that none went without warm socks or stockings and strong boots. But much more might be done. An immense improvement in the health and educational progress of the children in the elementary schools might be effected if local education authorities would start a "school uniform" for boys and girls respectively; that is to say, suitable underclothing, together with a tasteful and hygienic dress of simple pattern, not necessarily identical in cut or color, but analogous to that adopted in some of the best boarding schools for the children of the wealthy. This would necessitate a free gift of the new clothing, at any rate in the poorest schools or to any parents requiring it. But it would be the means of getting rid of the insanitary layers of dirty wool and of the "rags and tatters" to which so many of the children are now condemned. What a splendid use might thus be made of a time of unemployment to put the whole school population, even the whole of the children in any particular town or village, into clean and healthy and beautiful clothing!

It may be needful to induce local authorities and other large consumers ordering supplies of clothing as above suggested to give their orders to other firms than those which formerly monopolized the supply, since such firms are in some cases exceptionally pressed by orders from the War Office and our allies, e.g., firms supplying the clothing and boots required for soldiers are working day and night. The Government stated last November that they have spread their orders for khaki amongst two hundred firms, apart from local contracts.

Why We Cannot Set the Unemployed Women to Commercially Productive Work.

It is frequently urged that the Government, or the local authorities or relief committees, should open workrooms for unemployed women, and set them to produce any of the ordinary commodities for sale in the market. Thus, at the outbreak of the war in August, 1914, various philanthropic ladies started workrooms in which they employed women at wages *to make garments for sale*. Sometimes they importuned the War Office for contracts for shirts which would otherwise have been given to the usual contractors. Sometimes they begged their friends to give them orders instead of buying at the shops. Sometimes they sold the product to the wholesale dealers, who would otherwise have given out the work among their usual sub-contractors and home workers. Thus, the work done in these philanthropic workrooms was only *diverted from the ordinary channels of trade*. Absolutely no good was done to women as a whole. During that very month shirtmakers and tailoresses and dressmakers were being discharged all over the kingdom, or being put on "half time," because the orders which would ordinarily have been given in the usual course of trade were being greatly reduced.

A similar mistaken policy used to be pursued as regards women by the Central Unemployed Body for London, the authority for creating employment under the Unemployed Workmen Act, 1905. For unemployed men this body quite rightly avoided competition with employment in the ordinary course of trade, and put the men to work at useful tasks not yielding any commercial value and not sold in the market. For unemployed women, however, owing to some economic blundering at the Local Government Board which has never been explained, the Central Unemployed Body conducted between 1908 and 1914 sewing rooms for unemployed women, where garments were deliberately made for sale in the market, where the utmost possible output was insisted on at the lowest possible cost, and where the enterprise was ostensibly run on commercial lines. The result can only have been to throw other women out of work. Moreover, the workrooms naturally failed even to make the profits they aimed at, and incurred considerable loss.

All such action is, from the standpoint of doing something for the unemployed, a clumsy error, which ought not to be repeated, whether by local authorities, by relief committees, or by benevolent people. To engage women in productive work of ordinary commercial character, which is merely substituted for other production, does nothing more than put some women into work at the cost of throwing others out of work. The total demand for labor is not increased. The Local Government Board now recognizes the mistake it made between 1908 and 1914, and the new women's workrooms of the Central Unemployed Body were, in October, 1914, ordered to be run on quite different lines from the old ones.

New Trades for Women.

It may be asked, why should not the women take up new trades, in which they might produce for sale, and make their employment commercially self-supporting, without throwing other persons, or at any rate not other women in the United Kingdom, out of work? There is every reason why this should be done, *if and wherever it is possible*. But experience shows that there are great difficulties in the way. It needs no little ingenuity to discover any new manufacture or service that is both practicable and profitable. It is not easy to obtain the services of someone possessing the necessary managerial skill and the business knowledge that is required. It is often difficult to overcome the inertia and resistance of the ordinary wholesale trader or shopkeeper through whom the product has to be sold. The railway rates are found to make both the bringing of the raw material and the selling of the finished product very costly. Lastly, the women workers themselves require to be trained to the new occupation.

Such experiments are difficult, but there is every reason why they should be tried.

The pulping of fruit, with a view to its preservation and bottling or canning in jelly form, was started in September, 1914, at Studley Horticultural College, under the Board of Agriculture, by the aid of a grant from the Development Commissioners. The plant cost about £750, and the necessary working capital for the purchase of fruit, etc., amounted to £500. The women were engaged at regular wages by the aid of a grant from the National Relief Fund. No information is yet available as to the commercial results.

The bottling of fruit may be practicable in some districts where fruit would otherwise be wasted. This can sometimes be set up in a small way by zealous volunteers, and made to cover the wages given to the workers. But it is practicable only for a short period in especial localities, and cannot be regarded as a trade. The drying of vegetables for sale in a form in which they can be preserved was also started in Warwickshire in September, 1914. This cost £800 for plant and £300 for working capital. Dried vegetables have hitherto been supplied from the Continent. They are used for export and for the supply of the troops, as well as for ordinary consumption.

The revival of the ancient home industry of hand-knitting is to be commended, in so far as it supplies the market with goods of better quality, for which there is a genuine permanent demand, or goods not otherwise obtainable, such as the special sea-boot stockings knitted by "trawler" women.

Foreign branches of trade in fancy leather, stationery, and metal ware may, with great advantage, in future employ women in England.

The exodus of foreigners from the country should give considerable scope for English women in cookery, as waitresses, and in several of the higher branches of the catering trade if the embargo of sex be withdrawn. And the withdrawal of more than a million Englishmen from civil life has unavoidably left vacancies which duly qualified women must be found and trained to fill. The Report of the Board of Trade on the state of employment in the United Kingdom for December, 1914, mentions an increase of 25 per cent. in the employment of women in London banks since the war, and the existence of a similar state of things in some other city employments. In the Post Office also women are working in what were formerly men's departments; they are also entering the grocery trade as shop assistants, acting as lift attendants, finding increased employment in metal work, e.g., in Vickers-Maxim's shops, and undertaking artistic work hitherto done by men in the printing trade.

The making of toys and dolls, in substitution for those formerly obtained from Germany, was started last autumn in various quarters. The Women's Emergency Corps and some branches of the National Union of Women's Suffrage Societies, in particular, have managed to employ a number of women in this way, utilizing the taste and artistic skill that they possess. A large factory on ordinary business lines is now being started at Burton on Trent, and one (The Goblin Toy Factory) has already been started in Reading. It will ultimately employ 1,000 women, many of them skilled workers with artistic training, the majority ordinary factory hands. Handloom weaving has been suggested as an occupation in which women might find commercially remunerative work in the production of articles of special quality, for which a demand has revived. The artistic handicrafts generally, it has been suggested, might be revived with the same purpose.

No experiment in this direction ought to be discouraged. In particular, we should be on the look out for any opportunity for the development of talent or the exercise of taste among women thrown out of work in their own mechanical or monotonous trades. There is now an opportunity to enlarge the field of women's activities, and to fit them to take in future a share in a larger variety of paid occupations, and also, it may be hoped, a fair chance to win and keep a place amongst the better remunerated workers. But we must bear in mind that it is not enough to obtain orders from friends and sympathizers. It is of no use, *as provision for unemployed wage-earners in distress*, to suggest occupations (such as poultry farming, or indeed any other farming, or running a tea-room or keeping a shop) which may, at best, *afford a livelihood as employers* to individual women able to command considerable capital. For the purpose of doing something for the unemployed women wage-earners the question must be honestly faced of whether in the proposed new trade there is (i) a continuing demand, (ii) from entirely uninterested purchasers, (iii) at a price sufficient to cover all the expenses of production, and (iv) of a volume sufficient to find lasting employment at all seasons of the year for a substantial number of women wage-earners, or regularly at certain seasons as an alternative trade. Unless these four questions can be answered in the affirmative, the proposed "new trade" is a sham, a philanthropic fad, really only another form of charitable relief, or at best a temporary makeshift.

What can be Given to the Unemployed—Doles or Training?

A certain amount of unemployment among women wage-earners can be met by the development of new trades for women, but we cannot hope instantaneously at a time of crisis to provide in this way for the great mass of girls and women—to be numbered literally by the hundred thousand—now thrown out of employment by any severe depression of trade. There they are, in every large town in greater or smaller numbers, myriads of seamstresses and dressmakers of every grade, of tailoresses and milliners, and all the miscellaneous workers on articles of dress ; factory operatives of all grades from the "box" and "jam" and confectionery "hands," the packers and labellers and bottlers of every conceivable commodity; the workers in jute, and wool, and silk and worsted, right up to the "four-loomers" in the cotton weaving shed ; the charwomen and office cleaners ; the typists, the book-keepers and the clerks ; the nursery governesses and the "companions," all find their chances of employment contracting through no fault of their own. What are we to do for them ?

There are two answers. The first is the voice of despair—Give them alms.

The Evil Policy of Doles.

This is the easiest of all devices, the eagerly adopted remedy of the charitable, the "cheapest" way of getting the unemployed off the momentarily stirred consciences of the well-to-do. But, as everyone knows who has tried it, the distribution of money amongst those in distress—though we have perforce to resort to it in hard times if we are too stupid or too lazy or too unconscientious to find anything better—is the worst of all methods of relief, demoralising alike to giver and recipient. Hardly any character is strong enough to stand up against the subtle corruption of dependence on alms. The dole is practically never adequate for maintenance; it is never to be relied upon, and consequently never admits of provident housekeeping; yet the mere expectation of it deadens all exertion, initiative and enterprise in seeking new employment. The unaccustomed idleness, with its evil loitering and inevitable gossiping, is especially demoralising to women used to regular employment. Finally, there is the tragic dilemma of the "scale." If the weekly dole is large enough for really adequate maintenance in full health and vigor, it will be (as the nation has with shame to confess) considerably in excess of the earnings of women at work in half the women's trades; and it is not in human nature to resist the temptation of letting slip the chances of employment that involve an actual loss of income. If, on the other hand, the dole is made less than women actually earn at their work, it means slow starvation.

The Policy of Training.

The more sensible practical alternative to employment that is commercially productive is not doles but another kind of employment—employment of an educational character. Those women and girls whom we find it impossible to place in situations in the ordinary way, whom we cannot, even temporarily, take into our augmented municipal employment, and for whom we fail to discover new trades, we can at any rate set to work at their own improvement. The provision of "maintenance under training" for girls and women is a plain matter of justice. Far less has hitherto been done for the technical training of girls than for the training of boys. There are far fewer scholarships (of all sorts, at all ages) available for girls than for boys. And in the war emergency of 1914, the Government, for its own purposes, applied to the million and a quarter unemployed men the principle of "maintenance under training" on a gigantic scale, taking them into army pay, and providing them with clothing and boots and complete maintenance, whilst it trained and drilled them into the utmost physical and military efficiency. Nothing analogous to this was done for the three or four hundred thousand women thrown out of work, though they were just as much in need of physical and sometimes of professional training as the men, and the nation, also because of the war, was in urgent need of trained workers.

What Kind of Training.

When it is sceptically asked what kind of training could be given to unemployed wage-earners, and whether the women are not too old to learn, we become conscious of the amount of prejudice that lies behind the doubt whether it is of any consequence whether women are properly trained or not! As a matter of fact the problem of providing training for unemployed women offers fewer difficulties than the corresponding problem with regard to men.

In the autumn of 1914 the Central Committee on Women's Employment, formed by the Queen to devise schemes (Miss Mary

Macarthur, Hon. Secretary), worked out plans in some detail for exactly this work,* to which the seal of Cabinet approval was given. It was laid down, as a fundamental condition, that the work to be done "should not compete in any way with ordinary industry," and that "it should be of such a nature as to maintain or improve the efficiency of the unemployed women." What was aimed at was "education or technical training or instruction." This might, where possible, take the form of instruction in the processes of new trades. It might, on the other hand (and this was found more generally practicable), take the form of instruction in the making and renovation of clothing of all kinds, from cutting out to finishing. It was found that hardly any of the unemployed wage-earning women were competent at domestic dressmaking and needlework, even for their own requirements ; and of course hardly any of them proved to be able to dispense with instruction as to reshaping and renovating their own garments and hats. Every kind of mending and adapting furnished many useful lessons.

Simple domestic economy was also taught with great success. Practical cookery, home laundry work and even the elements of domestic hygiene and infant management could be made subjects of instruction. All this naturally requires organizing, and involves the engagement of competent, skilled instructresses in the different subjects—thus finding suitable employment for such persons who are themselves out of work—and these engagements have, of course, to be at comparatively high rates of pay. The Government rightly insisted, through the Central Committee on Women's Employment, that no attempt must ever be made to beat down the standard rates, whether of forewomen or instructresses, cooks or charwomen.

But the training given was by no means all of domestic utility. Workers already belonging to a skilled trade, or anxious to train for a skilled trade, were grouped for a special course of trade instruction provided by the local education authority, after consultation with the women's department of the Labor Exchange as to local demand for skilled workers.† About 150 girl clerks were sent to educational institutions to learn foreign languages ; 30 ex-factory girls, by their own desire, were sent to train in market gardening [an experiment reported in January, 1915, as very successful] ; some elder women were trained as sick-room helps for laid-up mothers of families. In January, 1915, the committee were giving grants to 55 work and training rooms (about 4,158 workers), carried on by local representative committees, and had 27 more under consideration, whilst their own experimental schemes were occupying and training 1,000 women, besides the 2,000 employed through their contracts branch or by the Central Unemployed Body for London.

* Memoranda on Schemes of Work for Women Temporarily Unemployed Owing to the War, issued by the Central Committee on Women's Employment, 8 Grosvenor Place, London, S.W. (W.E.R, 2, 3 and 4).

† The London Juvenile Advisory Committee is issuing a pamphlet showing which are the trades which, owing to the war, are needing an increased number of learners. (Board of Trade, Labor Exchanges and Unemployment Department, Queen Anne's Chambers, S.W.)

The experience of the autumn of 1914 by no means exhausts the possibilities of providing training for unemployed women. The problem need not always be dealt with on wholesale lines. When time permits, the cases should be considered one by one, and each girl or woman provided with the individual training best suited to her needs. In a large city the number of women thrown out of work in the different branches of the dressmaking and tailoring trades would allow of the selection of those suitable in age and otherwise to be sent to technical classes that would qualify them for the more skilled and more highly paid branches of their trades, from which they would otherwise remain all their lives excluded. Even three months expert technical training will often start a young woman in the progress from a mere " hand " at 8s. or 10s. a week into a machinist or a waistcoat-maker, who will presently be making twice or thrice that wage. In the crafts at which women already find employment, such as upholstery and bookbinding, most of them never get a chance of rising to the more skilled grades, at which some women earn relatively good wages. Even a few months instruction would put some of these excluded ones on an upward move. There are thousands of women who gain a living by cooking or laundry work, but there is constant scarcity of really trained cooks and an unsatisfied demand for the higher grades of laundry workers. Some of the unemployed women should be picked out for thoroughly expert technical instruction in these relatively well-paid occupations. Indeed, there seems no reason why selected women should not be put through the necessary training for dairy and other agricultural work,* for sick nursing, for dispensing, for midwifery, for the work of health officer and sanitary inspector, even for the understaffed medical profession, where there is such urgent permanent need for women's services, while so many suitable girls, who have had a good secondary education, cannot afford the needful five years of training. Once the idea is grasped that the best way to spend the time of unemployment is in training, and that the best form of provision for the unemployed for whom we cannot find situations is maintenance while they are being taught, there are endless opportunities of instruction and improvement to be discovered.

Experience, alas! shows that it is very difficult to get this principle of " educational training and maintenance " into the heads of town and county councillors and members of local relief committees, male or female. In the autumn of 1914 the Central Committee on Women's Employment seems to have found it expedient to compromise with those members of the Cabinet and those mayoresses and other " committee ladies " who did not " hold with " education, and were always hankering after some way of " getting the women to work "! In order to satisfy this yearning for " production," it was found expedient to allow part of the time to be devoted to " making things in which it was difficult to pretend that the workers were in any way benefiting, either by acquiring new skill or by otherwise

* The Board of Agriculture is actively organizing classes for women and girls in butter-making and other branches of dairy and other work connected with agriculture.

improving themselves." It was then necessary, if this misguided waste of time had to occur, to see to it that the work of the women, at any rate, did no harm in putting other women out of work. It was therefore sternly insisted on that under no circumstances were supplies to be sent to the soldiers or sailors for the diminution of the War Office or Admiralty orders, and that the produce was never to be sold in any way. What was produced had to be given away to the very poorest, who could not possibly have otherwise been purchasers. In this way a number of women were kept at work making maternity outfits and articles of clothing for gratuitous distribution. As the women learned nothing by this work, and were thus in no way aided to obtain better employment than heretofore, whilst the commercial value of what they produced was inconsiderable and, of course, enormously below what was paid to them in maintenance, this plan of making things for the poor is not to be recommended. It ought only to be a concession to the ignorance or prejudices of the committee when the members cannot be made to see reason.

Payment or Maintenance.

It is obvious that what the women receive who are thus given training or instruction, or who are put to work, not at their own trades, in producing maternity outfits or garments for gratuitous distribution, is not in the nature of wages, and much misunderstanding is caused when that term is used for it. What ought to be provided for those unemployed for whom we fail to find productive work is not wages, but *maintenance until situations at wages can be discovered for them.* We want to get them back to regular wage-earning—if possible in a higher grade of work than that which they left—at the earliest possible moment.

What can properly be paid as maintenance? The Central Committee on Women's Employment decided, after careful consideration, that the amount could not safely be put at more than 10s. a week as a maximum for women over eighteen, and for this sum five days attendance (or forty hours) at the educational institution or women's training centre (or women's workroom, as it was sometimes less aptly termed) should be required. Where tramway fares or other travelling expenses have to be incurred, the amount of these might be added. It is desirable that dinners and teas should be supplied on the premises, where convenient, at a very small charge, the women taking it in turns to be taught the very best way of preparing these meals. The maintenance allowance of 10s. per week is, of course, for the woman alone. Whenever she has children, or other dependants, a separate allowance for their maintenance, according to the approved scale, is supposed to be made by the local relief committee. For girls between sixteen and eighteen thrown out of work, and in attendance at the training centre, an allowance of 1s. a day was suggested.

These amounts are far lower than could be wished, and they were much complained of by hasty critics. But there can be no doubt that the decision of the Central Committee on Women's Employment was right; and it is to be noted that it received the unanimous endorsement, after careful consideration, of the War Emergency Workers' National Committee, representing the Labor Party, the Trades Union Congress, and the principal women's trade unions. It is absolutely essential, if maintenance is to be offered to the 5 or 10 per cent. who are unemployed, that this should not actually be more than what is being earned as wages by the 90 or 95 per cent. who are still at work. If a person, merely by becoming unemployed, could get more money than by continuing at work, experience shows that there is real danger of the provision that we are striving to make for the involuntarily unemployed being swamped by a rush of workers throwing up their jobs to get the larger income. Ten shillings a week is little enough. But, unfortunately, there are many hundreds of thousands of women whose wages are less than this sum. Indeed, it was found necessary to add that where a woman habitually earned less than 10s. a week at her work, she must be restricted to fewer than five days a week attendance, so as to prevent it being so attractive to her that she would be in no hurry to get again into employment. It is, of course, of the utmost importance to raise the deplorably low rates of wages common in women's employment; but it is of no use trying to do so by giving more to unemployed women for maintenance than they can earn as wages when they are at work. What we have to secure is an extension of the Trade Boards Act to all trades in which less than (say) 30s. a week is paid to man or woman, and such a raising of the legal minimum wages fixed under that Act as will secure a much higher standard of life than the humbler grades of workers are now permitted to enjoy.

The Dependants of Women Workers.

One main cause why public opinion is so careless of the sufferings of wage-earning women is that few persons realize the extent to which the female members of the family amongst the working classes contribute to the family income. It is quite untrue, as is commonly supposed by men of all ranks and by most women of the middle and upper classes, that women workers differ from men workers in having no one to support by their exertions but themselves. Although everyone knows cases of daughters in domestic service who are sending money home regularly, or of factory girls, living at home, who are paying part or all of their wages to their parents, or of married women going out to work, or taking work at home, to help to supply the needs of the family, few persons deduce anything from these facts. Few realize that when large numbers of women workers are unemployed it means a great increase of poverty in working-class homes throughout the country, as well as the distress of the unemployed women themselves.

A careful statistical enquiry of the Fabian Women's Group, extending over thousands of cases, in practically the whole range of women's occupations, showed that *about half* the women wage-earners canvassed were supporting, wholly or partially, either children or parents, or brothers and sisters, or disabled husbands or other dependent relatives. Among laundresses, over 75 per cent. were so contributing ; among cotton weavers, 66 per cent. ; among needle-women, 60 per cent. ; among domestic servants, 53 per cent. ; and among nurses, 52 per cent.

Among women who have received a university education the returns showed 43 per cent. as helping to support others ; and in a similar investigation undertaken among themselves by the women employees in the Post Office, 42 per cent. of the women of over ten years service were returned as contributing to the support of others.

From enquiries in a very poor neighborhood in Outer London among some 750 workers, the majority of whom were girls of about 16-18 years of age, with an average wage of 7s. a week, 84 per cent. were shown to be entirely supporting themselves, and nearly 62 per cent. contributing to the family income over and above their own cost of living.

In Northampton and Warrington particulars have been obtained from cards kindly lent by Dr. Bowley, which contained the results of an investigation made by him into some 1,300 working class house-holds, in which are over 600 female workers, 30 per cent. of whom may be said to be contributing to the upkeep of the family. In both these towns the family wage is fairly high.

From information supplied by the Women's Industrial Council, it was found that out of 578 married women working in gainful occupations, only 53 were not self-supporting, that 97 (or 16·78 per cent.) were the sole support of the family, and that at least 64 per cent. were contributing to the support of their children. In an article on "Working Class Households in Reading," Dr. Bowley says that in 609 households canvassed, "The statistician's normal family of man (at work), wife (not working), and three dependent children only occurs thirty-three times" (*Royal Statistical Society's Journal,* June, 1913).

The fact that, as is indicated by the above examples and figures, a large proportion of the six million women workers must pro-vide for dependants, is of the greatest importance. *It means that probably at least two millions of gainfully occupied women are res-ponsible for the maintenance, wholly or in part, of others besides them-selves.* This is one more reason, and a crucial reason, why serious attention should be given by the Government and by the public to the conditions of women's employment and the needs of unem-ployed women.

PART II.—WOMEN AND THE CONTROL OF INDUSTRY AND SUPPLY.

There are many causes, besides the carelessness of the public, why women's unemployment and the resultant distress commands so little attention. Everywhere the economic position of women is changing with the times, and not only do men fail to grasp the fact and its implications, but women do not understand their own present position themselves.

In England—the European country where agrarian and indus-trial life has most completely changed during the last hundred and fifty years—the anomalies and contradictions of women's economic position lie thickest. Hence the war crisis caught British women at a peculiar disadvantage. They had in readiness no trained and organized expeditionary force to join issue at once in the economic battle. They were quite unprepared to step into the breach caused in the normal economic life of the nation by the diversion of the energies of increasing numbers of men from the creation of wealth to its destructive expenditure. For nowadays Englishwomen, with very few exceptions, normally take no effective part in directing the business life of the country.

How British Women are at a Disadvantage.

In France, in Germany, in Austria, in Galicia, where a large pro-portion of the population is engaged in agriculture, and where small peasant holdings still abound, women, deprived of their menfolk, have been able to carry on the work of producing food for their people at large as well as for their own families. It is an occupation in which, mind and body, they have been accustomed to take active part. The business of the small holding is as much theirs as their husbands', and many of them also do seasonal field work for wages, e.g., in the beet fields. Therefore, when the withdrawal of the men left them wofully shorthanded, these women were able *to direct their own labor* and to meet the economic strain by gallant exer-tions. In August the French Government appealed to the women of France to keep agriculture going and to feed the army, and splendidly they have done it. Never have corn harvest and vintage been more successfully gathered in the undevastated districts.

No such simple course of action has been open to the women of England. We have now few small holdings. Women have gradu-ally been dropping out of all share in farm management, even in their ancient kingdom, the dairy, and in the south scarcely any women are now even seasonally employed in agricultural work. Our great-great-grandmothers would have had little difficulty in exerting themselves to supply the serious shortage of labor dreaded by our farmers ; but, as things are, the help south-country women could give would be wholly unskilled, and farmers are demanding that little boys, who at least have some idea of farm work, shall be taken from school to do it.

Agriculture is no longer our main industry or source of supply, but Englishwomen are also at a tremendous disadvantage with re-gard to all the great industrial and commercial undertakings upon which our national maintenance depends. They have next to no part or lot in the organization, direction, and control of these enter-prises, though by millions they are employed in them. In France women normally take an active share in the management of a family business, and therefore when the invasion of 1914 called fathers, sons, and husbands to the colors, many mothers, daughters, and wives could and did carry on the concern, thus materially helping to minimise the stagnation and dislocation resulting from the war. But amongst our seven million women in gainful occupations very few indeed have the business knowledge and experience to carry on successfully even the smaller trades. Except those in domestic service—the most unorganized and chaotic of industries—most of our female workers for gain are simply units in the vast army serving male employers ; and, with few exceptions, they are as helplessly ignorant of the business management and finance of the enterprise they serve as of the larger economic conditions determining their employment.* What part, for instance, do women take in the business management and direction of the cotton industry, in which the majority of skilled operatives are women? Englishwomen are as eager to help their country as are Frenchwomen, but they have lost touch with the guidance of its economic life ; consequently an appeal from the English Government to any female section of our industrial population, such as that addressed by the French Government to the women agriculturists of France, would be sheer farce. Our seven millions of gainfully occupied women have little or no control over the arrangements conditioning their occupations. Amongst the too few women trade unionists and the handful of women serving on Trade Boards business aptitude is very slowly developing, but amongst women born in the employing classes—except, perhaps, amongst small shopkeepers—the tendency has been to ignore business, even a business carried on by the men of the family, and girls who have entered of conscious purpose upon a breadwinning occupation have usually launched forth in some other direction.

Family and National Housekeeping.

If this be the case with regard to the seven million gainfully occupied, it is equally applicable to the millions of unpaid British women occupied in organizing consumption in detail, each in her separate household. At least half of these have no grasp, often scarcely the vaguest conception, of national housekeeping or the relation of their own unit with national supply. Our wholesale distribution, like our great industries, is organized and directed by men ; women have been content to remain in ignorance of its larger aspects, to say nothing of controlling them. Consequently, like their gainfully occupied sisters, millions of "home makers" have no knowledge enabling them intelligently to help their country at an economic crisis, or to deal with the economic distresses of the workers of their own sex, who supply or serve them. Here, however, the light is beginning to dawn—and again, as amongst the wage-earners, the solution is coming from the toilers themselves.

Some three million married working women belong to the co-operative movement, probably about half being actual shareholders, while the remainder are wives of shareholders. In industrial co-oper-

* See figures of women working employers for England and Wales, p. 3. Both mistresses and servants are now beginning to make some attempts to organize domestic work in accordance with modern economic conditions.

ative societies distribution is controlled by the people for the people. In some towns it is already customary for women to attend the quarterly business meetings of the societies, and thus take their share in the control of these societies, which do a trade of nearly £80,000,000 annually. There is a slowly growing movement for placing women on the management committees of societies, and there are now eighty-nine women on fifty-six of these committees, including some of the largest, such as Leeds, with nearly 50,000 members, Manchester, Bristol, etc.

The distributive societies have combined to form the English and Scottish Co-operative Wholesale Societies, doing a trade of £28,000,000 annually. Women are beginning to be sent by their societies as delegates to the business meetings of these societies and thus gain a knowledge of wholesale trading.

The war has proved conclusively the value of the co-operative societies to the consumers. In the panic at the outset they refused in most cases to raise prices, meeting the demand by supplying only the weekly amounts their members were accustomed to purchase. By this action the general rise of prices in capitalistic shops was checked to a considerable extent.

The Co-operative Wholesale Society was able to give valuable information to the Government as to stocks and prices by which they were able to check the statements of capitalistic traders.

In co-operative societies goods are sold at the ordinary market prices, and the surplus, which in capitalistic trade goes as profit to the shareholders, is divided amongst the purchasers in proportion to their purchases, after paying a fixed interest on capital.

By joining a co-operative society and attending its business meetings every woman can obtain a knowledge of distributive and wholesale trading and can share in its control. To enable themselves to do this more intelligently, London members of the Women's Co-operative Guild are attending classes on distribution and supply.

At the universities also, some few girls are seriously studying the economics of supply and its control in relation to consumption. Still the fact remains that British women have much ground to traverse before they can take their proper place as effective members of the greatest industrial community in the world.

Women and the Control of Capital.

Another aspect of the economic position of Englishwomen is the curious anomaly that, in spite of their lack of control over industry, supply and the conditions of employment, a large amount of wealth is now entirely at their personal disposal. A British woman, married or single, be she the mistress of hundreds of thousands of pounds, a small shareholder in a co-operative society, or a post office depositor, a physician in large practice, or a charwoman at half-a-crown a day, has now a complete legal control over her possessions and earnings. Like a man, she is free to spend her income and manage her own affairs as she pleases. She need not consult her husband or anyone else ; and of course she has the legal and moral responsibilities of an economically independent person. The war subscription lists are a current illustration of the large amount of money thus at the disposal of women.

This money owned by women is part of the capital financing British industry and commerce. Yet the economically independent women of to-day seem to have less practical control over the work supplying national necessities than had, for instance, the working mistress of an English farm in the eighteenth century; though in those days a married woman had no legal right to keep or spend even her own earnings without her husband's consent. Since the decline of agriculture and of the system of domestic industry, and the advent of production and distribution on the grand scale in this country, our women seem to have dropped the slender guiding rein they once held in matters economic. Indeed in the textile industries, when the female "hands" followed their work from home to factory, the female directing brain was already atrophied. Whilst women have continued to crowd into paid employment, they have failed to obtain any grip of the new forces directing our complex business life, despite the great increase of their personal economic freedom and the opening out of ever widening opportunities of education and of work.

Why Women Have Stood Outside Modern Business Life.

It is not a natural lack of aptitude for business in the female brain : witness the organizing and administrative ability manifested by many women at the head of institutions, schools, societies, and large households, and the capacity and initiative shown in the present crisis by so many who in suffrage and other women's societies, or as trade union or co-operative guild organizers, have gained experience in conducting business on their own responsibility. Neither is it lack of intellectual grasp : witness the brilliant achievement of women who take economics as a university subject. Yet many a man has initiated, organized, and directed a flourishing business concern with far less opportunity than many women get, or might get if the normal, average, modern Englishwoman, especially in the employing classes, had not developed the habit of holding herself aloof from business and even the management of her own affairs.

This attitude in the women of the employing, and now of many of the employed, classes seems to have arisen as the direct result of the great Industrial Revolution, which so completely altered our economic life. One of its results was the supremacy of money, so that, instead of the old system of production for use and exchange in kind, supplies were bought and products were sold to an ever increasing extent, and personal wealth was capitalized for machinery and wages. This capitalization of wealth, in the then state of the law with regard to married women's property, meant that the control of capitalist production fell entirely to men. Sir Frederic Eden, in his monumental work on the "State of the Poor," in 1797, opines that married women had grown slack in working to provide their share of the family income because of the injustice of the law which deprived them of the disposal of their own earnings. Whether he was right or not about the poor, there was probably a great deal of truth in his suggestion as applied to the wives of the growing classes of large farmers and manufacturers. The great industries separated not only work, but the control and direction of work, from home activities. Husband and wife no longer consulted over the details of daily occupations in pursuit of common interests centring round the homestead, and, moreover, the growing wealth of the middle classes made it less and less necessary for the whole family to work.

Superabundance of wealth fostered the idea that it is "genteel" and "womanly" for the women of a family to live in more or less idle and ignorant dependence on the income and exertions of its men, an idea as foreign to the English farmers, craftsmen, and small traders of the eighteenth century as to the laboring folk. Gradually it spread from the upper to the middle classes, and thence downward. To women it was enervatingly easy, and men encouraged and approved it, partly from kindliness, partly because it flattered their vanity, partly from an inclination to dominate, and a delusion of self-interest.

Ever since the modern awakening of womanhood began, the feminine outlook on the economic side has been confused by two opposite currents of social feeling and opinion : the downward current toward gentility, which regards paid work for women as a miserable necessity for the poor and the unfortunate, and even now has by no means wholly spent its force ; and the upward current toward conscious recognition of the right and duty of all women, as of all men, to work and to be fairly remunerated. This second current is still mainly individualist in tone, and still splits on the obstacle of marriage, and its course is as yet by no means clearly defined ; but the shock of the war, with its revelation of their lack of control over the economic forces that sway national life, has been a rude awakening for intelligent Englishwomen. They feel that their present economic position is an anachronism, and are bitterly conscious of failure and shortcoming ; perhaps never so bitterly as when men are praising their zeal in knitting "comforts," whilst they are becoming more and more aware that thereby they have been taking bread out of their unemployed sisters' mouths. Suppose for a moment that the share of control once possessed by women in the textile industries—a share so real that for centuries statutes dealing with the cloth trade explicitly included clothiers of both sexes—had developed with the industry, instead of perishing utterly a century or more before the Industrial Revolution. Our Government might in that case have been able to make, in the present emergency, just such an appeal to Englishwomen as the French Government made to the women of France. It might have appealed to our women clothiers to carry on one of the industries most essential to the well-being alike of the troops and of the civil population, whilst the men who usually shared in the work went forth to fight. And our women cloth manufacturers might then have organized the absorption into the growing needs of the trade of every unemployed woman capable of the work required.

After the War.

Alas for the might-have-been! But the future is our own, and already it bristles with challenge. When the war is over the question of women's employment and unemployment will become more difficult and more acute than now. Not only will there be many young widows, but a considerably larger proportion of the girls of the rising generation than of the young women of to-day will be, not only fatherless and brotherless, but husbandless and childless. Are girls of the upper and middle class to continue to grow up work-shy and unskilled? Is employment to be open to them and to the daughters of the manual workers only in certain limited directions? Is it to be confined to the lower grades of trade and industry? Are the wages of women always to remain inadequate to their needs? Or will the women of Britain rise to the occasion and insist on a thorough technical training for girls of all classes? Will they declare that a little instruction in baby-craft, and housecraft, and needlework at elementary and secondary schools will not meet the case of women who must earn a livelihood? "Vocational training" of this sort will not fit our ablest girls to win their way to a place in the direction of national industry, or to influence its future developments. Yet, that they should do so is, above all else, the need of to-day, and will be still more the need of to-morrow. Women must make up their minds to meet it. Business men must be persuaded to train a daughter as they would a son to help and to succeed them. Girls must be taught to manage their own affairs, and expected to do so. Mothers must grasp the fact that henceforth women are called to take active part in the business life of the country, not merely to work for a living if they cannot catch a husband, and that they must be trained accordingly.

To meet the future on the economic side it will not suffice for women to obtain Parliamentary Enfranchisement and adequate representation on Local Governing Bodies. It will not suffice for them to obtain free admission to the middle and upper grades of the Civil Service and of Municipal Employment; it will not suffice that large opportunities of a professional career in the Medical and Health Services, and other honorable and profitable callings, are opening before girls able to take advantage of them. None of these important things will suffice to put the economic position of our womanhood upon a sound basis, unless women in general alter their whole attitude towards business, and conceive it to be their bounden duty, and an act of social service, not merely to study economics, but to set and accustom themselves to take an active share in the practical administration of business and industrial enterprise. There are indications that this drastic change is already beginning to take place—a splendid enthusiasm, a tentative activity in many directions is stirring amongst women. When it takes definite and permanent shape, and not until then, will the problems of women's employment and unemployment be adequately dealt with.

Summary.

We have seen that the unemployment among women wage-earners demands consideration independently from that among men; and that it ought to be prevented, as far as practicable, by the same increase of public employment to balance the decrease of private employment. Local authorities ought to take all possible steps to increase the number of the women and girls for whom they provide either wages or scholarships. The opportunities for immediately increasing the volume of public employment are less easy to find in the case of women than in the case of men. Other provision for unemployed women has accordingly to be made. We should strive to set going new trades for women. Apart from this difficult task, we must provide, for the women still unemployed, *not productive work of commercial character* which would result only in throwing other women out of work, but *maintenance under training*. All sorts of training might well be provided, and the experience of the Central Committee on Women's Employment in the autumn of 1914 affords valuable guidance. The fullest standard rates of wages should be paid to all persons employed (forewomen, instructresses, clerks, typists, charwomen, etc.). What is provided for the unemployed women themselves is not wages but maintenance. This cannot safely be put at more than the women habitually earn, and the sum of 10s. per week, for five days attendance, is found to be as much as can be given without risk of the whole experiment being swamped. Separate provision must, however, be made for travelling expenses and for the maintenance of dependants. Women workers have others dependent upon their exertions to an extent at present unrecognized, and their unemployment is a widespread source of destitution.

Women's employment, its conditions, its remuneration, its vicissitudes, should be the vital concern of women; not only when their own livelihood is involved, not merely as a matter of philanthropic interest, but because it is essential to the well-being of the womanhood of the country, and therefore of the whole people, that women should take an intelligently active share in the economic life of the nation. Though so large a proportion of British women work to produce our wealth, though so many are occupied in organizing its consumption in detail, and so many own a considerable share of it, women have failed to take their proper part in skilled labor and in the responsible direction of industry and supply. The economic crisis of 1914 has revealed this failure. For women, as for men, the war has brought a call to be up and doing.

$\frac{4}{\sqrt{}}$F **ABIAN SOCIETY.**—The Fabian Society consists of Socialists. The Annual Report with the Rules and a list of publications can be obtained at the Office, 25 Tothill Street, Westminster, London, S.W.

FABIAN ESSAYS IN SOCIALISM. Paper 6d.; cloth 1/6; post. 2½d. and 4d.
WHAT TO READ on Social and Economic Subjects. 1s. n. and 2s. n.
THE RURAL PROBLEM. By H. D. HARBEN. 2s. 6d. n.
THIS MISERY OF BOOTS. By H. G. WELLS. 3d., post free 4d.
FABIAN TRACTS and LEAFLETS.
Tracts, each 16 to 52 pp., price 1d., or 9d. per doz., unless otherwise stated. Leaflets, 4 pp. each, price 1d. for six copies, 1s. per 100, or 8/6 per 1000.
The Set of 77, 3/6; post free 3/11. Bound in buckram, 5/-n.; post free 5/6.

I.—General Socialism in its various aspects.
TRACTS.—169. The Socialist Movement in Germany. By W.S.SANDERS. 2d. 159. The Necessary Basis of Society. By SIDNEY WEBB. 151. The Point of Honour. By RUTH C. BENTINCK. 147. Capital and Compensation. By E. R. PEASE. 146. Socialism and Superior Brains. By BERNARD SHAW. 142. Rent and Value. 138. Municipal Trading. 121. Public Service v. Private Expenditure. By Sir OLIVER LODGE. 107. Socialism for Millionaires. By BERNARD SHAW. 139. Socialism and the Churches. By Rev. JOHN CLIFFORD, D.D. 133. Socialism and Christianity. By Rev. PERCY DEARMER. 78. Socialism and the Teaching of Christ. By Dr. J. CLIFFORD. 42. Christian Socialism. By Rev. S. D. HEADLAM. 79. A Word of Remembrance and Caution to the Rich. By JOHN WOOLMAN. 72. The Moral Aspects of Socialism. By SIDNEY BALL. 69. Difficulties of Individualism. By S. WEBB. 51. Socialism: True and False. By S. WEBB. 45. The Impossibilities of Anarchism. By BERNARD SHAW (price 2d.). 7. Capital and Land. 5. Facts for Socialists. 132. A Guide to Books for Socialists. LEAFLETS—13. What Socialism Is. 1. Why are the Many Poor? WELSH TRACTS—143. Sosialaeth yng Ngoleuni'r Beibl. 141. Translation of 139. 87. Translation of 78. 38. Translation of 1.

II.—Applications of Socialism to Particular Problems.
TRACTS.—177. Socialism and the Arts of Use. By A. CLUTTON BROCK. 175. The Economic Foundations of the Women's Movement. 2d. 173. Public versus Private Electricity Supply. By A. C. BAKER. 171. The Nationalization of Mines and Minerals Bill. By H. H. SLESSER. 170. Profit-Sharing & Co-Partnership: a Fraud and Failure? By E. R. PEASE. In cover. 164. Gold and State Banking. By E. R. PEASE. 163. Women and Prisons. By HELEN BLAGG and CHARLOTTE WILSON. 2d. 162. Family Life on a Pound a Week. By Mrs. REEVES. In cover, 2d. 161. Afforestation and Unemployment. By A. P. GRENFELL. 160. A National Medical Service. By F. LAWSON DODD. 2d. 157. The Working Life of Women. By Miss B. L. HUTCHINS. 155. The Case against the Referendum. By CLIFFORD SHARP. 154. The Case for School Clinics. By L. HADEN GUEST. 153. The Twentieth Century Reform Bill. By H. H. SLESSER. 152. Our Taxes as they are and as they ought to be. By R. JONES. 2d. 150. State Purchase of Railways. By EMIL DAVIES. 2d. 149. The Endowment of Motherhood. By H. D. HARBEN. 2d. 131. The Decline of the Birth-Rate. By SIDNEY WEBB. 145. The Case for School Nurseries. By Mrs. TOWNSHEND. 140. Child Labor under Capitalism. By Mrs. H. DALE. 136. The Village and the Landlord. By EDW. CARPENTER. 144. Machinery: its Masters and Servants. By H. H. SLESSER and C. GAME. 128. The Case for a Legal Minimum Wage. 122. Municipal Milk and Public Health. By Dr. F. LAWSON DODD. 125. Municipalization by Provinces. 124. State Control of Trusts. 83. State Arbitration and the Living Wage. LEAFLET.—104. How Trade Unions benefit Workmen.

III.—Local Government Powers: How to use them.
TRACTS.—176. The War and the Workers: Handbook of Measures to Prevent Unemployment and Relieve Distress. By SIDNEY WEBB. 172. What about the Rates? By S. WEBB. 156. What an Education Committee can do (Elementary Schools), 3d. 62. Parish and District Councils. (Revised 1913). 137. Parish Councils and Village Life. 109. Cottage Plans and Common Sense. 76. Houses for the People. 82. Workmen's Compensation Act. LEAFLETS.—134. Small Holdings. 68. The Tenant's Sanitary Catechism. 71. Ditto for London.

IV.—General Politics and Fabian Policy.
TRACTS.—158. The Case against the C.O.S. By Mrs. TOWNSHEND. 108. Twentieth Century Politics. By S. WEBB. 70. Report on Fabian Policy.

JOHN RUSKIN AND SOCIAL ETHICS - - -

By EDITH J. MORLEY.

Biographical Series No. 6.

—

Published and sold by the Fabian Society, at the Fabian Bookshop, 25 Tothill Street, Westminster; & by George Allen & Unwin, Ltd., 40 Museum St., London, W.C. ~ Price 2d.

JOHN RUSKIN AND SOCIAL ETHICS.

(1819—1900.)

Introductory.

R USKIN not only denied that he was a Socialist : he asserted that the Socialistic ideal of human equality was unattainable and undesirable. He even wrote of "liberty and equality," that he detested the one, and denied the possibility of the other ("Time and Tide," chap. xxii, § 141). He proclaimed himself a "violent Tory of the old school," and an "Illiberal," and it is certain that, for a clear exposition of Socialistic doctrine, we must look elsewhere than in the volumes of Ruskin.* Moreover, economists tell us that many of his theories are unsound. and that his attempts to work them out in detail are as unpractical as the ill-starred Guild of St. George.

It is probably true that any movement to remodel society precisely on the lines he laid down would be foredoomed to failure. It is at least equally true that to ignore his teaching becomes every day more impossible and disastrous. For Ruskin, who is accepted neither by Socialist nor by practical political economist, nevertheless strikes at the very root-disease of modern "civilisation" when he condemns commercialism and the struggle for mere material possessions, showing that life is the only true wealth, and that the richest man is he whose existence is the most useful, many-sided and helpful.

Ruskin himself says "that in a science dealing with so subtle elements as those of human nature, it is only possible to answer for the final truth of principles, not for the direct success of plans ; and that in the best of these last, what can be immediately accomplished is always questionable, and what can be finally accomplished inconceivable." ("Unto this Last," Preface). Though we may frequently refuse to accept the special application of Ruskin's principles ; though in a good many instances we are forced to regret that those applications were ever made, yet concerning the principles themselves there can be but one opinion. They may be summed up in his own statement that "Life without Industry is Guilt; Industry without Art is Brutality" ("Lectures on Art," III).

Whatever the particular phase of human activity which he might be considering, Ruskin revealed its relation to the ultimate truth and meaning of life. He showed, and in no narrow didactic spirit, the necessary connection between art and ethics; he traced the links between morals and sociology, and pointed out that scientific economics

* See, on the other hand, Collingwood's "Life of Ruskin," Book III, chap. iv. "For when, long after 'Fors' had been written, Ruskin found other writers advocating the same principles and calling themselves Socialists, he said that he too was a Socialist" (and *ante*, p. 242. 1/- edition).

are inevitably bound up with the reform of the individual. Above all, he proved incontrovertibly that increased prosperity, whether national or individual, industrial or social, must go hand in hand with increased capacity and with a desire for a prosperity and advance which are above and beyond all these. "It is open, I repeat, to serious question . . . . whether, among national manufactures, that of Souls of a good quality may not at last turn out a quite leadingly lucrative one." In all the many forms of teaching which he undertook, this manufacture of souls, this awakening of the spiritual in the material, was John Ruskin's chief end and aim. In art and in economics he applied the same touchstone, for it was his distinction to see life always as a whole and to refuse to divide it into the water-tight compartments beloved of specialists.

Childhood and Early Life.

Ruskin was of opinion that the study of a man's work should begin with an attempt to become familiar with his life and character, more especially as these were shaped and developed in his childhood. Thus, in his autobiography, "Præterita," he dwells in great and loving detail on his early life and upbringing, but discontinues the story soon after the completion of "Stones of Venice," and before the beginning of his campaign of social reform. A similar disproportion may, therefore, be excused in a tract which essays only to give a brief account of his aims in that campaign. But these cannot justly be appraised unless we understand something of the man who devoted the best of himself to their achievement, and realise something of his passionate concentration, his intense emotional nature, and of his " unusual moral principle and self-command."

John Ruskin was born, of Scottish parentage, at 54 Hunter Street, Brunswick Square, W.C., on February 8th, 1819. His father was a well-to-do wine-merchant, hard-working, energetic and successful in business, and " entirely honest," as his son later on described him, in words of praise which meant much coming from that source. He was also cultured and intelligent, with a real appreciation of scenery and travel, and a lover of art and literature. His wife, who was some years older than her husband, held a more puritanical view of life, and it was she who took the lead in the early upbringing of their precocious and not very robust little son. Her methods were as stern as they were affectionate and careful ; he was allowed no toys but a cart and a ball and two boxes of well-cut wooden bricks ; he had few or no playmates, and he was taught to rely on himself for amusement and occupation. " I . . . could pass my days contentedly in tracing the squares and comparing the colours of my carpet. . . . The carpet, and what patterns I could find in bed-covers, dresses, or wall-papers to be examined, were my chief resources." It sounds a lonely and self-centred life for a small boy, though doubtless it resulted in the powers of concentration and accurate observation which were to distinguish him later on.

Ruskin, in his own summary of the " blessings " of his childhood, puts first the fact that he had never heard his parents' voices raised in anger, nor seen any disorder in any household matter. Thus, he early learned·" the perfect meaning of Peace, in thought, act, and word." On the other hand, he complains that he had no one to love or assist or thank, and nothing to endure. " My strength was never exercised, my patience never tried, and my· courage never fortified."

In 1823, his parents moved to Herne Hill, and, from this time onwards, his outdoor recollections were of the garden where he played and of the surrounding country in which he delighted. It is tempting to linger over these early days, and to trace in the child the father of the man. Narrow and conventional as was his home in many ways, it was in other respects unusually cultured and intellectual. From his babyhood, long before he was supposed to care to listen, he heard great books read aloud by his parents for their own amusement—the eighteenth-century novelists and Byron, as well as the authors usually considered more suited to the family circle. Above all, his imagination was awakened by the yearly journeys all over Great Britain, and, later, on the Continent, which gave him his first introduction to the beauties of nature. His father "travelled" for his own orders, and wife and child accompanied him on the pilgrimages, which combined pleasure and sight-seeing with business. The happy weeks spent on these driving tours gave Ruskin just the education he needed. Old buildings stirred his interest in the past ; beautiful scenery and, above all, mountains, stimulated the love of nature which, at the age of three and a half, already led him to ask for a background of " blue hills " when his portrait was painted by Northcote. A little later he was enquiring of what the mountains were made, and soon he was poring over minerals, beginning his study of geology, and pulling to pieces every flower he could pluck, until he knew " all that could be seen of it with child's eyes."

Very early in life he learned, after his own fashion, to read and write, and he soon began to imitate his father by keeping a journal, in which every detail of his travels was set down. Thus, naturally, the habit of descriptive writing was acquired. Doubtless, Ruskin was right in supposing that his extraordinary command of rhythm and language was largely due to his mother's training. From the time he could read, until he was fourteen, and about to start on his first continental journey (1833), morning after morning, year by year, they read together two or three chapters of the Bible, completing the whole, from the first verse of Genesis to the last verse of the Apocalypse, only to begin once more at the beginning. Every day, too, the child committed to memory some verses of the Bible and of the Scottish paraphrases, and was compelled to repeat them over and over again until not a syllable was missed or misplaced, not a sentence wrongly accented. To this daily discipline he rightly attributed " the best part of his taste in literature," his appreciation of the music of words, and also his capacity for taking pains.

Pope's Homer, Walter Scott's poems and novels, " Robinson

Crusoe," "Don Quixote" and "Pilgrim's Progress," were his other "text-books" of literature, but these from choice, not compulsion.

Human companions he had few: his Scotch cousins, one of whom became his adopted sister, his cousins at Croydon and a boy friend at Herne Hill, are all that he mentions, and we know that he was not allowed out except under supervision, that he was not sent to school until he was fourteen, and then only to a small private class to which every day he was personally conducted by his father, and where he remained less than two years. There is no doubt that he suffered from this mode of upbringing in so self-contained a household. He was over-fostered and over-cared for, " safe against ridicule in his conceit," his "father and mother in their hearts caring for nobody in the world but me." He developed prematurely in many directions; he wrote too much, both of prose and verse; he exerted his mind more than was wholesome, and he became too self-opinionated.

The first disturbance in his sheltered life came when, somewhere about the age of seventeen, he fell in love with the young daughter of his father's French partner, Mr. Domecq. The passion was not requited, and four years later, in 1840, the girl married Baron Duquesne. The effect of the disappointment on a lad of Ruskin's temperament was great. "Men capable of the highest imaginative passion are always tossed on fiery waves by it," he writes; and again, in referring to the evil consequences of his isolated childhood, "when affection did come, it came with violence utterly rampant and unmanageable, at least by me, who never before had anything to manage." We know that the young man broke down in health and spirit as a result of this unfortunate experience, which darkened several years of his life.

Meanwhile he had been prepared for Oxford at King's College, London, and, in 1836, he matriculated as a gentleman-commoner at Christ Church, going into residence in the following January. Already he had made his appearance as the defender of Turner in *Blackwood's Magazine* (1836), and earlier than this he had seen his verses in print in *Friendship's Offering*. But his regular academic studies were less advanced, and his lack of accurate scholarship was a drawback to him at college, and a hindrance all his life. Yet he did well at Oxford, not only taking the Newdigate Prize for English Verse as he had intended, but winning a reputation as a writer and student, and raising hopes that he would secure a first class. Then at the critical point, when all seemed going well, and in spite of the care of his mother, who had followed him up to Oxford in order to watch over him, the crash came and his health broke down. For two years he was more or less an invalid, threatened with permanent lung trouble. Foreign travel restored his health, but all idea of an honours degree had to be abandoned. In 1841 he went up for the pass examination and did so well that he was granted the highest distinction possible—an honorary double fourth class in honours—always a most unusual, and nowadays an impossible, reward of merit.

Ruskin as Art Critic.

By this time (1841-2) his ill-health, combined with his interest in art, changed his plans for the future, and Ruskin finally abandoned the idea of taking Holy Orders. He settled down to serious art study, and it was in this same year that an attempt to sketch a tree-stem with ivy upon it, forced upon him the consciousness of his vocation. Suddenly he realized that it was his mission to preach the gospel of sincerity in art, "to tell the world," in the words of Mr. Collingwood's " Life," " that Art, no less than other spheres of life, had its Heroes ; that the mainspring of their energy was Sincerity, and the burden of their utterance, Truth."

It was many years before Ruskin passed from the rôle of art-critic to that of social reformer and preacher, and there is no room in the limits of this tract to trace in detail the process of the evolution. But a cursory investigation is enough to show that it was by a natural course of development, and not by any sudden change of idea, that the author of the first volume of " Modern Painters " (1843) became the inspired prophet of " Unto this Last " (1860) and " Munera Pulveris " (1862). Because, not in spite of, his study of art, Ruskin was bound to grow into a student of sociology. The underlying principles of his teaching develop, but fundamentally they remain the same. The foundations of his creed, whether in art, in thought, in morals, or in sociology may be expressed in his own words : "Nothing can be beautiful which is not true." Sincerity is the foundation of all true art ; honesty of purpose in the artist, truth and beauty in the thing portrayed ; and to Ruskin, art, religion and morality are different only in so far as they reveal different aspects of the same thing. Hence " all great art is praise," that is to say, it is the result of the artist's instinctive reverence and delight in the beauty, which it is given him to see more truly and accurately than other men, and which it is his supreme mission to reveal to others. He sees more truly and must make others see too ; he must be faithful to nature, representing with exactitude that which he perceives. But there is a spiritual as well as a physical perception,— the insight which pierces through externals to the essential truth that is beyond, and is the result of intuition, inspiration, enthusiasm and of all that is implied by the word "imagination." To Ruskin, as to other great critics of the nineteenth century, imagination is the interpreter, the power which transforms or transfigures reality, but without destroying the basis of ordinary perception. It does not change facts, but, by rendering them imaginatively, it forces them to yield something beyond themselves. It is this "putting the infinite within the finite" that differentiates art from "imitation," which can be only of the material.

Essential truth is, then, for ever inconsistent with imitation. "Ideas of truth are the foundation, and ideas of imitation the destruction of all art "; for, in the words of Goethe, "The *spirit* of the real is the true ideal." This being so, it is not difficult to understand how Ruskin came to connect morality with art: he shows us the links between the two when he writes that art is an inspiration, "not a teachable or gainable thing, but the expression of the mind of a God-made great man"; and again, from a somewhat different angle, art "declares the perfectness and eternal beauty of the work of God, and tests all work of men by concurrence with or subjection to that." Art unites the real, the ideal, the moral and spiritual, and by this union it is serviceable to man. "All art which involves no reference to man is inferior or nugatory. And all art which involves misconception of man, or base thought of him, is in that degree false and base." In other words, art must be brought to the test of life, and is worthy, as all other work is worthy, when it is of use, though the kind of usefulness is of course quite different from that of the things which, as Ruskin says disdainfully, "only help us to exist." It is by presenting noble ideas nobly that art fulfils its function of service.

By criticism on these lines he justly claims that the distinctive character of his "essays on art is their bringing everything to a root in human passion and human hope." He holds that art exists for the service of man, and is greatest when its service is greatest; without this motive no true art can come into being.

A study of "Modern Painters," shows that Ruskin was early led to the belief that the nature of the work of art depends primarily on the character of the artist. Later, he came to the conviction that a nation's art is the expression of its life and character, the individual artist being moulded by his surroundings and by the age in which he lives, so that, if these be unclean, the resulting art will be, like Renaissance architecture, decadent and unpure. Thus, he writes in "On the Old Road" (§ 276) : "Let a nation be healthy, happy, pure in its enjoyments, brave in its acts and broad in its affections, and its art will spring round and within it as freely as the foam from a fountain ; but let the springs of its life be impure and its course polluted, and you will not get the bright spray by treatises on the mathematical structure of bubbles." And again, in "Lectures on Art" (§ 27) : "The art of any country *is the exponent of its social and political virtues.* . . . The art or general productive and formative energy of any country is an exact exponent of its ethical life." From this position there was no very startling transition to the famous chapter "On the Nature of Gothic" in "Stones of Venice" (1851-3), which contains in embryo all his later sociological and economic teaching. From teaching art and from the promotion of culture, both ethical and intellectual, Ruskin passed to the final phase of his life-work, and that which he considered by far the most vital.

Ruskin's Later Life and Work as Practical Reformer.

In the years which had elapsed since his graduation as M.A., and his subsequent settlement with his parents at Denmark Hill in 1843, Ruskin had succeeded, in spite of violent opposition, in establishing himself as the leading critic and exponent of painting and architecture.

A series of provocative and brilliant volumes* had gained him this
position ; his defence of the Pre-Raphaelites had won for him the
affection of Rossetti (whom he helped in a characteristically quixotic
fashion), Millais, and their circle, while of the older men, Turner,
Carlyle, and Browning were among his friends. Lastly, he had
secured devoted adherents among his pupils and fellow-teachers at
the Working Men's College ; while his own old College had recognized
his achievements by the award of an honorary studentship of Christ
Church in 1858. Thus, though his marriage had been brief and
unhappy (1848-1854), and his private disappointments many ; though
his violent assertion of his opinions had aroused enmity and detrac-
tion, it nevertheless seemed by this time that he had outlived the
period of storm and stress, and might look forward to a future of
happy and successful work as an art-critic. But from 1860 onwards,
that is, from the time when the last volume of " Modern Painters "
was published, he no longer made art his main theme. Art he
believed to be the outcome of a true and elevated national life, and
he had been forced to realise that English national life was neither
pure nor elevated. Social evils went too deep for philanthropic
tinkering, and he therefore set himself to plan a complete scheme
for social reorganisation. This scheme, unfortunately never systematically developed, has as its leading feature the banishment of
utilitarianism and materialism, for which it substitutes the beauty
which is also justice and truth. It insists that there is no necessary
antagonism between industry and art ; that, on the contrary,
both are indispensable elements of the social organism, though
they can be combined in various ways in order to fulfil various
functions. But unless work is beautiful, it is not true work, and
unless the life, even of the humblest worker, is beautiful, it is not a
true life.

It is difficult to speak quite dispassionately and temperately
about this last development of Ruskin's teaching ; difficult, too, to
realise what was entailed by his change of plan. For years, he had
struggled single-handed, against enormous odds, in his endeavour to
revivify English thought about art, and to overcome its insincerity
and conventionality. Now, when any success he could desire seemed
within his grasp, he came to realise that his most important work
was still before him, and the battle still to wage. Never for a
moment did he flinch or hesitate. He allowed his books on art to
run out of print, that attention might be concentrated on the new
message he had to deliver ; while he withdrew into the solitude of
the seer and prophet, upon whom are laid the burden and the consciousness of a great mission. " The loneliness is very great," he
cried ; " I am . . . tormented between the longing for rest and
lovely life, and the sense of this terrific call of human crime for
resistance and of human misery for help, though it seems to me as

* Of these, the chief are : " Modern Painters," five vols., 1843-1860 ; " Seven
Lamps of Architecture," 1848-9 ; " Notes on the Construction of Sheepfolds," 1851 ;
" Stones of Venice," 1851-3 ; " Lectures on Architecture and Painting," 1853-4 ;
" The Political Economy of Art," 1857 ; " The Two Paths," 1859.

the voice of a river of blood which can but sweep me down in the midst of its black clots, helpless."

It is not necessary to dwell in much detail on the outward circumstances of the remaining years of Ruskin's life. His father, who had loyally endeavoured to understand his vagaries in art, was bitterly distressed by his heresy in economics, while his mother was wholly out of sympathy with his falling away from religious orthodoxy. At home, as abroad, he had to submit to misunderstanding.

From his parents, Ruskin inherited £157,000 in money, as well as houses and land. The whole of this property he expended during his life-time upon the promotion of reforms in which he was interested, while he lived for many years solely upon the proceeds of his books. Much of his money went to the foundation of the St. George's Guild, which was intended to prove the possibility of uncommercial prosperity in a society contented to get its "food . . . out of the ground and happiness out of honesty." (See " Fors," Letter LVIII, for the creed of the Guild). What it did prove was Ruskin's lack of success in the management of men and of detailed and complicated business affairs. .

Again, he gave liberally to many individuals, educating promising young artists, or subsidising craftsmen and their crafts ; he founded and arranged a model museum at Sheffield ; gave pictures to the Universities of Oxford and Cambridge ; established a drawing-school at Oxford ; and bestowed collections of drawings and of minerals on museums, colleges, and schools.

His belief that all children should be taught to draw, as a means of training eye and hand and mind ; his pioneer work in founding the Art for Schools Association ; and his sympathy with the education of women, are other instances of his practical wisdom. Similarly, his suggested reforms in education, which are founded on the assumption that every child has the right to be properly housed, clothed, fed, trained, and taught until it reaches years of discretion, are for the most part now generally accepted, at any rate in theory. Ruskin was, for example, the pioneer of technical education in England ; and even his road-making experiment with the Oxford undergraduates, which brought him so much ridicule, was the result of a sound educational ideal.

Ruskin also spent much time and money on sociological innovations, which have since been generally approved and imitated. For instance, he gave Miss Octavia Hill the means to manage house-property by a system of helping the tenants to help themselves. In pursuit of this aim he himself became a slum-landlord. Moreover, he never ceased his demand for the provision of decent accommodation for the working classes, though his agitation for housing reform made him many enemies. Another of his enterprises was the establishment of a model tea-shop ; yet another, a scheme for the organised relief of unemployment and for the training of the unemployable.

Indeed, it is scarcely an exaggeration to say that almost every modern measure of social improvement may, either directly or indirectly, trace its origin to the precepts and example of John Ruskin.* Thus, nothing can be more fallacious than to regard him as merely capricious and fanciful in matters of practice, or to forget his proposals for definite schemes of social regeneration, because he blinds us with the lightning of his zeal, or deafens us with his moral fulminations.

"He was like the living conscience of the modern world," says Sir E. T. Cook, his editor; and his health, never robust, was eventually undermined by the strain of his exertions and disappointments. The last twenty-five years of his life were clouded by frequently recurring attacks of illness, which sapped his powers and added to the misery of private grief and mental overstrain. The first grave collapse occurred in 1878, and soon afterwards he resigned his Oxford professorship (1870-1879) and retired to the peace of Brantwood on Lake Coniston. The retirement was not absolute : he wrote much and gave many lectures during the ensuing ten years, and from 1883-1884 he was even well enough to return to Oxford ; while as late as 1888 he went once more abroad—his farewell journey to France and Switzerland and Italy. But from that date onwards until the end he was in a state of mental decay, when "his best hours were hours of feebleness and depression." Death released him on January 22nd, 1900, and he lies buried, as he wished, in Coniston churchyard.

When, in 1860, Ruskin ceased to devote himself to pure art, and turned instead to the problems of sociology, when he abandoned the search for abstract beauty, in order that a little more beauty might be brought into unlovely human lives, then by that sacrifice of inclination and of popularity he enrolled himself among the lonely thinkers whose message is not accepted by their own generation, and whose lot in this world is aching disappointment. Ruskin had tasted the joys of popularity and friendship ; he had known the smoothness of a life of wealth and ease ; above all, he possessed the artistic and poetic gifts which made the strife of the arena particularly hateful to him, and rendered him peculiarly sensitive to harsh criticism. These facts give the measure of his sacrifice and of his faith. They explain, too, the emotional strength of his social criticism, and of his demand for social regeneration. It was no Utopian dreamer, no armchair-philosopher, who proclaimed insistently the old truth that whosoever will save his life shall lose it. This man had made the supreme offering, and he spoke from the certainty of his experience.

The Meaning of "Wealth."

The warmth of Ruskin's pleading misled the so-called practical men of his generation, who accused him of unlawfully confusing sentiment with business. But passionate earnestness is not necess-

* "National Education, National Hygiene, National Dealing with the Housing of the Poor, even National Succour for those who fall by the way in the toilsome march of the Army of Labour, National Dealing with Land, National Dealing with Trade, with Colonisation, with all the real National Interests—all these measures, so long denounced without distinction by the old sham political economy of the past, he advocated, and now they are within or at our doors,"—YORK POWELL,

arily fanaticism, nor does burning hatred of wrong inevitably lead to distortion or even exaggeration of fact. To apply everywhere and always the test of humanity and of life, rather than the test of money-gain, may, even from the commercial standpoint, in the long-run be the most profitable course. Certainly, if Ruskin's standard be the right one, if "the essence of wealth is in its power over man, and the grandeur of wealth is to make men better and happier," then it may reasonably be accepted "that the final outcome and consummation of all wealth is in the producing as many as possible full-breathed, bright-eyed and happy-hearted human creatures." The most hard-headed business man cannot, at any rate, controvert the next statement: "Our modern wealth, I think, has rather a tendency the other way; most political economists appearing to consider multitudes of human creatures not conducive to wealth, or at least conducive to it only by remaining in a dim-eyed and narrow-chested state of being."

It is not easy to formulate a systematic body of sociological teaching from Ruskin's writings, for he never arranged his doctrines with scientific clearness and logical consistency. Yet the underlying principles are, as we have seen, laid down with perfect simplicity. His political economy is founded on the conviction that "there is no wealth but life—life including all its powers of love, of joy and of admiration. That country is the richest which nourishes the greatest number of noble and happy human beings." Those who deal with the science of mere getting and spending, who conceive of "wealth" as mere material possession, have no just claim to be called political economists. At best, they are interested only in a science of avarice, a mercantile economy, which ignores human welfare and has no right to arrogate to itself the title "political," i.e., belonging to the citizens who form the State. At worst, their teaching is wrong, even in so far as it deals with buying and selling, since it deliberately starts from the false premise that men are moved, permanently and essentially, by nothing but their desire for material gain.

Now Ruskin interprets life always in terms of humanity, and is consequently impervious to arguments which postulate an "economic man," "a covetous machine," in whom "the social affections are accidental and disturbing elements." On the contrary, he proclaims, in the words of Wordsworth, that "We live by admiration, hope and love," and that it is for ever unsound and unscientific to ignore these permanent attributes of human nature. The individual cannot separate his work from his human feelings on the one hand, or from his physical capacities and desires on the other. What is true of the individual is true also of society, which is made up of individuals, and cannot, therefore, satisfactorily be regarded as an abstract theoretical entity. Any competition or money-grabbing that injures the individual, at the same time reacts against the State and is opposed to civic and social welfare.

Again, things which cannot be bought and sold in the market-place—e.g., love, friendship, self-sacrifice, capacity, truth—do nevertheless, and must inevitably, have a very real influence even on supply and demand. Ruskin shows for instance, in an unforgettable paragraph in the first chapter of "Unto this Last," that "all right relations between master and operative and all their best interests ultimately depend" on the "balances of justice, meaning in the term justice to include affection—such affection as one man *owes* another." Since a workman is not a machine who is moved by steam "or any other agent of calculable force," but "an engine whose motive power is a Soul," it is obviously impossible to deal with him as if the so-called economic man were separable from the emotional man. Even from the lowest point of view, the greatest material result of his work will be obtained if he serves his master gladly, i.e., if his "soul" enters into his work. To treat him as a machine, as something less than a man, is to lower the economic worth of his work, which is best done when, valued and valuable for its own sake, a blessing and not a curse, it calls into activity all the noblest human energies and emotions. (This argument does not apply to purely mechanical operations. But these, Ruskin would, precisely on this ground, reduce to a minimum, as tending to the destruction of the real wealth, which is life and has no relation to market-value.) It must be admitted that, if this be sentiment, it is sentiment of a very practical, reasonable kind. Similarly, it is illogical and misleading to make a science of industrial wealth and to ignore "real wealth," i.e., human welfare in the widest and deepest interpretation. Thus the statement that "There is no wealth but life" is again a literal statement of fact, a common-sense doctrine which is intended for the plain business-man and not for the idealist. Wealth, according to Ruskin, does not depend on market-value ; the worth of any object cannot be determined by the price that may be obtained for it; and on the other hand, as we have seen, many inestimably valuable things can neither be bought nor sold. "A thing is worth precisely what it can do for you, not what you choose to pay for it. . . . The thing is worth what it *can* do for you, not what you think it can." ("Queen of the Air," § 125.) Thus a miser, with hoards of money and jewels, is not really wealthy in any accurate sense of the term. His store benefits no one, himself least of all. Again, there is all the difference in the world between the value of a field of corn, and of a factory full of costly and death-dealing implements of war, or between a cheap edition of Shakespeare's works and an edition de luxe of the latest fashionable small poet : the corn is worth its weight in gold, Shakespeare's plays are priceless wealth—and the other things are not really valuable at all. For "there is no wealth but life" ; wealth-giving things are those which "avail towards life." Whether we do or do not desire them, whether there is "demand" for them, does not affect their worth. A picture by Whistler is no more valuable now, when it fetches thousands in the auction-room, than when it first left the unknown artist's brush to be reviled by Ruskin. The worth, as distinct from the exchange-value, is not to be estimated by passing whims on the subject, nor by the price paid, but by the intrinsic power to be of service if rightly used. So that the wealthy man is he who possesses useful things and also the power and capacity to use them: wealth is the "possession of the valuable by the valiant": "usefulness is value in the hands of the valiant" (or availing). Things which are desired for base purposes and which pander only to the lower nature, are "illth," not wealth, "causing devastation and trouble around them in all direction," having no *use* at all, since they avail not for life, but for death. Wealth promotes life and all the life-giving, wholesome desires which are natural to healthy men and women. "Perhaps it may even appear after some consideration that the persons themselves *are* the wealth."

The above argument of Ruskin is open to certain objections which have tended to obscure the essential truth of his contention. In the first place, as he says himself, though he does not always remember it, the potentiality for good, i.e., the "value" of anything depends invariably on the owner's capacity to use it. Certain things have no life-giving power, except under certain conditions of culture. For instance, the beads given to savages by travellers are, both actually and potentially, valueless; but Shakespeare's plays or Whistler's pictures would not give so much pleasure or produce equal effect. The *actual* worth does not vary, but the *effective* worth does. To that extent it is untrue that "evil and good are fixed . . . inherent, not dependent on opinion or choice." ("Modern Painters," § 33.) Ruskin states the case better when he writes that "a horse is no wealth to us if we cannot ride, nor a picture if we cannot see, nor can any noble thing be wealth, except to a noble person" ("Modern Painters," § 14, and *cf.* "Munera Pulveris," § 35.) Secondly, though Ruskin ignores the fact, even the potential value of things varies in inverse ratio to their quantity. Thus, in spite of its intrinsic, life-giving quality, corn becomes potentially useless if there is a glut of it, and already more bread available than can be consumed.

Even more misleading, though this is not altogether the fault of Ruskin, is the fact that, as we have seen, he refuses to use the term "value" in any current economic sense. Thus he implies by it, neither market-value, nor worth to an individual, but, almost invariably, "life-giving quality." Now the ordinary science of political economy is concerned very little with "wealth" as measured by any life-giving properties. It deals simply with demand and supply, that is, with what men actually want at any given moment, and the means of satisfying their desires. Ruskin, on the contrary, insists that every demand for commodities is, of necessity, a demand for life or for death—a demand, that is, for things both in themselves and in the nature of their production, either good or evil, promoting human welfare or human misery. Thus it makes a very real difference whether money is exchanged for shoddy cloth or for hand-woven material; for penny-dreadfuls or for the romances of Scott.

The Meaning of "Political Economy."

Thus, Ruskin substitutes a human life-standard for a money-standard. Political economy, since it has to do with living men and women, must treat them as such, and not as money-producing and money-spending and calculating machines. Here, as everywhere else, he bases his deductions on an ethical foundation—refusing to discuss theories which leave out of sight the fundamental factors of right human nature. What *is*, cannot be made a satisfactory starting-point for the determination of what ought to be : men do not always want what is best and most desirable, but a true scientific political economy must raise them up to worthy desires, not pander to their most degraded instincts and the brute desire to over-reach one another. It must, therefore, insist that " In true commerce, as in true preaching or true fighting, it is necessary to admit the idea of occasional loss . . . sixpences have to be lost as well as lives, under a sense of duty ; . . . the market may have its martyrdoms as well as the pulpit, and trade its heroisms as well as war." The merchant's business is to provide for life, and if necessary, like the members of the other great intellectual professions, to *die* for it ; his function is to provide for the nation, not merely to get profit for himself. " This stipend is a due and necessary adjunct, but not the object of his life," if he be a true merchant. That object is, to produce the best commodity at the lowest possible price compatible with making himself responsible for the kind of life led by the numerous agents who necessarily work under his direction. For cheapness must not be obtained at the fatal cost of human lives or human character : the work required must be beneficial to the worker as to the consumer. In any commercial crisis, the merchant, like the captain of a ship, is bound to share the suffering with his men. Thus must he prove that he cares most for the state or commonwealth, and that he understands the real meaning of political economy, the economy of the " polis," which, if it be true to its name, is a social and not an individual science.

The Cost of Production and of Consumption.

Such being the case, Ruskin is careful to point out that " production does not consist in things laboriously made, but in things serviceably consumable : and the question for the nation is not how much labour it employs, but how much life it produces "—and life includes more than meat ; it includes wisdom, virtue, salvation, the right and opportunity to be " holy, perfect, and pure." " The presence of a wise population implies the search for felicity as well as for food." Hence the authoritative command : " In all buying, consider, first, what condition of existence you cause in the producers of what you buy ; secondly, whether the sum you have paid is just to the producer, and in due proportion, lodged in his hands ; thirdly, to how much clear use, for food, knowledge, or joy, this that you have bought can be put ; and fourthly, to whom and in what way it can be most speedily and serviceably distributed."

If production consists in things serviceably consumable—tending to obtain and employ means of life—then, naturally, the use of the things produced is at least as important as their actual production. This leads Ruskin to a statement which is startlingly unlike that of most political economists, viz., that "consumption is a far more difficult art than wise production. Twenty people can gain money for one who can use it ; and the vital question, for individual and for nation, is never 'how much do they make ? but to what purpose do they spend ?'" What has been done with the potential wealth that has been produced ? If it has been hoarded up, not used, it has been wasted, and has never really become wealth at all. "The true home-question to every capitalist and to every nation is not, 'How many ploughs have you ?' but 'Where are your furrows ?'" Thus, "to use everything and to use it nobly" is the final object of political economy. "The essential work of the political economist is to determine what are in reality useful or life-giving things, and by what degrees and kinds of labour they are attainable and distributable." Wealth can be estimated only by discovering the remaining amount of utility and enjoyment—the life-giving properties—after the cost of production has been deducted. "Cost" is "the quantity of labour required" for production, and in so far as this implies loss of life to the worker, the worth of the work is diminished. When the cost includes the physical or spiritual degradation of the worker, then it can never be worth while to produce such goods, for no function of use or enjoyment which they fulfil suffices as a set-off to the harm committed in their manufacture. To produce such goods can never be "profitable." "Labour is the *suffering* in effort. . . . It is that quantity of our toil which we die in."

If, in such production, suffering outweighs the desirableness of the thing produced, then such labour is death-bringing—and " there is no wealth but life." It is wholly and eternally different from work and effort, the application of power (opera) ; that, in its noblest form, whether in physical action or mental, intellectual striving, is pleasurable and recreative. "It does not matter how much *work* a thing needs to produce it ; it matters only how much distress. Generally, the more the power it requires, the less the distress ; so that the noblest works of man cost less than the meanest." Thus interpreted, work, as distinct from labour and suffering, is salutary and beneficial to the worker. Ruskin realises the impossibility of doing away with all unpleasurable labour, but at the same time he points out that its amount may be decreased in various ways.

The Mechanisation and Division of Labour.

For instance, he shows that in manufacture the interest is diminished and the monotony, i.e., suffering, increased, when the worker continually carries out the same process without seeing any visible result of his labour. It is true that division of labour lowers the money-cost of many manufactured articles, but it is often soul-destroying to the producer. Less wages are obtained by the tailor who spends his life in stitching button-holes, than by the skilled workman who is capable of making the whole garment or any part of it. But to counterbalance the reduction of wages, it is necessary to remember the lowered standard of workmanship, and also the lessening of power, efficiency, and well-being of the workman. It does not really "pay," even in the lowest sense, to degrade human skill and taste, and to decrease healthy interest in the work done. This fact, almost unrealised either by economists or employers when Ruskin first stated it, led him to condemn both machine-made goods and also that over-specialisation which is the tendency of modern life. Just as the artist's personal touch differentiates a picture from the best photograph ever taken, so, in lower kinds of creative work, the maker's individuality must be expressed if the thing made is to be, in the best sense, valuable. There is an eloquent passage in one of Ruskin's books, in which he explains that no two specimens of great Venetian glass ever were, or could be, exactly similar, though modern Venetians turn out vase after vase exactly to pattern. The moral he deduces is universally applicable—namely, that the human standard alone is the true test of efficiency. Machine-made things are inferior in quality, whatever the ease with which they can be produced; purely mechanical labour is inferior, though the wages required to command it be never so low.

Hence, Ruskin's reintroduction of hand-loom weaving and handicrafts of every kind; hence, too, his tirades against steam power and steam engines. He hated them, because they necessitate all sorts of degrading labour in mines and in factories, and because, at the same time, they destroy the beauties of nature. For he believed "that a nation is only worthy of the soil and the scenes that it has inherited, when by all its acts and arts it is making them more lovely for its children."* Moreover, since beautiful work can be produced only by people who have beautiful things about them, if the workers are surrounded by chimney-pots and smoke, their ears deafened by steam whistles, and their hearts saddened by a grey and dismal life of toil, they will create nothing which contains even the elements of beauty.†

In spite of the common belief, Ruskin did not wish indiscriminately to destroy all railways and all factories, and very often his complaints against them were eminently reasonable and right, as when he objected to spoiling beautiful Swiss valleys by running trains through them for excursionists who were too lazy or too hurried to enjoy them wisely. He would have allowed railways only where their presence tended definitely to broaden men's minds and to facilitate the production of ideas; he would have subordinated them everywhere and always to the real "wealth" and "utility," which no money advantages can outweigh. Here, as everywhere, he applied the human instead of the commercial standard. This does not imply that he never exaggerated his complaints or went wrong in his condemnations. Much of what he said, for example, of hand-

---

* Cf. "Lectures on Art," § 123 : "Find places elsewhere than in England, or at least in otherwise unserviceable parts of England, for the establishment of manufactories needing the help of fire . . . reduce such manufactures to their lowest limit." And see "The Two Paths," §§ 89, 90.

† Love of beauty "is an essential part of all healthy human nature and . . . . is itself wholly good—the direct adversary of envy, avarice, mean worldly care, and especially of cruelty."—" Lectures on Art," III ; and see infra §§ 25, 26.

weaving, was the result of imperfect knowledge. No life could well be more brutalising than that of an eighteenth century loom-worker; and in the same way, the lot of an agricultural labourer was not, from any point of view, more attractive in the days when the whole of his labour had to be accomplished by hand. But mistakes of this kind do not in reality detract from the truth of Ruskin's main contention, that the mechanisation of labour and of life is an evil which needs remedy, in so far as it destroys individuality and wholesome enjoyment in men's work and in their surroundings. As long as human skill and understanding are necessary in order to guide the machine, as long as man is its master, not its servant, so long may its use be justifiable. As soon as it is possible to put in raw material at one end to come out manufactured goods at the other, without any further attention than that which is purely a matter of routine, such as stoking or turning a handle, the workman deteriorates and the kind of labour is harmful. It cannot be right, for it is degrading to press a button and let the machine do the rest.* The tests of wise work are, that "it must be honest, useful, and cheerful": work that ruins the worker can be none of these things. To be occupied solely with mechanical work is necessarily and inevitably to lose in individuality and in humanity—to sacrifice soul, the development of which is the most "leadingly lucrative" of national manufactures. When such labour is unavoidable, the hours of toil should be correspondingly short, in order that the workers may have ample time for recreation and for the development of their powers and sympathies.

The Morality of Taste.

Moreover, from another point of view, mechanical work produces mechanical results which, as Ruskin has shown in much detail and in various places, are almost, if not quite, as bad for the consumer as for the producer, since they destroy taste. This brings us to one of Ruskin's most startling assertions, which is also one of the most vital elements in his teaching. He insists upon the *morality* of taste. "Good taste is essentially a moral quality . . . not only a part and an index of morality; it is the *only* morality. . . . Tell me what you like and I'll tell you what you are" ("Crown of Wild Olive," § 54); and again, "Good taste is the instantaneous preference of the noble thing to the ignoble." Happily, it may be acquired and developed, and not least by the influence of our surroundings, natural and artificial. But since the converse is equally true, a smoke-begrimed or ugly environment has a far-reaching influence for ill. For,

* *Cf.* "Crown of Wild Olive," § 45: "What! you perhaps think, 'to waste the labour of men is not to kill them.' Is it not? . . . It is the slightest way of killing to stop a man's breath. Nay, the hunger, and the cold, and the whistling bullets— our love-messengers between nation and nation—have brought pleasant messages to many a man before now: orders of sweet release. . . . At the worst, you do but shorten his life, you do not corrupt his life. But if you put him to base labour, if you bind his thoughts, if you blind his eyes, if you blunt his hopes, if you steal his joys, if you stunt his body, and blast his soul, and at last leave him not so much as strength to reap the poor fruit of his degradation, but gather that for yourself, and dismiss him to the grave, when you have done with him . . . . this you think is no waste, and no sin!"

"what we *like*" (or endure) "determines what we *are* and is the sign of what we are ; and to teach taste is inevitably to form character."

If Ruskin was right, it is small wonder that he protested against shoddy and machine-made goods, and against the ugliness of the modern industrial system and its productions. For to be satisfied with quantity instead of quality is a sign and precursor of worse evils which lurk behind. If we suppose, as he contended, that national taste be indeed the expression of national character, severe judgment must be passed not only on the Venetians, but on all nations who are content to exist without art or with inferior art. For they are proved incapable of delight, that is, in the true sense, uneducated, unable to be "glad justly." Yet enjoyment is a right which belongs to all in a well-ordered society,—a right sadly curtailed for most people under present economic conditions, when they are taught neither what to like nor how to like it.

Lack of taste results, too, in the wrong use of labour and the substitution of commercialism and competition for honest work.

Competition and the Problem of Right Payment.

It is not too much to say that for commercial competition of all kinds Ruskin had an utter loathing. Thus his treatment of the wages-problem is unusually enlightened. At the beginning of "Unto this Last," he insists that the question of supply and demand ought not to affect the wages paid in one sort of work more than another. A doctor's fees, quite rightly, do not vary in accordance with the amount of illness at a given time. A cabman is not allowed to ask higher fares because it is raining and his services are much in demand. Nor, in a dry season, is he expected to accept less. All work is worth a certain wage and should, in Ruskin's opinion, be paid at a fixed rate, irrespective of other factors. Bad and good workmen, who are entrusted with the same task, should receive equal pay : in this respect Ruskin is entirely in accord with modern trade-unionism. A bad workman should not be allowed to undercut prices "and either take the place of the good, or force him by his competition to work for an inadequate sum." "The natural and right system respecting all labour is that it should be paid at a fixed rate, but the good workman employed and the bad workman unemployed." We do not choose our doctor because he is cheap—provided, that is, that we have money—but because we think him efficient. The same principle should be applied in choosing a bricklayer or any other worker. No other form of wage-competition is justifiable.

Again, it is infamous that a man's necessities should determine the amount he is paid for his work : he should be paid what it is worth—that amount, neither more nor less, he ought to have. Moreover, to cheapen labour is in every sense bad economy, since it results in bad workmanship and inferior workers. From the lowest point of view, it does not pay to keep men down to a barely living wage ; it is wise policy, even from a selfish standpoint, to let good workmen benefit from the increased goodness of their work.

When Ruskin advanced this theory it was laughed at, like so

much else which he stated almost for the first time. Nowadays practical business men are coming more and more to adopt what their predecessors termed a "sentimental" doctrine, which after all amounts to little more than that it is in the long-run more profitable to pay a higher wage to an efficient, than a lower wage to an inefficient workman. In this instance, as in many others, Ruskin's prophetic insight helps him to the vision of a very practical and far-reaching reform.

In spite of this, Ruskin later, in "Arrows of the Chace," II, 97, makes a claim which might lead to dangerous results. He is far ahead of his time in his demand that salaries shall be determined by a standard of life instead of by competition. He asks for a definitely prescribed, uniform income or wage for each type of worker, that is, as he defines it, "the quantity and kind of food and space of lodging . . . approximately necessary for the healthy life of a labourer in any given manufacture." Doubtless this is a better method of payment than that resulting from blind obedience to "supply and demand," since at least it secures a minimum of comfort to all workers, irrespective of competition. But Ruskin does not appear to recognise that this definitely prescribed, uniform wage might be a maximum as well as a minimum. It is not enough, as he himself implies in "Unto this Last," "Munera Pulveris" and elsewhere, that the workman shall be paid at a fixed wage. He has the right to raise his standard of life as the average product of his community increases in value ; and he, as well as the capitalist-employer, ought to profit by industrial improvements.*

Competitive industry is not merely bad policy in so far as the workers are concerned. Its ill effects are felt in every direction, and perhaps chiefly in that it lays the main stress on "profit" rather than on utility and good workmanship. For it is simply untrue that rivalry promotes excellence of manufacture. On the contrary, it causes that mechanisation of labour which results in the evils to which we have already referred,—the deterioration of the worker and the degradation of work by the production of cheap and nasty goods which are palmed off on the consumer, whenever he can be deceived, as equivalent to something better. Advertisements tell their own tale, and are a sure indication of the dangers of trade competition. Ruskin may overstate his case and ignore everything that can be said in favour of modern commerce. Certainly he makes no reference to the social qualities sometimes developed in the struggle for life— enterprise, industry and self-sacrifice for example, all of which qualify a man for service as well as for the attainment of personal ends. But he is right in recognising the moral and material waste which normally results from the system of fraud upon which trade, to a lamentable extent, depends ; and in anathematising the selfishness of the struggle and the loss of power which result from individualism.

* Compare his own assertion ("Time and Tide," § 8): "It is the merest insolence of selfishness to preach contentment to a labourer who gets thirty shillings a week, while we suppose an active and plotting covetousness to be meritorious in a man who has three thousand a year."

Ruskin's Views about Interest.

He is not equally incontrovertible in his attack on interest, which, in the latter part of his life, he denounces as indefensible. In his earlier writings he is content to condemn usury : in " Fors,'' and especially in Letter xviii, he makes no distinction between this, which is rightly called extortion, and the interest on commercial capital. There is nothing surprising in the fact that Socialists accept his position, since they detest the capitalist system, which allows wealth to accumulate in the hands of the few and to be used for their personal advantage. For Socialists hold that all wealth should be created and expended for the common good, and that the conduct of the community's business for private profit is prejudicial to the body politic. But Ruskin never goes so far as this, though he advocates the increased ownership and control of industry by the State (" Time and Tide," § 81), and its organisation for social service. Consequently, his condemnation of reasonable interest on capital cannot be substantiated. He argues that interest is a forcible taxation or exaction of usury, adding that, since money cannot produce money, there is no sense in the claim that savings ought to be increased by interest. " Abstinence may, indeed, have its reward nevertheless ; but not by increase of what we abstain from, unless there be a law of growth for it unconnected with our abstinence." This is plausible, but unsound reasoning. It is easy enough to see the evil of usury, of profiting by the need of an individual, and losing all charity in the process. But if, as Ruskin rightly maintains, money consists merely of counters symbolising command of commodities and of labour, then the use of capital in production does result in an increase of the product, and investment of money in enterprises needing capital is a social service, for which (so long as there is not enough capital for its unlimited use) the consumer of the product may fairly be charged. So long as society relies, for obtaining capital, on its accumulation by individual owners, there is reason in this charge for its use, which is included in the price of the commodity.

Consequently there is an essential difference, in a capitalistic community, between reasonable interest on capital and the exaction of usury. A labour-basis of exchange and social service, instead of profit, are not feasible ideals until society has been reconstructed on a more satisfactory basis. And of this reconstruction, Ruskin refused to hear. He believed in a capitalistic society, and did not altogether condemn the private control of industry for individual profit ; as a result, his attacks on interest are unreasonably ferocious. Until industry is deliberately organised by the State for the common good, social saving is desirable, and, until borrowed capital is no longer needed for commercial enterprises, interest is both permissible and inevitable.

Society is an Organic Whole.

While Ruskin refused to go the whole way towards the nationalisation of capital and of the means of production, yet the reforms he advocated tended always towards the promotion of economic equality; and he had a real horror of the unlawful accumulation of personal possessions. No one has ever more clearly recognised the fact that society is an organic whole, and that injury to an individual is therefore injury to the State. But he believed that industry could be saved from the slough of commercialism only by reforming individual capitalists and members of the ruling classes. He had a touching faith in the doctrine of *noblesse oblige*, but no hope of any reform that could come from the people and from democratic rule. In this we hold that he was doubly mistaken. However enlightened and virtuous the individual capitalist or manufacturer, it is, in the nature of things, impossible for him to revolutionise commercial conditions. Ruskin himself was forced to defend his own possession of money and acceptance of interest, by pointing out the indubitable fact that an individual can do no good, and probably will do much harm, by tilting, as an isolated Don Quixote, at the windmill of commercialism. Similarly, though Ruskin did not recognise the truth, an individual manufacturer or merchant would simply land himself in the bankruptcy-court, while benefiting nobody, were he, as an individual, to refuse to conform with the conventional conditions of trade. Individual efforts must be supplemented by social co-operation and State action; similarly, the progress of all must come through all, that is, "the State" should be the expression of the whole of society, and not of any one section thereof.

It is strange that Ruskin failed to recognise this fact. He was hindered, as Carlyle had been hindered, by his acute realisation of the natural inequalities of men, both mental and moral. These convinced him that it was the duty of the strong man to govern, and of the ordinary man to reverence and obey his superiors. On the whole, it seemed to him that the existence of a powerful aristocracy was the safest form of government, since all social order must be built on authority. But the aristocracy he upheld was to be "the assured measure of some kind of worth (either strength of hand, or true wisdom of conduct, or imaginative gift)." Position was in no way to be purchasable with money, but to be obtainable only by superior intellect and energy. Hence he was conscious that, if ruin were to be arrested, there must be "repentance of that old aristocracy (hardly to be hoped), or the stern substitution of other aristocracy worthier than it." Yet in the very next sentence comes the startling and short-sighted admission : "Corrupt as it may be, it and its laws together, I would at this moment, if I could, fasten everyone of its institutions down with bands of iron, and trust for all progress and help against its tyranny simply to the patience and strength of private conduct."

Obedience may be, as he held, "an inherent, natural, and eternal inheritance of a large portion of the human race," but there is no duty of obedience to the laws of primogeniture, nor to mere wealth and social advantages. It is true, and no modern Socialist will deny the fact, that men's capacities differ along with their functions, and that equality among millions of individually developing units is as inconceivable as identity. There are, as Ruskin says, "unconquerable differences in the clay of the human creature." But this does not warrant any individual in using his unequal powers as a means of injuring or oppressing those who are inferior to him. Nor ought the State to permit him to use his superior capacity in such a way as to build up either riches or dominion. Moreover, equality of opportunity ought to be secured for each individual, and for this no man has more earnestly pleaded than Ruskin himself, who even stated, in so many words, that "this enormous difference in bodily and mental capacity has been mainly brought about by difference in occupation, and by direct maltreatment." Let every child have his chance, and the right spirit of reverence for superiority will not disappear : rather will it grow and develop in those who have no cause for envy or hatred, but only for the "admiration, hope and love" by which we live.

And, indeed, in "Time and Tide," Ruskin propounds a theory of government by co-operation and fellowship among nations, as among separate peoples, which is conceivable only in a world from which the evils of commercialism and tyranny have disappeared, and in which all men have been protected both from the unnatural inequalities born of oppression and from any misuse of the natural superiorities of others.

The Nationalisation of Land.

Ruskin's opinions about the possession of land are in some respects remarkably modern, and although not identical with the latest Socialist doctrine on this question, they come surprisingly near to the view that land held by occupying owners for agricultural purposes belongs to the category of tools, and is therefore quite properly in individual ownership.

Ruskin is clear that land and water and air, "being the necessary sustenance of men's bodies and souls," must not be bought or sold. Yet he believes, up to a certain point, in the hereditary private possession of land by occupying owners, superintended by State overseers and paying a tax to the State as State tenants—the amount of land thus owned being strictly limited by the capacity to make good use of it. Apparently he has in mind a sort of peasant-proprietorship ; in cases where larger tracts of land are granted in perpetuity to "great old families," "their income must in no wise be derived from the rent of it." Land must never become a source of income to such owners ; its possession is a trust and "should be, on the whole, costly to them . . . made . . . exemplary in perfection of such agriculture as develops the happiest peasant-life." (See e.g. "Time and Tide." Letter XXIII.)

The Organisation of Labour.

Perhaps he is most a pioneer in his demand for the complete organisation of labour and his belief in the right to work and to the best possible training and education for its accomplishment. His system of selecting the suitable worker for a particular job, and of utilising every potential labourer, is complete and satisfactory. All children are to be taught the laws of health, habits of gentleness and justice, and the calling by which they are to live. All those who are out of employment are to be received at once in government-schools or labour-colonies and set to such work as they can do, or trained for such work as they are fit. For the old and destitute, comfort and home are be provided. "A labourer serves his country with his spade, just as a man in the middle ranks of life serves it with sword, pen or lancet. If the service be less, and, therefore, the wages during health less, then the reward when health is broken may be less, but not less honourable; and it ought to be quite as natural and straightforward a matter for a labourer to take his pension from his parish, because he has deserved well of his parish, as for a man in higher rank to take his pension from his country, because he has deserved well of his country." (Preface to "Unto this Last.") The case for old-age pensions has never been more trenchantly stated.

Lastly, he demands either government-workshops or trade guilds which shall set the standard of price and of workmanship for every commodity, "interfering no whit with private enterprise,"* except in so far as their productions are "authoritatively good and exemplary." Ruskin's desire for some such guild system, self-governing in its constitution but vocational and voluntary in its composition, brings him nearer to the aspirations of Guild Socialism than to the achievements of Collectivism, but in any case, and in spite of his denials, his ideal is definitely Socialistic in its trend.

The Results of Ruskin's Economic Teaching.

Omitting, as we must, within the limits of a tract, a more detailed description of Ruskin's actual plans, and ignoring his somewhat perverse attitude on the subject of a fully democratic suffrage, we are now in a position to summarise something of what Ruskin effected by his economic teaching, and to estimate his influence on the nascent Socialist movement of the second half of the nineteenth century.

In the first place, he justifies his claim that "honest production, just distribution, wise consumption" are the reforms that it is most necessary to enforce. For these reforms, radically instituted, would go far towards the establishment of what to-day still beckons to us as a far-off Utopia.

But more important than any particular means that he advocates, is his whole attitude towards social problems, and, indeed, towards life itself. Above all else, he acts as a stimulating power, a disturber of the vulgar modern complacency which he hated, an awakener of ideals, of higher motives and more generous resolves. Everywhere and always he applies the test of humanity; he breaks down the barriers which divide one human activity or instinct from another, and insists on the interrelation of all social and individual

* It is interesting to note that the establishment of such government-workshops, as a means to secure a high standard of workmanship and to prevent or reduce adulteration, is an "original" panacea recently proposed by Mr. Emil Davies, who would, however, also use them as a method of obtaining additional revenue for the State.

interests. The supreme moral and spiritual teacher of his age, he penetrates everywhere to first principles and ultimate truths ; and whether his ostensible subject be art or economics, he attempts to alter men's aim and motive in life, to uproot evil however manifested, and to bring a little nearer "the true felicity of the human race," by showing wherein nobility, wealth, and beauty consist.

Thus, while errors and extravagance are to be found in his teaching, and while he may justly be accused of lack of system in the presentation of his ideas about social reform, yet the abiding impression left by his work is not of these. It is rather a conviction of the breadth and vividness of his sympathies, and of his clear vision of essentials. His belief that no system of economics can be of permanent value, if it fails to develop "souls of a good quality," the insight which enables him to recognise the ultimate connection between economics and morals—these are perhaps his most important contribution to social science. But, greater even than the great lessons which he taught, the man's own nobility of purpose shines forth in all his writings—a beacon-light for future ages.

AUTHORITIES.

THOMAS BARCLAY (arranged by). "The Rights of Labour according to John Ruskin." W. Reeves. 1d.

W. G. COLLINGWOOD. "The Life of Ruskin." Methuen. 1s.

FREDERIC HARRISON. "John Ruskin." English Men of Letters Series. Macmillan. 1s.

J. A. HOBSON. "John Ruskin ; Social Reformer." Nisbet and Co. (This is the standard work on this aspect of Ruskin's teaching. The tract here presented is deeply indebted to it.)

P. GEDDES. "John Ruskin : Economist."

F. YORK POWELL. "John Ruskin."

J. M. ROBERTSON. "Modern Humanists."

The works of Ruskin, which are mainly relevant, are :—

"Stones of Venice." The chapter "On the Nature of Gothic." 1851.

"Unto this Last." 1861.

"Munera Pulveris." 1862.

"The Crown of Wild Olive." 1866.

"Time and Tide." 1867.

"Fors Clavigera." 1871-81.

The standard library edition of Ruskin is that by Cook and Wedderburn. (Thirty-nine vols. 1903-12.) There are various cheaper editions, one at 1s. the volume, which includes all the above-mentioned works, except the last. This is obtainable in The Pocket Ruskin, in four volumes at 1s. 6d. each. The publishers are, in every case, Messrs. Allen & Unwin, Limited.

THE PHILOSOPHY
OF SOCIALISM - -

By A. CLUTTON BROCK

Published and sold by the Fabian Society at
the Fabian Bookshop, 25 Tothill Street, Westminster, S.W.1. . . Published September, 1916;
reprinted' January, 1919. . . Price One Penny.

THE PHILOSOPHY OF SOCIALISM.

What is the Aim of Civilization?

SOCIALISM is the attempt to put a certain theory of human nature into political practice. If it is separated from that theory, it loses all its virtue and its sense of direction. It becomes a mere mechanical expedient, and might easily produce that Servile State about which its opponents are always talking.

My aim in this tract is to state that theory, and to show how Socialism owes its virtue to it and its sense of direction.

We are all agreed that we have attained to a certain amount of civilization, and that we wish to attain to more of it. We are also agreed that civilization has an aim—in that it differs from barbarism, which has no aim—but there are two opposed theories about the aim of civilization, and they may be stated shortly thus : the one theory says that the aim of civilization is to organize the struggle for life ; the other that it is to transcend the struggle for life.

Each theory is based upon a certain view of human nature. The first assumes that human nature is, and always must be, controlled by the struggle for life. Men have been made what they are by that struggle, and it is, necessarily, the only business of their lives. The best they can do is to wage it efficiently ; and the aim, the only possible aim, of civilization is to wage it so.

That phrase, *the struggle for life*, is often misunderstood by those who wish to misunderstand it for their own purposes. It does not mean, necessarily, a struggle between men. It does not mean that life is a substance of which there is not enough to go round, so that one man must always be fighting with another for it. A man struggles for life when he fights with a disease ; and men certainly have discovered that they can carry on the struggle for life better by co-operation than by fighting with each other. When, therefore, this theory says that men are controlled by the struggle for life, it means, not that they must necessarily be always struggling with each other, but that their final aim is to go on living, and that civilization is an organized and co-operative effort to go on living.

Quantity or Quality of Life.

There is one obvious objection to this theory, which seems fatal at first sight, namely, that, as a matter of fact, individual men are often ready to sacrifice their lives for others. But the answer made to that objection is that there is in men, not only an instinct for self-preservation, but also an instinct for race-preservation. It is this instinct for race-preservation which gives us what we call our higher values. We value in men those qualities which make for race-preservation more highly than those which make for self-preservation. But, according to this theory, all our values are ultimately survival values, though we may not know it. Those

emotions which seem to us the noblest are aroused in us by whatever makes for the preservation of the race. There is some power
in us which, unknown to ourselves, always aims at that, and which
imposes illusions upon us so that our instinct of self-preservation
may be subordinate to our instinct of race-preservation. For, without those illusions, the man who has risen superior to self-preservation would care nothing for race-preservation. The good man, as it
seems to us, prefers quality of life to quantity. Without quality life
would be worthless to him. But this quality is all an illusion. He
only gets the sense of quality in life by doing that which secures
quantity of life for others. He holds life cheap for himself so that
he may have the glory of giving that which he holds cheap to
others. And those others, too, can only have the sense of quality in
their own lives if they are ready to sacrifice them so that yet others
may have quantity. Ultimately there is nothing but quantity of life
to be lived for, however much we may disguise the fact to ourselves.

So civilization must be an organization of the struggle for life,
since there is nothing else to be struggled for. This is a universe in
which living consists of the effort to go on living, whether the individual makes that effort for himself or for the community. Civilization would induce him to make it for the community, but only so
that the community, now or in the future, may have that quantity
of life which the individual is trained to despise for himself ; and
civilization will persist and improve only if men are continually
trained to despise that which alone is worth having.

Socialism is for Quality of Life.

The other theory, as I have said, holds that the aim of civilization is to transcend the struggle for life, and it is based upon the
belief that men are not ultimately controlled by the struggle for life,
and that their proper business in life is to escape from the control of
it as completely as possible. It denies that all our values are survival values, or that those emotions which seem to us the noblest
are aroused in us by what makes for the preservation of the
race. A man does not love truth or spend his life in seeking it
because it makes for the preservation of the race, but because it is
truth, and therefore to be loved for its own sake. He does not do
what is right because it makes for the preservation of the race, but
because it is right, and therefore to be done for its own sake. He
does not make beautiful things for the preservation of the race, but
because they are beautiful, and therefore to be made for their own
sake. And his proper business in life is to do all these things for
their own sake, and to live, not that he may go on living, but that
he may do them.

To the question why they should be worth doing for their own
sake, there is no answer, because they are worth doing for their own
sake. They are absolutes, and cannot be expressed in terms of anything else. Man is of such a nature that he desires to do those
things for their own sake, and the universe is of such a nature that
they are worth doing for their own sake. If he asks what is right,

the answer is that which he permanently finds worth doing for its own sake, and not so that he may go on living. For life itself is not an absolute, but merely a condition of action. We must think of life in terms of those things which we do for their own sake, and not of those things in terms of life. And the more we do things for their own sake, the more clearly we shall see what things are to be done for their own sake. If we think that the aim of life is to go on living, we shall not see anything clearly at all.

There is no Safety in Altruism.

This theory is dogmatic, but not more dogmatic than the other ; and its appeal is to experience, whereas the appeal of the other is mainly to facts observed about savages or animals. But my object in this pamphlet is, not so much to defend one theory or to attack the other, as to show which is consistent with Socialism and which is not. Socialism, I believe, is necessarily based upon the theory that the aim of civilization is to transcend the struggle for life ; and, unless it is based upon that theory, it loses its virtue and its sense of direction.

It might be contended that each theory will lead to altruism, and therefore that it does not matter practically which theory you hold. An altruistic organization of society, a Socialistic organization, is the logical result of both. But altruism is an ugly word, and may mean a very ugly thing. If you believe that the proper aim of civilization is to organize the struggle for life, that quantity of life for the race is the highest thing that a community can aim at, then the individual has no rights for you. Not only may he sacrifice himself, but he may also be sacrificed, for the community. Quantity of life is the only absolute ; and everything else, including all our morality, is to be thought of in terms of it. There is nothing to stop you from killing a minority so that a majority may live longer. There is nothing to keep you from attempting to breed a race of over-men, at the expense of all those whom you consider under-men, if you believe that life for the race of over-men will be longer and more secure. All this you may do quite altruistically, in that you do it, not for your own advantage, but for the better preservation of the race. If quantity of life is your final aim, you will have no desire to provide quality of life for the individual, unless you think that quality for him means quantity for the race ; and there is no certainty whatever that you will think this, since quality of life is to you a mere illusion. As for pity and virtues of that kind, they will not be virtues to you at all, if they seem to you to endanger race-preservation. You will think altogether in terms of the race, and not at all in terms of the individual ; and altruism may lead you, if you have the power, into a tyranny which will be utterly ruthless because you think it scientific.

The Sanctity of the Individual.

But the theory that the aim of civilization is to transcend the struggle for life is a theory which necessarily implies the sanctity of the individual. For if the aim of civilization is to transcend the struggle for life, its aim is that every individual here and now shall transcend it ; and, so far as any one man is prevented from transcending it, there is failure of civilization. According to this theory there are desires in every man, which we may call desires of the spirit ; a desire to do what is right for its own sake, a desire to discover the truth for its own sake, and a desire to make things as beautiful or as well as they can be made for the sake of making them well. And the proper object of life is to satisfy these desires, not to go on living. Further, Society is an association of human beings with the object of giving to all of them the opportunity to satisfy these desires. If it has not that object, it is vicious and perverse in its whole constitution. It must have other objects, of course, such as defence and the better organization of the struggle for life ; but these are subsidiary to its main object, which is to give freedom to satisfy the desires of the spirit.

Now this is the only theory upon which what we call social justice can be securely based, for, if the aim is to give all men freedom to satisfy the desires of the spirit, it follows that some men must not have freedom at the expense of others. It is necessary that a mass of work should be done so that men may live ; but, if all are to have an equal freedom, all must do their fair share of this work. And it will be a further aim of Society that men shall, as far as possible, satisfy the desires of the spirit in the work which they have to do. The test of all work which is not absolutely necessary will be—whether the worker can take pleasure in doing it well for its own sake. If he can, then it is worth doing ; if he cannot, then it is an offence against civilization to force him to do it. It is not strict laws against luxury which are needed for civilization, but a sense of the iniquity of unnecessary and joyless labour. And this sense can only be based upon a belief in the sanctity of the individual, in his right to the satisfaction of his spiritual desires.

The other theory will not give social justice, because it will not aim at it. It will not assert the right of the individual to satisfy his spiritual desires, because it does not believe in the existence of spiritual desires. It only believes in existence itself without any further aims. It has no value for anything except existence itself, and all our other values it necessarily reduces to a value for existence and nothing more.

The Sacrifice of the Individual for the Race.

In practice, of course, there are few or none who carry this theory to its logical conclusion. But the theory is always with us and is always affecting our thought about social and political matters. It produces a kind of altruism which is dangerous because it necessarily denies the sanctity of the individual. For the only altruism which is consistent with this theory is an altruism which neglects the individual for the race, which exalts the struggle of the race for existence above the struggle of the individual. You cannot attain to altruism at all through this theory except by giving up the individual

for the race, except oy valuing the race instinct for preservation more
than the individual instinct. This valuing of the one more than the
other is your religion, the principle upon which all your morality is
based ; and there is nothing whatever to limit it in your theory. So
it may become a fanaticism as cruel as any of those religious fanatic-
isms of the past which were based upon a belief in the paramount
importance of salvation. For them there was nothing but the
struggle for eternal life ; for this theory there is nothing but the
struggle for temporal life. For both the individual, and his sanctity
and freedom, are nothing compared with the struggle, and he may
be sacrificed in any way which the struggle demands.

The German Error.

The only alternative which this theory permits to such inhuman
altruism is the instinct of self-preservation with its merely barbaric
selfishness. There is nothing in politics between anarchy and a
State in which the individual has no rights. If anyone would say
that the theory does not exist, or that it has no practical influence
in any existing State, I would draw their attention to Germany at
the present moment and to our own country for the last hundred
years. Germany has developed that inhuman altruism for which the
individual has no rights. Her whole conception of the State is that
it is a unit in the struggle for life to which all individual rights must
be sacrificed. The aim of the State, Treitschke says, is power ; but
power to do what ? Power to survive as a State ; and to this power
every individual and every individual conscience must be sacrificed.
It does not matter that the Germans themselves consent to this
sacrifice. You do not remain free because you willingly give up your
freedom for something else. You do not keep your conscience
because you have conscientiously surrendered it. The Germans talk
of their idealism and their Kultur, but in their political life both are
subordinate to the struggle for life itself, a struggle carried on with
an altruism the more ruthless and the more dangerous both to themselves and to others, because it is altruism and not selfishness,
because it has sacrificed the claims of the individual to the claims of
the race.

It matters not that this altruism is for the German race and not
for the human. That is, perhaps, merely a want of logic in detail ;
or it may be that they think the human race has the best chance of
surviving if the German race is supreme. In any case their altruism
is based upon a belief that the individual must be sacrificed to the
race ; their Socialism, so far as they are Socialists, is an organization
of the struggle for life and not an attempt to transcend it. Needless
to say, there are many attempts in Germany, as elsewhere, to transcend the struggle for life, but these are attempts of individuals. The
theory of the State is not their theory, as the present war has proved.

The English Error.

In England, on the other hand, we have inclined more to anarchy
than to the organization of the struggle for life, because we have

trusted rather to the instinct of self-preservation than to the instinct of race-preservation. We have, very justly, disliked and distrusted the ruthless altruism which will allow no rights to the individual; but we have based all his rights upon his instinct of self-preservation. We, no less than the Germans, have seen something holy in the struggle for life itself, believing it to be the ultimate and controlling fact of life. Politically, we too have believed that all values are only survival values. The only difference is that, for us, it is the survival of the individual that matters. It is his struggle that is holy and the source of all virtues.

"Competition is the soul of trade" and also the soul of the universe. We would rather carry on the necessary and holy war with each other individually than as a drilled and regimented nation with other nations. That is why the Germans despise us and we despise the Germans. We see the wickedness of their altruism, they see the wickedness of our individualism. They talk about our slums and we about their shambles; and we are both right. At the present moment their altruism is a danger to all the world and must be withstood. But our individualism is a danger to ourselves always; and the source of the danger in both cases is the same doctrine, that doctrine which says that there is nothing worth having in life except life itself.

But if you believe that life is worth having only for certain things that can be done in life, if you desire quality of life rather than quantity, you will not think the struggle for life holy, whether a struggle of individuals or of larger units such as nations. For life is not worth having on the terms that it alone is worth struggling for. It is merely a condition precedent to the doing of those other things which are worth doing; and the State exists not for its own power, which means the survival of its members or some of them, but so that its members may all be able to do those things which are worth doing. We have discovered by experience, if we do not all know it in our hearts, that those things which are worth doing for their own sake are best done in co-operation, can indeed only be securely and persistently and largely done, when men are able to forget the struggle for life in co-operation; for it is only co-operation which enables them to forget the struggle for life for one moment. Every State, every degree of civilization, aims at a certain amount of co-operation, and is kept in being only because men are able to forget themselves in co-operation. The question is therefore, the ultimate political question, why shall they co-operate? No indvidualist can give a clear answer to that question. No Socialist can be logically and thoroughly a Socialist, unless he gives the right answer—which is that they shall co-operate so that they may, as far as possible, escape from the struggle for life to the doing of those things which are worth doing for their own sake.

The Proper Purpose of Co-operation.

Co-operation itself is one of the things that are worth doing for their own sake. It is morally right, as conflict is morally wrong. It is true, of course, that men may co-operate for a wrong purpose, but even then they get some moral or spiritual satisfaction in their co-operation, in their self-forgetfulness. The German Army, because of its co-operation, is not morally as low as a footpad. The individual members of it do display certain virtues, and often very high ones, which they could not display if they were footpads. But their co-operation is a danger to the world because its purpose is bad, because it does not aim at something which is worth doing for its own sake, but merely for national success in the struggle for life. There is not complete self-forgetfulness in it, but only self-forgetfulness for the sake of a national egotism in which every German self has a part.

As co-operation implies self-forgetfulness, so its ultimate aim should be one in which self is forgotten, one free from egoism, national as well as individual; otherwise it will be dangerous because of its power, and will raise up a desperate opposition against itself. One can easily imagine a world of highly organized States rushing to a conflict far worse than the present one, and destroying all civilization in the course of it, if their Socialism was controlled by national egoism, if the aim of their co-operation was power, and not the doing of those things in which men forget all egoism. Co-operation, however far it is carried, must be dangerous, and must raise up enemies and provoke conflicts, unless its aim is the doing of those things which are worth doing for their own sake. So long as that is its aim, there is no danger in it, either of tyranny within the State or of aggression upon other States; and with that aim it may be carried as far as possible without fear of tyranny or aggression.

That, therefore, is the test of Socialism. Is it consistent co-operation that it aims at, a co-operation which means self-forgetfulness both in its process and in its ultimate aim, or is it an inconsistent co-operation, in which men forget themselves so that they may ultimately in some way satisfy their egotism? If the latter, it is dangerous in proportion to its efficiency. Aiming at power, it leads to war; aiming at comfort, it leads to stagnation. But if the former, there is no danger in it, since the more men forget themselves, the more they wish to forget themselves, and in forgetting themselves they can do no harm to each other. But they can only consistently and completely forget themselves if they are aiming at those things which are worth doing for their own sake, at doing what is right for the sake of doing it, at discovering the truth for the sake of the truth, at producing what is beautiful for the sake of what is beautiful.

Men have a desire to do what is right, and that, not for any ulterior benefit to themselves, but simply because it is right. When they see it to be right, they wish to do it. That is what we mean by doing right; it is not right if we do it for some ulterior purpose. So they have a desire for the truth, and they wish to discover it because it is the truth, and for no other reason. When we say that a man has a love of the truth, we mean that he loves it for its own sake, and not because he hopes in some way to profit by it.

The Imposition of Morality on the Poor.

Now, in our pursuit of all these things for their own sake, we are constantly hindered by the struggle for life. The mass of men, by reason of their poverty, have hardly any chance at all of exercising their intellectual or æsthetic faculties, and we take it for granted that they ought to be satisfied with exercising their moral faculties. The business of the poor is to be good. But a man cannot be good if he is confined to the exercise of his moral faculties alone, and we cannot be good if we confine him to it. Spiritual health consists in the exercise of all spiritual faculties, the intellectual and the æsthetic as well as the moral. If we wish the poor only to be good, we may be sure that we wish them to be good for our own profit. Their goodness to us means such conduct as will make us most comfortable, which is not goodness at all, but merely submission to a moral code imposed upon them. If we wish them to be good for our profit, we misunderstand the very nature of goodness and cause them also to misunderstand it. If we are to understand the nature of goodness ourselves, or to give them a chance of understanding it, we must not see their goodness in terms of our convenience. Our aim must be to release them from the pressure of the struggle for life, so that they may exercise all their spiritual faculties, so that they may have that freedom in which alone a man can do what is right for its own sake, can pursue truth for its own sake, and can enjoy and produce beauty for its own sake.

That freedom is very far off from all of us at present, from the rich no less than from the poor. In a society like ours the rich fear truth and are stinted of beauty, and their very conception of goodness is perverted by their fear of truth and by the general penury of beauty. They, anxious to maintain their position, are subject to the struggle for life no less than the poor. The only difference is that they exact more from life than the poor do, and therefore struggle for more. But their sense of the absolute, of those things which are worth doing for their own sake, is just as weak as if they were poor themselves. It is not spiritual freedom that they aim at, but success in the struggle for life; and therefore, not aiming at spiritual freedom, they cannot attain to it.

Yet we can aim at spiritual freedom, and we can understand that it is only to be reached if we aim at it for all. A man cannot enjoy a private spiritual freedom in a society based upon injustice any more than he can enjoy health in a plague-stricken town. The very desire for spiritual freedom must arouse in him a desire that all shall have it. If he wishes to do what is right for its own sake, he must wish that all should have the chance of doing what is right for its own sake. If he wishes to know the truth for its own sake, he must wish that all should have the chance of knowing it. If he wishes to make things beautiful for the sake of their beauty, he must wish that all should have the chance of making them so. And where the mass of men have not this chance or this desire, he finds himself continually thwarted in his own aims. Right is wrong, truth is falsehood, beauty is ugliness, to a society which does not desire these things for their own sake. We must desire them for their own sake, if we are to know what they are; and we must wish for a society in which every man shall desire them for their own sake, a society in which the obstacles to spiritual freedom shall be removed.

The Desire for Spiritual Freedom is the Basis of Socialism.

So the desire for spiritual freedom is the basis, the only basis, of Socialism. Without it co-operation will mean merely tyranny; it will be a means by which some will exercise their "will to power" over others. It will be a change in the organization of society, but merely one that will give those who start rich more power than ever over those who start poor. There is in everyone a will to power, just as there is a sexual instinct. But this will to power is, if indulged, more of an enemy to spiritual freedom than the sexual instinct. If I am possessed by the will to power, I cannot be a saint or a philosopher or an artist; I cannot even wish to be any of these. I shall wish for nothing except to exercise my own will; and, because I have no sense of the absolute, I shall not know what to exercise it upon. Even if I think that I aim at the truth, my sense of the truth will be continually perverted by my will to power. I shall aim at freedom to do what I want to do, but what I want to do will not be dictated to me by a desire for spiritual freedom; and this wilful freedom of mine will mean slavery for others.

Hence the extreme importance that the fundamental doctrines of Socialism should be clearly defined and held by all Socialists; that Socialism should be desired for the right reason, not for the wrong; that it should mean to every Socialist spiritual freedom, and not an organization by which he shall be able to work his will upon other men. Before the desire for Socialism, there should be the desire for spiritual freedom. And Socialism should endeavour to prove that it is the natural and inevitable product of the desire for spiritual freedom. We wish for a society in which all men shall have the chance of doing what is right for the sake of doing it, of seeking truth for truth's sake, of producing beauty for beauty's sake. We believe that in every man there is the desire to do those things, that no man can be happy except through the satisfaction of this desire. Further, we believe that this desire can only be satisfied in common and in a society whose chief aim is the common satisfaction of it. Without that aim a society is blind. It has no test by which to distinguish progress from reaction, civilization from barbarism, freedom from tyranny. It may be engaged in incessant changes and adjustments, all of which will be merely the exercise of the will to power by one class or another. It may organize itself into a very high state of efficiency, and then, in its pride at that efficiency, become only a unit in the struggle for life, and provoke against itself a continued opposition that will destroy it.

The Logic of Socialism.

There is, in fact, no theory of man's nature, or of the nature of the universe, upon which any social organization can be logically founded, except the theory that men do above all things, and beyond all things, desire spiritual freedom, and that they know how to use it when they have got it. And Socialism is the logical expression of this theory in political practice. It would carry the organization of society further than individualism would carry it, not merely because it believes in efficiency or any such meaningless abstraction, but because it believes that men do desire spiritual freedom above all things, and that they will aim at spiritual freedom individually whenever they have enough control of the struggle for life to do so. This is the faith of Socialism, a faith in the mind of man, not in mere mechanical efficiency, a belief that when men are all reasonably prosperous they will not fall in love with a dull prosperity. For it is not in man's nature to fall in love with dull prosperity. When he seems to do so, it is not because he is Philistine by nature, but because he is afraid to lose what he has. All those evils of prosperity about which reactionaries tell us are evils of insecurity or of unjust excess. No man, not even·a poet, is the worse for a good meal of wholesome food. He will write poetry better on it than if he is over or underfed. Prosperity demoralizes men only when it is unusual. If it were common and equal, it would be to them a necessary condition of their spiritual activities.

But, further, we believe that a common and equal prosperity can be attained to only if society aims at spiritual freedom for all. To aim at prosperity alone will be to lose the way to it; therefore means to prosperity must not be imposed upon the unwilling poor by masterful philanthropists. Socialism is not, as its cleverer enemies pretend, a method of regimentation; although a capitalist tyranny might learn much from Socialism, if it were clever enough, and might even call itself Socialist. But the difference between such a tyranny and Socialism would always be in aim. It is difference of aim and difference of faith that produce difference of result. That is why we need to insist upon the importance of the Socialistic faith and to define it with almost theological precision. Unless it is so defined and held by all Socialists, Socialism will become what its enemies say it is, merely a method which an intelligent despot could use better than anyone else. He, of course, would ignore the logic of Socialism, or would apply it only so far as suited his own purposes, but that would matter little to him. To the Socialist, on the other hand, the logic of Socialism should be everything. It should·connect his conception of the nature of man and of the universe with every detail of political action; otherwise Socialism will be to him also only a method and one in which his faith may easily be shaken.

Why is it that so many men, in their youth ardent Socialists, afterwards become reactionaries and yet do not know that they have changed? It is because they have never grasped the logic of Socialism, because it has never been to them anything but a method which they can apply to any purpose. There is logic in Socialism only when it is a faith, not in method, but in the mind of man and the nature of the universe, and when this faith expresses itself in a method which is Socialism. I will not say that Socialism is a religion, any more than I would say that art is a religion. But Socialism and art are themselves only when they make or express certain affirmations about man and the universe in common with religion. Religion is an affirmation of absolute values. It tells us that we are to value certain things because they have value in themselves and not because they help us to go on living. It tells us that we live to do what is right because it is right, to discover truth because it is true, to make what is beautiful because it is beautiful, and that the purpose of our lives is not to go on living. So Socialism is the application of these affirmations to politics. It is an effort to attain to a state of society in which every man will be able to make these affirmations in practice as well as in theory ; and it is based upon a religious belief that every man desires to make them and will make them if he is freed from the tyranny of circumstance. This belief may seem forlorn in our present society ; it often does seem forlorn to us when we look at other men of a different class or nation. Yet it never seems forlorn to us when we look at ourselves. We make these affirmations about ourselves, and we are angry with a society which does not allow us to practise them. This anger, without logic, produces a belief in aristocracy. There are a few, ourselves among them, who ought to rule the world so that they may practise these affirmations, of which the vulgar herd are incapable either in theory or in practice. But, with the logic of religion, which tells us that other men are to themselves what we are to ourselves, it produces Socialism. We know that to be released from the pressure of the struggle for life would not demoralize us ; why then should it demoralize the mob, which is only a name for men seen hostilely and in the mass ? We want material freedom so that we may attain to spiritual freedom ; and so do all other men, even those who think they can attain to it only at the expense of the mob. We all have the same desire ; but there are some who think that this desire is peculiar to themselves and a few other aristocrats like them ; and there are some who have forgone their desire from fear or from the tyranny of circumstance. For one reason or another they lack faith and the logic of faith. Their politics are disconnected from their desire and they are not Socialists. But the politics of the Socialist are connected with his desire and with his religion. He believes about other men what he wishes them to believe about himself. That is why he is a Socialist, why he is not afraid of trusting mankind as he himself would wish to be trusted. But unless he has this belief and this trust he is not a Socialist, whatever he may call himself.

When Peace Comes:
The Way of
Industrial Reconstruction

By Sidney Webb.

Price Two Pence.

The Fabian Society, 25, Tothill Street,
Westminster, London, S.W.   October, 1916.

THE HISTORY of the FABIAN SOCIETY.

By EDW. R. PEASE.

Price Five Shillings net (postage 5d.).

TOWARDS SOCIAL DEMOCRACY?

A Study of Social Evolution during the past
three-quarters of a century.

By SIDNEY WEBB.

Paper cover, 48 pp.   Price 1s. net, postage 1d.

HOW TO PAY FOR THE WAR.

Being ideas offered to the Chancellor of the Exchequer
by the Fabian Research Department.

Edited by SIDNEY WEBB.

Cloth, 6s. net.   Postage 5d.

INTERNATIONAL GOVERNMENT.

Two Reports by L. S. WOOLF on How War may be
Prevented, and How International Government is Actually Coming into Existence: together with a Project
by a Fabian Committee for the Prevention of War.

Cloth, 6s. net.   Postage 5d.

The Fabian Bookshop, 25 Tothill Street,
Westminster, London, S.W.

WHEN PEACE COMES—THE WAY OF INDUSTRIAL RECONSTRUCTION.*

I.—THE GREAT DISBANDMENT.

The difference between the Outbreak of War and the Outbreak of Peace is that we did not expect the former and we do expect the latter. War sent the whole nation scurrying round like scared rabbits trying to prevent dislocation from spelling unemployment and starvation. The Declaration of Peace will entail an even greater dislocation of industry and of wage-earning than did the Declaration of War. If we let it come upon us without adequate preparation, it will be much more difficult to deal with, and much more socially disastrous, than anything that we have yet had to face. It will create much more discontent and angry feeling, for thousands who would cheerfully die for their country in the stress of war will furiously resent going hungry in time of peace. But we can see the trouble coming, and we can, if we choose, prepare for it. Great will be the responsibility of the Cabinet if the nation presently discovers that proper preparation has not been made for what we can all see is a certainty.

When War Wages Cease.

To-day at least seven millions of our wage-earners (probably not far short of half the total wage-earning population) are engaged on "war work," either in the Army and Navy and their innumerable subsidiary services, or in the four thousand factories making munitions, or in the countless other establishments working on Government orders of every kind. These millions, together with their managers and officers, and the shareholders and other capitalists who are living on their labours, are being fed from the five million pounds per day that the Treasury is disbursing. From the very moment that peace is assured the Treasury will do its utmost to stop that expenditure, and to reduce it as rapidly as possible to the

---

* This tract is reproduced, with slight additions, from half-a-dozen articles in the "Daily News" (which appeared July 28, August 3, 12, 19, 26, and September 5, 1916), with permission of the proprietors. Many of the facts, figures, and proposals will be found more fully stated in "Great Britain After the War," by Sidney Webb and Arnold Freeman, price 1s. net (supplied by the Fabian Bookshop, 25, Tothill Street, Westminster).

few hundreds of thousands per day that will represent the future normal outlay on these services. This means, under the system on which we have chosen to conduct our industry, the stoppage of the earnings of nearly half our manual working population. No such economic convulsion has ever menaced the inhabitants of these islands. And we know that it is coming; we can foresee its approach, and we can, if we choose, take the action necessary to prevent it from resulting in distress and demoralisation and starvation. If our people have any political capacity—if those whom we have put in high places to rule over us have any "gumption" and any sense of public duty—let them show it now, or dire will be our fate. What is approaching in all the belligerent countries, so far as the mass of the people are concerned, is more like an Indian famine than like any ordinary depression of trade.

The War Office Promises.

So far as is known, the Government has come to practically no decision on the Problems of Demobilisation; and the preparation of the Great Peace Book, about which Mr. Asquith was talking about six months ago, has in September, 1916, resulted only in the secret appointment of a score of different committees, not all of which have yet got under way. We learn from Lord Newton's answers in the House of Lords in December, 1915, and from a stray reference or two elsewhere, that the War Office has come to certain provisional conclusions about the disbandment of the soldiers. The return of some three millions of men from all the various theatres of war, and their discharge from the Army, must necessarily be gradual; but it is to be proceeded with, under Treasury pressure, as promptly and rapidly as possible. Moreover, the mass of the men are enlisted only "for the duration of the war"; and they will nearly all eagerly claim an early discharge. The disbandment will be governed exclusively by military considerations, without reference to the position of the Labour Market. It must take place, so the War Office declares, by entire military units, irrespective of the needs of particular industries or the desires of individual men. The only concession that the War Office will make to those who are troubled about getting these millions of soldiers back into civil employment is to promise that a form shall be filled up for each man, stating his occupation, the town to which he intends to proceed, and whether he desires a place to be found for him. This form is to be forwarded through the War Office to the Labour Exchange of the town which the soldier has designated at least one month before he will be discharged. Every soldier will be given at the port of disembarkation a free railway ticket to any station in the United Kingdom; and he will be allowed a month's furlough, during which pay and separation allowance will be continued. He will be awarded a gratuity of an amount not yet fixed. (After the South African War the men received five or six pounds each.) And, as if with a magnificent gesture washing its hands of the whole problem, the War Office promises to every discharged soldier, for a whole year after his discharge, that he shall be entitled, whatever his occupation, whenever he is out of work, to call at the Labour Exchange and receive Unemployment Benefit (for which, if he belongs to an insured trade, he has already been paying), to an amount not yet definitely fixed, but probably ten or twelve shillings per week.* It is believed that the Admiralty will not refuse to do the same for the couple of hundred thousand sailors whom it will dispense with.

Finding Situations.

Now this provision, which leaves the War Office astonished at its own munificence, and to which, it is feared, the Treasury had not then given its consent, is considerably in excess of any previously made. It does not, as will be explained later, go far to ensure the soldier civil employment. But, so far as merely disbanding an army goes, it is on the right lines. It is quite a good innovation to send forward the soldier's application for employment a whole month before he can possibly take up a job, although it may be doubted whether this will, in most cases, lead to any engagement in advance. In spite of the fact that the Board of Trade has hardly kept faith with the trade unions in the matter of Supervisory Committees of the Labour Exchanges—there are such committees, but they have been formed in secret, usually for impossible areas; they hardly ever meet; they are given next to nothing to do; and they are carefully prevented from knowing anything of the daily operations of the Labour Exchanges—it is absolutely necessary to entrust the Exchanges with the finding of situations. The Board of Trade ought promptly to make its Trade Union Advisory Committees into realities; to constitute them, as at present, to the extent of one-half of representative local trade unionists; to have a separate one for each town or county district; to let them meet regularly and control their own secretaries and agendas; and to enable them to see exactly how the Exchange is being run. After all, these committees are only advisory. They can do no harm. The timid secretiveness of the Board of Trade over this matter arouses a quite unwarranted suspicion and distrust of the really fine work that the 400 Exchanges are doing. They have at present accommodation and staff adequate to deal with fifteen or twenty thousand cases per day. The task thrown upon them by the receipt within a few months of these millions of applications for situations will be immense. It can be satisfactorily accomplished only if the Exchanges are adequately strengthened by the Treasury, generally utilised by employers, and trusted by the trade unions, and if their work is better understood by the

---

* It is to be noted that these are definite promises by the Government, which Lord Newton publicly announced on their behalf that he was authorised to make; and voluntary recruiting took place on this basis. It would therefore be a grave breach of faith if these pledges were in any detail departed from.

public. But, with all their shortcomings, the Labour
Exchanges are far more efficient and far more trusted by
the workmen than any philanthropic committees would be. There
has been an influential backstairs movement going on to get the
whole business of finding situations for the soldiers handed over to
a series of charitable bodies, working on Charity Organisation
Society lines. This, it is believed, is now scotched. In view of the
fact that the important thing is not to get the ex-soldiers into employment *at any price*, but to do so without in any way lowering
the Standard Rate, the intermeddling of the philanthropists would
be simply disastrous. The only appropriate answer would be an
immediate labour revolt.*

Soldiers and Savings Banks.

A very serious question—not, it is believed, yet answered—is how
the War Office is going to pay these three millions of soldiers their
gratuities. What the Army Pay Department wants to do is what it
has done before—apparently merely because it is what it has done
before—namely, pay each man his five to ten pounds in cash when
he is given his railway ticket at Folkestone or Southampton or
Plymouth! We hope that the strongest protest will be made against
any such insensate endowment of the local publican. Why should
the Government incur the unnecessary expense—no inconsiderable
item—of paying over in cash three million separate sums of money
to the aggregate amount of twenty millions sterling? It was all
very well at the end of the eighteenth century wars, when there
were but scant banking facilities, and these were not understood by
the soldiers of the time. But to-day the Post Office stands ready
with 25,000 branches, eager to do the business. The Postmaster-
General would jump at the chance of opening three million special
accounts in the Savings Bank. The War Office would supply a list
of names and amounts, and would pay the twenty millions to the
Postmaster-General in a single cheque. Each soldier would be told
to call at the Labour Exchange of the place to which he was returning, and would there be handed—along with any news as to employment—his new Savings Bank book, showing the gratuity and
balance of pay standing to his credit, withdrawable from the local
post-office at his will. All that the Army Pay Department need do
is to accompany the railway ticket with a one-pound note as "journey money." All the rest ought, in the twentieth century, to be
done through a bank (as it has long since been done for the officers).
The saving in cost to the Treasury might be as much as 5 per cent.
on the sum to be handled—a clear million sterling! The saving to
the three million men themselves would be inestimably great.

---

* The schemes of the Social Welfare Association of London, though doubtless
well-intentioned, are wholly inapplicable, because they show no comprehension
of the supreme national importance of maintaining the Standard Rates of
Wages. They actually take for granted that wages must be left to supply and
demand!

What about the Munition Workers?

But all this relates only to half the problem of disbandment. The three or four million men, women, boys and girls now working on Government orders will also be summarily disbanded. For their immediate necessities the Government has, so far as is known, yet made no provision. Probably a quarter of a million of them are directly in the pay of the Minister of Munitions, the Admiralty, or the War Office in the hundred or more national factories already at work. Nearly three millions are working in the 4,000 odd controlled establishments, at rates of wages fixed or controlled by the Government, and they are legally forbidden to relinquish their employment in order to take up more permanent jobs, as some of them would wish to do. The Government, in fact, is as responsible for their discharge, when it comes, as for that of the soldiers. The Treasury will be just as insistent in its demands for immediate stoppage in the one case as in the other. Yet we can learn nothing of any decision as to their fate. What has just been done is—not to provide for their disbandment—but to start levying $2\frac{1}{2}$d. per week upon their wages (the employer having to contribute a like sum), so as to bring them, in six months' time, into eligibility for Unemployment Benefit when they are out of work (but only so long as they remain in these "insured" trades), to the extent of seven shillings per week for a limited number of weeks. Even this limited provision is refused to the poorly paid workers for the Government in the food and confectionery trades; and the textile and the boot industries, with some others, have also been omitted at the request of the employers and the better-paid sections of the workers—to the loss of the badly paid youths and women and unskilled workers, who have not been consulted. This Unemployment Insurance is in itself a good thing, which might well be made universal, except where the trades make other adequate provision for themselves; but it is not provision for demobilisation. We hear nothing as yet of (1) securing these munition workers, like the soldiers, a gratuity on discharge, or a month's furlough, or even any prescribed notice of dismissal; or (2) providing free railway tickets (for which the Government would not have to pay any fares) to enable them to get back to their former homes, or some place where alternative employment can be found; or (3) ensuring that particulars of their needs as to new situations are supplied to the Labour Exchange one month before they are discharged. Why cannot these things be done by the Ministry of Munitions for the army of men and women which has worked for us in overalls just as well as by the War Office for the Army of about equal numbers which has worked for us in khaki?

The Need for National Organisation.

The machinery and the provision for the disbandment of the three or four million munition workers, no less than of the three or four million soldiers and sailors, are of vital importance, because of their influence on all the Problems of Demobilisation. These seven million men and women have to be helped to sort themselves out afresh. They have to be got as quickly as possible into appropriate civil employment. The send-off is half the battle. It is very largely upon the organisation that we devise for discharging them from war service that will depend our success in getting them back to wealth-producing service without loss of time, loss of health, loss of character, and loss of temper. For it is upon a sea of troubles that we shall be discharging them. What will be the state of trade after the war, immediately or eventually, no economist dares to predict. What is certain is that the sea of employment will be " choppy "; that even if a large proportion manage to keep afloat in trade revival, the tides will leave many hundreds of thousands on the rocks; and that nothing but national foresight and national organisation on the largest scale will save us from calamitous and long-continued unemployment. This demands a separate section.

II.—THE PREVENTION OF UNEMPLOYMENT.

What the Government is presently going to do—it is as well to re-state the position clearly—is, as soon as possible after the Declaration of Peace, to bring to an end the war employment, and to stop the wages of nearly seven million men and women, equal to not far short of half the industrial wage-earning population of these islands. It is the most gigantic " turning off of hands " that the world has ever seen. And the Government will, of course, be right in this step. The sooner we can take our people off this " unproductive " war work, and get them back to wealth-production, the less will be the burden of debt that the nation has to shoulder. But the dismissal of these six or seven million wage-earners from the Army and the munition works—the sudden stoppage of the means of subsistence of possibly one-third of the families of the community —will be one of the most momentous economic decisions ever taken by a Government.

The Disbanded Millions.

Now, this is not an unnecessary warning. On no previous occasion, when similar but much smaller dislocations have been imminent, has the Government admitted any particular responsibility in the matter. The Treasury, it is believed, still clings to the old-fashioned economic doctrine that the " labour market " will in due course " absorb " those who are unemployed, and that it would be contrary to all financial precedent to admit any obligation to find situations for the disbanded millions. On this occasion, however, it will be the deliberate act of the Government that will produce the crisis. It will be a Cabinet decision that will summarily bring to an end the incomes of these millions of families. The nation ought to insist—I think the nation will insist—on the Government taking as much trouble to prevent the occurrence of unemployment after the peace, as it is now being practically driven to take over the mere disbandment of the Army.

It is not as if there need be any lack of employment after the war. There will be work enough for a whole generation in repairing the ravages of war, and replacing the enormous mass of commodities that have been destroyed. We know that every one of the seven million wage-earners can produce at least the value of his or her subsistence; and, indeed, a great deal more, as is shown by the tribute of rent and interest that the mere landlords and capitalists actually derive from the industry of those who labour by hand or brain. But we know also that, if we "let things alone" the process of "absorption" by the labour market may take a long time; and that it will certainly mean a great amount of more or less prolonged unemployment, the slow starvation of men, women, and children, the lowering of the rates of wages, even of those fortunate enough to get employment; and the Degradation of the Standard of Life of a large proportion of the population. That is what happened after the Peace of 1815, because the Government of that time "let things alone." That is, quite certainly, what will happen after the coming peace until a different policy is adopted.

Trade After the War.

What will be the "State of Trade" in the first, the second, and the third year of peace? No one can predict with any confidence how things will go on the whole. We know, on the one hand, that there will be millions of men and women simultaneously running up and down seeking for new employment. We shall have looking for jobs the disbanded soldiers and sailors (together with 50,000, or it may be 100,000, partially disabled men); the displaced substitutes; many of the ousted women. There will be sudden slumps, too, not in "war trades" alone, but also in all the diverse industries that have been producing substitutes for the things that we could not get during the war—just as there will be local slumps in the present congested "munition towns," and at those ports (including London and Liverpool) to which traffic has been artificially diverted.

On the other hand, there will immediately be local trade expansions at the ports which have been largely closed to Continental traffic, and at other towns characterised by the reviving trades. The industries repairing war damage will become suddenly busy. The shipbuilding yards will go on working continuously at their fullest strength for the next few years at least. The world-scarcity of warm clothing will long keep the woollen and worsted industries occupied. The makers of marine-engines, of agricultural machinery, of automobiles, and of sewing-machines and many other engineering mechanics will be in demand. The devastated areas all over Europe will require iron rails, bridges, rolling stock, and every kind of railway equipment; they will need every builder's requisite and all sorts of raw material; they will .have to import coal, and, for a long time, food, for all of which their Governments will have to find the necessary purchasing power.

Thus, we shall have the strangest possible mixture of local booms and local slumps, with the most unforeseeable " repercussions " and " reverberations " at a distance; some trades suddenly reviving in more or less lasting spurts of activity, whilst others simultaneously go down into the dumps of depression; pressing demands for additional labour in some places for some purposes, whilst other places will have crowds of men and women who can find no situations. It is emphatically a case for national organisation.

The Prevention of Unemployment.

What, then, can the Government do? It can, if it chooses, prevent the occurrence of unemployment. It is emphatically not a case for merely relieving the unemployed. That is a poor business, always unsatisfactory in its working and its results, and unnecessarily very costly; but inevitable when the Government has failed in its duty of preventing unemployment. It is plainly better to prevent the occurrence of unemployment (as of cholera) than to let it occur and then relieve the sufferers. And though it is not pretended that every individual case of unemployment can be prevented —any more than we can prevent individual cases of cholera—it is now known that it is quite within the power of the Government, by nothing more recondite than using the huge orders of the various public authorities in such a way as to keep at a fairly uniform level the aggregate national demand for labour within the kingdom as a whole, actually to prevent any widespread or lasting involuntary unemployment in any part of it.

The first step in organising the Labour Market lies in systematising the disbandment. That is why it is so important (as already indicated) to provide in the same sort of way for the three or four million munition workers as for the three or four million soldiers— to secure them all pay or gratuity during a brief spell of leave, as well as adequate notice of their coming dismissal; to arrange for them all to be looked after at the Labour Exchange before their dismissal, so as to stay the aimless wandering in crowds after " will of the wisp " rumours of vacancies that will otherwise ensue; and to promote mobility by a free railway ticket (the Government being still in control of the railways). It is plainly imperative to strengthen the 400 Labour Exchanges, which are now staffed to deal, in the aggregate, only with fifteen or twenty thousand applicants per day, and which will certainly, in the first year of peace, have to grapple with soldiers and munition workers discharged in successive batches of hundreds of thousands within single weeks. A calamitous breakdown of the official machinery will only be averted by a timely addition to the staff and the premises, so considerable as probably to take away the breath of the Treasury!

But the Labour Exchange is dependent, at present, on the

goodwill and intelligence of employers, most of whom neglect to make known their labour requirements in advance of the vacancies, and many of whom still refrain from notifying them at all. It may not be practicable to make it compulsory on employers to use the Labour Exchange, though the provisions of the Merchant Shipping Act, obliging shipowners to complete all engagements of seamen through the Mercantile Marine offices (provisions found most successful in preventing unemployment among seamen) afford a useful precedent.* But would it not be possible for the Government to request the principal employers in the kingdom—notably, all the 4,000 "controlled establishments"; all the railway companies; all the dock, harbour, gas, water and electricity undertakings; all the firms seeking Government contracts in any industry; all the mines; all the factories and workshops to which the Factory Acts and the Trade Boards Acts apply; and all the firms with which the Board of Trade is in friendly communication over statistics, etc. —to agree, as an act of patriotism, in the colossal "general post" of workers that is about to take place, at least to notify all their labour requirements to the Labour Exchange?

Organise the Public Work.

The Labour Exchange, however, cannot find situations that do not exist; and we know that there is going to be a shortage, in particular trades and at particular places, of longer or shorter duration, until the revival of trade becomes sufficiently general to take off all the six or seven millions who will have to find jobs. Now, at this point trouble will arise. There are those who want to see the difficulty dealt with on what we may not unfairly call C.O.S. lines—the getting of particular men and women into places by philanthropic influence and personal favour; in short, by kindly jobbery. Against this idea every Trade Union will protest, and rightly protest. What will become of the Standard Rate if it is to be left to kindly charity to get people into work? The right course is quite otherwise. The number of situations can, if only the Government chooses, be made equal to the number of applicants for them. There should be no question of "making work for the unemployed." There need be no unemployed. What is required is to maintain at a constant aggregate the total demand for labour, by systematically organising with this object the extensive orders that the local and central Government authorities will, during the ensuing five or ten years, certainly be giving. Let us note one or two of these inevitable developments.

---

* To make the use of the Labour Exchange as compulsory as is that of the Mercantile Marine Office does not mean, as is often supposed, that no worker will be permitted to get a situation otherwise than through the Labour Exchange; or that an employer may not take on any man he pleases. All that it would involve would be that the employer would be required to notify to the Labour Exchange how he had filled the vacant place.

Housing.

The nation will need to lay out a very large sum—possibly as much as a couple of hundred millions--in housing. The building of workmen's cottages and blocks of dwellings, very largely suspended as a builder's speculation since about 1905 because it could not be made to pay, and actually prohibited during the war, has left us with a ten years' shortage in town and country. We shall not get enough farm labourers unless we build a couple of hundred thousand new cottages.* We shall not be able to face the widespread rise in rents that will be made by the town landlords of weekly property, when the present Rent Restriction Act expires soon after the end of the war, unless the Local Authorities have actually increased by several hundreds of thousands the supply of dwellings in all the congested areas. We know, from the Census of 1911, how many hundreds of thousands of families were then living in an overcrowded condition. We know how many had only one room. We know how many had only two when the minimum requirements of decency were three or four. Great Britain needs, it may be thus calculated, at least five million additional rooms, in cottages or town tenements before the humblest third of its population can be said to be housed up to a bare minimum standard. But the Local Authorities cannot now build without a subsidy; and objectionable as a subsidy is, the Government has definitely adopted this policy. In Ireland, which has less than one-tenth of the population of Great Britain, it will be remembered that some 40,000 cottages—healthy, but unfortunately very ugly—have already been built wholly at the Government expense. This precedent is now to be partially followed for Great Britain. As long ago as November 24, 1914, the Chancellor of the Exchequer proclaimed, in a long and careful statement, how the Government would not only advance the necessary capital on the most favourable terms, but would also render it possible for Local Authorities to build without involving any charge on the rates *by making a free grant of a substantial percentage of the total cost.* Since that date nearly a dozen towns have received these free grants for housings (in addition to loans), to the amount of about 20 per cent. of the cost; and have thus been enabled to build without any charges on the rates.

What ought now to be done is for the Local Government Board to put pressure on all the Local Authorities, urban and rural, to secure sites and at once prepare plans for cottages, up to a possible total expenditure even of a couple of hundred million pounds, so as to enable as many as a million cottages, if need be, to be put in hand on the very morrow of the Declaration of Peace; and to be proceeded with in batches, quickly or slowly, according as the

---

* As to the rural shortage of cottages, see "The Rural Problem" (Constable, 1913), being the Report of the Fabian Society's Committee on Land Problems and Rural Development, edited by H. D. Harben.

Board of Trade reports unemployment to be setting in. Conditional on these preparations being now made by the Local Authority, the Government might renew its promise of free grants in aid of the capital cost so as to make the enterprise involve, with rents deemed " reasonable " in the locality, no charge on the rates. In no other way are we likely to get the workers decently housed. What is more urgent, in no other way can we avoid very serious disturbances when the Rent Restriction Act expires.

Schools.

There is no need to enlarge on the necessity for the same procedure of timely preparation and promise of grants (in this case, of loans and the ordinary maintenance grants), to enable every local education authority to put in hand, the very morning after peace is declared, the necessary making-good of two or three years' arrears of buildings, repairs, school furniture, books, etc.; and it is to be hoped, of the promised great new developments in education. To name only one item, the calamitous shortage of teachers ought to lead to the taking into the University and other training colleges immediately peace is secured of at least 20,000 young men and women with adequate Maintenance Scholarships. These educational developments will be further discussed on a subsequent page. For the moment we need note only the opportunity they offer for keeping the aggregate volume of wage-earning employment approximately level from year to year.

" Preparedness."

Nor need we do more than mention the very considerable orders that will necessarily be given by the War Office and Admiralty during the next few years in order that the nation may have in store, in case of any sudden need for reconstituting " Kitchener's Army," enough khaki uniforms, sailcloths, blankets, boots, belts, rifles, etc. These orders for equipment to be laid up in store should be given, not just as the War Office and Admiralty think fit, but at dates deliberately arranged, just when unemployment shows signs of occurring, with a view to prevent it.

Keep the Wage-total Even.

It is, in fact, easy to foresee that in every branch of the public service there will have to be, at any rate, within five years, the same bound forward. What is needful to prevent the occurrence of unemployment is only to put brains and forethought into the work. The Government should (1) authorise, here and now, these bounds forward, which it can be foreseen must occur, and get the plans ready; (2) deliberately control the time and rate of putting all this public work in hand (including the extensive orders of all the public departments and local authorities) in close correspondence with the amount of the contemporary labour demands of the private capitalists, and in such a way as to keep the total aggregate of weekly wages paid in the kingdom approximately at a level.* There would then be—apart from individual cases and particular trades and localities in exceptional circumstances—no involuntary unemployment. It can be done, and done even by the present Board of Trade, if the Cabinet would consent. And this mere rearrangement and control of the public orders, it is now statistically demontrated, would, by the endless reverberations that it would set up, automatically prevent any unemployment on a large scale, or for any long period.

But although the Government knows how to prevent unemployment, and thus save themselves all trouble about dealing with the unemployed, and although the officials realise exactly how it can be done, the Cabinet is not prepared yet to give the necessary orders. The Chancellor of the Exchequer does not want to be committed to finding all the capital that the local authorities would need, or to making the necessary increase in their grants in aid. There are still some Ministers who hope, after the war, actually to cut down the public services (such as Housing and Education), instead of expanding them as is required, because they wish to reduce the supertax! The general opinion of employers is against the Government taking steps to prevent the occurrence of unemployment—they honestly cannot bring themselves to believe that there will be any more men at their factory gates than will be convenient for their foremen! The result is that the Cabinet has, so far, come to no decision on the subject; and the President of the Local Government Board has merely asked the local authorities to tell him what works are likely to be put in hand.

Unless "Labour" wakes up, and insists on the proper steps being taken in time, this Government will do what every other Government so far has done, namely, let the unemployment occur (which it knows how to prevent); and then, in the most wasteful way, grant sums of money merely to relieve the unemployed!

Yet this time the importance of preventing unemployment is greater than ever; because, as Mr. Gosling said in his presidential address to the Trades Union Congress in September, 1916, this Prevention of Unemployment is actually the key to the very serious industrial problem with which the Government is confronted.

III.—THE INDUSTRIAL CONFLICT.

Reluctant though we may be to face the fact, there is the gravest danger that peace on the battlefield will be followed by tension between employers and employed at home—indeed, by spasmodic and possibly widespread industrial war. Employers are counting on being able to secure a heavy fall in wages, when several millions of men and women will be simultaneously seeking employment. But unless prices come down with a run, the conditions to meet

---

* One imperative need is for an Act enabling Local Authorities to secure sites for schools, housing schemes, etc., without the present interminable delays.

which war bonuses and war rises were granted *will not have changed;* and every Trade Union will fight its hardest against any reduction of rates, *which have nowhere risen in proportion to the cost of living.* Now freights are going to remain high, owing to the shortage in ships; and practically all raw materials owing to the renewed demand from Central Europe. All woollen clothing will be dear; and meat and milk may go to famine prices when Germany begins to replace its slaughtered herds, and the American Meat Combine once more gets hold of the refrigerating ships. (Why should not the Government retain its present control of these?) Rents are, to say the least of it, not likely to be lowered. All over the world the currency will long remain inflated; and this in itself causes high prices.

No More Cheap Bread.

Though bread may fall by a penny or two per loaf, it is not within human foresight likely to go back to the fourpence or five-pence per quartern of previous decades. We cannot hope to get rid of heavy taxation on tea and petroleum at least. We are accordingly in for years of dear living. Yet, unless very drastic action is taken by the Government to ensure that the aggregate number of situations is kept approximately equal to the aggregate number of applicants for them, employers will undoubtedly seek to beat down wages. The Majority Report of the recent Committee on Agricultural Employment almost openly relies on unemployment and distress in the towns to compel men to become farm labourers at the insufficient wages of the past. When the separation allowances cease, and the overtime earnings—when the school children and the grandfathers are no longer adding to the household incomes, and even the adult man goes on short time—any fall in wage-rates would seriously aggravate what may anyhow prove to be a socially disastrous Decline in the Standard of Life of the mass of the people.

Restoration of Trade Union Conditions.

But the tension will not be confined to the attempts that will be made to lower wages. The men in the engineering workshops have, at the instance of the Government, patriotically given up the regulations and customs—often originating in the shop and quite unconnected with any trade union—which they had built up in resistance to the employers' continual attempts, by "speeding up" and cutting piece-work rates, to lower the rate of payment for each unit of effort. They have (and not in the engineering industry only) submitted to autocratically determined piece-work rates without Collective Bargaining; they have yielded up their places to women and labourers, and allowed their skilled jobs to be subdivided and brought down to unskilled level; they have accepted the utmost possible acceleration of work without guarantees against the maximum output of piece-work intensity being presently converted into task-work at virtually time-work earnings. The Government has sworn itself black in the face, and pledged its honour, and Parliament has endorsed the guarantee by express words in a statute, that all these new departures shall be uncondi-tionally reversed and undone at the conclusion of the war.

Employers and Pledges.

The employers are laughing at the pledges, and openly saying that the restitution of the old conditions is physically impossible, even if it were desirable; and that, from the standpoint of maxi-mising production and minimising expense, it is so undesirable that nothing will induce them to consent to it. Moreover, some of the leading "captains of industry" are going further. They make no secret of their intention to insist on complete control over their own factories; they will henceforth brook no interference with their decisions as to the machines to be used, the "hands" to be put to any kind of work, the speed to be maintained, the hours to be worked, the holidays to be allowed, and the piece-work rates to be given. They propose, so they declare, to treat the workmen fairly; but they intend to deal with each man or woman as they choose. This means, as they realise, a death-blow to trade unionism. They have made up their minds that, in competitive factory industry on a large scale, the only "scientific management" is autocracy.

It is doubtful whether the Government, if it decides simply to adhere to its plighted word, can enforce on the employers the *status quo ante;* especially as this might involve ousting many tens of thousands of women and labourers, and "scrapping" the machines constructed for them. What we are in danger of is the proposal of some specious alternative, privately suggested by the employers, to which some trade union leaders may be persuaded to agree, in despair of finding anything better, but which will not satisfy the members of the Amalgamated Society of Engineers—the represen-tatives of the Government then retiring from the dispute, and quibbling over the exact terms of the Government pledge—and an era of local strikes, demarcation disputes, sullenness and anger; pos-sibly the destruction of trade unionism in the engineering industry, and the revival of the objectionable tricks of restriction of output, and refusal to make the best of machines, which are the angry workman's reprisals when he feels himself baffled and cheated.

Canon Barnett's Suggestion.

What can be done to avert such a calamity? There comes to my mind a remark of one of the nation's wisest teachers, the late Canon Barnett, of Toynbee Hall, very shortly before his death. Admira-tion was being expressed of the late Sir Henry Campbell-Banner-man's successful audacity in the grant of Constitutional Govern-ment to a South Africa lately in rebellion. He had triumphed, it was said, not by any great political genius, but because of his simple faith in ". Liberal principles," and his honest determination to apply them. I well remember Canon Barnett turning suddenly round, and asking, " Cannot we apply Liberal principles to the Labour problem ? "

Will the Government have the courage to declare that autocracy can no more be allowed in the factory or the mine than on the throne or in the castle? That after a century of Factory Acts, Mines Regulation Acts, and Minimum Wage Acts, the claim of the employer to "do what he likes with his own " has long been obso. lete; and that the time has come, as the only means of averting social disaster, to *grant a Constitution* to the factory; and quite frankly to recognise and insist that the conditions of employment are not matters to be settled by the employer alone, any more than by the workmen alone, but in joint conference between them; and not even for each establishment alone, but subject to the National Common Rules arrived at for the whole industry by the organised employers and employed, in consultation with the representatives of the community as a whole? The principle of conjoint control is already embodied at various points in our industrial legislation— for instance, in the checkweighman and pithead baths clauses of the Mines Regulation Acts, in the Joint Boards fixing wages under the various Minimum Wage Acts, and, again, the other day, in the clause in the Act providing for welfare work. On the other side, the employers in each great industry may presently be organising themselves, as Mr. Ernest Benn suggests,* in a National Association for the better management of scientific research, representation in foreign countries, standardisation of production, and other parts of their business.

What is needed now is for the Government, supported by the House of Commons, very definitely and decidedly to negative the claim that employers are once more making to autocracy; to insist that any National Associations of Employers cannot be allowed to refuse a constitution to their employees; to set up the necessary machinery of workshop committees and national industrial committees, formed from the trade unions concerned; and to give the decisions of these committees (which would not, any more than do the Factory Acts, compel any employer to engage in business, or any workman to accept employment) as to the minimum conditions upon which the industry shall be carried on, all the backing of law, administration, and public opinion.

A Workers' Constitution.

Such a grant of a constitution to each industry would go far to allay the discontent that may presently flame up into anger. But the mere establishment of constitutional machinery to deal with difficult problems does not in itself find solutions for them. The employers are already at work with their plans for such a factory

---

* "Trade as a Science." By Ernest Benn. Jarrold. 2s. 6d.

reorganisation as shall give them the largest possible profits. What
are the Trade Union proposals for factory reorganisation? It is
imperative that the workmen, if they are not eventually to be
"done" in the deal, should have thought out separately for each
industry and prepared in detail their own solutions of such problems as the effect of piece-work on the standard rate, the rates to
be fixed for labourers, women, and boys in relation to those for
skilled men, the avoidance of disputes as to demarcation, the maintenance of the standard minimum per unit of effort, and so forth.
We ought to hear that each Trade Union Executive and every local
Trades Council has appointed its own committee to solve these difficult problems from its own standpoint.

What the workman wants is status and security and freedom, as
well as better conditions of life. But, after all, one of the biggest
immediate issues will be the amount of wages that his work will
bring to him. Now on this issue five general principles stand out
as of national even more than of individual importance, upon which
the Government and the House of Commons and public opinion
ought to insist, and for the enforcement of which in all industries
every adminstrative device and social pressure ought to be employed:

1.—Prevention of Unemployment.

There must be (as already explained) an actual Prevention of
Unemployment.

2.—Maintenance of Standard Rates.

There must, in the second place, be a very authoritative maintenance (and a very definite security for maintenance) of the existing standard rates. A degradation of the standard of life is the
worst calamity that can happen to a nation.

3.—Security Against Cutting Piecework Rates.

There must be, in particular, wherever any form of piece-work
remuneration is adopted, some effective means of protecting the
scale of piece-work payments against the insidious degradation of
the pay per unit of effort, whether by the progressive "cutting of
rates," or by various forms of "speeding up," to which (as a whole
century of experience has shown) unregulated individual piecework is prone.

4.—No Limitation of Output, or Hindrance to Machinery or to New Classes of Workmen.

On the other hand, we cannot as a nation afford to permit, for
this or any other purpose, anything in the nature of limitation of
output, or restriction on the best possible use of machinery or new
materials or processes, or hindrance to the employment of any individuals or classes for any work of which they are capable. We
must simply find some other way of achieving the object.

5.—Universal Enforcement of the National Minimum.

Finally, we cannot as a nation afford to let any of our workers remain at wages, or under conditions, which do not allow of the maintenance of their strength and of a continued healthy family life. We must, perforce, start from existing conditions, inexcusably bad as in many cases they are; and only gradually build up whatever may be prescribed as the national minimum of subsistence, sanitation, education, and rest, below which no employer and no worker can, in the interests of the community as a whole, be permitted to descend. But build it up we must, at whatever cost of capitalists having to forgo some of their possible profits. It was Mr. Asquith himself who said that "every society is judged, and survives, according to the material and moral minima which it prescribes to its members." Huxley warned us a quarter of a century ago that "any social condition in which the development of wealth involves the misery, the physical weakness, and the degradation of the worker is absolutely and infallibly doomed to collapse." We all admit it in general terms. But how to apply these five principles in the prevention of the industrial conflict with which we are threatened must be left for another section.

IV.—THE TWO MAIN PUZZLES: WOMEN IN INDUSTRY AND "SCIENTIFIC MANAGEMENT."

We have seen that, whilst the grant of a constitution to the factory and the mine may be the only way to prevent the industrial conflict to which the autocracy of the employer will inevitably bring us, no constitutional machinery, however perfect, will in itself supply a solution of the problems of industrial organisation. We are warned by a whole century of experience that not even the most effective democratisation of control will prevent a disastrous lowering of the standard of life without the adoption of regulations, and especially of systems of remuneration, that will automatically counteract this constantly working tendency of competitive employment. Not even the fullest representation of the workers on joint committees will avail to prevent the recrudescence of such anti-social devices as Limitation of Output, Demarcation Disputes, and the exclusion of those "who have no right to the trade" on the part of workmen who, owing to the failure of their representatives to solve the problem, feel their accustomed livelihood slipping from them. The two main difficulties which the Government has to face in any reconstruction that will not only prevent industrial strife, but also, in the words of Mr. Asquith's new pledge, "secure a fairer distribution amongst all classes of the products of our industries," are the entrance into occupations hitherto monopolised by skilled craftsmen of women and other new workers, and the great extension of the piecework which is an element in what is known as "Scientific Management."

Now, it is not irrelevant to observe that the difficulty of solving both these problems will be enormously increased or diminished according as the Government fails or succeeds in preventing unemployment. If the influences now at work to dissuade the Government from undertaking the " very serious responsibility " of daring to touch "the labour market " should prevail; if the Cabinet should decide against such a deliberate organisation of the housing, school-building, road-making, and the mass of other public orders that must anyhow be given sooner or later as will keep the aggregate demand for wage-labour approximately level, and thus substantially *prevent unemployment*, then any satisfactory solution of the two main puzzles may well be impossible. The Prevention of Unemployment is, in a very exact sense, the key to the position. Against being thrown into a sea of unemployment all the trades will fight like tigers.

Six-and-a-Half Million Women Workers.

Let us take first the case of the women and other newcomers in the skilled trades. There are now probably six and a-half million women " gainfully occupied " in the United Kingdom, as compared with five and a-half millions five years ago. There are apparently nearly 300,000 more than just before the war in the principal industries; over 200,000 more in commercial establishments; over 9,000 on the railways, and 7,000 in other transport work; over 63,000 more directly in the national and municipal departments—altogether perhaps 650,000 who have come in during the war, but 100,000 of these have merely shifted from domestic service, etc. Thus the war has merely increased the total number of "gainfully occupied " women by as many in two years as they increased during the preceding four or five years of peace. But, besides this not very important quickening of the pace, there has been a new opening of gates. Women have been put to many kinds of work hitherto supposed to be within the capacity of men only; and they have done it, on the whole, successfully. In the same way many thousands of unskilled labourers have been put to new jobs, many of them hitherto reserved for skilled men; and they have rapidly become expert at these tasks. The women will not all wish to remain in industry when peace comes; but a large proportion—perhaps a majority—of them certainly will. None of the labourers promoted to skilled jobs will want to relinquish them. Yet the Government has definitely promised that they shall do so.

Keeping up the Standard Rate.

Whether or not we can get over this difficulty peaceably depends, it is necessary to repeat, on whether or not there are in the first year of peace thousands of men walking the streets unemployed. If the Government lets this happen (as it need not) the unemployed men will naturally not be satisfied with anything less than the fulfilment of the nation's solemn pledge, and the ousting of the women and the newly introduced labourers from their avowedly temporary employment, the scrapping of the new machines, and the reversion in all respects to pre-war conditions, as the Government has guaranteed. This many employers will resist or evade, even to the extent of setting up new factories, and calamitous will be the resultant bitterness. On the other hand, if there is still work to be done, and no competent skilled men are unemployed, it would be difficult to argue, after the war as during the war, that the services of the women and of new classes of men should not be utilised. What the workmen would then mainly object to would be the chance—indeed, the certainty—of the women and the unskilled men being used as a means of undermining and reducing the Standard Rate. If the Government take steps (as it quite well can if it chooses) to make such a misuse of female or unskilled labour impossible, as well as to prevent unemployment, the Trade Unions might properly agree to release the Government from fulfilling its pledge. But not unless.

Women's Wages.

It comes, therefore (with unemployment prevented), to a question of the terms on which the new workers should be employed. Now, apart from exceptional cases, we cannot, unfortunately, usefully insist that women should be paid the same as men. To enact this would mean the exclusion of women from the majority of industrial employments, because the typical woman is worth less to the employer than the typical man. It is true that the employer finds her more "docile" and more "conscientious." But she is not usually available for night-work; she does not do so much overtime, and she often works shorter hours, which suit her better. She is, on an average, absent from ill-health more than a man. She is unable, on account of physical or other incapacity, to do certain services that are occasionally required. She is usually unwilling to remain long years at her work, or to undertake additional responsibility; and she is less eligible for promotion. Where both sexes are employed, additional expense is involved for superintendence, lavatory accommodation, "welfare work," etc. Thus, at equal time wages, men would nearly always oust women. Even at equal piecework rates, if the men and women really execute the same tasks, men would be usually preferred. Now we cannot ask the six million women to propose terms which would mean to many of them —perhaps to most of them—the loss of their situations. The women simply will not ask for wages equal to those of the men. What is required is—to use the words of that wonderful shilling's worth, the "Labour Year-Book" *—"the fixing of a rate for men and women which shall be in equitable proportion to any less degree of physical endurance, skill, or responsibility exacted from the women, or to any additional strain thrown on the men, and which shall neither exclude women on the one side, nor blackleg men on the other." It

* Published by the Labour Party. Post free from the Fabian Bookshop, 25, Tothill Street, Westminster, for 1s. 5d. paper, or 2s. 11d. cloth.

is this delicate adjustment that the Government will have to make, perhaps by one of the devices suggested below (*prescribing minima only*, and securing by law the rigid enforcement of the minimum rates thus fixed). Only at this price can very serious trouble be averted. The same principle applies to the newly introduced unskilled men. It could equally be applied in solution of the difficulties presented by Demarcation Disputes, and by the admission of outsiders to a trade. If once the skilled craftsmen are secured against unemployment (as the Government can, if it chooses, secure them), their quarrel as to the employment of women, labourers, and men of other trades concerns only the Maintenance of the Standard Rate. This the Government can, if it chooses, also secure.

No less grave and no less complicated is the difficulty presented by the employers' insistence on what they call " scientific management." This American invention (as to which Hoxie's " Scientific Management and Labour " should be consulted †) aims at greatly increasing output. As to much of it that concerns the greater use of machinery, the provision of the very best appliances, the better organisation of the factory so as to avoid waste of time or discontinuity of work—all this amounting to a severe indictment of the knowledge and capacity of our own factory managers—we need say nothing here. Nor need we criticise the application of brains to find out how each job can be most efficiently done, least of all the discovery of the proper intervals of rest and change of motion so as to minimise fatigue. What is dangerous is the introduction (and this is an integral part of the scheme) of payment by the piece, without any guarantee for the maintenance of the standard rate. One of the changes under the Munitions Acts, which the Government has pledged itself to reverse, is a vast extension of piecework, in one or other form, to jobs formerly paid for by time rates.

Piecework.

What is the workmen's objection to piecework—an objection in which they are now upheld by all instructed economists? It is that, however liberal may be the piecework rates fixed at the outset, managers and foremen cannot refrain, and never do refrain, as is proved by a whole century of experience in all countries, from sooner or later " cutting " the rates, when the workmen have increased their output (and the intensity of their effort). This is, of course, a fraud on the workers, who have been tempted to substitute piecework intensity for timework intensity; and then eventually find themselves giving piecework effort for no more than their old timework earnings. Against this every workman revolts. The standard rate of pay per unit of effort is thus subtly lowered. The result is, if not a series of embittered strikes,

---

† Published by Appleton and Co., New York. To be got at the Fabian Bookshop, 25, Tothill Street, Westminster. See also " Great Britain After the War," by Sidney Webb and Arnold Freeman, price 1s. net (on sale at the same address).

sullen resistance to "speeding up," more or less concerted limitation of output, refusal to make the best of machines, "ca' canny" in all its forms—in short, the parlous state into which this ill-considered and, in fact, fraudulent action of the employers had brought some of our factories prior to the war.

Now, workmen do not really object to piecework as such—they usually prefer it, and more than half the Trade Unions, including some of the most powerful and most successful, actually insist on it. But what every instructed Trade Unionist fights against is a system under which the piecework rates (a) are autocratically fixed by the employer; or (b) are not settled by Collective Bargaining; and (c) do not embody some effective safeguard against a subsequent "cutting of rates," either for the same or similar jobs, or for all the work of the trade, contrary to the implied agreement to maintain the Standard Rate *per unit of effort.*

What has to be discovered and adapted to the special circumstances of each industry is some permanent and automatically acting brake on the successive lowering of the piecework rates—not in order to ensure that the individual workman shall take home undiminished earnings (comparatively a minor matter), but in order to maintain undiminished for all the workmen in years to come the Standard Rate per unit of effort. *The problem has been solved in some industries;* in fact, a whole wealth of experiment, hitherto usually ignored by employers and Trade Unionists in other industries, as by the economists, lies open to the inquirer.

Piecework Lists or Independent Rate-fixers.

The devices found successful in safeguarding the Standard Rate, whilst allowing piecework or "premium bonus" systems, seems, fundamentally, to fall into three classes. There is the collectively-bargained-for "List of Prices," unalterable by the employer, however much the workmen may earn. These piecework lists, of which hundreds are published by the Board of Trade,* are often (as in the cotton trade) of great complexity, and (as in the boot trade) successfully applied to jobs varying in minute details. Where the variations are incessant, almost every job differing from the last, the device of a salaried and disinterested Rate-Fixer, or couple of Rate-Fixers—in practice, usually the officials of the Trade Union and Employers' Association—has been found successful (as among the brassworkers and some of the coal-miners), "pricing" each new job on the agreed basis of a percentage above a standard time-rate. Where women are employed, there ought to be a pair of such Rate-Fixers, one of each sex. Failing such independent rate-fixing, an automatic brake on the employer's constant reductions was found, a quarter of a century ago, by some of the branches of the Amalgamated Society of Engineers (have they now forgotten it?) in the Guaranteed Time and a Quarter, a standing agreement with the

---

* The latest volume so published is Cd. 5366 of 1910, price 2/2.

employer that, "whatever the piecework rates, every workman in the shop should always be guaranteed a minimum earnings *each week* of 'Time and a Quarter.'" The importance of this rule lay, not in preventing all cutting of rates, for this it did not achieve, but in the fact that the employer found that it did not pay to "cut" the piecework rates or premium bonus times below such a minimum level, because in such case *he failed to evoke the piecework intensity that he desired.* The workman dropped back to timework speed whenever he found he was not making "Time and a Quarter" at least.

There may well be other devices equally effective. But, in one or other way it is vital to Industrial Reconstruction to make it impossible for the employer to use either the labour of women and unskilled men, or the substitution of piecework for timework, as a means of reducing the Standard Rate of remuneration, not merely per hour, but also per unit of effort. We must not only replace the autocracy of the employer by a constitution for the factory and for the trade, but also place in the hands of the representative Workshop Committee or Trade Board some device effective in preventing, whether by the employment of women or the use of piecework, any degradation of this Standard Rate.

V.—THE NON-ADULT.

The nation does not realise to what an extent its boys and girls are helping to win the war. Among the three million workers in controlled establishments and firms fed by war orders there are literally hundreds of thousands of "non-adults," from 13 upwards. The hundred or so National Factories already at work have on their wage-rolls boys and girls between 13 and 18 to the number of tens of thousands. At Woolwich Arsenal alone there is believed to be a larger working force of boys—I will not state the number of thousands—than in any other industrial establishment in the world. Less creditable to us as a nation is the fact that boys and girls of 13, 12, and even 11 years of age are being allowed to absent themselves from school, to the number, in the aggregate, of many tens of thousands, in order to earn a few shillings a week in industry or agriculture. We have, in the stress of war, called in even the children to help the State. How are we going to make it up to them?

The non-adults will bear their full share in the suffering that peace is destined to bring by industrial dislocation. The boys and girls now serving as inadequate substitutes for men will be discharged when men can be got; the swollen pay-rolls of the 4,000 munition factories will rapidly shrink, and the boys and girls will lose their present highly paid jobs; there will be a sudden besieging of the juvenile departments of the Labour Exchanges, which (unless the Treasury sanctions a gigantic expansion of staff and premises) will be unable to deal with the rush of applicants for places; and whilst employers will be glad enough to pick up smart youths for new occupations at "improvers'" wages (if the Trade Union does not revolt against it), there will be at least as great a risk of unemployment—indeed, the same certainty of slumps in particular trades and in particular localities—for the non-adult as for the adult.

Unemployment Among Youths.

The sudden unemployment among youths in East and South-East London will be extensive and lasting. And the failure of the boy between 16 and 21 to get immediately into a new situation when he loses his job is nothing less than a national calamity. Unemployment is bad enough, cruel enough, demoralising enough in the grown man, but any prolonged unemployment for the average manual working youth in our great industrial centres is soul-destroying. Forty per cent. of all the crime in the kingdom, so the Chairman of the Prison Commission informs us, is perpetrated by youths between 16 and 21. It is literally the fact that 80 per cent. of all the inmates of our prisons are found, on investigation, to have gone to prison for the first time before they were 21. *In the vast majority of cases their first offence was committed whilst they were unemployed.* The inference is that, important as it is that the Government should take the necessary steps to prevent unemployment among the adults, it is still more important—nay, absolutely vital for national health—that the Government should take the necessary steps to prevent unemployment among the youths who will be discharged by the thousand when peace comes (how many thousands from the Government's own factories?).

But we cannot deal only with the particular non-adults who happen to have been engaged in "war work"—these cannot be saved from unemployment and destruction except by the means that will save equally the other workers of their own age. What the Government has to reconstruct, in order to solve this particular Problem of Demobilisation, is, in fact, our social machinery for dealing with the non-adult—what we call, for short, our educational system.

A System in Ruins.

It sounded an exaggeration when Sir James Yoxall declared in the House of Commons that "the elementary school system of this country is in ruins." But there is a sense in which this startling statement is quite true. It is not merely that the children are slipping out of school-attendance, that hundreds of school buildings have been taken for Army needs, and that the supply of teachers has been knocked on the head. What is even worse is the demoralisation of the Local Education Authorities, the "slipping up" of the machinery for securing attendance, and the sudden loss of faith in the validity of the structure which Whitehall has been painfully building up. The nation is half-conscious of the ruin. Public opinion, as yet very little concerned about preventing unemploy. ment, is already whole-hearted about improving our educational system. Nothing meets with more acquiescence (outside the house- holds of Lord Midleton and Lord Cromer) than the boldest demands for educational reconstruction. The nation is prepared for an authoritative lead, and will eagerly adopt any reasonably plausible Government plan, if it is only large enough! And we have come to the point when, as Mr. Henderson emphasised in moving the vote for the Board of Education, we know that " it is a question of money, more money, and still more money." We are spending only eighteen millions of national and eleven millions of local funds on education of every kind—less than threepence per week per head! After the war the vote for the Board of Education will need to be trebled.

The Home Child.

What social provision do we need for the Non-Adult? Let us begin at the beginning. At present our Local Education Autho- rities are hampered because the material on which they have to work is largely spoilt when it is handed over to them. The physical wreckage among the children under school-age, due simply to social neglect, is appalling. The Local Government Board and the Board of Education are now making a good start with their schemes of maternity provision and infancy care, their " Baby Clinics " and Schools for Mothers. Up to twelve months old in most towns the Health Visitors more or less successfully look after the infants; and infantile mortality has already gone down by 30 per cent.! The unguarded tract is now between the ages of one and five. Only in one or two pioneer boroughs does the Local Health Authority at all systematically look after the children in these perilous years, in which the lives of tens of thousands of our future citizens are wrecked. The London Education Authority has distinguished itself by using the device of excluding the " under fives " to turn 50,000 of them out of the infant schools into the gutters. We need (i.) to make the maternity and infancy provision, now elaborately pre- scribed in the L.G.B. circulars, obligatory on all Local Health Authorities; (ii.) *to extend its scope right up to school age;* (iii.) to pay at least 80 per cent. of the whole cost by grant in aid in order to overcome municipal apathy.

The School Child.

So calamitous are the results of our social neglect of the Home Child that when it becomes a School Child 15 per cent. of all the millions we spend on its schooling are wasted. The Chief Medical Officer of the Board of Education tells us that a million of the children at school are in so bad a state as to be unable to get any reasonable amount of benefit. So tragic a waste demands an immediate development. of the School Feeding and School Medical Treatment services.

A determined Minister of Education with anything like a free hand from the Cabinet would put such pressure on the Local Education Authorities, by honours and rewards to those who did well, no less than by holding up to public opprobrium and by reducing the grant to those who lagged behind, that he might (a) make elementary schooling genuinely obligatory and universal, even in Ireland; (b) insist on having enough really qualified teachers at decent salaries; (c) compel such a reorganisation of schools and classrooms as had already been adopted in principle at London and Bradford to bring down the maximum class to not more than forty, and the average per teacher to fewer than thirty; (d) make the leaving age everywhere effectively 14; (e) secure by-laws limiting much more severely than at present the employment of children out of school-hours; (f) get everywhere an adequate provision of Maintenance Scholarships to enable not merely the budding geniuses but all bright children to continue their education; and (g) induce every local authority to complete its numerical quota of secondary schools and training colleges.

Our Anæmic New Universities.

What would do most to invigorate and vivify the feeble score of Universities, which is all that this nation at present affords (and most of the newer among these are anæmic from a shortage of students having both brains and enough to eat), would be the establishment at each of them of at least 100 national scholarships of the value of £150 a year, given in open competition to the ablest young people of each adjacent area proposing to follow one or other brain-working occupation. Such a system of national scholarships would cost only £300,000 a year—less than ninety minutes of the war!

This sounds like an extensive programme. But it is literally true that the whole of it needs no alteration of the law. It requires only a wisely imaginative use of the grant in aid; the tactful distribution of knighthoods to mayors, chairmen of education committees and local education officers who push their local authorities on in advance of the ruck; the incessant harrying of the laggards, with an organised campaign of persuasion of the obstructive local potentates; and the effective local publication of really stinging reports on the authorities that are most backward, with a demonstration of the injury done to the ratepayers in the shape of substantial reductions of the grant in aid. If the Minister of Education was as keen about getting his job done as the Minister of Munitions is, can anyone picture what a change there would be? What Parliament needs to do, besides at least doubling the present Education Votes, is to raise the school-leaving age, at any rate to 15.

Half-time for Adolescents.

Such education proposals are, however, the stalest of common.
places. What will strike the ordinary citizen as revolutionary is the
demand now made on all sides—by the practical teachers, by the
Government health experts, by the economists, by Lord Haldane
every time he speaks—for the rescue of the precious years of
adolescence from enslavement in wage-earning. These years, from
14 to 21, must now be claimed for production in the highest sense
—not, as at present, absorbed in the making of material things, but
dedicated primarily to the building up and training of the man and
woman. We cannot create healthy and productive citizens so long
as we let our boys and girls be wholly swallowed up by industrial
or agricultural wage-earning at 13, or 14, or even 15. Nor will our
evening class system ever suffice, in which tired teachers try to teach
youths exhausted by a factory day. There is universal agreement
that, if we are to have an efficient or even a healthy community, we
must rescue some of the youth's time from competitive industry.
*We see now that there must be, in some form, half-time for
adolescents.* Even employers are coming round to agree, provided
that the measure is made universally applicable throughout the
kingdom, so as to prevent any competitor from taking advantage of
the backwardness of his own local authority. We must re-enact, in
principle, the present half-time clauses of the Factory Acts—merely
substituting new ages for those now in the Act—and prohibit employers from employing youths under 18 (or even under 21) for more
than thirty hours per week; with possible alternative systems,
allowing the devotion to training of whole months at a time, for
agriculture, seamanship, etc.

The Halving of Boy Labour.

From the standpoint of Labour, this would mean, virtually,
halving the number of boys in industry; and the consequent stop.
page of the misuse of boy-labour for other than apprenticeship pur.
poses. A period at which it is all-important to prevent unemploy.
ment, and especially unemployment among youths, is just the time
for such a revolution. Its gradual introduction would in itself
enable the Government absolutely to prevent all unemployment
among young people. From the standpoint of education, the change
would involve the preparation of the best possible curriculum for
some millions of boys and girls at the most formative period; attending, according to the industry in which they were engaged, either
alternate half-days or days, or alternate weeks, months, or seasons,
for a duly organised mixture of physical and technical and intellectual training. This might be completed by whatever training in
drill and the use of arms is deemed requisite. Meanwhile *there need
be no interruption of industrial employment, wage-earning, or home*

life. The farmer's boy, the van boy, the errand boy, the news-paper boy, the "glue boy" of the carpenter's shop, the shipyard rivet boy—if these are really the best uses to which employers can put boys—might still unfortunately continue; but the nation would at least be doing its best, by their Half-time Training, to prevent them from graduating as hooligans and unemployed corner-boys into the gaol. We want, it need hardly be said, for all our bright boys and girls an abundance of Secondary Schools and Maintenance Scholarships. But more important than these is Half-time Con-tinuation Schooling—physical, technical, and intellectual—up to at least 18 for those whom we now permit the employers to take wholly into their service at 14. And now is the time, just when the Government, as we may believe, is concerned to prevent the occur-rence of unemployment, especially unemployment among youths, for the preparation of such a scheme of Half-time for Adolescents, to be put in force as soon as Peace is declared.

VI.—THE CONTROL OF CAPITAL.

Two unspoken anxieties haunt many of us. Shall we, amid all this destruction of wealth, have enough capital to maintain the nation's industrial pre-eminence? How can we, in face of our war losses and a staggering National Debt, afford to pay for the social readjustments required?

Now it may seem a paradox, but the economic student will at once realise its truth, that this war, like all wars, is carried on, substantially, out of national income, not out of national capital; and that there is every reason to believe that this country will come out of it with its industrial capital almost undiminished. The land is all there, with its buildings and improvements, happily exempt from any more devastation than a few bomb explosions. The machinery and plant of all kinds have actually been increased. There is no prospect of any shortage of raw materials or of food. Our herds of horned cattle are greater than ever before. We shall, it is true, have lost some of our merchant shipping. We shall have neglected many works of maintenance and repair, thus deteriorating our roads, railways, buildings, etc.; and some appreciable work will be needed to adapt our whole industrial machine once more to a peace production. But, taking all this into account, it is doubtful whether the lessening of material capital has yet been greater than the current increase. And if it be objected that "credit" will be lacking, or currency, or banking facilities, let it be noted, once for all, that all this is merely a question of organisation, which can be indefinitely increased up to any extent found genuinely useful by ordinary Government action.

What is happening is that those who can spare any part of their incomes, after paying the heavy taxes and the high prices, are lend-

ing these savings to the Government.* At the end of the war the
Government will probably owe to various individuals 4,000 million
pounds, involving a mortgage on our earnings, for the benefit of
those who lent the money, of 200 millions a year. But the aggregate
capital within the kingdom is not affected by these paper transactions.

The Proprietary Class.

But although the nation's capital will still be there, substantially
undiminished, we have to take account of the fact that we have
allowed nearly all of it—practically all but the thousand million
pounds' worth or so that is administered by the national Govern_
ment and the municipal authorities, together with the fifty or sixty
million pounds' worth of the co-operative movement—to be counted
in law as the personal riches of private individuals, nine-tenths of it
belonging to a class of about a million families, or one-tenth of the
community.† We are accordingly dependent on the proprietary
class, which we have thus artifically created, for permission to use
the land, the buildings, the railways, the shipping, the machinery,
and the stocks by means of which the nation lives. Thus, although
there is no reason to anticipate any deficiency in capital, the capital
will not necessarily be available for the purposes for which the
nation may deem it most urgently required. The owners may prefer
to invest it, in its mobile form, in South America; or, for that
matter, in Germany or Austria, which will be offering high rates of
interest. Last century we were told to trust to the workings of the
enlightened self-interest of the capitalist; to believe that where the
highest rate of interest was offered for a loan (allowing for insurance against loss), there the capital was most urgently required in
the public interest; that, consequently, extravagant Sultans and
corrupt South American Republics, foreign armament firms, or
enemy shipowners ought to be allowed to compete freely for capital
with home needs; and that, as between home needs, the capitalist's
preference for whisky distilleries and automobile factories over
arable farming and cottage building proved that the nation did not
really require the latter so much as the former.

We know now—even the economists—that this system of *laissez-
faire* cannot be relied on to secure the devotion of the national
capital to the national needs in anything like the proper order or
the proper proportion. The capital may be there, but it will not
necessarily flow where it is most urgently required—according to

---

* At the same time, those of us who own securities of Neutral States are
exchanging these for British Government securities. These mortgages will
henceforth be on the production of the United Kingdom, instead of on that o
the Neutral States. This transfer of mortgages equally leaves unchanged th⁰
amount of capital in the United Kingdom.

† See Fabian Tracts, No. 8, "Capital and Land"; and No. 5, "Facts for
Socialists," for the most authoritative statistics on this point.

any public estimate of requirement—*unless the Government takes care that it shall do so.* That is why we have had, during the war, a great deal of control of capital, and we see now that we ought to have had much more. *Can we afford to relinquish that control when peace comes?*

The Export of New Capital.

Take, for instance, overseas investments. At present the Treasury temporarily prohibits all public raising of capital for investment abroad, unless in exceptional cases. If, after the war, there is any doubt or difficulty about getting enough capital for (i.) the full restoration of all our home productive force; (ii.) the execution of the extensive programme of public works, national and municipal, which the Government is actually now beginning to consider, and which (let us not forget it) alone can enable the Government to prevent the occurrence of unemployment; and (iii.) all the " preparedness " that the nation deems necessary, in the way of storage of food and materials, against the chance of a future submarine blockade—then·the question arises: Why allow the export of capital? Of course, there are advantages in leaving property-owners free; the capital exported goes away largely in the shape of. machinery and other goods, and thus momentarily benefits particular home industries; the development of other countries through our capital is indirectly of some use to us at home; the interest on the foreign investments of our capitalists comes in commodities, and thus benefits our shipowners and import merchants; and it seems, at any rate, more profitable to the proprietary class. All this, as we have realised during the past two years, counts for very little against the public interest in having enough capital at home. There is a great deal to be said, at any rate as a temporary measure during the Great Reconstruction that the Government has to undertake, for an extension *to all new investments of British capital overseas,* public or private, of Mr. McKenna's additional income-tax on the foreign securities which the Treasury wishes to buy or to borrow. It is found quite easy to enforce such a tax by special assessment on the dividends or interest coming from the· penalised source. Moreover, we ought all to be required to produce a complete list of all our investments. If any capitalist abstracts his capital from the work of national reconstruction, preferring to lend it to foreigners at higher rates of interest, let us not only stigmatise such action as unpatriotic, but also penalise it by an additional income-tax of 2s. in the £. At any rate, until such step is taken no Minister can pretend that shortage of capital stands in the way of any desirable. measure of reconstruction.

Railways and Canals.

Particular forms of capital obviously need special measures of control. The railways, for instance, cannot be left as·they are nor yet be allowed to revert to private control. To buy out all the private interests at full Stock Exchange prices would cost little over 800 millions in Government Bonds; and would permit of the organisation of an entirely disinterested Public Service of Railway and Canal Transport, managed by the ablest technical experts, henceforth concerned only to serve the public and give proper treatment (including a share in control) to the employees; expending all the economies of amalgamation and improvement on better conditions of transport and of service; and yielding a fixed amount to the Treasury sufficient only to cover interest and sinking fund on the railway debt.*

Housing.

To put a stop to insanitary housing and (a far-reaching evil) indecent occupation, the nation probably needs, as has been suggested, the prompt building of a million new cottages and town tenements. This will not be done by the capitalists, who gave up this form of investment ten years ago for rubber planting and petrol production. It will be done only if the Government stirs up the·local authorities, and *renews the offer already made*, not only of favourable loans, but also of free grants sufficient to enable the municipalities to build without charge on the rates. Possibly a couple of hundred millions will be required in this way, in loans or grants, as part of the Programme of Reconstruction.

Agricultural Land.

Consider, too, our agricultural land, which, as the Board of Agriculture has just told us (Cd—8305, price 4d.), produces per 100 acres of cultivated area less than half as much corn as the German land, one-fifth as much potatoes, less than two-thirds of the milk, *even slightly less meat*, and next to no sugar, of which Germany produces a great deal. It feeds, in short, only two-thirds as many people. Why? Fundamentally because the Germans have invested many millions in fertilisers and in arable cultivation. Our farmers have found it more profitable to themselves, though not to the nation, to invest little capital and to " let the grass grow." The result is our perilous dependence on the uninterrupted arrival at our ports of our food ships. Nor will any import duty on corn or guarantee of price secure the end. We shall not get our landlords and farmers to plough up their worst four million acres of grass without definite control—either by peremptory legal obligation on the private owners and farmers to cultivate; or by public ownership and leasing, under strict covenants to maintain the cultivation that the nation requires, or, finally, by State farms.

---

* See the fully worked out scheme in "How to Pay for the War," to be obtained from the Fabian Bookshop, 25, Tothill Street, Westminster, at 6s. net; or the reprint of the chapter, "A Public Service of Railway and Canal Transport," price 1s. net.

The Coal Supply.

Can we afford any longer to leave our coal mines in private hands? These 3,300 pits, belonging to 1,500 companies, are worth at the present inflated Stock Exchange prices perhaps 200 million pounds, or only six weeks' war; but they employ one-tenth of the community, and upon their uninterrupted working our very life depends. It would be well for every householder—certainly every Trade Union Branch—to learn how we could nationalise our coal production and municipalise our coal distribution; paying out every capitalist interest at full price and securing uniformly improved conditions for all the million colliers; and supply every family in the kingdom with all its coal for domestic use at a fixed and uniform National Price for Household Coal, no more liable to variation than the penny postage stamp, of one shilling per hundredweight delivered to cellar.*

National Factories.

Before the war the Government had made itself dependent on the private capitalist ("the Armament Ring," etc.) for very nearly all the supplies that it needed—the output of Woolwich Arsenal and other public factories having been reduced to the smallest possible dimensions deliberately in order to permit more contracts to go to the capitalist firms. Now the Government possesses altogether between one and two hundred factories of its own, producing many kinds of war stores. Most of these are newly built and equipped, regardless of cost, in the most efficient manner. When peace comes the Government will want to get rid of these, and it intends at present to hand them over to private capitalists! This must not be permitted. Why should fresh opportunities for profit-making be given to private capitalists at the expense of public funds? We ought to insist on all these National Factories being retained by the Government, and kept running to their full capacity, in order to supply the national needs. When their lathes and other machines are not wanted for shells, they should be used (as are the engineering shops of the Hungarian State Railways) for making agricultural implements or motor-cars.

Can We Afford to Pay?

We come now to the second anxious inquiry: Can we afford to pay for the social readjustments required? Fortunately the war has answered this question. We see now that when Ministers postponed Old Age Pensions for nearly twenty years because the nation could

---

* See the completely elabor·ted scheme in "How to Pay for the War," to be obtained from the Fabian Bookshop, 25, Tothill Street, Westminster. at 6s. net; or the reprint of the chapter, "The Nationalisation of the Coal Supply," price 1s, net.

not afford twelve millions a year, when Lords Goschen and St. Aldwyn shrieked with horror at the rise of the Grants in Aid, when Chancellors of the Exchequer—from Gladstone downwards—deliberately starved the Education Estimates to avoid having to increase the National Revenue—either they "did not know their job" or they were shielding the rich from bearing their share of taxation. Even the "Morning Post" sees that it will never again do for any Chancellor of the Exchequer to pretend that "the nation cannot afford it." "We are at least sure," declares that organ of the wealthy, "that the working classes who are fighting side by side with those who once had leisure and wealth will never again believe that there is not sufficient money in the country to provide sufficient wages and good houses." The Chancellor's revenue for the current year is over 500 millions sterling. The Government, which is the sleeping partner in every business firm, and the mortgagee of every private proprietor, ought never to budget for a less sum. *To reduce taxation whilst leaving urgent social needs unprovided for means that we prefer to endow the taxpayers rather than meet the social needs.* Not that we can keep the War Budget unchanged. We must, at any rate, abolish the sugar tax and reduce the tea duty. We shall, unfortunately, be urged to repeat the temporary Excess Profits Tax; though, as it only hits excess profits— profits in excess of those of the most profitable years known to British industry—there seems no reason why some similar tax should not be imposed. We must promptly remedy the shocking unfairness of the Income-tax, and especially its immoral and anti-eugenic special penalisation of lawful matrimony and an adequate family.

But, after making all proper allowances, the systematic regraduation of the Income-tax and super-tax on the scale suggested by so moderate a statesman as Lord Courtney of Penwith—beginning, say, with a penny in the pound on the small incomes, and rising to 16s. in the pound on those of £100,000 a year—would yield, in the fairest way, all that the Chancellor of the Exchequer will need to maintain a 500 million Budget.* It is, as we·see very well, mere pretence to say that the nation "can't afford it." It has shown that it can afford it *when it chooses.* Any hesitation over measures of social reconstruction, any denial of social justice on the ground that the nation cannot afford it, means henceforth only this, that the Government, *speaking for the payers of super-tax*, does not wish to afford it.

---

* See "A Revolution in the Income Tax," price 1s. net; or "How to Pay for the War," 6s. net.; to be had of the Fabian Bookshop, 25, Tothill Street, Westminster.

Printed by
St. Clements Press,
Portugal Street,
Kingsway, W.C.

FABIAN RESEARCH DEPARTMENT.

How to Pay for the War.

Edited by SIDNEY WEBB.   6/- net.

Five of the chapters of this volume, prepared by the Fabian Research Department, have been reprinted in pamphlet form as under :—

The Development of the Post Office.

Suggests such new enterprises as daily newspaper delivery in country districts, "collection on delivery," postal banking accounts with cheques, investment agency, bookselling, debt collecting, and other reforms, many of them already in operation in other countries, and an international form of remittance, available on demand to any amount.

A Public Service of Railway and Canal Transport.

This is a carefully worked out scheme full of details, showing how much would be gained to the public by abolishing our almost unique system of private ownership.

The Nationalisation of the Coal Supply.

Proposes national production and municipal distribution, together with a fixed and uniform national price for household coal of 1/- per cwt. delivered.

A State Insurance Department.

Proposes a State guarantee for all existing policies and future bonuses, a State department for all future life insurance business, and an absolutely universal funeral benefit.

A Revolution in the Income Tax.

Evasions are to be stopped, and the unfairness of the present tax remedied by assessment of *family* incomes, so as to recognise the obligations of parents ; graduation is suggested from 1d. in the £ on £131 up to 15s. 7d. on incomes over £100,000 a year.   A tax so amended would yield twice the present revenue with half the personal hardship.

Price of each Pamphlet, 1/- net ; postage on one copy, 1d. (except that on Coal, 1½d.) ; per dozen, 10/-, postage 7d.
Special Terms to Trade Unions to be obtained on application.

Published at the FABIAN BOOKSHOP, 25, Tothill Street, Westminster, S.W., and by GEORGE ALLEN & UNWIN, Ltd., 40, Museum Street, London, W.C.

ROBERT OWEN, IDEALIST

By C. E. M. JOAD

Biographical Series No. 6.   Price 2d.
Published and sold by the Fabian Society,
at the Fabian Bookshop, 25 Tothill Street,
Westminster, S.W. 1. - - - June, 1917.

ROBERT OWEN, IDEALIST.

THE main facts about Robert Owen's career as successful business man, and his endeavours to bring about social reform by
means of State action, have been already described in a previous
Tract treating of "Robert Owen, Social Reformer." Finding politicians unsatisfactory, the public thick-headed, and his attempts to
create a Utopia on the basis of existing institutions impracticable,
Owen diverted his eloquence, his energies, and his wealth to the
task of setting up model communities which should realise those
ideals of a rational life founded upon communal ownership of property which were peculiarly his own.

The amazing optimism with which he continuously prophesied
sudden and complete moral and social revolutions, and the unflagging enthusiasm which led him to embark on new communities
after repeated failures, spring from, and were in the main conditioned by, that particular view of human character for which he is
perhaps most famous. It was because he believed that human
nature was entirely malleable to impress, that he so continually
strove to impress it with his own mark. It was because he was convinced that men could be made to lead any kind of life, that he
never tired of preaching the life he wanted them to lead. Hence
his practical efforts at community-forming arise directly from his
psychological view of character-forming—otherwise their persistence
would seem incredible.

The objects of this Tract are therefore twofold. Firstly, to give
some account of Owen's peculiar view of human nature. Secondly,
to describe the more important communities which resulted from
that view.

PART I.

Owen's Psychology. The Five Fundamental Facts.

Owen was one of the most thoroughgoing materialists who ever
lived. That is to say, he conceived of human consciousness as a
purely incidental phenomenon occurring in a world of matter, and
not as the essential underlying reality of the universe. He would so
define the world as to leave man's soul upon it as a sort of outside
passenger, or alien, as opposed to the spiritualist conception which
insists that the intimate and human must surround and underlie the
material and the brutish. Thus he tended to regard sequence as
proceeding always from the inanimate to the animate. Whereas we
most of us agree that the inanimate may have a limiting influence
on the actions of the animate, Owen thought that the phenomena of
consciousness were entirely caused and explained by the influence of
the inanimate.

With regard to the old opposition of character and environment in the total human compound, he was continually emphasising the importance of environment, and belittling that of character. He carried this attitude to the point of denying absolutely that character was in any sense formed or controlled by the individual. It was formed for the individual by external circumstances independently of his will.

The view that the individual is in any way responsible for his character is regarded by Owen as the fundamental delusion, the arch-error, which is responsible for all the ills of society and the sufferings of the human race. He speaks of it in the fiercest terms. It is "this hydra of human calamity, this immolater of every principle of rationality, this monster which has hitherto effctually guarded every avenue that can lead to true benevolence and active kindness."

Once dragged to light by Owen's writings, this principle, "conscious of its own horrid loathsome deformity, will instantaneously vanish, never more to appear." In contradistinction to this principle, which has hitherto reigned paramount both in ethics and politics, Owen asserts his five fundamental facts, which explain the basis of human nature. The statement of and implications arising from the facts, repeated in various connections, form the contents of Owen's gospel of character, " The New Moral World."

The facts are :—

1. That man is a compound being whose character is formed of his constitution or organisation at birth, and of the effects of external circumstances upon it from birth to death : such original organisation and external circumstances continually acting and reacting upon each other.
2. That man is compelled by his original constitution to receive his feelings and his convictions independently of his will.
3. That his feelings and his convictions, or both of them united, create the motive to action called his will, which stimulates him to act and decides his actions.
4. That the organisation of no two human beings is ever precisely similar at birth, nor can art subsequently form any two human beings from infancy to maturity to be precisely similar.
5. That, nevertheless, the constitution of every individual, except in the case of organic disease, is capable of being formed into a very inferior or a very superior being, according to the qualities of the external circumstances allowed to influence his constitution from birth.

Implications of the Facts.

I. EDUCATION.

Conjoin the fifth fundamental fact, and the principle that characters are formed for individuals not by them, and the supreme importance of education in Owen's system is immediately apparent.

"The Government," he says " of any community may form the individuals of that community into the best, or into the worst characters."

"That great knowledge," therefore, with which it is Owen's privilege to enlighten the world, is that "the old collectively may teach the young collectively to be ignorant and miserable or to be intelligent and happy."

Instruction of the young becomes the keystone of his system, for, unless children are rationally trained, the State cannot hope to produce citizens sufficiently intelligent to appreciate the truth of Owen's system.

The then existing education must be "scrapped" utterly. "Reading and writing do not in themselves constitute education: they are the instruments by which knowledge, true or false, may be imparted." Thus, "according to the present system children may learn to read, write, account, and sew, and yet acquire the worst habits and have their minds irrational for life."

The true object of education is to teach the young to reason correctly, to develop their critical faculty, and to enable them to sift the true from the false. Only their memories, he says, are exercised under the present system, and these are only used to retain incongruities. The most controversial religious questions, for instance, are solved in a phrase, and the answer is taken on trust. "Children," he says, "are asked theological questions to which men of the most profound erudition cannot make a rational reply; the children, however, readily answer as they had been previously instructed, for memory in this mockery of learning is all that is required."

In his conviction that children must be taught primarily to think for themselves, Owen anticipated many educational reformers. To carry out his system of education, the most capable persons in the State were to be appointed teachers. State seminaries were to be established for the instruction of the teacher, and the children to be given uniform attention in community schools.

Owen rarely condescends to details, but a sketch of the various stages in a child's education is to be found in "The New Moral World."

There are to be four classes of children in the model community:

I. From birth to the age of five. They are to acquire the primary characteristics of Owen's system: confidence in others, unselfishness, toleration, with knowledge of simple objects. These qualities will be inculcated by the automatic action of a healthy environment.

II. Class II, from five to ten, will "discard the useless toys of the old world." Education will be confined to handling objects, and conversations with older persons. They will help in domestic arrangements, but there will be no tasks. They will work only for "amusement and exercise."

III. From ten to fifteen:

(a) Children from ten to twelve will instruct and supervise the work of those in Class II.

(b) From twelve to fifteen they will learn the more advanced arts and handicrafts.

They will also receive instruction in the mechanical sciences.

IV. From fifteen to twenty, the Communists will be engaged in becoming "men and women of a new race, physically, intellectually, and morally." They will instruct the class below, and become "active producers on their own account."

A sketch of the future activities of the model Communist may as well be inserted here. His life is divided into eight stages, of which we have already described four.

V. From twenty to twenty-five, the members, aided by the inventions of science, will be engaged in producing all the wealth required by the community. Further, they will be general directors in every branch of education and production.

VI. From twenty-five to thirty, the main activities of the Communists will be directed to the distribution of the wealth produced by the lower classes, but this only for a few hours a day. For the rest, they will engage in study and intercourse.

VII. Those between the ages of thirty and forty will govern the internal affairs of the community, settle disputes and administer justice.

VIII. The eighth class, between forty and sixty, will undertake the duties of exchange of goods with other Communists, and the maintenance of friendly relations ; in the course of these duties they will spend much of their time in travelling, partly on pleasure, partly on communal business.

Thus Owen maps out the whole life of man.

II. Tolerance and Charity.

A conviction that men are in no way responsible individually for their characters will engender a universal tolerance for the shortcomings of others.

People will no longer be rewarded according to their deserts, for they are no longer responsible for their deserts. Distinctions of wealth will go the way of distinctions of birth, which are, of course, entirely irrational. Pharisaism will disappear with intellectual snobbery. Anger, jealousy, and revenge will give way to regret, perhaps, that other people's instincts are so unfortunate, but never to reproach.

"With insight into the formation of character, where is there any conceivable reason for private displeasure or public enmity?"

With this doctrine Owen lays one of the foundation stones of community life. Remove anger, jealousy, and revenge, and there is really no reason why people should not live happily together in communities, with common aims and common ownership of all property.

To remove those differences between individuals which operate in the main to create malice and enmity, Owen's system of education will act in two ways :—

First, children trained under a rational system will exhibit few shortcomings. More especially, the desire to overreach one's neighbour in competition, which makes the majority of persons unfitted for community life, will disappear. Secondly, even if such shortcomings do exist, we shall find no cause of offence, for "rationally educated children will realise the irrationality of being angry with an individual for possessing qualities or beliefs which, as a passive being during the formation of these qualities, he had no means of preventing."

Prisons will disappear in company with workhouses. Illuminated addresses and knighthoods will be thought as illogical as satires and sermons.

Instead of blaming, "we shall only feel pity for individuals who possess habits or sentiments destructive of their own pleasure or comfort."

The problem of what to do, assuming these opinions, with the burglar who is caught stealing your silver will be solved by the considerations, firstly, that the burglar will have no incentive to steal, will, in fact, become extinct, and, secondly, that in stealing my silver he will be stealing the community's silver, whtch already belongs to him as much as it does to me.

Thus Owen's doctrine of character seemed to him to abolish at one blow the corrective and retributive functions of government, with all the difficulties they carry in their train.

III. The Laws of Nature.

Owen is continually reiterating the assertion that while all other systems, previous and present, have done violence to the laws of nature, his alone is in conformity with them.

"We undertake to explain the principles of nature," he says in the preface to "The New Moral World."

He conceives, in fact, of the present system of society as of something artificially imposed upon human nature which should be, and, in point of fact, has been at some period of the world's history, exempt from it. The Greeks' thought that society was necessary to man, because it was only as a member of society that he could realise all that he had it in him to be. Owen felt, on the other hand, that the social structure, as it existed in his time, so far from developing, restricted the development of human nature.

Thus "it will be obvious," he says, "to children rationally educated that all human laws must be either unnecessary, or in opposition to nature's laws."

Like the Social Corttract writers of the seventeenth and eighteenth centuries, Owen envisaged a kind of Golden Age, existing before the institution of society, in which everybody did precisely what they pleased. One characteristic of this age was the fact that everybody lived according to Owen's principles, although, perhaps, they were never formulated. Owen's system, then, was an attempt to revive the freedom of the Golden Age, with the added advantages of a communal society somehow tacked on to it. So, under Owen's system, "none will be engaged in administering laws, at once an improvement and a return, in opposition to the laws of nature ; or in adjudging artificial rewards and punishments to counteract those of nature, which are all wise and all efficient."

The sequence of the argument then proceeds as follows. The laws of nature are also the laws of the nature of individuals. But the laws of nature are not to be counteracted ; therefore no restriction is to be imposed upon human action, or check upon human feeling. Hence, "justice will be done for the first time to human nature by every feeling, faculty, and power inherent in each child being cultivated for its work to its full extent." It follows logically that every law which conflicts with individual pleasures, or violates any individual belief, is tyrannical and contrary to nature ; for it is Owen's belief that pleasures, being formed entirely independently of our will, "every individual is so organised that he must like what produces agreeable sensations in him."

Human laws, therefore, either (*a*) express our beliefs and pleasures, in which case they are expressing the laws of nature and are superfluous, or (*b*) conflict with them, in which case they are wrong. Owen never thought out all the implications of this doctrine. The following, however, which he recognises and accepts, appear as cardinal points in his system.

IV. (1) MARRIAGE. (2) PROPERTY. (3) COMPULSION.

(1) *Free divorce:* for there is no reason why people should continue to live together when it violates their feelings or proclivities to do so ; in fact, Owen sometimes speaks as if he accepted the full Platonic doctrine of the possession of wives in common.

(2) *No distinction of individual property.* In a state of nature things were held in common. The principle of the division of property is, further, the basis of the principle of division in the community, of the distinction between rich and poor, of poverty, of jealousy and of war. That harmony, therefore, which Owen claimed for his system can only exist if the institution of private property is abolished. There will be no difficulty about this, however, in Owen's state. Harness the inventions of science to the service of the community, and you will produce more than enough for all. Owen was tremendously impressed by the advance of scientific discovery. "In the time of your ancestors, sire," he writes to King William IV, "fifteen millions of men could produce enough to supply the wants of fifteen millions, and no more. But now, a population of twenty-five millions can, with the same expenditure of energy, supply the wants of six hundred millions." Thus, "wealth being made abundant beyond the wants or the wishes of the human race, any desire for individual accumulation or inequality of condition will consequently cease."

(3) "*No compulsion.*" Since no compulsion is possible where free play is to be given to every individual feeling we can say nothing either to the criminal or to the debauchee. Owen at times accepts this implication, looking to his system of education to abolish both. At others we find him faltering. Thus, although we are told that

pure affection and unreserved knowledge of each other's character is sufficient reason for any and apparently any number of sexual unions, he makes provision in "The New Moral World" that marriage shall be formal, and shall not be entered into without three months public notice, and that no separation shall take place under a year of union, and six months further notice, *i.e.*, eighteen months in all.

V. EUGENICS.

At times, moreover, a tendency to flirt with Eugenics is difficult to reconcile with free play to nature and to individual choice. "We have learnt to improve the breed of the lower animals," says Owen, " but in the much more important matter of breeding human beings we are content to leave all to chance." Regulations are therefore laid down to prescribe only the unions of the fit; which seems rather unfairly to penalise the unfit for what of course they are not responsible. Such minor inconsistencies abound in Owen's work. It would, however, be wasted labour and captious criticism to continue to score academic points against a system which appears as an ebullition of Quixotic enthusiasm, and yet, strangely enough, a movement of sound common sense, rather than as a logical structure, watertight in every compartment, propounded to delight Dons.

PART II.

The Community Ideal.

It is undoubtedly to Robert Owen that the conception of the community in the modern sense must be attributed. The promulgation of his ideas forms a landmark; it is the beginning of modern Socialism. The idea arose directly out of the distress caused by the cessation of the European war in 1815. In 1816 a public meeting of the "Association for the Relief of the Manufacturing and Labouring Poor" appointed a committee to enquire into the prevailing distress, under the presidency of the Duke of York. Of this committee Owen was a member. Having impressed himself upon the committee by a powerful speech, in which he ascribed the prevalent distress as due to (1) the cessation of the extraordinary demand occasioned by the war, and (2) to the displacement of human labour by machinery, Owen was commissioned to draw up a report to the committee. This report, also called the "Plan for the Regeneration of the World," embodies for the first time a definite statement of the community theory. Any successful plan which takes into account the present demoralisation of the poor must, says Owen, "combine means to prevent the children from acquiring bad habits, and . . . provide useful training and instruction for them; it must provide proper labour for adults, direct their labour and expenditure so as to produce the greatest benefit to themselves and society, and place them under such circumstances as shall remove them from unnecessary temptations and closely unite their interest and duty."

To serve these ends the working class are to be gathered together into an establishment ; not too small, or else the cost of superintendence would be too high ; not, on the other hand, too large to be effective. Hence the community of 500 to 1,500 persons. The community should be self-sufficing, and its members were therefore to engage in various branches of agriculture and manufacture. All were to work at suitable tasks, according to their ability. The necessary capital to build the required establishment was to be raised by voluntary subscription or advanced by the Government. Thus three main advantages are aimed at in the communistic scheme : —

(1) It is the simplest and most effective method for educating the children of the poor.

(2) It enables a greater population to be supported in a given area than under any other conditions.

(3) It is so easy to put in practice that it may more conveniently be started than a new factory.

The original plan, then, in germ aimed simply at finding employment for the poor. Owen's optimism once having grasped the idea, saw far and quickly. A month later we find him stating not only that the community system was the only possible form of society for the whole world, but that, when it had once been promulgated by himself, "the principle and plan are so fixed and permanent that hereafter the combined power of the world will be found utterly incompetent to extract them from the public mind. Silence will not retard their course, and opposition will only give increased celerity to their movements."

The scheme was put forward under fashionable patronage, the papers were not unfavourable, and Owen was ingenious enough to propitiate the press as a customer and propagandise the country as a prophet at a single stroke by buying 30,000 copies of the papers containing his plan and distributing them to the clergy of every parish in the kingdom.

In 1819 the Duke of York held a meeting to appoint a committee to report on Owen's plan. The report whittled away the full-fledged communism of the plan to a joint-stock enterprise on a large scale. According to the report, the workmen would indeed feed in common and be housed in the same building, but "they will," says the committee, "receive their wages in money, and the mode in which they would dispose of them will be entirely at their own option."

A wealth of criticism and controversy centred not only round the extreme measures of the original plan, but even the milder recommendations of the other. The main point of vantage of the attack was the economic one.

Were Mr. Owen's communities, it was asked, to be self-sufficing or not self-sufficing? If they were to be the former, the number of workmen would not be sufficient to secure the sub-division of labour essential to modern processes, and the cost of production would be increased; if the latter, and barter and exchange were permitted with other bodies, the community would lose many of those exclusive advantages for which alone it had been formed, and would become subject to the commercialism and fluctuations of ordinary markets.

Owen met such objections by emphasising the enormous ease and wealth of production which modern machinery had made possible, the importance of which, as we have already seen,* he continually tended to exaggerate. The colonists were to labour in a "community of interests." There would be no disputes either about the division of property or with neighbouring communities, because all "would produce the necessaries and comforts of life in abundance." Nobody, at present, says Owen, wants more than his fair share of air and water, simply because we have these things in abundance. The same would happen to property if society were rationally organised.

Despite, however, Owen's continual propaganda, despite the elaboration of his scheme contained in the "Report to the County of Lanark," the country still remained incredulous, and it was left to America to be the recipient of the first model Owenite community.

New Harmony.

Early in 1825 there assembled at New Harmony, Indiana, several hundreds of persons drawn from various parts of the United States to make a practical experiment in Communism. New Harmony had previously been the abiding place of a religious sect, the Rappites, who, cemented by a narrow and intense religious creed, had themselves not unsuccessfully grappled with the problems of Communism. The land was fertile, the climate good. Owen in 1824 had paid £30,000 down for the village as it stood.

The society was to be open to all the world except "persons of colour." The existing situation of the houses would not permit the establishment of an ideal community in all its completeness forthwith, nor would the inhabitants be able to adjust themselves to Communism without training. The society was at first to achieve only temporary objects; it was to be a half-way-house on the road to the communistic goal, in which materials were to be collected and preparation made for the final burst from "the chrysalis stage of semi-individualism into the winged glory of full Communism."

Accordingly, although at first there was to be pecuniary inequality in view of the superior talents or capital which certain members were bringing into the society; although members were to bring and to keep their own furniture and effects; although individual credit was to be kept at the outset for each member at the public store for the amount of work done and against it a debit registered for the amount of goods supplied: although, in short, these clogging traces of an obsolete individualism were still temporarily to cling to the embryo community, Owen hoped and stated that within three years the

---

* See section on "Community of Property," above.

members would be prepared to constitute a community of equality "and so for ever bury all the evils of the old selfish individual system."

The response to the appeal for members was somewhat overwhelming at first, both in quality and quantity. Robert Dale Owen, the founder's son, describes them as a "heterogeneous collection of radicals, enthusiastic devotees to principle, honest latitudinarians and lazy theorists, with a sprinkling of unprincipled sharpers thrown in." Of many it seems to have been true that their only credentials for the ideal world to come were constituted by their total failure in the world that is. A few of the most unsatisfactory were weeded out, but, in pursuance of Owen's principle, no general process of selection seems to have been exercised.

In spite of this, however, Owen on his return to New Harmony in January, 1826, after a visit to England to collect men of science and learning to leaven and instruct the community, found the experiment so far advanced that he was induced to cut short the period of probation and constitute immediately the finally developed community.

A committee of seven were elected to draw up a constitution. It will be as well to give the main articles of "Union" in full, as they embody fairly well what may be taken to be the main tenets of the community ideal, whether realised or not, aimed at in all the Owenite experiments.

Objects of New Harmony.

"All the members of the community shall be considered as one family, and no one shall be held in higher or lower esteem on account of occupation.

"There shall be similar food, clothing, and education as near as can be, furnished for all according to their age and, as soon as practicable, all shall live in similar houses and be accommodated alike.

"Every member shall render his or her best service for the good of the whole."

The governing body was to be constituted as follows:

Agriculture.
Manufactures
Literature, Science,
  Education.
Domestic Economy.
General Economy.
Commerce.

Should each form one department. Each department should again be divided under intendants. Each intendant was to choose four superintendents. All the officers with the addition of a secretary were to form the executive council. The real estate was to be vested in the community as a whole.

We shall have cause to comment on the amazing intricacy of the governing body when we come to consider the community ideal in general. In the meantime it may be considered that complete communism was established. There was to be no discrimination between one man's labour and another's, and no buying and selling within the bounds of the community. Each was to give of his labour, according to his ability, and to receive food, clothing, and shelter according to his needs.

Success of the Community.

For the year following the emergence of the society into full communism all went well. A paper called the *New Harmony Gazette* gives a glowing account of the activities of the society. "The society is gradually becoming really as well as ostensibly a community of equality, based on the equal rights and equal duties of all. Our streets no longer exhibit groups of idle talkers, but each one is busily engaged in the occupation he has chosen for his employment."

Robert Dale Owen, arriving in 1826, is particularly enthusiastic. There were concerts, weekly dances, and all manner of social intercourse in the community hall; there were weekly discussions, and complete freedom of view was allowed. The housing, it is true, was of the simplest, and the fare of the rudest, while there was plenty of hard work to do. But there does seem to have been a real spirit of unity and enthusiasm pervading the community in the early days. Many distinguished persons also came to visit and observe the settlement.

Signs of Breaking-up.

From one of these latter, the Duke of Saxe-Weimar, we have the first note of discord. He observed in particular two disquieting signs : the extreme frugality of the living, and the difficulty of amalgamating the different social grades. This last is significant. We are told that at the dances the "working men did not join in the dances in the public hall, but used the newspapers scattered on the table." . . . While, when partners were assigned for the cotillion, "the young ladies turned up their noses at the democratic dancers who often fell to their lot." In the lectures, the work, and the amusements alike, the better educated classes kept together, and eschewed their social inferiors. Some such social divergence was probably the real cause of the split of the main community into two smaller ones, Macluria and Feiba Peveli. Robert Owen finds only cause for increased optimism in this duplication of communities. Both societies contemplated pure Communism, it is true, and we find Owen saying that "the formation of communities is now pretty well understood among us, and is entered upon like a matter of ordinary business." But it is to be feared that Owen was gilding his facts to reflect his expectations. Divergence in the main community cannot be looked on as a healthy sign, and by 1827 no less than seven different communities had evolved from the parent society in a similar manner.

Already in 1826 we hear of dissension in the society. The real estate of the society was to be transferred from Owen to twenty-five representatives. Apparently, however, so much confusion arose in the financial affairs of the community that the transfer was never accomplished. The members complain that they are stinted in food allowance (two meals a day, costing, on an average, about threepence in all, constituted their diet), while Owen is sumptuously regaled at the tavern. The accounts are complicated, and far too large a proportion of the members are engaged in the unproductive drudgery of clerkships. Thefts of community money occur.

Three changes of constitution took place during the next year, 1827, and an editorial in the *Gazette* of 1827 practically owns the scheme a failure.

We hear that "the whole population, numerous as they were, were too various in their feelings and too dissimilar in their habits to unite and govern themselves harmoniously in one community." Again, and very significantly, the admission is made that " the deficiency of production appeared immediately attributable in part to carelessness with regard to community property ; in part to their want of interest in the experiment itself—the only true incitement to community industry ; and these, again, were to be traced to a want of confidence in each other, increased by the unequal industry and discordant variety of habits which existed among them."

In fact, all the bogeys visioned and marshalled in critical array by the Individualist, when making orthodox assault on Communism, do really seem to have appeared, and in May, 1827, the parent community was formally dissolved.

Dissolution of Community.

At the dissolution of the parent society into five separate villages, the inhabitants of which voluntarily selected each other, Owen offered land and pecuniary assistance to anyone who wished to settle on the estate. Of the inhabitants, all who did not join one or other of the daughter communities were warned that they must either support themselves by their own industry or leave New Harmony. "Under the circumstances," says Owen, " many families left New Harmony with their feelings more or less hurt." Even now Owen's faith does not fail him. "The cheering prospects before the daughter communities," he tells us at this time, "induce a belief that nothing can prevent a spread of the social system over the United States."

After this we hear little of the future history of New Harmony. In April, 1828, Owen, after a visit to England, returned to the place, and in a public address to the inhabitants practically confesses that the great experiment has failed.

Speaking of the leases of land that had been made a year previously to the daughter communities, he says : " Upon my return, I find that the habits of the individual system were so powerful that the leases have been, with a few exceptions, applied for individual purposes and for individual gain, and in consequence they must return again into my hands. This last experiment has made it evident that families trained in the individual system, founded as it is upon superstition, have not acquired those moral qualities of forbearance and charity for each other which are necessary to promote full confidence and harmony among all the members, and without which communities cannot exist." This confession on the part of the founder sounded the death-knell of New Harmony. In June,

1828, Owen bade farewell to the place, and the relics of the community soon lapsed into complete Individualism.

Queenwood.

After an interval of some dozen years, marked by several abortive attempts to establish communities, and by numberless societies formed for that purpose, the ideal once more materialised in the settlement of Queenwood, at Tytherly, in Hampshire. Queenwood was started and financed by the "Community Society," founded by Owen. Each branch of this society which subscribed £50 for the enterprise was entitled to nominate one of its members to join the community. In 1839 the members, to the number of some sixty, entered upon possession of a large farm at Tytherly. Once again, however, no real process of selection appears to have been exercised. Dissension took place in the first few weeks in the community, members were asked to resign, and the chosen residue, some nineteen in all, were entrusted with the whole management of the experiment. After numerous early struggles, mainly financial, into which it is unnecessary to enter, the community was fairly established in an apparently flourishing state by 1842. They were in full possession of a magnificent building, costing some £30,000, some six hundred people had now been collected to inhabit it, and a sketch of the life of the place at the time, given by a visitor, who writes in the *Morning Chronicle*, signed "One who has Whistled at the Plough," is full of interest.

After a description of the fields, garden, and outside of the building called Harmony Hall, we hear next of the kitchen. When the writer entered, three or four women were washing dishes with incredible speed and the aid of a mechanical contrivance. The kitchen was fitted up with every modern convenience, and communicated with the dining hall by a tunnel, along which ran trucks containing plates, dishes, etc. A bathroom and the sleeping accommodation are also described. On the estate itself we are told of the activities of builders, gardeners, brickmakers, roadmakers, and shepherds. Labourers had been hired from the neighbouring villages, and were paid at nine shillings a week, a wage apparently considerably in excess of the normal rates for Hampshire at that time.

An account of the behaviour of the Queenwood Socialists is given in a letter refuting the doubts recently expressed by the Bishop of Exeter respecting their morality :—

They are bringing, from all parts of the kingdom, the best improved implements and methods of working. . . . Amid a poor population they are creating and enjoying wealth ; amid an ignorant population they are dispensing education ; amid an imperfectly employed population they are spreading employment ; amid a population not remarkable for moral conduct they are showing themselves an example which compels the respect of all who know them, and who at first distrusted them. If their principles are as dangerous to society as has been often said, what is to be done to counteract them ? The anathemas of the bishops neither sink their thousand acres in the sea nor set a blight upon their crops.

Another Socialist visitor gives us a description of their meals. "Coffee without cream and buttered bread form the breakfast, puddings and dainty vegetables the dinner. Meat is not eaten." The visitor fed on cauliflower with sauce, a turnip nicely prepared, a potato moulded into tempting shapes, and home-made bread. Certainly the Socialists did not expend their substance in riotous living. And yet, in 1844, the committee are faced with a deficit of £2,900 on the year's working, and new managers, "business men," are elected. Even they could not stave off the impending financial bankruptcy, and by the summer of 1845 the residents had melted away and the enterprise ended.

Only the fees from the community school had kept the settlement going for as long as six years ; and before we examine some of the causes which led to the failure of New Harmony, Queenwood, and similar enterprises, we may pause a moment for a brief view of Owen's educational ideals working in practice in the communities we have described.

Community Schools.

Owen held that the individualistic tendencies of men and women, as he found them, were largely grown and fostered by the competitive spirit prevalent in the normal school. The one incentive to work was to do better than your neighbour. If you did notably better than your neighbour—or, as Owen would say, over-emphasised your individuality at the expense of his—you were given a prize ; if notably worse, the cane. Had he known of Nietzsche's " Will to Power," he would have recognised in the existing school system a good example of its working. Hence, in the New Harmony Schools no rewards and no punishments were permitted. The boys, a lawless lot, were restrained and disciplined by sheer commonsense and good will on the part of Robert Dale Owen, the head-teacher. As the interest of the work itself was the only incentive recognised for the doing of it, it was plain that dull and informative textbooks would not succeed. In this matter, again, Owen held peculiarly enlightened views. He recognised that teaching does not necessarily involve a conception of a child's head as an empty box which you fill with facts as you fill a jar with jam. It was possible, he felt, to take into account the aptitudes of each individual child, and to let them to some extent dictate the teaching, instead of laying down a uniform curriculum for all ; while a sense of discipline could be inculcated by setting the older children, as a reward of proficiency, to instruct the younger.

Hence we are told that the boys and girls at New Harmony " have a very healthy look, are cheerful and lively, and by no means bashful. The girls are as little oppressed as the boys with labour and teaching. These happy and interesting little children were much more employed in making their youth pass as happily as possible."

Each boy was taught a definite trade from the very first, and the rest of his education moulded accordingly. Apparently the children were not overfed, rose at five o'clock, saw their parents not more than once a year, and were otherwise subjected to a Spartan discipline.

At Queenwood a school was started on Owen's principles, the fees for which were £25 a year, including clothing, and to which the children of people who were not members of the settlement were admitted. The school was one of the few financial successes of Queenwood. In 1844 it numbered ninety-four children, of whom sixty-four were paying fees The curriculum embraced the widest range of subjects, including astronomy, chemistry, anatomy, painting, vocal and instrumental music, land surveying, French, and German. The school, however, came to an end at the collapse of the settlement. This apparent failure does not impair the excellence of the system on which the schools were based. In education, perhaps, more than any other subject, Owen saw far in advance of his time, and it is only to-day that we are tentatively beginning to pay practical tribute, in the shape of schools on Owenite lines, to the merits of a system which has been loudly acclaimed in theory for years past.

Orbiston.

The Community of Orbiston, though prior in date to the Queenwood venture, has not been described hitherto, as Owen himself was not directly concerned with the founding of the community. He was, however, interested in the experiment, which drew its inspiration from his teaching, and he once visited the place.

In 1825 Abram Combe, a successful Edinburgh business man, who had become an ardent convert to Owen's system, associated himself with two or three sympathetic capitalists, and purchased the estate of Orbiston, about nine miles east of Glasgow.

An enormous stone building was here planned for the accommodation of a projected community, of which the left wing only, holding some three hnndred persons, was ever finished

On Saturday, April 8th, 1826, the new settlers took possession, although the building was still incomplete. The objects of the community were practically identical with those already described at New Harmony and Queenwood. Each adult was to have a private room, but all the cooking and eating arrangements were to be in common.

A special feature of interest, however, was introduced in the provisions with regard to children. In each of the other communities we have noticed, the care and education of the children was to be a charge on the community. At Orbiston it was agreed that each child should be debited with the entire cost of his maintenance and education, in the confident expectation that, on growing up, the children would willingly repay the sums expended on their education out of the profits of their labour. Unfortunately, as the community only lasted for a year and a half, it was never possible to judge whether these optimistic expectations were justified.

As at New Harmony, no principle of selection with regard to the members of the community appears to have been exercised. "A worse selection of individuals—men, women, and children—could scarcely have been made," said one of their number. They were described as " a population made up for the most part of the worst part of society."

Combe, however, justified his action in admitting all comers by insisting on the truths of Owen's system. He explained : " We set out to overcome ignorance, poverty, and vice ; it would be a poor excuse for failure to urge that the subjects of our experiment were ignorant, poor, and vicious." As Combe maintained the strictest adherence to the Owenite ideals of no compulsion and *laissez faire*, the communists were at first left without organisation or direction of any kind. Each was to act on his own account, and the only incentive to work was that of loyalty to the community. In these circumstances the familiar traits of individualism began at once to reappear. Those who wished appropriated to themselves the fruits of their labour ; those did not, acted on the principle of taking as much from the community and giving as little to it as possible.

Conseqeuently, Combe was forced, in order to keep the community going, to take in hand some measure of organisation. Squads were formed from among the communists, according to the capacities of the workmen. There was an iron foundry, a horticultural company, a dairy company, and a building company, whose first task was to complete the unfinished community buildings. Similarly, there were squads of hatmakers, clothworkers, and shoemakers, the necessary capital for each of these industries being provided as loan by the initiators of the community.

The domestic arrangements were divided among the women in a similar way. Payment for work done was given at ordinary market rates by book credit at the communal store, and the members were at first permitted to hire their labour to outside employers. In September, 1826, however, the members passed of their own accord the following resolution, affirming the principle of equal remuneration for all kinds of labour, according to the time given :—

That all the members of the society unite together to produce a common stock' out of which all our common expenditure, hereafter to be agreed upon, will be paid ; and that an equal share of the surplus of our labour be placed to the account of each member of the community, according to the time occupied by each.

At the same meeting the members agreed to take over the ownership of the land and premises from the proprietors, paying them five per cent. interest on their outlay, and ultimately the whole of the capital advanced, so that the community should be in every sense the owners of their dwelling-place.

By the spring and summer of 1827 the community appears to have attained a very real measure of success. The external aspect of the settlement had considerably improved. Roads had been made, and the gardens were well kept. The iron foundry was doing well, and the domestic arrangements under the squads of women were running efficiently. The boys, at first unusually unruly, had been reduced to cleanliness and order, without any grave departure from Owen's principles. The communists were, above all, remarkably happy. One lady member writes : " It is like another world. . . . I have been at a meeting last night, and such mirth I never knew. There is dancing three times a week. Indeed, there is nothing but pleasure, with the best of eating and drinking." Nor did the stress of making ends meet preclude leisure for the cultivation of the arts. The boys were taught music, preparatory to the formation of an orchestra; and, as a crowning achievement, a theatre was actually built, and plays performed by the members. At this stage (summer, 1827) Owen paid a visit to Orbiston, and found the community afloat on the high waters of success.

Break-up of Orbiston.

Signs of disaster were not wanting, however, even while matters presented so fair an outward show.

It has already been noticed that all comers had been admitted at the opening of the settlement, and many abused to the full the privileges granted by the communist system. The method by which credit at the communal store was entered to the account of each member, according to the number of hours work returned, was particularly open to abuse. Members were constantly cheating the timekeeper by returning more hours than they had actually worked, and so inflating their credit at the store.

A large section of the communists worked just sufficiently to procure a requisite amount of food and clothing at the common store, for the remainder of their time hiring out their labour for wages to outside employers. Thus they were enabled to live in what was comparatively a state of luxury, while the more conscientious members were labouring and stinting to maintain the public burdens. Thus, in June, 1827, out of two hundred and ninety-eight persons, only two hundred and twenty-one fed at the public mess. The remaining seventy-seven fed privately, being enabled by their outside earnings to purchase at the store food superior both in quantity and quality to that which fell to their more public-spirited fellow-members. It is further hinted that some of the surplus food purchased by the individualistic seventy-seven was exchanged with outsiders for commodities which the exchangers would have been better without.

In August, 1827, Combe, the founder, died. His brother William endeavoured to carry on the community for a few weeks after his death, but from September, 1827, onwards our records cease entirely. All we know is that William Combe, probably under pressure from the mortgagees, gave all the members notice to quit the premises in the autumn of 1827, and that the whole concern was shortly afterwards sold by public auction.

There can be no doubt that financially the community was a great failure, that two at least of the founders lost all their money in the experiment, and that lack of capital accounted for the abrupt close of the venture.

Co-operative Societies.

The communities described above were by no means the only expression of the effects of Owen's teaching. Another important development is now to be traced which resulted in the formation of co-operative societies. The rise of these societies, as contrasted with the parallel growth of communities, seems to have been due to the feeling that, assuming the validity of the main contentions of Owen's doctrine, it was still true that any attempt on the part of the working classes to better their condition must, to ensure success, originate among themselves. The communities had been artificial structures, in the sense that they had been founded from outside, and subsisted on funds provided by a few wealthy men. When outside support was withdrawn the communities went smash.

Referring to such attempts and their wealthy promoters, the *Co-operative Magazine* says : "Since their way is not our way, there could hardly be that unanimity and boundless confidence in a community established by them that there would be in one founded upon a system of perfect equality, every member of which may say, 'This is ours and for us.'"

Between 1820 and 1835 a considerable number of co-operative societies were formed, implicitly or explicitly, as a result of this conviction.

Their immediate objects are defined by the editor of the *Brighton Co-operator* as follows, though there were, of course, numerous varieties : "To protect their members against poverty, to secure comforts for them, and to achieve independence." The means to these three ends are, first, a weekly subscription from the members to secure capital to trade with ; second, the manufacturing of goods for themselves ; "lastly, when the capital has still further accumulated, the purchase of land and living upon it in community."

The immediate method by which profit was to be secured for the co-operators, and the chief advantage of the co-operative system, lay in the exclusion of the middleman. William Thompson, author of the "Distribution of Wealth," one of the ablest exponents of Owen's system, had done much to inspire the movement by his insistence on the doctrine that, as all wealth is the product of labour, the labourer has an indefeasible right to the whole of what he produces. He then goes on to define the primary object of a co-operative community formed of the producing classes to be the acquisition of the whole of the fruits of their labour by means of "mutual co-operation for the supply of each other's wants, and equal distribution amongst all of the products of their united industry."

Thus two more or less distinctive stages can be traced in the development of these societies :—

1. They were joint-stock trading enterprises, the goods produced by the members being accumulated in a common store. These goods were to be retailed to the members at practically cost-price, and to the outside public at a considerable profit, which was to go to a common fund. Thus the middleman and the capitalist were abolished together.

2. Out of the profits so realised, and an accumulation of weekly subscriptions, land was to be purchased and a community formed, wherein all the more revolutionary tenets of Owen's system, more

particularly with regard to the education of children, were to be put in practice. In this second stage incomes were to be pooled and all possessions held in common.

The first of these societies to be noticed, the London Co-operative Society (1824), placed in the forefront of its activities the popularisation of Owen's views. The "Crown and Rolls," in Chancery Lane, the headquarters of the society, witnessed nightly debates between Owen's followers and the individualist members of the young Liberal Party, including John Stuart Mill.

A plan was formed for the establishment of a community within fifty miles of London, and suitable farms were advertised for. Only Owen's return from America was awaited to put the project into operation.

As in the case of the Dublin Co-operative Society (1826), which was formed with the same object, and to which some thousands of pounds were subscribed, it does not appear that this project ever passed beyond the stage of optimistic anticipation.

The Devon and Exeter Co-operative Society of 1826, financed by a Mr. Vesey, seems to have been the first whose plans for a community passed beyond the paper stage. A small estate near Exeter was actually purchased, and thirteen co-operators started to prepare buildings for the expected communists. A month later twelve cottages were ready. Mr. Vesey, however, soon after this period withdrew his financial support, and the original settlement was abandoned.

In August, 1827, a fresh farm was purchased, crops were harvested, and several trades started. Although no new recruits for the society could be obtained, the prospect was regarded as not by any means discouraging. From this point, however, all record of the society in our only authority, the *Co-operative Magazine*, ceases.

In 1826 a more hopeful venture, independent of outside support, entitled the Co-operative Community Fund Association, was started. The objects of this association were identical with those already mentioned. The new departure lay in their method of obtaining the funds. £1,250 was the requisite capital aimed at, to be raised by means of fifty shares of £25 each. The shares were to be obtained by a weekly subscription of not less than four shillings from each member. When £500 had been thus accumulated, the purchase of land for a community was contemplated. The children of the members were to be supported at the common charge, and the government of the contemplated community was to be strictly democratic, consisting of committees elected from the members by the members, and sitting for short terms of office only.

With the establishment of the Auxiliary Fund by the London Co-operative Society in 1827, a new departure was made. From this time forward the characteristic feature, both of this and of the other societies whose course we are tracing, is the development of co-operative trading enterprises. Henceforward the second of the two objects noted above, the community ideal, tends to become more and more subordinated to the first. The general store or shop, financed by the Auxiliary Fund of the Co-operative Community Fund Association, is the first step in a course of developments which ended in the famous Owenite labour exchanges.

The general store was primarily designed for the sale of articles produced by the members of the association. Before long, however, provisions and other goods in common use, by whomsoever manufactured, were admitted into the store and sold to the members at wholesale prices.

The store was very successful, and great hopes were formed of extending it. An optimistic prophecy contemplated the association as being in possession of one such repository in each of the main thoroughfares of London, which, by diverting the tide of riches from its present tendency to flood the pockets of capitalists and middlemen into the pockets of the producers, i.e., the members of the association, would "emancipate the millions from the control of the units."

The Union Exchange Society, 1827, was also formed about this time. The members agreed to meet together once a month, and sell each other such goods as they could command, ten per cent. being levied on the sales and handed over to a common fund, which was to be distributed equally among the members. Tea, bread, flour, boots, umbrellas, and brass and tin ware were sold in this way.

The Brighton Co-operative Provident Fund Association, founded with the same objects as the Union Exchange Society, had a much longer life. It started with a membership of one hundred and fifty, each member paying a penny a week subscription into the common funds. Shortly afterwards this was transformed into a trading association, with a capital in £5 shares, forty of which were taken almost at once. The association issued a circular, stating that they regarded "the real cost of all commodities to be the amount of labour employed in preparing them for use."

In order, as far as possible, to secure that the exact cost of production and no more should be paid, a joint store, repository, or exchange was established, "in which a confidential agent will receive from members of the association such articles as they produce, and, according to a scale authorised by a committee or council of work, give them an order for other commodities in store to an equal value at prime cost, or a note for the value of so much labour as is brought in, which note may be cancelled when articles of that value are issued for it, so that the labour notes may always represent the quantity of goods in store and work unrequited" (*Co-operative Magazine*, November, 1827).

It will be seen that it was but a step from a project of this kind to the complete labour exchange system.

Little more remains to be said of the co-operative societies. The Brighton Association, whose objects have just been described, is considerably the most important. It lasted for several years, started the earliest provincial co-operative magazine, the *Brighton Co-operator*, and exercised the greatest care in the selection of its members, to which fact in particular its success was attributed.

By 1830 there were no less than three hundred co-operative societies in the United Kingdom. In 1831 the first co-operative congress was held. In 1832 the number of societies had risen to from four to five hundred. These societies were becoming more and more directly simply co-operative trading associations, and the legitimate development of this aspect of the movement into labour exchanges soon followed. It is interesting to note, however, that these early co-operators never thought of competing for profit with capitalist enterprises. They were simply anxious that each man should receive the due reward of his labour, and for the great majority the immediate necessity of getting a living thrust the more inspiring aims of Owen's teaching into the background. Trading bazaars and labour exchanges took the place of communities.

The Labour Exchanges.

It is in the Report to the County of Lanark that we first find Owen suggesting that as "the natural standard of value is human labour," a standard labour unit should be established for purposes of exchange.

The inadequacy of the monetary currency system, which became a subject of acute controversy between 1830 and 1834, and was regarded by many reformers as an important factor in the prevailing poverty of the masses, together with the possibilities opened up by the stores and bazaars of the co-operative societies, combined to direct Owen's attention about this time to the question of evolving some satisfactory system of labour currency. Owen was at this time the editor of a paper called the *Crisis*, and in an editorial for June, 1832, thus states the theory which inspired the labour exchanges: "Hundreds of thousands of persons of all the various trades in existence rise every morning without knowing how or where to procure employment. They can each produce more than they have occasion for themselves, and they are each in want of each other's surplus products." He goes on to point out that the usual course then pursued is (1) to convert the goods into money by selling them to a middleman, and (2) with that money to buy the articles required again from a middleman, who thus intervenes at two points in the transaction, and diminishes the real value of the labour expended by the profits he keeps for himself.

"Now there is no necessity for the middleman," says Owen. "Producers can do without him if they merely want to come in contact with each other, and they can exchange their respective produce to their mutual advantage and to the advantage of the general consumer."

A standard of value and a medium of exchange is, however, required. The argument then proceeds as follows: All wealth proceeds from labour and knowledge. Labour and knowledge are generally remunerated according to the time employed. Hence time should be the standard or measure of wealth, and notes representing time or labour value will be the new medium of currency.

In practice the doctrine lost something of its simplicity in view of the fact that different kinds of labour were paid at different rates, and an hour's labour expended by a skilled mechanic was more valuable than an hour's labour on the part of a navvy.

When the labour exchanges were actually working, the value of a man's labour was assessed as follows : The average day's labour was regarded as ten hours ; the average rate of pay at sixpence an hour. Required, to value different kinds of labour according to this standard.

Mr. Podmore gives the following illustration : "If a cabinet maker, whose value in the open market was paid for at the rate of a shilling an hour, brought a chest of drawers to the Equitable Labour Exchange to be valued, its price in labour hours would be computed as follows : First, the value of the raw material would be set down in vulgar pounds, shillings, and pence ; then the value of the labour would be added in the same base medium. The whole would then be divided by sixpence, and the quotient would represent the number of hours to be entered on the labour note." Clearly a purely artificial result, and not representative of anything in particular !

On Monday, September 17th, 1832, the first " National Equitable Labour Exchange " was opened in the Gray's Inn Road, near King's Cross. The deposits of goods produced, in exchange for which labour notes were issued, were during the first few days so numerous that the pavement outside the exchange was blocked. The goods stored at the Exchange were sold on receipt of cash as well as of labour notes issued by the exchange ; but in the former case a small commission was charged, in order, as far as possible, to discourage the use of money.

For a time it looked as if the labour notes system was likely to spread. They were accepted as payment for tickets at the social festivals given at the institution run in connection with the Exchange, and many local tradesmen put up notices in their shop windows to the effect that labour notes would be accepted as payment for goods. During the remainder of the year 1832 the popularity of the Exchange continued to grow, the chief depositors being tailors, cabinet makers, and shoemakers. For the seventeen weeks ending December 22nd, the deposits represented 465,501 hours, and the Exchanges 376,166 hours, leaving a balance in stock representing 69,335 hours, i.e., £1,733. 7s. 6d.

The greatest difficulty lay in valuing the pile of diverse goods deposited, and there is no doubt that in some cases anomalies resulted. A tailor, for instance, wrote to the *Times*, stating that he had paid thirty-six shillings for cloth and trimmings to make a coat, made it, and took it to the Exchange, where it was valued at thirty-two shillings. Owen replied, justifying the assessment, on the ground that a low valuation of all goods had been purposely adopted in order to compete with outside traders ; and that the tailor had suffered no real loss, inasmuch as all the goods at the Exchange were valued at the same low standard : an explanation which was clearly not very satisfactory to the tailor.

The following week, however, another tailor also wrote to the

Times, stating that he had received the full market price at the Exchange for a coat and trousers, both of which were clearly misfits and unsaleable elsewhere, so that it is pretty obvious that some of the assessments tended to be capricious.

The first Exchange, in the Gray's Inn Road, was brought to an untimely end by a dispute with the landlord, and moved to new premises in Fitzroy Square. Here, however, it passed under entirely new management ; and whereas it had started as a kind of clearing house for the products of individuals, it now became a mart or bazaar for the exchange of the products of various co-operative societies.

This change took place in the following way. In 1833 a new body had been formed, entitled the United Trades Association. This association comprised societies numbering among their members representatives of all the chief producers. The main object of the association was to find employment for the out of work members of the societies. A weekly contribution provided a fund to procure material and workroom accommodation for unemployed members. The goods produced were sent to the Labour Exchange to be valued by persons elected by the societies from among themselves. In most cases the products were exchanged direct at the Exchange. Thus notes appear in the *Crisis*, the successor to the *Co-operative Magazine*, to the effect that the Surrey Society had made a quantity of clothes, for which they had received in exchange a quantity of leather. The carpenters likewise report that they have engaged to fit up a shop for the shoemakers, who have promised shoes in exchange.

It soon became apparent, however, that something was inherently wrong with the financial arrangements of the Exchange. For a considerable time the accounts were kept straight by entering on the credit side large amounts received from the lectures and festivals held by the different societies, many of the lectures being given by Owen, while at the same time a considerable amount of business continued to the transacted at the Exchange.

During the latter half of 1833 the deposits averaged over 10,000 hours a week, but by January, 1834, this figure had diminished to 5,284 hours. During the early part of 1834 the deposits continued to shrink at an alarming rate, and we find that many articles were sold for three-fourths cash payment and only one-fourth notes, so that the peculiar currency system of the Exchange seems to have been falling into disuse.

By the summer we find the affairs of the Exchange to be in such a bad way, and the surplus stock in hand so small, that the secretary of the association, who was in direct charge of the management, writes to Owen, recommending that the affairs of the Exchange be wound up. After this we hear no more of the Exchange, and the various subsidiary Exchanges that were opened about the same time in some of the provincial towns appear to have closed down also.

The immediate cause of the failure of all these Exchanges was simply that they did not pay. Their financial difficulties were, according to William Lovett, who had been at one time storekeeper to one of the London associations, caused by "religious differences, the want of legal security, and the dislike which the women had to confine their dealings to one shop." Owen's rationalistic lectures appear to have caused much disturbance among the more religious members of the co-operating societies, and were ultimately the cause of many withdrawing their support from the Exchange.

The Exchanges had no legal safeguards, as they were not enrolled societies, and could not obtain legal redress when their servants robbed them. Love of shopping on the part of the women, and the unwillingness they felt for their husbands to be acquainted with the exact extent and nature of their purchases, precluded much enthu-siasm on their part for the experiment.

Owen, however, never appears to have been heart and soul in favour of the Exchanges. He explains in the "New Moral World" that it was not his wish to start a Labour Exchange at the time and in the manner chosen, and speaks of the experiment as being forced upon him by the inexperience of impatient friends. There appears to have been always at the back of his mind the feeling that mere buying and selling arrangements were a trivial matter in comparison with the complete revolution he contemplated, and unworthy of the attention of a comprehensive reformer.

Syndicalism and Guild Socialism.

The position of Owen in the history of social reform and legisla-tion is comparable to that of Plato in the history of philosophy. The germs of all subsequent movements can be found in his teach-ing. There is no single measure of social or industrial reform which has since been advocated about which he did not have something to say. Thus he has been acclaimed as the apostle of many contra-dictory things, and among others of Guild Socialism.

We have seen how the co-operative societies were, to begin with, miscellaneous associations of men of different trades. They dis-charged the functions now performed by the sick and benefit funds of a trade union, and during a certain stage of their development frequently maintained a Labour Exchange for the employment of their out of work members. As time went on it was found more convenient and more profitable for members of the same trade to associate together. As such the societies became to all intents and purposes trade unions, and during the disturbed times of 1832-1834 indulged in strikes for better conditions and more wages, mainly un-successful, on modern lines. The policies of these trade unions were directly inspired by Owen's teaching, and, though he disapproved of their more militant aspect, he made great efforts to capture the leadership of the whole movement.

These early trade unions rapidly took on some of the functions with which the modern National Guild movement is anxious to endow them. Thus in 1834 the operative tailors address a circular manifesto to their employers, stating that they have decided to in-troduce some new regulations into the trade. The circular con-cludes: "Your workmen, members of the society, will cease to be employed by you should you decline to act upon the new regulations. In that case they will no longer consider it necessary to support your interest, but will immediately enter upon the arrangements prepared by the society for the employment of such members for the benefit of the society."

A Grand National Guild of Builders was actually formed in 1834, and set to work on building a guildhall in Birmingham. The guildhall was, however, eventually finished by the landlord, as the association lacked the necessary funds to complete the work.

Owen seized upon the opportunity provided by these tentative experiments as the occasion for delivering a lecture, in which he outlined all the fundamentals of the modern Guild Socialist scheme. "We have long since discovered," he said, "that as long as master contends with master, no improvement either for man or master will be possible. There is no other alternative, therefore, but national companies for every trade. All trades shall first form associations or parochial lodges, to consist of a convenient number for carrying on the business." These parochial lodges should send delegates to county lodges, and so on, up to the Grand National Council. "This is the outline for individual trades. They shall be arranged in companies or families; thus all those trades which relate to clothing shall form a company, such as tailors, shoemakers, hatters, etc., and all the different manufactures shall be arranged in a similar way. No secret shall be kept from public knowledge. Any information respecting costs and profit shall be freely communicated, and shall be done by a gazette."

Owen later made it clear that he contemplated unions, including not only operatives, but also masters and manufacturers, and ultimately the Government itself.

As a result of this propaganda there was founded in 1834, under Owen's auspices, a "Grand National Consolidated Trades Union of Great Britain and Ireland," which in a few weeks time is said to have enrolled between half a million and a million members, with auxiliary branches—"lodges," they were called—in all the large industrial towns.

The programme of the union and the objects it set out to achieve are insufficiently recorded in the evidence available on the subject, but it appears that in some rather vaguely defined way it aimed at securing control of the conditions under which its members worked in all the leading industries, the strike being the weapon contemplated in the case of recalcitrant employers.

The Grand National caused profound alarm among the propertied classes, but its career was lamentably brief. The first of its activities was the organisation of a monster procession to present a petition to the Government against the sentence of transportation passed upon six Dorsetshire labourers for an alleged offence against an out of date Act with regard to the administering of illegal oaths (the swearing of oaths was a preliminary formality to joining a trade union lodge). But the Government was determined to break the strength of the movement, and acted with a high hand. Several unsuccessful and costly strikes on the part of various unions followed. We hear incidentally that the Potters' Union expended £6,223 2s. 11d. in strikes during ten months, 1833-1834. There seems at length to have been a growing weariness of strikes among the unions, and a desire to return to the earlier method of co-operative trading and exchange, and the Grand Lodge was accordingly shortly remodelled on co-operative lines.

In August, 1836, a special meeting of delegates was convened in London under Owen's presidency. Owen stated in his address that the union "had experienced much more opposition from the employers of industry and from the wealthy portion of the public, as well as from the Government, than its promoters anticipated."

It was then resolved that the name of the union should be changed to "'The British and Foreign Consolidated Association of Industry, Humanity, and Knowledge,' that the initiatory ceremony of membership should be dispensed with so as to conform with the law, that effective measures should be adopted to reconcile the masters and operatives throughout the kingdom, and that a charter should be applied for from the Government."

At the same time Owen, in an editorial in the last number of the *Crisis*, announces that the "awful crisis" in human affairs is now happily terminated ; that the old world will pass away "through a great moral revolution of the human mind, directed solely by truth, by charity, and by kindness."

Henceforth, Owen drifted further and further away from the trade union movement. His distrust of reform springing from the people themselves left him at bottom out of sympathy with the fundamental doctrines of what we should now call Guild Socialism. At the same time his attitude was often akin to that of the modern Syndicalist.

A Syndicalist tendency is manifested in Owen's distrust of political measures as a means of engineering the revolution. He was not, for instance, in favour of enlarged political rights for the masses, and refused to co-operate with the Chartists. "The Owenites," says Bronterre O'Brien, "seek every opportunity to speak sneeringly and contemptuously of their possession (the vote) as a consideration of no value."

Owen was impatient of the slowness of all agitation on political lines, and refused, for instance, to work with Oastler for his propaganda in support of an eight hour day. Such things were mere palliatives ; they delayed the revolution by chloroforming the workers. "Why waste your time in useless theories," he says, in a manifesto to the Chartists, "instead of going staight forward to the immediate relief of your wants—physical, mental, moral, and practical ? You, the Chartists, have been gradually stimulated to expect the most unreasonable and impracticable results from the Charter. If it were to be obtained to-morrow and its workings known, there are none who would be more disappointed with its effects than the Chartists themselves. It is not any mere political change in your condition that can now be of any service to you or society." The true remedy, he intimates, can only be found in the Socialist Community at Queenwood.

Bureaucratic Tendencies.

On the other hand, Owen's whole attitude towards the people whom he desired to reform was strongly bureaucratic. He always tended to regard the community ideal as something imposed on the people from without, not arising spontaneously from within. In effect he said to them : " You can lead a better life than the life you are leading : to wit, the community life as I have pictured it. But you are so stupid and ignorant that unless I keep urging, teaching, and directing you, you will never discover this for yourselves."

He distrusted a spontaneous movement for social betterment because he was convinced of the ignorance of the people. At present they were not fit ; they must be remade. He was convinced of the practicality of his own proposals because his view of human nature told him that people could be remade ; his view of his own, that he could remake them. He could not tolerate half measures. He preached the revolution on the Owenite plan or nothing ; but this is quite intelligible when we remember his belief that nothing could prevent the revolution on the Owenite plan. He is said to have stated in an interview, explaining his high-handed conduct on a committee, that " we must consent to be ruled by despots until we have sufficient knowledge to govern ourselves."

To Metternich, Prime Minister of Austria, he reports himself to have said that " it will be much easier to reform the world by Governments properly supported by the people than by any other means. Let Governments once be enlightened as to their true interests in promoting the happiness of their peoples, and they will lend their willing assistance and powerful aid to accomplish this ever to be desired result."

Such a view constitutes the very antithesis of the conception of a spontaneous movement among the people towards self-government. Owen never seems to have recognised the almost theoretic impossibility of devising an efficient government which is truly representative of the people, and it is on this rock that his community ship was found ultimately to split.

Reasons for Failure of Communities.

The really important question that arises for consideration from this short sketch of Owen's efforts to found communities is whether the actual failure and break-up of every community that was founded was due to incidental defects of bad management in each successive case, or to anomalies inherent in the community ideal itself, which made it unworkable in practice. Did the communities fail simply because all communities must fail, or because these particular communities were badly organised, insufficiently financed, unwisely selected as to membership, and so forth ?

Now the most thorough and comprehensive scheme of Communism ever put before the world is that contained in the Fifth

Book of Plato's "Republic." Theoretically perfect and logically complete, it embodies an ideal so inspiring and comprehensive that we cannot but believe that Owen endeavoured to model his own attempts at realisation closely upon it.

Against this plan for a communistic society Aristotle makes certain criticisms, which derive great interest from the significant manner in which they were borne out by Owen's experiments.

In the first place, the distribution of the common property, says Aristotle, will be a perpetual source of dispute. Members will protest that they are not receiving in proportion to their worth.

Secondly, compulsory association with others will not bring harmony, but friction.

Thirdly, common property, inasmuch as it belongs to nobody in particular, will be apt to be neglected by everybody.

Fourthly, it is obviously better to share voluntarily with others what is your own than to hold it compulsorily in common. Communism destroys generosity and hospitality by making them unnecessary.

Fifthly, unless the community is very small, there will be no real self-government by the members.

Now the truth of nearly every one of the strictures is exemplified by the course of events at New Harmony and at Queenwood. Taking the last point first, we have been struck already by the extraordinary elaboration of the governing committee at New Harmony. With a community of a thousand persons, some kind of delegation and representation was obviously necessary; but in a community of equality, the mere existence of superintendents and intendants, a group of officials, who might conceivably act as a check upon one another, but were officially uncontrolled during the period of office by the community, constituted a grave inequality.

Hence the parent community is found to split up into daughter communities. Dissension and distrust prevailed among the members, we are told, because they had no real voice in the governance of their affairs; the committee of government was delegated from above.

Again, New Harmony made it clear that a most careful selection of members was necessary before success could be achieved. Sharpers, unsuccessful speculators, and amiable visionaries do not form a good amalgam. There is no scourge for idleness, no incentive to work. All very well if you are a set of religious fanatics who, having abolished man-made law, will work owing to your possession of divine grace, and eschew material goods. In New Harmony, however, material goods were desired, but, being shared equally amongst all, went to the idlers equally with the workers. There were further social inequalities, religious and racial difference, yet the members were compulsorily associated. Hence we are told that "it was found much easier to assimilate a few with the same pursuits than many having different occupations."

Two lessons emerge: make your community small enough to be really self-governing, and make your members homogeneous, bound together by a common enthusiasm, preferably religious, and it may succeed.

So far we have pointed only to mistakes in the actual experiments ; we have not invalidated the ideal. To say that New Harmony was run badly is not the same as saying that a community cannot be run well. Is this latter statement true?

The Community Ideal.

Roughly, the community ideal may be said to rest upon the theory that there is a certain kind of good life that all men should lead, and that this life should be roughly the same for all men. Differences come from private property and the inequalities thereof. Abolish differences and inequalities of property, and a common kind of life may result.

Now, in the first place, equal participation in common property predicates a great degree of intimacy and power of getting on with each other among the participators. Intimacy and knowledge are required both to avoid squabbling and to ensure a proper selection of rulers. On the other hand, as soon as your community is extended beyond a small number, it is difficult to make the bulk of the members feel that they are taking part in the direction of their own property. Could you then extend those principles, which have had so little success even among small communities, to a large heterogeneous population, compelled to rely solely on itself for internal government and external defence? It seems unlikely.

Nor must it be forgotten that the disadvantages which attach to the administration by the members of property held in common are serious. It is open to question whether they do not outweigh its advantages.

The path of the individual in modern life is not a path, but a groove. He has little scope for expanding his personality or stamping his impress upon environment. His voice is a pipe in the world, but it may be a thunder in his own home. It is here alone that he may give expression to his own will and to the aspirations of his own personality.

If you give to each only according to his worth, you restrict his activities to definite tastes. On the other hand, the possibilities of falling into distress through lack of wisdom in management, and the contrary possibility of success by contrary conduct, are valuable elements in the life of the citizen. So long as private property exists, a man may, at least in that restricted sphere, possess the power of carrying out his own plans in his own way, and of displaying his own initiative. Under Communism he would simply do the State's work under regulations. It is only in the home that the capitalist may be said at present not to have got hold of the worker. Without the control of a certain amount of material property, then, a man cannot be said properly to give expression to his own will.

Finally, as Aristotle naïvely remarks, "the possession of private property is a source of harmless pleasure, and therefore desirable."

The Good Life.

The institution of Communism is not without objections; but it was not advocated as an end in itself. It was embraced and preached by Owen because he definitely desired to produce a certain kind of life in his citizens, and he considered that private property, by introducing the principle of difference, militated against it. We have already seen reason to doubt Owen's ethical principle that character and life may be formed for individuals, and not by them. We have noticed the distrust and opposition which his view of reform, as something imposed upon the worker from without, produced. Finally, we cannot subscribe to his principle that there is one kind of good life for all men. This was the Greek view, which lay at the basis of the Greek view of the State. The State, according to Greek thinkers, was the one organisation which made the good life possible for its members. It was only within the State that they realised their full nature. Similarly, in Owen's view, it was only in a community that man could realise all that he had it in him to be.

We, on the other hand, have come to hold, as the result of the individualist and democratic thinking of the last century, that neither the State nor any individual is in a position to predicate a certain kind of good life for others. We hold it vital that each man should judge for himself what he holds to be valuable in life; while, if we are to accept authority on such matters, it must be self-chosen. Hence modern Utopias have always inspired a feeling of repulsion, because men do not happen to want to live the life which the authors of these hopeful and aggressive works want them to live. It is here, I suspect, that we must look for the root reason of the failure of Owen's communities. The members did not all want to live one kind of life, nor was it the one kind of life Owen favoured. For the first and last time the hack anti-Socialist criticism hit the mark; "The Socialist did not take account of human nature."

Value of Owen's Work.

The communities were the concrete embodiment of all that Owen stood for. They failed, but their failure did not negative the value of his work. In an age when Individualism was rampant, Owen was the first to emphasise the need of State control.

The Individualism of the Manchester School of Liberals was based upon the view that man being fundamentally selfish, he himself was the person most capable of looking after his own profit and interests, without interference from his neighbours.

In a state of society with equality of power, wealth, and opportunity, this position may be sound; it is obviously better than to have everybody meddling with everybody else's affairs and the State poking its inspectors into every household. Economically, however, it rested on three fallacies:—

1. That each individual is equally farsighted and has an equal power of knowing what he wants.

2. That each individual has an equal power of obtaining it and equal freedom of choice.

3. That what all the individuals want is identical with the well-being of the community as a whole.

The results of Individualist policy were the hideous cruelties which necessitated the Factory Acts. It was seen that the State must step in to prevent some individuals exploiting their fellows in their efforts to satisfy their wants. As a result of his experiences at New Lanark, Owen realised this fact very clearly. The State must control its members; but, in order more efficiently to do this, it must delegate its functions to self-supporting communities, wherein men may be trained to govern themselves.

We have said above that only the communities which have banded themselves together for religious purposes have approached success, but it is fairly clear that to some of the settlers at Queenwood their community was a religion. An austere enthusiasm for the millennium was illuminated by a devoted veneration for their own community, which was pointing the way.

Hymns to community, a strange goddess, in the Socialists' Hymn Book, bear witness to the devotion of the early Communists to their ideal. And they worshipped Owen as a divinely inspired prophet. Amid much that is ridiculous, both in the man himself and in his followers, something cast in the heroic mould remains. Owen saw and thought far in advance of his age. But it is not in his intellectual creed that his greatness lies. Owen stands out permanently as a prophet and a dreamer. Pervaded by a real hatred of the iniquities of the social system as he found it, he combined the inspiration which he drew from this source with an unflagging enthusiasm in the pursuit of his ideals. It was the great force of sincerity which enabled him to appeal so strongly to the imaginations of men, and to suffuse his creed with a religious tinge. If he was a dreamer, he was not content to dream his life. He possessed that greatest of faiths, the faith to live his dreams.

NOTE.

The best life of Owen is entitled "Robert Owen: a Biography," by Frank Podmore, two vols. Hutchinson, 1906. It is out of print. Another is "The Life, Times, and Labours of Robert Owen," by Lloyd Jones, third edition, 1900. Allen & Unwin. 3s. 6d.

The most extensive bibliography available is published at 1s. net (54 pages) by the National Library of Wales, Aberystwyth, for the Welsh Bibliographical Society, "A Bibliography of Robert Owen, the Socialist, 1771-1858," compiled by A. J. Hawkes (1914). The best collection of Owenite literature is in the Goldsmiths' Company's Library of Economic Literature, University of London, Imperial Institute, S.W. 7, which contains a large part of the library of Owen's "Institute" in John Street, Tottenham Court Road.

The Reform of the House of Lords

By Sidney Webb.

Price One Penny.

The Fabian Society, 25, Tothill Street,
Westminster, London, S.W.1.   November, 1917.

THE REFORM OF THE

HOUSE OF LORDS.

At present the House of Lords is, constitutionally, in a position of suspense. By the Parliament Act of 1911 its right of absolute veto of the people's will, expressed in a Bill passed by the House of Commons, has been destroyed. But the entirely unrepresentative and accidentally selected assembly of 600 odd Peers of Parliament remains unreformed. It still possesses great powers of obstruction and delay. Its influence in emasculating all progressive measures with which its members disagree is still very great, and is all the more objectionable in that it is largely exercised through the Cabinet in secret, without the check of public opinion. Moreover, various party leaders, and the House of Commons as a whole, are more or less pledged, if only by the preamble to the Parliament Act, to an early reform of the Second Chamber. The question cannot, therefore, be ignored. The Committee of Peers and members of the House of Commons, which, in the autumn of 1917, has taken in hand the reconstruction of the Second Chamber, is strangely constituted. Lord Bryce, who patriotically consented to be chairman—after the Speaker, Mr. Asquith, and Lord Lansdowne has successively found it impossible to undertake the task—met with great difficulties in getting his Committee together. It has no constitutional or other authority. It is very far from being a convincing or even an impressive assembly. The genuine Liberals are far outnumbered by their opponents, and the unrepresentative complexion of the list is emphasised by there being only a single representative of the Labour Party. The Committee, which is as "unconstitutional" as was the Speaker's Conference which suggested it, can claim even less support from public opinion. It can justify its existence only in one way: by discovering a solution commanding general assent.

It may be doubted whether the reconstruction of the Second Chamber has yet been sufficiently considered by public opinion for any plan to which representative members of the House of

Lords are likely to agree to gain sufficient public support to enable it to be carried into law. But the present position of the House of Lords is too anomalous to permit of the question being indefinitely shelved; and the appointment of Lord Bryce's Committee has at any rate set the ball rolling. The reconstruction of the Second Chamber will be one of the issues on which candidates at each successive General Election must be required to declare themselves. The subject is, therefore, one on which not only members of Parliament, but also ordinary citizens, and particularly the Labour Party, must make up their minds.

Do we need, in the United Kingdom, any Second Chamber at all; and, if we do, what exactly do we need it for? Clear thinking about these questions is at present hindered by three subconscious prepossessions, one of them inspired by a haunting sense of history, another by indistinct visions of political geography, and the third by a vague fear of Democracy, basing itself on a bygone political science.

WHAT IS THE HOUSE OF LORDS?

The House of Lords, so far as history and the forms of the British Constitution are concerned, is not a Second Chamber at all. It is one of the few survivals in Europe of the once common separate Estates of the Realm. Of such " Estates " there used to be, in some countries, not two only, but three, four, or even five—the Nobles, the Clergy, the Municipalities, the Peasants, and the tenants on the Royal Demesne being entitled to be separately summoned to give the opinion of their respective orders upon the King's business. What happened was that, in the course of centuries, in this as in other countries, the majority of the separate orders were merged in a single assembly of " the Commons," which ceased to be an Estate of the Realm, and came to stand, in fact, though not always in form, for the whole community. Where any ancient Estate continued to sit separately, as in this country the Peers and Bishops did in the House of Lords, they did so (if we are to regard the substance of the Constitution), not as distinct Estates of the Realm, but—so far, at any rate, as the nineteenth century was concerned—as a Second Chamber. Since 1832, at least, the House of Lords has not been regarded by constitutional writers as having, *in fact*, whatever it may have had in form, any other functions than those of a Second Chamber; and it was in respect of its satisfactory exercise of those functions that the House of Lords was, by its friends, alleged to find its justification. The political crime or blunder committed by the Conservative majority of the House of Lords in 1909-10, when it rejected the Budget Bill passed by the House of Commons, lay in the explicit revival of the claim of the Peers and Bishops to act, not as a Second Chamber, but as a separate Estate of the Realm. The House of Lords did not oppose the Budget Bill in the form in which it was presented on the ground that it was so badly drafted as to fail in many of its clauses to express the

4

opinion of the Legislature, and that it therefore needed drastic revision—though this, as we now see, was abundantly true. Nor did the House of Lords seriously allege that the House of Commons, in passing such a Budget, was not acting with the acquiescence and support of a majority of the electorate—a point on which the Peers and Bishops might have been honestly mistaken. What made the action of the overwhelming majority of the House of Lords equivalent to its political suicide was the suddenly revived claim of their Lordships to act, not as a Second Chamber, but as a separate Estate of the Realm, by setting up, as against the will of the nation expressed by the House of Commons, their own personal opinions that the Budget was, in substance, a bad one; and by acting on those opinions so far as to assert their right to nullify, whenever they chose, the decisions made by the House of Commons, in which the voice of the whole community had come to be sought. The result was decisive. We may take it as definitely settled that, whatever else they may desire, the people of this country will not tolerate the revival of any separate " Estate " of persons or classes who are to be privileged to enforce, against the opinions of the majority of the nation, any views of their own order. Any reconstructed House of Lords must accordingly be quite definitely made only a Second Chamber, with the functions and powers appropriate to such an organ of the National Legislature, and no others.

DO WE WANT AN IMPERIAL SENATE ?

The question is, however, confused in the minds of some people by an indistinct impression of the Senate of the United States, and to a lesser degree of the Federal Council representing the Cantons of Switzerland, one or other of which has lately formed a model for other federal communities, notably Australia and South Africa. It is sometimes suggested that the reconstructed House of Lords should take the form of an " Imperial Senate," in which representatives of the various parts of the British Empire, including the United Kingdom, should sit as an Imperial Legislature, incidentally serving as a revising Chamber to all the subordinate Legislatures, including the House of Commons itself. This, to put it bluntly, is a dream, and a bad dream. The British Empire is not, and cannot now be made, a federal Empire with subordinate Legislatures. It is an Alliance of Free States, with a congeries of other dependencies, themselves progressing towards various forms of legislative autonomy. The self-governing Dominions have not the slightest intention of placing themselves, even for what are called " Imperial affairs," under a Senate in which they must for many generations form a minority. Neither Canada nor Australia, neither New Zealand nor South Africa, would for a moment consent to make their own Legislatures subordinate to an Imperial Senate formed out of a British Second Chamber. Nor has British Democracy any desire

5

to allow the British "Junkers" to call in Canadian and South African plutocracy to their aid. Constitution-making for the "Britannic Alliance" must take another form. Any representative " Council of the Empire " will, for as far ahead as can be foreseen, exercise powers of consultation and suggestion only, not of command or legislation. And any such " Imperial " organ would be quite unfit to serve as a Second Chamber for the British or any other constituent Legislature. These " federal" Senates, whether in Australia or South Africa, Canada or the United States, Switzerland or the German Empire, have nothing to do with our problem of a Second Chamber. We must accordingly dismiss the idea of any colonial representation, or the separate representation of Scotland, Ireland or Wales, in the proposed Second Chamber for the United Kingdom.

" THE HOUSE OF PROPERTY OWNERS."

The third source of confused thinking is the vague fear of Democracy, leading to the desire for some counterpoise to an all-powerful single Chamber. This prepossession, found to greater or less extent in nearly all property owners, is scarcely amenable to argument. It is plainly founded, to a large extent, on an illusion. The apprehended attacks on property must come in the main in the form of taxation in the annual or other money Bill; and it is just these money Bills that no Second Chamber, however constituted— not even the present House of Lords—can ever be allowed to touch. This was finally settled by the Parliament Act of 1911, from which there will certainly be no going back. Thus no Second Chamber can possibly save the property owner from taxation, however drastic. Moreover, property owners, like peers, cannot nowadays claim any position of privilege against the will of the Nation. Any real danger of unjust treatment can be met by the powers of revision and delay which constitute the proper function of a Second Chamber. What is abundantly clear is that, if it is really sought to create a rival power to the House of Commons, the intention must be carefully concealed from the Labour Party and the electorate, under pain of getting the whole scheme summarily rejected! It is too late to " go back on Democracy "; and apprehensive property owners would be well advised to place their trust in "the people," contenting themselves with ensuring that any serious innovation shall obtain a considered judgment, and not merely an impulsive decision, from the electorate.

WHAT KIND OF SECOND CHAMBER DO WE NEED ?

We come now to the question of what the nation really needs in place of the House of Lords. One thing is plain. We do not require, and public opinion will not tolerate, any rival to the House of Commons. Where it agrees with the popular Legislature such a rival is useless; where it disagrees, it is in the highest degree dangerous. This consideration quite negatives the project of an elected Second Chamber, which Mr. Asquith's Cabinet was contemplating before the war, but against which the House of Commons very decisively expressed itself before even the draft was published. The long and calamitous experience of an entirely elected Second Chamber in Victoria is conclusive against its imitation in any other unitary State. It is not the function of the Second Chamber in a unitary State to represent the people; this must be done, as well as it can be done, by the House of Commons. Whatever may be the imperfections of the House of Commons in this respect, they are not mended by setting up another Chamber claiming to be representative. This would be to get back to the mediæval system of rival and competing Estates of the Realm. We are free from the needs of a federal State which have compelled the United States and the Australian Commonwealth to incur the inconvenience and peril of such a legislative dualism. Similar considerations negative equally the fantastic project of a functional or stratified Second Chamber, elected by the whole electorate voting by trades, professions or occupations. All the arguments adduced for this by its advocates are valid—in so far as they have any validity at all—for the election of the House of Commons, that is to say, the Legislature itself; they have no relevance for a body which is not to be a Legislature but merely a Second Chamber.

THE PROPER FUNCTIONS OF A SECOND CHAMBER.

The essential function of a Second Chamber, it may be suggested, and the only one for which such a body is required or can be permanently useful, is that of revision in its largest sense. The Legislature proper may often be passing Bills which ought not to pass into law in the form in which they leave the popular assembly. There will be, in the first place, errors of drafting, and palpable mistakes and omissions. In the second place, there will not infrequently be a lack of consistency, either of legislation or of policy, in relation to other matters which the whole community would wish to see righted. Finally, there is on some measures the contingency of doubt as to whether the decision of the House of Commons would be upheld by public opinion. The House of Commons does not always represent the people. It may be under the dominion of an imperious temporary majority, itself controlled by a " party caucus," and dominated by a particular interest. The particular measure may have been finally carried only by one vote. It may enact an indefinite prolongation of the life of the Legislature. It may have been carried by a moribund House. It may have been rushed through all its stages in a few days, in a wild panic, or conceivably even by an anti-popular conspiracy, without public opinion becoming aware of what is happening. It may be of a nature to arouse irresistible popular opposition, only that opposition does not instantly manifest itself. British Democracy may well be in full agreement with the most apprehensive of property owners in not desiring to erect even its elected House of Commons into a position of supreme dictatorship. The case for a Second Chamber, *confined to the proper functions of a Second Chamber*, is as convincing to the Democrat as it is to the most timid of Conservatives, provided *only that it is not made an excuse for setting up some power by which any particular class or any particular political party can defeat the people's will.*

WHAT A SECOND CHAMBER OUGHT TO BE.

What is required for a Second Chamber is a position of independence of the Popular Assembly, well-defined functions of its own which it cannot extend, and sufficient power temporarily to " hold up " the Popular Assembly, without temptation or opportunity to compete with it. The Second Chamber needs to be composed of persons of ripe wisdom and judgment, not necessarily orators or popular electioneerers; known to and respected by the public for their personal qualities, but not necessarily the most widely known of notorieties; not representative of any one class or interest, not even of age or of property in general; and widely inclusive of legal and administrative training and experience. It must not be merely an " Order of Merit," an assembly of old men; least of all a sanctuary of the superannuated, a gathering of " Ex's," or persons who have retired from office as Cabinet Ministers, Judges or Colonial Governors. Popular election does not produce such an assembly as is required. Appointment by the King (that is, by the Prime Minister for the time being) has proved a failure in Canada and New Zealand, and is, from its inevitable partisan character, obviously unsuitable; there is no case for selection from the peerage any more than from the beerage; moreover, its members must not oppress us for life, but must be continually being renewed, so as to keep the Second Chamber always in touch with the opinions of the current generation.

It has sometimes been incautiously suggested that the only acceptable Second Chamber in a free State would be one formed by popular election. This requires further examination.

NO "LOADING OF THE DICE" AGAINST DEMOCRACY.

In the first place, it is not at all likely that the present House of Lords will sanction, or that the present Cabinet will propose, a Second Chamber chosen entirely by the popular electorate. There will certainly be claims that some, at least, of the present Peers

8

should sit as of right, or at any rate (like the existing Scottish and Irish Representative Peers) by the suffrage of their brother Peers. There will be attempts made to secure permanent seats for the holders of certain great offices, such as the Royal Princes, the Archbishops and Bishops of the Church of England, perhaps the leaders of Nonconformity, the heads of the so-called "learned professions," and, comically enough, the Right Honourable the Lord Mayor of the City of London! All these must be decisively negatived by the Labour Party. Whatever their pretext, they really represent underhand attempts to "pack" the Second Chamber with members who, whatever may be their other qualities, do not share either the feelings or the desires of the great mass of the population.

Any permanent reservation of seats in the Second Chamber, either for Peers or Ecclesiastics, the scions of Royalty or great Officers of State, the representatives of particular localities or of particular classes, means a "loading of the dice" against Democracy, which Labour (even if tempted by the offer of a few seats for distinguished Labour Leaders!) must absolutely reject.

NO "FAKED" ELECTION!

More plausible are the proposals that will be put forward—when it is found that public opinion will not tolerate a "faked" Second Chamber, which would (from the standpoint of Democracy) amount only to the resuscitation of a House of Lords under another name—for a Second Chamber "more or less" elected by the people. It may be proposed to form the Second Chamber, wholly or in part, of the Chairmen or other representatives chosen by the County Councils or the principal Municipal Corporations. We may find the Chambers of Commerce or the new Federation of British Industry asked to appoint representatives, the doctors and the lawyers, and even, to impart an appearance of fairness—really throwing a bone to the dog!—the Trades Union Congress graciously allowed to nominate one or two members among the whole crowd of so-called "superior people."

All these projects of indirect election are born of the distrust of Democracy; they are devised with the deliberate intention of hindering the House of Commons from carrying out the people's will. However ingeniously these systems are formulated, so as to hide their main purpose, they always reveal themselves as calcu-lated to produce a Second Chamber made up, almost entirely, of members of one or other of the old political parties; of representatives of the landlord or capitalist class; of employers and "business men"; of more or less wealthy property-owners. The one section that is always deliberately excluded, or else admitted only as a quite infinitesimal minority, are the four-fifths of the whole population who are manual working wage-earners. A

Second Chamber thus constituted—professedly by popular election!—would certainly contain, at most, only a handful of men of the wage-earning class. There would probably not even be any Payment of Members. Such a Second Chamber would suit the Conservative Party down to the ground. It might be nearly as useful to the Liberal Party. The Labour Party, even if it came to form a majority in the House of Commons, would find itself, with such a Second Chamber, in the same hopeless minority as is the present Liberal Party in the House of Lords. If that position is intolerable to the members of the Liberal Party, with what " face " can they propose to subject the Labour Party to the same impotence ? Moreover, from such a Second Chamber one whole sex would find itself either wholly excluded, or at best only represented by a small handful of carefully picked women. Any indirectly elected Second Chamber could not fail to be predominantly an Assembly of the wealthy middle-class, permanently biassed against really effective economic and industrial reforms.

NO ELECTED SECOND CHAMBER !

Matters are not much mended if (as Mr. Asquith and Mr. Runciman, Lord Crewe and Mr. McKenna are believed to have been ready to propose in 1913) the Second Chamber is formed entirely by direct election. Apart from merely federal bodies (like the Senates of the United States and the Australian Commonwealth), such Second Chambers as exist of this kind in unitary States (as in Victoria) have worked very badly. There is nearly always a higher franchise or a higher qualification, whether by property or age, than for the Popular Assembly. Or the same end is secured by making the Second Chamber much smaller than the Popular Assembly, and therefore elected by gigantic constituencies which, in this country, with large populations, could be adequately contested only at great expense, and with the aid of the most widely circulating newspapers which are all controlled by wealthy men. Thus, with our prospective electorate of 16 millions —certainly to be increased presently to at least 20 millions—a popularly elected Second Chamber of 100 members would mean single-member constituencies each averaging half a million population, with electorates each averaging from 150,000 to 200,000 men and women to be circularised and addressed ! Complicated systems of Proportional Representation (with grouped constituencies of a million or two electors !) would further increase the necessity— if a majority of the Assembly is to be secured, and not merely the return of an isolated representative of exceptional views—for expensive party organisation. One way or another it is always contrived, in all the plans that are suggested, that the elected Second Chamber shall be predominantly a " House of Wealth." This purpose is openly avowed. It is declared that, if numbers are to rule the Popular Assembly, " property " must be represented— *even out of all proportion to the numbers of property owners—*

10

in the Second Chamber. Against any such contention every earnest Liberal or Radical, every member of the Labour Party—indeed, every real Democrat—must enter an emphatic protest.

What does not seem commonly realised is that even the best possible elected Second Chamber necessarily and inevitably makes a bad Second Chamber—that is to say, a body so constituted as to perform very badly the essential duties of a Second Chamber. A popularly elected Second Chamber is, in this country, certain to be elected on "party issues," and to be organised on "party lines." The very intention with which such a Second Chamber is created is that it shall frequently, if not invariably, be made up, so far as its majority is concerned, so as to be in opposition to the Popular Assembly. Otherwise there would, in the opinion of those who advocate such a plan, be no profit in it! Whenever the majority of the Second Chamber is of another political party than that to which the Government of the day belongs, the temptation to the party leaders, the party organisers, the party newspapers and the party caucus to discredit the Government measures, to delay and obstruct their becoming law and even to throw them over for a General Election will be irresistible. Needless to say this political partiality would tend always to be exercised to the detriment of innovations; and therefore to the disadvantage of all but the Conservative, or "stand pat" Party. Once more the dice would be loaded, more skilfully than ever, against Democracy.

But there is another reason, of quite a different character, against an elected Second Chamber—a reason which is all the stronger when the proposal is to make the Second Chamber entirely elective, on a franchise as wide as that for the Popular Assembly, and with qualifications and other conditions no more restrictive. Such a Second Chamber—whether chosen by geographical constituencies or by industries or other classes—without being well qualified for the duty of revision of the measures sent up to it, could claim to be as truly representative of the People's Will as the Popular Assembly itself. *This is a fatal defect in a Second Chamber.* To set up a second exponent of the People's Will, in opposition or rivalry to the first, would inevitably be to create opposition, conflict and deadlock. What would be the use of such an Elected Second Chamber if it always agreed with the other House? How could differences of opinion between them on minor points, or unpopular causes, or abstruse issues, ever be decided? How could the quarrels between them be decided, even on great issues, without evil wrangling and long delay, and possibly the drastic remedy of a Double Dissolution, whenever there was a failure to agree? It is of the greatest importance to take care that the Second Chamber should be so constituted as to have no claim to be an exponent of the People's Will, any more than to be a medium for the expression of the will of particular Estates of the Realm or particular social classes. What the nation wants a Second Chamber for is not to pretend to the expression of any body's will—that is the business of the Popular Assembly—but

11

for the quite distinct function of acting as a criticising and revising body, coming to the help of the Popular Assembly in order to ensure a correct expression of the People's Will. We want to get an organ of criticism and revision that will not be swayed by party passion or party bias to oppose the measures sent up to it, merely because it does not like their contents; and yet will maintain a position of independence of the Popular Assembly sufficient to enable it temporarily to " hold up " that Assembly whenever it fails to express the People's Will.

THE RIGHT SOLUTION.

Surveying all the experience of the world with Second Chambers —municipal as well as legislative, unitary and federal—it may be suggested that the best expedient, and one which has, in fact, worked with singular smoothness and success, is that adopted by Norway, namely, election of the Second Chamber by the Popular Assembly. We suggest that the best plan of reconstructing the House of Lords as a Second Chamber for the United Kingdom is to enact that, immediately after each General Election, the House of Commons should elect, by the best system of Proportional Representation, a Second Chamber of, say, one hundred members, chosen from among persons (male or female) who are not members of the House of Commons. They should be irremovable during their tenure of office; should be made members of the Privy Council (and thus be styled Right Honourable); and should receive the same payment as Members of Parliament. Such a Second Chamber should be empowered to confer privately by committees with the House of Commons about the details of Bills, and to refer back to the House of Commons for reconsideration (but only if accompanied by a critical and detailed report expounding the revision suggested, and the reasons therefor) any Bill (not being the Annual other Money Bill as now defined) in which, whether or not its objects and purposes commended themselves, it was thought that specific amendments were required, in order either to make the measure more accurately express what the House of Commons desired, or to remedy what seemed to be omissions or inconsistencies within the measure itself, or to bring it into harmony with existing legislation in other departments. Moreover, the Second Chamber should be empowered, irrespective of its own views upon the propriety of the Bill, whenever it considered that a measure was of such a nature, or had been passed by the House of Commons under such circumstances, as to demand further consideration by the public opinion of the nation, either to refer the Bill back to the House of Commons for reconsideration in a subsequent session, explaining the reasons making such delay expedient, or (except in the case of the Annual Money Bill, or other legislation not brooking delay); in an extreme case, to suspend it for reconsideration by the House of Commons for a period not exceeding two years, or until the first session after the next ensuing General Election. No reference back of either sort should be permitted more than once for the same measure.

It is suggested that a Second Chamber of this sort, with powers strictly defined in the above sense, would exercise satisfactorily all the functions that are proper to a Second Chamber, and it could not practically usurp any others. It would be as free as is possible from the temptation—the greatest, to which a Second Chamber is exposed—to act from party spirit in a direction contrary to that of the majority of the House of Commons. It would be always in touch with every section of the House of Commons, and would yet be entirely independent of it. It would have at its command all the talent needed for revision in the largest sense, and none of the corporate ambition that might tempt its members to rivalry of what must, in any case, be and remain the supreme Legislature.

THE CUNNING AMENDMENT THAT WILL RUIN IT!

It is essential to the proper working of such a Second Chamber (in order to obviate the deflecting influence of party bias or party passion) that it should at all times correspond exactly, in the distribution of its members among parties, with the Popular Assembly for the time being. The cunning way to vitiate the proposal—an amendment certain to be proposed in the interests of the Conservative party and the property owners—is to make the term of office of such a Second Chamber longer than that of the House of Commons by which it is chosen; for instance, to say that its members should serve for the duration of two Parliaments, one half retiring at each dissolution. Such an amendment, specious as it is, must be strenuously resisted. However suitable it might be for a popularly elected Second Chamber, in which it was sought to secure an expression of the nation's permanent will, rather than of what might be only a momentary wave of feeling, it is quite out of place with regard to a Second Chamber which has not got to express the nation's will at all, but only to act as a Court of Revision. The cunning of the amendment lies in the fact that it would set up a bulwark against each successive House of Commons in which a relatively " progressive " majority had been returned. This would find itself baulked by the over-standing half of the Second Chamber representing the defeated party majority of the last previous House of Commons. The discredited Conservative or property-owners' majority, against which the nation had risen in revolt, and indignantly it hurled from office and power, would be enabled always to lay its dead hand on the measures that the nation had voted for! It is accordingly of vital importance that the Second Chamber should be wholly appointed by each newly elected House of Commons for a

13

term of office expiring at each dissolution. Nothing short of this ought to be agreed to by any member of the Labour Party or by any genuine democrat.

CONCLUSIONS.

Thus we come definitely to the following conclusions:—

The House of Lords must go.

The House of Commons must be and remain the Supreme Legislature.

There is good ground for the establishment of a Second Chamber.

But only if this is not made an excuse for enabling particular sections to defeat the People's Will.

An Imperial Senate is impossible, and would anyhow not form a suitable Second Chamber.

The nation will not stand a " House of Property Owners," or any revival of separate Estates of the Realm.

There must be no " faked " Second Chamber loading the dice against Democracy.

Nor do we want a sanctuary for the superannuated, an Assembly of Ex's, a Gilded Sepulchre for the Meritorious Aged.

Any " partially elected " Second Chamber would inevitably turn out to be packed with peers and dignitaries, millionaires and superannuated officials, in which the Conservative Party would have a permanent majority, and in which the Labour Party would find itself as hopelessly out-voted as is the Liberal Party in the House of Lords.

We must beware equally of any Second Chamber formed by indirect election, or nominated by County Councils, the learned professions and great interests—all of them devices for loading the dice against Democracy !

Beware, too, of the bribe to Trade Union leaders—even as many as six of them may be offered seats in a Second Chamber of rich men—how generous !

But the Second Chamber may be quite as deadly to Democracy if it is wholly elected by the people, as Victoria has found to its cost: it is easy, whether by a special franchise or by requiring high qualifications, or even merely by making colossal constituencies, to exclude all but wealthy men or the representatives of wealthy party organisations, as successfully as in the House of Lords.

A popularly elected Second Chamber would, in fact, always be a bad Second Chamber, because it could claim to be as much the representative of the people as the House of Commons, and would inevitably become a rival to it. The function of a Second Chamber is merely to help the House of Commons to express correctly the People's Will; not to baulk it.

By far the best way of forming a Second Chamber in this country would be the Norwegian system—let the House of Commons elect, after each General Election, by Proportional Representation, say 100 men and women outside its own ranks, to remain in office only for the term of that Parliament, to be paid the same as Members of the House of Commons, and to be styled Right Honourable.

Such a Second Chamber might be entrusted with power to refer back to the House of Commons, with a detailed critical report (but once only), any Bill (other than the Annual Money Bill) which the Second Chamber thought badly drafted or inconsistent with other legislation; or any such Bill, irrespective of whether or not it commended itself in substance, which seemed to require further consideration by public opinion.

But beware of the cunning amendment by which the Tory party, or the property-owners, will certainly seek to pervert even this proposal into a bulwark of the existing order. To enable the dead hand of the past to baulk the people's will it is only necessary to make the term of office of the Second Chamber longer than that of the House of Commons that nominates it. Any such cunning dodge to make the Second Chamber differ in party balance from the House of Commons for the time being must be strenuously resisted.

FABIAN PUBLICATIONS.

FABIAN ESSAYS IN SOCIALISM. Paper 6d.; cloth 1/6; post. 2½d. and 4d.
HISTORY OF THE FABIAN SOCIETY. By E. R. PEASE. 5s. n.
TOWARDS SOCIAL DEMOCRACY? By SIDNEY WEBB. 1s. n., post. 1d.
WHAT TO READ on Social and Economic Subjects. 1s. n. and 2s. n.
THE RURAL PROBLEM. By H. D. HARBEN. 2s. 6d. n.
THIS MISERY OF BOOTS. By H. G. WELLS. 3d., post free 4d.

FABIAN TRACTS and LEAFLETS.

Tracts, each 16 to 52 pp., price 1d., or 9d. per doz., unless otherwise stated.
Leaflets, 4 pp. each, price 1d. for six copies, 1s. per 100, or 8/6 per 1000
The Set of 77, 3/6; post free 3/11. Bound in buckram, 5/-n.; post free 5/6.

I.—General Socialism in its various aspects.

TRACTS.—184. The Russian Revolution and British Democracy. By JULIUS WEST. 2d. 180. The Philosophy of Socialism. By A. CLUTTON BROCK. 169. The Socialist Movement in Germany. By W. STEPHEN SANDERS. 2d. 159. The Necessary Basis of Society. By SIDNEY WEBB. 151. The Point of Honour. By RUTH C. BENTINCK. 147. Capital and Compensation. By E. R. PEASE. 146. Socialism and Superior Brains. By BERNARD SHAW. 142. Rent and Value. 138. Municipal Trading. 121. Public Service v. Private Expenditure. By Sir OLIVER LODGE. 107. Socialism for Millionaires. By BERNARD SHAW. 139. Socialism and the Churches. By Rev. JOHN CLIFFORD, D.D. 133. Socialism and Christianity. By Rev. PERCY DEARMER. 78. Socialism and the Teaching of Christ. By Dr. J. CLIFFORD. 42. Christian Socialism. By Rev. S. D. HEADLAM. 79. A Word of Remembrance and Caution to the Rich. By JOHN WOOLMAN. 72. The Moral Aspects of Socialism. By SIDNEY BALL. 69. Difficulties of Individualism. By S. WEBB. 51. Socialism: True and False. By S. WEBB. 45. The Impossibilities of Anarchism. By G. B. SHAW. 2d. 7. Capital and Land. 5. Facts for Socialists. 2d. LEAFLETS—13. What Socialism Is 1. Why are the Many Poor?

II.—Applications of Socialism to Particular Problems.

TRACTS.—183. The Reform of the House of Lords. By SIDNEY WEBB. 181. When Peace Comes—the Way of Industrial Reconstruction. By SIDNEY WEBB. 2d. 178. The War; Women; and Unemployment. 2d. 177. Socialism and the Arts of Use. By A. CLUTTON BROCK. 175. The Economic Foundations of the Women's Movement. 2d. 173. Public v. Private Electricity Supply. 171. The Nationalization of Mines and Minerals Bill. 170. Profit-Sharing and Co-Partnership: a Fraud and Failure? 164. Gold and State Banking. 163. Women and Prisons. 2d. 162. Family Life on a Pound a Week. By Mrs. REEVES. 2d. 161. Afforestation and Unemployment. 160. A National Medical Service. 2d. 157. The Working Life of Women. 155. The Case against the Referendum. 154. The Case for School Clinics. 153. The Twentieth Century Reform Bill. 152. Our Taxes as they are and as they ought to be. 2d. 149. The Endowment of Motherhood. 2d. 131. The Decline of the Birth-Rate. 145. The Case for School Nurseries. 140. Child Labor under Capitalism. 136. The Village and the Landlord. By EDW. CARPENTER. 144. Machinery: its Masters and Servants. 122. Municipal Milk and Public Health. 125. Municipalization by Provinces. 124. State Control of Trusts. 83. State Arbitration and the Living Wage. LEAFLET.—104. How Trade Unions benefit Workmen.

III.—Local Government Powers: How to use them.

TRACTS.—176. The War and the Workers. By SIDNEY WEBB. 172. What about the Rates? By S. WEBB. 156. What an Education Committee can do (Elementary Schools), 3d. 62. Parish and District Councils. (Revised 1913). 137. Parish Councils and Village Life. 109. Cottage Plans and Common Sense. 82. Workmen's Compensation Act. LEAFLETS.— 134. Small Holdings. 68. The Tenant's Sanitary Catechism. 71. Ditto for London.

IV.—General Politics and Fabian Policy.

TRACTS.—158. The Case against the C.O.S. By Mrs. TOWNSHEND. 70. Report on Fabian Policy. 41. The Fabian Society: its Early History. By BERNARD SHAW.

V.—Biographical Series. In portrait covers, 2d. each.

182. Robert Owen, Idealist. By C. E. M. JOAD. 179. John Ruskin and ial Ethics. B Prof. EDITH MORLEY. 16 . Francis Place. B ST. JOHN

The
Russian Revolution
and
British Democracy.

By Julius West.

Price Twopence.

The Fabian Society, 25, Tothill Street,
Westminster, London, S.W.1.   November, 1917.

The author, who is Russian by birth, and is a member of the Executive Committee of the Fabian Society, was sent by his colleagues to Petrograd in June, 1917, in response to a telegram from the Council of Workers' and Soldiers' Delegates, inviting the Society to send a delegate to discuss the then proposed International Socialist Congress at Stockholm.

The following paper was completed in August, 1917, before the author left for a second visit to Russia, and any later revision of it has not been possible.

THE RUSSIAN REVOLUTION AND BRITISH DEMOCRACY.

It is no easy task to estimate the value of the Russian Revolution for British democracy, but it is a very necessary task. There can be no doubt that when commonsense and experience have blown away the froth which now covers the surface of events, and when time has allowed the sediment to sink to its proper place, we shall see a nation greatly different from the distressed Russia of 1917. The process of settling down may take some years to accomplish, but nobody with any knowledge of Russia can doubt that before long she will take her place as one of the undisputed leaders of the great democracies. And if democracy is to make for lasting peace and for the welfare of the world, it is clear that there must first be mutual understanding, as a preliminary to mutual trust. The purpose of this pamphlet is to explain, with this object in view, some of the features of the new Russia which seem to have a bearing on her future relations with Britain.

THE RUSSIAN WORKING MAN.

Industrially, Russia is one of the youngest countries in the world, although factories made their first appearance there as far back as here. (E.g., " Under Catherine II. [1762-96] the workers sent to the Imperial Court three delegates, instructed to implore the Imperial protection against the abuses of employers. These delegates ' received each one hundred blows with the knout, had their nostrils burnt with red-hot irons, and were deported for life to Siberia.' "—From Alexinsky's *Modern Russia*.) But, in spite of the fact that Russia was enviously looked upon as an employers' paradise by many of the capitalists of Western Europe, the factory system developed slowly. In 1913 the total number of factory employees in European Russia under Government inspection was only about two and a-quarter millions, out of a population of about one hundred and forty millions. Even if we allow for the large number of persons employed in the factories which have been springing up at convenient points away from towns, especially over the south and south-west of Russia, the total industrial population in all that vast area will be very far short of that of England and Wales.

The factory workers, relatively few though they be, are in most cases of peasant origin; that is to say, that they have been born in the villages. They had been coming to the towns before the traditions of serfdom had been fully extinguished. In consequence they have put up with abominably bad treatment from employers and foremen, with insanitary and insufficient housing accommodation, and with ridiculously low wages, which made existence possible only on a diet of weak tea and black bread. From 1870 to 1905, in spite of brutal repression, serious strikes were taking place in all the towns. And, be it remembered, the Russian working man was generally illiterate, and had no means of improving his own condition. The Government came down heavily on all forms of self-organisation, thus making trade-unionism, co-operation or political action practically impossible. There was no Duma and no labour representation anywhere.

In the circumstances it is not surprising that the political theories which the Russian working man evolved for himself were generally based on the necessity for a violent revolution. In 1905 a great effort was made to produce it—very nearly with success. But the difficulties of existence prevented the general acceptance of any definite and detailed political and industrial programme. The task of carrying the revolution through was gigantic enough to absorb all the energies of the working man; he could not see beyond it. And, it is important to note, this faith in a revolution was not confined to a section of the working class. It was the creed of the whole working class. The separate representation of working men was provided for in the Electoral Law under which the members of the Duma were chosen. The experience of four general elections led Prof. Milynkov to say that " every representative of the working men is invariably a Socialist in Russia. Thus it is quite impossible for the capitalists to elect a non-Socialist member. Russia is the only place in the world, I suppose, where the ' bourgeois ' and the ' junkers ' are obliged to elect Socialist members " (in " Russian Realities and Problems," 1917).

The fact that the political creed of the working class, insufficient though it was, was so generally accepted created a feeling of class solidarity incomparably stronger than any counterpart which may be found in Great Britain. This class solidarity, in combination with the faith in revolution, led to the ready acceptance of the Marxist doctrine of the class war. In Russia the line between one class and the next was very distinctly drawn in the days before the Revolution. A Russian had to belong to one of five legally defined classes, which was named in his passport. The " bourgeois," or middle-class man, although scarcer in Russia than in Western Europe, was, in accordance with the theory of Marx, looked upon as the natural enemy of the working man,

4

or, at the outside, tolerated as a temporarily necessary but ultimately superfluous institution.

THE COUNCIL OF WORKERS' AND SOLDIERS' DELEGATES.

This explanation may clear up the attitude of the Russian revolutionist towards the world, after his success in March, 1917, when the Council of Workers' and Soldiers' Delegates became, for all practical purposes, the Russian Parliament. Here it may be as well to describe the origin and growth of this generally misunderstood assembly.

The revolutionary movement of 1905 came to a head with a general strike, about the middle of October. The strike was a political one. It began on the railways, and by the 14th of the month it had spread over the whole of Russia, the Caucasus and the greater part of the Siberian and Asiatic railways. The factories immediately followed, and fights took place between strikers and soldiers in many parts of Russia. The telegraph ceased to work; the Government was paralysed. On October 12 it was decided, at a meeting in Petrograd, to form a Council of Working Men's Deputies. Within four days it had branches in all the great cities, and a Press of its own. Within a week this body became the real Government—the only organisation with any power behind it. On October 17 the Emperor ostensibly capitulated and signed a manifesto granting Russia a Constitution. On the 20th the general strike was discontinued by order of the Council. This was its high-water mark. We need not concern ourselves here with the subsequent unsuccessful general strikes, the risings, military and civil, of 1905 and 1906, and the gradual suppression of the revolutionary movement by the army and the police. The leading members of the Petrograd Council were arrested at the end of November and the beginning of December, when the centre of the revolution shifted to Moscow, where the local Council of Workers' Deputies, with a revolutionary Council of Soldiers' Deputies, kept up a fierce struggle for a month or so before they were overpowered.

From the end of 1905 to March, 1917, the Petrograd Council of Workers' Deputies lived underground. On March 12, 1917, the Duma was apparently at last in control of the situation. On the morning of that day it had decided to ignore the Tsar's ukaze proroguing the Duma. The Petrograd garrison had united with the working men in armed resistance to the police. The Chairman of the Council, a Georgian member of the Duma named Cheidse, decided that the time had come. A meeting of the Council was hastily summoned at the Taurida Palace, the building occupied by the Duma, and on the same day a proclamation was published inviting the workmen and soldiers of Petrograd to elect representatives to a Council of Workers' and Soldiers' Delegates. This Council came into existence three days before the Provisional Government, and one of the strongest men in Russia, Kerensky, was a vice-chairman. The C.W.S.D. was strong enough to exert an influence on the composition of the first Provisional Government. When it (the C.W.S.D.) was only a week or two old it had already grown to such dimensions that it could crowd the Duma out of its own home and take possession of the Taurida Palace, where it remains.

Within a few days of the revolution local C.W.S.D.'s had sprung into existence over all Russia and Siberia, followed a little later by Peasants' Councils. The members of the C.W.S.D.'s are naturally all Socialists, but of a good many different shades. In July, 1917, the writer heard a man holding forth in a Petrograd street to this effect: "The mother of seventeen young children lies dangerously ill. Her brood is misbehaving, making a terrible racket in the house, quarrelling amongst themselves, and fighting. If the noise continues the mother will die, and the children will starve. Is it not right, therefore, that the children should compose their differences for a while, forgetting that their names are Esserr, Bolshevik, Menshevik, Internationalist, Anarchist, Cadet, and so on, until the old lady has recovered. For if the Motherland dies, what will become of the Revolution?"

The man was speaking extremely good sense. There are too many parties, and the nearer they are, curiously enough, the greater the distance between them. The insuperable goes arm-in-arm with the inseparable. A and B, two Socialists, in agreement on everything that matters, will find some point of detail on which to differ, and will form separate parties. Then C, a kindly theorist, will say: "Why this disunion? Let us unite." And a few of the followers of A and B will leave them and come under C's banner, thus making a new party. Half the parties in Russia are the result of somebody's efforts to unite the other parties. The people who try to compose sectional differences succeed only in decomposing the existing organisations.

THE SOCIALIST PARTIES.

To see how the Socialist movement in Russia has been affected by this tendency to split up in the name of unity, let us glance over the party make-up of the great All-Russian Conference of Workers' and Soldiers' Delegates of June, 1917—about as representative a body as one could hope to find. There were in all 1,090 delegates:

    285 Social Revolutionists.
    248 Mensheviks.
    105 Bolsheviks.
     32 Internationalists.
     73 Non-Party Socialists.
     10 United Social-Democrats (Bolshevik and Menshevik).
     10 Bundists (Jewish S.D. Party).
      3 The "Edinstvo" (Unity) Group.
      3 National Socialists.
      5 Labour Group.
      1 Anarchist Communist.

The total falls a good deal short of 1,090 because the list does. not include various representatives of provincial organisations, the. army, the navy, and the peasantry, who were not selected on a party platform.

*   *   *   *   *   *

It may be gathered, therefore, that the people who really matter are the Social-Revolutionists, the Mensheviks, and the Bol-. sheviks. All three groups are Marxian, especially the Bolsheviks. The other two recognise the, at any rate, temporary justification of. the existence of the middle-class, or bourgeoisie (a member of which rejoices in the name of "boorjooy"). The Bolsheviks, on the other hand, want to get rid of the boorjooys out of hand. The Social-Revolutionists (or Esserrs) base their views on the theory that you must begin on the bottom floor, which means the moujik. In their economic doctrine, as in Tolstoy's, one begins with the peasant and the land, the first holding the second in communal ownership. The Mensheviks and Bolsheviks are not quite so keen on the land. They claim that the revolution must be the work of the victims of capitalism, who are not the peasantry, but the working classes.

*   *   *   * .   *   *

About 1898 there was formed a party known as the Social Democratic Labour Party. In 1903 it split into two, called the Bolsheviks (or Majorityites or Maximalistes) and Mensheviks (or Minorityites or Minimalistes). The first party were the followers of Lenin. As the foregoing table shows, the Bolsheviks are now the minority, and vice versa. But both parties stick to their old names. No Menshevik wants to be called a Bolshevik, accuracy notwithstanding; to him the word has become a term of abuse more than a party description. The Mensheviks have provided the Socialist members of the Cabinet, and their party, working amicably with the Social-Revolutionaries, has been able to ensure a dependable majority in favour of the continuation of the war, and a sane policy generally. They meet, none the less they do not mingle. Plekhanov tried to get them to merge, and the result was the "Edinstvo" Group, the size of which is indicated by its three representatives at the All-Russia Conference. The Bolsheviks harmonise, so far as this is possible, with the Internationalists, who want to see the whole world follow the example of Russia.

The Peasant Councils are ostensibly non-party; they nevertheless practically accept the Social-Revolutionary programme. The vote of peasant soldiers was large enough to elect a Social-Revolutionary majority in the municipal elections held in Moscow in June, 1917.

LENIN.

The difference between the outlook of the British and Russian working man cannot be illustrated better than by reference to a well-known and generally misrepresented extreme case. Lenin

7

was an active member of the Social-Democratic Labour Party from the start, in Russia and in exile. Some people say that he is a German agent, but it is more likely that he is one of those curious products of the Russian revolutionary movement who have ceased to live on the moral planes of the rest of the world. So many revolutionists have turned out to be police agents, who in their own heart of hearts did not know which of their employers held the first claim on their allegiance. Azev, and Father Gapon, and the detective who shot the Premier, Stolypin, are all examples of the type. Messrs. Joseph Conrad and Maurice Baring have dealt with it. Lenin is probably under the same shadow. To him the future of humanity, and its realisation by his methods, are everything—matters infinitely more important than the sources of the subscription to his funds, or the character of his allies.

His career during his abode in Russia, between his return from exile in April and his escape in August, is only explicable on this theory of his character. He arrives in Russia from Switzerland, the country of his exile, viâ Germany, in a special train lent him by the Kaiser's Government. He arrives in Russia, and explains that it is his mission to fight Russian Imperialism as much as the German brand of the same article. He needs a headquarters in Petrograd; so an armed body of his followers descend upon the house of a well-known ballet-dancer, Mme. Ksheshinskaya, turn her out, and make themselves at home, remaining to this day in an admirably chosen strategic position. He needs a Press, so his armed followers come down on the editorial department of the Ministry of Agriculture. This used to publish a bulletin for distribution in vast numbers among Russian agriculturists, as well as pamphlets and leaflets galore. Lenin and Co. therefore come into possession of a ready-made newspaper office, with a huge stock of paper in hand and machinery of just the right kind. He starts a daily paper, and immediately attacks the Provisional Government. The latter remonstrates feebly, but Lenin does not budge. The *Pravdo (Truth)* comes out, with a swarm of local editions, a special edition for soldiers, and another for propaganda purposes at the front. The last, however, was soon suppressed.

Pravda remained until August, and was on sale everywhere. Its four pages contained, day by day, the essence of the pro-German and anti-Ally campaign. No lie was too blatant for *Pravda*, no argument too thin. Alone of the Petrograd Press it did not even mention the successful offensive of July 1—though its twin-brother, the *Soldiers' Pravda*, made the comment that the advance was a stab in the back of the German democracy! The word Allies was always printed in quotation marks in *Pravda*. Statements were made in every number with the purpose of discrediting the Allies. France, it was alleged, shoots Russian soldiers for faternising with the enemy, and England looks on Russia as a sort of India or China, to be exploited hereafter. All

8

English Socialists are false to Socialism; even MacDonald, because he has never fought the capitalistic imperialism of British " boorjoys." When there were joyful demonstrations, *Pravda* used to get up counter-demonstrations of dilapidated soldiers carrying banners: " We want to go home," " If we do not bring in the harvest the war is lost." The whole thing was an imposture, of course. The soldiers were already deserters to a man, and the principal reason why they could not go home is that their own people refused to have them there.

THE OUTBREAK OF FREE SPEECH.

The prevalence of such extremists, and of their opinions, is very largely to be attributed to the political conditions of the Old Russia. Before March, 1917, you could not for all practical purposes make a speech in Russia. It was fairly difficult even to find a speech to listen to unless it took the form of a lecture on some subject not too closely connected with politics. They do not preach much in the Russian Church, and the chances of achieving pulpit fame as a dissenter were, and still are, very limited. The Revolution removed the gag. Everybody began to talk at once, and is still at it. The importance of it all lies in the fact that the task of governing Russia has got mixed up with the very natural desire to address the meeting. Russia has contracted the habit of holding Conferences, several at once, and all the time. They last sometimes from 9 a.m. to 5 a.m., and then they start again. They go on for weeks and weeks. There have been Labour Conferences, Socialist Conferences, Professional Conferences, and the usual Party Conferences. Thousands of them. They have not all been on the beaten track. In May, 1917, there was a Conference of the Criminal Classes held in Odessa, and more recently a sort of rash broke out over the map of Russia of Children's Conferences. The latter seem to have been a source of deep annoyance to the older generation. The infants of several towns demanded the return of the Romanovs, and in one or two places they discussed the Future of the Family.

The writer was present at some of the meetings of the All-Russian Conference of the C.W.S.D.'s, reference to which has already been made.

One evening he heard an American Socialist, Charles Russell, of New York, welcome the Russian Revolution. He described the way in which the most peacefully disposed among modern democracies had been compelled to take up the sword, and he assured his audience that they, too, would find sooner or later that there could be no real peace while Germany was undefeated. The crowd cheered ecstatically. Then an officer read out an immense resolution, all about this being an imperialist, bourgeois, capitalist war, about Russia's desire for peace, and her disinclination to conclude a separate peace in case one side or other came out of the war stronger than she would otherwise do—a resolution which took at least ten minutes to read, bristling with self-contradictions, a resolution which might have been composed by everybody' in a crowded room saying what they thought about the war to a reporter who reported everything and forgot to work out an average. And the crowd cheered ecstatically. They admire speech as an art in itself. Their discussions are got up for the sake of the speeches, not the division on them. Most of the resolutions before the Conference in point seemed to be of academic interest. In the meantime the Executive Committee did all the work, settling strikes, negotiating with the Provisional Government, and so on.

An interesting sidelight on the fact that in Russia free speech is still in the nature of an imported luxury is thrown by a widely distributed pamphlet, calling itself "The Revolutionist's Pocket Dictionary," which explains about a hundred terms at present in vogue. About six of them are Russian, the others come from Western Europe. Words such as "annexations," "contributions," "internationalism," "lock-out," "boycott," "trade union," and, in fact, all the vocabulary of industrial warfare, and of Socialism, are borrowed from the countries where first these things were practical politics.

ARTELS AND TRADE UNIONS.

' The aspects of Russian Democracy described above are the more obvious ones, the thing which strikes the eye of the casual traveller, rather than those gradually evolved institutions which matter more, while they show up less.

At the bottom of Russian industrial and co-operative organisation is the artel, which has been described as follows by Dr. Harold Williams, in his *Russia of the Russians* (undoubtedly the best book published in recent years on the country). "An artel is a kind of mutual liability association. Workmen frequently form artels as a guarantee against loss. The porters on railway stations are organised in artels, so are the floor-polishers, so are the messengers and red caps who stand at the street corners in the cities, so are the messengers in banks and business houses. The artel is liable for all its members, so that if one of them steals or injures property the artel has to make the loss good. The members of the artel pool their money and share gains as well as losses. Peasants from a village community often form themselves into an artel when they go to work at a distance, and local patriotism seems to form the basis of membership in the big artels in the cities, the men of Yaroslav forming one artel, the men of Kostroma another, and so forth. The name artel is now used in the co-operative movement, and in this way a link of continuity is maintained with traditional Russian forms of association."

The development of the artel into the trade union was complicated by political conditions. The men who were responsible for the formation of the unions, in the 'seventies and again in 1905, wished to make them political rather than economic organisations. In order to counteract a tendency which might

10

work out to the danger of the existing order, the Government, from 1901 to 1906, actually encouraged the formation of trade unions of an economic type. The Chief of the Political Department of the Moscow police, named Zubatov, had the ingenious idea of nursing workmen's societies, in order that anti-Government feeling might be worked off on employers, and, incidentally, to give the police a chance of levying blackmail upon the factory-owners, who either had to pay up or see their workers come out on strike. This fake trade unionism was worked up all over Russia, and for a time it undoubtedly did a great deal towards choking a genuine movement. In the long run, however, it failed utterly, for Zubatov, having brought working men's societies into existence, necessarily taught their members how to organise themselves, and so paved the way towards the real thing. Zubatov's activities frightened the Government, and he was dismissed and banished to the Province of Arkangel. But he had set the ball rolling—and not at all in the desired direction. In 1907 there were said to be a quarter of a million organised trade unionists. Their numbers were subsequently reduced by repression; funds were confiscated, and when unions were allowed to exist, they were forbidden to federate. The Revolution has, of course, led to the formation of many great new unions. It is at present impossible to give any figures, as the unions are growing very quickly, and the process of amalgamation and co-ordination have not yet been clearly defined. The metal-workers' unions are attracting members by the hundred thousand, but as the number of workers at their trade has been artificially and perhaps temporarily inflated by the wholesale establishment of munition factories, it is at present impossible to trace the lines on which their organisations will develop. This much only is certain—the trade union will be a big thing in the new Russia.

A definition of the artel has already been given. It should be borne in mind, however, that there are several types of artels, which correspond to the various British forms of working-class economic organisation.

A. The most primitive kind of artel. The members supply only their labour; raw material and capital are not required—*e.g.*, a body of men form an artel for the purpose of hauling barges up a great river. The artel is paid in a lump sum, and divides it among its members in proportion to the amount of work done.

B. This type of artel requires capital, which is either found by its members or borrowed. It corresponds to the unsuccessful self-governing workshops which were set up by the Christian Socialists in England, and to a certain extent to the existing Productive Co-operative Societies where these are run by the workers themselves. Such artels do not require very considerable capital. The " Russian Peasant Industries " productions, which are now so popular in England, are generally manufactured in this way. Toy-making, for example, requiring no elaborate machinery, is largely conducted by this class of artel. Occasionally we find highly skilled work being turned out by artels. " The Co-operative Movement in Russia," by J. V. Bubnov, describes artels at some length, and mentions what is supposed to be the biggest one in Russia. This is at Pavlovo, in the Province of Nizhni-Novgorod, and employs about 300 men, of whom 125 are members; it is normally engaged in the manufacture of cutlery, but since the outbreak of war it has been making surgical instruments. Artels generally have a very much smaller number of members, and are naturally suffering from factory competition. In their present state they are doomed to extinction, but there are signs of their transformation into two · new types. The first of these is:

C. During the last three years a great many artels, engaged on war-work, have been capitalised by the Zemstvos, and have, in fact, developed into State workshops, run by the local rural and urban authorities. Some idea of the work of these will be obtained from the section on the Union of the Zemstvos.

D. Is another newish type. The artel here loses its original character and turns into a trade union, which consists of all the employees at a single factory. Such artels (the name is adhered to) are, of course, made possible by the incompletely capitalist organisation of Russian industry, and by the existence of isolated factories near villages, where the employees all know one another and are not easily displaced.

E. Finally, there is, practically, the joint-stock company, or the co-operative factory. The artel finds the capital, and takes on its employees in the usual way. The co-operators are the employers, not the employed.

CO-OPERATION.

This classification of the artel system will show that co-operative consumption and production are connected naturally with the previously existing types of organisation. There was no question of the acceptance of a new theory. Both the theory and the practice were already present; they merely needed a few business-like individuals to hitch them together. Some fifteen years ago the impulse came, and since then the growth of various forms of co-operation has been stupendous. The war has merely stimulated what was already a. prodigious growth. The progress of the co-operative movement since the Revolution (no figures are available) has been unchecked; indeed, it is possible that the predominant type of Russian production will be co-operative, just as the British type is joint-stock. Let us begin with consumers' societies—the Russian equivalent of the " co-op." stores. It is impossible to give any

12

up-to-date figure of their number and membership. According to Mr. Bubnov, there were on January 1, 1914, 10,080 consumers' societies, and three years later there were about 20,000. During the period of the war they have been forming at the rate of about ten a day. The total membership on January 1, 1914, was 1,450,000, and it must have more than doubled by this time. The "Co-operation" Society in Moscow had in June, 1917, 65,000 members. The provinces of Kiev, Podolia and Poltava are the principal centres of this form of co-operation. Here, again, there was already in existence an organisation of a lower type to simplify the evolution of the higher. A few years ago Russian factories frequently had an ostensibly co-operative store attached to them, run jointly by the management and workers. This system is now almost extinct; it seems to have had a good many of the disadvantages of the "truck" shop of the early part of last century, with some of the benefits of the co-operative store.

A type of co-operation which is doing very well in Russia to-day is represented by the sixteen or seventeen thousand Credit Associations, with their membership of over ten million householders. There are various types of these; their common object is to help the peasant smallholder (he must be an owner) to borrow money in order to purchase livestock, agricultural machinery, etc., on the security of his land and crops.

Lastly, there are the co-operative productive societies. These, again, vary greatly. The most characteristically Russian is the mass of associations of various types which come into the Union of Siberia Creamery Associations, formed in 1908. This has grown directly out of innumerable butter artels, and is now apparently in a fair way to gain a monopoly of the whole dairy business of Siberia. There are also productive bodies built up on a model similar to that of the English and Scottish Co-operative Wholesale Societies. The Moscow Union of Consumer Societies is the principal such body. During the last few years it has opened a great many factories all over Russia, and its activities have been stimulated rather than checked by the war. Then there are a large number of auxiliary bodies connected with the co-operative movement. The Moscow Narodov (People's) Bank is the principal financial organ of the movement, which also has an educational side. At the moment of writing Russian co-operation, although in a thoroughly healthy state, is too shapeless to be described in detail. While certain sections of the movement were regarded with suspicion by the pre-revolutionary governments, others (e.g., the Credit Associations) used to receive intelligent encouragement. Now that all unnatural restrictions upon their growth have been removed, the co-operative organisations are developing in unexpected directions. The high prices of food, the scarcity for which the late Government was largely responsible, and the consequent profiteering and uneven distribution, have largely discredited the private trader and given a great impetus to the co-operation.

13

THE LAND.

The movements which have been described in the course of this paper have been urban with the exception of the co-operative impulse, which has made itself felt in village and town alike. On June 7, 1917, the All-Russian Council of Peasant Deputies issued a statement on the land question, in the course of which the leading ideas which have been in vogue among the peasants since the abolition of serfdom are briefly expressed. Although the policy which this statement recommends has not been completely accepted by the Provisional Government, and will have to be decided in the long run by the Constituent Assembly, there is no doubt that its ideas are already being acted upon very largely both by Government Departments and by the peasants themselves. All lands, whether belonging to the State, the Church, or private persons, are to be handed over to the people, with no compensation to their present owners. The land administration is to be handed over to local agricultural committees, which are to be responsible for the cultivation. These committees are to have the power of requisitioning agricultural machinery where its present owners are not already using it to the national advantage. The committees are to gather in the harvest, regulate river fisheries, and control the output of timber. They are, further, to fix rents, prices, and wages in connection with these activities. The statement from which these points are taken concludes with the expression of the conviction that only under these conditions will it be possible to create a new social organisation worthy of Free Russia, an organisation which "will unite in one family of brethren, under the protection of one Government all the toilers on the land without distinction of nationality, religion, and social standing—the great Russian and the Ukraianian, the Christian and the Mussulman, the peasant and the Cossack, the Russian and the stranger within his gates, the villager and the courtier." This may read like the wildest Utopianism, but Russia happens to be the one country on earth where Utopian schemes are practical politics. The peasants' programme, as we shall see a little later, has already led to certain disorders. But it is also leading to a more intelligent peasantry, with a greater sense of responsibility for Russia. It is as well to be reminded that the peasants' programme will affect the destinies of about a hundred million persons.

*　　*　　*　　*　　*　·　*

The last of great Russian democratic organisations is

THE UNION OF THE ZEMSTVOS.

There used to be a legend—it is not dead yet—to the effect that Russian people were used to being autocratically governed. The people who held this view maintained that if the Russians were allowed to mind their own business instead of letting it be conducted for them by German officials and half-German Courts, there would be confusion, if nothing worse. This quaint theory is, of course, entirely baseless. Democracy as a living force has nowhere shown itself more wonderfully since the outbreak of the war than in Russia.

When war began it immediately became apparent that the Russian War Office was going to have its hands very full indeed. It also became pretty clear that the Russian Red Cross Society, admirable body though it is, was not strong enough to do the work laid down for it. A new organisation was needed to rectify the shortcomings which were immediately apparent, and a new organisation came into existence, without the help of the Government — actually for a time in opposition to the Government or to one member of it. Russia is divided for purposes of local government into what are known as Zemstvos, to which our county councils may be taken as equivalent. Many years ago, during the war with Japan, a Union of Zemstvos had been formed to supplement the very inadequate Red Cross Organisation. Almost immediately after Germany made war in 1914 the Russian Union of Zemstvos was revived, and was soon followed by a similar body on a smaller scale, the Russian Union of Towns, consisting of a federation of town councils. Early in August, 1914, the new organisation sprang into existence. The movement began in Moscow, and the rest of Russia quickly followed. The Cossacks of the Don contributed no less than £50,000 to the Union. Before the war was a month old the organisation was under way.

The Union of Zemstvos was supposed to play a subordinate part in the work of the sanitary organisation of the Ministry of War and of the Red Cross Society, and consequently the War Office, as well as the Red Cross, would not allow the Union to work independently for the evacuation of the wounded and to extend its activity to the battle line. The work was to be divided so that the Red Cross should be at the front, whilst the Union was supposed to relieve the wounded in the interior of Russia. According to these plans and in consideration of the very limited funds of the Union, provision was made for about 25,000 to 30,000 beds and for a few hospital trains which were to run in the interior of the Empire. But from the very beginning the circumstances necessitated not only the widening of the sphere of work as formerly planned, not only the extension of the Union's activity to the fighting line, but also to give over to the Union some functions that were purely Governmental, and were formerly undertaken by the Government alone.

It soon became evident that many needs, and some of them not directly connected with the relief of the wounded, had not been foreseen in peace time, and that neither the Sanitary Department of the War Office nor the Red Cross Society could supply those needs, especially when, owing to certain events developing unexpectedly, both these institutions had to devote all their energy for the medical work at the front. This created the necessity of erecting numerous hospitals, of collecting and distributing centres for the sick and wounded coming from the front. At those centres an adequate medical staff had to be appointed; all the equipment, as well as trains for the transport of the wounded, had to be provided. All that could be effected, and all these pressing needs could be met only by a close alliance between the Government and the public corporations, of which the Union of Zemstvos, possessing the confidence of all classes, and having at its disposal a well-trained staff, took the lead.

The Government was bound to accept its aid, and the General Committee was ready at once to assist the army with all its strength and with all its available means.

After organising hospitals, hospital trains and food providing units, the Union of Zemstvos extended its activity to the front; its first attempt proved a success, and the High Command laid on the Union the most varied tasks. New enterprises followed one after the other, more primitive ones were extended, and new duties were added. The units at the front increased in number, stores of various kinds, with their bases in the rear, accumulated at the front, and, in conjunction with the War Office, stations, medical organisations supplemented by canteens, bath houses and laundries, were established by the Union. The victualling of a host of over 300,000 men, engaged in war constructions in the immediate rear of the army, fell to the care of the Union. The medical sanitary work with numerous units for dealing with infectious diseases, units for vaccination, disinfecting units, bacteriological laboratories, medicinal stores at front and base, movable bath houses, developed rapidly. The Union of Zemstvos was required likewise to relieve the refugees, and responded by organising a net of canteens, medical institutions, registration and labour offices, refuges for children, workshops, etc.

Nor was this all. Little by little the Union of Zemstvos, always helped by the Union of Towns, found itself taking over the whole work of looking after the sick and wounded. At the beginning of 1916 it ran fifty hospitals. But it was not only Russia's sick and wounded who needed help. The War Office organisation was quite incapable of undertaking a campaign so enormous as that in which Russia found herself engaged. All sorts of essential articles were lacking. The Union began to provide clothes for the army, organising for that purpose the co-operation of the local authorities in every part of Russia. Funds were raised for the purchase of necessary articles abroad, especially in England and the United States. In February, 1915, the only tannery in Russia was requisitioned by the War Office and handed over to the Union. A little later, when the Union had succeeded in getting supplies of tanning extracts, a special leather factory was opened. Contributions for the great work came in readily. The local authorities found the greater part of the necessary funds. Private subscriptions were also forthcoming, and even the War Office came down with handsome contributions. When the great retreat of 1915 took place, it was the Union which had the task of dealing with the refugees, of whom there were no fewer than four millions on the south-western front alone.

A number of guides were appointed to help the refugees on their way. These took upon themselves the care of refugees travelling by railway. The necessity of rescuing the children brought into existence a great number of crèches and nurseries, to which more than 58,000 children were admitted on the south-western front alone. Apart from that, there were established, for the benefit of the refugees, labour exchanges, inquiry and registration offices, and many investigations were made with regard to the position of the refugees in different districts.

The extent of the Union's operations may be gauged from the fact that it had at the beginning of 1916 no less than 124 establishments in the Caucasus alone. So far the work which we have been describing has been of a character subsidiary to the War Office. But the Union did not stop at this.

In the spring of 1915, when the Russian army had suffered so badly from a deficiency of shells and ammunition, a general movement to give assistance to the army swept through the whole of Russian Society. At this very moment the Russian Union of Zemstvos took an active part in the work of providing the army with all the necessary materials. After the failures in Galicia in 1915 it became evident that there was a colossal inequality between the equipment of Russian troops and that of the Austro-Germans. The Government itself could see the necessity of calling upon all social forces for the sake of reinforcing the fighting power of the army. The Russian Zemstvos, of course, could not remain indifferent with regard to this work.

The meeting of the representatives of the Government Zemstvos, which took place in Moscow on June 5, 1915, decided to commit the charge of this enormous task of providing the active army with all necessaries, not to isolated Zemstvos, but to the Union of Zemstvos. In all the Zemstvos, government and district committees were formed, and these approached this work very earnestly. The first and most important task was the unification of small industries, the work of the peasants in their homes, and also the uniting of the isolated technical ability of the country.

In July, 1915, the Union of Zemstvos took orders from the military authorities for different articles of ammunition and army equipment, which amounted to many millions of roubles. Among these were not only articles of commissary-supplies (vehicles, harness, kitchens, wheels, horseshoes, tarpaulin, knapsacks, saddles, etc.), but articles for artillery and military equipment, such as shells, hand-grenades, entrenching tools, telephones. All these orders were immediately distributed among the local organisations of the Union of Zemstvos.

Simultaneously with the distribution of these orders among local committees, the General Committee set about the organisation of enterprises of its own; munition works for providing 3-inch and 6-inch shells, the erection of factories for making sulphuric acid, telephones, tarpaulin, and much besides.

17

With regard to supplying the army, the Union of Zemstvos co-operated from August, 1915, with the Russian Union of Towns. Both these Unions are working together, having formed a Special Committee for army supply.

All this marvellous organisation, it must be repeated and emphasised, has grown up independently of the Government departments. The Russian people alone, through their elected local authorities, have done the work. Can it be said any longer that they are incapable of self-government, fit only to be the subjects of an autocracy? *

ECONOMIC DIFFICULTIES.

For the present, however, the situation is ominous. English opinion is too much inclined to attribute the disorders on the other side to political causes. The British public is apparently under the impression that the trouble is mainly due to party disputes, with a certain amount of German propaganda thrown in. There is no doubt that these are very important factors in the situation, but by themselves they can hardly be held accountable for the increasing disorganisation of affairs in general. The root of Russia's present difficulties is economic and financial, and not political. So far as there is a political difficulty—and I do not for a moment deny that it exists and is serious—it is to a very large extent merely the reaction of the prevalent economic conditions.

The outward and visible sign of the troublesomeness of the situation is paper. Metal currency has ceased to exist. If you ask people where it has got to they shrug their shoulders and talk about hoarding. Illiterate peasants, it appears, dislike paper money, and have collected all the coin in circulation. During the last three years the Romanov Governments attempted to get out of their financial difficulties by printing vast quantities of paper money. This had the result of driving coins out of circulation and depreciating the rouble. In a country with an advanced banking system the effects would not have been so serious, but in Russia, where banks are mistrusted, the unrestricted issue of paper money provided an exceptionally easy descent towards national bankruptcy.

With a banking system such as exists in Russia there is no limit to the quantity of paper money which the country can absorb, and consequently to the liabilities which the Government can incur in issuing it. The smaller coins—30, 20, 15 and 10 copecks, and down to one copeck—have been replaced by a special issue of postage stamps, printed on specially thick paper. The one copeck note (now worth about the tenth of a penny) may be regarded as a pathetic symbol of Russia's difficulties.

This, however, is only one side of the difficulty. There is also the wages problem to be considered. The Russian town workman

---

* This account of the work of the Union of the Zemstvos is based upon the *Report*, published by Messrs. P. S. King and Son. 1s net.

was until quite recently in receipt of extraordinarily low wages, and accustomed to a terribly low standard of life. His wages, in English terms, often came to no more than a pound or two a month. He and his family lived on black bread and weak tea, and shared a room or a cellar with perhaps several other families. In the circumstances it is not surprising that he was seldom a particularly efficient workman. He was slow, and his employer generally called him lazy. Wages had been rising gradually since 1905, the year of big strikes, and they had been increasing fairly rapidly between the outbreak of war and the Revolution. But even so they were appallingly insufficient, especially in view of the extraordinary rise of prices during the latter period.

Consequently, when the Revolution came, the workmen felt they were justified in asking for an increase of wages, which sometimes came to as much as 300 or 400 per cent. And yet, in the circumstances of the case, the Minister of Labour, M. Skobelev, assured me that such demands could not always be regarded as unjustifiable. Immediately after the Revolution these demands for higher wages took place at virtually every factory. But it was found impossible to settle matters immediately on a satisfactory basis, as prices, after a temporary decline, started once more on the upward path. So that a succession of demands for higher wages took place, and in a good many cases the workmen felt that the food speculators were getting the best of them and that the only way of meeting them was to insist on the demands of wages out of all proportion to those which they had been receiving. Cases have been heard of when the workmen demanded as much as 800 per cent. over pre-Revolution rates.

This demand for higher wages naturally has not been accompanied by smoothness throughout. There have been innumerable strikes, although they have seldom lasted more than a few days. The dangerous element in the new movement has been the tendency towards syndicalism. Workmen have attempted to take control of factories and to dispense entirely with the so-called "bourgeois" management. In certain cases the workmen have very soon discovered that they could not carry on without their technical staff, which found itself reinstalled after a very few days.

The net result of this agitation has been an enormous decrease of production. It must be remembered that not only have the workmen been insisting on higher wages, but they have also been demanding (and they have obtained) a greatly reduced working day. Moreover, employees of a great many large factories have refused to go on working unless the management complied with certain almost penal conditions. For instance, men elected by their fellow-employees to serve on local councils of Workmen's and Soldiers' Delegates must continue to receive their wages, and time lost through disputes has also to be paid for.

In the circumstances it is not surprising to find innumerable undertakings shut down altogether. Factories engaged in the pro-

19

duction of munitions have in most cases been able to secure help from the Government, but those not directly engaged on war work have been having a very bad time.

There are, of course, no reliable statistics available as to the extent of the fall in production.* A few fortunate factories in Petrograd and Moscow have been able to report that they have not suffered to the extent of more than 20 per cent., but the majority, perhaps, place the figure at something like 50, and one hears occasionally of places where only 20 per cent. of the pre-Revolution output is maintained. I have heard of one unfortunate establishment engaged on Government work, employing many thousands of men and women, which turned out during the three months following the Revolution only 7½ per cent. of its output for the previous six months.

Add to these facts the very important consideration that transport is becoming more and more difficult, that the number of locomotives needing repair is something in five figures, while the number of locomotives actually undergoing repair is comparatively microscopical, and it must be realised that the economic situation is perhaps even more menacing than the military. A great many things which we had been in the habit of regarding as necessaries of life have virtually gone out of manufacture. In Petrograd and Moscow boots, shoes, and clothing cannot be obtained except at fantastic prices.

The refusal, for that is what it practically comes to, of the workmen to work, except on economically impossible conditions, finds its parallel not only in the behaviour of the Armies, but also in the attitude which is being taken up by the peasant in a great many parts of Russia. It is impossible to sum up the agrarian situation in a few words, and I shall not attempt to do so. But this much is certain: a great many peasants, with all the produce of particularly lucrative harvests turned under their cottage floors, have not recognised the necessity of seeing that this year's harvest should be a normal one. Production in this direction has also enormously dropped off, and sooner or later the pinch will be felt in consequence. Moreover, conditions of instability have asserted themselves in "expropriation," and in the large towns one meets a good many men and women who were wealthy landowners until the other day when their peasants reduced them to bankruptcy at a single blow. Here, as in the case of the town workmen, retributive justice has been at work no less than human folly. The employer who did his best for his men, and the landowner who always kept before him the interests of his peasants, have distinctly received preferential treatment. It is gratifying to know that among the former there are a number of British enterprises. In the long run, however, one is brought up against the fact that democracy is based upon discipline, and that in any state citizens which try to do without discipline simply cannot exist. But discipline in Russia is peculiarly scarce at the moment. Let me give one or two illustrations.

THE NEED FOR DISCIPLINE.

The Nevsky Prospect, the main thoroughfare of Petrograd, is the nightly scene of innumerable little meetings. You can hear workmen arguing their right to the whole produce of labour; you can hear impassioned ladies beseeching deserters to return to the front and to defend Russian "cultura," and you can hear innumerable unenlightened discussions on an extraordinary number of purely theoretical matters. The most interesting feature about these discussions, however, is the attitude of the deserters. Sometimes they repeat what is evidently a set speech as they heard it delivered by a Leninite. They assure their hearers that it is all one to them whether they are ruled by German capitalism, or, as at present the case, Anglo-French capitalism. When they are asked where is the latter they generally, I notice, begin again from the beginning. One hears officers beseeching deserters to return to the front, and one also hears deserters explaining to officers why the latter should follow their own example.

Take another example, also from the Army. General Brusilov, the Commander-in-Chief, orders a general offensive. The Council of Workmen's and Soldiers' delegates of the town occupied by General Headquarters sends a bitter protest to Petrograd and the Government against the General's refusal to discuss the conditions of the offensive with them beforehand, and this protest is widely circulated all over Russia, conveying the impression that the General was not entitled to order an offensive.

They are repeating a story in Petrograd a good deal just now. It may not be absolutely true, but it seems to sum up the situation in a perfectly admirable manner. As English readers will be already aware, the lines of the opposing armies on the Russian fronts have seldom been as close to one another as in Flanders; at some points, in fact, the lines have been several miles apart. When the hot weather came on an officer in command of a unit at the front decided that the present position of his men, which was in a swamp, was not healthy, and likely to become worse. In front of them was a hill, behind them was another. The officer ordered an advance. The hill in front could probably be taken without any loss of men, and an advance was ordered accordingly. The men thereupon held a meeting, and decided that they would not advance as they were not fighting a war of aggression. The officer thereupon suggested a move to the rear, any hill being healthier than the swamp. The men again met to consider the matter, and decided that as this was an offensive war they would not yield any ground. One almost feels justified in using the words: "and so they all perished miserably."

THE OUTLOOK FOR THE FUTURE.

Now what effect is all this slackness going to have on the future? The immediate prospect for Russia is distinctly uncomfortable. In the first place, the number of desertions is likely to grow rather than diminish when the cold weather sets in. Moreover, the increased difficulties of picking up a living will probably lead to various forms of brigandage which at present fortunately are rare. The problem is more than a purely military one. We must consider the effect which a demoralised Russia will have upon the state of feeling in Germany and the rest of Europe. Undoubtedly the effect will be to encourage the supporters of absolutism in all its forms throughout the world. If the Russian democracy cannot pull itself together it will make itself for many generations to come " the horrible example " to be quoted as an argument against any further democratisation.

And yet the Russian people themselves are hardly to be held to blame for the catastrophe in which they are unwittingly taking part. The most enormous, and at the same time the most ignorant of the European nations has suddenly found itself able to shape her own destinies. Up to the day of its liberation the Russian democracy had never been allowed to consider what it would wish its destiny to be. If Russia has fallen into the hands of theorists and extremists, it is because the practical, experienced administrator of Liberal principles had not been previously allowed to exist. The present débâcle is the legacy of the Romanovs, their last but deadliest insult to the intelligence of Europe.

Such is the situation in Russia to-day. The success of the Revolution is not yet assured. The new Russia has a magnificent foundation in its democratic institutions and in its genuinely democratic sentiment. The danger comes not only from indiscipline and treachery, but also from the apparently too materialistic outlook of many of the present leaders. The greatly talked-of " moral personality " of the Revolution is too often allowed to supersede the personal morality of the revolutionist. But no genuine democrat need despair; if democracy is indeed the spirit which makes a nation great, then Russia is safe.

What can the British Labour movement do to help Russia? Mutual knowledge is the first essential. The Russian co-operative movement has been making advances to the British movement, and it is clear that the two great people's organs are bound to become more closely associated in the future, possibly, as some Russian co-operators believe, to the point of interdependence. British co-operatively manufactured goods will certainly be exchanged against Russian agricultural produce through the media of the co-operative organisations.

Relations between British and Russian trade unions must depend upon the extent to which Russia avails herself of the help proffered by this country. In this case, at any rate, the youngest democracy has much to learn from the oldest.

The Labour and Socialist movements must keep in close touch. A useful start has already been made in this direction by the exchange of delegations. It is to be regretted that the opportunity of the Stockholm Conference was not whole-heartedly accepted, as the British Labour point of view on the war is generally misunderstood and often wilfully misinterpreted.

The British Labour movement can itself do much to bring about a better understanding with the foreign democracies by insisting on the appointment of Labour Attachés at British embassies and legations. (The idea, I believe, is Mr. Arthur Henderson's.) The selection of youngish men from the ranks of trade-union officials for such posts would have these desirable effects. First, the better mutual knowledge of the working classes of the civilised nations. Second, the education of the future trade-union leaders and Labour M.P.'s. Third, the breaking down of the social exclusiveness which tends to prevail at British embassies and legations. A Labour Attaché to the Embassy in Petrograd might be of the greatest service to both Britain and Russia.

The time is clearly coming when the Labour movements in all countries will have to appoint their own ambassadors. The representatives and plenipotentiaries of Labour will concern themselves with economic rather than with political questions; they will watch over international Labour legislation and make it effective; they will prevent the manipulation of tariffs in the interests of any particular body of manufacturers, and they will see that one country does not undercut another's industry by allowing sweated labour to continue. For the first time in European history Labour controls the government of a great nation. Whatever the blunders of the Russian Revolution, it has already demonstrated the possibilities for good latent in democracy.

The future peace of the world will depend very largely upon the relations of the great democracies to one another when the common cause of war has ceased to hold them together. Britain is united with the U.S.A. by ties of blood, and with France by a common tradition and a great memory. If these three nations conclude a people's pact with the Russia which will assuredly arise from the present disorders, the world will be able to afford to laugh at the lessening menace of the few remaining autocracies.

FABIAN PUBLICATIONS.

FABIAN ESSAYS IN SOCIALISM. Paper 6d.; cloth 1/6; post. 2½d. and 4d.
HISTORY OF THE FABIAN SOCIETY. By E. R. Pease. 5s. n.
TOWARDS SOCIAL DEMOCRACY? By Sidney Webb. 1s. n., post. 1d.
WHAT TO READ on Social and Economic Subjects. 1s. n. and 2s. n.
THE RURAL PROBLEM. By H. D. Harben. 2s. 6d. n.
THIS MISERY OF BOOTS. By H. G. Wells. 3d., post free 4d.
FABIAN TRACTS and LEAFLETS.
Tracts, each 16 to 52 pp., price 1d., or 9d. per dos., unless otherwise stated.
Leaflets, 4 pp. each, price 1d. for six copies, 1s. per 100, or 8/6 per 1000.
The Set of 77, 3/6; post free 3,11. Bound in buckram, 5/-n.; post free 5/6.

I —General Socialism in its various aspects.

TRACTS.—184. The Russian Revolution and British Democracy. By
Julius West. 2d. 180. The Philosophy of Socialism. By A. Clutton Brock.
169. The Socialist Movement in Germany. By W. Stephen Sanders. 2d.
159. The Necessary Basis of Society. By Sidney Webb. 151. The Point
of Honour. By Ruth C. Bentinck. 147. Capital and Compensation. By
E. R. Pease. 146. Socialism and Superior Brains. By Bernard Shaw.
142. Rent and Value. 138. Municipal Trading. 121. Public Service v.
Private Expenditure. By Sir Oliver Lodge. 107. Socialism for Millionaires. By Bernard Shaw. 139. Socialism and the Churches. By
Rev. John Clifford, D.D. 133. Socialism and Christianity. By Rev.
Percy Dearmer. 78. Socialism and the Teaching of Christ. By Dr. J.
Clifford. 42. Christian Socialism. By Rev. S. D. Headlam. 79. A Word
of Remembrance and Caution to the Rich. By John Woolman. 72. The
Moral Aspects of Socialism. By Sidney Ball. 69. Difficulties of In-
dividualism. By S. Webb. 51. Socialism: True and False. By S. Webb.
45. The Impossibilities of Anarchism. By G. B. Shaw. 2d. 7. Capital
and Land. 5. Facts for Socialists. 2d. Leaflets—13. What Socialism
Is. 1. Why are the Many Poor?

II.—Applications of Socialism to Particular Problems.

TRACTS.—183. The Reform of the House of Lords. By Sidney Webb.
181. When Peace Comes—the Way of Industrial Reconstruction. By
Sidney Webb. 2d. 178. The War; Women; and Unemployment. 2d.
177. Socialism and the Arts of Use. By A. Clutton Brock. 175. The
Economic Foundations of the Women's Movement. 2d. 173. Public v.
Private Electricity Supply. 171. The Nationalization of Mines and
Minerals Bill. 170. Profit-Sharing and Co-Partnership: a Fraud and
Failure? 164. Gold and State Banking. 163. Women and Prisons. 2d.
162. Family Life on a Pound a Week. By Mrs. Reeves. 2d. 161. Affor-
estation and Unemployment. 160. A National Medical Service. 2d. 157.
The Working Life of Women. 155. The Case against the Referendum.
154. The Case for School Clinics. 153. The Twentieth Century Reform
Bill. 152. Our Taxes as they are and as they ought to be. 2d. 149. The
Endowment of Motherhood. 2d. 131. The Decline of the Birth-Rate.
145. The Case for School Nurseries. 140. Child Labor under Capitalism.
136. The Village and the Landlord. By Edw. Carpenter. 144. Machinery:
its Masters and Servants. 122. Municipal Milk and Public Health. 125.
Municipalization by Provinces. 124. State Control of Trusts. 83. State
Arbitration and the Living Wage. Leaflet.—104. How Trade Unions
benefit Workmen.

III.—Local Government Powers : How to use them.

TRACTS.—176. The War and the Workers. By Sidney Webb. 172. What
about the Rates? By S. Webb. 156. What an Education Committee can
do (Elementary Schools), 3d. 62. Parish and District Councils. (Revised 1913). 137. Parish Councils and Village Life. 109. Cottage Plans
and Common Sense. 82. Workmen's Compensation Act. Leaflets.—
134. Small Holdings. 68. The Tenant's Sanitary Catechism. 71. Ditto
for London.

IV.—General Politics and Fabian Policy.

TRACTS.—158. The Case against the C.O.S. By Mrs. Townshend. 70.
Report on Fabian Policy. 41. The Fabian Society: its Early History.
By Bernard Shaw.

V.—Biographical Series. In portrait covers, 2d. each.

182. Robert Owen, Idealist. By C. E. M. Joad. 179. John Ruskin and
Social Ethics. By Prof. Edith Morley. 16 . Francis Place. By St. John

ian Tract No. 185.

The Abolition of the Poor Law

By Mrs. Sidney Webb.

Price One Penny.

The Fabian Society, 25, Tothill Street,
Westminster, London, S.W.1.   March, 1918.

THE POOR LAW.

For everything there is an appropriate time. There is a time to work and a time to play; a time to eat and a time to sleep. In the politics of the Labour Movement there is a time for speech and a time for action; a time for the declaration of our widest principles and purposes and a time for achieving particular reforms that are part of our programme. Now is the appointed time for securing one valuable and far-reaching improvement in our social organisation, which will put an end to much suffering and demoralisation, and open up the way to further emancipation. Now is the time when a determined effort by Trade Union Branches, Trades Councils, Co-operative Societies, the Women's Co-operative Guild, the Women's Labour League, Socialist organisations, and other progressive bodies from one end of England to the other would secure. nothing less than the total and complete

ABOLITION OF THE POOR LAW.

This has been recommended by a strong Government Committee, in which the Labour Movement was represented by Mr. J. H. Thomas, M.P. (National Union of Railwaymen), and myself. The Government is prepared to carry it promptly into law against all vested interests if the people declare themselves emphatically enough. The proposal is now submitted for the verdict of " public opinion."* It is the business of every section of the Labour Movement to express itself upon it promptly, loudly, and energetically. We can, if we like to take the trouble, at one blow, get rid not only of the Workhouse, the " Stone Yard," the Casual Ward, and the Board of Guardians, but also of the demoralising Poor Law itself, and of the very idea of " pauperism."

WHAT THE POOR LAW IS.

The English Poor Law, which dates from 1601, was in its time a notable expression of the right of the individual in distress to be helped by the community, and of the duty of the community to rescue from want even the weakest of its members. But the Poor Law and its administration became subject to grave abuses, which were drastically cut down in 1834. Unfortunately the system then adopted was one of limiting the public assistance to the " relief of destitution "; of refusing to help until " destitution " had set in; and of a rigid " deterrence " of all applications for relief by (a) making " pauperism " a disgrace; (b) treating applicants harshly and discourteously; (e) surrounding the relief by deliberately unpleasant conditions, such as " the offer of the Workhouse " and the imposition of penal tasks like picking oakum or " the Stone

---

* See the significant note by the Minister of Reconstruction prefixed to the Report of the Local Government Committee of the Ministry of Reconstruction on the Transfer of the Functions of the Boards of Guardians (Cd. 8917), which will be sent on application to the Fabian Bookshop, 25, Tothill Street, Westminster, S.W.1, enclosing 3½d. in stamps.

Yard." The result has been that the Poor Law is universally hated. The Workhouse, even when humanely managed, is looked on with detestation. The degrading treatment of homeless wayfarers in the Casual Ward is furiously resented by all honest travellers. The unemployed have repeatedly refused to be relegated to the tender mercies of the Boards of Guardians. Men sometimes go to prison rather than seek Poor Law relief. Every year a few starve to death rather than accept the Poor Law Guardians' bitter bread. Yet in many a rural district there is no other shelter for the homeless, no other place for the sick, no other maternity hospital, no other refuge for the orphans, and no other asylum for the feeble-minded, no other home for the helpless aged than the General Mixed Workhouse in which they are all interned.

"CITIZENS, NOT PAUPERS."

Meanwhile there has been growing up, especially under the Town Councils of the most progressive great cities, another system of meeting our needs, not as paupers, eating the bread of charity, but as citizens, supplying ourselves collectively with what would be beyond our reach as individuals. Through the Local Education Authority we provide for our children, not only schools and teachers, but also books for them to read—if they are ailing, also medical treatment—if they are hungry, even food. Through the Local Health Authority we provide hospitals for such of us as are ill, and help in maternity and infancy, not as a matter of charity, but as a matter of the public health, in which all citizens, rich or poor, are equally concerned. Through the Old Age Pensions Committee we issue pensions (as yet far too small in amount, and beginning too late) to such of us over seventy as are in need of them, as a matter not of favour but of legal right. In all these and many other municipal services there is no "stigma of pauperism," and nothing disgraceful. When we need this help we are dealt with, not as paupers, but as citizens. And whilst the Town Council administration is very far from perfect, this is found to be much the most successful way of dealing with the cases. The municipal hospitals, the municipal schools, the municipal arrangements for maternity and infancy have been proved to be far and away more successful in preventing disease and death, and illiteracy, than the rival Poor Law institutions—not because the Poor Law institutions are always badly managed, but because they have to be run, even by the kindest and most efficient Board of Guardians, under the cramping and demoralising Poor Law, and subject to the minutely restrictive regulations of the Poor Law Division of the Local Government Board.

WASTE OF MONEY.

Another result is, in most of the populous cities, a terrible waste of public money in the duplication of institutions and overlapping of services. The Boards of Guardians provide everywhere, in one way or another, for maternity and infancy, for children needing schooling, for the sick and infirm, for the feeble-minded and lunatics, for the aged, and for the able-bodied unemployed—provided that these come under the definition of "destitute." The Town Council has its own arrangements for helping the mothers and infants irrespective of destitution, runs its own set of schools, has its own doctors and nurses, administers its own hospitals, sanatoria and asylums, issues pensions to the aged, and even (through the Distress Committee) provides for the able-bodied unemployed. This double set of services and institutions for the same classes of people is wasteful and extravagant. It means an unnecessary multiplication of inquiries and officials. One or other—either the Poor Law system or the municipal system—must go. Which shall it be?

WHAT THE COMMITTEE RECOMMENDS.

The "Local Government Committee of the Ministry of Reconstruction" proposes that—

(a) The entire Poor Law, with all the Orders of the Poor Law Division of the Local Government Board, the whole system of "deterrence," and all "taint of pauperism" should come to an end;

(b) The Workhouse, the "Stone Yard," and the "Casual Ward" should be abolished; and

(c) The Boards of Guardians should cease to exist.

It is proposed that all the buildings and other property of the Poor Law Authorities should be handed over (with proper adjustments for differences of area and for debts) to the directly elected Town and County Councils, to be made use of for the services already administered by their Education, Health, Asylums, and other Committees, in whatever way these Councils find most convenient.

All the present officers of the Poor Law Authorities would either be offered situations at least equivalent in value to those they now hold, or else be liberally compensated for loss of office or for any diminution of emoluments of all kinds.

The Poor Rate would no longer be levied.

Thus the whole Poor Law system would be wound up and finally got rid of.

But we must take care that all the people now dealt with under the Poor Law are provided for, without disturbance or the break of a single day, not only as well as they now are, but better; and that their legal right to maintenance is preserved.

Let us first consider the case of the County Boroughs, the eighty-two large towns like Manchester and Birmingham, which are now wholly governed by their directly elected Town Councils.*

THE SICK AND INFIRM.

It would be the duty of the Town Council, acting through its Health Committee, to take under its care, and to provide for under the Public Health Acts, along with those whom it already looks after, all the sick and infirm persons (including maternity and infancy and the aged needing institutional care) whom the Board of Guardians now provides for. The Health Committee would enlarge its present staff of doctors, nurses, and health visitors under its chief medical officer; and would increase its institutional accommodation (probably by using for this purpose some of the buildings

---

*The complications presented by London and the other Administrative Counties are explained on a later page.

transferred to the Council) so as to be able to merge among its existing patients, without any distinction according to poverty or riches, all the various classes of sick and infirm persons now in the Poor Law institutions. The Health Committee need not interfere with any voluntary hospitals already existing in the town, although it would probably wish to enter into mutually advantageous arrangements with these hospitals for particular cases or classes of cases. Nor is it suggested for the moment that there need be any change in the work of the Local Insurance Committee or in that of the doctors on the panel. Any reform of the Insurance Act must be left to the future.

THE CHILDREN OF SCHOOL AGE.

It would be the duty of the Town Council, acting through its Education Committee, to make, under the Education Acts, all provision required for the children now under the Poor Law who are able to attend school. Already most of these boys and girls attend the Council's schools; but some of them are in residential (Poor Law) schools or "Cottage Homes," and where these exist they would be transferred, subject to proper adjustments for difference of area, to the Council, and become part of its ordinary educational machinery, available without distinction for all orphans and other children needing board and lodging as well as schooling. Other "pauper" children are now in "Scattered Homes," which would equally pass to the Council. Others are "boarded out," and would likewise be henceforth arranged for by the Council. No child would henceforth be a pauper.

THE PERSONS OF UNSOUND MIND.

It would be the duty of the Council, acting through its Asylums Committee (together with its Mental Deficiency Committee, if this exists separately), to make all the necessary provision for persons of unsound mind, including idiots and the feeble-minded, whether or not they are formally "certified" under the Lunacy or Mental Deficiency Acts (though without any power of compulsorily detaining those not so "certified"). The Asylums Committee would, therefore have to increase its institutional accommodation—not necessarily on the present expensive scale of regular lunatic asylums —so as to provide proper homes and treatment for the feeble-minded and mentally deficient folk now herded together in the General Mixed Workhouses. Some of the Poor Law buildings to be transferred to the Councils could doubtless be adapted to this purpose. All persons of unsound mind would be freed from the "stigma of pauperism," and would be properly treated without distinction of class in respect of their unfortunate mental infirmity, and not in respect of their poverty.

THE UNEMPLOYED.

Under the Poor Law there is nothing for the able-bodied man who seeks in vain for employment, except what is really imprisonment in the Workhouse—it may be. under worse than prison conditions, in an "Able-bodied Test Workhouse." If the labourer tramps away in search of work he finds shelter only under degrading conditions in the Casual Ward. Only in extreme distress will the Poor Law Authorities provide employment outside the Workhouse, and then only at stone-breaking or other valueless labour, not at wages, but on a starvation pittance. So futile and disgraceful is the Poor Law system with regard to the able-bodied that even the Conservative Government of 1905 had to abandon it, and by the Unemployed Workmen Act to set up Distress Committees (and in London the Central Unemployed Body), working in conjunction with the Borough Councils. But these Distress Committees, which organise " relief-works " and " farm colonies," are cramped in their powers. They are empowered neither to prevent the occurrence of unemployment by regularising the total demand for labour, nor yet find situations at wages for the unemployed, nor yet to provide " maintenance under training " for the unemployed, nor yet, frankly, to admit the demand of the Labour Party's " Right to Work " Bill.

What is now proposed by the Government Committee is that the whole business of dealing with the unemployment problem in each town should be placed, with new statutory powers, in the hands of the Town Council, which will be required to appoint a " Prevention of Unemployment and Training Committee," *on which " Organised Labour " is to have a special right to be represented.* This committee will be expressly empowered to prevent the occurrence of Unemployment by keeping the total demand for labour in the town as far as practicable at a uniform level; to find situations for men and women; to provide maintenance and training for any who are unemployed; to provide village settlements if required; to assist towards migration or emigration of families wishing to move elsewhere; and generally to do whatever can be done to deal satisfactorily with the difficulty. As the Workhouse, the Casual Ward, and the " Stone Yard " will have come to an end with the Poor Law itself, there can be no reversion to these barbarisms.

This is a most important reform. One of its most important features is the right to be conceded to " Organised Labour " to be specially represented on the committee. The Trades Council and the Trade Union Branches must see to it that this representation is effectively given, as, by explicit order of the Government, it has been given on the Local War Pensions Committees, by the Trades Council (where it is fully representative) or the principal Trade Union Branches in the locality *being allowed to nominate their own representatives.** Where this is not done, and the Town Council chooses what it considers to be "representatives of Labour " (as happened by a blunder of the Ministry of Food in the Food Control Committees), the result is nearly always failure. The Trade Unions must insist, therefore, on Labour having the right to nominate its own representatives on the " Prevention of Unemployment and Training Committee," as the Government intends and desires that it should do.

HOME ASSISTANCE.

There remains the large class of persons in need, for whom the best form of help is a weekly payment to " maintain the home." The widows with young children, the old people who can get

* See Report of the Parliamentary Committee of the Trades Union Congress, Bristol, 1916.

decently looked after, the men and women crippled by chronic disease, the workers left temporarily without resources through some misfortune—how harshly and cruelly they have often been treated by the Poor Law Guardians, sometimes by the direct instigation of the Poor Law Division of the Local Government Board, in pursuance of the policy of always " offering the Workhouse "and trying to prohibit all Outdoor Relief.

This is now to come to an end. The Poor Law Orders, including the Outrelief Regulation Order, will drop. There will be no question of Poor Relief. There will be no Workhouse with which to threaten the applicants. The Town Council is to appoint its own committee, the " Home Assistance Committee," which is, under new statutory powers, to be responsible for granting " Mothers' Pensions " to widows, under the name of " home assistance,".for all cases which can best be helped in this way. This committee is to seek admission to suitable hospitals for those who are sick and who need to go to hospital; to procure admission to appropriate boarding schools for orphan and other children requiring this; to see that the old people, and the chronically afflicted, and the feeble-minded are properly cared for; to become the guardian of orphan and deserted children; and to look after the interests of all the families who come to it for help. This " Home Assistance Committee " is to be concerned only with " maintaining the home," and—this is very important—is specifically not to have any institution of its own which it might be tempted to use as an alternative!

THE COUNTY COUNCIL.

In this way all the people now looked after by the Boards of Guardians under the Poor Law as paupers would henceforth be looked after as citizens by the Town Council itself through its several committees.

The same system would come into force in the administrative counties, with some necessary adjustments. In London, for instance, it is proposed that all the Poor Law buildings should pass to the London County Council, and that all necessary institutions for the sick and infirm, the persons of unsound mind, and the orphan and deserted children should be maintained by that Council—the Metropolitan Asylums Board and the Central Unemployed Body ceasing to exist, as well as the Boards of Guardians—whilst the Metropolitan Borough Councils would take over, under their own Health Committees and their own medical officers of health, the present outdoor medical staffs of the Boards of Guardians, and set up their own " Home Assistance Committees" to grant " home assistance " and " maintain the home." The London County Council would undertake by its " Prevention of Unemployment and Training Committee " the whole responsibility for preventing the occurrence of Unemployment by keeping the total demand for labour in London as far as practicable regular from year to year and throughout each year; and for providing in the most suitable way for the unemployed. And, in order to equalise the burden as between rich districts and poor, it is proposed that two-thirds of all the expenditure of the Metropolitan Borough Councils under these heads should, under proper rules, be repaid by the London County Council. In this way the poor districts would no longer be crushed by such heavy local rates, to the advantage of the richer districts.

In the Administrative Counties other than London much the same sort of arrangements are proposed. But all the places having 50,000 population which are not County Boroughs will, for this purpose, have the same complete independence as if they were County Boroughs. This meets the need of such places as Tottenham and Willesden and Rhondda. The children of school age will be provided for by the Local Education Authority, whatever it is. The persons of unsound mind will be dealt with by the Asylums Committee of the County Council. The County Council will set up "Prevention of Unemployment and Training" and "Home Assistance" Committees, and these, aided by District Committees in the different localities, on which the local councillors will sit, will look after all the cases. With regard to the provision to be made for the sick and infirm (including maternity and the aged requiring institutional care), it is suggested that the responsibility should be with the County Council, and that it should at once submit a scheme, showing how it proposes to make the necessary provision for all the various needs for all parts of the County. If any Borough or Urban District which is important enough to be a Local Education Authority very much desires to be independent as regards this new and enlarged Health service, and can show itself prepared to make proper provision without delay at the expense of its own rates, it is suggested that it might (under proper conditions of co-operation with the County scheme) be allowed to run its own hospitals and homes for the infirm aged, its own scheme of maternity and infancy care, and its own medical and nursing service. But no district is to be allowed to "contract out" in order to be free to neglect its duty.*

Such, in summarised form, is the plan for the breaking up of the Poor Law and the abolition of pauperism, which the Government is understood to be prepared to put before Parliament *if public opinion demands it*. Of its advantage to the poor, and also to the nation as a whole, it is unnecessary to speak. Three questions are asked about it.

CAN THE COUNCILS DO ALL THE WORK?

The answer is: Yes, easily, if the councillors set about it properly, and so organise their business that the elected representatives do the work of representatives, and do not attempt—a fault of many a councillor—to take upon themselves work which ought to be done by the salaried municipal officials, whom the elected representatives ought only to appoint, supervise, and direct. The existing Education, Health, and Asylums Committees will not find their work seriously increased merely because the numbers under their care have grown. But two new committees must be manned (the "Prevention of Unemployment and Training Committee" and

* The various incidental functions of the Poor Law Authorities are, of course, to be provided for. The administration of the Vaccination Acts and of those relating to the Registration of Births, Marriages and Deaths will pass to the Local Health Authority. The appointment of the Assessment Committee, where this is now made by the Board of Guardians, will go to the County Council, pending a complete reform of assessment and rating.

the "Home Assistance Committee"); and there will be, under the other committees, additional institutions to be looked after by new sub-committees. The need for more men (and especially for more women, and for both men and women of experience in the special work to be done) must be faced. The number of councillors cannot usually be increased with advantage or without making the Council itself too large for efficiency. There seems no alternative but to give the Council power to add to each committee a minority from outside the Council. This resort to unelected persons is sometimes thought to be against Democratic theory. But, after all, the Council itself has still the decision. The committee or the sub-committee can act only under the Council's orders. What is more important, this plan of Co-optation, within due limits, is found to work well. It has long been of great use in most large towns in the case of Libraries and Museums Committees. It was at first strongly objected to in the case of the Education Committee, but after fifteen years' trial very few Education Committees would now wish to abandon it. It would be of considerable value to have some representatives of the Local Insurance Committee on the Health Committee. The same thing would be of great assistance to the Asylums Committee, which has everywhere a most burdensome task, for which many of the councillors can with difficulty find time. And, in the case of the Prevention of Unemployment and Training Committee, *it becomes of very special value if it enables the Trades Council and the principal Trade Union Branches in the district to nominate their own representatives to this Committee.* If only for this reason alone, Organised Labour should think twice before it condemns the suggestion.

WILL IT RAISE THE RATES?

The reform ought to lower the rates, not raise them. The General Rate for the Town or County Council's expenditure will necessarily go up; but, on the other hand, *the Poor Rate will cease altogether.* There will have to be more spent in proper provision for the sick and on maternity and infant care; but, on the other hand, the present extravagant duplication of institutions and multiplication of officials will come to an end. Moreover, the Government has already agreed to propose to Parliament an extensive new Grant in Aid of all Health services, as well as increased Education Grants; and these ought to be sufficient at least to prevent any increase in the rates.

CAN SUCH A REFORM BE GOT THROUGH WHILST THE WAR LASTS?

It *must* be got through promptly, even whilst we are at war, because it is supremely important to put our social machinery in order before Peace is declared. The very day after Peace is assured the great industrial dislocation and "general post" of workers will begin. The munition workers will be suddenly and promptly dismissed. The millions of soldiers will be rapidly discharged to a labour market which will, at least, be disorganised, and may (owing to shortage of raw material) be calamitously overstocked. More than eight millions of men and women will lose their employment within a year or so. There will presently be hundreds of thousands of men and women seeking situations. And disease will increase. The close of a war has always been a time of increased sickness. Many thousands of "carriers" of disease from foreign countries will be scattered among the whole population. However optimistic we may be as to "Trade after the War," the nation cannot fail to have to face Unemployment, Disease, and Want in thousands of homes. We need to set our house in order before the time comes "Do it now" rather than "Wait and See."

The Ministry of Health Bill is waiting. The Maternity and Infancy ("Baby-saving") Bill is overdue. Would it not be the right course—one overcoming many objections—to insert the necessary clauses abolishing the Poor Law in the same Bill as the other two reforms, and thus put through the whole reorganisation at once.

You are requested—

1. To get resolutions passed by every organisation with which you are connected asking the Government promptly to carry the Abolition of the Poor Law.
2. To get such resolutions sent to the Prime Minister and also to the member of Parliament for the constituency.
3. To get deputations sent to your member of Parliament asking for his help in the matter.
4. To make it a test question at any Parliamentary Election.
5. To get it brought forward for discussion in your Town or County Council.
6. To write a letter to the local newspaper urging the necessity for the Abolition of the Poor Law.

APPENDIX.

For further information see the following, any of which would be sent on receipt of remittance by the Fabian Bookshop, 25, Tothill Street, London, S.W.1:—

Report of Local Government Committee of the Ministry of Reconstruction on the Transfer of the Functions of the Boards of Guardians (cd. 8917). Price 3½d., post free.

Poor Law Commission, 1905-9. Majority Report, 2 vols.; Minority Report, 1 vol. (The Minority Report, which was that of the Labour representatives on the Commission, contains a complete account of the Poor Law and the provision for the Unemployed, and remains still the best description of the whole system.)

English Poor Law Policy. By Sidney and Beatrice Webb. 6s net (postage 5d.). A detailed analysis of the changes between 1834 and 1907.

The Prevention of Destitution. By Sidney and Beatrice Webb. Price 7s. 6d. net (postage 6d.). ∴ policy and programme for actuall reventing extreme poverty

ALL ABOUT THE I.L.P. :

Its Origin, Its Policy, Its Methods, Its Objects, Its Inspiration, Its V ews on the War, Peace and the Settlement.

1d., post free 1½d.

THE NEW FRANCHISE ACT

Explained by PHILIP SNOWDEN, M.P.

1d , post free 1½d.

SOCIALISM AFTER THE WAR

By J RAMSAY MACDONALD, M P.

1/-, post free 1/2 ; cloth, 2/6, post free 2/10

THE MINSTRELSY OF PEACE

A collection of notable verse in the English tongue relating to Peace, ranging from the Fifteenth Century to the present day. Edited, with Notes and an Introduction on Poetry and War and Peace in English Poetry, by **J. BRUCE GLASIER.**

Cloth 5/- net, post free 5/5.

AFRICA AND THE PEACE OF EUROPE

A New Book by E. D. MOREL (Author of " Truth and the War," " Ten Years of Secret Diplomacy," &c.)

In this volume Mr. Morel brings his special knowledge to bear upon the African problem as it affects the Peace of Europe. The distribution of European sovereign rights in Africa, and the manner of their interpretation, are admittedly amongst the most difficult questions which the Peace Conference will be called upon to settle.

2/-, post free 2/4. Two maps.

THE FIGHT FOR DEMOCRACY

By J. A. HOBSON.

Contents: How to Break the Vicious Circle. The New Economic Situation. Two Problems for Labour. The Conquest of the State. The Close State and Internationalism.

1/-, post free 1/2.

SOCIALISM FOR PACIFISTS

By A. FENNER BROCKWAY (Editor of the " Labour Leader").

Contents: The Militarist and Socialist Ideals. War and the Economic System. Capitalist Interests which thrive on War. Trade and Financial Rivalry as a cause of War. The Socialist Movement and Peace. Socialism and the Labour Movement. The I.L.P., The War, and Peace. .

6d., post free 8d.

THE KEIR HARDIE CALENDAR

A quotation for every day in the year, compiled by R. C. WALLHEAD. 120 pp., printed in two colours, and containing a recent photograph of Hardie.

Paper covers 1/-; cloth covers 1/6; postage 4d.

JAMES KEIR HARDIE : A MEMORIAL

By J. BRUCE GLASIER.

100 pp., profusely illustrated. Paper covers 1/-; cloth covers 1/6; postage 4d.

" It will make those who are not of us understand Keir Hardie in his death as they never understood him in his life ; and it will deepen our own determination."

Published by THE NATIONAL LABOUR PRESS, LTD., 30, Blackfriars Street, Manchester, and 8 and 9, Johnson's Court, Fleet Street, London, E.C.4., and to be obtained at the Fabian Book Shop

Printed by ST. CLEMENTS PRESS, LTD., Portugal Street, Strand, W.C.2.

Central Africa

and the

League of Nations

By R. C. Hawkin.

Price Twopence.

The Fabian Society, 25, Tothill Street,
Westminster, London, S.W.1.   June, 1918.

S4

Central Africa and the League of Nations

By R. C. Hawkin

It should be taken as an axiom that in spite of all revolutionary change which may or may not supervene after this war, no one will ever propose to withdraw international rights which already exist. Now, the Free Trade zone in Central Africa was created by International Law, so there exist many such rights there, and I shall begin by exposing them as a basis for the development of an International State subject to the control of the League of Nations.

The story of the European occupation of Central Africa goes back to the times of Prince Henry the Navigator, a younger son of the usurper, King John I. of Portugal, by his marriage with Phillippa of Lancaster, the sister of our usurping King Henry IV.

Prince Henry was Grand Master of the Order of Christ, and his expeditions laid the foundations of Portuguese predominance and prepared the downfall of Venetian commerce: one of his proclaimed objects was to extend the Holy Religion of our Lord Jesus Christ and to bring to Him all the souls that wish to be saved, while incidentally he desired to secure help in the wars against the Mussulmans, and in consideration of these pious aspirations the Pope, in 1436, conceded to the Prince all the countries which he might discover south of Cape Bojador; furthermore, it was agreed that 20 per cent. of any trade profits should be paid to the Grand Master of the Order of Christ, so that arrangements could be made to convert the negroes.

The Pope as International Executive.

A Papal Bull was, of course, the then recognised method of securing a title to foreign possessions. William the Conqueror ruled England by virtue of a deal with the Pope, who required Norman military aid against the German Kaisers; and England rules Ireland to-day by virtue of such a title, so we are, I suppose, under a similar obligation to teach the natives of Ireland the Christian religion.

Now there are two theories on which all these Bulls rested: One you will find enunciated by Melchizedek in the 14th chapter

3

of Genesis, when he arbitrated with Abraham for the King of Sodom after the great world war between four Asiatic kings and five Phenician cities for the control of the Suez trade route. The Melchizedek theory was that all property belongs to an International God, and should be held subject to the payment of tithes to an earthly trustee, who would use his influence to settle disputes between rulers. Abraham thereupon paid the tithes and agreed to accept these principles, though his Amorite allies refused to do so.

This theory, however, was not very convenient to the Pope, because it upset the doctrines of conquest on which Imperial Rome was built; so it began to be argued that the Pope had acquired his rights over territory by virtue of a cession made to the Pope by the Emperor Constantine in return for a healing of his body and forgiveness of his sins. Thus the Christian Church came to recognise the theory of conquest, which is the negation of international right.

The Portuguese, however, had to enforce their title to Africa just as we have to do in Ireland, and this would have been a much more difficult matter if it had not been for the extraordinary influence of the Christian Religion over the natives.

John II. of Portugal carried on Prince Henry's work, and in 1516 the King of Congo admitted his subjugation to Portugal. This was entirely because he was willing to do almost anything in order to secure missionaries to teach his people religion, and one native chief became himself a fanatical propagandist. The Geographical Society of Lisbon have preserved records of a vast rebellion which broke out in Congo in consequence of a proclamation favouring monogamy, including a wonderful story of the sudden appearance of a Red Cross knight on a white horse, who caused the rebels to fall into their own ambush, and left a small band of Christians masters of the situation.

The Papal Collapse.

During the sixteenth century the missionary zeal of Portugal began to wane, and, after repeated failures to secure priests from Portugal, the Congolese at last applied to Spain. Philip of Spain excused himself on the ground that he was engaged in conquering England, so the Pope was applied to once more, and he decided that the Congo must in future belong to Spain, who must send the missionaries. Here, then, we again find the only international authority stepping in to decide a question of title in Central Africa. It seems also that the Pope (Sixtus V.) claimed the right to dispossess the Portuguese and to re-grant the overlordship to Spain. He was certainly not the kind of Pope to be afraid of creating a precedent, for he selected a Jew for his chief adviser, excommunicated our Queen Elizabeth, and published his own translation of the Bible. After the Reformation Protestant countries claimed the power to make grants of distant lands to chartered companies,

4

and during the Thirty Years' War (1616-1646) the Pope found himself unable to maintain his international status.

I am not able to say whether Portugal acquiesced in its loss of Central Africa. It seems as though she did, but probably the Congo sank back to its barbaric condition, oppressed by a neighbouring Emperor at the head of an army of women warriors, who selected their own husbands and left men to act as nurses.

Portugal had done fairly well out of the Slave Trade, but her glory was now passing. The British and Dutch East India Companies were in progress of foundation, and in 1644 the Slave Trade with Brazil was commenced, the Arabs lending a hand, and no international authority could interfere with those sea Powers who made money in this way. The conscience of England was at last aroused by the evangelical revival of the eighteenth century, followed by the democratic doctrines which swept over the world.

An American Theory.

There was then no international organisation for enforcing moral laws common to humanity; but America formulated a doctrine that land in the New World could be claimed by the first white occupier.

When the slaves were freed in America very grave practical questions arose, and in 1822 a Committee in Washington raised a fund and acquired a tract of land in Upper Guinea as a refuge for freed African Negroes. A Republic was constituted called Liberia, and Great Britain acknowledged her independence. Another similar Republic called Maryland was founded by the purchase of lands near Liberia, but Maryland was afterwards, by consent, annexed to Liberia. All this naturally introduced American influence into Africa, and aroused American interest in Africa as providing a possible solution for her black problems.

A New York daily paper had, therefore, no difficulty in raising the wind for Stanley's expedition through Central Africa, and he, of course, flew the United States flag as he went.

Like Prince Henry, he combined business and philanthropy, but the United States Government understood the difference between the two, and was never under any delusion as to the danger of the philanthropic side disappearing, so she soon began to watch Europe very carefully. Her new theory began to appear, which was the basis of land law in America, viz.: that African soil belonged to any European race which chose to claim and occupy it.

King Leopold of Belgium had by means of expeditions in 1882, 1883 and 1884 secured the signatures of various native chiefs to some documents purporting to cede rights to a society called the International Association of the Congo, which had been founded by King Leopold for the purpose of promoting the civilisation and commerce of Africa and for other humane and benevolent purposes. The Association published a declaration that a number of Free States were being established, and that the administration of the interests of the said Free States was vested in the Association, which would adopt a blue flag with a gold star in the centre. They undertook to levy no customs, to guarantee to all foreigners the right of navigation, commerce and industry, and to do all in their power to prevent the Slave Trade and to suppress slavery.

The World Conference of 1885.

England promptly recognised the International Association, and King Leopold then applied to all the world to do the same. For this purpose he summoned the Berlin Conference of 1885 to consider his proposition. All nations were invited, but the Pope, to his great chagrin, was refused a place at the Conference by Bismarck.

The first question which arose when the Conference assembled was the old problem, viz., by virtue of what right could such a Conference legislate for the world, and it was then agreed that the Acts should be issued in the name of Almighty God. So once more we see the quest for a moral sanction for International Law.

America at once played the principal part, as she claimed that the Congo was discovered by an American citizen flying the Stars and Stripes. America wanted the zone to be as big as possible, and got her way.

Free Trade was guaranteed to all nations; the principle of free navigation laid down by the Congress of Vienna in respect of the Danube was adopted for the Congo and Niger rivers; a declaration relative to the neutrality of the Congo Basin was made; perfect equality of treatment for the subjects of all nations regarding navigation rights was enacted. It was further enacted that this law should be recognised as forming a part of International Law; that any Power who had not signed the Berlin Act might at any time adhere to it; and that any Power which thereafter took possession of, or assumed a protectorate over, any coast land of Africa must notify all the signatories of the Berlin Act, in order to enable them, if need be, to make good any claim of their own. Portugal, therefore, claimed a good deal by virtue of her old title, and these claims were duly recognised.

America Protests.

Now, all this was to the good, but a grave difficulty arose over the neutrality clauses. Everyone was willing to bind himself to respect the neutrality of the Congo Basin, but the question arose as to what should happen if the Powers exercising rights of sovereignty or protectorates were engaged in war. How, then, was neutrality to be enforced? Who was to do the enforcing? It was proposed that all should agree to enforce neutrality, so that Central Africa should be guaranteed neutral even if war occurred elsewhere. One Power alone stood out against this scheme, and that was America. She was estopped by the Monroe Doctrine from undertaking to use force in Africa, even to enforce peace. It is true she had proclaimed her special interest in Liberia, and had refused to allow France to proclaim a protectorate thereover; but to join the other European Powers in guaranteeing peace in Central Africa was too much for the Senate, who unhesitatingly threw over their own representative at the Conference, and dissented from his view. The clauses were whittled down and modified, but all to no purpose, and the American ratification was refused. Bismarck was furious, and made caustic comments on the inability of a democracy to conduct foreign affairs.

The fact was that the Senate was thoroughly disconcerted over the whole matter, and found itself quite out of harmony with European opinion about God and Africa. The view of the United States was formally placed on record in 1890, when the Senate was ratifying the Brussels Act regarding the Slave Trade. It was to the effect that America disclaimed any intention to indicate any interest whatsover in the possessions or protectorates established or claimed by European Powers in Africa, or any approval of the wisdom, expediency or lawfulness thereof. This resolution was sent round to all the Powers, and certainly requires the closest attention at this moment from those who imagine Central Africa can be used as a counter in the negotiations after the war.

Evidence of the great gulf between the American and European point of view came only a few weeks afterwards, when King Leopold put the International Association of the Congo and Free States into the melting pot, and announced himself as Sovereign of the Independent State of the Congo.

International Bureaux.

In 1890 the Brussels Conference met to deal with the Slave Trade and to limit the importation of firearms for the use of slavers and natives, and the features of the Act were the foundation of a number of International Bureaux charged with administering the Act. One was to be at Zanzibar, where the Slave Trade was well understood; this was to collect all information regarding the Slave Trade. Another was a "Liberation Office"; there were to be auxiliary offices, with an international control office, attached to the Foreign Office at Brussels, and laws were made to suppress the trade and punish the offenders.

There have also been International Acts to limit the Liquor Trade in Central Africa, and it must be admitted that to some extent these laws have been effective; but it was not the Congo Free State which carried out these reforms; it was to a great extent

England, armed with the authority acquired from these general Acts. Our ships chased the slavers off the seas, and our shippers assisted in repressing the liquor traffic and the traffic in firearms. America appealed to the Acts when chiding Belgium for ill-treating the Congo natives, but there is at present no strong executive to see that the Acts are properly enforced.

Imperialism ousts Internationalism.

We note, therefore, the rise of a new theory of World Government, by which territory was granted by a World Conference, subject to certain International Laws, limiting the rights of the States so created and imposing conditions on the new governing authorities in this great area, as well as on part of the territory originally granted by the Pope. Unfortunately, however, there arose soon after the mad scramble for African territory which followed the discovery of gold in South Africa, and England, France, Belgium, and Germany all conceived ideas for acquiring African Empires. The British notion of a Cape-to-Cairo Empire was hampered by the effects of the Berlin Act, and Mr. Cecil Rhodes found his pet project held up by King Leopold, who had agreed to give France the right of pre-emption over the Congo Free State, and had made a will leaving all the property rights and privileges inherent in his Congo Sovereignty to Belgium. England and France had recently had trouble over Fashoda, and their relations were not good. Now Rhodes wanted in particular to run a telegraph wire along the Cape-to-Cairo route as the first step towards his goal; but the Kaiser was opposed to the whole project, and refused a request addressed to him by our Foreign Office for permission to cross German East Africa. In 1896 the Kaiser sent his famous telegram to Kruger, and to the ordinary diplomatist Rhodes' decision to try and square the Kaiser would doubtless have appeared to be of the wild cat order.

Inspiration came when in 1898 he visited Egypt to make certain proposals to Lord Cromer with regard to his Cape-to-Cairo scheme. The latter did not approve of Mr. Rhodes' ideas of finance, for he himself was engaged in trying to prevent speculators from exploiting Egypt; but, during a visit to the Assouan Dam on the Nile, Mr. Rhodes heard about the project for irrigating the rich plains of Bagdad by damming the Tigris and Euphrates, and he also heard of the Kaiser's celebrated visit to Syria and Jerusalem and his aspirations for a German Empire in Mesopotamia.

This idea was good enough for Rhodes, and he went straight off to Berlin, which city he reached on March 10, 1899. Next morning he sallied out to see the Kaiser at Potsdam and the flunkeys were surprised to see a travelling Englishman walk up to the Palace and offer his card, explaining in English that he wanted to see the Kaiser. They were probably still more surprised to find that the rules of precise German etiquette were all to be waived, and Cecil Rhodes was ushered into the august presence.

The Kaiser's deal with Rhodes.

Now there is only one record in this country as to what took place, and that was an account written by Mr. Rhodes himself and handed to the then Prince of Wales (Edward VII.), who asked Mr. Rhodes for a record: but various persons heard at various times various scraps of this most irregular diplomacy.

We know that the Kaiser referred to his telegram to President Kruger, and Rhodes explained that it deflected the British resentment felt against him to the Kaiser himself, because England resented the telegram. We know that the Kaiser brought out an atlas and at first resolutely refused to allow the Cape-to-Cairo wire to cross German East Africa. We know that at last it came to something like a row, during which Rhodes suddenly accused the Kaiser of wanting Mesopotamia, and that the Kaiser retorted: "What if I do?"

It was that reply that gave Rhodes his supreme diplomatic victory. He had won, for it was the admission by a responsible Sovereign that Germany was coveting territory owned by Turkey. Rhodes saw his advantage and changed his tone. Now he could talk plain English, and he dared to offer the Kaiser a free hand in Mesopotamia in return for a free hand in Africa.

The Kaiser was delighted; here was a man who offered him the chance of realising his glittering Oriental dream and swore that he could deliver the goods. The Kaiser took the bait.

I don't believe there was anything in writing, but each undertook to back the other. Three days later they met again at dinner, and the following day the Telegraph agreement was duly signed. The Kaiser told the British Ambassador that he only wished Mr. Rhodes could be his Prime Minister, as he personally was in favour of the Cape-to-Cairo wire, but that the Reichstag was not Imperial enough. Rhodes came back to England and delivered a great speech eulogising the Kaiser, and he added a codicil to his will by which five yearly scholarships of £250 per annum were established at Oxford for students of German birth, the nomination to be with the Kaiser; moreover, he announced his object to be that an understanding should grow up between America, England and Germany which would render war impossible, "because educational relations make the strongest tie." Rhodes then returned to South Africa and the Boer War began.

All this explains the reference in Prince Lichnowsky's recent revelations to what he calls "the programme of the great Rhodes."

It was a secret treaty made between two men, who merely trusted each other, and the following were the consequences. The Kaiser, on his side, first of all persuaded Queen Wilhelmina of Holland to urge President Kruger to give way to Rhodes' demand for franchise reforms in the Transvaal; he then urged Kruger to accept mediation by America. When Kruger had refused the

9

Kaiser's advice and war broke out, he proclaimed German neutrality and refused all invitations to join France and Russia against England. He refused to see Kruger when the old President reached Europe, and one of the last letters Mr. Rhodes ever received was from the Kaiser congratulating him on the fact that his telegraph wire had reached Ujiji in Central Africa. It must be admitted that Rhodes did well out of the business.

Meanwhile the Kaiser had called in Mr. Gwinner, the President of the Deutsche Bank, to draft a proposal for the Anatolian Railway Concession in Asia Minor.

A few weeks after the South African War broke out the Kaiser arrived in London with Prince Bulow, and during his visit, on November 27, 1899, the Bagdad Concession was authorised by the Sultan of Turkey; it was signed on the day before the Kaiser left England. The Reichstag doubled the size of the German Navy, but there was no protest from England. Turkey decided to re-arm her fleet, and called for tenders. A British firm tendered £80,000 less than a German tender, but, to everyone's surprise, it was announced that the tenders would be open a second time. The result was the same, but the German tender was accepted. Tenders were asked for the construction of the Bagdad Railway. A British firm was in competition with the Deutsche Bank. The latter was demanding from the Sultan twice the guarantee that was necessary to cover the cost of construction, but the Deutsche Bank got it. To pay the interest, the Sultan found himself obliged to pawn the tithes payable by the Armenian farmers, and Germany thus became the tax-gatherer of Mesopotamia. The Deutsche Bank secured the right to exploit the minerals near the railway, to cut the timber of the forests, to establish trading stations and a number of important trade monopolies. No wonder that Karl Liebnecht was punished for persistently interrupting Reichstag speakers with the words: " What about the Deutsche Bank ? "

At last Russia took fright and the Balkan War broke out, but it is clear from Prince Lichnowsky's Memorandum that Germany intended to press her claims against Turkey till just before the present war.

We need not stray into the Balkan quagmire, but it will, I think, be clear that March 11, 1899, when Rhodes saw the Kaiser, was an important date in history.

Now the establishment of a telegraph wire from the Cape to Cairo was a very reasonable thing, and we may ask whether there was any more reasonable way of getting it done?

Here was a work of great international importance, which would admittedly have opened out a rich and almost unpopulated country. Here were laws laid down at Berlin and Brussels, made with the object of developing trade and civilisation in Central Africa. These laws enacted Free Trade in the very territory through which the wire was to pass. They introduced the International Conven-

10

tion of the Universal Postal Union, revised at Paris in 1878, as a law of Central Africa. Germany had with the other signatories solemnly declared that she was animated by the firm intention of putting an end to the Slave Trade, and that the establishment of telegraph lines was one of the most effective means for accomplishing this end. She was pledged by International Treaty to give aid and protection to commercial undertakings in Central Africa, and yet when it came to the point Rhodes was unable to secure from a country which claimed to occupy German East Africa by virtue of a World Title simply a permit to run a telegraph wire through that country except on terms which in effect have laid the whole world under tribute, and more especially the unfortunate Turks.

The Remedy: A New Executive.

Will anyone deny that all this might have been saved if the Conference at Berlin had gone further and established an executive charged with considering only international interests instead of omitting to create any body to enforce these interests? Even the International Pope could excommunicate and put countries under interdicts; but Rhodes had no such way, and it is evident that the European Powers were really taking no notice of their international obligations under International Law.

England was by far the best: it really was keen on suppressing the Slave Trade, the liquor traffic, and on maintaining native rights, as the land laws of Nigeria prove; but France, Belgium, and Germany treated their Central African possessions as held by European feudal tenure, whereas the feudal system has not yet been formally accepted by the world as law in Central Africa.

The Berlin Act laid it down that foreigners without distinction should enjoy in Central Africa with regard to the protection of their persons and effects and with regard to the acquisition and transfer of their movable and real property the same treatment and rights as Nationals; at the same time, all the Powers exercising sovereign rights or influence bound themselves to care for the improvement of the conditions of the moral and material well-being of the natives. When Belgium formally annexed the Congo Free State she was supposed to take on her shoulders all the obligations of the International Association of the Congo, but the International Bureau at Brussels was practically a dead letter office, and the solemn laws promulgated by the world in the name of Almighty God were neglected and forgotten. It almost looks as if the old International God were thoroughly angry with us for having thus acted. Prince Bismarck told the Berlin Congo Conference in 1885 that the evils of war would assume a specially fatal character if the natives of Africa were led to take sides in disputes between civilised Powers; yet I am informed that on August 2, 1914, the Germans in German East Africa telegraphed to their military posts ordering the mobilisation of their native troops. A day or two afterwards England bombarded the German

11

port of Dar-es-Salaam, and these two acts smashed up the neutrality clauses of the Berlin Act providing that Central Africa should remain neutral in case of a European war.

Spain's Intervention.

Probably neither the German Commander in German East Africa nor our Admiralty knew anything about these laws, but Belgium did, and at once called on the Powers to respect them, and Spain, acting as a neutral signatory of the Berlin Act, took up the question. There were many conversations, but on August 6, 1914, France told Belgium that she wished to get back that part of the Congo which she had to give up during the Agadir incident, and that a success would not be difficult to obtain. On the following day England told Belgium that as German troops had already taken the offensive, England was sending forces to overcome all opposition, at the same time undertaking to prevent any risings of the native population in Belgian Congo.

The Spanish intervention, therefore, failed, and Germany complains that Spain never told her of the Belgian communication, because she would have acted differently had she known of the conversations among the Entente Powers and neutral signatories.

Germany, however, a week later conceived the same idea as Belgium, and approached President Wilson on the subject. The President replied that as the Senate had refused to ratify the Berlin Act, America would not depart from George Washington's doctrine of non-interference with European quarrels.

In the fall of 1915, however, the question came up again, and in the House of Commons Mr. Bonar Law told us that the military position in East Africa was largely one of stalemate, and England admitted the very great desirability of neutralising this region if only it were possible.

America and Holland held conversations on the question, but they came to nought; perhaps at that time Germany was pleased with the stalemate out there. This disappeared under General Smuts's influence, and to-day Central Africa is well nigh cleared of Germans. But it will never be the same as before the war—the influence of the tribal chiefs will disappear, the tribes will split up, the white man's influence will be different, and the missionary will have to battle with new ideas which are surging through the black mind.

Some natives will have seen England, some France; some will notice our strong points, some our shortcomings; and we are to-day faced with new problems as to the introduction of firearms and munitions into Central Africa, the growth of liquor abuse, the danger of tribal wars and the reconstruction of the Government in East Africa.

Now all these questions formed the subject of a lecture by Dr. Solf, the German Colonial Secretary, last December, in which he discussed the suggestion that Central Africa shall be inter-nationalised, and told his audience that England would be the strongest opponent of the proposal. Now I submit that in view of the fact that the Labour party and Trades Union Congress have included this proposal in their published Memorandum of War Aims, which Mr. Lloyd George has accepted, there is clear evidence that Dr. Solf is mistaken, but it is not necessary to wait until the war is over to take action in this matter.

The League of Nations should act.

Here is ready to hand all the machinery for summoning a meeting of the League of Nations to consider the present state of Central Africa. Any signatory of the Berlin Act can do so, but per-haps Spain is the most suitable Power to take the lead, as she took action before. What stands in the way is the fact that England has refused her former approach, and so England must let it be known that such a proposal will be reconsidered.

This is what I desire to persuade our Government to do, and if Mr. Lloyd George can be induced to assure Spain that, in view of the "all clear" signal in Central Africa, England will now reconsider Spain's 1914 proposal, then I see no reason why a World Conference on Central Africa should not meet at once.

President Wilson demands an absolutely impartial adjustment of colonial claims, the interests of the peoples concerned having equal weight with the claims of the Government whose title is to be determined. Here would be the chance of translating these words into practical politics!

Mr. Young, the ex-Secretary of the Lisbon Legation, has told us that a policy of internationalism would save Central Africa from German and other Imperialism, and that we can count on Portugal to contribute her part. Portugal has historic claims to be heard. I have read that Belgium maintains the views she expressed at the outbreak of the war. Let King Albert and M. Vandervelde speak for Belgium!

It is not necessary that Germany or Austria should attend They would be invited, of course, and the Conference should be convened at a city which they could reach. But the Berlin Act did not depend on Germany, and Central Africa will exist without her; but Dr. Solf's scheme for the development of Tropical Africa on international lines is so detailed that I cannot think he will be happy outside such a Conference. He will have the pleasure of arguing with Trotsky on equal terms.

General Smuts has suggested that the time may be ripe for an African Monroe Doctrine, and the Conference would be the very place for him to promulgate his doctrine. In 1883 Bismarck lodged a protest against the idea of an African Monroe Doctrine, which, he thought, might have the effect of excluding other Europeans from participating in the African pie.

Now no one that I know has ever dreamed of excluding Europeans from Africa any more than the original doctrine kept Europeans out of America; it recognised the existing dependencies of European Powers, but said that the interposition of Europe in America for the purpose of oppressing or controlling the young Republics of the New World would be to manifest an unfriendly spirit towards the United States, and President Cleveland reformulated the doctrine on the ground that he feared the introduction of European militarism into America. Now Africa is vitally concerned to exclude European militarism from Africa, and I believe that no more favourable moment for the clear examination of such a doctrine will exist than at a Conference of signatories of the Berlin and Brussels Acts, to be summoned forthwith. If we wait till the war ends, one side may suffer a knock-out blow, and concentrate all her thoughts on revenge instead of harmony.

Germany has on several occasions offered to abandon her military policy in Central Africa; so there is a clear basis of agreement. The Conference should amend the present Acts by forming an executive charged with carrying the International Laws into effect, and the Belgian Bureau is the germ of this Executive, which can be developed on the lines of the old Danube Commission.

The natives are in practice represented by missionaries just as Irish villagers regard the Priest as representative. There should be a Board of Trustees (as we already have in Natal), including such people as the Pope, the Chief of Cairo University, the President of Liberia, the South African Minister of Native Affairs, and some suitable American acting under a well drafted Trust Deed.

I think it is important that the Pope should be induced to exercise the remnants of his old international authority solely in the interests of the natives, and in return for this he should cease to recognise the doctrine of conquest, which incidentally has resulted in his losing all his territory.

This appears to me the best possible way of protecting native interests. By such means the natives of South Africa have advanced, so that the whites in Cape Colony have granted them a limited franchise, and one day the Trustees will doubtless advise some such experiment in Central Africa.

In its reply to the Inter-Allied Socialists' War Aims, " Vorwärts " tells us that the restoration of the *status quo ante bellum* on the Western front is the only peace solution it can support, and pleads that the surrender of Alsace-Lorraine to France would be a victory, not for Entente Socialism, but for Western Imperialism. Let England demonstrate her rejection of Imperialistic designs by accepting the International solution in Africa as a contrast to Germany's action in Russia.

The neutrals would attend and exercise a moderating influence, and Labour would not remain outside, nor allow the procedure of Brest Litovsk.

But best of all would be that the League of Nations would no longer be merely a theory, it would exist.

This is the proposal for which I venture to ask support.

The Temple,
    May, 1918.

THE FABIAN SOCIETY.

NEW FABIAN TRACTS.

No. 185. **The Abolition of the Poor Law.** By Mrs. SIDNEY WEBB. 1d.

No. 184. **The Russian Revolution.** By JULIUS WEST. 2d.

No. 183. **The Reform of the House of Lords.** By SIDNEY WEBB. 1d.

No. 182. **Robert Owen, Idealist.** By C. E. M. JOAD. 2d.

No. 181. **When Peace comes: The Way of Industrial Reconstruction.** By SIDNEY WEBB. 2d.

OTHER PUBLICATIONS.

The History of the Fabian Society. By EDWARD R. PEASE. 1916. 5s. net.

The Restoration of Trade Union Conditions. By SIDNEY WEBB. 1s. net. A statement of the nature and extent of the nation's pledge to the Trade Unions, coupled with an explanation of the revolution in factory conditions which makes a literal fulfilment impossible.

Towards Social Democracy. A study of Social Evolution during the past three-quarters of a century. By SIDNEY WEBB. Second Impression. Paper covers, 1s. net.

BOOK BOXES.

Book Boxes, containing 20 to 30 Books on Social and Economic subjects supplied for 10s. a year to any Trade Union Branch, Study Class, Club, &c. Write for prospectus and full catalogue to :—

THE FABIAN SOCIETY, 25, Tothill St., Westminster, London, S.W.1.

THE TEACHER IN
POLITICS

BY

SIDNEY WEBB

Price Twopence

The Fabian Society, 25 Tothill Street, Westminster, London, S.W.1 . . Published September 1918 ; reprinted February 1923.

THE TEACHER IN POLITICS.*

By SIDNEY WEBB.

"Prodeegius," we may imagine Dominie Sampson exclaiming if anyone could convey to him the news that one professional teacher was the official head of a nation of a hundred million people; and that another was the King's Minister responsible for the whole educational system of England and Wales. "Prodeegius" would Dominie Sampson have thought not only the extension of education, but also the rise in status and salary, in influence and public esteem, of the teaching profession during the past hundred years. Yet we all feel that there is much justification for the conclusion that it is because we have not sufficiently heeded the teacher, not given sufficient scope to education, not got the best out of the brains with which the nation is endowed, that we have so far made only an equivocal success of our national struggle. When we come to face the difficulties of peace the need will be still more apparent. It is plain that systematic education must play even a larger part in the world during the generation to come than it has during that which is past. And as systematic education is now more and more predominantly a Government function, and the bulk of the teaching profession is enrolled in one or other form of public service, we have necessarily to treat all educational projects as being, in the strict sense of the word, politics, and as politics of the highest national importance.

The Teachers' Entry into Politics.

Now, it is into politics in this sense that the teacher claims to come. The claim cannot be resisted. I venture to predict that during the ensuing decade (during which the public expenditure on education will almost certainly be doubled) the teacher in politics will play an increasing, and presently, so far as concerns the conditions under which education is carried on, it may be even a dominating part. The 300,000 men and women in the United Kingdom who, for the Census of 1911, described themselves as engaged in teaching, nowadays feel themselves to constitute, not only a substantial fraction, with their families, something like two

---

* An Address prepared for a meeting of teachers.

per cent. of the whole community, but also a distinct profession, conscious of itself as such; with its own peculiar service to render to the State, and its own exceptional needs, about which its members realise that they possess special knowledge. It has, consequently, a claim to exercise a professional judgment, to formulate distinctive opinions upon its own and upon cognate services, and to enjoy its own appropriate share in the corporate government of its own working life.

The Organised World of Teachers.

This is a new social phenomenon. Organisation in the teaching profession was slow to begin and slow to extend. Half a century ago it can hardly be said to have existed. A quarter of a century ago it was still only sectional and fragmentary, struggling for bare recognition. Even now public opinion is unaware of the extent to which the profession as a whole is organised and corporately self-conscious. Confining ourselves only to England and Wales, where there are possibly a quarter of a million teachers of all sorts and grades (and omitting the one-fourth of them who are merely private tutors or governesses, or the music, dance and drawing teachers paid by individual clients, and at work in their own or other people's homes) we discover that of the real " World of Teachers " in educational institutions at least 70 per cent. are already members of one or other professional association. On the one hand there stands out the powerful and now almost ubiquitous National Union of Teachers, with a membership approaching 100,000, claiming to comprise (besides other grades) about 90 per cent. of the elementary school teachers eligible for admission to its ranks. On the other hand, in a more complex organisation, but possibly including in its enrolment an equally large proportion of the aggregate of teachers in secondary schools, we have the Federal Council of Secondary School Associations, uniting the separate Headmasters' Conference, the Incorporated Association of Headmasters, the Headmistresses' Association, the Association of Assistant Mistresses, and—largest of all—the Incorporated Association of Assistant Masters, the whole representing a membership of some eight or nine thousand. There is, in addition, a bewildering array of small associations of specialist teachers and separate interests. But more important than all these in its promise for the future of the profession as a profession is perhaps the statutory body known by the inadequate title of the Teachers' Registration Council, in which the whole world of teachers, including all the separate associations referred to, has been given an officially recognised representative organisation, empowered, not merely to construct a Register of Teachers, but also to voice the opinions and exercise the influence of the profession as a whole. If the teachers are behind the lawyers in their achievement of professional self-government, they are, in their possession of a statutory representative Council, in a position to put themselves presently on a level with the doctors and the pharmacists; and, at any rate, in constitutional form, they may claim to be in advance of such other professions as the architects, the various kinds of engineers, and the chemists.*

Why do I recite these facts? It is because what we have to realise is that it may to-day be said that the Teaching Profession in England and Wales has at last become an organic whole, conscious of itself as a profession; that it is now organised, throughout practically all grades and kinds, as constituting a single profession; and that the time has come when it is both willing and able to assume a greatly increased measure of corporate responsibility for the conditions under which its services are rendered to the community. What is claimed by the Teaching Profession, in agreement with other professions in all countries, is that on the one hand, in mitigation of bureaucracy, and on the other in bringing before public opinion the distinctive needs of the profession, professional intervention and professional responsibility are, in themselves, distinctly serviceable and advantageous to the community as a whole; and are, indeed, as we now see, necessary elements in Demcratic administration, indispensable to the attainment or maintenance of the highest efficiency of the service which the profession has to render. This, and nothing less than this, is the meaning of the increasing participation of the organised teachers in public affairs. This, and nothing less than this, must be the sphere of the Teacher in Politics.

The Sphere of Professional Organisation.

Now I do not propose to embark on the whole philosophy of Vocational Participation in Public Administration, on which there is much that is interesting to be learnt and taught; nor yet to bore you with erudition as to the origin and the historical development of the claim of those engaged in each occupation to have a voice in the conditions under which it is carried on. More practical it seems to map out the proper sphere of action of a professional association; to make a hasty survey of the ground on which the influence of the Teacher in Politics is likely to be most useful; and to suggest some of the methods by which it may be most beneficially exercised.

The Protection of the Standard of Life.

The sphere of action of a Professional Association falls into two departments.† There is, first of all, the protection of the

---

* Detailed particulars of the origin, development, and present condition of the associations among teachers of all kinds and grades, with a statement of the problems before them, will be found in the monograph by Mrs. Sidney Webb, "English Teachers and Their Professional Associations," published as Supplements to *The New Statesman* of September 25th and October 2nd, 1915. (Fabian Bookshop, 25 Tothill Street, S.W. 1, price 2s. 2d. post free.)

† A detailed study of the Professional Associations of England and Wales, with a critical examination of their aspirations and achievements, will be found in the two Supplements of *The New Statesman* of April 21st and 28th, 1917. (Fabian Bookshop, 25 Tothill Street, S.W. 1, price 2s. 2d. post free.)

position of the individual member of the profession. We may frankly admit that, among the teachers, exactly as in all other professions, and all varieties of Vocational Organisation, an improvement in the status—usually taking the form of an increase in the remuneration—of the individual members assumes a foremost place. Teachers are human beings even as others are; and there is nothing to be ashamed of, nothing to apologise for, in the claim of their Professional Associations for a more adequate (and periodically rising) salary scale. One result of the general apotheosis of wealth and of the almost universal acceptance of pecuniary profit as the test of worldly success, which dominated the nineteenth century, has been the tendency, in all public bodies, acting in the spirit of the capitalist employer, to cut down salaries and wages to the lowest possible figure. The public is callous; it is glad to have its State and Municipal services done as cheaply as possible; it is not aware of the tyranny or the oppression of which it may be guilty; and the influence of "The Treasury" of the nineteenth century has gone far to make a cheeseparing parsimony the ideal of public administration. The result is a "downward thrust" of the community as a whole, against which the lowly and less well-organised classes of employees struggle in vain; often succumbing to remuneration so low and to conditions of employment so onerous and unfair, as not only to injure their own health and shorten their own lives, but also to make quite impossible any high standard of efficiency in service. Along with this is apt to go an autocratic tyranny, fortunately only sporadic and, we may hope, exceptional, against which the individual is practically defenceless. I need not remind you how severely the teaching profession has suffered in the past from such enormities. The time is not so far gone when the country clergyman treated the elementary school teacher as his menial servant; or when the humble "usher" in the contemporary secondary school was the most downtrodden of wage-slaves. Things are, even now, not by any means what they should be, in the more remote country schools, or among the lowlier grades of assistants. It is emphatically still necessary for the professional associations of teachers of all grades to formulate their own standard salary scales and their own standard conditions of engagement, dismissal, advancement, hours of service, freedom from extraneous tasks, holidays, etc.; to endeavour to get all teachers to adhere to them; to press for the universal adoption of these standard conditions by all employing authorities; and to use all their Parliamentary and local political influence to make them compulsory, as minima, from one end of the kingdom to the other. There is nothing "against Political Economy" in all this. There is nothing against the public interest. There is nothing derogatory to the dignity of a learned profession. We may agree that it is not legitimate for the Teaching Profession, any more than any other section of the community, to extort from the public the utmost reward for its services that its economic strength may enable it to obtain. That is now rightly stigmatised as profiteering; and it is encouraging to find such conduct denounced, to the bewilderment of the average ship owner or trader, as a disgraceful act of treason to the State. But it is, as we now see, not only legitimate, but actually a matter of public duty, for each profession very forcibly to point out to the community how gravely the public interests are suffering from every case in which a member of the profession is prevented from rendering his full service to the community by underpayment or oppression ; to insist, in season and out of season, on the greater advantage that would be gained by the community as a whole, if the circumstances under which the services of the profession were rendered were such as to promote of their greater professional efficiency ; and to propose, at every suitable opportunity, whatever widening of opportunity, whatever increase of influence, whatever rise in status is believed to be likely to promote the greater efficacy of the profession as an organ of the community. It is therefore not only permissible, it is actually the bounden duty of every profession to see to these things. There is no more honourable, as there is no more useful work for any teachers' representative in Parliament or on Local Governing Bodies, than in persistently upholding the prescribed professional Standard of Life, whether as regards salary, pension, conditions of service, security of tenure, or the resistance to oppression or tyranny. No case ought to be too obscure, no injustice too trivial, no victim too lowly for this persistent defence in the interests of the profession as a whole.

The Development of the Profession.

The other legitimate field for the operation of the Professional Association is in the development of the service of the profession It is, for instance, distinctly the duty of the teachers, through their professional organisation, to do what they can to promote national education. I need not remind you that each profession is an organ of the community, existing for the purpose of rendering to the community its own peculiar and specialised service. As a profession, it can have no object but to serve, no purpose but to increase its public usefulness. The community does not exist, and is not organised into a State, for the sake of the lawyers, the doctors, or the teachers : all these, and other vocations, exist for the benefit of the community, and therefore to serve the State. Social well-being depends on a duly proportionate allocation of the means and energies at the disposal of the community among all its varied needs and functions ; and therefore upon the due apportionment among the several professions of opportunity for this exercise of their respective services, and upon the efficiency with which, taken as a whole, these services are rendered. Now, it is an old observation that the shoemaker thinks there is nothing like leather. The community is not prepared to take teachers, any more than lawyers or doctors, at their own valuation. We can all see how biassed the other professions are in their estimate of the importance of their services to the community. Depend upon it, we are likely to be just as much biassed about the value of our own! This is why no community can properly grant, or is ever likely to grant, to any profession or vocation, either the right to determine how much of the means and energies of the community can be allowed to be put at the disposal of that particular calling; or what shall be its rights and privileges in comparison with those of other callings; or, in short, anything like complete powers of self-government. But it is now coming to be generally recognised that, whilst no profession can be allowed to decide these things for itself, because it is, by its very nature, incapable of forming a correct opinion of the needs of the community as a whole, yet no proper decision is likely to be arrived at, nor is the fullest advantage for the community likely to be ensured, unless the profession or vocation has a very full and free voice in the matter. We are slowly learning what an elaborate and complicated piece of social organisation is Democracy. A hundred years ago the best possible governmental machinery seemed (as to Bentham and James Mill) to be exclusively lay in its nature; to be, indeed, nothing more than an array of directly elected councils of popular representatives, controlling the policy put into execution by an exiguous and practically unspecialised bureaucracy. The ardent Socialists of a generation ago, with all their magnificent ideas as to the functions of a Collectivist State, had scarcely a more adequate vision than Bentham and James Mill of the government they desired; and often, indeed (as with William Morris, and I suspect also, in his hours of ease, Karl Marx) saved themselves the trouble of precise thought about so dull a subject as administrative machinery by toppling over into a Utopian Communism. We see now that even the most logically formed hierarchy of directly elected Councils, and the most perfecty equipped bureaucracy of salaried Civil Servants, will not, in themselves, give us either the general Consciousness of Consent or the universal Sense of Personal Freedom that we look for in Democracy; and, therefore, as we infer, they will not, in themselves, ensure us, in the long run, that aggregate maximum of personal development which alone can be accepted as the utmost civic efficiency. Accordingly, we nowadays look, for the most perfect democracy, to a higher degree of complication than either James Mill or Karl Marx ever contemplated—to a perpetual interaction, in council and in administration, between the representatives of the community of citizens or consumers, on the one hand, and on the other, the representatives of each vocation or profession, organised as producers of commodities or services.* The nation, organised as a united community, will necessarily insist on taking the final decision. But the community, great or small, is not itself endowed with any corporate consciousness, and its organs or instruments, whether popular legislatures or executive bureaucracies, are neither omniscient nor inaccessible to bias. They can decide only on what comes before them. Experience accordingly shows it to be necessary for each

---

* *Industrial Democracy*, by S. and B. Webb, pp. 818-823.

vocation or profession, like every other separate "interest," to stand up for itself; to bring vigorously to public notice the importance of its own particular function; to explain to a necessariiy uninstructed public opinion or to an official secretariat, what are the conditions of the fullest efficiency for its professional work ; to emphasise the claim of the profession to be allowed to render to the community all the service of which it is capable ; and, in particular, to demonstrate, as promptly and efficaciously as possible, the new developments and novel applications of its science and art, which the profession will be constantly discovering.

Service of the Entire Community.

On this point I have an observation to make which is applicable to all professions. It is, as I understand, the community as a whole that a profession has to serve, not merely those members of the community who happen to be its most profitable clients. As the brainworking professions successively arose, it was perhaps inevitable that their members, originally remunerated always by fees, should think of themselves primarily as serving those who paid them, and the classes to which these clients belonged. We do not find the lawyers—with honourable exceptions—troubling themselves much about how to make the law more serviceable to the poor who could afford no fees. The architects have sought, I am afraid, rather to improve the architecture of the relatively small proportion of buildings ordered by wealthy patrons, than to insist that the skill of the architect should be brought to bear on the common run of workmen's cottages, or on the mean streets hitherto put up by the speculative builder. Even the doctors, in their professional associations, have not been the most clamorous advocates of the sanitary legislation that would secure the health of the poor, or the most persistent agitators for such an organisation of the medical service as would guarantee to every family in the land, and not merely to those who can pay fees, the best available preventive and clinical attendance, and the most effective institutional treatment. We see now that it is the duty of each profession to take the needs of the whole community for its sphere, the whole kingdom for its province. It must claim as its function the provision of its distinctive service wherever this is required, irrespective of the affluence or status of the persons in need. It must emphatically not regard itself as hired for the service only of those who can pay fees ; and it must therefore insist on being accorded, by public authority and where necessary at the public expense, the opportunity and the organisation that will enable this full professional service being rendered wherever it is required. In view of the devoted and valuable services rendered to the poor without fee or reward by so many professionals of all kinds and grades, it would be manifestly unfair to describe the brainworking professions as the servants of the wealthy. But what I have seen of the activities during the past half-century of the professional associations of the lawyers, doctors, and architects in particular—to name no others—leads me to the suggestion that, in their corporate capacity, these typical professional associations. have not been sufficiently alive to what is distincly their obligation to the community as a whole—namely, to insist on their right and duty to be enabled to render their professional services to all who need them, irrespective of wealth or poverty ; and to be accorded the means and the organisation permitting this to be done.

The Danger of Class Fission.

The Teaching Profession is far less subject to this reproach than the lawyers, the doctors or the architects. The Professional Associations of Teachers have been, almost from the first, honourably distinguished by the claims they have made for the extension of education to the very poorest. They have always been foremost in pressing for its improvement, and for its provision irrespective of wealth or status. Teachers have always wished to be permitted to take the whole community as their pupils, and to enrol in their schools all sections and even all ages. This is as it should be with every profession. What the Teaching Profession needs, perhaps, to be on its guard against, is a tendency to class fission, leading, unconsciously, to the assumption that some kinds and grades of education may legitimately be restricted to those families which can afford to pay for them at rates yielding to the favoured professionals who serve this class higher scales of remuneration, and more agreeable conditions of service than are accessible to what tend to be invidiously regarded as humbler grades of the profession. Let us strive to insist that genuinely effective access to the whole field of education shall be the common heritage of every member of the community.

The Demand of the Labour Party.

This is the note struck by the Labour Party, which has, during the past few years, passed more resolutions, more insistently demanding specific educational reforms, than all the other political parties put together. It is, unfortunately, not the educated classes of this country, taking them as a whole, who are the advocates of educational progress. Resolutions demanding new Education Bills have not been favourites at either Conservative or Liberal Conferences. It is the newly reconstituted party of the workers "by hand or by brain"—not the Conservative or the Liberal Party—that nowadays supplies the Minister of Education with the driving force of educational reforms. What the conference of a thousand delegates from the branches of the Labour Party all over the country declared in June, 1918, was as follows :—

"That the Conference holds that the most important of all the measures of social reconstruction must be a genuine natioualisation of education, which shall get rid of all class distinctions and privileges, and bring effectively within the reach, not only of every boy or girl, but also of every adult citizen, all the training, physical, mental and moral, literary, technical, and artistic of which he is capable, and with due regard to its physical welfare and development, but without any form of military training.

"That the Conference, while appreciating the advances indicated by the proposals of the present Minister of Education, declares that the Labour Party cannot be satisfied with a system which condemns the great bulk of the children to merely elementary schooling, with accommodation and equipment inferior to that of the secondary schools, in classes too large for efficient instruction, under teachers of whom at least one-third are insufficiently trained; which denies to the great majority of the teachers in the kingdom, whether in elementary or in secondary schools (and notably to most of the women), alike any opportunity for all-round culture as well as for training in their art, an adequate wage, reasonable prospects of advancement, and suitable superannuation allowances; and which, notwithstanding what is yet done by way of scholarships for exceptional geniuses, still reserves the endowed secondary schools, and even more the universities, for the most part, to the sons and daughters of a small privileged class, whilst contemplating nothing better than eight weeks a year continuation schooling up to 18 for 90 per cent. of the youth of the nation.

"The Conference accordingly asks for a systematic reorganisation of the whole educational system, from the nursery school to the university, on the basis of (a) social equality, (b) the provision for each age, for child, youth, and adult, of the best and most varied education of which it is capable, (c) the educational institutions, irrespective of social class or wealth, to be planned, equipped, and staffed according to their several functions, up to the same high level for elementary, secondary, or university teaching, with regard solely to the greatest possible educational efficiency, and free maintenance of such a kind as to enable the children to derive the full benefit of the education given, and (d) the recognition of the teaching profession, without distinction of grade, as one of the most valuable to the community."*

The Teacher in Politics may, according to his knowledge or his temperament, belong to any political party. But when he presses for further advances in Education, or improved conditions of service for the profession, there can be little doubt on which side of the House of Commons he will find the greatest support.

The Duty of the Teaching Profession.

The resolution of the Labour Party is necessarily couched in general terms. It demands for the students of all ages and classes, and for the teaching profession, the very best that the nation can give. But what is the very best, and how can it, in actual fact, be given? This, as it seems to me, is where the Teacher in Politics should come in. One of the most important duties of the Professional Organisation of Teachers is to instruct those who move for educational reform—whether belonging to the Labour Party or to any other—what exactly it is that they should demand and press for. It is, as I have suggested, not for the Professional Association to decide the policy of the nation, and therefore the Professional Association must not presume to dictate the programme of reform, even with regard to its own service. But it is the standing duty of the Professional Association, as it seems to me, to tender advice—to counsel the legislature and the nation as to what the decision should be, and therefore to counsel those who seek reform as to what should be their programme. I can imagine each Professional Association vigilant about projects and proposals with regard to its own service, from whomsoever emanating; prompt to study

---

* Labour Party Conference, June 26, 1918.

every problem as it presents itself, so as to be prepared to formulate the conclusions, for the time being, of the profession as a whole; ready, therefore, with its advice and practical assistance to every reformer or political party prepared to take up the subject; and influential in its authoritative public criticism of every programme of reform that is not in accordance with its own conclusions. Can we say that the Organisation of the Teaching Profession yet discharges these duties? Where is the authoritative criticism of the Profession upon the various projects of Educational Reform? Why is it left to the Workers' Educational Association—essentially an organisation of manual working wage-earners—to formulate almost the only programme of reform of the nation's educational system which is at once comprehensive and detailed? Why is the eager Labour Party—to say nothing of the more stolid Liberal and Conservative Parties—left unsupplied with a statement of what the Teaching Profession believes to be required for the improvement of national education? How can we wonder at the blindness and the ignorance of the politicians, or be surprised at the blunders of our Town Councillors, with regard to the needs of all the professions, if the professions themselves do not take the trouble to supply the desired programme?

Unsettled Questions in Education.

Such a conception of the Teacher in Politics points to the need for more systematic and more continuous corporate study of the requirements of the educational service than the Professional Associations of Teachers have commonly yet undertaken. And the task cannot with impunity be neglected. Bills will be introduced, administrative changes will be made, worse still, defects will remain unremedied, and urgently required alterations will not be effected—none the less because the organised Teaching Profession is silent, or speaks only with discordant voices. Generation after generation of little ones passes beyond our reach, imperfectly taught, inadequately equipped, too often actually maimed and scarred by the experience of what should have been to them a positive enlargement of faculty and development of emotional impulses, because our educational system is not what it should be. With the Teaching Profession, which has the knowledge of what is lacking, must rest the blame, until the Professional Associations have cleared themselves by at least informing the nation of the reforms that are required. And the survey needs to be a comprehensive one. I should like to see the Teaching Profession determine, by a series of investigating committees and professional conferences, what is the deliberate judgment of the Profession upon all the unsettled questions of educational organisation. What, for instance, is required in the way of Nursery Schools for the millions of children " below School Age"? What is needed to make the Infant Departments more efficient? What can be done to redeem the Elementary School from its present almost invariable ugliness; to make it a place of really educational sense-impressions in form and colour, cleanliness and beauty; to make it positively attractive to the pupils? Are we satisfied with the condition of the school-room atmosphere—not to say also the condition of the pupils' minds— at the end of the day's work, and if not, what ought to be insisted upon in order to make children's sojourn in the school-room—they spend there quite a large proportion of their waking lives—actually healthful to them ; and not, as is at present too often the case, an adverse influence on their physical well-being, to be counteracted by open-air games and exercises? What is the real function of the Open-Air School? What changes are required in the school hours, the lesson intervals, and the term holidays to make the work most efficient ; what in the curriculum ; what in the school equipment and materials? What more is needed in the way of books, maps, pictures, specimens? Which is the best arrangement of subjects and classes, and how can the teaching of each best be organised? Is the distribution of functions (to say nothing of salaries!) between the Headmaster and the class or form or subject teachers exactly what it should be ; and what is to be said for a periodical rotation of duties among the entire teaching staff, coupled perhaps with equality of salary scales? How should the school life, from entry into the Nursery School right up to departure from the University or the Technical College, be divided among a hierarchy of different institutions ; at what ages should the transfer from one to another commonly take place, and what alternative roads for the student should be provided? What is to be done for the 5 or 10 per cent. of the non-adult population which is, in one or other way, sub-normal? What, on the other hand, should be our course with regard to the like percentage which is distinctly super-normal? Do we at present get as much as we should for the nation out of our Secondary Schools? And if not, what ought to be done to secure them a much larger recruitment, a longer average period of attendance, and more effective articulation with the Elementary School below and the Technical College or the University above?

Do We Teach the Right Subjects in the Right Way?

Are we quite sure that the curriculum of our Secondary Schools and Universities comprises all that with which the nation's brain-workers need to be provided ; and whether the slowly changing distribution of time—say, among the Latin and Greek classics, mathematics, the physical and biological sciences, geography and anthropology, and the languages, literatures and histories of the nations of the modern world respectively—is to-day, by some happy chance, precisely that required in the preparation for life of the citizen of the third decade of the twentieth century anno domini? What is required for the best professional or technical training of the doctor, the dentist, the pharmacist, the midwife, the nurse, the lawyer, the teacher, the historian, the scientific researcher, the social worker, the statesman and Civil Servant, the architect, the surveyor, the engineer, the journalist, the accountant, and the manager ; and how far do our existing institutions supply it?

These are but examples of the issues which present themselves to the educational administrators, local or national. Are we, as a profession, sufficiently alive to the new discoveries and fresh developments that are being made outside our own country, and sufficiently prompt in considering the lessons to be derived from them? Would it be too revolutionary an idea for the Professional Associations, not merely to appoint committees, but also to establish Travelling Scholarships, which would enable selected members of the profession to take a year off in order to survey what is being done in particular questions in other parts of the world, and present to the Profession a detailed, critical report of what they have seen? I do not think that either the Teachers' Registration Council or the Federation of Secondary Schools Associations or the National Union of Teachers is at present doing as much as might be expected to assist the Local Education Authorities, the Minister of Education, and the House of Commons to come to the best decision and to take the appropriate action in the matters with which they have necessarily to deal.

The Professional Association as Scientific Society.

I have suggested that the Professional Association ought to be, on one side, something in the nature of a Trade Union, protecting the Standard of Life of its members, and on the other side, something in the nature of a Political Association, promoting changes in the public organisation of the State—strictly confining itself, in both these aspects, to the service which it is ihe function of the Profession to render to the Community. Ought the Professional Association to be also that in which it in many cases began, namely, a Scientific Society or "Subject Association," aiming at the continuous improvement and extension of the science and art with which the Profession has to deal? We have, on the one hand, such examples as the Institution of Civil Engineers, which combines in one and the same organisation the protection of the interests of its members, the promotion of such changes in public organisation as are conducive to the development of the Profession, and the advancement of the science and art of engineering. On the other hand, we see in the medical profession the Royal Society of Medicine pursuing its special science and art, apart from the British Medical Association, which looks after its members' interests, and promotes or resists Governmental changes.

On the whole, I do not suggest that the Professional Associations of Teachers should, in their corporate capacity, aim at the promotion of Pedagogy, or investigate the possibility of improved methods of teaching languages or arithmetic. I think that experience shows that science is best pursued entirely for its own sake, in a spirit of detachment from the interests of persons or professions. A Professional Association cannot escape a bias in favour of its own profession, in favour of the technique to which its members have become accustomed, in favour of the result which the

Profession has been trained to achieve. This bias is no drawback to its Trade Union aspect—the Community, which develops astonishing powers of resistance, needs to have such sectional claims forcibly pressed upon it! It is no drawback to what I have called its political aspect—so great is the inertia that nothing is accomplished without a certain amount of exaggeration in the zeal of its promoters! But such a bias is a distinct drawback to a Scientific Society, which ought to be quite free to pursue lines of investigation that look like leading to entirely revolutionary discoveries, which would be destructive of existing technique, and subversive of customary objects or results. Moreover, it is not only one Profession that is interested in a science or an art, and not even a group of Professions alone. Other professionals, and even lay amateurs, need to be admitted to a Scientific Society, of which they often constitute the most useful members. Thus, the advancement of pedagogy, or of the art of teaching, is, or ought to be, of interest not only to school teachers, but also to psychologists, prison administrators and prison reformers, nurses, medical men, and the directors of large establishments of all kinds ; and some of these could throw very useful light upon teaching problems. My conclusion is that the Teachers' Associations are well advised to leave the work of the Scientific Society to such "subject associations"—mainly composed of teachers, but open to all who are interested—as the English Association, the Classical Association, the Mathematical Association, the Modern Languages Association, the Geographical Association, and the Historical Association, with which there should be associated an independent Pedagogical Society.

How Can the Teachers Influence Politics ?

In what way, it will be asked, is the influence of the Teacher in Politics to be exercised ? There is, in the first place, the direct participation, in council and in administration, of the Teachers' Representative, whether as an elected member of the County or Borough Council, or of the House of Commons, or as a co-opted member of the Education or of the Library and Museums Committee. During the eighteen years that I sat on the London County Council there was always on the Council, as an elected member, an officer of the London Teachers' Association ; and I am sure that all the Councillors came to appreciate the high value, to the Council itself as much as to the teaching profession, of Mr. Gautrey's services. When the Council took up Technical Education and appointed its Technical Education Board, it invited the Headmasters' Association, the Headmistresses' Association, and the National Union of Teachers to nominate, as full voting members, their own representatives to this Board, to which large executive powers were entrusted ; and the influence of these members proved of the utmost value. There will, no doubt, be an increasing number of such teachers' representatives on all educational bodies, whether elected or co-opted. But it is not by this method that I expect to see the influence of the Professional Associations of Teachers most effectively exercised.

Statutory Advisory Committees.

What I propose, for the improvement of education, and the increasing participation in its government of the teachers themselves, is a very great development of Professional Advisory Committees, to be attached to all Education Authorities, national and local. The Teachers' Registration Council should evolve into a Standing Advisory Committee to the Ministry of Education. Every Local Education Authority should be statutorily required to appoint a Local Advisory Committee, genuinely representative of all grades and kinds of teachers in the locality, to be nominated, as far as possible, by the local branches of the Professional Associations. These Advisory Committees—which ought to exist for other professions also, especially the medical—should be given no executive powers. Their function would be to advise and warn, to initiate and criticise, but not to decide. But they should have a statutory right to be consulted on all important changes which affected the profession or its service. They should be authorised to appoint Sub-Committees and to conduct investigations (a small sum being allowed them for expenses) ; and to report in whatever terms they chose, either confidentially or publicly. And they should not be prevented or restrained or hampered by any censorship, in reporting publicly to the ratepayers or to Parliament, whenever this was deemed necessary, however severely they felt called upon to criticise the Ministry of Education or the Local Education Authority, upon anything done or undone within the educational sphere. I believe that such a series of Professional Advisory Committees, constantly conveying to the official Authorities the responsible judgment of the Profession, would be of the greatest value. It would give a priceless education to the Councillors. It would greatly mitigate the undue authority which the Director of Education or other professional bureaucrat is apt to exercise over a lay commitee. It would inform the Town Council and the House of Commons of the opinion of the main body of the profession, in contrast with the views of particularly prominent individuals. And if the officials—perhaps even the Minister himselt—found this expert criticism inconvenient, whether in connection with administration or with legislative proposals, the remedy would be a more explicit argumentative justification of the official proposals, a public battle of wits between the bureaucracy and the professsion, upon which public opinion and the Legislature would decide.

Here, then, is room enough and to spare for the Teacher in Politics, without once approaching the party struggles between "Blue" and "Yellow" which some people, fondly deeming themselves educated, still imagine to be the whole matter.

NATIONAL FINANCE

AND

A LEVY ON CAPITAL

What the Labour Party Intends

BY

SIDNEY WEBB

A LECTURE—WITH CERTAIN MINOR AMENDMENTS BRINGING IT UP
TO DATE—DELIVERED IN THE FABIAN SOCIETY'S COURSE AT KING'S
HALL IN MAY 1918 ; IN A COURSE BY THE LIVERPOOL FABIAN
SOCIETY IN NOVEMBER 1918 ; AND ELSEWHERE.

PUBLISHED AND SOLD BY THE FABIAN SOCIETY,
25 TOTHILL STREET, WESTMINSTER, LONDON, S.W. 1.
PRICE TWOPENCE . . . . MARCH 1919

NATIONAL FINANCE AND A LEVY ON CAPITAL.

WHATEVER may be our predilections and prejudices, the pivotal question of politics, not only in April when the Chancellor of the Exchequer produces the Budget, but throughout the coming years, must inevitably be that of National Finance. There are those to whom the most important issue in politics seems always to be that of our contemporary foreign relations. To others the supreme issue appears to be this or that projected constitutional change. Others, again, are most keen about Social Reform, general or particular. For the next few years, at any rate, these three sets of people will all find themselves limited, and controlled by, and whether they like it or not, to a large extent grouped and classified according to their assumptions and proposals in the sphere of National Finance. It is over the Budget, I venture to predict, that Parliaments for some time to come will find the fundamental party cleavage. The nation finds itself charged with a National Debt which may, as Lord Leverhulme has rightly warned us, notwithstanding the termination of the war, possibly amount in gross figures (including all that the Government will find necessary in Reconstruction) to something like ten thousand million pounds; and committed to a governmental expenditure, including the necessary services of the Local Authorities, of something like a thousand million pounds a year— sums never heretofore even contemplated by the wildest of theorisers. The problem of how to deal with finance of this magnitude—involving, as it must, in the society of to-day, the sharpest issues between class and class—between those who, whether by hand or by brain, live by producing and those who live by merely owning—will presently dominate our politics.

The Labour Party is accordingly not wantonly or wickedly stirring up "class bitterness," or raising the "red spectre," when it discusses the present distribution of wealth, or propounds plans of taxation. It is merely facing an issue which cannot be avoided. But it is facing it publicly and democratically. It is asking the electors to consider the question for themselves, and themselves give a decision, so as not to leave it, year after year, when the Budget Day comes round, to a practically autocratic Cabinet and Chancellor of the Exchequer.

What is it, then, that the Labour Party desires and intends in this realm of National Finance?

No Currency Crazes.

Let it first be noted, for the comfort of those who are apprehensive of all sorts of unsound finance, that the Labour Party is exceptionally free from delusions in money matters. "Religion, love and currency," said Sydney Smith a hundred years ago, "fill all our lunatic asylums." They do not appear in the programme of the Labour Party. There is, at present, scarcely a trace in the British Labour Movement of "wild cat" ideas for solving all our financial difficulties by printing more and more paper money; or by some magic provision of universal bank credit; or by "Labour Notes" on the one hand or "Free Silver" on the other; or by any other Utopian manipulation of the currency. It does not enter into the heads of the adherents of the Labour Party that a simple way out of all our difficulties can be found by a "wiping of the slate." No one in the Labour Party suggests the Repudiation of the National Debt, or its redemption by an unlimited issue of international promissory notes guaranteed by all the Governments of the belligerents. I get projects of this kind sent to me from time to time, as doubtless other persons do; but they come, not from members of the Labour Party or from manual working wage earners, but usually from honest army officers, from simple-minded employers and business men of all sorts —some of them men of wealth—from perplexed country squires, and from lonely members of the Indian Civil Service. To whatever cause it may be attributed, it is a remarkable, and, as I think, a comforting fact, that on all this range of questions the British Labour Movement is, as Lombard Street would say, "as sound as a bell." We shall probably have in this country, as in the United States, a recrudescence of the currency crazes of past generations; but I see no sign that the British Labour movement will be infected by them.*

We must increase Production.

The British Labour Movement, which is, unlike the other political parties, made up almost exclusively of producers, is, indeed, quite keenly alive to the fact that the essential problem is that of production—*production, that is to say, not of profits or fortunes, but of the commodities and services by which the community lives.* We can replace the material wealth destroyed in the war only by new production. And we must therefore raise our national production —production, that is, of useful commodities and services—to its highest possible amount consistent with a humane and civilised life. It is a profound mistake to suppose that the Labour Party is indifferent to production. None of the revelations of the war is more keenly appreciated in the Labour Party than the lamentable failure that we now see that we have heretofore made, as a nation, in this

---

* Those who seek a commonsense and practical exposition of currency and its problems may consult one of the latest books, *Money, its connection with rising and falling prices,* by Edwin Cannan, Professor of Political Economy in the University of London (P. S. King & Son, 2/6 net); or *Gold, Prices and Wages,* by J. A. Hobson (Methuen, 2/6).

matter. Whether in agriculture or in manufactures, in industry or in commerce, in science or in social organisation, it is plain that we have, as a community, not produced anything like as much—I do not say of profits and wages, but of useful commodities and services —as we could have done, without any lengthening of the working day, or increase of strain, if the nation had really set itself to do its utmost. But I may make two observations which are usually not in the minds of those who talk about this slackness in production.

Private Capitalism.

First, it is against our whole system, not against individuals, that the gravest indictment must be brought. It is our agricultural system, the system under which we have done our importing and exporting, the system prevailing in our factories and mines, our system of wholesale and retail distribution, the system of our transport, our banking, our remittances—in short, our whole national organisation from end to end, that we now see to be, from the standpoint of maximum production of commodities and services, horribly imperfect. But this organisation in all its phases is the outcome of the private ownership of capital, guided by the individual striving for personal riches, and allowed a free run, under the impression that "competition" and the "law of supply and demand" would make the best of all possible worlds ! It is this that has become, in all classes, so generally discredited. There is coming to be a very general feeling, not by any means peculiar to the Labour Party, that, *speaking from the standpoint of maximum production*, this whole system has been proved to be a failure.

The Prevalence of " Ca' Canny."

My second observation is that one of the evil incidents of the system, intensifying its inherent disadvantages, has been the almost universal prevalence of what is called " Ca' Canny." Looking back on the years before the war, it really seems as if hardly anybody who was not driven by the hardest of taskmasters was habitually pulling his full stroke, or putting his whole energy into his production—again, let me say, production of useful commodities and services, as distinguished from the very different question of the amount of profits or wages that he could extract. We have heard a lot about the " Ca' Canny " of the manual wage-earner. It seems to me that the habit of " Ca' Canny " was even more characteristic and even more habitual among the brain-workers, whether salaried or profiteering, than among the manual workers. The Civil Service was certainly not doing its utmost—was not even officially allowed or encouraged to do its utmost. I do not mean to say that the Civil Servants, "like the fountains in Trafalgar Square," played only from ten to four. I mean that, from top to bottom, they were never even asked to put their brains into the task of *how to increase the efficiency of administration*. Ministers and Members of Parliament, so far as their official duties were concerned, lounged through life, taking long holidays, working only three or four days a week at their ostensible tasks, spending a vast amount of their energy, not on working at their administrative and legislative problems, but on political camouflage and all that side of political life that other people call social entertaining. They were, for the most part, not bent on making the State Departments as serviceable as possible to the public. And business men were just as guilty. Employers and managers, partners and directors were very seldom putting in a full week's work. Most of them, especially the more prosperous, were habitually taking long "week-ends." They spent, in the course of each year, endless time in golf, in shooting or in their motor cars. It seldom entered their heads to consider whether they were getting out of their intellect and their capacity for the captainship of industry —not profits, but *the maximum output of useful commodities and services.* And, turning to other spheres, I don't see how the lawyers justify, from this standpoint, their absurdly prolonged annual Vacation ; or for that matter, how the Universities can defend the laying idle of the educational plant that has cost many millions sterling for rather more than half the weeks in the year. And, to turn to another large class, consider the incredible aggregate of time spent, practically in social intercourse, by the entire class of tenant farmers in their largely unnecessary attendance on market day. The whole of British society, from top to bottom, was addicted to the habit, not of doing with all its might that which it had to do, but of doing only as much work, and putting only as much energy into its work, as it deliberately, for its own interest and pleasure, chose to do. And this habit of "Ca' Canny" was naturally far more restrictive of national production, and far more fatally effective in keeping down the aggregate output of commodities and services, when practised by the brain-workers, than when it was the manual workers who were in fault. It is not so much a question of the nominal length of the working day, as of intellectual integrity and the intensity of effort that is put into the work. I say nothing of the large class of the idle rich, who thought themselves (and, extraordinary as it may seem, still think themselves) exempted from the obligation of wealth production. This was (and is) merely so much dead loss, and it must necessarily raise the question to what extent we can afford to permit the inheritance of wealth by private persons. But the slackness of the organiser, the manager, the director, the administrator, the professional thinker, and the legislator, was even worse than the idleness of the idle rich, because it had a paralysing effect on the whole social machine. These things must cease. The Labour Party is keen on such a national reorganisation and such a reform, personal as well as social, as shall bring definitely to an end what John Stuart Mill called "... the great social evil of ... a non-labouring class " ;* such as shall stimulate to greater efficiency—measured by output of commodities and services—the producers of all kinds ; and such as shall give to our industry and government the organisation securing to the producers of all grades the highest development of body and mind. The Labour Party, far from believing that all

* *Principles of Political Economy,* p. 455 of People's Edition.

may be made right by any mere redivision of that which exists,: recognises—apparently, if we may judge from the timidity of their Reconstruction proposals, more vividly than either the Liberal or the Unionist members, or than that of the Coalition Party in which they have nearly all merged themselves—that it is essentially upon such an increase in the nation's aggregate output *of commoaities and services* that the nation's financial policy must depend.

The Cost of the War.

After this preamble, let us come to the figures. We cannot yet estimate how much our country will have spent on the War because the bills for the aftermath are not yet presented, but it is already clear that the War will have cost the nation, first to last, at least seven thousand million pounds (£7,000,000,000), which is equal to nearly half the private fortunes, before the War, of all the people in this country who owned land or houses or stocks. But it is quite incorrect to say that we have lost half our investments. The investors, taken as a whole, have lost nothing—very much the contrary, indeed. Their lands and houses and stocks and shares still belong to them, and (although these investments may, by the change in the price level, none of them sell for as much gold as they did in 1914) they can still be exchanged for each other in approximately the same ratio as before; and, what is more important, they yield to their owners as much rent or interest or dividend in money as they did before. In many cases, indeed, they are yielding more income. And they have greatly increased in volume or amount—the best estimate puts it at £5,000,000,000. This is the estimated increase in private fortunes since 1914.[*] It is, therefore, a mistake to suppose that the War will have lessened the sums annually drawn by the owners of land and capital (irrespective of any contemporary service rendered by them) from what is annually produced.

What will have happened, on the contrary, will be that the other great mortgage on our labours, known as the National Debt, will have increased more than tenfold. Instead of paying for the War as we went along, to the utmost possible extent, by taking what was needed in taxes, the Governments preferred, to an extent that the economists have criticised as unnecessary, to borrow the money from those who had it to lend, at high rates of interest, which the nation has now year after year to provide, and subject to an obligation of repayment of the capital, which the nation has eventually to honour. Thus, so far as we have financed the War out of loans, we have put off the evil day; but we shall have to pay for

[*] See the careful estimate of Dr. J. C. Stamp, of the Inland Revenue (author of *British Incomes and Property*), in *Economic Journal,* June, 1918. It may be pointed out that although the selling value of each old security has, since 1914, fallen by about twenty-five per cent. on an average, owing to the rise in the rate of interest, and in some cases has been further depreciated, the aggregate value of the whole volume of securities now quoted on the Stock Exchange has (owing to the creation of so vast an amount of new securities by the British and other Governments, and the exceptional appreciation of others) increased by thousands of millions sterling.

the War twice over, first in interest, and then in repayment. After the War, and after all the necessary expenses of the long period of demobilisation have been paid, together with the measures of Reconstruction that are being found to be imperative, the gross amount of the National Debt will probably be £10,000,000,000 ; and even allowing for recoupments, and for repayments from our Dominions and our Allies, it is difficult to estimate the annual net charge for interest and the necessary sinking fund at less than £400,000,000. This huge sum will have to be paid by the Government in our name to the investing classes, and it certainly constitutes an addition to their incomes, which goes far to explain their aggregate increase in capital wealth. And it is not evenly divided. In spite of Supertax and Excess Profits Duty, the rich, taken as a whole, have become richer, even if the poor have not become poorer. Those watchful silent officials at Somerset House, through whose hands now pass the detailed income accounts of the 30,000 families enjoying incomes exceeding £2,500 a year, know that, whilst the individuals to some extent shift, the class, as a whole, becomes steadily both more numerous and, in the aggregate, more wealthy. The official records show, without doubt, that this small class of 150,000 persons (including children), maintained on the 30,000 super-taxed incomes—drawing in 1918 probably £300,000,000 sterling, or about one-tenth of all our national production—has been, on the whole, greatly enriched by the War.

It may be said that the termination of the War, and the possible repayment of part of our expenditure by our Allies and our Dominions, a possible (but, in my own opinion, not very probable) recovery from the German Government of something by way of reparation or indemnity, and at any rate the sale of our own surplus stores (said to be worth as much as £1,000,000,000) will prevent our National Debt and the annual debt charge from reaching anything like so great a sum as Lord Leverhulme talked about. On the other hand, we have to add the very considerable expenditure in the way of capital outlay that the Government will have to incur under the head of Reconstruction. We must not leave out of account the fact that if the Government succeeds in doing what it has repeatedly promised to do, namely, put right the shortage of houses, and therefore within the first three or four years of Peace manages to build a million healthy and commodious cottages in the United Kingdom ; if we should think fit, as the basis of national reorganisation, and as the Government has already in principle decided, to expropriate all the shareholders and stockholders of our railway and canal companies ;* if, as the Labour Party urges, we should do the same with our coal and iron mines ;† if, in order to get the cheapest possible power, light, and heat, the Government sticks to its decision to nationalise the generation of electricity ; if we bring equally

* See *A Public Service of Railway and Canal Transport* (Fabian Research Department, price 1s.), reprinted from *How to Pay for the War*.

† See *The Nationalisation of the Coal Supply* (Fabian Research Department, price 1s.), reprinted from *How to Pay for the War*.

into public management and control the banks and the life asssurance companies,* in each case paying in compensation the full Stock Exchange value ; even if we thought it necessary, for the sake of reforming our farming, to resume possession of all the nation's agricultural land, buying out the British rural landlords as the Irish are being bought out, *all this would make a nominal addition to the* *National Debt of less than £3,000,000,000 sterling*, or not nearly half the amount piled up by the War. Any such addition to the gross debt would, of course, be merely nominal, as these services would at least pay their way as they now do. The very extensive, but somewhat indefinite, assets left in our hands, both in accumulated stocks and stores of all sorts, and in debts due to us from our Dominions and our Allies, must clearly be devoted to the expenses of demobilisation. Lord Leverhulme's figure of £10,000,000,000 for the gross National Debt is therefore one that we can take as a standard.

In addition to the interest and sinking fund on the National Debt, we have to provide for the ordinary expenses of Government. In the Budget for 1914-15 the various departments and services of the National Government (includihg the Grants-in-Aid) were to cost, in round figures, nearly 175 million pounds. We know that this will be increased after the War, owing partly to the increased cost of everything, partly to the heavy burden of War pensions, partly to the greater provision that must necessarily be made for health, education, housing, insurance, etc., and partly to the need for maintaining, at least for some time to come, an army and navy larger than in 1914. I venture to say that, on these heads alone, four hundred millions a year will not pay the normal bills of the Chancellor of the Exchequer. Thus, in all probability the gross total of the expenditure of the National Government, including the debt charge of 400 millions, will be 800 million pounds a year, together with at least 200 millions spent by the Local Authorities of the United Kingdom—making, in all, 1,000 millions, or four times as much as in 1913-14. Can the nation endure such a load (in addition to the levies of rent, interest and profits by the landlords and capitalists) without the poor being crushed into destitution ? This is the problem before us—not put by the Labour Party or wantonly raised by the Socialists, but imposed on all parties by the facts of the case.

How to get the Revenue.

Now the Labour Party approaches this problem with no other desire than that of discovering the solution most calculated to promote the well-being and prosperity of the community as a whole. As a party it accepts, as its guide, the highest and most authoritative science and wisdom on the subject wherever it can be found. It has no panacea of its own discovery. Why it is specially concerned—more concerned, apparently, judging from the speeches, than the Coalition Party—is that it remembers that, after every previous war,

* See *A State Insurance Department* (Eabian Research Department, price 1s.), reprinted from *How to Pay for the War.*

notably in 1815, as is now universally admitted and deplored, the
private interests of the landlord and capitalist classes have been
so powerful as to cause the adoption of financial measures which
have neither been warranted by economic science, nor yet determined
by any consideration of the well-being of the community as a whole.
There are, so the economists tell the Labour Party, three considerations to be borne in mind in deciding how the unprecedented taxation
shall be levied, which are of paramount importance. The first is that .
there is no calamity to a nation so great, and of such lasting injury to
the general well-being, as any general lowering of the Standard of
Life of the vast majority of folk who at present live on weekly wages.
The second is that no burden is so onerous to a nation as anything
that lessens its annual productivity, *not indeed of profits and wages,
but of commodities and services*; and that it is therefore vital to do
nothing to diminish either the powers of production or (without
necessarily depending on any particular system or motive of the
past) the springs of action that set the powers to work. And the
third consideration is that the way to make the national burden
press least heavily upon the community is to cause it to bear upon
us, not equally, at so much per head, not even proportionately at so
much per pound sterling of income or fortune, but, as far as may be
reasonably practicable, without flying in the face of other indispensable considerations, according to the principle of *equality of sacrifice*. I will add a fourth consideration of no less importance. It is
vital to our character that nothing should be done that would outrage, not justice, as to which there is no abstract definition of validity,
but the sense of justice of the community. This, I hold, is as essential
as the other three. I venture to believe that, whatever else he might
urge, no instructed person will deny the force or the scientific validity of these four considerations. It is upon these considerations that
the financial policy of the Labour Party will be based.

What do these considerations point to? I do not pretend to
formulate the Budget for what I predict will be a series of different
Chancellors of the Exchequer of the next few years. But we see at
once that the old controversies about Free Trade and Protection
have practically no relevance to this financial problem. Not even
the most infatuated supporter of a protective tariff has ever imagined
that it would yield more than ten or twenty or forty millions a year
to the Exchequer. What is this when we need to raise a thousand
millions? The same considerations dispose of those amiable people
who bother us with projects for taxes on cats, or on titles, or on the
pretentious names given to suburban villas, or on all the host of other
new taxes that are suggested each year to the Chancellor of the Exchequer. These imposts, all put together, would not yield enough
to meet the deficit of a single week in the year. There is no way
out but deliberately to submit to heavy taxation *upon persons*—that
is, upon ourselves, collectively—which is exactly what none of us
likes! There is no getting away from the fact that all taxes fall upon
people's wealth—that is to say, they leave people with less to spend
as they choose than if there had been no tax. We must not be de-
luded, therefore, by any idea of taxing "land," or "luxuries," "dia-

monds," or "imports," or "foreign-made articles." It is never a thing that we tax, but always a person, whom the Government thereby makes poorer in money than he would otherwise have been.

What the Government can earn.

There is, however, one proposal on which the Labour Party will insist, in order to enable this taxation to be as small and as little onerous as possible, and that is, on the Government making the best of the national estate. We want a rich and prosperous Exchequer, not a starved and bankrupt one. We want the Government, whilst paying to every person employed proper wages, to push the productiveness and to develop the serviceableness of every part of the public domain, so that it may yield the utmost possible profit to the community as a whole, even if this means that fewer opportunities for private profit are left to capitalist speculators. To take one instance among many, we want the Post Office to develop its profitable business in all directions, so as to employ for the public advantage its magnificent national organisation, instead of timidly stopping short, at this point or that, because the bankers, or the railway companies, or the carriers, or the remittance houses, or the insurance companies, prefer not to be competed with.* This is virtually to plunder the national Exchequer for the benefit of private profitmakers. We want the new national electricity plant—the score of super-power stations that are to give us electric heat, light and power for next to nothing —to go ahead for the public benefit, without regard to the feelings of the Standard Oil Company or of the gas shareholders or of the coalowners. What the Labour Party asks for is the abandonment of the tacit convention of the nineteenth century capitalists that all the opportunities for profitmaking should be left as their private monopoly. We must have a free hand for the Chancellor of the Exchequer, consistently with the proper treatment of the persons employed and of the public of consumers, to gain as large a revenue as he can from the public enterprises, even if this means that there are fewer opportunities for the piling up of private fortunes.

This "non-tax" revenue of the State after the war will necessarily be of vast dimensions. What with a Post Office doubled or trebled in the range and extent of its useful services ; with a united public service of railway, canal, road and also harbour transport—the harbour is only a peculiarly specialised bit of a line of communication, and should be dealt with as such—the whole organised with the single aim of national efficiency ; what with the national service of electricity generation, and of the coal supply, which plainly cannot be allowed to be monopolised against its largest consumers ; what with the extensive public enterprise in life assurance (for the sake of giving security to the policy-holders), and banking (to avert the consequences of the rapidly approaching monopoly) it is plain the Chancellor of the Exchequer should be able to look, for the interest of a quarter or a third of the National Debt of £10,000,000,000—being at least that portion represented by the compensation paid to bring

* See *The Development of the Post Office* (Fabian Research Department, price 1s. ; reprinted from *How to Pay for the War.*)

these services under public control—to the non-tax receipts that they will yield to him as the successor to the former shareholders. All the rest of his eight hundred millions a year the Chancellor of the Exchequer must get by taxes. We want the Local Authorities in the same way to develop to the utmost their own magnificent public services of gas and waterworks, of tramways and omnibuses, of ferries and docks, of markets and milk depots, of houses for the people and places for their recreation and entertainment.* They ought to yield them a considerable revenue. All the rest of their 200 millions (apart from Grants-in-Aid) they must get in rates. It is clear that we shall all have to pay a great deal more than we shall like. How can we make the burden most endurable, bearing in mind the four fundamental considerations that I have mentioned?

Who gets the National Income?

Let us first recall how our aggregate national product is shared. The national income—that is to say, the aggregate annual output of commodities and services—may perhaps be roughly estimated, at present prices, at three thousand million pounds. This, however, is at present very unequally distributed among the eleven million families of the United Kingdom. We have chosen so to arrange our society (largely by the purely artificial institution of private ownership of the means of production, and the equally artificial device of abandoning the management and control of our services to the guidance of private profit-making) that a small class of some 30,000 persons (including, with their families, only about one two-hundred-and-fiftieth part of the community)—the payers of the Supertax—enjoy incomes of between £2,500 and a million pounds a year per family, amounting in the aggregate to about three hundred millions (£300,000,000). A second great class, comprising nearly three million persons (including, with their families, between one-fourth and one-fifth of the community), enjoy incomes of between £130 and £2,500 per family per annum, averaging perhaps £500 per family a year, and amounting, in the aggregate, possibly to as much as fifteen hundred millions (£1,500,000,000). The great mass of the people, comprising more than two-thirds of the whole community, find themselves getting from a few shillings to a few pounds per week, the aggregate income from all sources of the humbler thirty-two millions of the population probably not reaching (including all income from investments, pensions, etc.) twelve hundred and fifty millions (£1,250,000,000); allowing thus, *on an average*, even at the new high level of earnings and prices, scarcely more than 15s. per week *per head of population*, men, women, and children, for all the needs of life, happiness, and citizenship. Of course, something like half the families have less than 15s. per head per week, and many much less. There are still many thousands, notwithstanding the rise of prices, "round about a pound a week."

Now it is the very emphatic deliverance of Political Economy that it is of vital importance to the permanent welfare of the com-

* See *What about the Rates?* or, *Municipal Finance and Municipal Autonomy* (Fabian Tract No. 172, price 1d.).

munity not to diminish the standard of life of the great mass of wage-earners. To take by taxation from scanty livelihoods averaging only 15s. per week per head, with the present excessive cost of living, must be, as far as possible, avoided. But, depend upon it, this will be attempted. Under every specious pretext—the desirability of making every elector feel that he is bearing his share, the equity of penalising working class luxuries, the convenience of concealing the levy by indirect taxation, the pretence that the foreigner can be made to pay Customs duties, the delusion that a Protective Tariff will make wages higher and employment steady—a very strenuous effort will be made to throw a large part of the burden on the poor. This will be for years to come the crucial issue of our home politics. There will be proposals for continuing the present excessive taxation on tea, coffee, sugar, cocoa, matches, and lamp oil instead of promptly abolishing it. There will be attempts to maintain the present high prices of commodities, so that the Government can in one or other way get revenue from them. There will be proposals for levying new taxes on all sorts of imports on the plea of protecting our trade against the foreigner—protection which, if it is necessary in the national interest, ought to be secured at the expense of those who can afford to bear taxation, not (in higher prices) at the cost of the poor.

The Wage-earner's Share of Taxation.

But shall the great mass of the manual working wage-earners be wholly exempt from taxation? It might be answered that they are anyhow by no means exempt ; that they contribute enormously, in proportion to their means, by the extraordinary abstraction from the produce of the vast tribute of rent and interest in which they, as wage-earners, have no share ; and that, in any systematic reorganisation of society, on a basis of equitable distribution of the product of our combined effort, there would be, instead of a tax-paper, a bonus or dividend to come to the wage-earner over and above his wages, as there occasionally is to this day to the burgher of a German commune. But we need not take up that position. The Labour Party does not assert, and has never asserted, that the wage-earning class should be wholly exempted from taxation. What we demand in the way of exemption (and that not at all exclusively for the sake of the exempted, but, according to the accepted orthodox teaching of the economists, in the interest of the community as a whole) is that there should be no encroachment by taxation on the necessary subsistence of the poorest family—no diminution, by any decision of the Government, of what is required to allow to the whole of the wage-earners their full development of body, mind, and character. This, so the Labour Party suggests, can be secured by confining any deliberate taxation of all the people below the Income Tax level to imposts on what are definitely luxuries, not necessary for this development ; and specially to those luxuries of which there is good reason for preventing the consumption in excess, and even also for restricting the consumption in moderation. Thus the Labour Party makes no protest against the Government obtaining the largest possible revenue from alcoholic drink and tobacco. It would not, as a party, if the State needed the revenue, resent the taxation of admission to race meetings, or any practicable tax on betting and gambling; and it would be disposed to consider favourably any plan by which any working class luxuries, which yield little or nothing in subsistence or refinement, could be made the vehicle of any necessary taxation. What we say is suicidal is any inroad on the Standard of Subsistence, and any hindrance to an advance of the average working class family in security, culture, and fulness of life. As a matter of fact, any such economically injurious taxation is unnecessary to make up the quota of taxation of the wage-earning class to any sum that could be justified by an honest apportionment, according to the principle of equality of sacrifice. It is, as experience indicates, quite easy to get, merely out of taxation of luxuries enjoyed largely by the wage-earning class, more than a hundred million pounds a year. This is one-twelfth of their aggregate income. If the whole revenue had to be raised by direct taxation, and if there were any genuine graduation on the principle of equality of sacrifice, no one would propose to get more than some such quota—equal, as it would be, to an Income Tax of something like one and eightpence in the pound—from the class below the Income Tax level. The Labour Party is accordingly fortified in its demand that any deliberate taxation of the class below the Income Tax level, carried out by the vehicle of Indirect Taxes, ought to be absolutely confined to luxuries not entering into the essential Standard of Life and unnecessary for the advance of the wage-earning family in security, culture, and fulness of life.

Apart from the development of revenue from the national estate and the taxation of the more questionable of the luxuries of the whole people, including the wage-earners, there are certain special sources of wealth that should be looked after by the Chancellor of the Exchequer as the mere assertion of a national claim. That the Direct Taxation of Land Values should be applied, at least to the extent of effectually diverting to the Exchequer the unearned increment of urban land values, is an old proposal, not of the Labour Party in particular, but of many of the political economists for three-quarters of a century. Even Mr. Gladstone, reactionary financier as he was, got so far as to talk about it. We have, at present, only such tentative and trivial applications of the principle as the Increment Duty on Land Values and the Mineral Royalties Duty. Mr. Bonar Law has applied the same principle to capital gains on the sale of ships, and now to profits on the sale of businesses and stocks of controlled establishments. Other countries have gone much further. There seems no reason why every realised accession of capital value should not be shared with the Government, which was long since declared to be—though our Chancellors of the Exchequer seem habitually to forget it—the sleeping partner in every undertaking, and the only righteous heir to every increment due to the progress of the nation in population and wealth.

With all these contributions, we are nevertheless left with an enormous deficit to be made good. The Labour Party suggests that this must necessarily be met by Direct Taxation; and that what we have to do is unflinchingly to apply the principle of equality of sacrifice, not, indeed, as between individual cases, which would make taxation arbitrary, and therefore inevitably outraging our sense of justice, but, as far as practicable, between different grades and kinds of "ability to pay."

Now, on this matter there is always a great scare, which the wealthy classes and the financiers for their own sakes foster, among the great army of the thrifty and industrious folk of narrow means. Just as the lord of broad acres is entrenched behind the peasant proprietor, and the millionaire owner of urban land values behind the man who is buying his house through a building society, so the man of ten or fifty thousand a year cowers behind the bulwark of the poor widow, the "lean annuitant," and the people who have laboriously accumulated a few hundreds in Government stock by way of provision for their old age. Speaking of this class as a whole, whether people earning by hand or by brain incomes between £130 and £1,000 a year, or humble annuitants, or men and women painfully purchasing their houses by instalments, or depositors in the Post Office Savings Bank, or holders of little lots of house property, it is not too much to say that, in this matter, their financial interests are really the same as those who are merely wage-earners. At present both are suffering in common. The political helplessness of the middle class has long made them the special prey of the Chancellor of the Exchequer. In all sorts of ways, some of which they feel but do not identify, they are at present taxed quite out of proportion with any principle of equality of sacrifice. Of course, they will again be mobilised against the Labour Party. They will be deliberately scared by false accusations that the Labour Party is going to repudiate the National Debt, confiscate all houses and land, forfeit everybody's shares in joint stock companies, seize all the savings bank deposits, destroy the Co-operative Societies, and, finally, as the crowning horror, conscript all the wealth of the country! I don't suggest that the Liberal or the Unionist candidates, who are all honourable men, will themselves say these things. But these things will be said, in the interests of these candidates, and for the protection of the rich—indeed, they are already being said.

No Confiscation.

Now, I wish to declare, very emphatically, that these allegations are untrue. The Labour Party has no project of taxation that will make things worse for the large class who are painfully saving to secure themselves a little independence. It has no sort of hostility to these small fortunes. On the contrary, what the Labour Party is out for is that every man and woman should have, for his or her own, not only the assured possession of a home, with all its paraphernalia, but also an equally secure provision for old age, in no stinted measure, and freedom to hand on this little family hoard, whether represented by house and garden, furniture and paraphernalia, insurance policy or invested savings, to family or other legatees.

To say that Socialism would destroy these little fortunes is simply untrue. It would make them more secure. The social danger of inheritance, which it will be necessary to avert by steeply graduated Death Duties, begins very much higher up in the financial scale than anything we are here contemplating.

Thus, what the Labour Party proposes in Direct Taxation, far from piling new burdens on this large class of thrifty folk, would actually redress some of the fiscal grievances from which they now suffer. How unfairly burdensome, for instance, are the heavy stamp duties levied on the man who buys a house or a little plot of land. How unwise it is to make the widow and orphans, who are left on the death of the breadwinner with no more than a thousand pounds or so, pay any Death Duties at all. With regard to the Income Tax, too, the Labour Party asks for nothing less than a revolution in the method of assessment, so that the burden is adjusted to the number of persons to be maintained. Moreover, the Labour Party will insist that every woman, married or unmarried, is treated for Income Tax as an independent human being, exactly as if she were a man. The Labour Party accepts the principle of differentiating in rate between earned and unearned income, and would carry it further.*

What the Labour Party expects, then, is a much greater use than at present of the Income Tax and Supertax with their existing unfairnesses remedied and a more equitable graduation introduced. If these taxes were assessed on a family basis, and the amount chargeable in each case fixed in inverse ratio to the number of persons to be maintained; if the net sum chargeable were taxed from, say, 1d. in the £ at the lowest level up to 16s. in the £ on incomes exceeding £100,000 a year; and if the present differentiation in rates between "earned" and "unearned" incomes were extended, *there seems no reason why the so-called rate of Income Tax, which only the holders of incomes above the highest Abatement level would pay, should ever fall below a nominal 10s. in the £.* Subject to the same conditions of graduation and differentiation, even this rate may not be sufficient to meet the whole charge of the National Debt.

The Capital Levy.

Here we come to the suggestion that has caused a quite unnecessary amount of alarm, namely, that of a tax assessed in proportion to each man's fortune or riches—called indiscriminately a Capital Tax or Capital Levy, and the Conscription of Wealth. I need hardly say that this is not specially an invention of the Labour Party. It is the expedient to which those who are facing the alarming financial situation ahead of us—bankers, economists, serious politicians—have for some time been considering. It is being proposed by financiers and economists in all countries. It has not been absent, as Mr. Bonar Law has revealed, from the considerations of the British Exchequer. When the sum to be annually levied is very large—suppose, for instance, that it came to equal fifteen shillings in the pound of the

* See *A Revolution in the Income Tax* (Fabian Research Department, price 1s.; reprinted from *How to Pay for the War*).

whole assessable income—the question inevitably arises whether it would not be easier and equitable, and more in consonance with the principle of equality of sacrifice, to apportion the assessment among the contributories partly upon the capital value of their several fortunes instead of wholly upon their incomes. There is every gradation —to take only the classes paying the full rate of Income Tax—between the business man or doctor earning £2,500 a year, and as yet without any appreciable accumulated wealth, and the owner of £50,000 in Government securities who is doing no productive work and earning nothing. At present it is literally true that both are made to contribute equally to Income Tax and Supertax.

There is an extraordinary delusion among the middle-class—a delusion fostered by the wealthy as one of their means of defence against being made to contribute equitably to the taxes—that the project of a Tax on Capital is put forward in the interests of the wage-earners, in order to spare the mass of the people from paying any taxes at all. But, as a matter of fact, it is not as a substitute for the taxation of the wage-earners that the Capital Tax is proposed. It is proposed as a substitute for a crushingly heavy Income Tax on the whole body of professional and business men. The alternative for the doctor or teacher or minister of religion to consider; for the farmer or shopkeeper or manufacturer or merchant to ponder over; for the man or woman living on an annuity or on the proceeds of scanty savings to reflect upon, is whether it is better to go on for all time paying an Income Tax at the nominal rate of fifteen shillings in the pound without a Capital Tax; or to have a properly graduated Capital Tax once for all, in order to get the Income Tax down to something like the pre-war rate.

One thing is certain. The high Income Tax and Supertax is what the millionaires, and generally all the wealthy families, very much prefer to a Capital Tax! And the reason is plain. If the Government must raise a very large sum by Direct Taxation it is very much more profitable to the owners of great estates and huge investments, if this large sum is levied entirely in proportion to people's *incomes*, than if any part of it is levied in proportion to people's *fortunes*. On the other hand, those people who have incomes without fortunes (or whose capital wealth is small in comparison with their incomes), stand to gain by getting part of the sum levied, not in proportion to incomes, but in proportion to capital wealth. Thus, practically all those who are earning incomes—the professional classes, the authors, the men actually engaged in business, and the great salaried class—would (unless they were already wealthy) benefit by the substitution of a Capital Tax for a great part of the crushing Income Tax that will otherwise be indispensable.

It will be realised that the imposition, once for all, of a Capital Tax, as an alternative to greatly increasing the Income Tax, is in strict accordance with the principle of equality of sacrifice. The man with £100,000 invested capital can more easily spare £50,000 once for all than the man earning £5,000 a year—dependent on his continuance in life and health, and contingent on all the chances of business—can spare an annual Income Tax of £2,500, or even £2,000 a year. Of course, the Capital Tax would be steeply graduated; probably charging nothing on little fortunes up to £1,000, or even up to £2,600, where the owner is now exempt from Income Tax; small percentage only (perhaps 1 per cent) up to £5,000; possibly 5 per cent up to £10,000; 10 per cent up to £20,000; and only rising to 50 per cent or upwards on the estates of the millionaires. Of course, too, all fortunes would be assessed at their present net value, after deducting all debts, mortgages, jointures and other charges.

Is it not the most sensible course to take? When a man is in debt, and subject to onerous annual charges for interest, it is nearly always economical for him to clear off his debts, even at the sacrifice of part of his property. It was not I but Mr. Bonar Law who suggested that it would be to the interest of the property owners of this country, as well as that of the community as a whole, that at any rate a large proportion of the National Debt should be repaid, once for all, soon after the war, rather than drag on for a whole generation, necessitating the payment, at the cost, year after year, of a colossal Income Tax, of much more than the actual expense of the war—that is to say, first the interest and then the repayment disguised in a Sinking Fund. In so far as the property owners have to pay this Income Tax, it would be more profitable for them to discharge the capital liability at once, and thus greatly reduce their own burden. This is the financial case for a drastic reduction of the National Debt, by means of a Capital Levy, perhaps down to a total no greater than is represented by the tangible or productive assets of the Government.

It has often been rashly asserted, by those who have given the matter no study, that the practical difficulties of a Capital Levy are insuperable. Such critics might remember that a universal Capital Levy was actually made by the German Government in 1914 and 1917. Or they might reflect that exactly the sort of Capital Levy that is now proposed is actually made in our own country every year in the shape of the Probate and Estate Duties, which yield over thirty millions annually. It is true that not all the property in the kingdom is simultaneously assessed in this way; in fact, only one-thirtieth of the wealth passes by death each year. A Capital Levy might be made without a new tax, if every person were, by statute, on some prescribed day, deemed for this purpose to be dead, and at the same time to be his own heir! Such a Capital Levy might probably involve thirty times as much trouble, and thirty times as numerous a staff, as the existing Death Duties necessitate. This cannot be supposed to be prohibitive. In reality, by prescribing that all securities should be taken at the Stock Exchange quotations, and that different classes of other property should be automatically taken to be worth so many years purchase of the income — according to the ascertained ratio of the last ten years' practice for Probate—with personal effects, pictures, jewellery, and so on, arbitrarily assessed in the light of the fire insurance policy, mitigated by such evidence as to cost as the owner chose to produce, the valuation could be reduced to little more than a matter of rendering an account. Once more, let it be said that the man who declares a Capital Levy to be impracticable, may any day find himself an executor, and he will then see the incredible actually existing, and the impossible going through the hollow mockery of taking place ! *

Sometimes it is urged that a Capital Levy would involve ruinous loss through the simultaneous necessity of realising land, houses, and securities in a depreciated market. There would be, it ought to be needless to say, absolutely no such realisation. During the War, it is true, the Government has needed cash, not wealth. But after the War, for this purpose of getting rid of the burden of the National Debt, the Government wants wealth, not particularly cash. It would therefore naturally be quite willing to take payment by instalments, even spreading the charge over ten years. It could offer, in the alternative, to take over all Stock Exchange securities (including the shares of companies quoted only on the Scottish and provincial markets) at the current valuation. They would be just as useful to the Government as to their present owners, and would be just as productive. It would equally accept, up to the amount of the levy, mortgages on lands and houses, ships and private businesses, if the contributory preferred not to pay in cash. It would not need to ask the taxpayers for a penny more in cash than they themselves preferred to pay. All these forms of wealth would be equally welcome to the Commissioners for the Reduction of the National Debt. The interest received on these securities and mortgages would year by year discharge the interest payable on an equivalent amount of War Loan. Gradually these securities would be unloaded, first, under the privilege of pre-emption during a certain time that might be accorded to the mortgagors ; secondly, by exchanges with holders of War Loan, who could be tempted by a slight bonus voluntarily to surrender their Government stock in return for these other securities ; and, thirdly, by gradual sale on a market for securities that would be continually expanding, to the extent of the simultaneous repayment of Government Debt with the proceeds of such sales.†

* It would be reasonable to make the Capital Tax a substitute for the *first* payment of Death Duties that falls due after its levy. It would thus take the form, to this extent, of an anticipation of the Death Duties to which all property is already liable on the death of the present owners. But the Death Duties (which yield about thirty millions a year) average only ten per cent. of the fortunes on which they are levied. The Capital Tax might be, on an average, in excess of that percentage.

It has been suggested that an alternative to a Capital Levy might be found in increasing the Death Duties four or fivefold, in the expectation that, with the greatly increased aggregate of private fortunes, of presently obtaining an income of £200,000,000 a year from this source. It is suggested that any such expectation is delusive, as Death Duties of such magnitude would be evaded by the rapidly increasing tendency to make transfers during life from parents to children. Such transfers would be of no avail against a Capital Levy, which would naturally be based on fortunes as they stood at a date prior to its introduction.

†For a careful examination of the whole financial position, and of the proposed Capital Tax, see *A Levy on Capital*, by F. W. Pethick Lawrence (Allen & Unwin, 1s. 6d.) ; see also *A Levy on Capital for the Discharge of Debt*, by F. Y. Edgeworth, Professor of Political Economy in the University of Oxford (Clarendon Press, 1s. net), and the articles in the *Economic Journal* for June and September, 1918.

And now I have given you all I know, in broad outlines, of the financial proposals of the Labour Party. There is nothing in them, so far as I can judge, that is in the nature of economic heresy, or the special invention of "wild Bolsheviks" in the Labour Party. They are, in fact, taken from the most orthodox political economists; they are distinguished from the financial proposals of the other political parties only by their candour and frankness, and by their resolute facing of the facts of the situation. They are based on the four fundamental considerations that I have named, which no instructed person can ignore or deny. There must be no lowering of the Standard of Life, and therefore no encroachment upon (and no undermining of) the necessary full and adequate subsistence of the people. There must be no impairment of production, rather a determined reorganisation of our industrial system, so as to secure an actual increase of production of useful commodities and services, and therefore no weakening of the springs of action necessary to set the powers of production to work. The huge burden that we have to bear must be adjusted according to the principle of equality of sacrifice. And nothing must be done that outrages the sense of justice of the community.

"No cake for anyone until all have bread."

What we must do is to develop to the utmost the revenue from the national estate, irrespective of the cupidity of the private profit maker.† We must levy taxation on those below the Income Tax exemption level only through the very large amount that the members of this class divert to luxuries of no social value. We must courageously intercept, for the benefit of the Exchequer, not only the growth of urban land values, but also every form of unearned increment. And we must rely, for our main source of revenue, on the Direct Taxation of Income and Property.

Fundamentally, the position is this. The nation must forego its fat. If we are to retain our health and strength, and keep up both our race and our production, we must imperatively—to use a liquidator's phrase—"marshal our assets," on the principle of "First things first," allowing the allocation of our possessions, in order to meet the most pressing requirements of the community, to whatever extent is necessary, *in the order of their urgency.* In the words of Ruskin, there is no wealth but life; and the nation must in all departments put its life above riches. In the hard and strenuous times before us there must be "*no cake for anyone until all have bread.*"

---

† *How to Pay for the War* (Fabian Research Department, 6s. net).

HISTORY OF THE FABIAN SOCIETY. By E. R. PEASE. 5s. n.
TOWARDS SOCIAL DEMOCRACY? By SIDNEY WEBB. 1s. n., post. 1d.
WHAT TO READ on Social and Economic Subjects. 1s. n. and 2s. n.
THE RURAL PROBLEM. By H. D. HARBEN. 2s. 6d. n.
THIS MISERY OF BOOTS. By H. G. WELLS. 3d., post free 4d.
FABIAN TRACTS and LEAFLETS.

Tracts, each 16 to 52 pp., price 1d., or 9d. per doz., unless otherwise stated.
Leaflets, 4 pp. each, price 1d. for six copies, 1s. per 100, or 8/6 per 1000.
The Set of 74, 3/6; post free 3/11. Bound in buckram, 5/-n.; post free 5/9.

I —General Socialism in its various aspects.

TRACTS.—184. The Russian Revolution and British Democracy. By
JULIUS WEST. 2d. 180. The Philosophy of Socialism. By A. CLUTTON BROCK.
169. The Socialist Movement in Germany. By W. STEPHEN SANDERS. 2d.
159. The Necessary Basis of Society. By SIDNEY WEBB. 151. The Point
of Honour. By RUTH C. BENTINCK. 147. Capital and Compensation. By
E. R. PEASE. 146. Socialism and Superior Brains. By BERNARD SHAW. 2d.
142. Rent and Value. 138. Municipal Trading. 121. Public Service v.
Private Expenditure. By Sir OLIVER LODGE. 107. Socialism for Millionaires. By BERNARD SHAW. 139. Socialism and the Churches. By
Rev. JOHN CLIFFORD, D.D. 133. Socialism and Christianity. By Rev.
PERCY DEARMER. 78. Socialism and the Teaching of Christ. By Dr. J.
CLIFFORD. 42. Christian Socialism. By Rev. S. D. HEADLAM. 79. A Word
of Remembrance and Caution to the Rich. By JOHN WOOLMAN. 72. The
Moral Aspects of Socialism. By SIDNEY BALL. 69. Difficulties of In-
dividualism. By SIDNEY WEBB. 51. Socialism: True and False. By S. WEBB.
45. The Impossibilities of Anarchism. By G. B. SHAW. 2d. 7. Capital
and Land. 5. Facts for Socialists. 2d. LEAFLETS—13. What Socialism
Is. 1. Why are the Many Poor?

II.—Applications of Socialism to Particular Problems.

TRACTS.—188. National Finance and a Levy on Capital. By SIDNEY
WEBB. 2d. 187. The Teacher in Politics. By SIDNEY WEBB. 2d. 186.
Central Africa and the League of Nations. By R. C. HAWKIN. 2d.
183. The Reform of the House of Lords. By SIDNEY WEBB. 181.
When Peace Comes—the Way of Industrial Reconstruction. By
SIDNEY WEBB. 2d. 178. The War; Women; and Unemployment. 2d.
177. Socialism and the Arts of Use. By A. CLUTTON BROCK. 175. The
Economic Foundations of the Women's Movement. 2d. 173. Public v.
Private Electricity Supply. 171. The Nationalization of Mines and
Minerals Bill. 170. Profit-Sharing and Co-Partnership: a Fraud and
Failure? 164. Gold and State Banking. 162. Family Life on a Pound
a Week. By Mrs. REEVES. 2d. 161. Afforestation and Unemployment.
160. A National Medical Service. 2d. 157. The Working Life of Women.
155. The Case against the Referendum. 154. The Case for School Clinics.
152. Our Taxes as they are and as they ought to be. 2d. 149. The
Endowment of Motherhood. 2d. 131. The Decline of the Birth-Rate.
145. The Case for School Nurseries. 140. Child Labor under Capitalism.
136. The Village and the Landlord. By EDW. CARPENTER. 144. Machinery:
its Masters and Servants. 122. Municipal Milk and Public Health. 125.
Municipalization by Provinces. 124. State Control of Trusts. LEAF-
LET.—104. How Trade Unions benefit Workmen.

III.—Local Government Powers: How to use them.

TRACTS.—185. The Abolition of the Poor Law. By Mrs. WEBB. 172. What
about the Rates? By S. WEBB. 156. What an Education Committee can
do (Elementary Schools), 3d. 62. Parish and District Councils. (Revised 1919). 137. Parish Councils and Village Life. 109. Cottage Plans
and Common Sense. 82. Workmen's Compensation Act. LEAFLETS.—
134. Small Holdings 68. The Tenant's Sanitary Catechism. 71. Ditto
for London.

IV.—General Politics and Fabian Policy.

TRACTS.—158. The Case against the C.O.S. By Mrs. TOWNSHEND. 41.
The Fabian Society: its Early History. By BERNARD SHAW.

V.—Biographical Series. In portrait covers, 2d. each.

182. Robert Owen, Idealist. By C. E. M. JOAD. 179. John Ruskin and
Social Ethics. By Prof. EDITH MORLEY. 165. Francis Place. By ST. JOHN
G. ERVINE. 166. Robert Owen, Social Reformer. By Miss B. L. HUTCHINS.

Fabian Tract No. 189.

URBAN DISTRICT COUNCILS:

Their Constitution, Powers and Duties.

BY

C. M. LLOYD, M.A.

PUBLISHED AND SOLD BY THE FABIAN SOCIETY,
25 TOTHILL STREET, WESTMINSTER, LONDON, S.W. 1.
PRICE TWOPENCE . . . . MARCH 1920

URBAN DISTRICT COUNCILS:

Their Constitution, Powers and Duties.

THE URBAN DISTRICT, as a unit of local administration, was established by the Local Government Act, 1894, superseding the old Urban Sanitary District. There are now about 800 of these Urban Districts in England and Wales, varying widely in population, area and wealth. Thus, at one end of the scale, we have Willesden and Rhondda, with populations of over 150,000 ; at the other end Grasmere or South Darley with less than 900, and the remarkable atom of Kirklington-cum-Upsland with 244. Willesden has a rateable value of something like £900,000, Grasmere of less than £8,000. On the other hand, Grasmere has an area of 7,332 acres, Willesden of only 4,383. The huge District of Rhondda covers 23,885 acres, or more than 37 square miles. The census of 1911 showed no less than 203 Urban Districts with populations of less than 3,000, and 203 others with less than 5,000, and it is clear that a very large proportion of the whole are really more rural in character than urban. It may be observed, however, that these small Urban Districts came into being for historical reasons ; new small districts are not now constituted.

An Urban District may apply to the Privy Council for a " charter of incorporation "—that is to say, to become a Municipal Borough.*

---

* The question often arises, in an Urban District with a population of 30,000 or 40,000, whether it should not seek to become a Municipal Borough. This involves an application to the Privy Council for a Royal Charter, which is only granted after considerable enquiry and delay, and is quite likely to be refused if the opposition from other authorities (especially the County Council) is strong. A Municipal Borough has practically the same powers as an Urban District ; but (if over 20,000 in population) it may be permitted to establish a police force of its own, instead of contributing to the County Force. A larger Borough may also be allowed its own Bench of Justices, its own Quarter Sessions, and its own Coroner. Its power of making bye-laws also is somewhat enlarged. Otherwise the only difference is that (a) the Chairman becomes a Mayor ; (b) the Clerk is styled Town Clerk ; (c) the Council appoints Aldermen, either from its own body or from outside ; (d) the Borough may escape from the audit of the Ministry of Health's District Auditor, and have its own Auditors, elective or appointed by the Mayor. A Borough exceeding 50,000 in population may apply to be made a County Borough, and thus become free of control by, or of contribution to, the County Council, and able to exercise within its area (and pay for) all the powers of a County Council as well as those of a Municipal Borough. Short of becoming a County Borough, the chief tangible advantage of an Urban District getting a charter of incorporation is said to be that of being able to raise loans on the Stock Exchange at a slightly lower rate of interest than is usually paid by an Urban District. But it may, of course, be argued that there will be a rise in status and dignity which may be of importance from a civic point of view.

A number of districts have obtained their charters during the last twenty-five years, among the most recent being Nuneaton, Fowey, Stourbridge, Buxton and Aylesbury. An Urban District with a population over 25,000 may petition the Home Secretary for a Stipendiary Magistrate.

Parishes or Rural Districts may be made into Urban Districts and the boundaries of Urban Districts may be altered by the County Council, under sec. 57 of the Local Government Act, 1888.

Constitution of Urban District Council.

The Urban District Council is in every case a corporate body with perpetual succession (*i.e.*, its life continues unbroken, irrespective of the individual members who compose it) and a common seal. Councillors must be residents in the District who are either (1) Local Government electors on the register, or (2) if not entitled to be registered as electors, owners of land or house property in the District, or have been residents in the Council's area for twelve months prior to nomination. There is no property qualification required. Voting is by ballot under rules made by the Ministry of Health. The franchise is wide ; for the persons entitled to be placed on the roll of Local Government electors comprise (1) every British subject, man or woman, over the age of 21, who is an occupier, as owner or tenant, of any land or premises (or as a lodger, provided he or she has taken rooms unfurnished) in the District on January 15th next before the election, and who has been such an occupier of any land or premises, either in the District, or in the County of which the District is a part, for the six months prior to that date, and (2) every woman over 30, who is the wife of a man entitled to be registered in respect of premises in which they both reside.

A Councillor sits for three years, and is re-eligible at the end of his term. As a rule, the whole Council does not come in and go out together ; one-third of the members retires each year, early in April, so that one-third are always "first year," one-third "second year" and one-third " third year " men (or women). It may, however, be arranged by Special Order of the County Council (in response to a resolution of the Urban District Council, passed by two-thirds of those voting) that the whole body retire *en bloc* every third year, and this is done in some Districts. The Chairman of the Council is elected by the Councillors, and he becomes, by virtue of his office, a Justice of the Peace. He need not be a Councillor himself, but may be chosen from outside. And the Councillors have power, if they wish, to choose a woman as Chairman, and in that case she will become a J.P., now that the Sex Disqualification (Removal) Act, 1919, has been passed. The Council may also appoint, and it generally does appoint, a Vice-Chairman, who must be a member of the Council. A District Council has no Aldermen and no *ex-officio* or nominated members. Councillors are unpaid.

Powers of Urban District Councils.

The powers and duties of the Urban District Council are very wide. They may be most conveniently grouped under the following heads :

(1) *Health*, including drainage and sewerage, scavenging and removal of refuse, treatment of infectious diseases, provision of hospitals, clinics, nursing, mortuaries, cemeteries, the inspection of slaughterhouses, bakeries, etc., and of articles of food exposed or prepared for sale, and the prevention of various nuisances.

(2) *Housing.*—Subject to certain powers exercised by the Ministry of Health, the Urban District Council is the authority for carrying out the provisions of the Housing and Town Planning Acts, which include not only the provision of new houses, but the clearing of slums and the ensuring that all dwellings in its area are fit for habitation, and the preparation of Town Planning schemes.

(3) *Education.*—Urban District Councils are, as mentioned below, the Authorities under the Public Libraries Acts, and they may spend what they please on libraries. They also have power to make provision for Higher Education. But they may not spend more than a penny rate for the purpose, and all but the largest Districts, therefore, are practically bound to work in co-operation with the County Council in this matter. As regards elementary education, the smaller Urban Districts (*i.e.*, those with a population less than 20,000 at the 1901 Census) have no real power at all ; their functions are practically confined to the appointment of two Managers to each " provided " and one to each " non-provided " school.

But in the case of the larger Districts (where, to be exact, the population of the District was over 20,000 in 1901), the Council has much greater powers. It then becomes the Local Education Authority for carrying out Part III. of the Education Act, 1902 (*i.e.*, all elementary education) and the additional duties imposed by the Education Act of 1918, while under Part II. it has power to expend up to a penny rate on education other than elementary. It is, however, permissible for an Urban District Council to relinquish these powers to the County Council, and one Urban District Council, that of Watford, has done so. There are now in England and Wales forty-eight Urban District Councils which are Local Education Authorities.

These three departments of Health, Housing and Education are, of course, of first-rate importance, but they will not be referred to in any further detail here. A full treatment of them will be found in three separate tracts. (See Fabian Tracts, " What a Health Committee can do " ; " What an Education Committee can Do " ; and " Housing.")

(4) *Highways.*—The Urban District Council is charged with the management of all streets and highways within the District. It repairs, paves, cleanses and lights the roads, and may name, re-name,

or re-number streets, or make new ones, and may put up clocks or statues in public places. Certain roads, however, known as " main roads" are in an anomalous position. Normally they are repairable and maintainable by the County Council. But the Urban Authorities were allowed in 1888, when the County Councils were created, to elect whether they would retain the control of any "main roads" hitherto under their jurisdiction. Furthermore, the County Council may require the Urban District Council to carry out the County's duty of maintaining and repairing any main road. In either case the Urban District receives an annual contribution from the County towards the cost, the amount being fixed by agreement between the two bodies, or, if they cannot agree, by the Central Authority, the Ministry of Transport. Many main roads, therefore, belong to the Urban District Councils, though the expense of maintaining them is only borne in part by the District ratepayers. Finally, the Ministry of Transport Act, 1919, allows the Ministry of Transport to make grants to an Urban District for the construction, improvement or maintenance of roads.

(5) *Parks, Recreation Grounds, Commons, etc.*—Under sec. 164 of the Public Health Act, 1875, any Urban Authority may make or lease or buy "public walks or pleasure grounds" and may make by-laws for their regulation. It has a practically free hand in the pro-vision of parks, recreation grounds, playing fields, and the like, and it is worth noting that the County Councils usually contribute about one-third of the cost in the case of large parks. Under the Commons Acts of 1876 and 1899, it may regulate and manage commons. Apart from its concern with the common from the point of view of recreation or amenity, the Urban District Council may also, with the consent of the County Council, aid persons in maintaining rights of common, even to the extent of taking legal proceedings, when the Council consider that the extinction of such rights would be prejudicial to the inhabitants of the District. It is the duty of the Urban District Council, too, under sec. 26 of the Local Government Act, 1894, to protect rights of way and to prevent encroachment on roadside wastes.

(6) *Allotments.*—Every Urban District Council has the duty of providing a sufficient supply of allotments for the inhabitants of any class (not now, as formerly, only for the working class), and for this purpose it may purchase or hire land. If the demand cannot be satisfied otherwise, the Council may, with the sanction of the Board of Agriculture, acquire the land compulsorily, and it may adapt, fence or drain it and equip it with suitable buildings for the allot-ment-holders. An allotment is a plot of land not exceeding five acres; but, in practice, of course, allotments are seldom, if ever, anything like that size, and it is not the duty of a Council to provide any allot-ment of more than one acre. A house may be built on any allotment of not less than one acre. The provision of small hold-ings, which may be larger (sometimes they may, in fact, be any-

thing exceeding one acre up to a limit of fifty acres)—is the business of the County Council, not of the U.D.C. But an Urban District Council may make representations to the Small Holdings Commissioners as to demand for, or desirability of, small holdings in the District. And a County Council may come to an agreement for delegating to an Urban District Council any of its powers in respect of acquiring, adapting or managing small holdings.

(7) *Public Utility Services.*—The Urban District Council may have its own gas or electricity undertaking, its own water supply, its own trams, though of these gas alone is ordinarily within the reach of the smaller districts. For services such as these Parliamentary or departmental sanction must be obtained. There are, however, two important matters in which the Urban District Council can act at its own will. These are the institution of (*a*) Libraries and Museums, and (*b*) of Baths and Washhouses. Any Urban District Council may, by a special resolution, adopt the Public Libraries Acts, and over 200 have done so. The Council may also adopt the Museums and Gymnasiums Act, 1891, for the provision of gymnasiums. It is worth noting that Authorities (*e.g.*, neighbouring Councils) may combine for the purpose of providing Libraries.

The Public Libraries Act, 1919, has made several very important changes in the law. It has abolished the restriction which formerly compelled a Local Authority to keep its expenditure on Libraries within the proceeds of a penny rate. It gives the County Council power to adopt the Public Libraries Acts for the whole or any part of a county, exclusive of any part which is an existing Library area. (In that case, a U.D.C., which has not already adopted the Acts will no longer have power to do so : the County Council will become the Library Authority.) It provides, furthermore, that a U.D.C. may relinquish its powers to the County Council, and if the U.D.C. is the Local Education Authority under Part II. of the Education Act, 1902, it may delegate its Library powers to the Local Education Authority (except the raising of a rate or borrowing of money).

The Baths and Washhouses Acts are also adoptive—*i.e.*, any Urban District Council may resolve to provide public baths and wash-houses. There is no restriction laid down by the law as to the amount that may be spent on this service out of the rates. A great many Urban Districts have their own public baths, and there is no reason why all but the smallest should not have them.

Public markets and slaughterhouses may also be established by the Council, and, where the District is a waterside one, public quays and wharves. In seaside Districts the Council may, and in some cases does, construct and own sea-walls, esplanades, piers, harbours, and sea-water supply works. And some Councils have "dust destructors," or installations for the disposal of refuse of various sorts, which enable them to convert waste into new raw material, often at a considerable financial profit.

(8) *Miscellaneous.*—The Urban District Council has besides a number of different powers or duties, which cannot be classified conveniently under any of the foregoing heads. These are as follows :

(i) *Advertisements.*—In Urban Districts with a population of 10,000 or upwards the Council may make by-laws for the regulation of advertisements in public places, on hoardings, etc.

(ii) *Diseases of Animals.*—The County Council may, if it chooses, delegate its powers under the Diseases of Animals Acts to the Urban District Council. The Urban District Council will then become the authority for dealing with swine fever, foot and mouth disease, cattle plague, anthrax, rabies, and various other diseases, with large powers of inspection, regulation, seizure and slaughtering.

(iii) *Employment of Children.*—The combined effect of the Employment of Children Act, 1903, and the Education Act, 1918, is that (a) no child under 12 years of age may be employed at all ; (b) no child under 14 may be employed in street trading, or in any factory, workshop, mine or quarry ; (c) no child between 12 and 14 may be employed on school days before the close of school hours, or on Sundays for more than two hours, or on any day before 6 a.m. or after 8 p.m. But Urban District Councils which are Local Education Authorities (under Part III.) may make by-laws modifying provision (c) and extending (b). They may permit under certain conditions the employment of children over 12 before school hours, and the employment of children by their parents, but such employment before 9 a.m. must be limited to one hour, and no child so employed before 9 a.m. must be employed for more than one hour in the afternoon. The Local Education Authority has the general power to prohibit or restrict any employment of a child which they are satisfied is prejudicial to his health. And by-laws may be made declaring street-trading illegal by any young person under the age of 16.

(iv) *Factories and Workshops.*—In workshops, including retail bakehouses, the law in regard to cleanliness, limewashing, ventilation, prevention of nuisances and overcrowding, etc., is enforced by the Council of the Urban District. A register of workshops in the District is kept by the Council. Factories are inspected by the Home Office; but the Home Office may, if it considers it necessary, demand the assistance of the Urban District Council.

(v) *Fire.*—The Urban District Council has, under the Town Police Clauses Act, 1847, and the Public Health Act, 1875, full powers of protection against fire, including the provision of engines, apparatus, stations, and the payment of firemen.

(vi) *Food Control.*—The Urban District Council appoints the local Food Control Committee, first set up by the Food Controller's Order in 1917. The members of the Committee are limited to sixteen (or twelve where the population is less than 20,000), of whom at least one must be a woman, and one a representative of Labour. None of them need be Councillors, unless the Council desires.

(vii) *Health Insurance.*—In Urban Districts with a population over 20,000, the Council is entitled to representation on the District Insurance Committee, which functions under the County Insurance Committee. The Urban District Council, as such, has, of course, no substantial power on the Committee, which is an entirely independent body. And the Council's representatives will be in a minority as against the representatives of insured persons, deposit contributors and doctors.

(viii) *Licensing, Registration, etc.*—The Urban District Council is the authority for licensing knackers' yards, game dealers, pawnbrokers, hackney carriages, horses or donkeys let out for hire, and pleasure boats. It registers and inspects canal boats, and old metal and marine stores. It licenses and regulates the keeping and selling of petroleum within the District. It makes by-laws for the regulation of the sanitary condition of tents, vans, and other "temporary dwellings." It may be licensed by the Postmaster-General to provide a system of public telephone communication, though with a national system in existence, it would, of course, not be likely to get such a licence. And finally it may, if it thinks fit, apply to the Home Office to abolish any fair in the District, or to alter the day for holding it.

(ix) *Old Age Pensions.*—In Urban Districts with a population of 20,000 or more, the Council appoints the Local Pensions Committee. The members of the Local Pensions Committee hold office for three years (or less, if so decided by the Urban District Council). They need not necessarily be members of the Council.

(x) *Profiteering.*—Under the Profiteering Act, 1919, an Urban District Council may, if it chooses, establish a Local Profiteering Committee (or Tribunal, as it is commonly called) of not less than seven and not more than twenty-five members. The members need not be Councillors. They must include two women, and at least three members of the Local Food Committee. And there must be "adequate representation of Labour" on the Tribunal. The business of the Tribunal is to investigate and hear complaints of alleged profiteering by local retailers, and either to dismiss the complaint, or to declare what is a reasonable price and order repayment of anything paid in excess of that price. Sec. 4 of the Profiteering Act allows Local Authorities to be authorised by the Board of Trade to buy and sell articles, but they are required to "proceed on a commercial basis, and not by way of subsidy at the expense of the ratepayers." But the ordinary expenses of the Tribunal may be met out of the rates.

(xi) *Shops.*—In Urban Districts with a population of 20,000 or more, the Council is the authority for enforcing the Shops Act, 1912. It appoints inspectors to see that hours of work are not exceeded for young persons, and that seats are provided for the assistants. The

Council may also make and enforce orders fixing the "Early Closing Day," and, subject to the sanction of the Home Office, fix times of closing for any class of shops in its District.

(xii) *Small Dwellings Acquisition Act*, 1899.—This Act, which, except in name, has nothing to do with the "housing question," was meant to facilitate the acquisition of ownership of small dwellings (formerly not exceeding £400 in value, but now, as amended by the Housing Act of 1919, £800) by the persons occupying them. For this purpose the Urban District Council is empowered to lend money to the occupier. In Districts with a population of less than 10,000, the sanction of the County Council is required, or of the Ministry of Health if the County Council refuses. The money lent must in any case be repaid within 60 years at most. A few Districts have made considerable use of this Act. Ilford especially claims to have helped a large number of residents to buy their houses.

(xiii) *Unemployment.*—The Unemployed Workmen Act, 1905, empowered the setting up of Distress Committees for the relief of unemployment in Urban Districts with a population of 50,000. The Distress Committee consists partly of Urban District Councillors, partly of Poor Law Guardians, and partly of " persons experienced in the relief of distress." About a dozen Urban Districts have Distress Committees—which enjoy a nominal existence, but are at present of no practical importance. When they did function some years ago, they depended almost entirely for the provision of their relief works on grants from the Exchequer, since the rates could not be used for the payment of wages on these works.

Urban District Finance.

The Urban District raises its revenue in two main ways. First, it has the General District Fund, which is derived from (1) rent or profits of property owned by the Council—*e.g.*, land, houses, markets, water and gas undertakings, cemeteries, baths and wash-houses—or the proceeds from the sale of waste from the scavenging department, or from the letting of public halls ; (2) penalties, such as fines for breaches of the Public Health Acts ; (3) grants from the County Council, or from the Central Exchequer paid through the County Council, for certain services. Such are the contributions towards the maintenance of roads, for salaries of officials, or for education. Secondly, there are the rates. (*See* Fabian Tract : " What About the Rates ? ") The General District Rate is made, levied and collected by the Urban District Council. The Council must prepare an estimate showing the total sum required, the value of the property on which it is assessable' and the amount of the rate per pound. It is assessed on the basis of the Poor Law Valuation, and is normally levied upon the occupiers of property. Where, however, the rateable value of the property assessed is less than £10, and the premises are let to weekly or monthly tenants, or in separate apartments, the Council may, if it chooses, rate the owner and not the occupier. If the owner and the Council agree to "compound" in respect of the property, whether it is occupied or unoccupied, the assessment must be reduced to one-half of the full rateable value. An Urban District Council, which is an Education Authority, gets its rate portion of the education expenses from the Overseers by precept.

Apart from the General District Fund and the District Rate, the Council has other financial powers. It may contract loans for various public functions (*e.g.*, the building of houses), with the approval of the Central Authority, the Ministry of Health (or the Board of Education, if the loans are for educational purposes or under the Libraries Acts, or the Ministry of Transport, if they are for roads, ferries, piers, tramways, etc.). These loans are repayable by instalments, and are a charge upon the rates. Further, it may incur expenditure for the benefit of particular inhabitants. For example, it may put Mr. Smith's house drains in order, or pave a *private* street, for which Messrs. Smith, Brown, Jones and Robinson, are responsible. In these cases the Council will send the bills in to Messrs. Smith, Brown, Jones and Robinson, and recover its expenses in the same way as if it were an ordinary contractor. But if the outlay has been heavy and only a few inhabitants have been benefited, the Council may declare the expenditure to be "Private Improvement Expenses." The repayment may then be spread over a number of years, not exceeding thirty, and the money will be collected by a "Private Improvement Rate," levied on the particular persons benefited. The accounts of the Urban District Councils must be made up to March 31st in each year, to be audited by a District Auditor appointed by the Ministry of Health.

Joint Services with other Local Authorities.

The Public Health Act, 1875, and the Local Government Act, 1894, allow certain services to be carried out by combinations of Local Authorities, and a number of Urban Districts are members of Joint Burial Boards, Joint Sewerage Boards, Joint Water Boards, Joint Hospital Boards or Committees. Thus, the Penistone U.D.C. unites with the Thurlstone U.D.C. and three Parish Councils to form a Burial Board. The Eastern Valleys (Monmouth) Joint Sewerage Board comprises six, and the Abertillery and District Water Board four, separate Urban District Councils. A Joint Hospital Board is formed in Kent by Beckenham U.D.C., Chislehurst U.D.C., Foots Cray U.D.C., Bromley Town Council, and Bromley Rural District Council. And Kettering U.D.C. combines with two other U.D.C.s and one Rural District Council to form a Joint Committee for the administration of the Dairies, Cowsheds and Milkshops Orders (under sec. 57 of the Local Government Act, 1894).

Officers.

A great part of the functions of a Local Authority is, of course, exercised through various officers. The principal officers in the employ of an Urban District Council are (1) Clerk, (2) Treasurer, (3) Medical Officer of Health, (4) Inspector of Nuisances, (5) Surveyor, (6) Collector. There may also, in a large District, be a School Medical Officer, Nurses, Midwives, Health Visitors, Superintendents of Baths, Gas and Electricity, Tramways, even a Veterinary Surgeon, and various others. All Urban District officials, except the Medical Officer of Health and the Inspector of Nuisances, are removable by the Council at its pleasure, which means that, in practice, they are generally subject to one month's notice of termination of their employment. As a rule, the Medical Officer of Health and the Inspector of Nuisances have their appointments sanctioned by the Central Authority, the Ministry of Health. Half of their salaries are then paid by the County Council, and their dismissal requires the approval of the Ministry. And the Surveyor will now be in a similar position, since the Ministry of Transport Act, 1919, provides that the Ministry may defray half the salary and establishment charges of the engineer or surveyor to a Local Authority responsible for the maintenance of roads (provided that his appointment and dismissal, and the amount of the establishment charges, are subject to the Minister's approval).

The duties of the principal officers are briefly as follows :

(1) The Clerk is the chief permanent official and secretary of the Council. He generally attends all meetings of the Council and Committees. He is responsible for the taking and circulation of the Minutes, and for the checking of the accounts before they go before the Committees. He has charge of the records and books and documents of the Council. He deals with correspondence, either as instructed by the Council, or in the course of his routine. His advice on all matters concerning the District, the powers of the Council and so on, is available at Council or Committee meetings. He is generally, and should always be when possible, a solicitor, and, if he has also had some financial training and commercial experience, it will be a great advantage.

(2) A Treasurer must be appointed by every Urban District Council, however small its finances may be. He is responsible for all monies paid out, and is usually, in practice, the Manager of the local Bank which keeps the Council's account. But it is only the Treasurer personally and not the Bank that the law recognises.

(3) Every Urban Authority must appoint a qualified medical man, or woman, as Medical Officer of Health, under sec. 189 of the Public Health Act, 1875, or must arrange that the County Council shall appoint one, the Urban District then paying a portion of the salary. The M.O.H. may be a "part-timer," and in the smaller Districts he generally is. But in the large Districts the work requires his whole

time, and in some cases that of assistants as well. If any middling sized District is hesitating between a whole-time and a part-time Medical Officer, it is pretty safe to say that they should decide in favour of whole-time. For the Medical Officer is, from the point of view of the public health—public health in the widest possible sense of the term—the most important person in the District. His functions do not fall within the province of this tract; they are fully explained in "What a Health Committee can do." It is a pretty general practice to combine the posts of Medical Officer of Health and School Medical Officer. Such an arrangement is strongly favoured by the Central Authorities, and it is obviously the right one.

(4) The Public Health Act, 1875, sec. 189, also requires that every Urban Authority shall appoint an Inspector of Nuisances. He has large powers as a sanitary officer, including the supervision of slaughter houses, cowsheds, dairies, workshops and factories; the disposal of refuse, the procuring of samples of food for public analysis, the serving of notices for the abatement of nuisances when the Council has decided to take action. He reports to the M.O.H., and in many matters he will work under him. And in all cases the Council should see that there is the utmost possible co-operation between these two officials.

(5) The Surveyor is the head of an important department, and keeps, or should keep, all plans, maps and records of public work and repairs. He advises the Council on plans for buildings and streets, inspects and passes drains and sewers, supervises the various operations undertaken by the Council, as well as the maintenance of the highways. In a large District the Surveyor will be a man with high professional qualifications; in the smaller ones his office may be combined with that of the Inspector of Nuisances.

(6) The Collector's task is the straightforward one of demanding and collecting the rates. Some Urban Districts have had conferred on them the power, under sec. 33 of the Local Government Act, 1894, to appoint an Assistant Overseer, and then the Collector of the General District Rate is also commonly appointed Assistant Overseer and Collector of Poor Rates. In some small Urban Districts the offices of Clerk and Collector are combined. But disapproval of this practice has been expressed by the Central Authority, on the ground that it is undesirable for the Clerk or other officer, employed upon or having access to the accounts, to be engaged also as Collector in receiving money on behalf of the Council. The larger Districts often have two or more Collectors; Willesden has as many as seven.

Committees.

The Urban District Council is required by law to meet at least once a month. It does not, of course, carry out all its work as one body. It divides itself into several Committees, each of which is responsible for a certain department, and only comes finally to the full Council for the approval and ratification of its decisions. The number of these Committees will naturally vary according to the amount and importance of the work and the services provided in the District. The most important Councils may have a dozen or more separate Committees. In the smallest the whole Council will sit as a Committee, and even in quite large ones the whole of the Councillors commonly form the General Purposes Committee. Certain statutory Committees (*i.e.*, Committees which the Council is bound by law to appoint) function, as has been mentioned above, quite independently of the Council—*e.g.*, the Local Pensions Committee. It should be noted also that the Libraries Committee may, if the Council chooses, consist of persons who are not members of the Council, and that Councils will find occasion to strengthen their Libraries Committee by the appointment of some outsiders whose assistance will be valuable to it. A point, which is often overlooked, is the importance of having the fullest possible co-operation between different Committees, so that the work of their departments may be properly correlated. It is obvious, for instance, that the Education Committee ought to be in touch with both the Parks Committee and the Libraries Committee. A second point, which is overlooked by all too many individual Councillors, is the importance of close attention to, and training themselves for, Committee work. Bernard Shaw once said very truly that "it is possible for a Councillor to be stupendously ignorant and shamefully lazy, and yet to be not only popular with his fellow Councillors, but—provided he is a tolerably entertaining speaker—with the ratepayers also. He passes for a very busy public man, when he is really only a sociable one, by attending all his Committees and doing nothing on them." Much of the work appears to be of a dull routine kind or a mass of tiresome details. But the dull routine and the tiresome details are the basis of an efficient public service. A member of a Highways Committee who thinks that a kind heart, or an acquaintance with Karl Marx, or a determination to " save the rates," are a good substitute for a knowledge of paving stones or the habits of contractors, had very much better not be there at all. The Committeeman who will "make good" on the Committee and in the Council is he who will aim at knowing as much as the Clerk or the officials themselves of the procedure, the details of the work, and the functioning and possibilities of the department.

The Duty of a good Councillor.

The efficiency of an Urban District Council, then, will depend largely on the character of its members. If the Councillors are keen and competent (which in a great many cases they are not) they will see, in the first place, that their officials are keen and competent. They will, in the second place, be constantly looking for improvements in all the work of the Council. This seems a trite thing to say, but it is important, because it opens up the whole question of finance. A large number of keen Councillors are merely keen to economise the rates. If they were competent as well as keen, they would know that spending rather than stinting may often be the truest economy. Thousands of municipal ships up and down the country are spoiled for a ha'porth of tar. A long list of examples could be given, not only from Public Health or Housing or Education Committee's reports, but from those of Highways and Parks and others. And one of the most fruitful causes of bad work is bad labour conditions—faulty organisation or underpayment of the employees of the Council or contractors. The larger Districts have now pretty generally accepted "Fair Contracts" clauses; some, but not all, have a decent minimum wage for their own workmen. But many of the smaller Councils are bad employers, many even of the larger ones are by no means as good as they ought to be. And this criticism refers, it should be remembered, to the underpaying not only of manual workers, but of clerks and even of higher officials, such as Medical Officers, Nurses, Librarians. Every Councillor ought to regard it as among the first of his duties to know the pay and the conditions of work of any servant of the Council, and to get them improved if they are not satisfactory.

But the keen and competent Councillor will not be satisfied merely with the efficient working of the existing services provided by the Council. He will ask whether there are not any new services that it might, or ought to, undertake. Reference has already been made to a number of communal enterprises of various sorts carried out by Urban District Councils.

It is possible that before long there may be added the supply of milk (not that limited supply, which, even now, the Council, as Health Authority, may provide in special cases, but the general supply of all consumers in the District), and the supply of coal. Socialists have long advocated municipal milk and municipal coal; the universal experience of profiteering during and since the War has at last begun to make a convert of the general public. It may even come to pass that we shall presently see the advantage of municipal pawnshops, such as exist in France and Italy and other continental countries. They would be a considerable advantage, at any rate, to large numbers of the "local government electors" by whom the pawnshop, under the present arrangement of society, is as regularly patronised as the Picture-palace. At present, however, there is no statutory power given to public authorities to embark on these enterprises.

But, as regards the larger public utility services, it is clear that the majority of Urban Districts are too limited in size or resources to undertake them. Nevertheless, there are few Districts in which there are not certain things, valuable, even if small, to be done for the public welfare. Outside the spheres of public health, housing and education, with which we are not concerned here, we may instance two matters, in which the majority of District Councils are content to do little or nothing. These are the provision of Libraries, and the provision of recreation or amusement. There are, no doubt, many Districts where it is alleged that there is no demand for a Library. But that will generally be found to mean that the Council grudges the expenditure, and few intelligent people will believe this ingenuous excuse for parsimony. If, however, there are places where the difficulty of raising funds, either by voluntary means or by a rate, is really a serious one, the County Council ought to be pressed, should pressure be necessary, to take up its powers newly conferred by the Public Libraries Act, 1919. As for recreation, much is waiting to be done in the little towns and large villages. There are hundreds of District Councils which could, for instance, make swimming baths in the open air or otherwise, improve their parks or playing fields, provide bands or concerts. Some of these things will not produce a revenue; some of them may even be a trifling " burden on the rates." But the wise Councillor will not be afraid of them on that account, since he knows that municipal enterprise and commercial enterprise are not and ought not to be the same thing.

SOME USEFUL BOOKS.

(Any of these will be procured and sent by the Fabian Bookshop, 25 Tothill Street, West-minster, on remittance of price and postage.)

(1) Legal.

District Councils. By H. D. Cornish. 1908. Stevens. 7/6.
The Local Government Act, 1894. By Macmorran and Dill. 4th Edition. 1907. Butterworth. 22/6.
Local Government and Local Taxation. By Wright and Hobhouse. 1914. King. 8/6.
Local Development Law. By H. C. Dowdall. 1919. Unwin. 10/6.

(2) Facts and Statistics.

The Municipal Year Book. (Published annually.)
The Reorganisation of Local Government. By C. M. Lloyd. 1919. Labour Research Department. 1/-.
Urban District Councils. By J. M. M'Lachlan. (*Out of print.*)
Fabian Tract. What an Education Committee Can Do.
———— What a Health Committee Can Do.
———— Housing.
———— What about the Rates ?

(3) General.

Local Government. By Odgers and Naldrett. 1907. Macmillan. 4/-.
The Commonsense of Municipal Trading. By G. Bernard Shaw. 1912. Fifield ; and Fabian Society. 1/-.
Local and Central Government. By Percy Ashley. 1906. Murray. 10/6.
The Municipal Manual. By. A. E. Lauder. 1907. King. 3/6.
Grants-in Aid. By Sidney Webb. 1911. Longmans. 5/-.
English Public Health Administration. By B. G. Bannington. 1915. King. 8/6.

FABIAN PUBLICATIONS.

FABIAN ESSAYS. 1920 Edition. 2/-

HISTORY OF THE FABIAN SOCIETY. By E. R. PEASE. 6s. n.

TOWARDS SOCIAL DEMOCRACY? By SIDNEY WEBB. 1s. n., post. 1d.

WHAT TO READ on Social and Economic Subjects. 1s. n. and 2s. n.

THE RURAL PROBLEM. By H. D. HARBEN. 2s. 6d. n.

THIS MISERY OF BOOTS. By H. G. WELLS. 3d., post free 4d.

FABIAN TRACTS and LEAFLETS.

Tracts, each 16 to 52 pp., price 1d., or 9d. per doz., unless otherwise stated.
Leaflets, 4 pp. each, price 1d. for six copies, 1s. per 100, or 8/6 per 1000.

The Set of 74, 3/6; post free 3/11. Bound in buckram, 5/-n.; post free 5/9.

I.—General Socialism in its various aspects.

TRACTS.—184. The Russian Revolution and British Democracy. By JULIUS WEST. 2d. 180. The Philosophy of Socialism. By A. CLUTTON BROCK. 169. The Socialist Movement in Germany. By W. STEPHEN SANDERS. 2d. 159. The Necessary Basis of Society. By SIDNEY WEBB. 151. The Point of Honour. By RUTH C. BENTINCK. 147. Capital and Compensation. By E. R. PEASE. 146. Socialism and Superior Brains. By BERNARD SHAW. 2d. 142. Rent and Value. 138. Municipal Trading. 121. Public Service v. Private Expenditure. By Sir OLIVER LODGE. 107. Socialism for Millionaires. By BERNARD SHAW. 139. Socialism and the Churches. By Rev. JOHN CLIFFORD, D.D. 133. Socialism and Christianity. By Rev. PERCY DEARMER. 78. Socialism and the Teaching of Christ. By Dr. J. CLIFFORD. 42. Christian Socialism. By Rev. S. D. HEADLAM. 79. A Word of Remembrance and Caution to the Rich. By JOHN WOOLMAN. 72. The Moral Aspects of Socialism. By SIDNEY BALL. 69. Difficulties of Individualism. By S. WEBB. 51. Socialism: True and False. By S. WEBB. 45. The Impossibilities of Anarchism. By G. B. SHAW. 2d. 7. Capital and Land. 5. Facts for Socialists. 2d. LEAFLETS—13. What Socialism Is 1. Why are the Many Poor?

II.—Applications of Socialism to Particular Problems.

TRACTS.—188. National Finance and a Levy on Capital. By SIDNEY WEBB. 2d. 187. The Teacher in Politics. By SIDNEY WEBB. 2d. 186. Central Africa and the League of Nations. By R. C. HAWKIN. 2d. 183. The Reform of the House of Lords. By SIDNEY WEBB. 181. When Peace Comes—the Way of Industrial Reconstruction. By SIDNEY WEBB. 2d. 178. The War; Women; and Unemployment. 2d. 177. Socialism and the Arts of Use. By A. CLUTTON BROCK. 175. The Economic Foundations of the Women's Movement. 2d. 173. Public v. Private Electricity Supply. 171. The Nationalization of Mines and Minerals Bill. 170. Profit-Sharing and Co-Partnership: a Fraud and Failure? 164. Gold and State Banking. 162. Family Life on a Pound a Week. By Mrs. REEVES. 2d. 161. Afforestation and Unemployment. 160. A National Medical Service. 2d. 157. The Working Life of Women. 155. The Case against the Referendum. 154. The Case for School Clinics. 152. Our Taxes as they are and as they ought to be. 2d. 149. The Endowment of Motherhood. 2d. 131. The Decline of the Birth-Rate. 145. The Case for School Nurseries. 140. Child Labor under Capitalism. 136. The Village and the Landlord. By EDW. CARPENTER. 144. Machinery: its Masters and Servants. 122. Municipal Milk and Public Health. 125. Municipalization by Provinces. 124. State Control of Trusts. LEAFLET.—104. How Trade Unions benefit Workmen.

III.—Local Government Powers: How to use them.

TRACTS.—185. The Abolition of the Poor Law. By Mrs. WEBB. 172. What about the Rates? By S. WEBB. 156. What an Education Committee can do (Elementary Schools), 3d. 62. Parish and District Councils. (Revised 1919). 137. Parish Councils and Village Life. 109. Cottage Plans and Common Sense. 82. Workmen's Compensation Act. LEAFLETS.— 134. Small Holdings. 68. The Tenant's Sanitary Catechism. 71. Ditto for London.

IV.—General Politics and Fabian Policy.

TRACTS.—158. The Case against the C.O.S. By Mrs. TOWNSHEND. 41. The Fabian Society: its Early History. By BERNARD SHAW.

V.—Biographical Series. In portrait covers, 2d. each.

182. Robert Owen, Idealist. By C. E. M. JOAD. 179. John Ruskin and Social Ethics. By Prof. EDITH MORLEY. 165. Francis Place. By ST. JOHN G. ERVINE. 166. Robert Owen, Social Reformer. By Miss B. L. HUTCHINS. 167. William Morris and the Communist Ideal. By Mrs. TOWNSHEND. 168. John Stuart Mill. By JULIUS WEST. 174. Charles Kingsley and Christian

Fabian Tract No. 190.

Metropolitan Borough Councils

THEIR CONSTITUTION, POWERS AND DUTIES.

BY

C. R. ATTLEE, M.A.

PUBLISHED AND SOLD BY THE FABIAN SOCIETY.
25 TOTHILL STREET, WESTMINSTER, LONDON, S.W.1
PRICE TWOPENCE . . . . MARCH 1920

Metropolitan Borough Councils.

THEIR CONSTITUTION, POWERS AND DUTIES.

The Metropolitan Borough Councils, 28 in number, were constituted under the London Government Act 1899 to take the place
of the chaotic collection of Boards of Works and Vestries, which
covered the 120 square miles of London, that had grown up round
the cities of London and Westminster. Of varying size, ranging from
Holborn, with under 50,000, to Islington and Wandsworth, with
over 300,000, they are of very different character. Some contain
90 per cent. of wage earners, others are almost entirely middle class.
Some are natural units of government, others like Lambeth are amal-
gamations of a number of communities with little common interest
to unite them. Some have a rateable value of only £5 or £6 a head
while Westminster has over £40. Westminster is a City and Kensington
a Royal Borough, while the City of London with its old constitution,
long traditions, great wealth, and practical independence, stands
apart from the London County Council on the one hand, and the
Metropolitan Boroughs on the other.

The Metropolitan Borough differs from the municipal borough
in the provinces in its powers and duties, which are more restricted,
the London County Council, the Metropolitan Asylums Board, the
Metropolitan Water Board, and the Port of London Authority performing some of the functions which in provincial boroughs of a similar
size and population would fall to the Borough Council.

CONSTITUTION.

A Borough Council consists of a Mayor, Aldermen and Councillors.
The Mayor is chosen by the Council, not necessarily from its members.
He holds office for a year from November 9th, but may be re-elected
any number of times. It naturally usually happens that the Mayor
is selected from the predominant political party in the Council. In
some cases, an honorarium, generally about £200, is paid by the Council
towards the expenses of the office. Aldermen form one-sixth of the
Council. They are selected by the Council, sometimes from its own
members of long service or failing health, to whom the hard work
of an election is an undue strain ; sometimes from the unsuccessful
candidates who secured the highest number of votes ; sometimes
from other persons of distinction or persons holding long records of
social service locally. With regard to the two last methods, something

may be said for each. On the one hand the selection of the most nearly successful of the rejected candidates is claimed as the more democratic expedient, as realising most nearly the ascertained wishes of the electorate. On the other hand, it is maintained by many, that all the best people will never be secured by the method of election, as the qualities that are valuable in administration are not necessarily those that are popular with an electorate, and, further, such persons may fail even to secure nomination, since their qualities make no strong appeal to the local political organisations, which naturally prefer a popular candidate and one who is committed heart and soul to their programme. Aldermen retain their seats for six years, one half retiring triennially but remaining eligible for re-election. Councillors may be either men or women, and must be local government electors or resident in the borough for twelve months, or be owners of property in the borough. They are elected on November 1st every three years by the local government electors. The qualifications to be on the electoral roll are :—

(a) A man who is on the last day of the qualifying period (six months), occupying as owner or tenant any land or premises and has so occupied it or them during the whole of the qualifying period. He must be 21 years of age.

(b) A woman as for a man and where she is the wife of a man so qualified. In the latter case she must be 30 years old.

The number of councillors varies with the size of the borough from 30 to 60.

The whole number retires every three years.

PROCEDURE.

The Council, like most other local authorities, transacts the greater part of its business through committees which meet fortnightly or monthly or when specially summoned. A committee is composed of from 10 to 24 members as a rule, and is presided over by a chairman, who is usually a member of the dominant party on the Council. Committees as a rule are composed in such a way as to reflect the composition of the Council as far as possible. They fix their own place and hour of meeting. Members of the Council may attend the meetings of any committee, but may only take part in the business by leave of the committee. The Mayor is *ex-officio* a member of all committees. Officials of the Council attend the various committees, but may be asked to withdraw at any time.

The only statutory committee is the Finance Committee, which has been given a very important position under Section 83 of the London Government Act, whereby no proposal to spend money can be considered by the Council except on an estimate submitted by this committee. The result of this provision is that all resolutions of a financial nature must pass the Finance Committee, and the most important items of the agenda are those embodied in the recommendations of this committee. The proceedings of the various committees are circulated to the members, and at the council the Chairman of each Committee is responsible for moving any resolutions from his committee and explaining them.

The meetings of the council but not those of committees are open to the public and the Press.

OFFICERS OF THE COUNCIL.

The chief officers of the council are the town clerk (always a lawyer), the borough treasurer, the surveyor, the medical officer of health (who is a qualified medical man and also generally holds the Diploma of Public Health), a number of sanitary inspectors, the borough librarian, and the heads of any public utility undertaking, such as electricity supply. Under the heads of departments work the rate collectors, assistant engineers, clerks, and other black-coated workers, and the council's workmen.

BOROUGH COUNCIL FINANCE.

The council derives the money required to carry out its administration from the following sources :—

(1) Income from property or trading enterprises.

(2) Grants from the Imperial Exchequer.

(3) Rates.

(1) Will be considered later under the head of permissive legislation.

(2) **Grants in Aid.**—As far as the actual work of the boroughs is concerned but little assistance is obtained from grants in aid beyond certain small payments under the Public Health Acts, including the salary of the Medical Officer of Health, and some contributions from the Ministry of Transport to roads, but indirectly the borough finance is relieved by the more extensive grants made to the larger London authorities without which their rates would be much higher.

(3) Rates are the principal source of income and are collected in a different method from that in provincial boroughs. Whereas in the provinces the money is obtained by precepts addressed to the overseers of the poor who make the rate, in London except where the unions concerned are not wholly contained in one borough, the borough council is the overseer and the boards of guardians obtain their money by precepts on the borough council.

The rating and valuation committee prepare valuations for the assessment of rates and the assessment committee fixes the assessment and hears appeals from the ratepayers against their decisions, and there is a further appeal, if desired, to the Justices in Quarter Sessions.

The chief work of the assessment committee occurs at the quinquennial assessment, and it is necessary to find members who can give up a lot of time in the day to this work. The same persons cannot be members of both the valuation and assessment committees, but it is useful to attend meetings of both in order to appreciate properly both branches of the work. The borough councils, besides the amounts required for their own work, collect the rates for all the other London authorities.

Rates vary greatly in the different boroughs, partly owing to differences in rateable value, partly to forward or retrograde policy, and partly owing to special local burdens. These inequalities are met to a very limited extent by the equalisation of rates fund made up from a rate of 6d. in the £ on the assessable value of London to which all boroughs contribute but from which they draw in proportion to population. A similar device is that of the Common Poor Fund whereby some equalisation of Poor Law expenses is obtained. In each of these cases in effect the rich boroughs pay and the poor boroughs receive.

ADMINISTRATION.

The functions of a Metropolitan Borough Council fall into two main divisions.

(1) The local administration of various acts or the determination of their local application through the council's representatives on other bodies.

(2) The initiation of measures for increasing the welfare of the community by the adoption of certain permissive legislation and the passing of local bye-laws in certain defined spheres of action, subject to ratification by the Home Office or the Ministry of Health.

Housing and Public Health.—The borough council is responsible, concurrently with the London County Council, for the initiation and pursuance of a housing policy. The borough council is the administrative authority for the execution of other provisions of the Housing Acts, the Infectious Diseases Notification and Prevention Acts, the Food and Drugs Acts, the Notification of Births Act, the Maternity and Child Welfare Act, and the sanitary provisions of the Factory and Workshops Acts. Their duties in these matters are performed through the sanitary inspectors who patrol the district on the look-out for breaches of the law. Offenders are usually warned in the first place, and given a chance of complying with the law. Prosecutions are initiated in glaring cases of wilful ignorance or transgression of the law or recalcitrance in remedying the illegalities pointed out by the inspectors. The borough council must provide or contract for the removal and disposal of refuse. This is either carted to barges; emptied into the river, used to make up marshy ground, or destroyed in an incinerator. Land made up in this manner should not be used for building* purposes. Some authorities classify their refuse and make a profit by selling the salvage. The drawback to this plan is the unsavoury and unhealthy raking over of the foul refuse by the work-people at the destructor. In some districts it is found possible to utilise the heat of the incinerator for warming the water for the bathing and cleansing stations. Sometimes the sludge can be made into paving slabs. Refuse should be collected at least twice weekly. A daily collection is the ideal. Sanitary iron bins with air tight lids should be and are now used by the best authorities. Some authorities arrange for the separation of the refuse by the householder by the provision of three or more receptacles, one for dust, one for tins, and one for food refuse. If the sorting has to be done at the destructor, mechanical contrivances should be provided as far as possible and special clothing and baths at the destructor supplied for workmen. The preventive side of this work is also carried on by the publication of leaflets and the promotion of lectures, etc., on hygiene. The subjects of Housing and Public Health are dealt with in detail in other Tracts.

Highways.—The Borough Council is charged with the duty of maintaining the highways. This includes the provision and super-vision of local drainage (the sewers of the main drainage system are managed by the London County Council), and the lighting, cleansing and paving of the streets. The occupier is responsible for cleansing the footway in front of his house. Some authorities have done much to brighten the streets by planting trees and cultivating flowering shrubs and hardy flowers in forecourts too small for use as public gardens, but there is still much room for improvement in the dinginess of the average London back street.

By the Private Street Works Act 1892 the Council may recover from the owners the expense of making private streets, and may decide to undertake this work wherever it is not satisfied with the condition of the street. The council may receive grants from the London County Council for widening main roads.

Tramway undertakings are under an obligation to keep in repair the surface of the road between and on either side of the track.

The borough council is also liable for the maintenance of foot-paths, whether or not by the side of a road. Bridges are entrusted to the London County Council. Under the Development and Road Improvements Act of 1909 and 1910 for improving road facilities, grants are payable in relief of the large expense incurred by some authorities in the upkeep of roads over which there is very heavy traffic by extra-local vehicles, and for subsidising experiments in new materials. The expenditure on roads in the Metropolitan boroughs which contain the docks and markets, is of course altogether dis-proportionate to the benefit which they receive directly from the traffic which wears them out. Trams pay a contribution to the rates of the boroughs through which their lines are laid, but motor buses, whose action is more devastating to the surface and who are free to choose and vary their routes and wear out one after another, at present make no direct local contribution except in respect of garages or other buildings in a borough. With the increasing number and weight of motor vehicles many serious difficulties of increasing urgency present themselves—the congestion of traffic during rush hours aggravated by lack of organisation for unloading vehicles from street to warehouse, the difficulty of securing a material which will withstand at once the sucking and grinding action of passenger and goods traffic. No doubt the new department of the Ministry of Transport will set to work on the relief of the congestion by laying out new routes and discovering new road material

REPRESENTATION ON OTHER BODIES.

Education in London devolves entirely on the London County Council, but the boroughs have the right to appoint one-third of the Managers of Provided Schools (those erected by the London County Council) and one-sixth of those of Non-provided (those erected and partially financed by a religious body in order to give sectarian religious instruction). The duties and rights of Managers are more apparent than real and are constantly being curtailed, but they provide an opportunity of becoming acquainted with the working and results of the elementary school system and limited facilities for gradual and slow penetration to the official mind and for the occasional initiation of minor improvements. It cannot be said, however, that the attitude of the London County Council to the suggestions of Managers offers much encouragement to an energetic person to devote himself to this work.

Distress Committees.—Under the Unemployed Workmen's Act, 1905, borough councils must appoint local distress committees which are to include co-opted persons, experienced in social work. The distress committee provides unskilled work for unemployed men and women and selects the applicants for it. Work is usually given to married people with large dependent families, for a few weeks at most, sometimes for a few days. It is difficult to devise work which does not still further depress the labour market by anticipating what would have been done on ordinary commercial lines at the fitting time, and owing to the inexperience of those assisted, such work proves more costly than when performed in the ordinary routine. Opinion is now favouring the provision of maintenance with training as successfully carried out in Queen Mary's Fund Workrooms during the period of distress at the beginning of the war. Those not in a position to profit by technical instruction can be taught the craft of a "handyman," or make things for themselves or other poor persons, who, as by reason of their poverty, they would not have the purchasing power to obtain them for themselves, will not disturb the stability of the labour market. Training can also be given in the elements of hygiene and the domestic arts. The local distress committees are subordinate to the Central Unemployed Body for London on which they are represented.

The council is also represented on two committees which have been recently established as the result of the War—the Local Food Committee and the Local Profiteering Committee. Both of these are composed partly of members of the council, partly of representatives of special interests, women, labour and discharged soldiers. The duty of the former is concerned mainly with considering prices and supply of food in the area and in giving permission to retailers to open shops. The latter is an attempt to check the exploitation of the consumer by the local retailers and restitution of improper charges can be ordered. Representations can also be made as to profiteering by wholesalers and producers.

Metropolitan Water Board.—This body, set up by the Metropolis Water Act, 1902, provides for the water supply of London and a large area of the environment (previously in the hands of a number of private companies). It has 68 members, 14 appointed by the London County Council, 2 from the City Corporation, 14 from outlying boroughs and urban district councils, 5 from other adjacent county councils and 29 from the metropolitan borough councils (Westminster sends 2). The Chairman and Vice-Chairman are co-opted and paid by the Board.

Old Age Pensions.—The borough councils take part in the administration of old age pensions through their representatives on the local pensions committees.

Police.—The police in London occupy an anomalous position over which the Londoner is apt to feel himself somewhat aggrieved. In the provinces the police are appointed and controlled by the standing joint committees of justices of the peace and county council members in the case of the county constabulary, and the watch committee (about one-third of members of the council and the mayor) in the case of borough police. One-half of the cost is defrayed by the Home Office, which inspects the efficiency of the force. In London, however, the police force is directly under the management of the Home Office and the local authorities have no control whatever over it, although they furnish half the cost of its maintenance.

London Traffic Advisory Committee.—As a result of representations by the Metropolitan Boroughs Standing Joint Committee, the Transport Minister has agreed to the appointment on the London Traffic Advisory Committee of a representative of the borough councils.

ADOPTIVE ACTS.

Open Spaces, etc.—Apart from the Royal Parks and those belonging to the City Corporation, the London County Council is the general authority for the maintenance of London's parks. By the Open Spaces Act, 1906, the local authorities may take over open spaces and burial grounds (including those disused) from trustees or corporations. Local authorities may also acquire and maintain open spaces and burial grounds and make bye-laws for their management. Many parts of London are very inadequately supplied with open spaces. Here, as usual, the bugbear of the rates blocks the path. The initial cost of laying out the space is considerable, though, in some cases, the cost could be diminished by having the work done through the unemployed under the distress committee. The maintenance, besides the cost of planting, would in most districts, have to include the payment of at least one and probably two park-keepers. Mention should be made of the use of the town hall, baths or other public buildings of the council for recreational purposes. It has been the custom in some boroughs to allow certain individuals to book up the halls, etc., for a number of dates, thus restricting the opportunities of other citizens for using them for recreational, political or educational meetings, while the hirer of the hall doubtless makes his profit. Councillors should be on the watch against this. There is no reason why the Council should not make its halls real civic centres and give free concerts, etc., there. In the same way, bands could be provided in the parks and open-air dances and organised games for the children arranged.

Libraries.—By the Public Libraries Acts, 1902–1919, the borough council can provide and maintain a library or libraries with reference and lending departments. Formerly owing to the restriction of expenditure to the product of a penny rate, now removed by the 1919 Act, councils were much restricted in their action and were often indebted to private philanthropists for the provision of libraries. The annual expenditure in the poorer boroughs was insufficient to admit of paying proper salaries and keeping the library in an efficient condition. With the removal of this obstacle considerable development should be possible.

Wherever possible, the " open access system " should be adopted. Where this obtains, borrowers may walk through to the shelves and examine and choose books at their leisure. In some cases, structural alterations to counters and passages would be costly, and opposition is sometimes raised on the ground of the difficulties of supervision and the chance of a dishonest reader decamping with several books. However, districts which have the system do not appear to find their losses appreciably increased. The names and addresses of borrowers are, of course, registered, and it should be possible to trace systematic theft. The system should encourage the growth of serious study and wide research—habits at present unfamiliar to the English temperament. Many councils have a special juvenile section, in which children still at school are allowed to have boxes of books kept during term at the school under the supervision of the teachers and lent by them to the children. It is thought that this system encourages the children to become library readers when they leave school. It is usual to keep a Suggestion Book, in which readers may ask for special books to be purchased. This arrangement does not appear to be so widely known to the public as might be expected. Library committees nearly always purchase a book asked for in this way unless its appeal would be to a very diminutive portion of ratepayers or its cost prohibitive, and in this way many students of navigation, engineering and other technical subjects may be helped to read books which it would be quite beyond their means to buy.

It is unfortunate that there is not more co-operation between borough councils in the provision of libraries. If boroughs would agree to specialize on certain subjects and allow the residents of other boroughs to use their libraries, a much wider selection of books would be provided.

Museums.—Where a part of the library can be used as a museum local patriotism, unfortunately, as a rule, so lacking in London as compared with the Midlands and the North, may be much stimulated. Many districts in London have sunk to their present mean aspect from a noble and stately origin, and past and civic pride may be again implanted by the remembrance of their former high estate. The museum would include any relics, coins preserved or excavated, old pictures and prints of old buildings or celebrities, the first railway trains used in the district, models of early sailing ships, etc.

Allotments.—Under the Small Holdings and Allotments Act, 1914, a Borough Council may provide allotments (the provision of Small Holdings—one acre to fifty acres—is in the hands of the County Council). An allotment must not exceed five acres, but is usually, of course, very much smaller—generally about ten poles. Any six registered Parliamentary electors or ratepayers may bring the matter to the notice of the Council, who must enquire into the extent of the demand. A considerable impetus was given by the war to the allotment movement, but now that the danger of actual starvation is past, it is to be feared that many Councils are seeking to revoke their grants of land or refuse further applicants. There are, of course, many districts where it is very difficult to find land for this purpose. The Vacant Lots Cultivation Society has done a great deal to make vacant building land temporarily available for agriculture. Experience has shown that crops will grow on the most unlikely-looking spots in London, and there is scope for valuable work in this direction.

Baths and Washhouses.—By the Baths and Washhouses Acts 1846, 1878, 1882, and 1899, any ten electors may petition the Council to provide the foregoing. The buildings usually include swimming baths, private hot and cold baths, including soap, towels, etc.,—usually termed slipper baths—and washhouses for family laundry work. The general supervision of the machinery, etc., is in the hands of the borough engineer; under him are the superintendent and matron, usually a joint appointment held by a man and wife. The superintendent is generally an engineer or naval stoker, or someone experienced in such matters. He and the matron are responsible for the routine efficiency and order of the baths, control the staff and arrange for the visits of other swimming clubs, galas, etc. It has lately been recognised that swimming baths may be a source of infection for diphtheria, typhoid and other diseases, and some authorities use a disinfectant in the water. The charge for swimming and private baths is usually from 2d. to 1s., according to the facilities and amenities provided. The charge at the washhouse section is usually 1½d. per hour. This generally includes continuous hot water, a trough sink for washing, mangle and wringer, hot air drying cupboard—one for the use of each person—which dries the clothes in about twenty minutes, and hot irons to complete the process. The washhouse is unquestionably an immense boon to those who have to live in a house with one kitchen-living-room almost totally devoid of facilities for laundry work, which makes the room hot and unhealthy and often causes bronchitis and chills to the children of the family. A difficulty is sometimes experienced in preventing the professional laundress from plying her trade by means of this subsidy from the ratepayers, and some authorities, in order to check this practice, limit the number of hours that may be worked by any one washer to what is supposed to suffice only for family washing.

Some authorities now provide facilities for mixed bathing at the swimming baths. This is generally much appreciated, opportunities for healthy athletics in London being all too few.

Baths and washhouses are now finding themselves in a difficult position owing to the high price and shortage of coal. Londoners do not usually appreciate a swimming bath under 70 deg., and the cost of raising a large volume of cold water to this temperature and maintaining a continuous flow of hot water in the washhouses is considerable. Some authorities are meeting it by opening only for a limited number of days per week.

MUNICIPAL TRADING.

This term is applied to the provision by a local authority of any service which shows a profit and loss account—as distinct from such services as public health or street paving, which, although necessary and beneficial, cannot be expressed in such terms. The advantages claimed are : the provision of a better and cheaper service, while profits go to the relief of the rates instead of to private employers and shareholders. The chief service provided in this way by the Metropolitan Borough Councils is electric power, lighting and heating, at a cost much below that of private companies. Another service provided in two or three cases is that of a municipal market. Since the outbreak of profiteering during the war many authorities have encouraged the promotion and semi-formalising of street markets, for which they charge a small rent per stall and afford protection and guarantee continuity of tenure.

Some authorities now give a bonus to all officials and workmen in the electricity undertaking. It is claimed that this gives them an "interest" in the success of the scheme and prevents slacking, carelessness with tools and machinery, and so forth. On the other hand it is manifestly unfair to employees in other departments—*e.g.*, public health, roads—which show no profit, and is thought to lead to quarrelling and jealousy among the workmen, every one watching his neighbour to see that he does his bit and pressing for his discharge if he seems likely to lower the standard of the fastest and cleverest workers. Labour representatives usually oppose this innovation.

THE BOROUGH COUNCIL AS AN EMPLOYER.

Labour and Socialist representatives have always been quick to see the value of the borough council as an agent in levelling up wages and conditions of labour. In many districts the borough council is about the largest employer of labour, and thus has the pick of the working population, and other employers must offer as good, or better, terms if they are to secure good workpeople. The wages of practically all the skilled or semi-skilled grades of workers are now fixed by conciliation agreements, and the only cases that are likely to prove difficult are those of employees who have no recognised occupational rate and are not organised in one union such as bath and lavatory attendants, dustmen, etc. It is very desirable that councils should get together and fix definite rates rather than that each should follow its own sweet will. Owing to London Government having been in reactionary hands so long there has grown up among municipal workers a habit of playing one authority off against the other, very understandable but very inconvenient for Labour Councillors. While it is, of course, necessary to give good conditions of labour, the rates paid should not, in general, exceed those paid to similar workers by the best firms in private undertakings. Most authorities, too, now have a "Fair Wages Clause" inserted in their contracts, by which all work executed for them must conform to Trade Union conditions, or, failing a Trade Union, to those customarily in force under good employers in the district. This is a powerful lever in improving conditions and in diffusing knowledge of the wages and hours obtainable. A word of warning must here be given on the position of the middle-grade and higher officials of the Council. Most Labour and Socialist representatives are ready to strain every nerve to obtain advances in wages for workmen, but are apt to think that officials should be paid the lowest sum for which anyone to fill the post can be obtained. Whatever the ethics of the case and the ideal desirability of a simpler and cheaper life for such officials, it must be insisted that it is impossible to have municipal work satisfactorily and successfully performed unless salaries are paid approximating to those obtaining in the private business world. Nor will the work of the Council run smoothly if its officials do it under a sense of injury and lack of appreciation. It is even more important that councils where labour is in control should secure the services of the very best men as officials since extended municipal enterprise, which they have advocated on the platform for so many years, is now on its trial, and if it fails, through lack of directive ability, may be discredited and get no similar chance of development, since high rates must be justified by high efficiency—for many years to come.

A rule has sometimes been made by local authorities that all their employees must live in the borough. The reasons given for this proviso are that those primarily interested in the borough as residents and ratepayers should have the first claim to employment there, and that a district deteriorates financially and socially if its more prosperous inhabitants in good regular work move away to be replaced by a poorer class of resident. It is doubtful how far this is a wise provision. It tends to check the natural flow of population, presses hardly in individual cases and, where the employee can afford it, can be easily evaded by renting one room in the borough but actually residing elsewhere. It is, of course, necessary that certain employees—*e.g.*, in the electricity undertakings—should live in the borough near to the work to attend to breakdowns, as a condition of their employment.

Many councils have a scheme of pensions and superannuations. There is much to be said for and against this plan. It is undoubtedly pleasant to think that the workman may look forward to old age without undue apprehension and may feel secure from the storms of the ordinary labour market. But a pension scheme aggravates the tendency to engage only young workers in the prime of life (in order to keep it actuarially sound), and thus adds to the already serious difficulty of the middle-aged man or woman in obtaining work if he has lost a permanent job through any misfortune. Further, it may lead to the retention of a comparatively slack or incompetent workman, because no one likes to be hard-hearted enough to deprive him of his expectation. And it may prevent a workman, discontented and believing himself capable of greater things, from leaving because " he doesn't want to give up something he has paid for."

Problems facing a Borough Councillor.—Probably all Labour representatives have observed the efforts made to promote the supply of electricity centrally by a company instead of through the machinery of the borough councils. It is claimed that a cheaper and more efficient service could be provided, and that this, as in the case of the provision of water by the Metropolitan Water Board, furnishes an instance of different authorities combining through representation to supply a service over a whole area which they jointly control. It may be doubted whether in the case of this or of the electricity proposals a case of the wisdom of each at the disposal of all would be illustrated, but pressure on these lines is threatening in the immediate future, and Labour representatives must study the question and take a definite stand on one side or the other. The present quality and price of gas supply a warning against trusting such services to a private company, even with the safeguards provided by special legislation.

Analogous to this is the conflict of opinion between the Local Government Devolution Party and the Centralisers. One may remember in this connection the recent proposal of the London County Council to take over all the public health powers of the borough councils, leaving them only those now exercised by the Poor Law Guardians. The Centralisers will point to certain backward local bodies, to the greater risk of bribery, corruption and intimidation in " parish politics " where secrets leak out more easily and interested parties know each other more intimately and can more readily exert influence; to the duplication of officials and administration. The devolutionist will point to the scandals and long overdue reforms to be found even in great central authorities, to the congestion of their business, which is almost a byword, and may claim that on the large scale on which their operations are conducted large frauds also are possible. On his behalf, too, it may be urged that the humbler sphere of the borough council provides a testing station for isolating and proving experiments which would not be attempted by a body with a larger area and greater responsibilities; that the control by the County Council, Ministry of Health and Home Office should suffice to keep their feet fairly well in the path of duty, and that the greater local knowledge and local interest available in a small district may be an advantage as well as a disadvantage.

THE BOROUGH COUNCIL AS A TRAINING GROUND.

The borough council is by no means to be despised as a training ground for the social reformer or the aspirant to Parliamentary honours. Perhaps had every legislator had the experience of following his laws home to roost, seeing the difficulties of enforcing them, the hardships involved to the conscientious, the loopholes through which the hardened lawbreaker will successfully slip, he would think at least twice before voting for the next new law. Local administration at least teaches the inability of an act of Parliament to make human nature good—unless it has been very skilfully framed ! On the other hand, his respect for the adaptability of the human brain would be greatly strengthened by seeing the success which attends the efforts, guided, of course, by their officials, and schemes of grocers, small manufacturers, labourers and those whom he would generally regard as " uneducated and ignorant " people. He would also gain the very human satisfaction of " getting things done " and " seeing them work," which is possible in a small area and the absence of which is the most depressing element in " national " work. Anyone with the time and interest for local problems will find his ambitions fulfilled in the work of a borough councillor. Sometimes in the past, no doubt from being only in an ineffective minority, Labour men have been inclined to interest themselves rather in securing better wages and conditions for workers than in mastering the larger problems with which they are faced. It is difficult to exaggerate the importance of a councillor's taking a real interest in the work that he controls—not only in the committee room and council chamber, but in the generating station, the disinfecting station, the work department. If he has a personal knowledge of the working out of the proposals he puts forward, he will be far more likely to carry his committee with him than if he had advanced them merely academically, and if he can convince officials that he has a genuine interest in their work for its own sake, and that he is not using his position simply as a vantage ground in the game of local politics, he will find that they will make it easy for him to acquire that personal knowledge. It is true that before any important alteration to the council's property can be carried out, the committee is taken to view the property—in a comfortable way in motor cars— but though this is important it is not nearly so valuable as a visit paid in the course of a normal working day.

A word should be added on the importance of a councillor attending committee meetings with regularity and being determined not to leave a meeting until the subject in which he is interested has been dealt with satisfactorily. Many a proposal has been carried in committee or council because its advocates were prepared to forfeit their suppers and its opponents were not.

VACHER & SONS, LTD., Westminster House, S.W.1.—7672b.

BOROUGH COUNCILS

Their Constitution, Powers
and Duties

BY

C. R. ATTLEE, M.A.

PUBLISHED AND SOLD BY THE FABIAN SOCIETY,
25, TOTHILL STREET, WESTMINSTER, LONDON, S.W.1.
PRICE TWOPENCE . . . . MARCH 1920

BOROUGH COUNCILS

Their Constitution, Powers and Duties.

THE Borough is one of the most ancient of all English units of Local Government and one of the most important. It is an urban community which has received a Charter of Incorporation from the Crown and is governed under the Municipal Corporations Acts, 1835–1882. It is not the purpose of this pamphlet to deal with the history of Town Government in this country or to trace the rise and decline of civic administration prior to 1832, but rather to deal with the borough as part of the machinery of local government at the present time. It is well, however, to recall that some boroughs are of very ancient origin and may have rights and privileges derived from charters and private acts of Parliament, owning property acquired many years ago, while others are the creation of yesterday, new communities that owing to their size and importance have obtained incorporation but derive their powers solely from statute.

From the fact of their origin it is not surprising that there is a great diversity of area and population among boroughs. Birmingham has a population of over 830,000, and Manchester an area of 20,000 acres, while Winchelsea has but 700 inhabitants, and Blandford only 145 acres. Boroughs, also, have differences of status among themselves, some of practical importance, others of sentimental interest ; thus some are Cities in virtue of being seats of bishops or possessing a grant from the Crown, others are allowed to style their chief magistrate Lord Mayor instead of Mayor, others have a more important distinction in the possession of separate Courts of Quarter Sessions and a paid judge, but the most important difference from the point of view of the student of local government and the practical administrator is that between County Boroughs and non-County Boroughs. The County Borough, which is in all but three cases a town of over 50,000 inhabitants, stands, for almost all purposes, outside the administrative county of which geographically it forms a part and has practically all the powers of a county council in addition to those of the most powerful municipal borough, while the non-county borough like the urban district divides its authority in its area with the county council. The county borough is the completest authority in English local government, and when the Boards of Guardians are abolished will be the sole authority in its area. At the present time there are 327 boroughs outside London in England and Wales, of which 80 are county boroughs. There is a certain amount of promotion among urban governing authorities, urban districts applying to the Privy Council may be incorporated and municipal boroughs and urban districts of more than 50,000 inhabitants may apply for county powers.

The Metropolitan Boroughs in London and the City Corporation will be.discussed in a separate pamphlet.

CONSTITUTION OF BOROUGH COUNCILS.

With the exception of the City of London and one or two Un-reformed boroughs, every borough owes its constitution to the Municipal Corporations Acts and is governed by a municipal corporation which enjoys perpetual succession and a common seal and consists of a Lord Mayor or Mayor, Aldermen and Councillors, the number of members varying according to the size of the borough. Councillors must be either (a) local government electors; (b) persons possessing property in the borough of a certain value; or (c) persons who have been resident in the borough for the whole of the 12 months previous to the election. There is no property qualification, and the councillors are elected by ballot on the first of November each year for three years, one-third of their number retiring each year.

The qualifications to be enrolled as a local government elector are:—(a) If a man, the occupation on the last day of the qualifying period (six months) as owner or tenant of any land or premises in the borough and their occupation for the whole of the qualifying period. He must be 21 years of age. (b) If a woman, the same qualification as for a man—or being the wife of a man so qualified. In the latter case she must be 30 years old. Aldermen are elected by the councillors from among their own number or from persons qualified to be councillors, and their number is one-third of the councillors. One-half of their number retire every three years.

The Mayor or Lord Mayor is elected by the councillors from the councillors or those qualified to be such. He may receive a salary, but aldermen and councillors are unpaid. The Mayor is a Justice of the Peace for his year of office and one year afterwards.

POWERS AND DUTIES OF BOROUGH COUNCILS.

The powers and duties of a borough council are derived.partly from its position as the representative body charged with the good governance of the town, partly from its being also an urban sanitary authority and in the case of a county borough a county authority, and partly from its being charged or empowered by the legislature to carry out certain duties by public or private Acts of Parliament.

These powers vary with the size of the borough, those with 10,000 population and those with 20,000 population having additional powers, while county boroughs have most of all. It will be most convenient to consider these differences when dealing with the various services performed by the councils which may be most easily grouped under the following heads.

(1) **As Municipal Authority.**—It administers corporate property: this is in many cases very considerable. Bristol derives £25,000 and Nottingham £30,000 from rents, while in the small but ancient town of Bodmin the income was enough to preclude the necessity of raising a borough rate until the present century. Other examples are Doncaster, Chester and Brighton that own race-courses, Colchester that owns oyster fisheries, and Bath and Harrogate that own baths. Labour councillors should look well to see that municipal property is being used to the best advantage, as cases have been known where the City fathers or grandfathers have leased corporate property to their friends for long terms of years at low rentals. The council also makes by-laws for the good governance of the town.

In addition to specific duties the borough council is the representative body of the town, and it is its duty to give expression to the wishes of the inhabitants and protect their interests. Thus it is the duty of the council to keep a careful watch on public and private bills introduced into Parliament, and where necessary obtain a *locus standi* and offer opposition to bills injurious to the borough. Under threat of opposition useful concessions can be obtained from railway companies and other bodies. If a railway company or the Postmaster-General fails to provide adequate services for the town it is the business of the council to make representations in the proper quarter.

The council should also be careful to do all it can to increase the amenities of the town. If a town hall or other public building is to be erected, it should be worthy of a city, not a mere ugly block.

(2) **Local Justice.**—The Mayor presides over the Borough Bench, and in boroughs that have a separate Commission of the Peace the J.P.'s are appointed by the Lord Chancellor on the advice of the Council, elsewhere by the advice of the Lord-Lieutenant of the County. Certain boroughs have obtained the appointment of a stipendiary magistrate, who is a paid justice appointed by the Crown on the advice of the Home Secretary. (There are 18 stipendiaries outside London.) The Crown may grant a separate Court of Quarter Sessions for a borough when the Recorder, who is a barrister appointed by the Lord Chancellor, sits as judge and is paid from the borough fund. There are 121 Recorders. There are also certain ancient courts in boroughs, such as the Salford Court of Hundred and the Guild Hall Court, Norwich. The council of a quarter sessions borough with a population of 10,000 or over, which is either a county borough or received its grant of quarter sessions before 1888, must appoint a fit person to be coroner. A few ancient towns are counties of cities or counties of

towns, and have power to appoint a sheriff, who must be elected annually by the council on November 9th.

(3) **Public Health.**—This, with Housing and Education, will be dealt with in detail in other Tracts. It is enough to say here that the council is the authority for drainage, sewerage, scavenging and removal of refuse, treatment of infectious diseases, provision of hospitals, clinics, nursing, mortuaries, cemeteries, the inspection of slaughter-houses, bakeries, food and drugs, and the prevention of nuisances. County boroughs will also administer the Midwives Act.

Under the National Health Insurance Acts, 1911–1918, the council of a county borough appoints one-fifth of the Insurance Committee. A district committee is also set up for the area of each borough with over 10,000 population.

(4) **Lunacy and Mental Deficiency.**—The county borough is the authority for carrying out the Lunacy Acts, 1890–1911. It is its duty to provide an asylum or asylums for the accommodation of pauper lunatics, and it may also make provision for lunatics who are not paupers. A Visiting or Asylums Committee is appointed by the council which manages the institutions and visits the inmates. The expenses are met from the borough fund as far as they are not covered by contributions from the Exchequer and the Boards of Guardians. Under the Mental Deficiency Act, 1913, the county borough council appoints a committee for the care of the mentally defective, composed partly of members of the council and partly of guardians and other persons with special knowledge ; some women must be appointed. As a general rule the Visiting or Asylums Committee, with the addition of at least two women, acts as the committee, or forms that part of it appointed by the council. The duties of the local authority include the ascertaining of what persons are defective, the provision of suitable supervision and suitable accommodation, and the provision of burial. The expenses are met from the borough funds or from the rates.

(5) **Housing and Town Planning.**—County boroughs are responsible for carrying out the Housing and Town Planning Acts in their entirety ; and other boroughs, subject to certain powers vested in the county councils, are similarly responsible for these duties, which include the provision of houses, the clearing of congested areas, the ensuring that all houses are placed and kept in a proper state of repair, and the preparation of town planning schemes.

(6) **Education.**—The county borough is the authority for Higher and Elementary Education, and boroughs with a population of over 10,000 are authorities for elementary education in their areas. Other boroughs are minor education authorities appointing managers for elementary schools, etc., but with little effective control. The borough council, where it is the local authority, appoints an education com-mittee, the majority of members of which must be councillors, but

there is power to co-opt on the nomination of other bodies and the inclusion of women is necessary. For higher education, including technical, all borough councils are authorities, although they can surrender their powers to or act jointly with the county councils.

(7) **Highways.**—Borough councils are responsible for the paving, lighting and cleansing of the roads in their area and for the general regulation, street numbering, tree planting, etc. Certain main roads although repairable and maintainable by the county are as a rule maintained and repaired by the borough councils receiving a contribution from the county councils. The latter may also make grants for the widening and improvement of local roads. The Ministry of Transport under the Act of 1919 may make grants to a borough council for the construction or improvement of roads.

The question of the distribution of the burden for the upkeep of main roads is a matter of some dispute at the present time, the burden falling heavily on places through which there is heavy traffic, and the possibility is being considered of some division of roads on a system analogous to that obtaining in France, whereby some roads would be maintained by the State, some by the larger and some by the smaller local authorities. County boroughs and boroughs over 10,000 population may make regulations as to the use of roads by heavy traffic, and councillors should not forget that they have power to make users pay for exceptional traffic. Borough councils also regulate by by-law the display of advertisements and licence hoardings and projections, etc., over the roadway. The council also maintains bridges and may contribute to the cost of construction by private persons.

(8) **Parks, Recreation Grounds, Commons, etc.**—Borough councils have power to purchase or lease land for the provision of parks, recreation grounds and open spaces, and to make by-laws for their use ; they may also provide boats for hire on lakes. Many boroughs, under private acts of Parliament, provide bands of music. The council may regulate commons and assist in maintaining rights of common and rights of way. In most towns there are neglected gardens in squares that have " gone down " which an alert council can obtain for use as open spaces or children's recreation grounds. The council can erect swings and gymnastic apparatus in these grounds.

(9) **Allotments and Small Holdings.**—Borough councils have power to acquire allotments, and if six ratepayers represent that they are required, must hold an inquiry, and if the representations are correct the council must purchase or hire sufficient land for the purpose. The land can, if necessary, be acquired compulsorily, and it may lie within or without the boundaries of the borough. A county borough may also provide small holdings. A small holding is a plot of land between 1 and 50 acres or larger if of small value. The council may purchase or lease land for the purpose of letting as small holdings, or may sell the land to the tenant or assist a small holder in purchasing

from a private individual. The council may appoint a small holdings committee. In the first three years of the 1908 Act county boroughs had acquired 1,655 acres.

(10) **Libraries.**—Every borough council has power to provide and maintain either alone or in conjunction with neighbouring authorities public libraries, but the restriction of expenditure to the product of a penny rate has previously prevented the adoption of the Act by small boroughs. This has now been removed by the Libraries Act of 1919. The new Act also gives power to the county council to act in boroughs where the Libraries Act has not been adopted, and where this is done the borough will lose its powers. Museums may also be established and maintained. There is power to co-opt outside members on the libraries committee.

(11) **Public Utility Services.**—A borough council may have its own gas or electricity undertaking, its own water supply, and may run a tramway service. Municipal slaughterhouses may be provided and public markets, provided that ancient market rights are not interfered with. These are the most usual services provided, but councils may and do carry on other undertakings to meet their special requirements. Thus watering-places frequently have piers, sea-walls, harbours and bathing places. Bradford has a municipal conditioning house for textile fabrics which pays its way. Manchester City Council was largely responsible for the Ship Canal and is a large shareholder, while Bournemouth has an hotel.

Baths and washhouses, which may be considered as part of the public health work rather than as a trading venture, are provided by most boroughs and are almost invariably run at a loss, the prices being fixed to attract users rather than to cover expenses. The baths are frequently utilised as public halls in the winter, and there is no reason apart from finance why they should not be utilised as civic centres for social life with free dances, etc., instead of being let to individuals.

(12) **Protective and Regulative Powers—**

(A) *Police.*—County boroughs and some municipal boroughs with over 10,000 population maintain their own police forces, but no new force can be set up in boroughs where the population is under 20,000. The force is controlled by the Watch Committee, consisting of not more than one-third of the members of the council and the Mayor. In other boroughs the police are under the Standing Joint Committee of the county council and justices. One-half of the cost of the pay and clothing of the police is contributed from the Exchequer on a certificate of efficiency.

(B) *Protection from Fire.*—The borough council may establish and maintain a fire brigade and the necessary appliances under the Town and Police Clauses Act, 1847, and provide for a supply of water, fire plugs, etc., under the Public Health Act, 1875, and where there is a local police force, may employ the constables as part of the fire brigade.

(C) *Employment of Children.*—The combined effect of the Employment of Children Act, 1903, and the Education Act, 1918, is that (1) No child under 12 years may be employed at all ; (2) No child under 14 may be employed in street trading or in any factory, mine or quarry ; (3) No child between 12-14 years of age may be employed on school days before the close of school hours or on Sunday for more than two hours, or on any day before 6 a.m. or after 8 p.m. But borough councils that are education authorities under Part 3 of the Act may make by-laws modifying provision (3) and extending (2). They may permit under certain conditions the employment of children over 12 before school hours and the employment of children by their parents, but such employment before 9 a.m. must be limited to one hour, and no child so employed before 9 a.m. must be employed for more than one hour in the afternoon. The above provisions of the law, it should be noted, are not yet in operation, but it is proposed to fix April 1st, 1920, " the appointed day " for their coming into force. In the meantime the local education authority have the power to prohibit or restrict any employment of a child which they are satisfied is prejudicial to his health, and by-laws may be made declaring street trading illegal by any young person under the age of 16.

(D) *Factories and Workshops*—In workshops, including retail bakehouses, the law in regard to cleanliness, limewashing, ventilation, prevention of nuisances and overcrowding, etc., is enforced by the borough council A register of workshops is kept by the council. Factories are inspected by the Home Office, but the Home Office may, if it considers it necessary, demand the assistance of the borough council.

(E) *Weights and Measures.*—County boroughs and boroughs with over 10,000 population are the authorities for putting into force the law relating to weights and measures. Standards of weights and measures must be provided and verified from time to time. The council appoints inspectors to verify and stamp weights and measures brought to them and to inspect those in use in the borough. It can also make by-laws regulating the sale of coal retail under the Weights and Measures Act, 1889.

(F) *Gas Meters.*—The testing and stamping of gas meters is carried out by county boroughs and municipal boroughs where the Sale of Gas Act, 1859, has been adopted, but where the council itself supplies gas, the matter is dealt with by the justices.

(G) *Shops.*—In county boroughs and boroughs with over 10,000 population the council is the authority for enforcing the Shops Act, 1912. It appoints inspectors to see that hours of work for young persons are not exceeded and that seats are provided for assistants.

The council may also make orders for early closing day and fix times of closing for classes of shops.

(H) *Diseases of Animals.*—County boroughs and boroughs with more than 10,000 population are the authorities for dealing with contagious diseases of animals and to prevent the introduction of destructive insects. The council elect an executive committee and appoint a veterinary inspector. The diseases dealt with are cattle plague, pleuro-pneumonia, foot and mouth disease, sheep pox, sheep scab, and swine fever, anthrax, rabies and other diseases. The council may also establish a place for the slaughtering of foreign cattle.

(I) *Licensing and Registration.*—The borough council is the authority for licensing knacker's yards, game dealers, pawnbrokers, hackney carriages, horses or donkeys let out for hire, and pleasure boats. It registers and inspects canal boats and old metal dealers and marine stores. It licenses and regulates the storage and selling of petroleum. It makes by-laws for the regulation and for the sanitary condition of tents, vans and other " temporary dwellings." It may be licensed by the Postmaster-General to provide a system of public telephones. And it may apply to the Home Office to abolish any fair in the borough or to alter the day for holding it. The county borough is the authority under the Explosives Act, 1875, and licenses the manufacturer and storage of fireworks and explosives. County boroughs also license emigration agents, race-courses, premises for the public performance of stage plays. Music and dancing licences are granted by the magistrates, except in county boroughs within 20 miles of the cities of London and Westminster, when they are granted by the Borough Council. Under the Fertilisers and Feeding Stuffs Act, 1906, a county borough may appoint an agricultural analyst and official samplers.

(J) *Food Control.*—The borough council appoints the Food Control Committee from within or without its own body, one member at least must be a woman and one a representative of labour. The duties of this committee includes granting permission to open retail shops.

(K) *Profiteering.*—Under the Profiteering Act of 1919 a borough council may establish a profiteering committee or tribunal of not less than 7 or more than 25 members, who need not all be members of the council. They must include two women and at least three members of the local food committee and there must be adequate representation of labour. The duty of the committee is to investigate and hear complaints of alleged profiteering by local retailers, and they have power to state what is a reasonable price and order repayment of excess charges. The local authority may buy and sell articles, but must proceed on a commercial basis and not by way of subsidy at the expense of the ratepayers. Ordinary expenses may be met out of the rates.

(13) **Inebriates' Reformatories.**—A borough council may provide or contribute towards the provision of an inebriate's reformatory and may establish or license a retreat under the Inebriates' Acts, 1879 and 1881.

(14) **Pensions.**—In county boroughs and boroughs with over 20,000 population the council appoints the local pensions committee. The term of office is three years or less if the council so decide. The council is also represented on the Soldiers and Sailors Pensions Committee.

(15) **Charities.**—The Ministry of Health may confer on a borough council the powers of a parish council, enabling them to administer non-ecclesiastical charities, and a county borough may pay the costs of an inquiry by the Charity Commissioners into the public charities of the district. This is worth considering by labour councillors, as there are often old charities with funds that might be put to far greater use than they are at present.

(16) **Fisheries.**—County boroughs and boroughs with a population of over 20,000 may apply to the Board of Agriculture and Fisheries for the creation of a fishery district under the control of the council and those engaged in the industry.

(17) **Unemployment.**—In county boroughs and boroughs with over 10,000 population the Distress Committee under the Unemployed Workmen's Act, 1905, consists partly of members of the council, partly of guardians and other persons experienced in the relief of distress. Their duty is to make themselves acquainted with the conditions of labour in their area. They may provide temporary employment and assist persons to emigrate.

FINANCE OF BOROUGH COUNCILS.

The expenses of a borough council are defrayed from three main sources :—

(A) Income from municipal property and from public utility undertakings such as gas, electricity, and tramways.

(B) Rates levied upon owners and occupiers of property within the borough.

(C) Contributions from the central government in the form of grants.

Two principal rates are levied in boroughs for council purposes, the Borough Rate and the General District Rate. In boroughs certain expenses such as the salary of the mayor, the costs of municipal elections, education, and libraries are primarily met from the borough fund, into which are paid the rents and profits of corporate property, fines, fees, etc., but when this is insufficient, as it almost always is, a borough rate is levied by the overseers in each parish upon a precept served upon them by the borough council. The overseers of the poor are appointed as a rule by the council and are substantial householders, generally two in number ; the actual work is done by the assistant overseer, who is a paid official. It is their duty to prepare the annual valuation list, which is then submitted to the assessment committee which is appointed by the Board of Guardians, or where the union is co-extensive with the borough, by the guardians and council in equal proportions. This committee hears appeals, and there is a further appeal from it to the justices. The overseers make and levy and collect the Poor Rate. The borough rate is collected as part of the Poor Rate and is based on the overseer's valuation, though the council may have a separate valuation made if it so desires.

The General District Rate is levied by every borough council directly and is generally based on the Poor Rate Valuation. The General District Rate is primarily levied to defray any expenses that cannot be met out of the district fund, which consists of monies received under the Public Health Acts.

Some boroughs levy special rates under private Acts of Parliament, and rates may be levied specially on occupiers of certain property where private improvements have been carried out.

Rates are levied on the rateable value of property which is the gross estimated rental, that is the sum at which the property might reasonably be expected to let, after deducting therefrom the probable annual cost of repairs, insurance and other expenses necessary to maintain them in a condition to command such a rent. The occupier pays the rates except in cases where the property is of low annual value, where the owner pays, the tenant paying his share in his rent. The question of rating cannot be dealt with here at any length as it is full of complications and there are various exemptions and reductions, notably in the case of agricultural land which is assessed at half its value.

The rates are the chief source of income of a borough council, and the amount levied in the £ varies very much between different boroughs according to their wealth and needs.

A penny rate in Southport will produce about £2,237, in Rotherham £1,128, though the population of the former is only 6,000 more than the latter, and a penny rate in Hedon will only produce £14, in Liverpool £21,030.

Grants-in-aid from the Central Government are made under various Acts and are distributed on principles that frequently conflict. Sometimes on rateable value when the rich boroughs profit most, sometimes on poverty. Sometimes unconditionally, sometimes as in the case of the Police Grant, on a certificate of efficiency of work done. Some of the grants-in-aid are paid from the local taxation account into which the product of certain taxes are paid and certain fixed sums under the Agricultural Rates Act, 1896, and the Tithe Rent Charge Rates Act, 1899. But of more importance are the numerous grants made directly in aid of certain services such as education, public health, etc. These are constantly growing, and over two-thirds of the money received from the central in relief of local government now consists of direct grants, and by 1915 the total grants received by all local authorities amounted to nearly £24,000,000.

It has been mentioned above that many boroughs have considerable corporate property, and to the amount received in this way must be added the profits on trading undertakings. The amount derived from this source will depend on the policy of the council, which may either keep the price charged for services, such as light and transit, low and take no surplus, or make their charges higher and relieve the ratepayers from the profits thus accruing, or use the surplus for further municipal activities.

LOANS.

For the purposes of carrying out works of a permanent nature and for financing undertakings such as tramways, water works, etc., a borough council may borrow on the security of the corporate property, funds or rates, with the consent of the Ministry of Health. The conditions of repayment are laid down in the various enactments empowering councils to carry out such works, and the amount that can be raised on the security of the rates under the Public Health Acts is limited to two years' assessable value. The limit of time for repayment is generally 60 years, though a longer period is allowed under the Housing and Town Planning Act. The Public Works Loan Commissioners lend money to local authorities on the security of the rates, but a council may also with the sanction of the Ministry of Health or in some cases under private Acts create stock.

AUDIT.

Borough accounts are audited by the Borough Auditors, two of whom must be burgesses and qualified to be but not being members of the council who are elected by the burgesses on the 1st of March each year, and the Mayor's auditor who is a member of the council nominated by the Mayor. Some boroughs are audited by the district auditor who also audits the accounts under the Education and Unemployed Workmen Acts for all boroughs.

BOROUGH COUNCIL WORK.

A borough council does its work through committees. Of these some such as the Education Committee are statutory, that is to say, the council must appoint them, others are set up for convenience in dealing with the business, and their number will depend on the extent of the council's activities. In committee the details of the work are thrashed out and the officials of the council are in attendance to give information. The council's by-laws lay down what subjects should be dealt with by each committee. Each committee makes its recommendations and those involving expenditure are submitted to the finance committee; the whole of the transactions of the committees with their recommendations are then sent out in the form of minutes and are discussed at the council meeting.

The personnel of the committees should reflect as far as possible the strength of the different parties on the council. Not all councils are divided on party lines, but in most of the more important boroughs the need for a policy and the necessities of election work have resulted in the formation of parties on much the same lines as in the national legislature, though there is a greater number of independent members.

The hardest and most valuable work of the borough councillor is done in committee, and the man who thinks that he can make a show by speeches in full meeting reported in the press without thoroughly mastering the work in committee will find himself disillusioned. While it is desirable to keep in close touch with all the council's activities, the work is so great that the ordinary councillor is well advised to devote himself to one or two branches of the work.

THE COUNCIL'S OFFICERS.

The Town Clerk is the chief executive officer and legal adviser of the council : he is a barrister or solicitor, and it is his duty to warn the council if their proposals are *ultra vires*. He is primarily responsible for seeing that the decisions of the council are put into effect.

The Borough Treasurer is head of the Finance Department. The Medical Officer of Health is the chief official for carrying out work under the Public Health Acts and is, of course, a medical man. He and the Inspector of Nuisances are appointed and removed subject to the approval of the Ministry of Health. The Borough Surveyor or Engineer is the executive officer for works, housing and highways, while the heads of the various trading undertakings are generally subordinate to him. Under the new Ministry of Transport Act he will be in the same position towards that authority as is the Medical Officer of Health to the Ministry of Health. Other important officials are the Director of Education, the Borough Librarian and the Chief Constable. The Recorder and Stipendiary Magistrate are paid judges in certain towns.

Beneath the officials comes the salaried staff, and then there are the numerous weekly wage earners employed in the various departments. Labour councillors may be trusted to see that good conditions are given to the council's workmen and that trade union rates of wages are paid by the council and its contractors, but they are not always so ready to recognise the claims of the black-coated officials and there is even sometimes a tendency to use the council as a means of advance to equality of remuneration for all. This is a very shortsighted policy, for it must be remembered that the council is not the only employer in the market and that failure to give the usual occupational rates will prevent the council obtaining and retaining the services of a really efficient staff. It is worth while paying a high salary to get a really good Medical Officer of Health or Engineer.

In addition, where possible the council should employ direct labour, for especially in an isolated town there will be a tendency for rings of contractors to be formed. If the borough is small it may well join with a neighbouring authority for the provision of various services, thus obtaining the advantages of the economy of production on a large scale.

CONCLUSION.

Generally it may be stated that the borough is a natural and useful governing body provided that it is big enough to have a separate life from the county, but there are very many small boroughs that are not nearly large enough for economical and efficient administration and their position will have to be considered in any scheme for reform of areas.

Vacher & Sons, Ltd., Westminster House, S.W.1.—76725.

FABIAN PUBLICATIONS.

FABIAN ESSAYS. 1920 Edition. 2s.
HISTORY OF THE FABIAN SOCIETY. By E. R. PEASE. 6s. net.
TOWARDS SOCIAL DEMOCRACY. By SIDNEY WEBB. 1s. net, post 1d.
WHAT TO READ on Social and Economic Subjects. 1s. net and 2s. net.
THE RURAL PROBLEM. By H. D. HARBEN. 2s. 6d. net.
THIS MISERY OF BOOTS. By H. G. WELLS. 3d., post free 4d.

FABIAN TRACTS AND LEAFLETS.

Tracts, each 16 to 52 pp., price 1d., or 9d. per doz., unless otherwise stated.
Leaflets, 4 pp. each, price 1d. for six copies, 1s. per 100, or 8s. 6d. per 1,000.
The Set of 74, 4s. 6d. ; post free 5s. 3d.   Bound in buckram, 7s. 6d. ; post free, 8s. 3d.

I.—GENERAL SOCIALISM IN ITS VARIOUS ASPECTS.

TRACTS.—184. **The Russian Revolution and British Democracy.** By JULIUS WEST.
2d. 180. **The Philosophy of Socialism.** By A. CLUTTON BROCK. 169. **The Socialist
Movement in Germany.** By W. STEPHEN SANDERS. 2d. 159. **The Necessary
Basis of Society.** By SIDNEY WEBB. 151. **The Point of Honour.** By RUTH C.
BENTINCK. 147. **Capital and Compensation.** By E. R. PEASE. 146. **Socialism and
Superior Brains.** By BERNARD SHAW. 2d. 142. **Rent and Value.** 138. **Municipal
Trading.** 121. **Public Service *v.* Private Expenditure.** By Sir OLIVER LODGE.
107. **Socialism for Millionaires.** By BERNARD SHAW. 139. **Socialism and the
Churches.** By Rev. JOHN CLIFFORD, D.D. 133. **Socialism and Christianity.** By
Rev. PERCY DEARMER. 78. **Socialism and the Teaching of Christ.** By Dr. J.
CLIFFORD. 42. **Christian Socialism.** By Rev. S. D. HEADLAM. 79. **A Word
of Remembrance and Caution to the Rich.** By JOHN WOOLMAN. 72. **The Moral
Aspects of Socialism.** By SIDNEY BALL. 69. **Difficulties of Individualism.** By
S. WEBB. 51. **Socialism : True and False.** By S. WEBB. 45. **The Impossibilities
of Anarchism.** By G. B. SHAW. 2d. 7. **Capital and Land.** 5. **Facts for Socialists.**
2d. LEAFLETS.—13. **What Socialism Is.** 1. **Why are the Many Poor ?**

II.—APPLICATIONS OF SOCIALISM TO PARTICULAR PROBLEMS.

TRACTS.—188. **National Finance and a Levy on Capital.** By SIDNEY WEBB. 2d.
187. **The Teacher in Politics.** By SIDNEY WEBB. 2d. 186. **Central Africa and
the League of Nations.** By R. C. HAWKIN. 2d. 183. **The Reform of the House
of Lords.** By SIDNEY WEBB. 181. **When Peace Comes—the Way of Industrial
Reconstruction.** By SIDNEY WEBB. 2d. 178. **The War ; Women ; and Unem-
ployment.** 2d. 177. **Socialism and the Arts of Use.** By A. CLUTTON BROCK. 175.
The Economic Foundations of the Women's Movement. 2d. 173. **Public *v.* Private
Electricity Supply.** 171. **The Nationalization of Mines and Minerals Bill.** 170.
Profit-Sharing and Co-Partnership : a Fraud and Failure. 164. **Gold and State
Banking.** 162. **Family Life on a Pound a Week.** By Mrs. REEVES. 2d. 161.
Afforestation and Unemployment. 160. **A National Medical Service.** 2d. 157.
The Working Life of Women. 155. **The Case against the Referendum.** 154. **The
Case for School Clinics.** 152. **Our Taxes as they are and as they ought to be.** 2d.
149. **The Endowment of Motherhood.** 2d. 131. **The Decline of the Birth-Rate.**
145. **The Case for School Nurseries.** 140. **Child Labour under Capitalism.** 136.
The Village and the Landlord. By EDW. CARPENTER. 144. **Machinery : its Masters
and Servants.** 122. **Municipal Milk and Public Health.** 125. **Municipalization by
Provinces.** 124. **State Control of Trusts.** LEAFLET.—104. **How Trade Unions benefit
Workmen.**

III.—LOCAL GOVERNMENT POWERS : HOW TO USE THEM.

TRACTS.—189. **Urban District Councils.** By C. M. LLOYD. 172. **What about
the Rates ?** By S. WEBB. 156. **What an Education Committee can do (Elementary
Schools),** 3d. 62. **Parish and District Councils.** (Revised 1919.) 137. **Parish
Councils and Village Life.** 109. **Cottage Plans and Common Sense.** 82. **Workmen's
Compensation Act.** LEAFLETS.—134. **Small Holdings.** 68. **The Tenant's Sanitary
Catechism.** 71. **Ditto for London.**

IV.—GENERAL POLITICS AND FABIAN POLICY.

TRACTS.—158. **The Case against the C.O.S.** By Mrs. TOWNSHEND. 41. **The Fabian
Society : its Early History.** By BERNARD SHAW.

V.—BIOGRAPHICAL SERIES. In portrait covers, 2d. and 3d. each.

182. **Robert Owen, Idealist.** By C. E. M. JOAD. 179. **John Ruskin and Social
Ethics.** By Prof. EDITH MORLEY. 165. **Francis Place.** By ST. JOHN G. ERVINE.
166. **Robert Owen, Social Reformer.** By Miss B. L. HUTCHINS. 167. **William
Morris and the Communist Ideal.** By Mrs. TOWNSHEND. 168. **John Stuart Mill.**
By JULIUS WEST. 174. **Charles Kingsley and Christian Socialism.** By C. E.
VULLIAMY.

Fabian Tract No. 192

GUILD SOCIALISM

BY

G. D. H. COLE, M.A.

A Lecture, revised by the Author, delivered in the Fabian Society's Course at King's Hall, London, in November, 1919.

PRICE TWOPENCE

LONDON:
THE FABIAN SOCIETY, 25 TOTHILL STREET, WESTMINSTER, S.W.1.
PUBLISHED MARCH, 1920. REPRINTED MARCH, 1922.

GUILD · SOCIALISM.

A GREAT change has come over the Socialist Movement in the course
of the last few years. When the propaganda of Guild Socialism
first began, especially so far as the Socialist Societies were concerned, we were working against the grain. The Socialist Movement had settled down into a certain body of doctrine, it had
learned to regard Socialism as an expression of consumers' organisation, it could not see beyond the conception of democracy as
an organisation of consumers. When we tried to introduce the
rival conception of an organisation of producers, people used to
tell us that we were not Socialists at all. Even in those days it
was much easier to appeal to a Trade Unionist than to the average
Socialist on Guild lines, because as far back as 1910-11 there was
beginning that remarkable awakening in the Trade Union Movement which has produced such an enormous change in its social
outlook. Gradually, the atmosphere in Socialism as in the Trade
Union Movement has changed and the path of Guild propaganda
become easier. When we insist on the importance of producers'
organisation we are no longer working against people's prejudices
and preconceptions. The Guild idea, whether accepted as a
complete doctrine or not, is now familiar and seldom encounters
hostility from a Trade Union or I.L.P. or other Socialist audience.
The change in Trade Unionism is much greater than it has yet
become in the Socialist movement itself. At any meeting of the
rank and file of the Trade Union Movement—of the conscious 10
per cent. or 20 per cent. which attends such meetings—the great
majority have got clearly the idea that they want, in some way
which they may not be able to define, the control of industry by
the workers. Very likely many of them know nothing of Guild
Socialism, and few may call themselves Guild Socialists; but
still they have in their minds this idea that their immediate aim
as Trade Unionist is to win the control or a substantial share in
the control of industry. Everybody who desires to understand
the present tendencies in the Trade Union Movement, who recognises the enormous strength Trade Unionism has gained, and the
great influence it is certain to exercise on the moulding of Society
in the very near future, must try to understand what this desire
to exercise control over industry means, and to find for that desire
legitimate expression in the organisation of the new Society.
The great majority of the Trade Unionists want to exercise a real

control over industry, and, that being not a theory but a fact, you have somehow to fit it into your idea of the social situation. It is no good saying that you think this control-of-industry idea does not matter. It matters for this reason, if for no other, that the great mass of the Trade Union Movement has become impregnated with it, that it is the most living force in Trade Unionism to-day.

Re-interpreting Socialism.

I want to make it quite clear that the Guild Socialism of which I am speaking is a form of Socialism—not an alternative to Socialism, not some new doctrine springing up altogether afresh as a challenge to the Socialist movement, but a new interpretation of Socialism, an attempt to make it a more complete and a more balanced doctrine, more completely expressive of democracy, a doctrine that will make democracy really effective economically as well as politically. It is an attempt to reinterpret the Socialist idea. The desire of the Guild Socialist is not to found a new school or a new organisation, but to convert the Socialist Movement as well as the Trade Union movement to its point of view ; to incorporate the new body of thought which the Guildsmen have brought into being in the general body of doctrine which belongs to the Socialist Movement ; to effect a change in Trade Union thought, not to bring about a break-away. That is the policy the Guild Socialists have always followed. They have not tried to found a new rival organisation, they have always striven, while creating their own small organisation for propaganda purposes, to remain inside and work through existing organisations.

The Control of Industry.

I profoundly believe that the factors that went to make the Guild Socialist Movement in this country are the same factors as have gone to make movements which are very largely parallel in other countries. If you look over not merely Europe but the whole of the industrialised countries of the world to-day, everywhere this idea of the control of industry is one of the governing ideas in present-day Society ; everywhere it is this idea that is driving forward industrial workers, and that is animating them in their attempts to change the existing system. You see the idea at work in Germany in the struggle between the Council system and the Government, and in Russia in the experiments in factory organisation. You see it at work in America in such new doctrines as the Railwaymen's proposal of the Plumb plan. All over the world the Trade Union Movement is gradually tending in the direction of making constructive and clear its demand for a real share in industrial control. That demand takes different forms. It shapes itself in different ways in the different countries of the world, but there is the same central idea, the same essential driving power behind it. That is a thoroughly healthy thing. You do not want exactly the same movement, exactly the same formal doctrine for all these different countries ; you want to get a certain central idea, driving forward the working-class movement over the whole world, but you want that idea to take different expres-sions, assume different forms, according to the different structure of economic Society in the various countries and the different temperaments of the various peoples of the world. You want the various democracies, the various proletariats, to be organising in such a way that they can effectively co-operate, not organising all the world over in accordance with some hard-and-fast mechanical system which ignores national differences.

Utopias and Realities.

I do not pretend, none of us Guildsmen pretends, that Guild Socialism is the right way for all the peoples of the world to tackle their economic problems. We believe it is the right expression for Socialism to take at this particular time in this particular country, and we believe that it includes ideas that are vital not only for this country but for the whole of the industrialised world ; but that these ideas will have to be worked out and applied in different ways according to different economic civilisations and national temperaments. We are not hard-and-fast dogmatists, believing we have some complete workable watertight system which can be applied to every Society. We are seekers after truth. We believe we have the central idea, and that we have a clear vision of some of the immediate steps that are necessary for the application of that idea ; but we do not believe that Guild Socialism, as we write it down in our books, as we have to describe it in answering questions, will ever exist in exactly the form in which we describe it. We know that Society does not work in that way. We know that, if you should predict a system and bring it into being exactly as you predicted it, it would inevitably be a wrong system, because by the time you had brought it into existence the social situation would have changed in such a way as to make that system unsuitable. But we do believe that it is worth while to try to foresee things as clearly as you can, to predict as clearly as you can the form of the future organisation ; not because you will be able to bring into being the precise form of organisation which you predict, but because your prediction will help you to see a way out of the problems with which you are faced. We believe you cannot take the immediate steps, cannot act effectively in facing the problems you are up against at the moment, merely by treating those problems as they arise. You have to face them with as clear an idea as you can get into your mind of the end at which you are aiming, and your vision of the end helps you in facing immediate problems. That is why we may be open to the charge of being Utopian, not because we believe in our Utopias as actual visions of the future Society, but because we believe that our Utopias are useful in enabling us to face the problems of to-day.

A Theory of Democracy.

I also want to make it clear that Guild Socialism is not a purely industrial theory. It is—certainly so far as I am concerned—rather an accident that Guild Socialism has taken a mainly industrial form. The reason why we are talking mainly about the organisation of industry is that industry is in such a beastly muddle that until you have straightened it out it is no good talking about anything else. That is why our National Guild doctrine appears mainly as a doctrine of industrial organisation. But the theory on which the Guild conception rests is much wider than any purely industrial theory. It rests fundamentally on a particular conception of democracy, essentially different from the conception of democracy which was almost generally accepted in the nineteenth century. Our conception of democracy is this : that it is nonsense to talk of one man representing another, or a number of others ; that there is no such thing as representation of one person by another, because in his very nature a man is such a being that he cannot be represented. But that is not a denial of forms of representative government properly understood ; it is merely to say that unless representative government conforms to certain canons, it will be misrepresentative government. Our next step is to try and lay down the canons to which representative government must conform if it is to be really representative. We say that the only way in which there can be real representation is when the representative represents not another person but some group of purposes which men have in common ; that you never ought to try to represent Smith and Jones and Brown by means of Robinson, but that if Smith, Jones, and Brown have a common interest in some particular thing, whether as producers or as football players or in any other capacity, it is quite legitimate for them to choose Robinson to execute for them and on their behalf their common purpose. That is to say, all true representation, if we are right, is not representation of persons, but only representation of common purposes ; or, to put it in other words, any real representation is necessarily functional representation. If that is so, then in social organisation, if it is to be democratic, you must follow this principle of function. If you want to have a democratic Society you can only get it by making Society democratic in all its different parts, in relation to all the various functions which have to be performed in that Society. Therefore you must treat the problem of industry as one problem, and see that you get it organised on democratic lines by itself. You must take the problem of politics and see that you get that organised on democratic lines by itself. You must take all the other problems that arise in Society, and see that in each of its compartments or departments Society is organised on a democratic basis. It is only then, by putting together these different democratic organisations which exist for the expression of particular groups of social purposes, that you can build up a really democratic Society. As long as you conceive of Society as finding its expression in some one form of representative institution, you will inevitably go astray and get a misrepresentative instead of a really representative institution, but as soon as you conceive of Society as a whole and try to make all the parts really democratic, you get your best chance and your only chance of making the whole democratic. We have worked out that theory mainly in relation to one part of social organisation—the industrial sphere, and we have concentrated on that sphere because, until you get the industrial organisation straightened out, you do not stand the faintest chance of straightening out anything else. As long as you have the present chaos in industry, as long as men and women live the sort of life they are living in industry to-day, as long as you have the present state of war between the various parties who are supposed to be co-operating in the task of production, it is no good expecting that your Society as a whole will function decently or that you will have any real democracy in any of its parts ; because the disorder in the industrial system is fatal to order in any part of the Society. Therefore that on which attention has first to be concentrated is straightening out as far as may be the industrial system, bringing it into harmony with real democratic principles, and then going on to introduce this new sanity into the other parts of Society as well.

Principles and Application.

This may seem a very long way of arriving at any attempt to describe Guild Socialism. I should not have gone this long way round unless I thought it would be the shortest way in the end ; because, unless I put clearly before you the essential principles on which we are working, I shall merely present you with the shell of an organisation without explaining why that organisation has been conceived, or why we believe it to be a useful thing. The principles behind Guild Socialism are far more important than the actual forms of organisation which the Guild Socialists have thought out. The thing that really counts is the principle behind the movement, and you might perhaps find ways of expressing that principle as alternatives to the ways we have devised. At any rate, having made clear what are the principles on which this conception of social organisation rests, I can go on and try to make clear the organisation itself.

What is a Guild ?

That brings me to the question, What is a Guild ? By Guild we mean something based upon Trade Unionism, but essentially different from present-day Trade Unionism in two particulars. First, even if a Trade Union is what is called an industrial union— that is to say, aims at including the whole of the workers in a particular industry—it is essentially an incomplete body, because even if it includes or tries to include all the manual workers in the industry, it very often makes no attempt to include the salaried or technical workers attached to the industry. In certain cases, Trade Unions do include professional and technical as well as other workers—the Railway Clerks' Association and to a less extent the National Union of Railwaymen are examples of that—in other cases, the salaried and technical workers have Trade Unions of their own, and these work in more or less close conjunction with the Unions representing the manual workers. But there is no case at present of a Trade Union body which does effectively and completely represent any industry and include the whole of the persons engaged in that industry who are essential to its efficient conduct. If you are to carry on an industry efficiently you must have the co-operation in the first place of the manual worker. The reason why industry is breaking down to-day is because the manual workers are not co-operating. That is why under the present system industry is bound to become more and more inefficient ; because the manual workers as they wake up to the real facts of the situation more and more refuse to co-operate in industry as long as it is carried on under the present conditions, and therefore industry will become increasingly inefficient as the workers become increasingly educated and class-conscious.

Workers by Hand and Brain.

For carrying on an industry you require in the first place these manual workers, but just as much for the efficient carrying on of an industry you require all the various classes of persons whose special technical or commercial training makes them useful for particular functions which the industry has to perform. Take the mining industry. Mining is every year becoming more and more an engineering problem. The mining engineer is becoming a more and more important person. The scientific problems of mining are every year increasing in importance, and that means that the mining engineers and the others, the skilled technicians attached to the mines, are constantly gaining in their relative importance to the other classes of workers in the industry. Now one of the ways in which a Guild, as we conceive it, would differ from a Trade Union is in that it would include the whole of the workers, by hand or brain, experts, brain workers, and manual workers of every kind— all the workers who are essential to the carrying on of that industry with efficiency as a public service. In our attitude towards the Trade Union Movement we have that object in mind ; we are always trying to create the sort of organisation that would be capable not merely of overthrowing capitalism—which is a comparatively easy job—but of replacing capitalism—which is a very much harder job. Therefore we are always trying, not merely to get the various sectional unions of manual workers amalgamated on industrial lines, but also to bring those unions into the closest possible relation with the unions of brain workers and technicians, with the ultimate object of bringing the whole of the workers in the various industries into a single organisation, which will not ignore the differences of function and capacity between the various grades, but will rest on a recognition by the manual workers of the distinctive function of the brain worker and technician, and by the brain worker of the rights of the manual worker. It is not an attempt to ignore the difference of function between the technician and the other workers; we are trying to provide for that difference, and get it fully recognised by both sides. At present you have snobbishness on both sides to contend with—the brain worker thinking he can get on without the manual worker, and the manual worker thinking that he does not want the co-operation of the brain worker, because the brain worker is the boss's man. You have to overcome both these forms of snobbishness, and to get the greatest possible effective co-operation between the manual worker and the technician, before you can have a Guild.

Turning out the Goods.

The second thing in which a Guild differs from a Trade Union to-day is that a Guild would be mainly concerned not with looking after the interests of its members in an economic sense but with carrying on the industry. The main job of the Guild would be not protection, not collective bargaining, not safe-guarding the standard of life of its members; it would be turning out the goods, seeing that the industry was efficiently conducted, actually running and administering the industry. That may seem a very big change from the Trade Unionism of the present time. It is a big change; but it is not a change for which there is no preparation, because as fast as a Trade Union gains in power or authority it does begin to stretch out its hands towards the control of industry. That is no new thing, it is a very old thing. It begins naturally in the way that is easiest for the workers. The Union begins with imposing restrictions on the right of the employer to organise industry in the way in which he chooses. It begins by saying, "You shan't do that, you shan't employ people in this industry unless you conform to such and such conditions," by hemming him round with negative restrictions, and of these negative restrictions many may tend, I quite agree, to hamper the efficiency of industry in many respects. I do not say in all respects, because very often the regulations imposed by the Trade Unions have actually helped industrial efficiency, but in many cases necessarily these regulations hinder efficiency. They do so for this quite simple reason. At present the Trade Union is kept outside the actual control of industry. It can't give orders, it can't say, "You shall do this," it can only say, "You shan't do that." That means that the Trade Union is always in the position of obstruction, in the position of obstructing other people from doing things as they choose. There, again, you have an example of the pulls of the classes which at present exist in industry : their pulling one against another hinders industry, makes industry necessarily inefficient under the present system. Now, as the Trade Unions go on gaining power, they more and more try to turn these restrictions which they have imposed on industry into a positive form. They try to pass beyond saying, " Thou shalt not " to " Thou shalt " ; not merely to check the way in which the employer does things, not merely to criticise and restrain, but actually to give orders and run things themselves.

The Shop Stewards.

Perhaps the most remarkable tendency in that direction in recent years is the growth of the Shop Stewards' Movement. It has been principally in the Engineering and allied industries, where it represents a definite attempt by the workers to convert their negative restrictions on industry into a form of positive control over industry. You may say that that was not consciously so. So far as many of the Shop Stewards are concerned it was not ; but I am dealing not with what was consciously present in the mind of every Shop Steward, but with the general tendency of policy behind the Shop Stewards' Movement as a whole. In that sense, what I say is undoubtedly true. During the present year the big control movements of the railwaymen and the miners have been obvious expressions of the tendency I have been describing. Both the railwaymen and the miners no longer content themselves with the imposition of restrictions on the way in which industry is run, but demand that they shall be admitted to a share in the control of industry, and shall have the right to a certain extent to lay down the conditions under which industry is to be organised in the future, and to share in the positive task of organising it. There is the second big difference between Trade Unionism as it has existed in the past and the Guild of the future.

From Trade Union to Guild.

Now, in the case of both these differences you can see that the bridge is being built by which Trade Unionism will pass from one stage to the other. There is already the tendency of the manual workers and the professional organisations to agree together and to come into closer contact. There is already the tendency for the organised workers not merely to demand, but to show themselves in a position to enforce their demand for, a real share in the control of those industries in which they are most strongly and best organised. In both cases you can see the bridge from the Trade Union to the Guild being built, and that process is likely to be immensely speeded up in the next few years, if the result of the movements which are going on in the building industry and the mines at present is a successful result. Suppose the miners succeed in securing the greater part of what they are now asking for, an enormous impetus will be given to the demands of the workers in other industries for similar concessions. As soon as we get the mines nationalised under conditions approximating to the demands which the miners are putting forward, some other industry will step into the place which the miners have left vacant. A crisis concerning nationalisation and democratic control will develop in some other industry, and the same battle will be fought out again ; only there will be this difference, that whereas now nationalisation and democratic control have the air of an untried experiment, then the workers who next demand it will have behind them the precedent which the miners will have created. That amongst other things is the main reason why the miners' battle is the battle of all the workers—the battle of everyone who cares for democratic organisation of industry, and why the whole Labour Movement ought to stand solidly behind the miners not only in their demand for national ownership but also in their demand for democratic control.

Rock or Sand ?

I have tried to make clear that in our idea of a Guild we are building upon something definite and tangible in the Trade Unionism of to-day. It is very easy to make theories, but it is of no use unless you have some definite means at hand of realising those theories. I could construct a better ideal of organisation than Guild Socialism standing on my head ; only it would not do any good, because there would be no way of getting it. When you are dealing with Guild Socialism there is a definite way of getting it, because it is built upon an existing organisation, because it can show the way in which that organisation can be adapted to the fulfilment of the functions suggested, because it can show already at work a very strong and definite tendency in the direction which it indicates. You never need take any notice of a theoretical movement unless it can say : Here is the organisation with which I am going to do this thing. At any rate, that is true in the economic sphere. Purely theoretical movements do not matter. The movements which are in the eyes of the authorities dangerous are movements which have definite organisations behind them. Guild Socialism has behind it first of all the functional organisation of Trade Unionism, and, secondly, and in a very important sense, the functional organisation of the Co-operative Movement.

The Guilds and the Community.

Then we come to what is undoubtedly the most difficult point in Guild Socialist theory to explain at all shortly or simply. As soon as you set forward your ideal for the control of industry by bodies of the kind which I have tried to describe, that is, by National Guilds, you are faced with the question, But won't these Guilds work for their own benefit, instead of working for the com-

munity as a whole ; won't they serve their own interests, instead
of serving the interests of the consumer? You are asked what
guarantee you can give that the miners won't strike under Guild
Socialism. I say at once, I cannot give you a guarantee, nor can
you give me a guarantee that you can devise any system on God's
earth under which the miners won't strike, because if the miners
don't want to go down the pit and get coal, there is no power on
earth that can make the miners go down the pit and get coal.
The thing you have to fall back on is the attempt to devise a system
under which miners will be prepared willingly to go down the pit and
get coal. That is where so many people who argue against theorists
like us make a mistake, because they always assume that under the
present system miners will go down and get coal—an assumption
which is steadily becoming less plausible and less true. If we do
not find some new way of persuading the miners to go down the
pits, then before long we shall find our houses even colder than they
are now, our factories stopping for lack of coal, and our whole
industrial system dislocated. It won't be a case of only the miners
not being willing to do these things for us, but of an increasing
unwillingness in every industry. Therefore it is not enough for you
to say that the Guild Socialist offers no guarantee that the miners
will produce for the community and not for themselves.

The Motive of Service.

You have, if you object to Guild Socialism, to show a system
under which they will be more likely to do that than they will
under Guild Socialism. I personally believe that a system under
which a man has a reasonable control of the conditions of his own
working life, and also, as a citizen, of the conditions of his political
life, offers the best guarantee that you can have, because it offers
the best opportunity for a man to give free service to the community and at the same time to express himself as a citizen and
as a consumer, as well as in his capacity as a producer. But I
certainly think you must rely, for securing that the various Guilds
will work for the public service and not for their own advantage,
mainly upon enlisting a new motive in industry and on making
a real appeal to the motive of public service, given under free
conditions. I do not want, and no Guild Socialist wants, the miners
or any other group of workers to own the industry in which they
are concerned. In the situation which has arisen to-day, we stand
with the Collectivists in the demand for national ownership of
industry. We believe the industries ought to be taken over and
owned by the public. The difference between our theory and other
theories that are put forward for the control of industry when
nationalised lies simply in our belief that when you nationalise an
industry that does not mean that the public has got to administer
it, or rather that the public has got to appoint bureaucrats to
administer it for them. We believe the right way of running an

industry is to hand it over to be worked by the people who know the best possible way of working it efficiently ; on the one hand by the technicians who understand how the industry is to be made efficient on its scientific and commercial side, and on the other hand by the manual workers without whose co-operation you cannot get the goods turned out.

The Case for Public Ownership.

We want public ownership of industry for this reason, that if any industry produces a surplus—or whatever surplus any industry produces—we desire that surplus to pass not into the pocket of the industry in question, but into the national exchequer, to become a part of the revenue of the whole country. In just the same way we do not desire the prices of commodities produced and of services rendered to be fixed by those who run those services or produce those commodities. We believe that the prices of commodities and services ought to be fixed by the community as a whole, that those are matters not for the body of working producers alone, but for the whole body of the people to determine, because the price of a commodity is something which affects the consumer even more nearly than it affects the producer. What we demand for the workers by hand and brain is not the entire control of the economic process right from production to consumption, but the control of the productive processes and the processes of distribution allied with production. We demand that the workers shall control those parts of the industry which are concerned with the way in which goods are turned out and services rendered, and that they shall organise themselves for the producing of those goods and the rendering of those services, but as soon as the producer comes into contact with the consumer, as soon as the consumer is directly affected, as he is in prices, as he is in the division of the surplus realised in the industry, then we recognise the consumers' right to make his voice heard. More than that, we recognise the right of the consumer to criticise to the full the way in which the productive processes are carried on by the producer, and, in the miners' recommendations to the Coal Commission, which are as good an expression of immediate Guild policy as you will find, that point of view is clearly and explicitly recognised in the proposal for a separate Consumers' Council related to the Mining Guild, and representing the community from the consumers' side. Therefore, we want communal control of industry and democratic control of industry. These are two sides of our programme which cannot be divided ; and they are equally essential for the creation of any Guild Socialist Society.

The Place of Co-operation.

I want to say a word as to the place which the Co-operative Movement would occupy in the Guild Socialist solution of industrial organisation. When you are dealing with the great industries and services, not only such services as mines, railways, and shipping but the other great productive industries also, then I believe that one by one all those industries will pass into the stage at which nationalisation combined with democratic control, roughly on the lines of the miners' scheme, will become immediate and practical politics. But when you are dealing with the retail distributive industry, and with small-scale industries closely in contact with the individual consumer, and producing commodities that are individually consumed in the home, then I am not so certain that many of the industries and services connected with that sort of domestic production will ever pass into the stage of national-isation as we ordinarily understand it. I think rather that you have to divide the various industries and services in the country roughly into three groups ; into the group which will pass into national ownership, including all the great industries and services of national extent ; the group which will pass into municipal ownership, or some other form of ownership by local authorities, including what we ordinarily call the Public Utility Services—gas and water and many more which will be added to them, including local transport, of course ; and then a third group that you may call the domestic industries, which I believe will pass into co-operative ownership, and will not pass through the stage of either State or municipal or any other form of ownership by a public authority. I believe it is in relation to this third group of industries—domestic industries—that Co-operation will find its survival in the Socialist community.

I am not speaking now of Co-operation in agriculture. There, again, Co-operation has probably a vast future for its activities, but so far as industry apart from agriculture is concerned, I believe the Co-operative Movement will find its place as the centre of the domestic industries, and that it will be related to Guilds organis-ing workers in those industries, in the same way as the State, or whatever replaces the State, will be related to the Guilds organising the great public industries and services, and in the same way as the municipality or other local authority will be related locally to Guilds organising the public utilities.

A Survey of Democracy.

The other great working-class movement besides Trade Union-ism is Co-operation. Any theory which ignores Co-operation, or unnecessarily puts up the back of Co-operation will inevitably and deservedly fail. In Russia, the Bolsheviks began with an attempt to subordinate Co-operation to their own theories. They failed. Co-operation was too strong for them, because it was a movement rooted in the producing sections of society : and in just the same way we shall have to face this problem of Co-operation, to find a real scope for Co-operation in the society of the future, and to run our social revolution by building jointly upon those two great working-class movements, and by finding for them a harmonious reconciliation. I believe that can be done. One of the things I would like most to see in the near future is not merely a survey of Co-operation, like the Co-operative Survey that has just been completed ; not merely a survey of Trade Unionism, like the survey we may get out of the proposals for a General Staff that are now being mooted, but a joint survey of Trade Unionism and Co-operation which would bring those two working-class movements together in theory as they are now rapidly being brought together in practice. If you could get those two movements working together, there is almost no limit to the power which they might exercise in Society.

Four Problems.

At the end of this lecture, I raise four big problems, not because I propose so much to deal with them separately, as because by putting them before you I shall be able to throw into relief that which should have been sticking out of what I have been saying all through my lecture. If Guild Socialism is a really living and vital doctrine it has to find satisfactory answers to these four problems. It has to show that it will provide a way of dividing national income, not necessarily on lines of absolute equality, although I personally believe in equality, but on lines at any rate of approximate economic equality and fairness. At the same time it has to show that it will provide for the making of fresh capital, that it will be able to divide the national production from year to year into two parts, one of which will go to satisfy the immediate needs of the population, and the other of which will go to replenishing the capital of industry, and make provision for future production. Under Guild Socialism, as under other forms of Socialism, saving becomes a business for the community as a whole, and not for the separate individuals in the community ; just as under Collectivist Socialism, so under Guild Socialism, the business of providing for the future is a business for the community as a whole. It is the business of those who budget in that community to say each year : We can afford to distribute so much in the form of income to our members, and we must put aside so much for future development. That presents exactly the same problem to Guild Socialism as it presents to any other kind of Socialism.

Guild Taxation.

Moreover, Guild Socialism provides, on the financial side certainly, the easiest basis for taxation that I know of. The basis of taxation under Guild Socialism would be taxation at source of the various industries, and we have always assumed that the main way of raising revenue, although not the only way, under Guild Socialism would be taxation at source imposed upon the various Guilds, which would incidentally be a very useful method of redressing any inequality which might remain as between the various Guilds, after the community had fixed the prices of their various products.

The Hope for Craftmanship.

Then as to the problem of Guild structure. As long as you have capitalism there is nothing for it but to centralise your forces more and more to fight capitalism ; but I believe as soon as the workers can get anything like economic freedom the first thing they will do is to begin to break up this enormous centralised industrial system that we have created. I do not mean that they will go around smashing machinery ; but I believe there will be a gradual reversion to localism, to smaller-scale production, to meet the gradual demand of the consumer for goods of higher quality. That will not be a sudden thing ; if it were sudden it would be a calamity. It will be a gradual process arising from the education of the worker, from the greater freedom which he finds in his work, from his desire to do better work. But that return to smaller-scale conditions of production cannot come about until you have installed some form of economic freedom, and until you have smashed the present capitalist system. Therefore, whether you believe ultimately in local or national or international Guilds, you have to concentrate on this problem of building up an organisation capable of overthrowing the present system and putting something in its place, capable of carrying on, even if it is not the final form of organisation you desire.

"Human Nature."

The last thing I want to say is a sentence or so about the problem of " human nature." It is impossible to lecture on almost any conceivable subject without being asked whether you believe that human nature has changed, and it is always wise to forestall some of the obvious questions in order to get on to the interesting ones. What, then, is the ordinary man really like ? That may seem rather a large question to raise at this hour. Many people would tell you the ordinary man does not want to be free, but only cares to be let alone, to get along with things without being too much interfered with. I do not believe that is true. I believe that the ordinary man might indeed very often say that all he wants is to be let alone. But if you let him alone I do not believe he would do decent work, or would enjoy himself ; he would very soon get extremely bored. What the ordinary man really does want is to have an opportunity of expressing himself if he desires to do so, to have many opportunities of expressing himself, in different directions, not because he will use those opportunities all the time or universally, but because he will be able to use them if he wants to. It is a very nice thing to feel that you have a ticket for this course of lectures, even if you don't come to all the lectures, and it is a very nice feeling that you have a sort of universal pass for human freedom, even if you are not particularly concerned in exercising human freedom in all its forms. I prefer to have a vote even when I would die sooner than vote for any of the candidates standing, and I believe my feeling is the common feeling.

The Man in the Street.

That is, I believe, a very important point that many people go wrong about. They say the ordinary man does not want really to control industry, therefore it does not matter whether he has a chance to do so or not. That is a profound mistake. We must organise industry on such a basis that every man does get a chance to control it, not because we believe that every man will take equal advantage of that chance, but because the whole atmosphere of industry will change if that chance is given, and because that will mean that the people who do actually control industry will be controlling it with the consent of the rest, and everybody will feel that he is really co-operating—that he really counts, and that the people who are controlling industry are doing their job under his direction. If we can only get into industry that feeling not merely of consent, but of co-operation, even if it is not the most active co-operation that can be desired, then we shall change to a great extent the spirit in which work is done. I believe the change will go much further, and that if we provide the right conditions, a very much larger proportion of people than now will be active and keen in exercising a real control over industry, although at the same time I believe no less that if you once get industry decently organised it will cease to occupy the disproportionate place that it occupies in men's minds to-day, and instead of being the main thing in our minds it will sink back into being a quite minor and humdrum thing about which we need not bother ; and I hope when we have got that feeling it will not be necessary for me to go on lecturing and bothering about industry. Certainly, I shall leave industry to look after itself, and get on with something else. Meanwhile, I suppose I must go on talking for a few years yet.

Trusting People.

Finally, the last problem of human nature is whether you are prepared to take the risk of trusting people or not. I remember the old Socialist question always used to be on the lines that you could not trust the people to work under conditions of industrial self-government. The Collectivists never did trust people a bit. I do not know whether they have changed now or not ; at any rate a few years ago, even if they did not trust the people, they had some hope of building through bureaucratic Socialism a sort of Society that would work. That hope has gone. There is no hope in bureaucratic Society, no hope that it would work, even if anyone still desired to bring it into existence. Nor is there hope or chance of capitalism lasting much longer. We have to find some new way of facing the problem of industrial organisation. Neither the old consumers' Socialism, nor Capitalism, is capable of turning out the goods. That puts it up to you either to accept what I am saying, or else to find some way by which you can induce men to go on producing, by means other than the means which were employed right through the nineteenth century—the means of hunger and fear. Almost the only reason why people have worked in the past, why people have consented to go on working under such miserable, unjust conditions, has been that they have been frightened, and that they have been starved. If that breaks down—and it is everywhere breaking down to-day—then either men won't go on working at all or else they will go on working for some quite different reason.

A Leap in the Dark.

I say plainly that the only reason I can see, the only appeal you can make to persuade men go on working, is the belief that in working they are really serving the community. If that conception won't work then nothing at all will work, and the world will come to an end. Not suddenly, which would not matter very much to any of us ; it will come to an end slowly and very uncomfortably for all of us, and we shall see year by year not merely industry growing inefficient, but everything growing more and more dirty and uncomfortable and nasty and hopeless, and more like a story by H. G. Wells. If we want to avoid that, if we want to build up a new Society before the old one cracks all round us, then we have to be quick in making experiments, and we have to make them on trust. Exactly what we must make is what Mr. Leslie Scott called in his case for the Coal-owners before the Coal Commission, " a leap in the dark."*

* For a fuller account of Guild Socialism, reference should be made to the publications of the National Guilds League, 39 Cursitor Street, London, E.C. 4.

THE FABIAN SOCIETY

25 TOTHILL STREET, WESTMINSTER, LONDON, S.W.1.

Those willing to join the Labour Party, or desirous of obtaining information about its Programme and Principles, are invited to communicate with the Secretary of the Fabian Society.

The Fabian Society has been, from the outset, a constituent body of the Labour Party; and membership of the Society carries with it full membership of the Labour Party; eligibility for nomination to all Conferences and Offices, and qualification for Labour Party, candidatures for Parliament and Local Authorities, without obligation to belong to any other organisation.

The Society welcomes as members any persons, men or women, wherever resident, who subscribe to its Basis (set forth below), and who will co-operate in its work according to their opportunities.

BASIS OF THE FABIAN SOCIETY.

(TO BE SIGNED BY ALL MEMBERS.)

(Adopted May 23rd, 1919.)

The Fabian Society consists of Socialists.

It therefore aims at the reorganisation of Society by the emancipation of Land and Industrial Capital from individual ownership, and the vesting of them in the community for the general benefit. In this way only can the natural and acquired advantages of the country be equitably shared by the whole people.

The Society accordingly works for the extinction of private property in land, with equitable consideration of established expectations, and due provision as to the tenure of the home and the homestead; for the transfer to the community, by constitutional methods, of all such industries as can be conducted socially; and for the establishment, as the governing consideration in the regulation of production, distribution and service, of the common good instead of private profit.

The Society is a constituent of the Labour Party and of the International Socialist Congress; but it takes part freely in all constitutional movements, social, economic and political, which can be guided towards its own objects. Its direct business is (a) the propaganda of Socialism in its application to current problems; (b) investigation and discovery in social, industrial, political and economic relations; (c) the working out of Socialist principles in legislation and administrative reconstruction; (d) the publication of the results of its investigations and their practical lessons.

The Society, believing in equal citizenship of men and women in the fullest sense, is open to persons irrespective of sex, race or creed, who commit themselves to its aims and purposes as stated above, and undertake to promote its work.

The Society includes :—

I. Members, who must sign the Basis and be elected by the Committee. Their Subscriptions are not fixed; each is expected to subscribe annually according to his means. They control the Society through the Executive Committee (elected annually by ballot through a postal vote), and at its annual and other business meetings.

II. Associates, who sign a form expressing only general sympathy with the objects of the Society and pay not less than 10s. a year. They can attend all except the exclusively members' meetings, but have no control over the Society and its policy.

III. Subscribers, who must pay at least 5s. a year, and who can attend the Society's Ordinary Lectures.

The monthly paper, *Fabian News*, and the Tracts from time to time published in the well-known Fabian Series, are posted to all these classes. There are convenient Common Rooms, where light refreshments can be obtained, with an extensive library for the free use of members only.

Among the Society's activities (in which it places its services unreservedly at the disposal of the Labour Party and the Local Labour Parties all over the country, the Trade Unions and Trades Councils, and all other Labour and Socialist organisations), may be mentioned :

(i.) Free lectures by its members and officers;

(ii.) The well-known Fabian Book-boxes, each containing about three dozen of the best books on Economics, Politics and Social Problems, which can be obtained by any organisation of men or women for 15s. per annum, covering an exchange of books every three months;

(iii.) Answers to Questions from Members of Local Authorities and others on legal, technical or political matters of Local Government, etc.;

(iv.) Special subscription courses of lectures on new developments in thought;

(v.) Economic and social investigation and research, and publication of the results.

Lists of Publications, Annual Report, Form of Application as Member or Associate, and any other information can be obtained on application personally or by letter to the Secretary at the above address.

TOWARDS SOCIAL DEMOCRACY? By SIDNEY WEBB: 1s. n., post. 1d.
THIS MISERY OF BOOTS. By H. G. WELLS. 6d., post free 7d.

FABIAN TRACTS and LEAFLETS.

Tracts, each 16 to 52 pp., price 1d., or 9d. per doz., unless otherwise stated.
Leaflets, 4 pp. each, price 1d. for three copies, 2s. per 100, or 20/- per 1000.
The Set of 74, 7/6; post free 8 6. Bound in buckram, 12/6; post free 13/6-

I.—General Socialism in its various aspects.

TRACTS.—192. Guild Socialism By G. D. COLE, M.A. 180. The Philosophy of Socialism. By A. CLUTTON BROCK. 169. The Socialist Movement in Germany. By W. STEPHEN SANDERS. 2d. 159. The Necessary Basis of Society. By SIDNEY WEBB. 151. The Point of Honour. By RUTH C. BENTINCK. 147. Capital and Compensation. By E. R. PEASE. 146. Socialism and Superior Brains. By BERNARD SHAW. 2d, 142. Rent and Value. 138. Municipal Trading. 121. Public Service v. Private Expenditure. By Sir OLIVER LODGE. 2d. 107. Socialism for Millionaires. By BERNARD SHAW. 2d. 139. Socialism and the Churches. By Rev. JOHN CLIFFORD, D.D. 133. Socialism and Christianity. By Rev. PERCY DEARMER. 2d. 78. Socialism and the Teaching of Christ. By Dr. J. CLIFFORD. 42. Christian Socialism. By Rev. S. D. HEADLAM. 79. A Word of Remembrance and Caution to the Rich. By JOHN WOOLMAN. 72. The Moral Aspects of Socialism. By SIDNEY BALL. 69. Difficulties of Individualism. By S. WEBB. 51. Socialism: True & False. By S. WEBB. 2d. 45. The Impossibilities of Anarchism. By G. B. SHAW. 2d. 7. Capital and Land. 5. Facts for Socialists. 3d. LEAFLETS—13. What Socialism Is. 1. Why are the Many Poor?

II.—Applications of Socialism to Particular Problems.

TRACTS.—196. The Root of Labour Unrest. By SIDNDY WEBB. 2d. 195. The Scandal of the Poor Law. By C. M. LLOYD. 2d. 194. Taxes, Rates and Local Income Tax. By ROBERT JONES, D.Sc. 2d. 188. National Finance and a Levy on Capital. By SIDNEY WEBB. 2d. 187. The Teacher in Politics. By SIDNEY WEBB. 2d. 186. Central Africa and the League of Nations. By R. C. HAWKIN. 2d. 183. The Reform of the House of Lords. By SIDNEY WEBB. 181. When Peace Comes—the Way of Industrial Reconstruction. By SIDNEY WEBB. 2d. 178. The War; Women; and Unemployment. 2d. 177. Socialism and the Arts of Use. By A. CLUTTON BROCK. 175. The Economic Foundations of the Women's Movement. 2d. 173. Public v. Private Electricity Supply. 170. Profit-Sharing and Co-Partnership: a Fraud and Failure? 164. Gold and State Banking. 162. Family Life on a Pound a Week. By Mrs. REEVES. 2d. 161. Afforestation and Unemployment. 155. The Case against the Referendum. 152. Our Taxes as they are and as they ought to be. 2d. 145. The Case for School Nurseries. 140. Child Labor under Capitalism. 136. The Village and the Landlord. By EDW. CARPENTER. 144. Machinery: its Masters and Servants. 122. Municipal Milk and Public Health. 124. State Control of Trusts. LEAFLET.—104. How Trade Unions benefit Workmen.

III.—Local Government Powers: How to use them.

TRACTS.—189. Metropolitan Borough Councils. Their Constitution, Powers and Duties. By C. R. ATTLEE, M.A. 2d. 191. Borough Councils. Their Constitution, Powers and Duties. By C. R. ATTLEE, M.A. 2d. 193. Housing. By C. M. LLOYD, M.A. 2d. 189. Urban District Councils. By C. M. LLOYD, M.A. 2d. 172. What about the Rates? By S. WEBB. 2d. 62. Parish & District Councils. (Revised 1921). 2d. 137. Parish Councils and Village Life. 2d. LEAFLETS.—134. Small Holdings. 68. The Tenant's Sanitary Catechism. 71. Ditto for London.

IV.—General Politics and Fabian Policy.

TRACTS.—158. The Case against the C.O.S. By Mrs. TOWNSHEND. 41. The Fabian Society: its Early History. By BERNARD SHAW.

V.—Biographical Series. In portrait covers, 2d. and 3d.

182. Robert Owen, Idealist. By C. E. M. JOAD. 179. John Ruskin and Social Ethics. By Prof. EDITH MORLEY. 165. Francis Place. By ST. JOHN G. ERVINE. 166. Robert Owen, Social Reformer By Miss B. L. HUTCHINS. 167. William Morris and the Communist Ideal. By Mrs. TOWNSHEND. 168. John Stuart Mill. By JULIUS WEST. 174. Charles Kingsley and Christian Socialism. By C. E. VULLIAMY.

Printed by G. Standring. 7 Finsbury St., London, E C. and published by the Fabian Society, 25 Tothill Street, Westminster, London, S.W.

Fabian Tract No. 193.

HOUSING

BY

C. M. LLOYD, M.A.

———

PRICE THREEPENCE.

THE FABIAN SOCIETY, 25, TOTHILL STREET, WESTMINSTER, LONDON, S W 1.
MAY, 1920.

HOUSING.

THE " housing problem " first came into public prominence about two generations ago. At that time, with the development of the factory system, the exodus from the country to the towns was in full swing. Vast populations were herding together in discomfort, squalor and misery. Overcrowding and disease were taking a heavy toll ; jerry-building was rampant. The municipalities were either indifferent or helpless before the magnitude of the task. Parliament had for some years been toying with the question, and the Statute Book was ornamented with Labouring Classes Dwelling-Houses Acts, Artizans and Labourers Dwellings Improvements Acts and the like. At last in 1884 a Royal Commission was appointed to inquire into the Housing of the Working Classes in the United Kingdom, and six years later a pretty comprehensive measure, The Housing of the Working Classes Acts, 1890, was passed. This Act was, of course, not an adequate solution of the problem, though it is only fair to say that if the Local Authorities had shown more public spirit in exercising the powers which it gave them, a vast deal more might have been done. The next important advance was not made till nineteen years later, when the Housing and Town Planning Act, 1909, was passed. But the results of this both in the towns and in the country fell far short of public expectation. Finally came the War, an almost entire cessation of building for five years, and simultaneously a quickening of the public conscience as to the conditions in which British citizens ought to live. It was officially admitted that, in England and Wales alone, half a million new houses were urgently needed. The Labour Party put the figure for the United Kingdom at a million, and early in January, 1919, Lord Astor, the Parliamentary Secretary to the Ministry of Health, announced that the revised estimate for England and Wales was now 800,000. The Government was compelled to place the question in the forefront of its " reconstruction programme," and, after a great deal of deliberation and, as it now appears, with decidedly inadequate forethought, the Housing, Town Planning, etc., Act, was passed on 31st July, 1919.

THE LAW AND THE AUTHORITIES.

The law relating to the housing of the working classes is, therefore, at present contained in a number of Statutes, of which the chief are the three above mentioned—The Housing of the Working Classes Act, 1890, The Housing and Town Planning Act,

1909, and The Housing, Town Planning, etc., Act, 1919. These Acts give large powers of providing new houses, of demolishing old ones or making them fit for habitation, and of town planning. The responsibility for these tasks falls primarily on the public authorities. (1) The Town (County Borough and Borough) Councils, Urban District Councils and Rural District Councils, and in London the London County Council and the Metropolitan Borough Councils, are, for housing purposes, the Local Authorities proper. All these Authorities are empowered to appoint a Housing Committee, to which may be delegated all the duties and powers in connection with housing, except the power to borrow money or make a rate. Persons who are not members of the Council may be co-opted on the Housing Committee, and some of these ought certainly to be women; but there must be a majority of Councillors. (2) The County Councils form what may be called intermediate authorities, with powers of acting in default of District Councils as well as certain independent powers of their own. Every County Council is bound by law to appoint a Public Health and Housing Committee. (3) The Ministry of Health is the national authority, having also powers to act in default and the general supervision of the work of the Local Authorities, and to some extent too, as we shall see presently, of that of private individuals or societies building houses. Part of this supervision is exercised through regional officers, called Housing Commissioners, each acting for one of the Districts into which England and Wales are divided for the purpose. In London—i.e., the Metropolitan Police District, which extends beyond the Administrative County, and includes a ring of outer Districts, such as Barnet and Cheshunt to the north, Bromley and Epsom to the south, Romford to the east, Staines and Uxbridge to the west—there is a London Housing Board, consisting of three Members of Parliament, instead of a single Commissioner. The function of the Commissioners (and of the London Housing Board) is to stimulate the provision of houses by the Local Authorities, to give advice to all who are building houses for the working classes, to perform as much as possible of the detailed work of the Central Authority in its relations with the localities. They may even, in certain circumstances, approve the plans of Local Authorities, without first submitting them to the Ministry. Similarly, as regards insanitary houses and unhealthy areas, the Commissioners may give the fullest assistance to the Local Authorities, even to the extent of temporarily lending inspectors on the regional staff for the carrying out of detailed investigations.

The Districts of the Housing Commissioners are as follows :—
A.' Cumberland, Northumberland, Westmorland and Durham.
B. Yorkshire.
C. Lancashire and Cheshire.
D. Wales and Monmouth.
E. Staffordshire, Shropshire, Warwickshire, Worcestershire and Herefordshire.

F. Lincolnshire, Nottinghamshire, Derbyshire, Leicestershire, and Rutland.

G. Gloucestershire, Dorset, Somerset, Wilts, Devon and Cornwall.

H. Hants, Isle of Wight, Sussex, Surrey and Kent (so far as not in the Metropolitan Police District).

K. London (Metropolitan Police District).

L. Berks, Bucks, Oxon, Northants, Bedfordshire, Hunts, Herts (so far as not in the Metropolitan Police District).

M. Cambridgeshire, Norfolk, Suffolk, Essex (so far as not in the Metropolitan Police District).

The exact functions and the relations of the Central and Local Authorities will appear as we discuss the powers and duties of each under the Acts. These powers and duties we shall, for the sake of clearness, deal with under the four separate heads of (A) Provision of new houses (including conversion of existing houses into flats, etc.) ; (B) Slum Areas ; (C) Unfit Houses ; (D) Town Planning.

(A) Provision of New Houses.

The Act of 1919 made it the duty of every Local Authority within three months (*i.e.*, before 1st November, 1919) to consider the need for working class houses in its area, and to submit for the approval of the Ministry of Health an outline scheme for the provision of such new houses as might be necessary. In cases where the circumstances make it desirable, two or more Local Authorities may combine in a joint scheme. And a County Council may, with the Ministry's consent, come into a joint scheme. All schemes must show approximately the number and kind of houses, the area of land, the number of houses per acre and the time expected for completion, and the estimated cost. The Ministry, if not satisfied with a scheme, may reject it or require amendments.

It does not follow, however, that the Local Authority is bound to undertake the building of new houses itself. What is required is that it (and the Ministry) shall be satisfied that the necessary houses are being provided. There are two other means of providing them. The first is by Public Utility Societies. A Public Utility Society is a Society registered under the Industrial and Provident Societies Act of 1893 (which, it is to be noted, is the Act under which Co-operative Societies are registered) for carrying on "any industries, businesses or trades specified in or authorised by its rules." It must have at least 7 members and a secretary, and no individual member must hold shares amounting to more than £200 in value (except in Loan Stock). It must not pay interest or dividends exceeding 6 per cent. A Society, then, "whose objects include the erection, improvement or management of houses for the working classes," and which satisfies the above conditions, may get financial assistance from the Government, or from a Local Authority or County Council, in the shape of subsidies as well as loans. (For this, see below, p.   ).

Secondly, the private builder may erect houses, which he may either retain in his own hands or, subject to the consent of the Ministry of Health, sell or lease to the Local Authority. In the latter case the Local Authority need only approve the site and the general outline of the scheme, and can then leave it to the private builder to obtain the detailed approval necessary at the various stages from the Housing Commissioners or the Ministry. In either case the private builder will be entitled to a subsidy from the State, under the Housing (Additional Powers) Act, passed in December, 1919, (See below p. 6)

LONDON.

In London (*i.e.*, the Administrative County) the powers and duties in housing matters are divided between the London County Council and the Metropolitan Borough Councils. If new houses are to be provided outside the Administrative County, the L.C.C. is the Local Authority charged with the duty, and the L.C.C. has, in fact, a large scheme in hand in the District of Barking. But each Metropolitan Borough is the Local Authority within its own boundaries, with two important provisos however. The L.C.C. may submit and carry out a scheme for the use of land in any Metropolitan Borough to meet the housing needs of districts outside the Borough. And secondly, the Ministry may order that any of the powers or duties of a Metropolitan Borough Council in regard to the provision of houses shall be transferred to the L.C.C. It may also transfer the powers or duties of the L.C.C to a Metropolitan Borough Council ; though this, of course, it is very unlikely to do.

As regards the City, the Common Council, which is the Local Housing Authority there, may enter into agreements with the L.C.C. for carrying out any scheme and for the apportionment of the expenses of it.

POWERS OF COUNTY COUNCILS, ETC.

If a Local Authority fails to carry out its duty to provide houses, or if it appears better that the County Council should prepare and carry out a scheme, the Ministry of Health may transfer the obligations of the Local Authority to the County Council. And, furthermore, the Ministry of Health may itself act in default of the County Council or of a Local Authority, if necessary. In the case of a joint scheme, the Ministry may either authorise the County Council to act in default of the Local Authorities, or may act itself.

But, apart from this, a County Council has certain limited powers of building for itself in the first instance. It may provide houses for any persons in its employment or paid by it—*e.g.*, for policemen, roadmen or teachers. And it may besides erect cottages in connection with Small Holdings which it provides. ●

A County Council also retains its old rights under former Housing Acts of (a) complaining to the Ministry if a Local Authority is not carrying out its duties ; (b) applying to the Ministry for an Order conferring on the County Council the powers of a Rural District Council to provide working class dwellings ; (c) holding a Local inquiry, on the complaint of a Parish Council or Parish Meeting or four inhabitant householders in a Rural District, into the default of the Rural District, and itself taking over the Rural District Council's powers, if satisfied that a case is made out.

CONVERSION OF HOUSES INTO FLATS.

Local Authorities have power to buy houses and convert them into working class dwellings. They may also assist a private owner who reconstructs, énlarges or improves buildings so as to make them suitable for working class dwellings, by making a loan to him, after the work has been satisfactorily carried out, of the cost incurred, not exceeding half the value of the property mortgaged.

FINANCE.

The problem of providing houses is now, whatever it was before, a national one, and it is evident that the Local Authorities could not possibly bear the whole of the cost. A Local Authority is only required by the Housing Act of 1919 to pay such a sum as will be produced by a penny rate, provided that the Ministry of Health is satisfied that the expenditure is reasonable and provided that the scheme is carried out by the 31st July, 1922, or such extended time as the Ministry may allow. The difference between this and the actual cost will be met by " moneys provided by Parliament "—i.e., out of the taxes.

Loans may be raised by Local Authorities, secured on the rates, at 6 per cent., and by Public Utility Societies also at 6 per cent., if repayable within 50 years. Companies and private persons, moreover, may similarly obtain loans at slightly less advantageous rates. A Public Utility Society may also get an annual subsidy from the State equal to 50 per cent. till March 31st, 1927, and after that 30 per cent., of the total loan charges (including interest and the payments for redemption of principal) during a maximum period of 50 years.

A County Council desirous of acquiring land to provide houses for its employees may negotiate a loan to be repaid within 80 years (instead of 30 years, as formerly), and it will receive an annual subsidy from the State equal to 50 per cent. till March 31st, 1927, and after that 30 per cent., of the annual loan charges. But this subsidy is subjéct to the conditions that the County Council's scheme has made such progress as is judged reasonable by the

Ministry of Health before the 31st July, 1920, and that it is completed before the 31st July, 1922, or such further period as the Minister may allow.

By the Housing (Additional Powers) Act, 1919, further incentives are offered to building. " Any persons or bodies of persons constructing houses," which satisfy the Ministry of Health, may receive subsidies from the State. It is laid down that the total sum to be paid for this purpose out of the taxes shall not exceed £15,000,000, the amount allowed for each house being £130, £140 or £160, according to its size. No grants will be made for houses with more than four bedrooms, or a superficial floor area of more than 1,400 feet, and the number of houses per acre will not be allowed to exceed eight in agricultural areas, and, except with the sanction of the Minister, twenty in urban areas (twelve being regarded as the normal standard).

Moreover, the Act provides that a Local Authority may, with the Ministry's approval, borrow money by the issue of " local bonds." These bonds are to be secured upon the rates, revenues and property of the Local Authority, and are to be issued for £5, £10, £20, £50 or £100, redeemable within periods of not less than five years.

THE PROGRESS OF " THE 500,000 HOUSES."

Having now shown briefly what can be done—on paper, let us see what has been done in fact. The amount of progress made has been a staggering disappointment. By 13th December, 1919, more than a year after the Armistice and four and a half months after the passing of the new Act—7,604 schemes, covering 75,170 houses, had been submitted to the Ministry of Health. Of these only 3,007 schemes, covering 59,964 houses, had been approved. The schemes of Public Utility Societies, which are included in these totals, amounted to 88, of which 27, covering 1,565 houses, had been approved. There was subsequently some acceleration; at February 14th, 1920, 8677 schemes, covering 121,660 houses, had been submitted, 4,471 schemes, covering 107.269 houses, had been approved. Public Utility Societies' schemes showed 115 submitted, and 43, covering 1,877 houses, approved. But down to March, 1920, comparatively few of the " approved " houses had been completed ; many had not even been begun.

What are the causes of this unsatisfactory state of things ? They can be put under six heads—(1) remissness of the Local Authorities, (2) remissness of the Central Authority, (3) difficulties in connection with building materials, (4) shortage of labour, (5) unwillingness of contractors to build, (6) financial difficulties. Of these the first two are probably the least important. There was at first a good deal of mutual recrimination between the Central and the Local Authorities. The Ministry accused the localities of being dilatory in producing schemes ; the localities complained bitterly that the red tape and the burdensome requirements of the

Ministry were thwarting and delaying them. Doubtless neither side has been entirely free from blame. Many of the Local Authorities have taken a long time to move. When they have moved, they in turn have shown impatience at the slowness of Whitehall. But a great deal of the withholding of approval by the Ministry has been perfectly proper from the public point of view. Often enough a Local Authority has submitted a scheme in which it proposed to pay a grossly exaggerated price for land, and the Ministry has acted fairly in insisting on an independent valuation by the Inland Revenue Valuers. Hundreds of thousands of pounds have thus been saved, which would otherwise have passed from the pockets of the taxpayers into those of greedy landowners. Again, the Ministry has held up schemes because the design was not satisfactory, generally in one or other of two ways. Either it was considered that it was not economical enough—that a saving of cost could be effected in some way which would not really impair the quality of the house. Or, on the other hand, the scheme of the Local Authority savoured too much of jerry-building. In either case the Ministry was justified in objecting to the scheme. At the same time there have been cases where the Ministry has tried to force the Local Authorities to save expense by putting up houses of a really inferior type. The gravest ground of complaint, however, which the Local Authorities have had, has been in connection with the financing of their schemes, as we shall see presently. But this is rather the fault of the Cabinet and the Treasury than of the Ministry of Health. Broadly speaking, it is futile to blame either the Central or the Local Authorities, because we have not got our houses quickly enough. It is the other difficulties which have been, and are, really serious.

DIFFICULTIES AS TO BUILDING MATERIALS.

It is not necessary to go into detail on this point. That there has been a shortage of building materials—bricks, lime, cement, timber, ·tiles, slates, corrugated iron and many other things—everyone knows. And the difficulty has been made worse by the lack of transport. All sorts of suggestions as to "alternative methods of construction" have been put forward. Local Authorities are allowed to relax their building bye-laws, and the Ministry of Health will now approve of such materials as chalk, clay and *pisê de terre* (*i.e.*, rammed or compressed earth) being used in place of bricks, or of wooden huts, timber frames, concrete blocks, and even of frameworks of houses "composed of the disused under-parts of motor cars, lorries, tram rails" and other surplus war materials. The huge increase of cost of all ordinary building materials has, of course, been a factor in the problem. Official figures recently published show that, between 1914 and 1919, the price of bricks increased by 170 per cent., of cement by nearly 200 per cent., of timber by 300 per cent., and of such articles as nails and kitchen ranges by from 250 to 400 per cent. Allegations have been made of heavy profiteering by rings of merchants holding up the supply and the price of various of materials. These allegations, though they have been hotly denied, have certainly not been disproved, and the public has learned enough about capitalistic " patriotism " during the war to have a fairly firm opinion on the point. It will await with interest the report of a Committee which was eventually appointed in February, 1920, to inquire into the matter.

The Shortage of Labour.

The number of operatives in the building industry is very much smaller than it was five years ago. A great many men have been killed or crippled in the war, and practically no new labour has been trained. It is probable that the diminution amounts to something like 100,000, a large percentage being skilled men, who cannot easily be replaced. Early in 1919 there were about 14 per cent. of building trade operatives unemployed ; twelve months later the percentage was five, and if we take only the skilled men, without whom nothing can be done, there was practically no unemployment at all. At the beginning of 1920 there were, according to the Secretary of the National Federation of Building Trades Operatives, only 134 out of 100,000 of his members in receipt of unemployment benefit. The Trade Unions, not unnaturally, in view of the obvious dangers and of past experiences, would not consent to " dilution," especially while the Government refused to release many skilled operatives from the Army. But, furthermore, it became only too clear during the autumn that a great number of the available workmen were not available for building new houses at all. Fifty or sixty per cent. of them were busy on repairs— some of them necessary, no doubt, but others quite unnecessary, and " luxury " work, such as cinemas, bandstands, restaurants and various industrial and commercial buildings which could very well wait for a year or two. The attraction of this repairing and " luxury " work goes far to explain another serious cause of delay—the unwillingness of contractors to embark on house-building.

Unwillingness of Contractors to Build.

The builders soon found that these jobs were highly remunerative. They could do their business at a minimum of risk and a maximum of profit. They could dominate the market in a way which was impossible under the pressure of competition before he war. Why then should they tender to Local Authorities or peculate in house-building on their own account ? When they id tender, it was pretty clear that the tenders were all too often on-competitive. If they were competitive we should not have e en, as we have seen again and again, variations of £200 or more between the lowest tenders in two districts in which the cost of labour and materials were on the same level. In short, the builders have not wanted to build unless at exorbitant prices.

FINANCIAL DIFFICULTIES.

Before the war a decent cottage could be built for £250 or £300 ; now the price ranges from £500 to £1,150, and few tenders are put in for less than £600. The following table, given by the Ministry of Health, tells its own tale.

COST OF HOUSES.

Cost of Houses of different types for which tenders have been approved and examined at the Ministry of Health up to 24th January, 1920. The cost of land, road making and sewering is excluded :—

Cost as approved	Non-Parlour Type.					Parlour Type.				Total Number of Houses
	Living-room, Scullery, and				Average cost per House	Parlour, Living-room, Scullery, and			Average cost per House	
	1 Bed-room	2 Bed-rooms	3 Bed-rooms	4 Bed-rooms		2 Bed-rooms	3 Bed-rooms	4 Bed-rooms		
					£				£	
£400 and under	—	—	24	—	400	—	—	—	—	24
£401 to £500	4	—	110	—	447	—	32	—	463	146
£501 to £600	—	216	561	—	569	13	160	—	572	950
£601 to £700	—	142	1623	6	658	—	135	—	670	1906
£701 to £800	—	4	1877	3	745	—	1912	73	762	3869
£801 to £900	—	—	323	4	833	71	2078	185	844	2661
£901 and over	—	—	—	—	—	—	343	79	929	422
	4	362	4518	13	£684	84	4660	337	£803	9978
	4897					5081				

The average cost of the 9,978 houses is £744.
The average cost of the 4,897 non-parlour houses is £684.
The average cost of the 5,081 parlour houses is £803.
Of the 9,978 houses :—
8,665 were in urban districts, and cost on the average £749 each.
1,313 were in rural districts, and cost on the average £699 each.
Throughout the autumn complaints were going up from the Local Authorities. The Chairman of the Housing Committee of the Rochdale Town Council observed that prices charged by builders were three-and-a-half times above pre-war prices. Sir J. Tudor Walters, the Paymaster General, said in the House of Commons on 8th December, that he believed that any contractor who wanted to, could build these houses for at least £300 less

than he was doing to-day. The builders indignantly deny profiteering, and Mr. Lloyd George has given them a testimonial of " integrity and patriotism." The plain citizen will draw his own conclusions.

But the problem of the Local Authorities has been rendered still more difficult by the requirement laid down by the Government that they shall charge a commercial rent for their new houses. In 1927 it is supposed that a normal level of prices will have been reached. Rents, therefore, it is suggested, should be fixed at a sum " which will be an economic rent on the probable cost of building in 1927," and this is to be reckoned at two-thirds of the present cost. What would this mean ? It would mean in many cases a prohibitive rent. One important Town Council in the North pointed out that on this basis the " economic rent " of a number of new cottages they were building would amount to £2 4s. apiece per week. Many other Councils would have to charge £1 or 25s. a week. And what would be the result of these enormous rents for the new houses ? The Increase of Rent (War Restrictions) Act, by which rents have been kept down during the war, would be repealed, and the rents of old houses would immediately leap up to the level of the new. That is to say, a handsome unearned increment would be presented automatically to house-owners all over the country. On the other hand, it is not likely that the working classes could, or would, submit to paying greatly increased rents without a corresponding increase of wages. The demand would be put forward for extra wages to meet the extra cost of living, and the demand could not easily be resisted. With wages risen, prices would rise, and the last state of the country would be worse than its first. Eventually the Ministry of Health has been forced by the pressure of criticism to issue revised regulations, making it clear that if it is not found reasonably possible to obtain a commercial rent based on the estimated cost of building in 1927, the Local Authority will not be penalised by the difference falling on the rates. The Local Authorities are still expected, however, to charge the highest rent they reasonably can. Any dispute on this point between the Ministry and the Local Authority is to be settled by a standing tribunal of five members, two appointed by the Ministry, two by associations of Local Authorities, with an independent chairman chosen by these four.

But another financial difficulty confronts the Local Authorities. They have to raise money for the capital expenditure on their housing schemes. At first the Treasury " particularly desired that Authorities should raise such loans in the open market " ; but later it was announced that the Government would be responsible for finding the money for the smaller Local Authorities, *i.e.*, those with a rateable value of £200,000 or less. But it soon appeared that the larger Authorities, thus left to their own resources, were not easily able to raise money in the open market, and it is evident that if their programmes of house building are to increase as they ought to increase, their embarrassment will become still greater. The remedy, which has been urged very strongly upon the Government, is a National Housing Loan—that is to say, that the Government should put all the Local Authorities, large as well as small, on the same footing, and thus make capital available where it is wanted at a fair rate of interest.

The Government's Remedies.

In December, 1919, when these difficulties could be no longer overlooked, the Government were forced to try to find some way round them. Their chief efforts are embodied in the Housing (Additional Powers) Act, to which we have referred above. They believe that the subsidy to the private builder (reinforced by the Prime Minister's touching appeal to his patriotism) will enormously stimulate building. And by the provision that a Local Authority shall have power to prohibit the erection of unessential buildings in its district, a good deal of labour will necessarily be directed from the "luxury" work on which it has hitherto been engaged. Labour has, of course, raised its voice strongly against this subsidising of private enterprise out of the public funds. But the Government pins its faith to the private builder. The Minister of Health, in reply to a question whether Municipalities should be allowed to construct new houses themselves by the direct employment of labour, said very guardedly that he was "prepared to consider proposals for the erection of houses by direct labour where it appears that economy is likely to result."

How much further towards "the million houses" this new plan will take us, remains to be seen. At present the builders do not appear to be highly enamoured of the proffered gift. Fears have been expressed that the standard of house that may now be built will be lower than that required of the Local Authorities, but Dr. Addison asserts that the Ministry of Health will take care that this shall not be so. He cannot, however, so easily insure that the new houses will be built where they are most needed. There is every danger that they will spring up haphazard in those places and on those sites which suit the contractor rather than the public. It is, in short, a retrograde step to relax at any point the control of the public authorities.

So far as the Local Authorities' own schemes are concerned, better progress may be made as a result of an agreement come to with the building trade by the Ministry of Health, under which builders will share out the work under a scheme, each undertaking a certain number of houses at a certain price. Dr. Addison has stated definitely to a deputation from the National Housing Council that Local Authorities might enter into arrangements with these builders for the erection of the required houses on the basis of prime cost plus a fixed charge to cover profit, use of plant and establishment charges. It is obvious that a costing system specially adapted to the needs of the building trade, with contracts at a price based on the actual cost of building plus a fixed profit (not a percentage on cost), opens up great possibilities. During the war costing systems were applied in the production of munitions, and saved hundreds of millions of pounds to the public. There is no reason why great economies should not similarly be effected in the production of houses. Moreover, such a system is desirable in the interests of efficiency in the building trade. A proper costing system, as the National Housing Council has urged, " will lay bare many cardinal faults. In some cases the plant will be found to be out of date, and in great need of additions. In other cases the management of labour will be such as to encourage and even develop slackness. In others the choice of markets for building materials will show lack of sound business acumen. But the best feature of all will be that the Government and the Local Authorities will be able to secure that, by the adoption of a good costing system, real facts instead of vague statements shall be available with regard to questions of speed in production and economy in the use of materials."

To the demand for a National Housing Loan the Government have not acceded. Dr. Addison is " inclined to be sceptical in regard to the representations of a number of great municipalities that they were unable to raise the money needed for housing schemes." That, of course, is not surprising ; to disbelieve in the complaints of its critics is the last refuge of a Government which has earned the distrust of everyone. However, the Local Authorities are to issue Local Bonds, which are to be gilt-edged securities and, the Government hopes, an attractive investment. They do not seem likely to be a good substitute for the National Loan ; their success is, to say the least, problematical. But they serve the purpose of preventing the spineless municipalities from " leaning up against the Chancellor of the Exchequer "—which is Dr. Addison's happy way of rebuking those who want the government to play a national hand in a matter of national concern.

Two other difficulties remain—the shortage of labour and of materials. As regards the first, all that the Government can do to increase the total supply is to release 20,000 or 30,000 men from the Army, and to hope that more operatives will be trained as quickly as possible. It is evident that the labour difficulty cannot be settled by a wave of the hand—even of the hand of so potent a wizard as Mr. Lloyd George. It is not likely to be settled until steps are taken to put the building trade on a proper footing, and to make proper provision against the disease of unemployment, with which it is cursed.

Meantime, considerable hopes have been raised by an independent move on the part of the Building Trade Unions. On the initiative of the Bricklayers, the operatives in Lancashire have formed a " Manchester Building Guild," embracing all the Unions in the area (and excluding employers), which has already agreed with the Irlam Urban District Council to erect a number of houses, and is in negotiation with the Manchester City Council for a similar undertaking on a still larger scale. The Guild charges the Local

Authority the cost of the job plus 10 per cent. to cover all overhead expenses—including provision against unemployment; for the operatives are not to lose their pay, if they are unable to work owing to weather or other causes. This scheme has attracted wide public notice, and it has inspired attempts at similar organisations in other towns. The Minister of Health has shown himself not unfavourable, and the experiment, if it proves successful, may have important consequences not merely in the better provision of houses, but for the future of the building industry as a whole. It is noteworthy that the Manchester Guild has declared itself in no sense hostile to the proposals for a National Building Guild. It has, indeed, definitely stated that it will be ready to merge itself in a National Guild, if such a body is established presently by the " Building Trades Parliament," or otherwise.

As for materials, there should be some improvement with the promised increase and speeding up of transport, and, for the rest, our hopes are to be centred in the blessed word " de-control." Optimists believe that, as a result of this, prices will soar for a time, but that the consequent increase in supply will presently bring them down, while the Profiteering Act will restrain gross exploitation. This is, indeed, a very rosy expectation! At the same time there is not much to be said in favour of the retention of control—certainly not of the feeble kind that we have had in the past. And a really rigid control of prices is, for various reasons, not a practical policy. The best method would be for the State to come in as a competitor in the production of some of the chief building materials.

WHAT THE LOCAL AUTHORITIES SHOULD DO.

The Local Authorities meanwhile ought obviously to get on with their proper task of municipal housing, despite the discouragement of the Government. They ought, wherever possible, to try to carry out their building by direct labour, with their own materials and their own plant, or through the " Guilds," when these are established. If they are bound to employ contractors, they ought, as far as possible, to make use of the cost plus profit system referred to above. They ought to exercise the greatest care in the public interest that there is no skimping or falling below standard in the work of the contractor. There is, despite official assurances, a real danger lest the Ministry, in its anxiety to see houses built, should allow, or even encourage, the Local Authorities to go on lowering standards. Labour Councillors at least will not forget that there is a problem of quality in housing as well as of quantity. The old policy was to save a few pounds—and the new policy is to save a few weeks—by means of the ancient art of jerry-building, by leaving out such useless incumbrances as parlours or front doors or baths, or, in short, by erecting " workmen's cottages " instead of houses. That policy ought to be resisted at all costs and in every detail. Every Local Authority should see that it has the assistance of an Advisory Committee of women in this matter—and the most important sort of women will be working women. Women's Advisory Committees have been formed in a good many places, and the Minister of Health is anxious to see them in every Urban District. The Local Authority might summon representatives of such organisations as the Women's Co-operative Guild, Women's Citizen Association, district nurses and midwives, women's sections of local Labour Parties, and so on, for the purpose of forming the Advisory Committee, or if it is in any doubt, it might consult the Standing Joint Committee of Industrial Women's Organisations as to the bodies to be approached for representatives. In Rural Districts, where it may not be possible to form permanent Advisory Committees, there should be a specially convened meeting of women in the parish concerned to give their advice on the plans of proposed houses.

(B) SLUM AREAS

A large proportion of the inhabitants of this country is housed, as everyone knows, under disgusting conditions. To prove, however, that we are a civilised nation, we have long been in the habit of passing admirable laws to remedy this scandal. But unfortunately it has been far easier to pass the laws than to get them properly carried out. It is true that many of the large-scale slums of a generation ago no longer exist. In Liverpool, for example, between 1901 and 1912, eighteen unhealthy areas were dealt with, involving 2,521 houses. And some years earlier (betwen 1893 and 1897), the London County Council had, by the famous Boundary St. Scheme, swept away fifteen acres of filthy and dangerous slums sheltering no less than 5,719 inhabitants. Yet there are still some of these plague spots left, as, for instance, the notorious Brady Street Area in Bethnal Green. This foul conglomeration has been denounced, disputed about, patched up, and tolerated for half a century or more. A Local Government Board inquiry in 1913 showed that it comprised 7 acres with 528 houses and tenements occupied by over 3,000 persons, and enjoying a death rate of 34.74 per 1,000 as compared with the rate of 16.71 for the whole Borough. Plans for dealing with it are still in course of preparation. There are also plenty of smaller slums ; there are vast numbers of back-to-back houses (though happily the erection of new back-to-backs was prohibited by the Act of 1909), packed tenement dwellings, and squalid little death traps all over the country. Many amiable persons would refuse to call all these " slums." But nobody but a fool, or one who considers the national welfare to consist merely in the saving of money, would dare to claim that they are healthy.

How does the law stand to-day ? Under Part I. of the Housing Act of 1890, strengthened by certain provisions in the Acts of 1909 and 1919, the Local Authorities have wide powers to clear or reconstruct large unhealthy areas.

The Medical Officer of Health will generally at his own initiative make an inspection of the area, and he is bound to do so on the request of a magistrate or six ratepayers. If he considers that an improvement scheme should be made, he must make a representation to the Local Authority. If he neglects to do so, then a Justice of the Peace or six ratepayers may get an inquiry by the Ministry of Health, and the Ministry may make an order equivalent to an official representation. The Local Authority, if satisfied of the truth of the representation and of the adequacy of their own resources, must order an improvement scheme. In default of the Local Authority, the Ministry of Health may order a scheme to be carried out. And if the Local Authority fail to comply with the Ministry's requirements within a fixed time, the Ministry may authorise the County Council to act, or may act itself.

Every Local Authority (except Rural District Councils and Metropolitan Borough Councils, which have not powers under Part I.) is now required to submit to the Ministry of Health, before 31st July, 1920, definite proposals for dealing with unhealthy areas.

What is an Unhealthy Area?

An "unhealthy area" is one in which the houses, courts, or alleys are unfit for human habitation, or the streets or houses so narrow, close, badly arranged or lighted or ventilated, so defective from a sanitary point of view or in such a bad condition, as to be dangerous to the health of persons living in or near the area. Such an area may be dealt with in one of two ways. Either some of the houses may be demolished, so as to enable the remainder to be made habitable, or the whole may be swept away. The first has generally been the favourite way, because it is cheaper, and only the poor live in "unhealthy areas." This "slum patching" will, of course, have to go on for the present, owing to the shortage of accommodation; but it is important that the Local Authority should only regard it as a temporary expedient.

Improvements in the Law.

In the past the Local Authorities have undoubtedly been seriously handicapped in dealing with this matter, especially by the great tenderness which the law has shown to the slum landlords, and by the idiotic requirements as to the re-housing of the persons turned out by an improvement scheme. Under the new law, however, the Local Authority is in a much better position. In the first place, if a slum area has to be cleared, the price to be paid is now the value of the land alone, without any compensation for the buildings. If the whole of the land to be cleared is required for re-housing, or partly for re-housing and partly as an open space, the price to be paid will be its value to a person who proposes to develop it for working class dwellings Formerly the Local Authority might have had to pay a price which it would have fetched for industrial or business premises, even though it was actually used for re-housing.

Secondly, though the law is not yet entirely satisfactory in the matter of re-housing, there has been a great change of public opinion, and it appears likely that the Ministry of Health will not follow the old reactionary Local Government Board by constantly insisting on " central re-housing." The Ministry, indeed, is already urging that Local Authorities should always carefully inquire into the genuineness of claims that residence very near to the place of employment is essential, and not allow the life-long attachment of the slum dweller to his slum to override the general good. They urge also the importance of open spaces, planted with grass or shrubs or trees, of playgrounds for children, and the like, where re-housing on the cleared site is carried out.

Thirdly, as in the case of building new houses, so in the case of destroying old ones and re-housing, the Local Authority is entitled to substantial assistance from the Exchequer, since it is only required to spend itself up to the limit of a penny rate. Furthermore, the Ministry may, under sect. 16 of the Act of 1919, for the purpose of assisting the preparation and execution of schemes, or of making immediate provision while schemes are being prepared, acquire and hold land and buildings, and erect, alter, enlarge, repair or improve buildings and dispose of any such lands or buildings.

On the other hand, the anxiety of any Local Authority to clear away its slums is unfortunately bound for the moment to be affected by the house famine. It will hardly be practicable in present circumstances to carry out immediately many large clearances. But every Local Authority can, and ought to, prepare without delay a comprehensive programme which can be put into force gradually, beginning at once with what is most urgent.

(C) Unfit Houses.

Apart from the slum areas, the Local Authorities have the very important task of dealing with individual houses (or small groups of houses) which are unfit for habitation. This is in one sense an even more serious and more exacting task. The slum area stares you in the face ; the unfit house will often have to be discovered. Constant watchfulness is required on the part of the Local Authority and its sanitary officers, and constant attention to detail. The owners will naturally not be anxious to expose the defects of their houses, and often enough the tenants will give little help. Any Local Authority which is remiss in this matter is guilty of a crime against society, for bad housing conditions are one of the causes of high death rates, and of an enormous amount of sickness, physical inefficiency and moral degradation. If statistics are wanted, they can be found in the Medical Officer of

Health's Reports and in almost any book on Housing, though it is well to remember that these must be taken with care, since other causes besides bad housing are operating in high mortality and disease rates. It is important, however, to call attention to the fact that the problem is not, as is sometimes supposed, entirely or even chiefly an urban one. Many of the "cottage homes" of rural England are little better than whited sepulchres. Many more of them, if not actually a serious danger to health, are not reasonably fit to live in. Here are some of the results of an inspection in the County of Somerset in the years 1911, 1912 and 1913. In the Rural District of Bath, out of 774 houses inspected, 58 or 7·5 per cent. were found to be unfit for habitation, 251 or 32·5 per cent. "defective though not unfit." In the Rural District of Williton 848 houses were inspected; 62, or 7·3 per cent. were unfit, and 603 or 71·1 per cent. defective. In the Rural District of Taunton 1797 houses were inspected; 171, or 9.5 per cent. were unfit, and 1,375 or 76·5 per cent. defective. Similar figures could be given for almost any County. Somerset is not singled out because it is particularly bad ; indeed it has an M.O.H., who is a well known and zealous housing reformer, and the County Council itself has shown much activity. But it is clear, in the face of such evidence, that there has been gross neglect in the past, and that the task of making " healthy homes for all " will be a long and heavy one.

What the Local Authorities can do.

The Local Authorities which are charged to deal with these unfit houses are, as laid down by Part II. of the Housing Act of 1890, the Borough and Urban and Rural District Councils, and the Metropolitan Borough Councils in London. The London County Council is not primarily concerned, except in a case where more than ten houses are included. The London County Council may, however, act, if it considers that the Metropolitan Borough Council is in default, or at the request of the Metropolitan Borough Council.

The Local Authority is required to make periodic inspections, and the Medical Officer of Health must, either of his own initiative or on the complaint of a Justice of the Peace or four inhabitant householders, make a representation to his Council as to any dwellings which are unhealthy. An " unhealthy dwelling house " is defined in the Housing Act of 1909, as one which is in a state so dangerous or injurious to health as to be unfit for human habitation (including every sleeping room of which the floor is more than 3 feet below the street level, unless it is seven feet high and complies with certain regulations). With such unhealthy houses the Act of 1909 also couples " obstructive buildings "—*i.e.*, buildings which, though not in themselves unhealthy, yet by reason of their position impede ventilation or conduce to the unhealthiness of other buildings or prevent the remedying of such unhealthiness.

The Local Authority, when satisfied that a dwelling is unhealthy, has several courses open to it. (1) It may make a closing order prohibiting the use of the house till it has been rendered fit for human habitation. Fourteen days are allowed for the owner of the house to appeal to the Ministry of Health against the closing order. If he does not appeal, or if his appeal is unsuccessful, the closing order becomes effective and the occupiers must move out, their cost of removal being in certain cases at the charge of the owner (see Act of 1909, sect. 17 (4) and (5), and Act of 1919, Schedule II.). (2) After a closing order has been in force for three months, the Local Authority, if they consider the house is not being made, or cannot be made, healthy, must issue a demolition order (from which the owner has a right of appeal to the Ministry of Health). If it appears that the house can and will be made healthy by the owner, the demolition order may be suspended for six months to allow him to carry out the work. (3) After a demolition order has been in force for three months, the owner must pull the house down. Failing him the Local Authority must pull it down at his expense. No house or other building which will be injurious to health may then be erected on the site. (4) Under sect. 28 of the Act of 1919, a Local Authority may serve a notice upon the owner of an unfit house requiring him within a reasonable time, not being less than 21 days, to make it " in all respects reasonably fit for human habitation." If the owner does not comply with the notice, the Local Authority may do the work at his expense, provided it can be done without reconstruction. It is important to notice that it is not necessary, before such an order for repairs can be issued, that the house should be in a state so dangerous or injurious to health as to justify a closing order.

As regards obstructive buildings, the Local Authority considers the cost of pulling them down and acquiring the land, and may after hearing the owner, make a demolition order (from which he has the right of appeal to the Ministry of Health). When the demolition order becomes operative, either the owner or the Local Authority must demolish the buildings, and the land may be retained by the owner or bought by the Local Authority.

When an area has been cleared by the demolition of unhealthy houses or obstructive buildings, and is too small for an " improvement scheme " under Part I. of the Act of 1890, then the Local Authority may, if it so desires, prepare a scheme under Part II. That is to say, reconstruction may be carried out by the minor authorities—Rural District and Metropolitan Borough Councils— on a small scale similar to that described above for a large slum area. The powers of the Ministry of Health to act in default, or to authorise the County Council to act in default, of the Local Authority are similar for schemes under Part I. or Part II.

A Local Authority is not, of course, bound to build new houses on a cleared site. It may, if it chooses, dedicate the site as a highway or open space, or exchange it for other land for workmen's dwellings.

It will be worth while now to examine in a little more detail what we mean by a house being reasonably fit for human habitation. It is, of course, useless at the present time to aim at Utopian ideals. A Local Authority is not a Harlequin in a Pantomime who can produce with a tap of his wand a wonderful transformation scene, and millions of citizens must continue to put up with discomfort, inconveniences and ugliness in their houses. But they need not be satisfied with anything that makes seriously for ill-health. Let us lay down certain minimum conditions of fitness.

Every house ought to be :—

(1) *Free from serious dampness.* Porous walls, the absence of gutter pipes, of a damp-proof course or of sub-soil drainage, the banking of earth against the walls, are some of the commonest causes of unhealthiness.

(2) *Properly lighted and ventilated.* It is worth remembering that the presence of a window, or what looks like a window, is not by itself a sufficient guarantee of ventilation. Proper ventilation means *through* ventilation.

(3) *Properly drained and provided with adequate sanitary conveniences, as well as with a sink and suitable arrangements for disposing of slop water.*

(4) *In good general repair.* Among the commonest defects under this head are bad paving in yards ; broken roofs, eaves, gutters, etc. ; cracked or peeling walls, dirty or loose wall-papers ; broken ceilings, floors, stairs ; rotten window frames ; warped doors ; stopped-up or broken ventilators and flues ; insufficient or defective cupboards ; broken or badly set grates, stoves or ranges.

(5) *Provided with a proper water supply,* and

(6) *With adequate washing accommodation (and in new houses, of course, a bath),* and

(7) *With a well-ventilated larder or store for food (if possible on the north or east side of the dwelling).*

This is not an exhaustive list. Many other matters, small, maybe, but important, will suggest themselves to any practical person. But how many Local Authorities maintain a decent standard on these seven points ? It is safe to say that there is not a town or a village in the kingdom where the conditions are satisfactory. It is idle to blame the law or the Ministry of Health ; it is the Local Authority, or perhaps the electors who elected it, that should be blamed. Civilised man has a marvellous propensity for choosing the wrong persons to represent him on public bodies. Is it to be expected that Councils consisting largely of wealthy manufacturers or shopkeepers, squires, farmers, landlords, builders and house speculators, will be particularly zealous about the closets and gutter pipes of the poor, or anxious to spend the rates or coerce property owners ? There are, of course, honourable exceptions among these classes, and there are some really public-spirited Local Authorities. But until the working class itself is serious about its own affairs, it will continue to be badly housed.

OVERCROWDING.

So far we have said nothing of overcrowding. Overcrowding is, in its magnitude as well as in the difficulty of dealing with it, the worst of the evils connected with the housing problem. It takes two forms—overcrowding per acre, *i.e.*, too many houses on any given area of land, and overcrowding of persons in any one house or room, These are distinct evils, though, of course, the two are often found together. Overcrowding per acre is evident to the naked eye in the poorer quarters of all our great towns ; but its full enormity will only be appreciated if the number of dwellers in some of these quarters is examined. It has been said that a healthy city ought not to have more than 25 people to the acre ; yet we find large areas all over the Kingdom with 200, 300 and more. As for overcrowding per room, this is widespread in town and country alike, and it has been enormously intensified by the house famine since the war. Both physically and morally it has disastrous effects. It is not confined to insanitary houses ; it was common, long before the abnormal shortage of accommodation, in homes otherwise healthy enough, for it is obviously a result, in part at least, of poverty. There are, as there always have been, hundreds of thousands of workmen with large families unable to pay the rent required for an adequate number of rooms.

Technically this form of overcrowding is a " nuisance," which can be dealt with under the Public Health Acts. The law is vague and unsatisfactory about it. There is no statutory definition of overcrowding. The Registrar General for the purpose of the Census Returns allows two adults to a room, counting a child under 12 as half an adult. Anything beyond that constitutes overcrowding, and in 1911 it was found that 3,139,472 persons, or 9.1 per cent. of the population of England and Wales were living in an overcrowded condition. In many places the state of things is utterly appalling, notably in the colliery areas. The evidence given before the Coal Commission in 1919 showed that in the mining district of Ashington, in Northumberland, 32·2 per cent. of the people were overcrowded, in Annfield Plain, Durham, 41·4 per cent., and in Leadgate, Durham, 43·6 per cent.

Most Local Authorities adopt the Registrar General's standard. Some take an even lower one ; the London County Council, for example, allows two adults per room and counts a child between 5 and 10 as half an adult, but does not count a child below 5 at all. It is, therefore, possible for two parents and seven or eight young children to live in a two-roomed L.C.C. tenement, the whole family sleeping in the one bedroom, and yet, in the eyes of the Public Health Authority, not to be overcrowded l In the case of lodging-houses we find other standards laid down by bye-laws, requiring a minimum cubic space per person. These minima vary from 240 c. ft. (for an adult, or 120 c. ft. for a child) to 450 c. ft. In Army barracks 600 c. ft. per man is the minimum, in the Metropolitan Police barracks 450 c. ft., and in Poor Law Institutions 500 c. ft. It is worth recalling that Professor Huxley many years ago fixed the quantity of cubic air space required for each adult at 800 c. ft.

Bad, then, as the overcrowding problem has long been on the low standard of two persons to a room, it is infinitely worse if we look at the prospects of raising that standard. Mr. E. D. Simon, of the Manchester City Council, recently made an inquiry into the conditions of a number of working class houses at Didsbury. Practically all of these were of the usual four-roomed type, two only of the rooms being bedrooms. Mr. Simon found house after house occupied by families—respectable families—of 5, 6, 7, 8, and even more persons. In some cases one bedroom was slept in by the parents and one and more children, the others by two or three other children, boys and girls indiscriminately. Sometimes there were a couple of beds squeezed into a room, one for the boys and young men, the other for the girls. Sometimes a lodger, male or female, formed part of this human *mélange*. Of the 71 houses examined only 4 were legally overcrowded. Mr. Simon submits that this is a scandal, and that $2\frac{1}{2}$ persons per bedroom should be regarded as a maximum, and that the separation of the sexes should be taken into account. Few decent people will disagree with his view. But on that basis nearly fifty per cent. of those houses were overcrowded! Didsbury is not an exceptional case, as everyone knows. Make some allowance, if you will, for the present shortage of accommodation, and build what hopes you will on the Government's " 800,000 new houses " ; and the problem yet remains serious enough. We cannot discuss it in more detail here ; it must suffice to say one thing—a higher standard than the Registrar General's ought to be adopted, if not immediately, as soon as is reasonably possible, and that standard ought to be enforced for all houses, old and new.

(D) Town Planning.

Town planning is not really a sub-division of the housing question, and it deserves a better fate than to be tacked on as a sort of tail to a Housing tract. . But since the legislature has thought fit to include it in the Housing Acts, it is necessary to touch briefly on it here, with the warning to the reader that it should be studied independently as a larger and profoundly important subject.

Town planning means the securing of proper sanitary conditions, amenity and convenience, in connection with the laying out and use of land. It ought to be regarded as one of the most urgent tasks of the Local Authorities. In point of fact, it has hitherto been most grossly neglected. In this country, throughout the nineteenth century, practically no attention whatever was paid to it. *Laisser faire* reigned triumphant, and the result is the hideous blotches that disfigure a great part of the land to-day. It was only in this century, after many efforts and experiments by private enthusiasts in the shape of Garden Cities, Garden Suburbs, and the like, and after the German municipalities had long shown the way, that the Public Authorities began to develop an interest in the idea. The Housing, and Town Planning Act, 1909, empowered Local Authorities to prepare town planning schemes in such cases as they thought fit. Few of them showed any disposition to " think fit," and those who did, were discouraged both by the bad regulations made by the Local Government Board and by the troublesome procedure involved in getting the Board's sanction for their schemes. In the nine years following the passing of the 1909 Act only one hundred Local Authorities prepared or decided to prepare schemes—to the number of 155 altogether, involving 279,184 acres of land. And only about one-tenth of these schemes have by 1920 got anywhere near a practical stage.

TOWN PLANNING UNDER THE ACT OF 1919.

The new Act marks a considerable step forward. The procedure for making schemes has been simplified. The Local Authority—(*i.e.*, in London the L.C.C., and outside London, every Borough, Urban and Rural District Council)—may now by resolution decide to prepare a town planning scheme for any area in its district, without having to obtain the authority of the Ministry of Health. To save unnecessary delay of development during the preparation of schemes, the Minister of Health may make orders prescribing the conditions under which the proposed development may proceed pending the making and approval of the schemes. After 1st January, 1923, the preparation of town planning schemes will be compulsory in all Boroughs or Urban Districts with a population of 20,000 or more. And in the meantime any Local Authority may be required by the Ministry of Health to prepare a town planning scheme for any area for which the Ministry considers that a scheme is immediately necessary. Furthermore, if a Local Authority fails to carry out its duties as regards town planning, the Ministry may act itself, or, in the case of a Borough or Urban District with a population of less than 20,000, or of any Rural District, may empower the County Council to act, at the expense in either case of the Local Authority. There is still need of an improvement in the law so far as the functioning of the Local Authorities is concerned. Joint Committees of neighbouring Authorities may be set up (see Act of 1919, Sect. 42 (2) (ii), but it is left to the discretion of the Authorities to decide whether they shall. Everyone, who is familiar with the practice and policy of the Local Authorities at the present time, will know that it ought not to be so left. There is a real need for the constitution of more or less permanent joint bodies for the purpose of town planning in many places. This is obvious enough in the case of " Greater London " and of a number of other large towns ; but it is also important, where it is not so self-evident, in a great many other districts. Now that we have the Housing Commissioners, with their defined areas, it ought not to be difficult to establish the proper machinery for co-ordinating town planning schemes.

THE PRESENT OPPORTUNITY.

Town planning, as we have already said, means the securing of proper sanitary conditions, amenity and convenience in the laying out and use of land. It is clearly a matter with which every member of a Local Authority, and every private citizen, ought to concern himself. And they ought to concern themselves with it now. New houses are to be built everywhere. It is necessary to see that in all these schemes the larger " amenities " and " conveniences " are not sacrificed to immediate haste for roofs and walls. The width and position of streets, open spaces, trees and grass, the proper sites for public buildings of all sorts, as well as for factories and workshops and offices, access to railway stations, docks, theatres and other busy spots—all these are matters to be taken into account in making a new town or altering an old one. They are matters which ought not to be considered piece-meal, but all together as parts of a whole plan. And it would be an agreeable innovation if a few Councillors, at the risk of being decried as cranks and sentimentalists, should insist that not only convenience but beauty is essential to a well-planned town.

SOME USEFUL BOOKS.

(Any of these will be procured and sent by the Fabian Bookshop, 25, Tothill Street, Westminster, on remittance of price and postage).

English Public Health Administration. By B. G. BANNINGTON. (1915). King. **8s. 6d.**

Garden Suburbs, Villages, and Homes. Garden City Press.

The Home I Want. By R. L. REISS. New edition. (1920). Hodder & Stoughton. **2s. 6d.**

The Housing Handbook. By W. THOMPSON. (1903). King. *O.P.*

Housing Up-to-Date. By W. THOMPSON. (1907). King. *O.P.*

Housing and the Public Health. By J. ROBERTSON. (1919). Cassell. **5s.**

The Housing Problem: Its Growth, Legislation and Pro-cedure. By J. J. CLARK. (1920). Pitman. **21s.**

Local Development Law. By H. C. DOWDALL. (1919). Fisher Unwin. **10s. 6d.**

Rural Housing. By W. G. SAVAGE. New edition. (1919). Fisher Unwin. **7s. 6d.**

The Working Woman's House. By A. D. SANDERSON FURNISS and MARION PHILLIPS. (1919). Swarthmore Press. **1s. 6d.**

The Case for Town Planning. By H. R. ALDRIDGE. (1915). National Housing and Town Planning Council. **21s.**

Town Planning in Practice. By RAYMOND UNWIN. (1917). Fisher Unwin. **31s. 6d.**

FABIAN ESSAYS (1920 Edition). 2s ; postage, 3d.
THE SICKNESS OF AN ACQUISITIVE SOCIETY. By. R. H. TAWNEY. 1s. n.,
post, 2d.
TOWARDS SOCIAL DEMOCRACY? By SIDNEY WEBB. 1s. n., post, 1d.
WHAT TO READ on Social and Economic Subjects. 1s. n.
THE RURAL PROBLEM. By H D. HARBEN. 2s. 6s. n.
THE MISERY OF BOOTS. By H. G. WELLS. 3d., post free, 4d.

FABIAN TRACTS AND LEAFLETS.
Tracts, each 16 to 52 pp., price 1d., or 9d. per doz , unless otherwise stated.
Leaflets, 4 pp. each, price 1d. for 3 copies, 2s. per 100, or 20s. per 1000.
The Set of 74, 4/6 ; post free, 5/3. Bound in buckram, 7/6 ; post free, 8/3.

I.—General Socialism in its various aspects.
TRACTS.—192. Guild Socialism. By G. D. H. COLE, M A. 180. The Philosophy
of Socialism. By A. CLUTTON BROCK. 169. The Socialist Movement in Germany.
By W. STEPHEN SANDERS. 2d. 159. The Necessary Basis of Society.
By SIDNEY WEBB. 151. The Point of Honour. By RUTH C. BENTINCK.
147. Capital and Compensation. By E. R. PEASE. 146. Socialism and Superior
Brains. By BERNARD SHAW. 2d. 142. Rent and Value. 138. Municipal Trading.
121. Public Service v. Private Expenditure. By Sir OLIVER LODGE. 107. Socialism
for Millionaires. By BERNARD SHAW. 139. Socialism and the Churches. By Rev
JOHN CLIFFORD, D.D. 133. Socialism and Christianity. By Rev. PERCY DEARMER.
2d. 78. Socialism and the Teaching of Christ By Dr J. CLIFFORD. 42. Christian
Socialism. By Rev. S. D. HEADLAM. 79. A Word of Remembrance and Caution to
the Rich. By JOHN WOOLMAN. 72. The Moral Aspects of Socialism. By SIDNEY
BALL 69. Difficulties of Individulism. By S. WEBB. 51. Socialism : True and
False. By S. WEBB 45. The Impossibilities of Anarchism. By G. B. SHAW. 2d.
7. Capital and Land. 5. Facts for Socialism. 2d. LEAFLETS —13. What Socialism
Is. 1. Why are the Many Poor ?

II.—Applications of Socialism to Particular Problems.
TRACTS—188. National Finance and a Levy on Capital. By SIDNEY WEBB. 2d. 187.
The Teacher in Politics. By SIDNEY WEBB. 2d. 186. Central Africa and the
League of Nations. By R C. HAWKIN. 2d. 183. The Reform of the House of
Lords. By SIDNEY WEBB. 181. When Peace Comes—the Way of Industrial
Reconstruction. By SIDNEY WEBB. 2d. 178. The War ; Women ; and Unemploy-
ment. 2d. 177. Socialism and the Arts of Use. By A. CLUTTON BROCK. 175. The
Economic Foundations of the Women's Movement. 2d. 173. Public v. Private
Electricity Supply. 170. Profit-Sharing and Co-Partnership: A Fraud and Failure ?
164. Gold and State Banking. 162. Family Life on a Pound a Week. By Mrs.
REEVES. 2d. 161. Afforestation and Unemployment. 157. The Working Life of
Women. 155. The Case against the Referendum. 154. The Case for School Clinics.
152. Our Taxes as they are and as they ought to be. 2d. 146. The Endowment of
Motherhood. 2d. 145. The Case for School Nurseries. 140. Child Labour under
Capitalism. 136 The Village and the Landlord. By EDW. CARPENTER, 144.
Machinery : its Masters and Servants. 122. Municipal Milk and Public Health.
125. Municipalization by Provinces. 124. State Control of Trusts. LEAFLET.—
104. How Trade Unions benefit Workmen.

III. Local Government Powers : How to use them.
TRACTS.—Metropolitan Borough Councils. Their Constitution, Powers and Duties.
By C. R. ATTLEE, M.A., 2d. 191. Borough Councils. Their Constitution, Powers
and Duties By C. R. ATTLEE, M.A. 2d 193. Housing. By C. M. LLOYD, M.A.
3d 189. Urban District Councils By C. M. LLOYD. 2d. 172 What about the
Rates ? By S. WEBB. 62. Parish and District Councils (Revised 1919), 137.
Parish Councils and Village Life. 109. Cottage Plans and Common Sense.
LEAFLETS.—134. Small Holdings. 68 The Tenant's Sanitary Catechism. 71.
Ditto for London.

IV.—General Politics and Fabian Policy.
TRACTS—158. The Case against the C.O.S. By Mrs. TOWNSHEND. 41. The Fabian
Society : Its Early History. By BERNARD SHAW.

V.—Biographical Series. In portrait covers, 2d. and 3d.
182. Robert Owen, Idealist. By C. E. M. JOAD. 179. John Ruskin and Social
Ethics. By Prof. EDITH MORLEY. 165. Francis Place. By ST. JOHN G. IRVINE.
166 Robert Owen, Social Reformer. By Miss B. L HUTCHINS. 167. William
Morris and the Communist Ideal. By Mrs. TOWNSHEND. 168. John Stuart Mill.
By JULIUS WEST. 174. Charles Kingsley and Christian Socialism. By C. E.
VULLIAMY.

Printed by the Broadway Press, and published by the Fabian Society, 25 Tothill Street,
Westminster, London, S.W.

Fabian Tract No. 194.

TAXES, RATES

AND

LOCAL INCOME TAX.

BY

ROBERT JONES, D.Sc.

PUBLISHED AND SOLD BY THE FABIAN SOCIETY,
25, TOTHILL STREET, WESTMINSTER, LONDON, S.W.1
PRICE TWOPENCE. . . . . JUNE, 1920.

THE FABIAN BOOKSHOP

25, Tothill St., London, S.W.1.

All books in print on Economics, Politics, Social and Industrial Questions and History as well as General Literature can be supplied.

Enquiries with regard to works on any subject will be replied to promptly.

Books and Pamphlets dealing with the aims and history of the Labour and Socialist Movement and of the Labour Party are the special features of the Bookshop.

The Fabian Society supplies to Socialist Societies, Co-operative Societies, Local Labour Parties, Trade Unions, Trade Councils, Labour Clubs, Reading Societies, Study Circles and Public Authorities,

BOXES OF BOOKS

on Political, Historical, Economic and Social subjects; both up-to-date new books and classical works. Each box contains from twenty to twenty-five volumes selected from a library of 5,000 books in accordance with the wishes of the subscribers.

For prospectus and application form write to :—

THE FABIAN SOCIETY, 25, Tothill Street., London, S.W.1.

Taxes, Rates, and Local Income Tax.

Local Finance.

THE whole business of local government stands in need of revision, and that revision must include a great deal of simplification. To no branch of local government does this apply more completely than to its finance. The present system is the result of a great number of laws, and its complications are not all of one kind. Some of them represent real differences in the proportion of local and national interests, others seem to have no justification whatever.

Central and Local Finance.

State subventions, in one form or other, have rapidly increased. Before Mr. Goschen formed the Local Taxation Account (1889), that is to say, " in the eighties," the State subvention was about one-ninth of the total local expenditure. In the pre-war period of this century, the proportion was about one-quarter. The tendency to increase the State subvention still continues. For the Education Act of 1918, it was fixed at one-half.

Principles.

There are no sound principles of local finance that differ, or can properly differ, from the principles of national finance. It is unfortunate that local affairs and local finance, being so complicated, should be so often considered by themselves. The trees hide the shape of the wood. This difficulty occurs along with another, which is similar in its effect—the slow growth of a knowledge of principles, and the long persistence of incorrect ideas, not only among the general public, but among large classes of the better instructed.

This slow fixing of sound principles is in part the result of natural human conservatism, and partly is caused by the fact that certain vested interests will grow around the incorrect view, strengthening it, finding reasons for it (a common and natural process), and upon occasion defending it with righteous anger. These causes are by no means small and subsidiary.

The following examples will illustrate the meaning and importance of what has been said above :

3

Some Examples of the " Time-Lag " of Knowledge :

(1) *The Nature of Taxation.*

Tribute, taxes, rates, impositions, in one form or another, have been levied for thousands of years. The principles of finance and of taxing have been discussed for twenty centuries. Yet no really correct definition of a tax appears until the first part of the nineteenth century. Now our ideas of the correct method of levying, collecting, spending rates and taxes depend very largely upon our idea of what a tax actually is. While people thought that a tax was a price paid for State protection, just as money might be paid to buy soap, they were likely to take an individualist view of public finance, and to judge of it as they judged business transactions in general. But rates and taxes are essentially communal, and not individualist, and it is just because this has not been properly grasped that certain people would find themselves startled by an imaginary conversation of this kind :

" London has got an immense and valuable property, able to yield hundreds of thousands a year—"

" It should be made as fully profitable as possible."

" The cash return from it is practically nothing. Yet a syndicate of capitalists could be formed to-morrow to take it over and pay a million or so a year for it."

" —And the rates bounding up ! Scandalous ! It should be disposed of at once."

" It is Hyde Park."

" Ah, well, of course—"

Now the gentleman who ends this imaginary conversation in such fashion would not have fallen into so simple a trap if his ideas of what is valuable, productive, profitable, had been built upon the communal, as well as upon the individualist meaning of those words.

In similar fashion, the old idea of a tax being a kind of price paid for State benefits received is only true in the communal sense. The total " payments " made to the local and central authorities, would not be made at all unless we had a belief—strong, even if confused—that very important benefits would result. But these benefits cannot be counted out, for each individual, in portions of so much for each £1 of rates or taxes. This confusion of communal with individualist ways of reckoning creates, in many directions, a series of false contradictions. Thus it is equally true to say that Hyde Park yields no income (dividend, profit, rent, cash), and that it yields a valuable income of health, education, happiness.

Taxes, as Mr. Sidney Webb puts it, represent the part of our incomes that we arrange to have spent for us by the community, and as the community directs. But a tax differs from an ordinary price in two respects : it is compulsory, and it is not proportioned to the "benefit" received in return. If sixpence buys a pound of soap, we expect a shilling to buy two pounds. But a doubling of rates or taxes by no means implies a doubling of the "benefit received." The parallel is truer in the case of the rate than in the case of the tax, though it is not correct for either of them. Rates, however, are in many cases linked with definite measurable services, such as road-mending or street lighting; and this is partly the reason why the old "benefit" idea has dominated local more completely than national finance. When a great part of local expenditure went to make improvements that increased the value of land, the idea of benefit to the landowner had a reality that sometimes got carried over, in mere confusion of thought, to the community in general. A century ago (1814) seventy per cent. of rates was levied upon land. On the outbreak of the war (1914) the percentage was twelve. The change was due chiefly to the increase in the value of buildings, and to the introduction of a new item, railways. It resulted partly, however, from the efforts of the landed interest to shift the burden to the taxpayer.

(2) Progressive or Graduated Taxation.

The change of public opinion in favour of graduated or progressive taxation illustrates both the slowness of the spread of a new idea (in finance as in other matters) and also, the speed of the spread of the same idea under an effective method of education. The third (1903) edition of our standard textbook on Public Finance (Bastable) still shows a distrust of graduated taxation, only less strong than that of the earlier editions. It reflects the sense of justice of the citizen of the nineteenth century, for our fathers honestly thought it unjust to tax an income of £2,000 a year at a higher percentage than an income of £200 a year. The basis of all rating and taxing must be the sense of justice or equity of the time, and this is a variable for which there is no fixed standard beyond the law of the land for the time being. We cannot apply that standard when it is a question of altering the law of the land, and that is what every change of taxation implies.

(3) Taxes upon Income.

The income tax is now the sheet-anchor of our national system. Many people are now discussing its application to local finance—an application already made, on the continent, and indirectly already adopted here, through our Grants in Aid. Yet Gladstone apologised for using an income tax in times of peace. He viewed it as an abnormal impost, only proper to such cases as the hard times of war. We think differently to-day.

5

Here again we see the educative force of actual practice. Just as to the ordinary citizen taxes should first of all be "fair"; just as to the economist they should not check the production of desirable goods, or encourage the production of undesirable goods; so to the Chancellor they should be productive; and no Chancellor lightly abandons any productive tax, once levied, however bitterly his party may have condemned it on its first appearance. It is scarcely credible to this generation that in 1816, the wealthy Whig party was able to get Wiltshire farm labourers—none of them earning so much as 10s. per week— to send resolutions to the House of Parliament protesting against the iniquity of continuing the income tax. The proposal was to continue the tax, reduced from 10% to 5%, on incomes over £150 per year. The national conscience, upon this instruction, was roused (!) and income tax disappeared from our Budgets. Only as an "exceptional tax" was it re-imposed (at sevenpence in the pound) in 1842.

(4) *Direct Taxation.*

The next example has an increasing interest just now, because the old dispute about direct and indirect taxation is re-emerging.

On the continent indirect taxes have long formed a part of local finance, as well as figuring in national systems,—the *octroi*, or tariff upon goods entering towns or districts; but so far (except in a few isolated cases) we have escaped town tariffs. The present Lord Chancellor wrote in 1909: "With characteristic arrogance, Mr. Lloyd George has thrown over the financial maxims of the past. Instead of an even balance between the two sets of taxes—direct and indirect—the direct burdens are more the heavier by about 7 per cent." But the economics of a Lord Chancellor-to-be are unknown to economists. The "even balance" is a myth that began to haunt the lobbies of the House when the proportion of indirect to direct taxes fell steadily from 73:27 (1840) to 50:50 (1900). The creators of the myth had simply "rationalised" their desire to check the movement. But the movement continued. The ratio of indirect to direct taxes was calculated, in 1917, as 18 : 82; and Mr. Austen Chamberlain, in April, 1919, stated the proportions of his budget taxes thus—Direct 75%, "Sumptuary," 17,91%, Indirect, 7,01 (essentially, Direct 75, Indirect 25). There is no reason known to the economist in favour of any particular ratio between them.

Indirect taxes by raising prices necessarily check consumption, and therefore check production. Hence they are best applicable to such commodities as in the opinion of the nation may at least be limited without any real harm resulting—whiskey and tobacco, for example. They should not be levied on food, on necessities, on any educative product or habit. They have the serious drawback

6

that they do not and cannot be.distributed according to " ability to pay." Further, they are not " progressive " in their graduation, but very often degressive. A tax on bread falls most heavily where it should fall most lightly. Finally, indirect' taxes make for a bad training in citizenship. All who exercise the rights of citizenship should share its duties, among which is to bear a just proportion of the national expenses. Representation without taxation is tyranny. No adult sane citizen should escape taxation ; and therefore no citizen should ever live at " bare subsistence " level ; for in that case, of course he—or she— is incapable of paying any tax. Lastly, every citizen should be aware of his citizenship, and take some pride in it. Indirect taxes hide from him the fact that he is paying at all. How seldom does an educated man, when he buys tobacco, realise that he is paying a tax ? How often, do uneducated men, who pay no taxes directly, think that they escape ? If a man pays rates embodied in his rent, and taxes only in the extra prices of the goods he buys, he loses a healthy continuous lesson in citizenship. A good State should ensure good citizens by these three methods, namely,

(a) By seeing to it that no citizen is incapable of contributing to the common fund ;

(b) By claiming from every citizen a contribution according to his abilities (which does not mean " in proportion to his income," although Adam Smith thought these two were one and the same, and others, with less excuse than he had, still can think nc more clearly. For a man with £1,000 a year is able to pay more than twice as much as another with £500 a year) ;

(c) By seeing to it, lastly, that the citizen not only pays, but knows that he pays, knows how much he pays, knows why he pays. If these things are hidden from him, or not clear to his mind, to that extent he is the less a good citizen.

It is a convenience to a Chancellor of the Exchequer if a tax, being disguised, arouses little opposition while providing a goodly sum. But it is a poor public spirit that grows from such ill statesmanship. Secret taxation is no more to be commended than secret diplomacy. Necessary or not, it is never admirable in itself.

These examples illustrate (1) the importance of keeping the main principles of finance in view ;

(2) the need of repeating them, and the comparative danger of assuming, in the detail of local affairs, that the general principles of finance may be taken for granted ; and

(3) the curious slowness in the spread of an idea, while it is still an " abstract idea," however good may be the reasons that support it ; and the equally curious speed at which a nation can absorb an idea when it has been translated into practice, by a Chancellor of the Exchequer for example.

Ratings.

Professor Cannan has pointed out that two principles have in the past controlled the development of local finance :

(1) That every inhabitant of a district should be made to contribute according to his ability ; and

(2) That everyone who receives benefit from the local expenditure should be made to contribute in proportion to the benefit he receives.*

"Applied to the same rate," he says, "these principles are obviously incompatible," and he goes on to show that a very fair approximation to rough justice is in fact reached by the counteracting effect of the two principles.

Rates are in effect taxes upon property rather than on income. It has often been pointed out that where two individuals, say a diamond merchant and a timber merchant, have equal incomes, it by no means follows, that they have equal holdings in fixed property,—land and buildings ; and that therefore it is absurd to assess their rates upon their properties. But the rates in both cases are really paid by the owners of the land on which the offices or timber yards are placed (except in the case of new rates or taxes). A fuller account is given under the heading "Local Income Tax," further on.

Rating is a method developed in connection, first of all, with the Poor Rate, and afterwards applied to other local purposes. The probable abolition of the Boards of Guardians in the near future will compel the setting-up of a revised system of assessment of the value of properties. The Overseers or the Boards of Guardians are still the valuers for rating purposes in many places, and even in some London Boroughs—Woolwich for example. The contrast between the relative unimportance of the Guardians, as illustrated by the apathy that marks their election, and the very great importance of the work of assessment entrusted to them, is one of the anomalies of local government. Highly responsible work should go to highly responsible bodies or individuals.

Newer Ideas of Finance.

Almost during the last generation, the following new ideas, proposals, or practices have come forward.

1. *Graduated scales.*—This was a re-emergence. Athens in the fourth century B.C. had a graduated scale of taxation.

* History of Local Rates in England in Relation to the Proper Distribution of the Burden of Taxation: Second Edition, 1912. P. S. King. 3s. 6d. net.

2. *The distinction between Earned and Unearned Incomes.*
Very largely this is an attempt to tax economic rents, or unproductive surpluses. Mr. J. A. Hobson has elaborated the whole idea in several recent books. *

3. *The Super Tax :* an extension of the ideas in (1) and (2), above.

4. *The Excess Profits Tax :* a well-meant but rather clumsy further extension.

5. *A Luxury Tax :* This might have been made economically useful, though in a small way. The temptation it offered to those who really desired more indirect taxation, or merely protectionism, proved stronger in action than any desire of economic purity. It was abandoned (1918).

6. The acceptance of the Tax on Income, in terms of Ability to Pay, as the " sheet-anchor " of our system.

7. The recognition of the Family as an economic unit. This has already expressed itself in the form of wife-and-children abatements. The assessment and taxing of the Family Income as a distinct unit, however, is yet only a suggestion.

8. *Municipal Enterprises.* This is a subject for a whole treatise. It has a long history of Beginnings,with a period of comparative disappearance, and a modern History of Emergence ; this last dating from the decay of the Individualist Period (18th—19th Centuries).

9. The general superiority of direct to indirect taxation.

10. The equity and practical wisdom of making exemptions and abatements, now applied to (a) life assurance, (b) children, (c) wives ; and, with vicissitudes that show the opportunism and empiricism of governments, to small incomes.

11. The definite relation of taxpaying to a sense of citizenship.

12. The right application of taxes upon income to local expenditure.

13. Taxes on persons in proportion to their wealth, fortune or " riches " as in the schemes for a Capital Levy.

Municipal Undertakings.

The extension of Municipal Undertakings, with their analogue, the Nationalisation of Industries, represents for the future a change in the nature of national and local finance so great as to dwarf all other developments. For national action, the way is open. The first " communally-minded " Parliament that meets will probably take two or three important steps of this kind,— unless, indeed, it is anticipated by a Parliament of shareholders who fear being bought out without " extra compensation for forced sale " or some similar formula.

* See the Industrial System ; Longmans, 1909 ; and his Taxation in the New State ; Methuen, 1919.

9

For local authorities, however, two preliminary steps are needed for the efficient development of municipal undertakings :

(1) The simplification of the present innumerable areas and authorities—possibly into Parish and Borough Councils only, with the County Council as the larger unit of area outside the County Boroughs ; and

(2) The grant of powers to the County and Borough Councils to do anything they wish except only those things that Parliament specifically forbids. At present, we are unable to see how droll we are in holding it ridiculous to force a company owning a private fleet of motor buses to get a special Act of Parliament passed, as a kind of certificate of birth, while insisting that if the same fleet of motor buses is to belong to the London County Council, a certificate of this kind (very costly upon occasion) must be insisted on. Profits, we seem to say, may go to profiteers or to profit-makers ; but only to profit sharers by an Act of Grace. Thus also the capital of a profit-making Company, when it is taken over by a public body, is to some good folk, no longer capital, but a burden of debt. Yet we smile at the Wiltshire labourers of 1816.

Central Control, Central Grants.

State Grants must always imply State control, and this will be good or bad according to the intelligence of the control department : but that is a limitation belonging to all human concerns. Broadly speaking, central control acts for the common good—

(1) When it encourages active and public-spirited local authorities ;

(2) When it maintains, against local apathy or ignorance, any necessary " National Minimum " ;

(3) When it leaves the door open for new ventures and experiments ;

(4) When it controls, and in extreme cases punishes, local bodies that through inefficiency or corrupt interests act against the public weal.

As a rule, action taken under (1) (2) and (3) is far more effective and valuable than the more sensational acts possible under (4). Here again the general law of human government applies, whether for nation, village, family, school, or any other group : that the methods of good government seek to prevent the need of punishment arising, just as good housing outvalues the best supply of medicines.

Scarcely any of the activities of a local authority are purely local in their effects ; so that the range of State subventions, or grants-in-aid, is a very wide one. The best method of payment is that adopted in the Education Act (1918) and likely to be extended to other branches of work. The Board of Education says in practice to the local authority : " If you go beyond the compulsory National Minimum of Education laid down for general use, then, whatever educational work you may undertake, whether experimental or not, so that you demonstrate that it is educational work, we will pay half your expenditure." But this should be accompanied, as was elaborately worked out in 1913-14, by a scale graduated so as to help even more liberally the districts of low rateable value in proportion to the necessary service.

Local Income Tax.

An extension of this method of Grants, together with a " free hand " for municipal enterprises and undertakings, would solve the difficulties of local finance so completely that the movement for a local income tax would probably cease. It would be merged into activities that would yield all that is being sought by the public-spirited people who are pressing for this particular change.

There is one hidden danger connected with a Local Income Tax that should have special mention. It is the danger that a Local Income Tax should replace part or all of the present system of rates. Every landowner and houseowner who is both selfish and intelligent ought to be an ardent supporter of the idea of sweeping away as much as possible of the present rates, and substituting a . Local Income Tax. The effects would work out somewhat in this fashion :

Any fixed charge upon land, such as tithe or rates, as soon as it is recognised as being fixed, must either be paid by the landlord at once, or, in the first instance, by the tenant. If by the tenant, he of course must reckon with it as with his rent ; if he is to pay £150 rent and £50 fixed charge in rates he has a clear item of £200 expenses to face. Suppose, now, the £50 rates removed, and a Local Income Tax on the whole community put in its place, the tenant paying, we will say, £10 towards this tax. Until his lease runs out, he will be paying £160 (£150 + £10) instead of £200 ; a gain to him of £40 per year. On the renewal of the lease, the landlord will ask for rent anything up to £190, for that will leave the tenant just as well off as before. Out of this £40 extra the landlord will pay his quota of the Local Income tax, which at the same rate will be less than £3 (the tenant paying £10 in £150, or one-fifteenth). If he pays at a higher poundage he may have to yield as much as £5 out of the £40. He is better off by £35 per year. The change would mean a gift to the holders of real estate, whether land or houses, running into tens of millions, even after allowing for the landowners' share in the new Local Income Tax.

11

Classification of State Grants.

The Goschen system of the Local Taxation account was intended to be the general and chief method of dealing with local finance. Fixed fractions of fixed taxes would go into a distinct fund, and from this fund payments would be allocated and made to the local authorities.* There were State payments, however, apart from this fund, notably payments for Education. These were at first held to be exceptional, but they have in fact become the most significant part of local finance. The direct grants are now double the amount paid from the Local Taxation Account, and they tend to increase still further. The Grants have been classified thus :

1. Amounts fixed : that is, not based on the present actions or activities of the local authority (*e.g.* the " Whiskey Money," or share in the Customs and Excise Revenue).

2. Amounts paid for the services or " efficiencies " of the local authority; being payments for services rendered and approved, but not proportioned in any way to the local expenditure.

3. Amounts calculated on a percentage of approved local expenditure. This promises to be the typical Grant, and the percentage now favoured is 50 (like the " Police Grant " of 1874, then raised to half the expenditure). But a higher percentage has been given in some instances, and there is no valid argument against 75 or even 85 per cent, instead of 50.

The practical solution of the national—local discussion, at the present day, comes briefly to this : a prescribed percentage share of the actual expenditure on all local services which the community wishes, for the common benefit of the nation, to see increased; with due provision for the needs of districts of low rateable value. On the side of direct finance, it would seem advisable to leave that solution to be further applied, and to help in its application. Side by side with this, local authorities should work for the " free hand " in municipal ventures. Such freedom is the likelier to be gained if the number of local bodies is reduced, and their position rendered more responsible. A practical "local authorities programme" would be :

1. Fewer authorities with more authority.

2. All powers except those definitely withheld by statute.

3. Acceptance and furtherance of the Grant in Aid method, of a percentage of actual expenditure for the immediate future.

* A diagram in Dr. Grice's book, *National and Local Finance*, P. S. King, 1910, illustrates the process.

A Single Tax.

We have all of us a natural tendency, when faced by any complicated system, to desire it simplified ; and if simplified into one type or method, so much the better. This feeling makes a part of all movements in favour of a single tax, whether on land or on income. The same feeling adds to the attractiveness of the idea of a local income tax ; for we have all moved towards a belief in these tenets :—

(a) Income is a better general test of wealth than is occupation of property, though less good than assessment in proportion to capital wealth or " riches."

(b) The tax on income is the best type of tax, because it is the most just (but consider the alternative of taxation in proportion to capital wealth).

(c) The income tax avoids all discussions of tariffs, preferences, bounties.

(d) Income and capital taxes can be assessed according to graduated scales with exemptions and abatements.

Against these must be put the fact, of which everyone knows examples, that people in certain occupations persistently evade income tax. This is a remediable weakness capable of steady reduction by improved administration. A less obvious danger, and one to be specially noted in discussing plans for a local income tax, has already been mentioned. No rates or taxes, such as those upon fixed property, should be removed in order that an income tax may replace them, for that would in effect be equivalent to making a disguised gift to the present holders of the property.

Our knowledge of economics and finance, and our experience of administrative methods, are a very long way from being so complete as to enable us to sweep away all our various rates and taxes in favour of any one tax, without, at the same time, very greatly benefiting some classes, or very unfairly hurting others, or both. To this there is but one possible limitation :

All " economic rent " can be taxed up to 100% without any injury whatever to the powers of production of the nation, for rent-takers, as such, give no services,—though they may do so in other capacities, if not as rent-takers. Now it is roughly possible to assess the " economic rent " of land, but it is not yet practicable to assess and tax all economic rents. Until that can be done, and is done, a mixed system of taxation is the most practicable one. Thus, a balance against the escape from income tax of certain groups may be found in a fuller and properly graduated tax upon transactions above a fixed amount— a method already in use in our " receipt stamps." This in turn, has the objection of being a tax on trade, and therefore a check upon production. It is only cited here to illustrate the difficulties of complete simplification.

The Demand for a Local Income Tax.

¶ The case for a Local Income Tax appears irresistible—until the difficulties are realised! The system of charging all the expenses of Local Government upon the occupiers of premises, approximately in proportion to the rental value of those premises, (i) fails to extract any direct contribution from the ground landlord or absentee owner of property; (ii) secures a quite unduly small contribution from the man with a big income occupying a small house; (iii) unfairly penalises the shopkeeper, the doctor, or the farmer, who pays in rent more than the average proportion of income; (iv) weighs heavily on the large family needing more rooms than the small family of like means; (v) operates as a discouragement to building additional houses; (vi) is specially unfair to the clergyman deriving his professional income from tithe, which (alone among professional incomes) is assessed to the rates; and (vii) makes the ratepaying occupiers disproportionately sensitive about any municipal improvements which involve a rise in rates. Moreover, the system by which each Local Authority has to provide, by rates levied on the occupiers within its area, for all the expenses of its administration, (a) weighs unduly on the " cities of the poor " with relatively low rateable value, and unfairly exempts the " cities of the rich " where rateable value is high; and (b) exacts from occupiers in the working-class districts an unfair share of the cost of the thoroughfares, the local drainage, the elementary schools, and the Public Health services, incurred in the common interest of the nation. Under this pressure the rates in some districts have risen even beyond " twenty shillings in the pound," whilst in others, no more economically managed, they are only a quarter of this rate.

What is a Local Income Tax?

It is accordingly suggested by some reformers that each Local Authority should be empowered to levy the whole, or some portion of the revenue that it requires, not according to the rental value of the premises occupied, but according to the incomes enjoyed by the several inhabitants, with provisions for the total exemption of very small incomes, and the mitigation of the impost on small incomes by Abatements, Wife and Children Allowances, etc., as for the National Income Tax. Such a Local Income Tax, it is urged, is in force in Germany and other countries.

A Local Income Tax Impracticable here.

Unfortunately, such a measure appears to be in this country both impracticable and inexpedient, at any rate in the form in which it is usually proposed, for the following reasons :
(A) The British Income Tax is, to the extent of more than two-thirds, " assessed at the source," in such a way as to make it

impossible to discover the total incomes of the inhabitants of each locality ; and this system is demonstrably so important in preventing evasion that it will certainly never be abandoned by any Government. Each Local Authority would, therefore, have to create its own machinery for assessment and collection of any Local Income Tax, which it would be extraordinarily difficult to institute and conduct with any accuracy or completeness.

(B) Even if this local machinery could be provided, the difficulty of deciding (i) where the income should be assessed, and (ii) how much of it should be assessed by each Local Authority, appears, in innumerable cases, insuperable. Consider (a) the common case of a man earning his income in the business area, and residing in the suburbs outside the Municipality ; (b) the case of a man maintaining several residences (*e.g.*, a cottage in the country as well as a house in the town) ; (c) the case of the proprietors of a business with different branches or " multiple shops " ; (d) the case of businesses making their incomes from a whole series of premises of different kinds, scattered over different Local Government areas ; such as a city warehouse ; various kinds of factories for different components ; stabling, wharfs, and offices in different places ; possibly also farms or grazing fields, and drying grounds. How would it be possible, for each of the many Local Authorities concerned, to decide how much of the aggregate income of the business, which could only be regarded as a whole, was to be deemed to be assessable at each point ? It seems as if the only possible way of dividing the income of such a complex case would be according to the extent and value of the premises employed in each place—which brings us back to the present basis of rateable value !

A Share in the National Income Tax.

In order to avoid these difficulties it is sometimes proposed that the assessment of Income Tax by the Inland Revenue Department for the whole nation should be adopted for local purposes ; and an additional penny, or two pence, should be added to the National Income Tax for the time being, the extra sum thus realised by the Inland Revenue being handed over to the Local Authorities in aid of their own finances. Each penny in the pound of Income Tax now yields, net, about four million pounds, which may be, approximately, equal to about a fivepenny rate. If a Local Authority could receive each year from the Inland Revenue the equivalent of a tenpenny rate, what a boon it would be to Councillors harassed by an impending rise in rates !

But this would not be a " Local Income Tax." It would not mean that each locality was getting the proceeds of the assessment of the incomes of its own wealthy residents. It would mean only that the National Income Tax, as we know it, had been increased by twopence in the pound ; and that the aggregate Grants in Aid to all the Local Authorities together were to be increased by eight million pounds. Thus, we come back to the present system of relying on Local Rates and relieving them by Grants in Aid.

How it Could be Distributed.

We should then have to face the problem of how to distribute among all the thousands of Local Authorities, rich and poor, apathetic and energetic, thrifty and extravagant, the additional Grant in Aid. If this were done on any common basis, such as proportionately to rateable value, or to population, or to superficial area, the result could only be the production of a new set of inequalities between the " cities of the rich " and the " cities of the poor," which would leave the problem essentially unsolved.

Moreover, it cannot be ignored that any such distribution, besides creating new inequalities, would bring the largest reduction in rates to the most apathetic or to the most stingy Local Authority, and the least reduction to the enterprising, energetic, and large-minded Local Authority that aimed at maintaining all the local services in a high state of efficiency. This would not make for Municipal Progress !

How to Help Local Authorities.

It is clear that what we want to do is to secure most relief to the rates in (a) those districts in which the necessary expenditure on local services is greatest in proportion to rateable value ; and (b) those districts which are actually providing most service of any desirable kind. A Local Authority which has a full supply of schools, a well-qualified and properly paid staff of teachers, an efficient public library, all the parks and open spaces that its inhabitants require, the best possible provision for Maternity and Infancy, and enough hospitals and convalescent homes for the sick, ought to receive much larger Grants in Aid than a Local Authority which neglects or starves all these valuable but costly public services. No system of Local Income Tax, or mechanical apportionment of an addition to the National Income Tax, makes this wise discrimination.

The Grant in Aid.

And so we come back to the plan of Grants in Aid calculated (a) proportionately to the actual expenditure of the several Local Authorities on all the various public services that it is considered desirable to encourage ; and at the same time (b) specially graduated so as to aid most those Local Authorities in which the rateable value per head of population is exceptionally low.

There is no advantage, but, on the contrary, great disadvantage, in making the aggregate Grant in Aid dependent on any particular source of revenue (such as the Spirit Duties or the Income Tax). The total Grant to Local Authorities ought to vary only with their needs, not according to the year's receipts from some particular tax. Hence the plea of local reformers should be, not for any share of the Income Tax, but simply for an Increase in the Grants in Aid and a proper reform of the System.

Bibliography.

Fabian Books: "*Fabianism and the Fiscal Question*," Edited by BERNARD SHAW, 1s. "*How to Pay for the War.*" Edited by SIDNEY WEBB, 6s.

Fabian Tracts: No. 121 "*Public Service versus Private Expenduture*," by SIR OLIVER LODGE, 2d. No. 152 "*Our Taxes as they are and as they ought to be*," by ROBERT JONES, 2d. No. 172 "*What about the Rates ?*" by SIDNEY WEBB, 2d. No. 188 "*National Finance and a Levy on Capital*," by SIDNEY WEBB, 2d.

ARMITAGE-SMITH, G. "*Principles and Methods of Taxation*," 1905. Murray, 5s.

BASTABLE, C. F. "*Public Finance*," 3rd edition, 1895. Macmillan, 16s.

BLUNDEN, G. H. "*Local Taxation and Finance*," 1895. Allen, 2s. 6d.

BOYLE, E., and G. HUMPHREYS DAVIS. "*Principles of Rating*," 1906. Butterworth, o.p.

CANNAN, E. "*History of Local Rates in England.*" New edition, 1912. King, 4s.

CLARKE, J. J. "*Outlines of Local Government*," 1914. Pitman, 1s.

DOWELL, STEPHEN. "*History of Taxation and Taxes in England.*" 4 vols., 1892. o.p.

EDGEWORTH, F. Y. "*A Levy on Capital for the Discharge of Debt.*" 1919. Clarendon Press, 1s.

FOXWELL, H. S. "*Papers on Current Finance*," 1919. Macmillan, 10s.

GIFFEN, SIR R. "*Economic Enquiries and Studies*," 2 vols., 1904. Bell, 25s.

GRAHAM, J. C. "*Taxation and Local Government.*" 4th edition, 1906. King, 2s.

GRICE, J. W. "*National and Local Finance.*" 1910. King, 12s.

HENRY, ROBERT. "*Who Pays? An Enquiry into the real Incidence of Taxation.*" 1912. Allen, 2s. 6d. and 1s. 6d.

HIGGS, HENRY. "*The Financial System of the United Kingdom.*" 1914. Macmillan, 6s.

HIGGS, HENRY. "*National Economy, an Outline of Public Administration,*" 1917. Macmillan, 3s. 6d.

HIGGS, HENRY. "*A Primer of National Finance,*" 1919. Methuen, 5s.

HOBSON, J. A. "*Taxation in the New State,*" 1919. Methuen, 6s.

JONES, ROBERT. "*The Nature and First Principles of Taxation,*" 1914. King, 7s. 6d.

KONSTAM, E. M. "*Rates and Taxes,*" 1906. Butterworth, 6s.

LAWRENCE, F. W. PETHICK. "*A Levy on Capital,*" 1918. Allen, 2s. 6d. and 1s. 6d.

MACBETH, A. D. "*The Rationale of Rates,*" 1912. Hogge (Edinburgh), 2s. 6d.

MALLET, SIR BERNARD. "*British Budgets, 1887-8 to 1912-13,*" 1919. Macmillan, 12s.

PLEHN, C. C. "*Introduction to Public Finance,*" 1909. Macmillan, 10s.

RAFFETY, F. W., and W. H. C. SHARP. "*The Nation's Income,*" 1909. Murby, 2s.

ROW-FOGO, J. R. "*Local Taxation in England,*" 1902. Macmillan, 6s.

SELIGMAN, E. R. A. "*Essays in Taxation,*" 1896. Macmillan, 21s.

SELIGMAN, E. R. A. "*The Income Tax,*" 1911. Macmillan, 16s.

SNOWDEN, P. "*The Socialist Budget,*" (Labor Ideal Series), 1907, 1s.

SNOWDEN, P. "*Finance and the Labour Party,*" 1920. Parsons, 4s. 6d.

TAUSSIG, F. W. "*Tariff History of the United States,*" (1789-1888). Revised edition, 1919. Putnam, 9s.

TURNER, HARTLEY (Editor). "*The repayment of Loans of Public Authorities,*" 1913. Sherratt and Hughes, 25s.

TURNER, S. H. "*The History of Local Taxation in Scotland,*" 1908. Blackwood, 5s.

WEBB, SIDNEY. "*Grants in Aid: a Criticism and a Proposal,*" 1911. Longmans, 5s.

WILLIAMS, W. M. J. "*The King's Revenue,*" 1909. King, 7s. 6d.

See also Report of the Machinery of Government Committee. Cd. 9230. 1918. 3d.

Reports and Evidence of the Royal Commission on the Income Tax. 1919-20.

Some of the Publications of the Fabian Society and the Labour Research Department. 19.

(Complete list of nearly a hundred on application).

The History of the Fabian Society. (1916) By Edw. R. Pease. 300 pp., with portraits. 6s. net.

The Wages of Men and Women : Should they be Equal ? By Mrs. Sidney Webb. 1s.

A Public Medical Service. By David McKail, M.D., D.Ph., and William Jones. 1s.

The Reorganisation of Local Government. By Capt. C. M. Lloyd. 1s.

Fabianism and the Fiscal Question. By Bernard Shaw. 1s. net.

How to Pay for the War. Being ideas presented to the Chancellor of the Exchequer by the Fabian Research Department. Edited by Sidney Webb. (June, 1916) 6s. net.

International Government, being two Reports by L. S. Woolf and a Project by a Fabian Committee for a Supernational Authority that will prevent war. (July, 1916) 10s. net.

Trade Unionism in Germany. By W. Stephen Sanders. With Preface by Sidney Webb. (1916) 7d. net.

Fabian Essays in Socialism. This is the celebrated collection of eight essays by G. Bernard Shaw, Sidney Webb, Sir Sydney Olivier, Graham Wallas, Hubert Bland, William Clarke and Annie Besant, of which over 50,000 copies have been sold, besides numerous foreign editions. 2s. Cloth, 4s.

This Misery of Boots. By H. G. Wells. A model propagandist tract. 3d.

Facts for Socialists (revised 1915). A collection of authoritative statistics. 137th thousand. 2d.

Public Service v. Private Expenditure. By Sir Oliver Lodge, F.R.S. 1d.

State and Municipal Enterprise. (1915). 1s. net.

Introduction to Trade Unionism. By G. D. H. Cole. (Nov., 1918). 5s.

The Commonsense of Municipal Trading. By G. Bernard Shaw. Cloth 1s.

The Payment of Wages. By D. G. H. Cole. (Nov., 1918). 6s.

Family Life on a Pound a Week By Mrs. Pember Reeves. 2d.

National Finance and a Levy on Capital. By Sidney Webb. 2d.

What to Read on Social and Economic Subjects. 5th edition. 1s. net.

Socialism and the Arts of Use. By A. Clutton Brock. 1d.

Women Workers in Seven Professions. Edited by Professor Edith Morley. 7s. 6d. net.

The Rural Problem. By H. D. Harben. 2s. 6d. net.

The celebrated Fabian Tracts (1d., 2d. and 3d. each). Nearly 100 still in print. Set, bound in buckram, 7s. 6d. net, 8s. 3d. post free.

THE FABIAN BOOKSHOP, 25, Tothill Street, Westminster, S.W.1.

FABIAN ESSAYS (1920 Edition). 2s. ; postage, 3d.

THE SICKNESS OF AN ACQUISITIVE SOCIETY. By R. H. TAWNEY. 1s. n., post, 2d.

TOWARDS SOCIAL DEMOCRACY? By SIDNEY WEBB. 1s. n., post, 1d.

WHAT TO READ on Social and Economic Subjects. 1s. n.

THE RURAL PROBLEM. By H. D. HARBEN. 2s. 6s. n.

THE MISERY OF BOOTS. By H. G. WELLS. 3d., post free, 4d.

FABIAN TRACTS AND LEAFLETS.

Tracts, each 16 to 52 pp., price 1d., or 9d. per doz., unless otherwise stated.
Leaflets, 4 pp. each, price 1d. for 3 copies, 2s. per 100, or 20s. per 1000.

The Set of 74, 4/6; post free, 5/3. Bound in buckram, 7/6; post free, 8/3.

I.—General Socialism in its various aspects.

TRACTS.—192. Guild Socialism. By G. D. H. COLE, M.A. 180. The Philosophy of Socialism. By A. CLUTTON BROCK. 169. The Socialist Movement in Germany. By W. STEPHEN SANDERS. 2d. 159. The Necessary Basis of Society. By SIDNEY WEBB. 151. The Point of Honour. By RUTH C. BENTINCK. 147. Capital and Compensation. By E. R. PEASE. 146. Socialism and Superior Brains. By BERNARD SHAW. 2d. 142. Rent and Value. 138. Municipal Trading. 121. Public Service v. Private Expenditure. By Sir OLIVER LODGE. 107. Socialism for Millionaires. By BERNARD SHAW. 139. Socialism and the Churches. By Rev. JOHN CLIFFORD, D.D. 133. Socialism and Christianity. By Rev. PERCY DEARMER. 2d. 78. Socialism and the Teaching of Christ. By Dr. J. CLIFFORD. 42. Christian Socialism. By Rev. S. D. HEADLAM. 79. A Word of Remembrance and Caution to the Rich. By JOHN WOOLMAN. 72. The Moral Aspects of Socialism. By SIDNEY BALL. 69. Difficulties of Individulism. By S. WEBB. 51. Socialism : True and False. By S. WEBB. 45. The Impossibilities of Anarchism. By G. B. SHAW. 2d. 7. Capital and Land. 5. Facts for Socialism. 2d. LEAFLETS.—13. What Socialism Is. 1. Why are the Many Poor ?

II.—Applications of Socialism to Particular Problems.

TRACTS—188. National Finance and a Levy on Capital. By SIDNEY WEBB. 2d. 187. The Teacher in Politics. By SIDNEY WEBB. 2d. 186. Central Africa and the League of Nations. By R. C. HAWKIN. 2d. 183. The Reform of the House of Lords. By SIDNEY WEBB. 181. When Peace Comes—the Way of Industrial Reconstruction. By SIDNEY WEBB. 2d. 178. The War ; Women ; and Unemployment. 2d. 177. Socialism and the Arts of Use. By A. CLUTTON BROCK. 175. The Economic Foundations of the Women's Movement. 2d. 173. Public v. Private Electricity Supply. 170. Profit-Sharing and Co-Partnership: A Fraud and Failure ? 164. Gold and State Banking. 162. Family Life on a Pound a Week. By Mrs. REEVES. 2d. 161. Afforestation and Unemployment. 157. The Working Life of Women. 155. The Case against the Referendum. 154. The Case for School Clinics. 152. Our Taxes as they are and as they ought to be. 2d. 146. The Endowment of Motherhood. 2d. 145. The Case for School Nurseries. 140. Child Labour under Capitalism. 136. The Village and the Landlord. By EDW. CARPENTER. 144. Machinery : its Masters and Servants. 122. Municipal Milk and Public Health. 125. Municipalization by Provinces. 124. State Control of Trusts. LEAFLET.— 104. How Trade Unions benefit Workmen.

III. Local Government Powers : How to use them.

TRACTS.—Metropolitan Borough Councils. Their Constitution, Powers and Duties. By C. R. ATTLEE, M.A. 2d. 191. Borough Councils : Their Constitution, Powers and Duties. By C. R. ATTLEE, M.A. 2d 193. Housing. By C. M. LLOYD, M.A. 3d. 189. Urban District Councils. By C. M. LLOYD. 2d. 172. What about the Rates ? By S. WEBB. 62. Parish and District Councils (Revised 1919). 137. Parish Councils and Village Life. 109. Cottage Plans and Common Sense LEAFLETS.—134. Small Holdings. 68. The Tenant's Sanitary Catechism. 71. Ditto for London.

IV.—General Politics and Fabian Policy.

TRACTS.—158. The Case against the C.O.S. By Mrs. TOWNSHEND. 41. The Fabian Society: Its Early History. By BERNARD SHAW.

V.—Biographical Series. In portrait covers, 2d. and 3d.

182. Robert Owen, Idealist. By C. E. M. JOAD. 179. John Ruskin and Social Ethics. By Prof. EDITH MORLEY. 165. Francis Place. By ST. JOHN G. IRVINE. 166. Robert Owen, Social Reformer. By Miss B. L HUTCHINS. 167. William Morris and the Communist Ideal. By Mrs. TOWNSHEND. 168. John Stuart Mill, By JULIUS WEST. 174. Charles Kingsley and Christian Socialism. By C. E. VULLIAMY.

Printed by The Broadway Press, London and Dartford, and published by the Fabian Society, 25, Tothill Street, Westminster, London, S.W.

Fabian Tract No. 195.

THE SCANDAL

OF THE

POOR LAW

BY

C. M. LLOYD, M.A.

PUBLISHED AND SOLD BY THE FABIAN SOCIETY, 25, TOTHILL STREET, WESTMINSTER, LONDON, S.W.1.

PRICE TWOPENCE.   JULY, 1920.

THE FABIAN · SOCIETY

25, TOTHILL STREET, WESTMINSTER, LONDON, S.W.1.

Those willing to join the Labour Party, or desirous of obtaining information about its Programme and Principles, are invited to communicate with the Secretary of the Fabian Society.

The Fabian Society has been, from the outset, a constituent body of the Labour Party · and membership of the Society carries with it full membership of the Labour Party, eligibility for nomination to all Conferences and Offices, and qualification for Labour Party candidatures for Parliament and Local Authorities, without obligation to belong to any other organisation.

The Society welcomes as members any persons, men or women, wherever resident, who subscribe to its Basis (set forth below), and who will co-operate in its work according to their opportunities.

BASIS OF THE FABIAN SOCIETY.

(To be signed by all Members.)

(*Adopted May 23rd, 1919.*)

The Fabian Society consists of Socialists.

. It therefore aims at the reorganisation of Society by the emancipation of Land and Industrial Capital from individual ownership, and the vesting of them in the community for the general benefit. In this way only can the natural and acquired advantages of the country be equitably shared by the whole people.

The Society accordingly works for the extinction of private property in land, with equitable consideration of established expectations, and due provision as to the tenure of the home and the homestead ; for the transfer to the community, by constitutional methods, of all such industries as can be conducted socially ; and for the establishment, as the governing consideration in the regulation of production, distribution and service, of the common good instead of private profit.

The Society is a constituent of the Labour Party and of the International Socialist Congress ; but it takes part freely in all constitutional movements, social, economic, and political, which can be guided towards its own objects. Its direct business is (*a*) the propaganda of Socialism in its application to current problems ; (*b*) investigation and discovery in social, industrial, political and economic relations ; (*c*) the working out of Socialist principles in legislation and administrative reconstruction ; (*d*) the publication of the results of its investigations and their practical lessons.

· The Society, believing in equal citizenship of men and women in the fullest sense, is open to persons irrespective of sex, race or creed, who commit themselves to its aims and purposes as stated above, and undertake to promote its work.

The Society includes :—

I Members, who must sign the Basis and be elected by the Committee. Their Subscriptions are not fixed ; each is expected to subscribe annually according to his means They control the Society through the Executive Committee (elected annually by ballot through a postal vote), and at its annual and other business meetings.

II Associates, who sign a form expressing only general sympathy with the objects of the Society and pay not less than 10s a year They can attend all except the exclusively members' meetings, but have no control over the Society and its policy

III. Subscribers, who must pay at least 5s a year, and who can attend the Society's Ordinary Lectures

The monthly paper, *Fabian News*, and the Tracts from time to time published in the well-known Fabian series, are posted to all these classes. There are convenient Common Rooms, where light refreshments can be obtained, with an extensive library for the free use of members only.

Among the Society's activities (in which it places its services unreservedly at the disposal of the Labour Party and the Local Labour Parties all over the country, the Trade Unions and Trades Councils, and all other Labour and Socialist organisations), may be mentioned :

(i.) Free Lectures by its members and officers ;

(ii) The well-known Fabian Book-boxes, each containing about three dozen of the best books on Economics, Politics and Social Problems, which can be obtained by any organisation of men or women for 15s per annum, covering an exchange of books every three months ;

(iii.) Answers to Questions from Members of Local Authorities and others on legal, technical or political matters of Local Government, etc. ;

(iv) Special subscription courses of lectures on new developments in thought ;

(v.) Economic and social investigation and research, and publication of the results.

Lists of Publications. Annual Report, Form of Application as Member or Associate, and any other information can be obtained on application personally or by letter to the Secretary at the above address.

THE SCANDAL OF THE
POOR LAW.

FIFTEEN years ago a Royal Commission was appointed to inquire into the working of the Poor Laws and the methods adopted for meeting distress due to unemployment. Its investigations dragged into the light not only the perpetual degradation and misery of a large section of the people, but also the futility and wastefulness of the whole Poor Law system in dealing with the destitute. The system was, and still is—theoretically at any rate—based on the famous " principles of 1834 " : (1) that relief should not be offered to able-bodied persons and their dependents except in a well-regulated Workhouse, and (2) that the lot of the able bodied should be made " less eligible " than that of the independent labourer outside. But the Royal Commission found that these principles had become, by the beginning of this century, mere shadows of their former selves. The relief of the able-bodied was very far from being confined to the Workhouse, nor were the pauper inmates always by any means " less eligibly " treated than those outside. The Workhouses for the most part were not well-regulated. They were too often shelters for an indiscriminate host of men, women, and children, able-bodied and infirm and feeble minded, of good character or bad, with little in common except their destitution and their disgrace. In a few cases the old hard theory of deterrence was still applied. In others the Workhouse had been transformed into a palatial institution, whose expensive grandeur served to conceal the wretchedness of its inmates and the stupidity of the whole policy of " parish relief." If the Workhouse that the Commission examined was, generally speaking, less uncomfortable than it was, and was intended to be, in the middle of last century, it was certainly not less detested. As for outdoor relief, it had, by the pressure of a humaner public opinion, grown to enormous dimensions. It was often given without any proper investigation ; it was capricious, and as a rule inadequate for a healthy subsistence, and being, as it frequently was, a mere temporary dole to the chronically destitute, it simply helped to perpetuate a pauper class. Moreover, there was an incredible waste of effort and of money, due to the fact that the Boards of Guardians were everywhere in competition with other public bodies engaged in making provision for the sick, the feeble-minded, the children and the able-bodied. Overlapping and duplication of administrative machinery was universal, and the development of the good policy of the Local Health or Education Authorities was retarded by the conflict with the bad policy of their rivals, the Destitution Authorities.

Let us look for a moment at the picture which the Reports of the Royal Commission presented.

THE PAUPER CHILDREN.

It was found that there were in the United Kingdom some 300,000 child paupers. Nearly 20,000 of these were actually being brought up in the Workhouses, subject to all the demoralising influences which life in such an atmosphere must produce. The birth-rate in the Poor Law Institutions was nearly 15,000 annually, and the infant death-rate was appallingly high. Bad as the Workhouse was as a birthplace, it was often worse still as a nursery. Many of these wretched children were tended by imbeciles, and kept in dark and unwholesome rooms, from which they were seldom or never taken into the open air. Nor was the case of the " outdoor " infant paupers and their mothers much better. The starvation pittances of relief given to expectant and nursing mothers, and the restriction of midwifery orders, spelt misery or lingering death for thousands of women and children. Of the children of school age some, it is true, had a happier lot ; for in many Unions they were " boarded-out " or brought up in separate institutions—Cottage Homes or Poor Law Schools. But a great number of the " boarded-out " children were without proper supervision, and paying the penalty of the inadequate sums allowed for their maintenance—sums often as low as 2/6 a week. And the condition even of those in the Homes and Schools was unsatisfactory ; for apart from the stigma of pauperism resting on them, their education was impaired by the constant passage of the " in-and-out " children, the indiscriminate mixture of children of different grades of intelligence and the difficulty of getting good teachers.

But the crying scandal was the case of the children on outdoor relief, numbering nearly 200,000. Tens of thousands of these, the Royal Commission reported, were being brought up in insanitary or drunken and immoral homes, while the great majority were chronically underfed, insufficiently clothed, badly housed, and often suffering gravely from want of proper medical attention. It was with a shock of surprise and pain that the public read that many Boards of Guardians were allowing sums of 1/6 or 1/- a week to a mother to provide for a child, sometimes even with nothing at all for herself.

THE SICK PAUPERS.

"Sickness," said the Majority Report, "is admittedly one of the chief causes of pauperism . . . . We estimate that at least one-half of the total cost of pauperism is swallowed up in direct dealing with sickness. To this burden we must add the indirect contributions of sickness, viz., the widows, children, and old people, cast upon the rates through preventable deaths of bread-winners, and the host of degenerate, imbecile, maimed and blind, with whom disease helps to populate our workhouses. It is probably little, if any, exaggeration to say that, to the extent to which we can eliminate or diminish sickness among the poor, we shall eliminate or diminish one-half the existing amount of pauperism." But the Poor Law system is a system which, by its very principles, can only deal with those who have fallen into destitution. It thus actually deters the sick from getting the earliest and best treatment of their disease, which is hardly the most promising way to " eliminate or diminish sickness among the poor." It was estimated, after an inquiry into the ravages of tuberculosis, that nearly 60 per cent. of the consumptives in the Poor Law infirmaries were paupers because they were consumptives, and not consumptives because they were paupers. The majority of these sufferers come to the Poor Law when their disease is well advanced, and it is too late to effect a cure. Apart from this fundamental failure, due to the fact that the Guardians are compelled to restrict treatment to the destitute, there were particular evils which called forth the strongest condemnation of the Royal Commission. In many Unions there was the " grave public scandal " of the retention of the sick in the General Workhouse. Even where there were separate infirmaries, these, like the ordinary Workhouse wards, were commonly understaffed both as regards doctors and nurses. As for Outdoor Medical Relief, it was shown to be a tragic farce. " From first to last," said the Minority Report, " it has no conception of the Public Health point of view." The parish doctors were generally underpaid and overworked, with the very natural result that the poor could seldom expect proper treatment. One Poor Law Medical Officer, indeed, in his evidence before the Commission, actually stated that " we are forced to treat the people not as patients, but as paupers ! "

THE FEEBLE-MINDED PAUPERS.

Out of the great host of feeble-minded persons maintained at the public expense, it was found that there were " detained in the General Mixed Workhouses of England. Wales and Ireland, and, to a lesser degree, those of Scotland, no fewer than 60,000 mentally defectives, including not a few children, without education or ameliorative treatment, and herded indiscriminately with the sane." The Minority Commissioners describe how they have themselves seen, " what one of the Local Government Board Inspectors observe is of common occurrence—idiots who are physically offensive or mischievous, or so noisy as to create a disturbance by day and by night with their howls, living in the ordinary wards, to the perpetual annoyance and disgust of the other inmates. We have seen imbeciles annoying the sane, and the sane tormenting the imbeciles. We have seen half-witted women nursing the sick, feeble-minded women in charge of the babies, and imbecile old men put to look after the boys out of school hours. We have seen expectant mothers, who have come in for their confinements, by day and by night working, eating and sleeping in close companionship with idiots and imbeciles of revolting habits and hideous appearance." And besides all these, certified or uncertified, of various degrees of mental deficiency, maintained by the Guardians in the workhouses, there were another 12,000 or so on outdoor relief, all more or less free to produce at the public expense further generations of imbecile paupers.

The Aged and Infirm Paupers.

The Royal Commission found that the " Aged and Infirm " were a mass of diverse individuals of all ages and of different mental and physical characteristics, making up about one-third of the entire pauper host. The lack of classification, shown in the lumping together in a single category of all these different groups with different needs, was in itself strong evidence of one of the chief defects in the Poor Law administration. For their treatment the majority of the Boards of Guardians made no other provision than the general Workhouse, or indiscriminate, inadequate and unconditional out-relief—" forms of relief cruel to the deserving, and demoralisingly attractive to those who are depraved." In one particular class—the aged—the Old Age Pensions Act, which came into force after the Royal Commission had reported, did, of course, produce a considerable reduction during the following years. But even so, thousands of old men and women over 70 remained still in the Workhouse or on outdoor relief, because. they were too feeble or too friendless to live independently on their pensions. And a still larger number under 70 must continue their pauper existence, a very few in the comparative comfort of separate " Homes " provided by a Board of Guardians here and there, the majority in the Workhouse or on doles of out-relief.

The Able-Bodied Paupers.

In certain Unions the Royal Commission discovered an attempt to carry out the strict deterrent principle of 1834. The " Able-bodied Test Workhouses," maintained at Manchester, Sheffield, and elsewhere, were little other than penal institutions, employing what were regarded as more brutal and stupid methods than any humane prison system would care to acknowledge ; whilst the " Stoneyards," opened in times of exceptional distress, offered a spectacle of the crudest and most uneconomic " relief work." In the majority of Unions, however, the ordinary way of dealing with the " unemployed " was to put them in the " able-bodied wards " of the Workhouse. These were characterised by the Commissioners as " places of sloth and utter degradation of character, will and intelligence." " Of all the spectacles of human demoralisation now existing in these islands," said the Minority Report, " there can scarcely be anything worse than the scene presented by the men's day-ward of a large urban Workhouse during the long hours of leisure on week-days, or the whole of Sundays. Through the clouds of tobacco smoke that fill the long, low room, the visitor gradually becomes aware of the presence of one or two hundred wholly unoccupied males of any age between fifteen and ninety—strong and vicious men ; men in all stages of recovery from debauch ; weedy youths of weak intellect ; old men too dirty or disreputable to be given special privileges, and sometimes, when there are no such privileges, even worthy old men ; men subject to fits ; the feeble-minded of every kind ; the respectable labourer prematurely invalided ; the hardened, sodden loafer, and the temporarily unemployed man who has found no better refuge . . . . all free to associate with each other, and to communicate to each other, in long hours of idleness, all the contents of their minds. In such places . . . . there are aggregated, this winter, certainly more than 10,000 healthy able-bodied men."

There is, however, yet another recipient of the Guardians' hospitality. This is the vagrant. The Casual Wards, where the tramps, in return for a night's lodging and a portion of bread and cheese and water, were put to a useless task of stone-breaking, corn-grinding, or oakum picking (with sometimes incarceration for thirty-six hours in a small cell), were condemned as " brutalising and demoralising." They were, indeed, patently cruel to the honest workman on the tramp for a job, whilst they could do little to deter, and nothing to reform, the wastrel or the " workshy."

THE DESTITUTION AUTHORITIES.

Such, then, briefly summarised, was the Poor Law system ten years ago. And such, in its essentials, as we shall see presently, it remains to-day. But there was another significant fact which the Commission laid bare. All this business of pauperism, covering in the course of a year something from one and three quarter million to two million individuals in the United Kingdom was, and is, administered by 1,600 or 1,700 *ad hoc* Destitution Authorities—640 Boards of Guardians in England and Wales, 154 in Ireland, and between 800 and 900 Parish Councils (with 70 or 80 Poorhouses) in Scotland—at an annual expenditure, out of the rates and taxes, of about £17,000,000. But the Local Destitution Authority, thus trying to cope with the problems of infancy and education, of sickness and lunacy and unemployment, was found to have a whole set of other Local Authorities competing with it in every department. In 1834 the Poor Law was the only public agency for dealing with any form of destitution. By 1909 not one of the five different classes which came under the Poor Law was left to the Poor Law alone. The Local Health Authorities were providing hospitals, dispensaries, clinics, nurses, midwives and health visitors. The Local Education Authorities were giving meals and medical treatment and (in Scotland) clothes to necessitous children. The Local Lunacy Authorities maintained their own asylums, and boarded-out mentally defectives. The Local Pensions Authorities were paying old age pensions, and were soon actually to take scores of thousands of aged persons out of the hands of the Guardians. A Local Unemployment Authority had been created in 1905 by the Unemployed Workmen Act with its Distress Committees, which, by means of Farm Colonies, relief works, women's workrooms, the payment of travelling expenses, and even of the expense of emigration, deliberately set out to save decent workmen in distress from falling into the clutches of the Poor Law. Even the Police Authority overlapped with the Poor Law, with its gifts of clothing out of the " Police Aided Clothing Fund " and (in Scotland) the provision of a night's lodging for vagrants. All this, as we have said, was significant. There was obviously a squandering of public money in maintaining this elaborate duplicate machinery, even supposing that the Destitution Authorities and their rivals were both administering their services as economically as possible. But it was also pretty obvious that the administration of the Boards of Guardians was not economical in any real sense, though. it was certainly miserly in all too many Unions. And the very fact of the development of the new services of the Local Authorities, and their steady encroachment on the Poor Law, was a sign that the Poor Law was a failure, and that public opinion was more and more recognising that failure.

The Reports of the Royal Commission.

When the Royal Commission reported in 1909 it was unanimous in its condemnation of the System as it stood, and urgent for large reforms, though as to the practical shape which these reforms should take, there was a division of opinion. Both the Majority and the Minority recommended the abolition of the

Boards of Guardians, and the transfer of their duties to the County and County Borough Councils. But the Majority were in favour of retaining an *ad hoc* Destitution Authority—a Statutory Committee of the County or County Borough Council, practically independent of the Council, though able to draw on it for funds, and appointing Public Assistance Committees to function under it in smaller areas (*e.g.*, Rural or Urban Districts, or groupings of these). The Public Assistance Committee would (in co-operation with Voluntary Aid Committees and other agencies) undertake the executive work hitherto carried out by the Guardians. The Minority Commissioners, on the other hand, were totally opposed to the idea of a Destitution Authority. It was not, they said, merely destitution that the victims of the Poor Law were suffering from. What was required was treatment of each individual according to his special needs. And the proper authorities, therefore, were those which were dealing with a particular class—*e.g.*, the Local Education Authorities, the Local Health Authorities, the Local Lunacy Authorities. Moreover, these authorities alone could, and do, pursue a policy of prevention and not of mere palliation. And the right method of coping with destitution is to prevent its occurrence, and not to relieve it after it has occurred.

Of the controversy that ensued between these two policies it is not necessary to say anything here; it has only a historical interest. It is sufficient to recall that the propaganda set on foot by the National Committee for the Prevention of Destitution very rapidly convinced the country that the Poor Law must be broken up, and its functions handed over to the appropriate Local Authorities. There was, of course, opposition by the defenders of the existing order—the vested interests of Bumbledom, from the President of the Local Government Board down to the ordinary reactionary Guardian or self-satisfied Workhouse official. But the Labour Party was solidly behind the Minority Report, as also were the majority of the Liberals and many Conservatives, and it was confidently expected, shortly before the outbreak of the war, that the Government would legislate.

Pauperism During and after the War.

With the declaration of war in August, 1914, there was a new situation. The prospect of the Government taking up the question of Poor Law reform was, of course, indefinitely postponed. During the early autumn there was a large increase of distress owing to the rapid and widespread dislocation of industry and commerce, and despite the many agencies, public and private, which sprang into being to combat this distress, a considerable number of people were driven to the Poor Law for relief. The total of pauperism within three weeks of the outbreak of war was as much as 41,621 higher than that for the corresponding date in 1913, and a month later it had risen by another 115,000. There was before long, however, an equally rapid recovery, and as more and more men were absorbed into the Army or the manufacture of munitions, and with the influx of women into industry, the figures of pauperism decreased. Many of the Poor Law Institutions—workhouses, infirmaries and the like, were taken over as military hospitals or depots, their inmates being transferred to other buildings or boarded out in neighbouring Unions. Nevertheless, there remained a large residue of pauper sick and infirm, feeble-minded, aged and children.

The following figures show the numbers in receipt of Poor Law relief in England and Wales at the end of the September quarter in each year :—

	1914	1915	1916	1917	1918	1919
Ordinary Paupers (in workhouses, institutions and on outdoor relief) ..	641,028	566,725	516,876	483,436	446,665	463,009
Casuals	5,587	3,799	3,321	1,849	1,195	1,857
Outdoor Medical Relief	17,521	14,238	14,169	13,661	12,794	12,274
Lunatics	100,941	102,975	100,182	97,356	90,718	83,172
Total ..	765,077	687,737	634,548	596,298	551,262	560,312

It will be seen that the figures for 1919 show an increase. This is due to the dislocation which followed the Armistice and the demobilisation, and resulted in widespread unemployment, with strikes and lock-outs. At the beginning of 1920 the volume of pauperism was clearly returning to its pre-war proportions, and although industrial conditions are more settled than they were a year or six months ago the numbers in receipt of Poor Law relief tends to rise week by week. In January, 1920, the total of indoor paupers in over 30 of the largest industrial areas in the Kingdom showed an increase of 2,642 (or 2·3 per cent.) over that of December, and the total of outdoor paupers (exclusive of vagrants and of persons receiving outdoor relief) an increase of 1,374 (or 1 per cent.). By March there was a further rise of 1·8 per cent. in the indoor figures, and 2·4 per cent. in the outdoor. As compared with a year earlier, the increases were, in the case of indoor paupers, 6·2 per cent., in the case of outdoor, 11·2 per cent. In London there were 9,500 more paupers on April 24th, 1920, than on the corresponding day in 1919.

Reforms in the Poor Law.

But, it will be asked, have there not been reforms in the Poor Law administration in the last five years, and even before the war, subsequent to the Reports of the Royal Commission ? Is the state of the Poor Law as described by the Royal Commission a true picture to-day ?

There have indeed been reforms. But let us examine them, and see how much change they have made in the Poor Law system. In the years following the publication of the Reports, Mr. John Burns, then President of the Local Government Board, did his best to whitewash the Poor Law. He admitted that amendments were required here and there ; but these could safely be left to him—" the fairy godfather of the poor," as he modestly called himself ! He was soon proclaiming that he had introduced sweeping " ameliorations," and that, " if reform by revolution has been denied us, revolution by reform in adminis- tration has been most efficiently secured." This revolutionary administrative reform proved, on examination, to amount to very little. An Outdoor Relief Regulation Order was issued, introducing a case-paper system. But in 1912 the doles of out relief in a great number of the Unions were as inadequate and as unsatisfactory as they had been before and as they have been since. Many of the Workhouses were still crowded with indis- criminate herds of paupers, as they had been before and as they have been since. The lot of the feeble minded remained practi- cally unaltered, and the improvement of the miserable Medical Service of the Poor Law only moved by inches. Some of the aged certainly, as has already been said, were being rescued, but the Old Age Pensions Act could hardly be claimed, save in a very ironical sense, as a reform in Poor Law administration. The " able-bodied " problem, except in so far as it was affected by the Insurance Act (which, again, was not a Local Government Board reform) was still the same problem. The hardened tramps, how- ever, were " reformed " by the remarkable device of putting all the twenty-eight Casual Wards of the Metropolis under the management of the Metropolitan Asylums Board. Thus, said Mr. Burns, " we shall be able to keep a register of all the vagrants, and devise a means by which the decent men amongst them can be put upon their feet, re-instated in the industrial sphere, and by which those who are not quite so good can be dealt with either by medical, curative or preventive methods." There is not, it must be confessed, much evidence that these dazzling hopes have been fulfilled. And, in any case, the possibility that the Metropolitan Asylums Board may succeed in rehabilitating a few hundred of these unfortunate wretches and " workshys," is not a very solid proof that the Poor Law is a satisfactory method of dealing with unemployment. In one department certainly Mr. Burns did make some useful efforts, though the process of reform took a long time. He put pressure on a number of the more reactionary Boards of Guardians to move their children from the Workhouses. Even in this, however, he was only partially successful, for a considerable number still remain to this day in their old surroundings. There was also a Boarding-Out Order in 1911, which did a little to improve the lot of the boarded-out children. But in many Unions it was very far from being honestly carried out. Altogether it is safe to say that Mr. Burns was the only man in the Kingdom who could discern any important difference between the " reformed " Poor Law of 1912 and the " unreformed " Poor Law of 1909 !

But there have been further reforms since 1912. It is not worth while to discuss them in detail. We have, indeed, only referred at some little length to Mr. Burns's activities in order to show the hopelessness of expecting any change of the Poor Law system from within. Of the most recent changes two only can be called important. These are the supersession of the reactionary Local Government Board by the Ministry of Health, and the removal, by the Representation of the People Act, of the disqualification which prevented a man from voting if he had received parish relief in the previous year. Both these, it will be noticed, were measures carried by Parliament ; both point clearly, to the general contempt for the Poor Law and its administration. For the rest, there has been, in some Unions, a better classification of paupers, a slight improvement in the treatment of sickness, and a further effort to deal with the " tramp " problem by the establishment of County Vagrancy Committees (which are, in fact, only local combinations of Boards of Guardians). And there is no longer a Workhouse ; it is now generally called "The Institution" (though the name "Workhouse" must still be used for certain legal purposes). This trivial joke, which Bumble and his champions take quite seriously, is again significant of the popular feeling about the Poor Law and its degrading associations.

THE POSITION TO-DAY.

What, then, is the sum total of all these reforms of the last ten years ? It would be unfair to deny that some Boards of Guardians have honestly tried to remove abuses, and that in the best administered Unions the standard of provision is as high as the law will allow. But in all too many cases the old evils, which were so unsparingly criticised by the Royal Commission, still flourish. The new Institution and the old Workhouse are as like as two peas. Outdoor relief is still, over a large part of the Kingdom, a synonym for inadequate doles dispensed in the old way. The outdoor scales have, of course, risen, but so also has the cost of living, and the old person or widow who receives 10/- or 11/- to-day cannot make it go any further than 4/6 or 5/- would go formerly. And some Boards, despite the great enhancement of prices, have not raised their doles beyond 7/6. The Guardians are little better equipped than they were for the treatment of disease, for maintaining the mentally defective or for educating children. Many of them, as we have already said, still keep their children in the " Institution " despite the laments of the Ministry of Health. There were, in' fact, on January 1st, 1920, over 3,000 inmates of the mixed Workhouses between the ages of three and sixteen (not more than one-third of whom could be said to be there only temporarily, pending their removal to some other place). As for the Medical Service, such reform as has been introduced has been largely superficial, and limited generally to the larger Urban Unions. Even there, it has not been universal. In one important town in the Eastern Counties, for instance, we find the Medical Officer complaining to the Guardians that " the nursing staff is inadequate and insufficiently paid, there are 120 people in the Infirmary, 83 of them bedridden, with only one certificated nurse and about three ward-maids."

Nor is there any sign of the Guardians having performed a miracle for the able-bodied. The Yorkshire Vagrancy Committee had 11,681 admissions to its Casual Wards during the fourth quarter of 1919. The Warwickshire Vagrancy Committee reports for the March quarter, 1920, an increase of 636 admissions over the previous quarter, and of 3,081 over the corresponding figure in 1919. The tramp, in fact, is again on the road, and the grim old farce will be repeated despite the County Vagrancy Committees.

Meanwhile, the encroachment on the Poor Law by the Local Authorities has grown apace. The Local Health Authority has of late enormously extended its provision for infancy and maternity and for sufferers from various diseases, notably tuberculosis and venereal disease. Moreover, it is in many places in open conflict with the Guardians on the question of hospital provision. The insufficiency of accommodation has become a serious problem. Boards of Guardians are asking the Minister of Health to let the ratepayers come as paying patients to the Poor Law Infirmaries ; for in many of these Institutions there are empty beds, whilst the non-Poor Law hospitals, already over-crowded, have long lists of patients waiting their chance to come in. At Bradford the Poor Law Infirmary has actually been handed over to the Corporation, with the approval of the Ministry of Health, to be run as a municipal hospital, and it seems probable that a similar policy will be carried out elsewhere. The Local Education Authority, with its School Medical service, now doctors thousands of children who formerly were treated (if they were treated at all) by the Poor Law. The Insurance Committees, too, have further diminished the importance of the Poor Law Medical service. And the war gave us yet another authority, the Local Pensions Committee, to add to the confusion.

The ugly picture, then, of the Poor Law system that was drawn by the Royal Commission in 1909, remains in all essentials, if not in its details, a true picture in 1920. There have been reforms ; some of the worst scandals have been removed, or partially removed, and large numbers of the poor have been rescued from the fear of the " parish." But the fundamental cause of the Poor Law's failure has not been removed, and a thousand " administrative reforms " could not remove it. An *ad hoc* Destitution Authority, which cannot take any steps to prevent destitution before it occurs, and which, furthermore, is forced to regard those who come to it primarily as destitute persons rather than as individuals in need of specialised treatment, is a hopeless anachronism. The demand for the break-up of the Poor Law is as urgent to-day as it was ten years ago.

Further Proposals for the Abolition of the Poor Law.

But that demand has now been strongly re-inforced. In July, 1917, the Ministry of Reconstruction appointed a Committee " to consider and report upon the steps to be taken to secure the better co-ordination of Public Assistance in England and Wales. Its members were : Sir Donald Maclean, M.P. (chairman), Mr. R. J. Curtis, Mr. Robert Donald, Sir G. Fordham, Lord George Hamilton, Mr. G. Montagu Harris, Mr. Spurley Hey, Sir Robert Morant, Mr. R. C. Norman, Mr. H. G. Pritchard, Sir Samuel Provis, Dr. John Robertson, Mr. A. V. Symonds, Mr. J. H. Thomas, M.P., and Mrs. Sidney Webb.

Its Report (Cd. 8917, 1918, commonly known as the " Maclean Report ") issued in December, 1917, was unanimous (with certain reservations, which need not be discussed here, by one or two members), and the following are its principal recommendations :

(1) Boards of Guardians should be abolished and all their functions transferred to the Councils of Counties, County Boroughs, and Boroughs and Urban Districts with populations over 50,000.

(2) Provision for all the sick and infirm (including the aged requiring institutional care, and maternity and infancy) should be made by these Authorities under the Public Health Acts suitably extended.

(3) The Ministry of Health should have power, on the application of any Borough with over 10,000 population, or any Urban District with over 20,000, to " direct that such functions as the Ministry may determine " shall be exercised by the Town or Urban District Council instead of by the County Council.

(4) The children should be dealt with by the Local Education Authorities, the mentally deficient by the Lunacy Authorities.

(5) Every County or County Borough (or Borough or Urban District Council with population over 50,000) should set up (*a*) a Prevention of Unemployment and Training

Committee (on the lines of the Education Committee, and including representatives of employers and Trade Unions) ;

(*b*) A Home Assistance Committee (on the lines of the Education Committee), to inquire into the economic circumstances of all applicants for public assistance, to supervise them, to administer all relief given in the home, to recover expenses for maintenance, treatment, etc., and to keep a private register of all such applicants and their families and of the assistance given.

(6) County Councils should appoint Committees for Districts or combinations of Districts, to which various functions of the Home Assistance Committee and the Prevention of Unemployment Committee would be delegated.

These District Committees would consist of (*a*) members of the County Council, (*b*) Town or District Councillors, (*c*) persons experienced in the work to be done.

(7) London should have a special scheme, in which the duties would be divided between the L.C.C. and the Metropolitan Borough Councils.

(*a*) The Borough Councils would appoint Home Assistance Committees, and would also carry out vaccination and registration of births and deaths.

(*b*) The L.C.C. would exercise the rest of the functions transferred (through its Public Health, Education, Asylums, and Prevention of Unemployment Committees). It would also appoint a Central Assistance Committee, which would lay down policy and rules of local administration for the Home Assistance Committees in the Boroughs.

(8) Poor Law officials should be transferred to the Local Authorities (provided both they and the Local Authorities agreed), and compensated for any pecuniary loss incurred by the change.

(9) The cost of all functions transferred should fall on the new Authority (the Administrative County, County Borough, Borough or Urban District), and in London mainly on the County, except for Home Assistance, which would be a charge on the Borough (but the L.C.C. would repay two-thirds of this, if satisfied of the efficiency of the Borough's staff and administration).

These recommendations, it will be seen, represent the acceptance of the principle on which the Minority Commissioners in 1909 were so emphatic—the abolition of the *ad hoc* Destitution bodies and treatment of each individual according to his needs by the appropriate Local Authority. There are two particular points, however, on which they diverge from the Minority Report, and on these they are open to some criticism.

Unemployment and The Local Authorities.

The first is the proposed local Unemployment and Training Committee. To this the objection has been made that it presents considerable administrative difficulties for the County Councils, and further that, in any case, a County is not a satisfactory area for dealing with unemployment. It must be confessed that there is a good deal in this contention. The problem of unemployment is primarily a national question. It might, no doubt, be dealt with in some measure on a " regional " basis—*i.e.*, by taking a group of counties as a unit. But single Counties are not convenient units. It is worth noticing, however, the exact words of the Maclean Report. It is proposed that the Prevention of Unemployment and Training Committee should supersede both the Board of Guardians and the Distress Committee set up under the Unemployed Workmen Act of 1905. It would " exercise the powers of the Council as to (i) preventing unemployment (so far as practicable, and subject to service requirements and due economy) by procuring such a re-arrangement of the Council's rules and services as to regularise the local demand for labour ; (ii) facilitating through the Employment Exchanges the finding of situations ; (iii) making use of any form of educational training in co-operation as much as possible with the Education Committee ; (iv) assisting migration ; and (v) creating and administering, whether by itself or in federation with other Local Authorities, any specialised provision of the time required by the unemployed.

The scheme, it will be observed, is not altogether clear, and it is difficult to pass a final judgment until its details are put in a more concrete shape. But this much, at least, may be said. In so far as it means a definite obligation imposed on a Local Authority to play its proper part in the organisation of industry, it points in the right direction. The prevention of unemployment will not be achieved without the carefully devised co-operation of the Local Authorities with the State for meeting the great industrial depressions which unhappily recur every few years. But is it necessary for this purpose to set up a new Committee of the Council, with a separate staff and machinery, and whose function will be not to manage any service of its own, but rather to interfere with those of other Committees ? In another aspect, again, it appears to duplicate the machinery of the Employment Exchanges. The Employment Exchange, for instance, is already able to assist migration. Is it necessary to charge a County Council also with this duty ? And why this elaborate Committee to " facilitate the finding of situations " through the Employment Exchange ? Push the idea but a little further and we shall have other Committees charged with facilitating the getting of Old Age Pensions from the Post Office, or Maternity Benefit from the Insurance Committee ! A third point is the provision of training. This, of course, may be of the highest importance. But it does not appear that the new Unemployment Committee is to maintain institutions of its own, but rather to see that men are properly placed in existing farm colonies, or trade schools or workshops. As for any " detention colonies " that may be created for " won't works," the Maclean Report does not propose to entrust these to the Local Authority at all, but " either to some one existing Government Department or to a special body on which the various Government Departments concerned would be represented." That is evidently right; but it is also evidently one reason the less for the establishment of the Prevention of Unemployment and Training Committee. Altogether, it is very questionable whether a case is made out for this new piece of local machinery.

" HOME ASSISTANCE."

Secondly, there is the Home Assistance Committee. Here, again, administrative objections have been raised on the part of the County Councils. The County, it is urged, is not properly equipped for this work ; it would be better done by the Boroughs and Districts on their own responsibility. But may it not also be asked whether some of it, at least, had better not be done at all ? The Maclean Committee was impressed, rightly enough, by the need of co-ordination among the various authorities giving assistance in money or kind out of public funds—often to different members of the same family, and without any common register of cases. There is thus, they argue, " a complex evil, involving (a) unnecessary expenditure on assistance and administration ; (b) unnecessary multiplication at enquiry offices and pay clubs ; (c) annoyance to the recipients of repeated inquiries from different authorities ; (d) failure in many cases, owing to lack of organisation and staff, to make the payments promptly or regularly ; and (e) the temptations to fraud afforded to the applicants by the failure of the overlapping authorities to discover what each is doing. And they add that it seems desirable that to the one Committee, which is to manage all the work of co-ordination, shall also " be assigned certain duties of general supervision, for the reason that it is the only unspecialised Committee and deals with all classes of applicants for assistance in the above sense . . . This supervision should apply to families where any member is in receipt of any form of assistance in money, kind, or service, wholly or partly provided out of rates or taxes, eligibility for which is dependent on the pecuniary need of the person or family concerned, or for which payment is legally recoverable. Have we not here peeping out the cloven hoof of the Charity Organisation Society? Obviously co-ordination, including a proper register of cases, is necessary. But why should this " unspecialised " Committee, on the plea of " co-ordination," interfere with the work of the specialised

Committees? Doubtless, too, some supervision is necessary. But supervision is a blessed word which too often covers a multitude of inquisitions. Why should a whole family be supervised by a new and "unspecialised" Committee, (a goodly proportion of whose members are co-opted "persons experienced in the work to be done"—an ominous category!) because grandmother gets an Old Age Pension, or little Jane a pair of spectacles? Did not the Minority Report, in a word, go as far as was necessary in suggesting a Registrar of Public Assistance to co-ordinate the work of the Education and Health and other Committees? This personage came in some years ago for a large measure of abuse as a sinister bureaucrat. But he would be at least an official with defined powers, with routine functions, and under democratic control. At the very worst, he might have chastised the poor with whips; the Home Assistance Committee, with its co-opted members "experienced in the work to be done," would chastise them with scorpions! The proposal, in short, as it stands, looks suspiciously like a concession to our old friend the professional philanthropist, who, convinced at the bottom of his heart that destitution is a "moral disease," will "learn the poor to be better."

THE GOVERNMENT'S PLEDGE.

But these two recommendations are, after all, details, which can easily be modified in the legislation that will abolish the Poor Law. The significance of the Maclean Report is that it heals the old breach between the partisans of the Majority and Minority of the Royal Commission, and unites them in the demand for the complete disappearance of the Board of Guardians. What, then, has the Government to say to this demand? The Government has accepted it. It has promised to legislate at the earliest opportunity. The Minister of Health has continually proclaimed the urgency of carrying out this great measure. When will the opportunity arise? Why not immediately? It is a large question to deal with, but it does not present the difficulties which it presented before the war. The Ministry of Health is in favour of reform, and not, as was its predecessor, the old Local Government Board, against it. There is even less popular support for the Poor Law than there was ten years ago—and there was very little then. A devoted band of reactionary Guardians and Bumbles, great and small, will die in the last ditch to save the system. But their plea for what they naively call the "splendid machinery of the Poor Law," so cheap at the price of £15,000,000 to £20,000,000 per annum, will hardly persuade an infant in arms. Nor will their own proposals for "genuine reform," in the shape of "re-adjusted" local Destitution Authorities "for the purpose of co-ordinating further assistance," commend itself to any intelligent person. The efficiency of such a scheme of glorified Boards of Guardians is no more credible than the efficiency of the present "splendid machinery." For the rest, the Government has no opposition to fear, and no excuse for its inaction. It is idle to pretend that time cannot be found for this important task ; the time of Parliament and of the Government is constantly occupied in less pressing business. No such pretence would be made if the public chose to bestir itself. Let the public, therefore, take careful stock of the facts of the last ten years and the position to-day.

The Poor Law to-day is a crying scandal. It is a scandal because it applies mischievous principles of deterrence where it ought rather to encourage treatment. It is a scandal because it inflicts needless humiliation and suffering upon a vast mass of the poor. It is a scandal because it interferes with the development of good local government. It is a scandal because it expends each year, for an utterly inadequate return, millions of public money. It is useless to tinker with it ; it cannot be " reformed." For the system does not fail merely because Boards of Guardians are not doing their duty : some of them are, in fact, doing all that is possible as the law stands. It does not fail because the " wrong people " are elected to administer it. It would fail if all the Guardians in the country were Archangels or Labour men—and that for the very simple reason that it is a system of Destitution Authorities, attempting to relieve those who have fallen into destitution instead of preventing them from falling into it. It is a system which is repellent alike to educationists, to public health reformers, to the victims who suffer under it, and to the democratic sentiment of the age. There is only one way to deal with it, which is to abolish the Boards of Guardians, the Poor Law Unions, and the Workhouses; to make the Local Health Authorities responsible for all the sick, the infants and the infirm aged ; to make the Local Education Authorities responsible for all the children of school age ; to make the Local Lunacy Authorities responsible for all the feeble minded ; to establish such an " organisation of the labour market " and such reforms in industry as will provide, through the State, the Local Authorities and the Trade Unions against the distress caused by unemployment.

All this was recommended by the Royal Commission eleven years ago and again by the Maclean Committee, whose proposals the Government pledged itself to carry out. It is high time to insist that the Government shall honour its pledge.

FABIAN ESSAYS (1920 Edition). 2s. 6d. ; postage, 3d.
THE SICKNESS OF AN ACQUISITIVE SOCIETY. By. R. H. TAWNEY. 2s. n.,
post, 4d.
TOWARDS SOCIAL DEMOCRACY? By SIDNEY WEBB. 1s. n., post, 1d.
WHAT TO READ on Social and Economic Subjects (in preparation).
THE RURAL PROBLEM. By H. D. HARBEN. 2s. 6s. n.
THE MISERY OF BOOTS. By H. G. WELLS. 3d., post free, 4d.
FABIAN TRACTS AND LEAFLETS.
Tracts, each 16 to 52 pp., price 1d., or 9d. per doz., unless otherwise stated.
Leaflets, 4 pp. each, price 1d. for 3 copies, 2s. per 100, or 20s. per 1000..
The Set of 74, 4/6; post free, 5/3. Bound in buckram, 7/6; post free, 8/3.

I.—General Socialism in its various aspects.

TRACTS.—192. Guild Socialism. By G. D. H. COLE, M.A. 180. The Philosophy
of Socialism. By A. CLUTTON BROCK. 169. The Socialist Movement in Germany.
By W. STEPHEN SANDERS. 2d. 159. The Necessary Basis of Society.
By SIDNEY WEBB. 151. The Point of Honour. By RUTH C. BENTINCK.
147. Capital and Compensation. By E. R. PEASE. 146. Socialism and Superior
Brains. By BERNARD SHAW. 2d. 142. Rent and Value. 138. Municipal Trading.
121. Public Service v. Private Expenditure. By Sir OLIVER LODGE. 107. Socialism
for Millionaires. By BERNARD SHAW. 139. Socialism and the Churches. By Rev.
JOHN CLIFFORD, D.D. 133. Socialism and Christianity. By Rev. PERCY DEARMER.
2d. 78. Socialism and the Teaching of Christ. By Dr J. CLIFFORD. 42. Christian
Socialism. By Rev. S. D. HEADLAM. 79. A Word of Remembrance and Caution to
the Rich. By JOHN WOOLMAN. 72. The Moral Aspects of Socialism. By SIDNEY
BALL. 69. Difficulties of Individulism. By S. WEBB. 51. Socialism : True and
False. By S. WEBB. 45. The Impossibilities of Anarchism. By G. B. SHAW. 2d.
7. Capital and Land. 5. Facts for Socialism. 2d. LEAFLETS.—13. What Socialism
Is. 1. Why are the Many Poor ?

II.—Applications of Socialism to Particular Problems.

TRACTS.—194. Taxes, Rates and Local Income Tax. By ROBERT JONES, D.Sc.
188. National Finance and a Levy on Capital. By SIDNEY WEBB. 2d. 187.
The Teacher in Politics. By SIDNEY WEBB. 2d. 186. Central Africa and the
League of Nations. By R. C. HAWKIN. 2d. 183. The Reform of the House of
Lords. By SIDNEY WEBB. 181. When Peace Comes—the Way of Industrial
Reconstruction. By SIDNEY WEBB. 2d. 178. The War; Women; and Unemploy-
ment. 2d. 177. Socialism and the Arts of Use. By A. CLUTTON BROCK. 175. The
Economic Foundations of the Women's Movement. 2d. 173. Public v. Private
Electricity Supply. 170. Profit-Sharing and Co-Partnership: A Fraud and Failure ?
164. Gold and State Banking. 162. Family Life on a Pound a Week. By Mrs.
REEVES. 2d. 161. Afforestation and Unemployment. 157. The Working Life of
Women. 155. The Case against the Referendum. 154. The Case for School Clinics.
152. Our Taxes as they are and as they ought to be. 2d. 145. The Case for
School Nurseries. 140. Child Labour under Capitalism. 136. The Village and
the Landlord. By EDW. CARPENTER. 144. Machinery : its Masters and Servants.
122. Municipal Milk and Public Health. 125. Municipalization by Provinces.
124. State Control of Trusts. LEAFLET.— 104. How Trade Unions benefit
Workmen.

III. Local Government Powers : How to use them.

TRACTS.—Metropolitan Borough Councils. Their Constitution, Powers and Duties.
By C. R. ATTLEE, M.A. 2d. 191. Borough Councils : Their Constitution, Powers
and Duties By C. R. ATTLEE, M.A. 2d 193. Housing. By C. M. LLOYD, M.A.
3d. 189. Urban District Councils. By C. M. LLOYD. 2d. 172. What about the
Rates ? By S. WEBB. 62. Parish and District Councils (Revised 1919). 137.
Parish Councils and Village Life. 109. Cottage Plans and Common Sense.
LEAFLETS.—134. Small Holdings. 68. The Tenant's Sanitary Catechism. 71.
Ditto for London.

IV.—General Politics and Fabian Policy.

TRACTS.—158. The Case against the C.O.S. By Mrs. TOWNSHEND. 41. The Fabian
Society: Its Early History. By BERNARD SHAW.

V.—Biographical Series. In portrait covers, 2d. and 3d.

182. Robert Owen, Idealist. By C. E. M. JOAD 179. John Ruskin and Social
Ethics. By Prof. EDITH MORLEY. 165. Francis Place. By ST. JOHN G. IRVINE.
166. Robert Owen, Social Reformer. By Miss B. L HUTCHINS. 167. William
Morris and the Communist Ideal. By Mrs TOWNSHEND. 168. John Stuart Mill,
By JULIUS WEST. 174. Charles Kingsley and Christian Socialism. By C. E.
VULLIAMY

Printed by The Broadway Press, London and Dartford, and published by the Fabian Society,
25, Tothill Street. Westminster. London. S W.

Fabian Tract No. 196.

THE ROOT OF LABOUR UNREST:

AN ADDRESS TO EMPLOYERS AND MANAGERS.*

BY

SIDNEY WEBB.

* An Address to a representative private gathering of Employers, Managers and Foremen in 1919 ; reproduced as delivered with bibliographical footnotes added. Reference may be made to *The Works Manager To-day*, by the lecturer (Longmans : 7s. 6d. net).

PUBLISHED AND SOLD BY THE FABIAN SOCIETY, 25, TOTHILL STREET, WESTMINSTER, LONDON, S.W.1.
PRICE TWOPENCE.   NOVEMBER, 1920.

THE FABIAN SOCIETY

25, TOTHILL STREET, WESTMINSTER, LONDON, S.W.1.

Those willing to join the Labour Party, or desirous of obtaining information about its Programme and Principles, are invited to communicate with the Secretary of the Fabian Society.

The Fabian Society has been, from the outset, a constituent body of the Labour Party : and membership of the Society carries with it full membership of the Labour Party, eligibility for nomination to all Conferences and Offices, and qualification for Labour Party candidatures for Parliament and Local Authorities, without obligation to belong to any other organisation.

The Society welcomes as members any persons, men or women, wherever resident, who subscribe to its Basis (set forth below), and who will co-operate in its work according to their opportunities.

BASIS OF THE FABIAN SOCIETY.

(To be signed by all Members.)

(*Adopted May 23rd, 1919.*)

The Fabian Society consists of Socialists.

It therefore aims at the reorganisation of Society by the emancipation of Land and Industrial Capital from individual ownership, and the vesting of them in the community for the general benefit. In this way only can the natural and acquired advantages of the country be equitably shared by the whole people.

The Society accordingly works for the extinction of private property in land, with equitable consideration of established expectations, and due provision as to the tenure of the home and the homestead ; for the transfer to the community, by constitutional methods, of all such industries as can be conducted socially ; and for the establishment, as the governing consideration in the regulation of production, distribution and service, of the common good instead of private profit.

The Society is a constituent of the Labour Party and of the International Socialist Congress ; but it takes part freely in all constitutional movements, social, economic and political, which can be guided towards its own objects. Its direct business is (*a*) the propaganda of Socialism in its application to current problems ; (*b*) investigation and discovery in social, industrial, political and economic relations ; (*c*) the working out of Socialist principles in legislation and administrative reconstruction ; (*d*) the publication of the results of its investigations and their practical lessons.

The Society, believing in equal citizenship of men and women in the fullest sense, is open to persons irrespective of sex, race or creed, who commit themselves to its aims and purposes as stated above, and undertake to promote its work.

The Society includes :—

I. Members, who must sign the Basis and be elected by the Committee. Their Subscriptions are not fixed ; each is expected to subscribe annually according to his means. They control the Society through the Executive Committee (elected annually by ballot through a postal vote), and at its annual and other business meetings.

II. Associates, who sign a form expressing only general sympathy with the objects of the Society and pay not less than 10s. a year. They can attend all except the exclusively members' meetings, but have no control over the Society and its policy.

III. Subscribers, who must pay at least 5s. a year, and who can attend the Society's Ordinary Lectures.

The monthly paper, *Fabian News*, and the Tracts from time to time published in the well-known Fabian series, are posted to all these classes. There are convenient Common Rooms, where light refreshments can be obtained, with an extensive library for the free use of members only.

Among the Society's activities (in which it places its services unreservedly at the disposal of the Labour Party and the Local Labour Parties all over the country, the Trade Unions and Trades Councils, and all other Labour and Socialist organisations), may be mentioned :

(i.) Free Lectures by its members and officers;

(ii.) The well-known Fabian Book-boxes, each containing about three dozen of the best books on Economics, Politics and Social Problems, which can be obtained by any organisation of men or women for 15s per annum, covering an exchange of books every three months;

(iii.) Answers to Questions from Members of Local Authorities and others on legal, technical or political matters of Local Government, etc.;

(iv.) Special subscription courses of lectures on new developments in thought;

(v.) Economic and social investigation and research, and publication of the results.

Lists of Publications, Annual Report, Form of Application as Member or Associate, and any other information can be obtained on application personally or by letter to the Secretary at the above address.

THE ROOT OF LABOUR UNREST

By SIDNEY WEBB.

The subject that I have been asked to speak upon is capable of more than one meaning. What I propose to do is to endeavour to convey to those here what I think is at the bottom of the mind of the workman. I am not going necessarily to justify, or even to adopt as my own, everything that I shall say, nor can I pretend that what I shall say will be found anywhere, either in the printed documents of any labour organisation, or, for that matter, in the speech of any workman. The workman, like many of us, is an inarticulate person, and you will not discover all that he is thinking from any programme to which he may give his assent. You will not even discover what he is thinking from anything you can get out of him in a brief interview. I am going to try and describe to you the ideas which he is scarcely conscious of himself, but which seem to me to lie at the bottom of the present industrial unrest. I am here as an interpreter to you of something which I think to be the real explanation, or the fundamental cause, of the phenomenon that we commonly speak of as labour unrest. Of course, this " new spirit " in industry is not, in one sense, really new. I have had occasion, when my wife and I were writing the " History of Trade Unionism,"* to try and trace the underlying motives and causes of industrial combination and industrial revolt for the last two hundred and fifty years, and the spirit which I am going to describe to you is to be detected a very long way back. It is thus very far from being merely a result of the war. What is new is its extent, I might even say its universality. It has spread more suddenly and rapidly in a year or two than any of us believed possible. Secondly, if I may say it without offence, another new element in the situation is the recognition by employers and managers that there is such a thing as this spirit. The unrest was there a hundred years ago, but it was ignored, denied, and refused any recognition. It has now forced itself upon the minds of the employers, because they, too, have experienced a certain change of heart. They have spontaneously recognised the existence of this spirit, and its unprecedented growth has coincided with their discovery of it. I need hardly say what I am talking about is not a demand for

---

* *The History of Trade Unionism*, by S. and B. Webb, new edition, enlarged and extended to 1920. (Longmans : 21s. net.)

higher wages. That is as old as history itself. There is nothing surprising in the demand for a rise in wages on one ground or another, and at present the demand is based on firm ground, not only on the continual rise in the cost of living, but also on the relatively considerable amount of the employers' profits in practically every industry whatsoever. At no time in the history of the British Empire have the aggregate profits of industry been so large as at the present time, so far as can be ascertained from the very imperfect statistics available. Whether you meet the demand of the workmen by saying that the rise in the cost of living is not quite so great as they represent it to be, or by telling them that your industry cannot afford the rise, you have a particularly weak case. And, as an actual fact, the rise is usually granted almost as soon as it is demanded. But, of course, there have often been general rises in wages before, from the 14th century onwards.

Nor is there anything new in the demand for shorter hours. That claim, too, has long been with us, and the normal working day has gone down from twelve hours—if there was any normal day at all 150 years ago—to ten, nine and eight hours. Now, employers and moralists pretend to be shocked if anyone proposes a day of six hours ; and yet there is no sanctity about any one of these numbers. There is no more reason *a priori* why men should sell their labour for ten hours a day than for eight, or for eight hours than for six. Each particular generation of employers clings desperately to some accustomed standard, but there is no finality.* I am quite sure myself that the work of the world, and all the present production, if properly arranged, could easily be done in much less than eight hours a day. We could get all that is required by very much shorter hours of labour than are at present worked. Incidentally, it might mean that every healthy adult (as Ruskin long ago suggested) would have to work—a terrible consummation, no doubt, for certain people. When we hear of it in Russia, we think the end of the world has come.

Putting it briefly, the most pressing claim of the workman at the present time is, as Lord Robert Cecil quite rightly observed, for partnership in industry. Unfortunately, Lord Robert Cecil, who can hardly be expected to know very much about it, assumed that partnership meant profit-sharing. Let me warn you straight away that profit-sharing is looked on by the workman as either a fraud or a futility. It is not infrequently a fraud, and always a futility. I cannot stop to prove that, but I am expressing the workman's point of view, and any attempt to smooth over labour unrest by proposals for profit-sharing stamps the man who makes them as an ignoramus. He has not taken the trouble to learn by experience, or even to theorise on the basis of what has happened. Naturally, I do not mean to imply that profit-sharing is always meant as a fraud: that, of course, is not the case. But we are bound to realise that, in all profit-sharing schemes, the

---

* The economic argument for prescribed hours of labour, as well as for a shorter working day, will be found in *Industrial Democracy*, chap. vi., " The Normal Day," by S. and B. Webb, edition of 1920. (Longmans : 21s. net.)

employer secures for himself a preferential claim to a fixed interest on capital, the amount of which is either not defined in advance, or is defined arbitrarily by the employer himself. The capital of a firm is often a purely imaginary figure, and you can put on as many noughts as you please. The workman is invited to agree to an arrangement by which, as a first charge, a fixed rate of interest shall be paid upon an amount of capital which he has had no share in defining and no means of verifying, and over which he has no power of control. Moreover, the proceeds are always subject to the prior deduction of sums for reserves and depreciation, and also for the salaries of the partners, or of the directors and managers, over the scale of which the workman is not allowed any control. Then, after all these deductions have been made, if there is anything over, the workman gets, in successful years, five or six per cent. addition to his wages. If he is getting £2 a week, under a successful profit-sharing scheme he may receive something like 2s. a week more in his share of the profits. This is nothing like good enough. Of course, any Trade Unionist would ask : " How do I know that I am not foregoing much more than 2s. a week on my standard rate ? Have I any security that the 2s. is a real addition at all ? "

PROFIT-SHARING REJECTED.

Suppose a workman invited to agree to a profit-sharing scheme was prudent enough to ask a solicitor : " Am I justified in going into this sort of partnership ? " If the solicitor gave the advice which he would give to a capitalist inquiring about a partnership, he would point out to the workman that he was putting himself entirely into the employer's hands, and pledging himself to accept the latter's estimates blindfold. In short, the solicitor would advise him to reject the proposal entirely.*

What the workman is asking for at present is a more genuine partnership. He does not want part ownership of the capital, except as a member of the community in a sense which I will afterwards explain. He does not want a share in the profits, because he does not think that profits (as distinguished from the wages of management) ought to exist. But he wants to be admitted on equal terms as a partner in the management and direction of the concern. What he objects to is the autocracy, the arbitrary power, to which he is asked to submit. Mr. Galsworthy, in one of his novels, describes the dwellers of a country house as people who got up when they liked, had what they liked for breakfast and lunch, did precisely what they liked during the day, and, when they liked, went to rest again. Then he describes an agricultural labourer, who had to get up at a certain time and go to work that he did not like, because he was ordered to do so ; he lived in a cottage that he did not like and his whole life was spent in an inevitable routine ; he was removed, when ill, to a workhouse that he did not like, and eventually died—to the last, under compulsion. Galsworthy's point is that

---

* See Fabian Tract No. 170 : *Profit-Sharing a Fraud and a Failure?* by E. R. Pease. (Fabian Society : price 1d.)

we have one class passing its whole existence in giving orders, and another class passing its whole existence in receiving them.

The workman objects to being placed perpetually in the second category. It is not the unjust distribution of the wealth of the world that, at the moment, he has in mind, but the unjust distribution of the world's power, in this sense of personal auto-cracy. That is the explanation of something that will seem to employers extremely unfair. They all understand the objection to slavery—and they look upon it as human degradation, degrading to the slave-owner as well as to the slave. Yet they find that the existing system of industry is called wage slavery ! But let them try to realise the point of view of the workman whose destiny is to pass his whole life in obeying another human being. He is bound to feel himself a slave. That is why profit-sharing strikes him as futile, if it is not worse. That is why, I am sorry to say, he resents a great deal of philanthropy. I am using the word "philanthropy" as a shorthand expression to cover many schemes, such as welfare, good housing, etc. The minor reforms which a kindly employer wishes to carry out are seldom received with gratitude, and they do not allay labour unrest. But if you recall my analysis, you will see the reason of this. It is the power of the employer which the workman resents, and his philanthropy, of course, is a manifestation of his power. The fact that it is exerted on the work-man's behalf does not placate him.

"LIBERTY, EQUALITY, FRATERNITY."

I have sometimes thought that the three words which we still see on public buildings in France—Liberty, Equality, Fraternity—are profoundly significant in their order. The French Revolution did not achieve those ideals, although it attempted to do so, but the important point is the order in which the three ideals are presented to us. Liberty, Equality—and when we have these,—Fraternity. Now, it is clear that if we attempt to begin with Fraternity, the prescription will not be so healing as if we adopted the original sequence. I suggest that we cannot have a genuine fraternity without equality, nor any genuine equality without liberty. Therefore, I think we must try to begin with liberty and equality.

This is a hard saying for the good employer, or the considerate manager, or the well-mannered foreman. It seems to them that equality and liberty are inconsistent with the present organisation of industry, and the present capitalist system, and they may be, on that account, all the more eager to be brotherly to the workers. They sincerely think this possible—that is, the man in a superior position thinks it possible to be brotherly to an industrial inferior. I like him for thinking so, but I am afraid that as a rule we shall only achieve a very thin kind of brotherliness on those lines. Let us assume that we secure for everybody adequate wages, short hours of work, considera-tion, welfare and the like. After all, that only amounts to treating the workman as though he were a horse. The wise owner of a number of horses will see to it that they are adequately fed and decently housed and have properly limited hours of labour. He will treat them with consideration. As a matter of fact, very often, he has looked after them much better than he did after his men. He recognised that it paid him to do so ; and he is only now coming to realise that it pays him equally well to take care of the human workers. But that is not the point. To-day, men are not content to be treated as well as horses. They want something different. The solution cannot be put on a "fodder basis;" as Mr. Bevin said the other day. At the present moment unfortunately, there are still hundreds of thousands of workmen who are not treated as well as horses, in spite of the rise of wages. They are not getting the short hours of work, the shelter, or the subsistence which well-kept horses receive. But even if they were, labour unrest would remain. What the workers resent is their virtual exclusion from the circle of—shall I say, human beings ? They do not under-value the advantages of good material conditions, but they want to go much further.

THE BAD MANNERS OF EMPLOYERS.

Let me emphasise a point at which we obviously fail—the manners of management. They are still, it seems to me, pretty bad. Before the war, I remember a young workman telling me what made his blood boil with anger. It was not that he only got a certain wage, or had to work so many hours. It was the foreman's habit of going round in the afternoon and saying : "You stop to-night,"—to certain men by way of telling them they had to work overtime. This young man knew that there must be overtime in certain emergencies, but he rebelled against the imperative order that he should remain when he had done the work that he contracted for. He might have a W.E.A. class, or some other engagement, but it did not matter. The foreman treated him as a horse.

This is one example of the habitual manners of management— and it is difficult to drive into the mind of the ordinary employer that it is "bad form," thus to claim to be entitled to exceed his con- tract. A workman regards the agreement into which he enters with the employer as pledging him to do a definite quantum of service. It is a defective form of agreement, of course ; it is ambiguous, ragged at the edges, and open to misconception. Still, the worker regards it as binding on him only within certain fixed limits of time and speed and exertion. But the employer imagines that he has bought the whole time and energy of the workman, and that his claim upon him can be indefinitely extended beyond normal working hours, the normal pace, or the normal intensity of effort, without so much as a "by your leave." It is the view of the slave-owner.

Now, into that kind of one-sided agreement the workman does not enter. He never consciously sells himself in that way ; he merely engages to render a certain amount of service, nor would he consider that he was behaving disloyally if he refused to work overtime, or in some other way failed to promote the employer's business interests, with which he has, under the contract of service, absolutely no concern. We must get rid of that difference of view between the two parties to the so-called contract—which really was never a contract at all because the parties were not agreed—and so long as we cling to the capitalistic system we shall certainly have to adopt the workman's standpoint. In future there must be some reciprocal and mutual engagement, in which one party buys and the other sells, certain definite, clear-cut services with a precisely fixed quantum.

To come back to my rebellious young friend, who objected to being told to work overtime. The foreman, of course, was obviously wrong. Instead of saying, " You stop to-night." he should have said, " Would it be convenient for you to stop to-night ? " What a difference that would have made ! Or he could have explained to the whole workshop that it was extremely important to get a certain job done, and that six or ten men were needed, and asked who could stop most conveniently to themselves. I do not know that I am particularly polite, but I always speak like that to my parlour-maid ; and why should not foremen speak in the same way to workmen ? They lose no authority by it. The officers who had most command over their men in the late war were those who treated them in a considerate way. To put it briefly, I plead for an enormous improvement in the manners of management, and I cannot believe that it is not possible to run a factory in a spirit of genuine partnership and mutual consideration. When I once expressed an opinion on military matters, a certain Major-General replied to me—" I cannot make an army in that way." I was rude enough to say, " I know *you* can't, but someone else might do it." Now, if you think what I am saying impracticable, ask yourself whether the real obstacle does not lie in our own conventional modes of thought. Someone else may find it practicable.

EQUALITY OF STATUS.

There is another thing. Even to treat the workman with the utmost consideration is not to solve the problem. What he is asking for is equality of status in industry. Now, is that quite impossible ? Status is very largely a matter of social distinction. Is there any reason why we should habitually think of the capitalist owner of the factory as belonging to one social class, and the workman in the factory as belonging to another ? Such social distinctions sting very much, and I do not think they are necessary. Of course, we can never make people equal, or identical, in capacity or in attainments, or even in refinement. But these innate or characteristic differences generally cut right across our differences of social status. Certainly they afford no warrant for ordinary class distinctions. Why does an employer or a foreman habitually address a workman by his surname " Jones " ? He would be very much surprised, except in the old-fashioned days in Lancashire, if the workman addressed him in that way. Washington was seen taking off his hat to a negro, and when asked why he did so,

he said, " I do not want the negro to be more polite than I am." There
are really no good manners without reciprocity and equality. There are
in England what used to be called the line officer's manners, which
meant a grovelling servility to those who were considered superiors,
and insolence to those who were considered inferiors. A gentleman
never measures his manners. He is equally courteous to everybody.

Consider, too, the horrible dirt, roughness and lack of amenity
with which many workmen are surrounded. Even the office clerk
is made far more comfortable than the ordinary manual worker—I
say nothing of the directors' Board Room. But true consideration and
the ideal of equality would lead us to give workmen surroundings as
pleasant as those of the clerks, while the clerks were treated as well as
the directors. I have heard of one factory in which, when a workman
calls to ask for a job, he does not go to the works gates, but is
shown into a properly furnished room and given a courteous reception,
just as if he had been a customer come to give an order. How is it
that we don't feel it imperative on us to treat manual workers courte-
ously, if we are gentlemen ? Perhaps we are not. Perhaps there are
no gentlemen in industry, in which case the first thing for employers
to do is to become gentlemen. We ought to show to everyone the
consideration which we regard as due to ourselves. Don't under-rate
the need for politeness. It is like an air-cushion ; there may be nothing
in it, but it eases the jolts considerably.

CIVILISATION IN THE FACTORY.

I venture to prophesy that, at no distant date, every factory will
have (as the Zeiss works at Jena already have) an adequate installation
of hot baths, a complete set of secure lockers for a suit of clothes and
private dressing-rooms, so that every workman will leave the premises
at the end of the day fit to enter his wife's parlour. If you think this
extraordinary, remember that it is what any educated employer
expects in his own case. Do we really mean to refuse to our workmen
the civilised amenities that we claim for ourselves ?

But more is needed than to supplement good material conditions
by courteous treatment. What the miners, for example, resent at
the present time is the fact that a toll is levied on their industry by
people who are contributing nothing to its value. They do not object
to the high salaries of the manager or the active employer, or to their
large share of the profits. Their objection is to the idle shareholder, or
royalty owner, or landlord who is regularly drawing a tribute from the
enterprise. This is, of course, good orthodox economics on the part of
the miners. The functionless shareholder or landlord was receiving,
every year before the war—roughly speaking, about a quarter of the
entire produce of the country.* He is probably receiving more to-day,
because the financial result of the war has been to augment the

* See for the relevant statistics, giving authorties, Fabian Tract No. 5,
Facts for Socialists, revised down to 1915. (Fabian Society : price 2d.)

share of the functionless shareholder at the expense of the portion
of those who do fulfil some definite function in industry. This
is, I need hardly say, an injustice against which the worker
furiously rebels. I am sometimes amused by the naïve gentlemen
who write to the " Times " or the " Morning Post " periodically,
to ask why we do not start an organisation to teach the working men
political economy ? The workmen are often far better instructed in
political economy than the people who write to the " Times," and
speaking generally, than the average man in the employing class. The
workmen, in the course of the past generation, have learned their
economics, whilst the employing classes, as a whole, have despised
the economist. We shall arrive at no ultimate settlement until we
take account of that fact. Take this question of the exaction of a
tribute. Speaking to people who are interested in business rather than
in land-owning, I think I may win my way to your acquiescence if I
point to the case of the landlord. It is always better to dwell on some
other case than our own. The workman cannot see that the landlord
has either created the land or created its enormous increment of value.
We pay about twenty million pounds a year in London for the bare
privilege of building houses, and squatting on the marshy ground by
the Thames, a work in which the landlords have given us no help.
It is easy to see that something is wrong with regard to the landlord,
but not so easy to see it in regard to the functionless shareholders, to
which class we all, more or less belong. They flatter themselves that
they contribute the capital, on which, of course, we are dependent
for keeping our business going. Without investigating that point
too closely. let us assume that the capital of a particular business has
been furnished by the shareholders, who have thereby rendered a
service for which some payment may be made. But no one ventures
to suggest that the amount which the shareholder gets to-day has any
relation to the sum that it is necessary to offer in order to induce the
saving of sufficient capital. How unnecessarily great it is we cannot
compute, but even the most orthodox economists have given up asserting
that it is no more than sufficient to evoke the necessary saving. To
pay a tribute of interest for ever and ever because a useful service was
once rendered is like paying a perpetual pension all down the ages to
the heirs of someone who once told you which was the road to London.

So far I have been endeavouring to portray to you what is in the
workman's mind. He intends to alter the present state of things,
and he intends as a rule, to use democracy as his instrument. He
understands by democracy something very different from what the
ordinary employer in this country or in America understands by it.
You will very often be told that this is a democratic country, and it will
be pointed out to you, by way of proof, that a large number of employers
and managers were originally workmen, and that men may rise from
the ranks. But democracy means more than opportunity, more even
than equality of opportunity. It means that no control over others
shall be exercised by individuals, but only by the community. Our
notion of political democracy is not that it shall be open to anybody

to become Prime Minister, but that the Prime Minister shall express and execute, not his own will, but the will of the people. Therefore, when the workman proposes to apply democracy to industry, he does not mean that he wants an equal chance to become a millionaire. To use an historic phrase, he wants that which concerns all to be decided by all. Now, nothing concerns the workers more than the way they get their livelihood, and this must therefore be decided democratically. But, whilst it is a difficult business to apply democracy to politics, it is still more difficult to apply it to industry.* We have hardly yet begun to think about the matter, and our suggestions are very crude. We have a long road to go, and it will be travelled gradually. Yet, if we adapt ourselves, as employers, managers, and foremen, more and more to this old constitutional ideal of democracy, we shall be putting ourselves in tune with the universe, and pulling with the stream instead of against it.

THE FUTURE OF INDUSTRY.

I do not want to leave you in any uncertainty, so I will put the matter in a more concrete way. It is, in my judgment, quite inevitable that individual ownership of industry and the means of production shall, in the main, and gradually, give place to collective ownership. The latter will take a great many forms. There will be certain great nationalised industries and services. In a few years it will be a commonplace for canals and railways to be run, not for the shareholders, nominally by orders of the shareholders, but for the benefit of the whole community by the will of the whole community. The same thing will happen with such essentially national services as coal-mining. Many other services by which we live will be organised and controlled by our local government, while, as for the great mass of commodities which we consume, they will obviously come within the sphere of the consumers' co-operative movement, which already operates far more successfully than any capitalistic enterprise that I ever heard of. It is now supplying nearly two hundred million pounds' worth of goods annually, and has a membership of one-third of the families in the Kingdom. It undertakes every kind of business, and is actually manufacturing something like fifty million pounds' worth of goods a year. In all this we eliminate the functionless shareholder and the landlord, but we do not get rid of management; and in this connection the workman is still very much at sea. As I have often tried to explain, even with the most complete democracy, and the utmost equality, management remains as indispensable as ever. In fact, it becomes even more indispensable, as enterprise becomes more complicated. In an orchestral concert there must be a conductor who gives the time and somebody must choose the tune. But the conductor is not the proprietor of the orchestra and usually not even of the musical instruments.

---

* This will be found, tentatively worked out in elaborate detail, in *A Constitution for the Socialist Commonwealth of Great Britain*, by S. and B. Webb. (Longmans: 12s. 6d. net.)

He is not in a different social class from the players, nor does he necessarily get a larger salary than the first violin. They are really all partners in a co-operative enterprise. Nevertheless, there is management, and, in a sense, autocracy, because the conductor's beat is law, and all the players recognise that it is only by obedience to the necessary direction that the co-operative product can be made. It seems to me that every business enterprise resembles an orchestral concert in which all the players must, for the time being, adjust their movements to the conductor's direction. That is a very appropriate picture of a factory, where, though neither private ownership nor the functionless shareholder is essential, we must have co-ordination and control.

I suggest to you that two things are going to solve the problem of industrial re-organisation. They are quite homely things, not new inventions; but we must apply them, as we have never yet thought of applying them, to industrial operations. In the first place, industry, as far as possible, should dispense with peremptory orders. In a choral society there is a great deal of give and take, of consultation and mutual arrangement. This should be the case in industry, where far more must be done by way of consultation among all the parties concerned. But I come back to my old Major-General, who said " I cannot make an army in that way," and I am quite prepared to hear employers tell me " We cannot run a factory in that way." My retort is the same : " If you cannot, perhaps somebody else can, and even run it better, for aught you know."

CO-OPERATION IN MANAGEMENT.

At present, the workers have only the vaguest idea of what the management or direction of an enterprise really is. They are not yet competent to undertake it, because they do not know what is involved. Nevertheless, as regards intellectual and moral competence, they compare quite favourably with the ordinary run of directors of companies, from whom we do not expect much as a rule. Yet, we consult our directors, or we do them the courtesy of seeming to consult them. Let us make a point of consulting the workmen—they will teach us something, perhaps more than we imagine. Consultation, in a business, means many things—such as Works Committees and the admission of representative workers to the Board of Directors. Those enterprises which have tremblingly put one or two workmen on their Board of Management have never regretted the step ; indeed, they only regret not having taken it before.

When I was responsible for a good deal of education in London, I said : " We are going to take all the teachers into counsel, and they shall as far as practicable sit on the Board." Perhaps that policy did not alter the steering to any great extent, but it enabled the ship to go with much greater smoothness. What this means, however, is that personal autocracy must go. I was told of a big firm at Birkenhead which suddenly announced a change in the workmen's dinner hour. There was a strike immediately, which cost the firm a lot of money.

Now, very likely the proposed change was wise, but it affected the men's households and all their domestic arrangements, and to introduce it autocratically, without consulting them, was an insane proceeding. Personal autocracy has been banished from the throne, the castle, and the altar. I do not think that it is going to survive in the farm, or the mine, or the factory. It may be necessary in dealing with horses, but not in dealing with men who are advancing rapidly in education and common sense. It must be superseded by a genuine democracy, which is quite compatible with the fact that the conductor gives the beat and chooses the tune. The employer must recognise that he is the servant of all, like the conductor in the orchestra. Where will the authority go? When I was on the London County Council, we of the Progressive Party took ourselves very seriously. We were democratic in spirit, and we thought we governed London. We certainly interfered a good deal; and out of our deep wisdom we decided to build a new bridge over the Thames. But we could proceed no further without calling in an engineer. He produced plans, and we had to accept them—there was nothing else for it. We found we could discuss little more than the colour the bridge was to be painted. Even on that point we consulted the artists, but they failed us, because they all advised different colours! So, finally, that decision was really left in our own hands. After all, in nearly every case, in the last resort, it is the facts that decide, and they can be interpreted only by the men who know the facts. There should be no more personal autocracy in industry than there was in the case of the bridge. It will be the facts that will decide, as interpreted by the common sense of all. But that would mean great changes in our industrial system; and not before it is time! Personally, to-day, I am amazed at the extraordinary inefficiency with which the productive work of this country and every other country is carried on. Think of our engineering shops at this moment. Think of the very best shops in the industry and the shortcomings existing even there—and then think of the chaotic conditions of the worst of them.

Industry will be transformed by two new principles, Measurement and Publicity. We shall have enormously more exact scientific measurement. Remember the ordinary foreman to-day, and his notions about a job. How very little exact measurement there is, either of the time it should take, the time it actually does take, or the time each part takes. But that is not the only sphere of measurement. The whole of costing is dependent on it. The majority of employers in this country do not even know what their own goods are costing, and we cannot have costing without exact measurement. As to the extent of the varied needs for their products; the degree to which what is made really satisfies the need; what is being done in other factories, in other industries and in other countries to increase the demand or to improve the product—on all this there is available as yet, even to the vigilant manufacturer, little more than the vaguest hearsay. You may think it unfair if I say that, in all these respects, the failure of Capitalism is egregious. It may have brought science into its mechanical processes, but it has certainly not done so in its business organisation. It is apparently to be left to Socialism to apply science to the organisation of production and distribution, industry by industry, from the standpoint of supplying, to the uttermost, the consumers' needs.

The second essential is publicity. That may seem a hard saying to some, because so frequently it seems as if secrecy were the soul of successful business. But this is only tantamount to saying that, to-day, the soul of business is perverted. There is no reason, however, why it should continue to be so. I imagine that employers are afraid that a policy of frankness would militate against their profits. But, of course, the object of business is not profits at all, but output. I suppose there are still some people who think that the object of business is profits, but that is bad economics. The only object of business is production. It is for the sake of the utmost possible productivity that we want the industrial machine to act with the utmost smoothness, and when an employer gauges his industrial success by the amount of profits he makes, he reminds me of a man who measures the perfection of his car by the amount of lubricating oil required to keep it running. There is no advantage whatever, but actual waste, in using more lubricating oil than need be. Equally, there is no advantage to the community at all, but actual injury, in any profit being more than the bare minimum that is required to keep the machine going. In future, we shall judge a business by its efficiency in production. We do not estimate the achievements of a doctor by the amount of his fees, but by the extent of his cures. Similarly, the business man will be judged by his efficient fulfilment of his function of production, and not by his profits, which are merely the lubricating oil allowed him at present but which in the interests of efficiency must be reduced to a minimum.

My vision of the function of management in industry in the years to come is a very exalted one. But this management, far from being autocratic, will be dependent very largely on the reports of disinterested experts. Of course, there will still be emergency decisions, but management on its higher level will probably come to be more and more a competent weighing of expert evidence involving both measurement and publicity. Think, for instance, what it would mean to a particular factory to receive a report from an efficient outside costing expert, and to find out exactly what each component and every process was costing in comparison with what it cost in previous years, and with its cost in other factories in this country and elsewhere. Similarly, comparative statistics will show the management how each separate part of the concern is running in relation to other parts, and how it compares with all the other factories in the world. Other reports would keep the factory up to date, in matters of health and education, and would make it acquainted with the latest inventions, in its own industry, and in analogous industries. What we need in industry, as in science, is to universalise knowledge, and to disseminate it with the very minimum of delay. At present every employer works in the dark ; and the worst of it is that he is so thoroughly accustomed to the darkness, like the blind fish in the pools of the Styrian caves, that he does not realise that he is in the dark! He declares that the darkness in which he gropes is the only sun-light!

My belief is that in the future the efficiency of production will increase very greatly, simply through industry being carried on under the glare of a group of searchlights, playing on every process from many different angles. As for the operators who manipulate the searchlights, they will not be dependent on the goodwill of the factory under observation. Their function will be fulfilled when they have given their advice. The sphere of the brain-working professional will be a great one.

The actual decisions will be arrived at in committees. Those people who say that industry cannot be managed by committees are evidently unaware that this is precisely how nearly all our present industry is managed. Why, even of Boards of Directors there are, to-day, in the United Kingdom, more than 66,000. The extent to which every large business is already managed by committees would astonish the village blacksmith if any such person happens to survive. We shall have more and more of this government. Committees are fruitful both in suggestion and criticism, and the representation of the workers upon them will be of tremendous value. But their main function is to bury personal autocracy.

To sum up, I began by putting before you my conception of what is at the bottom of the new spirit in industry. It is the demand of the workman for a partnership in the direction and management of the business in which he is engaged : partnership not with the functionless shareholder, or even in profit, but with the technicians and managers of all grades, with the community as owner. This change must come, and it is coming, and we must find out a way of introducing it successfully without upsetting the machine.

Secondly, I have suggested that production must be facilitated, not by secrecy, but by the widest possible knowledge of every relevant fact. Such knowledge will involve both scientific management and publicity, and the latter will very largely result from the use of the reports of professional experts, on whose services all great business is relying to an ever-increasing extent.

Thirdly, it is just this transformation of business by Measurement and Publicity that will enable business men to become professional men and gentlemen, instead of mere shopkeepers.

Finally, it is by the combination of the conception of partnership among all those concerned in each enterprise, and the conception of the function of industry—to produce not profits, but products—with the devices of measurement and publicity coupled with an early elimination of all mere " passengers " in the industrial ship, who now actually pride, themselves, as landlords or functionless shareholders, on " living by owning " and of committee government upon a universalised knowledge of the facts as to the industry as a whole, that we can safely make the transition from Industrial Autocracy to Industrial Democracy, which alone will allay Labour Unrest.

VACHER & SONS, LTD., Westminster House, S.W.1.—83913.

Fabian Tract No. 197.

THE

INTERNATIONAL LABOUR ORGANISATION

OF THE

LEAGUE OF NATIONS

BY

WM. STEPHEN SANDERS

PUBLISHED AND SOLD BY

THE FABIAN SOCIETY

PRICE TWOPENCE

LONDON:
THE FABIAN SOCIETY, 25 TOTHILL STREET, WESTMINSTER, S.W.I.
JUNE 1921

The International Labour Organisation of the League of Nations.

THE International Labour Organisation of the League of Nations is the outcome of reiterated demands on the part of the working classes of the chief industrial countries throughout the world. At International Congresses and Conferences of the organised workers the pressing need for an institution of this kind has been repeatedly urged, and resolutions calling for its establishment have been carried again and again. During the war the interest in the subject deepened, and its importance for the future welfare of the workers became still more widely recognised. The Inter-allied Trade Union Conference held at Leeds in 1916 demanded the creation of an International Labour Commission with the object of "controlling the application of legislation on social insurance, immigration and emigration, hours of labour, hygiene and protection against accidents." The same Conference insisted upon the necessity of the co-ordination and development of statistical studies and enquiries into the conditions of the workers by means of an International Labour Office. The Stockholm Conference of 1917 came to the same conclusions, and, in 1919, the Berne Conference urged the drafting of an International Charter of Labour to be applied by an International Labour Office. Thus it was in accordance with the emphatically expressed desires of the working classes that the statesmen and diplomatists who drew up the Treaty of Peace included within it the provisions relating to Labour which form Part XIII. of the Treaty.

Labour and the Treaty of Peace.

To Part XIII. of the Treaty there is the following preamble :—

"Whereas the League of Nations has for its object the establishment of universal peace, and such a peace can be established only if it is based upon social justice;

"And whereas conditions of labour exist involving such injustice, hardship and privation to large numbers of people as to produce unrest so great that the peace and harmony of the world are imperilled; and an improvement of those conditions is urgently required: as, for example, by the regulation of the hours of work, including the establishment of a maximum working day and week, the regulation of the labour supply, the prevention of unemployment, the provision of an adequate living wage, the protection of the worker against sickness, disease and injury arising out of his employment, the protection of children, young persons and women, provisions for old age and injury, protection of the interests of workers when employed in countries other than their own, recognition of the principle of freedom of association, the organisation of vocational and technical education and other measures;

"Whereas also the failure of any nation to adopt humane conditions of labour is an obstacle in the way of other nations which desire to improve the conditions in their own countries ;

"The High Contracting Parties, moved by sentiments of justice and humanity as well as by the desire to secure the permanent peace of the world, agree to the following ': (here follow the articles establishing a permanent organisation for the promotion of the principles set out in the preamble) *'

Statement of Principles.

Further, in Article 427, the Treaty lays down the following general principles with regard to the treatment of labour :—

1st. The guiding principle . . . . that labour should not be regarded merely as a commodity or article of commerce.

2nd. The right of association for all lawful purposes by the employed as well as by the employers.

3rd. The payment to the employed of a wage adequate to maintain a reasonable standard of life as this is understood in their time and country.

4th. The adoption of an eight hours day or a forty-eight hours week as the standard to be aimed at where it has not already been attained.

5th. The adoption of a weekly rest of at least twenty-four hours, which should include Sunday wherever practicable.

6th. The abolition of child labour and the imposition of such limitations on the labour of young persons as shall permit the continuation of their education and assure their proper physical development.

7th. The principle that men and women should receive equal remuneration for work of equal value.

8th. The standard set by law in each country with respect to the conditions of labour should have due regard to the equitable economic treatment of all workers lawfully resident therein.

9th. Each State should make provision for a system of inspection, in which women should take part, in order to ensure the enforcement of these laws and regulations for the protection of the employed.

This declaration of the principles which should "inspire the policy of the League of Nations" may be said to constitute a kind of Labour Charter such as was demanded by the International Trade Union Conference at Berne.

---

* For a complete statement of the constitution, powers, duties and standing orders of the Organisation, see "Permanent Labour Organisation : Constitution and Rules." (The London Office of the International Labour Office, 26 Buckingham Gate, S.W. 1.) Also "Labour and the Peace Treaty," with an introduction by the Rt. Hon. G. N. Barnes, M.P. Issued by the Ministry of Labour. (H.M. Stationery Office.)

Principles and Practice.

But, in order to secure the well-being, physical, moral, and intellectual, of industrial wage-earners, which has been the aim of the workers' organisations, and is the declared intention of the signatories of the Treaty of Peace' as embodied in the Labour clauses of the Treaty, it is necessary to have something more than declarations. The experience of the past justified the insistence of the workers upon the necessity for a Permanent International Organisation, whose duty it should be to see that the "Charter" was actually carried out in all countries which agreed to its provisions. There have been attempts, such as the Conferences at Berne of 1906 and 1913, to arrive at an international agreement with regard to certain branches of labour legislation. But in these instances action arose simply through the chance initiative of some State specially interested in the subject, which issued an invitation to other States (which they could accept on conditions or refuse altogether) to send officials to a Conference which, when dispersed, might never be called together again. Such spasmodic and un-authoritative consultations, valuable as they may have been as tentative experiments in international co-operation for industrial legislation, would have to be greatly improved upon if the principles of the "Charter" were ever to be put into universal practice.*

The Permanent International Labour Organisation.

(1) The International Labour Conference.

Realising this, the authors of the Treaty of Peace decided to set up a permanent International Labour Organisation as a part of the League of Nations, thus meeting the oft-repeated demand of the organised working classes. The Treaty provided that "the original members of the League of Nations shall be the original members of this Organisation, and hereafter membership of the League of Nations shall carry with it membership of the said Organisation."

The Permanent Organisation consists of (1) a General Con-ference of representatives of the members, and (2) an International Labour Office controlled by a Governing Body. The General Conference consists of representatives of each of the fifty States belonging to the Organisation. The only great States remaining outside it are the United States of America, which, up to the present, has not signed the Treaty, and Russia still in the throes of revolution.

---

* "The International Labour Organisation : a Comparison," issued by the International Labour Office (The London Office of the International Labour Office, 26 Buckingham Gate, S.W. 1), gives a short account of previous attempts to promote and co-ordinate labour legislation on international lines by means of the International Association for Labour Legislation.

All States, whether large or small, have equal rights at the Conference. Each is represented by two Government delegates, one Employers' delegate and one Workers' delegate. Each delegate votes individually ; if they so desire the Workers can vote with the Workers, and the Employers with the Employers of all nationalities. The Employers' and Workers' delegates have to be "chosen in agreement with the industrial organisations, if such organisations exist, which are most representative of employers or workpeople " in each country. Thus the Workers' representative of Great Britain is selected in agreement with the Parliamentary Committee of the Trades Union Congress, the body having the greatest number of affiliated industrial workers' organisations. In addition to the delegates, technical advisers may be appointed to assist in the discussions of subjects on which their expert knowledge would be valuable.

The General Conference meets as occasion may require, and at least once in every year. Two meetings have already been held— one at Washington in November, 1919, and the other at Genoa in June, 1920, the latter being specially devoted to maritime questions. The results of these gatherings are given in detail later on. The third meeting of the Conference will take place at Geneva, October, 1921, and will deal mainly with questions concerning labour in agriculture.

The General Conference, which may justly be called an " International Social Parliament," cannot pass legislation. Each country remains jealous of parting with any portion of its sovereignty ; but the Conference votes Draft Conventions, by which States agree to observe strictly certain regulations and recommendations which should be taken as guides in passing national legislation or in issuing administrative orders. These may, it is true, vary in different countries, but they have to conform to one and the same principle.

The Ratification of Conventions.

The Parliaments of the various States are not bound to adopt the Conventions agreed to by the Conference, but Governments and Parliaments are always subject to the influence of public opinion, which can bring pressure to bear upon them for the purpose of securing ratification. A large number of States have already drafted Bills dealing with the ratification of Conventions ; some of them have already been ratified.* Once the Conventions have been ratified by a State and the Recommendations have been the subject of special legislation, those States are bound to respect them. Any violation brings the International Labour Office, its Commission of Enquiry, and the International Court of Justice into action, and these possess definite powers for obtaining proper enforcement. Here again economic penalties can be applied.

---

* Information relating to the progress in the process of ratification of Draft Conventions by the member-States is given in the Bulletin of the International Labour Office, which is issued at intervals of about one week. This publication also records the activities of the Office. The English edition of the Bulletin can be obtained from the London Office of the International Labour Office, 26 Buckingham Gate, S.W. 1.

The Permanent International Labour Organisation.
(2) The International Labour Office.

The International Labour Office is under the control of a Governing Body consisting of 24 persons, 12 of whom represent the Governments of the States which are members of the International Labour Organisation, six elected by the delegates to the General Conference representing the Employers, and six elected by the delegates to the General Conference representing the Workers. Of the 12 persons representing the Governments, eight are nominated by the States which are of the chief industrial importance, and four are nominated by the States selected for the purpose by the Government delegates to the General Conference, excluding the delegates of the eight States mentioned above. The period of office of the Governing Body is three years. The headquarters of the Office are at Geneva, the seat of the League of Nations.

The functions of the Office include the collection and distribution of information on all subjects relating to the international adjustment of industrial conditions of life and labour, and particularly the examination of subjects which it is proposed to bring before the General Conference with a view to the conclusion of international Conventions, and the conduct of such special investigations as may be ordered by the General Conference*. It is entrusted with the duty of receiving complaints with regard to violations or ratified Conventions, and the Governing Body can, if they think fit, apply to the League of Nations for the institution of a Commission of Enquiry to investigate any such complaint. If a complaint is found to be justified, further measures are provided in the Treaty for securing a remedy.

The preparation of the Agenda of the General Conference is also a duty of the Office.

International Labour Office and the Individual Citizen.

It will thus be seen that the International Labour Office can affect beneficially the conditions of life and labour of every worker in every country. Not only so, but, on the other hand, every worker can, if he so wills, help to influence and direct the activities of the Office. The subjects dealt with by the periodical meetings of the General Conference are drawn up by the Governing Body of the Office, upon which, as already stated, are representatives of the great national working class industrial organisations. These organisations can put forward proposals to be brought before the Conference. It is, therefore, quite possible for any individual member of a body affiliated to the Parliamentary Committee of the Trades Union Congress to

---

* A considerable number of publications consisting of a monthly periodical, *The International Labour Review*, and studies and reports on questions vitally concerning labour have already been issued by the Office. A full list can be obtained from the London Office of the International Labour Office, 26 Buckingham Gate, S.W. 1.

request, through the usual channel of his local branch, that his organisation should ask the Parliamentary Committee to propose that a given question of international importance relating to labour should be placed upon the Agenda of the General Conference. Members of employers' organisations are given the same opportunity of having subjects which interest them discussed.

The First International Labour Conference.

The first meeting of the General Conference, held in Washington from the 29th October to the 29th November, 1919, proved to be a gathering of the greatest significance for the future of industry, and demonstrated the value of the new International Labour Organisation as an instrument for securing far-reaching reforms in the conditions of labour. The Conference was attended by the representatives of forty countries. The United States had no official delegate, as the Peace Treaty had not been ratified by the Senate, but the Conference was presided over by Mr. W. B. Wilson, the United States Secretary of Labour. Three important States were, unfortunately, not represented. The delegates of Germany and Austria were unable to be present owing to the difficulty of securing passages to America, and there was no representative from Russia. Apart from these exceptions, however, the Assembly was a fully representative international gathering. The delegations, in normal cases, included, as provided by the constitution of the General Conference, representatives of employers and workpeople as well as of Governments. Each delegate was free to cast his vote as he thought best on every occasion and irrespective of the fact that he belonged to a particular nation, or represented a particular class ot interests. The fact that in a body of this character it was possible to secure agreement on detailed proposals for international action augured well for the success of the whole movement for international labour organisation.

The Representatives of the United Kingdom.

The United Kingdom was represented by the Rt. Hon. G. N. Barnes, M.P., and Sir Malcolm Delevingne, K.C.B., Assistant Under-Secretary for State for Home Affairs, on behalf of the Government; Mr. D. S. Majoribanks, C.B.E., Managing Director of Messrs. W. G. Armstrong, Whitworth & Co., Ltd., on behalf of the employers; and Mr. G. H. Stuart-Bunning (Postmen's Federation and ex-President of the Trades Union Congress) on behalf of the workers. Attached to the delegates were groups of technical advisers. Accompanying Mr. Stuart-Bunning in this capacity were the Rt. Hon. C. W. Bowerman, M.P. (Secretary of the Parliamentary Committee of the Trades Union Congress); Mr. A. Onions, M.P. (South Wales Miners' Federation); Mr. T. Shaw, M.P. (Weavers' Association); Mr. J. Sexton, C.B.E., M.P. (National Union of Dock Labourers and Riverside Workers); Miss Margaret Bondfield (National Federation of Women Workers); and the late Miss Mary Macarthur (National

Federation of Women Workers). Several of the advisers acted as representatives of the delegates on special commissions, and during the discussions in the full Conference of the questions on which they were expert!

Women and the Conference.

A feature of the Conference was the claim of the women for special representation. This was met under the constitution which, as already mentioned, allows technical advisers to replace delegates on occasions when questions in which they are specially competent arise. In accordance with this provision, Miss Bondfield represented the British Labour Delegate on the Commission on the employment of children and the late Miss Mary Macarthur represented him on the Commission on childbirth and maternity, while Miss Constance Smith (Senior Lady Inspector of Factories, Home Office) replaced Sir Malcolm Delevingne on the latter Commission. In the preparation of the Conventions, especially on these two subjects, women took a prominent part.

The Results of the Conference.

The Conference adopted six Draft Conventions and six Recommendations. The Draft Conventions dealt with :

(1) The application of the principle of the eight hours day and the 48 hours week.
(2) The prevention of or provision against unemployment.
(3) The employment of women before and after childbirth.
(4) The employment of women on night work.
(5) The minimum age of employment of children in industry.
(6) The employment of young persons on night work.

The Recommendations related to :

(1) Public Employment Exchanges.
(2) Reciprocity of treatment of foreign workers.
(3) The prevention of anthrax.
(4) The protection of women and children against lead poisoning.
(5) The establisment of Government Health Services.
(6) The application of the Berne Convention of 1906 on the prohibition of the use of white phosphorous in the manufacture of matches.

The various Conventions and Recommendation were prepared by the Commissions of the General Conference, and much useful discussion between experts on the particular subjects took place on these Commissions. Differences of national interest and difficulties between employers and workers' representatives had to be faced, and drafts arrived at which could be placed before the plenary meetings of the Conference. Conventions were so thoroughly discussed in the Commissions, and such a degree of agreement was arrived at, that with comparatively few alterations they were adopted by the General Conference.*

---

* "International Labour Conference, 1919. Draft Conventions and Recommendations ; with an Introduction." (H.M. Stationery Office.)

The Convention on Hours of Labour.

The most important Convention is the one dealing with the hours of labour. It was naturally not easy to arrive at an agreement on this matter. Eventually, however, the representatives of the employers and the workers accepted the principle of the eight hours day, but with the conditions in regard to its application made fairly elastic. The Convention as finally passed involves an agreement of the countries concerned to introduce legislation for securing an eight hours day and a 48 hours week for all workers in industrial undertakings, including mining and quarrying, manufacturing, building and construction work. It was agreed that the provisions relative to transport by sea and on inland waterways should be determined by a special conference. Each country may adopt modifications within certain limits in the application of the principle of the eight hours day to their industries. But all Governments have to report to the International Labour Office the regulations which they adopt and the modifications they permit. The peculiar conditions prevailing in Oriental countries rendered it necessary to make special provisions with regard to India and Japan. In the former country the hours of labour are to be generally 57 in the week, in the raw silk industry 60 for adults, and for persons under fifteen and all miners, of whatever age, 48. In British India the hours of labour in factories, mines and railway works are to be limited to 60 in the week. These provisions represent for these two countries greater progress than the other provisions do for Western lands.

The Convention on Unemployment.

The Convention on unemployment involves an international scheme for securing information from all countries with regard to the problem, the establishment of free public employment agencies where not already in existence, and for mutual benefits for emigrants in regard to unemployment insurance. Further, the Conference recommended that every Government should prohibit new private employment agencies, and permit existing agencies to operate only under a licence ; that the recruiting of foreign labour should be only by agreement between the countries concerned and after consultation with the employers and workers ; that there should be in every State unemployment insurance ; and that public work ought to be allocated to periods of unemployment, or to districts affected by it. It was also recommended that foreign workers should receive the protection and the rights of organisation possessed by the native workers, by mutual arrangements between the States concerned.

The Conventions on the Work of Women.

The Conventions on the work of women workers laid down that for six weeks after confinement women shall not be permitted to work in industry or commerce, and shall have the right to cease work six weeks before confinement, being paid in both periods full benefits for maintenance. Further, a nursing mother shall have half an hour twice a day for nursing her child. Dismissal is not to take place during the two rest periods before and after childbirth. Night work for women in industry is prohibited, the night being defined as normally a period of eleven consecutive hours, including the period from 10 p.m to 5 a.m. In the case of India and Siam a special form of legislation is provided; and certain general exceptions are allowed.

The Conventions on the Work of Children and Young Persons.

The Conventions relating to the employment of children and young persons fixes fourteen as the minimum age at which a child should enter industry. Exceptions were made in the cases of Japan and India, where the age is to be 12. Persons under the age of 18 are not to be employed during the night, although persons over 16 may be so employed in continuous process industries, as in the manufacture of iron and steel, glass, raw sugar, paper, and in the reduction of gold. Certain exceptions in particular industries and countries are permitted.

Diseases of Occupation.

Diseases of occupation were also the subject of discussion, and it was recommended that wool infected with anthrax spores should be disinfected ; that women and children should be excluded from certain employments involving the risk of lead poisoning ; and that certain other occupations should be permitted only if proper appliances were used certain and regulations observed. It was also recommended that health services, in addition to factory inspection, should be introduced by all Governments.

The Pioneer Work of the Conference.

The results of the Washington Conference are generally recognised as being of permanent importance. In reviewing the work accomplished, the great problems that had to be encountered should be borne in mind. It was the first Conference of its kind, and it had to meet and surmount all the difficulties which confront the pioneer. Language obstacles, well known to those acquainted with international gatherings for the transaction of business, were prominent. It is, therefore, remarkable that in the complicated negotiations inseparable from the drafting of Conventions and Recommendations language difficulties were overcome, and that complete agreement was reached on so many complex subjects. By some the Conventions may be considered moderate in their provisions, but it must be remembered that the degree of progress in reforms intended to be world-wide in extent is determined in some measure not by the most advanced country, but by the most backward ; and that the great aim of the Conference was to make provision for the gradual or, in some cases, rapid raising of the more backward countries to something approaching the level reached by the more advanced nations after many years of social effort.

British Labour and the Washington Conference.

In Great Britain the Washington Conventions are now known in Labour circles as the "International Labour Charter." The views of the Labour delegates, members of workers' organisations of Great Britain, are interesting as showing the importance they attach to the Conventions :—

> Whilst we should have liked to have seen stronger and more far-reaching Conventions and Recommendations, we feel sure that in the circumstances more was accomplished than we could have expected. At a first Conference of such a character, it would not have been surprising had it failed to do more than set up machinery with a view of working in the future, but not only were we able to do this, but to carry through the Conventions and Recommendations mentioned above.*

The Parliamentary Committee of the Trades Union Congress, in commenting upon the Report of the delegation, states :—

> The Washington Conference was not only unique from the international standpoint, but without parallel, and, as will be seen from the short statement of the Conference's work appearing in another portion of this Report, the results exceeded expectations. It was indeed remarkable that, with representatives of the most backward nations (from an industrial standpoint) brought into consultation for the first time with representatives of the most highly developed nations, questions affecting the industrial workers of the world should have been discussed with such keenness and with a genuine desire on the part of the former to bring their countries into line industrially with the more advanced and better organised countries. Common agreement was realised on many points, and it now remains for the various Governments to give legislative effect to Recommendations from the Conference.†

The Genoa Conference.

The second session of the General Conference was held at Genoa in June and July, 1920. The conditions of the work of seafarers was the sole subject of discussion ; but it proved so complex and refractory that it was not possible to arrive at a definite conclusion on the chief question : that of the application of the eight hours working day to seamen. The Commission which considered the problem succeeded, after long and strenuous debates, in framing a Draft Convention. But this failed by a fraction of a vote to secure the necessary two-thirds majority when it came before the General Conference, and hence, no decision on the subject was reached. Draft Conventions, however, were agreed to on the following questions :—

(1) The minimum age for the admission of children to employment at sea.

---

* Report of the Parliamentary Committee of the Trades Union Congress adopted by the Trades Union Congress, Portsmouth, 1920.
† *Ibid.*

(2) Unemployment indemnity in case of loss or foundering of the ship.

(3) The establishment of facilities for finding employment for seamen.

Further Recommendations were passed dealing with :

(1) Limitation of hours of work in the fishing industry.

(2) Limitation of hours of work in inland navigation.

(3) The establishment of national seamen's codes.

(4) Unemployment insurance for seamen.

Further, a Joint Maritime Commission, consisting of representatives of shipowners and seamen, was elected to consider the drawing up of an International Seamen's Code and other questions affecting seafarers.*

How the Work Can be Perfected.

The results of the Washington and Genoa Conferences are, however, only the beginnings of a tremendous task, for the completion of which the International Labour Office is responsible. To carry out this responsibility successfully, the Office requires the steady and vigorous support of public opinion in every country, and especially that of far-seeing employers who realise the economic necessities of the times, and of the workers who have repeatedly demanded the establishment of international machinery for promoting systematic and universal industrial reforms. International labour legislation, even when Conventions and Recommendations have been secured, depends, like national legislation, entirely on the citizens of each country. By persistent and methodical action the industrial organisations of employers and employed can obtain from the Parliaments of their countries the ratification of Conventions already agreed upon and ensure that they are faithfully observed. Moreover, through the International Labour Office and the International Labour Conference they can achieve by further measures the fulfilment of the programme drawn up in the Treaty of Peace, which requires that the conditions of labour should be brought to an ever-increasing extent into conformity with justice.

---

* Following the Session of the General Conference at Genoa the International Seafarers' Federation requested the Director of the International Labour Office to endeavour to bring about an unofficial conference between the shipowners' and seafarers. Steps were taken by the Office to carry out this request, with the result that a Conference between the International Shipping Federation and the International Seafarers' Federation was held at Brussels on January 25 and 26, 1921, under the chairmanship of the Director of the Office. This Conference elected two Committees to discuss the whole problem of working hours in the seafaring industry, with the view of arriving at a practicable solution of the question. A further Conference is to meet to discuss the reports of the Committees.

SELECT BIBLIOGRAPHY.

BARNES, G. N. The Industrial Section of the League of Nations. (Barnett House Papers. No. 5. Milford, London. 1s.)

BRITISH YEAR BOOK OF INTERNATIONAL LAW, 1920-21. (Frowde & Hodder & Stoughton.)

INTERNATIONAL LABOUR OFFICE (These publications may be obtained from the London Office of the International Labour Office, 26 Buckingham Gate, S.W.1) :
Constitution and Rules.
Labour Provisions of the Peace Treaties.
Report presented to the Peace Conference by the Commission on International Labour Legislation.
Bulletin. Vol. I. (in preparation.)
Bulletin. Vol. II.
Official Bulletin. Vol. III.
Reports prepared by the Organising Committee for the International Labour Conference, Washington, 1919.
International Labour Conference. First Annual Meeting, Washington, 1919.
Reports prepared for the Seamen's Conference. Genoa. June, 1920.
International Labour Conference. Second Annual Meeting, Genoa. (Daily Record.)
International Labour Review. Monthly. 3s. No. 1. January, 1921.
Leaflets.
Studies and Documents. Series A. No. 8 : The International Labour Organisation : a Comparison. 1920.

BURNS, C. DELISLE. The League and Labour. (League of Nations Union, 1s.)

BUTLER, H. B. The International Labour Organisation. (The League of Nations Starts: An Outline by its Organisers. Pp. 140. Macmillan & Co., Ltd., London, 1920. 10s. 6d.)

DELEVINGNE, SIR MALCOLM. The International Regulation of Labour under the Peace Treaty. Manchester University. Labour and Industry ; a series of lectures. Pp. 169. (Longmans, Green & Co., 1920.)

HENDERSON, ARTHUR. League of Nations and Labour. Oxford Pamphlet, 1919.

HETHERINGTON, H. J. W. International Labour Legislation, 1920. (Methuen, London. 6s. net).

LABOUR PARTY. Memoranda on International Labour Legislation : The Economic Structure of the League of Nations. London, 1920. 1s.

SANGER, SOPHY. The New International Labour Organisation. (International Law Association. Report of the 29th Conference. Pp. 329. Sweet & Maxwell, 1920.) 30s.

———— Labour Legislation under the League in Problems of Peace and War : Papers read before the Grotius Society in the year 1919. Pp. 145. (Sweet & Maxwell. 6s. net.)

SOLANO, E. JOHN (Ed.) Labour as an International Problem. A series of essays, comprising a short history of the International Labour Organisation and a review of general industrial problems. (Macmillan & Co., London, 1920, 18s.)

THOMAS, ALBERT. The International Labour Office (The Quarterly Review. No. 466, p. 191. January, 1921.)

U.K. MINISTRY OF LABOUR. Labour and the Peace Treaty, 1919. London. H.M. Stationery Office.

International Labour Conference, 1919. Draft Conventions and Recommendations, 1920. London, 3d. H.M. Stationery Office.

International Labour (Seamen's) Conference, 1920. Draft Conventions and Recommendations, with an Introduction. 1921. London, 3d. H.M. Stationery Office.

THE FABIAN · SOCIETY

25 TOTHILL STREET, WESTMINSTER, ·LONDON, S.W.1.

Those willing to join the Labour Party, or desirous of obtaining information about its Programme and Principles, are invited to communicate with the Secretary of the Fabian Society.

The Fabian Society has been, from the outset, a constituent body of the Labour Party ; and membership of the Society carries with it full membership of the Labour Party, eligibility for nomination to all Conferences and Offices, and qualification for Labour Party candidatures for Parliament and Local Authorities, without obligation to belong to any other organisation.

The Society welcomes as members any persons, men or women, wherever resident, who subscribe to its Basis (set forth below), and who will co-operate in its work according to their opportunities.

BASIS OF THE FABIAN SOCIETY.

(TO BE SIGNED BY ALL MEMBERS.)·

(*Adopted May 23rd*, 1919.)

The Fabian Society consists of Socialists.

It therefore aims at the reorganisation of Society by the emancipation of Land and Industrial Capital from individual ownership, and the vesting of them in the community for the general benefit. In this way only can the natural and acquired advantages of the country be equitably shared by the whole people.

The Society accordingly works for the extinction of private property in land, with equitable consideration of established expectations, and due provision as to the tenure of the home and the homestead ; for the transfer to the community, by constitutional methods, of all such industries as can be conducted socially ; and for the establishment, as the governing consideration in the regulation of production, distribution and service, of the common good instead of private profit.

The Society is a constituent of the Labour Party and of the International Socialist Congress ; but it takes part freely in all constitutional movements, social, economic and political, which can be guided towards its own objects. Its direct business is (*a*) the propaganda of Socialism in its application to current problems ; (*b*) investigation and discovery in social, industrial, political and economic relations ; (*c*) the working out of Socialist principles in legislation and administrative reconstruction ; (*d*) the publication of the results of its investigations and their practical lessons.

The Society, believing in equal citizenship of men and women in the fullest sense, is open to persons irrespective of sex, race or creed, who commit themselves to its aims and purposes as stated above, and undertake to promote its work.

The Society includes :—

I. Members, who must sign the Basis· and be elected by the Committee. Their Subscriptions are not fixed ; each is expected to subscribe annually according to his means. They control the Society through the Executive Committee (elected annually by ballot through a postal vote), and at its annual and other business meetings.

II. Associates, who sign a form expressing only general sympathy with the objects of the Society and pay not less than 10s. a year. They can attend all except the exclusively members' meetings, but have no control over the Society and its policy.

III. Subscribers, who must pay at least 5s. a year, and who can attend the Society's Ordinary Lectures.

The monthly paper, *Fabian News*, and the Tracts from time to time published in the well-known Fabian Series, are posted to all these classes. There are convenient Common Rooms, where light refreshments can be obtained, with an extensive library for the free use of members only.

Among the Society's activities (in which it places its services unreservedly at the disposal of the Labour Party and the Local Labour Parties all over the country, the Trade Unions and Trades Councils, and all other Labour and Socialist organisations), may be mentioned :

(i.) Free lectures by its members and officers ;

(ii.) The well-known Fabian Book-boxes, each containing about three dozen of the best books on Economics, Politics and Social Problems, which can be obtained by any organisation of men or women for 15s. per annum, covering an exchange of books every three months ;

(iii.) Answers to Questions from Members of Local Authorities and others on legal, technical or political matters of Local Government, etc.;

(iv.) Special subscription courses of lectures on new developments in thought ;

(v.) Economic and social investigation and research, and publication of the results.

Lists of Publications, Annual Report, Form of Application as Member or Associate, and any other information can be obtained on application personally or by letter to the Secretary at the above address.

FABIAN TRACTS and LEAFLETS.

Tracts, each 16 to 52 pp., price 1d., or 9d. per dos., unless otherwise stated.
Leaflets, 4 pp. each, price 1d. for three copies, 2s. per 100, or 20/- per 1000.
The Set of 74, 4/6; post free 5/3. Bound in buckram, 10/-; post free 11/-

I.—General Socialism in its various aspects.

TRACTS.—192. Guild Socialism By G. D. COLE, M.A. 180. The Philosophy of Socialism. By A. CLUTTON BROCK. 169. The Socialist Movement in Germany. By W. STEPHEN SANDERS. 2d. 159. The Necessary Basis of Society. By SIDNEY WEBB. 151. The Point of Honour. By RUTH C. BENTINCK. 147. Capital and Compensation. By E. R. PEASE. 146. Socialism and Superior Brains. By BERNARD SHAW. 2d. 142. Rent and Value. 138. Municipal Trading. 121. Public Service v. Private Expenditure. By Sir OLIVER LODGE. 2d. 107. Socialism for Millionaires. By BERNARD SHAW. 139. Socialism and the Churches. By Rev. JOHN CLIFFORD, D.D. 133. Socialism and Christianity. By Rev. PERCY DEARMER. 2d. 78. Socialism and the Teaching of Christ. By Dr. J. CLIFFORD. 42. Christian Socialism. By Rev. S. D. HEADLAM. 79. A Word of Remembrance and Caution to the Rich. By JOHN WOOLMAN. 72. The Moral Aspects of Socialism. By SIDNEY BALL 69. Difficulties of Individualism. By S. WEBB. 51. Socialism: True and False. By S. WEBB. 45. The Impossibilities of Anarchism. By G. B. SHAW. 2d. 7. Capital and Land. 5. Facts for Socialists. 2d. LEAFLETS—13. What Socialism Is. 1. Why are the Many Poor?

II.—Applications of Socialism to Particular Problems.

TRACTS.—196. The Root of Labour Unrest. By SIDNEY WEBB. 2d. 195. The Scandal of the Poor Law. By C. M. LLOYD. 2d. 194. Taxes, Rates and Local Income Tax. By ROBERT JONES, D.Sc. 2d. 188. National Finance and a Levy on Capital. By SIDNEY WEBB. 2d. 187. The Teacher in Politics. By SIDNEY WEBB. 186. Central Africa and the League of Nations. By R. C. HAWKIN. 2d. 183. The Reform of the House of Lords. By SIDNEY WEBB. 181. When Peace Comes—the Way of Industrial Reconstruction. By SIDNEY WEBB. 2d. 178. The War; Women; and. Unemployment. 2d. 177. Socialism and the Arts of Use. By A. CLUTTON BROCK. 175. The Economic Foundations of the Women's Movement. 2d. 173. Public v. Private Electricity Supply. 170. Profit-Sharing and Co-Partnership: a Fraud and Failure? 164. Gold and State Banking. 162. Family Life on a Pound a Week. By Mrs. REEVES. 2d. 161. Afforestation and Unemployment. 157. The Working Life of Women. 155. The Case against the Referendum. 154. The Case for School Clinics. 152. Our Taxes as they are and as they ought to be. 2d. 149. The Endowment of Motherhood. 2d. 145. The Case for School Nurseries. 140. Child Labor under Capitalism. 136. The Village and the Landlord. By EDW. CARPENTER. 144. Machinery: its Masters and Servants. 122. Municipal Milk and Public Health. 125. Municipalization by Provinces. 124. State Control of Trusts. LEAFLET.—104. How Trade Unions benefit Workmen.

III.—Local Government Powers: How to use them.

TRACTS.—189. Metropolitan Borough Councils. Their Constitution, Powers and Duties. By C. R. ATTLEE, M.A. 2d. 191. Borough Councils. Their Constitution, Powers and Duties. By C. R. ATTLEE, M.A. 2d. 193. Housing. By C. M. LLOYD, M.A. 2d. 189. Urban District Councils. By C. M. LLOYD, M.A. 2d. 172. What about the Rates? By S. WEBB. 2d. 62. Parish and District Councils. (Revised 1919). 137. Parish Councils and Village Life. 109. Cottage Plans and Common Sense. LEAFLETS.—134. Small Holdings. 68. The Tenant's Sanitary Catechism. 71. Ditto for London.

IV.—General Politics and Fabian Policy.

TRACTS.—158. The Case against the C.O.S. By Mrs. TOWNSHEND. 41. The Fabian Society: its Early History. By BERNARD SHAW.

V.—Biographical Series. In portrait covers, 2d. and 3d.

182. Robert Owen, Idealist. By C. E. M. JOAD. 179. John Ruskin and Social Ethics. By Prof. EDITH MORLEY. 165. Francis Place. By ST. JOHN G. ERVINE. 166. Robert Owen, Social Reformer By Miss B. L. HUTCHINS. 167. William Morris and the Communist Ideal. By Mrs. TOWNSHEND. 168. John Stuart Mill. By JULIUS WEST. 174. Charles Kingsley and Christian Socialism. By C. E. VULLIAMY.

ted by G. Standring. 7 Finsbury St., London, E.C. and published by the Fabian Society 25 Tothill Street, Westminster, London, S.W.

Fabian Tract No. 198.

SOME PROBLEMS OF EDUCATION.

BARBARA DRAKE.

·Published and Sold by

THE FABIAN SOCIETY.

PRICE SIXPENCE.

LONDON:
THE FABIAN SOCIETY, 25 TOTHILL STREET, WESTMINSTER, S.W. 1.
PUBLISHED MAY, 1922.

CONTENTS.

INTRODUCTION.

THE object of this pamphlet is to present a short survey of public education for the use of members of local education committees and practical educationists. Under cover of national economy, the parties of reaction, inside and outside of Parliament, are preparing an attack on the people's education, which threatens, not merely to destroy the promise of the Education Act of 1918, but to undo to a great extent the achievement of the Act of 1902. Hence, lovers of education have to arm themselves for the children's defence on one side with a knowledge of facts, on the other side with a practical policy. There has been no attempt to cover all the ground, but rather to fix attention on certain central problems. The various matters connected with medical inspection and care of physical health have been purposely omitted from the reference, as these subjects are discussed in other Fabian publications. Nor does the writer pretend to originality of views, but the pamphlet is mainly composed of abstracts from official and Labour Party publications, or from various documents, a list of which is given in the bibliography. If, however, the pamphlet should succeed in strengthening the hands of educationists against forces of reaction in ever so small a measure, it would not have wholly failed in its purpose.

The thanks of the writer are due to officials, directors of education, school teachers and others, who, while taking no responsibility for the opinions expressed, have given generous assistance in correcting and revising the draft.

SOME PROBLEMS OF EDUCATION.

The Building of Schools.

PUBLIC ELEMENTARY SCHOOLS. — According to the Annual Report of the Board of Education for the year 1919-1920 there are 20,971 public elementary schools in England and Wales, of which 8,705 are provided by local authorities and 12,266 by voluntary agencies. There is a total accommodation for about 7,000,000 pupils. There are in addition 478 " special schools " for physically infirm and mentally defective children, with places for about 35,000 scholars, and 53 " certified efficient schools." It is incumbent on a local education authority to provide school accommodation for every child of school age within its area, but a rising standard of efficiency, together with fluctuations of population, do not make this duty an altogether simple one. While in some districts there is an accommodation considerably in excess of present needs, elsewhere nearly every school has too many children. Similarly, in some large areas with a total excess of accommodation, there is a deficiency in certain parts of the area. Moreover, owing to the awkward arrangement and unwieldy size of class-rooms in the older schools, the nominal accommodation is often no real guide to the effective accommodation.

A general survey of school premises has not been published by the Board since the year 1908-1909. The Annual Report for that year states that information furnished to the Board indicated that in the case of about 2,000 schools, or 3,000 departments, in England and Wales, the school premises were more or less seriously unsatisfactory, and 660 schools were condemned unconditionally. These figures did not include cases in which the only objection to the premises was the fact that three or more classes were taught in a single undivided room ; nor cases in which the only ground for objection was the absence or insufficiency of playground accommodation ; nor cases of schools where the accommodation was merely insufficient for the number of scholars taught, and enlargement was the only improvement required. Moreover, the standard embodied in the Board's Building Regulations, which is applicable to new schools, was not employed in judging existing buildings. Such a procedure would have resulted, according to the Board, " in the condemnation of a large number of school buildings erected within the last twenty or thirty years, and could not in the present state of public opinion be carried to a successful issue."

Since the year 1908-1909 about 1,200 new schools in England and Wales have been opened, or have taken the place of old ones, making a net increase of 238 schools. The whole advance took place before 1915, for the building of new schools was almost entirely held up by the circumstances of the war. Between 1915 and 1919 there was actually a net decrease of 120 in the total number of schools. In the year 1919-1920 the Board of Education had "under consideration how best to meet not only arrears of building caused by the war, but also the new requirements of the Education Act, 1918, especially as regards the instruction of older children." The year saw the opening of 51 new schools, but the figure represents barely more than a quarter of the average output of schools in the five years before the war. Less than nothing has been done to make good the war-time arrears. The Board has embarked on a policy of so-called economy, and the prospects of building are about as bad as they can be.

It is common knowledge that, in areas where the population is increasing, there is serious congestion in the matter of school accommodation, accompanied by the usual tendency to deterioration. Under the Board's Building Regulations a new school should have " no undesirable surroundings " ; a good playing-ground, with a portion covered for shelter in wet weather ; a central hall for general assembly ; a number of class-rooms such that there is never more than one teacher working in each ; as a rule there should be not less than two class-rooms for every hundred scholars and not less than 10 square feet of floor space for each scholar in the class-room ; class-rooms should be well lighted from the left of the pupils, well ventilated and warmed ; there should be wide corridors and safe staircases and exits, adequate cloak-rooms where clothes can be dried, well-provided lavatories for necessary washing, and a good supply of drinking water. Schools erected, however, before 1900 fall far short of modern requirements. Even before the war the standard adopted by the Board in condemning schools was a very low one indeed compared with the modern ideas of school planning, and condemned premises have been allowed to continue in use for years because a new building has not been available. It is not unusual in old-fashioned schools to find cramped surroundings and no proper playground, no separate hall which is not used as a class-room, class-rooms made to accommodate 60 to 100 children, and sometimes one large room in which four or more classes are taught together. Even passages and exits are known to be used as class-rooms. The Education Act of 1918 requires that suitable provision should be made by local authorities for " practical instruction," but the lack of accommodation in backward areas makes this out of the question. Some local authorities, such as the London County Council, had arranged before the war to rebuild or remodel systematically a certain number of schools each year, but these schemes are now held up indefinitely. Local authorities are not merely permitted by the Board, but deliberately advised to make do with premises which do not comply in the least with the Board's building requirements. Even in the case of a new school, the Board has actually forbidden the provision of a practical room, although the provision of such a room is a statutory obligation. There is practically no new building except in cases where the conditions are actually injurious to health, or the congestion is so great that children are walking the streets. The Board has recently arranged for the purchase by local authorities of disused army huts, and a large number of these are being used as temporary accommodation; but makeshift premises of this kind are necessarily unsatisfactory to run, and tend to cost more in the end than the building of efficient schools. It is true that owing to the decline of the birth-rate during the war, the number of children proceeding to school in the next few years will fall below the normal. There will be for a time a decrease rather than an increase in the demand for elementary school accommodation, but this is no reason why children should be taught in unsuitable premises. The Board of Education ought to carry out the survey of existing school buildings which was begun before the war, and should put pressure on local education authorities to make good deficiencies by giving notice that after a reasonable interval it will decline to pay grant on account of schools held on premises which are obviously unsuitable. At the same time, labour members of local education authorities should call for regular reports on the school accommodation of their area, and should press for the erection of new schools in place of those which are condemned. Educationists may reasonably claim that the rebuilding or remodelling of the schools in the coming year should be at least equivalent to the average achievement in the five years before the war.

NURSERY SCHOOLS.—The advent of nursery schools, provided for under the Education Act of 1918, seems as far off as ever. Under the new Act, local education authorities are expressly empowered to make arrangements for "supplying or assisting the supply of nursery schools (which expression shall include nursery classes) for children over two and under five years, or such later age as may be approved by the Board of Education, whose attendance at such schools is necessary or desirable for their healthy physical and mental development." The Board issued its regulations in respect of nursery schools in January, 1919, twenty-nine such schools being recognised up to March, 1920, but of these only three have been provided by local authorities. During the last twelve months the Education Committee of more than one town has been offered as gifts suitable and substantial buildings for use as nursery schools. Owing to the fact that the Board of Education would be required to contribute annually their proportion of the cost for carrying on the school, the Board has refused to approve the acceptance of buildings for nursery school purposes.

"GRANT-AIDED" SECONDARY SCHOOLS.—"The primary need of the moment," the President of the Board of Education has declared, "is the multiplication of secondary schools." The total number of grant-aided secondary schools in England and Wales is 1,140, with places for about 308,000 pupils, and 206 other schools are recognised by the Board "as efficient." The comparative prosperity among certain classes of workers during the war resulted immediately in an increasing demand for secondary education, a fact which refutes the middle-class contention that working-class parents do not appreciate the value of education. Secondary schools became rapidly filled to overflowing, with the result that thousands of would-be scholars, among them intending teachers, have to be refused admission because there are no places for them. In 1910 the London County Council arranged to establish a number of " central" schools with the object of providing advanced instruction for children over 11. At the end of 1921, there were fifty-one such schools in being, with accommodation for 17,000 children, and the Council proposed to extend the scheme so as to bring up the total number to 100 schools, with 40,000 places, but the scheme is held up with every other reform. The Board has found it necessary to suspend its rule limiting the size of classes to thirty-five pupils, and it is admitted that " the enforced stoppage of building " has caused serious overcrowding in the great majority of secondary schools. The clamant need for a large increase in secondary school accommodation is discussed in a later chapter.

The standard of accommodation and equipment required by the Board's Building Regulations in "grant-aided" secondary schools is higher than in elementary schools, as regards both class-rooms and playing-fields, but "higher elementary schools" and schools of the type of the L.C.C. "central schools" are required to "be planned in accordance with the principle applicable to an ordinary public elementary school."

The Law as to School Attendance.

WHOLE-TIME SCHOOL ATTENDANCE.—It is estimated that in 1919 the total number of scholars on the books of public elementary schools in England and Wales was 5,419,137, with an average attendance of 5,123,526 per day. The age-limits of compulsory whole-time school attendances are fixed by law, but these may be varied by local authorities to some extent. Section 8 (1) of the Education Act (1918), which has not yet, however, been brought into operation, requires that "no exemption from attendance shall be granted to any child between the ages of 5 and 14 years." Under the same section labour certificates must not be granted to children under 14, but the local authority may, if it pleases, raise the higher age limit of school attendance to 15. Further, the Board of Education may, on the application of the local authority, "authorise the instruction of children in public elementary schools till the end of the school term in which they reach the age of 16, or (in special circumstances) such later age as appears to the Board desirable." Thus there is nothing in the terms of the Act to prevent school authorities from providing education for children up to 16. Children over 15, it is true, cannot be legally compelled to attend school, but parents may be persuaded to let them remain. Not merely does whole-time school attendance up to 16 exempt young people between 16 and 18 from part-time attendance at continuation classes, but local authorities are empowered to provide allowances for maintenance in the case of children over 12, so that there need be no hardship to poor families from the loss of children's earnings. The payment of fees in public elementary schools, which was the practice until recently in some voluntary or "non-provided" schools, was finally abolished by the Education Act of 1918.

Unfortunately, however, the Education Act of 1918 is in a state of suspended animation. The Act comes into operation on a day appointed by the Board, different days being appointed for different purposes. For the purpose of raising school age it was laid down that "the appointed day shall not be earlier than the termination of the present war." Month after month the Board refused to take action, pleading in excuse the long delay over the Turkish settlement. Now, however, that the termination of the war has been officially proclaimed, the Board can no. longer hide the fact of its ignominious surrender to the pressure of reactionary forces. The baby has been thrown to the wolves, and there seems no immediate prospect of a change of policy. Meanwhile, the earlier law remains in operation. Under previous Education Acts, local authorities are obliged to make bye-laws regulating school attendance for children between 5 and 14. In London, there is compulsory attendance up to 14, but local authorities can and do grant "labour certificates" to children over 12 who have reached a certain standard in school, or children over 11 in agricultural areas, exempting them from whole-time or part-time attendance. The consequence is that a number of promising young scholars who would benefit greatly from another year of schooling leave school at 13. It is significant of this tendency that the number of children between 13 and 14 on the books of public elementary schools is only about two-thirds of the number in the age-group from 12 to 13. Nor is the Board relieved from responsibility by the passing of the Employment of Women, Young Persons, and Children Act, 1920, which prohibits a child under 14 from employment in "an industrial undertaking." The term covers mines and quarries, factories and workshops, works of construction and transport, excepting transport by hand, but children over 12 may be employed in shops, domestic service, agriculture and in casual occupations, and the effect of the new industrial legislation may be merely to prohibit their employment in a regular trade. Pending action by the Board, local authorities would be well advised to make bye-laws enforcing whole-time school attendance on children between 5 and 14. This measure would be preparatory to raising the higher age-limit to 15, when the Education Act of 1918 comes eventually into operation.

SPECIAL REGULATIONS FOR INFANTS.—Children under 5 cannot be obliged to attend school, but under the Education Act of

1918 local authorities may provide education for children over 2 and under 5 in nursery schools or nursery classes.. The number of children under 5, however, attending elementary schools in England and Wales does not amount in all to over 2c0,000, and all progress is effectually checked for the time being by the lack of school accommodation. In the case of children under six, the local authority may make a bye-law relieving parents from their obligation to cause the child to attend school, but regard must be had to "the adequacy of the provision of nursery schools for the area," and any ten parents of children attending public schools in the area may require the local authority to hold a public enquiry "for the purpose of determining whether the bye-law should be approved." It is usual for the infant class to break up in the afternoon half an hour or an hour before other departments, and there is some feeling among parents in comfortable home circumstances that children under seven should not be obliged to attend school in the afternoon. On the other hand, mothers with several young children and perhaps an infant in arms, would find it extremely inconvenient to have children under seven half the day on their hands, and would be thankful in most cases to send infants over two to a nursery school. Experience shows that children coming from poor and crowded homes may greatly benefit, not merely in training, but in health, from early attendance at school. In the case of children under seven, while local authorities should make proper provision, it seems desirable that a certain option should be allowed to parents in the matter of school attendance. The setting up of parents' committees—an experiment which has been made with success in Scarborough—deserves the attention of progressive school authorities.

PART-TIME ATTENDANCE AT CONTINUATION CLASSES.—Under the Education Act of 1918, it is obligatory on local authorities to organise a system of part-time education for young people between 14 and 16 (and after the lapse of seven years from the " appointed day " between 14 and 18) in their respective areas. The Act provides that young people of these ages shall attend continuation schools, at such times and on such days as the local authority may require, for 320 hours in the year, distributed as regards time and seasons as may best suit the circumstances of each locality. Within a period of seven years of the "appointed day" the number of hours can be reduced to 280, but only by a special resolution of the local authority. Further, attendance must take place between 8 a.m. and 7 p.m., and not on Sundays or on any customary holiday or half-holiday. In short, attendance must take place in working hours. A local authority may, if it pleases, recognise " works schools " as giving "suitable and efficient part-time instruction," but a young person cannot be compelled to attend a "works school" against his will. Nor is it a sound proposition that a school connected with a private commercial or industrial undertaking, and run for business purposes, should be recognised by the local authority as a suitable place of education.

The Board intended originally to invite local authorities to draw up schemes of continued education, and to fix the "appointed day" for each area as the local authority was ready to carry out its duties. A few local authorities, including Manchester, began the organisation of a voluntary system of day continuation classes, while London set to work with a compulsory scheme, and the "appointed day" for the area was fixed as from January, 1921. At the end of a month 90 per cent. of the young people notified had enrolled under the scheme, but the experiment had hardly been tried when the Board decided to change its policy, and local authorities were advised to draw in their horns. In London, a one year's course has been substituted for a two years' course, the size of classes has been swollen beyond the limits, not merely of good teaching, but of ordinary discipline, and the scheme is not given a fair chance. Local authorities ought to act in advance of the Board, and invite young people between 14 and 16 to attend at continuation classes for at least 320 hours per annum, or else offer them the equivalent in some other and better form of secondary education.

The Scope of Elementary Education.

CHILDREN UNDER 7.—It is now generally recognised that in elementary education there are three distinct phases, the first covering the period of a child's life from admission to school to 7, the second the period between 7 and 11, and the third the period from 11 to 14, or so long as the child remains at school. The broad lines of the school curriculum are laid down in the Board of Education Code of Regulations, but these admit of considerable variety of interpretation, depending largely on the qualifications of the teaching staff and the nature of the school equipment. The tendency of recent years has been to abolish the system of examinations, and to give teachers as much freedom as possible in framing their curricula.

The period of school life up to 7 is spent in the infant school. According to the Code, the aim is to provide for the free development of mind and body, and for the formation of habits of obedience and attention. Physical exercises should take the form of games, or singing and breathing exercises rather than of set drill. Younger infants should be encouraged "to employ their eyes, hands, and fingers in suitable free occupations," to talk and to ask questions. The teacher should tell stories, leading the children to form ideas and to express them in simple language of their own. Older infants should be trained to listen carefully, to speak clearly, to cultivate their powers of observation, and to do simple things with their hands ; they should begin to read and write, to count and to sing simple songs. In up-to-date schools an improvement has taken place in methods of teaching infants which amounts almost to a revolution in the last twenty years.

CHILDREN BETWEEN 7 AND 11.—At 7 the child usually passes into the main school. There are in towns separate departments for boys and girls, but departments are "mixed" in rural districts, and in some schools where all children are under 11. At 11 the normal child is supposed to be able to read and write fluently, and to be familiar with the simple rules of arithmetic. It is a matter of regret to some teachers that in this country, unlike in America, handwork, except in the form of drawing, receives too little attention during the four or five years between the infant classes and the upper standards, when the child is preparing to leave school for industry. There is, however, no question that the education provided in the junior departments of efficient elementary schools does reach a high level of excellence and produce admirable results. The quality of the instruction may be judged, not merely from the number of elementary school children who at the age of 11 win scholarships in first-rate secondary schools, and hold their own in competition with children who have far greater home advantages, but in the high standard of average intelligence. It is suggested in the Report of the Departmental Committee on Scholarships and Free Places that some 75 per cent. of elementary school children in junior departments are intellectually capable of profiting by further whole-time instruction up to 16 or beyond.

CHILDREN OVER 11.—The instruction of children over 11 gives rise to more difficult problems. The child is now qualified to study a growing variety of the subjects which equip him for "the work of life." The Code requires that the curriculum should be developed in the direction of history, geography, literature, elementary science and nature study, and further it is incumbent on local authorities to make adequate provision in their areas, as part of the ordinary provision of elementary education, for practical instruction appropriate to the needs of the pupils and the circumstances of the schools. Teaching in the past has been often dull and perfunctory, but teachers are now keenly alive to the fact that the main value of instruction lies in the interest evoked as much as in the actual knowledge acquired. "There has," the London Education Committee reports, "within recent years been a distinct movement towards strengthening the appeal of literature, art, music and drama by an imparting of the spirit rather than an insistence on the letter. Instead of parsing Shakespeare plays, as was the practice a quarter of a century ago, the children now go to see them acted. Instead of listening to a recital of dry facts about Dickens and his writings they read "David Copperfield" and "A Tale of Two Cities." In many London schools, teachers in the upper standards are specialists in their own subjects, and scholars in their final year, more especially pupil teachers, are encouraged to concentrate on studies for which they have particular aptitude, and to work individually or in small groups at intensive courses. The L.C.C. has opened ten "home workrooms" as an experiment, so that children from poor homes may have the opportunity for private study, and so successful is the venture that it has been decided to open ten more in the immediate future.

The practical side of education is largely inspired with the same spirit. Practical subjects may include handicraft, cooking, laundry work, housewifery, dairy work, gardening, and " all such subjects as the Board may declare to be subjects of practical instruction." In London over 92 per cent. of the accommodation necessary for practical instruction of boys over 11 has already been provided. The majority of the centres are for woodwork lessons, but about 20 are for metal work, some of these being furnished with power machines. In other parts of the country there have been successful experiments in using such crafts as printing and bookbinding. Gardening is mostly practised in rural areas. " The work of a rural school," the Board advises, " should centre round such practical subjects as are suited to the occupations of the locality, mainly gardening, handicraft and domestic economy, and associated with these should be subjects teaching the principles underlying the practical instruction, such as arithmetic, drawing, and rural science." *Practical instruction* which aims at developing intelligence by the use of hand or eye should not be confused with *vocational training*, the primary object of which is to fit the child for his adult occupation.

Nevertheless, it has long been felt by teachers and inspectors that all is not well in the upper part of the elementary school. Teachers are faced with the impossible task of crowding into three short school years instruction in a range of subjects which should properly occupy at least a five years' course. Even such extension of school hours as may be afforded by part-time continuation classes would relieve the congestion to some extent. For example, it has been proposed by the London Education Committee to simplify the teaching of history and geography, as these subjects " must be taught in future as subjects preparatory for higher work in continuation schools," a consideration which " applies in a less degree to the whole of the elementary school curriculum." Moreover, the ordinary elementary teacher, who is required to take a class through all or the greater part of the time-table, does not, as a rule, possess the wide grasp of a subject which would enable him to inspire enthusiasm in his pupils. Nor is there always the proper equipment for specialised work. The lack of equipment for practical work in many areas has been a serious hindrance to undertaking it.

The London Education Committee has proposed to attack the problem in two ways. The first proposal is to develop the system of " central schools," namely, schools providing more or less advanced instruction for selected children over 11, a proposal which has been held up for the time being by the practical embargo on building. The second proposal is to simplify the curriculum in the upper standards for children who remain behind in the ordinary elementary schools, and to specialise in practical work to a greater extent than hitherto. Teachers would be encouraged by means of "refresher courses" to take up practical subjects, and so far as possible a practical workshop would be attached to each school. "If all the pupils," the London Education Committee observes, "capable of profiting by the more advanced courses of instruction associated with secondary and central schools are removed from the ordinary elementary schools, the problem of dealing with the remainder is greatly simplified and an opportunity is presented for breaking with many old traditions." The weakness of the scheme lies partly in the fact that it does not go far enough. Witnesses before the Departmental Committee on Scholarships and Free Places estimated that 75 per cent. of elementary school children are "capable of profiting by the more advanced courses of instruction associated with secondary and central schools," and the scheme does not propose to provide for more than 20 per cent. at most. Thousands of children will be given mainly practical diet, whose intellectual capacities demand stronger meat. Another serious objection to the scheme is that "central schools" do not offer, as a rule, genuine secondary education, but are provided "with a view of giving suitable pupils a course of instruction with a bias to some kind of industrial and commercial work." Educationists are now commonly agreed that education in adolescence should be solely determined by a child's capacity to profit by it, and not by the needs of his adult occupation.

The Scope of Secondary Education.

THE RELATIONSHIP BETWEEN ELEMENTARY AND SECONDARY EDUCATION.—Public elementary education, we are told by the Education Advisory Committee of the Labour Party, was originally established by the governing classes for the children of "the independent poor." It was designed as a special kind of education, suited to "the conditions of workmen and servants." It had no connection with secondary education, which was the education of the well-to-do, and there is still organised opposition from employers' bodies, such as the Federation of British Industries, to education "which would unfit children for employment they will eventually enter." Old artificial barriers are, however, breaking down before the pressure of social changes and modern conceptions of education. It is not only school authorities who are aware that the later years at the elementary school are largely wasted, but parents complain that between the ages of 12 to 14 a child is mostly marking time, while the child himself is sick of schooling. The Advisory Committee points out the essential futility of an elementary course which is not related to the laws of a child's natural development. It proposes to throw over the old pernicious doctrine that elementary education is "a special kind of education designed for the children of a particular class," and to substitute a system under which it would form "the preparatory stage in a course extending through childhood and adolescence."

This modern view of education is recommended by the Committee for adoption by the Labour Party as an essential part of a progressive programme. "The Labour Party is convinced that the only policy which is at once educationally sound and suited to a democratic community is the one under which primary education and secondary education are organised in two stages in a single and continuous process; secondary education being the education of the adolescent and primary education being the education preparatory thereto. Its objective, therefore, is the development of public secondary education to such a point that all normal children, irrespective of the income, class or occupation of their parents, may be transferred at the age of 11 from the primary or preparatory to the secondary school and remain in the latter till 16." The Labour Party holds that all immediate reform should be carried out with that objective in view and in such a way as to contribute to its attainment. In particular it regards all "central schools," "junior technical schools and part-time continuation classes" as at best transitional arrangements, which must on no account be allowed to conflict with "the creation at the earliest possible date of a system of free and universal secondary education." The general lines of the Labour Party scheme for giving practical effect to these views may be briefly indicated under the following headings.

THE CONTINUATION SCHOOL.—From the educational point of view, part-time attendance at continuation classes forms a miserably inadequate substitute for full-time secondary education. From another standpoint, non-labour members of the L.C.C. have declared that "the continuation school stops employment and ends discipline without adequate result," and that it would be more satisfactory to keep the children full-time until a later age. Similarly, parents protest that the loss of children's earnings is not sufficiently compensated by a few hours a week of instruction, or mere physical drill or dancing in an overcrowded class-room. Half a loaf is, however, better than no bread. Local education committees are advised by the Labour Party to extract what good they can from the Education Act of 1918, and to press forward voluntary schemes of continuation classes, but to keep always in mind that the ultimate goal of any scheme is whole-time secondary education. Not merely there should be provision for at least 320 hours per annum, but schools should be staffed and equipped up to the standard of "grant-aided" secondary schools.. The curriculum should be framed on broadly humanistic lines, and narrowly vocational subjects should not be taught to children under 16.

HIGHER ELEMENTARY SCHOOLS.—By the mere practical necessities of the situation, local authorities have found themselves committed now for many years past to the organisation of some form of post-primary education, which they have tacked on to the elementary school under such names as "higher elementary schools," "higher

grade schools," " higher tops," "junior technical schools " or
" central schools." The type of " central school" which in London
is superseding the earlier forms of " higher elementary school"
provides instruction of a comparatively advanced grade, the time-
table including at least one foreign language. Nevertheless, in
general academic standing, these schools fall definitely below the
standard of a " grant-aided " secondary school, and are modelled
on somewhat different principles. The general characteristic of the
" central school" is inferiority to secondary schools in teachers'
qualifications and salaries, in the ratio of staff to pupils, in school
buildings and equipment, and in surroundings and playing-fields,
while the curriculum is framed with a vocational bias and children
do not generally remain at school after 15. " Central schools " are
favoured by school authorities, partly because the vicious doctrine
persists that a child's education should be determined by the needs
of his adult occupation, but principally for the sake of cheapness.

" We have not yet gone so far," the Director of Education for
Darlington has declared, " as to establish vocational schools for intending doctors, lawyers, and those who intend to take up the higher
branches of engineering. A good general education is essential
whatever calling a boy or girl proposes to follow." From a broad
statesman-like point of view it is bad economy on the part of a local
authority to provide schools of a type which offer merely a cheap
substitute for secondary education, and would certainly have to be
scrapped when the nation faces seriously the problem of education.
As opportunity occurs, higher elementary schools should be remodelled on the lines of a true secondary school, and transferred to
the proper authority, where separate local authorities are responsible
for elementary and secondary education. The methods of staffing
and equipment should be approximated so far as possible to the
secondary school model, and the curriculum freed from a vocational
bias. Pupils should be encouraged by means of maintenance grants
to remain at school until 16.

THE SECONDARY SCHOOL.—The Education Act of 1902-1903, by
placing responsibility for secondary as well as elementary education
in the hands of county and borough councils, made it possible for a
child to pass on from the elementary to the secondary school, and
in some rare cases from thence on to the university. The L.C.C.
awards annually 1,700 junior county scholarships to elementary
school children, tenable for three or five years, and there are similar
schemes in operation elsewhere. A ladder of this kind is, however,
reserved to children of exceptional talent and ability. It is estimated that something under 9 per cent. of elementary school children
between 11 and 12—the normal age of transfer—pass on to secondary
schools, and the majority of these children leave school before
they reach 15. Fresh powers and new duties were conferred by
the Education Act of 1918, and local authorities are under the
obligation of using their powers in such a way that " adequate pro-

vision shall be made to secure that children and young persons shall not be debarred from receiving the benefits of any form of education of which they are capable of profiting through inability to pay fees." For the first time the provision of secondary education has been made a statutory duty, and local authorities have to hold themselves responsible for the failure of suitable candidates to gain admission to secondary schools. The Departmental Committee on Scholarships and Free Places has revealed that in all probability as many as 75 per cent. of elementary school children are intellectually capable of profiting by full-time instruction up to 16 or beyond. It is significant that in 1919-1920 over 8,000 children were refused admission to secondary schools because there were no free places, and over 9,000 children because there were no means of accommodation at all. Nor do these figures represent by any means the full extent of the demand. In hosts of cases a child does not apply for admission to a secondary school, for the simple reason that there is no such school within reasonable access of his home. And these are not the worst difficulties. Apart from the payment of fees, few working-class parents can afford to maintain children over 14 at school without hardship to other members of the family, and the present provision of allowances for maintenance is quite inadequate to the need. The total number of children who receive maintenance grants may be roughly estimated at 30,000, the average grant being about £8 10s. per annum. Further, there is a tendency for a higher standard of intellectual acquirements to be required from children of poor parents than from children of the well-to-do. The London Education Committee has made the amazing proposal that, " in the interests of the community," the children of fee-paying parents should be admitted to public secondary schools on easier intellectual terms than children who apply for free places, while a still higher standard should be required from children whose parents are so poor as to claim an allowance for maintenance.

For practical reasons it would be idle to suggest that the present shortage of secondary schools should be made good all at once. The Advisory Committee of the Labour Party has therefore put forward the very moderate proposal that local authorities should provide places for at least twenty children between 11 and 16 for every 1,000 of the general population in their areas. This is the standard laid down by the Departmental Committee on Scholarships and Free Places " as the basis of a reasonable development," and one which has been recommended for adoption in the scheme of the York Education Committee. From this basis the number of places could be increased each year until it covered all children capable of profiting by secondary education. The proportion among elementary school children has been variously estimated by educational experts as from 75 to 90 per cent. So as to make the most of existing accommodation, it is proposed that the preparatory departments of " grant-aided " secondary schools should be abolished. These departments now provide about 10,000 places for fee-paying children under '10' and could be turned to the better use of providing for children over 11. The remodelling of higher elementary schools would be another means of providing further secondary school accommodation. In sparsely populated areas, where secondary schools are few and far between, a motor service could be organised for the conveyance of pupils to and from school. The normal age of transfer from the elementary to the secondary school would be 11, and children would norm ally remain at school until 16, but provision should be available for late developers up to the age of 14.

Students' fees in grant-aided secondary schools, under the Labour Party proposal, would be abolished straight away. Bradford has already taken this step, while Durham has prepared a scheme under which the number of free places would be systematically increased each year until all places would be free at a given date. There should be a generous system of allowances for maintenance. Children in need of this assistance should receive it as a matter of course, and the grants should be adequate in amount, the scale rising automatically with the child's age and growing expenses. Under the Education Act of 1918, local authorities have power to make grants for maintenance in respect of children over 12. Finally, there should be one uniform test of admission to "grant-aided" secondary schools, and children of poor parents should not be required to exhibit exceptional intellectual attainments. The central purpose of the Labour Party scheme is that secondary education, from being the privilege of a few specially intelligent or fortunate children, should become the right of every child of normal intelligence.

UNIVERSITY SCHOLARSHIPS.—It would be premature to consider a general scheme for the development of public university education. Apart from special arrangements for ex-service students, the Board established in 1920 a scheme offering 200 university scholarships to students in grant-aided secondary schools in England and Wales, but this scheme is now suspended. Present holders of scholarships only are allowed to complete their course. There are other scholarships provided by local authorities for poor students at the universities and various places of higher learning, but the total provision is too small to affect seriously the problem of education for the general mass of young people.

Miscellaneous Provisions.

SIZE OF CLASSES.—The excellent work of teachers in elementary schools is too often handicapped by the unduly large number of pupils in a class. The following table shows the number of adult teachers of various grades for every thousand scholars in average attendance for the year 1919-1920 :—

	Head Teachers.	" Certificated " Assistants.	" Uncertifi- cated " Assistants.	Other Adult Teachers.	Total.
London	3·7 ...	24·3 ...	·3 ...	·3 ...	28·5
County Boroughs...	4·0 ...	19·0 ...	4·6 ...	·5 ...	28·0
Boroughs	5·3 ..	15·5 ...	8·4 ...	1·2 ...	30·4
Urban Districts ...	3·8 ...	19·4 ...	4·8 ...	·5 ...	28·7
Counties	9·2 ...	9·3 ...	9·9 ...	5·4 ...	33·7
Total	6·0 ...	15·8 ...	6·3 ...	2·3 ...	30·4

These figures indicate that the average size of a class does not
greatly exceed 30 pupils, but head teachers are not supposed to take
a class in any but very small schools, so that the average size of
classes is larger than the figures would suggest.   Nor do the
figures refer to the number of children on the register, but to
the number in average attendance, and the attendance on full
days would be considerably above the average.   Further, the
average is reduced by the inclusion of small rural schools.   In urban
areas the size of classes is considerably above the average.   On
the other hand, the proportion of " uncertificated " or supplementary teachers in village schools is nearly twice as large as for the
country as a whole.

The Board's Code of Regulations requires that the number
of scholars on the register of any class, or group of classes, under
the instruction of one teacher should not exceed 60 ; while " in no
case will a staff be considered sufficient if, in the aggregate, it is not
at least equivalent for the average attendance of the school or department, measured by the following scale " :—

Head teacher	35 children
Each certificated assistant teacher ...	60 ,,
Each uncertificated assistant teacher ...	35 ,,
Each student teacher	20 ,,
Each supplementary teacher	20 ,,

In the old-fashioned type of school, however, where class-rooms
are built to seat as many as 80 or 100 pupils, local authorities
are hampered in carrying out even the minimum prescriptions
of the Code.   The L.C.C. adopted a scheme in 1912 under which
the size of classes in existing schools would be reduced at the end of
fifteen years to the limits prescribed by the Council in new schools,
namely, 40 children in senior departments, and 48 children in infant
departments, and in the last ten years the number of classes with
from 50 to 60 pupils has been reduced by about 200.   Nevertheless,
there were in London no fewer than 4,800 classes of this size in
1920.   Meanwhile, the recent restrictions on building have caused a
general suspension of new schemes, and there is already a noticeable
tendency to discharge teachers and increase the size of classes.   For
example, Sheffield has proposed to economise by a general inflation
of classes to a 50-60 standard, and also to relax the rule by which
the head teacher is relieved from the ordinary duties of teaching.

In the spring of 1922 it was stated in the House of Commons that, out of 150,000 classes in elementary schools in England and Wales, 39,000 classes had between 40 and 50 pupils, 31,000 classes between 50 and 60 pupils, and nearly 7,000 classes over 60 pupils.

Classes in "grant-aided" secondary schools are subject to special rules. The Board prescribes a limit of 30 pupils, but, owing to the present lack of accommodation, it has recently been decided to raise this limit to 35. There are no special rules as regards higher elementary schools, but, broadly speaking, the ratio of pupils to teachers is greater than in secondary schools, but not as great as in an ordinary elementary school. By swelling the size of classes beyond their proper proportions, so that teachers and pupils alike find that their best efforts are discouraged, local authorities do not achieve economy, but merely a waste of public time and money. Moreover, teachers in elementary schools should not be required to teach under conditions which would not be tolerated in other schools. Local education authorities would be well-advised to reduce the size of classes in elementary schools to at least the standard of a "grant-aided" secondary school.

SPECIAL CLASSES FOR BACKWARD CHILDREN.—In a report by Mr. Cyril Burt to the London Education Committee, it is estimated that about 10 per cent. of elementary school children, though not mentally defective, may be classed as backward. For children of this type it is necessary to provide either special classes, or special schools. Mr. Burt is in favour of special classes, on the ground that there is no hard and fast line in the case of backward children, who ought not to be completely segregrated from their normal school-fellows. Backwardness in many cases may be traced to underfeeding, illness or similar physical cause, or merely to perpetual "migration" from one school to another, so that there is no continuous education. Many backward children develop later so as to reach the full normal standard. Mr. Burt advises that classes for backward children should be limited to 30, and that the curriculum should be predominantly manual in character, and for older children adapted to their probable future employment. For children of limited intelligence there seems an actual advantage in early vocational training. It is observed that backward children are by no means deficient in æsthetic appreciation, and may be keenly susceptible to music and drama.

PHYSICAL TRAINING.—The Code of Regulations requires that children should be afforded every opportunity for the healthy development of their bodies, not merely by training them in appropriate physical exercises, but by encouraging them in organised games. Instruction and practice in swimming may be included in the time-table. For the proper encouragement of organised games the London Education Committee advises that additional playing-fields inside and outside the county are badly needed, and it is most desirable that more use should be made of the royal parks and the parks belonging to the L.C.C. and the Borough Councils. The Committee has in view proposals for the provision of additional school swimming baths, these classes being most popular among the pupils, but the Board's present policy of economy has thrown back every development in this direction. In some areas organised games have been restricted to one hour instead of four hours a week, so that all the time is taken up in going to and from the playing-fields, and organised games are practically cut off altogether. It is not necessary to believe that "Waterloo was won on the playing-fields of Eton" in order to realise the importance of physical exercises and games for growing boys and girls.

THE "PREFECT" SYSTEM.—"It is incumbent on the school," the London Education Committee states in a memorandum on the " prefect system," not only to see that the child has every opportunity for full development as a child, but to see also that the training shall be a real preparation for future duties and responsibilities, social, utilitarian and cultural. Perhaps one of the greatest needs of the time is the development of a social conscience and a keen sense of corporate life in the schools. "With these ends in view older pupils are invited by enterprising school authorities to take an active part in the good government of the school. Prefects are appointed by the head teacher in some cases, but in schools where the tone and discipline are of a higher order it is preferred that prefects should be selected by the scholars within certain limits on a democratic basis. Each school has to work out its own scheme, but there seems unanimity of opinion as to the educational value. "One head teacher after another," the Director of Education for Warwickshire has stated, " tell of its marvellous results : how it has made manly boys and womanly girls of children who, at the best, had kept their good to themselves, how the whole school has easily responded ; how swearing and foul talk and smoking have disappeared, or nearly so ; how manners in the street and road have been metamorphosed by the new code of honour which has appeared ; how the parents have risen up and blessed it ; how corporal punishment has nearly gone ; how new activities of school life have appeared spontaneously ; how the whole relationship of teachers and children has been changed."

SCHOOL LIBRARIES AND PICTURES.—"There is," the London Education Committee reports, " great need for the establishment of a really good library in each school, for nothing is likely to have a real influence on the older children than to place at their disposal a wide range of stimulating literature." Something has already been done by the Committee in developing a system of circulating libraries. Sets of carefully chosen books are circulated among the schools, the sets being so arranged that each child in each class has three or four books every term, and there are now about two million volumes in circulation under the scheme. In Sheffield and in some other boroughs and districts there is useful co-operation between the school libraries and public libraries, and teachers act as vouchers and advisers to boy and girl readers. There seems room for further development in this direction.

Teachers interested in stimulating a child's natural love of beautiful things attach a great importance to the educational influence of school decoration. Reproductions of famous pictures and statues may be purchased at a comparatively low cost. In Buckinghamshire the local authority has recognised a voluntary organisation, which will lend pictures to a school in return for a small annual subscription. The pictures are changed each year, so that a child may become familiar with a wide variety of styles during his school life.

SCHOOL JOURNEYS.—According to the Code, " time occupied by visits paid during school hours to places of educational value and interest, or by field work or by rambles " may be reckoned as school attendance, and academic teaching in art and science may be supplemented by this means from living experience. The London Education Committee puts aside habitually a certain sum each year for expenses of this sort. Children have been taken in school term for journeys in the country, extending in some cases for a fortnight, so that they may have experience of camp life. They have visited museums and picture galleries and been taken to the theatre. Elementary school children have formed some of the most enthusiastic audiences of the classic performances at the "Old Vic," and the Committee assisted recently in organising in various parts of London special performances of Shakespeare plays. The latter expense, however, was subsequently disallowed by the District auditor. The matter was referred to the Courts, which upheld the auditors' decision, and the judge further questioned how far a child's attendance at the performance of a play in a theatre could be brought within fair interpretation of the term " visits to places of educational value and interest." Children may derive from good drama, not merely exquisite delight, but keen stimulus to imagination and intellectual activity ; and this unfortunate judgment, together with the policy of stringent economy preached by the Board, has resulted in a real deprivation to London children. The L.C.C. has decided to cease its expenditure on school journeys for the coming year, thereby saving a round sum of £13,500. It is left to the enthusiasm of the teachers to raise a voluntary fund and to keep the system going.

The Supply of Teachers.

THE SHORTAGE OF TEACHERS.—On the supply of teachers depends the future of education. There are in England and Wales something over 166,000 adult teachers of all sorts in elementary schools. The supply of qualified teachers is already insufficient for present needs, and the general shortage would be immediately apparent under conditions of normal development. In the event of the Education Act of 1918 being brought fully into operation, it is estimated that there would be a deficiency of at least 20,000 teachers. Even before the war teaching was, in fact, a "decaying trade," the number of entrants each year being $_{too}$ few to replace the normal wastage caused by death and retirement. It is significant of the present tendency that the number of persons recognised by the Board of Education for the first time as intending teachers was 9,614 in 1908, but had declined to 6,088 in 1918. The falling-off in numbers since 1914 can no doubt be partly attributed to war circumstances. At all events, there was a certain recovery after the Armistice, so that the figure was raised to 6,604 in 1919, but this reversal of the general tendency may have merely a passing significance. Meanwhile, the shortage of teachers has had disastrous effects, not merely in hindering natural development, but in giving countenance to the employment of unqualified persons, and dragging down the standard of the service. At the present moment nearly one-third of the total adult staff in elementary schools are "uncertificated" or supplementary teachers. In London the proportion is only about 2 per cent., but the figure rises to nearly one-half in rural areas. Under healthy conditions, it should be as impossible to employ an "uncertificated" teacher as an unqualified medical practitioner.

In secondary schools there is not quite the same acute problem. The superior conditions of service attract, not merely a good proportion of university graduates, but the cream of students from State-aided training colleges—further depleting the supply of elementary teachers. It is, however, obvious that a multiplication of secondary schools would depend on the multiplication of secondary school teachers, and the present supply would have to be largely increased so as to meet the needs of a reasonable rate of progress. The causes of the present decline in the supply of elementary teachers may be grouped under two heads according to whether they relate to difficulties experienced by candidates during the stage of preparation, or to the ultimate prospects of the profession.

TRAINING OF ELEMENTARY SCHOOL TEACHERS.—The system of training elementary school teachers, as it stands to-day, cannot be said to exhibit any definite unity of plan. Rather less than one-half of the teachers in elementary schools have undergone a course of instruction in a training college beginning at the age of 18 or over, while about one-third have received the Board's certificate without going through a training college. The remainder are composed of persons who have only passed an examination of inferior grade, and are known as "uncertificated" teachers, or they belong to the anomalous unqualified class which goes by the name of "supplementary" teachers.

There are, broadly speaking, three types of training college, namely, residential colleges provided by private initiative and having mostly a religious and denominational character ; day colleges attached to a university ; and residential or day colleges provided by local authorities, either as independent institutions or in connection with a university or other place of higher learning. The students' fees amount to about £30 per head per annum, impecunious students being usually assisted by their local authority in this respect. These fees are supplemented by grants from the Treasury, and colleges have to conform to certain requirements laid down by the Board. For example, half the places in a denominational college must be open to students not belonging to the denomination of the college. At the head of each college there must be a responsible principal of university standing, and at least two-thirds of the teaching staff must consist of persons holding academic qualifications approved by the Board. The principal of a woman's college should be a woman, and a woman vice-principal should be appointed where there is a woman's department. Students are still partly recruited from pupil teachers who have had considerable practice in teaching, but whose general education has been, as a rule, incomplete and unsatisfactory. The majority, however, have now received a substantial period of secondary education. Thus, the training college has to perform a double function. It has to continue the general education of students as well as to train them in the principles and practice of teaching. There is normally a two years' course, but a limited number of students reading for university degrees remain for a third or fourth year ; or an extra year may be allowed for a special course at a school of art or science, or for foreign travel. Further, a small number of " certificated " teachers or university graduates take a one year's course of professional training. The Board's final examination is normally taken at the end of a two years' course, and students who pass are recognised as "certificated" teachers, but university degrees and various university examinations not necessarily leading up to degrees are accepted by the Board as equivalent to the " certificate" examination. Men students receiving grants from the Board are required to pledge themselves to serve for seven years as teachers in a " grant-aided " school within a period of ten years following training, and women for a term of five years within a period of eight years.

The system of training for elementary teachers has undergone important changes in recent years, and facilities have been largely increased since the Education Act of 1902. There are, however, wide gaps which still remain to be filled. Most serious of all is the lack of secondary school accommodation. Though the majority of free places in " grant-aided" schools are occupied by prospective teachers, there are not nearly enough places to go round. The Board has made certain proposals for the attendance of rejected candidates at pupil teacher centres or at higher elementary schools, but cheap makeshifts of this sort do not take the place of true secondary education. It is clearly undesirable that intending teachers should be confined through childhood and adolescence

within the close atmosphere of the elementary school, where they
expect to remain as adults, and the whole system of boy and girl
pupil teachers should be completely abolished. A generous provision of secondary school accommodation is the preliminary step
in a sound system of training, and incidentally would act so as
largely to increase the supply of potential teachers.

Other defects of the present system are due to the limitations
of the training college, which has to perform the double function of
providing both higher education and professional training within
the limited space of two years. The curriculum has been lately remodelled, so as to give opportunity for a more liberal course of study
to two-year students than had previously been allowed, but the mere
fact of so short a course practically prohibits the average student
from undertaking advanced studies in special subjects. The number
who do so falls admittedly below the needs of the schools. So far
back as 1846 it was the intention of the Education Department to
provide a normal course of three years, but this ideal has never
been realised for any but a small minority of students. The time
seems already overdue for establishing a minimum three-years'
course, and encouraging the rank and file of students to read for
university degrees. Students who are intellectually not up to the
university standard should not, as a rule, be admitted to the teaching profession. Further, there are defects of training due to the
isolated circumstances of intending teachers. It has been recognised
by the Board for many years past, in principle if not in practice,
that a system which segregates students for two years in a residential training college tends to develop an unduly narrow and
professional outlook. It was, in fact, realisation of this defect which
led to the movement for establishing day training colleges attached
to a university. For the first time students were privileged to take
part in the general social and academic life of a university, where
they were brought into touch with teachers who were men of
eminence in their subjects, and capable of kindling intellectual
enthusiasm, as well as able to secure passes at examinations. Day
training colleges have, however, been found wanting in other
respects. Apart from the difficulties of students who live at a
distance from the college, young people living at home, or in cheap
lodgings, do not enjoy the privacy and facilities for uninterrupted
study which are afforded in a residential college. Another serious
danger which threatens municipal training schemes is the danger
of excessive provincialism. It is not good that teachers should
have been brought up, educated and trained within a single county
or borough, and for this reason some local authorities arrange to
draw part of their school staff from outside areas. There is, indeed,
no royal road to training so long as higher education is closed
to students capable of profiting by it, and the immediate need is
for a generous provision of university scholarships. Under an
efficient system young people would not be called upon to decide

on a profession, but would pass on as a matter of course from the preparatory school to the secondary school, and from thence on to the university, intending teachers mixing freely at every stage with students of all types. The training college would be reserved to graduates who required a period of professional training at the end of the academic course. It is the survival of the old pernicious doctrine that elementary education is a special kind of education designed for the children of a particular class which is the root of all trouble. The training of elementary school teachers should, in fact, not differ substantially from that of secondary school teachers, who are already largely drawn from the universities. It is a condition of progress that the student of to-day shall be trained so as to teach in the school of to-morrow.

TEACHERS' SALARIES.—In comparing the various hindrances to a proper supply of teachers, the Board has expressed its opinion that by far the most important and fundamental of these have arisen from insufficient ultimate prospects. The slight increase in the number of candidates since 1919 is principally attributed to the fact that "substantial progress has been made in the direction of improving these prospects by the provision of more adequate salaries, and better pensions and disablement allowances." A Standing Joint Committee, composed of representatives of the various associations of local education committees on one side and of the National Union of Teachers on the other side, was appointed in 1919 under the chairmanship of Lord Burnham. A national agreement was drawn up, prescribing scales of salaries for elementary school teachers, which was unanimously adopted by the Committee and approved by the Board. These scales are as follows :—

Scales for Certificated Assistant Teachers (Two Years College Trained) in Elementary Schools :—

Scales.	MEN.			WOMEN.		
	Minimum.	Annual Increment.	Maximum.	Minimum.	Annual Increment.	Maximum.
	£ s.	£ s.	£ s.	£ s.	£ s.	£ s.
Standard Scale I. ...	172 10	12 10	325 0	160 0	12 10	260 0
Standard Scale II...	172 10	12 10	340 0	160 0	12 10	272 0
Standard Scale III.	182 10	12 10	380 0	170 0	12 10	304 0
Standard Scale IV.	200 0	12 10	425 0	187 10	12 10	340 0

· Scales for Uncertificated · Assistant Teachers in Elementary Schools :—

| | MEN. | | | | WOMEN. | | | |
| | | | Maximum. | | | | Maximum. | |
Scales.	Minimum.	Annual Increment.	Appointed on or after 1st April, 1914.	Appointed before 1st April, 1914.	Minimum	Annual Increment.	Appointed on or after 1st April, 1914	Appointed before 1st April, 1914.
	£ s.	£ s.	£	£	£	£ s.	£	£
Standard Scales I. & II.	103 10	7 10	160	204	96	7 10	150	164
Standard Scale III. ...	109 10	7 10	180	228	102	7 10	160	182
Standard Scale IV. ...	120 0	7 10	200	255	112	7 10	170	204

The scales vary according to the district, Scale I. relating to rural areas, and Scale IV. to London and the extra metropolitan areas. Certificated teachers who have completed a three-years' course of training, or are university graduates, receive one increment in addition, or two increments in the case of four-year students. An assistant teacher who is appointed as head teacher, or a head teacher who is promoted to a higher grade school, retains his or her existing salary, and receives in addition a " promotion increment " of £20-£25 for men and £15-£20 for women. The maxima for head teachers vary again with the size of the school, Grade I. including schools with not over 100 pupils, and Grade V. schools with over 500 pupils.

Maxima for Head Teachers in Elementary Schools :—

| | GRADE I. | | GRADE II. | | GRADE III. | | GRADE IV. | | GRADE V. | |
Scales.	Men.	Women.	Men.	Women.	Men.	Women.	Men.	Women.	Men.	Women.
	£	£	£	£	£	£	£	£	£	£
Standard Scale II....	374	300	408	328	442	356	476	384	510	412
Standard Scale III.	418	335	456	366	494	397	532	428	570	459
Standard Scale IV.	467½	374	510	408	552½	442	595	476	637½	510

.Corresponding scales were drawn up by a second Standing Joint Committee for teachers in " grant-aided " secondary schools, viz. :—

Scales for Assistant Teachers in Secondary Schools :—

	Men.	*Women.*
Graduate assistant teachers	£240—£500 ...	£225—£400
Non-graduate assistant teachers	£190—£400 ...	£177 10s.—£320

In the case of secondary school teachers, there is an addition of £50 for men, and about £40 for women, who are employed in and about the London area, and certain other additions for teachers with special qualifications. Owing to the variety in the type of school and differing local conditions, there is no fixed scale of salaries for head teachers in secondary schools, but it was agreed by the Committee that the minimum commencing salary should be £600 for a head master and £500 for a head mistress.

Teachers were notoriously underpaid before the war, and the new scales when agreed did little more than compensate the rise in the cost of living. The scales were, in fact, only accepted by the teachers' side of the Standing Joint Committee in the expectation of an immediate fall in prices, and it was agreed by the Committee, with the approval of the Board, that salaries should not be revised until September, 1925. It would be in the highest degree unfortunate should the new economies to be effected by the Board now hinder in any way local authorities from observing their part of the agreement. Not merely a grave injustice would be done to the present generation of teachers, but so gross a breach of faith would have disastrous and far-reaching effects on recruiting.

The Departmental Committee on Teachers' Salaries which considered the question of " equal pay " for men and women teachers rejected the proposal as impracticable. The Committee took the view that a salary which would attract a woman would not necessarily attract a man with similar qualifications, owing largely to the fact that, under existing social and fiscal conditions, financial liabilities fall on a man in connection with his family which do not fall on a woman to the same extent, and that a difference between the scales of men's and women's salaries is inevitable. The War Cabinet Committee on Women in Industry, after considering this report, advised that, " in order to maintain the principle of ' equal pay for equal work ' where it is essential to employ men and women of the same grade and capacity, but where equal pay will not attract the same grade, it may be necessary for the State to counteract the difference of attractiveness by a payment for the services rendered to the State in connection with the continuance of the race, or, in other words, by the payment of children's allowances to married men." It seems worth while to give the proposal a trial, provided that women's salaries are levelled up to the men's standard, and not men's salaries levelled down to the women's standard. It is, however, important that local authorities should be under no temptation to prefer unmarried teachers. For this reason the whole of the additional cost of the children's allowances should be borne by the Treasury. The practice of discharging women teachers on marriage, though admittedly fit for their work, has been universally condemned by women teachers and all women's organisations as socially unjust and economically unsound. It cannot be urged too strongly that this practice should be discontinued, and women teachers receive the same allowances as men for dependent children.

The Regulation of Children's Employment.

RESTRICTIONS ON EMPLOYMENT.—Children's employment is regulated under the Factory Acts, and by various special legislation. Under the Women, Young Persons and Children's Act (1920), a child under 14 may not be employed in "an industrial undertaking." The latter term covers mines and quarries, factories and workshops, works of construction and transport, excepting transport by hand. Further, children's employment is restricted by the law of school attendance, and local education authorities have wide powers of regulating conditions for children of school age not coming under special industrial legislation. Under the Employment of Children Act (1903), the local authority may prescribe for children employed in any occupation the age below which employment is illegal, the hours between which employment is illegal, the maximum number of hours to be worked per day or per week, or may prohibit employment in a specified occupation. There are certain statutory requirements. A child under 12 may not be employed for longer than two hours on Sunday, or for longer than one hour before and one hour after school on any day when he is required to attend school. Also, a child under 14 must not be employed between the hours of 8 a.m. and 6 p.m., or in street trading, or in public performances without a licence from the local authority. It is these statutory requirements which form the basis of local bye-laws, but local authorities may exercise a wide discretion over and above the statutory minimum. In London and in most large towns, local authorities have used their powers to prohibit children's employment in the sale or delivery of intoxicants, in lathering or similar processes in barbers' shops, and have taken advantage of their option to prohibit street trading for girls up to 16. Children's employment is prohibited in different localities, in such various occupations as billiards or bagatelle marking, the sale of programmes or shifting of machinery in theatres and cinemas, working in hotel and restaurant kitchens, acting as messenger, tout, or agent to bookmakers, soliciting for the letting of apartments, sorting rags or refuse, and cleaning door-steps.

The weakness of the Employment of Children's Act lies in its mainly permissive character. Backward local authorities, not only neglect to make suitable bye-laws, but seem unable to enforce such legal restrictions as exist. Moreover, the reports of school medical officers reveal that any employment out of school hours, beyond the lightest errand work, tends to impair the child's physical development. The obvious remedy would be that a child under 14 should be unconditionally prohibited by law from employment for wages. The simplicity of such an enactment would give it the further advantage of being comparatively easy to enforce. During a recent revision of local bye-laws by the L.C.C., some members interested in education brought forward a proposal to the effect that " a child shall not be employed on any day when the school is open," but the motion was defeated by the reactionary parties. It has not been clearly established in the courts that local authorities have power to make a general order prohibiting children's employment, but they may achieve practically the same result by prescribing the strictest limits to employment, and by a rigid enforcement of bye-laws.

The need for raising the age of school attendance, and for abolishing labour certificates in the case of children under 14, have been discussed in a previous chapter.

CHOICE OF EMPLOYMENT.—Under the Choice of Employment Act, 1910, local education authorities have power "to make arrangements, subject to the approval of the Board of Education, for giving boys and girls under 18 years of age assistance with respect to the choice of suitable employment, by means of the collecting and communicating of information and the furnishing of advice." About 600,000 boys and girls leave the public elementary schools each year, and of these a large and increasing number seek help, either from local employment committees acting as sub-committees of the local education authority, or from juvenile advisory committees appointed by the Ministry of Labour. Unfortunately, however, the existence of this dual authority has led to conflicts between the Ministry of Labour and local authorities, which have seriously jeopardised the success of the service. Young people between 14 and 18 are in a period midway between the educational life of the child and the industrial life of the adult. It is necessary to consider their interests from both points of view, and the alternative is, either a system of local administration by local education committees, reinforced by assistance from the Ministry of Labour, or a centralised system where the Ministry of Labour is the supreme authority, acting in co-operation with local education committees. Following the Chelmsford Report, the most recent proposal is that local education authorities should within a specified period declare, whether or not, they will undertake in their areas the duties under the Choice of Employment Act. If a local authority decides not to act, then the Minister of Labour can, and presumably will, take action instead. The policy is that there should be an organisation of some kind in each area, but it has always been recognised by the authorities on both sides that "the employment of juveniles should be primarily considered from the point of view of their educational interests and permanent careers rather than from that of their immediate earning capacities." Local education authorities neglect a great opportunity who do not make efficient use of their powers under the Choice of Employment Act.

UNEMPLOYMENT.—" When there is unemployment among adults," the Labour Party has laid it down as a general principle, " the entry of juvenile workers into industry should, as far as possible be arrested, provision being made by means of adequate system of maintenance allowances to prevent the family suffering from loss of earnings." The opposite effect has, however, been achieved by the policy of the present Government in holding up the Education Act of 1918 regardless of the growing volume of unemployment. It is a common practice among employers in some industries deliberately to discharge adult men or women in preference to young people who are content with low wages. The Labour Party proposes that powers of emergency should be conferred on local authorities to raise whole-time school age from 14 to 15 (this being the highest age-limit under the Education Act of 1918), at times of acute unemployment in their areas. Further, local authorities should open special training centres, and provide suitable instruction and maintenance for unemployed young people.

The Cost of Education.

Precise figures as to the actual expenditure on education from central and local funds are not available for any recent year. The following summary figures are computed from the published estimates of the Board of Education and the local education authorities as to their expenditure in the year ending March, 1922. They are, of course, approximate only.

ESTIMATED PUBLIC EXPENDITURE ON EDUCATION IN ENGLAND AND WALES IN THE FINANCIAL YEAR ENDING MARCH 31ST, 1922.

A.—*Elementary Education.*

1. Net Expenditure of Local Education Authorities :

    (a) Salaries of teachers £43,795,000

    (b) Other expenditure £19,853,000

               Total £63,648,000

2. Grants from the Board to Local Education Authorities :

    £36,900,000

3. Grants from the Board to other Bodies : £98,000

B.—*Higher Education.*

(Including Secondary Schools, Technical Schools, Training Colleges, etc., but not Universities).

1. Net Expenditure of Local Education Authorities £13,469,000

2. Grants from the Board to Local Education Authorities £6,647,000

3. Grants from the Board to other Bodies ... £2,130,500

C.—*Total of A and B.*

1. Total Net Expenditure of Local Education Authorities £77,117,000

2. Grants from the Board to Local Education Authorities £43,547,000

3. Other Grants to Local Education Authorities (Local Taxation Grants, etc.) £950,000

4. Difference to be met by Local Education Authorities from rates £32,620,000

D.—*Other National Expenditure on Education.*

1. Pensions to Teachers £1,575,000
2. Grants to Students—ex-Service Students ... £2,248,000
   Other Students £192,000
3. Expenditure on Universities £1,500,000
4. Other Expenditure by the Board (Museums, Administration, etc.)... ... ... £722,000

E.—*Total Public Expenditure on Education.*

	1913-14.	1921-22.
1. Grants from the National Exchequer	£15,320,000	£53,400,000
2. Local Rates	£16,190,000	£32,600,000
Total Local and National Expenditure	£31,510,000*	£86,000,000

* Actual expenditure.

Between the years 1913-14 and 1921-1922 there was an increase of 168 per cent. in the total sum of public expenditure on education. The rise is most acutely marked in the amount of national grants, the national exchequer bearing at present a substantially greater proportion of the total expenditure than before the war, but the figures taken as a whole do not represent an excessive rate of advance. They err rather on the side of moderation. Apart from special items of expenditure in the estimates for 1921-1922, such as provision for ex-service students, and a fall of at least 100 per cent. in the value of money, there has to be taken into account the necessities of growth in an undeveloped but vital public service. Broadly speaking, it is true to say that the progress of a nation in civilisation may be measured by the sum of its expenditure on education.

The primary need of the moment, Mr. Fisher has told us, is the multiplication of secondary schools. The Labour Party scheme, put forward as "a basis of reasonable development," would involve a net additional expenditure of about £15,000,000 per annum. This estimate, which takes into account the corresponding saving on elementary schools, would cover the abolition of fees in grant-aided secondary schools, places for at least 20 children between 11 and 16 for every thousand of the general population, and maintenance grants for children over 14. The immediate cost would be a comparatively small one, and there is no better time than to-day to undertake this and other schemes entailing the building or rebuilding of schools. There are at the time of writing as many as 150,000 building operatives out of work, and at least a part of the outlay on building would be compensated by a corresponding saving of public money on unemployment benefit and poor law relief. For this reason building schemes undertaken immediately should be generously financed by the Treasury. Nor is it desirable on other grounds that fresh burdens should be thrown on local rates, which are so high in some poor localities that local authorities find their best activities paralysed. Not merely " the poor pay for the poor " in working class areas, but rents have been forced up to a point which practically prohibits the provision of decent working-class dwellings. Under the present rating system, local rates amount virtually to a single tax on housing, which presses necessarily more heavily on the poor man than on the rich man, and with the utmost severity on large families. A further rise in local rates would be the cause of grave injustice and hardship to hundreds of thousands of poor tenants. There is an overwhelming case that further expenditure on education should be met by increased grants from the national exchequer. The London Labour Party has proposed that at least 75 per cent. of the cost of education should be borne by the Treasury, and the proportion seems a fair one. In respect of measures directly undertaken for the relief of unemployment, the proportion of national expenditure should not be less than 90 per cent.

For the time being, however, forces of reaction are paramount in Parliament. "Education," Lord Inchcape has told us, "is an excellent thing in its way, but there is a limit to its economic usefulness." Hence, the Geddes Economy Committee, of which Lord Inchcape is a member, advises the Government to cut down the education estimates for the coming year by no less a sum than £16,000,000, or nearly one-third of the total national expenditure on education. The Committee makes no attempt to discriminate between one public service and another, and would cut down the education estimates by about the same proportionate amount as the swollen army estimates. Its members view apparently with complacency the total exclusion from school of children under 6 regardless of home convenience, enlarging the average size of classes in elementary schools to 50 or 60 pupils, a drastic curtailment of the school health services, a breakdown of the scholarship system, so that the number of children who now pass from the elementary school to the secondary school or to the university would be still further diminished, together with the wholesale discharge of teachers and a general reduction of salaries contrary to the "Burnham" agreements. And this saving of money on public education the Committee proposes to devote to the purpose of relieving taxation on private incomes. In short, the business man's idea of national economy is to shift the burden of paying for the war from off his own broad back on to the shoulders of the poor man's child!

The signs of unexpected public indignation at the ruthless attack on the people's education, together with the prospect of a general election, seem to have had their influence on the Government, which has rejected the more sensational of the Geddes proposals. The reductions foreshadowed in the education estimates for

1922-1923 do not exceed £6,000,000. The outlook is nevertheless a sufficiently grave one. Working-class opinion has so far been conciliated that children between 5 and 6 are not to be excluded from school without their parents' consent, but there are to be economies where staffing is on a lavish scale, and a number of teachers are to be discharged. This method of economy is preferred by the Government to a reduction of teachers' salaries. Pensions are to be placed on a new contributory basis, but the Burnham scales are to be maintained intact. In spite of unemployment, school feeding must be kept within normal limits, and necessitous children referred to the Poor Law. Similarly, the quality of entrants into secondary schools is to be narrowly watched, and there is practically an end to progress. The general policy of the Board is, however, not to make specific proposals for cutting down of this or that branch of the educational services, but to ration local authorities up to a fixed maximum grant in aid of local expenditure. The policy of percentage grants which was condemned by the Geddes Committee as a "money-spending" device, has been referred by the Government to a separate committee for further consideration, but seems in effect to have been already abandoned. Local authorities will be obliged either to cut down their expenditure or else to raise local rates, and so spare the taxpayer at the expense of the rate-payer.

There is, of course, a limit to "economic usefulness," in education as in everything else. It is a question of degree, and the first step towards a sound system of economy is a proper sense of economic values. The product of education is "brains," which from the most commercial point of view are the nation's most valuable asset. To save on education, while vast sums are spent on less "excellent" things, such as tobacco, drink, or armaments, which are not conspicuous for "economic usefulness," or money is lavished on mere wanton luxury, this is not economy but waste.

The business man has, however, his own axe to grind, and he is not such a fool as he seems. The manner of his attack on the workers' education and his desperate anxiety to thrust it back within the old limitations "suited to the conditions of workmen and servants," suggests, indeed, that he appreciates its significance for himself, not too little, but too well. Education is a double-edged tool. It makes good servants but bad slaves, and capital is afraid of losing its hold over labour. It is possible that a reactionary Government may succeed in cutting down the people's education so that the effects would be felt for a generation or longer, but this is not the political broom which will sweep back the rising tide of democracy. For men do not wait to seize power merely because they may not be "fit to govern." The danger which threatens democracy is that radical social and economic changes may take place unaccompanied by a forward movement in the schools.

SUMMARY OF PROPOSALS.

I. School Premises.—Local authorities should proceed at once with their schemes for the building or rebuilding of schools in accordance with the Board's Building Regulations and the requirements of the Education Act of 1918. These schemes should make provision for a proper number of nursery schools and for increasing the number of secondary schools. The provision for building in the coming year should be at least equivalent to the average achievement in the five years before the war.

II. School Attendance.—Pending the operation of the Education Act of 1918, local education committees should enforce whole-time school attendance for children between 5 and 14, and the higher age-limit should be raised to 15 as soon as the new Act comes into force. Nursery schools, or nursery classes, should be available for children between 2 and 5, but a certain option should be allowed to parents as regards the attendance of children under 7. Local authorities should forestall action on the part of the Board of Education and invite young people between 14 and 16 to attend continuation classes for at least 320 hours per year, or offer them an equivalent in some other and better form of secondary education.

III. The Scope of Elementary Education.—As regards children under 11 the curriculum should be framed in accordance with the Board's Code of Regulations. For children over 11, there should be provided advanced courses of instruction of the type generally associated with secondary education. It should be the ultimate goal of local education committees that all children of normal intelligence should pass as a matter of course from the elementary school to one type or other of secondary school about the age of 11. Provision should, however, be available for late developers up to the age of 14.

IV. The Scope of Secondary Education.—Local authorities should immediately provide secondary school accommodation for at least 20 children between 11 and 16 for every thousand of the general population in their areas, the number of places being increased each year until all children of normal intelligence are provided for. Meanwhile, continuation classes and higher elementary schools should be developed so far as possible on the lines of true secondary education, and vocational subjects should not be taught to children under 16. Students' fees in grant-aided secondary schools should be abolished, and adequate maintenance grants provided for children over 14.

V. Miscellaneous Provisions.—(1) The size of classes in elementary schools should approximate so far as possible to the standard of secondary schools and be limited to 30 pupils. (2) Special classes should be arranged for backward children, and instruction in their case given a practical bias. (3) Playing-fields should be enlarged and public parks opened so as to encourage children in physical exercises and organised games. (4) Increased attention should be paid to school libraries and pictures. (5) The prefect system should be encouraged in senior departments. (6) Increased facilities should be given for school journeys and visits to places of educational value and interest.

VI. The Supply of Teachers.—The supply of teachers may be encouraged (*a*) by increasing the facilities for training, and (*b*) by improving the ultimate prospects of the profession. Training schemes should provide for full-time secondary education up to 18 and a three years' course in a training college, or preferably at a university, to be followed by a period of professional training. Teachers should be assured against any breach of the agreements of the Standing Joint Committee in respect of salaries, and the present scales should be gradually raised so as to compare not unfavourably with earnings in other learned professions. The Standing Joint Committee should consider a proposal for "equal pay" to men and women teachers, to be supplemented by children's allowances.

VII. The Regulation of Children's Employment.—Pending an amendment of the law so as to prohibit children under 14 from employment for wages, local education authorities should make bye-laws restricting children's employment within the narrowest limits, and in every area should make efficient use of their powers under the Choice of Employment Act. At times of acute unemployment local authorities should be given power to raise school age from 14 to 15, while suitable training with maintenance should be provided for unemployed young people.

VIII. The Cost of Education.—The burden of fresh expenditure in order to meet the growing needs of education should not be thrown on local rates, but met by additional grants from the national exchequer. At least 75 per cent. of the total public expenditure on education should be borne by the Treasury, the proportion being raised to 90 per cent. in respect of measures undertaken for the relief of unemployment.

SELECT BIBLIOGRAPHY.

Annual Reports of the Board of Education, 1908-1909 to 1919-1920.

Provisional Code of Regulations, 1919.

Building Regulations, 1914.

Suggestions for the Consideration of Teachers and Others Concerned in the Work of Public Elementary Schools. Board of Education, 1912.

Interim Reports of the Committee on National Expenditure, 1922.

Report of the Departmental Committee on Scholarships and Free Places, 1920.

The Organisation of Education in London, L.C.C. 1919.

Report on Development of Education in Public Elementary Schools, L.C.C. 1919.

Report on Instruction of Children over 11 in Ordinary Elementary Schools, L.C.C. 1919.

Time Tables of Schools, L.C.C. 1921.

Report on the Prefect System in Elementary Schools, L.C.C. 1921.

Report on the Provision for Backward Children, L.C.C. 1918.

Reports of the Standing Joint Committee on Standing Scales of Salaries for Teachers in Public Elementary Schools and in Public Secondary Schools. 1921.

Juvenile Employment Inquiry. Lord Chelmsford. 1921.

Continued Education under the New Education Act. Labour Party. 1920.

Local Education Schemes. Labour Party. 1921.

Secondary Education for All. Edited by R. H. Tawney, for the Education Advisory Committee of the Labour Party. 1922.

Industrial Legislation. Labour Party. 1920.

Unemployment: A Labour Policy. Labour Party and Trades Union Congress. 1921.

FABIAN ESSAYS. (1920 Edition). 2/6; postage, 3d.
KARL MARX. By HAROLD J. LASKI. 1/-; post free, 1/1½.
FROM PATRONAGE TO PROFICIENCY IN THE PUBLIC SER-
VICE. By WILLIAM A. ROBSON. 1/-; post free, 1 1½.
SOCIALISM AND CHARACTER. By HENRY STURT. 7/6; postage, 5d.
THE WHITLEY SYSTEM IN THE CIVIL SERVICE. By J. H.
MACRAE-GIBSON. 1/-; post free, 1/1½.
WHAT TO READ on Social and Economic Subjects. 2s. n.
TOWARDS SOCIAL DEMOCRACY? By SIDNEY WEBB. 1s. n., post. 1d.
THIS MISERY OF BOOTS. By H. G. WELLS. 6d., post free 7d.

FABIAN TRACTS and LEAFLETS.
Tracts, each 16 to 52 pp., price 1d., or 9d. per dos., unless otherwise stated.
Leaflets, 4 pp. each, price 1d. for three copies, 2s. per 100, or 20/- per 1000.
The Set of 74, 7/6; post free 8 6. Bound in buckram, 12/6; post free 13/6.

I. —General Socialism in its various aspects.
TRACTS —192. Guild Socialism By G. D. COLE, M.A. 180. The
Philosophy of Socialism. By A. CLUTTON BROCK. 159. The Ne-
cessary Basis of Society. By SIDNEY WEBB. 151. The Point of
Honour. By RUTH C. BENTINCK. 147. Capital and Compensation. By
E. R. PEASE. 146. Socialism and Superior Brains. By BERNARD SHAW. 2d.
142. Rent and Value. 138. Municipal Trading. 121. Public Service v.
Private Expenditure. By Sir OLIVER LODGE. 2d. 107. Socialism for Mil-
lionaires. By BERNARD SHAW. 2d. 139. Socialism and the Churches. By
Rev. JOHN CLIFFORD, D.D. 133. Socialism and Christianity. By Rev.
PERCY DEARMER. 2d. 78. Socialism and the Teaching of Christ. By Dr. J.
CLIFFORD. 42. Christian Socialism. By Rev. S. D. HEADLAM. 79. A Word
of Remembrance and Caution to the Rich. By JOHN WOOLMAN. 72. The
Moral Aspects of Socialism. By SIDNEY BALL 69. Difficulties of In-
dividualism. By S. WEBB. 51. Socialism: True & False. By S. WEBB. 2d.
45. The Impossibilities of Anarchism. By G. B. SHAW. 2d. 7. Capital
and Land. 5. Facts for Socialists. 3d. 41. The Fabian Society: its
Early History. By BERNARD SHAW.

II.—Applications of Socialism to Particular Problems.
TRACTS.—198. Some Problems of Education. By BARBARA DRAKE. 6d.
197. International Labour Organisation of the League of Nations. By
WM. S. SANDERS. 196. The Root of Labour Unrest. By SIDNEY WEBB. 2d.
195. The Scandal of the Poor Law. By C. M. LLOYD. 2d. 194. Taxes,
Rates and Local Income Tax. By ROBERT JONES, D.Sc. 2d. 188. National
Finance and a Levy on Capital. By SIDNEY WEBB. 2d. 187. The
Teacher in Politics. By SIDNEY WEBB. 2d. 186. Central Africa
and the League of Nations. By R. C. HAWKIN. 2d. 183. The
Reform of the House of Lords. By SIDNEY WEBB. 181. When
Peace Comes—the Way of Industrial Reconstruction. By SIDNEY WEBB.
2d. 177. Socialism and the Arts of Use. By A. CLUTTON BROCK. 175. The
Economic Foundations of the Women's Movement. 2d. 173. Public v.
Private Electricity Supply. 170. Profit-Sharing and Co-Partnership:
a Fraud and Failure? 164. Gold and State Banking. 161. Afforestation
and Unemployment. 155. The Case against the Referendum. 152. Our
Taxes as they are and as they ought to be. 2d. 145. The Case for School
Nurseries. 140. Child Labor under Capitalism. 136. The Village and
the Landlord. By EDW. CARPENTER. 144. Machinery: its Masters and
Servants. 122. Municipal Milk and Public Health. 124. State Control
of Trusts. 158. The Case against the C.O.S. By Mrs. TOWNSHEND.

III.—Local Government Powers : How to use them.
TRACTS.—190. Metropolitan Borough Councils. By C. R. ATTLEE, M.A.
2d. 191. Borough Councils. By C. R. ATTLEE, M.A. 2d. 193. Housing.
By C. M. LLOYD, M.A. 3d. 189. Urban District Councils By C. M. LLOYD,
M.A. 2d. 62. Parish & District Councils. (Revised 1921). 2d. 148 What a
Health Committee can do. 2d. 137. Parish Councils & Village Life. 2d

IV.—Biographical Series. In portrait covers, 2d. and 3d.
199. William Lovett, 1800 1877. By BARBARA L. HAMMOND. 3d. 182.
Robert Owen, Idealist. By C. E. M. JOAD. 179 John Ruskin and
Social Ethics. By Prof. EDITH MORLEY. 165. Francis Place. By ST. JOHN
G. ERVINE. 166. Robert Owen, Social Reformer By Miss B. L. HUTCHINS.
167. William Morris and the Communist Ideal. By Mrs. TOWNSHEND. 168.
John Stuart Mill. By JULIUS WEST. 174 Charles Kingsley and Christian
Socialism. By C. E. VULLIAMY.

Printed by G. Standring, 7 Finsbury St., London, E.C. and published by the Fabian Society,
25 Tothill Street, Westminster. London S.W.

Fabian Tract No. 199.

WILLIAM LOVETT

1800-1877

By Mrs. L. BARBARA HAMMOND

Biographical Series No. 8.   Price Threepence.
Published and sold by the Fabian Society at
the Fabian Bookshop, 25 Tothill Street, Westminster, S,W. 1.   . . .   Published May, 1922.

WILLIAM LOVETT

1800-1877

WILLIAM LOVETT was born at Newlyn, a mile from Penzance, in the year 1800. His father, a Yorkshireman, captain of a small trading vessel, was drowned before his birth. His mother, a Cornishwoman, left to her own resources, supported herself, the child, and her own mother by hawking fish and doing various odd jobs in Penzance. As a child Lovett showed no signs of the passion for learning that marked him in later life, for no dame's school in the town could succeed in teaching him to read, though he consented finally to learn his alphabet from his great grandmother, an old lady of 80. Later on he learnt at school "to write tolerably well, and to know a little of arithmetic and the catechism, and this formed the extent of my scholastic acquirements." His mother, an ardent Methodist, was kind and indulgent except where religious duties were concerned. The Sundays of his childhood were long remembered by Lovett with horror—three services at chapel, "the reading of texts, prayers, and portions of Scripture" in between the services filled up the gloomy day. One Sunday when the boy played truant and ran off to play with other boys on the sands he was unlucky enough to sprain his ankle. His mother, concerned for his body, but even more concerned for his immortal soul, pronounced it a judgment on him for breaking the Sabbath, but nevertheless sent for the doctor.

When he was about thirteen Lovett was apprenticed for seven years to learn ropemaking. During his apprenticeship he led a hard life, for his mother made a second and unhappy marriage, and he and his grandmother lived together on the five shillings a week he was paid, helped out by what little she could earn in the fishing season. His work was laborious and involved carrying great weights and, what he minded more, the walking along lonely roads by night, for the terror of his early childhood, the cry, "The press gang is coming," was now succeeded by an overwhelming fear of ghosts and goblins that lasted till London life made him a sceptic. Fond though he was of reading, he had nothing to read except "the Bible, and Prayer and hymn book, and a few religious tracts, together with fragments of an old magazine," and occasionally a nonsensical pamphlet about "giants, spirits, goblins, and supernatural horrors." There was no bookshop in the town and no opportunity for intellectual improvement, but the future writer of manifestoes and addresses found some scope for his gifts in composing love letters for his young neighbours. His leisure was busily spent in making " gimcracks of every kind," boxes, birdcages, a machine for spinning twine, a turning lathe and so on, and he was allowed to play about and pick things up in the shop of a friendly carpenter, a privilege that ultimately proved of great importance, for at the end of his apprenticeship he found himself, at the age of 20, master of a skilled trade in which there was no work. Chains had begun to supersede ropes, and, except for a few weeks in the winter, there was nothing in Penzance for a ropemaker to do. For one season Lovett tried a fisherman's life ; the opening was promising, for he had the offer of succeeding to the fishing business of a great uncle, but he could not overcome his sea-sickness, which attacked him even before he got on board at the mere thought of the " short cross loping waves," and so when the season was over he renounced all thoughts of becoming a fisherman, and obtained work at a neighbouring car-penter's. But the regular apprenticed carpenters of Penzance objected, and he had to leave. In despair of obtaining employment of any kind at home, he determined to try his fortune in London. By making a lady's workbox with secret drawers and a pair of tea caddies he raised about 50s. ; another workbox paid for part of his passage money on a small trading steamer, and he found himself in London in 1821, aged twenty-one, with 30s. and some letters of introduction to ropeworks in his pocket.

Early Struggles in London.

In London the prospects of work seemed at first no brighter than in Penzance. The ropeyards needed no hands, and attempts to obtain employment in the company of some carpenters from the country were no more successful. His sailor's dress, as worn by the young men of Penzance, told against him. For weeks he was reduced to a penny loaf a day and a drink at the pump. Then he got one or two odd carpentering jobs, but when these were finished and the money they brought exhausted, the half-starved youth determined, in spite of sea-sickness, to take a situation as ropemaker on board an Indiaman. Before finally engaging himself he went to see his carpenter friend from Penzance, who, after failing in business, had come to London and obtained work in a carpenter's shop in Somers Town. This friend's master, seeing probably a chance of cheap labour, agreed to take Lovett on as well, and for several months employed him making furniture. Though the pay was poor, Lovett managed to provide himself with more conventional clothes and a few tools. Soon, however, the pay ceased altogether, and the master after being sent to the Fleet Prison for debt, and persuading his workmen to finish their work on the understanding that it would be paid for when sold, turned out to be a thorough rogue, and they never received a halfpenny of the six or seven pounds due to each of the three. Lovett was again in low water ;

he lived in a damp unhealthy back kitchen and fell seriously ill. When he recovered he tried in vain to earn a living by making and selling small bits of furniture, and when this failed ·decided to try his luck as a cabinet maker, in which line he had now some experience. He was fortunate enough to be given a job at a small repairing shop, where he met a Scotchman, David Todd by name, " one of the most intelligent, kindhearted, and best disposed men I ever met with." Todd urged Lovett to join the Cabinet Makers' Society, but the Society very naturally rejected him as he had not served the five years required by their rules. Todd then procured him a situation at a small cabinet maker's for twelve months at a guinea a week. Though it was not a Society shop, his fellow workmen threatened to oust him because he had not been apprenticed. Lovett thereupon called a meeting and put his case before them, and they agreed to let him stop on, charging him heavily for help in different parts of the work. Once started as a cabinet maker Lovett succeeded in getting employment at different shops, and after he had served the required five years was admitted a member of the Cabinet Makers' Society, of which he afterwards became President.

Intellectual Development.

When Lovett first came to town he was too much absorbed in attempts to earn his bread to have much leisure or energy for other things, though a fellow lodger, a kind old schoolmaster, helped him during this time by correcting his " provincialisms and bad English," and by advising the study of Lindley Murray's Grammar, a book which became his pocket companion. His first real intellectual awakening came after he was in regular work, when he was introduced by chance to a small society called " The Liberals," composed mostly of working men, who had a circulating library, and met twice a week in Gerrard Street for discussion. Lovett had never officially joined the Methodist connection, though for a short time under the influence of some female preachers he had become a " converted member " of an obscure sect called the Bryanites ; but when he came to London he still thought that impromptu speaking, which he had never heard except in the pulpit, was a " kind of inspiration from God." To his astonishment, at the meetings of " The Liberals " he found the members making speeches, and good speeches, about the soul. He was at once fired by the desire to defend Christianity, and, with the help of David Todd, became a member of the society in order to study for this purpose. Political questions were also discussed at the meetings and roused his interest. " In short, my mind seemed to be awakened to a new mental existence ; new feelings, hopes and aspirations sprang up within me, and every spare moment was devoted to the acquisition of some kind of useful knowledge. I now joined several other associations in its pursuit, and for a number of years seldom took a meal without a book of some description beside me." The youth who had often wondered in vain in Cornwall about "the causes of day and night, the seasons and the common phenomena of nature," joined the Mechanics' Institute, and was soon discussing scientific theories. On other evenings he would attend the debates in coffee houses and listen to the heroes of past campaigns, such as Gale Jones and Richard Carlile. The vicissitudes of his love affair with his future wife stimulated his intellectual pursuits. She was a lady's maid, and he first saw her in Marylebone Church. He managed to make her acquaintance, and all went well till she asked him to take the sacrament with her. Lovett, whose religious views had been considerably affected by a year or two of London, explained that this was impossible for him. She then decided that she could not marry him and they parted, she returning with her mistress to the continent, he endeavouring to drown his grief in associations "literary, scientific, political." "And this means," he wrote later, "of diverting the mind from the object that preys upon it, I would venture to recommend to all those who may experience a similar heartrending disappointment." He resigned himself to a bachelor's life, but unnecessarily, for a year later the young lady relented, and after some "controversial correspondence" on the subject of the sacrament they were married on June 3, 1826, the various associations were given up, and for a time Lovett led a purely domestic life, devoting himself to his wife and interesting her in all his pursuits. He was firmly convinced that much of the unhappiness and failure of working class life came from the men's habit of expecting their women to be on a lower level of intelligence and omitting to share their intellectual interests with them. In his own case the opposite policy brought great happiness. "My wife's appreciation," he wrote later, "of my humble exertions has ever been the chief hope to cheer, and best aid to sustain me." All through his long life he retained the enthusiastic feminism of his early days. In 1856 he published a poem, written in 1842, called "Woman's Mission," of which the sentiments, though not perhaps the verse, are admirable. One stanza runs :—

> " Would man in lovely woman ever find
> His best adviser, lover, truest friend,
> .   .   .   .   .   .
> He must at once his gothic laws annul,
> Fling back her dower, strive only for her love,
> And proudly raise her up all rights to share."

Owenism and Politics.

Lovett's studies in London led him to become an ardent Owenite. The accumulation of property in the hands of individuals seemed to him to be the root of all evil : community of property the key to human happiness. Owen and his followers were flooding the world with schemes for the regeneration of mankind. Of one of these, the first London Co-operative Trading Association, founded during Owen's absence in America, Lovett became storekeeper in 1828. For two years after his marriage in 1826 he had been in good work at his trade ; he had then made an unfortunate venture in a pastrycook's business. On getting rid of his business, though not his debts, he accepted the storekeeper's post, at some financial sacrifice, but in the belief that " the gradual accumulation of capital by these means would enable the working classes to form themselves into joint stock associations of labour, by which (with industry, skill, and knowledge) they might ultimately have the trade, manufactures and commerce of the country in their own hands." But so far was the London Trading Association from fulfilling these expectations that it could not even pay Lovett's salary, and in a few months his wife was asked to take his place at half his pay. Lovett went back to his trade with his optimism undaunted, for he became hon. secretary of the British Association for Promoting Co-operative Knowledge. But these various co-operative societies only lasted three or four years, failing, according to Lovett, from want of custom, want of legal security, and from the over-strong meat provided in Owen's Sunday morning lectures, which alarmed "the religious portion of their members."

Lovett's Owenism did not prevent him from being critical of Owen the man and autocrat, or from taking part in Radical campaigns. Amongst these was the " Unstamped Agitation," described by him afterwards as " one of the most important political movements that I was ever associated with." At that time every newspaper was bound by law to have a 4d. stamp on it. Henry Hetherington, the protagonist of the movement, started publication in 1830, in defiance of the law, of an unstamped paper called the *Poor Man's Guardian*. The Stamp Office soon proceeded against the publisher and the booksellers who sold it ; volunteers then came forward for the work of distribution, some for love, others for the reward of a stock of papers and £1 a month during imprisonment. A "Victim Fund" was started for the sufferers, and Lovett became secretary of the Committee of Management. The campaign lasted five years. Over 500 persons in different parts of England suffered imprisonment. Hetherington himself when not in prison was " on the run," and his business was nearly ruined. In 1836, in consequence of the agitation, the 4d. stamp was reduced to 1d. Curiously enough, the *Poor Man's Guardian*, over which the battle had been fought, was finally declared by Lord Lyndhurst to be a strictly legal publication.

In the years before the passing of the famous Reform Bill of 1832 there were three schools of opinion amongst advanced working class thinkers about the question of reform. First, there were Owen and his followers, who despised political action, believing that mankind would be' saved by other means. Secondly, there was the group of Radicals, who believed that universal suffrage (by which they meant, as a rule, adult male suffrage), and nothing less than universal suffrage, was the necessary preliminary to all social improvement. This school was joined by many Owenites, who came to believe that democracy must precede communism, and gradually dropped their communistic dreams. Thirdly, there were the Radicals like Francis Place, who believed in taking the Bill as it stood, or with such amendments as were possible, and treating it as an instalment of a larger measure.

Lovett belonged to the second group. His conversion from Owenism to political reform was no doubt hastened by his acquaintance with Henry Hunt, the veteran reformer, whom he first met about 1828. For some years he continued working for the two movements side by side : one day he would be discussing the founding of an incipient community on the plan of Mr. Thompson, of Cork ; another day he would be helping to found the Metropolitan Political Union, to obtain effectual and radical reform in the Commons. Not content with these activities, he became " greatly interested in the temperance question," and in 1829 drew up a petition for the opening of the British Museum on Sundays. "Your petitioners," ran the opening sentence, " consider that one of the principal causes of drunkenness and dissipation on the Sabbath is the want of recreation and amusement." All the time, too, he was working at his trade of cabinet making. By 1831 his Radical convictions were so strong that on being drawn for the Militia he refused to serve or to pay for a substitute on the ground that he was unrepresented in Parliament. The authorities seized his little stock of household furniture, which his wife suffered to go "without a murmur"; but the protest had its effect, for discussion on the subject in the House of Commons and fear of an epidemic of "the no-vote no-musket plan" brought the balloting system to an end. Lovett had become a public character.

The Reform Bill.

In 1831 Lovett joined the newly founded National Union of the Working Classes and Others, which, amongst other objects such as " the repeal of all bad laws," aimed at " an effectual reform of the Commons House of Parliament." When the Whig Reform Bill was produced Lovett and Watson drew up a declaration of the principles of the National Union, headed by a quotation from Thales, calling for nothing less than adult male suffrage, voting by ballot, the abolition of property qualification for Members of Parliament, and annual Parliaments, thus comprising four of the six points of the future Charter. The National Union was an active body ; besides holding many small meetings for discussion under class leaders, it held public meetings, of which those at the Blackfriars Rotunda were the most important, and from these meetings its adherents were often called " Rotundanists." It attracted some violent spirits : " could the violence and folly of the hot-brained few," wrote Lovett later, " have been restrained, a far larger amount of good might have been effected. But, as in almost all associations that I have ever been connected with, our best efforts were more frequently directed to the prevention of evil by persons of this description than in devising every means and in seeking every opportunity for the carrying out of our objects." But whilst Lovett was blaming the " hot-brained few," Place was blaming Lovett and his friends. Place and those who thought with him formed a society called the National Political Union, with the object of supporting the Whigs in carrying their Reform Bill. They were bitterly opposed by the Rotundanists, who objected to being made the " tools " of the middle classes. Both sides tried to mobilise working class opinion. Lovett moved a universal suffrage amendment at the first public meeting of the National Political Union, but it was drowned by the " noise and clamour " of the opposing side, though a later proposal that half the. Council should consist of working men was carried. The Rotundanists, however, found themselves pitted against a past master of strategy and intrigue in Place, who managed to secure for the Council the election of " respectable " working men untainted with Rotunda heresy.

Another blow to the Rotundanists was the proclamation of their proposed public meeting to ratify the declaration drawn up by Lovett and Watson. In vain, Lovett, Watson and the secretary waited on Lord Melbourne to assure him of their peaceable intentions.. Lord Melbourne, receiving them with a barrier of chairs in front of him and a posse of police in the next room, assured them that their meeting was illegal, and that attendance at it would be high treason. The meeting was abandoned.

It cannot be said that the National Union of the Working Classes, or Rotundanists, were conciliatory in their methods. When the Government ordered a general fast for the cholera in March, 1832, the National Union, on the grounds that the cholera was largely due to underfeeding, decided to celebrate the day by providing a good dinner for their members, to be preceded by an orderly procession through the streets, headed by Lovett, Watson and Hetherington. The police interfered with the procession, using their bludgeons freely, and a few days later Lovett, Watson and the veteran and violent Benbow were arrested and charged with having " made a great riot, tumult and disturbance . . . . and caused great terror and alarm." All three were triumphantly acquitted by the jury, but Lovett and Watson withdrew from the Committee of the National Union as a protest against what they considered Benbow's unscrupulous conduct in connection with the expenses of the trial.

In spite of the efforts of the Rotundanists, the Reform Bill was passed in June, 1832. The National Union of the Working Classes and Others continued to exist for a time, but Lovett took little part in its activities, though a police spy did his best to entrap him into attending a meeting of whose objects he disapproved. The agitation for the " unstamped press " was absorbing his energies.

The twenties, thirties and forties of last century produced a bewildering procession of organisations and associations. The National Union of the Working Classes and Others was succeeded by the remarkable though short-lived movement known as the Grand National Trades Union of 1833-1834, a movement due largely to the reaction amongst the working classes against political intervention after the Reform Bill, and described by Mr. Hovell as " militant Owenism." The object of the Grand National was to obtain better conditions of life by means of combinations and strikes. Lovett joined it, and tried in vain to make it declare in favour of universal suffrage. By the end of 1834, after a series of unsuccessful strikes, it was dead.

In 1834 Lovett left his trade and made a second venture in business. He opened the premises of one of the defunct Co-operative Stores as a coffee house. Its conversation room and debates were well attended, but its financial side was a failure. After struggling with it for two years at a loss, Lovett gave it up. Opposite the coffee house was a school for poor music boys, opened by Mazzini, with whom Lovett became acquainted.

London Working Men's Association.

It was in the year 1836 that Lovett did the most important work of his life, the founding of the London Working Men's Association. What kind of a man was he at this time ? Place, a critical friend, described him as " a tall, thin, rather melancholy man, in ill-health, to which he has long been subject ; at times he is somewhat hypochondriacal ; his is a spirit misplaced." To his upright character and to his gentleness, all his contemporaries bear witness. Place wrote to Lovett urging him to overcome his melancholy, and to be less troubled by the miseries of mankind. " When youth and strength and flow of spirits," answered Lovett, " have been wasted in unrequited toil and poverty, and when after years of great physical and mental exertions, after a life of sobriety and industry, you find yourself losing your physical energies (so necessary for those who have to depend on their labour), and getting more and more involved in difficulties inextricable, and having the cares of a family in whose welfare is your highest hope, you need not be surprised if my tone and manner correspond with my situation. Perhaps the scenes I have had to encounter in my journey may have increased my sympathies for my fellow men ; and while I believe with you that this is the best world of which I have any hope, yet when I feel conscious of how much could be done to make it a comparative paradise of happiness instead of the hell of toil, of poverty and crime we find it, I cannot help lamenting that the wise and intelligent few do not carry their views of reformation beyond making

comfortable slaves of the many to pamper and support the few."
Lovett had only one child, a daughter, a second daughter having
died in infancy.

Fifteen years experience of London life and political campaigns
had brought a certain disillusionment. He no longer pictured his
fellow workmen as waiting eagerly for opportunities of study and
regeneration. They were more inclined "to croak over their
grievances with maudlin brains, and to form and strengthen their
appetites for drink amid the fumes of the tap room" than to put
Lindley Murray's grammar in their pockets. But their shortcomings
were due to the "circumstances and constitution of society, and not
to the organisation of man." Salvation, he felt convinced, must
come not from above, but from the workers themselves. They must
cease to look up to leaders, they must educate themselves. He complained that "a lord, a M.P., or an esquire was a leading requisite to
secure a full attendance and attention from them on all public occasions"; this must cease, and they must develop "discrimination and
independent spirit in the management of their political affairs."
With this object the London Working Men's Association was started.
Its membership was confined "as far as practicable" to the working
classes : it aimed at mental improvement as well as at equal political
and social rights. The ideal of the founders was expressed in an address
as follows : "Imagine the honest, sober and reflecting portion of every
town and village in the kingdom linked together as a band of brothers,
honestly resolved to investigate all subjects connected with their
interests, and to prepare their minds to combat with the errors and
enemies of society—setting an example of propriety to their neighbours, and enjoying even in poverty a happy home." Political
rights were not to be aimed at as an end in themselves ; "when we
contend for an equality of political rights, it is not in order to lop
off an unjust tax or useless pension, or to get a transfer of wealth,
power or influence for a party ; but to be able to probe our social
evils to their source, and to apply effective remedies to prevent,
instead of unjust laws to punish."

The London Working Men's Association exercised an influence
on public affairs out of all proportion to its membership. Quality,
not quantity, was aimed at. Between its foundation in June, 1836,
and 1839 only 279 members were admitted, in addition to some
35 honorary members. But missionaries were sent into the country,
and a hundred and fifty kindred associations sprang up elsewhere.
Lovett, who was secretary of the London Association, found full
scope for his passion for drafting addresses and manifestoes. Attention was not confined to domestic affairs, urgent though these might
have seemed ; the importance of international affairs was fully
recognised. The workers of Belgium were sympathised with over
the persecution of Jacob Katz ; in the course of an exhaustive view
of foreign politics the working classes of Europe, and especially the
Polish people, were assured that it is "the ignorance of our brethren

which generates and fosters the despot "; the Canadians were encouraged in their opposition to Whig coercion : " It gives us great pleasure to learn, friends, that you are not so easily scared *by proclamation law*—by the decree of a junta against a whole nation. Surely you know and feel, though Governor Gosford may not, that ' A NATION NEVER CAN REBEL ' "; the Americans were congratulated on their republican institutions and on the heights of political liberty to which they had attained, but were asked the searching question, " Why, after sixty years of freedom, have you not progressed further ? "

A long address on education, a subject dear to Lovett's heart, contained a scheme of schools of various grades to be provided by public money and managed by local school committees elected by universal suffrage, and ended with an appeal to Christians .to rise above sectarian jealousies in the matter of religious education. An address on " The Rotten House of Commons " gave a scathing description of the personnel of the existing House, and urged on working men the duty of demanding equal political and social rights so that they might send working class representatives to Parliament.

The Charter.

But the most important work of the Association was the preparation of the Charter, with its famous six points. At a public meeting at the Crown and Anchor in the Strand, on February 28, 1837, a petition to Parliament was adopted embodying the six points : (1) universal suffrage, (2) the ballot, (3) payment of members, (4) annual Parliaments, (5) equal electoral districts, (6) the abolition of property qualifications for M.P.s

The petition was entrusted to Roebuck for presentation, and he suggested enlisting the support of other Radical M.P.s. A joint meeting of eight members of Parliament and various members of the Working Men's Association accordingly took place. The Radical members of Parliament, fresh from the chilly atmosphere of the House, showed little enthusiasm, and were taken severely to task by Lovett, who charged them with thinking more of their seats than of their principles. O'Connell retorted that Lovett was impracticable. The result of this and of a later meeting was the formation of a committee, consisting of six members of Parliament and six members of the Working Men's Association, to draw up a Bill embodying the six points, to be known as " the People's Charter."

This committee was hardly appointed when William IV. died, Parliament was dissolved, and the members disappeared to their constituencies. The business of drawing up the Bill was in consequence postponed for several months. Lovett's pen was busy in the interval with an Address to Reformers on the elections and with an Address to Victoria on her accession. This latter Address the Association proposed to present in person by a deputation of six, but they were deterred by the necessity of appearing in Court dress. " With every respect for those forms which make personal cleanliness and respectful behaviour necessary qualifications to approach her Majesty, we have neither the means nor the inclination to indulge in such absurdities as dress swords, coats and wigs," wrote Lovett to Lord John Russell. If Victoria ever read the Address she must have been somewhat bewildered by the exhortation contained in it to distrust alike Whigs and Tories, who " have for many years past succeeded in making Royalty a mere puppet of their will," and to instruct her Ministers to prepare a Bill for universal suffrage.

When Parliament reassembled the committee of twelve appointed Roebuck and Lovett to draw up the proposed Charter. Roebuck was too busy with Canadian affairs to help, so the task fell to Lovett. In such leisure as his trade left him he compiled a rough draft which he then submitted to Place, who suggested alterations. In the first draft of the Bill provision was made for women's suffrage, but it was afterwards decided to omit this on the ground that it would " retard the measure," a decision that Lovett regretted. In a composite document the question of authorship is a nice one, and both Place and Lovett afterwards claimed to have composed the Charter. Place's were not the only amendments, and the physical work of writing and rewriting the document several times—no light task—was Lovett's. It was finally published in May, 1838, accompanied by an address composed by Lovett, in which he characteristically dwelt on self-government as a means to " enlightenment." " When a knowledge of their rights and duties shall have taught the people that their own vices and ignorance are the chief instruments by which they are bowed to the dust, titles, privileges and wealth will lose their potency to enslave them."

The Charter itself had nothing simple or popular about it except its name. It was a long and complicated Bill entering into the minutest details about arrangements for registration and elections. Never has so dull a document had such sensational effects. Within twelve months over a million persons had signed a petition in its favour, and the middle classes were quaking at the very name of Chartism.

The Charter was published at a crucial moment, and succeeded in focussing heterogeneous movements of discontent. (1) The Birmingham Political Union, which had done yeoman service for the Reform Bill of 1832, had lately been revived under the leadership of Attwood, described by Disraeli as " a provincial banker labouring under a financial monomania." Attwood's panacea for the ills of society was the creation of unlimited paper money, but he and his followers were ready to press for suffrage reform as a means to this end. The Birmingham Association drew up what came to be known as the National Petition, and the Working Men's

Association agreed to adopt it as the petition for the Charter. It was from the Birmingham Association, too, that the suggestion came of a General Convention of the Industrious Classes, which was to create and extend public opinion in favour of the principles of the People's Charter, and present the monster petition to Parliament. It was decided to hold the General Convention next year, and meanwhile to procure signatures for the Petition.

(2) The agitation in the North in favour of Factory Reform and against the new Poor Law was also all swept into the stream of Chartism. The audiences which had acquired the habit of being lashed into frenzy by Oastler, Stephens, and O'Connor had now a fresh object for excitement and enthusiasm. The Charter was to be the cure for economic evils. " Universal Suffrage," said Stephens, " is a knife and fork question, a bread and cheese question." " Six months after the Charter is passed," declared O'Connor, " every man, woman and child in the country will be well fed, well housed, and well clothed." " The furious appeals to the passions of the multitude "; " the violent ravings about physical force," as Lovett called them, were now transferred to the Chartist campaign. Henceforth, though Lovett and his friends may have launched the boat, the new crew controlled her course. The *Northern Star*, O'Connor's organ, which shrieked out denunciations week after week, was a brilliant success with a huge circulation, " a melancholy tribute," it has been called, " to the low intelligence of its readers." (Hovell, The Chartist Movement). On the other hand, the *Charter*, started in London by the intellectuals of the movement, was a dismal failure and died early, leaving debts behind it.

No two men could have been more antagonistic to each other than Lovett and Fergus O'Connor, who now began to play an important part in the Chartist agitation ; O'Connor, the horn demagogue with his unscrupulous appeals to the emotions ; Lovett, the composer of innumerable addresses directed to the reason of his fellow men. " We are of opinion," wrote Lovett, " that whatever is gained in England by force, by force must be sustained : but whatever springs from knowledge and justice will sustain itself." O'Connor preferred to rouse his audiences by vague threats of " fleshing swords to the hilts," though when opportunity offered he showed no disposition to draw the sword from the scabbard. The two men had already had a bitter encounter over the Committee on the Combination Act, a Parliamentary Committee appointed early in 1838 largely as the result of attacks on Trade Unions by Daniel O'Connell. O'Connor falsely accused Lovett and the Working Men's Association of engineering the appointment of the Committee out of hostility to Trade Unions. In reality, Lovett had been appointed by the Trade Unions to watch over their interests in connection with it. In his answer to O'Connor's attack, he showed that it was not only the Northern demagogues who could use vituperation. " You tell the country," he wrote, " that you alone have organised the Radicals of London"—and tell the Londoners the wonders your genius has performed in the country. You carry your fame about with you on all occasions to sink all other topics in the shade—you are the great "I AM" of politics, the great personification of Radicalism—Fergus O'Connor."

The Convention.

To avoid prosecution under the infamous Six Acts of 1819, it was necessary to elect the delegates for the proposed Convention at public meetings. These meetings gave ample opportunity for the mob orators of the North to exercise their gifts. At the London meeting the speakers were specially warned by the Working Men's Association, but warned in vain, so far as O'Connor was concerned, to avoid "every abusive or violent expression which may tend to injure our glorious cause." The moderates were already suffering for the ebullitions of the physical force party in the alienation of middle class opinion. "But the meeting of the Convention," wrote Lovett afterwards, "was now fast approaching, and so strong was the hope reposed in that meeting by the Chartist body, that the great majority of them manifested the strongest desire to sacrifice their peculiar feelings and convictions for the sake of union. A few hot-brained enthusiasts, however, were not so patriotic; union was naught with them compared with their own blustering harangues about arming and fighting ; these and their daily invectives against everything bearing the resemblance of moderation, preparedness, or intellectual and moral effort, served to create constant irritation in our ranks, and ultimately to cause distrust and disunion."

The Convention met in London on February 4, 1839. It was composed of 53 delegates, a few of whom never sat. It met in an atmosphere of wild hopefulness combined with a certain vagueness as to its objects. Lovett was appointed secretary, a post from which O'Connor, who was not present at the election, tried in vain to oust him. His literary facility and business-like ways made him the obvious choice. As the first business of the Convention was to promote the Petition, missionaries were sent out to procure signatures from districts hitherto untouched. In the meantime the Convention showed an unlimited capacity for discussion of topics like "the suffering in the manufacturing districts," "the new Rural Police Bill," "the factory system." Outside, its supporters grew restive : one association declared "that if the Convention did its duty the Charter would be the law of the land in less than a month." Inside, O'Connor and his party became so violent in their language and methods that in March the Birmingham delegates and others of the moderate party seceded from the Convention. By May 6 the great National Petition was ready to be taken to Attwood for presentation to Parliament. It contained 1,283,000 signatures, was nearly three miles long, and was escorted to his house by the members of the Convention, marching two by two.

The presentation of the Petition was postponed by the dissolution of Parliament, and meanwhile the Convention on May 13th moved to Birmingham, in hopes of securing immunity from arrest and more sympathetic surroundings. The question of what was to be done if Parliament rejected the Petition became acute, for rejection seemed only too probable. Discussion of this question produced the famous " Manifesto of Ulterior Measures," drawn up by Lovett from notes of the conclusions arrived at in an unofficial meeting of delegates, and formally ratified by the Convention after they reached Birmingham. The manifesto contains probably the most violent language that Lovett ever penned. " I believe that I did an act of folly in being a party to some of its provisions," he wrote in later life. Ignorance of the world outside London and close association with men who claimed to speak for multitudes ready to rise seem to have made him for a time almost a convert to physical force. At any rate, he pressed for the adoption of the manifesto on the grounds that the Convention ought to give a lead to its followers. (Hovell, p. 149.) " Shall it be said, fellow-countrymen," runs the manifesto, " that four millions of men, capable of bearing arms, and defending their country against every foreign assailant, allowed a few domestic oppressors to enslave and degrade them ? " " We solemnly believe that the Radical Reformers are the only restraining power that prevents the execution of an outraged people's vengeance." " We have resolved to obtain our rights, ' peaceably if we may, forcibly if we must '; but woe to those who ibegin the warfare with the millions, or who forcibly restrain their peaceful agitation for justice—at one signal they will be enlightened to their error, and in one brief contest their power will be destroyed." After these threats the methods suggested for enforcing the people's will read rather like an anti-climax. " Simultaneous public meetings " are to be asked if they are prepared (1) to draw out their money from the banks, (2) to convert their paper money into gold, (3) to give effect to the proposed " sacred month," that is, to have a general strike and to " go dry " for a month. They are further asked (4) whether " they have prepared themselves with the arms of freemen " according to their old constitutional rights, (5) whether they will provide themselves with Chartist candidates at the next election and treat them as M.P.s if elected by show of hands, and (6) deal exclusively with Chartists, and finally (7 and 8) work for the Charter and obey the Convention.

A few days after adopting the manifesto, the Convention adjourned till July 1st, and the " simultaneous meetings " were held during Whitsuntide. Thanks to the wisdom of General Charles James Napier, who had been put in command of the Northern district, the demonstrations were peaceful. The Convention had tried to leave the decision as to " ulterior measures " to the people, but when it met again it was clear that the " simultaneous meetings " had given no lead. What was to be done? Were the "arms of freemen " to be used or only kept in the background? How were the workers to be supported during the "sacred month "? Lovett proposed that as a preliminary test one or two trades should be called on to stop work and a fund be raised to support them. Benbow, one of the wilder spirits, talked of " the cattle upon a thousand hills " as the best strike fund. The aim of the Convention was described by a Scottish delegate : " We must shake our oppressors well over hell's mouth, but we must not let them drop in." Whilst plans for the shaking were being discussed, a serious blow was dealt at the Convention by the arrest of Lovett.

During the agitation for the Reform Bill of 1832 Birmingham reformers had been in the habit of meeting in the Bull Ring. When the Chartist agitation began the Bull Ring was again used as a place of meeting. These Chartist meetings were prohibited by the magistrates, some of them ex-reformers of 1832. The Chartists took no notice of the prohibition or of the spasmodic arrests, and continued to meet. The Birmingham authorities thereupon sent for police from London, who proceeded on their arrival to attack a peaceful crowd in the Bull Ring. The crowd, exasperated, tore up the railings from a neighbouring churchyard, and ugly retaliation on the police was only prevented by the intervention of two members of the Convention, Dr. Taylor and Dr. McDouall. Dr. Taylor was arrested by the police. Next morning the Convention received an appeal from some of the frequenters of the Bull Ring. Lovett, whose personal courage never failed, drew up three resolutions condemning the police, which the Convention passed unanimously, ordering them to be placarded throughout the town. The first and strongest resolution declared " that a wanton, flagrant, and unjust outrage has been made upon the people of Birmingham by a bloodthirsty and unconstitutional force from London." " Characteristically enough, Lovett insisted that his own signature alone should be attached, so that the Convention should run no risk. Characteristically enough, the Convention was quite willing to sacrifice him." (Hovell, p. 157.) On July 6th, when the placards appeared, Lovett and Collins, who had taken the draft to the printers, were both arrested.

Lovett and Collins were committed for trial at the next assizes, and though bail was fixed at £1,000 each, the magistrates made great difficulties about their sureties, and detained them in prison for nine days. During those nine days they were subjected to great indignities, which Lovett made the subject of a petition to both Houses of Parliament. Stripping, dirt, infection were among the things complained of, and the House of Lords was moved to merriment by the idea of Lovett's hair being cropped by a common felon, merriment that Brougham very properly rebuked. On the day on which the two prisoners were released on bail, there was another more serious riot in the Bull Ring, the culmination of a succession

of collisions between police and people. Shops were burnt and the
military called in, and though Lovett and Collins had nothing to
do with the affair, the weapons used by the rioters were produced,
to their prejudice, at their trial.

Two days before the riot, on July 12th, the long-expected
debate on the Petition had taken place in the House of Commons.
Attwood, supported by Fielden, proposed that it should be taken
into consideration. Forty-six members only voted for him, 235
voted against him. The Petition's parliamentary career was over.

The later history of the Convention, from which Lovett was,
of course, absent, is soon told. They reassembled in London, and
blew hot and blew cold about "ulterior measures." August 12th
was fixed on as the day for beginning the "sacred month," but
further enquiries showed that most of the would-be strikers had no
work to strike against. The "sacred month" was abandoned, and
after some futile recriminations the Convention was dissolved on
September 6th, 1839.

A successful popular agitation in England uses physical force as
an ally in the background, but is careful not to produce the ally for
too close an inspection. The more violent Chartists made the
mistake of parading their ally till his weakness was apparent to
everyone. The abortive rising in November at Newport, when
twenty-eight soldiers successfully routed what was called a Chartist
army, was a final proof of the futility of their threats. One after
another the leaders had been clapped into prison, and the first
Chartist agitation had collapsed.

Trial and Imprisonment.

On August 6th Lovett was tried before Mr. Justice Littledale, at
the Warwick Assizes, for publishing a "false, malicious, scandalous
and seditious libel" on the police. Four persons had previously
been condemned to death for the second Bull Ring riot (the death
sentence was afterwards commuted to imprisonment through the
exertions of Joseph Sturge), and Collins had been tried and found
guilty the day before. Collins was defended by counsel, Sergeant
Goulbourne, a Tory, who, to Lovett's disgust, regarded it as "a
glorious opportunity of having a slap at the Whigs." Lovett
defended himself in an able speech, pleading justification, and appealing to public opinion. The resolutions, he argued, were true and
not malicious, they were public censure of a public act. "My lord,
it is for directing public attention to a flagrant and unjust attack
upon public liberty that I am brought as a criminal before you."
His condemnation was a foregone conclusion; two of his jury had
been heard to wish that all Chartists were hanged. He and Collins
were sentenced to twelve months imprisonment in the county gaol.

During his imprisonment Lovett suffered severely, both physically
and mentally. A diet of gruel with blackbeetles in it disgusted him
with his food and gastric trouble set in. The society of companions,

one of whom planned the robbery of his own mother and the division of the spoils with a fellow prisoner shortly to be released, whilst another described how he had thrown down a woman and kicked her on the face and eyes, was torture to a sensitive man. The chaplain and the doctor seem to have been caricatures of their type in fiction, the former consigning men to the refractory cell for coughing in chapel, the latter depriving the prisoners of half their scanty allowance of meat because it made the soup too rich. None of the ordinary privileges of political prisoners were granted the two Chartists. Application to the visiting magistrates was referred to the Secretary of State : application to the Secretary of State was referred to the visiting magistrates. It was with the latter that the power really lay, but Lovett and Collins had prejudiced their case by exposing the way in which they had been treated before trial, an exposure which had obliged the magistrates to provide sheets and more hygienic bathing arrangements. Ultimately, though other privileges were withheld, pen, ink, and paper were given to the two prisoners, and Lovett, with the help of Collins, set about writing a book called " Chartism, or a New Organisation of the People." Lovett and Collins were offered the remission of the last three months of their sentence if they would be bound for good behaviour for a year. This they refused to accept, considering it to be an admission of past guilt. By the end of their year the portly Collins had become a thin man, and the thin Lovett a weak emaciated wreck.

Lovett and Collins were released in July, 1840. Lovett was too ill to attend most of the festivities arranged in their honour, and after one public dinner in London set off for Cornwall in hopes of regaining his health. Funds for the journey to Cornwall were provided by friends, who had also supported Lovett's wife and daughter whilst he was in prison. It would be interesting to know whether his Chartism or his scepticism about the supernatural excited more surprise in his native place, where his visit was preceded by that of a ghost, who walked about without a head. After some months of rest he returned to town, and being still too weak to work at his trade, opened a small bookseller's shop in Tottenham Court Road— his third venture in business, and, like the other two, unsuccessful.

Knowledge Chartism.

Lovett's views on policy had undergone some modification after his experiences in the Convention and his imprisonment. Now, as always, an enlightened people was his ideal, and the enactment of the Six Points the means to that end and not an end in itself. But the Six Points seemed more difficult to achieve than in the early days of the Convention, and he began to lay greater stress on a preliminary enlightenment of the people as the means by which the Charter itself would be won. The Charter itself when won would in its turn be the means to " political and social reform."

It was the same idea of education at which the Working Men's Association had aimed, but Lovett had now given up the idea of a purely working class movement, and appealed to " the wise and good" of all classes to unite and to "labour and reason together to work out the social and political regeneration of man." They must " redeem by reason what had been lost by madness and folly," and the middle classes must not stand "apart from the name and principles of the Charter " because of " the intolerant and mischievous conduct " of certain Chartists. The workers, whilst " labouring to obtain the Charter," should be " instructing themselves, so as to realise all its advantages when obtained," and no longer "be engaged, as reformers have heretofore been, in periodically arousing the public mind to the highest state of excitement, suddenly to sink into apathy, *with* or *without* the attainment of their object . . ."

This ideal was to take practical shape in a " National Association of the United Kingdom for Promoting the Political and Social Improvement of the People." This Association was to work for the Charter, and it was also to subsidise missionaries, circulating libraries, tracts, public halls and schools—a vast programme with an Owenite ring about it. As for funds, Lovett suggested that if each signatory to the petition for the Charter gave a penny a week, this would bring in £256,000 a year, of which £240,000 could be used for the erection of 80 halls or schools at £3,000 each, and the rest be spent on the libraries, missionaries, tracts, &c.

Lovett had outlined this scheme with Collins' help in the thesis on " Chartism " that he wrote in jail and smuggled out to Place, with the request that it should be published on the day of his release. Place, thinking the scheme grandiose and impracticable, threw cold water on it, and hence publication was delayed—a delay that Lovett resented bitterly. After his release he and Collins published the book, following it up in March, 1841, with an address setting out the plan for the National Association. Many leading Chartists signed this address, but when the plan came under the ban of O'Connor, who attacked it with virulence in the *Northern Star*, some of the signatories withdrew their signature ; the second edition of the book failed to sell, and by the time the National Association actually came into being, in October, 1841, the scheme was fore-doomed to failure. O'Connor, as an ally, might have made success impossible, but as an enemy he made success equally impossible.

Working class support, such as it was, lay behind O'Connor and the National Charter Association, a body formed in July, 1841, in Manchester, to restart the agitation after its ignominious collapse. This body.Lovett refused to join, though he disclaimed all hostility to it. Its illegal constitution was given as the reason for his refusal, and by the time the constitution had been amended his relations with O'Connor were too bitter to make co-operation between the two men possible.

Complete Suffrage Movement.

As his scheme fell flat, so far as working class support went, Lovett was driven more and more to the middle classes, and he took a prominent part in the attempt in 1842 to amalgamate the middle class and the working class movements for suffrage reform, known as the Complete Suffrage Union, and associated with the name of Joseph Sturge of Birmingham. Lovett, unlike O'Connor, was a Free Trader, but he thought the suffrage more important than the repeal of the Corn Laws, which were " only one of the effects of the great cause we are seeking to remove." Hence he resented the anti-Corn Law agitation as side-tracking enthusiasm for the Charter. Sturge, who belonged to the anti-Corn Law League, came to a similar conclusion, and in April, 1842, he organised a conference in Birmingham of middle-class democrats, including John Bright, drawn largely from the ranks of the anti-Corn Law League, together with working class representatives such as Lovett and Collins. To every-one's surprise, complete unanimity was reached on the Six Points, and the substance of the Charter was adopted, though its name was studiously avoided. Its name had now too many sinister associations for the middle class delegates to allow its use. Lovett pleaded hard for a motion that the actual Charter should be considered at a future meeting, but the question was shelved, the Conference agreeing to a resolution that " any documents which embody the necessary details" should be considered. Meanwhile, on Lovett's motion, the Complete Suffrage Union was formed.

The future looked promising enough for the new body. Local associations sprang up : a petition promoted by the Union was discussed in Parliament, and though it obtained only 67 votes as against 226, all the Radicals and Free Traders voted for it, including Cobden, and, of course, Bright. But, again, O'Connor's ban was on the project, and he threatened to swamp the coming Conference. To checkmate him, and to keep discussion off the tabooed subject of the Charter, the middle-class members of the Council resorted to what seemed to Lovett a piece of sharp practice. They drafted a new Bill, called the Bill of Six Rights, containing the Six Points, but avoiding the name of Charter, and this Bill they presented to the Conference as the basis of discussion. This rejection of the actual Charter, the symbol for which men had fought and suffered and died, roused Lovett's indignation, and drove him to make common cause with O'Connor. He proposed a motion, seconded by O'Connor, that the People's Charter should be discussed. It was carried by 193 to 94, but the middle classes thereupon withdrew from the Conference and co-operation was at an end. Lovett's lip was said to have " curled in scorn," whilst O'Connor poured flattery on his ally. It was the only occasion after the 1839 Convention on which the two men worked together, and their co-operation did not outlast the day.

Whilst Lovett was working for the Complete Suffrage project, the National Charter Association had occupied itself in promoting another monster petition to Parliament. This second petition, six miles in length, with over three million signatures, was presented in the House of Commons in May, 1842. The activities of its "physical force" members, which usually found scope only in breaking up meetings of the anti-Corn Law League and other societies, a policy abhorred by Lovett, were given a real opportunity in the summer of 1842, when a series of strikes spread through the North and the Midlands. It was a chance for the Chartists to dominate the situation. An attempt was made to call on the workers to remain on strike till the Charter was won, but not only was the response half-hearted, but the "physical force" Chartists themselves were in two minds about it; O'Connor disavowed the action, and the Government promptly packed away most of the leaders in prison. Lovett, during the strike, had issued a characteristic address urging the strikers to avoid violence.

One more effort was made to close up the ranks and produce co-operation between Lovett and O'Connor. When O'Connor diverted the Chartist agitation to his ill-fated land scheme, Lovett was asked, in 1843, to become its secretary. He refused, and published his letter of refusal, with its bitter indictment of O'Connor and of the mischief he had done. " Previous to his notorious career there was something pure and intellectual in our agitation. There was a reciprocity of generous sentiment, a tolerant spirit of investigation, an ardent aspiration for all that can improve and dignify humanity, which awakened the hopes of all good men, and which even our enemies respected. He came among us to blight those feelings, to wither those hopes. . . . . . By his great professions, by trickery and deceit, he got the aid of the working classes to establish an organ to promulgate their principles, which he soon converted into an instrument for destroying everything intellectual and moral in our movement."

Lovett made a last effort in 1845 to induce the Chartists to change their ways, and to eschew " violence and folly." " Be assured," he wrote, "that those who flatter your prejudices, commend your ignorance, and administer to your vices, are not your friends. ' Unwashed faces, unshorn chins' and dirty habits will in nowise prepare you for political or social equality with the decent portion of your brethren. . . . . Empty boastings, abusive language and contempt for all mental and moral qualifications will rather retard than promote your freedom." Using his favourite phrase about a combination of "the wise and good," he urged them once more "to rise into vitality and strength." But his appeal fell on deaf ears. After the failure of the Complete Suffrage agitation, Lovett had, in fact, become a publicist and not a politician. He continued to compose addresses, including appeals to the working classes of France and America against war, and could organise a successful meeting of protest in 1844 against the reception in England of that "active, scheming, wily tyrant," Nicholas of Russia, but he had no following, and the societies he tried to found, such as " The General Association of Progress " and the " People's League " were failures. After 1846 he became for a time publisher of *Howitt's Journal*, which he used as a vehicle for fresh manifestoes.

Later Life.

Henceforth his main work in life was as an educationalist, fostering those " mental and moral qualifications " which he felt to be the basis of all improvement. The National Association, though it failed to fulfil the dreams of the writer of " Chartism," and sometimes seemed to exist only to afford him a platform from which to address the public, had managed in 1842 to open one, though only one, of the proposed National Halls. The hall was in Holborn, where a music hall now stands. It started in debt, and it remained in debt, and much of a testimonial of £140 given to Lovett by friends in 1848 went in payments connected with it ; but, though a constant source of pecuniary worry, it gave opportunities for educational experiments ; a Sunday school was opened there in 1843, at which Lovett taught ; and in 1848 a regular day school was started under Lovett's superintendence. Later on, in 1851, he began to do most of the teaching himself.

It cannot be said that he was a disappointed man. Few men who have led movements have cared less for leadership. His denunciations of the evils done by relying on leaders were sincere. He neither possessed nor desired the gift of swaying multitudes. That one man should influence others, except by helping them to use their own reason, seemed to him a vicious thing. The work of education was congenial to him—his whole life had been an attempt to help the working classes to educate themselves—and he threw himself with as much zest into writing elementary school books on anatomy and physiology as he had shown for his studies in his early twenties. At the age of sixty-four he was engaged on a text book about vertebrated animals, but found the subject so important that he " determined to treat of the invertebrated animals also." Nor can a man be called disillusioned who, after Lovett's experiences, could at the age of fifty-six seriously send a petition to the House of Commons, urging the need for a higher intellectual and moral standard for members of Parliament, to be obtained by a compulsory examination for all candidates, or could advocate that the clergy should be turned into an instrument of progress by inducing them to teach elementary astronomy on Sundays. But he was a sad man, as, indeed, he had always been, and it was a sombre old age. The closing of the National Hall, and, in consequence, of his school in 1857, was a heavy blow. He taught elementary science at other schools afterwards, and continued writing text books, which sometimes found and sometimes did not find a publisher, but he could not support himself, and was forced to accept help from a generous friend. " Such kindness, indeed," he wrote, " has been rarely witnessed towards a stranger as that which I have received from my noble-hearted friend. Bnt while I know that all this kindness is extended towards me freely and ungrudgingly, it does, however, jar upon my feelings to think that, after all my struggles, all my industry, and, I may add, all my temperance and frugality, I cannot earn or live upon my own bread in my old age."

As an old man he lived with his devoted wife and his grand-daughter, the only child of his daughter, and wrote his " Life and Struggles," a book in which he strung together the addresses and manifestoes of his earlier days, adding long comments on later events. He died on August 8th, 1877, aged seventy-seven, and was buried at Highgate.

Fabian Tract No. 200.

THE STATE IN THE NEW SOCIAL ORDER

By HAROLD J. LASKI

With a Note by EDWARD R. PEASE dealing with
the history of the Fabian Tracts, on the occasion of the
issue of No. 200 of the series.

Published and sold by the Fabian Society at
the Fabian Bookshop, 25 Tothill Street, Westminster, S.W. 1. Dec. 1922. Price Twopence.

FABIAN TRACTS.

FABIAN TRACT No. I was printed in 1884, a few. months after the foundation of the Society ; the publication of Fabian Tract No. 200 in 1922 affords an occassion for some reflections on the series. Probably no other organisation, certainly no other English political society, has ever before issued a continuous series of Tracts, all in the same format, with a total of two hundred spread over a period of thirty-eight years. Very few of the little group which prepared Tract No. I are still alive, and the present writer is the only one of them who is still an active member of the Society. But the work started by that little group has been carried forward chiefly by others who soon joined it, and has accomplished more than its founders anticipated.

Fabian Tracts have been the instrument of much of the activities of the Fabian Society. After the first and enduring success of "Fabian Essays," we have achieved but little by larger publications. Our members have written innumerable books, but the Society has had but little to do with them. It is as a producer of Tracts that the Society will be remembered.

The two hundred Tracts are a miscellaneous collection. The largest class deals with the application of the principles of Socialism to particular subjects, Education, Poor Law, Agriculture, etc. Another class describes the organs of local government, Parish Councils, Town Councils, County Councils, and explains how their powers can be used for social amelioration. Our "best seller" was a penny pamphlet describing the Workmen's Compensation Act, 1896. Trade Unions bought it by the thousand to distribute amongst their members. A good second is "Facts for Socialists," first published in 1887, and still selling vigorously in its twelfth edition.

The number of Fabian Tracts issued to the public between 1890 and 1922 is 2,775,000. For a short time we gave away propaganda leaflets, but the cost of this soon proved prohibitive. Apart from the copies of new publications supplied to members, the above figures represent sales. Pamphlets, unless by Prime Ministers, are not a commercial proposition, but Fabian Tracts have on the whole nearly paid their way. Their success may be attributed in the main to two causes, the use of a single format enabling sets to be bound in a volume, and each number in the series to advertise the others ; and in the second case, to the great care exercised by the Executive Committee that a high standard of literary excellence, and extreme vigilance for accuracy in statements of fact should always be maintained.

Some of the early Tracts are still in print in new and often revised editions, but very many are altogether out of date for the excellent reason that the legislative reforms which they recommended have long ago become law.

EDW. R. PEASE.

THE STATE IN THE NEW SOCIAL ORDER.

THE English political scene has always changed its perspective after a crisis in the national fortunes. The civil wars of the fifteenth century produced the centralised despotism of the Tudors. The sense of national confidence gained from the victory over Spain led the Puritans to resist the Stuart attempt at further usurpation ; and the ultimate result of the Great Rebellion was to put the Crown in fetters. War always transforms the foundations of national thought, and the scale of our last experiment has been vast enough to leave no institution or doctrine untouched. It is clear already that its onset marked a new and pronounced epoch in our affairs. Just as the Napoleonic struggle freed the commercial classes from the last remnants of aristocratic control, so, in the long run, it is probable that the main result of the recent conflict will be to bring the working classes to a new position in the state.

The emergence, indeed, of the Labour Party as the main Parliamentary Opposition is not the least important index to the new temper. It means that the Third Estate has ceased to associate the idea of government with the ownership of property. Exactly as the main consequence of the Reform Act of 1832 was the destruction of those political privileges which separated the middle classes from the seat of power, so, it may be suggested, the result of the Reform Act of 1918 will, in the background of war-experience, be the slow destruction of those economic privileges which prevent the access of the workers to the moral assets of the state. It is not, of course, likely that the process will be either logical or straightforward. The English people is not accustomed to make a direct highroad to its intellectual goal. The national method is rather to mitigate the evils we have than fly to obvious benefits of which doctrine can demonstrate the substance. But, based upon the reforms of 1832, the ultimate character of nineteenth century legislation in England was to make a world in which the profits of business men were economically possible and legally secure. So upon the basis of the reforms of 1918 it will be the tendency of legislation in our own day to make a world in which men who have no commodity to sell save their labour will share in a fuller way in the riches that civilisation can offer.

The directions in which that effort will be made are already becoming clear. There is abroad, however half-heartedly, a new sense of the significance of education. If the democracy is to be master in its own house, it must be adequately equipped for its task. Control of the sources of knowledge is the one sure road to power ; and it is evidence of high import that the workers themselves are foremost in demanding an educational system which gives them access to that control. Hardly less urgent is the feeling that basic monopolies, coal, power, transport, land, must be directly managed by the people themselves. Nationalisation is a word that has manifold interpretations ; but nationalisation, in some form, of the obvious basic monopolies is an inevitable corollary of democratic government. Not less certain, as the future expands, will be the conference upon the workers of definite institutional security against the tragedy of unemployment. That the resources of the state must be used to safeguard its citizens against the hazards of trade is already a commonplace ; and since the principle was admitted in the Insurance Act of 1911, it is rather with its administrative application than its legislative substance that the next age will be concerned.

Second only in importance to education, and in large part dependent upon it, is the growth of industrial self-government. It has become intolerable that the mass of men should be the mechanical recipients of orders they are compelled to execute without scrutiny. It has become finally clear that the release of individuality—after all, the ultimate purpose of the state—is utterly impossible so long as the control of industry is confided to a small number of men whose decisions need not take account of the wills of those who work under them. It may be admitted that the transformation of industrial control presents immense difficulties. The mass of the workers has not been trained to work that is instinct with responsibility. The capitalist régime has sought not the men who think but the men who obey. It has subordinated to the acquisitive impulse whatever spirit there is of service and creativeness in those who are subject to its dominion. It has obscured the processes by which it governs. It has so divorced the actual work of production from the business of direction as to leave the industrial pattern unintelligble to those whose lives are dependent upon its right arrangement. So complex have its mechanisms become that no single formula—guild socialism, consumers' co-operation, the multiplication of small peasant proprietorship—has any but a limited application. In the discovery, therefore, of institutions which enable the industrial worker to be something more than a tender of machines it is inevitable that there should be hazardous experiment ; and the corollary of experiment is failure. But that feeling of unfreedom which Mr. Justice Sankey discovered among the miners, which interferes with the quantity and quality of their work, is typical of labour as a whole. It demands, as is now recognised, channels of response which will minimise its intensity.

These are, of course, predominant currents of effort in their largest outline. There is no aspect of our social life which remains unaffected by the impact of new desires. The Industrial Revolution turned urban England into a slum, and since Mr. Sartorius, ably seconded by Sir Alfred Mond, shows no sign of abdication, he is destined, sooner or later, to be supplanted by a community at last awakened to its responsibilities. Housing is the bedrock upon which the health of the nation depends. Parallel with its improvement, there is certain to be a realisation that the development of the medical services is a vital public concern. What are now half-casual and half-starved amenities, the public libraries for instance, are bound, as education developes, to be regarded as charges upon the public income not less fundamental to the general well-being than the army and navy. Nor can such amenities be adequately enjoyed unless the working-day is adjusted to meet their claims. The worker cannot respect the obligations of citizenship if he is simply and solely an unreflecting unit in the productive system. It is, moreover, becoming probable that the centre of importance for most men in the future will be the period of leisure rather than the period of work. In that aspect, the limitation of the hours of labour is fraught with deep consequence to them at a vital point. Nor can the substance of our civilisation remain unaffected by the changing prospects of women. Marriage for most has meant a position akin to that of a trusted servant in an upper-class family, with the added right to frequent the sitting-room, in the rare cases where there is one, when the day's work is done. But women have not only invaded industry in wholesale fashion ; they have also come to see that they may make of marriage a career as significant as the bar or the church. They have thus come to regard it in a sense very different either from the faded spinsters of Cranford or the genteel harpies of Jane Austen. What influence their views will have upon our social economy we cannot yet tell; it is clear only that it will be profound and decisive.

Nothing of all this implies either that such changes are immediately impending, or that their path will be easy and straightforward. Their consequences go too deep into the fabric of the state for most of them to be welcome. They involve an assault upon tradition which will invoke the resistance of all the forces of conservatism and inertia. They imply a change in the property-relation so vast as to alter in their implication the very purpose of the state. They will have to proceed piece by piece, advancing here, there suffering defeat, until most of them become in turn traditions. Then, perhaps, in typical English fashion, because they have become institutions to which we have grown accustomed, we shall regard them as the necessary foundations of society. They will, in part, be dependent upon the possibility that we can avoid revolution, on the one hand, and foreign warfare upon the other. If we recognise sufficiently the inevitable basic infirmity in all human institutions so as to be convinced that with all its slowness the path of reason is preferable to the path of violence, that the inadequate good of peace may be preferable to the cost of ideal good attempted by war, an atmosphere of constructiveness may emerge from the present reaction. But only upon the condition of peace. For it is clear that the resources now at the command of conflict may, if utilised, destroy any possibility of civilisation. If force should triumph over reason in the next age, ideas such as these may well pass into dim memories; and, as in Mr. Wells' dramatic picture, some ancient survivor of the struggle may seek to explain them to grandchildren who do not understand even the primary notions of civilised life.

But if we may count—it is a large assumption—upon a peace as long and as extensive as that given to England in the Victorian age, we may be confident that social theory will undergo a radical transformation. A new world will arise from the ashes of the old ; and a new political science will be necessary to the statement of its meaning. Already, it is possible to discern some at least of the elements that will go to its making. It is likely, in the first place, to be far more complex than the old. The sanction of our institutions will not be divine right, as with the Royalists of the seventeenth century, or fear, as with Hobbes, or the facile simplicity of direct and omnipresent consent, as with Rousseau. It is likely to come from the slow development of a social psychology based upon inductions about human nature far wider than in any previous time. It will take account of the magistral demonstration by Marx thalt political power is the handmaid of economic power ; and it wi l therefore insist as integral that the existence of great wealth and widespread poverty in the same state are incompatible with the attainment of social good. It will seek to discover the largest way commensurate with national efficiency of associating the creative energies of men with the actual business of government. It will realise that the main reason why social systems have decayed in the past is their inability to make adequate response to the primary impulses of men. For the onset of revolution does not mean the existence of a will to wrong in the people. It is they who always, and most deeply, are the sufferers from disorder. Revolution never comes from the effort of chance conspirators or malevolent ideas. It is the outcome always of wrongs that have become too intolerable to be borne ; and the moral judgment it involves is decisive against the government which has failed to see in reform the only real safeguard against it.

The coming of the democracy to power involves a change in the purpose of the state. It means placing the riches of civilisation at the disposal of that democracy. But, still more, it means a change in the methods by which that effort is made. In the aftermath of the Industrial Revolution, it was believed that the conflict of private interests would result in a well-ordered commonwealth. The duties of government were the duties of a police force. The atmosphere of the courts—always the surest index to the temper of the governing class—was mainly an insistence that in nothing was the public welfare so essentially protected as in the safeguarding of industrial private rights ; and the classic case of *Mogul Steamship Co.* v. *McGregor*[1] was evidence that restraint upon freedom of action in

---

[1] (1888) 21 Q.B.D. 544 ; [1892] A.C. 25.

the name of public policy was regarded as a definite evil. It was somehow assumed that since every person is, in the main, the best judge of his own happiness, the larger the boundaries of freedom of contract, the greater would be the happiness of the nation. It was not understood that there is a difference between judging what is for one's happiness, and having the means to effect it. Freedom of contract only begins, as Mr. Justice Holmes has said, where equality of bargaining power begins; and there is no real equality of bargaining power, so far as the means of adequate subsistence are concerned, unless there is approximate equality of property. When Bentham and his disciples set an individualistic perspective to the theory of the state, what in reality they did was simply to put that state at the disposal of the owners of political and economic power. The second half of the nineteenth century was mainly occupied with the effort to relax the rigours of an individualistic régime, while retaining an active and profound faith in its main assumptions. Such measures as Factory Acts, Employers' Liability Acts, Housing Acts, were, at bottom, concessions made to humanitarian sentiment which shuddered at the cost of *laissez-faire*. They did not involve a belief that it is the business of the state to see that the citizen realises the full power of moral development which is in him.

Until, roughly, 1870, Benthamism held practically unmitigated sway over the English mind. From then onwards, T. H. Green and the Oxford idealists wrought something akin to revolution in the English theory of the state. Trained in a Platonism sharpened by contact with Hegel, they recognised that the Benthamite opposition between state and individual was at once artificial and dangerous. The individual was a citizen, and he therefore had no meaning apart from his citizenship. Unless, then, the state could guarantee to each man the powers without which he could not realise himself, it became devoid of ethical content. The state was, for them, an instrument through which and in which its citizens realised themselves; and it was thus its main function to secure to each such rights as would achieve his full moral development. There can be no doubt of the high service rendered by the idealist philosophy in destroying the notion that state-intervention is, in its nature, an evil thing. Unfortunately, the failure of idealism lay in its inability to differentiate between state and government. It did not with any sharpness disentangle the acts of principal and agent, with the result that it confused the temporary acts of the latter with the permanent purpose of the former.

The idealist philosophy of the state so highly exalted its power that individuals and societies obtained their meaning, and, therefore, their rights, only by its permission. It was so occupied with the theoretic purpose of the abstract state that it hardly, T. H. Green apart, regarded the actual achievement of concrete states. It did not see that a purpose abstractly noble may, in the hands of human agents, be stripped of every whit of moral splendour. By insisting that every institution was the incarnation of a spiritual principle idealism failed to develop a theory of moral values, and was therefore unable to distinguish between degrees of right. It thus provided no solution for the situation where social obligations conflict. It so confounded the actual motives of social agents with the ideal purpose by which they ought to have been informed, that it detected the existence of benevolent progress where none in fact existed. It beatified Imperialism, for example ; and the noble picture of the white man's burden blinded the eyes of its devotees to the natives who were in fact bearing it. It did not help a miner called upon to choose between his union and the Prime Minister to be told that the latter represented an institution whose abstract end was good. It afforded no real direction to a Quaker who believed in the moral wrong of war to be informed that war might be exalted when the state undertook it. Idealism, in short, tended to beatify things as they are. It was too occupied with abstract ends to be sufficiently critical either about the time-factor in the process of their achievement, or the methods by which they were effected. It asserted, and with justice, that right and truth ought to prevail; but its actual result, in the hands of its chief exponents, was to identify right and truth merely with the decisions of the governmental authority legally competent to make them. It did not penetrate beyond those decisions to the sources from which they were derived.

It was possible, in the years before the war, to see that idealism as a political creed was rapidly losing ground. It had become a commonplace that the authority of the state, neither in its forms nor in its achievement, justified the allegiance it demanded. Socialism came in its varied guises to offer proof that the state did not secure either the freedom or the happiness of its members. Churchmen like Figgis came to see that its assumed pre-eminence might deprive voluntary organisations of powers necessary to the fulfilment of aims not less noble than its own. Lawyers like Maitland urged that the state was merely one form of human association, and that it could make no moral claim to sovereignty other than that which it could prove on the ground of moral achievement. The survival of its power, especially in the background of European revolution, has become dependent, in part upon the national inertia of men, in part also upon its ability to respond to new wills and new demands that had, before the war, been hardly organised or articulate. It is true, of course, as Mr. Barker has said, that the state being with us, we must make the best of it. But what has moved into the hinterland of doubt are the motives which underlie its institutions and the forms they use for their expression.

The society in which we live is organised upon the basis of property. Ownership confers rights, and rights are legally unrelated to the performance of service. The society towards which we are moving will be organised upon the basis of functions, and the rights it will confer will be dependent upon the functions we perform. For it is obvious to anyone who scrutinises the present social order that the one thing it has secured is a continuously larger production. It has not regarded equity in the distribution of the product. It has not achieved even a minimum level of decent existence for the mass of the producers. It has never, above all, sought to stimulate at their highest level the creative energies of men. But the test of social institutions is the extent to which they develop those creative energies for social ends. If we assume a moral ideal that is capable of being aimed at by the state, each individual is clearly entitled to those rights which enable him to contribute to its attainment; he must be enabled, that is to say, to fulfil his moral vocation as a man. But the outstanding feature of the present society is that most men have, substantially, no rights at all, while those who do possess them are not bound to the service that they ought to involve.

The consequence may be seen in the absence of a common purpose binding men together in the state. There is, of course, common dependence in the sense that if an employer secures orders, his men secure work; and that he, in turn, depends upon their labour for the fulfilment of his contract. But the absence of any principle in the method of distribution leaves the partition of the product simply to the pressure of opposing forces, and the result is what is called the class-war. So long as that social disharmony persists, the currents of social activity can never so flow together as to converge into a single channel. Nor can any institution which is touched by that disharmony really attract the motives which promote civilisation. For the absence of principle at the root is bound to affect the upper branches of the tree. If we start, not from the assumption that property has rights because it is property, but that socially valuable functions require rights in order that the individuals fulfilling those functions may achieve their end, in proportion as those ends are realised, the foundation of disharmony disappears. We then move to the conception of a minimum basis of civilisation secured to each individual in order that his citizenship may be possible. Beyond that, because the interest of the state in the happiness of its members is equal, we attempt the maximisation of equal opportunity. We do not, that is to say, associate opportunity with a status that is mainly economic, but with the mere fact that the individual, as a member of the state, must be given the fullest chance to prove his worth.

It is perhaps worth while insisting that this is not an effort after identity. Equality of opportunity is simply the admission that unless each citizen has an equal access to the heritage of the state, the persistence of disharmony, with the internecine warfare it entails, is certain. It is, moreover, clear that men will very variously avail themselves of the equal opportunities conferred. Their tastes are not the same. Some are by nature leaders; to others, the temptation to inert acceptance of direction is irresistible. In particular, it does not seem probable that the increase of interest in politics will be as intense as is usually supposed. The social nature of men must always be carefully distinguished from the political nature of some few. The average member of Parliament, even, is not there because he has a love of state-building. He is there, like Sir Frederick Banbury, to defend an economic interest threatened from within, or, as in the case of many retired business men, because the House of Commons is an avenue towards certain social distinctions that are prized by their class. Equality of opportunity will undoubtedly multiply the number of citizens fit for polical function. But the two important possibilities it opens are, first, that the state becomes informed by a common purpose, and, second, that it is enabled to utilise the reservoir of talent that, with the present disparity, is bound to remain largely undiscovered.

Nor does this doctrine involve the abolition of property as such. It simply limits the rights of ownership by insisting that they shall be conditioned by the performance of service. It must, of course, further limit those rights by organising social institutions in such a fashion that they leave each citizen who desires the sense of freedom in their working to perform, where he has the capacity, responsible functions. It involves, that is to say, the democratisation of industrial control, and the decentralisation of political control. It means for the mines such a form of organisation as that, for instance, which Mr. Justice Sankey has depicted. There, at least, in pit, in district, and in the industry as a whole, the abolition of private ownership would remove barriers which now stand in the path of service and achievement. The miner who could convince his fellows that he was competent to direct their labours could test his powers in an increasingly wider field. So, too, in another sphere, with local government. At present, the amenities the latter can secure are limited by parliamentary enactments devised at every point in the interest of ratepayers and ground-landlords. If, apart from the need of general reorganisation, a compulsory minimum were fixed centrally, and the degree of effort beyond that minimum left to the local authority, many of the shadows that now lie across the face of English life would disappear. For the truth is that, in the eyes of property owners, extravagance is not the sin of Poplar, but the desire of its councillors to make the lives of their constituents less empty of the aids to well-being that Belgravia can afford. It is the notion of using the national resources for the purpose of promoting equality against which the defenders of the present system are adamant. Yet, whether in industry or politics, democratisation tempered by *expertise* is the only path to creativeness.

In any philosophy which seeks the grounds of national co-operation, a thorough grasp of the significance of such equality is fundamental. The miners who went on strike in 1921 knew not less well than other citizens that they imperilled by so doing the foundations of the economic security afforded by the present system. But because that system was unequal in its operation they had the less interest in the maintenance of its stability than those who, owning it, denounced them. Just as, during the war, the system of rationing produced better health in the nation because the food consumed, though less in quantity and quality, was more fairly distributed, so in the general organisation of social life, men who feel that the product is equally available in return for equal service will be willing to serve gratefully and in full measure. Let it be added, too, that equality implies a higher standard of knowledge and effort than can now be secured. Democracy, it is obvious, has as much need to test the standards of its performance as the chemist to test the accuracy of his balance. Equality must always be conditioned by the establishment of criteria of qualification for the performance of functions. But these criteria will not be resented where they bear equally upon all. Where they are destructive of social solidarity is in their inequality of operation. The son who inherits his father's business because he is the accident of an accident, the nobleman who becomes a company director, the judge's son who becomes clerk of assize, are examples of the acquisition of status without qualification which imperil the co-ordination of effort. The average working-man does not begrudge the standards of entrance to the civil service; but he rightly resents the inequalities of an educational system which, practically speaking, prevents his children from being able to attain that standard. The absence of an equal interest in the assets of the state inevitably begets an inferior interest in the maintenance of its foundations; and it is the obvious lesson of our experience that the inferior interest of the many is the active hatred of the few. No state can long survive in which a group of citizens aim, through profound moral conviction, at its overthrow. That is why the movement towards equality is the one sure safeguard against revolution.

It is doubtful, indeed, if ends such as these can in any full measure be attained through the classical institutions of representative government. We have evolved the great society without any real effort to see that our political methods keep pace with the changes in social and economic structure. No one who examines the large outlines of the English governmental system can point to any capital discovery in the past fifty years. The emergence of the Labour Party has altered the general perspective of their effort. The transference of the centre of importance from the House of Commons to the Cabinet, the consolidation of that pre-eminence given by Mr. Gladstone's long career to the office of Prime Minister, a superb improvement in the quality of the civil service, these, and things like these, have an importance beyond denial. But the normal assumptions which, for example, Bentham had in mind in the prophecies he made for the future of the representative system have ceased to work. The private member is a pale ghost of his former self. Debate has become utterly unreal; and divisions merely register mechanically decisions the real grounds of which are rarely determined in the House of Commons. The old system of party government has lost its mainspring; and the suspicious inertia of those who are not active in the machine itself is a commonplace. Nor is all this true of England alone. In France, in Italy, and in the United States, the same disharmony between political method and the social process may be detected. The legislative assembly is not merely overburdened by the pressure of its work; it is, in its classic form, unfitted to carry out the functions for which it exists.

It is, of course, possible to improve the actual machinery we have. Members of Parliament could be given direct contact with the business of administration by the creation of committees to watch the work of each department. They might be in part organs of consultation, and in part an effective and necessary *liaison* between the bureaucrat and the House of Commons, The transformation of the present committee-stage of bills into a process akin to the working of committees upon municipal bodies would not only destroy much deliberate obstruction, but it would also ensure to the private member a more real understanding of the measures upon which he votes, and a more real consideration than he now receives. A reduction in the size of the Cabinet has become clearly essential to the vital habit of corporate decision ; and it is at least equally clear that there does not exist in the civil government any body whose business it is to undertake the investigation and research that are necessary to the proper working of policy. Nor are the functions of t he different departments allocated upon any coherent principle. Until each department has before it a properly organised field of acti vity, there is bound to be waste and confusion. At present, there is overlapping and cross-division to a degree that makes officials surrender to contests for control with other officials time that should be given to creative work. No one can doubt that the serious consideration of political institutions could result in inventions for their improvement of capital importance.

Yet even if these and similar changes were effected the modern legislative system would be inadequate to its task. That there are many functions, the provision of law and justice, the maintenance of the national health, the provision of public education, defence and foreign policy, which require an undivided communal organ for their general direction, is clear enough. But when we pass from functions such as these, which concern men as citizens rather than men as producers, analysis makes it obvious that the simple formulæ of representative government do not apply. What we need, then, is to take the services that have to be performed and devise institutions for their government. We have so to devise them that we may secure to each function the rights without which citizenship is impossible, and, within the boundaries of that limiting principle, to free the general legislative assembly from the task of intimate and incessant supervision. It is not, in any case, fit for such a task ; for, as Mill long ago pointed out, a popular assembly is in its nature unfitted to administer or dictate in detail to those who control administration. Here it becomes necessary to depart from the narrowly geographical habit of our political thinking. We must learn to think of railways and mines, cotton and agriculture, as areas of government just as real as London and Lancashire. They are relatively unified functions which need, just as much as geographical units, organs of administration. Clearly, of course, it is easier to give a simple form of institutionalism to an industry like mining, which is susceptible of immediate nationalisation, than to a industsy like cotton-spinning, in which the formulæ of nationalisation are far more dubious. But, granted the conference of powers to a representative assembly for the cotton industry, granted, also, the principles of citizenship within which it must work, it is not difficult to imagine mechanism through which a constitutional system of government might work there. As with the mines, it is necessary to give representation in such a functional assembly to interests which need special protection —the consumer, the technician, allied industries in a special sense related to cotton. It is necessary, also, to use such associations as the trade unions and the employers' federations as the basis upon which selections of personnel must be made. Nor should any barriers be put in the way of joint consultation between industry and industry. Whether a national economic council is implied in such a scheme as this it is very difficult to say. The problem of its constitution is extraordinarily complex ; and the solution of general industrial questions is, as a rule, really the solution of problems of citizenship which come within the scope of Parliament. Their administration is almost always a special problem of a particular function, and is better left to the function for settlement. When the German Economic Council has had a longer life we shall be better able to judge the possibilities it involves.

It may be useful at this stage to indicate the institutional pattern implied in a social philosophy of this kind. We visualise a Parliament with the taxing power, which lays down fundamental rules, and administers, through the Cabinet, the matters of general citizenship. Below it would be territorial and functional institutions. The one would be concerned with the normal subject matter of local government ; and, under the revised areas of control, they would possess that greater complex of powers characteristic of the first-class German municipality, rather than the narrow delegation inherent in the British system. Each industry would possess an industrial council in which management and labour, technicians and the representatives of allied industries, together with the representatives of the public, would take their place. Such a council would have as its business the application to the industry it controlled of the minimum basis of civilisation we have suggested as now fundamental. It would consider all questions affecting industrial relations within its scope of reference. It would issue decrees, perhaps of the nature of provisional orders, where it was desired to go beyond the principles of the national minimum. It would undertake research ; and it would have a special costings and audit department of which the task would be to secure complete publicity upon the details of the business process within the trade. It is possible, also, that a National Industrial Council would be required; but it is doubtful whether it is possible to build it, and uncertain whether the questions it would seek to resolve are not, in fact, problems with which the ordinary Parliament is better able to deal.

At the back of all this lies an implied insistence upon education as the main channel of hope in our ultimate relief. For if the object of the state is to enrich the social heritage through the enlargement of individual personality, then individual personality must be given that power of adequate expression which comes through knowledge to make its needs known. At bottom, therefore, the problem is the instruction of individual wills, and the building, as in our institutional pattern, of channels through which those wills can flow. It is not suggested that wills can or should function equally, since abilities are unequal. But it is suggested that the general environment in which these wills function must be at a certain minimum level. It follows, therefore, that the charges of maintaining and raising that level are the first national burden to be borne; and the whole concept of property must undergo a radical change to that end. For, ultimately, the real implication of a national minimum is the replacement of the spirit of acquisitiveness by the spirit of service. That may not mean destroying the legal notion of property; but it does mean spiking its guns.

If we approach in this way the central problem of the state we make it, as Plato made it, that notion of justice which is the right ordering of human relationships. It involves the view that each citizen has an equal claim on the common good in respect of equal needs; and the corollary is therein implied that differences in response to claims are differences that the common good itself requires. This would, in all likelihood, rule out any rigorous scheme of communism on the ground that it leaves no room for the recognition of the social importance of individual differences; though we must ceaselessly remember that the tribute paid to those differences has its marginal utility. It would also allow the payment of a monopoly-rent to ability only when we can be certain that a social need can be satisfied in no other fashion. Broadly, then, justice implies equality where human beings are equal in their needs. But justice must function in that psychological atmosphere in which we get the best out of our ablest men. The principle of the payment for service, the standard, therefore, by which property can be justified, is a measure of remuneration which harmonises individual interest with the common good. It ought here to be emphasised that the importance of profit-making as a motive has been greatly exaggerated, and that experiment with its replacement could not effect other than benefit. The state owes to each of us the opportunity of useful service; but it does not owe us the occasion to spend the substance of other men's lives.

We are seeking to visualise a state in which the individual citizen is entitled to an effective voice in collective decisions. Admittedly, of course, the power he can have is limited by the inherent needs of large-scale organisation. But it ought still to mean that the ordinary man can help to select his rulers and to get himself elected if he can. It ought to mean his right to unfettered criticism. It should involve the right to be informed of all important decisions and the consequent opportunity to revoke, in concert with his fellows, the mandate to government. So, in the economic sphere, every capable individual must have a right to work, with, of course, the corollary that it is his duty to work well. Within the limits of social requirement, he ought to have the opportunity, as few now have, to choose and to vary his occupation. If he has merit, he ought to be able to advance by it. If he has initiative, he ought to be able to exercise it through the structure of his function. He should be able by his work to purchase a reward of service that meets all material needs ; and from the accidents of unemployment and sickness, as from the cares of old age, he should be protected. This, at least, is what the state in substance means ; and if its institutions have so far failed to give content to that meaning, it seems to follow that they stand in need of change.

The political science of the next generation will be mainly occupied, if it is to be fruitful, with the explorations of channels through which this end may be attained. It will seek to discover ways in which the individual may be made significant. It will have to remember that he is not absorbed by the state ; within the mind of every man there are reserves into which organisation does not, and ought not to, enter. Society is the harmony of a system of selves, not a harmony over and above them. It is the *milieu* in which they live; it is not itself the life. Control is social because individuals act directly upon each other, and it is necessary, therefore to have criteria of right action. Here, we have argued that control must not lie in any vocation, or area, or rank, but in the citizen-body as a whole. For, otherwise, the lives of the many lie at the disposal of the few ; and they are used, as history makes evident, not for the common good but a perversion of it. Our business is to give to the common man that access to his inheritance of which he has hitherto been deprived. Of that inheritance he has become aware; and the future most largely depends upon the response we make to his awareness. Our complex civilisation is being tested by men who do not judge it by the thought and effort that have gone in its making, but by the happiness it brings to ordinary men and women. It is only by endeavouring to meet their desires that we shall be able to await their judgment with confidence.

FABIAN PUBLICATIONS.

FABIAN ESSAYS. (1920 Edition). 2/6; postage, 3d.
KARL MARX. By Harold J. Laski. 1/-; post free, 1/1½.
FROM PATRONAGE TO PROFICIENCY IN THE PUBLIC SER-
VICE. By William A. Robson. 1/-; post free, 1/1½.
SOCIALISM AND CHARACTER. By Henry Sturt. 7/6; postage, 5d.
THE WHITLEY SYSTEM IN THE CIVIL SERVICE. By J. H.
Macrae-Gibson. 1/-; post free, 1/1½.
WHAT TO READ on Social and Economic Subjects. 2s. n.
TOWARDS SOCIAL DEMOCRACY? By Sidney Webb. 1s. n., post. 1d.
THIS MISERY OF BOOTS. By H. G. Wells. 6d., post free 7d.

FABIAN TRACTS and LEAFLETS.
Tracts, each 16 to 52 pp., price 1d., or 9d. per doz., unless otherwise stated.
Leaflets, 4 pp. each, price 1d. for three copies, 2s. per 100, or 20/- per 1000.
The Set of 74, 7/6; post free 8,6. Bound in buckram, 12/6; post free 13/6-

I.—General Socialism in its various aspects.
TRACTS.—192. Guild Socialism By G. D. Cole, M.A. 180. The
Philosophy of Socialism. By A. Clutton Brock. 159. The Ne-
cessary Basis of Society. By Sidney Webb. 151. The Point of
Honour. By Ruth C. Bentinck. 147. Capital and Compensation. By
E. R. Pease. 146. Socialism and Superior Brains. By Bernard Shaw. 2d.
142. Rent and Value. 138. Municipal Trading. 121. Public Service v.
Private Expenditure. By Sir Oliver Lodge. 2d. 107. Socialism for Mil-
lionaires. By Bernard Shaw. 2d. 139. Socialism and the Churches. By
Rev. John Clifford, D.D. 133. Socialism and Christianity. By Rev.
Percy Dearmer. 2d. 78. Socialism and the Teaching of Christ. By Dr. J.
Clifford. 42. Christian Socialism. By Rev. S. D. Headlam. 79. A Word
of Remembrance and Caution to the Rich. By John Woolman. 72. The
Moral Aspects of Socialism. By Sidney Ball. 69. Difficulties of In-
dividualism. By S. Webb. 51. Socialism: True & False. By S. Webb. 2d.
45. The Impossibilities of Anarchism. By G. B. Shaw. 2d. 7. Capital
and Land. 5. Facts for Socialists. 3d. 41. The Fabian Society: its
Early History. By Bernard Shaw.

II.—Applications of Socialism to Particular Problems.
TRACTS.—198. Some Problems of Education. By Barbara Drake. 6d.
197. International Labour Organisation of the League of Nations. By
Wm. S. Sanders. 196. The Root of Labour Unrest. By Sidney Webb. 2d.
195. The Scandal of the Poor Law. By C. M. Lloyd. 2d. 194. Taxes,
Rates and Local Income Tax. By Robert Jones, D.Sc. 2d. 188. National
Finance and a Levy on Capital. By Sidney Webb. 2d. 187. The
Teacher in Politics. By Sidney Webb. 2d. 186. Central Africa
and the League of Nations. By R. C. Hawkin. 2d. 183. The
Reform of the House of Lords. By Sidney Webb. 181. When
Peace Comes—the Way of Industrial Reconstruction. By Sidney Webb.
2d. 177. Socialism and the Arts of Use. By A. Clutton Brock. 175. The
Economic Foundations of the Women's Movement. 2d. 173. Public v.
Private Electricity Supply. 170. Profit-Sharing and Co-Partnership:
a Fraud and Failure? 164. Gold and State Banking. 161. Afforestation
and Unemployment. 155. The Case against the Referendum. 152. Our
Taxes as they are and as they ought to be. 2d. 145. The Case for School
Nurseries. 140. Child Labor under Capitalism. 136. The Village and
the Landlord. By Edw. Carpenter. 144. Machinery: its Masters and
Servants. 122. Municipal Milk and Public Health. 124. State Control
of Trusts. 158. The Case against the C.O.S. By Mrs. Townshend.

III.—Local Government Powers : How to use them.
TRACTS.—190. Metropolitan Borough Councils. By C. R. Attlee, M.A.
2d. 191. Borough Councils. By C. R. Attlee, M.A. 2d. 193. Housing.
By C. M. Lloyd, M.A. 3d. 189. Urban District Councils. By C. M. Lloyd,
M.A. 2d. 62. Parish & District Councils. (Revised 1921). 2d. 148. What a
Health Committee can do. 2d. 137. Parish Councils & Village Life. 2d.

IV.—Biographical Series. In portrait covers, 2d. and 3d.
199. William Lovett, 1800-1877. By Barbara L. Hammond. 3d. 182.
Robert Owen, Idealist. By C. E. M. Joad. 179. John Ruskin and
Social Ethics. By Prof. Edith Morley. 165. Francis Place. By St. John
G. Ervine. 166. Robert Owen, Social Reformer By Miss B. L. Hutchins.
167. William Morris and the Communist Ideal. By Mrs. Townshend. 168.
John Stuart Mill. By Julius West. 174. Charles Kingsley and Christian
Socialism. By C. E. Vulliamy.

Printed by G. Standring. 7 Finsbury St., London, E.C. and published by the Fabian Society.

CPSIA information can be obtained
at www.ICGtesting.com
Printed in the USA
BVHW040552101118
532319BV00026B/95/P